JAMES JOHNSON
PLACE NAMES
OF ENGLAND
AND WALES

TO

SIR JAMES A. H. MURRAY

HARDEST OF WORKERS

AS A MEMENTO OF A CONNEXION

OF OVER THIRTY YEARS

JAMES JOHNSON
PLACE NAMES
OF ENGLAND
AND WALES

BRACKEN BOOKS

LONDON

Places Names of England and Wales

First published in 1915 by John Murray, London

This edition published in 1994 by Bracken Books, an imprint of
Studio Editions Ltd, Princess House, 50 Eastcastle Street,
London W1N 7AP, England

Copyright © this edition Studio Editions Ltd 1994

ISBN 1 85891 133 8

Printed in Guernsey

PREFACE

A FEW words of preface seem necessary, especially for the sake of those who wish to make serious use of this book. Let it, then, be clearly understood at the outset that it makes no attempt or pretence at completeness. In so vast a subject this would scarcely be possible for any man, no matter how accomplished or favourably situated. Least of all has it been possible for the writer, a busy minister working absolutely single-handed in a Scottish provincial town, with the oversight of a large congregation which has had the first claim upon all his time and energy and has always received it. Why, then, attempt such a task at all ? Because it seemed so needful to be done. No proper conspectus of the whole subject has appeared hitherto; and the writer does think that through the gatherings of fully twenty years he has been able to do something. He would humbly hope he may receive a little thanks for what he has done, rather than censure—all too easy to utter—for what he has left undone. Every student may at once discover omissions, perhaps a good many mistakes also, though the writer has done his best: he can only cherish the hope that at least he has made the pathway easier for the more thorough men who are sure to come after.

Consultation of works only to be found in large libraries— Domesday, the O.E. charters, the Rolls, and Chroniclers—has all had to be done during brief and occasional visits to Edinburgh and Glasgow, where even the best libraries are far from perfect in this respect. Still, one has been able to gleam not a few valuable forms, especially from the more recent issues of the Close and Patent Rolls (which have hardly been touched by others yet), and from several of the early chroniclers. Unless it be in the notes to *Anecdota Oxoniensia*, next to nothing of permanent value on English place-names appeared until so recently as 1901, when the lamented Dr. Skeat issued his brochure on Cambs. The gazetteers and guide-books, even the best of them, are nearly all useless on our subject; generally a great deal worse than useless from a scientific point of view: and we cannot even exclude the latest edition of the *Encyclopœdia Britannica*. But invaluable help has been received from the numerous works of Dr. Skeat, and from not a little private correspondence with him, in which the Cambridge professor of Anglo-Saxon showed himself aboundingly generous, up to within a fortnight of his death. Much is owed both to the books and to the private help of the late Mr. Duignan, who was also most kind. One of the best place-name books yet issued is Wyld and Hirst's book on Lancashire, to which the writer is very deeply indebted. The book is marred only by a few serious omissions (like Bacup), and by a rather overfondness for Scandinavian, and an oversuspiciousness of Keltic origins, which occasionally leads to curious results, as in the case of Condover. Mr. M'Clure's book has been found to contain much splendid material with some weak admixture. Baddeley's Gloucester is a first-rate bit of work; the writer's only regret is that it came so late into his hands. He has a similar regret with regard to the work of Dr. Mutschmann. Several others, containing valuable information, were unfortunately issued just before or after his own MS. was completed in November, 1913; they will be found in the Bibliography. The stern exigencies of space have forbidden many other acknowledgments of indebtedness.

The number of Domesday forms given is by no means complete, and the identification in a few cases may be a little uncertain owing to lack of local knowledge. But the information given is certainly fuller than is available elsewhere. All village names not important enough to be mentioned in the *Postal Guide* have been passed over, except in cases of special interest. *Postal Guide* spellings have usually been taken as the standard.

Wales has been a great difficulty. Accessible and trustworthy literature has proved very scarce (see p. 66). Letters have been exchanged with a number of kindly correspondents; but hardly anybody has been found able and willing to give real help, except that excellent antiquary, Mr. Palmer of Wrexham, and Sir Edward Anwyl, whose all too scanty communications have proved of great value. As to Cornwall, the writer worked diligently for three weeks in the Public Library at Falmouth, and was fortunate in being able to supplement his studies from the valuable Cornish library of the Rev. Wilfrid Rogers. R. O. Heslop, Esq., of Newcastle, has given useful hints about names in Northumberland, and Rev. Charles E. Johnston, of Seascale, has helped with those of Cumberland. Numerous other correspondents must be gratefully acknowledged in a body. Their help has been none the less real, and the writer's gratitude is just as hearty, though it is impossible to mention all their names.

Professor Ernest Weekley, of Nottingham, our best living authority on English personal names, has read all the proofs and has enriched nearly every page with some valuable suggestion, though, of course, he is responsible for no statement in the book. The writer tenders to him his warmest thanks. Fresh information and accredited corrections of any kind will always be welcome.

JAMES B. JOHNSTON.

St. Andrew's Manse, Falkirk.
    June 15, 1914.

CONTENTS

THE PLACE-NAMES OF ENGLAND AND WALES

INTRODUCTION

CHAPTER I

THE USE AND VALUE OF PLACE-NAME STUDY

To many this needs an apologia; it is such a useless, dryas-dust study this, they say. And yet the apologia is easily writ, because:—

1. Place-name study helps to satisfy a widespread and very natural curiosity; and everything which helps to satisfy a legitimate and intelligent curiosity is good, and deserves some meed of commendation, not a frown. But this, if the first is perhaps the lowest of the uses, we shall name.

2. It is one of the most valuable and readily available of our sidelights on history. The history of the far past is as a rule dim enough, and needs every beam of light, even the faintest, which we can throw upon it. In England, it so happens, we have records of place-names in abundance long before we have regular history in abundance. Often where the direct record is of the meagrest, the most tantalizingly scanty sort, place-names may be practically the only definite evidence we have on certain important points. The early history of Cumberland is a good case in point. Moreover, place-names help much to indicate the breadth and depth of the impact of the foreign invader, and England had invaders not a few.

3. Our study helps not a little to reveal and illustrate racial idiosyncrasies, modes of thought, feeling, and taste. Tastes Keltic were, and are, very different from tastes Saxon. Our names, *e.g.*, show what men or class of men each race admired

1

and revered most, the men whose memories they sought most eagerly to perpetuate. In the case of Angle, Saxon, and Dane, they tell at least a little, perhaps not a great deal, as to who were their favourite heroes; whilst in the case of the Kelt they show who were his favourite saints. The bluff Saxon seldom troubled himself much about saints, at least so far as to enshrine them in a place-name; though one or two instances, like CHADKIRK or KEWSTOKE, might be cited to the contrary.

4. It gives most valuable evidence as to the processes of phonetic change and decay, and the lines on which those changes proceed. The laws, once found and firmly established, are wellnigh as sure and helpful as those in the most exact of the physical sciences. It is often of extreme interest to the philologer to trace these sound-changes; and our place-name records often afford valuable supplement to the dictionary, supplying missing links, and giving, in a good many cases, earlier evidence of the use of a word than any surviving literary record. Examples of this will be found *passim* (see, *e.g.*, BISHOP BURTON, HATHERLEIGH, REACH, RYE, etc.).

5. Lastly, we need not hesitate to add, the study of place-names is a useful discipline, a taxing exercise of scholarly patience, in a department where much has already been done, but where a vast amount of hard work still awaits the doer. In a much-traversed, much-contested territory like England and Wales, the student needs to remove each successive layer of names as carefully, and to scrutinize them as diligently, as a Flinders Petrie when he is digging down into one of Egypt's ancient cemeteries, or as a Macalister exploring one of the great rubbish mounds at Gezer or Lachish. And the place-name student has his own little joys of discovery,[1] his own thrills over a much-tangled skein at last unravelled, as well as a Schliemann at Mycenæ, or a Flinders Petrie at Abydos. He also has his own sure retribution if he neglect the laws of his

---

[1] *E.g.*, Professor Kuno Meyer's recent discovery, in an old Irish MS., of the name 'Ard Echdi' (height of the horse), the exact Irish or Gaelic equivalent of the *Epidion akron* of Ptolemy, c. A.D. 150, Ard Echdi is said to be 'in Kintyre,' which confirms the supposition long since made, that Ptolemy's name stood for the Mull of Kintyre. This discovery also confirms our belief in Ptolemy's accuracy, whilst it shows that, in his day, Kintyre was inhabited by Kelts of the *p* group, not by Kelts of the *c* or *k* group, as all Scottish Kelts are at this day.

study, and dogmatize upon unsufficient evidence. Bad guesses are sure to bring to him shame and confusion. But in this study sober conjecture is not to be despised, even if it afterwards prove wrong. It is often the only resource which lies open. But one must use all the evidence available, and one must know and remember the rules, which nine out of every ten place-name guessers do not.

CHAPTER II

ROMAN AND LATIN NAMES

WRITTEN record of British history before the arrival of Julius
Cæsar's legions in 55 B.C. there is all but none. True, the
Cassiterides—*i.e.*, ' tin islands '—are referred to by Herodotus,
the father of history himself, as well as by Strabo; and these
Cassiterides must have included part of the mainland of
Cornwall as well as the Scilly Isles. There is a Cassiter Street
in Bodmin at this day. The general name, BRITAIN,[1] also
goes back to Aristotle. For the rest there yawns a vast
blank.

On Rome in Britain we shall be very brief; the subject has
already been discussed so often, with such fulness and care,
by more competent pens. We get many names in England
in Ptolemy's well - known *Geography*, written in Greek *c.*
A.D. 150. So far as Britain is concerned it is not first-hand
knowledge, but a pure compilation, and, except in the case
of a few rivers, Ptolemy's names can rarely be identified with
certainty with names still in use. We get a large number of
town names along the routes given in the *Antonine Itinerary*, a
document only put into its final shape *c.* A.D. 380. We get
a good many more in the *Notitia Dignitatum*, which dates about
twenty years later. All the evidence afforded by these, our
three chief authorities for Roman names in England, will be
found set forth and discussed in scholarly fashion in M'Clure's
British Place-Names. Of course, we have a few names, a
mere handful, which come in earlier. Only in very rare cases
do these represent names which still survive. Cæsar gives us
Cantium or Kent, Tameses or Thames, Mona or Man. Vectis
or Wight goes back to Pliny, A.D. 77. His name for England

---

[1] The printing of a name in capitals always means, See details in
the List.

is Albion, possibly 'the white (L. *albus*) land,' from the white
chalk cliffs about Dover. Tacitus, a little later than Pliny, is
the first to mention Londinium or London, and the Sabrina or
Severn, also a R. Avona (probable reading), and that is about
all—a very meagre array. The Roman Itineraries cover the
whole country from the Scottish Border to Exeter, or Isca
Damnoniorum. Rome made little mark S. and W. of that.
But the Itinerary names are seldom identifiable with existing
names, and have given rise to endless controversy. A good
many of them will be found discussed in our List, s.v. Carlisle,
Dover, Manchester, Worcester, and the like. But the names
which have come down to us from pre-Saxon times, though
writ in Latin, are practically all Keltic, or pre-Keltic, and so
fall, properly, to be dealt with in our next chapter.

Chester or CAISTOR, as we find it alone, -caster, -cester, or
-chester as we find it in combination, is usually thought to be
the sure sign manual of the Roman, and proof of the existence
of a former *castra*, camp, or fort. But numerous though these
'caster' names be, none of them really go back as names to
Roman times. Names like Alia Castra for Alcester are spurious
inventions. CHESTER itself comes in as a name quite late, and
few if any 'casters' are earlier than the beginnings of the O.E.
Chronicle. GLOUCESTER is found in a grant of 681 as Gleawe-
ceasdre, and WORCESTER is nearly as early. Thus, -caster.
O.E. *ceaster*, is a Saxon rather than a Roman appellative.
There are also one or two names which embody the L. *colonia*,
'a settlement,' usually of veteran soldiers. LINCOLN is certainly a case in point, and COLCHESTER, O.E. Colenceaster, is
confidently given as another, with fair reason too. But
very possibly it means no more than 'camp on the R. COLNE,'
and this river name must be Keltic or pre-Keltic. In either
case the present names, Lincoln and Colchester, seem to have
been of Saxon, not of Roman, make.

Thus, of real Latin names in England there are almost none.
Skeat will not even admit SPEEN, Berks, to be the L. Spinæ.
But Catterick, S. Yorks, is known to be the L. *cataracta* or
'waterfall,' and Pontefract is the same region, though first
found in Norman documents, may have come down all the
way from the Romans. But Centurion's Copse, Brading, is a
silly modern corruption for 'St. Urian's copse'; and AQUILATE,

Staffs, is not *Aqua lata*, but comes from Aquila, Latin rendering of the Norman surname L'Aigle. Monkish Latin has certainly had to do with a few of our present names. MONKSILVER, *e.g.*, must be from *silva*, ' a wood '; MEREVALE is Mira valle, and Gaia Lane, Lichfield, is med. Latin for 'jay,' Nor. Fr. *gai, gay ;* whilst the earliest known spelling of DEVIZES seems to be Divisis, which we venture to translate—the Latin is barbarous —place ' at the borders ' or ' divisions.' The history of AUST is also very interesting.

The great fact remains that in Britain, unlike neighbouring Gaul or Spain, no Roman language has been spoken for 1,500 years. The Britons kept, and still keep, their own mother-tongue. Only a few townsfolk and wealthier landowners would ever speak Latin at all. Hence it is that this chapter so soon comes to an end.

CHAPTER III

THE KELTIC ELEMENT

OF all the problems connected with the place-names of England there are few so interesting or so intricate as those connected with the Keltic element — how much, or perhaps we should rather say, how little, of the old British speech still survives in English place-names. On this subject much nonsense has been asserted, even by learned men who ought to have known better, or who, at any rate, should have been more careful about their facts before making such large claims for the Keltic element as they have. The truth is, the deeper and the more thorough the investigation, the smaller seems the sure Keltic residuum, whilst very small indeed now is the group of names of which we can make nothing sure at all, though convinced that they must either be Keltic or pre-Keltic. There must be several pre-Keltic names in Wales, but in England they are confined chiefly, and possibly altogether, to a handful of river names. There are, *e.g.*, two or three names in Cheshire which are hard nuts to crack, rivers like the Biddle, Bollin, Croco, and Etherow; whilst Kennet, a river name in both Berks and Cambs, is another of the rare insolubles. It is such an age since these long-skulled, dark-haired, dark-eyed pre-Kelts (probably also pre-Aryans) ceased to speak their own tongue on British soil, that their names, as well as everything else belonging to them, except a few skulls, have been practically wiped out; and time spent in speculating on their language or their names can be little else than time wasted.

Not a great many centuries before Julius Cæsar, the great Aryan family of Kelts began to arrive on our shores. The Goidels or Gaels, because to-day in force in Northern Scotland, Ireland, and Man, must, it is generally supposed, have arrived first. But of Goidels in England we now know exceedingly

7

little.   Their very existence there, once upon a time, is proved
by not much else than a few inscriptions, commonly called
Ogams.   There have been none found E. of Devon or Wales,
only one in Cornwall, and barely fifty altogether.   But these
Ogams can only date from late in the Roman occupation, and
seem to suggest that the makers of them had crossed over from
the S. of Ireland, perhaps from about Waterford, to Pembroke.
Th?re was also an Irish invasion or immigration into Cornwall
in early historic times.   But of the earliest Goidels in England
we know almost nothing.   Next came the Brythons, the *p*
group as scholars call them, as opposed to the *k* or *q* group, the
Goidels.   Comparison of the abundant remaining skulls of the
Neolithic Age in Belgium and in England, seems to indicate
that the English Kelts we know best came from the tribe of
the Belgæ, and crossed over to us where the sea was narrowest.
The Belgæ were akin to the Gauls, and the Gauls were undoubtedly nearer of kin to the Brython than to the Gael, so
far as their very scanty linguistic remains show.   The Picts,
who were akin to the Brythons, especially to the Cornish, seem
to have been confined to Scotland, though in Searle's *Onomasti-*
con we find nine names of men compounded with Peoht or
Pict—*e.g.*, Peoht-helm, -red, -wine, -wulf, etc.

However, over a large area of England we now know for
certain that there are next to no Keltic names at all.   Where a
competent investigator has been at work, like Dr. Skeat
among the names of Berks, Cambs, or Herts, we can now say
confidently that there are no surviving Keltic names except
those of two or three rivers; a very different story this from
what was supposed not so very long ago.   All over the S.E.
of England, and indeed in the whole region along the coast
from Tyne to Solent, Keltic names are extremely rare.   It is
doubtful if in that section there be thirty such names all
told.   In Lincoln, Norfolk, Suffolk, Essex, Middlesex, Surrey,
Sussex, the Keltic element seems represented by only five,
three, or possibly even one name each; for in Middlesex, apart
from London and Thames, which it shares with other counties,
what is there save Brent ?   In the Midlands, too, Keltic
names are few and far between, except on the Welsh border.
In Bucks, Bedford, Oxford, Warwick, there are next to none.
And what is stranger and more unexpected, even in the far

N., in Westmorland and Durham, hardly a single true British name survives. Of the original English Goidel our place-names preserve scarce one footprint. It is doubtful if in all England, outwith the borders of Northumberland and Cumberland, there can be picked out a single clearly Goidelic name,[1] and, of course, the Border names are probably due to the filtering S. of the Scottish Gael.

On the other hand, as is well known, in districts where the Saxon invader arrived late, in Cornwall, 'the horn of the Welsh,' and in Monmouth, Keltic names are still in an overwhelming majority. In Cornwall there are perhaps no true English names of any consequence, except modern upstarts like New Quay, and two names on the very eastern edge— Launceston and Saltash. Next to Cornwall and Monmouth, *the* region for Keltic names is, very naturally, that along the Welsh border, and in what was the old Brythonic kingdom of Cumbria—*i.e.*, Lancashire and Cumberland—also, as we have already noted, all along the Scottish Border. In Hereford, Salop, and Cheshire, and in these three northern counties, Welsh names (or Gaelic names) of rivers, of hills too, and villages and towns, are still fairly plentiful. Many river names in Devon and Somerset, and quite a handful in Stafford, are Keltic; so also is a fairly numerous group of towns or villages in Somerset and Dorset. Whenever we find such village names surviving, it is pretty clear proof that extermination or driving out of the Brython at the hand of Saxon or Angle had not been so swift or ruthless as in most other parts. It is curious, however, that Keltic village names are so lacking in Devon.

It is the Welsh dictionary which is our chief aid in searching out the Keltic names. English Keltic names are certainly for the most part of Brythonic type. But, as we have already noted, near the Scots Border we have a few purely Goidelic, interesting as showing that the present Border was once upon a time by no means the southern border of the Gael. There is a W. *glyn* as well as a G. *gleann ;* but we can scarcely err in

---

[1] Perhaps the best attempt has been, to show the G. *crioch, criche,* ' boundary, limit,' in the numerous names in Creech and Crick, and even PENKRIDGE. But the evidence which will be found *s.v.* CREECH, CRICK, CRICKHOWELL, etc., seems conclusive against it.

holding that all the Glens in Northumberland are of Gaelic origin. Near Haltwhistle alone we find three—a Glencune, a Glendhu, and a Glenwhelt. Glencune reappears in Cumberland, near Ullswater, as Glencoin. Both are clearly derived from the G. *cumhann* or *comhann*, with the *mh* mute through 'eclipse,' as it is called. Glencoe, the far-famed, has the same origin; it is spelt Glencoyne in 1500, and Glencoan in 1623. Another Glen, with a very Highland smack about it, lies E. of Keswick, GLENDERAMACKIN, which is pure Gaelic for 'glen of the stream with the bulbs or parsnips.'

The Kielder Water near the Northumberland border is as clearly G. *caol dobhar* (*bh* mute), 'narrow-stream.' The G. *ao* in names has run through nearly all the vowel sounds. We have it taking on the long *ee* of Kielder away up in Eddrachilis, W. Sutherland, pronounced Eddrahéelis, G. *eadar-a-chaolais*, 'between the straits or narrows.' Pure Gaelic, too, is Mindrum, Coldstream, G. *min druim*, 'smooth hill ridge.' In Cumberland such names are rarer, but we have a few very interesting samples, like Cardurnock, on the shore S. of Bowness, G. *cathair* (*th* mute) *dornaig*, 'fort at the pebbly place,' the same word as Dornock on the other side of the Solway, and as the better known Dornoch in the far north. Culgaith, Penrith, is unmistakable Gaelic too, *cul gaoith*, 'at the back of the wind,' the *th* being preserved here, whilst in Gaelic for many a generation *th* has gone dumb. As already noted, of clearly Gaelic names farther south there are perhaps none at all, unless it be CANNOCK.

By far the most important group of Keltic names in England are the names of *rivers*. No first-class river in England, absolutely none in Wales, has an English name. One writer instances as probably English these six—Eamont, Loxley, Swift, Waveney, Witham, and Wyth-burn. The first three, all quite small streams, probably are; and, as we shall see by-and-by, there are plenty more. But the last three we may pretty confidently conclude to be Keltic (see the List). Why the rivers should be so tenaciously Keltic it is not quite easy to say, for the same rule by no means holds true about the other unchanging natural features of the land, the hills, the bays, etc. But a hill belongs to one district only, a river of any size to several. It would thus be fairly easy to change the name of a hill, but to change the name of a river would often have caused great confusion, and so the Saxons kept the old names on, and adapted their tongues to them as best they could.

It is worthy of note how intensely commonplace and unimaginative the bulk of our river names are. When examined they are very often found to mean 'river' or 'water,' and nothing more. Phonetics, not imagination, has lent the variety. To take the commonest first, the name AVON; there are seven Avons in all, three of them tributaries of the one R. Severn. The earliest known form, that of Tacitus, Avona, already gives us the spelling of to-day; but reference to the List will show that spellings with *b* and *f* pro *v* are early found too, clearly showing the connection between W. *afon* and G. *abhuinn* or *obhuinn*, both meaning 'river,' and nothing more. In England Avon is generally pronounced with ă, but sometimes, as in Shakespeare's Avon, with *œ*. In Scotland we find the same thing, the pronunciation usually ăvon, but in S. Lanarkshire always ævon, as in Strathæven or Stræven. This last pronunciation is also seen in fair Ravenglass, S. Cumberland, of which many absurd and law-defying interpretations are current, but which is simply W. *yr afon glas*, 'the greenish' or 'bluish river.' We probably get it again in the Norfolk R. WAVENEY, where a common English diminutive ending has tacked itself on. In Scotland, but not in England, the G. *amhuinn* or *abhuinn* reappears more than once as Almond. In England, however, we have various other forms. In Salop the root shows itself in OUNY or Onney, and we have it again in the Oun-dle of Northants, Bede's Un-dalum, forms paralleled in old Keltic Gaul, as in the Garonne, Rhone, Saone, and the like, whilst with Ouny we may also compare ŏwn, the pronunciation of G. *abhuinn* in some districts; and the form Onn-ey (English diminutive ending) probably has its parallel in such a familiar Scottish name as Carr-on.

Still more protean in its shapes is that root for 'water' or 'river,' variously spelt in different regions, Axe, Esk, Exe, Usk; the Romans spelt both Exe and Usk, Isca, and Ux-bridge certainly, Ox-ford possibly, represents the same word. This is the old Keltic *uisc*, the G. *uisge*, as in the famous usquebaugh or 'eau de vie.' Simeon of Durham (*c.* 1130) writes of Exeter as 'Britannice Cairuisc, Latine Civitas Aquarum.' Whitley

Stokes held that Esk is Pictish, cognate with O.Ir. *esc*, ' marsh,
fen.' But in face of the evidence, it seems very superfluous
to talk of Pictish in England, even in S. Cumberland (R. Esk
and Eskdale). We cannot prove that Ox- in Oxford is the
same root; still it is quite likely that OXFORD, R. Ock, Berks,
and Ockbrook, Derbyshire, are all cognates. The Latin name
of the Thames at Oxford is Isis, already so given by Leland
c. 1550, but exactly 200 years earlier we find it in Higden's
Polychronicon as Ysa. It seems most likely that Isis also is
related to *uisc* and to the R. OUSE. A plausible O.E. origin
can be suggested for the Ouse, which is partly confirmed by
the forms given under Great OUSE. But Oxnam, on the
Roxburgh border, though already, *c.* 1150, Oxeneham, stands
upon a little burn called the Ousenan ; and this hilly region can
never have been very suitable for oxen, so that Ox- as well as
Ouse, which appears four times in England, may well mean
' river ' too.

The Cheshire Dee, Ptolemy's Deva, the modern W. Dwfr
Dwy (' two rivers '), likewise means ' river,' whilst the R. Dove,
Derby, and R. Dovey or Dyfi, S. Wales, are both forms of
this W. *dwfr* or *dwr*, O.W. *dubr ;* and the same root, W. *dwr*, or
G. *dobhar* (*bh* mute), is also seen as forming half of such stream
names as Ad*der* or Ad*ur* (there are three such rivers), *Der*went
(three also), *Dar*wen, and Kiel*der*. The Westmorland R.
Lowther is probably but Keltic for ' canal ' or ' trench.' The
R. Alde, Suffolk, seems cognate with the G. *allt*, ' a burn,' seen
pure and simple in the Alt, Lancs, and as a compound in many
a Scots name—Aldourie, Garvald, etc. Then Wey, a river-
name both in Surrey and in Dorset, is plainly W. *gwy*, ' a river,'
especially a slow-flowing one, probably seen again in the Sutherland G. *uidh*. And, of course, we have the same root in the
R. Wye, Domesday's Waia, and in the Gowy, a little Cheshire
tributary of the Mersey. TYNE, too, may mean ' river ' and
little more. All this, when summed up, forms a remarkable
mass of evidence in proof of the statement with which we
began, that English river names very often mean plain ' river '
or ' stream,' nothing else.

Again, there is a considerable group of names which mean
simply ' quiet, smooth,' or, possibly, ' broad river.' The forms
in the group vary a good deal—Taff (and Llan-daff), Tame

(and Tam-worth), Tamar, Tavy, Taw, Teme (tributary of Severn), Thame, Thames; almost certainly Tone (and Taunton) and Tweed, too. A similar group is formed by the three rivers, Leven, Lancs, Leaven, Yorks, and Levant, S.W. Sussex, all from W. *llev*, which likewise means 'smooth'; but these English Levens can hardly have the same origin as the many Levens (*q.v.*) of Scotland. As for the rest of our Keltic river names, many of them are very hard to explain, and a good many may remain for ever insoluble, their history has been so completely lost. Only a few English river names—Ribble, *e.g.*—can confidently be claimed as evidence of the certainly widespread river-worship of our Keltic ancestors. What there is to say will best be noted in our chapter on Wales. Rivers like the Lug, a case in point, are common to both.

If the meaning of our river names be often difficult to unravel, we are in a far worse plight about many of the names of our most conspicuous hills and mountains, largely because in so many cases we have no early record of the spelling, and so we have been delivered over to much guesswork, more or less sober. Nobody, *e.g.*, seems to know where the name Pennines came from, and about such an attractive name as Helvellyn we can only make guesses. But, as with the rivers so with the heights, many of our Keltic hill names either mean simply 'height,' or else are compounds including that. *E.g.*, the W. *mynydd*, 'hill,' may crop up alone in Mint, Westmorland, and Munet, Salop,[1] but it is surer in compounds, such as Long-mynd, Ok-ment Hill (Devon), and Stad-ment (Hereford). Brean, on the Somerset coast, is but the plural of W. *bre*, 'a hill, a brae'; and the Northumberland Carrick, like its Scottish and Irish kindred, means simply an outstanding rock, whilst Tor in Torbay and Torquay, Cat Tor, etc., is another word for 'a (tower-like) hill.'

There are two places called simply Penn, which is W. for 'head, height,' very common in Cornwall too. This *penn* in combination recurs in numerous cases from Cumberland to Worcester and Somerset. The Chevin, Yorks, is a manifest corruption of W. *cefn*, 'a ridge'; whilst the Peak of Derbyshire is one of our very oldest names, and almost undoubtedly British, though, curiously enough, we can only make shots at its

---

[1] On the Forest of Dean Mcends, see Baddeley, *Gloucestersh.*, app. iii. See also Mindton.

meaning. The inquirer ought to consult the *Oxford Dictionary*, *s.v.* Names in England (not in Scotland) with the prefix Dun- are almost always Saxon, not Keltic; but we get the Keltic or W. form in Dinmore Hill, Hereford, W. *din mawr*, 'big hill,' whilst Dinder, Wilts, is apparently *din dwr*, 'hill by the river.' *Moel*, the W. for 'a bold, conical hill,' G. *maol*, is very common in W. hill names; but we probably see it also in the Cumberland Millbreak, 'speckled hill,' and in MALVERN, 'hill of alders,' whilst the Lickey Hills near by do but give us the W. *llechau*, pl. of *llech*, 'a rock, a stone.' Pure Welsh hill names have seldom survived amongst English shires, but there is one con- spicuous exception in PENNYGANT, a name of many modern, but few or no ancient, spellings, representing either *penn y gwant*, 'height of the butt or mark,' or *y gwynt*, 'of the winds.' The well-known Somerset Quantocks yield us a very interesting name. In an old charter long before the Conquest they are spelt Cantuc, in *Dom.* Cantoche, which is at once decipherable as W. *cant uch*, 'upper, higher circle.'

As to valleys, we have several examples of the Keltic *glen* in Northumberland, and at least one, GLENCOIN, in Cumberland. Besides it is now generally admitted that the common English *combe* is a loan-word from the W. *cwm*, 'a hollow'; and this last is still to be seen in quite a group of names in Cumberland. Unfortunately, in this former home of the Brythons, surviving evidence, dating before the twelfth century, is exceedingly scanty. Indeed the only Cumberland Cum- which seems to be known early is CUMDIVOCK, found in one of the very few early charters, *c.* 1080, as Combedeyfoch. The prefix here certainly wears its English form, but the name seems pure Keltic none the less. We cannot identify deyfoch with any English root. Except Cumcatch ('valley of Cæcca'), and probably Cumwhitton, all the rest of the Cums- appear Keltic— Cumlongan, Cumrangan, Cumraw, Cumwhin-ton, and the rest.

On our sea-coast the after-coming and more sea-loving Saxon and Norseman have allowed the Kelt to leave little mark. Of inlets of any consequence with Keltic names there are very few, the chief exceptions being the HUMBER, which must be an aspirated form of Cumber, W: *cymmer*, 'a confluence,' and the SOLENT, another difficult name, though probably con- taining the Keltic *sol*, 'tide.' Morecambe Bay is plainly a reproduction of Ptolemy's Μορικάμβη, but the name seems to have appeared, or reappeared, quite recently, and must be due to the antiquaries, a very rare state of matters with a place-name.

When now we proceed to town and village names, we do find a considerable number indisputably Keltic, but not nearly so many as has commonly been thought. Still, a few of the very greatest names in England, both in Church and State, are Keltic, not Teutonic: LONDON, to begin with, and York and Carlisle, with Jarrow and Truro a little less notable; great travellers' rendezvous also like Dover and Crewe, as well as Carlisle and York, whilst ancient dwelling-places like DORCHESTER and LIN-COLN are half Keltic, half Roman (or Saxon). There has been a good deal of debate about several of these names, not least about London, which, through its commercially commanding site, is probably the oldest, whilst still the greatest, of British cities. These debatable names will be found fully discussed under their proper headings. YORK looks very English in its present shape, but it is nothing else than a Saxon re-spelling of a Keltic Eburach. Lincoln is often associated with *lindens*, but, as it is as old as the second century at least, the Lin- must be Keltic. DOVER, with its cognates CONDOVER, Salop, and DOVERCOURT, Harwich, is a very interesting name, being simply British for ' water ' or ' channel of water,' W. *dwfr*, G. *dobhar*, the true British sound being still preserved for us by our French neighbours, who call it Douvre(s).

Apart from the sporadic names just cited, Keltic towns and village names occur in any considerable numbers only in ten counties: Northumberland, Cumberland, Lancashire, Cheshire, Salop, Hereford, Monmouth, Somerset, Dorset, and Cornwall; Durham, York, and Devon have strangely few, all things considered; whilst several counties, like Westmorland, Rutland, Norfolk, Suffolk, Cambridge, Huntingdon and Hertford, seem to have practically no sure Keltic names at all. This is so far as the present writer has noted. Only, for present purposes, he has seldom found it possible to go beyond the ordinary good atlases and books of reference, the Postal Guide and Bradshaw. Cheshire he has specially investigated, and for this reason probably he has found there more Keltic town and village names than in any other shire (except, of course, Monmouth and Cornwall), about twenty-two in all; not a very large number wherewith to head the list, and several of these are too insignificant to find place in any ordinary map or gazetteer. Next come Cumberland with eighteen, and Salop and Hereford with sixteen; but a minute investigation would certainly produce more in these last cases. Dorset, it is remarkable, has at least seven. Only on the Welsh border and in Cumberland do we find names of the regular W. or Keltic type—names like CARDURNOCK or PENRUDDOCK, Cumberland; Bettws y Crwyn, GOBOWEN, Trefonen, or Buildwas in Salop; and Pontrilas or Rhiwlas in Hereford.

But more interesting, and always surrounded with some perplexity, even doubt, are the solitary names which occur, like islets in the ocean, in purely English regions—names like PENGE (Surrey), WENDOVER (Bucks), QUEMER-ford (Wilts), or YALE (Derby). It is difficult to account for such isolated survivals from the old British days, except where the names embody a river, as is the case with Wendover and Quemer-ford, this last being W. *cymmer*, 'confluence,' the same name as the well-known Quimper in Bretagne. The number of still remaining Keltic names in Somerset and Dorset indicates a long and not altogether unsuccessful struggle of Briton against Saxon.

The O.W. and G. *lann*, mod. W. *llan*, Corn. *lan*, cognate with our own Eng. *land*, occurs, as is well known, a good many times on the English side of the Welsh border. Its original meaning is 'a level spot,' then 'an enclosure,' then 'a sacred enclosure, a church-yard,' and then, as it usually is to-day, 'a church'; just as the common G. *cille* or *cil*, so frequent in Scottish and Irish names in Kil-, means 'graveyard' before it means 'church,' though in this case the *cille* comes from L. *cella*, 'a chamber,' and then 'a (monk's) cell.' In England this *cille* is found perhaps only in KYL-OE in the extreme North. The earliest recorded English Lan- seems to be Lantocal (*B.C.S.* 47), in a charter which is dated 680. It is described as near Ferramere, a place unknown. It *may be* the same name as Landicle, Cornwall, 'church of St. Tecla.' The only Lan- in Domesday seems to be Landican, West Cheshire, which is possibly W. *llan diacon*, 'church of the deacon,' though it is not now a parish church. Crockford's Directory gives only Llandecwyn, Carnarvon. Of the soft *ll* or *thl* there is no trace till long afterwards. But there are at least five regular *llans* in Hereford. Elsewhere there seems only one, Llanymynech, Salop, ' church of the monk ' (L. *monachus*). There is also in Hereford a spurious Llan- (a modern notion, countenanced by His Majesty's Post-Office), Llangrove, Ross, which all old spellings, as well as its present appearance, prove to be neither more nor less than Long Grove !

The names of our English counties also present a large pre-Saxon element, often with a Latin ending, as, *e.g.*, Glou-cester, Lan-caster, Lei-cester, Lin-coln, Wor-cester, and even the simple Chester or Cheshire; more rarely with a Saxon ending, as in Corn-wall and Dor-set, Mon-mouth and War-wick. Not seldom, however, the shire name is pure British, as in York, Kent, and Devon, whilst fair claim for a Keltic origin may also be put in for BERKS and WILTS, as well as for both Ox-ford and CAM-bridge. Thus, out of the forty shires, only twenty-three have names clearly post-Keltic in their ancestry, a very noteworthy fact. The origin of several of our shire names is highly disputable; they will be found discussed as far as possible under their proper headings.

Considering that England and Scotland were peopled at first by the same two Keltic races, the Goidel and the Brython, it is surprising how few Keltic place-names are common to both. Of town and village names there are all but none. There is a Crewe near Granton, Edinburgh, but it seems modern. There is a Currie, Midlothian, as well as a Curry, Somerset. Press, Coldingham (Berwickshire), is very near to Prees, Salop, and Clun, Salop, is very near to the common Scottish Clunie. There is a Troon, Camborne (Cornwall), in addition to the well-known golfing resort on the Ayrshire coast; and the puzzling name BLYTH occurs both N. and S. of the border; so does Glass (Glass Houghton, as well as Glass, Huntly). But Ross, while a town name in England, is name of no town in Scotland. Aught else worth mentioning there appeareth not. With river names, of course, it is quite diffcrent. We have Adder, Allen, Alt, and Avon, all common to both; so, too, are Dee, Don, Douglas, Eden, Esk, and Leven, and perhaps others; whilst the Scots R. DEVON is considered to have the same origin as that of the English shire.

PROVISIONAL LIST OF KELTIC PLACE-NAMES IN ENGLAND.

(Monmouth and Cornwall excluded.   Names before the line in each county are natural features ; names after it towns and villages.)

NORTHUMBERLAND.

Allen.
Alne.
Alwyn.
Amble (?).
Blyth (?).
Breamish (?).
Carrick.
Carter (Fell).
Cheviots.
Glen, R.
Glencune.
Glendhu.
Glenwhelt.
Kielder.
Kinkry Hill.
Lindisfarne.
Till.
Tippalt (Burn).
Tweed.
Tyne.
Usway-ford.

Amble (?).
Cambo.
Cambois.
Carvoran.
Kyl-oe.
Mindrum.
Ogle.
(East) Ord.
Pressen.

CUMBERLAND.

Alne or Ellen, R.
Croglin.
Derwent.
Eden.
Esk.

Gelt.
Glaramara.
Glencoin.
Glenderamackin.
Helvellyn.
Irt.
Irthing.
Mellbreak.
Old Man (?).
Wampool.

Arrad (Foot).
Blencow.
Cardurnock.
Carlisle.
Carnarvon.
(Castle) Carrock.
Culgaith.
Cumdivock.
Cumrangan.
Cumran-ton.
Cumrew.
Cumwhin-ton.
Durdar.
Lasket.
Lindeth.
Pelutho.
Penrith (?).
Penruddock.
Ravenglass.

WESTMORLAND.

Lowther.
Winster.

Mint (?).
Pendragon (Castle).

DURHAM.

Fendrith Hill.
Tees.

Coundon.
Jarrow.
Pencher.

LANCASHIRE.

Alt, R.
Darwen.
Douglas.
Duddon.
Glaze-brook (?).
Hesketh (?).
Hodder.
Irwell.
Leven.
Lune.
Morecambe (Bay).
Pendle (Hill).
Ribble (?).
Wyre (?).

Cart-mell.
Colne.
Darwen.
Manchester.
Penketh.
Penwortham.
Preese.
Roose.
Treales.
Werneth.
Wigan (?).

YORKSHIRE.

The Chevin.
Derwent.
Don.
Gorple Water.
Hodder.
Humber.
Ouse.
Pennines (?).
Pennygent.
Pinnar (Pike).
Ure.
Whern-side.

Alne.
Crayke.
Glass (Houghton).
Nidd.
Rathmell.
Roos.
Thirsk (?).
York.

CHESHIRE.

Biddle.
Bollin.
Cat Tor.
Croco.
Dane or Daven.
Dee.
Duddon.
Etherow.
Gowy.
(Knolton) Bryn.
Mowl (Cop).
Walwern.
Weaver (?).
Wheelock.

Carden.
Carlett.
Condate.
Crewe.
Daven-port.
Duddon.
Frith.
Ince.

Kerridge.
Lach Dennis.
Landican.
Leese.
Liscard.
Macefen.
Pettypool.
Rowarth.
Tallarn Green.
Tarvin (?).
Tidnock.
Tor-side.
Wervin.
Wincle (?).

LINCOLN.

Glen, R.
Witham.

Kyme.
Lin-coln.

DERBY.

Bull (Gap).
Derwent.
Erewash (?).
Noe.
Ock Brook.
Winster.

Crich.
Pentrich.
Yale.

STAFFORD.

Barr (Beacon).
Blythe (?).
Churnet.
Ocker (Hill).
Stour.
Tame.
Tean.
Trent.
Weaver (Hills) (?).

Bre-wood.
Cannock.

(Great) Barr.
Hints.
Keele.
Mon-more.
Morfe.
Onn (High and Little).
Penkhull.
Penkridge.
Pensnett.
Ridware.
Talke.
Trysull.

SALOP.

Caradoc.
Ceiriog.
Longmynd.
Ouny.
Roden.
Severn.
Teme.
Wrekin.

Bettws-y-Crwyn.
Buildwas Abbey.
Clun.
Clungun-ford.
Condover.
Gobowen.
Hints.
Kinver (Forest).
Knockin.
Llanymynech.
Munet' (?).
Myddle (?).
Prees.
Trefonen.
Wem (?).
Wenlock.

NOTTS.

Devon.
Dover-beck.
Leen.
Mann or Maun.
Soar.

LEICESTER.
Bar-don Hill.

Glen (Magna).

RUTLAND.
Guash (?).

NORFOLK.
Ant.
Ouse.
Tass.
Waveney.
Wilney (?).
Yare.

Trunch.

CAMBRIDGE.
Cam or Granta.
Kennet.

Tydd (?).

HUNTS.

NORTHANTS.
Ise, R. (?).
Nen.

WARWICK.
Alne.
Arrow (?).

Coundon.
Crick.

WORCESTER.
Dover-dale.
Dur-bridge.
Gladder Brook.
Lickey Hills.

Corse Lawn (?).
Kyre.

Malvern.
Mamble.
Mathon.
Pencrick-et.
Pendock.
Pensax.
Pinwin.
Rhyd y Groes.
Tump.

HEREFORD.
Dinmore (Hill).
Howle (Hill).
Lugg.
Wye.

Dilwyn.
Ewyas.
Foy.
Llancillo.
Llanfaino or -veynoc.
Llangarron.
Llanwarne.
Llowes.
Madley.
Pencoyd.
Pencraig.
Pontrilas.
Rhiwlas.
Ross.
Stadment.
Trumpet.

SUFFOLK.
Alde.
Blyth (?).
Deben.

BEDFORD.

BUCKS.

Chet-wode.
Kimble (?).
Wendover.

OXFORD.
Chilterns (?).
Isis.
Thame.
Thames.
Windrush.

GLOUCESTER.
An dover-ford.
Bream.
Carant.
Cam.
Churn.
Doverle.
Leaden.
Sarn-hill.

Dymock (?).
Glou-cester.
Lancaut.
Meon.
Newent (?).
Penpole.
Tump.
Turk-dene.

ESSEX.
Ouse.
Pent.
Roding.
Writtle.

Chich St. Osyth.

HERTS.
Colne.
Rib (?).
Ver (?).

MIDDLESEX.
Brent.

London.

BERKS.

Kennet.
Kimber.
Loddon (?).
Ock.
Thames.

Bedwin (?).

KENT.

Inlade.
Kent.
Limen.
Medway.
Stour.
Teise.
Thanet.

Appledore (?).
Dover.
Lynne or Lymne.

SURREY.

Wandle (?).
Wey.

Penge.

SUSSEX.

Arun.
Dove.
Levant.
Ouse.

HANTS.

Anton.
Avon.
Boldre.
Exe.

Hamble (?).
Meon.
Solent.
Test or Tees.
Wight (Isle of).
Yar.

Andover.
Burgh(clere).
Cendover (?).
Chute (Standen).

WILTS.

Adder or Adur.
Avon.
Wiley.

Calne.
Knook.
Knoyle.
Quemer-ford.

DORSET.

Allen.
Brit.
Cerne.
Divelish.
Stour.
Tillywhim (Caves).

Creech.
Dewlish.
Dor-chester.
Pensel-wood.
Pentridge.
Pimp-erne.
Warminster (?).
Winfrith.

SOMERSET.

Axe.
Brean.

Brue.
Carey.
Creech Hill.
Frome.
Mendips.
Parret.
Quantocks.
Tone.

Badcox.
Chilcott (?).
Creech (St. Michael).
Curry.
Dunster ?
(East and West)
    Chinnock.
Frome.
Kenn.
Pennard.
Wookey.

DEVON.

Axe.
Creedy.
Exe.
Lewdown.
Lid.
Lundy I.
Okment (Hill).
Plym.
Tamar.
Taw.
Teign.
Torridge.

Appledore (?).
Clovelly.
Clyst.
Dawlish.
Quither.
Tor-quay.

POSSIBLE PRE-KELTIC NAMES.

Awre.	Croco, R.	Sow, R. (2).
Biddle, R.	Etherow, R.	Stour, R.
Blythe.	Itchen, R. (2).	Teign, R.
Bollin, R.	Ithon, R.	Trent, R.
Cheviots.	Kennet, R.	Wrekin.
Cole, R.	Meon.	Writtle, R.
Colne, R.	Severn, R.	

Etc.

CHAPTER IV

THE ENGLISH ELEMENT

THIS is, out of sight, *the* element in the place-names of South Britain, but it will be needless to tread again the well-trod path of early English history. We only need to repeat for the sake of the place-name student a bare skeleton of facts and dates to furnish a little clearness and coherence to his thoughts. As everybody knows, the Teutonic races of Middle Europe, who gradually swarmed over to our England, were chiefly three in number—Jutes, Angles, and Saxons. To these we must add a fourth race closely allied to the Saxons, the Frisians of Holland, all the way from the Scheldt to the Ems and Weser in N.W. Germany; probably our own nearest kinsmen by blood. For, 'Good butter and good cheese is good English and good Friese.' Herdsmen, husbandmen, traders, and also sea-rovers were these our special ancestors; and it was the piratical raids of the Frisians that first brought the Teuton to our shores, which were just opposite their own. It was in A.D. 287. Soon after their inconvenient attentions became so serious that the Romans, still in power in this island, had to appoint a 'Count of the Saxon Shore' (*comes litoris Saxonici*) to superintend and insure their repulse. None, however, settled down on our shores so early as that. When they first did so we do not know. Skene thought it was very early, probably before the traditional date, 449. Frisians certainly may already have reached Lothian before 500.[1]

By A.D. 410 the last of the Romans had left us, but the native Brython was not allowed long to enjoy his native land to himself. In 449—there need be little doubt about the date

---

[1] For examples of Frisian names see DEARNE, FAWLEY, NAR, RYDE, TIRLE, WHISTLEY, WISKE, etc. Skeat finds clear traces of a Frisian settlement in Suffolk.

—the first Teutonic invaders with any intention of becoming settlers appeared off the coast of Kent—Jutes from Holstein in the S. of Denmark. A little later these same Jutes also settled down in the Isle of Wight and part of Hants. We cannot tarry over these dim bands, because we hardly know what exactly their speech or dialect was, and we can point to almost no definite trace of their influence. Though we may conjecture with at least some probability that one or two names, like BAPCHILD and HONEYCHILD in Kent, and BON-CHURCH, Isle of Wight, may have had a Jutish origin.

Next came the Saxons (L. *Saxons*, Ger. *Sachsen*, the High-lander's *Sassenach*, or Englishmen), a race first named by Ptolemy in the far E. of Europe, but already located on either bank of the Elbe when they made their first spring across the North Sea, and landed in 477 on the shore of what was ever after called SUSSEX, or South Saxon land. The first arrival of the third set of invaders of our isle, the Angles, the men who succeeded in giving their own name to all ENGLAND, is an event which cannot now be precisely dated. But probably before 540 they had landed in East Anglia, sailing over from that district of Holstein, which seems to have been called Angul because it was shaped like an ' angle ' or fish-hook. The king-dom of East Anglia was afterwards split into the ' North folk ' or ' South folk.' This last name, however, does not emerge till 1076, after the Norman Conquest, whilst the shire name Norfolk is first found in Domesday. But the great region of the Angle was in the North, from Humber right up to Forth; and by 547 we find Ida as Anglian King of this Northumbria or North-humber-land. The original Anglian speech is now best represented by Lowland Scots and by the burr of the Northumberland miner. Before 1400 the same tongue was heard all the way from Hull to Aberdeen. But distinctively Anglian elements cannot be said to be prominent anywhere in our names.

In 577 Ceawlin, King of Wessex or of the West Saxons, won the Battle of Dyrham (Gloucester), and so became master of the lower Severn—*i.e.*, of Gloucester and of part of Somerset and Dorset. Thus early was the much weaker Brython driven out of his home even so far West. Æthelfrith of Northumbria, who sat his throne from 593-617, defeated the Brythons, or

Welsh, and the Scots at Chester, and so added from Dee to
Ribble to the sway of the Anglian sceptre. Then, after a long
interval, the great Offa of Mercia, 757-796, makes Shrewsbury
an English, no longer a Welsh, town, drives the Welsh out of
the mid-Severn valley, and builds a dyke from the mouth of
the Dee South to the mouth of the Wye. This is the district of
England where the Welshman's tongue is still required oftenest
to interpret the place-names. Not till 924 did King Edward
the Elder, son of Alfred the Great, and his successor as King
of England, become ' father and lord ' over Cumbria and
Strathclyde.

When the Brython remained so long in power in the North-
West, we do not wonder that true English names are few in
Cumberland, and we do wonder that he has left so few place-
names in N. Lancashire. Twelve years later than the English
lordship over Cumbria, Athelstan, King of Wessex and Mercia,
succeeded in absorbing Cornwall. But linguistically that far
Western ' horn ' was hardly absorbed at all, and to this hour
purely English names are very rare in Cornwall. By 936, then,
all modern England was nominally English, except Monmouthshire, which is practically Welsh still. We may therefore
affirm with some confidence that our real English place-names,
except the few demonstrably medieval or modern, grew up
between the sixth or seventh and the tenth century.

The vast majority of our names of any consequence are
as old as Domesday Book, whilst our contemporary charter
evidence goes back in some cases to the end of the seventh
century. Kemble, Birch, Napier, and Stevenson have printed
for us a great store of O.E. charters, which yield us most
valuable, and often unmutilated, forms for about the whole of
the S.E. half of England, the N. and W. limits running
round by Warwick, Stafford, and Gloucester. Pre-Domesday
charters N. and W. thereof are, alas ! more than rare. Domesday Book itself is a complete survey of most of England, its
manors and villages, made by order of William the Conqueror
in 1086-87, and is a wonderful standby. But it is very
unfortunate that we have no *Dom.* for Monmouth, except a
scrap, or for any part N. of Yorks in the E. The S. part of
Lancashire is given under Cheshire, whilst N. Lancashire
and the barony of Kendal, Westmorland, come under

Yorks. For the rest *Dom.* wholly fails. Exon Domesday is
a special transcript of the record for Wilts, Dorset, Somerset,
Devon, and Cornwall, with slight variations. Domesday is a
priceless document. The pity is that any proper index to it
is still so inaccessible even in many of our best libraries.

Domesday, in some ways, reads strangely modern. Here
we find, to a most surprising extent, the same names and landmarks, the same manors, parishes, and homesteads, as we do
to-day. The analysis of Sir Henry Ellis, in his laborious *Intro-
duction to Domesday*, also shows that there were in William the
Conqueror's time about 1,400 tenants in chief, including
ecclesiastical owners, and of under tenants 7,871. Of these
last a surprisingly large proportion are Saxon, not Norman.
Thus it is that we find so few names of Norman lords embedded
in the names of our towns to-day. The vanquished has been
more enduring than the victor; the Saxon, like the Sicilian,
absorbed the Norman. Domesday also records some 1,700
churches, whose distribution seems passing strange; the record
cannot be complete, for it gives 364 in Suffolk, 243 in Norfolk,
222 in Lincoln, but only 1 in Cambs, and none in Middlesex
or Lancashire. Of all these 1,700 Domesday churches there
is no proof that any one existed in England before the English
arrived, unless we except LANDICAN, which is just on the Welsh
border of Cheshire, and a few in Cornwall.

As to the spelling of Domesday, it will help the searcher much
to remember that Domesday has no *j*, *v*, or *y*;[1] that it almost
always has *ch* for *k*; that initial *th* is almost always written *t*,
and medial *th* always *d*; whilst the Domesday scribes hate all
gutturals, *h*, *ch*, *gh*, and very often boldly change them into *st*,
a fact which yields the clue to many a puzzle, as we shall find
passim. The truth is, the Norman could not himself pronounce
gutturals, nor did he find *sh* easy either, and so he usually
writes plain *s*, or else as often he prefixes an *e*. The Norman
knew very little of the English tongue and much disliked it,
and so his English spelling is often inaccurate. Still he had
rules of his own, as we have been trying to tell, and these rules
once mastered, much of the seeming inaccuracy disappears.
Thus it is quite according to rule that we have in Domesday
cherche or chirche, and not *kirk*, and Chingeslei instead of

---

[1] In these cases he will look instead for *ge, i, u,* or *w*.

Kingsley; *torp* and not *thorpe*, Torentun not Thornton; *orde* or *vrde* always instead of the common ending -worth; Liste-corne instead of LIGHTHORNE ('thorn-tree with the light hung on it'), and Bristoldestune for BRIGHTWALTON ('Beorhtwald's town'); Sorewell for Shorwell, Escafelt for SHEFFIELD, and Eseldebourne for SHALBOURNE.

The Norman scribe has his common errors, too—*e.g.*, the putting of *ll* for *ld*, especially in -field—Gamesfille for GANFIELD, Licefelle for LICHFIELD, etc. More rarely we have *ll* for *dl*, as in Celle for Cedle—*i.e.*, CHEADLE. Other little peculiarities the regular student discovers by degrees for himself. But, we must repeat, on the whole in Domesday we have the same names as to-day. A map of Domesday's England would show the parishes, manors, and landmarks much the same as we find them to-day. How very different it would be were the map one of eleventh-century Germany or France!

There is no Domesday for Durham, but the lack is considerably alleviated by the Boldon Book, a survey of the See of Durham made in 1183, which gives us all the town and village names of Co. Durham, and a good many in Northumberland, only a century later than Domesday. For this latter county we have also a good many references in the Coldingham (Berwickshire) charters, which begin but a very few years after Domesday. The copious nomenclature of Simeon, monk of Durham (d. 1130), also does much to atone for the failure of the Conqueror's Survey to reach the farthest north. For Cumberland and Westmorland we are particularly badly off, except for the Kendal district. Their record is poorer even than that of most of the Scottish counties, where as a rule we are far worse off for early records than in England. For N.W. England we have little till we come to the Pipe Rolls (enrolled accounts of the sheriffs, etc.) of the latter half of the twelfth century, and they mention but a handful of the place-names.

But once we get well into the twelfth century we find great masses of evidence of all sorts waiting for examination. A good inkling of the variety of available evidence may be got by glancing at such a laborious and scholarly compendium as Wyld and Hirst's *Place-Names of Lancashire*. But a serious difficulty about using the place-name forms found in our O.E. charters is the corrupt and illiterate spelling in which so many

of them are found, especially if they date after A.D. 1000. We
have already noted that anything in the way of peculiarly
Anglian or Northumbrian forms is rare. But the difference
between Mercian and Wessex forms is pretty considerable.
Classic O.E. is the Wessex speech of the time of Alfred the
Great, *c.* A.D. 900—the speech then spoken all the way from
Kent to Devon. It is according to this classic Wessex tongue
that our O.E. dictionaries are arranged; so are all the spellings
in Searle's laborious *Onomasticon*, or manual of O.E. personal
names.

But many of our charters are Mercian—*i.e.*, they belong to
what was once the central Saxon kingdom of England, the
kingdom of Offa, and the rest. The many charters quoted
by Duignan in his valuable books on Stafford, Warwick, and
Worcester are all Mercian. The Mercian district stretched
from Ribble to Bristol Channel, and from Humber to Thames;
Suffolk names, *e.g.*, are distinctly Mercian. Remains of true
Mercian before the Norman Conquest are rare, and until
quite recent years their idiosyncrasies were little studied or
understood. A brief but valuable statement thereanent will
be found in Skeat's *Our English Dialects*, 1911, chap. viii., and
a study of the parallel lists on pp. 71, 72 will be found helpful.
We there see in special that the Mercian was inclined to dis-
pense with those diphthongs of which the West Saxon was so
fond. He said *eall*, the old Mercian said *all*, even as we do at
this day. The Wessex man said *sceap*, the Mercian *scep*,
which we have softened into *sheep*. In Wessex they said *geoc*,
in Mercia *ioc*, which we have made into *yoke*. The Wessex
scribe wrote *gyrd*, the Mercian *ierd*, we write *yard*. Such things
need to be borne in mind when we are hunting through the
O.E. dictionary to trace the meaning of a Mercian charter
name, and it will easily be seen that the spelling of many a personal name becomes much shorter than we find it in Searle's
classically spelt *Onomasticon*. The Beorhtwealds and Earn-
beorns and Heathubeorhts get clipped down into Berthold
and Arnbiorn and Eadbert, and even into forms still shorter
and less easy to recognize.

The student will thus perceive that the careful study of
place-names at least helps, though not a great deal, in the
study of our English dialects. Names at times take the regular

dialect forms, as in Zeal Monachorum (Devon) or Zoy (Somerset), where we have the regular West Country *z* instead of the normal *s* ; or as in the Gloucester Yatton, ' town at the *yat* ' (*cf.* Simmon's Yat), called in the North *yett*—*i.e.*, ' town at the gate, or opening, or pass.'

The Kelt had a long start of the Englishman, and had ample time and occasion to give names to all the great natural features of the land. Thus, as we already know, all our chief rivers still bear Keltic or pre-Keltic names. But minor rivers, much more numerous than is generally supposed, bear purely English names, some of them very interesting. Here is a rough list of the chief, one or two a little doubtful: Anker, Bure, Coquet, Dearne (S. Yorks), Eamont, Ember, Harris (Yorks), Idle, Irk (S. Lancs), Ivel, Lark, Leam, Linnet (Suffolk, ' a play name '), Lyme, Manifold (Staffs), Mite, Ousel, Ray, Rea, Rede, Rye (Yorks), Soar, Stort, Swift, Waver, Wythburn. To take the first three only by way of illustration, Anker is a unique name of its sort, and commemorates the dwelling of *ancres*, or female anchorites, at Nun-eaton. The Bure is possibly Frisian in name, its root the same as O.E. *borian*, to bore, Sc. *bure* and Du. *boor*, an auger; while the Coquet is the Coc-wuda or ' cock wood ' of the very old history of St. Cuthbert. England has few mountains, a good many hills. As is but natural, most of these have Keltic names, though one has always to be on guard against traps. INKPEN BEACON, S. Berks, *e.g.*, looks very like a tautology, with English beacon (O.E. *bécn, beácen*) = W. *penn*. But it is not so, for Inkpen is ' Inga's pen ' or sheep-fold, just as Inkberrow, Worcester, is pure English for ' Inta's hill.' Beacon we find again several times, as in Worcestershire Beacon, etc. The regular O.E. word for ' a hill,' and then ' fort on a hill '—most hills once had their forts—is *dún*, seen in ' the Downs,' and in a good many names like Dunham, Dunmow, etc. *Hill* itself, in the Midlands *hull*, is good English from the earliest times; but the common endings for ' hill,' like ' fell ' and ' pike,' are generally Norse; -ridge is half and half. Pure English are such curious names as Harrison STICKLE, and all the BARROWS and Berrows and Brows, as in BERRY BROW; so likewise the Tippings, Roseberry, Blackham, etc., Tipping, in the E. Riding.

The English influence on our nomenclature may perhaps best be studied further in connection with the common endings, detailed in our chapter on Endings (p. 46). We there learn how many of our names once described a lea or meadow (-ley, -leigh), how many a meadow by a river (' a holm '), how many a ' haugh,' or flat land by a river (O.E. *healh*, dative *hale*, ' a corner, a nook '), found in hundreds of names now as -hall; though this has nothing to do with our modern English *hall*. But we must beware of concluding too hastily that any name with an English-looking ending must be English; -dale and -holm look English enough, but will often, the former perhaps always, be found to be Norse. Very common is -mere, ' a lake '—ten times in Cheshire alone—often now -mer, as in Cromer, Dunmer, Walmer, etc.; while the -mere may be attached to a non-English name, as in WINDERMERE; and nowadays in the south the mere has generally disappeared, altogether drained long ago. The endings -grave and -barrow often survive to tell of an old place of sepulture—Belgrave, Gargrave, etc.—whilst -or and -over are also common, representing two distinct O.E. words, *ora* and *ofr*, both meaning ' bank, edge, shore.' CUMNOR is the former, *e.g.*, and HADSOR the latter. The *ofr* often gets clipped down into -er, as in HASLER, WOOLER, etc.

There is almost no commoner ending than -ford, showing the extreme importance of the ford in the early bridgeless days. Ford and caster are much the commonest endings in Bede, whilst names in -bridge are very rare before the Norman Conquest. Among the very few exceptions are BRIDGENORTH and QUATBRIDGE, (Salop), and CAMBRIDGE, found in O.E. Chron., 875, as Grantebrycge. Agbrigg (S. Yorks), Sawbridge (Daventry), Bridgford (Staffs), and Slimbridge (Glo'ster), are already in Domesday, but not many more. In shires like Berkshire and Cheshire there are no early names in *bridge* at all.

The origin and boundary-making of the shires with English names has not yet been fully worked out; but this much is clear: that the five great Danish boroughs—Derby, Leicester, Nottingham, Lincoln, and Northampton—and the districts around them which ' obeyed ' them, as the Chronicle often says, formed the nucleus of the five modern counties with these names. Similar Danish influence organized Hunts, Cambridge,

Bedford, and Herts. 'Each of these counties had a *jarl*, or
earl, whose headquarters were at the "borough."' Thus
most of the counties in old Mercia shaped themselves naturally
rather than 'artificially,' as Freeman puts it. In Wessex the
counties still retain the names of the princedoms founded by
the successors of Cerdic. In some of them there was no outstanding borough, and even though the shire may contain a
town of the same name, it was seldom called directly after that
borough. 'Local divisions in Wessex were not made, but
grew.'

When we come to town and village names, by far the most
important item in our répertoire, we find that they are over-
whelmingly English, and, for the most part, tell us over and
over again, with aggravating monotony, how that an Englishman's house was and is his castle. To understand this group
of names, one must first master what has to be said about
-burgh or -bury, about the two -hams, about -ton (always interchanging with -don and -stone), and about their compound
HAMPTON, all of which originally implied an enclosure, probably always at first fortified or capable of defence. One must
also learn about -ing which gives a tail as well as a tale to
so many English names, and is not by any means always a
patronymic. Thence we learn that the overwhelming majority of our place-names teach us simply that this was So-and-
so's town or home. The chances always are that the first part
of an English town or village name denotes the name of some
man or woman, its founder or former owner. WOLVERHAMP-
TON has nothing to do with wolves, but with the Lady Wulf-
runa. CHILLINGHAM has nothing to do with 'chilly,' but with
a man *Cilla*, just as CARDINGTON is from a man *Carda*, and
SUNNINGHILL is 'hill of the Sunnings.' A good many town
and village names indicate their stance upon a river—names
like Cheltenham, 'home on the Chelt'; Chorley, 'meadow on
the Chor'; Crediton, 'town on the Creedy'—though it is always
to be remembered that the present names of rivers and brooks
are often back formations, and that Chelt and Creedy may
have originally been names of men. In like manner, Pin is
but a recent back-formation from PINNER, Rom from
ROMFORD, Yeo from YEOVIL, as well as Chelmer from
CHELMSFORD.

Our great business, then, in connection with most names, really is to find out what man's name is therein denoted or included. Here some such guide as Searle's *Onomasticon* is indispensable, to be used, of course, after learning the phonetic lessons already insisted on. Searle took enormous pains to render his work as complete as possible, and yet the investigator is for ever finding how incomplete it still is. A run through any part of our list will soon show this. To take one example, Searle gives no name Elk or Elc, and yet we find two Elkstones, which make it extremely likely that Elk must have been a proper as well as a common noun. Many cases are more certain than this; *e.g.*, the old forms of that puzzling-looking Cambs name BABRAHAM make it certain there must once have been a woman called Badburh, though Searle knoweth her not. He gives us no Beorc, but it is certain that Birch was very early the name of a man as well as the name of a tree (see BARKING and BARKLEY). It would be easy to multiply such examples indefinitely.

The way in which O.E. proper names have become distorted or corrupted is very extraordinary, though Dr. Skeat always insisted that everything moved and worked according to phonetic law; so that even such a desperate change as SEACOURT, Berks, for ' Seofeca's worth,' or farm, was shown to be all correct ! Though names like that are indeed a warning against all rash attempts to guess without evidence. Not far from Seacourt is Courage, and Courage is really ' Cusa's ridge ' ! And who would ever think that Ellastone, Staffs, was originally ' Æthelac's town '; that Shareshill in the same shire was once ' Sceorf's hill '; or Stramshall once ' Stranglic's hill '; or that ABERFORD, ADDERBURY, and HARBURY all embody the one protean name Eadburh ? It has always to be borne in mind, also, that two villages with the same title to-day may have been derived from two quite different names yesterday. The very first names in our List show us how wary we need to be. ABBERLEY actually was born as ' Eadbeald's lea,' whilst Abberton, in the same shire, was at first ' Eadbeorht's town,' and its modern twin near Colchester comes from a woman Eadburh. Even more extraordinary is it to find that such a name as ADBASTON, Salop, came originally from the same man's name as Abberley.

But the disappointing thing is, that when, after much patient labour, we do find out the correct personal name embalmed or embodied in the place-name, that is nearly always all we get for our pains. *Stat nominis umbra*. The Saxon, unlike the more modest and poetic Kelt, dearly loved to commemorate himself, or, at any rate, his own family name, in a manor or farm or village. But, in a few generations, the history of the name is totally forgotten, and posterity can tell naught thereof. Only in a very few cases can we tell the story of the lord or lady, the abbot or monk, founder or name-giver, to the place. MALMESBURY, TEWKESBURY, WOLVERHAMPTON, are such cases; there are not many altogether. Kingly names, like those of the great Alfreds, Edwards, and Harolds, are, strange to say, scarcely represented at all. It is interesting to note, however, how often very old personal names, first found in some out-of-the-way place-name, still survive, and are in use to-day. Examples are—the personal name Gammell or Gemmel, found in GANTHORPE, Domesday Gameltorp; Gentle or Gentles, in Gentleshaw, Rugeley, where a Jo. Gentyl is known in 1341; Gilling in Gillingham, 1016 Gillingaham; Gould or Gold in Goldsborough, Domesday Goldeburg; and so on.

Some of our simple names, names of towns and hamlets, not called after any princess or thane or any other person, are extremely common. Few can be aware how common some of them are; here are some calculations which have been made: There are in England, it is said, 87 Newtons (47 in combination, 40 alone), not reckoning Newtowns; 72 Suttons (36 in combination, exactly half); 63 Stokes; 52 Westons (also exactly half in combination); 47 Thorps (26 in combination); Walton, Upton, and Stone occur over thirty times each; there are 21 Kirbys and 21 Leighs; and Hutton, Kingston, and Thornton are very common too.

Seebohm, in his *English Village Community* (1883), p. 362, speaks of 'the hasty conclusion that the Saxons were totemists.' Yet not a little evidence *seems* at least to point that way. It is certain that many a village was called after the name of a beast—boar, lamb, ox, sheep, whale, wolf, etc. The only question is, Was the beast's name first applied to a man before it became applied to the village? (See such names as EVERTHORPE and EVERTON, WHALLEY, etc.)

Of modern whimsical names, like Four Throws, Hawkhurst, or Besses o' th' Barn and ¦Clock Face (Lancs), England has singularly few—fewer far, in proportion, than Wales.

The Common Element.

Before we proceed to the study of the second great Teutonic element in our place-names, the Scandinavian, it will be interesting and instructive to remind ourselves how large is the element common not only to our Norse and purely English names, but common also to our Continental neighbours in the homes of our ancestors. At least a few of our name-endings may have originated either on Saxon or on Scandinavian lips—*e.g.*, the common -thorpe and -hope; but when careful scrutiny is made, -thorpe will be found almost always Danish, and -hope almost always pure English. Thorpe is, of course, the cognate of the German *dorf*, 'village,' as in Düsseldorf, Waldorf, etc., found in Schleswig in the form Gottorp, and in Dutch as Apel-dorp, Leydendorp, etc., though -dorp is not nearly so common as our English -thorpe; in S. Africa, however, it is common enough—Krugersdorp, etc. *Holm* may come from either branch too; but if it mean 'a meadow,' it will probably be English, whilst if it mean 'a flat island,' just as in Bornholm, Saltholm, and many another such name in Denmark, it will be Danish.

One of our commonest endings is -burgh or -bury; it is just as common both in Germany and Scandinavia. In Germany it is usually -burg, as in Hamburg, Magdeburg, and scores of other cases. In Denmark it may be -burg, as in Flensburg, or -borg, as in Viborg; and -borg is as common all over Sweden and Norway. In Holland it is -burg, as in Doesburg, Elburg, etc.; or else -berg, as in Geertruidenberg, 's Heeringberg, etc. In Norse names, -ham, 'home,' is not so common as in England; but we have well-known cases like Stal-heim and Trond-hjem. In Sweden it appears as Lofta-hammer,[1] Sand-hammer, etc. (Icel. *heim-r*, 'village'). In Germany the ending -heim is exceedingly common—Hildesheim, Mannheim, etc.; in Holland we have a few places ending as in England—*e.g.*, Den-ham (Overyssel), as well as names like Arn-hem, Deutic-hem,

---

[1] Some hold that here *hammer* means a square-shaped rock.

etc. Names like Denham suggest a Frisian origin for our common -ham.

The common English -stead is, of course, even commoner in Germany as -stadt, where it is one of the most frequent endings for ' town '; as -stadt it is almost equally prominent in Scandinavia and Dutch S. Africa, though hardly so in the Dutch motherland. The specially frequent English -ton does not seem represented on the Continent; but the less common and often intermingled -stone is very conspicuous on the map of Germany as -stein — Ehrenbreitstein, Oberlahnstein, etc. Havens are naturally common in most Teutonic lands—Bremerhaven, Cuxhaven, etc., in Germany; Kjöbnhavn (Copenhagen), Frederikshavn, etc., in Denmark; in Sweden it is often -hamn (Icel. *höfn*), as in Slitehamn, Soderhamn, etc.; but in Holland it occurs, though rarely, as with ourselves— Brouwershaven, etc. Holland, perhaps alone, gives us a counterpart of the common English -wick or -wich, ' dwelling,' as in Harder-wijk, Steen-wijk, etc.; but if -kirk is common in N. England, names like Nijkerk or Neukirch are common alike in Holland and Germany; whilst the similar North of England -dale is common everywhere in Scandinavia as -dal, and in Germany as -thal, ' valley '—Neanderthal, etc. England has only one firth, that of Solway; but the common Norse -fjord reappears in Wales as Haver-ford, Milford, etc. The ending -by in England vies for frequency with -ton; and it certainly is represented abroad, especially in Sweden. In the one little island of Öland there are five marked on an ordinary map. (See also CHIPPING, etc.)

CHAPTER V

THE SCANDINAVIAN ELEMENT

In England, as in Scotland, the Scandinavian element is not only important, but obtrusive. To-day Denmark, Sweden, and Norway are each separate kingdoms, with separate languages, though these are closely akin, and, to a large extent, mutually understandable. But in the days when our place-names were in the making, practically the same tongue was spoken all over Scandinavia, in Iceland and the Faroes too. The dictionary which we need chiefly to consult is the Icelandic, which is, to all intents and purposes, Old Norse; though sometimes it is modern Danish which yields the most helpful forms for our exegesis. We commonly call the people who spake this tongue Norsemen; the Old English chroniclers mostly call them Danes; whilst, when they went away south and settled on the north coast of France, or far away in Sicily, we generally find them called Northmen or Normans. Need, hunger, lust for booty and adventure, and the scantness of their arable fields at home, combined to drive these hardy sea-lovers wide and far. And, though they always came at first with coat of mail and battle-axe, often they speedily settled down among us, and made admirable colonists, diligent practitioners in the arts and crafts of peace.

Into all the details of the Viking's many invasions of England, Wales, and Man we need not go again. The student can easily learn what he wants in the proper histories. Here, for our purposes, we need give but the barest outline of facts and dates. The first Danish invasion might, perhaps, be termed that of the coming of the Jutes to Kent in 449. But it is at least doubtful if these Jutes ever lived in Jutland; and, in any case, they were, in blood and speech, much nearer to the Angle and Saxon than the Norse. When the first Viking beached his boat on English sand we do not know; but men from the Hardanger landed near Dorchester in the reign of Beorhtric of Wessex, 786-802; and the first dated invasion is the sacking of Lindisfarne, in the extreme north, in 793. Vikings were very fond of sacking monasteries and seizing their sacred spoils, as many a Columban monk to his cost did find; and, having come once, they oft came again.

Glamorgan saw them in 795, and rocky little Iona in 802; whilst already by 830 they had paid visits as far away as Cornwall. Before 850 they had overrun East Anglia (Norfolk and Suffolk), whilst in 855 Danes first wintered in Sheppey. Stronger and stronger they grew in our midst, as sore-pressed King Alfred was made to feel. But by-and-by the tide turned, and in 886 Alfred made his well-known treaty with Guthrun, King of the Danes. In it the boundary between English and Danish rule was agreed to be, the R. Thames from its source east to the source of the R. Lea, then north-west to Bedford, and up the R. Ouse to the Roman Watling Street, and so by it probably west all the way to Chester. All north of this line was the Dane's, all south thereof Alfred's. The latter, be it noted, held Chester. Had the Danes held it, it would have been called Caster to-day (see p. 49). In 954 the English overthrew the Dane's rule in Deira (Yorks), whilst, be it carefully noted, Cumbria and Bernicia (Northumberland and Durham) never really came under Danish dominion at all.

It is well known that this rule revived again in England under King Swegen, who came from Norway with a huge fleet and army, 1013-14, and reigned here for one year only. Then, after three years of strife, great King Cnut was able to seat himself on England's throne for eighteen years, and Danish influence was strong among us, though Cnut thought it wise to send the bulk of his Danish troops back to the lands from whence they came. Cnut was succeeded by the two brothers, Harold Harefoot and Harthacnut. With the death of the latter in 1042, the Danish sceptre passed for ever from our midst. We may add, St. Clement Danes was the church of a large Danish settlement in London, of whom we are told by Ralph de Diceto.[1]

Such are the bare facts which the annalist tells: of battle

[1] Vol. i., p. 186, ed. Stubbs.

and bloodshed much, but of the actual nature of the Danish settlement very little. Here the study of place-names comes in to offer at least some help. What it has to say about Wales will be found on pp. 71 and 72. To begin with, we find that Norse names are often strangely rare where the Norseman was once only too attentive, in the ancient kingdom of Bernicia e.g., from Tyne to Forth. In all Northumberland we can set eyes on the merest handful of Norse names. LUCKER is sure, BRINKBURN and NEW-BIGGIN-BY-THE-SEA are probable. On the Borders we have a number of 'fells'—Carter, Fairwood, Girdle, and Peel Fells; but as a rule it is only the 'fell' which is Norse, not the rest of the name. There are a rare -gill or two, and a few dales—Allendale, etc.—but that is all.

On the other hand, place-names clearly show Danish settlement where there never was Danish rule—viz., in Cumbria proper (Cumberland and Westmorland), which simply teems with names Danish rather than Norse, of all sorts; perhaps the Danes first came over from their little kingdom in the Isle of Man. In Cumbria, Dane and Gael or Brython must have been in close contact for many a day; and occasionally the Scandinavian borrowed a word from the Kelt. The best-known instance is the G. *airigh*, 'a shieling, a shepherd's or herdsman's hut,' which the incomers shaped into -argh, -ark, or -ergh, as in ARKLID and PAVEY ARK, SIZERGH (Kendal), and as far south as GRIMSARGH, Preston. Final -gh in Gaelic is now generally mute, but it does at times become guttural. The purely Scandinavian endings -beck, -by, -fell, -force (*fors*, 'waterfall'), -gill, -thorpe, -thwaite, are found everywhere in this region; it would be superfluous to give examples. Moreover, some of these are almost or quite peculiar to it and to the closely neighbouring parts—*e.g.*, -beck, -fell, -force, -gill, -thwaite. This would seem to indicate that some special division of the Scandinavian race must have been the settlers here. Yet it is very difficult for us now to say which or what it was, because, as we have seen, Old Norse was so largely a homogeneous language. Sweden, at any rate, may be ruled out. Runes show that some Swedes did settle in England, but only as individuals, never in force; and, as for the rest, medieval chroniclers never seem to know any difference between *Dani* and *Nordmanni*. (It is usually held, however, that East

Anglia and the region of the five boroughs—Derby, Leicester,
Lincoln, Nottingham, and Northampton—were peculiarly
Danish).

An ending like -beck occurs farther south as -bach or
even -beach, only now as English; and -force, it may be said,
is so rare in the south, because waterfalls are so rare there
too; the same reason might, perhaps, be urged as to -fell.
But why should an ending like -gill be confined almost, though
not altogether, to the north ?   And, even more singular, why
should -thwaite—' an enclosed or cut-off piece of land '—
never seemingly be found farther south or east[1] than the
neighbourhood of Huddersfield ?   All we can say is, the many
-thwaites in such a hilly, rocky land as Cumberland is very
fair proof that the Danish settlers there as a rule must have
been, not blood-thirsty pirates, but peaceful and most industrious peasants, eager to make the best of things, just like their
Norse kinsmen to-day.

Another thing indicated by our surviving place-names is
this: that Scandinavian influence in England remained strong
enough to give and establish many names long after the Danish
sceptre had fallen down; and that means a good deal.   In proof
of this, we point to such facts as these: that in Cheshire to-day
we can still find at least fifteen Norse names; but of these only
four seem to be found in Domesday, compiled 1086-87.   This
seems to show that a good many of these fifteen names did not
come into being until a good while after the Norman Conquest.
In Cambs, which has curiously few Danish names, out of the
five given by Skeat, four are in Domesday; and, what is noteworthy, one of these four, STAINE, has clearly been renamed
by Danish lips, *after* Domesday.   Duignan has not worked out
the Norse influence in his books on Stafford and Warwick, and
it is stronger in N.E. Staffs and in Warwick than his readers
might think.   We have traced eight clear cases in Staffs and
about eleven in Warwick; six of the Staffs cases are in Domesday, in Warwick three, whilst other two are found in O.E.
charters; but RUGBY and Monk's Kirby have been altered by
Danish tongues after Domesday.

On the other hand, whilst history distinctly tells of Viking
visits to Cornwall in the middle of the ninth century, one could

[1] But EASTWOOD, Notts, used to be Easthwaite.

scarcely have guessed it from the present-day names of that peninsula. This is all the more curious seeing that Norse names are so common on the south coast of Wales. All over the south coast of England, however, such names are very rare, until we come round east to Kent. There seems one curious exception in BONCHURCH, Isle of Wight (Domesday, Bonecerce), which must surely tell of some Norse landing; or can it be a real old Jute name ? In Kent Norse names re-appear sparsely. We have two or three -gills, and two well-known -nesses, though it is possible that both DUNGENESS and SHEERNESS may be pure English. NORE is Norse, clear enough ('a bay with a narrow entrance'); and then there are the names in -child, to which M'Clure has called pointed atten-tion, especially BAPCHILD, found in O.E. Chron., 694, as Baccan celde or 'Bacca's well.' This is interestingly, even pro-vokingly, early. But the -child of Bapchild must be the same as the common ending -keld (O.N. kelda) in the north—Salkeld ('salt spring'), Threlkeld, etc. This, strange to tell, is also the root of St. Kilda, which, as is now well known, is no saint's name at all. In a Kentish charter of 858 we also find a Hwyte Celda, or 'white well'; and there is still in Romney Marsh a HONEYCHILD ('honey-sweet well'). Such names may well be claimed for the Norsemen; and reference to the Jutes, who arrived in Kent in the fifth century, seems hardly in place, because, so far as we know, the Jute speech was English in type, not Norse. So, then, there were Norse settlers in Kent c. 694, of whom we have no direct historic record. With them we may venture to associate the men who named the few sur-viving 'gills' in Surrey and Sussex—Gill's lop, Heron's Ghyll, etc.

When we come to survey as a whole the surviving evidence of the presence of the 'hardy Norseman' in our midst, we find that it corresponds nearly, but by no means quite, with what we should expect from the historic evidence. The Danelagh, or that region of England where Danish law did rule, is said to have comprised at its widest all the shires from Yorks south to Essex, Beds, Herts, and Bucks, and west to Notts, Derby, Leicester, and Northants. Now, Worsaae, in his *Danes in England*, estimated that of 1,373 Danish names in all, over 400 are in Yorks, 292 in Lincoln, 90 in Leicester; in Norfolk and Northants about 50 each. These are all Danelagh shires. But Cumberland and Westmorland have about 150 each too, and Lancashire, he says, about 50. But Mr. Sephton has, much more recently, estimated the Scandinavian names in Lancs at about 90. What he says is, that of 500 Lancs names on record before 1500, about 80 per cent. are Low German, 18 per cent. Scandinavian, and only 2 per cent. Keltic. Worsaae estimated that 14 other counties had 130 Danish names between them, and 18 counties none at all; or, to put it otherwise, about 1,000 of our Danish names lie within the old Danelagh, and only about 400 outside.

So far as Yorkshire is concerned, mark and sign of the Dane, in place-name ending, is so ample that it would be a superfluity to dwell upon it. The same is true of Lincoln, most Scandinavian of all our shires, though little Rutland is very Danish too. As we come south, however, the mark and sign grow less clear, and in Hunts, Beds, Cambs, and Herts the trace is very slight indeed. The most useful endings to take as guides or clues are -bie or -by, -caster, and -thorpe, and perhaps -toft. The ending -by, signifying simply 'a house, dwelling, or little settlement,' is ubiquitous. In Lincoln alone we find it 212 times; in Norfolk there is quite a cluster round Great Yarmouth, the cluster extending as far as Barnaby, south of Lowestoft, in Suffolk; in the rest of Suffolk sign of Dane is rare to see.[1] But -by holds on along the coast as far south as Kirby Cross and Kirby-le-Soken, near Walton-on-the-Naze, Essex. Then it seems to disappear, and not to emerge again until we reach the many inlets of Pembroke. Inland, -by ranges south to Badby, south of Daventry (Northants), and west to Rugby (Warwick)—a shire not reckoned in the Danelagh. But, common though the ending be, there is not a single specimen in Cambs or in any of the southmost counties of the Danelagh, which shows how brief and shallow Danish influence there must have been. At the Danes' northern limit, Co. Durham, -by is said to occur four times, no more.

The ending-caster is also somewhat of a guide to the Dane's presence, but by no means one so sure or serviceable as -by. Norse tongues alone preserved the Roman hard c in *castrum* or *castra*. On the lips of the Saxon, aided by the Norman, the

---

[1] But *cf.* THINGOE, etc.

c has always softened into -cester or -chester. *E.g.*, the form
is always -chester even in Durham (Chester-le-Street, etc.) and
Northumberland (the Chesters, Hexham, etc.). But in Cumberland we find the form to be Mun-caster; in Lancashire, Lancaster itself; in Yorks, Don-caster; in Lincoln, An-caster; and,
as far south as the north-west corner of Norfolk, we have one
example in Bran-caster. But, as showing that Danish influence
was far from all-powerful, even in its own territories, we have
such well-known names as Lei-cester, Chester-field, and Manchester, as well as Rib-chester, north-east of Preston. The
ending -thorpe is also interesting and instructive to work with.
Many would say that *thorpe* is quite an English word, and no
sure token of Danish residence at all. But, as the *Oxford Dictionary* will show, *thorpe* in any form is a very rare word in older
English; and, in any case, the true English form is *trop* or
throp, found in place-names in almost purely English quarters;
only, very rarely. We have, *e.g.*, Adlestrop, Chipping Norton,
Pindrup, Upthrup, Westrip, and Wolstrop, all in Gloucester,
and Staindrop (' stone-built village ') in S. Durham; also at
least once in Yorks, Wilstrop; besides, we have Thrupp both
in mid-Oxford and S. Northants; and we have a Throope
away down beside Christchurch, Hants. We have Thorpes,
too, where any other Danish forms are very uncommon—*e.g.*,
Thorpe Thowles, north of Stockton-on-Tees; Thorpe-le-Soken,
Essex; Thorpe Morieux, Bury St. Edmunds; and plain
Thorpe, Leiston, Suffolk. But the only Thorpe in the *Postal
Guide*, which is in a distinctly English district, is Thorpe,
Chertsey. We thus are pretty safe in taking -thorpe as a mark
of the Dane. It is particularly common in Yorks and Lincs
(there are sixty-three in all), and quite common in Norfolk;
but as an ending it is very rare south thereof. Its other
southern[1] and also its western limit seems to be Eathorpe,
Leamington, another proof of Danish influence outside the
Danelagh; and we have Thorpe Constantine near Tamworth.
Not so common an ending as -thorpe is -toft (' homestead '),
though common enough in Yorks and Lincs. In five cases it
stands alone, and it occurs not only in the most Danish parts

---

[1] But also note, Upthorpe, Hunts, which seems to have been
Upeforde in *Dom.* Astrope (Herts), ' East Thorpe,' gives us the English,
not the Scandinavian, form.

of the Danelagh, but also in Cambs and Suffolk, and in un-Danish Durham, in Toft Hill, Bishop Auckland.

In Wales the Viking has left his permanent stamp on many a bit of the coast; not so in England, because it is conspicuous for its absence of bays and fjords, unless it be in Essex and Cornwall. To Sheerness, Nore, and Dungeness in the south-east we have already referred. There seems little else in the way of name with Danish cast upon our seashore, until you reach the very Borders, where SOLWAY FIRTH is a doubly Norse name. The name Solway, though it has been much disputed, is almost certainly the O.N. *söl-vag-r* ('muddy bay,') the ending being often paralleled in Scotland (in Stornoway, Scalloway, etc.) Some of the many nesses or headlands between Lincoln and Kent—Skegness, Winterton Ness (Norfolk), the Naze, etc.— *may* have been named by the Vikings, but perhaps not in a single case is this certain—not even SKEGNESS, which is a tautology, Skeg- being O.N. and -ness O.E. for 'headland.' One should perhaps refer here also to such a name as AIRMYN, near the mouth of the Yorks Ouse, which is 'mouth of the R. Aire' (also a N. name), from O.N. *munn-r*, 'mouth.' On the north coast of Scotland *goe* (O.N. *gjá*, 'gap, cleft') is very common. In smooth-shored England we seem to have none, though inland, near Carlisle, there stands Cargo (? 'rock-gap'); but old forms are needed here. It may well be 'Carig's hoe' or 'how.'

The chief mountain ending which comes to us from a Norse source is -fell, very common in the south of Scotland for a ' bare ridge, a stretch of waste hill land,' and no less common on the Borders in Northumberland, Cumberland, and Westmorland, and down as far as Littledale Fell, south-east of Lancaster. Beyond that *fell* does not seem to go.

Of rivers in England with Scandinavian names we have but few. River-names, as we have found, are usually very ancient, and are 'sweer,' as the Scots say, to change their names. There are, or were, in England, at least three rivers called Fleet; the London one has now disappeared. And Fleet might be O.N. *fljót* as well as O.E. *fleót*, 'river, stream,' in either case the root idea being 'fleet, swift.' But probably all three, as well as Fleetwood, Lancs, are not Norse; Fleet, Hants, certainly is not. However, we do have a few clearly Danish-named streams—the Aire, Greta, and Wharfe, in Yorks; the

Mease and Tern, in Staffs; and there may be others. The names just mentioned will each be found explained *s.v.* The old fords on our rivers far oftener show sign of Danish visitors than the rivers themselves. When this is so the Danish tongues have softened *ford* into *forth*—a very common ending in Cumbria and Yorks—but also found farther south, as in Handforth, N. Cheshire, and even at Forth End, Chelmsford; whilst Marlingford, Norwich, was Marlingforth as late as 1482.

The chief Scandinavian endings not yet fully commented on are -beck and -with, found together with another character-istic ending -shaw, in Beckwithshaw, Harrogate, a hybrid name, where O.E. *scaga* is = Norse *with*, 'a wood.' The Scan-dinavian -beck is very close to the English -bach, and runs into it in S. Lincs (see *s.v.* -beck). Becks, or 'brooks,' are common in the north-west, whilst in Durham we have Harwood Beck and Beechburn Beck. WANSBECK, the only one in Northum-berland, is a modern corruption. South of Lincoln they are not found. The ending -with (O.N. *við-r*, Dan. *ved.*, 'a wood ') is common in Yorks, as in Askwith, of course the same name as that of our present Prime Minister and of our peerless arbi-trator; also in Beckwith and Skipwith (which occurs again in S.E. Cumberland); yet even in very Danish Lincoln it now occurs but once, though it may recur in, or rather, there *may* have been similar Danish influence in, CHARNWOOD Forest, Leicester; *c.* 1165 Charnewid.

Clear traces of Scandinavian mythology in our nomenclature are not frequent. Thor, the brave thunder-god, and Odin, ruler of heaven and earth, are commemorated often enough. But *Thor* in our place-names seems generally found originally in its Saxon form *Thunor*, as it certainly is in Thundersley, and as it probably is in all names in Thur-: THURLEIGH, THUR-LOW, etc. Similarly, *Odin* is found in our names perhaps only in his Saxon or Teutonic form Wodin (also Waden, Weden; in Simeon of Durham, however, Othan); but in this shape it occurs frequently. Names of ordinary Norsemen crop up continually, especially in names ending in -by north of the Trent. The names in Butter-, like BUTTERMERE, probably conceal or reveal a good many cases of Norse settlement. We may even find a Norseman in WINDERMERE too, as well as in— to take, for example, a group at the end of O- — Osbournby,

Osgathorpe, Osgodby, Osmotherley ('meadow of Osmund-r '!), Oughtrington ('town of Authgrim-r '!). In such places the Norsemen's names have become greatly disguised and distorted—twisted, indeed, almost out of recognition—by tongues which knew not the men or the race which owned the names. GAMSTON and GANTHORPE, both from Gamel ('gamle Norge '!), are other interesting cases in point; so is Gothersley, for 'Goodrich's lea '; and the subject has by no means been fully worked out yet.

ROUGH LIST OF SCANDINAVIAN NAMES IN THE SHIRES WHERE THEY ARE NOT FREQUENT.

CAMBRIDGE.—Bourne, Brink-ley, Carl-ton, Staine, Toft.

CHESHIRE.—Ayre (Point of), Chad-kirk, Frankby, Greasby, Helsby, ? Helstry, Irby, Kirby West, Ness, Pensby, Quoysley, Raby, Thing-well, Toft Hall, Whitby.

DURHAM.—Butterby, ? Newbiggin, (Pontop and West) Pike, Raby, Roker, Tantobie, Toft (Hill), Wasker-ley.

NORTHUMBERLAND.—Brink-burn, Lucker, New-biggin-by-the-Sea; also the endings -dale, -fell, and -gill in several names each.

STAFFORD.—Carr, Cheadle, Crake-marsh, Leek, Tern R., Thorpe (Constantine), Uttoxeter, Yarlett.

WARWICK.—Biggin (2), Brinklow, (Monk's) Kirby, Prinsthorpe, Rugby, ? Tardebigge, Toft, Wibtoft, Willoughby.

WORCESTER.—Clent, ? Hag-ley, ? Sme-ster.

CHAPTER VI

THE ENDINGS

In the case of English place-names a knowledge of the endings is quite half the battle; and so we now set forth the chief of these in some detail. The student will find this section well worth mastering. He should first consult the Abbreviations, p. 87.

-age is a rare and always puzzling ending, often not a true ending at all. In WANTAGE, *e.g.*, it seems quite modern, whilst in BURBAGE the ending is really -bage, modern form of O.E. *bece*, ' brook.' The sequence is -beck, -back, -bach, -batch, -baitch, -bage; and all these forms are found represented among our names and their pronunciations. In COCKNAGE and STEVENAGE the -age is O.E. *h)æcce*, ' hatch '; whilst SWANAGE is O.E. Swanawic, ' swan's haunt '; and BROOMAGE, Larbert, Scotland, is 1458 Bruminche, or ' broom, gorse links,' or ' meadow.' CRANAGE may be like Swanage, ' crane's abode,' but CRESSAGE seems to be ' crest edge.'

-ay, -ea, -ey, -y.—These all represent, though -y only sometimes, the O.E. *íg*, ' island '; *íg* is Wessex, the Anglian and O. Mercian is *ég*, in M.E. *-ei*, *-ey*, from O.E. *éa*, ' stream, river, brook '; so that the root idea is ' watery place,' not only an island, but a peninsula—as often, Selsea, Bawdsey (Hollesley Bay), etc.—or any place surrounded with brooks or streams, or even a marshy place. Most places now with this ending can never have been true islands. Berks, *e.g.*, has nine examples; and we not only have the Isle of ANGLESEA (O.E. Chron. Angles ege), but also an Anglesea Priory, Cambs. Places like Pevensea,

Swansea, etc., are also cases in point. In the north -ey
may be the O.N. *ey*, Dan. *oe*, with the same meaning
But few English names in -ey are certainly Norse. The
ending -y certainly sometimes represents 'island,' as in
Lundy Island; and Skeat gives Coveny and Wendy in
Cambs, but he refused ELY, Bede's Elge, or 'district'
not 'island of eels;' *ge* being rare O.E. = Ger. *gau*,
what Bede calls 'regio.' In Marrick, *Dom.* Marige,
N. Yorks, -ige has seemingly hardened into -ick; this
is rare.

-bach, -beach, -beck.—O.N. *bekk-r*, Sw. *bäck*, 'a brook, a stream.'
Not in Northumberland, where WANSBECK is a recent corruption of Wannys pike; but we have a 'Bolebec,' in 1157
Pipe Roll, Northumberland. It is found still, however, in
Durham, in some tributaries of the Wear, where we even
have a Beechburn Beck! It is common in Cumbria and
Yorks—Holme Beck, Troutbeck, etc.—but perhaps not
farther south than Lincs. One of the most southerly is
PINCHBECK, Spalding; but as that is already found in an
810 *charter* Pyncebek, the -beck here is probably the O.E.
bece or *bœc*, found in this same charter in Holebech or
Holbeach, in the same district, with the same meaning.
Bach, also bache, and -batch, is a regular dialect name for
'brook,' common especially in Cheshire—Bache, COM-
BERBATCH, Sandbach, etc.; whilst in *Dom.* we have here
a Bachelie. The O.N. gen. of *beck*—viz., *bekkjar*—is
found in the two BECKERMETS, 'mouth of the brook';
whilst, as we noted above, BURBAGE is, in 961, Burhbece.

-borne, -bourne, -burn.—This last is now only northern, but all
three are forms of O.E. *burna, burne, burn*, O.N. *brunn-r*,
originally 'a spring, a fountain,' then 'a brook, a rivulet.'
In Northumberland -burn is common, as in Scotland,
Hartburn, Otterburn, Warkburn, etc.; in Cumberland it
is rarer—Greensburn, near the Border, etc. Tributaries of
the Wear vary between -burn and -beck; south thereof
-burn ceases, and -borne or -bourne becomes common
nearly everywhere. In old spellings in Berks, Cambs, etc.,
we have -burn or -burne, but not now. In Mary-le-*bone*,
London, the *r* of bourne has vanished.

-boro', -borough, -burgh, -bury, all variants of O.E. *burӡ, burh,* 2[1]
bure(g)h, beriӡ, 3 *buri,* 3—4 *borh, boru* (for other forms
see *Oxford Dictionary*), ' an enclosed or fortified town '
(or village), rather than a simple fort or castle like
dún, though *cf. c.* 820 *Kent. Gloss.,* ' ad arcem, to burӡe.'
The ending is very common all over, especially as -bury;
-burgh, so common in Scotland, is rare in England; even in
the north it is rather -borough—Bamborough, Flamborough, Middlesborough, etc. But we have Burgh-on-
Sands, on the Solway, pron.[2] Bruff, and Burgh, E. Lincs.
The ending has come down to -ber in BRAMBER (*cf. harbour*
and its forms in *Oxford Dictionary*). The northern ending
-bergh, as in Caldbergh, Sedbergh, etc., is not from -burgh,
but is a variant of BARROW. But FARNBOROUGH at least
three times in *Dom.* ends in -berg(e; and in Denmark
to-day we have -berg, -borg, and -burg all representing our
burgh. On the other hand, Crowborough, Leek, is *c.* 1300,
Crowbarwe, perhaps dative of O.E. *bearu,* ' a wood '; and
Hillborough, Warwick, is, in 710, Hildeburhwrthe, ' farm
of Hildeburga.'

-by, -bie.—North. O.E. *bý,* probably adoption of O.N. *bœ-r,*
bý-r, Sw. and Dan. *by,* ' dwelling, village,' from O.N. *búa,*
' to dwell,' same root as in North. *big,* ' to build.' Mawer,
Vikings, p. 124, says it indicates Dan. rather than Norse
settlement; but this contradicts his own statement (p. 11)
that Northumbria was Norwegian; and Yorks is crammed
with -bys. However, there are only four north of Tees—
Butterby, Durham, being one of the northmost—and
there are none in Northumberland. We get the *bœ-r* form
in Canisbay and Duncansbay, Caithness, but not in England. The ending runs as far south as Badby and Kilsby,
south of Rugby. There are none in Cambs or Herts, but
there are several in Norfolk and Suffolk round the mouth
of the Yare, and we have Kirby Cross and Kirby-le-Soken
in N.E. Essex. There is also a Laghenbia, in *Dom.*
Essex, ? where. There are at least eight in Cheshire, but
perhaps none in the west to the south of Cheshire. The

---

[1] The meaning of these figures is explained at the end of the
Abbreviations.

[2] Pronounced.   (See Abbreviations.)

ending reappears in Jersey—Hougie Bie, 'dwelling on the mound.'

-caster, -cester, -chester.—L. *castrum, castra,* ' a camp, a fortification '; not always a proof of Roman work, though, along with *-ford, -ceaster* is the commonest of all the endings in our earliest historian Bede. Outside the Danelagh the *c* usually softened into *ch,* or from hard *c* to soft. Thus we get many -chesters even in the north—CHESTERFIELD (1165 still Cestrefelt), MANCHESTER (1421 still Mamecestre), and even RIBCHESTER, north-east of Preston. Yorks is full of -casters; and we even have Muncaster, in Danish Cumberland; but in Durham and Northumberland the form is always -chester—Binchester, Ebchester, and Rochester (Northumberland). The hard -caster comes as far south as Brancaster (King's Lynn), a very Danish locality, but not farther; Warwick has none. The form -cester occurs rarely within the Danelagh, as in LEICESTER, and is the regular form in the more southern parts— BICESTER, CIRENCESTER, GLOUCESTER, WORCESTER, etc.— all these cited being much more contracted on modern lips. O.E. *ceaster* has also become -xeter = cseter, as in EXETER and WROXETER (this form seems late), but not UTTOXETER. Once we find the ending as -cetter, in MANCETTER, Atherstone. (On the origin of the O.E. forms, see CAISTOR.)

-comb, -combe.—Common also in Cumberland as a prefix—Cumdivock, -rangan, -ranton, -whinton, etc.—or separately, as in Combe Down, Combe Florey, Combe Martin, etc. The proximate root is O.E. *cumb,* ' a hollow thing '; hence ' a bowl,' and then ' a (deep) valley ' or ' a hollow in the flank of a hill.' In origin it is probably Keltic, and cognate with W. *cwm,* ' a hollow.' As suffix, it is found chiefly in the south, especially in Somerset, Dorset, and Devon—in the first commonest of all. In Berks there are four, in Cambs none, in Warwick only Walcombe (no old forms), in Cheshire only Seacombe, which is at least as old as the days of Henry VI.; there is also Holcombe, near Manchester; and the suffix reappears in the north in Cumberland, Gillercombe, and Glaramara and Langdale Combes, etc.; also at least once in Durham, Escomb (Bishop Auck-

land). But in the north one must be careful to differen-
tiate from coom *sb*[2] (*Oxford Dictionary*), ' a domelike hill,'
of uncertain origin, as in Black Combe, White Combe, and
Hen Comb, Cumberland, and Comb Fell and Combhill,
Northumberland. SACOMBE, Herts, is a corruption, being
Sueuechamp in *Dom.*

-dale.—O.E. *dæl*, or, perhaps nearly always in old names, O.N.
dal-r, ' a dale,' the root meaning being probably ' deep,
low place ' (*cf.* Gothic *dalath*, ' down.'). Found from the
Scottish Border south to Derbyshire, but much commoner
in the north, where Norse influence was strong, and there
usually ' a river-valley between hills, a glen '—Allendale,
Borrowdale, Ennerdale, etc. The southmost instances
seem to be Darley Dale, Matlock, and Coalbrookdale,
S. Salop. The simple Dale recurs in Pembroke, a very
Norse locality; but -dales farther south, like Begdale,
Cambs, Skeat looked on as merely modern—*e.g.*, also Sun-
ningdale, Berks, a recent coinage, suggested by the ancient
Sunninghill near by. A pure English southern instance is
Doverdale, Droitwich, in 706 Dourdale, 817 Doferdæl.
Rarely -dale becomes -dle, as in CHEADLE; and once at
least it has been corrupted from -hale, ' nook ' (see -hall)—
in Dinsdale, Yorks, *Dom.* Digneshale—unless *Dom.* be in-
correct.

-dean, -den, -dene.—These suffixes usually stand for O.E. *denu,*
' a valley,' same root as *den*(*n*), ' a den.' A ' dean ' now
generally is a valley deep, narrow, wooded. The suffix
occurs all over Great Britain; -dene is rare and southern
(*cf.* North Denes, Great Yarmouth). O.E. *den*(*n*), or *dœn,*
means not only ' den, cave, lair,' but ' woodland pasture
for swine,' seen in Denford, Berks, and perhaps in Forest
of Dean. The suffixes -den and -dean are continually
interchanging with -don or -dune, as in Basilden or -don,
Burdon, *c.* 1130 Byrdene, Croxden, 1237 Crokesdun, Eversden or -don, Morden, *c.* 1080 Mordune, Yattenden or
-don, etc. Sometimes the -den may have an entirely
different origin, and be a part of -warden, *q.v.*, as in
CARDEN, HAWARDEN, etc.

-er (see *-or, -over*).

-et (see BARNET, COQUET, FARCET, HODNET, etc.).

-fell.—O.N. *fiall*, Dan. *fjeld*, ' a mountain, a hill,' also in north
of England, ' a wild stretch of waste hill land, a moorland
ridge.' In either case the name is found only from the
Northumberland Border through Cumberland and Westmorland, south to Littledale Fells, south-east of Lancaster; perhaps not elsewhere.

-ford, -forth.—One of the commonest, widest-spread, and
earliest of our suffixes, a ford being such an important point
in early days, when bridges were rare or non-existent.
In Bede -ford and -ceaster are the commonest of all endings. It is O.E. *ford*, from the common Teutonic root *far*,
' to go '; it is cognate with L. *port-us*, ' harbour,' and W.
rhyd, O.W. *rit.*, ' ford '; also with O.N. *fiorð-r* or *fjord*.[1]
Probably it is to Norse influence we owe the soft form
-forth so common in the north; examples in un-Scandina-
vian districts are rare; but note Gosforth, north of Newcastle, Marlingford, Norwich, 1482 Marlyngforth, and
Forth End, Chelmsford, probably all due to Norse tongues.
The *Postal Guide* has four places simply called Ford; in
Cheshire we have seven fords—five already in *Dom. ;* in
Cambs, eight—seven in *Dom. ;* in Berks, no less than
eighteen, all dating from Saxon days, though only eight
seem in *Dom.* Duignan gives twenty-six -fords in Warwick, nearly all very old, and at least fourteen as old as
Dom. But the ending has its traps; especially does -ford
tend to replace -worth, as in Duxford and Pampisford,
Cambs, Beeford, Driffield, Whiteford, Bromsgrove (*Dom.*
Witeurde), Offord, Warwick, etc. (see those names). Boxford, Berks, was originally Boxore, ' box-tree bank ' or
' shore.' In Devon -ford is asserted to stand as a rule for
W. *ffordd*, ' road, passage '; in Stirlingshire -ford, which is
fairly common, never stands for what we now call ' a ford.'
McClure, p. 242, has a useful note on the different kinds
of -ford, those whose names tell their nature—Mudford,
Sandford, Stamford, etc.; those which tell what animals
used them—Oxford, Shefford (' sheep-ford '), etc.; those
which tell what kind of helps you will find there—Bam-
forth (' beam ford '), Stafford, etc.

[1] Sometimes -ford directly represents *fjord*, as in HAVERFORD, MIL-
FORD, ORFORD.

-gill.—O.N. *gil, geil,* ' a deep glen.' *Oxford Dictionary* does not class this with ' fish *gill,*' as is often done.   In later English it comes to mean ' a narrow stream, a rivulet,' but in names it usually signifies ' a narrow, slit-like glen or opening.' Rare in Northumberland, it is fairly common elsewhere in the north—Bullgill, Dallowgill, Ivegill, Lowgill, Ramsgill, etc.—and especially common around Grasmere.   *Gill* is also used in the dialects of Kent and Sussex, but there gives name only to obscure places like Heron's Ghyll, Lewes, Gills lop (' leap,' O.N. *hlaup*), on the N.E. Sussex border, etc.   Sometimes -gill is curiously disguised, as in ALD-WINKLE, 1137 Aldwin gel, or ' Ealdwin's gill.'   This village, near Thrapston, Northants, is one of the most southerly instances.   We get -gill less disguised in Winskill, the man ' Wine's ravine.'

-hall, -all, -ell.—A very important and much debated suffix. There is a genuine O.E. *heall,* ' a palace, court, royal resi-dence,' then ' a mansion, a hall '; and probably a few of the many hundred names ending in -hall are derived therefrom. *E.g.,* we have Croxall, Lichfield, in 773 *charter* Crokes-halle, *Dom.* Crocheshalle; and in *Dom.* we have Buben-halle, Brunhala, Crenhalle, Chenihalle, for Bubbenhall, Broomhall, Crewe Hall, and Killinghall respectively; and these all *may be* from *heall.*   But far the most plainly come from O.E. *healh,* ' a nook, a corner,' then ' a flat meadow by a river, a haugh,' which last is its modern representa-tive.   In charters and *Dom.* the ending is usually -*hale,* a Mercian dative; more rarely -*heale,* the ordinary O.E. dative.   The ending is by far the commonest in old Mercia or the Midlands.   In Cheshire alone there are over 250 places with names ending in -hall or Hall (the latter often, not always, quite modern).   We get the simple Hale (*sic* in *Dom.*), near Altrincham and Liverpool, and in the plural, as Hailes, Gloucester; whilst it is preserved as an ending in Enhale, Cambs, in O.E. *charter* Eanheale.

The *h* easily drops away, and so we get -all, as in Bignall, Birdsall (York), Gnosall (still 1298 Gnoddeshale), Walsall, etc.; or else we get -ell, as in Beadnell, Bracknell (the only case of *hale* in Berks), Bucknell; or even -el, as in Ellel, *Dom.* Ellhale; whilst the *hale* is even more merged in Paull,

Dom. Pagele. The endings -hall and -hill often run into one another, not seldom in the Midland form of *hill*—viz., *hull*—e.g., Minshull Vernon, Cheshire, is *Dom.* Manesshale or Manessele; Stramshall, Staffs, is *c.* 1300 Strangeshull; and GOXHILL, HODNELL, and SUGNALL lend further illustration.

-*ham*, -*am*.—This very common suffix represents two distinct words, and only when we get O.E. charter evidence can we be sure which word it is. (1) O.E. *hām(m)*, *hom(m)* in the oldest charters often *haam*—e.g., 692-93 *Essex chart.* Bedden-haam and Deccen-haam (Degenham)—found also in all the Frisian dialects as *ham(m)*, *hem*, *him*, ' a pasture, a meadow enclosed with a ditch '; Duignan adds, ' at the bend of a river,' so as to connect with the human *ham*, which is caused by the bend of the knee. In England the meaning is ' enclosed ground, generally pasture.' So far as we know, this by a good deal the rarer of the two suffixes— *e.g.*, there are in Berks seventeen names ending in -ham, of which only five are clearly *hamm*, because we find in charters ' æt Bennanhamme,' for Beenham, etc. In Cambs there are twenty-four -hams, but in no case do they clearly come from *hamm*, though Skeat cites abundant evidence from the eleventh century onwards. There is a Chippenham, Cambs, *c.* 1080 Chipenham, but the place of the same name in Wilts is O.E. Chron. 878 Cippanhamme. The same rarity seems to hold true elsewhere. There are several Hams on the Severn, and a few on the Wye and Trent, from *hamm*. (2) O.E. *hām*, our ' home,' whilst *hāmm*, with its long *a*, represents an English *hem*. This is one of our very commonest endings, often clipped down into -am (*cf.* CHEAM), or more rarely into -um, as in Bilsum, Gloucester, *c.* 955 Billesham; but in the north largely replaced by the Norse -by, except in Northumberland, where -ham is common and -by non-existent. We have a fair number of northern -hams—Askham, Brigham, etc., Cumberland, Bispham, Kirkham, etc., Lancs. But the inquirer always needs to be wary, because in the north, especially in Yorks, -ham or -am frequently represents an O.E. locative or dative—*e.g.*, HALLAM, *Dom.* Hallum, O.E. *healon*, ' on the slopes '; HULAM, *Sim. Dur.* Holum, O.E. *holon*, ' at the

holes '; also see ILAM, KILHAM, LYTHAM, etc.   Even -holme
may at times represent simply an O.E. locative, as in
HIPPERHOLME, *Dom.* Huperun; -holm and -ham often tend
to interchange, as in DURHAM, etc.

Though -ham is certainly abundant after the patronymic
-ing, *q.v.*, Isaac Taylor's statement that, in the O.E.
charters, *ham* is found united with names of families, but
not with the names of individuals, is abundantly incorrect
(*cf.* Skeat, *Place-Names of Cambs*, p. 20); see, *e.g.*, BECKEN-
HAM, BEENHAM, BIDDENHAM, BOXHAM, etc.

-*hampton*—*i.e.*, *ham-tún*—' home town,' as in Bathampton, etc.,
is a very common suffix also.   Duignan cites seventeen in
Ombersley and Astley, Worcester, alone — five now
vanished.

-*holm* see HOLME.

-*hope*, -*op*, -*up*.—O.E. *hóp*, ' a piece of enclosed land, generally
among fens and marshes; waste land.'   Also, especially
in N.E. England and S. Scotland, ' a small enclosed valley,
branching off a larger one, a blind valley '; same root
as O.N. *hóp*, a ' haven, place of refuge '; but we have no
seaboard names in England akin to St. Margaret's Hope,
Orkney and Queensferry.   In Northumberland no less
than seventy-three places end in -hope, and forty in Durham.   We have Easthope, Hope Rowdle, and Rattling-
hope as far south as S. Salop, and a Woolhope in Hereford.
But as this ending comes south, it tends to become -op;
already in Dunsop and Clitheroe, also in GLOSSOP Worksop; but Hatherop (Gloucester) is 1294 Haythorp.   Even
Kershope, on the Cumberland border, has become Kirsop as
a personal name.   Rarely we find -up, as in BACUP, Blake-
up, *sic* 1604 (a hill on the Borders), and the personal
name Kirkup = ' valley with the church.'   There are no
-hopes in Berks, Cambs, or even Cheshire; but in Pembroke we have Lydstep, which stands for ' Lud's or Llyd's
hope.'

-*how*.—This is O.N. *haug-r*, ' mound, cairn,' a rather rare suffix,
and only in the north—Brant How, Great How, etc.   It
may shrink into -oe, as in ASLACOE or THINGOE (this in
Suffolk); or even into -o, as in Duddo, 1183 Dudehowe, and
as, perhaps, in Cargo, N. Cumberland.   But Brisco, in the

same shire, is, in its charter form, Birkescagh—*i.e.*, birk shaw or 'birch wood.' The same word appears again Frenchified, in the Channel Islands, as Hogue and Hougue.

-ing, in our oldest charters often -incg. This is one of the most interesting and important of all our suffixes; in its way unique, being absolutely *personal* in its reference, not local. The idea conveyed is one of possession, or intimate connection with; hence 'son of, descendant,' as in Æthel-ing, 'son of the ethel, the noble-born,' Cerdicing, 'son of Cerdic,' etc. We even have in the O.E. of Luke iii. 38, Adaming, 'son of Adam.' There are many place-names ending in -ing, like Barking, Basing, Reading, Woking, which originally meant, 'the sons or descendants of Beorc, Bassa, Read, Woc,' and only thereafter 'place where these descendants dwelt.' In a name like Centingas it can never mean anything but 'men of Kent'; the suffix in O.E. charters is often found as -ingas, which is nominative plural or -ingum, genitive plural, as in Bede's Berecingas (Bark-ing), or O.E. Chron.'s Readingum (Reading). This patro-nymic -ing, though so common, is not universal, and chiefly southern; in Cheshire there are none, in Cambs. only two; in Stafford and Warwick Duignan gives none, unless WATLING ST. be called an exception; but in Norfolk -ing is fairly common—Hickling, Horning, etc.; whilst Horsfall Turner enumerates twenty-two for Yorks— Gembling (*Dom.* Ghemelinge), Kipling (*Dom.* Chipelinge), Pickering, etc. In Yorks there are, of course, the three Ridings—*i.e.*, third-ings or third parts; only this comes from the equivalent O.N. -ung rather than the O.E. -ing, the O.N. being thrithjung-r; in *c.* 1066, *Laws of Edw. Confessor*, trehingas. The same ending reappears in Holland in such a name as Appingadam. Sometimes, but very rarely, the -ing is now -inge, as in E. and W. Ginge, Berks, in O.E. charters Gaeging and Gaincg, *Dom.* Gainz, 'place of the sons of Gæga.' This softening into the modern *j* sound (-inge = -inj), is also found in such modern pronunciations as Nottinjam, Whittinjam, etc., fairly often heard. Also, very rarely, the -ing may be dropped in course of time, as in Cudeley, Worcester, in 974 Cudinc-lea.

If names ending in -ing are rare in some parts, names compounded with this patronymic suffix are found everywhere.

Generally the ending is -ingham or -ington, more rarely -ingford, -ingwell, or the like. In many cases these are genuine patronymics, denoting the home or village of somebody's descendants—Beddingham, ' home of the Beadings '; Bennington, ' home of the Bennings '; and so on; it is needless to multiply examples. But, unless the evidence for the -ing goes back to O.E. times, we can never be sure that we have before us a true patronymic. Many years ago, *e.g.*, the writer pointed out that in Scotland, where there are a good many names in -ingham and -ington, not more than two or three are real patronymics. One needs to be hardly less wary in England, because very often the -ing is but a later softening of the O.E. genitive in -*an* or -*en*, usually the masculine gender in -*an*, as Barrington, *c.* 1080 Barentone, ' Bæra's village '; or Bedingham, O.E. charter Beddanham, ' Bedda's home.' Take the very first case that comes to us, ABINGDON; it is 699 charter Abbendune, ' Abba's ' or ' Ebba's hill '; whilst Abington, Cambs, is *Dom.* Abintone, ' Abba's town '; not patronymics at all. Sometimes the -ing arrives very late; Marchington, Uttoxeter, is 907 Mærcham, ' home on the march or boundary '; 1004 Merchamtune, or ' March Hampton '; not till the thirteenth century have we Marchynton, and the -ing is later still. Sometimes, too, the -ing is a pure corruption, as in ALMINGTON for ' Alchmund's town,' or ARDINGTON for ' Eadwine's town.'

Besides, we have always to beware of names in -ing, which have nothing patronymic about them; names like Holling Hall, where Holling is but M.E. for ' holly,' or like Stocking Lane, Staffs, where, Duignan says, Stocking means ' grubbing up, clearing of wood or wild land '; whilst STOCKING, Haresfield, is an O.E. locative, *stoccan*, ' at the tree-stocks.'

Dr. H. Bradley (*English Historical Review*, October, 1911) seems to have made out a strong case for -ing or -inge being also sometimes an ending to denote a place on a river or stream, of which AVENING, EXNING, GUYTING, TWYNING, etc., would be examples.

-leigh, -ley, -lie, -ly.—These are all modern forms of O.E. *léah,* dat. *leage,* ' a bit of cultivated ground, a meadow, a lea.' This is one of our commonest endings, especially as -ley; there are fifty-three in Cheshire alone, thirteen in Berks, twelve in Cambs—these two last small counties. The form -ly is rare,[1] but we have EARLY, Berks, etc.; -leigh, which represents the dative, is not common except in a few parts like Devon; there are none in Berks or Cambs. But Leigh alone occurs twelve times in the *Postal Guide,* from Lancashire to Kent. Two or three times in Yorks we find the suffix as -laugh, Healaugh (' high meadow'), SKIRLAUGH, etc.; and in Cheshire it takes the form -lach, as in SHOCKLACH. Traps in connection with this ending are few; but we have Cookley, Kidderminster, 964 Culnan clif.

-low, and, in the north, *-law.*—O.E. *hláw, hlǽw,* ' a hill,' then, ' a burial-ground, barrow, tumulus.' The ending is common in the south—Challow, Hounslow, Marlow, etc.; but -low is found in the north too, in Yorks at least three times—Barlow, Bierlow, and Chellow (*Dom.* Celeslau), but Barlow is *Dom.* Berlai (= lea). In the north, where the form is -law, it is usually written separately—Collier Law, Durham ; Black and Kilhope Laws, S. Northumberland ; etc. J. H. Turner gives no -law now in Yorks, but there were several formerly—Chellow, as we have seen, also Ardsley, and Tinsley, in *Dom.* Erdeslau, and Tirnes- or Tineslawe. We see the same tendency, -ley replacing -low, farther south, in Staffs, where Moxley was, *c.* 1400, Mockeslowe, and Muckley, *c.* 1600, Mucklow.

-minster.—This and -caster form our only Latin endings. It is late L. *monasterium,* later L. *monisterium,* O.E. *mynster,* originally ' a monastery '; but, as a place-name suffix, -minster seems always to mean ' the church of a monastery,' then ' any church,' generally a large one. It is now found chiefly in the south—Axminster, Bedminster, Sturminster, Westminster, etc.; but, of course, we freely speak of York Minster, Beverley Minster, etc.; and in an

---

[1] Also *cf.* ACLE, etc.

inscription of 1056-1066 in Kirkdale Church, Yorks, we read of 'S̄c̄s̄ Gregorius minster.' The O.N. form *mustari* does not seem represented among our names; but in Menstrie (Alloa), Scotland, we get a Gaelicised form, from G. *mainistreach*, 'pertaining to a monastery.' This is very like the form in AYMESTREY, Hereford, *Dom.* Eiminstre. Musters, Durham, is 'de Monasteriis.'

-or, *-over*, also *-er*.—The ending *-or* represents two distinct words: (1) O.E. *ōra*, 'margin, bank, shore,' cognate with L. *ora*, found by itself as a name in Oare, Berks; but common as an ending too, as in BOGNOR, 'Bucga's shore,' CUMNOR, KEYNOR, and WINDSOR, whose early charter form is Wendles ore, which Skeat thinks may be 'the Vandal's bank.' But (2) *-or*, with *-er*, and its fuller form *-over*, represents O.E. *ofer*, O. Fris. *overa*, *overe*, M. Fris. *over*, E. Fris. *över*, *öfer*, Ger. *ufer*, 'border, margin,' hence 'seashore,' and especially 'river-bank'; by *c.* 1205 *Layamon*, it has become *oure*. We get this word as a name in OWRAM, Yorks, in *Dom.* Overe, Oure, and Ufrun, which are locatives singular and plural, Ufrun becoming OWRAM after the type described under ham (2). The full form *-over* is still retained in Ashover, BOLSOVER, etc. But it has often been shortened into *-or*, as in Baddesley Ensor (or EDENSOR), HADSOR, *c.* 1100 Headesofre, and HASELOR, *c.* 1300 Haselovre; and we get it as a prefix in Orgrave, N. Lancs, *Dom.* Ourgreve, 'grave on the bank.' Most names in *-er* also have the same root, though this has not hitherto been much recognized; especially those named from trees—Asher, 'ash-tree bank'; Beecher, Hasler, 'hazel-bank'; Pinner, 'pine-tree bank'; and Thorner, as well as Iver, Uxbridge, which is probably 'ivy bank'; and HEVER, 'high bank'; and even WOOLER, which has nothing to do with 'wool,' but is 1197 Welloure, 'well bank.'

-thorpe, *-torp*, *-trop*.—This is O.E. *c.* 725 *throp*, *c.* 800 *ðrop*, later *thorp*, O.N. *thorp*, N. *torp*, O.Fris. *thorp*, *therp*, 'farm, hamlet, village.' It is very rare in O.E., and in place-names is due almost solely to Norse influence. It is found as a name simply as Thorp(e), five times in the *Postal Guide*, and often in combination—Thorp Arch, Thorpe

Abbotts, Thorpe-le-Soken, etc.; also as Throop (Christ-church), and Thrupp, Mid Oxon and S. Northants. These last forms will be pure Eng., as are also the rare occurrences of the ending outside the Danelagh—ADLESTROP, Eastrip, Somerset ; HUNTINGTRAP, Worcester ; etc. Gloucester, a purely English county, contains many remarkable variations of *throp*—Hatherop, Pindrup, Puckrup, Westrip, Wolstrop, and even Upperup. Wilstrop, W. Riding, *Dom.* Wilestrop, is one of the very few cases of -trop in a Danish region, whilst Thorpe, Chertsey, is one of the very few cases of thorpe outside such a region. The ending -thorpe is common in Norfolk, and occurs three times in Warwick, in which cases it is certainly due to Norse influence; it does not occur at all in Cambs or Cheshire, once each in Hunts, Beds, and Herts. In Denmark to-day the ending -trup is very common.

-thwaite.—O.N. *pveit, pveiti,* ' a piece of land, a paddock ' (lit. ' a piece cut off,' a piece ' thwited ' or whittled off). This suffix is found only in the north-west, chiefly in Cumberland; also, rarely, in S. Scotland. The limits seem to be— Seathwaite, Broughton-in-Furness, Satterthwaite, Ulverston, Linthwaite (' flax plot '), and Slaithwaite, Huddersfield, and Hunderthwaite, N. Yorks (*Dom.* Hundredestoit, or ' bit cut off the hundred '). Modern lips have clipped Slaithwaite down to Sló-at. We have one -twight in Norfolk, Crostwight, *Dom.* Crostueit; and see EASTWOOD.

-toft. See TOFT.

-ton ranks with -ley as the commonest of all our suffixes. Dr. Lee estimated that about one-eighth of all the names in the first two vols. of Kemble's *Codex Diplomaticus* had this ending, whose root idea is ' enclosure,' ' my property '; whereas, singular to note, this same root is never used as a place-name ending anywhere on the Continent. It is O.E. *c.* 725, ' *tuun* cors ' (= cohors, L. for ' court '), later *tún,* O.N. *tún,* ' enclosure, homestead, farm '; *toun* in Scot., *town* in W. Somerset, and *tun* in Norw. dialects are still used for ' a single farm.' In Cornwall *town* and *town-place* are still applied to the smallest hamlet or even to a farmyard. Then, probably after the Nor. Conquest, *tun* came to mean ' a town '; long before

that it meant ' a village.' The root is often said to be akin to Keltic *dún*, ' a fort,' as in the old ending -dunum. But this is doubtful, as *dún* means first, ' a hill,' and then, ' the fort which so often crowned the hill.' True, the forms -don and -ton do sometimes run into one another, as in Bishopston, 1016 Biscopesdun, Farndon (Cheshire), *Dom.* Ferentone, GAMSTON, Larton (Cheshire), *Dom.* Lavorchedone, etc., also Dunstall and TUNSTALL.

One needs to be careful about the common confusion with -stone, as in ATHERSTONE, BEESTON Castle, BRIGHTON, BRIXTON, etc., whilst Elkstone, Leek, was 1227 Elkesdon (*cf.*, too, the common interchange of Johnston and Johnstone). Perhaps oftenest, in these cases, the original ending was O.E. *stan(e)*, ' stone '; but not in Johnston. An example of the reverse case is Woolstone, Berks, which is the O.E. Wulfricestun. Sometimes the *s* is the genitive of the preceding personal name; and of course *e* may be added at the end of almost any old name. There are also some curious corruptions, like Austerson, Cheshire, which is *Dom.*'s Alstanton, whilst Enson, Staffs, is *c.* 1300 Eneston and Enson. In rare cases, as in COTTON, Cambs, the ending -on may be the old locative, ' at the cots,' the same ending which in Yorks so often becomes -un, -um, and then -am; see -ham; so that -ham and -ton may mean the same thing, and yet not ' dwelling ' at all ! In rare cases -ton is, or was, used to give a Saxon look to a Keltic name—*e.g.*, Clyst, Exeter, was 1001 O.E. Chron. Glistun, *v.r.* Clistun, whilst we also have a ' Clistune ' in *Dom.* Worcester, all probably being originally W. *glwys*, ' a hallowed place, a fair spot.' In MITTON, which occurs several times, the -ton is corrupted from O.E. *mythan*.

-*warden*, -*wardine*, -*worth*, -*worthy*, are best all taken together, being in root the same. Very common is -worth, O.E. *worth, weorth, wurth, wyrth*, ' open space, piece of land, holding, farm, estate,' akin to our Eng. *worth*. In *Dom.* it is usually found as -orde, or -vrde, -worde. Examples are so numerous that they need not be cited. J. H. Turner cites thirty-one cases, past or present, of the ending, in Yorks alone. Occasionally we meet a corruption, as in BISHPORT for ' bishop's worth,' and, more serious, SEA-

COURT near Oxford, which was once Seovecwurde or
'Seofeca's farm.' Who would ever guess that? In a few
cases -worth has been replaced by -ford, as in DUXFORD and
PAMPISFORD, Cambs ; OFFORD, Warwick, and Tudworth,
Yorks ; where *Dom.* has both Tudeworde and Tudeforde.
We see the reverse case in Brinsworth, Rotherham,
Dom. Brinesford, and Wigglesworth, E. Yorks, *Dom.*
Wiclesforde. In either case the transition form was -vorde.[1]

-worthy is an ending purely S. Western. It is O.E.
worthig, seen more fully in WORTHING; root and meaning
the same as -worth. Seemingly it is not a diminutive
but an extended form as in -warden. Examples are
Badgeworthy, Holsworthy, King's Worthy, etc.

-warden, -wardine, is an ending very common in Salop,
whilst a few cases occur in the surrounding counties; elsewhere it is unknown. It is Mercian O.E. *worthign*, extended form of *worthig* and of *worth ;* see above, and
meaning, as before, ' farm, holding, place of worth.' In
Dom. Salop we have a simple Wrdine; but instances of
the ending are also abundant in that shire—Belswardine,
Shrawardine, etc. In N. Hereford we have Leintwardine
and Pedwardine, in Worcester Bedwardine (' the monk's
table farm '), and Tollerdine, in Flint Hawarden, whilst
we have contracted forms in CARDEN, Cheshire; and
HARDEN, Staffs; as well as Ellerdine, Salop. Gloucester
gives us Ruardean, *c.* 1281 Rowardin, and Shepherdine. It
is interesting to note that Lapworth, Warwick, is in an 816
charter Hlappanwurthin and in *Dom.* Lapeforde. In
Holland we have names like Leeuwarden (Dutch. *leeuw*,
' a lion '), where we seem to have the same ending; but
there is no Dutch *warden* or *worden* in Calisch's Dutch
Dictionary.

-wich, -wick.—This is O.E. *wic*, ' dwelling, village,' borrowed
from L. *vicus*, ' village,' same root as Gk. οἶκος, ' house ';
also borrowed in Corn. as GWEEK, found in place-names
there. One of the very earliest recorded instances of
-wich is ' the port of Quentawic,' in Bede iv. 1, *i.e.*,
St. Quentin, Picardy. In the South *wic* is usually softened
into -wich—Greenwich, Harwich, Sandwich, etc. In the

---

[1] The natives now call Deskford, Banffshire, Deskurd.

north it remains hard, as -wick—Alnwick, Berwick,
Cheswick, Withernwick, etc. But the hard -wick is also
found in the south. We have both Berwick St. James
and St. John near Salisbury, as well as one near Shrewsbury, and we have Chiswick near London as well as one
in the far North. In Cheshire and Worcestershire -wich
or -wych is popularly interpreted as indicating a brine
or salt spring (*cf.* 716 charter ' In wico . . . Saltwich,' Worcester). But there is no O.E. authority for this, even
though Nantwich is in W. Yr Heledd gwen, ' the white
place for making salt.' Droitwich is in O.E. Chron. simply
Wic. We get the hard form in Salwick, Preston, which
can hardly mean ' salt bay,' O.N. *vík*, but rather, ' village
where salt was made.' It is doubtful if any -wick in
England means ' bay ' (though *cf.* SANDWICH), whilst
such are common in the north of Scotland. Skeat thought
the -wick in Saltwich, Droitwich, etc., was the N. *vík*,
' a small salt creek or bay '; and that the change to
' brine-pit ' would be easy. But to some of us this seems
very unlikely indeed, down inland at Droitwich, and só
early as 716. In Yorks *wíc* becomes Wike, *Dom.* Wic,
and Heckmondwike, etc. The O.E. ending -*awic* sometimes becomes -age, *q.v.*

-*with.*—O.N. *vith-r*, Dan. *ved*, ' a wood,' is common in Yorks.
J. H. Turner cites eleven cases—ASKWITH, Beckwith,
Bubwith, etc., where *Dom.* spells *vid, wid, uid,* and *vi,*
always avoiding *th*. It is doubtful if -with ever really
interchanged with -wick. We do have SKIPWITH twice
in *Dom.* as Schipewic, and again in 1200 Scippewic, also
Butterwick, Yorks, in *Dom.* both Butruic and Butruid;
but as a rule in such cases *c* will be the common scribe's
error for *t*. Occasionally -with is found changing into
-worth; whilst Langwith, Derby and Notts, and Lang-
worth, Lincs, all ended with -wath, ' ford,' in thirteenth-
century charters.

CHAPTER VII

THE NORMAN ELEMENT

THE pure Norman period in England was but short—from the Conquest in 1066 to the accession of the Angevin Henry II. in 1154. However, from the marriage of Æthelred to Emma, the Duke of Normandy's sister, in 1002, Normans began to find homes in our land and to influence our affairs, an influence which lasted on till the accession of Edward I. in 1292, first of our Kings with an English name since fatal Senlac, and an Englishman out and out. Hallam has well pointed out that Norman influence in England has often been exaggerated. Sir Henry Ellis's enumeration of the nearly 8,000 *mesne* tenants in Domesday shows how very large was the number of purely Saxon lords of the manor at that date; whilst it should be better known that French was never used among us for deed or law until the reign of Henry III., 1216-1272. Still, considering the wide power of Norman lords and landholders, and the large use of French among all educated Englishmen, Norman place-names in England are wonderfully few.[1] Here the stolid Saxon peasant fairly extinguished the proud Norman peer.

But there is one pretty large group of Norman names in England, those beginning with Beau—or, before a vowel, Bel- (feminine, belle), 'beautiful, lovely,' a common prefix for a spot chosen because of its fine outlook or natural beauty. There are among us two Beaudeserts or 'lovely wilds,' a Beaulieu, 'lovely spot,' reappearing corrupted in BEWDLEY and in LEIGHTON BUZZARD; also two Beaumonts and two Belmonts, 'fine hills.' There are two Belchamps, 'fine plains,' better

[1] Of course the Normans profoundly influenced both the spelling and pronunciation of many English names, both local and personal. See p. 26, and names like CERNE, OSGODBY, etc.; but wholly Norman names in England are few. The whole subject is carefully worked out in Zachrisson's *Anglo-Norman Influence on English Place-Names*, 1910.

known to us in the shape of Beauchamp or Beacham; then there
is not only a modern Belle Vue, ' fine view,' but an old Belvoir,
' fine to see,' whilst the Beaurepair, ' lovely haunt,' of the
Chron. of Lanercost, has now become transformed into Beau-
park, Ebchester; but it remains as Belrepeir in Gloucester, and
appears again in Derby as BELPER. BELFORD, BELGRAVE, and
a good many other names in Bel-, have an English, not a
Norman, origin.

ANTROBUS, Nantwich, is of an almost unique type for an
English name; but it surely must be Fr. *entre buis*, ' among
the box-trees '; in *Dom.* it is Entrebus. Almost its only
parallel so early is MONTGOMERY, of which, and of other
Norman names, we shall have something to say in the
chapter on Wales Another old name in Mont- we have
in Montacute, ' sharp hill,' brought in the Conqueror's days
from Normandy to S. Somerset. A few of our abbey
names also are Norman. It is not to be wondered at, so
many French monks and clerics swarmed over to England
with William I.; hence JERVAULX and RIEVAUX. These, however, are only half French, the first half in both cases being
English; but *vaux* or *vaulx* is the plural of Fr. *val*, ' a valley.'
Bois, Fr. for ' a wood,' has been preserved in a few place-names,
Chesham Bois, Bucks; Theydon Bois, Epping Forest, etc.; but
not CAMBOIS. Forest, too, as in New Forest, Forest of Dean,
etc., is, of course, French. Then it should be noted that all our
names with the suffix -market are due to Norman influence—
Newmarket (4), Stowmarket, etc. About the earliest record
of such names which we have found is in the Pipe Roll
for 1179-80, Yorks, De Novo Mercato (Latinized form of
O.Nor. Fr. *mercat*), now Newmarch, which gives us the modern
Fr. *marché*, with the same meaning.

Norman personal names are very commonly appended to
real old English names—*e.g.*, BOVEY TRACEY, HURSTMONCEUX,
Milton Deverel, Sutton Mallet, and Montis, etc. A run through
Duignan's county books will show, however, that these double-
barrelled names rarely came into use until well on in the Middle
Ages. More rarely the Norman name (in most cases the pro-
prietor's) is prefixed, as in GUYHIRN, ROYSTON, etc. A real
Norman name, long a puzzle, is BARNET, first found *c.* 1200,
Barnette. It is almost certainly a diminutive of Fr. *berne*

or *berme*, ' a narrow space, a ledge, a berm.' Boulge, Suffolk, is also worth referring to, because it preserves an old Norman word for ' a heathery waste.' In the same region is DOVER-COURT, which goes back to *Dom.*, and so gives us the word *court* more than 200 years earlier than it is recorded in our English dictionaries.

A church or ecclesiastical building among us is usually denoted by -church in the south, -kirk or kir- in the north, or else by -minster. But Normans have their share here too. The O.Nor. Fr. *capele*, late L. *cappella* (lit. ' a little cape '), is now usually Chapel, which goes to form fourteen names in the *Postal Guide*—Chapel Allerton, Chapel Amble, etc. They may not all go back to Norman days, but such a name as Chapel-en-le-Frith certainly does; so do the four Capels, two in Kent and near Dorking and Ipswich, whilst there are ten Capels in Wales. There is likewise a Chappel in Essex. Very few of our names in Castle come in before 1300; but Castle Holdgate, Salop, occurs as Chastel Hollgod in the thirteenth century, and must be Norman.

Three curious specimens of quasi-Norman names may bring this brief chapter to a close: Lappal, Halesowen, is in 1335 Lappole, which must mean ' the pool '; while in 1342 we read of ' Thomas atte Pole.' Surtees, Co. Durham, is in 1211 Super Teisam, the L. *super* having been changed into Fr. *sur ;* and the name, of course, means (place) ' on the Tees,' Beachy Head, Sussex, if correctly interpreted, is unique in its way as an English cape name. It is always thought to be the Fr. *beau chef*, ' fine head ' or ' headland '; and there is a Beauchief near Sheffield. The French article *le*, ' the,' still remains in a curious number of cases—Chapel-le-Dale, Chester-le-Street, Newton-le-Willows, etc.

CHAPTER VIII

THE NAMES OF WALES, MONMOUTH, AND CORNWALL

GREAT progress has now been made in the study of the names of England and Scotland, still greater with the names of Ireland and of Man. As to the wealth of Keltic names in Cornwall much remains to be done, largely because Cornish is now so utterly a dead language. It has dictionaries, but none satisfactory to the place-name student; and perhaps nobody now alive knows enough about it to do the subject justice, unless it be Mr. Henry Jenner. We have, indeed, a great store of Cornish names in Domesday, including twenty-eight which begin with Lan-, or 'church.'[1] But, with rare exceptions, like BODMIN or LAUNCESTON, Domesday's names are not those familiar to most of us to-day. So, for lack of anything which we feel worth saying—we confess it with regret—we pass on.

With Wales, and its very Welsh neighbour, Monmouth, the case is altogether different. Welsh is a tongue exceedingly alive. In 1911, 43·5 per cent. of the people still spoke Welsh, though that showed a decrease of 47,542 in ten years. On the other hand, only 14 per cent. of the people of Ireland then spoke Erse, and just over 4½ per cent. of the people of Scotland spoke Gaelic. Excellent Welsh scholars abound, yet almost nobody seems to have fairly tackled the host of intricate and interesting Welsh names which await explanation. Men like Professors Rhys and Anwyl have given scattered hints; and one very solid contribution we do have—the Cymmrodorion Society's edition of Owen's *Pembrokeshire* (1603), edited by H. Owen, with huge blocks of notes in small print by himself, Mr. Egerton Phillimore, Professor Rhys, Mr. W. H. Stevenson,

---

[1] Out of the 200 old Cornish parishes, no less than 145 are called after Keltic saints—Irish, Welsh, Breton, or Cornish.

etc., notes which often display acutest learning and insight concerning names all over Wales, but arranged with a terrible lack of method, and sadly unhandy for the busy student. The only book dealing with the whole subject seems to be Mr. Thomas Morgan's *Place-Names of Wales*, second edition, 1912. The author was prize-winner at the Newport Eisteddfod in 1897 for a *Dictionary of Welsh Names in Monmouth*, so it may be taken for granted that he knows spoken Welsh thoroughly, and he has collected a lot of useful material. But he omits many important names, even Glamorgan, and he hardly refers to any mountain or hill, not even Plynlimmon. Worse still, Mr. Morgan has had no scientific training, and so, on many points, his little book is a very unsafe guide.

Something might have been expected from the new edition of the *Encyclopædia Britannica*, that wonderful monument of well-arranged learning. The article 'Wales' gives a long list of Welsh words for river, hill, and dale, with specimen names derived from them. But the list is such that any tyro could easily compile it out of a dictionary for himself; and no attempt is made to analyze or explain a single one of the hundreds of difficult Welsh names. Rarely, an article like 'Cardiff' makes some effort to deal with the philological problems. But, from a place-name point of view, many of the separate articles are deplorable. All we are told—*e.g.*, under 'Denbigh'—is: 'Din in Dinbych' (the Welsh spelling) means 'a fort.' But, as we shall see, the strong probability is that DENBIGH is a Danish, and not a Welsh, name at all. Under WREXHAM, another puzzling name, we are told that the original name 'in the Anglo-Saxon Chronicle,' is 'Wrightesham.' This last is not the original name, and Wrexham is never mentioned in that Chronicle at all.

As we have referred to Cardiff, the history of the great seaport's name is quite worth telling before we proceed further. The *Britannica* article gives a very imperfect record of the early forms of the name. But in all probability it is correct in holding that the usual explanation 'fort on the Taff' must be wrong. No early writer ever calls it Caerdâf, (which would be the proper Welsh spelling if this were so), unless we make exception of the English antiquary Leland, in the days of Henry VIII., and he was only writing down his own guess.

The earliest spelling now known is of date 1128, Kardi; a little later we find Kardid, whilst in the Pipe Roll for 1158-59 we have Cardif. The modern Welsh is Caerdydd, pronounced Caer déeth. These forms suggest the meaning 'fort, castle of Didius.' Within the last few years it has become certain that Cardiff stands on the site of a Roman fort; and so this Didius will probably be that Roman general who, in A.D. 50, fought against the Silures, the British tribe who inhabited this region. If this conjecture be right, Cardiff will take rank as one of the earliest known Roman stations in the British Isles.

It is generally agreed that Wales was originally peopled by a non-Keltic race, almost certainly pre-Aryan, and now practically wiped out, though it has left its mark in the skulls of many of its successors. Next, it is agreed, came the Goidels or Gaels, Kelts pure enough. They probably spread over nearly the whole of modern Wales, and a little farther east, except where, near the Salop border, the Brythonic Ordovices became firmly fixed. Their leading tribes were the Silures in the south-east and the Demetæ in the south - west. Brythons came in successive waves after the Gaels; and while the Saxon was busy driving the native Briton westwards out of England, the Brython was as busy in Wales conquering the Gael, the conquest being all but complete about A.D. 500. Legend and tradition make it well-nigh certain that the Gaels were once in large force in Wales, and, in early historic times, were aided against the Brythons by counter invasions of Gaels from the south of Ireland. But, as they were completely conquered before civilization had made any great advance, they have left behind only a few inscriptions, rare and precious, in South Wales, especially Caldy Island, Pembroke, in Ogam characters. There are no such inscriptions in Mid Wales, and only one in the north. Of clear trace in Welsh place-names the Gael has left singularly little. It is difficult to say now what must be truly Goidelic. The fact—e.g., that glyn, our Scottish glen—seems commoner in Glamorgan than else-where might perhaps seem to point that way. But the fact e.g., that we have a Clyne (modern Welsh clun, G. claon, 'a meadow') both in Glamorgan and in Sutherland, is hardly convincing proof that the Welsh Clyne must be a name left behind by the now vanished Gael. But to one interesting pair we may venture to point—ROSEMARKET and Rhosmarket, both in Pembroke. Their old forms are Rossmarken and Rosavarken, for which no explanation is forthcoming in modern Welsh. The names must surely be the same as Rose-markie, Fortrose (*c.* 1228, Rosmarkensis Episcopus), where Dr. W. J. Watson takes the ending to be G. *marcnaidh*, old genitive of *marcnach*, ' place of horses '; and so the whole name is probably Goidelic for ' moor on which horses were kept or stabled.'

About Rome, too, and the tramp of her many legions through Wales, surviving place-names tell us sadly little, though Rome most certainly was here. There are no -casters or -chesters to be found; caer- or car- everywhere takes their place. For early place-name material we are worse off in Wales than anywhere else in our British Isles. In Wales—*e.g.*, no Roman inscriptions have yet been found, though they are found every-where else, one or two even in Cornwall. We have already told how that Cardiff was probably a Roman fort soon after A.D. 50. But, as matter of fact, no Roman writer mentions any place in Wales till we come to Tacitus, who, in his Life of Agricola, *c.* A.D. 90, refers to Mona, the Welsh Mona or Anglesea, not Julius Cæsar's Mona, the Isle of Man; whilst in his Annals, at least ten years later, Tacitus mentions Mona again and also Sabrina, the River Severn. Soon after Tacitus comes the famous Geography of Ptolemy, *c.* 150, who describes all Britain in ample detail; and yet, perhaps, the only existing Welsh name identifiable in Ptolemy is Maridunum, which must be CAERMARTHEN. This last seems, indeed, to be a translation of Maridunum, ' fort, castle by the sea.' In Welsh ' the sea ' is *mōr*, but in G. it is *muir*, genitive *mara ;* so that this, too, may probably be taken as a Goidelic name.

The present name we find first in Nennius, *c.* 800. He spells it Cair mardin, a spelling exactly preserved in (perhaps) its next mention, the Pipe Roll, 1158-59, whilst Giraldus, *c.* 1188, has Cairmardhin, or -merdhin. In Welsh *ll* has come to have the soft or hissing *thl* sound, and so, at least since the twelfth century, Welshmen have taken the same to mean ' fort of Merlin,' the mighty magician of King Arthur's court. His name in modern Welsh is Myrddin; but already by 1148 we find it in its Latin form Merlinus. One of the earliest known instances of the Welsh *ll*, written as *thl*, is in the Rolls of Parliament, I. 463/1, not later than 1300, where we find a very familiar name spelt Thlewelyn.[1]

For a few other Roman names in Wales we can turn to the Itinerary or Road Book of Antonine (see p. 4). There were plenty of Roman roads in Wales, and wherever one finds *sarn* in a place-name, one may hopefully search for traces of a Roman road. But in the Antonine Itinerary we can identify only three known names of to-day, and there is doubt even among these—Gobannio (certainly ABERGAVENNY), Nid (which may be NEATH), and Leucaro, possibly LOUGHOR, Caermarthen; all three on the Roman highway from Uriconium (Wroxeter) to Caermarthen. In the Ravenna Geographer, *a.* 700, we can probably identify Canubio with R. CONWAY. That seems to exhaust our stock for the early centuries.

The Saxon has left a much deeper mark on the surface of Wales than his Roman predecessor, but, unfortunately for us, not in his Chronicle nor in his charters. In the Anglo-Saxon Chronicle we find nothing in the shape of a Welsh place-name before the Conquest, save BUTTINGTON, Montgomery, in 893, BRECKNOCK in 916, and RHUDDLAN in 1063. We have now mentioned all our available documentary evidence up to Domesday; because the dates of the present text of Skene's *Four Ancient Books of Wales* are far too uncertain to found almost anything upon. To refer to Domesday now may be to anticipate; but we may finish this survey of our meagre data before 1100 by saying that a handful of place-names in Flint and Denbigh are mentioned in the Conqueror's survey of Cheshire, 1086-87—Hawarden, *e.g.*, also Bersham, Broughton, Halkin, and Rhuddlan, here Roelent; but probably not BAGILLT, though so careful an antiquary as Mr. A. Palmer of Wrexham confidently identifies it with Domesday's Bachelie. This seems as phonetically impossible as Mr. Morgan's Welsh derivation, *bu- geillt*. The first syllable has always been Ba-, and seems to represent W. *bach*, G. *beag*, 'little'; the second means 'hills' or 'cliffs.'

Salop's Domesday contains, perhaps, no Welsh name except Montgomery just on its border. But several names around

---

[1] But also *cf.* Cardeol (= *caer Lleol*), spelling of CARLISLE by Ordericus Vitalis, *c.* 1145; and for an instance in 1246, see CEFN LLYS.

Monmouth are in the Domesday of Hereford. From 600 onwards the Welsh march or frontier was a very unfixed quantity—has always been so, we may say, up to the present hour. Monmouthshire, nominally in England, is still Welsh in nearly everything but name; whilst Hereford and Monmouth were once called West Wales. The fluctuating frontier is well illustrated by the fact, often referred to in recent disestablishment controversies, that, at points, the jurisdiction of the Bishops of St. Asaph and Llandaff runs right into England, whilst something like four parishes of the See of Hereford are in Wales. West of the River Wye Hereford names are largely Welsh, whilst east of it they are purely English; and in that West-of-Wye region, Welsh was largely spoken not more than sixty years ago. On the other hand, the Saxons were always pushing their spears into Wales, especially the redoubtable Offa who, before 800, finally hunted the Welsh out of Pengwern (henceforward known as Shrewsbury), and built the famous dyke all the way along from the mouth of the Dee to the Wye, so making this quite an English region, even, *e.g.*, a good piece of what is now Denbigh.

Thus it is only as one might expect, that English placenames are to be found in considerable numbers over about two-thirds of St. David's Principality, historic and ancient place-names too. The most purely Welsh of the twelve counties are Cardigan, Merioneth, and Caernarvon, all in the west, where, curious to relate, in all three, perhaps the only Old English name is the highest mountain in the land, Snowdon, ' the snow-capped hill,' a name found as early as the Norman chronicler, Ordericus Vitalis, who, at Lisieux, *c.* 1140, wrote of Mons Snaudunus. Doubtless the name goes back to Saxon days. The natives have their own name, Y Wyddfa, ' the Tomb,' or ' Tumulus.'

Almost as early in Wales as the Saxons were the Norsemen. The hardy Norseman was always prowling about the Irish Sea and St. George's Channel, from the beginning of the ninth century to the end of the thirteenth; and for long there were Norse or Danish Kings in Dublin and the Isle of Man. It was impossible, therefore, that Wales should escape their usually unwelcome attentions; though, it must be added, when once they settled down, very peaceful and industrious settlers

they did make.   So far as place-names go, they have left little
mark in Wales, save among the bays and islands of Pembroke,
which are so like their own much islanded, much indented,
rocky shores.   In Pembroke we have Norse footprints in abundance—Caldy I., Colby, Dale, Fish-guard (= garth or yard),
Flatholm, Gellyswick, Hakin, Haverford, Milford Haven,
Skokholm, Stack Rocks, and Tenby, with quite a number
more, which all testify to Viking visitors, though it is impossible
in almost any case to give to these a precise date.

The French-speaking, domineering Norman was in great
force along both north and south coasts, and along the border,
from the Conquest, or a year or two later, right on to the days
of Edward I., whose little son, the first Prince of Wales, was
born at Caernarvon in 1284.   Both William the Conqueror
and his son Rufus personally led expeditions into Wales, the
latter no less than three, on one occasion marching as far as
Snowdon.   Indeed, only the rugged north-west was left un-
touched.   South, in Glamorgan, we can still decipher not a
few of the heavy footmarks of the great Sir Robert Fitzhamon,
one of the Conqueror's chief knights, who, with his leading
retainers, coined many new names for the hamlets in the Vale
of Glamorgan, because their Norman tongues could not pro-
nounce the Welsh ones.   Altogether, these landlords from France
have left behind a very interesting and somewhat important
little group of place-names—*e.g.*, the Welshman's Mōn has
now an English name, Anglesea, with a French name for its
capital, Beaumaris—or Beumarish, as it is earlier spelt.   The
natives called it Rhosfair, 'moor of Mary.'   However, in 1293
Edward I. came hither, built a castle on the low-lying land by
the shore of the Menai Straits, that so the castle might communicate with the sea; and, because of the suitability of the
site, called the place Beau marais, or 'fine, beautiful marsh!'
MOLD, in Flint, is another remarkable Norman name, well
disguised.   The Kelts termed it Gwyddgrug, 'conspicuous
mount,' from the great heap still to be seen near the chief road.
The Normans translated this into *Mont halt* (mod. Fr. *haut*),
'high mount'; and we find Roger de Monalto here in 1244.
Mont hault, with a transition stage in Moalt, has now been
squeezed down into Mold, just as Mowbray was originally
Munbrai.

As interesting is the name Montgomery. A border castle was built at this place just after the Conquest, by one Baldwin; hence its present Welsh name Trefaldwyn, 'Baldwin's house.' The castle was soon captured by Roger de Montgomery, who had been made Earl of Shrewsbury in 1071; and ever since the spot has borne his name. We find it in a Latin form in Orderic, *c.* 1145, Mons Gomerici, 'hill of Gomeric,' which must have been the name of somebody in Normandy, now lost in oblivion. Already in Domesday, its first mention, the name is spelt not only Montgomeri, but also Muntgumeri, which shows how early *o* was slurred into *u*.[1] Of pure French is Beau Pré[2] or 'Fine Meadow' House, in Glamorgan, on the site of another Norman castle, whilst Fleur de Lys is just across the border in Monmouth. Beaufort, Brecon, seems to be modern; but Hay near by is true Norman (Fr. *haie*, 'a hedge'). We have already heard (p. 65) that names in Capel must be Norman too; and there are at least ten chapel sites in Wales with this name, Capel Curig, Capel Saron, etc.

When we come to examine the true Welsh names as a whole, as we now have them, we find, as we should expect, that the river-names are all Keltic, or else pre-Keltic. Many of the former, as well as of the latter, are difficult to interpret, however early we get their forms. The subject still requires much investigation, and as yet clearly pre-Keltic names seem few. Some river names are easy enough, like Usk, which goes so readily with Axe and Exe. Indeed, a good many are names common to both England and Wales, and have already been treated—Dee, *e.g.*, and Wye, and Avon (Glam.), where also we find the parallel form Aman, just as we have in Gaelic both *abhuinn* and *amhuinn*, the latter seen in such a Scottish name as Cramond, originally Caer Amond. The River Amman, Caermarthen, though spelt with two *m*'s, is more likely to be the same word than to come from *aml*; whilst the River Conway goes with Wye, being W. *con gwy* (*con*, 'together'), *i.e.*, 'chief stream.' Cynon may be similar, *q.v.* Before we go farther, it ought to be noted that the Severn, biggest and

---

[1] In Norman French *o* regularly becomes *u*, especially before a nasal.
[2] It may be added here that the Beaurepair, 'lovely haunt,' and Belper of England reappear in Keltic Cornwall as Barrepper, Borripper or Brepper.

earliest recorded river of all, is probably now insoluble. The
native Welsh name is Hafren, which the Romans turned into
Sabrina and the Saxons into Sæfren—quite according to rule;
as, in like manner, the Greek ἕξ and ἑπτά are the Latin sex
and septem, our six and seven.

We have also in Wales, as in England, a good many Keltic
names, as well as Avon, which mean simply ' water ' or ' river '
—e.g., Dovey, W. dwfr, seen again in the Derbyshire Dove;
whilst a common river ending is -on, which also means nothing
but ' stream,' as in Aeron, Cynon, and Avon itself; also in
Scottish rivers like the Carron, and French ones like the
Gar-onne; L. Garumna, where the -umna is clearly the
G. amhuinn and L. amnis—or, rather, a root akin thereto.
The old Keltic deities were largely local or identified with
places. Thus we are not surprised to note that a good many
Welsh rivers, in the view of scholars like Sir Edward Anwyl,
show in their names survivals of river-worship—e.g., Dwy ffor
and Dwy ffach, which, says Anwyl, mean ' great ' and ' little
goddess,' whilst the Merioneth Dyfi probably means ' goddess '
alone. The goddess of war may be commemorated in the
AERON, and the god of the metal-workers or smiths in GAVENNY
(where -y = gwy, ' river '). Yet another god seems to be
buried, or should we not rather say drowned, in the River
LUGG.

The River TAWE is probably the same root as the English
Thame and Thames, only aspirated, all meaning ' smooth,
quiet.' TAWY may be the same; but the TOWEY must be
another root, implying ' to spread out '; and the Cardigan
Tivy may have the same notion hid within it. The derivations
of many of the Welsh streams given by Mr. Morgan are pure
guess-work. Everything here needs careful sifting by a good
Keltic philologist.

The Welsh mountain names are all Keltic too, with the one
notable exception of Snowdon. Some of these mountain names
hide quite a story, if only we could draw it out—Cader Idris,
e.g., ' the chair ' or ' seat of Idris,' who is said to have been
a Welsh hero and a great astronomer. Unfortunately, for
early forms or spellings of these mountain names, our best
and earliest authorities almost entirely fail us; we mean *Liber
Landaviae* or the *Book of Llandaff, c.* 1130, and the bulky

works of Giraldus Cambrensis, the famous Pembrokeshire Norman, *c.* 1180-1200.

But when we turn to counties and coastline we find a quite different state of matters. It is somewhat remarkable that five out of the twelve Welsh counties now bear non-Welsh names. First there is ANGLESEA, usually interpreted as Old English for 'the Isle of the Angles,' a name which goes back to the Norman Conquest. But Mr. W. H. Stevenson prefers to derive from O.N. Öngulsey, 'island of the fjord' (the Menai Straits); the Welsh always call it Ynys Fōn—*i.e.*, their Isle of Man. Then comes DENBIGH, a name over which much nonsense has been talked, largely because, from its earliest mention (? *c.* 1350), the name·is always found in its Welsh spelling, Dinbych, Dynbiegh, or the like, with a final guttural. Dinbych would literally mean 'hill of the wretched being'; while Mr. Morgan holds out for *din bach*, 'little hill,' which it certainly is. But Din bach it is never called; and there can hardly be any doubt that the English pronunciation gives the true name, Den-by, 'Danes' dwelling.' The ending -by is one of the commonest in Great Britain, whilst Dane has become Den- just as in Den-mark. The name is thus identical with TENBY at the opposite corner of Wales; *d* and *t* continually interchange in Welsh names. Next is FLINT, also debated; but it must be the English *flint*, and be called from some rocky peculiarity about the town or county, even though what we technically term 'flint' does not seem at all common here.

The fourth is MONTGOMERY, already dwelt upon; as a county name unique in either Wales or England, being called after a Norman. Lastly, there is RADNOR, as plainly English as Flint, though few people seem clear about it. Mr. Morgan tells us, the shire's name was given to it in the reign of Henry VIII., and that it means 'red district.' The fact is, the name, though not the shire, is as old as Domesday, and is the Old English Radan ora, probably meaning, 'at the edge of the road,' presumably the Roman road which ran from Wroxeter south to Abergavenny and Caerleon. The native Welsh name is Maesyfed or -hyfed, probably for *maes hyfaidd*, 'field of the dauntless one.'

As to the seven other counties with pure Welsh names, it is notable that no less than five commemorate a national hero—

Brechyn, Ceredig, Merlin, Merion, Morgan. This is greatly different from the practice of the Scottish Kelt, who rarely puts either himself or any other human being into his place-names. The two exceptions among the seven are PEMBROKE, which is corrupt Welsh for 'head of the sea-land'; as Giraldus has it, 'Pembrochia caput maritimæ sonat'; and then CAERNARVON, 'fort opposite Mōn' or Anglesea. There is another Carnarvon in Cumberland, with the same meaning. Only in this case the Mōn (aspirated Fōn, pron., Von) is our Isle of Man.

The Welsh have been allowed even less say in naming their own coastline than in naming their counties. A study of the map shows that, except round Cardigan Bay, it is the Norse-man or the Saxon who has named all the headlands of impor-tance. Beginning at the north-east corner and going round, we find—e.g., Point of Ayre, Great Orme's Head, Strumble Head, St. David's Head, Hook Point, St. Gowan's Head, Scar Point, Nash Point, Oldcastle Head, the Nose and Worm's Head (*Worm* being another form of *Orme*, 'the Snake'). The common or map names of the islands are almost all Teutonic, too, though, of course, the Welsh have names of their own— Anglesea, Holy Island, Skerries, South Stack, Puffin Island, Bardsey, Ramsey, Skomer, Skokholm, Grassholm, Caldy, etc.; where, of course, the endings -y, -ey, and -holm are all Norse for 'island,' in its English form -ea. The bays, too, are very largely English Even in very Welsh Anglesea we have a Church Bay and a Redwharf Bay, whilst farther south we have Fishguard Bay, Milford ('sandy fjord') Haven, Oxwich, and Swansea Bays.

Examination of Welsh town and hamlet names reveals several curious and interesting things. The Kelt has always been a devout man, and it is only what one would look for to find that the Church has had a large say in Welsh nomen-clature. Of churches called after the Virgin Mary alone (Llanfair, etc.) we have about 150. Of course, by far the commonest prefix here is *llan*, 'a church,' originally 'an enclosed bit of land,' found once in Scotland in Lhanbryde, 'church of St. Bride.' The *Postal Guide* registers less than half the total, and of its 221 *llans*, four are in Hereford. Crock-ford's *Clerical Directory* enumerates about 465 in all, to which must be added Lampeter, ' St. Peter's church,' and LAMPHEY, formerly Llandyfei, and so, not as commonly thought, 'church of faith,' but ' church of St. Tyfai.' Crockford also gives ten places named Capel and sixteen named Bettws, to which we shall return. But meantime we feel compelled to decline discussing the patron saints of Welsh churches. It would be an endless task, a very perplexing one too. There are so many saints of the same name, whilst about so many exceedingly little is known. It only remains to add, that the student who wishes to know more of British hagiology, and to assure himself who is the saint referred to in Bettws Cedewen, Bettws Garmon, etc., or in any of the 460 *llans*, will do well to consult Smith's well-known *Dictionary of Christian Biography*, where he will find practically all that is really known, set forth in compact form. Only, of course, the student always needs to be on the outlook for spurious saints like St. ISHMAEL'S, or saints in disguise, like Tyfai, who lies buried in the afore-mentioned name LAMPHEY.

We cannot but note, however, that modern Nonconformity has had a share in the naming of villages, which makes a fair second to that of the ancient Catholic Church. In the most Welsh of shires we find a number of hamlets now styled Bethesda or Beulah, Hebron, Nazareth, or Pisgah, after some popular Baptist or Methodist chapel in their midst. It is rather humiliating to add that the public-house comes close on the heels of the Nonconformist chapel in its effect on Welsh place-names, and, little as one would expect it, has had more say in Wales than in any other part of Britain. Tavern Spite marks the site of an inn reared on the ruins of a hospice for pilgrims to the shrine of St. David's. Spite, W. *ysbytty*, is a compound of the L. *hospis, -itis*, ' a guest,' and W. *ty*, ' a house.' This is unobjectionable; but names like the Three Cocks, Brecon; Stay Little, Montgomery; and Tumble, from a TumbledownDick, in Caermarthen, do not sound very dignified.

But, as we promised, we are not yet done with the Church. In addition to all the Llans, there are at least two or three Capels, or Chapels, in almost every shire—Capel Garmon, from the much commemorated St. Germanus, and the like. We need not again comment further on this Norman prefix. But to many a reader it will be a surprise that the familiar W.

bettws is a purely English word with a Welsh frock on. 'We
come now to Bettws—that is, a warm, comfortable place.'
So the word means in Welsh, or else simply 'a house, a place
of shelter.' But though Mr. Morgan mentions ten different
suggested derivations, there can be little doubt that *bettws* is
nothing other than the English *bead-house*, O.E. *bedhus*, 'a
prayer-house.'[1] Phonetically this exactly suits the case. In
English a 'bead-house' came to mean an almshouse, whose
inmates prayed for the repose of the soul of its founder. But
in Welsh a *bettws* seems to have been a prayer-house erected
on one of the great pilgrim highways for the use of devout and
weary pilgrims. It is scarcely questioned that Bettws y Coed,
and all places of like name, date from after—indeed, probably
a good deal after—the Norman Conquest. Dyserth in Flint,
like Dysart in Fife, is the L. *desertum*, 'a desert,' then 'a hermit's
cell,' and then, like Bettws, 'a pilgrim house.'

As with the headlands and islands, so also the chief sea towns
have been named by Norse or English lips (except Cardiff)
—Swansea, *e.g.*, and Newport, Milford, Fishguard, and Holyhead. Because of its present pronunciation, some have thought
that this last must be Holly head; but it is found as 'Le holy
hede' before 1490. The Welsh call it Caergybi, in honour of
Gybi or Cybi, a British saint who, after visiting Gaul and
opposing Arianism, returned *c.* 380, to found a monastery on
this remote isle. Even a number of the favourite watering-
places are non-Welsh in name: Tenby, *e.g.*, and Oystermouth
or Mumbles, and the Cardigan New Quay, which, like its Cornish
namesake, and like Port Madoc, is quite a modern affair. We
must add BARMOUTH, really a corruption of Aber Mawddach,
'at the mouth of the Mawddy,' or 'the broad, expanding river.'
But by the sailors it was deliberately changed to its English
form in 1786, that they might have an English name to mark
upon their vessels. Aber-, by the way, is a very common
prefix in Wales. It was much used by the Brythons and also
by the Scottish Picts. But its Goidelic equivalent Inver-, so
common all over Scotland, and not rare in Ireland, is never
found in Wales. The *Postal Guide* mentions forty-four Abers-
in Wales and Monmouth.

---

[1] Possibly Corn. *botus*, 'a parish,' may be the same word; see BOTUS-
FLEMING.

There are, as we have noted, perhaps no original Roman names left, but there are two Welsh abbeys still with names in medieval Latin—Valle Crucis, 'the Valley of the Cross,' and Strata Florida, 'the Flowery Way,' in Cardigan, called the Westminster Abbey of medieval Wales. *The* county for non-Welsh names is Pembroke, where the town and village names run about half and half. A rough calculation of the names of any consequence gives about seventy Welsh and seventy non-Welsh. Many of these last are known to be due to the batch of Flemings whom Henry I. imported from the Netherlands in 1111, and whom he settled here to help to cow the native Welsh, who could ill brook the iron-handed Norman in their midst. Johnston, Reynoldstown and Rogeston, are cases in point. William Rufus had planted a like colony in Gower in 1099; but Freeman thought these must have been Wessex men brought over from Somerset. All place-name study is full of pitfalls and snares, and Wales is no exception. The student therefore must always be on his guard against names which are not what they seem. There are many real English names on Welsh ground, but not a few masqueraders too, like Valley in Anglesea, which is really the Welsh *maelle*, 'place of trade,' with the often aspirated *m*; whilst Watford, Glamorgan, seems to be a corruption of the Welsh Y Bodffordd, 'the house by the road.'

Of all the real Old English names in Wales not yet descanted upon, perhaps the most important—anyhow, the most perplexing—is WREXHAM, now in Denbigh, but in Saxon days a frontier town of the kingdom of Mercia. We have seen nowhere an accurate account of this name; and we have found that even prominent and highly educated dwellers in Wrexham believe its name to be Welsh, because it has a so-called Welsh name, Gwrecsam, for which some extraordinary explanations have been given. But Gwrecsam is an obvious corruption of the English name, which, in its early spellings, is a little puzzling. It occurs first in the Pipe Roll for 1160-61 as Wristlesham. The *st* at once betrays the pen of a Norman scribe. These men, as we already know (see p. 26), detested gutturals, and practically never wrote them down. When we hunt in Searle's monumental *Onomasticon Anglo-Saxonicum* for a name likely to be represented by Wristles-ham, we find only one, Wrytsleof, 'dux,' at Crediton in 1026.   Wryt- will be for Wryht-, and in all probability the original name is 'Wryhtsleof's home.'   The next recorded spelling is in 1222, in the charter of Madoc ap Gruffydd—Wrecheosam; in 1236 it is Wreccesham or Wrettesham; whilst in 1316-17 is given as Wrightlesham, by far the nearest approximation to the original form.   Beaumont and Fletcher, as is well known, clipped it down to Rixum.

CHAPTER IX

PHONETIC NOTES ON THE ALPHABET AND ITS MUTATIONS IN ENGLISH PLACE-NAMES

a tends to become æ, or reversely—Abba, Æbba; Alfred, Ælfred, etc. The -*an* of the masculine O.E. genitive often becomes -ing—Æbbandune, now Abingdon; Aldantun, now Aldington, etc. We see a reverse process in Ælfredinctun now Alfreton. Medial *eo* in classic O.E. regularly becomes *a* in Mod.E.—HARKSTEAD, 'place of Heorc,' etc.

b may become its fellow labial *p*; but rarely—Abetone is now Apeton, Ebbasham is now Epsom. It also intrudes itself like *p*, but much more rarely—Gamesford is now Camblesforth, Gamelesbi is Gamblesby, Ghemeling is Gembling, etc.

c in Danish regions generally remains hard, but elsewhere tends to soften into *ch*; cf. -*caster*, -*cester*, -*chester*. Sometimes, though rarely, *c* softens into *s*; cf. BRACEBOROUGH, and Shadwell, thought to be 'Chad's well,' whilst already in 1236 we have Ceffton for Sefton.

d interchanges sometimes with its fellow dental *t*—Belford is, c. 1175, Belifort. It even slides on into -*th*; many of the northern -fords are now -forths. It is one of the letters which frequently insert themselves, as in Bewdley for Beaulieu, Brindle for Brinhill, Windrush for Wenrisc, etc.

e in M.E. may appear almost anywhere. It is often a worndown *a* as in Essebi for Ashby, or represents some other almost lost inflexion; but very often, as an ending, it has no significance.

f in Welsh sounds *v*—Afon is Avon, etc.; *ff* sounds *f*, though often the modern final -*ff* is no true *f*, as in CARDIFF, LLANDAFF, etc.

g in Welsh freely interchanges with *c*—Gaerwen for Caerwen, etc. Sometimes it does so in Teutonic names too— Gisburn is, 1197, Kiseburn, etc. Initial *g* tends to drop away, leaving *I* or *Y*, as in Ipswich, the old Gippeswic, Great Yarmouth, once Gernemuth, etc.

h is an elusive aspirate, which freely prefixes itself all over— Abbertune is now Habton, Yorks; Addingham was once also Hatyngham; whilst Aldermaston is found spelt Heldremanestuna.

i and *j* are rare initials in old names. These will generally be found under *g*.

k. In O.E. we only have *c*, in O.N. only *k*. *Dom*. rarely has *k* except in Suffolk, and, more rarely, in Norfolk.

l. This liquid is always disappearing; indeed, the liquids *l*, *m*, *n*, *r*, above all other letters, need watching. Aldworth by 1225 has become Audeworth, and Alnwick, by *c*. 1175, Audnewic (Norman spelling), whilst to-day it is pronounced Annick. *l* is also constantly appearing where it has no right to be, as in ISLINGTON, SCAGGLETHORPE, WALNEY, etc., or as in Hartlepool for 'hart's pool.' We even get Harlington for an orignal Herdington. The *l* may not seldom be replaced by its sister *r*, as in Abberley for 'Eadbeald's' lea '; Barnacle for Barnhangre shows the reverse process; whilst it is the liquid *n* instead of *r* in Ecchinswell for Eccleswell, and in DROMONBY.

ll is a peculiarly Welsh combination. Its soft *thl* sound was reached soon after 1200. The first instance we have noted is in the *Patent¯Roll* for 1246—Keventhles, now Cefn Llys, Radnor. About fifty years later comes *Rolls Parliament*, i. 463, 1,where we have Thlewelyn for Llewelyn. But up to at least Giraldus, *c*. 1200, there is no trace of this. In him we always get *lan*, *e.g*., and no trace of *llan*. We find *c*. 1620 the interesting form Flanteclex for Llanteglos, with which compare FLETHERHILL.

m and *n*, being closely kindred liquids, tend to interchange, as in several cases of Dum- for Dun-.

n is specially liquid, and tends to vanish. See ALNEMOUTH, now Alemouth, Quarrington, etc. It may also interchange with any of the other liquids. See Allerdale for Allendale, Holsingoure, now Hunsingore; Hildrewelle, now Hinderwell; and Baltersbergh, now Baltonsborough. As curious a case as any is the name now RICKMANSWORTH, originally 'Ricmær's worth.'

p. As already said, *p* interchanges with *b*, but rarely. Perhaps in no sure case in aber-, though in old spellings in Scotland we do certainly find apor-. *Cf. Dom.* Ypestan now Ibstone. The letter *p* is a common intruder; see BAMPTON, HAMPTON, etc.

qu as in old Scots is *=wh*, as Whaplode, old Quappelode; Wheldale, old Queldale; Whenby, old Quennebi; etc.

r. See already under the other liquids *l* and *n*. Of course, it often disappears, as in ' fine English ' pronunciation to-day —Abbey Dore is really Aberdore, Heigham Potter should be H. Porter, and Mary-le-bone is properly Mary-le-bourne. It can intrude itself too, as in BARDON, ULVER-STONE, etc.; whilst Derrington, Staffs, was regularly Doddington, or the like, up to 1318. Note that *re* in old spellings is always sounded *er*. This often helps to unravel a knot.

s. The O.E. *sc-*, of course, becomes *sh-*, as in Shalcombe, Shalfleet, Shanklin, etc. More rarely *sh-* may be fr. O.N. *sk-*, as perhaps in Shap and Sheerness. This *sk-* usually remains hard. The plural *s* or *es* is often modern. *Cf.* Coates, Mumbles, Staithes, etc.

th, as we know, is almost always *d* as a final in *Dom.* We find the same change in modern names too, as in Cottered, where -red stands for -rith, ' stream.' Initially *th* is sometimes a mere Norman superfluity, as in Thames, whilst the Th in Thanet is also quite late. *Dom.* usually writes initial Th as T. *Th-* also makes a singular and remarkable change into *f*, as in Fenglesham, Deal, which was in 831 Thenglesham, Felbridge, old Thelbrig, and, conversely, *Dom.* Freschefelt is now Threshfield, Yorks.

v is a genuine element in very few English names.

y is usually for O.E. *ge-* or *g*, as in Yarmouth, Norfolk, for Gernemuth, Yardley for Gyrdleahe, Yarnfield for Gearn-feld, Yatesbury from a man Geat, etc. But *Dom.* often has nothing to show for the *y* sound, as in Yarlett, *Dom.* Erlid, and Yarmouth, Isle of Wight, *Dom.* Ermu.

z is South-West English for *s*. Zoy, *e.g.*, is Soweie, ' sow island,' etc. In *Dom.* it often replaces *s*—Cranzvic for Cranswick, Branzbi for Brandsby, etc. In Ginge, Berks *Dom.* has Gainz, ' where *z* has the sound of *ts* or *dz*, and only approximately represents the English sound of a palatalised *g* (like modern English *j*).'—Skeat.

EXPLANATORY LIST OF
THE CHIEF PLACE-NAMES
OF ENGLAND AND WALES

ABBREVIATIONS

2-4, or such-like figures before an English word denote the centuries in which it is so spelt; *e.g.*, 3-7 *nelde* means that *needle* is found so spelt from the thirteenth to seventeenth centuries.

ABBERLEY (Stourport). *Dom.* Edboldlege, *c.* 1200 Albo(l)desleye, 1275 Albedeleye. *Cf. c.* 1350 *chart.* Aberleye, prob. Lincs. ' Meadow of *Eadbeald*' or '*Ædbold*,' a very common O.E. name. See how one liquid, *l*, glides into another, *r!* *Cf.* next and **ABRAM**, also Ablington, Bibury, *c.* 855 *chart.* Eadbaldingtune. See -ley.

ABBERTON (Pershore and Colchester). Pe. A. 969 *chart.* Eadbrigtincgtune, *Dom.* Edbritone, 1275 Edbriston (*st.* Norman), 1538 Aburton. ' Dwelling of (the sons of) *Eadbriht*' or '*Eadbeorht.*' *Cf.* **ABBERLEY**, and *Dom.* Salop, Etbretone, and Ebrington (Glouc.), *Dom.* Bristentune, *c.* 1300 Ebricton. But Co. A. is *Dom.* Eadburghetun, ' dwelling of (the woman) *Eadburga.*' *Cf.* **ABERFORD.** See -ing and -ton.

ABBEY DORE (Pontrilas). Corrup. of *Aber Dore*, ' place at the confluence of R. **DORE**' and Monnow; W. *aber*, O.G. *aber*, *abber*, *abir*, ' confluence.' The other places in **ABBEY** denote a former abbey—*e.g.*, **ABBEY HULTON** (Burslem), or ' Hill town,' where a Cistercian abbey was built in 1223.

ABBOTS BROMLEY (Rugeley). 1004 Bromleag, -lege, *Dom.* Brunlege, *c.* 1400 Bromley Abbatis, Abbottes Bromley. It belonged to Burton Abbey. See **BROMLEY.**

ABBOTSBURY (Dorset). *Dom.* Abbodesberie, 1155 Abbedesberi, *c.* 1180 *Bened. Peterb.* Abbotesbiria. 'Burgh, of the abbot,' O.E. *abbod. Cf.* 1167-68 *Pipe* Glostr., Abotestun. A Benedictine abbey was founded here in 1044 by the steward of K. Cnut. See -bury.

ABBOT'S KERSWELL (Newton Abbot). *Dom.* Carsewelle, -svelle, 1158-59 *Pipe* Carsewell. 'Watercress well,' O.E. *cærse, cerse,* now 'cress,' Sw. *karse. Cf.* CRESSWELL and KERESLEY. For the Abbot see NEWTON ABBOT; also *cf.* 940 *chart.,* Abbodes wyll, Wilts.

ABBOTS LANGLEY (Herts). 'Abbot's long meadow,' O.E. *lang léah.* Close by is King's Langley.

ABBOTSLEY (Hunts). 1225 Aiboldesley, *c.* 1256 Abboldesley, 1340 Abbodesley. '*Ealdbeald*'s' or '*Albold*'s meadow.' Fine lesson in caution, and in the liquidity of *l.* See -ley.

ABBOTS RIPTON (Hunts). 960 *chart* Riptone. Prob. not 'harvest village,' O.E. *rip,* 'harvest, reaping'; but, 'village of *Rippa.*' *Cf. K.C.D.* 1361, Rippan leah (now Ripley, Woking), and REPTON.

ABBOTTS ANN (Andover). *Dom.* Anne. It is on the R. *Anton,* of which Ann seems to be a contraction; though there is no early record of the form *Anton;* and Anne may be a contraction of W. *afon,* 'river.' See Introd., p. 11, and ANDOVER.

ABER (N. Wales). In W. Aber -gwyngregyn. W. *aber,* 'confluence,' or 'place at the mouth of' (here) a beautiful glen. Nennius speaks of an Oper linn liuan where the Llivan, a tributary, joins the Severn; and Irish *Nennius* speaks of an Operuisc, now Caerleon. *Cf.* ABER (Sc.) at mouth of R. Endrick. *Aber* in G. is often pron. *obair;* in O.G. it is also *apor. Gwyn gregyn* is W. for 'of the white shells,' sing. *cragen.*

ABERAMAN (Aberdare). 'Confluence of the R. Cynon with R. *Aman,*' which is prob. an unaspirated var. of *afon,* 'river.' *Cf.* R. ALMOND (Sc.) and G. *amhuinn,* 'river.' There is also a R. Amman, Carmthn.

ABERANGELL (Dinas Mawddy). W. *angel,* 'an angel'; and see ABER.

ABERARTH (Aberystwith). 'Confluence at the height'; W. and Corn. *arth.*

ABERAYRON (Cardigan). 'At the mouth of R. Ayron.' See AERON.

ABERBARGOED (Rhymney). 'Confluence of the R. Rhymney with R. Bargoed.' This last, the *P.G.* spelling, should be W. *bar coed,* 'height with the wood'; but the more correct spelling seems to be *Bargod,* which means 'a march, a boundary.'

ABERBEEG (Pontypool). ? 'Little confluence'; O.W. *becc,* W. *bach,* G. *beag,* 'little.'

ABERBRAN (Brecon). On Bran see BRANCASTER. In W., Ir., and O.G. *bran* is ' a crow.'

ABERCANAID (Merthyr). ' At the mouth of the Canaid,' a rivulet here; W. *cannaid*, ' white, gleaming.'

ABERCARN (Newport, Mon.). ' Confluence at the cairn or mound '; W., O.Ir., and G., *carn*.

ABERCONWAY (N. Wales). *c.* 1188 *Gir. Camb.* Aberkonewe, -coneu; 1295 Aberconewey. See ABER and CONWAY.

ABERCRAVE (Neath). ' Confluence of R. Tawy with the brook Craf '; fr. W. *craf* (*f* pron. *v*), ' claws, talons '; *crafu,* ' to scratch or tear up,' referring to the action of the stream.

ABERDARE. ' Confluence of the R. Cynon with R. Dâr '; Cynon may mean ' chief brook,' whilst Dâr is prob. W. *dar,* ' an oak.'

ABERDARON (Pwllheli). ' At the mouth of the R. *Daron,*' which is said to mean 'noisy river '; the ending -on may quite well stand for ' river,' as in CARRON (Sc.), Garonne, etc., and as in Cynon, see above.

ABERDULAIS (Neath). ' Confluence of the dark, black stream '; W. *du glais. Cf.* DOUGLAS and DOWLAIS.

ABEREDW (Builth). ' Confluence of the R. *Edwy,*' of which the Ed- may be fr. W. *eddu,* ' to press on, to go,' whilst the -wy is = WYE or ' river.'

ABERERCH (Pwllheli). ' Confluence of R. Erch '; W. *erch,* ' dun-coloured, dark.'

ABERFFAN (Merthyr). ' Confluence of the brook *Fan,*' with R. Taff. Said to be fr. W. *ban,* ' high.'

ABERFFRAW (W. of Anglesea). *a.* 1196 *Gir. Camb.* Aberfrau, 1232 *Close R.* Abbefrau, *c.* 1350 Aber(i)frowe. Ffraw is thought by H. Bradley to represent an orig. Frāma, later Frōm (name of R. FROME in *O.E. Chron.* 998), which would develop on Brit. lips to Frauv, and later to Ffraw. The earliest recorded form of R. Frome actually is Fraau (*O.E. Chron.* 875). Meaning doubtful; some think it means ' agitated, active, swift ' river.

ABERFORD (Leeds). *a.* 1200 *Pipe* Ædburgforth, Ædburford Nothing to do with *W. aber,* ' confluence '; but ' ford of ' (the lady) *'Eadburh,'* gen. *-burge,* as in ABBERTON (Essex). See -ford.

ABERGAVENNY. *c.* 380 *Anton. Itin.* Goban(n)io, *a.* 1196 *Gir. Camb.* Abergavenni, -gevenni, *c.* 1200 *Gervase* Bergevene, 1281 and often later, Bergeveny, 1610 *Holland* Aber- Gevenny. Local pron. Aber-venny. In W. Abergefni or Y Fenni. ' Confluence of the Gavenny ' and Usk. *Gobann* is gen. of *goibniu,* ' a smith,' in Ir. a proper name = Smith and GOVAN (Sc.) and Gowan. In late W. legend Gofannon is patron god of metal-workers. The a- in aber- is rarely lost, as in many old forms here; but *cf.* BARMOUTH, BERRIEW, etc.

ABERGELE (N. Wales). Pron. -gáyly. Perh. *c.* 1350 *chart.* Abergelon. 'At the mouth of the R. Gele'; prob. W. *gele*, 'a leech'; leeches used to be common in the estuary here.

ABERGWILI (Carmarthen). *Gwili* is a river name. Here it is prob. the same root as R. WILEY. Some derive fr. W. *gwyllt,* 'wild.'

ABERGWYNFI (Bridgend, Glam.). 'Confluence of the brook Gwynfi'; Thos. Morgan says Gwynfai means 'blessed plain'; W. *gwyn ffau* would mean 'clear cave.' The writer cannot learn if there is one here.

ABERGWYNOLWYN (Towyn). 'Confluence of the white swallow;' W. *gwinnol gwyn.* But the name seems better spelt Abergwernolwy(n). The river here is the Gwernol, W. for 'swampy, boggy.'

ABERKENFIG (Bridgend, Glam.). 'Confluence at KENFIG Hill.'

ABERLLEFNI (Merioneth). The -llefni is very doubtful. W. *llefnau* means 'ruins'; some think of W. *llech feini*, 'slate stones.' Thos. Morgan inclines to the form Llwyfeni, as the name is spelt by *Ifan Tew;* this means 'elm-trees,' still found on the bank of the river. *Cf.* LEVEN (Sc.) and Aberllynfi, 1233 *Close R.* Abberlewin, Abrelenuith.

ABERLLEINIOG (Anglesea). *c.* 1205 *Brut re* ann. 1096, Aberlleiniawc. 'Confluence of the Lleiniog,' a mere brook. The name seems connected with W. *lleinio*, 'to blade,' *lleiniad*, 'a putting forth of blades,' fr. *llafn*, 'a blade.'

ABERPORTH (Cardigan). W. *aber porth*, 'confluence at the harbour.' *Cf.* LANGPORT.

ABERSYCHAN (Pontypool). 'Confluence of the *Sychan,*' which may mean, a brook that runs dry in summer; fr. W. *sych*, 'dry'; *sychin*, 'drought.'

ABERTEIVI (Cardigansh.) *Sic a.* 1196 *Gir. Camb.;* he also has Aberteini, -theini (? mistakes, *n* for *u*) ; also Abertewi (? the same place). See TIVY.

ABERTILLERY (Pontypool). 'Confluence of the R. *Tillery,*' perh. a pre-Keltic name. To derive fr. a reputed *ty O'Leary*, or 'O'Leary's house,' seems ridiculous; nor is it likely to be fr. O.W. *twyllawr, -lwr,* 'a cheat, a deceiver.'

ABERYSTWITH. *c.* 1196 *Gir. Camb.* Aberescud; 1461 *Lib. Pluscard.* Abirhust Wiche –a bad shot by an ignorant scribe. W. *ystwyth* is 'pliant, flexible,' a likely name for a river. But -escud suggests W. *ysgwd*, 'a thrusting forward,' or *ysgod*, 'a shadow,' or *ysgoad*, 'a starting aside.'

ABINGDON. *Sic c.* 1540 ; 699 *chart.* Abbendune; 1051 *O.E. Chron.* Abbandune, Æbbandune; *c.* 1180 *Benedict Peterb.* Abbendonia;

c. 1377 *Piers Pl.* Abyndoun. O.E. *Æbban dún.* ' Ebba's hill ' or ' fort.' *Abba* or *Ælbba* is a common Wessex name. In Yorks the Abbetune of *Dom.* has become Habton. See -don.

ABINGER Common and Hammer (Dorking). Pron. Abenjer, *cf.* BIRMINGHAM. *Old* Abingworth, Abingerth. O.E. *Abban worth,* ' Abba's farm,' rather than ' Abba's yard ' or ' garth,' O.E. *geard.* See HAMMER. *Dom.* Surrey has only Abinceborne. See -bourne and -ing and -worth.

ABINGTON (Cambridge and Northants). Cam. A. *Dom.* Abintone, 1302 Abyntone. Nor. A. *chart.* Abintone. O.E. *Abban tun,* ' village of Abba.' ABINGTON (Sc.) is 1459 Albintoune.

AB-KETTLEBY (Melton Mow.). *Dom.* Chetelbi, *c.* 1350 *chart.* Abbekettelby. The *Dom.* form is simple—' dwelling of *Cetel* ' or ' *Kettel,*' a common O.E. name. The Ab- is difficult; perh. the name intended is *Ælfcytel,* a fairly common one, of which a var. *Ælbcytel* occurs. There is also a name *Aba,* seen prob. in ' Abegrave ' in *Dom.* of this same shire. *Cf.* ' Abblinton,' Lincs, in *Roll Rich. I.,* and ABLOAD, Glouc., 1189 *Pipe* Abbelada; also KETTLEBURGH. See -by.

ABRAM (Wigan). 1190-1322 Adburgham, 1212 Edburgham, 1372-1481 Abraham. ' Home of *Eadburh* ' or ' *Eadburga,*' a common O.E. woman's name. Of course the later forms have been modified through supposed connection with *Abraham.* *Cf.* ABBERTON, BABRAHAM, and WILBRAHAM.

ABY (Alford). *Dom.* Abi. ' Dwelling, village on the stream '; O.N. *á-bi.* *Cf.* ABRIDGE, Romford, and 1166-67 *Pipe,* Hants, Abrigge, Hamonis; only in this last the A- will be O.E. *eá,* ' river.' See -by.

ACASTER MALBIS (York), and A. SELBY. Both in *Dom.* Acastra, -stre, also ' Acastra, other Acastre '; 1166-67 *Pipe* Acastra. Prob. N. *á-caster,* ' camp, fort by the stream.' See -caster. The *Malbysse* family dwelt at A. Malbis for some centuries after the Conquest. It is on R. Ouse.

ACCRINGTON. 1258 Akerynton, 1277 Acrinton, *a.* 1300 Alkerington, Akerington, *c.* 1350 Alcrynton; *cf. Dom.* Worcr. Alcrintun. This seems to be ' town, village of *Ealhhere* '; also spelt *Alcher* and *Ahhere.* or, of his descendants. The name is very common in O.E. See -ing and -ton.

ACKLAM (York). *Dom.* Aclun, 1202 Aclum, 1528 Acclame, 1530 Acclome. A little puzzling. Said by some to be an old loc. of O.E. *ác,* ' at the oaks.' *Cf.* KILHAM. But how account for the *l*? The first part must be the name of its owner, given in *Dom.* as *Ulchel,* or *Ulkel,* short for the common *Ulfcytel;* the *Onom.* also gives a form or name *Achil.* The ending may be a loc., ' at Ulkel's,' afterwards assimilated to -ham, *q.v.* *Cf.* Acklington, Morpeth, where old forms are needed, and ACOMB.

ACKLETON (Wolverhampton). Old forms needed. Prob. '*Aculf's*
or *Acwulf's* town '; but *cf.* above, and ACLE; and see -ton.

ACKLEY (Kent). [789 *O.E. Chron.* Acleah, and *Sim. Dur.* ann. 851
Aclea, in Northumbria.] *a.* 1000 *chart.* Acleah, O.E. = ' oak-
lea, oak-meadow.' *Cf.* ACLE and OCKLEY. But ACKSLEY
(Dorset) is *K.C.D.* 706 Accesleah, ' meadow of *Acca.*' Ackholt,
Kent—*i.e.,* ' oak-wood '—is 1232 *Close R.* Achalt, -holt.

ACKWORTH (Pontefract). *Dom.* Acewrde, 1204 Acworth, which is
O.E. for ' oak place.' See -worth.

ACLE (Norwich). *Sic* in *Dom.* A rare type of name, O.E. *ác léah,*
' oak mead '; -ley is rarely slurred into -le. But *cf.* Oakle, Minsterworth, *old* Okkele, Ocle; also *cf.* ACK- and OCKLEY.

ACOMB (Hexham and York). Hex. A. *old* Oakham, mod. pron.
Yekhm. Yor. A. *Dom.* Acum, Acun. This seems to have
nothing to do with -combe ' valley,' but to be an old loc.,
O.E. *ácun,* ' at the oaks '; afterwards influenced by -ham. *Cf.*
ACKLAM and KILHAM.

ACONBURY (Hereford). 1218 *Patent R.* and 1285 *Close R.* Acornebury. ' Burgh of ' ? *Acorn,* used as a personal name, not in
Onom. The sb. is O.E. *æcern,* ' fruit of the acre,' *i.e.,* ' unenclosed land.' *Oxf. Dict.* does not give the form *acorn* till
1440. Very likely, however, Acorn- may be corrup. of *Ecebearn*
or *Ecgbeorn,* a name found in Worc. *c.* 1055.

ACREFAIR (Ruabon). ' Acre ' or ' field of Mary '; W. *Fair* (*f* is
aspirated *m* in W.).

ACTON (London, Suffolk, Nantwich, etc.). Lond. A. *c.* 1300 Acton;
Suff. A. *a.* 1000 *chart.* Acantun; Nant. A. *Dom.* Actune. O.E.
ác-tun, ' enclosure, village, with the oaks.' But Acan- must be
the gen. of *Aca* or *Acca,* a common O.E. personal name. In
S. Yorks the Actone of *Dom.* is now Ackton, whilst in E. Riding
Dom.'s Actun has become AUGHTON.

ACTON BURNELL (Shrewsbury). *Dom.* Achetone, 1271 Actone
Burnel. The *ch* in *Dom.* is the habitual softening of the Nor.
scribes. See ACTON. Sir Robt. *Burnel,* tutor to K. Edward I.,
and made by him Ld. Chancellor and Bp. of Bath and Wells,
was given the manor here *c.* 1270. *Brunel* is the same name.

ACTON TRUSSELL (Penkridge). 1004 Actun, *Dom.* Actone; and
ACTON TURVILLE (Chippenham). See ACTON. A *Tourville* or
Turville came over with Wm. the Conqueror, and is found on
the roll of Battle Abbey. One is found at Normanton-Turvile,
co. Leicester, *temp.* Hen. II. The *Trussells* were also a Nor.
family.

ADBASTON (Eccleshall). *Dom.* Edbaldestone; *later* Adbaldestone,
Alboldestun, Albaldiston. ' Town, village of *Eadbeald,*' a
common name. *Cf.* ABBERLEY and ADBOLTON (Notts) *Dom,*
Alboltune.

ADDER or ADUR R. (Wilts). *a.* 420 *Notitia* Portus Adurni—*i.e.*, Aldrington on this river. Nothing to do with *adders;* but Kelt., Corn. *dour,* W. *dywr,* 'water.' The A- is doubtful. The Sc. R. ADDER is prob. aspirated fr. G. *fad dobhar* or *dūr,* 'long stream.' There is a R. Adur both in Sussex and Cornwall.

ADDERBURY (Banbury). *a.* 1000 *K.C.D.* 1290 Eadburgebyrig, *Dom.* Edburgberie, 1229 *Close R.* Eadburebir', 1230 *ib.* Eburbir', 1270 Abberbury, 1288 Adburbur', 1428 Addurbury. 'Burgh, town of the lady *Eadburh,*' gen. *-burge.* To-day it is the *d,* not the *b,* which has survived, as in ABBERTON and ABBER-FORD. But we still have the *d* in St. Adborough's Ditch, Cotswolds. See -bury.

ADDERLEY (Mket. Drayton). *Dom.* Eldredelei, 1284 *Close R.* Addredeleye; 'Meadow of the woman *Aldreda,*' in O.E. *Æthel-thryth,* a common name. See -ley.

ADDINGHAM (Leeds). *c.* 1130 *Sim. Dur.* Addingeham, v.r. Hatyng-ham, 'Home of the descendants of *Adda,*' a common O.E. name. See -ing and -ham, and *cf.* next.

ADDINGTON (Bucks, Croydon, Maidstone, Northampton.). Croy. A. *Dom.* Edintone, Nor. A. *chart.* Adyngton(a), *Dom.* Edintone, whilst *Dom.* Kent is Eddintone. 'Village of *Adda* or *Edda,*' or his descendants. *Cf.* above, and -ing.

ADDISCOMBE (Croydon). *Old* Adscomb, Adgcomb; not in *Dom.* '*Adda's* vale,' O.E. *cumb*(e). *Cf.* above. But ADDISCOTT, S. Tawton, is 1228 *Close R.* Eilrichescot, 'cottage of *Elric,*' var. of the common *Ælfric.*

ADDLE or ADEL (Leeds). *Dom.* Adele, Ecton's *Liber Regis* Adhill. 'Hill of *Ada,*' 2 in the *Onom.* Possibly the -ele represents -hale or -hall, *q.v.*

ADDLETHORP(E) (W. Riding and Burgh, Lincs). *Dom.* Yorks, Ardulfestorp, Lincs, Arduluetorp. '*Ardulf's* village.' *Cf.* Addle-stone (Chertsey), and see -thorpe.

ADISHAM (Canterbury). 616 *Grant* Adesham, v.r. Edesham. '*Ada's*' or '*Edda's*' home. *Cf.* ADDINGHAM, and see -ham.

ADLESTROP (Stow-on-Wold). *Dom.* Tedestrop, Thatlestrope, 1198 Tadelesthorp, *Feud. Aid.* Tatlestrop. This must be orig. '*Tædald's*' or '*Tædweald's* village'; one such in *Onom.* The name is very interesting for (1) the rare dropping of initial *T,* and (2) the preserving of the true O.E. form *t(h)orp,* very rare in Eng. names, except in this shire. *Cf.* Westrip, *old* Westrop, and Wolstrop, *old* Wulvesthrop. See -thorpe.

ADLINGFLEET (Goole). [Perh. *O.E. Chron.* 763 Ælflet ee; ee = O.E. *ige,* 'isle.'] *Dom.* Adelingesfluet, *c.* 1080 Athlingfleet, 1304 Athelingflete. 'Stream of *Atheling,*' the O.E. *æðel-ing,* 'descen-dant of a noble family,' spelt 1387 *Trevisa* 'adelyngus.' *Cf.*

Ger. *adel*. The -fleet is O.N. *fljót*, 'stream, river,' cognate with *fljót-r*, 'fleet, quick.' The Adelingestorp of *Dom.* is now Ellinthorpe, S. Yorks.

ADLINGTON (Chorley and Macclesfd.). Chor. A. 1184-90 Edeluinton, Adel-, Aldeventon, Adelinton, Athelington, 1294 Adelingtone, 1286 Edlington. Macc. A. *c.* 1250 Adelvinton. The name is the very common O.E. *Æthelwine*, in its L. form, *Adelwinus ;* but some of the spellings were evidently influenced by the O.E. *œðeling*. See above, and -ton.

ADMASTON (Rugely and Wellington, Salop). Rug. A. *a.* 1200 Edmundeston, Admerdeston, *a.* 1300 Admundestan, Edmundestone. Wel. A. *a.* 1300 Ademon(e)ston. 'Town, village of *Eadmund'* (or '*Eadmœr*'). The forms show how both the liquids *n* and *r* can vanish.

ADSTOCK (Winslow). *Dom.* Edestocha. 'Place of *Ada, Ædda*, or *Æddi*' *;* -stock is = STOKE. *Cf.* ADWICK, and ADSETT (Glouc.), 1221 Addesete, '*Adda*'s settlement.'

ADUR R. See ADDER.

ADVENT (Lanteglos, Cornwall). May be fr. *Advent* Sunday, day of the consecration of the Church here; or fr. St. *Adwen*, daughter of a W. saint and king, 4th cny.

ADWALTON (Bradford). 1202 Athelwaldon; 'Town, village of *Æthelweald*,' or its equally common var., '*Eadweald*.'

ADWICK - LE - STREET (Doncaster) and **ADWICK - ON - DEARNE** (S. Yorks). Both *Dom.* Adewic., 'Dwelling of *Ada*.' *Cf.* ADSTOCK, and see -wick. For Dearne see WATH-ON-DEARNE.

ADWYRCLAWDD (Wrexham). W. *adwy r' clawdd*, 'gap, breach in the dyke'—*i.e.*, Offa's Dyke, close by.

AERON or **AYRON R.** (Cardigansh.). Possibly fr. *Agriona ;* Kelt. goddess of war, W. *aer*, 'battle.' W. *air* is 'bright, clear,' whilst -on is contraction of *afon*, 'river.' *Cf.* CARRON (Sc.).

AFFPIDDLE (Dorchester). *Dom.* Affapidele. Prob. 'puddle' or 'puddly stream of *Affa*'; 2 called *Affa* and 2 *Afa* in *Onom.* See PIDDLE.

AFON ALAW (Anglesea). W. = 'river of water lilies.' Afon in W. is, of course, pron. AVON.

AFONWEN (Holywell). W. *afon gwen*, 'very clear, bright river.'

AIGBURTH (Liverpool). 1190-1256 Aykeberh, 1329 Aikebergh. O.N. *eik-berg*, 'oak-clad hill' or 'rock'; the endings have been influenced by the forms of what is now *Barrow* sb[1] *Oxf. Dict.*, O.E. *beorg*, 3 *berhg*, 4 *bergh*, *burgh*. *Cf.* EAKRING.

AINDERBY (Northallerton). *Dom.* Aiendrebi, Andrebi, 1208 Enderby. 'Dwelling of *Andar*' or '*Ænder*,' though the only forms in *Onom.* are *Andhere* and *Andahari*. *Cf.* ANDERBY, and see -by.

AINSDALE (Southport). *Dom.* Einuluesdel, 1199 Annovesdala, 1190-1206 Aynuluisdale, 1201-02 Ainolvesdale, 1206 Einonesdal. 'Valley of *Einwulf*,' one in *Onom.* *Cf.* ARMTHORPE and EYNESBURY.

AINSWORTH (Bolton). 1190-1216 Haineswrthe, 1244 Ainesworth, *c.* 1514 Aynsworth. Doubtful. It may be 'farm of *Eginulf*' or '*Einulf*,' as in AINSDALE. It prob. is 'farm of *Hagena*' (now Haines); or perh. 'of *Egon*,' as in EYNSHAM. AINSTABLE, Armathwaite, Cumbld., is 1210 Einstapeleth, which may be '*Einwulf's* market,' *cf.* BARNSTAPLE. See -worth.

AINTREE (Liverpool). 1244-92 Eyntre, 1296 Ayntre. Perh. '*Æne's* tree.' *Cf.* the 'Aynburg' in *Sim. Dur.*, BRAINTREE, etc. But Wyld says, O.E. *an treow*, 'one tree,' *one* in N. dial. being *ane*, 5-6 *ayne, ain.*

AIRE R. (Yorks). 959 *chart.* Yr., 1314 Hayr. Prob. O.N. *eyri,* 'tongue of land, gravelly bank.' *Cf.* AYR R. (Sc.), which prob. has the same origin.

AIRMYN or ARMYN (Goole). (? *Dom.* Amuine.) 1314 *chart.* Hayrminne, 1317 Ayremynn, *a.* 1400 Ayermynne. Aire -munn is 'confluence of the R. AIRE' and the Ouse; fr. O.N. *minni*, N. *munn-r*, 'mouth.' *Arminni* is common in the Sagas for 'a confluence.' *Cf.* STALMINE.

AIRTON (W. Riding). *Dom.* Airtone. 'Town on R. AIRE.'

AISHOLT (Bridgewater). Not in *Dom.*, but it has in Somst. Aissecote and -forde. O.E. *æsc-holt*, 'ash-wood.' *Ash* is round *a.* 1300 as *asse*, *c.* 1450 *aish.* *Cf.* Great Aish, South Brent. But AISTHORPE, Lincs, is 1233 *Close R.* Austorp, prob. 'east village.' *Cf.* AUSTERFIELD.

AISLABY (Sleights, Yorks). *Dom.* Aslachesbi. 'Dwelling of *Aslac*.' *Cf.* ASLACKBY, and see -by.

AKELD (Wooler). O.N. *eik-kelda*, 'oak-tree spring'; *cf.* LITTLE SALKELD. Possibly the name is purely O.E. *Cf.* O.E. *ác* ('an oak'), and BAPCHILD.

ALBERBURY (Shrewsbury). *Dom.* Alberberie. Prob. '*Ealdbeorht's* burgh' or 'fort.' Several men of that name known in Mercia. *Cf.* Albur-, Alber-wyk in a charter of Edw. III., and Elberton (Glouc.), 1230 Albricton. There is in 1160-61 *Pipe* N'hants, an Albodeston, or '*Ealdbeald's* town,' which *may* be the same name as ALBASTON, Tavistock; old forms needed. At any rate we have 1166-67 *Pipe*, Glouc., Abbdeston, Abbedeston, also found as Albedeston. *Ealdbeald* is more commonly *Eadbeald*, v.r. *Ædbold.*

ALBOURNE (Sussex). (? *Dom.* Aldingeborne.) *Cf.* 931 in *B.C.S.* II. 358 *q.v.* Æt aleburnan æt þam lytlan egilande [near Clare, Hants]. The Al- is doubtful. *Cf.* ALBURGH; and see -bourne.

ALBRIGHTON (Shrewsbury and Wolverhampton). *Dom.* Salop, Albricstone. [823 *chart.* 'Aldberhtingtun in occidente Stur,' near Canterbury.] 'Town' or 'village of *Ealdbeorht.*' *Cf.* Elburton, Plymouth: on the -st in *Dom. Cf.* p. 26.

ALBURGH (Harleston) and ALBURY (Guildford and Bps. Stortford). Guil. A. *a.* 900 *chart.* Aldeburi, whilst Bps. S. A. is still spelt Aldboro'. O.E. *eald* (M.E. *ald*), *burh,* 'old burgh, fortified place.' *Cf.* negro *ole* for *old,* ALDBOROUGH and ALDEBY; also see -burgh.

ALCESTER (Redditch). 1166-67 *Pipe* Alecestr', 1178 *ib.* Alencestra, 1217 *Patent R.* Alencestre, 1538 *Leland* Aulcester. 'Camp on R. ALNE.' It certainly was a Rom. camp. Close by is Great Alne. See -cester.

ALCONBURY (Hunts). 1232 *Close R.* Alcmundebir', *a.* 1300 Alkemundebyri. 'Burgh of *Alchmund.* But Aconbury, Hereford, is 1218 *Patent R.* Acornebury, seemingly fr. a man called *Acorn,* O.E. *œcern,* 'acorn.' See -bury.

ALDBOROUGH (S.W. Essex, Norwich, and W. Riding). No. A. *Dom.* Aldebga, York A. 1203 Vetus Burgum, L. for O.E. *eald,* Mercian *ald burh,* 'old burgh,' or 'fortified place.' A. in Yorks is, *e.g.* Roman (L. Isurium). *Cf.* next and ALBURGH. For ALDBOROUGH HATCH (Ilford) see HATCH.

ALDE R. and ALDEBOROUGH (Suffolk). *Sic* 1298, but *Dom.* Aldebure. This, unlike the above, is 'town on R. Alde,' W. *allt,* 'side of a hill, wooded crag,' cognate with G. *allt,* which in Sc. names is often Auld. In Scotland it usually means a stream, or the high banks through which a stream flows; thus = L. *altus. Cf.* ALT.

ALDEBY (Beccles). Not in *Dom.* North.O.E. *eald bý,* 'old house' or 'hamlet.' *Cf.* ALBURY, and -by. This cannot be a Norse name, as Norse used only *gamel* for 'old,' positive degree.

ALDENHAM (Bushey). *Sic* 969, but 785 *chart.* Ældenham, *a.* 1000 Ealdenham. *Dom.* Aldeham, 'Home of *Ealda*'; several so called in *Onom.*

ALDERBURY (Salisbury). Not in *Dom.* Prob. O.E. *aler-burh,* 'town of the alder-tree,' O.E. *alor, aler,* as early as Chaucer. *alder. Cf.* ALDERFORD (Norwich) and ALDERHOLT (Salisbury), O.E. *holt,* 'a forest, a wood'; and see next.

ALDERLEY (Crewe, Manchester, Leek, etc.). Cr. A. *Dom.* Aldredelie. Le. A. 1129 Aldredeslega. 'Aldred's lea' or 'meadow,' O.E. *léah.* There are many *Ealdreds* in Mercia in *Onom.* But in some cases it may be simply 'alder-meadow'; *cf.* above. With Alderley Edge, Manchester, *cf. Dom.* Suffk. Ethereg, now the name Etheridge

ALDERMASTON (Reading). *Sic c.* 1540. *Dom.* Eldremanestune and Heloremanestune (scribe's error), 1166-67 *Pipe* Alder-mannestun, 1316 Aldermanston; also Aldremanneston. ' Village of the alderman,' O.E. *ealdormann.* The *n* has been lost through its liquidity.

ALDERMINSTER (Stratford-on-Avon). 1275 Aldremoneston, -mes-ton. Not in *Dom.* Corrup. of ' *alderman's* town,' as in above, influenced by -minster.

ALDERNEY (Channel Islds.). *a.* 380 *Ant. Itin.* Riduna. Fr. Aurigny, 1218 Aurennye, 1219 Aureneye, 1224 Alnere. As it stands the name is ' alder-tree isle,' O.E. *œlren-ige. Aldern* is an adj. already found, 1001, as *œlren.* Riduna might repre-sent a Keltic *rid dun,* ' reddish hill.' *Cf.* W. *rhydd, rhudd,* ' red.'

ALDERSHOT. *Shot* is a broad way or glade in a wood, through which game can dart or shoot. *Cf.* SHOTOVER and COCKSHUTT. Similarly, ALDERSHAW (Lichfield), *c.* 1300 Alreshawe, is ' alder wood,' O.E. *sceaga,* M.E. *schawe.*

ALDERTON (Beckford, Chippenham, Felixstowe). Ch. A. *Dom.* Aldritone. Fe. A. *c.* 1150 Alretun. ' Alder-tree village.' *Cf.* ALLERTON.

ALDFORD (Chester). ' Old Ford,' O.E. *eald,* Mercian *ald.*

ALDIN GRANGE (Durham). Prob. fr. the very common *Aldhun* or *Ealdhun ;* one was bp. at Chester-le-Street, Durham, *c.* 990. *Cf.* GRANGE.

ALDINGTON (Hythe and Worcester). Hy. A. *a.* 1124 *Eadmer* Ealdintune. Wor. A. 709 *chart.* and *Dom.* Aldintone. *K.C.D.* 61 Aldantune, ' Town, village of *Alda* ' or ' *Ealda,*' gen. -*an. Cf.* Aldingbourne, Chichester, and Aldingha' in *Dom.* N. Lancs.

ALDRIDGE (Walsall). *Dom.* Alrewic, *a.* 1200 Alrewich, Allerwych. O.E. *alr wic,* ' dwelling, village among the alders.' *Cf.* ALDER-BURY and PENKRIDGE.

ALDRINGHAM (Saxmundham). Not in *Dom.* Perh. ' Home of the elders or parents,' M.E., *c.* 1300, *eldryng.* But old forms might reveal that it comes fr. some personal name. See -ing and -ham.

ALDRINGTON (on R. Adur, Wilts). *a.* 1300 Aldrinton. Prob. now ' Village of the elders.' *Cf.* above. But orig. it came fr. the river on which it stands, *q.v.*

ALDWARK (Easingwold). ' Old fort ' or ' bulwark '; O.E. *worc,* an ' outwork,' a fortification. *Cf.* WARK.

ALDWINCLE (Northampton). 1137 *O.E. Chron.* Aldwingel; 1166-67 *Pipe* Aldewincle, 1298 Audewyncle. Nothing like -wingel in O.E. So this will be ' *Ealdwine-geil,*' The former is a common O.E. name, *cf. B.C.S.* 1280 Aldwines barwe; the latter is O.N.

geil, gil, ' a deep glen or ravine, a gill '; not found in Eng. till 1400 ' gille.' *Cf.* Winskill, Langwathby; and see -gill.

ALDWORTH (Reading). *c.* 1225 Audeworth, 1316 Aldeworth. ' Old farm '; O.E. *eald,* Merc. *ald.* But ALDSWORTH, North-leach, *Dom.* Aldeswrde, is ' farm of *Eald* ' (the old man). See -worth.

ALFORD (Lincs and Somst.). Lin. A. *Dom.* Alforde, Som. A. perh. *Dom.* Aldedeford. These names are uncertain; perh. O.E. *eald ford,* ' old ford.' But ALFORD, Hants, is *K.C.D.* 1035 Ælwelford—*i.e.,* ' *Ælfweald, Alfwold,* or *Æthelweald*'s ford.' All these names are common in *Onom.*

ALFRETON (Chesterfield). 1002 *chart.* Ælfredincgtun. ' Hamlet of Alfred's descendants.' See -ing.

ALFRISTON (Polegate). *Dom.* Alvricestone, 1288 *Close R.* Alver-icheston. ' Village of *Ælfric* ' or ' *Alfricus,*' both in *Onom. Cf.* ALFRIC (Worc.), said to be for Alfredeswic, and 1167-68 *Pipe,* Devon, Ailricheston.

ALGARKIRK (Boston). 810 *chart.* Algare. ' Church of *Ælfgar,* v.r. *Alger,*' a very common name. It may be fr. Earl *Algar,* 9th cny., a brave opponent of the Danes.

ALKBOROUGH (Doncaster). *a.* 1100 (in *Grant* of 664) Alkebarue, 1359 Alkebarowe. ' Burial mound of *Alca,*' one in *Onom.* This is O.E. *elch,* M.E. *alce,* L. *alces,* ' an elk.' *Cf.* next and BAR-ROW; also ALKHAM, Dover.

ALLAN R. (Bodmin and St. David's), and ALLEN R. (S. Northbld. and Dorset). Keltic *aluin.* ' fair, lovely.' See ALN, and *cf.* ALLERDALE. The Alwyn, trib. of Coquet, is, of course, the same name.

ALL CANNINGS (Devizes) and ALL STRETTON (Church Stretton). Prob. the *all* is for *hall,* O.E. *heall ; cf.* HALTON. See CAN-NINGTON. Stretton is ' street town,' ' village on the (Roman) road.'

ALLER (Somerset). 878 *O.E. Chron.* Alor; perh. *Dom.* Alra. O.E. *alor,* ' the alder-tree.' *Cf.* COULTER ALLERS (Sc.), also 808 *chart.* Alercumb, Somst.

ALLERDALE (Cumberland). *c.* 1080 Alnerdall. ' Valley of the alder-trees '; see above and ALDERNEY. Only, through it flows the R. Alne or Ellen, near whose mouth is Alneburg or Ellen-borough, for which see ALLAN. The liquids *r* and *n* easily inter-change. See -dale. ALLERDEN (Nthbld.), is 1099 Elredene, ' alder dean '; see -dean.

ALLERTHORPE (York). *Dom.* Alwarestorp. ' *Ealdweard*'s village.' *Cf.* ALVERTHORPE and ELLERBY, and see -thorpe.

ALLERTON (Axbridge and 3 in Yorks.). *Dom.* Yorks, Alreton, -tun, including Northallerton twice; Chesh., Salop, and Worc.

Alreton(e). Perh. = ALDERTON, 'village in the alder-trees.'
But Axb. A. may be *a*. 1199 *Roll Rich. I*. Alurinton (in
Somst.), where the first part may represent a man's name,
it is uncertain what. And ALLERSTON, Pickering, is *Dom*.
Alurestan, Alvrestain, Alvestun, 'town' or 'stone of *Alfere*,'
late form of the common Ælfhere, fr. which also comes NORTH-
ALLERTON. *Cf*. ELLERTON.

ALLESLEY (Coventry). *Sic a*. 1300, and ALLESTREE (Derby).
Prob. 'lea, meadow,' and 'tree of *Ælla*,' a common name.
But ALLESTON, Pembk., is *old* Ayllewarston, or '*Æthelweard*'s '
or *Ælfweard*'s town.'

ALLINGTON (Grantham). *Dom*. Ellingetone. *Cf. Dom*. Chesh. Alen-
tune. Prob. 'town of the sons of *Ælla*.' See -ing.

ALLITHWAITE (Grange). 'Place of *Alli*.' a man found in *Onom. ;*
and *Alla* was K. of Northumbria in 560. See -thwaite.

ALLONBY (Maryport). *c*. 1350 Alaynby. 'Dwelling of *Alayn*,
Allo, or *Allon*.' There was an *Allo,* gen. *Allonis*, dux *c*. 800;
and Allon is still a surname. Of course, the name may be,
'dwelling near the R. ALNE or Ellen'; but this would not be in
accordance with analogy in names ending in -by, *q.v.*

ALLTWEN (Swansea). W. *allt gwen,* 'bright, clear hill-side or
wooded crag.' *Cf*. ALDE.

ALMELEY (Eardisley). *c*. 1200 *Gervase* Almelege. O.E. *elm-leáh*,
'elm-meadow.' O.E. *elm,* O.N. *alm-r*. Sw. and Dan. *alm,*
'elm.' No man *Alm* or the like in *Onom.*

ALMINGTON. See AMINGTON.

ALMONDBURY (Huddersfield) and ALMONDSBURY (Bristol). Hud.
A. *Dom*. Almaneberie, 1202 Aumundebir. Br. A. *Dom*.
Almodesberie, 1233 Alemundebere. Nothing to do with *almond*
or Sc. ALMOND; but 'burgh, town of *Almund, Alemundus,* or
Ealhmund,' a very common name. See -bury.

ALN R. (Northumbld.), ALNE R. (Warwk.), ALNE or ELLEN R.
(Maryport), and ALNE (York). Nor. A. prob. *c*. 150 *Ptolemy*
Alaunos, with Alauna, ? Alnwick, *c*. 730 *Bede* Aln, Alna; War.
A. *B.C.S*. 1227 *re* the year 723, Ælwinnæ, 1178 Alen; Yor.
Alne., *sic* in *Dom*. All these names are apt to run into ALLAN,
ALLEN, and, like those in Scotland and Ireland, are all Kelt.;
though not always with the same meaning, for the Sc. and Ir.
Allans are often fr. *ailean,* 'a green plain.' But the Eng.
names are prob.= Sc. R. ALE, *c*. 1116 Alne. W. *alain, alwyn,*
alwen, G. *aluinn, ailne,* 'exceeding fair, lovely, bright.' *Cf*.
ALCESTER and ALNEMOUTH.

ALNEMOUTH (Northumbld.). Often locally pron. Alemouth. See
above.

ALNEY (R. Severn). Prob. 1016 *O.E. Chron.* Olanige; *a.* 1200 *Wm. Newbury* Alnewich. ' *Olla's* isle '; see -ey. *Cf.* OLNEY and ALNE.

ALNWICK, pron. Annick. *c.* 1175 *Fantosme* Audnewic ; *c.* 1180 *Bened. Peterb.* Alnewic ; *c.* 1463 Annewyke. ' Dwelling on the R. ALNE.' See -wick.

ALPHINGTON (Exeter). *Dom.* Alfintone. Prob. ' town, dwelling of *Ælfin* '; one was bp. at Athelney in 1009.

ALRESFORD (Colchester and Hants). Col. A. *Dom.* Alreforda, *a.* 1200 *chart.* Ælesforda. Hants A. *c.* 830 *chart.* Alresforda, 1286 Alresford. Form *a.* 1200 may be a scribal error; but *cf.* AYLESFORD. Prob. ' ford of the alder-tree,' O.E. *aler, alr, olr,* M.E. *aller. Cf.* ALLERSTON.

ALREWAS (Lichfield). *Sic* 942 and *Dom.* 1284 Allerwas. Pron. Allr-wass. O.E. *alr, alor wáse,* O.N. *ölr vcisa,* ' alder fen ' or ' marsh.' *Cf.* ALDERBURY, BROADWAS, Rotherwas, Herefd., and *Oxf. Dict. s.v.* OOZE sb[2] 1280 *Close R.* has ' Alrewasheles,' ? in Northbld.

ALSAGER (Stoke-on-Trent). Pron. Al-sæ'jer. Old forms needed. *Cf.* ' Alsiswich,' Herts, *a.* 1199 *Roll Rich. I., Alsi* is a contraction for *Ælfsige* or *Ælfswith,* both very common O.E. names. This latter part is doubtful.

ALSTON (Stafford and Carlisle), and ALSTONFIELD (Ashbourne). St. A. *Dom.* Alverdestone—*i.e.,* ' *Ælfweard's* town.' But another Alston (Staffs), is *a.* 1200 Aluredstone, where *Alured* is var. of *Alfred ;* whilst Alstonfield is *Dom.* Ænestanfelt — *i.e.,* ' field of *Æne's* stone.' Note, too, that Austonley (S. Yorks) is *Dom.* Alstanesleie. How needful and important early forms are ! *Cf.* BEER ALSTON and ATHELSTANEFORD (Sc.).

ALT R. (S. Lancashire) = ALDE. On it is ALTCAR, fr. CARR sb[2] in *Oxf. Dict.,* ' a bog, a fen '; it is Norse; Norw. *kjœr, kjerr,* ' pool, marsh, wet copse.'

ALTARNUN (Launceston). Pron. altar-nún, as if Eng. 1294 Ecclesia de Altar Nun, 1536 Alternone, Corn. *altar Non,* ' altar of St. Non,' sister of Gwen of the three breasts, and mother of St. David, *a.* 550.

ALTHORNE (Maldon). Not in *Dom.* Prob. ' old (O.E. *eald*) thorn.' *Cf.* ALBURY. Only ALTHAM (Lancs), is *old* Alvetham, Elvetham —*i.e.,* ' home of *Ælfgeat.*'

ALTHORPE (Doncaster). Not in *Dom. a.* 1100 *chart.* Alethorpe. Perh. ' Ale place,' ' ale-house '; O.E. *alu, ealu,* in 2 *ale ;* but prob. ' village of a man *Æla* ' or ' *Ala,*' both forms in *Onom. Cf.* Alatorp, *Dom.* Norfk., and Altofts, Normanton, (see -toft), in *Dom.* it is simply Toftes.

ALTON (Dorset, Hants, etc.). Hants A. *c.* 880 *chart.* Æweltun, Aweltun, 1166 *Pipe* Aultona, which looks like O.E. *awel-tun,* 'village shaped like an awl,' O.E. *œl, eal, awel, awul.* M'Clure says = 'Ea-well'—*i.e.,* 'spring-ton' or 'river-source.' *Dom.* Surrey has Aultone. Some of the others may be 'old town'; *cf.* ALBURY and NORTON. But ALTON or Alveton (Uttoxeter), is *Dom.* Elvetone, *c.* 1300 Alneton (*n* for *v*), which is prob. 'town, village of *Ælf*' or '*Ælfa,*' one each in *Onom.* The 'Alton' in *Dom.* Yorks is now HALTON.

ALTRINCHAM (Manchester). Pron. Al'tringham. Named fr. some man; there are *Aldran* and *Aldrannus* in *Onom.;* or perh. 'home of the elders,' O.E. *eldran,* comp. of *eald,* 'old,' *c.* 1440 *elther.* There is a personal name, Eltringham; also see -ing.

ALVANLEY (Warrington). Not in Wyld and Hirst. It may be 'meadow of *Alfa,*' or 'of *Ælfheah*'; *cf.* 1294 Alvedene, also in Lancs, and ALVINGHAM. See -ley.

ALVECHURCH (Birmingham). 780 Ælfgythe cyrce, *Dom.* Alvieve-cherche. 1108 Ælfithe cyrce, *a.* 1200 Alviethechurch. Now pron. Allchurch. 'Church of *Ælfgith*'; but *Dom.*'s form is influenced by *Alveva* or *Ælvive,* late forms of *Ælfgifu,* a very common woman's name in *Onom. Cf.* Alvecote (*sic a.* 1300), Tamworth.

ALVELEY (Bridgnorth). 1160 *Pipe* Aluielea 1231 Alwithel'. See above and -ley.

ALVERMERE (Worcester). *K.C.D.* 120 Ælferamære, '*Ælfhere's* lake.' But ALVERTHORPE (Wakefield), not in *Dom.* is prob. = ALLERTHORPE.

ALVERSTOKE (Gosport). *Dom.* Alwarestoch, '*Alward's* place.' *Cf.* next, and *Dom.* Essex, Alueraina; and see -stoke.

ALVERSTONE (Sandown). *Dom.* Alvrestone, and ALVERTON (Notts and Penzance). 'Town of *Alfer,*' late form of the common *Ælfhere.* The two 'Alvretone' or 'Alvretune' in *Dom.* Yorks, have now become ALLERTON Mauleverer and NORTH ALLERTON. But Notts A. is *Dom.* Aloretun, but *c.* 1190 Alvrington, Auvrington, which seems to be a patronymic. *Cf.,* too, Ailvertune, *Dom.* Norfk. See -ing and -ton.

ALVESCOT (Bampton). *Dom.* Elfegescote, 1216 Elephescote, 1274-79 Alfays-, Alfescote, 1276 Aluescot. 'Cottage, cot of *Ælfheah.*' *Cf. Exon. Dom.* Ailesvescota.

ALVESTON (Thornbury). *c.* 955 *chart.* Ælfes-, Ælvestun, *Dom.* and *c.* 1097 *Flor. W.* Alvestan, 1158-59 *Pipe* Alvestan 1229 Alewestan. 'Dwelling of *Ælfe*' (the elf); *Cf. Sim. Dur.* ann. 1093 Alwestan, ELSTON and OLVESTON. See -ton, which often interchanges with -stone. But A. (Stratford-on-A.) is 985 *chart.* Eanulfestune, 988 *ib.,* *Dom.* Alvestone, 'town of *Eanwulf.*' For ALWESTON, Sherborne, old forms are needed; perh. it is 1166-67 *Pipe* Alfwieteston, which may be, 'town of *Ælfswith,*' a common female name.

ALVINGHAM (Louth), old forms needed, and ALVINGTON (Lydney and I. of W.). Ly. A. 1221 Alwintone, 1223 Elvetun, *later* Elvynton. I. of W. A. *Dom.* Alwinestun. Prob. all. ' home ' and ' town of *Ælfwynn* ' ; but, in last case perh., ' of *Ealhwine* ' or ' *Alwinus*,' names in *Onom.* It should also be at least noted here, that O.E. *ælf, elf*, 3 *alve* is ' an elf,' and O.E. *ælfen, elfen,* ' a female elf.' See -ing, -ham, and -ton.

ALWALTON (Peterboro'). Said to be 955 *chart.* Æthelwoldingtune— *i.e.*, ' dwelling town of Ethelwold's descendants.' But *a*. 1100 *chart.* and 1230 *Close R.* Alewalton, which may be ' old, walled town.' *Cf.* ALBURY and WALTON.

ALWEN R. (N. Wales). W. *al-(g)wen*, ' very white, very bright '; same as ELVAN Sc. *c.* 1170 Elwan, Alewyn. *Cf.* ALWIN.

ALWIN R. (Rothbury) =ALWEN. On it is ALWINTON.

ALWOODLEY (Leeds). 1288 *Close R.* Athewaleley ' *Æthelweald*'s meadow.' See -ley.

AMBERGATE. Not in *Dom.* Prob. ' pitcher-road '; fr. O.E. *amber, omber*, ' a pitcher. a bucket,' and *geat*, ' gate, way,' denoting the road to a well. There are many names in Amber-; *Dom.* Bucks Ambretone suggests a man, ? *Amber ;* so even more does *Dom.* Ambresdone, now AMBROSDEN; only it is prob. fr. *Ambrosius.* Amber Hill, Boston, will be fr. O.E. *amber,* fr. its shape.

AMBERLEY (Stroud, Marden, Herefd., and Arundel). St. A. 1166 Umberleia, *later* Umberley. Ma. A. *Dom.* Amburlege, Ar. A. *Dom.* Ambrelie. ' Meadow of the pitcher,' see above; *cf.* OMBERSLEY. Some derive fr. a man *Amber* or *Amalbeorht.* See -ley.

AMBLE (Acklington). Old forms needed. Perh. W. *am pwl*, ' round about the pool.' But *cf.* AMPLEFORTH. AMBLECOTE. Stourbridge, is *Dom.* Elmelecote, *a.* 1300 Amelecote, ' cottage of *Hemele*,' a common O.E. name, still found as Hamil. *Cf.* AMBLESTONE.

AMBLERTHORN (Halifax). Old forms wanted. Not in *Dom.* Perh. fr. a man *Amalbeorht*, a name in *Onom.*

AMBLESIDE. Perh. ' *Hemele's* seat '; *cf.* AMBLECOTE and next: -side is corrup. of Icel. *sœti, set.* which means ' a seat ' in either modern use.

AMBLESTONE (Pembroke). In W. Tre amlod, of which Amblestone is a translation, ' house ' or ' town of *Hamill*,' said to be one of the vikings who founded the Norse colony here. Hamil is still an Eng. surname; *cf.* HAMILTON *Sc.*, also *Dom.* Surrey ' Amelebrige,' and above.

AMBROSDEN (Bicester). *Dom.* Ambresdone. Prob. ' den, haunt of *Ambrosius* ' Aurelianus, Damnonian chief, leader of the Britons against Hengist, *c.* 450 A.D. *Cf.* AMESBURY, and

Ambresbury Bank, Epping. In *c.* 800 *Nennius* we read of
'Ambros, British Embres guletic,' which last, W. *gwledig*, means
'a leader, a general.' The Epping place is or was also called
Amesbury and Ambers' Banks, and is reputed the site of Q.
Boadicea's final defeat.

AMERSHAM (Rickmansworth). 1218 *Patent R.* Aumodesham, 1231
Agmodesham, 1280 *Close R.* Agmundesham, 1291 Amundesham.
An interesting corrup., '*Agmund-r*'s home'; *cf.* AMOTHERBY.

AMERTON (Stafford). *c.* 1300 Embricton, later Ambric-, Am-
brighton. 'Town of *Eanbriht*' or '*Eanbeorht*.'

AMESBURY (Salisbury). 995 O.E. *Chron.* Ambresbyri(g); *Dom.*
Ambresberie; *c.* 1160 *Gest. Steph.* Abbesbiriensis (prob. scribe's
error); *c.* 1180 *Bened. Peterb.* Ambres-, Ambesbiria, 1280 Aum-
bresbir'. 'Fort. town, of *Ambrose*.' See AMBROSDEN and -bury.

A(L)MINGTON (Tamworth). 889 *chart.* Alchmundingtuun, *later*
Alhmundingtun. 'Abode of the descendants of *Alchmund*.'
But Almington, Mket. Drayton, is *Dom.* Almontone, *a.* 1300
Alkementon, which is simply, 'town, village of *Alchmund*' or
'*Ealhmund*.' See -ing and -ton.

AMLWCH (Anglesea). *c.* 1451 Amlogh. W., meaning 'a circular
inlet of water'; the *lwch* is cognate with G. *loch*.

AMMANFORD (Caermarthen). 'Ford on the R. *Am(m)an*.' See
ABERAMAN.

AMOTHERBY (Malton). *Dom.* Edmundrebi, Aimundrebi; *c.* 1350
Aymonderbi, 'dwelling of *Agmund-r*.' *Cf.* OSMOTHERLEY and
next. *Dom.* says Edmund-, because *Agmund-r* was an un-
familiar name to the Nor. scribe. But *cf.* next and see -by.

AMOUNDERNESS (Preston). *Dom.* Agemundrenesse, *Sim. Dur.*
ann. 1123, Agmunderness; *later*, Ackmounderness. 'Cape,
promontory of *Agmund-r*.' *Cf.* above. But in *chart.* dated
705 it is Hasmunderness, fr. *Asmund* or *Osmund*, well-known
N. names. *Cf.* OSMOTHERLEY. See NESS.

AMPLEFORTH (York). *Sic c.* 1505, but *Dom.* Ampre-, Ambreforde,
1166 A'pleford, 1202 Ampleford, 1298 Ambelforde. 'Ford of
the pitcher.' See AMBERGATE and -forth. The name is a
lesson in phonetics.

AMPNEY CRUCIS (Cirencester). The Ampney is a river, *Dom.*
Omenie, -nel, *later* Omenai, Ameneye, -anell. This name is
a tautology, the *p* as often being a late intrusion, *cf.* HAMPTON.
Amen or Omen is simply O.Kelt. for 'river' (see p. 11), whilst
the -ie or -ey is O.E. *éa*, 'stream.' Here stands the Early Eng.
church Santæ Crucis, 'of the Holy Cross.''

AMPTHILL (Bedford). *Sic* 1454, and *c.* 1350 Ampthull, but *Dom.*
Ammetelle. 'Ant-hill,' O.E. *æmete*, *æmyte*, 3-4 amte, 4-6 *ampte*,
'an ant or emmet.'

AMRATH, -ROTH (Pembroke). *c.* 1130 *Lib. Landav.* Amrath, 1603 *Owen* Amrothe. Prob. W. *am Rhath,* ' on the Rath,' the river *Lib. Land.* calls the Radh. *Cf.* Cilrath and Penrath near by, and *llan am ddyfri* = LLANDOVERY. W. *rhath* is ' a mound, a hill,' as prob. in Roath, Cardiff.

AMWELL (Ware). *Dom.* Emmewelle, 1281 Amewell, *later* Emwell. There is in *B.C.S.* 801 an Ammanuuelle, but not this one. ' Well of *Amma.'* *Cf. B.C.S.* 1110 Amman broc.

ANCASTER (Grantham). *c.* 1190 *Gir. Camb.* Anecastrum. This must be ' *Anna's* camp.' *Anna* is an O.E. man's name. See next and -caster; and *cf.* Anwick, Sleaford.

ANCROFT (Beal). *a.* 1128 Anacroft, *later* Anecroft. This must be ' *Anna's* croft ' or ' field.' *Anna* is a fairly common O.E. name, and *croft* a real O.E. word. *Cf.* ANCASTER. We have *croft* also in *Dom.* Cornw. Croftededor.

ANDERBY (Alford) and ANDERTON (Northwich). ' Town of *Andar'* or ' *Andhere,'* names in *Onom. Cf.* AINDERBY and ' Andrelav,' *Dom.* Salop and ' Andrebi,' *Dom.* Holderness; and see -by and -ton. But ANDERSFIELD, Somerset, is 1233 *Close R.* Eldredesfeld, fr. the common *Ealdred.*

ANDOVER (Hants). 994 *O.E. Chron.* To Andeferan, -faran, -efron; *Dom.* Andovere, *c.* 1120 *Hen. Hunt.* Andovre, 1155 *Pipe* Andieura. Andover is now on R. Anton, but no early forms of this name seem on record; and the earlier forms seem to have been Ande or Anne (see ABBOTTS ANN). The O.E. form has been interpreted as ' fare ' (*cf.* thoroughfare) or ' passage, ferry, over the Ande.' But the O.E. word is *fær, faru,* inflected *fare,* not *fara ;* the root being *faran,* ' to go, fare, make one's way '; so this is doubtful. More likely is it *Ande-ofer,* ' on the bank of the Ande,' -over, *q.v.,* being a very common ending. The similar-looking names WENDOVER (Bucks), and Cen- or Candover (Hants), tempt to a derivation fr. the old British DOVER, W. *dwfr,* ' a stream.' In that case An- might be the Kelt. *an* ' the.' In any case the river-name Anton, Ande, or Anne, is doubtful. It *may* have some connection with *Ann'* mother of the gods among the Kelts—*e.g.,* in ' The Two Paps of Ana,' Kerry. But the R. Ant, S. Norfolk, must be the same root; then what of the *t* or *d ?* ANDOVER(S)-FORD (Cheltenham) is 759 *chart.* Onnanford, *c.* 800 *ib.* Annanford, *c.* 1270 Anneford, which Baddeley derives fr. the O.E. man's name *Anna.* It is also 1266 Andevere, *c.* 1270 Andovere, where he makes the latter part = Dover, and the former he leaves doubtful. In W. *on,* pl. *onn* is ' an ash-tree.' *Cf.* AMPNEY.

ANERLEY (Norwood). Not in *Dom.* ' Meadow of *Aner.' Cf. B.C.S.* 910 Aneres broc. See -ley.

ANGARRACK (Gwinnear Road). Corn. *an carrack*, ' the rock,' G. *carraig*.

ANGERTON (Morpeth). ' Town of *Anger*.' M.E. *angard, ongart*, ' boastful, arrogant.' There is one *Angerus* in *Onom.* *Cf.* the mod. name Ainger.

ANGLE or NANGLE (Pembroke). *c.* 1190 *Gir. Camb.* Angulus, 1594 Nangle. The Eng. sb. *angle* is fr. Fr. There seems no W. equivalent name. It lies in an angle; but W. H. Stevenson thinks it may be O.N. *öngull*, ' a fjord,' fr. *ang-r*, O.E. *eng*, ' narrow.' *Cf.* ANGLESEA. Nangle is for *an angle*.

ANGLESARK (Lancs). ' Shieling, hut of the *Angle* ' ; *argh, ark*, or *ergh*, is a N. corrup. of G. *airigh, airidh*, ' shepherd's hut.' *Cf.* ARKLID, GOLCAR, GRIMSARGH, etc. Final -gh in G. is now usually mute. The fuller form is seen in Airyholme, N. Riding, which was Ergun in *Dom.*, whilst Eryholme, also in Yorks, was Argun in *Dom.* The -un is sign of the loc. plur.

ANGLESEA. 1098 *O.E. Chron.* Angles ege—*i.e.*, ' isle of the *Angle*,' or Englishman. But in W. *ynys Fôn*, ' Mona's Isle,' *cf.* MAN, and see -ey. The same name is found in Cambs, 1270 Angleseye. However, W. H. Stevenson thinks the orig. name was O.N. Öngulsey, ' isle of the fjord ' (see ANGLE). It is so named *c.* 1225 in *Orkney. Saga*.

ANGMERING (Worthing). *c.* 885 *Alfred's Will*, also in 2 charters, Angemæringtun, *Dom.* Angemare. ' Place of the descendants of *Angemœr*.' See -ing.

ANKER R. (Nuneaton). O.E. *ancra*, 3-6 *ancre*, 4-7 *anker*, ' an anchorite, an anchoress, a nun.' Evidently so called from the Benedictine nunnery on its banks—almost a unique river name in its way. *Cf.* ANKERWYKE, Staines, where a Benedictine nunnery was founded, in 12th cny.; also ANKERDINE Hill, Bromyard, 1275 Oncredham, *c.* 1300 Ancredam, and -ham; prob. also fr. *ancre ;* for its ending see -den; the O.E. would be *ancran denu*.

ANLABY (Hull). *Dom.* Umlouebi, Unl-, Umloveby. ' Dwelling of *Unlaf* ' or ' *Anlaf*.' *Cf.* Anlafestun *B.C.S.* 1128. One *Anlaf* was K. of Northumbria, 941-52. See -by.

ANNAITSFORD (Newcastle). *Anait* is Kelt. for ' a parent church.' *Cf.* ANNAT, *Sc.* Possibly Annait- is corrup. of a man's name. There is nothing in *Onom.* nearer than one *Enefœt*. It may be Annette, dimin. of *Anne*.

ANNEAR or ENNOR (Cornwall). Corn. =' *the* earth,' *an* being the article, and *nōr*, ' earth.'

ANNESLEY (Nottingham). *Dom.* Aneslei. ' Lea, meadow of *Anna* ' or ' *Ana*.' Several of this name in *Onom.* One was K. of East Anglia, 636-54. *Cf.* Ainley and N. and S. Anston, Yorks, which in *Dom.* are Anele and Anestan, also ANCASTER, etc.

AN ORS (rock, Lizard). Corn. = ' the bear,' L. *ursa*, Fr. *ours*.

ANSLEY (Atherstone). *Dom.* Hanslei, *a.* 1500 Anstéley, -lay. Doubtful, but prob. ' meadow with the narrow pathway.' See next and -ley. However, ANSLOW (Burton-on-T.) is 1004 Ansythlege, Eansythlege, Ansideleye, *c.* 1300 Ansedesleye. ' Meadow of *Eanswyth*,' possibly a female saint. ANSDELL (Lytham) is not in *Dom.*, and doubtful too.

ANSTEY (Alton, Buntingford, Leicester, Tamworth), and ANSTYE CROSS (Hayward's Heath). Alt. A. 1157 *Pipe* Anestiga. Tam. A. *Dom.* Anestie, *a.* 1300 Anesty, Anestleye; O.E. *anstiga*, *-ge*, ' a narrow path, a pass,' lit. ' one footway.' In *Dom.* Yorks, we have Ainesti, Annesti Wapentac, 1179-80 Ainsti, now Ainsty Wapentake.

ANTROBUS (Nantwich). *Dom.* Entrebus. Prob. Fr. *entre buis*, ' among of the box-trees.' Fr. *antre*, ' a cave,' is not recorded till 1564. Nor. names are very rare so early in this locality. *Cf.* WARBOYS and 1215 *Close R.* Grambus = Fr. *grand bois*.

APETHORPE (Stamford) and APETON (Stafford). *Dom.* Abetone, *a.* 1300 Abbe-, Abe-, Apeton. ' Place ' and ' village of *Æbbe*,' a common name, found also as *Æbba*, *Ebba*, and *Eappa*. *Cf.* next, EPSOM and ' Apetun,' *chart.* Hants. The ape is found in O.E. as *apa*, *ape*, but is hardly likely here. *Cf.* Apes Dale, Bromsgrove, 1552 Apedale. See -thorpe.

APPERLEY (Leeds). 1201 Appeltreleg—*i.e.*, ' apple-tree meadow.' A. (Tewkesbury) is 1221 Happeley, 1413 Appurley, prob. also fr. O.E. *æppel*, ' apple-tree.' But the common *Eadbeorht* has once *Eappa* as var, so this may be ' *Eadbeorht*'s meadow,' as in ABBERTON. See -ley.

APPLEBY (Westmorland and Doncaster). We. A. 1131 Aplebi, 1174 *Pipe* Appelbi, ' Apple-town,' O.E. *æppel*, *æpl*, O.N. *epli*, O.Sw. *æpli*, ' an apple '; and see -by. Also APPLEBY MAGNA (Atherstone), ' great Appleby '; *cf.* Ashby Magna, etc. The ' Aplebi ' of *Dom.* Yorks is now Eppleby in the N. Riding. The Don. A. is not found there. However, the local pron. of this Westmorland name is Yæpplby, which favours a derivation fr. *Hiálp*, a name known in the Sagas ; and certainly in a Danish region ' Hialp's dwelling ' would be more in accord with analogy.

APPLEDORE (3 in Devon, and S. Kent). Crediton A. 739 *chart.* Apuldre, and -dran; whilst S. Appledore, Halberton, is *ib.* Suran Apuldran, *Exon. Dom.* Surapla. ' sour apple-tree.' Bideford A. *Dom.* Appledore. Kent A. 893 *O.E. Chron.* Apulder, *Dom.* Apeldres, *c.* 1200 *Gervase* Apeldre, 1439 *Will* Apuldr. Some of these (esp. at Bideford) prob. were orig. O.W. *apul dur* (or *dwyn*), ' at the confluence of the streams '; *apul* being for *apur* or *aber* (*q.v.*); the liquids *l* and *r* easily interchange; *cf.* APPLE-CROSS (Sc.), *c.* 1080 Aporcrosan. But very early Apuldre was thought to be simply ' apple-tree.' *Cf.* MAPLEDURHAM and

APPERLEY. There is an 'Appel doucham' 1217 in *Patent R.;* and there is still an Appledram or Apuldram near Chichester; *cf.,* too, 940 *chart.* Appildore (Wilts).

APPLEFORD (Abingdon). 892 *chart.* Æppelford, *Dom.* Apleford. 'Ford at the apple-tree.' But *cf.* APPLEDORE.

APPLESHAW (Andover). 'Apple-wood,' O.E. *scaga,* 'a wood.' *Dom.* Hants has only Aplestede.

APPLETON (7 in *P.G.*), also APPLETON WISKE (Northallerton, *Dom.* Apletune). 1179-80 Appelton, 1202 Apelton (both in Yorks). 'Town of the apples'; O.E. *æp(p)el,* 2-7 *appel.* Wiske, not in *Dom.,* is now the name of a little R. here, 1212 Wisc, which is prob. O. Keltic *uisg,* G. *uisge,* 'water, stream,' hence *whisky; cf. L. Isca,* USK, and KIRBY WISKE. But it may be E. Frisian *wiske,* 'a small meadow,' Ger. *wiese,* 'a meadow,' in Eng. usage seemingly one moist and low-lying. *Cf.* WHISTLEY, in O.E. *chart.* Wiscelea, Wisclea.

APPLETREE (Derby). 1298 *Writ* 'Henrico de Apletrefelde.' This tree was the meeting-place of the hundred (or shire-division). *Cf.* GARTREE, GREYTREE, Plumtree (Notts), and APPERLEY.

APPLEY BRIDGE (Wigan). Not in W. and H. Prob. O.E. *æpl-leáh,* 'apple-tree meadow.'

APPS COURT (Surrey). *a.* 1000 *chart.* Æpse; also Abbs. O.E. *æspe, æps,* 'the asp or aspen tree.' *Cf.* M.E. and dial. *claps* for *clasp.*

APSLEY (Bedford). *Dom.* Aspeleia, but 969 *chart.* Æpslea, which is O.E. for 'aspen-tree meadow'; see above. Or else, 'meadow of *Æppa* or *Eppa*'; *cf.* EPSOM and IPSLEY, also *a.* 810 *Nennius* 'Episford,' in our tongue 'Set thir gabail,' where gabail must surely be the same as G. *gabhal,* or *gobhal,* 'a fork.' Apsley, Tanworth, is better ASPLEY; but *a.* 1300 Apsele.

AQUILATE (W. Staffd.). 1129 *Pipe* 'Matilda de Aquila,' *a.* 1300 Aquilade, *a.* 1400 Aquilot, *a.* 1600 Acquilat. Called after the Nor. family L'Aigle, L. *aquila,* Eng. *eagle.* The Matilda of 1129 was widow of Robert de Mowbray, Earl of Northumberland, and has also conferred her name on Winford Eagle, Dorset. The ending is quite doubtful. It may have been suggested by *lade,* 'channel,' O.E. *ge lád,* see CRICKLADE; hardly by *lot,* O.E. *hlot,* which is not applied to land till quite late; though *loot mede* or 'lot meadow' is found as early as 1553.

ARAN MOWDDWY (mtn., Merioneth). W. *aran mwddi,* 'peaked hill with the arch or vault.' This is (1590) Spenser, *Faerie Queen's* 'Under the foot of Rauran mossy hore'; Rauran being yr Aran, 'the peak.'

ARBORFIELD CROSS (Reading). *c.* 1540 Arburfeld. Dr. Skeat informed the writer that a charter has recently been found showing that this is orig. '*Eadburh's* field,' Eadburh being a woman. Another warning against guessing !

ARCHENFIELD, ARCHFIELD, or IRCHENFIELD (Herefordsh.). *c.* 1130 *Lib. Landav.* Ergyng, and prob. *c.* 380 *Ant. Itin.* Areconium, *c.* 1147 *Geoff. Mon.* Erging. Very doubtful; perh. *erging* may suggest W. *ergryn,* 'terror, horror.'

ARDDLEEN (Oswestry). W. *ardd llion,* 'height on the streams,' *llion* pl. of *lli.* *Cf.* CAERLEON.

ARDEN and ARDENS GRAFTON (Alcester, Warwk.). *a.* 1199 Arden. The first part is prob. a contraction of one of the numerous O.E. names in Eard-. The 'Forest of Arden' is an invention of Shakespeare, in allusion to the Ardennes, Belgium; so Duignan.

ARDINGLEY (Hayward's Heath), not in *Dom.,* and ARDINGTON (Wantage and Surrey). Wa. A. *Dom.* Ardintone, 1316 Ardynton. Sur. A. 1233 Eard-, Erdendon. Prob. 'meadow' and 'town of *Eardwine,*' 2 in *Onom.* *Cf.* the mod. surname Harding, and ERDINGTON; and see -ley and -ton.

ARDLEIGH (Colchester); also ARDLEY (Bicester). *Dom.* Ardulveslie, 1149 Ardusley, 1229 Ardolvesl,' 1259 Erdulffey, 1316 Ardele. 'Meadow of *Eardwulf,*' or '*Ardulf.*' The Colch. name may not be the same; old forms needed. *Cf.* 1297 *Writ* Arderne, Essex. See -ley.

ARDSLEY (Barnsley, Wakefield, etc.). 1202 Ardislawe, 1208 Erdeslawe. Prob. 'Eard's lea' or 'meadow,' *Eard* being short for *Eardwulf,* a very common O.E. name. But -lawe is, of course, not 'meadow,' but 'hill'; see -low.

ARDWICK (Manchester). 1282 Atheriswyke, 1502 Ardewyk. A case of dissimilation; at least, as Wyld suggests, Ather- prob. represents some O.E. name in Æðel-; there are many. *Cf.* ATHERSTONE and ATHERTON. 'Arduuic' *Dom.* S. Yorks is now HARDWICK.

ARENIG (Bala). ? dimin. of W. *aren.,* 'a kidney.'

ARGOED (Tredegar). W. *ar coed,* 'ploughed land by the wood.' *Cf.* BARGOED.

ARKENDALE (Knaresboro'). *Dom.* Archedene, Arghendene; and ARKENGARTHDALE (Richmond, Yorks). Doubtful. Prob. the Arken- is a contraction fr. some of the many names in *Earcan-* or *Eorcon-* in *Onom.* Possibly it might be 'valley of the arks' or 'chests,' O.E. *earc, arc.* *Cf. Dom.* Herefd. Archenfeld, and Arkinholm, old name of Langholm (Sc.). The O.E. *dene,* see -dean, has been changed by N. influence to -dale. The -garth is O.N. *garð-r,* O.E. *geard, a.* 1300 *garth,* 'enclosure, field, yard.'

ARKESDON (Newport, Essex). *Dom.* Archesdana. This Ark- or Arch- here may be contraction fr. the common *Arcytel* or *Arkil;* there is no recorded *Arc.* Or the name may be: '(wooded) valley of the chest'; O.E. *earc, arc.* *Cf.* ARKLEBY and ARKSEY; and see -den.

ARKHOLME (K. Lonsdale). *Dom.* Ergun. ' Hut on the meadow. Norse G. *argh.* See ANGLESARK and -holm. In *Dom.* -un represents -am or -ham rather than -holm—indeed, is a loc., generally made afterwards into -(h)am; so Ergun will be ' at the huts.'

ARKSEY (Doncaster). *Dom.* Archeseia. Prob. as in ARKESDON, ' isle of the chest,' or ' of *Arc.*' See -ey.

ARKLEBY (Aspatria). [*Cf. c.* 1215 Arkilleshow, S. Lancashire.] ' Dwelling of *Earcil, Arcytel,* or *Earcytel,*' a common O.E. name. See -by.

ARKLID (Cumberld.). Gaelic-N. *argh,* G. *airigh, airidh,* ' a shieling, a hut '; and N. *hlið.* ' a slope.' *Cf.* ANGLESARK and PAVEY ARK; also GOLCAR, GOOSNARGH, etc.

ARLECDON (Cumberld.). Old forms needed. Perh. hybrid = HARLECH and O.E. *dún,* ' a hill, a fort.'

ARLESEY (Hitchin). *Dom.* Alriceseie. ' Isle of *Ælric* or *Ælfric.*' But ARLESCOTE (Wwk.) is 1080 Orlavescoth, *Dom.* Orlavescote, 1123 Ordlavescot: ' *Ordlaf's* cot.' ARLESTON, Salop, is 1284 *Close R.* Ardolfeston, ' town of *Eardwulf,*' a common name. Three places in Arles-, and all different ! See -ey.

ARLEY (Bewdley and Northwich). Bew. A. 994 Earnleie, *Dom.* Ernlege, *a.* 1300 Erlei, Arnlegh. ' Meadow of the eagle,' O.E. *earn ;* though Duignan prefers to think of a contraction fr. one of the numerous names in Earn-, Earnbald, -grim, etc. *Cf.* 1179-80 *Pipe* Erlega (Cumbld.) and *c.* 1537 ' Erleghecote haythe ' (Furness) which seem to come fr. *earl.* See above; also ARNCLIFFE and EARLY; and ARLE (Cheltenham), *old* Alra —*i.e.,* O.E. *aler,* ' alder-tree.'

ARLEY REGIS or A. KINGS (Bewdley). *Dom.* Ernlege, *c.* 1275 Ernleie. See above. *Regis* is L. for ' of the King.' It belonged to the Crown in the Mid. Ages, having twice escheated.

ARLINGHAM (Stonehouse). *Dom.* Erlingehā. ' Home of *Arling* ' or ' *Erling* '—*i.e.,* ' the descendant of the earl.' But ARLINGTON (Bibury and Barnstaple) is Bi. A. *Dom.* Aluredintune, 1221 Alwintone; Ba. A. prob. not in *Dom.* ' Town, dwelling of the sons of *Alured.*' Searle does not equate this with *Alfred.* See -ing, -ham, and -ton.

ARMATHWAITE (Cumberld.). A little doubtful. It may be ' place of ' some man, with a name in Eorm-. Eormenburh, -frith, etc., and here contracted. But it may be O.N. *arm-r,* ' an arm,' and then, ' the spur of a valley.' *Cf.* ARMLEY, ARMTHORPE, and ARMADALE (Sc.); and see -thwaite.

ARMITAGE (Rugeley). *a.* 1300 Hermitage; in Eng. 1290 *ermitage,* 5 *armitage ;* O.Fr. *hermitage.* There was one here in the 13th cny.

ARMLEY (Leeds). *Dom.* Ermelai. Prob. '*Eorm*'s meadow.' See ARMATHWAITE, and -ley.

ARMTHORPE (Doncaster). *Dom.* Ernulfestorp, 1202 Arunthorp, 1212 Ernetorp. 'Village of *Earnwulf*'; the latter unaccented syllable often drops away. See -thorpe. ARMSCOTT (Shipston-on-Stour) is actually 1275 Edmundescote !

ARNCLIFFE (Skipton). *Dom.* Arneclif, and Gerneclif. Perh. 'Cliff of the erne or eagle,' O.E. *earn.* But possibly Arn- represents a man's name; *cf.* above and ARMLEY. *Cf.* ARNCOT (Oxon), which is *K.C.D.* 1279 Earnigcote, *Dom.* Ernicote—*i.e.,* 'cot of *Earnwig*' or '*Arnwi*.'

ARNESBY (Leicester). 1160 *Pipe* Ernesbi. 'Dwelling of *Arni*' —*i.e.,* 'the eagle.' *Cf.* above, and ARNISORT (Sc.); and see -by.

ARNOLD (Nottingham). *Dom.* Ernehale. 1157 *Pipe* Erneshala, 1316 Arnall, 'Nook of *Earne*' or, ' of the eagle'; see above and -hall. The present, quite late form has been influenced by the common name *Arnold.* On the excrescent *d* see p. 81. *Cf. Dom.* Arnodestorp, now Arnoldstoft, N. Riding. See -toft.

ARNSIDE (Carnforth). 'Eagle-slope,' *cf.* above. *Side,* O.E. *síde,* here has the sense of 'the slope of a hill or mountain.' *Cf.* AMBLESIDE.

ARRAD FOOT (Ulverston). Prob. W. *aradiad,* 'tillage,' fr. *aradr,* 'a plough'; L. *aratrum.*

ARRAM (Beverley). *Dom.* Argun. The Arg- is Norse G. *argh,* 'hut, shieling'; see ANGLESARK. The -un is a loc.; see ARKHOLME.

ARRETON (I. of Wight). *Sic* 1285. Not in *Dom.* Hants, but in Sffk. Are-, Aratona; 'town, hamlet of *Ara*,' or '*Are*,' names in *Onom.*

ARRINGTON (Royston, Camb.). *Dom.* Erningetone, *chart.* Ærningetune, 1270 Arington, 1307 Arnington. 'Village of the sons of *Erne* or *Ærn*,' O.E. *earn, œrn,* 'an eagle.' Armingford, also in Cambs, has the same origin. Skeat thinks the change to Arrington arose through association with Barrington near by.

ARROW R. (Warwksh.), ARROW Brook (Wirral, Chesh.). A. River *a.* 800 *chart.* Aro. Prob. same root as W. *aru,* 'to plough.' The river seems nowhere like ' an arrow,' O.E. *arewe.*

ARTHINGTON (Otley). Not in *Dom.* 1204 Arthigton. Further old forms needed. May be ' village of *Earthegn* or *Ertein*.' The name is in *Onom. Cf.* Hartington, Buxton.

ARTHOG (Barmouth). Dimin. of W. *arth,* ' a height '; ' little hill.'

ARTHURET (Carlisle). Wh. Stokes thought this the same as Verteris in *c.* 400 *Notit. Dign.,* which is prob. of same root as W. *gwerthyr,* 'fortification.' But K. *Arthur* was a real Keltic King none the less, and his name prob. influenced the form of this. The name is first found in Juvenal *Sat.* 3, 29, Artorius. This, says Rhys, is early Brythonic *Artor,* gen. *Artōros.*

ARUN R. (Sussex). Perh. named fr. a neighbouring hill, W. *aran*, ' a peaked hill.'

ARUNDEL (Sussex). *Dom.* Harundel; 1097 *O.E. Chron.* Arundel; *c.* 1175 Arandel. ' Dell, dale (O.E. *dœl*) of the ARUN.' Very early the Arundel family had on their arms the swallow or *hirondelle*, a Fr. word found in Eng. *c.* 1600 as ' arrondell.' Of course, this is only heraldic etymology.

ASCOT (Berks), *a.* 1300 Escot, also Ascote; ASCOT-under-Wychwood (Oxford; see WYCHWOOD), ASCOTE (Southam) *a.* 1300 Astanes-cote. ASCOTT (Shipston-on-Stour), no old forms. Ascot or Escot may be *east cot*—*cf.* ASTLEY; but is prob. =Ashcott, Bridge-water, ' cot, cottage made of ashwood,' O.E. *œsc*—*cf.* ASHFORD, *Dom.* Asford. Ascote is ' cot of *Ælfstan*,' a ' faithful man ' re-ferred to in a grant by Oswald, Bp. of Worcester, in 991. *Dom.* Bucks has an ' Achecote.'

ASFORDBY (Melton Mowbray). Not in *Dom.* ' Dwelling of *Asford*,' bailiff at Croyland. See *Onom.*, and -by.

ASGARBY (Lincolnsh.). 1154-66 *charts.* Asgerbi, Ansgesbia; *a.* 1200 Asgerebi. ' Dwelling of *Asgar* or *Asgaer* '; so in *Onom.* *Cf.* ASKERSWELL, and see -by.

ASH R. (Wilts). 712 *chart.* Æsce, which is O.E. for ' ash-tree.' But almost all our river names are Keltic, and so this is prob =Ax or ' water.'

ASH (Aldershot, Sevenoaks, Sandwich). Prob. O.E. *Æsce*, ' ash-tree.' The *c* has remained hard in Aske, Yorks; *Dom.* Hasse.

ASHBOURNE (Uttoxeter and Derbysh.). Der. A. *Dom.* Esseburne, 1162-65 *chart.* Esseburna; ' ash-tree stream,' *bourne* =Sc. *burn ;* O.E. *burna*, Icel. *brunn-r*, ' a brook, a stream.' *Ash*, the tree, is given as 3 *asse* and 5 *esche*.

ASHBRITTLE (Wellington, Som.). Not in *Dom.*, and old forms needed. The origin of the Eng. *brittle* is doubtful; see *Oxf. Dict.* But prob. this has nothing to do with *brittle ;* prob. it is ' *Æsc-beorht*'s hill.' *Cf.* *B.C.S.* 624 Æscbyrhtes geat, and ASTLE, *a.* 1300 Asthulle.

ASHBURNHAM (Battle). *K.C.D.* 930 Ashbornham, ' home at the ASHBOURNE.' There is also an ' Esburnehā ' in *Dom.* Bucks.

ASHBURTON (S. Devon). Prob. *Dom.* Essebretone. ' BURTON, fortified hamlet, by the ash-tree '; or, ' of ' a man ' *Æsc* ' or ' *Æse* '; the names are in *Onom.* *Cf.* next and ASHDOWN.

ASHBURY (Berks and Okehampton). Ber. A. *c.* 931 *chart.* Æscæs-byrie, 953 *chart.* Æscesburh, 960 Æscesburuh. O.E. for ' burgh, fort of *Æsc*,' perh. he who was the son of Hengist. *Æsc* means ' an ash,' and Ash(e) is still a common surname. There is an ' Asseberga ' in *Dom.* Worc., which is prob. ' burgh of *Asa*,' a name common in *Onom.* *Cf.* ASHDOWN.

ASHBY (Doncaster) and ASHBY DE LA ZOUCH. Don. A. 1179-80 Essebi, Dɔ la Z. A. *c.* 1300 *Eccleston* Esseby (the E. Anglian pron.; *cf.* ASHWELL). 'Dwelling of Æsc' or 'Asa,' see above; and afterwards of the Nor. family La Zouch. See -by.

ASHBY PUERORUM (Horncastle). [Prob. 1292 Parva Askeby.] 'ASHBY of the boys'; L. *puer,* 'a boy.'

ASHBY ST. LEDGERS (Rugby). See above. St. *Ledger,* in Fr. St. *Léger,* is *Leodegarius,* a famous Fr. saint and martyr, Bp. of Autun in France; d. 678. *Cf.* the Doncaster St. Leger, which already, in 1567, had reached its popular corrup. 'Sellinger' or 'Selenger.'

ASHDOWN (Berksh.). 673 *chart.* 'In Escesdune LV in loco qui vocatur Earmundeslea.' *O.E. Chron.* ann. 661 Æscesdune, ann. 871, Æscesdun; also *sic* in *a.* 910 *Asser,* who (or an interpolator) explains the name as *mons fraxini.* 'hill,' or 'hill-fort of the ash-tree.' But, on the analogy of *Æscæs* byries Sudgeate or 'South gate of Ashbury' (*c.* 931 *chart.*), this may be 'hill' or 'fort of Æsc.' There are 3 called *Æsc* and one *Æsca* in *Onom.* *Cf.* ASHBURY.

ASHELDHAM (Southminster). Not in *Dom.* Prob. 'Home of *Ashild,*' a Norse female name. But ASHELWORTH (Glouc.), *Dom.* Esceleuuorde, 1260 Asselworth, is either 'farm of *Æscelf,*' one in *Onom.;* or else fr. the common *Aschil, Ascil,* or *Ascytel.* See -ham and -worth.

ASHEY DOWN (Ryde). The only adj. in *Oxf. Dict.* fr. *ash,* the tree is *ashen;* yet this Ashey is prob. fr. it also. See -down.

ASHFORD (Kent, Laleham, etc.) and ASHFORD CARBONEL (Ludlow). Lal. A. *Dom.* Exeforde; also *old* Echeleford, Eckleford, fr. the little R. EXE or *Echel* here. As. Carb. *Dom.* Asford. Prob. they all mean 'ford on the river.' See ASH R., and *cf.* ASHBOURNE. A Sir John *Carbonell* is mentioned in Norfolk, 1422, in *Paston Lett.*

ASHINGTON (Morpeth and Pulboro'). Pul. A. *Dom.* Essingetune (*cf.* 1298 'Johannes de Asshendene'). Prob. 'town, vlliage of the *Ashings* '; on this family or dynasty see *Bede,* ii. 5. See, too, ASSINGTON.

ASHLEY (many). *E.g.,* in *Dom.* Ascelie (Chesh.), Esselie (Cambs and Staffs), Achelei (Bucks). 'Ash-tree meadow.' Some may come fr. a man *Æsca,* as we have Ashley (Staffs), *a.* 1300 Assinge-legh. *Cf. Dom.* Worc., Escelie. See -ing and -ley.

ASHMANSWORTH (Hunts). *a.* 1200 *chart.* Æscmeres weorth, which is 'farm beside the mere or lake of the ash-tree '; a curious corruption. But there is both an *Asman* and an *Æscmann* in *Onom.* *Cf.* RICKMANSWORTH, and see -worth.

ASHMORE (Salisbury and Lichfield). Li. A. *c.* 1300 Estmcresbrok, Asschmorebroke, Ashmeresbroke. Prob. ' brook of *Æscmær.*' *Cf. B.C.S.* 1227 on Æscmæres hammas. Sal. A. *may* be ' ash-tree moor.'

ASHORNE (Warwick). 1196 Hasshorne, 1370 Asshorne. Perh. ' ash-tree nook.' O.E. *æsc,* M.E. *asse, esse,* ' an ash,' and O.E. *hyrne, hern,* ' nook, corner.' But -horn in WHITHORN (Sc.), etc., represents O.E. *erne,* ' house.'

ASHOVER (Chesterfield). *Dom.* Essovre. ' Ash-tree bank,' fr. O.E. *obr, ofr,* M.E. *overe,* ' border, bank of a river.' *Cf.* BOLSOVER, etc., also Asher.

ASHOW (KENILWORTH). *Dom.* Asceshot (-shot prob. error, but *cf.* ALDERSHOT), *a.* 1300 Ascesho, Ashyho, Asshisho. ' HOE, out-stretching point of land, with the ash-tree.' See above, and ASHBURY.

ASH PARVA (Whitchurch). ' Little Ash,' L. *parvus,* ' little.' *Cf.* ASHBY MAGNA, etc.

ASHREIGNEY (Chulmleigh). Not in *Dom.* Reigney seems to be the S.W. dialect *reen, reene, rhine,* ' a ditch, an open drain.' prob. fr. O.E. *ryne.*

ASHRIDGE (Bucks). Prob. 1376 Assherugge. *Ridge* in the N. usually takes the form *rigg.,* O.E. *hrycg,* Icel. *hrygg-r. Cf.* ASKRIGG.

ASHTON (Northampton, etc.). *c.* 955 *chart.* Æsctune, Bristol. 963 *O.E. Chron.* Æsctún, ? which. ' Ash-tree village.' Ashton in *Dom.* is sometimes Estun as well as Essetone, but that will here mean the same.

ASHURST (Southampton). (*Dom.* has Eisseburne.) ' Ash-tree grove,' O.E. *hyrst,* Sw. *hurst,* ' a wood.' *Cf.* CHISELHURST, etc.

ASHWELL (Herts). *a.* 1300 *Eccleston* Assewelle (for this spelling *cf.* ASHBY DE LA ZOUCHE). ' Well by the ash-tree.'

ASKAM (Carnforth). O.E. *æsc-hám,* ' dwelling, village by the ash-tree,' the hard *c* being retained in North. Eng. *Cf* ASKHAM. The *Æsc* may well be a man's name here. *Cf.* ASHBURY.

ASKERN (Doncaster). Not in *Dom.* O.E. *æsc-erne,* ' house built of ash-wood.' *Cf.* WHITHORN (Sc.).

ASKERSWELL (Bridport). Not in *Dom.* ' Well of Asgar '; several named *Asgar, Asgær, Esgar,* in *Onom. Cf.* ASGARBY.

ASKHAM (Penrith and Yorks). Yorks, more than one, *Dom.* Ascam, Ascha'. =ASKAM.

ASKRIGG (Bedale). North. form of ASHRIDGE.

ASKWITH (Westmld. and Yorks). *Dom.* Yorks, Ascuid, -vid; 1201 Ascwith. O.N. *ask-r við-r* (Dan. *ved*). ' Ash wood or forest.' *Cf.* ASKAM and BECKWITH. This is, of course, the same name as Asquith.

ASLACKBY (Folkingham) and ASLACTON (Long Stratton). *Dom.* Aslachesbi. ' Dwelling of *Aslac* '; several in *Onom.* *Cf.* next and AISLABY; and see -by.

ASLACOE (Lincoln). *Dom.* Aslacheshou. ' Hoe or how or moct-hill of *Aslac* '; see above. *Hoe*, as in MORTE HOE, also means ' an island,' as this may once have been.

ASLOCKTON (Nottingham). *Dom.* Aslachetone. ' *Aslac's* village.' See above.

ASPATRIA (W. Cumberland). Local pron. Spatry. 1224 *Patent R.* Estpateric. Said to be fr. *As-* or *Gos- patrick*, first lord of Allendale, or fr. *As* or *St. Patrick*, predecessor of Kentigern, and patron St. of the church here. In time of K. John we find a ford near here called Wath-Patrick -weth. *Ass* in O.N. means a sort of demi-god, one under the patronage of a god, usually Thor. But possibly the first syll. is the obs. Eng. *este*, O.E. *ést*, O.N. *ást*, ' delight, good pleasure, favour '; so the name would mean ' The delight of St. Patrick,' which is more in ac-cord with analogy than to call a place after a man alone.

ASPENDEN (Buntingford). *c.* 1280 Apsedene, *Feud. Aids* Aspedene, O.E. *œspe denu*, ' aspen-tree vale.' See -den.

ASPLEY (Huddersfield, and 2 in Staffs; *Dom.* Haspeleia, 1227 Aspeleg, Eccleshall; and 2 in Warwk., both 1272 Aspeley; but one *a.* 1300 Apsele), and ASPLEY GUISE (Woburn), 1232 Aspel'. ' Lea, meadow (O.E. *léah*) of the asps or aspens,' O.E. *œspe*. *Cf.* APSLEY, and Asps, 1196 Aspes (Warwk). *Guise* may or may not show connection with the well-known ducal family of Lorraine; at any rate *Guises* held property here.

ASPULL MOOR (Wigan). Prob. =' asp-hill ' or ' aspen-tree hill,' O.E. *œspe*, ' an aspen '; *hill* is found spelt 2-5 *hull.* *Cf.* ASPEN-DEN and SOLIHULL.

ASSELBY (Yorks). *Dom.* Aschilebi. ' Dwelling, village of *Aschil* or *Ascytel*,' a common O.E. name. *Cf.* HAISTHORPE; and see -by.

ASSINGDON or ASSINGTON (Colchester). 1016 *O.E. Chron.* Assan-dun; *c.* 1115 *Henry Hunt.* Esesdun. This place-name is cor-rectly translated by *Flor. Worc. c.* 1097, ' mons asini,' ' hill of the ass,' O.E. *assa*, gen. *assan*, ' a male ass.'

ASTBURY (Congleton). Not in *Dom.* Prob. ' burgh, town of *Ast*,' given as ' 956 regulus Worc.' in *Onom.* However, O.E. *ast* is ' an oast or kiln.' *Cf.* next.

ASTLE HALL (Macclesfield). *a.* 1300 Asthulle. ' Ast-hill,' O.E. *ast*, ' an oast or kiln ': *hill* is spelt 2-5 *hull.* *Cf.* ASPULL and SOLIHULL.

ASTLEY (5 in *P.G.*). Nuneaton A. *Dom.* Estleia, *a.* 1300 Est(e)ley. 1327 Astleye. Stourport A. *Dom.* Eslei, *a.* 1200 Æstlege, *a.* 1300 Estley. Astle, Estelc. The *Oxf. Dict.* gives no spelling of *East* as *ast*, yet old forms show that many names in Ast-must come fr. *East*. See below. So this name is, ' East lea ' or ' meadow.' See -ley.

ASTON (Herts, Bucks, Staffs, Warwk., Yorks, and Nantwich). All *Dom.* Eston or Eastun(e)—*i.e.*, ' east-town.' It may at times be ' ash-tree-town.' *Cf.* ASHFORD, in *Dom.* Asford. Duignan says one Aston was in O.E. *Æsctun*, but does not say which.

ASTON MAGNA (E. Worcestersh.). Prob. *K.C.D.* 616 Eastune, 1275 Estone. ' Magna ' is ' great.'

ASTON TIRROLD (Wallingford). *Dom.* Estone—*i.e.*, ' East-town.' *Cf.* ASTON. Tirrold ? fr. Walter *Tirel* or *Tirrold*, who shot Wm. Rufus in New Forest. *Tirweald* was a common O.E. name; it is the same as the mod. Eng. name Thorold.

ASWARBY (Folkingham). *Dom.* Asuuardebi. ' Dwelling of *As-ward.*' *Onom.* has only one *Asuert*. See -by.

ATCHAM (Shrewsbury). *Dom.* Atingeham; later Attingham. ' Home of the sons of *Ata*,' 2 in *Onom.* For the present form *cf.* Whittingham, now pron. Whittinjem.

ATHELNEY (Taunton). 871 *O.E. Chron.* Æðelinga ég or eigg—*i.e.*, ' island of the Athelings,' or princes or noble-born men, fr. *æðel*, ' noble ' and -*ing*, ' belonging to.' M'Clure thinks the name purely personal, and meaning ' descendants of some man called Æthelbeorht, Æthelræd,' or the like. See -ey.

ATHERSTONE (Nuneaton, on-Stour, and Somerset). Nun. A. *Dom.* Aderestone, 1246 Edrideston; also Aldredestone. Stour A. *Dom.* Edricestone, 1248 Athericstone, 1249 Athereston. The former is either ' *Eadred*'s ' or perh. ' *Ealdred*'s town '; it may be ' stone,' see -ton. The latter is fr. a man *Æthelric* or *Ethric*.

ATHERTON (Manchester). *Sic* 1258-59; but 1265 Aser-, Adserton, 1320 Athyrton. This must have been orig. ' town of *Asser* '; or, in its O.N. form, ' *Atser.*' *Cf.* AZERLEY.

ATTENBOROUGH (Trent). Not in *Dom.* *c.* 1200 Adigburc, *c.* 1240 Hadinbur, 1291 Addingburg, *c.* 1500 Addyngborough. ' Burgh, town of the sons of *Ead(d)a.*' See -ing and -borough.

ATTERCLIFFE (Sheffield). *Dom.* Ateclive. ' Cliff of *Ata*.' The letter *r* tends to insert itself, as in KIDDERMINSTER etc. Here it has been influenced by *otter*, which is found in M.E. as *atter*.

ATTLEBOROUGH (Norfolk and Nuneaton). Nun. A. 1155 Attele-berge, *a.* 1400 Atleborowe, Attilburgh. Nor. A. *Dom.* Atlebure, *c.* 1456 Attylburgh. Perh. ' Burgh, town of *Athulf* or *Æthelwulf* '; several in *Onom.* of that name. But there is a known *Attile* in *Dom.*

ATTLEBRIDGE (Norwich). *Dom.* Ate-, Attebruge, *c.* 1465 Attyl-brigge. ' Bridge of *Athulf* '; see above. O.E *brycg*, North. and Sc. *brig*, ' a bridge.'

ATWICK (Hull). Not in *Dom.* Seems to be ' at the dwelling-house,' O.E. *wíc. Cf.* Atcombe, **ATLOW** (Derby), 1285 Attelawe, ' at the law ' or ' hill,' Atworth. Melksham, not in *Dom.* and Attewell, now only a surname, but 1281 *Close R.* Ettewell, Notts. *Dom.* often has Adewic, but always for **ADWICK**.

AUBOURNE (Lincoln). *Dom.* Aburne, 1208 Audeburn. Prob. ' old burn or brook ' as in **AUDLEM**; presumably an old channel superseded by a newer one. There is also an **AUBURN** or **AWBURN** near Bridlington; *Dom.* Eleburn, ' brook of *Ealla* ' ; a liquid sound like *al* easily slurs into *aw. Cf.* next.

AUCKLAND. See **BISHOP AUCKLAND.**

AUCKLEY (Doncaster). *Dom.* Alcheslei, Alceslei, Alchelie. ' Meadow of *Alca.*' *Cf.* Awkley, Notts, 1278 Alkelaye. See **ALKBOROUGH**, and -ley.

AUDENSHAW (Manchester). 1190-1212 Aldenshade, Aldensawe, 1240-59 Aldensagh, *later* Aldwynschawe, 1523 Aldewynshaw, ' Wood of *Alda* ' or ' *Ealda* ' ; O.E. *sc(e)aga,* ' a wood.' Shaw is still common in North. dial. and Sc.

AUDLEM (Nantwich). *Dom.* Aldelime. Prob. O.E. *ald elm,* ' old elm-tree '; *elm* is found in dial. as *elem, ellum ;* whilst *old* is 4-6 *aulde, awld,* dial. *awd, aud, aad. Cf.* next, and Thorp Audlin, W. Riding, not in *Dom.* except as Torp.

AUDLEY (Newcastle, Staffs. and Saffron Walden). New. A. *Dom.* Aldidelege, 1217 Aldidelee, 1218 Aldithelee. 1223 Alvithelegh, 1280 Aldithel'. ' Meadow of *Aldgith* ' or ' *Ealdgyth.*' See -ley.

AUGHTON (Ormskirk and Rotherham). Orm. A. *Dom.* Acketun, 1285 Aghton. Roth. A. *Dom.* Actun. O.E. *ác-tún.* ' Oaks' town.' *Cf.* **ACTON.**

AUST (Tockington). 691-2 *chart.* æt Austin, 794 *ib.* æt Austan, *Dom.* Austreclive (' cliff '), *c.* 1100 Augusta, 1285 Awste, Hawste, 1368 Augst. Not ' East,' as often thought, but the Roman *Augusta,* name also given to Caerleon by *Rav. Geogr. Cf.* Aosta, Piedmont and **EASTBURN.**

AUSTERFIELD (Bawtry). 702-05 Ouestrefelda, Eostrefeld. ' East field,' O.E. *éaster feld ; éaster* being compar. of *éastan,* ' East.' *Cf.* 1156 *Pipe* Austurcarii, and 1166 *ib.* Austerbi, both Lincs. But the **AUSTRELLS**, Aldridge, is *a.* 1300 Asterhull, ' hill of the hearth ' (forge or furnace), M.E. *astre,* O.Fr. *astre, aistre,* mod. Fr. *âtre. Cf.* Aisthorpe, 1233 Austorp.

AUSTERSON (Nantwich). *Old* Alstanton—*i.e.,* ' Athelstan's town,' a curious study in liquids. *Cf.* **ATHELSTANEFORD** (Sc.).

AUSTREY (Atherstone). 958 *chart.* Alduluestreow, *later chart.* Aldulfestreo—*i.e.,* O.E. for ' Ealdwulf's tree '; *Ealdwulf* is a common name in *Onom.,* also found as *Aldwulf, Aldulf ;* and *cf.* **OSWESTRY.** A name like this shows how hopeless it often is to guess, without old forms to guide. As late as 1327 it is Aldulvestre.

AUSTWICK (Settle). *Dom.* Oustewic, 1202 Austwic. 'Eastern dwelling,' O.E. *éastan* (O.N. *aust-r*) *wic*. *Cf.* AUSTERFIELD.

AUTHORPE (Louth). *Dom.* Avetorp. Prob. ' village of *Eawa*,' 2 in *Onom.* *Cf.* 1155 *Pipe* Auton, Hants; and see -thorpe.

AVEBURY (Calne). Perh. *Dom.* Avereberie, 1740 (and ? still) Abury. If orig. Avereberie it may be ' burgh of *Ælfhere*,' a very common O.E. name, found once as *Ælfuere*. More old forms needed; it may be ' burgh of *Æffa*' or ' *Æffe*,' also a common name. *Cf.* AVETON. See -bury.

AVELEY (Purfleet). *Dom.* Auileia, 1285 Alvetheley. ' Meadow of *Ælfgyth*,' a common woman's name. One was abbess of Barking in 11th cny. See -ley.

AVENAGE (Bisley, Glouc.). 1337 Abbenesse. Prob. ' *Abba*'s ash-tree.' AVENHAM (Preston), not in W. and H., may be fr. the same man, or else fr. *Æffe*, *-en*. To-day Avenage is called Avon Edge. *Cf.* next and ASHTON.

AVENING (Stroud). 896 *chart.* to Æfeningum (dat. pl.). *Dom.* Aveninge, 1221 Evening. On R. AVON, with -ing or -inge here as a river-ending. *Cf.* TWYNING, etc.

AVETON GIFFORD (Kingsbridge). *Dom.* Afetone. ' Town, village of *Afa*' or ' *Æffe*.' *Cf.* AFFPIDDLE, AVEBURY, etc.

AVINGTON (Alresford). 961 *chart.* Afintune; 1316 Aventon. Prob. ' Town of *Afa*,' 2 in *Onom.*

AVON R. (7, 3 tribs. of R. Severn, also AFON Wrangon, S. Wales). Sev. A. *Tacitus* Avona, 704-9 *chart.* Afen; 793-6 Aben, *a.* 1196 *Gir. Camb.* Avenina, Avenna; Wilts A. *c.* 380 *Ant. Itin.* Abone; *c.* 650 *Rav. Geogr.* Abona; *a.* 910 *Asser* Abon; O.E. *Chron.* ann. 653 Afene, Afne; also *charts.* Afene, Auena, Eafen, Hafene. W. *afon*, G. *abhuinn*, ' river.' The name is found in Sc. both as AVON and ALMOND. *Cf.* RAVENGLASS or *yr afon glas*.

AVONMOUTH (Bristol). 918 *O.E. Chron.* Aftena muða, 1067 *ib.* into Afenan muðan.

AWLISCOMBE (Honiton). *Dom.* Avlescome, 1282 Haulescumbe. Prob. ' Valley of *Eawulf*' or ' *Æthelwulf*,' a very common name. *Cf.* ALTON, *c.* 880 Æweltun. See -combe.

AWRE (Newnham). *Dom.* and 1223 Aure, 1160-61 *Pipe* Aura. *Dom.* Devon has Avra. W. *awr* means ' golden '; but this scarcely seems to satisfy. *Oxf. Dict.* gives *awre* as var. of OWHERE, ' anywhere.' But the Old English never made jokes with their names !

AWSWORTH (Nottingham). *Dom.* Eldesvorde, 1316 Aldesworthe; ' farm of *Ealda*.' The change is quite according to rule, so far as phonetics go. See -worth.

AXE R. and **AXMOUTH** (Somerset). *c.* 708 *Grant* Axa; *O.E. Chron.*
755 Asca; 944 *chart.* Exa, 1049 *O.E. Chron.* Axamutha. Keltic
for 'water, river' = Ex, Usk, etc. *Cf.* ASHFORD. We prob.
have the same name in the Fr. R. Aisne, L. Ax -ŏna, the-ona
being the common Kelt. ending for 'stream.'

AXHOLM (N. Lincoln). *c.* 1180 *Bened. Peterb.* Axiholm. For Ax-
see above; this was a very marshy region. A *holm* is properly
' an island in or near a river '; see -holm. Possibly it is ' holm of
Æcci,' a known name.

AXMINSTER. *O.E. Chron.* 755 Axan-, Ascanmynster, *Dom.* Axe-
minstre, ' Monastery on the R. AXE '; O.E. *mynster*, ' a monastery,' then ' a (cathedral) church,' fr. L. *monasterium.*

AYCLIFFE (Darlington). *a.* 1130 *Sim. Dur.* Heaclif—*i.e.,* O.E.
heáh clif, ' high cliff.' But School Aycliffe is 1183 *Boldon Bk.*
Sculacle, -ley, and 1130 Acheleia, 1211 Aclai—*i.e.,* O.E. *ác léah,*
' oak meadow '; this looks as if there had been a transition
form, aik lee, and the meaning of *aik* being forgotten, it was
' improved ' into Aycliffe. But the existence of the double old
form is puzzling.

AYLBURTON (Lydney). 1224 Aylbricton, 1288 *Close R.* Albrith-
ton. Prob. ' Albert's town ' or ' village '; O.E. *Ealdbeorht* or
Alberht, of whom there are many in *Onom. Cf.* Elberton
(Thornbury), *Dom.* Eldbertone, 1175 *Pipe* Alberton, 1346 Ayl-
berton.

AYLESBEARE (Exeter). *Dom.* Eilesberge. ' *Ægil's* wood,' O.E.
bearu. See AYLESBURY, and *cf.* BEER, LARKBEARE, and next.
The -berge (= BARROW) of *Dom.* is prob. an error for -bere.

AYLESBURY. *O.E. Chron.* ann. 571 Ægelesburh, Æglesbyrig;
1154-61 *chart.* Aeilesbiria. ' Ægil's burgh ' or ' fortified place.'
Ægil is the sun-archer of Teutonic mythology. See -bury, and
cf. AYLESBEARE and Ailsbury (Warwk.) 1272 Ayllesbury.

AYLESFORD (on R. Medway). *O.E. Chron.* 455 Ægelesford, also
Ægelsthrep ; *c.* 1120 Æglesforda, Æilesforda; *Sim. Dur.* ann.
1016, Eagelesford, 1160 *Pipe* Ailesfort, ' *Ægil's* ford.' See
AYLESBURY.

AYLESTON (Stratford, Wwk.) and **AYLESTONE** (Leicester). Str.
A. *Dom.* Alnodeston, 1095 Elmundestone, *a.* 1200 Alvodestone.
Either ' *Ælfnoth's*,' later ' *Alnod's* town,' or ' *Ealhmund's* town.'
For Leic. A. old forms needed. *Cf.* AYLESBURY; and on -stone,
see -ton. AYLWORTH, Glouc., *Dom.* Eleurde, Baddeley would
derive fr. the name *Æthel.*

AYLMERTON (Norwich). *Dom.* Almartune. ' Town, village of
Aylmer.' There are several called *Ælfmær* or *Elmer* in *Onom.*

AYLSHAM (N. Norfolk). 1157 Ailesham, 1443 Aylesham. ' Home,
of *Ægil*'; see AYLESBURY, and -ham.

AYLSTON (Hereford). *c.* 1030 *chart.* Ægilnothes stane—*i.e.*, ' stone of *Ægilnoth* or *Ægil.*' See AYLESBURY.

AYMESTREY (N. Herefordsh.). *Dom.* Eiminstre. Prob. ' island-minster ' or ' church.' See -ay and -minster. *Cf.* MENSTRIE (Sc.) fr. G. *mainistreach,* ' belonging to a monastery,' in 1263 Mestreth. Aydon, Corbridge, is 1285 *Close R.* Eyden.

AYNHO (Banbury). *Dom.* Aienho. ' Hoe or hill of *Egon* ' or ' *Æga* ' ; *cf. B.C.S.* 226 Æganstan; there is also a Bp. *Æine* in *Onom. Cf.* ASLACOE and EYNSHAM.

AYOT ST. LAURENCE and ST. PETER (Welwyn, Hatfield). *Ayot, ait, eyot* is ' a small island,' prob. a dimin. of O.E. *ig,* ' island.' See *Oxf. Dict. s.v.* AIT.

AYR, POINT OF (Wirral). O.N. *eyri,* ' tongue of land, gravelly bank ' =AIRE.

AYSGARTH (Bedale). *Dom.* Echescard. 1202 Aikeskerth. ' Garth, enclosure, court, yard of *Æcce* or *Æcci,*' names in *Onom.*

AYTHORPE RODING (Dunmow). Not in *Dom.* Old forms needed. The Ay- may mean ' high ' as in AYCLIFFE, or it may mean ' egg-place, egg farm,' fr. O.E. *æ3,* M.E. *ay* ' an egg.' See -thorpe, and RODING.

AYTON (Cleveland, Pickering, etc.). Cl. A. 1202 Haitone. Pi. A. 1208 Aton. There are several Aytons in Yorks; in *Dom.* all are Aton, Atun, or Atune. This is prob. ' river-town,' O.E. *éa,* M.E. *æ,* ' river,' running stream. But *cf.* EYTON.

AZERLEY (Ripon). *Dom.* Aserla, Asserle, 1281 *Close R.* Atherley, Azarlay. ' Meadow of *Atser* ' (O.N.) or ' *Asser* ' (O.E.), as in ATHERTON. *Onom.* has the forms *Adser, Azer, Azor,* all as var. of the common *Atser.* See -ley.

BABBA- BABBICOMBE (Torquay). ' Valley of *Babba* ' or ' *Bebba,* ' several in *Onom. Cf.* Bablake, Coventry, 1344 Babbelak, and Bablocklithe, Oxon, which mean ' *Babba's* pool ' (O.E. *lac,* see *Oxf. Dict.* lake *sb*⁴ 2), and ' the landing stage ' or ' HYTHE ' beside it. See BABWELL and -combe.

BABCARY (Somerton). *Exon. Dom.* Babakari, Babba cari, *Dom.* Babecari. Prob. ' *Babba's* forts,' W. *caer,* pl. *-rau* (pron. -ray), ' a fort, a castle.' See BABBACOMBE, and *cf.* CASTLE-CARY (Sc.).

BABRAHAM (Cambridge). *c.* 1080 *Inquis. Camb.* and 1166 *Pipe* Badburgeham, *Dom.* and 1286 Badburgham, 1450 Baburgham. This must be fr. a woman *Badburh,* gen. *-urge,* not in *Onom.* See -ham.

BABWELL (Bury St. Edmunds). *Dom.* has only Babenberga. 1289 *Contin.* of *Gervase,* Balbewelle. ' Well of *Babba.*' There are 5 *Babbas* and one *Baba* in *Onom.* In form 1289 *lb* is a

common scribe's error or 'trick' for *bb*. *Cf.*, too, Babthorp
(Yorks); *Dom.* Babetorp.

BACKBARROW (Ulverston). *Barrow* is O.E. *beorg*, 2 *beoruh*, 6 *barow*,
'a mount, a hill,' then, 'a grave mound, a tumulus.' The
Back-, as in BACKFORD, is doubtful; it may be Icel. *bakki*, Dan.
bakke, Sw. *backe*, 'a hill-ridge,' and so the name will signify
'long, ridged hill.'

BACKFORD (Chester). The meaning of back- here is uncertain.
It may just be 'back'; less likely ='hill-ridge,' as prob. above;
very possibly =*bach* or *beck* as in SANDBACH, *Dom.* Sanbec, and
so, 'ford over the beck or stream.' *Cf.* BACTON and Backworth,
(Newcastle-on-T.).

BACONSTHORPE (Holt, Nfk.). *Dom.* Baconstorp, 1346 Baconthorpe.
'Place, village of *Bacon*.' a name which seems not otherwise
recorded in England till 1200. It is an O.Fr. accus. of a Ger-
manic *Bacco*. See -thorpe.

BACTON (N. Walsham and Stowmarket). N. Wal. B. *Dom.* and *c.*
1150 Baketun(e), *a.* 1310 Baketon. St. B. *Dom.* Bachetuna.
Prob. 'village, town of *Bacca* or *Becca*.' *Cf. Dom.* Essex,
Bacsteda, and Baxby, Yorks, *Dom.* Backesbi. But also *cf.*
BACKFORD.

BACUP (Lancs). Local pron. Báykop. *c.* 1200 *chart*. Ffulebachope,
c. 1470 Bacop, 1507 Bacope, 1579 Baccop. *c.* 1200 clearly is
'foul bach hope,' or 'enclosed valley of the foul, dirty brook';
see -hope. Bacup stands at the centre of four valleys or
'hopes.' Bach or bache (see *Oxf. Dict. s.v.*), is a rare var. of
beck, O.E. *bœce*, *bece*, O.N. *bekk-r*, 'brook, rivulet,' which also
becomes *batch*, as in Comberbatch. SANDBACH (Cheshire), is
Dom. Sanbec. *Cf.* ECCUP and FULBECK; 'foul' is O.E. *fúl*,
2-5 *fule*.

BADBURY (Berks), *chart*. Baddanbyrig, and BADBY (Daventry)
Dom. Badebi. 'Burgh' and 'dwelling of *Bada*' or '*Badda*,'
a name common in *Onom*. See -bury and -by.

BADCOX (Frome). Not in *Dom.* Perh. W. *bedd coch*, 'red grave'
or 'grave mound,' with Eng. plur. *s* (*cs* =*x*).

BADDESLEY CLINTON and ENSOR (Atherstone). *Dom.* Bedeslei,
1327 Baddesleye Endeshover. '*Badda*'s meadow.' *Cf.* BADBY
and Badenhall, Eccleshall, *Dom.* Badenhale. See -ley. Ensor
is contraction of EDENSOR. The 'Ednesovre' family owned
the Warwk. manor *a.* 1300. Clinton is fr. the De Clintons of
Coleshill.

BADGEWORTH (Cheltenham). 872 *chart*. Beganwurtha, *Dom.* Beiwrde,
c. 1150 Begeword, and BADGEWORTHY (Lynmouth) local pron.
Badgery. *Dom.* Bicheordin, 1167-68 *Pipe* Badewurth. The
man's name is a little uncertain, but prob. both mean '*Bœcga*'s
farm.' *Bicca* is also a fairly common O.E name, and the

phonetic change fr. Biche- to Badge- is exactly illustrated in
BURBAGE, also found as Burbidge, now a personal name. The
endings are in root all the same, O.E. *worth*, with its extended
forms *worthig* and *worthign*, ' farm '; see -worth and -wardine.
Cf. Bageridge, Wolverhampton, 1286 Baggerugge.

BADINGHAM (Framlingham). *Dom.* Badincha. [*Cf.* 902 *O.E.
Chron.* ' Baddanbyrig,' near Wimborne, and *a.* 1100 *chart.*
' Badingtun ' near Melton.] ' Home, dwelling of the sons of
Badda.' *Cf.* BADDESLEY; and see -ing.

BADLESMERE (Faversham). *Sic* 1363, but *Dom.* and 1283 Badeles-
mere. ' Mere, lake of *Badela.*' *Cf. K.C.D.* 714 Badelan broc.

BADMINTON (Gloucester). 972 *chart.* Badimyncgtun, *Dom.* Mad-
mintune (*M* an error); ' town, village of *Beadumund* or *Bade-
mund,*' names in *Onom.* It may be a patronymic; Baddeley
thinks it is fr. *Beaduhelm,* a very rare name. See -ing.

BADSEY (Evesham). 709 *chart.* Baddeseia, 714 *ib.* Baddesege, *Dom.*
Badesei; and BADSWORTH (Pontefract). *Dom.* Badesworde.
' Isle ' and ' farm of *Badda.*' *Cf.* BADDESLEY; and see -ey and
-worth.

BADWELL ASH (Bury St. Edmunds). (709 *chart.* Badeswelle,
? Worc.). Not in *Dom.* Prob. ' *Badda*'s well.' *Cf.* above; not
likely fr. *bad* adj. *Cf.* BARKSTON ASH.

BAGBOROUGH (Somerset). 935 *chart.* Bacgingberghe, ' burgh,
fortified place of *Bacga.*' *Cf.* BAGLEY and BAGENDON, Cirencester, *Dom.* Benwedene, *a.* 1300 Bagindon. See -burgh and -don.

BAGBY (Thirsk). *Dom.* Bagebi. ' Hamlet, town of *Bacga* ' ; *cf.*
above and *B.C.S.* 924, ' Bægan wyrth '; See -by. But,
BAGGABY BOTTOM, Pocklington, not in *Dom.*, is 1202 Bagothebi,
where *Bagoth* seems a corrupt form of *Beagnoth,* a common
name in *Onom.*; or else it is fr. *Bagot,* a surname prob. fr. O.Fr.
Bottom, O.E. *botm,* is found with the meaning of ' valley, dell
low-lying land,' from *c.* 1325.

BAGDEN (Reigate). Not in *Dom.* Prob. ' *Bacga*'s den,' or else
' dean '—*i.e.*, (wooded) valley. Certainly nothing to do with
badger, as some imagine. *Cf.* BAGBOROUGH and BAGLEY.

BAGILLT (Holywell). A difficult name; evidently a W. corrup. of
some Eng. name. The oldest sure form is Bagilde. By some
it is identified with the Cheshire *Dom.* Bachelie, later Bakley.
But it is not certain that this is the same place, and the identification is phonetically difficult. Bachelie would prob. represent ' *Bacga*'s lea,' as in next. Quite possibly the name is W.,
bach gallt (pl. *gelltydd*), ' little cliff.'

BAGLEY (Berks). *a.* 1100 *chart.* Bacganleāh, O.E. for ' *Bacga*'s
meadow.' *Cf.* BAGDEN and BAGWORTH. There is also a
BAGNOR (Donnington). ' *Bacga*'s bank or edge '; O.E. *ora.*

BAGNALL (Stoke on T:). *a.* 1200 Baggenhall, *a* 1300 Bagenholt Baghinholt, *a* 1400 Baknold. There has been a mingling here of '*Bacga's hall*' and '*B.'s holt,*' O.E. *holt*, 'a wood' See above and -hall.

BAGSHOT (Camberley). Prob. '*Bacga's* shot' or 'glade through a wood' See BAGDEN and ALDERSHOT. The old forms are numerous—Baggeshott, Bagshat, etc ; but also Bagshet, Bakeshet, Bakset, Baggeshete, which Skeat says must be, O.E. *bœc sceat,* 'back nook or corner.' A wood near Winkfield is called Bac-sceat in *Chron. Abingdon,* temp. Wm. I.

BAGULEY (Stockport). *c.* 1320 Baggulegh. '*Bago's* lea' or 'meadow.' There is a Bago in *Onom.* See -ley.

BAGWORTH (Leicester). *O.E. chart.* Bæganwyrth, 1442 Baggeworth. '*Bœga's* or *Bacga's* farm.' *Cf.* BAGLEY and BAYWORTH, also 1155 *Pipe* Bagewurda, 1160-1 Beggewurda, Somerset, and 1158-9 *ib.* Beggewurda, Wilts; and see -worth.

BAILDON (Shipley). *Dom.* Beldone. Prob. O.E. *bœl dún,* 'hill of the fire or funeral pile.' In later Eng. it is 4-*bale,* 4 *baile,* 5 *belle,* 6 *bele ;* see *Oxf. Dict. s.v.* BALE *sb.*[2] and BALE-FIRE.

BAILEY GATE (Wimborne). Bailey is found in Eng. *a.* 1300 as *bailly.* It is O.Fr. *bail,* 'wall of the outer court of a feudal castle.' *Cf.* the Old Bailey.

BAINBRIDGE (Bedale). Not in *Dom.* Perh. 'Straight bridge.' O.N. *beinn,* 'straight, direct,' M.E. *bayn* (though not in this sense), North. dial. *bane, Whitby Gloss.* 'That way's the banest'—*i.e.,* the shortest. But perh. fr. a man *Baga,* as in next.

BAINTON (Driffield and Stamford). Dr. B. *Dom.* Bagentone. 'Town of *Baga, Bacga,* or *Becga,*' gen. *-an. Cf.* Baynhurst, Cookham, and 1157 *Pipe* Lincs, Baenburc.

BAKEWELL (Derbysh.). 924 *O.E. Chron.* Badecanwylla, v.r. Badecan wiellon; 1280 *Close R.* Bathekewell, 1287 *ib.* Bauquell, 1297 Baukwelle. '*Beadeca's* well,' O.E. *willa, wylla,* 'a fountain, a well.' There is one *Beadeca* in *Onom.* Birch says 949 *chart.* Badecanwell is Bucknall cum Bagnall, Staffd. *Cf.* Baginton, Coventry, *Dom.* Badechitone.

BALA. W. *bala,* 'a shooting-out,' *bala llyn,*' 'the outlet of a lake.'

BALBY (Doncaster). *Dom.* Ballesbi. Prob. 'village, hamlet of *Bald, Beald,* or *Bealda*'; here already seen in its more mod. form, *Ball. Cf* BALDON, and Balcombe, Hayward's Heath.

BALDERSBY (Thirsk) and BALDERTON (Newark). *Dom.* Baldrebi. The original *Balder* was son of Odin, and hero of one of the most beautiful myths in the Norse Edda. See -by and -ton.

BALDOCK (Herts). *a.* 1200 Baudac, -oc, 1287 Baldak, Baudak. An amazing name, given as a fancy name by the Knights

Templars, its founders—Ital. Baldacco, the Eng. Baghdad !
Cf. Eng. *baldachin*, older *baudekin*, a fine embroidered stuff also
named fr. Baghdad.

BALDON (Oxford). 1054 *chart.* Bealdan hama. ' *Bealda's* home.'
Note the contraction, and *cf.* BALBY and BEEDON.

BALE (Holt, Norfolk). Not in *Dom.* O.E. *bœl*, O.N. *bál*, 'a funeral
pyre, a bale-fire.' *Cf.* BAILDON.

BALKING (Uffington, Berks). 948 *chart.* Bedalacing; 963 *ib.*,
Badalacing, Bathalacing; *later* Bethelking. The *Onom.* has only
the names *Badeca* and *Badela.* But this seems to be a patronymic, denoting the ' place of the descendants of some man
Bedalac,' or the like. See -ing.

BALLINGDON (Sudbury). Not in *Dom.*, but *cf.* 704-709 *chart.*
Balgan dun, Shottery. This last is ' hill ' or ' hill-fort of *Balga.*'
But the name as it stands means ' hill of the sons of *Ball,*' a
known Eng. name; in O.E. *Beald* or *Bealda*, the ' bold,' not
' bald,' man. *Cf.* BALBY and Ball's Cross, Petworth. See -don.

BALMER (Sussex). *Dom.* Burgemere; *later*, Bormer. A curious
example of the easy interchange of liquids, and the result of
' Cockney ' pronunciations. The orig. name would mean ' mere
or lake beside the burgh,' or fortified place.

BALNE (Doncaster). Not in *Dom.* Possibly a loc. of O.E. *bœl*, or
O.N. *bál*, ' at the funeral pyres or bale fires.' *Cf.* HOXNE,
formerly Hoxon, and BAILDON.

BALSALL HEATH (Birmingham) and BALSCOTT (Banbury). 1226
Belessale, 1327 Balesale, *Dugdale* Balshall ; prob. ' *Ball's* nook '
and ' cottage.' *Cf.* Bram(h)all, Cheshire, *Dom.* Bramale, and
BALBY, and see -hall.

BALSHAM (Cambridge). 974 *chart.* Bellesham, *Dom.* Belesham,
c. 1120 *Hen. Hunt.* Balesham. ' Home of (prob.) *Ball.*' See
BALLINGDON, and -ham.

BALTERLEY (Newcastle, Staffs). 1004 Balterytheleage, *Dom.*
Baltredelege, *a.* 1300 Balterdeleye, Baldridele, -trydelegh.
' Meadow of *Bealdthryth* '; she of this lea is the only one in
Onom.

BALTONSBOROUGH (Glastonbury). 744 *chart.* Baltersberghe, *Dom.*
Baltunesberge. 1610 Balsboro'. Another case of the inter-
changeableness of the liquids *r* and *n.* The orig. name was
' burgh, fortified place of *Balter,*' a name found in *Onom.* as
Baltherus or *Baldred* or *Baldhere.* They are all the same name.
See -borough.

BAMBER BRIDGE (Preston). Omitted by Wyld and Hirst. Old
forms needed. *Cf.* Baumber, Horncastle, not in *Dom.*, and
next. *Bamber* is also found as a surname. The -ber may be for

-burgh or -bury *q.v.*, O.E. *burg, burh,* and *berig,* dat. *berie,* 'a fort, castle, or fortified town'; as it is in *Dom.* Caldeber. now Caldbergh, N. Yorks.

BAMBOROUGH (Belford). Founded *O.E. Chron.* ann. 547; 709 *Eddi* Bebbanburg; 1119 Bawmburgh. *a.* 1130 *Sim. Dur.* Babbanburch; *c.* 1175 *Fantosme* Banesburc; 1197 Banburc; 1213 Baenburc; 1221 Bamburg; 1281 Baumburgh. *Bede,* iii. 16, says the place was called 'ex Bebbae quondam reginae vocabulo.' Bebbanburh is O.E. for 'Bebba's burgh or castle'; and *Bebba* was perh. wife of K. Ida, its founder.

BAMFORD (Rochdale and Sheffield). Roch. B. *sic* 1228, 1282 Baumford. Bam- will either be O.E. *béan,* 'bean,' or *béam,* 'a tree.' *Cf.* BAMPTON, and next. The Sheff. B. is not in *Dom.*

BAMFURLONG (Wigan). 1205-23 Bonghefurlong, Bonke-, Bancfurlong, 1200-20 Benfurlong, 1200-68 Benefurlong. The latter forms are 'bean-furlong,' lit. *furrow-long,* properly the name of an unenclosed field of indefinite size. But the earlier forms seem to be fr. *bank,* M.E. *banke,* Icel. *bakki,* 'a ridge, eminence, or bank of a river,' first in Eng. in *Ormin, c.* 1200; in 4 *bonke, bonc.* *Cf.* Ashfurlong, Sutton Colfield, 1242 Hasfurlong.

BAMPTON (Oxford, etc.). *O.E. Chron.,* ann. 614, Beandun; 1155 *Pipe* Bentune; 1298 Bamptone. *Bean-dún* is O.E. for 'bean hill.' For change of *n* to *mp, cf.* Sampton, 833 'Sandtun.' See -don and -ton.

BANBURY. *Dom.* Banesberie; 1155-62 *chart.* Bannebiria; 1298 Bannebury. 'Burgh, fortified town of *Bana.*' *Cf. B.C.S.* 1219 Banan wyl. See -bury.

BANDON (Croydon). Not in *Dom.* Prob., like BAMPTON, O.E. *bean-dún,* 'bean hill.' *Cf.* BANSTEAD and Banham, Attleborough.

BANGOR. *Sic* 1250 *Layam.,* but *c.* 1120 *Hen. Hunt.* Banchor, *Sim. Dur.,* ann. 1102, Bancorensis, *a.* 1196 *Gir. Camb.* Bangorensis ecclesia; also see next. There are several in Wales, two in Brittany, and more than one in Ireland. Ir. *benn-chor,* 'a row of points or peaks,' either a circlet of rocks or a row of hills, as Joyce has shown. W. *bangor* now means 'an upper row of rods,' then 'a coping, a battlement'; W. *bann,* 'high'; Bret. *ban,* 'an eminence.' It so happens that several Bangors are lofty sites of churches or monasteries, but this is accidental; and the common derivation, 'high choir,' is now abandoned. *Cf.* BANCHORY (Sc.), the same name.

BANGOR ISYCOED (Wrexham). *Bede* Bancornburg. See above. W. *iscoed* means 'under the wood.'

BANKYFELIN (Caermarthen). Might be W. *banc y Ffelin,* 'table of Felin or Velyn.' *Cf.* STIRLING (Sc.), orig. Ystrevelyn, and HEL-

VELLYN. But simpler is the derivation ' bank, slope of the mill,' *melin*, aspirated *felin*.

BANNINGHAM (Aylsham). 'Home of the Bannings.' 'Banningas nomen populi,' in *Onom*. See -ing.

BANSTEAD (Epsom). 727 *chart*. Benstede; *Dom*. Benestede; 1280 Banstede. O.E. *béan-stede* 'bean place or store.' 'Bean' is O.E. *béan*, 3-6 *ben*, 4-6 *bene*. *Cf*. BAMPTON and BANDON.

BANWELL (Somerset). *Chart*. Banawell. Bannwille, *Dom*. Ban-welle. Prob. O.E. *bána-wœl*, 'pool of the bones.' M'Clure thinks *bena-wille*, 'prayer-well.'

BANWEN (three in Glamorgan). J. B. Bury thinks one of these represents Bannauenta or Vicus Bannavem, the home of St. Patrick. See his *Confessions*, c. 450 A.D. This is very doubtful. W. *ban gwen* is 'fair, clear hill.'

BAPCHILD (Sittingbourne). Not in *Dom*. Said to be *a*. 716 *chart*. K. *Wihtred* Baccancelde, which is '*Bacca*'s spring'; O.N. *kelda*, 'a spring, a well.' See *keld* in *Oxf. Dict*. There is no likely name with a *p* in *Onom*., and that letter remains unexplained. But *celde* here must be genuine O.E., and not Norse, as M'Clure thinks. *Cf. Dom*. Bucks, Celdestane, 'stone at the well.'

BARBON and B. FELLS (Kirby Lonsdale). *Dom*. Berebrune. Prob. O.N. *barr* or *berr brunn-r*, 'bare-looking burn or stream.' Liquid *r* is easily lost. Or the Bar- may be O.N. *barr*, O.E. *bere*, 'barley.' *Cf*. BARBRIDGE and BARFORD. The 'Barebones' Parliament,' 1653, was called after 'Praise God Barbon,' a Fleet Street leather-seller, reputed to have sprung from this district.

BARBRIDGE (Nantwich). Most of the names in Bar- are doubtful. The *sb*. 'bar,' O.Fr. *barre* (origin unknown), occurs in Eng. as early as *c*. 1175, but it may not enter into any of them. Some-times Bar- may represent a man's name, a corrup- of O.E. *Boerht* or *Beorn* or *Bearn*, as in Barthorpe Bottoms, Yorks, 1208 Barkesthorp; sometimes, especially where Norse influence is likely, as in BARBY, it will be O.E. *bœr*, O.N. *berr*, Dan. *bar*, 'bare.' Then sometimes it may be for O.N. *bar-r*, O.E. *bere*, 'bear or barley,' as in BARFORD; sometimes, too, for O.E. *beor*, *bear*, 'beer,' as in BARHAM. Old forms are always needed to ensure certainty.

BARBURY HILL (Ringwood, Hants). Prob. *O.E. Chron*., ann. 556, Beranbyrg; also Byranbyrig, Berin Byrig. 'Burgh, fort, af *Berin*,' perh. *Berinus*, in Bede, a foreign bishop who came to Wessex A.D. 635. But see also BURBURY HILL; and -burgh.

BARBY (Rugby). *Dom*. Berchebi is = BARKBY. But BARDEN, Yorks, is *Dom*. Bernedan, 'valley of *Björn*,' or 'the Bear.' See -dean.

Bardney (Lincoln). *Bede* Beardeneu; *O.E. Chron.*, ann. 642, Bardanige, Barðanig; 1230 Bardenay. ' *Barda*'s or *Bardi*'s isle,' O.E. *ig, ige*, M.E. *ey, ay*, 'island.' *Cf.* BARNSTAPLE, also a 'Bardunig' or ' Barðanig,' in *chart. c.* 680, and B ardsley, Ashton-under-Lyne.

Bardon (Leicester, Haltwhistle). Leic. *Dom.* has only Bartone, see BARTON. Perh. O.E. *bœr dún*. 'bare hill.' ' Bare ' is 3 *bar*, 4-5 *baar*. But Duignan says Bardon Hill, Stratford, Wwk., is 704 *chart*. Baddan dun, ' *Badda*'s hill.' For intrusion of *r, cf.* KIDDERMINSTER.

Bardsea, -sey (Leeds, Ulverston). Le. B. *Dom.* Berdesei, ' Isle of *Bardi*.' See BARDNEY. *Cf.* 1387 Trevisa *Higden I.* ' At Nemyn in North Wales a litel ilond . . . hatte Bardeseie,' which may be 'isle of the *bard*,' not found in Eng. till 1449. But M. B. is *Dom.* Berretseige, ' isle of *Berred, Beorred*, or *Burgred*,' names in *Onom.* See -ea, -ey. For Bardsley (Glouc.), see BARNSLEY.

Bare and **Bare Lane** (Morecambe). *Dom.* Bare, (?) 1094 and *a.* 1200 Bar. Prob. W. *bar*, ' top '; Corn. *bar, bor*, ' summit '; G. *barr*, ' a height.' It can hardly be O.E. *bœr, ber*, ' a bier.'

Baregain (farm, Cornwall, etc.). This may simply indicate a small holding. For other conjectures, see M'Clure, p. 272.

Barford (Warwick, on Tees, etc.). War. B. *Dom.* Bereford; Tees B. 1183 Bereford. ' The barley ford.' See BARBRIDGE.

Bargoed (Cardiff). See ABERBARGOED.

Barham (Canterbury and Linton, Cambs). Cant. B. is 805 *chart*. Beorahame, 809 Bereham, *Dom.* Berham; O.E. *beor-hám*, ' beer-house ' or ' brewery '; O.E. *beor, bear*, 3-4 *ber*, ' beer.' It is urged that Barham or Berham Court belonged to the Fitzurses, or ' sons of the bear,' O.E. *bera*, 2-7 *bere*. But, of course, they come in far too late here. Camb. B. is *c.* 1080 *Inquis. Camb.* Bereham, *Dom.* Bercheham, 1210 Berkham, 1302 Bergham, 1346 Berugham, O.E. *beorh-hám*, ' home on the hill or BARROW.' Barmoor, co. Durham, is in *chart*. Beyrmor, (?) ' bare moor.'

Barkby (Leicester). *Dom.* Barchebi, ' dwelling of *Beorc* or *Berc*.' See next, and *cf.* BARKHAM, Wokingham, 952 *chart*. Beorcham, *Dom.* Bercheham. which could mean ' home by the birch-tree ': but Birch, like Ash, Beech, etc., is certainly also a personal name.

Barking (Essex). 693 *chart*. To Bercingon, *Bede* Bercingas, Bercingas, *Dom.* Berchinges. *a.* 1100 *Wm. Poitiers* Bercingis. Patronymic, ' place of the descendants of *Berc*,' the modern name Birch. In *Onom.* the only forms found are *Bercta, Beorga, Beorht. Cf.* BIRKIN, and see -ing.

BARKSTON (Nottingham), BARKSTONE (Grantham), and BARKSTON
ASH (Yorks). Yo. B. *Dom.* Barcheston, 'town, village of
Beorc.' See BARKING.

BARKWAY (Royston). Not in *Dom.* 1450 Berkewey. Prob.
'road laid with *bark*,' found in Eng. *a.* 1300, O.N. *börk-r*, Dan.
bark.

BARLASTON (Stoke-on-Trent). 1004 Beorelfestun, *Dom.* Bernulve-
stone, *c.* 1200 Berlaston, Berlewston. 'Town, village of *Beornwulf* or *Bernulf*' ('brave wolf'). BARLESTONE, Nuneaton, is
the same name, *Dom.* Berulvestone.

BARLBORO' (Chesterfield). 1287 Barleburgh, and BARLBY (Selby).
Dom. Bardulbi. 'Burgh, fort,' and 'dwelling of *Bardolf.*' in
O.E. *Bardwulf.* See -borough and -by.

BARLING (Shoeburyness) and BARLINGS (Lincoln). B. Linc. 1233
Barling. Patronymics, 'place of the descendants of ?' See
above and -ing.

BARLOW (Selby, Manchester, etc.). Man. B. 1259-60 Berlawe, 1325
Barlawe, *Dom.* Bucks, Berlaue, 1183 *Boldon Bk.*, Berleia, Durham.
Man. B. seems *bere-lawe*, 'barley-covered hill.' *Cf.* BARTON.
But all the names may not be the same. See -low.

BARMBOROUGH (or BARN-, Doncaster) and BARMBY Moor and on
the Marsh (Yorks). Don. B. *Dom.* Barneburg, Berneborc.
Marsh and Moor B. *Dom.* Barnebi (this name is eleven times in
Dom. Yorks). 'Burgh, fortified town,' and 'dwelling of *Bearn,
Beorn*, or *Beorm.*' *Cf.* BARNBY and BIRMINGHAM; and see
-borough and -by.

BARMING (Maidstone) and BARMINGHAM (on Tees). 1214 Bermige-
ham. Patronymics, 'place of *Bearm*'s or *Beorm*'s descendants.'
Cf. above and BIRMINGHAM, also Bermintona in *Dom.* Devon;
and see -ing and -ham.

BARMOUTH. In W. Abermaw. Eng. corrup. (adopted in 1768) of
Abermawddach, 'mouth of the R. *Maw.*' For loss of the initial
a, *cf.* old forms of ABERGAVENNY, also BERRIEW. Mawddach is
fr. W. *mawdd*, 'that which fills or spreads out.' Colloquially
the name at times gets clipped down to Bermo.'

BARNACK (Stamford). *a.* 1100 *Grant of* 664 Bernake. O.E. *berne-
ác*, 'barn oak.' 'Barn' is O.E. *ber-ern*, *a.* 1000 *berne*, 'barley-
house.' BARNACLE, Nuneaton, is *Dom.* Bernanger, 'barn in the
hanging wood,' O.E. *hangre.* See CLAYHANGER, etc.

BARNARD CASTLE. 1200 de Castello Bernardi; 1305 Villa de Castro
Bernardi. Built, 1112-32, by *Bernard* Baliol, ancestor of John
Baliol, King of Scotland. Bernard in O.E. is Beornheard. There
is a 'Biornheardes lond' in 808 *chart* (Kent).

BARNBY (Beccles, etc.). Newark B. *Dom.* Barnebi =BARMBY.

BARNES (London). *Dom.* Berne; also *old* Bernes. 'Barns,' O.E. *berne,* 'a barn.' *Cf.* BARNACK.

BARNET (N. of London). [1199 *chart.* Bergnet is spurious] *c.* 1200 *chart.* Barnette, 1278 La Bernette, 1428 Barnette. This is Nor. Fr., and a dimin. of *berne* or *berme.* 'a narrow space, a ledge, a berm,' prob. cognate with O.N. *barm-r,* 'brim, edge.' A very rare name for England.

BARNETBY (Lincs). *Dom.* Berned-, Bernetebi. Prob. 'dwelling of *Beornheard*' or '*Bernard.*' See -by.

BARNHAM (Bognor, etc.). Bo. B. *Dom.* Berneham. 'Home of *Bearn* or *Beorn,*' though possibly 'house with the barn.' *Cf.* BARNACK and BARNWELL.

BARNOLDSWICK (Colne). *Dom.* Bernulfeswic. 'Dwelling, village of *Beornwulf* or *Barnulf,*' a common O.E. name. See -wick.

BARNSBURY (N. London). It is said to be Bernersbury, fr. Juliana *Berners,* prioress of Sopwell Nunnery, near St. Albans, *c.* 1400. This is for several reasons doubtful. Otherwise it might be 'baron's burgh or fort,' fr. *baron, a.* 1200 *barun,* 6 *barne.*

BARNSLEY (Yorks and Cirencester). Yor. B. *Dom.* Berneslai. 'Meadow of *Beorn*'; *eo* regularly becomes *a.* But Ci. B., also spelt BARDSLEY, is *c.* 802 *chart.* Bearmodeslea, 855 *ib.* Beorondeslea, *Dom.* Berneleis, *a.* 1300 Bardesle otherwise Barnsley, and must be fr. a man *Beornmod.* See -ley.

BARNSTAPLE. 930 *chart.* Beardastapole, 1018 *chart.* Beardestaple, *Dom.* Barnestaple, *c.* 1160 Gest. *Steph.* Bardestapula, 1167-68 *Pipe* Berdestapl', *c.* 1200 *Gervase* Bernestapele. As early as 1397 contracted Barum (*m* and *n* commonly interchange). The orig. name was '*Barda*'s market,' O.E. *stapel,* 'a prop, a post'; then 'a fixed market.' *Cf.* BARDNEY. But in some abnormal way it was early changed into '*Beorn*'s or *Bearn*'s market.' perh. because it is in the hundred of Branton (Bearn-ton). *Cf.* BARMBOROUGH. There is also a 'Berdestapla' in *Dom.* Essex.

BARNSTON (Birkenhead and Dunmow), BARNSTONE (Nottingham), and BARNTON (Northwich). First three in *Dom.* Bernestone, -tuna. Perh. all mean '*Bearn*'s or *Beorn*'s town or village.' *Cf.* above. But Barnton, not in *Dom.*, may come fr. *barn. Cf.* BARNHAM.

BARNT GREEN (Birmingham). 'Burnt Green,' fr. *burn,* O.E. *beornan, bearnan,* past t. 1 *bearn, barn,* 3 *barnde, bearnde,* mod. *burnt. Cf.* Barnhurst, Wolverhampton, *a.* 1400 Barnthurst, also BURNTISLAND (Sc.).

BARNWELL (Oundle and Cambridge). Oun. B. *a.* 1100 *Grant of* 664 Bernewell, which might be 'well beside the barn.' O.E. *berne,* earlier *ber-ern,* 'bear or barley house.' But Camb. B. is 1060 *chart.* Beornewell, *c.* 1250 Bernewell. 'well of *Beorna* or *Beorn,*' O.E. for 'warrior.'

BARRAS (Kirby Stephen) and BARRASFORD (Wark). O.Fr. *barras*, M.E. *c.* 1375, *barras*, ' a barrier or outwork in front of a fortress '; then ' the lists for knightly tournaments '; fr. Fr. *barre*, ' a bar.' *Cf.* BARRASSIE (Sc.).

BARR BEACON (Walsall). *c.* 1200 Barr(e). W. *bar, bor, bur,* ' top, summit '; G. *barr,* ' a height '; *Beacon,* O.E. *béacn,* is a common name for a commanding hill—Worcestershire Beacon, Dunkery Beacon, Exmoor, etc. — but *Oxf. Dict.*'s earliest quot. is 1597.

BARRINGTON (Cambridge). *c.* 1080 *Inquis. Camb.* Barentone, 1210 Barntone, 1428 Baryngtone. ' Village of *Bara, -an.*' But B. (Glostrsh.) *Dom.* Bernin-, Bernitone, *c.* 1245 Bernington, is prob. ' village of *Beornwine.*' There are two others. *Cf.* BERRINGTON and the surname Baring. See -ing and -ton.

BARRIPPER (Camborne). Not in *Dom.* There are elsewhere in Cornwall also Bereppa, Brepper, and Borripper, which good authorities think all come fr. Fr. *beau repaire,* ' fine haunt or lair.' *Cf.* Belrepeir, Haresfield, *c.* 1220 Bewper, *a.* 1470 Beaurepaire; and see p. 64.

BARROW (nine Barrows in *P.G.*), also BARROWDEN (Stamford) and BARROWFORD (Nelson). Chesh. B. *Dom.* Bero. Worc. B. 1275 Barew. O.E. *biorg, beorh,* ' a hill '; after 1576 *barrow* is often applied also to a grave-mound, a tumulus. It is a common name of hills in the S.W.—Bull Barrow, Dorset, etc. In the N. usually it is a long, low hill—*e.g.,* Barrow near Derwentwater, Barrow Hill, Chesterfield, etc. *Cf.* BERROW and next, and BURROW.

BARROWBY (Kirkby Overblow, Yorks, and Grantham). Yor. B. *Dom.* Berghebi, ' dwelling by the hill,' or ' tumulus.' See above. ' Berghebi ' in *Dom.* is often BORROWBY. See -by.

BARRY (Cardiff). In W. Y Barri. ' the Barry.' The island belonged to the family of Giraldus de *Barry,* lords of the island. The du Barry family is well known, or rather notorious, in later Fr. history. There is also a Barry, *sic* 1603, in Pembk.

BARSTON (Birmingham). *Dom.* Bereestone, Bertanestone, *a.* 1300 Berstonestun, 1327 Berstanston. ' Town, village of *Beorhtstan* ' or ' *Beorht.*' See -ton.

BARTESTREE (Hereford). *Dom.* Bertoldestreu. ' Tree,' O.E. *treow,* ' of *Beorhtweald,*' a very common O.E. name. *Cf.* OSWESTRY. BARTHERTON or Batherton, Nantwich, is 1283 *Close R.* Bercherton, prob. fr. a man *Beorhtheard* or *Berehthart,* nàmes in *Onom.*

BARTHOMLEY (Crewe). *Dom.* Bertemlea. ' Lea, meadow of *Bertram* or *Beorhthelm,*' a very common O.E. name. See -ley.

BARTLEY (Southampton and Birmingham). ' *Beorht*'s meadow.' *Cf.* BARTESTREE. Duignan omits. See -ley.

BARTLOW (Cambridge). 1303 Berklawe. 1316 Berkelowe, 1428 Berklowe. ' Hill of *Beorht, Beorh,* or *Beorc,*' all the same name. *Cf.*, too, **BARHAM** (Cambs.) See -low.

BARTON (16 in *P.G.*). Leicetser B. *Dom.* Bartone ; *Dom.* Sffk. Bertune. Barton-on-Humber is thought to be *Bede,* iv. iii. ad Barve, which Bede renders ' at the wood.' Barton Regis is *Dom.* Bertune apud Bristou; and Barton - on - the - Heath (Warwk.) is *Dom.*Bertone. Barton-under-Needwood is the same. But Barton le Street (Yorks) is *Dom.* Bartun(e), and so is Barton le Willows. Barton is O.E. *bere-tún,* ' grange or enclosure for bear or barley or other corn, farmyard.' *Cf.* **BARWICK.**

BARTON BENDISH (Norfolk), **BARTON-IN-THE-CLAY** (Ampthill), etc. There are forty-five such names compounded with Barton in *P.G.* Bendish is said to be for *fen-ditch,* but phonetically that is very unlikely. It is prob. a family name.

BARWICK-IN-ELMET (Leeds). *Dom.* Berewich. O.E. *bere-wic,* ' house for bere or barley ' = **BERWICK** and **BARTON.** Elmet, sic *Nennius, Bede* and *Dom.* Elmete, *a.* 800 *chart.* Elmed sætna (' dwellers in '), was a British kingdom, now the W. Riding of Yorks. Origin unknown.

BASCHURCH (Shrewsbury). *Dom.* Bascherche. ' Church of *Bassa.*' See Llywarch Hen's elegy. *Bassa* or *Bassus,* a valiant soldier of K. Edwin of Northumbria, is mentioned in Bede. (*Cf.*, too, the mod. surname Bass, though it may be fr. Le bas.) Similar is Bascote, Southam, *sic a.* 1300, and the 2 Basfords, *Dom.* Notts, Baseford.

BASILDON or **-DEN** (Wallingford). *Dom.* Bastedene; 1241-42 Bastilesden; also Basteldene. *Cf. B.C.S.* 565 Bestles ford. ' **DEAN,** (wooded) valley of *Bœstel* or *Bestle.*' *Cf.* **BISHAM.**

BASINGSTOKE (Hants). 871 *O.E. Chron.* Basingas; *Dom.* Basinge stoch(es), 1238 Basyng. Patronymic, ' Place (O.E. *stóc*—lit. ' stake '), ' of the *Basings,*' or ' descendants of Bass.' *Cf.* **BASCHURCH.** But Old Glossary *Basincge, melotae,* ' in goat-skins.' Bessingby (Yorks), is *Dom.* Basingebi.

BASINGWERK (Flint). *sic* 1277, but *a.* 1196 *Gir. Camb.* Basingeworc— *i.e.,* ' outwork, fort of the *Basings.*' See above, and **BASCHURCH.** There is a ' Basingewerc,' 1160, in *Pipe* Notts and Derby.

BASLOW (Chesterfield). 1156 Bassalawa. ' *Bassa's* hill.' See **BASCHURCH** and **-low.**

BASSALEG (Newport, Mon.). Thought to be *c.* 800 *Nennius* Campus Elleti (*t* common scribe's error for *c*), and so = the mod. W. name Maesaleg, ' plain ' (W. *maes*) ' of *Ælloc*' or ' *Aloc,*' names of men in *Onom.* Close by is *maes Arthur,* ' plain of Arthur.' But it is *c.* 1130 *Lib. Landav.* Ecclesia de Bassalec. Kuno Meyer derives this fr. L. *basilica,* Gk. βασιλική, ' royal residence, courthouse,' in L., after 4th cny. A.D., 'cathedral, church,' found in O.Ir. as *baisleac*. But there seems no sure evidence or analogy for this, and it contradicts the evidence given above. Moreover, the church here is dedicated to St. *Basil*, and the -lec or -leg might easily represent the common O.E. *léah, léaʒ,* see -ley, and so the name be 'Basil's meadow.' Only, Eng. names so early as 1130 in this region are very unlikely. The present W. pron. varies between Macsaleg, Mashalyg ('field of willows '), and Maeshalog (said to be 'salt-field '), showing that the natives are all at sea; and the rest of us are not much better !

BASSENTHWAITE (Keswick). 'Place of *Bassa* ' (the -*en* is a gen.). See BASCHURCH, and -thwaite.

BASSETLAW (a wapentake of Notts). *Dom.* Bernedeselawe, ' Hill of *Beornheard* ' or '*Bernard*,' a common O.E. name. But 1155 *Pipe* Desetlawa, 1189 *ib*. Bersetelaw. *a.* 1199 Basselaw (*d* or *t* prob. omitted in error). As Mutschmann says, the orig. name prob. was, O.E. *bearu-sœtena-hláw,* 'mound of the forest-dwellers'; *cf.* DORSET, and see next. In 1155 D is an error for B. See -low, -law.

BASSETT (Southampton). *Dom.* Bessete. Difficult. Perh. 'heath of *Besa, Bassa, Bass*, or *Basso*,' all names in *Onom.* The ending -et is generally puzzling ; but for the suggested origin here *cf.* the forms of HATFIELD, Herts, and HODNET. The Bassetts were Nor. lords of Drayton Bassett, Tamworth, and elsewhere, for several generations. So possibly the name is O.Fr., though not probably. Fr. *basset* means ' of low stature,' and gave name to a Nor. family very early in Notts.

BASSINGBOURN (Royston, Camb.), also **BASSINGHAM** (Newark). 1202 Bassingburn; 1298 Bassingburn, -borne; *a.* 1300 *Eccleston* Bissingburne (Norfolk pron.). 'Burn or brook of Bass's descendants.' *Cf.* BASCHURCH and BASINGSTOKE. See -bourne and -ham.

BASTON (Market Deeping). *Sic* in *chart.* of 806. 'Town, village of *Bass*.' See BASCHURCH, etc.

BASTWELL (Blackburn). 1288 Baddestwyssel, 1329 Battistwyssel, 1322 Batestwysel, 1594 Bastwell. A remarkable contraction— ' the TWIZEL,' or ' confluence of *Badda*.' *Cf.* HALTWHISTLE and *Dom.* Norfolk, Bastwic.

BATCHWORTH HEATH (Rickmansworth). 1007 *chart.* Bæcceswyrth. Prob. ' Place of *Bacca* or *Becca*,' both names in *Onom. Cf.* BETCHWORTH, and BLETCHLEY fr. *Blecca*. But possibly fr. *batch*, var. of *bache*, ' a river-vale.' See *Oxf. Dict*. It is the same root as *beck, cf.* COMBERBACH and Pulverbatch, Salop. Skeat inclines to the meaning, ' farm in the river-valley.' The sign of the gen. in the *chart.* is against that. See his own *Pl. Names of Berks*, p. 35. *Cf.* The Batche, Forest of Dean.

BATCOMBE (Bath, etc.). *a.* 900 *chart.* Batancumb, 940 *chart.* Batecombe. *Cf.* 1298 ' Thomas Botencombe.' ' Valley of *Bata*,' a name in *Onom.* See -combe.

BATH. *c.* 380 *Ant. Itin.* Aquæ Solis. 781 ' at Beathum; 796 *chart.* ' Celebri vico qui Saxonice vocatur æt Baðum '; 1088 *O.E. Chron.* (Peterb.) Baðon, 1130 *ib.* Bathe, *c.* 1160 *Gest. Steph.* Batthentona, also ' Batta quod Balneum interpretatur.' O.E. *bœð,* ' a bath.'

BATHEALTON (Somerset). *Dom.* Badeheltone, BATHEASTON (*ib.*), (?) *Dom.* Estune, ' east town,' and BATHWICK, ' dwelling near Bath.' See -wick. In all three cases, of course, the first part is BATH. The -ealton may be O.E. *eald tún,* ' old town.' *Cf.* ELTHAM. But it may be ' town of *Ela, Eli,*' or ' *Ella,*' all names in *Onom. Cf.* ELTON.

BATLEY (Dewsbury). *Dom.* Bateleia, Bathelie; 1202 Battelege; 1298 Bateleie. ' Pasture lea or meadow,' fr. O.N. *beit,* ' pasture '; *beita,* ' food, bait '; or else ' *Bata*'s lea.' *Cf.* BATCOMBE and *Dom.* Norfk. Bathele, Notts, Badeleie (now Bathley).

BATLEY CARR (Dewsbury). See above. Carr is North. O.E. *carr* (*c.* 950 in *Lindisfarne Gosp.*), ' a rock.' *Cf.* the CARR Rocks, Berwick, and REDCAR.

BATTERSBY (N.E. Yorks). *Dom.* Badresbi. ' Dwelling of ' some Norseman, prob. *Beaduheard* or *Badherd,* common in *Onom. Cf.* BUTTERMERE, and see -by.

BATTERSEA (London). 693 *chart.* Batriceseye; *Dom.* Patricesy; 1308 Badricheseye. ' St. Patrick's ' or ' St. Peter's isle '; *Peter* and *Patrick* are often interchanged. See -ey. It belonged to the Abbey of St. Peter of Westminster. *Cf.* PADSTOW. Change fr. *P* to *B* is not common, and M'Clure suggests ' Beadurich's isle,' and compares Beadorices Uurthe, old name of St. Edmund's Bury in *Ethelwerd's Chronicle.*

BATTLE ABBEY (Hastings). Begun 1070, four years after the battle of Hastings. *Dom.* Ecclesia de labatailge (O.Fr. *bataille,* ' battle '). 1297 *R. Glouc.* ' Ycleped in Engelond abbay of þe batayle.'

BATTYEFORD (Normanton). Not in *Dom.* Prob. fr. some man. The surname *Batty* is well known, and there is *Beata* in *Onom.*

BAUGHURST (Basingstoke). *B.C.S.* 624 Beaggan hyrst. ' Wood of *Beagga.*' See -hurst.

BAWDESWELL (Dereham). *Dom.* Baldereswella. ' Well, spring of *Bealdhere,*' 5 in *Onom.* The change to Bawde- is quite according to phonetic law. *Cf.* BAWDSEY.

BAWDLANDS (Clitheroe), not in W. and H., and BAWDSEY (Felixstowe). Old forms needed for the first; prob. fr. *bawd* sb.[2], ' a hare.' The second is *Dom.* Baldereseia, Baldeseia. ' Isle of *Bealdhere.*' *Cf.* BAWDESWELL, and see -ey.

BAWDRIP (Bridgewater). *Dom.* Bagetrepe. 'Drop of *Baga*,' or '*Bæga*.' There is The Drip near Stirling; the Sc. verb is *dreep*, 'to drop down from a height.' It occurs in M.E. as *dripe*, and in O.E. as *drýpen*, but is not found in either as a *sb.* Cognate with *drip, droop*, and *drop*. *Cf.* Bawtry, Yorks, not in *Dom.* ? '*Baga*'s tree.'

BAXENDEN (Accrington). 1332 Bakestonden; also *cf. B.C.S.* 917 Beaces hlaw, and *B.C.S.* 906 Bacgan broc. A somewhat rare combination—'town of *Beaca*,' + -den, *q.v. Cf.* BAXBY, Coxwold par., Yorks, *Dom.* Bachesbi, 1201 Baxeby.

BAXTERLEY (Atherstone). 1327 BAXTERLEYE. A unique name. 'Meadow of the *baxter*,' still a common Sc. surname. O.E. *bæcestre*, M.E. *baxter*, 'a baker.'

BAYDON (Lambourne). Prob. O.E. *Beagan dún*, 'Beaga's (or Bacga's) hill,' *cf. B.C.S.* 882 Beagan wyl. *Cf.* BAYTON and BAYWORTH. *Bay* = 'bay-coloured,' is O.Fr. *bai*, and is not found in Eng. till 1374. BAYFORD (Hereford) will have a similar origin.

BAYLHAM (Ipswich). *Dom.* Beleham, 1453 Beylom, 1456 Boylom. Prob. O.E. *Bæl-hám*, 'home, house of Bæl' or 'Bayle'; *cf. B.C.S.* 1316 Bælles wæg. Not so prob. fr. O.E. *bæl*, O.N. *bál*, 5-9 *bail*, 'a blazing pile, a bonfire, a funeral pyre.'

BAYNARDS CASTLE (Horsham). Said to be fr. *Bainiardus. Bainardus.* or *Baignardus*, tenant of the abbot of Westminster, named in *Dom. Cf.* BAYSWATER. The final -ard in personal names, like Bernard, Reynard, etc., is usually O.E. *heard,* O.H.G. *hard*, 'strong (in counsel).'

BAYSTON HILL (Shrewsbury). *Dom.* Begestan. 'Town, village of *Begha* or *Baega*,' same name as ST. BEES. *Cf.* BAYWORTH; -stan *i.e.*, -stone often interchanges with -ton, *q.v.*

BAYSWATER (London). 1653 *Grant*, 'At Paddington, near to a place commonly called Baynard's Watering.' But in 1720 clipped down to Bear's Watering.

BAYTON (Cleobury Mortimer). *Dom.* Betune, *a* 1200 Bertune, 1275 Beyton, 1339 Baynton. Some confusion here, but Duignan is prob. right in making it O.E. *Bægan tun*, 'Baega's town.' *Cf.* BAYDON and next.

BAYWORTH (Abingdon). 956 *chart.* Bægen weorthe; Bægan wyrthe; *Dom.* Baiorde; *a.* 1200 *Hist. Abindgon* Baigeuuortha. 'Farm of *Baega* or *Begha*,' same name as ST. BEES. *Cf.* BAYSTON and BAGWORTH, and see -worth.

BEACHAMWELL (Swaffham). *Dom.* has Becheswella, 'well, spring of *Bæcca, Beac*,' or '*Beocca*,' all in *Onom. Dom.* also has Becham, Bicham, which is prob. 'home on the beck,' O.E. *bæce, bece, cf.* BACUP, but may also be '*Beac*'s home.' This

Beacham can hardly be the same as Beauchamp (pron. Beécham) Court, Worc., *Dom*. Bello Campo, which is Fr. and L. for 'fine field' =BELCHAMP. BEACHLEY, Tewkesbury, is *old* Betesle, fr. a man *Beta* or *Betti*.

BEACHY HEAD (Sussex). Fr. *beau chef*, 'fine head or headland.' There is a Beauchief near Sheffield.

BEACONSFIELD (Bucks). Old forms needed. *Cf*. BACONSTHORPE. *Dom*. has only Bechentone and Bechesdene, fr. *Becca* or *Beco*, names in *Onom*.

BEADLAM (Helmsley). *Dom*. and 1202 *Yorks Fines* Bodlum, -lun. Older forms needed. See -ham. But Bodlum suggests corrup. of O.E. *botlon*, loc., 'at the dwellings.' *Cf*. HALLAM, KILHAM, etc. O.E. *botl* is O.Fris. *bodl*. *Cf*. HARBOTTLE etc.

BEADNELL (Bedford). [*Cf*. *B.C.S.* 936 Beaden heal.] Prob. '*Beada*'s nook' or 'hall,' as in charter cited. *Cf*. BEDNAL and BEDWIN, and see -hall.

BEAL (Northbld.). *chart*. Behil, Beyl. Prob. O.E. ʒe, *bi*, *hil* or *hyl*, 'by the hill,' as in Biddick, Durham 1183 Bedyk. Bydyk, 'near the (Roman) Wall,' and Biwere, 'by the weir.' *Inquis. Eli*., p. 190, 'Hec sunt piscaria monachorum . . . Vttrewere ('outer weir'), 'Landwere . . . Biwere, Northwere, etc.' Beaford, Torrington, may also mean 'by the ford'; old forms are wanting, but we have *Dom*. Worc. Beford. On the other hand, see BEAWORTHY in the same county. The ending in Beal may be -hale (see -hall). BEALL (Knottingley) is *Dom*. Begale, which is prob. '*Bega*'s nook.' *Cf*. BAYDON and BRILL.

BEALINGS, Great and Little (Woodbridge). *Dom*. Belinges. and B. parva. Patronymic; 'place of the sons of *Bella*' or '*Beola*,' both in *Onom*. Prob. =BILLING.

BEANE R. (Hereford). *c*. 1120 *Hen. Hunt*. Beneficia. This yields a curious conundrum.

BEAR- BERSTED (Maidstone). 1005 *chart*. Berhamstede, and so same name orig. as BERKHAMSTED; or else as in BERSHAM, 'stead, place, farm of *Ber*.'

BEARLEY (Alcester). A changed name. *Dom*. Burlei, 1327 Burlege, *a*. 1600 Byrley. 'Burgh on the lea'; see -burgh and -ley.

BEAUDESERT (Henley-in-Arden and Cannock). Hen. B. *c*. 1135 Beldesert, *a*. 1400 Beaudesert. Can. B. *a*. 1300 Beaudesert, *a*. 1400 Bellum Desertum. This is Fr. for 'beautiful wild '; *desert* in Eng. is often used for 'wild, mountain or forest land.' Henley B. was in *Dom*. Donnelie.

BEAUFORT (Brecon). Fr. *beau fort*, 'fine fortress.' Called after the Fr. Beaufort, near Angers. It belonged to the Lancaster family in the 14th cny. and from them the Dukes of Beaufort are

descended. BEAUPRE House. Cowbridge, Fr. for ' fine meadow,'
is on the site of a Norman fortress. See also *s.v.* BEAUMARIS.

BEAULIEU (Southampton). Pron. Bewly. *c.* 1246 de Bello Loco Regis
(*i.e.*, John), 1289 *Contin. Gervase* Bellum-locum. Fr. *beau lieu,*
' beautiful place '; founded by K. John for the Cistercians
in 1204. *Cf.* Beauchief (Sheffield), BEAULY (Sc.), and BEWDLEY.

BEAUMARIS (Anglesea). *Old forms* Bumaris, Beumarish, Byw-
mares. The old W. name was Rhosfair, ' moor of Mary.' In
1293 Edward I. built a castle on the low-lying land by the shore,
that so the castle ditch might communicate with the sea.
Because of this suitability of site the King called it *Beau marais,*
(O.Fr. *mareis*), which is Fr. for ' fine marsh ' or ' low-lying,
swampy ground.' *Cf.* BEAUDESERT. In W. to-day it is pron.
Bliwmaris, just as Beaufort, (Mon.) is pron. Bluefort. Maresden
(Glouc.) is also fr. *mareis.* But Beamish, Co. Durham, is *old*
Beaumeis, ' fine dwelling,' fr. O.Fr. *mes,* ' a manse, a mansion.'

BEAUMONT (Lancs., Colchester, and Jersey). La. B. 1230 Bello
Monte, 1316 Bealmont. 1494 *Fabyan,* ' The castell of Beaw-
mount.' Fr. *beau mont,* ' fine hill ' = BELMONT. But Bowmont
Water, Cheviots, is *a.* 1000 Bolbend, of doubtful meaning; it
cannot be fr. *bend* sb[4].

BEAUSALE (see BEOLEY).

BEAVER (Ashford). Old forms needed. It may be = BELVOIR (pron.
beever). Fr. for ' fine outlook ' or ' view,' = *beau voir. Cf.*
BEACHY HEAD.

BEAWORTHY (N. Devon). *Dom.* Bicheordin. ' Farm of *Bica* '
(*ī* = *ee*). The ending is O.E. *worðige,* a dat.; see -warden and
-worthy. *Cf.* Beaford (Devon), old forms needed.

BEBINGTON (Birkenhead). [*Cf.* 1298 Willelmus de Bibington.]
' Town, village of *Bebba,*' or of his descendants. *Cf.* BAM-
BOROUGH, and see -ing.

BECCLES (Lowestoft). *Sic Dom.* 1157 *Pipe* in Becclis, 1298 Bekles,
1443 Bekelys. An abnormal name. Possibly O.E. *bi, be*
ECCLES, ' by, beside the church.' *Cf.* BEEFORD, BIX, etc.
But prob. one of those rare cases of a man's name in the gen.
standing alone for a place-name, as in BEEDON, BRAILES,
COVEN, etc., and so ' (place of) *Beoccel.' Cf. B.C.S.* 1117
Beocceles put. *Dom.* Suffk. has also Abecles, and *Dom.* Nfk.
Breckles, Breechles.

BECKENHAM (Kent). O.E. *chart.* Beohhahamme, -hema, *Dom.*
Bacheham, *a.* 1200 *Text. Roff.* Becceham. A little doubtful;
prob. not *'Becca*'s home,' as in Beckbury (Shifnal), nor ' enclosure
on the *bach* or *beck,* as in BACUP; but prob. ' enclosure of
Beohha,' though we should have expected some sign of the gen.
Cf. Dom. Essex, Bacheneia; and see -ham, ' enclosure.'

BECKÉRMET (Egremont and W. Riding). Eg. B. 1189 *Pipe* Bekir-met, *a.* 1200 Becchiremond. W. Rid. B. not in *Dom.*, but *old* Beckermond; O.N. *bekkjar muð-r,* 'mouth of the beck or brook.' Beck occurs again in Albecq, Guernsey; prob. O.N. *áll-bekkr,* 'ed brook.' 'Mouth' in O.N. is *munn-r, muð-r.* Dan. *mund;* and N. *nd* regularly becomes *th* or *t* in Eng. names. *Cf.* AMOTHERBY, OSMOTHERLEY, and MITE. Also *cf.* 1183 *Boldon Bk.* Becchermore, 'moor of the brook,' in Durham.

BECKFORD (Tewkesbury). 803 *chart.* Beccanforda—*i.e.*, 'ford of *Becca*'; 1158-59 *Pipe* Becheford. *Cf.* Beckbury (Shifnal) and Becesworde, *Dom.* Surrey.

BECKINGHAM (Gainsboro' and Newark). *Dom.* Notts Beching(e)-ham, [Lincs Bechebi]; and BECKINGTON (Bath). *Dom.* Beching-tone. 'Home' and 'village of *Beca*'s descendants.' *Cf.* above; and see -ing, -ham, and -ton.

BECKWITHSHAW (Harrogate). *Dom.* Becvid. It seems a tautology. 'Wood on the beck or brook.' *Cf.* BECKERMET. For -with is Icel. *vith-r,* 'a wood, shrubs' (*cf.* ASKWITH); and -shaw is O.E. *scaga,* 'a wood' (*cf.* AUDENSHAW).

BEDALE (Northallerton). *Sic* in *Dom.* It is on R. Ure. Analogy would make this, O.E. *be dal,* 'by, near the dale.' *Cf.* BEAL and BEEFORD. Of course, it might be 'bee dale,' O.E. *béo;* prob. not.

BEDDGELERT (Carnarvon). W. = 'grave of *Gelert*,' the famous and faithful dog of Prince Llewellyn, in the legend, killed by him by mistake. Some, however, say the orig. name was Bwth Cilarth or Bethcelert, and say it orig. was 'house, booth of *Celer*,' patron saint of Llangeler.

BEDDINGHAM (Lewes). 810 *Grant* Beadyngham, 'Home of the *Beadingas*.' *Cf.* BEEDING, BEDINGHAM, and next.

BEDDINGTON (Croydon and Hants). Croy. B. *c.* 905 Beddinctun, *Dom.* Beddintone. Prob. patronymic like the above, and so 'town, village of the *Beadingas*.' *Cf.* 854 *chart.* Beaddingbroc. But both this and the above may be fr. a man *Bedda*.

BEDFONT (Middlesex). *Dom.* Bedefunde, -funt. '*Beda*'s font,' O.E. *font,* 2-6 *funt*(e). *Cf.* Bedfield, Framlingham, and CHAL-FONT.

BEDFORD. There is also a Bedford near Manchester. *The* Bed-ford is in W. Rhydwely, which prob. means 'ford on this torrent,' W. *gweilgi.* *O.E. Chron.* 577 Bedecanford; 1011 *O.E. Chron.* Bedanfordscír, 1016 *ib.* Beadaford scire. *c.* 1150 Bedefordia. 'Ford of *Bedeca*.' *Cf. B.C.S.* 1307 Bedecan lea. The Man. B. is 1296 Bedeford, '*Bœda*'s ford.'

BEDINGFIELD (Eye and Notts). Eye B. *Dom.* Bedinge-, Bedinga-fielda, Bading-. Not. B. Not in *Dom., a.* 1199 Bedingefeld.

Prob. both patronymics like BEDDINGHAM. But BEDINGHAM (Bungay). *B.C.S.* 81, Beddenham, is 'home of *Bedda.*' See -ing.

BEDLINGTON (Northumberland). *Chart.* Betligtona, Bellintona, *c.* 1155 Bellingtonesir (-shire). 'Town, village of *Bedling,*' a name found in *Onom.*, prob. a patronymic. *Cf.* BIDLINGTON, Sussex, *a.* 1100 Bedelingstone. See -ing.

BEDLINOG (Glamorgan). W. *bedd llwynog,*' grave of the fox'; but T. Morgan thinks rather, *bedw llwynog.* 'place with a grove of birch-trees'; they are plentiful here.

BEDMINSTER (Bristol). *Dom.* Betminstre, 1155 Bedmenistre. '*Beda's* minster' or '*church.*' *Cf.* BEDFONT, and see -minster.

BEDMONT (Herts). Not in Skeat. '*Beda's* mount' or 'hill.' O.E. *munt*, L. *mons, -tis,* 'a mountain.'

BEDNAL (Stafford). *Dom.* Bedehala, 1271 Beden hulle (= 'hill'), *a.* 1300 Bedan- Baden hale. '*Bede's* nook' or 'hall' = BEAD-NELL. *Cf.* BETHNAL GREEN, and 1160-01 *Pipe* Nthbld. Bedehal.

BEDWAS (Cardiff). O.W. *bed gwas,* 'grave of the servant.'

BEDWIN, -WYN, GREAT and LITTLE (Hungerford). 778 *chart.* Bedewind, *Dom.* Bedvinde, 1155 *Pipe* Estbedewind. As *wind* in O.E. simply means 'wind,' this would seem to be W. *bedd gwynn,* 'fair, beautiful grave.' Though it is said to be *O.E. Chron.* 675 Bedan- or Biedenhafod—*i.e.*, '*Bieda's* head' or 'headland.' But the two names cannot be the same.

BEDWORTH (Nuneaton). *Dom.* Bedeword. '*Beda's* farm' *Cf.* BEDMINSTER, etc., and see -worth.

BEEDING (Steyning). *Dom.* Bed(d)inges (nom. plur.). Patronymic. See BEDDINGHAM.

BEEDON HILL (Newbury). *Chart.* Bedene, Bydene; *Dom.* Bedene; 1316 Budeneye; 1428 Budene, Bedene. Skeat thinks this must be simply O.E. *Bedan,* 'Byda's or Beda's,' 'home' to be supplied. *Cf.* BIDDENHAM. This is a rare type of name, but see BALDON, BENSON, and WIGAN.

BEEFORD (Driffield). *Dom.* Biworde. 'Beside the farm or estate'; O.E. *bi worth;* -worth and -ford often interchange. Also *cf.* BEAL and BIDEFORD.

BEENHAM or BENHAM (Reading). 956 *chart.* Bennanhamme; *Dom.* Benneham, Beneham. 'Home of *Benna*'; see -ham. In *Calend. Inquisit.* I. we find 'Benham manerium' among lands held by Adomarus de Valencia or Aymer de Valence; hence the full name B. Valence.

BEER (Axminster), *Dom.* Bere, BEER ALSTON, and BEER FERRIS (Devon). *Dom.* Bere, Bera. O.E. *bearu,* 'a wood'; and see ALSTON. The other name is better written Bere Ferrers. F. was a crusader, whose tomb is in the church here.

BEESBY (Alford). *Dom.* Besebi. 'Village, dwelling of *Besa.*' One in *Onom.* See -by.

BEESTON (Leeds, etc.). Leeds B. *Dom.* Bestone, 1202 Bestona. Notts B. *Dom.* Bestune. Chester B. *Dom.* Buistane. Perh. Bovis in *Ant. Itin.* The Ches. B. looks as if fr. N. *bui*, 'a goblin'; but the others are prob. fr. the name *Begha* or *Bees. Cf.* above.

BEETHAM (Westmorland). *Dom.* Biedun, which may be '*Bede*'s hill'; it is very rare for *dún* to become -ham.

BEETLEY (Dereham). *Dom.* Betellea. Doubtful, more old forms needed. Prob., as above, fr. a man *Beta.* But perh. 'beet-root meadow,' fr. O.E. *bete ;* whilst Betel- might also stand for *Bethild* or *Betweald,* names in *Onom.*

BEGELLY (Pembksh.). *Old* Bugeli. It is thought to be a tribal name, fr. W. *bugail,* G. *buachail,* 'a shepherd'; or perh. a man's name, *Bugail ; cf.* Merthir ('martyr') Buceil in *Lib. Land.,* once near Bridgend, Glam.

BEIGHTON (Rotherham and Norwich). Ro. B. not in *Dom.* Nor. B. *Dom.* Begetona, 1450 Beyton, Boyton. '*Begha*'s town.' *Cf.* ST. BEES.

BEKESBOURNE (Canterbury). Not in *Dom.* '*Beca*'s' or '*Becca*'s brook. See -bourne, and *cf.* BECKBURY.

BELBROUGHTON (Stourbridge). 817 *chart.* Belne, et Brocton, *Dom.* Bellem, Brotune, *a.* 1200 Beolne, 1275 Belne-Bruyn, Brocton, *a.* 1400 Belne-Brocton, -brotton, Bellenbrokton. A curious compound. BROUGHTON is plain enough; but 'Belne' seems at present insoluble.

BELCHAMP ST. PAUL and BELCHAMP WALTER (Suffolk). *Dom.* Belcamp. O.Fr. *bel champ,* 'fine field or plain.' Same name as Beauchamp or Beacham. *Cf. Dom.* Bucks, de Belcamp, 1160 *Pipe* 'Belcāp,' Hereford. and BEACHAMWELL; also 1281 *Close R.* Belcham, Essex.

BELCH- or BELSHFORD (Horncastle). *Dom.* and 1281 Beltesford. Prob. 'ford of *Bealda,*' two in *Onom.* But *cf. Dom.* Essex Belcham. *Onom.* has one *Balchi.*

BELEY (Glostrsh.). 972 *chart.* Beoleahe, =BEOLEY.

BELFORD (Northumberland). *c.* 1175 *Fantosme* Belefort; there is in *B.C.S.* 454 Bellan ford. Perh. O.Fr. '*bel fort,* 'fine fort,' as in Belfort, Alsace. But prob. 'ford of a man *Bella*'; *cf.* BELLINGHAM.

BELGRAVE (Leicester). Old forms needed. Not in *Dom.* Prob. '*Bella*'s grave,' O.E. *graf. Cf.* above. From this comes BELGRAVIA, London.

BELLBUSK (Leeds). Not in *Dom.* 'Bell-bush,' referring to an inn sign. 'Good wine needs no bush,' which is M.E. *busk,* O.N. *busk-r,* 3-7, and still in Nthn. dial., *busk.*

BELLEFORD (Dartmoor). Old forms needed. ? *Dom.* Boleborde (*b* for *f*, or else *v*, and so =-worth, with which -ford often interchanges). ? 'ford of *Bola*,' two in *Onom.* *cf.* BOLSOVER and BELFORD. All Dartmoor names in -ford are said by some to be fr. W. *ffordd*, ' a road, a way.' This is doubtful.

BELLERBY (Bedale). *Dom.* Belgebi. 1166-67 *Pipe* Beleg'ebi, Berlegerbi ; perh. ' dwelling of *Bealdgær*,' one in *Onom.* More old forms needed. The name may still survive in the surname Bellairs. See -by.

BELLE VUE (Manchester). Mod. Fr. = ' fine view.' *Cf.* BELVOIR and Belvedere, Erith, which is Ital., with similar meaning— ' fine to see,' or ' fine view.'

BELLINGHAM (N. Northbld., Notts, and Kent). Notts B. *sic* 1230 *Close R.*, ' Home of *Belling*' or ' of the sons of *Bella*.' *Cf.* *Inquis. Camb.* Belincgesham, and BILLINGSGATE. Also BELLINGTON (Worcestrsh.), *Dom.* Belintones, 1275 Belinton. See -ing and -ham and -ton.

BELMONT (Bolton and Surrey). Fr. = ' fine hill.'

BELPER (Ambergate). Not in *Dom.* *Cf.* BELREPEIR, Haresfeld, *c.* 1220 Bewper, *c.* 1450 Beaurepaire, which last is Fr. for ' lovely haunt'; O.Fr. *bel.*, Fr. *beau,* ' fine, beautiful.' *Cf.* BARRIPPER.

BELSAY (Newcastle). ' *Bell*'s or *Bella*'s island. *Cf.* BELFORD, and see -ay.

BELSTONE (Okehampton). *Dom.* Bellestham. Here the ending has changed fr. *hám* to *tún* or -ton. The name of the man intended by the first part is a little doubtful, but is prob. *Bella.* *Cf.* BELFORD and *Dom.* Beleslei, Salop. *Dom.*'s form may be a scribal error.

BELTON (Doncaster, etc.). Prob. not ' town with the bell,' O.E. *belle*, but ' *Bella*'s town.' BELTHORP, Helmsley, is *Dom.* Balchetorp (*cf.* BELCHFORD); but Belby, York, is *Dom.* Bellebi. *Cf.* BELFORD.

BELVOIR CASTLE (Grantham), pron. Beever. *c.* 1540 *Leland* Beavoire, Bever. O.Fr. = ' fine to see,' or ' fine view.' *Cf.* BELLEVUE and BELVEDERE.

BEMBRIDGE (Ryde). Old forms needed. Bem- may be O.E. *béam*, a tree, a ' beam.'

BEMERTON (Salisbury). *Dom.* Bimertone. ' Town, village of the trumpeter,' O.E. *beamere, bymere.*

BEMPTON (Flamborough). *Dom.* Bentone. Prob. =BAMPTON— *i.e.*, O.E. *béan-dun,* ' bean hill.' It is 3-6 ben. See -don and -ton.

BENEFIELD (Oundle). *a.* 1100 *Grant of* 664, Beinfelde, *c.* 1200 *Gervase*, Benigfelde. Doubtful. Possibly ' field of *Beonna*,' or *Benna*,' a common O.E. name, in one case Latinized *Benignus.* It might even be O.E. *béan-feld*, ' bean field.'

BENENDEN (Staplehurst). *Dom.* Benindene. 'Den or dean or haunt of *Benna* or *Beonna*,' gen. *-an.* *Cf.* above and BIDDEN- DEN, close by.

BENFLEET, N. and S. (Essex). 893 *O.E. Chron.* Beamfleót (*c.* 1120 *Hen. Hunt.* Beamfled), which is O.E. for 'tree river,' ? river lined by trees. It is *Dom.* Benflet, 1166-67 *Pipe* Bemflet. See FLEET.

BENGEO (Hertford). *Dom.* Belingehon, 1210 Beningeho, Benigho, 1291 Beningho. 'Hoe, hoo or high ground of the *Bennings*,' or 'sons of *Ben(n)a*'; O.E. *hóh, hó,* 'high ground, hill.' *Cf.* BLETSOE and next. As to *Dom.*'s form, *cf.* BENNINGTON. *Dom.* is always confusing the liquids.

BENGEWORTH (Evesham). 709 *chart.* Benigwrthia, 714 *ib.* Benincgworthe, 780 *ib.* Benincwyrthe, *Dom.* Benningeorde, Bennicworte. 'Farm of the sons of *Ben(n)a*.' *Cf.* BENEFIELD, BENGEO, and BENNIWORTH; and see -ing and -worth.

BENHALL GREEN (Saxmundham). *Dom.* Benehal(l)a. '*Benna*'s or *Beonna*'s nook.' *Cf.* BEENHAM and BENSON. and *Dom.* Benehale, Salop. See -hall.

BENHILTON (Sutton, Sussex). Not in *Dom.* *Old* Benhill Town. Prob. '*Benna*'s or *Beonna*'s hill.' *Cf.* above.

BENINGTON (Boston), BENNINGTON (Stevenage), and BENNIWORTH (Lincs.). Bos. B. *Dom.* Beninctun, Beningtone, *c.* 1275 Benig- ton. St. B. *Dom.* Belintone. 'Town' and 'farm of the *Bennings*,' a patronymic. *Cf.* BENGEO and BENTON; and see -ton and -worth.

BEN RHYDDING (Leeds). 'A modern coinage.' Ben is G. *beinn,* 'a mountain, a hill,' W. *penn.* W. *rhydd* is 'red.'

BENSON, more fully BENSINGTON (Wallingford). *O.E. Chron.* ann. 571 Bænesingtun, 1155 *Pipe* Bensentun. 'Town of the *Bensings*.' There is a Dan. chief *Benesing* in 911 *O.E. Chron.* For the contracted or dropped ending, *cf.* BALDON and BEEDON; and see -ing and -ton.

BENTHAM (Lancaster and Badgeworth). La. B. *Dom.* Benetain (scribe's error). 'Home among the bennet or bent-grass,' O.E. *beonet, c.* 1325 *bent. Cf.* next and CHEQUERBENT; and see -ham.

BENTLEY (Doncaster, Walsall, Atherstone, on Severn, Suffolk, etc.). Don. B. *Dom.* Benedlage, -leia, Benelei, 1298 Bentele, Wa. B. *a.* 1200 Benætlea, Benetlegh. Ath. B. *Dom.* Benechelie, *a.* 1300 Bentley. Sev. B. 962 *chart.* Beonet læage, 1017 *ib.* Beonetleah. Suff. B. 1455 Bentele. 'Meadow of the bent- grass or bennet,' see above. *Cf.* Bentworth, Hants. In some cases perh. fr. *Benet* for *Benedict.* See -ley.

BENTON (Newcastle). 1311 *Durham Reg.* Benton, Benington. This is clearly a contracted patronymic, 'Town, village of the

Bennings'; *cf.* BENINGTON. Other 'Bentones' have become BAMPTON or BEMPTON.

BENWELL (Newcastle). *a.* 1130 *Sim. Dur.* Bynnewalle—*i.e.*, 'within the (Roman) wall.' O.E. *binnan,* 2-4 *binne* 'within, inside of.' *Cf.* BINBROOK, and the Sc. '*ben* the house,' where *ben* is, says *Oxf. Dict.,* var. of *binne.*

BENWICK (March). *Ramsey Chart.* Benewick. Prob. '*Ben(n)a*'s or '*Beonna*'s dwelling.' See -wick.

BEOLEY (Redditch). 972 *chart.* Beoleahe, *Dom.* Beolege, 1327 Beleye. 'Meadow of the bees,' O.E. *béo.* *Cf.* BELEY, Beobridge, Claverley, Salop, and Beausale, Warwk., *Dom.* Beoshelle or 'bees's nook,' see -hall; also see -ley.

BERDEN (Bp's. Stortford). *Dom.* Berdane. Prob. 'barley dean' or 'den' or 'glen.' O.E. *bere* 'bear or barley.' *Cf.* BERWICK; and see -den.

BEREA (Haverfordwest). Fr. *Acts* xvii. 10. Welsh Nonconformists love to name their chapels, and the villages around them, so. Hence we also have Bethel, Beulah, Horeb, etc.

BEREPPA (Cornwall). See BARRIPPER.

BERE REGIS (Wareham). O.E. *bearu* 'wood.' L. *regis* 'of the king.' *Cf.* BEER and LYME REGIS.

BERGH APTON (Norwich). *Dom.* Berc, Berch. Merc. *berh.*, O.E. *beorh, beorg,* 'hill, grave, barrow.' Apton is 'town, village' of '*Apa, Ape, Appa, Appe,* or *Appo*'; all these forms are found in *Onom.* Baddeley derives LA BERGE, Glostrsh., fr. *beorg* also.

BERGHHOLT (Colchester). *Dom.* B'colt, Bercolt. See above. Holt is O.E. and Icel. *holt,* 'a wood, a grove.'

BERKELEY (Sharpness). 824 *chart.* Beorc-, Berclea, 1088 *O.E. Chron.* Beorclea, *c.* 1097 *Flor. W.* Beorchelaum, *a.* 1142 *Wm. Malmes.* Bercheleia, 1297 *R. Glouc.* Berkele. Prob. 'meadow of the birch-trees,' O.E. *beorc, byrc.* *Cf. Dom.* Worc., Berchelai. B. HERNESS, in same shire, Baddeley derives fr. O.E. *hyrne,* M.E. *hürne,* 'corner, district'; it is *Dom.* Berchelai hernesse.

BERKHAMSTED. 1066 *O.E. Chron.* Beorhhamstede; 1155 Berkhamstede, *a.* 1200 *chart.* Berhamstead; 1501 *Will* Gret Berkehamstede. Prob. O.E. *beorh-hám-sted,* 'sheltered-home-place,' or fortified farm. Perh. 'home-place of *Beorht,*' a very common O.E. name. *Cf.* BERSTEAD.

BERKSHIRE. 931 *chart.* Be(a)rruc-scire; 1011 *O.E. Chron.* Bearruc-scir; *Dom.* Berrochescire, Berchesira; 1297 Barcssire; *c.* 1325 Barkschyre (which is still the pron.). 'Box-tree-shire,' O.E. *bearroc;* though some, without sure evidence, would derive fr. the tribe *Bibrŏci,* Caesar *B.G.* v. 21; or even say it is 'bare oak shire'! *Bearruc* is a dimin. of *bearu,* which means simply 'a wood, a grove'; the meaning 'box-tree' is a later and perhaps mistaken idea.

BERKSWELL (Coventry). *Dom.* Berchewelle; *a.* 1400 Bercleswelle. It seems 'well of *Beorht* or *Berct,*' but form *a.* 1400 points to an earlier *Beorcol,* 4 in *Onom.*

BERMONDSEY (London). ? *a.* 715 Vermundsei, 'isle of *Fœrmund* or *Pharamond.*' But *Dom.* Bermundesye; *c.* 1180 *Ben. Peterb.* Bermundsheia. '*Bermund*'s' or '*Bermond*'s isle.' *Cf.* 'Bearmodes lea,' Worcestersh. in *Grant, c.* 802; and see -ey.

BERNEY ARMS (Yarmouth). ? fr. the Fr. *Bernay* near Evreux. Villages called after public-houses are common all over England, and not less so in Wales.

BERNWOOD FOREST (Bucks). 921 *O.E. Chron.* Byrnewudu—*i.e.,* O.E for 'Beorn's' or 'Byrne's wood.' O.N. *björn* means 'a bear.'

BERRIEW (Montgomery). =Aber-Rhiw, 'confluence of the R. Rhiw' with the Severn. In W. *rhiw* is 'a break out'; also 'a slope.' *Cf.* BARMOUTH.

BERRINGTON (Tenbury and Shrewsbury and Glostrsh.). Te. and Sh. B. *Dom.* Beritune. Te. B. 1275 Beriton. Gl. B. 1273 Byrton. Possibly =BURTON; quite as likely, 'town of *Bœra.*' *-an,* now become Berry. *Cf.* BARRINGTON and BURBURY; and see -ing.

BERROW (Burnham and Ledbury). Var. of BARROW.

BERRY BROW (Huddersfield). Berry, like the above, is perh. a variant of BARROW, 'a hill, a mound,' M.E. *berghe, berie.* But BERRY or BURY HILL, Stone, is *a* 1300 Le buri; see -bury. Brow, O.E. *bru,* is found used for 'brow or edge of a hill' as early as *c.* 1435. In North. dial. it commonly means 'a slope, an ascent,' as in Everton Brow and Shaw's Brow. two steep streets in Liverpool. *Cf. Dom.* Warwk. and Worc., 'Bericote.' The Yorks *Dom.* Berg has now become Baragh and Barugh.

BERRYMEAD PRIORY (Acton, Middlesex). 'Mead or meadow with the mound or hillock.' See BERRY BROW and BARROW.

BÉRRYNÁRBOR (Ilfracombe). Old forms needed. Not in *Dom.,* and all is doubtful. The first part is prob. O.E. *biorn, beorn,* 4-5 *beryn,* 'a hero, a warrior.' As to -arbor, it might quite possibly be for *harbour,* the M.E. *herberg,* in 6 *harbor,* which means orig. 'any kind of place of shelter or sojourn.' Not so likely fr. *arbour,* which is fr. Fr. and first in Eng. *c.* 1300 *herber.*

BERSHAM (Wrexham). Old forms needed, *cf. Dom.* Sffk., Barshā; but prob. 'home of *Ber,*' a man named in Chesh. *Dom.*

BERSTED (Sussex). 680 *chart.* Beorganstede, O.E. for ' *Beorga*'s place '; 2 *Beorgas* in *Onom.*

BERWICK (on Tweed, etc.). 700-15 *chart.* *Wihtred* Bereueg (Kent); 1060 *chart.* Uppwude cum Ravelaga berewico suo '; Ber. on Tw. 1097 Berwick, *a.* 1150 Berewic, Berwich, 1187 Suthberwyc (as contrasted with North Berwick, Sc.). Shrewsbury B. *Dom.* Berewic. O.E. *berewic* ' a demesne farm,' fr. *bere*, ' barley,' and *wic*, ' dwelling, village.' *Cf.* BARTON, also Berwick St. James and St. John, Salisbury.

BERWYN (Llangollen) and **BERWYN MTN.** W. *aber gwyn*, ' clear, bright confluence.' For loss of *a-* *cf.* ABERGAVENNY and BERRIEW.

BERYAN (Cornwall). *Sic* 1536. Called after *Buriena*, pretty daughter of Aengus, K. of Munster, time of St. Patrick.

BESCAR LANE (Southport). Old forms needed. Not in Wyld and Hirst. Possibly it is =BESSACAR, Cantley, Yorks, 1202 Besacre, which, though it might be ' *Besa*'s acre ' or ' field,' is prob. ' *Besa*'s rock,' Anglian O.E. *carr*. But Bes- may represent many things. See below.

BESCOT (Walsall). *Dom.* Bresmundes cot, *a.* 1300 Ber (e)mundescote, Bermondscote, Bermonscot, *a.* 1400 Berkmondescote, Berkescote. This is an extraordinarily contracted form, fr. O.E. *Beorhtmundes cot.*

BESTHORPE (Attleborough and Newark). At. B. *Dom.* Besethorp, Ne. B. Bestorp. ' *Besa*'s village.' *Cf.* BEESTON and BESCAR, and see -thorpe. Bessingby, Yorks, was *Dom.* Basingebi.

BESWICK (Manchester and Beverley). Man. B. 1327 Bexwyk. ' *Becc*'s dwelling.' But Bev. B. is *Dom.* Basewic, which is prob. ' *Bassa*'s dwelling.' *Cf.* BASCHURCH and BASTWELL. See -wick.

BETCHLEY (Tiddenham). *Old* BETTISLEY, ' lea of *Betti*.' *Cf.* BEACHLEY, BATCHWORTH, and Betchworth, Surrey (? fr. *Becca*).

BETHANIA (Bl. Festiniog), **BETHEL** (Carnarvon), **BETHESDA** (Bangor), and **BEULAH** (Brecon) are all Bible names for villages called after Nonconformist chapels. *Cf.* BEREA.

BETHNAL GREEN (London). *a.* 1600 Bednall Green. Said to be ' Bathon's hall,' fr. the family *Bathon*, who had lands in Stepney, temp. Edw. I. But BEDNAL is *Bedanheál* or ' Bede's nook or hall.' See -hall.

BETLEY (Crewe). *Dom.* Betelege, *a.* 1200 Betteleg. ' *Beta*'s lea or meadow.' O.E. *béte* also means ' beet root '; but this would give Beetley. *Cf.* BITTON.

BETTISFIELD (Whitchurch). *Dom.* Beddesfeld. ' Field of *Beta*, *Betti*, or *Bettu*,' all names found in *Onom*. *Cf. Dom.* Bucks, Betesdene

BETTWS (8 in *P.G.*). W. *bettws*, ' a place of shelter and comfort,' ' a (prayer) house.' Common in Wales, and there are two in England, B. Y CRWWYN (O.W. *crewyn*, ' pen. sty, hovel '), S.W. Salop. and B. NEWYDD (' new '), Newport. Mon. It seems now agreed that W. *bettws* phonetically and actually represents Eng. *bead-house*, c. 1160 *bed hus*, ' prayer-house, almshouse.' Bettws is said to have been first applied to a W. parish church in 1292, *Taxat. of Benefices*. But how is it that Wales has so many ' bead-houses ' among her place-names, and England none ?

BETTWS CEDEWEN (Montgomery). *Cedewen* is prob. *Cedwyn*, a Welsh sixth cny. saint.

BETTWS GARMON (Caernarvon). ' House of St. *Garmon*' or *Germanus*. twice a visitor of Britain, and perh. the man who sent St. Patrick to Ireland. *Cf.* Capel Garmon and LLANARMON.

BETTWS-GWERFUL-GOCH (Corwen). ' House of Red *Gwerful*,' who must have been a W. saint. *Cf.* Ffynon gwerfil, ' Gwerfil's well.' a farm, Cardigansh.

BETTWS-Y-COED (N. Wales). W. ' house in the wood.'

BEVERE(GE) (island in Severn). *Chart.* Beverege, *a.* 1100 Beverie. O.E. *beofer-ige*, ' beaver-isle.' The beaver was not extinct in England till *c.* 1100. *Ige* as an ending in Eng. names has usually become -ey, *q.v.*

BEVERLEY. *Dom.* Bevreli, Beurelie; c. 1180 *Bened. Peterb.* Beverlacum; 1387 *Trevisa*, ' Beverlay . . . the place or lake of bevers.' O.E. *beofer* or *byfere-léah*, ' beaver-meadow '; though both Bened. and Trevisa seem to think the ending may be O.E. *lac*, ' pool.' *Cf.* FILEY. Beverley is also the name of a brook at Wimbledon, 693 *chart.* Beferith, where *rith* is ' stream.' *Cf.* above.

BEVERSTONE (Tetbury), 1048 *O.E. Chron.* Beofres stan.—*i.e.*, ' the beaver's rock,' *Dom.* Beurestone.

BEWCASTLE (Carlisle). O.Fr. *beau castel*, ' fine castle.' *Cf.* BEAULIEU pron. Bewley, and next.

BEWDLEY (Kidderminster). 1304 Beaulieu, *c.* 1440 Bewdeley. Fr. *beau lieu*, ' beautiful spot,' as in Beaulieu, Hants, pron. Béwly. Also *cf.* BEWSBORO', Kent, 1228 *Close R.* Beausbergh.

BEWHOLME (Hull). *Dom.* Begun, 1202 Beighum. Prob. ' *Begha's ham*,' or ' home.' The endings -ham and -holme, ' meadow,' *q.v.*, often interchange. Possibly *begun* may be loc. of O.E. *beg*, ' at the rings.' This loc. is common in Yorks. See -ham.

BEXHILL (Hastings). *Dom.* has only Bexelei. ' *Becca's* hill.' *Cf.* next. *B.C.S.* 309 Beccanford, and *Dom.* Bucks, Bechesdene.

BEXLEY (Kent). *Dom.* Bix; *a.* 1200 *Text. Roff.* Bixle; later Bekesley; also *cf. Dom.* Hants, Bexeslei. ' *Bica's*, *Bicca's*, or *Becca's* lea or meadow.' All these names are found in *Onom*. *Cf.* BEXHILL and BIX.

BEYTON (Bury St. Edmund's). *Dom.* Begatona, 1288 Beyton. '*Begha*'s town.' *Cf.* BAYWORTH.

BIBURY (Fairford, Glostr.). *c.* 740 *chart.* Beagan byrig, *Dom.* Beche-, Begeberie. This must be as above, 'burgh, fortified town of *Begha*.' See -bury.

BICESTER (Oxon). *Dom.* 1307 Bernecestre, ? 1149 Burcetur, 1216 Burnecestr', 1414-31 Burcestre, 1495 Bysseter, 1612 Bisceter, 1634 Bister, the present pron. 'Camp of *Beorn*,' in N. *Biörn*. A fine study in the disappearance of liquids ! See -cester.

BICKENHILL (Birmingham). *Dom.* Bichehelle *a.* 1200 Bychen hulle, Bigen-, Biken hull, O.E. Bicanhyll, 'hill of *Bica*,' 3 in *Onom.* *Cf.* BICKMARSH, Alcester, 967 *chart.* At Bicanmersce. It is just possible it is 'beacon-hill,' O.E. *becen*, *becun*, Wyclif *bikene*, S.W. dial. *bick'n*. This is not confirmed by BICKMARSH, Honeybourne, *Dom.* Bichemerse, 1608 Bickemershe.

BICKER (Boston). *Dom.* Bichere. Doubtful. Prob. not M.E. *biker* (1297 *R. Glouc.*), origin unknown, 'a bicker, a skirmish'; nor O.N. *bikarr*, 'a beaker, an open cup or goblet,' used here to describe the shape of the site ; but prob. var. of O.N. *bekk-r*, 'a brook.' Also *cf.* next.

BICKERSTAFFE (Ormskirk). *c.* 1200 Bikerstat, 1230 Bykstat, *c.* 1260 Berkerstat, *c.* 1280 Bekirstat, 1292 Bykerstath. 1267 Bikerstaff. The Bicker- is a little uncertain. The Eng. *bicker*, 'a quarrel,' is of unknown origin, and not found till 1297, so is unlikely here. The old forms seem to waver between O.N. *bekkjar.* 'of the brook,' *cf.* BECKERMET, and *bjarkar*, gen. of O.N. *bjork*, 'birch.' The ending is curious; it also wavers between O.N. *stað-r*, 'place,' and O.E. *stæp*, 'shore, river-bank'; this is still preserved in the personal name Bickersteth. *Cf.* Bickershaw, Wigan, and Bycardyke, 1189 Bikeresdic, Notts.

BICKERTON (Wetherby and Cheshire). Weth. B. *Dom.* Bickretone, Bichreton. Ches. B. *Dom.* Bicretone. As *bicker* is not found in Eng. till 1297, prob. 'brook-town.' See above and BICKERSTAFFE.

BICKERY (Glastonbury). 971 *chart.* 'In insulis' (*i.e.*, the low lands often forming islands in flood-time) . . . *Bekeria*, which is called 'parva Ybernia,' or 'little Ireland'; fr. O.Ir. *bec Eriu*, 'little Erin,' *Erinn* being gen. of *Eriu*. Off Wexford is Beggary-island, really the same name; M'Clure, p. 205.

BICKINGTON (Barnstaple and Newton Abbot). *Dom.* Bichentone. 'Town, village of *Bic(c)a*,' gen. -*an*. See above. *Cf.* BEXLEY, and 1167-8 *Pipe* Devon, Bichingbrige. See -ing.

BICKLEIGH (Tiverton) and **BICKLEY** (Kent). Both in *Dom.* Bichelei. '*Bicca*'s' or '*Bica*'s meadow.' *Cf.* Bickford, Penkridge, *Dom.* Bigeford, 1334 Bikeford, prob. fr. *Bica* too; also *Dom.* Chesh. Bichelei, and Devon Bicheford.

BICKNACRE (Chelmsford). 'Field of *Bica*,' *-an*. Acre is O.E. *œcer*, *acer*, 'a plain, open country'; L. *ager*, 'a field.' *Cf.* BICKENHILL, and next.

BICKNOLLER (Taunton). *Dom.* has only Bichehalle. '*Bica*'s alder'; or else perh. 'Beacon-alder-tree,' O.E. *alor, aler, alr, olr,* 'an alder.' See above and BICKENHILL. BICKNOR on Wye, *Dom.* Bicanofre, 1298 Bykenore, is clearly '*Bica*'s bank.' See -or, -over.

BICKTON HEATH (Shrewsbury). *Dom.* Bichetone, also *ib.* Bichedone (Bucks). [*Cf.* 1298, 'Thomas de Bikebury.'] '*Bicca*'s town or village.' *Cf.* BEXLEY and BICKLEIGH.

BIDDENDEN (Staplehurst) and BIDDENHAM (Bedford). *Old* Biden-, Bedenham. '*Bidda*'s' or '*Byda*'s wooded valley' and 'home.' *Cf.* BEEDON, and Bidboro', Tunbridge Wells; and see -den and -ham.

BIDDESTONE (Chippenham). *Dom.* Bedestone, '*Bedda*'s' or '*Bidda*'s stone' or 'town.' See -ton; and *cf.* BIDSTON, *Dom.* Chesh. Bedesfeld, and above.

BIDDLE R. (Congleton). Doubtful, as so many Eng. river names are. ? W. *bedw-dol*, 'birch-tree meadow.'

BIDDULPH (Congleton). *Dom.* and later Bidolf. This is an O.E. personal name, *Beadulf* or *Beaduwulf.* Such are very rarely applied to places without a suffix; but *cf.* CRANTOCK, Snitter, Northbld., TYDD, etc.

BIDÉFORD. *Dom.* Bedeford, *a.* 1300 Bydyford, Budeford. The form 'Bytheford' is also found early; but this is mere 'popular etymology.' The name is 'ford of *Bede, Buda*,' or '*Byda.*' *Cf.* BIDDESTONE and next. Possibly -ford may be for *fjord*, as in HAVERFORDWEST. Waterford, Wexford, etc. The Norsemen came all round the Bristol Channel.

BIDFORD (Stratford-on-Avon). 710 *chart.* Budiforde, *Dom.* Bedeford, *a.* 1600 Bidford. 'Ford of *Buda*,' 3 in *Onom.*, which has also 2 *Bydas. Cf.* above, and Bidfield, For. of Dean, *old* Budefield.

BIDSTON (Birkenhead), and BIEL. See BIDDESTONE and BEAL.

BIERTON (Aylesbury). *Dom.* Bertone. Prob. 'bear' or 'barley -town.' O.E. *bere*, 6-8 *beer*. Hardly fr. O.E. *bœr, bér*, 'a bier for carrying a corpse.' North Bierley (Yorks), *Dom.* Birle, looks as if Eng. -ley had been attached to O.N. *bý-r*, 'house, hut, byre.'

BIGBURY (Kingsbridge). *Dom.* Bicheberie. Not fr. 'big,' *adj.*, which is unknown in Eng. till *c.* 1300, but '*Bica*'s or *Biga*'s burgh,' or 'fort.' *Cf.* BIGSWEIR on Wye, 1322 Bikiswere. See -bury.

BIGGIN (Coventry and Rugby) and BIGGIN HILL (Westerham, Kent). The only old form we have met is Cov. B. 1327 Bugginge. *Biggin* is North. word for 'building, house,' O.N. *byggja*, 'to dwell, to build,' already found in 1153 Newbigginghc, Oxnam, Roxbgh.; but prob. it only filtered late South into Warwick. In Kent it seems most unlikely; there *biggin* may be Fr. *béguin*, 'a child's cap,' found in Eng. fr. 1530, whose shape might easily be thought like that of the hill; or else fr. a man *Biga, -an.*

BIGGLESWADE (Beds). *Dom.* and 1132 Bicheleswade, -da., 'Ford,' lit. 'wading-place of *Bichel*' or '*Beccel*.' Perh. he who was servant of St. Guthlac of Croyland; -wade is O.E. *wæd*, M.E. *wath*, 'a ford.'

BIGHTON (Alresford). *Dom.* Bighetone. '*Bigha*'s, *Biga*'s, or *Begha*'s town or village.'

BIGNALL END (Staffordsh.). Not in Duignan. Prob. '*Biga*'s' or '*Bigo*'s nook' or 'hall.' *Cf.* BEADNELL and BEDNAL. The *n* is the sign of the gen. See -hall.

BIGRIGG (Carnforth). Possibly 'Big ridge'; see -rigg. *Big* is an adj. of unknown origin, and does not come into Eng. until *Havelock, a.* 1300. The *big* may also be O.N. *bygg*, 'barley,' found in Eng. and Sc. fr. *c.* 1450.

BILBROUGH (York). In *Dom.* Mileburg (? fr. a man *Milo*). 'Burgh, fortified town of *Billa*,' as in Bilham and Bilton also in Yorks, *Dom.* Bileham and Bil(l)etone. *Cf.* BILSBOROUGH, Bilborough, Notts, *Dom.* Bileburg(h), and *Dom.* Essex, Bilichangra, 'steep slope of *Bila*.' See -burgh.

BILLESDON (Leicester). '*Billa*'s dune' or 'hill,' or 'fort.' *Cf.* BILBOROUGH, and BILLESLEY (Warwk.), 704 *chart.* Billes læh, *Dom.* Billeslei, 1157 *Pipe* Bileslega; and see -don.

BILLING (Wigan). Patronymic. There are two *Billings* in *Onom.* It may mean 'descendant of *Belin*.' On 'blissful King Belyn' see *c.* 1205 *Layamon*, 4290 *seq.* *Cf.* Billingford, Dereham, Billingham, Stockton, and next; also BEALINGS.

BILLINGHAY (Lincoln). 1285 'Waltero de Billingeye' (found in Norfolk). See above; -hay is O.E. *haga*, Icel. *hagi*, 'an enclosed field,' same root as *hedge*.

BILLINGLEY (Yorks). *Dom.* Bilingeleia, 1178-80 *Pipe* Billingslea, and BILLINGSLEY (Bridgnorth). Perh. 1055 *O.E. Chron.* Bylgesleg. '*Billing*'s meadow.' *Cf. a.* 1100 'Belnesthorpe,' Lincs. See -ley.

BILLINGSGATE (London) and BILLINGSHURST (Sussex). 1250 *Layamon*, Belynes ʒat. See BILLING, and -hurst, 'a wood'; also *cf* 1155 *Pipe* Bilingete, Hants.

BILLINGTON (Stafford), *Dom.* Belintone, and BILLINGTON LANGHO (Whalley). *Sim. Dur.* ann. 798 Billingahoth. 'Town of the *Billings*,' see BILLING. The -hoth in *Sim. Dur.* may represent the -ho in Langho. Hoe, as in Plymouth Hoe, is O.E. *hóh, hó*, 'a hill, high ground.'

BILNEY, EAST (Dereham). *Dom.* Bilenei, 1298 Bilneie. ' Isle of *Bil(l)a*.' *Cf.* BINLEY, and see -ey.

BILSBOROUGH (Preston), and BILSBY (Alford). *Dom.* Billesbi. =BILBROUGH. '*Billa*'s burgh or fort,' and 'dwelling.' See -borough and -by.

BILSTON. 994 Bilsetnatun, -netun, *Dom.* Billestune, *a.* 1300 Bilestun, -tone. '*Billa*'s town' or 'village.' See BILBROUGH and BILLESDON. In 994 -setna is gen. pl. of *sœtan*, 'a settler, dweller in.' *Cf.* DORSET, SOMERSET, etc.

BILTON (Knaresboro' and Rugby). Knar. B. *Dom.* Billetone, Bileton. '*Billa*'s town.' See BILBROUGH. But Rug. B. is *Dom.* Beltone, 1236 Belton, 1327 Beultone. Duignan says this is O.E. *Beolantun*, 'town of *Beola*,' only one in *Onom.*

BINBROOK (Market Rasen). *Dom.* Binnebroc. Prob. 'within the brook.' O.E. *binnan*, M.E. *byn*, ' within, inside.' *Cf.* BENWELL, BINFIELD, etc. But Binneford (Stockleigh, English) is 739 *chart.* Beonnan ford, 'food of *Beonna*,' perh. he who was father of St. Sativola of Exeter.

BINCHESTER (Bp. Auckland). *c.* 380 *Anton. Itin.* Vinonia. Here the Bin- or Vin- prob. represents W. *gwyn*, 'white, clear '; in 1183 *Boldon Bk.* it is Byn cestre, -chestre, 1197 Bincestr'. *Cf.* BENWELL. See -chester, 'camp.'

BINEGAR (Shepton Mallet). Old forms needed. Not in *Dom.* Perh. corrup. of *bin acre*, 'within the field.' O.E. *œcer, acer,* L. *ager*, a' field.' *Cf.* BICKNACRE, BINFIELD, and BESSACAR.

BINFIELD (Bracknell). 1316 Benefeld; but earlier Benetfeld, Bentfeld. This is 'field of *bent* or bennet '—*i.e.*, a coarse grass. O.E. *beonet*. *Cf.* BENTLEY. But by temp. Hen. VIII. it had become Bynfeld, which by analogy should mean ' within the field.' *Cf.* BENWELL, BINBROOK, etc.

BINGHAM (Notts). *Dom.* Binghehā, Bingehamhou Wap., 1230 *Close R.* Bingeham. It seems hardly to be fr. O.N. *bing-r*, 'a heap,' found in Eng. *c.* 1325 as 'bing,' and though there seems no name in the *Onom.* which suits, form 1209 in next suggests a man *Binge* or *Binga*. *Cf.* BENGEWORTH. Mutschmann derives fr. *Benning*; see BENNINGTON.

BINGLEY (Keighley). *Dom.* Bingheleia, Bingelei, 1209 Bingelege. Doubtful. See above; -ley is O.E. *leáh*, 'meadow,' and Binge- is prob. some man's name.

BINLEY (Coventry). *Dom.* Bilnei, Bilueie, 1251 Bilney. Prob. O.E. *Billan ige*, 'isle of *Bil(l)a*.' See -ey. *Cf.* BILNEY. Change fr. *ln* to *nl* is uncommon.

BINNEFORD. See BINBROOK.

BINSTEAD (Ryde and Sussex), and BINSTED (Alton, Hants). Suss. B. 1280 *Close R.* Benested. Ryde B. *Dom.* Benestede, which

may either be ' bean place ' or, less likely, ' prayer place,' fr.
O.E. *béan*, 3-6 *ben*, 4-6 *bene*, ' a bean,' or *bén*, 2-4 *bene*, ' a prayer,
petition, boon '; and *stede*, ' farm-yard, steading.' *Cf.* homestead. Not fr. *bin* or *binne*, O.E. *binnan*, ' within.' This never
seems spelt with a central *e*.

BINTON (Stratford, Wwk.). 710 *chart.* Bunintone, *Dom.* Benintone,
Benitone, *a.* 1200 Buvintone, 1325 Bunynton. ' Town of
Buna,' 3 in *Onom.*; but the form *Bynna* is much commoner.
Dom. Yorks, Binneton, is now Binnington.

BIRCHAM (King's Lynn). *Dom.* Brecham, 1489 Brytcham. *Cf.*
Dom. ' Bercham,' Warwick. Prob. ' house, home built of birch.'
O.E. *beorc*, *berc*, *byrce*, *birce ;* though the first part may be the
name of a man *Beorht* or *Berh*, as in *Dom.* Yorks, Berceworde,
now Ingbirchworth.

BIRCHANGER (Bp's. Stortford). ' Birch-slope.' O.E. *hangra, angra*,
once said to be ' a meadow '; but M'Clure thinks ' the slope of
a hill,' and Duignan, more exactly, ' a wood growing on a hill-
side.' *Cf.* CLAYHANGER, Alderhanger (Worcestersh.), HUNGER-
FORD, and RISHANGLES.

BIRCHILLS (Walsall). *a.* 1600 Birche leses, Burchelles, Byrchylles,
Byrchells. ' Birch hills.' O.E. *berc, beorc*, 5-6 *byrche*.

BIRCHOVER (Matlock). *Dom.* Barcoure. ' Birch brink or bank,'
O.E. *ofr, obr*, ' brink.' See BIRCHAM, and -over.

BIRDHAM (Chichester). *Dom.* Bridehā, and BIRDHOLME (Chesterfield). ' Bird home ' and ' bird meadow.' See -holme. *Bird*
may be a man's name, *cf.* next. Bird in O.E. is *brid*, Northumb.
bird ; and *Brid* is a name in *Onom.* *Cf.* BIRDSALL.

BIRDINGBURY (Rugby). Pron. Birbury. 1043 *chart.* Burtingbury;
K.C.D. 916 Birtingabyrig juxta Aven, *Dom.* Berdingberie.
Derbingerie (blunder) *a.* 1300 Burdingbury. ' Burgh, fort of
the sons of *Beorht*,' or ' *Birht*.' Patronymic. See -bury.

BIRDLIP (Gloucester). Not in *Dom.*, 1221 Bridelepe, 1262 Brudelep.
Prob. ' bird's leap,' O.E. *hlýp(e)*, 3 *leep, lip*, 4-6 *lepe*. *Cf.*
HINDLIP and ISLIP. Here, again, *Bird* may be a man's name.
W. H. Stevenson points out, *hlýp* must sometimes mean not
' a leap,' but ' an enclosed space.' *Cf.* Lypiatt (Stroud), *old*
Lypgate, Lupeyate, ' gate into the enclosure.'

BIRDSALL (York). *Dom.* Briteshale, Brideshala, 1208 Brideshale.
' Nook of *Brid, Briht*, or *Beorht*,' all names on record, and prob.
all the same name too. Change of *r* is common, as in board
and broad, etc. *Cf.* BIRKBY and BIRTLEY, and see -hall.

BIRKBY (Co. Durham and Huddersfield). *Dom.* Yorks, and 1197
R. Bretebi, Durham. ' Dwelling of *Beorc* ' or ' *Beorht*,' of
which *Bret* (*t*) is a later form. *Cf.* BIRDSALL; and see -by.

BIRKDALE (Southport). *Birk* is N. Eng. and Sc. for *birch*, O.E.
beorc, byrce, birce, berc. Cf. Birkacre (' field '), Chorley.

BIRKENHEAD. *Sic* 1282, but *a.* 1100 Byrkhed. 'Head, promontory covered with birch,' O.E. *beorc, berc, byrce, birce.* The adj. *birchen,* North. *birken,* is not given in the *Oxf. Dict. a.* 1440; so that this name, in 1282, seems the earliest known instance of it.

BIRKENSHAW (Leeds). 'Birch wood,' O.E. *scaga,* a wood; see above. Now a personal name in this district.

BIRKIN (Normanton). *Dom.* Berchinge, Berchine. A patronymic. 'Place of the descendants of *Beorht.*' *Cf.* BARKING; and see -ing.

BIRLING (Maidstone) and BIBLINGHAM (Pershore). 972 Byrlinghamme, *Dom.* Berlingeham, 1275 Byrlyngham. 'Place of the descendants of the cup-bearer or butler,' O.E. *byr(e)le.* The -ham, *q.v.,* in this case means 'enclosure.' *Cf.* BURLINGHAM.

BIRMINGHAM. *Dom.* Bermingeha', 1158 Brimigham, 1166 Bremingeham, 1255 Burmingeham, 1333 Burmyncham, *c.* 1413 Brymecham, *c.* 1463 Bermyngham, 1538 Bermigham, also Bromieham. 'Home of the *Beormingas,*' or 'sons of Beorn.' Duignan makes the original family *Breme,* 'illustrious,' and connects with BROMSGROVE; see his full art. *s.v.* For the mod. pron. Brummajem *cf.* Whittingham, pron. Whittinjem, and 'Nottingjam' is also heard.

BIRSTALL (Leeds). *Dom.* thrice Beristade (? -ade, error for -ale) Berist- seems to be for '*Beorhtsige's*' or '*Byrcsige's,*' a very common O.E. name; and -ale is 'nook,' see -hall. Close by is BIRSTWITH, fr. O.N. *vith-r,* O. Dan. *wede,* Dan. *ved,* 'a wood.' *Cf.* ASKWITH, etc.

BIRTLEY (Herefordsh., Chester-le-Street, and Wark.). Ch. B. 1183 Britleia, Birdeia, 'Meadow of *Brid,*' or '*Bird,*' or 'of the birds.' Transposition of *r* is common; *cf.* BIRDSALL and Birtwistle (see TWIZEL). BIRTS MORTON, Glostersh., is *a.* 1350 Morton Brut, 1407 Bruttes, -tis, fr. Walter *le Bret,* known as living here, 1275, or some one earlier. The name means 'the Breton.'

BISCOVEY (Par.) Not in *Dom.* Might be Eng., 'Biso's cave'; the names *Besa, Besi, Bisi,* and *Biso* are all found in *Onom.;* whilst the O.E. for 'cove or inlet' is *cofa.* But Bis- looks like Corn. *bes, bis, bys,* 'a finger.' *Cf.* BISSOE.

BISHAM (Marlow). *Dom.* Bistesham; 1199 Bistlesham; later Bestlesham, Bustleham. 'Home of *Bestel,*' *cf. B.C.S.,* i. 108, ii. 206, Bestlesford, Bæstlæsford, near Bradfield, also BASILDEN.

BISHAMPTON (Pershore). *Dom.* Bisantune, *a.* 1100 Bishamtone. 'The home-town or village of *Bisa,*' see BISCOVEY. The mod. -hampton may here be a corrup. of -antune.

BISHOP AUCKLAND, also NORTH and WEST AUCKLAND (Co. Durham). 1183 *Boldon Bk.* North Alcland and Aclet, West Aclet, Alcletshire, v.r. Aukelandschire, 1305 Auke-, Aucland. Auckland is

O.E. *ác land*, ' oak land '; but the form Alclet is puzzling.
M'Clure thinks it is O.E. *halc clet*, ' haugh, river-meadow rock ';
but *klett-r*, ' a rock,' is O.N., not O.E. at all, nor even English,
save late in Scotland. The -let *may be* a var. of O.E. *hlíth*,
' a slope,' *cf.* YARLETT, and so the name be ' river-meadow slope.'
But this is doubtful. The Bishop is, of course, the Bishop of
Durham. Also *cf.* AUCKLEY.

BISHOP BURTON (Beverley). *Dom.* Santriburtone, ' Bishop's burgh-
town,' or ' fortified village '; ? fr. St. John of Beverley, Bishop of
Hexham and York. The Santri- in *Dom.* must be a corrup. of
sanctuary, O.Fr. *saintuarie*, spelt in Eng. in 6 *santuary ;* but not
given in *Oxf. Dict.* as Eng. till *a.* 1340.

BISHOP MONKTON (Ripon). *Dom.* Monuchetone. O.E. *monuc*,
munuc, munec, fr. L. *monachus*, ' a monk.' *Cf.* MONKTON.

BISHOP'S CANNING (Devizes). *Sim. Dur.* ann. 1010 Canninga merse
(*cf.* MERSEY). Canning is a patronymic, fr. *Cana* or *Cano*, in
Onom.

BISHOP'S CAUNDLE or CAUNDLE BISHOP (Sherborne). *Dom.* Candel,
-dele, -delle. Caundle is O.E. *cendel*, 1-4 *condel*, ' a candle.'
Cf., too, *Florio*, 1611, ' *Fungo* . . . that firy round in a burning
candle called the Bishop.'

BISHOP'S CLEEVE (Cheltenham). *Bede* and *c.* 780 *chart.* Clife,
Dom. Clive. Cleeve is M.E. *cleve*, var. of *cliff*, O.E. *clif. Cf.*
CLEVELAND. It is called ' Bishop's ' to distinguish it fr. Prior's
Cleeve.

BISHOP'S FONTHILL (Salisbury). *Dom.* Fontel; but *chart.* Funt-
géall; O.E. *font, fant,* (L. *fons, -tis*), O.Fris. and in Eng. 2-6
funt, ' a font, a fountain '; but in Dicts. *gealla* has only the
meaning of ' bile ' or ' a gall in the skin,' so it may be an error
in the charter, perh. for *héal,* ' hall.' *Cf.* Fontley, Fareham.

BISHOP'S HULL (Taunton). Hull is west midl. for ' hill.' See
ASPULL.

BISHOP'S ITCHINGTON (Leamington). 1043 *chart.* Ichenton, 1111 *ib.*
Yceantune, *Dom.* Icetone. ' Town on the R. ITCHEN.' It
belonged formerly to the Bps. of Lichfield and Coventry.

BISHOP'S LYDEARD (Taunton). See LYDIARD.

BISHOP'S NYMPTON (S. Molton). *Dom.* Nimetone, ' Town of
Nima.' Onom. has only *Numa* and *Nunna.* On the common
intrusion of *p, cf.* BAMPTON.

BISHOPSTOKE (Southampton). ' Bishop ' (of Winchester's) ' place.'
See STOKE.

BISHOPSTON (Stratford, Warwick, and Glam.), also BISHOPSTONE
(5 in *P.G.*). Str. B. 1016 *chart.* Biscopesdun—*i.e.,* ' bishop's hill '
—but *c.* 1327 Bisshopeston. See -don and -ton.

BISHOP'S STORTFORD. *Dom.* Storteford. Skeat thinks the R. *Stort* may mean 'pourer.' *Cf.* Dan. *styrte*, ' to rush, to spring,' cognate with *start*.

BISHOP'S WALTHAM (Hants). 1001 *O.E. Chron.* Wealtham. The Bp. of Winchester's 'home in the *weald* or forest.' See WALTHAM.

BISHOPSWORTH, contracted BISHPORT (Bristol). 'Bishop's farm.' See -worth.

BISHTON (Rugeley, Tidenham, Newport, Mon.). Ru. B. *Dom.* Bispestone, *a.* 1300 Bissopestune, Ti. B. 956 *chart.* Bispestune. 'Village of the bishop' of Lichfield or Llandaff, O.E. *biscop*, though possibly fr. a man *Bisp*, found *a.* 1200. *Cf.* BISHPORT and BISPHAM.

BISLEY (Stroud, Coventry, Woking). St. B. 896 *chart.* (late MS.) Bislege, *Dom.* Biselege, 1156 Bissclega. Co. B. *a.* 1200 Bisselei. Skeat thought there must have been an O.E. *bisse*, 'a bush'; *cf.* Bushwood (Stratford, Wwk.), *a.* 1300 Byssewode, 1404 Biswode. But this is prob. 'mead of *Bisi*' or '*Biso*,' both in *Onom. Cf. Dom.* Worc., Biselege, and BISHAM. See -ley.

BISPHAM (Preston). *Dom.* and *c.* 1141 Biscopham—*i.e.*, 'bishop's home.' *Cf.* BISHPORT.

BISSOE (Perranwell, Cornwall). Doubtful. *Dom.* has a 'Beveshoe,' which may be this, and may stand for 'how, hollow of *Beffa*,' 2 in *Onom.* It may be fr. a man *Bissa. Cf.* BISCOVEY and BENGEO.

BITTERNE (Southampton). Perh. *c.* 380 *Anton. Itin.* Clausentum. '*Bitta*'s or *Bitto*'s house,' O.E. *erne*, 'a house.' *Cf.* next, and WHITHORN (Sc.).

BITTESWELL (Lutterworth). ? *Dom.* Betmeswelle. [*Cf. c.* 1200 *Gervase* 'Bittesdene,' Northants.] ? '*Bitta*'s well.' *Cf.* above.

BITTON (Kingswood, Glos.). *Dom.* Betone, 1158-59 *Pipe* Bettune. Prob. 'town, village of *Beta*,' 2 in *Onom.*, or 'of *Betti*,' also 2 in *Onom. Cf.* BETLEY.

BIX (Henley). *Dom.* Bixa, 1216-1307 Bixe, -a, 1300 Buxe Jelwyni (fr. the *Gelwyn* family). Doubtful. Alexander compares Box, Herts, not an exact parallel, and derives fr. O.E. *bixen, byxen*, '(place) of the box-tree'; this is far from certain. The form *bixen* is very rare, and for the *sb.* there seems only *box*. Nor does there seem any good analogy. BEXLEY (Kent) is also Bix in *Dom.*, and seems to mean 'Beca's' or 'Bica's lea.' As likely as not Bix is *bi Ex*, 'by the river.' *Cf.* BEEFORD, BEAL, etc., and EXE.

BLABY (Leicester). *Sic* 1298. O.N. *blá-r bi*, 'blue, blae-looking hamlet.' *Cf.* BLADON, and see -by.

BLACKAWTON (Dartmouth). (*Dom.* has Blache-berie, -grave, -pole, etc.). Old forms needed. Perh. '*Blaca*'s HAUGHTON' or 'village on the haugh or river-meadow.'

BLACKBOYS (Uckfield). Not in *Dom.* Old forms needed. One may conjecture '*Blaca*'s boss' or 'knoll.' *Boss* is found in Eng. *a.* 1300 meaning 'a hump,' and in 1598 meaning 'a hump-like hill'; whilst it is spelt in 5-6 *boys*(*s*). But all this is quite doubtful. *Cf.* Blachestela, *Dom.* Surrey.

BLACKBURN. *Dom.* Blacheburne; also *chart.* Blagborn. 'Black brook,' O.E. *blaec, blac, c.* 1190 *blache ;* and see -bourne. *Cf.* 833 *chart.* 'Blakeburnham,' Kent.

BLACKER (Barnsley). Old forms needed. Not in *Dom.* As a rule -er is contracted fr. -over, 'bank.' *Cf.* ASHOVER, HASLER, WOOLER, etc.; so this is prob. 'black, dark bank.'

BLACKHEATH (London, etc.). Lond. B. *c.* 1420 *Lydgate*, Blakeheth. *Cf.* Blachefelde, *Dom.* Surrey.

BLACKPILL (Swansea). *Pill* here is corrup. of Eng. *pool*, W. *pwl.* In S. Pembrokesh. *pill* is quite common for 'a little bay, a creek.' *Cf.* next.

BLACKPOOL. Modern. *Cf. B.C.S.* 834 Blæccanpol—*i.e.*, '*Blacca*'s pool.'

BLACKROD (Chorley). 1199 Blackeroade, 1292 Blakerode. Either '*Blaca*'s road,' or 'dark, black road,' O.E. *rád*, North. Eng. and Sc. *rodd. Cf.* BLACKBURN.

BLACKWALL (London). 1377 Blakewale, 1480 'the wall called Black Wall,' along the bank of the Thames.

BLADNEY (Somerset). Not in *Dom.* Prob. *c.* 712 *chart.* Bledenithe. '*Bleda*'s' or '*Blædda*'s HYTHE.' A *hithe* is 'a landing-rise.'

BLADON (Woodstock, both river and village). *O.E. chart* Blædene, Bladaen, *Dom.* Blade, 1216-1307 Bladen(e), 1272 Bladone. Cannot be '*blae* hill,' because *blae* or blue-looking is O.N. *blá.* But it may be contr. for '*Blædda*'s hill.' *Cf. K.C.D.* 721 Blæddan hlæw. See -don. Baddeley thinks that this, as a river name, must be pre-English.

BLAENAU FESTINIOG. W.= 'highlands of Festiniog.' *Cf.* next.

BLAENAVON (Monmouth). W. *blaen afon,* 'source, hill source of the river'—*i.e.*, the R. Avon, Glamorgan.

BLAENGARW (Glamorgan). W.= 'rough fore-part,' *blaen* means both 'source' and 'fore-part,' whilst its plur. *blaenau* means 'highlands.' W. *garw* or *geirw,* 'rough,' is the same as G. *garbh,* so common in Sc. names; whilst in Sc. we also have BLANTYRE.

BLAENLLECHA (Pontypridd). W.= 'projecting rocks or stones.' *Cf.* BLAENGARW.

BLAEN-Y-FFOS (Pembroke). W.='source of the ditch' or 'little brook,' W. *ffos*, L. *fossa*.

BLAGDON (Bristol and Taunton). *Dom.* Blachedone. O.E. *blac dún*, 'dark hill'; *cf.* Blagborn, old form of BLACKBURN. BLAISDON, Glostr., is 1200 Blechedun, prob. 'hill of *Blæcca*,' which may be the origin of Blagdon too.

BLAINA (Monmouth). W. *blaenau,* 'highlands.' *Cf.* BLAENGARW.

BLAKEDOWN (Kidderminster and Kenilworth). 'Black down' or 'hill'; O.E. *blæc, blec, blac*. Duignan has no authority for saying that *black* here means 'uncultivated, running wild.'

BLAKENALL (Walsall) and BLAKENHALL (Nantwich, Wolvermptn.). Nan. B. *Dom.* Blechenhale, Wo. B. *c.* 1300 Blakenhale, '*Blecca*'s or *Blaca*'s nook.' *Cf.* next and BLETCHLEY, and see -hall.

BLAKENEY (Newnham, Glos., and Norfolk). Not in *Dom.* Ne. B. *c.* 1280 Blacheneia, '*Blæca*'s' or '*Blaca*'s isle.' *Blæca* is the mod. surname Blake, which may either be fr. O.E. *blæc, blac,* 'black, dark man,' or fr. O.N. *bleik-r,* in Eng. *c.* 1205 *blake,* 'pale, wan.'

BLAKENHAM, GREAT (Ipswich). *Sic* 1298, but *Dom.* Blachehā. '*Blaca*'s or *Blæca*'s home,' *Cf. Dom.* Surrey, Blachingelei, a patronymic, and Blakesley, Towcester.

BLANCHLAND (Corbridge). Land paid for in 'white' or silver money, *Fr. blanc, blanche,* 'white.' 'Blanch farm' or 'blench ferme' is a common legal term.

BLANDFORD. *Dom.* Blane-, Bleneford. Difficult to say what the *Dom.* forms stand for; whilst O.E. *bland* is 'a mixture, a blend,' and our adj. *bland* is quite mod. BLANDSBY (Pickering), *Dom.* Blandebi, must be 'dwelling of a man *Bland*'; *Onom.* has only *Blandmund* and *Blandwinus.* More light needed for Blandford. See -by.

BLANKNEY (Lincoln). *Dom.* Blachene. 'Isle of *Blaca*,' here nasalized *Blanca,* gen. -*can.* See -ey.

BLATCHINGTON (Brighton). Prob. *Dom.* Bechingetone (*l* omitted in error). The present name represents an O.E. *Blæccan tun,* '*Blæcca*'s town.' *Cf.* BLETCHINGLEY.

BLATHERWYCK (Kingscliffe). 1166-7 *Pipe* Blarewic, *c.* 1350 *chart.* Blatherwyk. 'Dwelling of *Blithgœr, Blithhere,* or *Blithmœr.*' All these names are in *Onom.* For omission of *th* in 1166-7 *cf.* 'Brer Babbit' for 'Brother R.' See -wick.

BLAWITH (Ulverston). O.N. *blá vith-r,* 'dark blue, blae-looking wood.' *Cf.* ASKWITH.

BLAXHALL (Tunstall). '*Blæcca*'s nook' or 'hall.' *Cf.* BLATCHINGTON; and see -hall.

BLAYDON-ON-TYNE.   Prob. ' dark blue, blae-looking dune or hill,'
O.N. *blá,* North. Eng. and Sc. *blae.   Cf.* next.

BLEADON (Weston-s.-m.).   ? 975 *chart.* Bledone and *a.* 1100 *Winchr.
Ann.* Bleodona.   Prob. ' coloured hill,' O.E. *Bleo dún,* fr. *bleoh,*
' hue, colour.'   *Cf.* BLEWBURY, BLOFIELD, and *Dom.* Bucks,
Bledone.

BLEAN or BLEE (Canterbury).   *Dom.* Blehem, *c.* 1386 *Chaucer* Ble(e).
Prob. ' *Blih*'s home,' one *Blih* in *Onom.*   For the contraction
cf. BEAL; but it is rare to find the unstressed final syll. falling
quite away.   See -ham.

BLEASDALE (Garstang).   1228 Blesedale, 1540 Blesedale.   Possibly
fr. a man, but seemingly ' dale, valley of the blaze or beacon-
fire,' O.E. *blase, blæse,* 3-6 North. *blese.*

BLEA TARN (Westmld.).   1256 *Assize R.* Blaterne.   ' Blae, bluish
mountain lake,' O.N. *blá-r*; and see TARN.

BLEDDFA (Radnor).   Perh. W. *blaidd fau,* ' wolf's cave.'   But the old
form is Bleddfach; where the ending is doubtful.   *Bledd* is ' a
plain,' and the latter part may be *ffag,* ' what unites or meets in
a point.'

BLEDINGTON (Chipping Norton).   *Dom.* Bladintone, 1221 Bladyn-
tone.   ' Town on R. BLADON.'   See -ing, as river-ending.

BLEDLOW (Bucks).   *K.C.D.* 721 Blæddan hlæw; *Dom.* Bledelai,
? 1297 *Scot. Chancery Roll* ' Johannes de Bledelawe.'   ' *Blœdda*'s '
or ' *Bledda*'s hill.'   BLEDISLOE, Awre, *Dom.* Bliteslau, is prob.
fr. a man *Blith.*   See -low.

BLENCOW (Penrith).   ? W. *blaen cu,* ' dear source or promontory ';
cf. BLAENGARW and GLASGOW (Sc.), also 1210 Blenecarn,
Cumbld., ' headland with the cairn.'

BLENNERHASSETT (Aspatria).   1189 *Pipe* Blendherseta, 1354 *Carlisle
will* Alan de Blenerhayset, 1473 *Paston Lett.* Blaundrehasset
and Blenerhasset (as a personal name).   This seems to be
' seat, dwelling of *Blandhere*' or ' *Blender,*' an unknown man.
Cf. DORSET, etc.   But this leaves the -hass ill-accounted for.

BLETCHINGLEY (Red Hill), BLETCHINGTON (Oxford).   *Dom.* Bleces-,
Blicestone, 1139 Bleche-, Blachedon, 1216-1307 Blecchesdon
(see -don); and BLETCHLEY.   ' Meadow ' and ' village of *Blecca,*'
or his descendants.   *Cf.* BLATCHINGTON; and see -ing and -ley.

BLETSOE (Bedford).   *Dom.* Bleches-, Blachesou, *a.* 1199 Blacheho.
' *Blecca*'s mound.'   *Cf.* THINGOE; and see -how.

BLEWBURY (Didcot) and BLEWBURY DOWN.   944 *chart.* Bleobyrig.
Dom. Blitberie, *a.* 1450 Bleobery.   One would expect this to
be fr. some man; but there is no name in Bleo- in *Onom.*   So
the first part may be as in BLEADON, ' bright borough,' lit., as
Skeat puts it, ' show-borough.'   *Cf.* Fairfield, etc.

BLICKLING (Norfolk). *Dom.* Blikelinga, 1450 Blyclyng. A patronymic; but it is not easy to give the root. *Onom.* gives no help.

BLIDWORTH (Mansfield). *Dom.* Blideworde, -vorde. ' *Blœdda*'s farm.' *Cf.* BLEDINGTON; and see -worth.

BLINDLEY HEATH (Red Hill). Old forms needed. Not in *Dom.* ? ' blind lea ' or ' meadow '; *blind* being here used in its meaning of ' obscure, dark, concealed.' A place ' Blindsyke ' is found in a Dumbartonsh. charter as early as *c.* 1350.

BLISLAND (Bodmin) and BLISWORTH (Northants). *Dom.* Blidesworde, 1158-9 *Pipe* Blieswurda. ' Land ' and ' farm of *Blida* ' (or ' *Blih* '). See -worth. Pike o' Blisco, Westmld., will be ' peak of Blida's or Blih's wood '; -sco or -scough for SHAW, *cf.* BURSCOUGH.

BLOCKLEY (Moreton-Henmarsh). 855 *chart.* Bloccanleah, *Dom.* Blockelei. ' *Blocca*'s lea.' *Cf.* BLOXHAM.

BLOFIELD (Norwich). *Dom.* Blafelda, 1157 Blafeld, 1452 Blofield. ' Leaden-coloured, bluish field.' M.E. *c.* 1250 *blo*, O.N. *blá*, ' livid,' cognate with *blae* and *blue*. *Cf.* BLEADON and BLOWICK.

BLOOMSBURY (London and Birmingham). Lo. B. *c.* 1537 Lomes-, Lomsbury. The history of this name is very obscure, and more evidence is needed. Possibly the Lome- represents *Leofman*, a fairly common O.E. name. See -bury.

BLORE HEATH (Staffs). *Dom.* and later Blora. *Blore* is an onomatopœic word meaning ' a violent gust or blast '; not found in Eng. *a.* 1440.

BLOW GILL (Helmsley). 1200 Blawathgile. O.N. *blá wath*, ' leaden-coloured, bluish ford,' in the ravine. See -gill. *Cf.* LANGWATHBY.

BLOWICK (Southport). ' Leaden-coloured, bluish dwelling.' See BLOFIELD and -wick, which must be Eng. here and not N., as Blowick is inland and can have no ' bay.'

BLOXHAM (Banbury). *Dom.* Warwk., Lochesham (error), 1155 *Pipe* Blochesham, 1231 Blokesham. ' Home of *Blocca*.' *Cf.* BLOCKLEY.

BLOXWICH (Walsall) and BLOXWORTH (Bere Regis). *Dom.* Blocheswic, *a.* 1300 Blockeswich, Blokeswyke. ' *Blocca*'s dwelling ' and ' farm.' See -wich and -worth.

BLUNDELL SANDS (Liverpool). Perh. fr. Randulph de *Blundevill*, Earl of Chester in 1180. *Blundell* has been a common Lancashire name from at least the 17th cny. *Cf.* next and -hall, which the -ell may represent.

BLUNDESTON (Lowestoft). Not in *Dom.* ' *Blunda*'s town or village.' The name is now Blunt, Fr. *blond*, Nor. Fr. *blund*, ' fair, flaxen.' *Cf.* next, and *Dom.* Essex, Blundeshala.

BLUNTISHAM (Hunts). *Dom.* Bluntesham. ' Home of *Blunti* ' or
' *Blunt*,' which last is still a common surname. *Cf. Dom.* Wilts,
Blontesdone, *K.C.D.* 666 Bluntesige, and Bluntington, Worc.
Blunham, Sandy, prob. represents the same name.

BLYBOROUGH (Kirton Lindsay). *Dom.* Bliburg. Prob., as in
BLISWORTH, ' burgh, fort of *Blida*,' but it may be ' of *Blih*.'
Cf. 1157 *Pipe* Norfk. Blieburc. See -borough.

BLYMHILL (Shifnal). *Dom.* Brumhelle (*r* for *l*, one liquid confused
in sound with the other), *a.* 1200 and later Blumonhull. Prob.
' hill of the *blooms*,' or molten masses of metal, O.E. *blóma*,
-an, then, curiously, not found till 1600 *bloom;* but 1584-5
blomary, or *bloomery*, a forge for making blooms. One must
have stood on this hill, which is in an iron-producing district.

BLYTH(E) (Northumbld., Warwk., Notts, and Rotherham), BLYTHE
BRIDGE (Stoke-on-T.). Roth B. *c.* 1097 *Flor. W.* Blida; Notts,
B. *Dom.* Blide, 1146 Blida, *c.* 1180 Blya, 1298 Blythe. The Eng.
blithe never refers to places; so this *may* be connected with
W. *blythair*, ' a belching,' *blythach*, ' a bloated person,' and
blwth, ' a puff, a blast.' There are two rivers in Northbld., and
one each in Staffs, Notts, and Suffk., all called Blyth(e), and
nearly all Eng. rivers are Kelt. in origin; though what that
was is now lost. On the Staff. Blythe are Blithbury, *a.* 1200
Blith(e)burie, and Blithfield, *Dom.* Blidevelt. In Northbld we
find 1208 Snoc de Bliemus—*i.e.*, ' snout, projecting headland
of Blythmouth '—1423 Blythe-snuke, *a.* 1800 Blyth-snook,
fr. O.N. *snok-r*, ' a mark stretched out,' *hnuk-r*, ' a little mountain, a rock '; *cf.* ' The Snewke or Conny-warren ' in Blaeu's
map of Lindisfarne.

BOARSTALL (Bucks). Popular etymology. See BORSTAL.

BOBBER'S MILL (Nottingham). *Bobber* in mid. dial. means ' a
chum.'

BOBBINGTON (Stourbridge). *Dom.* Bubintone, *a.* 1200 Bobintune;
cf. 798 *chart.* ' Bobing-sæta,' Kent. ' Town, village of *Bobba* '
(or his descendants), mentioned in a Worcester chart. of 759.

BOCKHAMPTON (Lambourn and Dorchester). Both *a.* 1300 Boc-
hamton. ' Beech-built HAMPTON,' or ' home-farm '; O.E. *bóc*,
O.N. *bók*, ' a beech.' *Cf.* BUCKLAND and GREAT BOOKHAM;
also *Dom.* Norfk., Bocthorp.

BOCKING (Braintree). *Dom.* Bochinges. Patronymic, ' place of
the sons of *Bocca* '; *cf.* 806 Bokenhale, ? near Croyland. *Onom.*
gives only *Bacca* and *Bacco.* See -ing.

BOCKLETON (Tenbury and Salop). Te. B. *Dom.* Boclintun, 1275
Boclinton, *a.* 1400 Bocklington, Bokelinton. Sa. B. 1321
Bochtone (an error), 1534 Bucculton. ' Town of *Boccel*.' *Onom.*
gives only one *Beoccel.*

BODEDERN (Anglesea). W. *bod edyrn*, 'residence of sovereignty,' or 'royal house'; but T. Morgan says, 'abode of *Edern*,' son of Nudd, warrior and poet.

BODELWYDDAN (Flintsh.). W. *bod-el-gwyddan*, 'residence of the wood-spirit' or 'satyr.'

BODENHAM (Leominster and Salisbury). *Sic* 1202. '*Boda*'s home.' O.E. *boda*, 2 *bode*, is 'a herald, a messenger,' one who 'bodes' or forebodes. *Dom.* Wilts, has Bodeberie, and *Dom.* Nfk., Bodenham. *Cf.* BODDINGTON on Chelt, *Dom.* Botintone.

BODFARI (Denbigh). Perh. *c.* 380 *Ant. Itin.* Varis. But now W. *bod Fari*, 'house of Mary,' the *m* being aspirated.

BODFFORD (Anglesea). W. *bod ffordd*, 'dwelling by the road or passage.'

BODHAM (Holt, Nfk.). *Dom.* has both Bodhā and Bodenham. 'Home of *Boda*' or '*Boddus*.' See -ham.

BODICOTT (Banbury). *Dom.* Bodicote, 1216-1307 Bodicot. '*Boda*'s cottage.' *Cf.* above.

BODMIN. *Dom.* Bodmini, *Exon. Dom.* Bodmine; *c.* 1180 *Ben*; *Peterb.* Bothmenia; *c.* 1200 *Gervase* Bomine; 1216 Bodminium. 1294 Bodmin. Corn. *bod* or *bo* is 'a house,' the second half is more uncertain; it may be 'house of stones,' Corn. *min, myin* (*cf.* next), or 'on the edge,' *min,* or 'on the hill,' *mene.*

BODVEAN (Pwllheli). W. *bod faen*, 'house of stone.' *Cf. cist faen*, 'a stone coffin.' As houses in Wales and Cornwall usually are of stone, the reference will prob. be to some 'Druidical' erection.

BOGNOR. Not in *Dom.*, but 680 *chart.* Bucgan ora—*i.e.*, '*Bucga*'s edge' or 'brink' or 'shore'; three *Bucgas* in *Onom.* In 1166-7 *Pipe* it is Begenoura. See -or.

BOLDON (Jarrow). 1183 Boldona. Prob. O.E. *botl-dún,* 'hill, dune with the dwelling on it.' *Cf.* BOLTON and BOLE.

BOLE (Gainsborough). *Sic* 1316, but *Dom.* Bolun. (*Dom.* Lincs has Bolebi, 'dwelling of *Bola*.') This may be O.N. *ból,* 'house, dwelling' (with -un an old loc.), if not *bol-r,* 'bole, trunk of a tree.' *Cf.* BOLFORD, Kendal, *Dom.* Bodelforde, 'ford at the house'; see BOLTON. Also *cf.* next, and *Dom.* Salop and 1157 *Pipe*, Northbld., Bolebec. 1160-1 *Pipe*, Sussex, Bulebech, may not be the same.

BOLE HILL (Wirksworth). *Oxf. Dict.* bole *sb*⁴, 'a place where miners smelted their lead.' Not found *a.* 1670, and origin unknown.

BOLINGEY (Truro). Prob. 'isle of the *Bolings*,' or 'descendants of *Bola*,' a name in *Onom.* We have 'Bullingbrooke' already in the time of Wm. the Conqueror, 1166-7 *Pipe*, Billingeburc and Bull-, 1233 Bulingbroc, Lincs, hence the name Bolingbroke.

BOLLINGTON (Macclesfield and Altrincham). 'Town, village on the R. *Bollin*,' which may be connected with same root as W. *bol, boly,* 'the belly,' and so 'swollen river.' See -ing as river-ending.

BOLNEY (Hayward's Heath) and BOLNHURST (St. Neot's). Not in *Dom.* 'Isle' and 'wood of *Bola*,' *-an. Cf. Dom.* Bucks, Bolebech (= bach, 'brook'), Devon, Bolewis, Yorks, Bolesford; also Bollesdon (Newent), *old* Bolesdone, Bullesdone, whilst *Dom.* Yorks, Bolebi is now Boulby. See -ey and -hurst.

BOLSOVER (Chesterfield). *Dom.* Belesovre, 1166-67 *Pipe* Bolleshoura, 1173-74 *ib.* Castella de Pech et de Bolesoura, *c.* 1180 *Bened. Peterb.* Boleshoveres. '*Bola*'s bank or brink'; O.E. *ofer, obr ;* M.E. *overe,* 'border, bank of a river.' *Cf.* ASHOVER, and see BOLNEY, etc.

BOLSTERSTONE (Sheffield). Not in *Dom.* Not likely to be fr. Eng. and O.E. *bolster,* but prob. a tautology, fr. O.N. *ból-staðr,* 'dwelling-place' or 'farm'; so common in Sc. names as -bister, -buster, and -bster; Scrabster, Ulbster, etc. Bolster will have been taken for a proper name, and -ton added; for the final *e cf.* Johnston and Johnstone, both meaning 'John's town.'

BOLTBY (Thirsk). *Dom.* Boltebi, 1209 Bolteby. 'Dwelling of *Bolt*,' a name not in *Onom.* Hardly fr. bolt *sb*[1]; but perh. a tautology, fr. O.E. *bóld,* 'house, dwelling,' and -by.

BOLTON (nine in *P.G.*). *Dom.* Boletone, 1208 Bollton (on Swale). Other B's in *Dom.* Yorks and Lancs are Bodeltone. We get an interesting set of forms for the Sc. Bolton (Haddingtonsh.), *c.* 1200 Botheltune, Boteltune, Boweltun, 1250 Boulton, 1297 Boltone. O.E. *botl-tún,* 'dwelling-enclosure, collection of houses, village'; influenced by O.N. *ból,* 'a house, a dwelling-place.' It is according to its rule for *Dom.* to spell Both- or Bot- as Bod-. *Cf.* BOOTLE.

BOMER(E) HEATH (Shrewsbury). *Earlier* Bolemere. 'Mere or lake,' O.E. *mere,* 'of the bull,' not in O.E., but O.N. *bole, boli ;* in Eng. *c.* 1200 *bule,* 3-5 *bole. Cf. Dom.* (Yorks) Bolemere, 1166-67 *Pipe* Bulemā, now Bulmer; also The Bolmers, Castle Bromwich, and the Bullmoors (Shenstone), and Boll Bridge (Tamworth), 1313 Bollebrigge.

BONBY (Hull). Either a man '*Bonda* or *Bondo*'s dwelling,' or 'dwelling of the peasant'; O.E. *bónda ;* O.N. *bonde;* *d* readily disappears. But *Dom.* (Yorks) Bonnebi (twice) is now Gunby. See -by.

BONCATH (Pembroke). W. *boncath* means 'a buzzard'; but *bon cath* is 'tree stump of the cat.'

BONCHURCH (Ventnor). *Dom.* Bonecerce. Bone- must be O.N. *bón,* 'a prayer, a boon'; in Eng. 2-7 *bone,* 3-4 *bon. Cf.* BUNWELL. There is no man named *Bona* or *Bonna* in *Onom.* The O.E. for a prayer is *bén,* so that, curiously, this must be a Norse name, the indication of a forgotten early N. settlement here. This is confirmed by *Dom.'s* ending -cerce, the hard *c*'s having quite a N. look. *Dom.* nearly always has -cherche, chirche, 'Alvievecherche,' 'Bascherche,' etc. *Dom.'s* form is also our earliest Eng. example of *boon ;* the earliest in *Oxf. Dict.* is *c.* 1175 *bone.*

BONINGTON (Notts and Kent). *Sic* 1297-98, but *Dom.* Bonintone (Kent), Bonnitone (Notts), 1296 Bonigtone (? where). Doubtful. It should mean ' *Bona*'s town,' but there is no such name in *Onom. Cf.* BONNINGTON (Sc.).

BONSALL (Derby). Perh. *Dom.* Bunteshale. Prob. ' nook, corner of *Bunda* or *Bonda*,' both in *Onom.* But *cf. Dom.* (Bucks) Bonestov, ? ' place of *Bone*,' still a surname. *Cf.* BUNNY, and see -hall.

BONTDDU (Dolgelly). W. *pont du,* ' black bridge.'

BONTNEWYDD (Caernarvon). W. ' new bridge '; W. *pont.*

BONVILSTON (Cardiff). *Bonville,* Fr. for ' good town,' as well as *Melville,* ' bad town,' occurs as a surname in Britain. In W. it is Tresimwn, ' house of Simon Bonville,' chief steward of the Norm. Sir Robt. Fitzhamon. There is a Hutton Bonville (Yorks). We find -ville common in the Channel Isles.

BOOSBECK (Yorks). Not in *Dom.* Prob. ' brook with the cow-stall beside it '; O.N. *báss ;* M.E. *boose,* ' a cow-stall.' See -beck.

BOOT (Ravenglass). O.N. *búð ;* Dan. and Sw. *bod,* ' a hut, a dwelling.' *Cf.* G. *both* or *bot,* ' a house.'

BOOTHBY (Grantham). 1298 Bothebi. Prob. ' dwelling of *Botha* or *Bota*.' Booth is still a common surname. *Cf.* Bootham (York). See -by.

BOOTHROYD LANE (Dewsbury). Called after a man Boothroyd, where -royd is prob. fr. rod *sb*,[2] 6 *roid,* ' a path, a way.'

BOOTLE (Liverpool, Cumbld.). Li. *B. a.* 1540 Bothul. *Dom.* for N. Lancs. has Bodele and Fordbodele (now washed away). O.E. *botl,* ' a dwelling, a house.' *Cf.* BOLTON and NEWBATTLE (Sc.).

BORDEN (Sittingbourne). Not in *Dom.* ' Boar's den '; O.E. *bár,* 3-7 *bor.* The wild boar was not extinct in England till at least the 17th century.

BORDESLEY (Birmingham). 1156 Bordeslega, 1158 -lea, in 1275 also Bordeshale. ' *Borda*'s lea ' or ' meadow.' *Cf.,* too, *B.C.S.* 739 Bordeles tun. See -ley.

BOREHAM (four in *P.G.*). *Dom.* (Surrey) Borham. ' Boar's home.' See BORDEN. *Boar* may here be a proper name. *Cf.* Borley Green (Sudbury). But BORLEY House (Upton-on-Severn) is *Dom.* Burgeleye, or ' fortified place in the meadow.' See next, and BURLEY. BOREFLEET is the old name of Brightlingsea Creek, earlier found as Bordfliet, Berfliet, and Balfleet; prob. FLEET or ' river of the boar '; O.E. *bár,* 3 *ber,* 4-7 *bore.* Dr. Diekin postulates an O.E. *bord,* ' border,' which does not exist; and *bore,* ' tidal wave,' is not found till 1601.

BOROUGHBRIDGE (York). 1380 Ponteburg. ' Fort-bridge ' or ' fortified bridge,' fr. O.E. *burh,* ' a fort, castle, or burgh.' *Cf.* PONTEFRACT, ' or broken bridge,' and Borough Green (Cambs).

BORRODAIL (Cumberland). N. *borg-dal-r,* 'dale, valley with a fort in it.' *Cf.* next and Borrowstonness or Bo'NESS (Sc.).

BORROWASH (Derby). Not in *Dom.* 'Burgh ash-tree.' *Cf.* above and next.

BORROWBY (several in Yorks). All in *Dom.* Berg(h)ebi. 'Fortified dwelling-place,' fr. O.N. *borg* or O.E. *borh, borg, burh,* 'fort, burgh.' *Cf.* BARROWBY, BORWICK, and BORRODAIL; and see -by.

BORSTAL or BOSTAL (Rochester). *Dom.* Borcstele, Borchetelle; *a.* 1200 *Text. Roff.* Borestella, Borgestealla. O.E. *beorh-steall,* 'seat, place, stall on the hillside.' Or Bor- may be O.E. *borh, borg, burh,* 'fort, burgh.' *Cf. Pipe* 1157 Burchestala, prob. in Beds.

BORTH (Cardigan). W. *bordd, burdd,* 'a board or table.'

BORWICK (Carnforth). *Dom.* Borch and Bereuuic (second *e* an error). O.E. *borh-wic,* 'fort-dwelling, fortified house.' *Cf.* BORROWBY.

BOSAHAN (Falmouth). Pron. Bow-sane. Corn. *bod, bos, bo,* 'house, dwelling,' G. *both,* common in Corn. names, as in BOSCAWEN, 'house beside the elder-tree,' *scawen,* Boslowick, Bosistow, etc. The latter half is often now uncertain, but Bosahan may be fr. *sawan,* 'a hole in a cliff beside the sea.' None of these in *Dom.*

BOSBURY (Ledbury). *Flor. Worc. and Sim. Dur. re ann.* 1056. Bosanbyrig, 'Burgh, castle of *Bosa.*'

BOSCASTLE (Cornwall). Prob. '*Bosa's* or *Boso's* castle'; names in *Onom.* But Corn. *bos* also means 'moor.' *Cf.* BOSAHAN.

BOSCOMBE (Bournemouth and Salisbury). Sal. B. *Dom.* Boscumbe. '*Bosa's* valley.' See above and -combe.

BOSHAM (Chichester). *Bede* Bosanham, 1048 *O.E. Chron.* Bosenham, 1167-68 *Pipe* Boseham. '*Bosa's* home.' *Cf.* BOSBURY.

BOSHERSTON (Pembroke). Modern. *Bosher* is an English surname, prob. fr. Fr. *boucher,* 'a butcher.'

BOSLEY (Macclesfield). *Dom.* Boselega. '*Bosa's* lea or meadow.' *Cf.* BOSHAM.

BOSTON. Not in *Dom.* 1090 *chart.* Ecclesia sancti Botulphi, *a.* 1200 *Hoveden* Sti Botulphi, *c.* 1250 *Dame Siriz* Botolfston in Lincolneschire, *Leland* Botolphstowne, and Boston. Linking forms seem curiously lacking. The copious *Hist. of Boston,* 1856, by Thompson, mentions none; but the name was St. Botolph's in Eng. or in Latin, rather than Boston, till after 1400. We have found 'Boston' first in 1391, Earl Derby's Exp. (Camden), 23. Of the origin there can be no doubt, as *O.E. Chron.* ann. 654 says, the hermit *Botwulf* (L. *Botulphus*) built the minster at Icanho, the earlier name of Boston. A similar contraction is perh. seen in BOSSALL (Yorks), whose church is also dedicated to St Botolph. But here *Dom.'s* forms are puzzling—Boscele and Bosciale. The ending is certainly

-hall, *q.v.*; but Bosc- does not suggest *Botulph*. The only name near it in *Onom.* is one *Bascic*. *Cf. Dom.* (Hunts) Botulves-brige.

BOTHAMSALL (Newark). *Dom.* Bodmescel(d), 1180 Bodemeskil, 1278 Bodmeshill, 1302 Bothemeshull, 1428 Bothomsell. Now '*Bothelm's* nook' or 'hall.' *Cf.* BONSALL, etc., and see -hall. But the orig. ending was either late O.E. *cell*, 'a small monastery or nunnery,' Med. L. *cella*; or, more prob., O.N. *kelda*, 'a spring, a well.'

BOTLEY (Hants and Henley-in-Arden). Han. B. *Dom.* Botelei. Hen. B. *Dugdale* Botle. Prob. '*Botta's*' or '*Botto's* lea or meadow.' Possibly O.E. *botl-léah*, 'meadow with the hut or house on it.' *Cf.* BOTLOE (Dymock), *Dom.* Botelav (see -low); also *Dom.* (Cambs) Botestoch (O.E. *stóc*, 'a place ').

BOTTISHAM (Cambridge). *Dom.* Bodichesham, 1210 Bodekesham, 1372 Bodkesham, 1400 Botkesham, 1428 Bottesham. 'Home of *Bodeca*.' See -ham.

BOTTLESFORD (Pewsey, Wilts). Not in *Dom.* [c. 1190 *chart.* 'Botlesford,' Notts.]. ? 'Ford of *Botwulf*' or '*Botweald*.' Only, in 796 *chart.* (Wilts), we have a Butlesleye, which must represent a name *Butela*, or the like.

BOTUSFLEMING (Cornwall). Corn.= 'parish of the Flemings' or men from Flanders. *Cf.* Flushing opposite Falmouth. *Botus* may be= W. *bettws*, corrup. of Eng. *bead-house*, 'house of prayer'; but this is uncertain. *c.* 1175 *Lambeth Hom.* has *bode, beode*, for *bede*, 'prayer, petition.' *Cf.* Bacchus (Glostrsh.), 1304 Bakkehuse, 'the back house.'

BOUGHTON (nine in *P.G.*). *Dom.* (Notts, Nfk., Northants) Buche-tone, -tuna. 1179-80 *Pipe* (Yorks) Bouton. Some conceivably might be 'town at the bend,' M.E. *bought*, same root as *bight*, 'a bay.' But B., Notts, 1225 Buketon, is fr. a man *Bucca*. Boughton (Worc.) is 1038 *chart.* Bocctun, 1275 Boctone, which is certainly 'town of the beech-trees, O.E. *bóc*.' The phonetics here are as in BROUGHTON.

BOUGHTO(U)N-UNDER-BLEE (Canterbury). *Sic* Chaucer, *c.* 1386. See above and BLEE.

BOURNE (Cambs and Lincoln). Cam. B. *Dom.* Brune, 1171 Brunne, 1210 Burne. B. Linc. *c.* 1200 *Gervase* Brunne. O.N. *brunn-r*, 'a brook'; O.E. *burn(a)*, 'a spring, a well, a stream,' the Sc. 'burn.'

BOURNEMOUTH. Perh. *c.* 1150 *Gaimar*, re ann. 1066 Brunemue. See above.

BOURTON (seven in *P.G.*). Glos. B. 949 *chart.* Burgtune, *Dom.* Bortune. Rugby B. *Dom.* Bortone. Bath B. *c.* 1160 Burton; also *B.C.S.* i. 506 Burgton (Berks). = BURTON, 'fortified town.' See -bury and -ton.

BOVERTON (Cowbridge). Prob. O.E. *bi-ofer-tún,* ' town, village, by the brink or edge.' *Cf.* ' Bovreford ' (Hants) in *Dom.;* also BEEFORD, BOLSOVER, etc.

BOVEY TRACEY (S. Devon). Pron. Buvvey. *Dom.* Bovi. Prob. ' *Bofa's* isle ' ; see next, and -ey. On Tracey *cf.* WOLLACOMBE TRACY.

BOVINGTON (Hemel Hampstead). 1298 Bovyngton. ' *Bofa's* town,' or else ' *Botwine's* town.' This last is a common name in *Onom. Cf. Dom.* Bouinton, 1205 Buvintone (in Yorks), now Boynton; and *Dom.* (Wilts) Boientone. *Boving* may be a patronymic. See -ing.

Bow (London). Early often called ' De Arcubus,' fr. a bridge arched or ' bowed,' built here in the time of Q. Maud, the first in England.

BOWES CASTLE (Yorksh.). *c.* 1188 *Gir. Camb.* Beoves. Prob. fr. a man *Bofa* or *Beofa ;* several Bofas in *Onom.* The *s* will be the gen.

BOWNESS (Cumberland). *c.* 1200 Bowenes. ' Ness or naze (O.N. and O.E. *næs,* ' cape, nose ') at the bow or bend '; O.E. *boga.*

BOWNHILL (Stroud). Not in *Dom.* Some think this is *Bede's* Mons Badonicus. But old forms are needed; meantime doubtful. Baddeley can throw no light.

BOWTHORPE (Menthorpe, Yorks). *Dom.* and 1199 Boletorp. ' Village of *Bola,*' two in *Onom. Cf.* BOLNEY; and see -thorpe.

BOXFORD (Newbury and Colchester). New. B. *B.C.S.* i. 506 Boxora, *Dom.* Bovsore, Bochesorne. The present form seems quite mod. *Box-ora* is O.E. for ' edge, river-bank lined with box-trees.' *Cf.* WINDSOR, etc. Box HILL (Surrey) was early famed for its box-trees. Close by is Box Hurst or ' box wood.'

BOXLEY (Maidstone). ? *Dom.* Bogelei, 1155 *Pipe* Boxel', *c.* 1188 *Gir. Camb.* Boxletha, 1289 Boxleya. Prob. O.E. *box-leáh,* ' box-tree meadow.' There are no names in *Onom.* like *Boc* or *Bocca;* but *cf.* next. The -letha might be for O.E. *hlið, c.* 1200 *liðe,* ' a slope.'

BOXWORTH (Cambridge). *Dom.* Bochesuuorde, 1228 Bukeswrth, 1256 Bokesworth. ' Farm of the he-goats.' Icel. *bokk-r,* Sw. *bock ;* also O.E. *buc,* ' a buck, a he-deer,' fr. which comes form 1228. *Cf.* BOXWELL (Charfield), *Dom.* Boxewelle, 1316 Bockeswelle.

BOYNTON (Bridlington). See BOVINGTON.

BOYTON (Launceston). *Dom.* Boye-, Boietone. ' *Boia's* town or village.' Several of this name in *Onom. Cf.* Boythorp (Yorks), *Dom.* Buitorp.

BRABOURNE (Kent). *Dom.* Bradeburne. O.E. *brád burna,* ' broad stream.' See -bourne.

BRACEBOROUGH (Stamford). *Dom.* Braseborg, and BRACEBRIDGE (Lincoln), *Dom.* Brachebrige, 1298 Bracebrigge. Prob. ' burgh, fort,' and ' bridge of *Bracca,* or *Breca,* or *Brece.*' But as to the latter note also 1483 *Cathol. Angl.* ' A brace of a bryge or of a vawte, *sinus, arcus,*'= ' span.' *Cf.* next, and BRACEWELL (W. Riding), *Dom.* Braisuelle.

BRACKLEY (Northampton). *c.* 1188 *Gir. Cambr.* Brakelega, Bracheleia. ' *Bracca*'s lea or meadow.' *Cf.* BRACKENTHWAITE (Cockermouth), 1202 Brakinthweit; see -ley and -thwaite.

BRACKNELL (Winkfield). 942 *chart.* Braccan heal. There can be little doubt this means ' nook of *Bracca.*' There is no word like the mod. *bracken* in O.E., and in any case ' bracken nook ' is not the likely meaning according to analogy, though it is supported by Skeat. See above and -hall. There is also a BRACKEN (Yorks), *Dom.* Brachen, which must be ' *Bracca's* place.' *Cf.* BEEDON, COVEN, etc.

BRADBURY (Durham). *a.* 1130 *Sim. Dur.* Brydbyrig. *Broad,* O.E. *brád,* never takes the form *bryd* or *brid,* so this is prob. ' Burgh or castle of the bride '; O.E. *brýd,* 3-4 *bryd.* See -bury.

BRADDEN (Towcester). 1221 Braden is ' Broad valley.' See BRADON, and -den. But for BRADDN see VRADDAN (Lizard).

BRADENHAM (Thetford and High Wycombe). *B. C. S.* 877 Bradanham. [*Cf. c.* 672 *Grant* ' Bradanfeld ' (Berks), and 1298 ' Thomas de Bradenston.'] ' *Brada*'s home.' The name is common in *Onom.* But Skeat holds that Bradanfeld, now BRADFIELD, is a weak dative fr. O.E. *brád,* ' broad.'

BRADESTON (Norfolk). (*Dom.* has only Bradehā.) 1298 Bradenston, 1422 Breydeston, 1450 Brayston, 1451 Braydeston. ' *Brada*'s town.' *Cf.* BRADENHAM. Form 1298 will then show a double gen.

BRADFORD, *Dom.* Bradeford; and BRADFORD-ON-AVON (Wilts). *O.E. Chron.* 652 Æt Bradanforda be Afne. ' Broad ford.' *Cf.* BRETFORD, and *Dom.* (Yorks) Bradfortun, Bratfortone, now Brafferton.

BRADING (I. of Wight). *Dom.* Berarding. This must be ' place of the descendants of *Beorhtweard,*' later *Beorhward, Berard.* See -ing.

BRADLEY (Keighley, and 7). *Dom.* (Yorks) several, Bradeleia; Bilston B. *Dom.* Bradeley; Stafford B. *Dom.* Bradeleia. 778 *chart.* Bradan leaȝe (? which), ' Broad lea or meadow,' or possibly ' *Brada*'s meadow.' *Cf.* BRADESTON.

BRADON (a district W. of Swindon). Sic *O.E. Chron.* 904. O.E. *brád dún,* ' broad hill.' *Cf.,* too, ' Bradene,' *Dom.* Somerset— *i.e.,* ' broad dean ' or ' valley.'

BRADSHAW (Bolton and Halifax). Not in *Dom.* Bol. B. 1313 Bradeshagh. O.E. *brád scaga,* ' broad wood.'

BRADWELL (5 in *P.G.*). *Dom.* Bradeuuelle (Bucks)., Braintree B. *a.* 1300 Bradwall—*i.e.*, ' broad well or spring.' *Cf.* 1160 *Pipe* Bradew'h, in the same region. But *Dom.* Bradewell (Yorks), is Braithwell (Doncaster).

BRADYAIR (Cumberland). *c.* 1141 Bradjere. O.E. *brád ȝeard,* ' broad yard.'

BRAFFERTON. See BRADFORD.

BRAFIELD (Northampton). *Dom.* Bragefelde. *a.* 1130 Braufield. ? ' Field on the brae or brow or hill slope,' O.N. *brá,* O.E. *bráew, bréaw*; lit. ' the eyelid.' But *Dom.* suggests ' field of ' an unrecorded ' *Braga.' Onom.* has only *Broga.*

BRAILES (Banbury). *Sic* in *Dom.* and 1248. A unique and puzzling name. Prob. some man ' *Brail's* ' (village), as in Brailsford (Derby). The name is otherwise unknown; it might be contr. fr. *Breguweald,* 2 in *Onom.* We have similar names, only with O.E. gen., in BEADON, COVEN, etc.

BRAINTREE (Essex). *Dom.* Branchtreu; *later* Branktry, Brantry. This must be ' tree of *Branc,*' the same name as in Branksome (Bournemouth), Branxton (Coldstream), and Branxholm (Hawick); *a.* 1400 Brancheshelm. The *ch* in *Dom.* and in this last are due to the habitual softening of Norman scribes. *Cf.* OSWESTRY.

BRAITHWAITE (Keswick). 1183 *Boldon Bk.* Braitewat, Braithewath, perh. in Durham. ' Brae-place.' See BRAFIELD and -thwaite. But BRAITHWELL (Doncaster) is *Dom.* Bradewell. See BRADWELL.

BRAMBER (Shoreham). ? *Dom.* Branbertei, which suggests an unrecorded ' Brandbeorht's isle.' See -ey. *Old* Brymmburg; also *cf. Grant* of 672 Brember wudu (Salisbury). The first part is doubtful. It may be O.E. *bróm,* ' the broom,' *cf.* next, or *bréme,* 3-6 *brem,* ' famous.' The -ber seems to be for *burh, cf.* BAMBER, and see -bury. *Cf.* Kirk Bramwith (Doncaster), 1201 Bramwith, where the ending is O.N. *vith-r,* ' a wood.'

BRAMCOTE (Nottingham and Nuneaton). Not. B. *Dom.* Bron-, Brunecote, *c.* 1200 Brancote. Nun. B. *Dom.* Brancote, *a.* 1300 Brom(p)cote, *a.* 1400 Bramkote. Duignan says ' cot in the broom ' or ' gorse,' O.E. *bróm.* Mutschmann thinks of *brand cote,* ' cot on the place cleared by burning.' Neither is certain. *Cf.* the other names in Bram-; also CASTLE BROMWICH.

BRAMHAM (Tadcaster); *sic* 1202, and BRAMHAM (S. Yorks). *Dom.* Bramha, Brameha. See above and next. The Bram- here is doubtful. BRAMSHALL (Uttoxeter) is *Dom.* Branselle, *a.* 1200 Brumeshel, *a.* 1300 Bromsholf, -sulf. Both look certainly as if fr. a man *Bram, Brom,* or *Brum.* The *Onom.* has *Brand, Bron, Brum,* and *Brun,* the last common. For the present ending see -hall; but -sholf, and -sulf point to O.E. *scylfe,* 'a shelf, a shelving piece of land.'

BRAMPTON (7 in *P.G.*). Nfk. and Suffk. B. *Dom.* Brantuna. Hants B. 1121 *O.E. Chron.* Bramtun, 1149 Brantona; 1238 *Close R.* Brampton, ? which. Prob. 'town of *Brand* or *Brant.*' · *Brand* is common in *Onom. Cf. B.C.S.* 712 Brantes wyrth. But BRANTON GREEN (Aldborough) is 1202 Brankstona. *Cf.* BAMPTON for common intrusion of *p.*

BRANCASTER (N.W. Norfolk). *a.* 450 *Notitia* Bransdunum. 'Castle, camp of *Bran.*' Ir. and O.G. *bran,* 'a raven'; in Breton 'a crow.' A chief *Brán* is found in *Bk. of Taliessin,* while Nant Bran, vale of Glam., is *c.* 1130 *Lib. Land.* Nant Baraen.

BRANDESTON (Wickham Market). *Dom.* Brantestuna. 'Town of *Brand*' (common in *Onom.*), or '*Branti.*' *Cf.* Bransburton, (Yorks), *Dom.* Brantisburtune, and BRANSTON.

BRANDON (Hereford and Durham, Coventry, Salop, and on Little Ouse). May be same name as *Rav. Geogr.* Branogenium. Cov. B. *Dom.* Brandune, 1227 Brandon, 1273 Braundon. Another, *a.* 1200 Brandune. 'Hill of *Brand,*' a common O.E. name. See -don. BRANCOT (Stafford), is often Bromcote in the 14th cny—*i.e.,* 'cot among the *broom.*' See BRAMPTON and BRANCASTER.

BRANSCOMBE (Axminster). *Chart.* Brancescumb. *Dom.* Branchescome. '*Branca*'s valley.' *Cf.* Brantin Green (Aldborough), 1202 Brankstona, and next. See -combe.

BRANSTON (Burton, Grantham, Lincoln). Bur. B. 771 *chart.* Brantistun, 978 Brantestun, *Dom.* and later Brantestone. 'Town, village of *Brant* or *Brand*'; the names are the same. *Cf.* BRANDESTON. BRAN(D)SBY (N. Riding), has been identified with 910 *O.E. Chron.* Bremesbyrig. This cannot be. See rather Bromsberrow. This is *Dom.* Branzbi, 'dwelling of *Brant.*' See -by.

BRANT FELL and BRANT HOW (Bowness). O.E. *brant, bront,* 'high, steep, sheer'; while How is O.N. *haug-r,* 'mound, cairn.' *Cf.* Great How, and MAESHOW (Sc.). See -fell.

BRANTINGHAM (Brough, Yorks). *Dom.* Brentingeha', Brentingham, Brendingham. *c.* 1180 *Ben. Peterb.* Brentingeham. 'Home of the *Brentings,*' or descendants of Brent. *Branting, Brenting,* and *Brant* are all in *Onom. Cf.* R. BRENT.

BRANTON (Alnwick). *Cf.* 1157 *Pipe* Brantona (Devon). 'Town of *Brant.*' See above.

BRAUNSTON (Oakham and Rugby). Not in *Dom.* 1298 Braunteston. *Cf. B.C.S.* 712 Branteswyrth. 'Town of *Brant* or *Brand.*' *Cf.* above and BRANSTON.

BRAWBY (Malton). *Dom.* Bragebi. 'Dwelling of ?' See -by.

BRAWDY (Pembroke). *c.* 1188 *Gir. Camb.* Breudi. Prob. W. *brwyd,* 'full of holes.' T. Morgan conjectures O.W. *brawd dy,* 'judgment house' or 'court.'

BRAY (Maidenhead). *Dom.* Brai; *later* Braie, Broy, Bray. Perh. = Sc. *brae.* See BRAFIELD. Skeat agrees with this, and connects with O.E. *bráw;* Mercian *brēg,* ' an eyebrow.'

BRAYTON (Carlisle and Selby). Sel. B. *Dom.* Bretone, Brettan. Perh. ' Brae-town.' See BRAY.

BREAGE with GERMOE (Helston). Fr. St. *Breaca* and her companion who landed forcibly, as missionaries from Ireland, at the mouth of the Hayle R., *c.* 500.

BREAN DOWN (Weston-s.-M.). Tautology. W. *bre,* ' a hill, a brae '; pl. *breon.* The R. BREAMISH, Northbld., prob. contains this root, or else *bryn,* a' slope '; *n* so easily changes into *m,* and will mean ' slope, brae, with the stream ' or ' water.' *Cf.* G. *uisge,* pron. ūshge, ' water.' There is also The BREAM, For. of Dean, *old* Le Breme. *Eng. Dial. Dict.* gives for *bream* ' an elevated place exposed to wind,' which quite suits *breon.*

BRECKNOCK or BRECON. 916 *O.E. Chron.* Brecenanmere, 1094 *Brut y Ty.* Brecheniauc, *a.* 1100 Brechennium, *c.* 1188 *Gir. Camb.* Brecheniauc, Brekenniauc, *c.* 1540 *Leland* Brekenock, Brecknock. These last are just Eng. spellings of the orig. W. name as seen in 1094. The name comes fr. *Brychan,* son of Anlac—*i.e.,* ' the speckled ' or ' tartan-clad.' He was an Ir. prince who conquered all this region *c.* 430. The town is called both Brecknock and Brecon in 1606; but the town's W. name now is Aberhonddu, being at the confluence of Honddu and Usk. One of K. Arthur's battles in *c.* 800 *Nennius* was Cat Bregion, near the mountain Breguoin. Some hold that these are the same names as the above. The -ock prob. represents a W. dimin.

BREDON (Tewkesbury) and BREDON FOREST (Wilts). *Bede* Briudun, 781 Breodune, *Dom.* Breodun, *c.* 1188 *Gir. Camb.* Briodun. Tautology, W. *bre,* and O.E. *dún,* ' hill.' But B. Forest is 905 *O.E. Chron.* Bradon, Braeden; which may mean ' hill with the brow or brae or cliff.' See BRAFIELD.

BREDWARDINE (Hereford). ' Farm of *Brid,*' 2 in *Onom.* See -wardine.

BREEDON-ON-THE-HILL (Ashby-de-la-Z.). *a.* 1100 Bredun. A triple tautology, for W. *bre,* O.E. *dún,* and Eng. *hill* all mean the same.

BREMHILL (Calne). 940 *chart.* Brembelwerna must have been quite near here, fr. O.E. *brémel, brembel,* ' the bramble or blackberry,' and Bremhill *might* be corrup. of this. Only it is prob. *Dom.* Breme, for which see BRAMBER.

BRENT R. (Middlesex) and BRENTFORD. 705 *Lett. Bp. Waldhere,* Breguntford ; 918 *O.E. Chron.* Braegent forda ; 1016 *ib,* Brent forda. This first half is W. *bre,* a ' hill,' a ' brae '; the second may be *gwyn, gwen,* ' clear, bright '; but perh. more prob. fr. W. *gwantu*, 'to sever,' or *gwant*, 'a butt, a mark.' The name of the tribe *Brigantes*, who dwelt N. of Humber, looks like the same name.

BRENT KNOLL (Axbridge). *c.* 708 *Grant K. Ine* Mons qui dicitur Brente. O.E. *brant, bront*, 'high, steep, sheer'; and *cnol*, 'knoll, knowe, hill.' Not the same as next. But Brand or Brent Ditch (Cambs), is the same word. Rhys inclines to connect the Brents with O.W. *breni*, 'a prow.'

BRENTWOOD (Chelmsford). Not in *Dom.* Prob. 'burnt wood,' fr. *burn* vb, 4-6 *brenne*. *Cf.* Brandwood (Rossendale), *c.* 1200 Brendewod, and **BURNTWOOD**.

BREPPER (Cornwall). See **BARRIPPER**.

BRERETON (Rugeley and Sandbach). *a.* 1300 Breredon. 'Brier, bramble hill,' O.E. *brer, brœr*, 3-9 *brere*. See -don.

BRETFORD (Coventry). *Sic* 1180, and **BRETFORTON** (Honeybourne). 709 *chart.* Bretferton, 714 Brotfortun, 860 Bradferdtun, *Dom.* Bratfortune, 1275 Bretforton. A little doubtful; it may be = **BRADFORD** -ton. But quite likely 'Ford of *Bret*' or '*Briht*.' *Brett* is still a common, personal name. *Cf.* Brettell, *sic* 1614, Kingswinford. It may simply mean 'Briton.' *Cf.* **BRAFFERTON** and **BRITFORD**.

BRETTENHAM (Suffolk). *Dom.* Bretenhame, and **BRETTON** (Wakefield). Wa. B. *Dom.* Brettone. 'Home' and 'town of the Briton,' O.E. *Bret. Cf.* **BRITAIN**.

BREWOOD (Stafford). *Dom.* Brevde, *a.* 1200 Breo-, Brewude, *a.* 1300 Brewode. Hybrid; W. *bre*, 'a hill,' and -wood. The Sc. *brae* is fr. O.N. *brá* '(eye) brow.'

BRIDGENORTH. 912 *O.E. Chron.* Bricge, *c.* 1120 *Hen. Hunt.* Bruge; *a.* 1145 *Orderic* Brugia, all meaning 'bridge.' *North* prob. added *c.* 1090 by Robert of Bellesne, to distinguish this place from his father's castle at Quatbridge, 3 miles to S. We have *c.* 1350 *chart.* Brugenorth.

BRIDGERULE (Bude). Not in *Dom. Old* Lan Bridget, or 'church of St. *Bridget*, or *Brigida*, or *Bride*,' of Kildare, A.D. 453-523. It was granted at the Conquest to one *Raoul. Cf.* **ABBOTRULE**, (Sc.)

BRIDLINGTON. *Dom.* Bretlinton (4 times); *Sim. Dur.* contin. ann. 1143 Brellintun; 1200 Bridlinton. Prob. named fr. a man, but his name is doubtful. Prob. O.E. *Bretelan tun*, 'town of Bretel,' one such in *Onom.* See -ton.

BRIDPORT. 1156 Bridep't. 'Harbour on the R. *Brit*,' which is prob. W. *brith*, 'spotted, parti-coloured.' Connexion with **BRITAIN** is uncertain. We get the root again in Little Bredy, near by. *Dom.* Litelbride.

BRIDSTON (Herefordsh.). Not in *Dom.* 'Town, village of St. *Bridget*.' See **BRIDGERULE**.

BRIGG (Lincolnsh.). Not in *Dom.*, but ' Bruge ' (Cheshire). O.E. *brycg*, Sc. *brig*, ' a bridge.' *Cf.* Briggate (Leeds and Knaresboro').

BRIGHAM (Cockermth. and E. Riding). E. Rid. B. *Dom.* Bringeha'. Prob. ' home of *Brine*.' *Cf.* BRININGHAM.

BRIGHTLINGSEA (Colchester). Local pron. Bricklesey. 1223 *Patent R.* Brichtlingese; 1521 Bryghtlyngsey. ' Isle of *Beorhtling*,' not in *Onom.*, where we have only noted *B.C.S.*, 1282 Brihtulfing tun; whilst *Dom.* has Brictriceseia, fr. the common *Beorhtric.* The *r* here has changed into its kindred liquid *l*, and the patronymic -ing has been added, after *Dom.* No less than 193 variants of the name are said to have been enumerated. See -ea.

BRIGHTON and BRIGHTHAMPTON (Oxon) and BRICKHAMPTON (Gloster). All three practically the same name ! Brighton is *Dom.* Brichelmestone, Bristelmeston (on the *st* see p. 26), ' Stone of *Brihtelm*,' var. of the common *Beorhthelm.* There was a *Brithelm*, Bp. of Chichester, in 956. Called Brighthelmstone as late as 1834, and Brighton as early as 1660. B. Oxon is *old* Brighthelmstone, and B. Gloster is *c.* 1230 Brithelmetun. But Breighton, (E. Riding) is *Dom.* Bricstune Briston, fr. *Bricsi* or *Beorhtsige, cf.* BRIXTON. See -ton which often inter-, changes with -stone.

BRIGHTWALTON (Lambourn). 939 *chart.* Beorhtwaldingtune; 1086 Bristwoldintona; *Dom.* Bristoldestone; also Brictewalton. 'Town of the descendants of *Beorhtweald*,' very common in *Onom.* *Bristwoldus*, is known var. of *Beorhtweald. Cf.* next. *Dom.* regularly writes *st* for a guttural.

BRIGHTWELL (Wallingford and Oxon). Ox. B. 947 *chart.* Beorhtan wille; also æb Berhtanwellan, which *chart.* translates ' declaratam fontem '—*i.e.*, ' clear, bright well.' O.E. *beorht, berht,* ' bright.' Wa. B. *Dom.* Bristowelle (*Dom.* always avoids gutturals and usually has *st* for *gh*). *Later* Brictewell.

BRIGSTOCK (Thrapston). 1160 *Pipe* Brichestoc. ' Place of *Brica* '; one in *Onom. Cf.* BRIXWORTH, and *Dom.* (Bucks) Bricstoch; and see -stock.

BRILL (Thame). 1155-57 *Pipe* Bruhella, -hulla; 1231 Brehull. ' Hill,' or else ' nook' (see -hall) ' on the brow or brae '; lit. the eyelid, O.E. *bráew, bréaw. Cf.* 1158-59 *Pipe* Northbld. Briehelle, *Dom.* Essex, Bruheleia, and BEAL.

BRIMHAM ROCKS (Harrogate). ' *Brim*'s home.' *Cf. B.C.S.* 64 Brimes dic. Locally, *brim* means ' a high place exposed to weather,' cognate with Eng. *brim*, first found *c.* 1205 *brimme;* origin doubtful. *Cf.* next.

BRIMPSFIELD (Glostrsh.) and BRIMSCOMBE (Stroud). *Dom.* Brimesfelde. *Old* Brimmescombe. ' Field ' and ' valley of *Brim*.'

Cf. a. 1000 *chart.* Brimhirst (Leicestersh.), Brimstage (Chesh.), BOOMSBERROW, and above. The man's name is a little uncertain. See -combe.

BRIMPTON (Reading). 944 *chart.* Bryningtune, *Dom.* Brintone, *a.* 1300 Brimpton. 'Town of the sons of *Brini.*' *Cf.* BRINGTON. For interchange of *n* and *mp cf.* BAMPTON.

BRINDLE (Chorley). 1227 Brimhill, 1228 Burnehull, 1254 Brunhull, 1356 Burnhull, 1584 Brindle. The *d* is thus quite late, and the name is 'hill of the burn' or 'brook,' O. E. *bryn*, var. of *burna.* *Cf.* -bourne. There is also a Brindle Heath (Salford). BRINE-TON (Shiffnal) is *Dom.* Brunitone; *a.* 1300 Bruneton, which is prob. 'town of *Brun*' or 'Brown.' *Dom.* Yorks, Brinitun and Brinnistun is now Burniston.

BRINGTON (Hunts). *Dom.* Breninctun. 'Town of the sons of *Brini*' or '*Brine.*' *Cf.* BRIMPTON and next; and see -ing.

BRININGHAM (Norfk.). *Dom.* Bruningahā. 'Home of *Bruning*' or 'of the sons of *Brun*'; both names common in *Onom.*, which also has *Brine,* and *Brin* as var. of *Beorn.* *Cf.* BRIGHAM; and see -ing.

BRINKBURN (on R. Coquet) and BRINKWORTH (Chippenham). 1150 Brink(e)burne, 1183 Brenkburna; 1065 *chart.* Brinkewrtha. 'Brook' and 'farm,' at the edge' or '*brink,*' a N. word. See *Oxf. Dict. s.v.* The above are the earliest instances of it in Eng. There is no name like *Brink* in *Onom.*, though there is a *Brica, -an.* But *Brink* is a Du. quasi-personal name, as in the well-known Prof. Ten Brink; *brink* in Du. has the same meaning and root as the Eng. word. Thus the above names might mean 'brook' and 'farm of Brink.' However, the 1183 form Brenk-leans towards O.N. *brekka,* 'hillside, slope,' Dan. *brink,* 'steepness, precipice, declivity.' See -bourne and -worth.

BRINKLOW (Rugby). *Cf.* above. *a.* 1200 Brinchelau, 1251 Brinck-lawe; also thought to be the 'Bridelawe,' *c.* 1188 in *Gir. Camb.* If so the form will be corrupt, and also nasalized since that time. *Brink* is Norse, and means, 'edge, border of a steep place'; here a huge tumulus or burial-mound, O.E. *hlœw.* See -low, and above.

BRINSCALL (Chorley), BRINSCAR (Lancs), 1228 Brunesgare, BRINS-FORD (Wolvermptn. and Lutterworth); Wol. B. 994 Bruns-, Brenesford; 1227 Bruneford; 1381 Bruynesford. Lut. B. *old* Brunesford; BRINSLEY (Notts); *Dom.* Bruneslei, and BRINS-WORTH (Rotherham), 1202 Brinesford. Prob. all fr. men named *Brun* or 'Brown,' a common O.E. name. One *Brun* was *Dom.* tenant of Brownsover ('bank'), Rugby. Brins-call's ending, without old forms, is uncertain, but -ear is O.N. *kjarr,* 'copsewood, brushwood'; or N. *kjœrr, kjerr,* 'marsh, wet copse.' Wyld and Hirst omit both Brinscall and Brinscar, but give BRINDLE in the same district. For the other endings see -ford, -hall, and -worth ('farm').

BRISTNALL (Smethwick). *a.* 1300 Brussenhulle, which is prob. ' bursten' or ' broken hill.' O.E. *berstan,* ' to burst,' past tense 4-6 *briste, brust,* pa. pple., 4-5 *brusten, brosten;* dial. *brossen.* *Cf.* BURSTWICK. See also -hall.

BRISTOL. 1052 *O.E. Chron.* (Worc.) Brycgstow, *Dom.* Bristou. *a.* 1142 *Wm. Malmesb.* Bristow, *c.* 1160 *Gest. Steph.* Bristoa; *c.* 1188 *Gir. Camb.* Bristollum. *Brycg-stow* is O.E. for ' bridge-place.' It is interesting to see the *-ow* change into the liquid *-ol.*

BRITAIN. 345 B.C. *Aristotle* αἱ βρετανικαὶ (*v. r.* Πρετ-) νῆσοι, 55 B.C. *J. Cæsar* Britannia, *c.* 50 B.C. *Diod. Sic.* Βρεττανία, A.D. 43. *Lett. of Claudius* κατὰ Βρετάννων. *O.E. Chron.* ann. 495 Bretene, ann. 755 Bryttisc (= British). W. *inis Prydain,* ' isle of Britain.' *Prydain* is the Brythonic form of Ir. *Cruithni,* usual Ir. name of the Picts; but whether this is really connected with the name *Britain,* and what that name means, is doubtful.

BRITFORD (Salisbury). 1065 *O.E. Chron.* Brytforda, Brytan forda; *a.* 1100 Brethevorde. ' Ford of the *Briton* '; the *th* in the latest form cited is a common Norm. softening. *Cf.* BRET-FORD.

BRIXTON. *K.C.D.* 940, Brihtricestan, ? which. Surrey. is *Dom.* B Brici-, Brixistan, ' stone of *Beorhtsige,*' a common name, found also as *Byrcsige, Brehtsig, Bryxie,* and *Brixius.* Plymouth B. *Dom.* Brictricestone, Bedricestone. ' Stone of *Beorhtric,*' another common name, found also as *Brychtrich, Brihtrig,* and *Bricxtric.* The endings -stone and -ton, *q.v.,* often interchange. BRIXTON DEVERILL (Warminster), is not in *Dom.,* but see DEVERILL. *Cf. Dom.* Bricsteuuelle, near Wallingford, ' *Beorht-sige's* well.' In *Dom.* we regularly have *st* for guttural *h* or *ch.* *Dom.* Yorks Bricstune, Briston, is now Breighton.

BRIXWORTH (Northampton). *Dom.* Briclesworde. This is prob. ' farm of *Beorhtel*' or *Berhtel,* or else *Beorhtgils,* all found in *Onom.* 1160 *Pipe* Northants has Brichestoc. *Cf.* BRIGSTOCK; and see -worth.

BROADWAS (Worcester). 779 *chart.* Bradeuuesse, -wasse, *K.C.D.* iii. 386 Bradewasan, 1218 Bradewas. O.E. for ' broad, stagnant pool.' O.E. *wase,* mod. *ooze.* *Cf.* ALREWAS.

BROADWATER (Sussex). *Dom.* Bradewatre. O.E. *brád,* ' broad.'

BROADWAY (Worc. and Ilminster). Worc. B. 972 *chart.* Bradwege and Bradanwege (a dat.). *Dom.* Bradeweia. It is on the road between London and Worcester.

BROCHURST (Warwksh.) and BROCKENHURST (Hants). War. B. 1327 Brochurst, Han. B. 1157 *Pipe* Brocheherst. ' Wood of the badger.' O.E. *broc.* *Cf.* next; and see -hurst.

BROCKLESBY (Lincs). *Dom.* Brochesbi, ' dwelling of *Brocwulf.*' *Dom.* is very careless of the liquids. *Cf.* BROXTED; and see -by.

BROCKLEY HILL (Edgeware). O.E. *Broc- léah*, 'badger meadow.' *Cf.* 674 *grant* Brocces broc and BROXBURN (Sc.). Similar is BROCKTON, Much Wenlock, *Dom.* Broctune, Brochetune, and three BROCTONS (Staffs), all *Dom.* Broctone. In all 3 Duignan prefers O.E. *bróc*, 'a brook.' Only the *o* here is long. *Cf.* Brockhill Dingle, Alvechurch, 1275 Brochole, BROCKHAMPTON (Glostrsh.), old Brochamtone, Brechampton (see HAMPTON), and BROCKWORTH, *ib. Dom.* Brocowardinge, Brockwordin; see -worth and -wardine, 'farm.'

BROKENBOROUGH (Malmesbury). [737 *chart.* To brocenan beorȝe.] 1298 Broukenbury, 1324 Brokeneberwe. 'Broken'—*i.e.*, presumably 'rugged hill.' O.E. *beorg. Cf.* BARROW.

BROMFIELD (Wigton and Salop). Wig. B. *c.* 1215 *chart.* Brunefeld; 1610 Brumfield. Fr. O.E. *bróm*, 'broom, gorse,' rather than *brún*, 'brown.' *Cf.* next; *m* and *n* freely interchange.

BROMLEY (Kent, Stafford, etc.). 862 *chart.* Bromleaȝ (near Langley). Staf. B. 1004 *chart.* and *c.* 1097 *Flor. Worc.*, Bromleage, -lege. *Dom.* Brunlege. Kent B. *Dom.* Brunlei, Bronlei. As above, 'broom meadow' and not 'brown meadow.' There is also KING'S BROMLEY (Lichfield), 942 *chart.* Bromlege, Bromli, *Dom.* Bromelei.

BROMPTON (London and Northallerton). Lon. B. *a.* 1016 *Ordinance Ethelred I.* Bromdun. Nor. B. *a.* 1130 *Sim. Dur.* Bromtun. 'Broom, gorse village,' or else 'hill.' For intrusion of *p cf.* BAMPTON and HAMPTON. See -don and -ton.

BROMSBERROW (Ledbury). 910 *O.E. Chron.* Bremesbyrig; *Dom.* Brunmeberge; *c.* 1120 *Hen. Hunt.* Brimesbirih; v.r. Brunesbirih, Brismesbirith; 1284 Brommesberewe. Confusion here in both halves. The man's name in the first may either be *Brunman*, a fairly common name, or *Brem(e)*; also in *Onom.* The ending is either what is now -bury—*i.e.* '(fortified) town,' or O.E. *beorg*, 'hill,' now represented by -berrow or BARROW; *Cf.* BERRY BROW and BROMSGROVE. BROM'S ASH (S. Herefd.) is 1228 *Close R.* Bromes heff, where *heff* is 'accustomed pastureground of sheep,' same root as *heft.* See *Oxf. Dict.* s.v. *heaf,* where the earliest quot. is *c.* 1525.

BROMSGROVE. 830 *chart.* Bremes grafa, 1156 Bremes-, Brimesgraua, 1166 Bromesgrava. '*Brem*'s grove.' O.E. *gráf. Cf.* above and BIRMINGHAM.

BROMWICH. See CASTLE BROMWICH.

BROMYARD (Worcester). *Chart.* Bromgeard, O.E. for 'field covered with broom.'

BRONDESBURY (London). 1766 *Entick* Bromesbury. Prob. 'burgh, castle of *Brom* or *Brem*.' *Cf.* BROMSGROVE. *M* and *n* often interchange. *Cf.* Dum- and Dunbarton, etc.; and *d* often intrudes.

BRONGWYN (Caermarthen). W. for 'fair, clear breast,' or 'breast-like hill.' *Cf.* W. *bron goch*, 'Robin redbreast.' The W. for 'hill' is *bryn*, but both *bron* and *bryn* are used in Cornwall.

BROOK (Ashford and Godalming). *c.* 1290 *S. Eng. Legend* Robert de Brok. O.E. *bróc*, 'a rivulet.' BROOKWOOD (Woking). 1289 contin. *Gervase* Brokwode.

BROOMFIELD (Bridgwater, Salop, etc.). Sal. B. *a.* 1196 *Gir. Camb.* Brumfeld, Brid. B. 1297 *R. Glouc.* Brumefeld, 'broom-clad field.' *Cf.* 909 *chart.* Brombricge, which will be called after a man *Brom.* or *Brem. Cf.* BROMSGROVE.

BROSELEY (Salop). Not in *Dom. Old ' Burhweard's* lea,' still seen in full in Burwardsley (Chester). *Cf.* BURSLEM.

BROTHERTON (Ferrybridge, Yorks). Not in *Dom.*; but *cf. Dom.* (Norfk.) Brodercros, 'town of *Broder* or *Brother*,' 'brother' being used as a surname.

BROTTON (Yorks). *Sic* 1179-80; but *Dom.* Brotune. Prob. O.E. *broc-tún*, 'badger village.' *Cf. Dom.* Bucks Brotone.

BROUGHAM CASTLE (Appleby). Thought to be *c.* 380 *Ant. Itin.* Brocavo or Brovonacæ. But more old forms are needed. Prob. like BROUGH (Yorks), *Dom.* Burg, fr. O.N. *borg;* O.E. *burh*, 'castle, fort, 'a broch,' with the common transposition of the *r*, and so = ' castle home. *Cf.* BROUGH FERRY (Elloughton), 1202 Burgum.

BROUGHTON (14 in *P.G.*). Broughton Hacket (Pershore), 972 and *Dom.* Broctune. Edinburgh B. 1128 Broctuna. Prob. all like that in Warwk., 1285 Brocton, ' badger town.' O.E. *brŏc* is 'badger,' *brōc* is 'brook.' Duignan seems certainly wrong in deriving from *brook*, a word never used in Sc., though we have two Sc. Broughtons as well as Broxburn and Broxmouth. Broctune occurs 14 times in *Dom.* Yorks, and represents several Broughtons. Of course *Broc* may be a man's name, now Brock. However, Broughton (Eccleshall) is *Dom.* Hereborgestone, plainly a contraction fr. '*Hereburh's* (gen. *-burge's*) town.' *Cf. K.C.D.* 710 and 1298 Hereburgebyrig.

BROWN WILLY (Camelford). Said to be Corn. *bron geled*, 'conspicuous hill.' *Cf.* BRONGWYN. Perh. Willie is for Corn. *gelli* or *celli*, 'a grove.' Yet another guess is 'hill of shackles,' W. *huel* or *hual*. Names in Brown—like Brownshill (Stroud, Glouc.), and BROWNSOVER (Rugby), pron. Brownsor; see -over) —will all come fr. a man *Brun. Cf.* BRINSFORD.

BROXTED (Dunmow) and BROXSTOWE (Notts). No. B. *Dom.* Brocholvestou, Brochelestou, 1457 Brocholwestouwa, also Broweston. Both prob. ' place (Stead and STOW both mean that) of *Brocwulf.*' *Cf.* BROCKLESBY.

BROYLE, Forest of the (W. Sussex). 1399 la Broile. O.Fr. *bruill, broil ;* Mod. Fr. *breuil*, ' an enclosed piece of brushwood or matted underwood.'

Brue R. (Somerset). ? Cognate with W. *bru,* 'womb, belly'; as likely fr. a similar root to G. *bruith,* 'to boil.' *Cf.* Bruar (Sc.). For old forms see Bruton.

Bruen Stapleford (Tarvin, Cheshire). Prob. *Dom.* Brunhala, or '*Brun*'s nook,' or 'hall.' See -hall. But said to be called after the *Le Brun* family, settled here in 1230. There is a ' Brunhelle ' in *Dom.* Bucks.

Brundall (Norfolk). *Dom.* Brundala, 1460 Brundehale. ? ' *Brand's* ' or ' *Brond's* nook.' See -hall. But *cf. Dom.* Cheshire, Brunford, prob. 'ford over the bourne or burn,' and Brundala may be ' dale with the bourne '—O.N. *brunn-r dal-r.* Horsfall Turner seems to identify all the numerous Bruntons or Brunetonas in *Dom.* Yorks with Bromptons. But one Brunton (Yorks) is 1166-67 *Pipe* Birunton, ' town of *Birun* ' or ' *Byron.*' The Buruns, or Biruns, held lands in Notts, Derby, and Lancs as early as *Dom.*

Bruton (Somerset). *Dom.* Breuutona, 1471 Brewton. ' Town on the R. Brue.'

Bryncoch (Neath). W. = ' red hill.' W. *bryn,* O.G. *brun,* Corn. *bron, bryn,* ' a hill.' *Cf.* Brongwyn, and Brynmor, ' hill slope by the sea.'

Bubbenhall (Kenilworth). *Dom.* Bubenhalle. ' Hall of *Buba* ' or ' *Bubba.*' See -hall.

Buckerell (Honiton). Not in *Dom.* 1166-67 *Pipe* Bucherel. More old forms needed. Perh. ' nook of *Bucard,*' one in *Onom.* The -el could be fr. *hale* or -hall, *q.v.*

Buckingham. 915 *O.E. Chron.* Buccingahám, 1154-61 *chart.* Buchingham, 1297 Bukingham. ' Home of the *Buccings.*' Patronymic, fr. *Bucca* or *Bucco,* both in *Onom. Cf.* 1179-80 *Pipe* Parva et Magna Bukesbi (Yorks).

Buckland (9 in *P.G.*). Faringdon B. *B.C.S.* iii. 205 Boc land, 1292 Bokeland. Devon B. *Dom.* Bochelanda. Betchworth B. *Dom.* Bochelant; also *Dom.* Glostr. and Bucks, Bocheland. O.E. *bóc-land,* ' book land,' land granted by a ' book ' or written charter to a private owner. *Cf.* Bockhampton.

Bucklebury (Reading). *Dom.* Borgedeberie, 1316 Burglildeburg, ' burgh of *Burghild* '; perh. daughter of Cenwulf, King of Mercia, 796-819. The old Icknield St., between Saintsbury and Newcomb, and also N. of Bidford, is called now Buckle Street, 709 *chart.* Buggildstret, 860 *ib.* Buggan stret, ' road of *Burghild.*'

Bucknell (Oxford and Salop). Ox. B. *Dom.* Buchehelle, 1149 Buckenhull (= hill), 1216-1307 Bikehell, Buckehull. Sal. B. *Dom.* Buche -hale, -halle. O.E. *Buccan hale,* ' nook, corner of *Bucca* '—*i.e.,* the He-goat. *Cf.* Buckingham. Bucknall cum

BAGNALL (Staffs) is not 949 *chart*. Badecanwell, as Birch says, but *Dom*. Buchenhole, *a*. 1300 Bukenhale, Bokenhowe, *a*. 1400 Buchenhole, and so the same as above. Only here the ending varies between -hale (see -hall) and -hole, softened into -howe. O.E. *hol, holh,* ' a hollow.'

BUDE HAVEN (N. Cornwall). Not Budecalech (see BUTLEIGH). Prob. same root as W. *bwth,* ' a hut,' G. *both,* ' a house '; Eng. *booth,* first found *c*. 1200 as *bode.*

BUDLEIGH SALTERTON (Devonsh.). *Dom*. Bodelie, ' *Boda's* lea ' or ' meadow.' See -leigh. *Cf*., too, 693 *Grant* Budinhaam, prob. in Essex, BUDBROOK (Warwick), *Dom*. Budebroc, and *Dom* Essex, Budcerca. BUDBY (Notts), *Dom*. Butebi, and 1166-67 *Pipe* Butebroc (Essex) are fr. a man *Butti,* a N. name.

BUDOCK (Falmouth). *Sic* 1536. Prob. a Keltic dimin. = ' little hut.' *Cf*. BUDE.

BUGSWORTH (Stockport). ' Bugga's farm.' *Bugga* is said to be a pet contraction of St. *Eadburga. Cf*. Bugthorp (E. Riding), *Dom*. Bughetorp, 1166-67 *Pipe* Buit-, Buttorp, also Bugbrooke (Weedon). See -thorpe and -worth.

BUILTH (Llandrindod). *a*. 1000 Buelt, *c*. 1100 *Ir. Ninnius* Boguelt, *a*. 1196 *Gir. Camb*. Bueld, *a*. 1600 Byellt. In W. Llanfair Ym Muallt. W. *buw-allt,* ' steep place, cliff (L. *altus,* ' high ') of the cattle.' The Nennius form will be fr. W. *gallt= allt.* Buelt was that part of Powys between Wye and Severn. *Cf*. BUILD-WAS (O.W. *gwas,* ' a servant '), Abbey, Wroxeter. This abbey dates fr. 1135.

BULKINGTON (Nuneaton). *Dom*. Bochintone, 1232 Bulkintone. Doubtful; but prob. ' town of *Bulca*.' *Cf*.*B.C.S*. 225 Bulcan pyt.

BULL GAP (Derbysh.). Thought to be a tautology. Bull= W. *bwlch* (G. *bealach*), ' a gap, a pass, a broken cut.' *Gap* is an O.N. word, not recorded in Eng. till *c*. 1380, which makes the idea of a tautology decidedly doubtful. BULL HOW (Westmld.) is thought to be fr. a Norseman, *Böl*—i.e., ' The Bull '; O.N. *bole, boli.* How is ' mound, hill.' See -how.

BULLINGDON (Oxford and Hants). Ox. B. ? *c*. 1097 *Flor. Worc*. ann. 1053 Bulendun, 1216-1307 Bulen, -Bulingden, Bolinden. Han. B. ? *Dom*. Bolende. ' Hill of *Bula*.' *Cf*. 1233 *Close R*. Buleworthy (Devon) and BULLEY (Glostrsh.), *Dom*. Bule-leye. See -ing and -worthy.

BULMER (York and Suffk.). See BOMERE.

BUNGAY (Suffk.). Not in *Dom*. 1460 Bowunggey. Prob. Skeat is right in deriving fr. Icel. *bunga,* ' a round hill, a bing,' and *ey,* ' island, peninsula.' The site supports this. Certainly it is not Fr. *bon gué,* ' good ford.' 1460 might suggest derivation fr. some unknown man, perh. a nasalized form of *Buga. Cf. Dom*. Sussex, Bongetune. See -ay.

BUNHILL (London). *Old* Bonhill. Doubtful. *Cf.* BONCHURCH, BONSALL, and BOWNHILL.

BUNNY (Nottingham). *Dom.* Bonei, 1228 *Close R.* Boneya, 1284 Boneye. Might be O.N. *bón-ey,* ' prayer isle.' *Cf.* next. But perh. fr. O.E. *bune,* ' a reed, the stem of the cow-parsnip '; it is only once given with an *o,* in 1388. See *bun* sb[1]. However, we have 1166-67 *Pipe* Boueneia (Oxon), which must be ' isle of *Bofa,*' gen. *-an,* a fairly common name. See *-ey.*

BUNWELL (Norfolk). Not in *Dom.* 1444 Bonewell, 1477 Bonwell. ' Prayer-well '; O.E. *bén,* O.N. *bón,* ' a prayer '; in Eng. 2-7 *bone,* 3-4 *bon. Cf.* BONCHURCH and above.

BURBAGE (Buxton, Hinckley, and Marlboro'). Hin. B. *Dom.* Burbece (also in *Dom.* Sussex). Mar. B. 961 *chart.* Burhbece; O.E. for ' burgh, castle on the beck ' or ' brook '; *Dom.* Burbetce. The more regular form would be Burbeck, still a surname; but *Oxf. Dict.* gives *beck* as a name found only in those parts of England once in Danish or Norse occupation. See *-bach, -beck.*

BURBURY HILL (Swindon). *O.E. Chron.* ann. 556 Beranburh or -byrig (see BARBURY HILL), which is perh. meant. May be fr. a man, *Beorga* or *Berga,* or *Bæra.* But BURCOTE (Bromsgrove) is *Dom.* Bericote, 1275 Byrcote. Prob. O.E. *bere-cote,* ' cot for storing bere or barley.' *Cf.* BERWICK.

BURDEN (Durham). *a.* 1130 *Sim. Dur.* Byrdene, 1197 Bireden. ' Dean, (woody) valley,' O.E. *denu,* ' with the house,' O.E. *búr,* the mod. Eng. *bower,* and Sc. *byre.*

BURFORD (Oxford). *O.E. Chron.* ann. 752 Beor-, Beorgford; *chart.* Bergford; *c.* 1120 *Hen. Hunt.* Bereford, 1231 Bureford. O.E. *burg, burh,* O.N. *borg,* ' a shelter-place, fort, burgh '; fr. O.E. *beorgan,* ' to protect.' See *-burgh.*

BURGH (Lincoln, Westmld., etc.). Lin. B. *Dom.* Burg. West B. *c.* 1175 *Fantosme* Burc, *c.* 1180 *Bened. Peterb.* Burgus. ' Castle, fortified dwelling.' See above. *Cf. Dom.* Surrey Berge, ? ' the Borough '; and *ib.* Essex, Burghstede.

BURGH CASTLE (Gt. Yarmouth). *Bede* Cnobheresburg id est, ' Cnobher's Town.' See BURFORD.

BURGHCLERE (N. Hants). *B.C.S.* 674 Clere, and *Dom.* often Clere. These may represent this place, or Highclere or Kingsclere near by. The Eng. adj. *clear* is fr. Fr., and is not found till 1297. This must be W. *clegr, clegyr,* ' a rock.'

BURGH-ON-SANDS (Carlisle). *c.* 1175 Burc; 1356 *Scalacronica* Burch sure le Sabloun (Fr. *sablon,* ' sand '). Now pron. Bruff. Thought to be *Sim. Dur.* ann. 792 Aynburg. *Cf.* AINTREE. Brough (Yorks) is *Dom.* Burg.

BURLEY (Leeds, Oakham, Hereford, Ringwood). Le. B. *Dom.* Burghelai. He. B. *Dom.* Burlei. ' Meadow with the *burgh* or castle.' See above and *-ley.*

BURLINGHAM (Norwich). *Dom.* B'lingahā, 1452 Byrhyngham, 1454 Suth birlyngham. 'Home of the *Birlings*.' See BIRLING and -ham.

BURMINGTON (Shipston-on-Stour). *Dom.* Burdintone, 1413 Burmynton. Doubtful. Duignan thinks ' *Burhman's* town.' A *burh-* or *burgman* was one who lived in a burgh or town.

BURNHAM (Chiltern). *Sic c.* 1018 *chart., Dom.* Burne-, Bernehā. Prob. O.E. *burna-hám,* ' house, home beside the spring, well,' or ' stream.' See -bourne.

BURNTWOOD (Lichfield). *a.* 1600 Brend-, Brandwood. *Brand, brent,* etc., are M.E. pa. tense of *burn. Cf.* BRENTWOOD and BARNHURST. In 1262, says Duignan, a Forest jury find ' a certain heath was burnt by the vills of Hammerwich (Burntwood's parish), to the injury of the King's game.'

BURRAGE TOWN (Plumstead). 1355 'Bartholomew de Burghest,' 1370 Burwash; also Burrish, Borage. The first syll. is prob. O.E. *burh,* ' fort, burgh '; but the ending is quite uncertain. Earlier forms are needed.

BURRINGHAM (Doncaster) and BURRINGTON (Bristol and Chumleigh). Old forms needed. Chu. B. *Dom.* Buretone. Donc. B. (not in *Dom.*) might be fr. Ralph de *Burun* (now *Byron*), who had lands in Notts in *Dom.* In *Onom.* we also find the names *Burwine* or *Beornwine,* and *Burro,* which are all possible origins; so is *Burga,* gen. *-an.* See -ham and -ton.

BURROUGH (Melton Mow.). *Dom.* Burgo. Prob. *burgh-hoe,* or ' castle hill.' See -burgh and HOE. BURROW (N. Lancs) is *Dom.* Borch = BARROW.

BURRY PORT (Carmthn.). Possibly the Eng. *burgh* or -bury, *q.v.* But it might easily be W. *bur gwy,* ' wild, frothy water '; whilst W. *bur* is var. of *bar,* ' top, summit.' Indeed, it is close to Penbre, ' head of the hill.'

BURSCOUGH (Ormskirk). *Sic. c.* 1200, but 1189-96 Burscogh, 1292 Burskew, 1306 Burscow. ' Wood of the *burh* ' or ' fort '; O.N. *skog-r,* Dan. *skov,* ' a wood.' See SHAW. For ending -scough *cf.* Swinscoe (Ashbourne), *a.* 1300 Swyneskow, -eschoch. See -burgh.

BURSLEM. *Dom.* Barcardeslim (scribe's error), *a.* 1300 Bur-, Borewardeslyme, *a.* 1400 *Tunstall R.* Borewaslym. O.E. *Burhweardes hlimme,* ' Burward's stream.' *Cf.* BURWARDSLEY and LYME.

BURSTALL (Ipswich). *Cf.* 1157 *Pipe* Burchestala (? Beds.). ' Place of the burgh ' or ' castle '; O.E. *steall, stæl,* ' place, stall.' See -bury. BURSTON (Diss), *Dom.* Burstuna, has presumably a similar origin. Or it may be fr. a man, *Burh* or *Burg.*

BURSTON (Stone and Diss). St. B. *a.* 1200 Burweston, *a.* 1300 Burceston, Buregeston, Bureweston, *a.* 1400 Bureston. *Dom.* has

Burouestone, almost certainly this place, though in the wrong Hundred. It must mean ' town of *Burga*,' one in *Onom. ;* or Burege-, Burwe-, may be a contraction of *Burgweard,* or some other of the many names in Burg-. Old forms needed for the Diss name.

BURSTWICK (Hull). *Dom.* Brostewic, Brocstewic. ' Burst or broken dwelling.' See BRISTNALL and -wick.

BURTON (23 in *P.G.*) Warwk. B. *Dom.* Bortone, Salop. B. *Dom.* Burtune. Pembroke B. *c.* 1188 *Gir. Camb.* Bertune. There are 29 instances in *Dom.* Yorks, all Burtone, or -tun. Also BURTON-ON-TRENT. *c.* 1180 *Bened. Peterb.* Burtona; monastery founded here, 1004. They are all O.E. *burh-tún,* ' fortified dwelling-place.' *Cf.* BO'NESS (Sc.) and BURGH. BURTON AGNES (Yorks) is 1281 *Close R.* Anneys-burton. However, Burton, Bamboro', is originally Burnulfeston.

BURWARDSLEY (Chester). 1280 *Close R.* Borewardesleye, ' Meadow of *Burhweard.*' *Cf.* BURSLEM and BURWARTON (Bridgnorth); and see -ley.

BURWELL (Cambridge). *Dom.* Burewelle, 1346 Burgewelle, 1521 *Bury Wells* Berwill. Prob. ' burgh well '; with form 1521 *cf.* Bertune, old form of BURTON. It prob. stands where K. Stephen afterwards built a castle; *burge* is gen. of O.E. *burh.*

BURY, also BURY ST. EDMUNDS. 1066 *O.E. Chron.* Byrtune (= BURTON). *Dom.* ' In Beccles villa abbatis sancti Edmundi,' also, ' burgo ht abb. sci edmundi '; 1450 Bury Seynt Edmond, 1480 *Bury Wills* Bury. Bury is O.E. *burh,* ' castle, burgh.' St. *Edmund* is Edmund the Martyr, K. of the East Angles, slain at Hoxne by the Danes in 870. *Cf.* BROUGHAM.

BUSCOT (Lechlade). *Dom.* Boroardescote, *c.* 1540 Burwardscott. ' Cot, cottage of *Burgweard.*'

BUSHBURY (Wolverhmptn). 994 Biscopesbry, *Dom.* Biscopesberie, (Warwk.), *c.* 1300 Bishbiri, Bischbury, ' Bishop's burgh,' a curious corruption. It is still pron. Bishbiry. See -bury.

BUSHEY (Middlesex). *Dom.* Bissei. ' Byssa's isle ' or ' peninsula.' Both *Byssa* and *Bisi* are found in *Onom.* See -ey.

BUTCOMBE (Wrington, Somerset). Not in *Dom.* 1298 Butencumbe, which is O.E. for ' without the valley.' O.E. *butan,* M.E. *buten, bute,* ' without.' *Cf.* BINBROOK. No *But(t)a* in *Onom.* See -combe.

BUTLEIGH (Glastonbury). *c.* 725 *chart.* and *c.* 1130 *Wm. Malmes.* Budecalech, 801 Bodecanleighe, *Dom.* Bodech-, -uchelie, *Exon. Dom.* Bodecaleia. ' *Bodeca*'s lea or meadow.' See -leigh.

BUTLEY (Tunstall, Suffk.). *Dom.* Butelea. This may be ' outside the meadow.' *Cf.* Butelege, *Dom.* Cheshire, and BUTCOMBE.

BUTTERBY (Durham). BUTTERKNOWLE (Co. Durham, O.E. *cnoll-* 'hill-top, hillock, knoll,' 7-9 *knowle*), BUTTERMERE (Cocker, mouth), BUTTERSHAW (Bradford). We have grouped the names in Butter- in two sets, and give first those which almost certainly have nothing to do with *butter* sb., but come fr. some Danish or N. settler, *Butter* or *Buthar* (*Onom.* gives only one *Buterus*); he may even have been sometimes a Saxon, as we have already in 931 *chart* and in *Dom.* a Butermere (Wilts). Or some of these names, if late, may come fr. M.E. *bitoure*, O.Fr. *butor*, the bird *bittern*, in Sc. *butter*, as in Butterdean (E. Berwicksh.). Buttergask (Dunkeld), however, is G. *bothar gasc*, 'causeway-hollow'; whilst Butterstone near by is plainly fr. a man. BUTTERTON, there are 2 in Staffs, stands in debatable ground. It is *a*. 1200 Buter-, Boterton, Buterdon, 1200 Buter-, Boterdon, 1223 Butterdon, Buterden, *a*. 1300 Botredon, *a*. 1400 Butterton. The endings -don and -ton often interchange, but it is more than likely that -don is the original here. If so, a hill would much more prob. be called after a man than after *butter*. See -by and -shaw.

BUTTERLEIGH (Cullompton), BUTTERLEY (Derby), BUTTERWICK (Boston, Penrith, etc.); also BUTTERTON. See previous article. Boston B. *Dom.* Butruic, 1216 Butterwyck, 1274 Boterwyke, *c.* 1275 Boturwyk, 1410 Boterwick. *Dom.* Yorks Butruic, 1183 Buterwyk (Co. Durham). There is also a BUTTERWORTH (Rochdale). These all prob., though not certainly, mean 'meadow, dwelling, farm or village where they made butter.' O.E. *butere*, 3 *buttere*, 4 *boter*(*e*), *botter*, 5 *buttyr*, *botyr*, 4 *-butter*. See -ley, -ton, -wick, -worth, and above. With Butterwick *cf.* CHISWICK, and with Butterworth *cf.* CHESWARDINE.

BUTTINGTON TUMP (Montgomery). 893 *O.E. Chron.* Buttingtún. *c.* 1120 *Hen. Hunt.* Budingtun. *Cf. K.C.D.* 746 Bottanige. Prob. patronymic; 'town of the descendants of *Botta* or *Butta*.' Tump is W. *twmp*, 'mound, barrow.'

BUXHALL (Stowmarket). *Dom.* Bukessalla, *a.* 1200 *chart.* Bucysheal. *Cf. Dom.* Buchehalle (Salop) and BUCKNALL. '*Buca's* nook.' See -hall.

BUXTON. 1572 Buckstones. *Enc. Brit.* says prob. *Dom.* Bectune (3 times); if so, Bec- must be error for Buc-. The *Enc.* also gives as old forms Buestanes (where again Bue- must be error for Buc-) and Bawdestanes, a form which cannot represent Buxton. Prob. 'stone of the buck,' O.E. *buc*, *bucca;* and see -ton for -stone. But more evidence is needed.

BWLCH (Breconsh.). W. for 'pass, gap,' G. *bealach* or Balloch. BWLCH GWYNT (Pembk.) is 'pass of the winds,' in *old charter* Windy yete, where *yet* or *gate* also means 'pass, gap.' BWLCH-Y-FFRIDD (Newtown) is 'gap in the forest.'

BYFLEET (Weybridge). 727 *chart*. Byflete, O.E. for ' by the river.'
Cf. BEEFORD and FLEET.

BYLAND WITH WASS (Coxwold, Yorks). *Dom*. Begeland, 1156 *Pipe*
Beland, 1199 Beilande, 1228 *Close R*. Begheland, 1242 *ibid*. Bey-
land. ' Land of *Bœga* '; *cf*. BAYTON, etc. Wass is O.E. *wáse*,
' a marsh, a fen.' *Cf.* ALREWAS.

BYLEY-CUM-YATEHOUSE (Middlewich). *Old* Biveley. Doubtful.
Perh. ' meadow of *Beoba*,' 3 in *Onom*. *Cf*. Bevington, Alcester,
1316 Byvinton, *a*. 1400 Beovynton. Bive- suggests connexion
with O.E. *bifian*, O.N. *bifa*, M.E. *bive*, ' to shake, to tremble.'
See -ley. Yate- is Gate-. *Cf.* YETHOLM (Sc.).

BYTHAM PARVA (Lincs). *Dom*. Bitham, 1228 *Close R*. Bi-, By-
hamel, 1292 Parva Byham. Prob. ' by the home,' O.E.
hám. *Cf*. BYFLEET, BEEFORD, etc.; also Attewell = ' at the
well.' *Parva* is L. for ' little.'

CADAIR IDRIS (mtn., Central Wales). W. = ' seat of *Idris*,' a Welsh
hero and a great astronomer. W. *cader, cadair*, is ' a chair,'
but in O.W. and Corn. ' a cradle, a framework.' The *c* has
become *g* in Llyn-y-Gader hard by.

CADBURY (Crediton and Wincanton). Cr. C. *Dom*. Cadebirie, *c*.
1540 Cadburi. Win. C. *Dom*. Cadeberie. ' Fort, burgh of *Cada*,
Cadda, or *Ceadda* '; several so named in *Onom*. *Cf*. *Dom*.
Cadenhov (Essex) and Cadnam (Hants). See -bury.

CADNEY (Brigg). *O.E. Chron*. 675 Cedenac (late MS.), ' Isle of
Ceadda,' gen. -*an*, or ' Chad.' See -ey.

CAE ATHRAW (Caernarvon). W. = ' Field of the master or doctor ';
cae, ' a field, an enclosure.' *Cf*. Caeglas, and the curious Cae
Llwyn Grydd, Carnarvon, which is ' field of the bush of the
red wall,' *y gaer rudd*, referring to an old castle now in ruins.

CAERAU (Bridgend, S. Wales). Pl. of W. *caer*, ' fort, castle '; O.W.
also *gaer*, Bret. *ker*, G. *cathair*, ' a fort.' *Cf.* CAERLEON and
CAREW.

CAERGWRLE (Flintsh.). An old castle here, and perh. once a Rom.
station. Said to be W. *caer gwr lle*, ' castle, fort at the boundary
place '; *cwr* or *gwr*, ' a boundary '; but the ending is decidedly
doubtful.

CAERLEON-ON-USK, pron. Karleén; in W. Caer Llion ar Wysc. *c*.
800 *Nennius*, ' city of Leogis ' or ' Cair Lion,' *Dom*. Carleion'
Castell; prob. *c*. 1145 *Geoffr. Mon*. Civitas Legionum, 1167-68
Pipe Carliun, *c*. 1205 *Layamon* Kair-luine and Kair Uske, in
edit. *c*. 1275 Ceyr-lyon, 1241 Karlyun. From early times
thought to be W. *caer lleon*, ' camp of the (Roman) legions ';
and the second legion, the Augusta, is said to have been stationed
here. But the true ' city of legions ' is CHESTER, which Nennius

calls Cair ligion. So this name is 'fort on the streams'; W. *lli*, pl. *llion*, ' a flood, a stream.' There is also a Caer Leon, St. David's. The present surname Carlyon is pron. Kar-líon. *Cf.* CAERDON (Sc.).

CAER-, CARMARTHEN. In W. Caerfyrddin, *c.* 150 *Ptolemy* Μαριδύνον, *c.* 800 *Nennius* Cair merdin, 1158-59 *Pipe* Cairmerdin, *c.* 1188 *Girald* Kairmardhin, -merdhin, *c.* 1205 *Layam.* Kair Merðin, 1240 *Close R.* Calverdin, 1242 *ib.* Kaermerdin, *c.* 1330 *R. Brunne* Kermerdyn. In W. *ll* has the soft *th* sound; hence the idea which arose early that the name is 'fort of *Merlin*,' the famous wizard at K. Arthur's Court. The L. form *Merlinus* is found as early as 1148; the Mod. W. is *Myrddin*. The orig. name of Merlin's Bridge, S. of Haverford W., was Mawdlen's or Magdalen's Br. It is doubtful what this name meant in Ptol.'s day; perh. ' castle by the sea.' The *dun* is certainly = *caer*, and *mari* may be Kelt. for ' sea '; in W. *mŏr*, but in G. *muir*; gen. *mara*.

CAERNARVON or CAR-. Also in Cumberland, Beckermet, with the same meaning. In W. Caernarfon. *a.* 1196 *Gir. Camb.* Kair-, Kaerarvon; in his *Itin. Camb.* 'Dicitur Arvon, provinicia contra Mon' (or, Monia insula); 1307 Carnaruan, *a.* 1340 Kaernervan, Llywelyn's *Survey* Caer yn Arvon. W. *caer 'n arfon*, 'fort opposite Mona' or 'Anglesea'; but in the Cumbld. case the *Mona* is the I. of Man.

CAER RHUN (Carnarvonsh.). W. = ' fort of *Rhun*,' son of Maelgwyn Gwynedd, a prince of the 6th cny.

CAERWENT (Chepstow). *c.* 380 *Ant. Itin.* Venta Silurum. The -went may be W. *gwant*, ' a butt, a mark.'

CAISTOR (Norwich and Lincoln). *Dom.*, both, Castre, also Castra. Li. C. *c.* 1188 *Gir. Camb.* Castrum apud Lindeseiam. The root is, of course, L. *castra*, neut. pl., ' a camp.' But this in *Bede* is always *caestir*, and in Mercian *cester*. Mr. Anscombe has shown this implies origin rather fr. late L. *castra*, fem. sing; the Wessex *ceaster*, the Merc. *cester*, and Northumb. *caestir* all coming normally from the inflected form *castrae* through an unrecorded *caestri*.

CALBOURNE (I. of Wight). Pron. Kaalbourn. 826 *chart.* Cawle-burne, *Dom.* Cauborne. O.E. for ' burn, brook of the fish-baskets or creels '; O.E. *cawel*, *cawl*, ' a basket '; still used in Cornwall as *cawell* or *cowel*. *Cf.* PORTHCAWL. See -bourne.

CALDECOTT (Cambs) and CALDICOT(E) (Newport, Mon., and 2 in Wrwksh.). *Dom.* Cambs., Bucks, Wrwk., and Chesh., Calde-cote, which is O.E. for ' cold cot ' or ' dwelling.' Skeat says Calde- is a remnant of the dat. of O.E. *cald*, *ceald*. *Dom.* Yorks Caldecotes is now Coldcotes. *Cf.* CAULDCOTS (Sc.), and *Dom.* Norfk. Caldanchota.

CALDER R. (Cumbld. and Lancs). Prob. O.N. *kald-r,* ' cool, cold.' *Cf.* CALDBERGH (N. Yorks), *Dom.* Caldeber; see BARROW.

CALDY (Tenby). In W. Ynys Pyr. 884 *Wrmonoc* Insula Pyrus. *c.* 1188 *Gir. Camb.* Caldei; also *a.* 1196 *ib.* Enis Pir, Insula Pirri. This *Pir* must be some man. *Cf.* MANORBIER. But Cald-ei is Norse or M.E. for ' cold island.' See -ey. There is also a CALDY in Cheshire, which *may* be *Dom.* Calders, which may be connected with CALDER.

CALF HEATH (Cannock.). 994 *chart.* Calfre heie, O.E. for ' Calves' hedge.' CALDON, (Cheadle) in the same shire, is 1004 Celfdun, ' calf hill.' *Cf.* 940 *chart.* Chealfa dune (Wilts.).

CALLINGTON (Cornwall). *c.* 988 *chart.* Cællwic, *Dom.* Calwetone. *Ex. Dom.* Caluuitona. ' Town of ' ? The nearest names in *Onom.* are *Caldewine* and *Calwinus.* The charter form seems to mean ' dwelling of *Cæll.*' CALLERTON (Nhbld.) is 1073 Calverdon, 1242 Cauveredon. See CALVERTON and -don.

CALLINGWOOD (Burton-on-T.) is an unique word. *c.* 1280 Calynge-wode, Chalengwode ; in L. deeds Boscum calumpniatum; *a.* 1600 Challengewood. O.Fr. *calenge, chalenge, -onge* (fr. L. *calumnia*), ' a reproach, an accusation, then a challenge.' In Eng. *a.* 1300 *Cursor Mundi,* ' chalange.' *Cf.* THREEPWOOD (Sc.) and in Northumbld. and Cheshire, fr. *threap,* 'a (scolding) contest.'

CALLOW HILL (Blithfield, Staffs, Chippenham, etc.). Bli. C. *a* 1300 Calu-, Kalewhull, *a.* 1400 Kalughulle. O.E. *calu, calwe,* L. *calvus,* ' bald, bare.' *Cf.* Caludon, Coventry, 1327 Calwedone. There are also 3 places called Callow (Wirksworth, Hereford, and Worcestrsh. (more than one).

CALNE. *c.* 996 Calna, 1387 Calne. Doubtful. Possibly fr. W. *calen,* ' a lump, a whetstone '; or even *calon,* ' heart, centre.' COLNE (Lancs) is the same. *Cf.* CAUNTON.

CALSTHORPE (Louth). *Dom.* Caletorp, 1233 Kaltorp. ' Farm, place of a man *Calla* or *Ceolla,*' the latter a common name. See -thorpe.

CALVERTON (Nottingham and Stony Stratford). *Dom.* Notts and Bucks, Calvertone. ' Town, village of *Ceolweard.*' But Mutsch-mann prefers O.E. *calfre tún,* ' calves' town.' See -ton. But CALVERLEY (W. Riding) is *Dom.* Caverleia, -lei; it may, how-ever, be fr. the same name; or else fr. what ? *Cf.* CALLERTON, and 1160-61 *Pipe* Nhbld. Calualea. See -ley.

CAMALLAN R. (Bodmin). Corn. for ' crooked ALLAN '; the Allan and Camallan unite to form the Hayle. *Cam* is ' crooked ' in W., Corn., and G.; in W. the fem. is *gam.* But R. Cam is quite different. See CAMBRIDGE.

CAMBERWELL (London). *Dom.* Ca'brewelle; thereafter *b* is rare till 17th cny; 1199 Camwell; Camerwell, Cambwell, and Kamwell are

also found.　Doubtful; *camber*, 'slightly arched,' is impossible.
See *Oxf. Dict.*　W. *cam ber*, 'crooked pike or spit,' might be
possible, if Kelt. names were not so very rare hereabouts.
Prob. it is 'well of *Coenbeorht*,' a common O.E. name; and this
is phonetically quite admissible.　*Cf.* ALBERBURY fr. *Ealdbeorht.*

CAM R. and CAMBRIDGE.　Possibly *c.* 380 *Ant. Itin.* Camborico;
prob. O. Kelt. *camb or*, 'crooked river' (*cf.* CAMBO and ORR,
Sc.), with *ic-* adjectival.　No doubt this Rom. name influenced
scholars long after to fix the name as it now is—Cambridge.
But orig. they had no connexion.　*c.* 700 *Felix Crowland*
Gronta flumen, *Bede* Grantacastir (the mod. Grantchester is
2½ miles fr. Cambridge); prob. *a.* 810 *Nennius* Caer Grauth (for
Grant), *O.E. Chron.* 875 Grantebrycge, 1011 *ib.* Granta-
brycgscir, *a.* 1145 *Orderic* Gruntebruga, 1142 Cantebruggescir,
a. 1153 *Hist. Eli.* Cantebrigia, 1150-61 Cantabrigia, 1436 Can-
brigge, 1449 Kawmbrege, 1462 Cambryge, 1586 *Camden* Camus.
Granta is the old name for the stream now called Cam.　The
two names have gradually become assimilated, *Gr* having orig.
become *C* through Norm. mispronunciation.　Granta may be
cognate with G. *grànda*, 'ugly.'　*Cf.* ALLT GRAND (Sc.), also
GRANTOWN (Sc.); or it may perh. be connected with W. *grwnan*,
'to hum, to drone.'　*Cf.* GRANTLEY There is also a little
R. Cam, trib. of Severn, Dursley (Glostr.), 1177 Camme, 1221
Kaumne, which is Keltic *cam*, 'crooked'; and on it there is a
Cambridge, too.

CAMBO (Morpeth).　1298 Cambhou, Camou.　*Cf.* CAMBO (Sc.), 1327.
Cambou.　Keltic *camb ou*, 'crooked stream'; the *ou* is same
root as in L. AWE (Sc.), and in Eu (Normandy), *c.* 1110 Owe.
Cf. next.

CAMBOIS (Blyth), pron. Kamis.　1183 *Boldon Bk.* Camboise, -bous,
Camhus, Cammus; *later* Commes.　This is not Fr., but G.
camus, 'a bay,' as in CAMBUS (Sc.). fr. G. *cam*, O.G. *camb*
'crooked.'　*Cf.* above and Aldcambus, (Cockburnspath) 1212
Aldchambos, Aldecambus (ald = G. *allt*, 'burn ').

CAMBORNE.　*Sic.* 1536.　Prob. Corn. *cam bron*, 'crooked hill.'
Transposition of *r* is a common phenomenon.

CAMDEN TOWN (N. London).　Called, after 1791, fr. Baron Camden
of *Camden Place*, Chiselhurst (Kent), where Wm. Camden,
b. 1551, author of *Britannia*, resided.　The name may be Keltic,
cam din, 'crooked hill '; but where was the original Camden ?
Perh. Staffs, to which W. Camden's father belonged.

CAMEL R. (Cornwall, and name of village, Somerset.) and CAMEL-
FORD (N. Cornwall).　*c.* 1145 *Geoffrey Mon.* Cambula, *c.* 1205
Layamon Camelforde.　Camel is perh. Kelt. for 'crooked
stream,' in G. *cam allt*.　*Cf.* CAMBO, and GAMESCLEUCH (Sc.).
But prob. fr. a Kelt. god, *Camulos*, a deity found both in Gaul

and Britain, and giving name to Camulodunum, or COLCHESTER. Keltic rivers are much associated with deities. *Cambula,* 'crooked river,' suggests a quite possible origin for the much-disputed name Campbell. *Cf.* CAMPBELTOWN (Sc.). With Camelford *cf.* GALFORD. Near the Som. C. lay Camelot, *c.* 1440 *Lancelot* Kamalot. Here the final syll. is perh. W. *lloed,* 'a place.' It seems first mentioned *c.* 1170, in Chrétien de Troyes' *Chevalier de la Charrette. Cf.* next.

CAMERTON (Bath). *Dom.* Camelerton, 'town on the R. *Camelar'* (*sic* in 961 *chart.*). See CAMEL. The -ar is quite uncertain. But the first part is almost certainly the god *Camulos.*

CAMPDEN (Glostr.). *Dom.* Campdene. 'Wooded vale with the battle site.' *Camp* is an early loan fr. L. *campus,* 'a plain.' *Cf. Eynsham Cart.* 'To Campsetena gemæra.' See -den.

CAMROSE (Pembksh.). 1324 Kameros. W. *cam rhōs,* 'crooked moor.'

CANDOVER (Hants). Prob. 707 *chart.* (*K.C.D.* v. 40) Cendefer, 1238 *Close R.* Candevre. W. *cefn dwfr,* 'ridge by the stream.' *Cf.* CENARTH and CONDOVER.

CANÉWDON (hill, S. Essex). 1240 *Close R.* Canewedon' (and Calewedon), but *Dom.* Carendun, which Freeman thinks must be an error. The name is prob. '*Canute's* hill' or *dun.* It lies close to the site of K. Canute's or Cnut's victory at Assandun, 1016.

CANKLOW (Rotherham) and CANK THORN (Cannock). 1595 Canck Thorne, Cannock Thorne. The Cank- in both cases must be the same, one would think, as CANNOCK. If so, Canklow (not in *Dom.*) is a tautology; Kelt. and Eng. = 'hillock' or 'mound.' See -low. In Midl. dial. *cank* means 'gabble or cackle,' as of geese.

CANNINGTON (Bridgewater). *Dom.* Candetona. Prob. named fr. some man, but both his name and the present name must be much corrputed. There is nothing in *Onom.* nearer than *Coenheard.*

CANNING TOWN (Plaistow). So named from the former principal employer of labour there.

CANNOCK CHASE (Staffs). *Dom.* Chenet, 1130 Chnoc, *a.* 1200 Canot, Chenot, Chnot, Cnot, 1238 Canoc, *a.* 1300 Canok, Kannock, *a.* 1500 Cank. *Dom.* regularly spells O.E. *cn* as *chen;* and in all old MS. *c* and *t* are constantly confused. So this must be that rarity a Goidelic Eng. place-name, G. and Ir. *cnoc,* gen. *cnuic,* 'a hill, a knoll,' so common in Sc. and Ir. names. Eng. and W. place-names in Knock- are very rare, perh. only KNOCKIN. There are also KNOOK and KNUCKLAS, but they are fr. W. *cnuc* rather than G. *cnoc.* There is no trace of *u* in all the many old forms of Cannock. *Cf.* CANKLOW. Chase is O.Fr. *chace,* 'chasing, hunting, a hunting-ground, wild park-land,' not found in Eng. in this sense till 1440. *Cf.* CHEVY CHASE.

CANTERBURY. [In *Bede* iv. 5 ROCHESTER is also called Castellum Cantuariorum, *O.E.* versn. Cantwaraburhge.] *a.* 810 *Nennius* Cair Ceint [also Cantguaraland]; *O.E. Chron.* 754 Cantwareburh, *ib.* 1011 Cantwaraburh ; *Dom.* Cantorberia, *c.* 1100 *Anselm* Cantuarberia, 1258 Kant'bur', *c.* 1330 *R. Brunne* Canterbirie, 'Kent men's burgh,' *wara* meaning ' dweller in.' *Cf.* Lindiswara, Mersewara (dwellers in Romney Marsh) and Wihtwara. See -bury. In Rom. days it was called Durovernum (W. *dwr gwern,* 'river with the alders ').

CANWELL (Birmingham). *a.* 1200 Canewelle; later Cane-, Canwall, Kanewall, -well. The name may be ' well of St. *Cain* ' or '*Keyne*' or '*Keigwin.*' There was a priory and a spring here, the latter dedicated to St. Modan; but there is no note of any connexion with St. *Cain. Cf.* KEYNSHAM. W. *can, cain,* 'beautiful, clear,' seems impossible here. But the first syll. may be O.E. *canne,* a ' vessel for liquids, a can.' *Oxf. Dict.* gives only one quot. fr. O.E., and then nothing till *c.* 1375, 'a vatir-cane.' The name must thus be left doubtful; prob. it is fr. *can.*

CAPEL CURIG (Bettws y coed). *Chapel* dedicated to *Curig,* son of Ilid or Julitta; the mother shares the dedication with her son. The form Capel, O.N.Fr. *capele,* ' chapel,' late L. *cappella,* orig. ' a little cloak or cape,' reappears in CAPEL ST. MARY and ST. ANDREW (Suffk.). There is also a Capel (Dorking), as well as a *Dom.* Herefd. Capel. In Pembk., 1603 *Owen* gives Capell Castellan and C. Colman (Irish Bp. of Lindisfarne, 661).

CARÁDOC or CAER CARADOC (Salop). W. *caer Madoc,* or else *Cadoc* ' fort of St. *Madoc,*' or ' of St. *Cadoc.*' Either *M* or *C* must have been lost by aspiration. *Madoc* or *Modoc* was a disciple of St. David in Wales, and lived 558-625. *Cf.* KILMADOCK (Sc.). *Cadoc, Cadocus,* or *Docus,* another Keltic saint, lived some years in Central Scotland, and is also commemorated in Landoc (Cornwall).

CARDEN (Malpas). *Old* Carwarden; the personal name Carwardine is still found. ' Farm of *Car* ' or '*Cari,*' both in *Onom.* For a similar contraction *cf.* HAWARDEN, now pron. Harrden. See -warden.

CARDEW (Dalston, Cumbld.). *c.* 1080 Carðen. W. *Caer Dewi,* ' fort of David '; or possibly fr. *Tiw,* the Northern god of war.

CARDIFF. 1126 Kardi, 1158-59 *Pipe* Cardif, *a.* 1150 Kardid, Cairti, *a.* 1196 *Gir. Camb.* Kaer-, Kerdif, 1218, Kaerdif, 1298 Kerdife, dyf, *c.* 1450 Cayrdife. Usually said to be ' fort on R. TAFF '; but early forms make this more than doubtful. In Mod. W. it is Caerdydd, pron. Kaerdaeth. This suggests ' fort of

Didius,' general of the Romans against the Silures, the British tribe of this region, A.D. 50. This is confirmed by the fact that we now know Cardiff was a Rom. fort. The form Caer Dāf (Taff) is found only in Leland, *c.* 1550, though Caer Dyv does occur. However, there are 2 Cardeeths in Pembroke; and the learned editor of Owen's *Pembroke* declines to suggest any etymology either for these or for the plainly cognate Cardiff.

CARDIGAN. *c.* 1188 *Gir. Camb.* Ceredigion, Kerdigaun; *Brut y Tywsy.* ann. 991 Ceredigion ; 1218 Kaerdigan, 1298 *Writ* Cardygan. Said to be fr. *Caredig* or *Ceroticus,* a Welsh prince, to whom St. Patrick wrote, denouncing him for his cruelty in Ireland.

CARDINGTON (Church Stretton). *Dom.* Cardintune. 'Town, village of *Carda.*' *Cf. B.C.S.* 877 Cardan hlæw.

CARDURNOCK (Bowness, Cumbld.). G. *cathair,* W. *caer,* 'fort,' and G. *dornag,* 'by the pebbly place '; a pebble being a stone easily held in the 'fist,' G. *dorn,* gen. *dùirn. Cf.* DORNOCK (Annan, Sc.).

CAREW (Pembroke). *c.* 1188 *Gir. Camb.* Kaereu, Kerreu. The same name is pron. Cárey in Cornwall, because this is for W. *caerau,* pl. of *caer,* ' castle, fort,' where the *au* is pron. *ăy.*

CARHAM (Kelso). *a.* 1130 *Sim. Dur.* Carrum, prob. O.E. loc. ' at the carrs ' (O.E. *carr*) or 'rocks.' *Cf.* Harlow Car, Harrogate. But see -ham.

CARISBROOKE (Newport, I. of Wight). 1217 *Patent R.* Carebroc, 1218 Kaerbroc, 1224 Carrebroc, *c.* 1350 Caresbrok; but *O.E. Chron.* 530 Wihtgaræsbyrg, or -garabyrg, which means 'Wight-dwellers' burgh ' or 'castle.' It does look as if the *Wiht* had been dropped, and the rest transformed into Carisbrooke; but this is contested by Stevenson in his *Asser,* and by M'Clure. In *Dom.* the name seems to be Bovecombe. There is in 1199 *chart.* a 'Carsbrok ' near Launceston—*i.e.,* ' brook of the fort.' Possibly the first syll. is CARR *sb*[2], or CARSE, O.N. *kjarr,* ' copse-wood ' then ' bog or fen,' and not Keltic *caer,* 'fort.'

CARLETON (Pontefract and Skipton) and CARLTON (22 in *P.G.*). *K.C.D.* iv. 288 Carlatun, *ib.* 300 Carletun. *Dom.* Carlentune (Cambs.), Careltune, Carentune (Notts), Cerletune (Chesh.), Cerletone (Salop), Ceorlatona (Devon); and in Yorks, 16 times, Carletun. *a.* 1130 *Sim. Dur.* Carltun, Stockton, 1189 Karlatun (Cumbld.). O.N. *karla,* or O.E. *ceorla tun,* ' carls', churls', serfs' village.' *Cf.* CARLETON (Sc.). *Cearl* or *Ceorl* is also a personal name.

CARLISLE. *c.* 380 *Anton. Itin.* Luguvallum, *Bede* Lugubalia, *a.* 810 *Nennius* Caer Ligualia, *Taliessin* Caer Lliwelydd (so in W. still), 1092 *O.E. Chron.* (Peterb.) Carleol, *c.* 1120 *Hen. Hunt.* Carleol quae a populis Anglorum corrupte Luel vocatur, *Sim. Dur.* ann. 1122 Lingua Britonum Cairlel quae nunc Carleol

Anglice appellatur, 1129 Chaerleolium, *a.* 1145 *Order. Vit.* and *Waverley Ann.* Cardeol, *c.* 1175 *Fantosme* Karduil, 1330 *R. Brunne* Carlele, 1617 Carliell. W. Stokes says, Luguvallum is 'wall of the god Lugus.' See Lugg. And Llewellyn, of which Luel or Leol is a contraction, is prob. mod. W. for Lugu-belinos. The same name is seen in Lugdunum or Lyons. Carlisle is, of course, ' castle of *Leol.*'

CARMEL (Holywell and 2 others, Wales). Presumably all W. *caer moel,* 'fort on the bare, round hill.' T. Morgan gives none. 1160-61 *Pipe* Herefd, Cormel (*o* error for *a*) is almost certainly the same name.

CARN or CORN CAVALL (mtn., Builth). W. *carn Cabal,* ' cairn of Cabal,' K. Arthur's dog.

CARNABY (Bridlington). *Dom.* Cherendebi. 'Dwelling of' some unknown person. The nearest in *Onom.* seems *Ceolwen,* a widow; *eo* regularly becomes *a,* and liquid *l* easily turns into its kindred *r.* Another possible name is *Carthegn* or *Carthen.* See. -by.

CARNFORTH (N. Lancashire). *Dom.* Chreneford. *a.* 1250 Kerneford. Prob. ' ford of *Crina* ' or ' *Crin,*' names in *Onom.* See -ford, -forth.

CARPERBY (N. Yorks). *Dom.* Chirprebi. 'Dwelling of' some Norse man unknown. His name may perh. be represented by the mod. surname Capper, the liquid *r* having vanished; though Prof. Weekley does not think so. Very likely the orig. name is the common *Ceolbeorht,* which would suit phonetically. *Cf.* CARNABY. See -by.

CARRINGTON (Manchester and Nottingham). No. C. *Dom.* Caren-Caretune; 1179-80 *Pipe* Carenton. Seems to be ' village of *Car* or *Cari* '; both forms in *Onom.* See -ing and -ton.

CARSHALTON (Mitcham). Pron. Casehalton, Casehorton. *Dom.* Aultone, *c.* 1200 Crossalton; also Kresalton, Kersalton, Case Horton. Orig. ' old town,' O.E. *ald tún,* then ' Cross old town '; *r* continually gets transposed. With this case *cf.* Bean cross for Bean corse or Bean carse (Falkirk). CARSE (Sc.), ' low-lying land beside a river,' is found in Scotland *c.* 1200, but not in Eng. till much later, if really at all. CARSINGTON (Wirksworth) *c.* 1460 Karsynton, must be fr. some unrecorded man, *Carsa,* or the like.

CARSWELL (Newent and Gower). Ne. C. *Dom.* Crasowel, 1221 Karswelle, 1303 Cassewalle; plainly = CRASSWELL, CRESSWELL, ' water-cress well.' Go. C. is also spelt Caswell, and is prob. the same. Dr. G. Henderson, however, thinks this name to be N., with the ending N. *völl-r,* ' field,' *cf.* SCATWELL (Sc.), and the former part presumably = CARSE (Sc.). In face of the evidence above this is doubtful. There is also Karswell (**Dursley**).

CARTER FELL (Cheviots). *Sic a.* 1540. Contract. fr. G. *cearta-chair,* ' a regulator, an adjuster,' fit name for a lofty hill, fr. *ceart,* 'right, just.' Prob. also the origin of the Dhu Heartach lighthouse, Colonsay. See -fell.

CARTMELL (Ulverston). *Sic a.* 1130 *Sim. Dur.,* 1224 Kertmel. Cart is prob. connected with G. *caraid,* ' a pair ' (*cf.* CART, Sc.)—because Cartmell Fell stands in the triangle between the two streams which unite to form the R. Winster, just as the Black and White Cart unite to form the Cart in Renfrewshire. The -mell is Norse for a ' sand dune ' or ' sandbank.' See MELLIS. If Cart- be Norse too—O.N. *kart-r,* ' a cart '—it may refer to a sandbank found firm enough for a cart to cross. However, CARTWORTH (W. Riding) is *Dom.* Cheterwrde, or 'farm of *Kater.*' *Cf.* KETTERING, and see -worth.

CARY R. (Somersetsh.). 725 *chart.* Kari, *c.* 1160 Carith. Prob. W. *carth,* 'scouring ' river, the root which Dr. Mc Bain suggested for R. CART (Sc.). *Cf.* CASTLE CARY.

CASSOP COLLIERY (Coxhoe, Durham). 1183 Cazehope, ' enclosed valley of *Casa* '; one in *Onom.* See -hope. But *Dom.* Salop Cascop will be ' *Casa*'s cop '; O.E. *cop, copp,* 'top, summit, crest of a hill.' 1160-61 *Pipe* Devon has a Cassewell, ' *Casa*'s well.'

CASTERTON (Kirby Lonsdale). *c.* 380 *Antin. Itin.* Calacum; possibly *Dom.* here and Chesh. Castretone. Hybrid fr. L. *castra,* O.E. *ceaster,* ' a camp.' But CASTERNE (Ilam) is 1004 *chart.* Coetes thyrne, ' *Coet*'s thorn.'

CASTLE BROMWICH (Birmingham). *Dom.* Bromwic (under Northants), *a.* 1200 Bramewic, Bromwich, *a.* 1400 Castel Brom wych; O.E. *brom wic,* ' dwelling among the broom.' See -wich. *Castle* (*sic*) is found in Eng. as early as 1137 *O.E. Chron.* (See also p. 61.)

CASTLE CAREY (Somerset). *c.* 1120 *Hen. Hunt.* Castellum de Cari, *c.* 1160 *Gest. Steph.* 'Duo castella, Carith videlicet et Harpebren.' The personal names Carey and Carew, prob. derived from this, are interchangeable. In Cornwall Carew is pron. Carey; and we find in Berks *a.* 1300 a Nicholas Carew or Cary. See CARY. The Sc. CASTLECARY is a tautology.

CASTLE CARROCK (Carlisle). 1222 *Patent R.* Castel Kayroc. Prob. = CARRICK (Sc.). G. and Ir. *carraig,* ' a rock, a sea-cliff.' Carrick (Ayrsh.) is in *Taliessin* Carrawg.

CASTLEFORD (Yorks). Prob. 948 *O.E. Chron.* Ceasterforda. O.E. *ceaster,* L. *castra,* ' a camp.' *Cf.* Castley (Yorks), *Dom.* Castelai.

CASTLE RISING (King's Lynn). 1224 *Patent R.* Castra de Risingis, 1450 Rysyng. *Rising sb.* is not found in *Oxf. Dict.,* with the meaning of ' rising ground, hill-slope, hill,' until 1565. So prob. this is a patronymic, like Barking or Reading, ' place of the descendants of *Rhys,*' a well-known British name. *Cf.* RISBY. Its Eng. form is Rice.

CASTLETON (I. of Man). Manx *Balla Chastal*, which means the same thing. Balla is G. and Ir. *bail, baile*, 'farm, village.'

CASTON (Attleborough). *Dom.* Cas-, Kastetuna. Difficult to say what Caste- represents, unless it be that the liquid *r* has dropped, and it is -caster, *q.v.* This would be abnormal. No likely name in *Onom.*

CASTOR (Peterborough). *Dom.* Castre, 1154-61 *chart.* Castra. See CAISTOR.

CATERHAM (Croydon). *c.* 1210 Katerham, 'Home of *Kater.*' Still found as a surname. *Cf.* KETTERING, and Catterton (Yorks), *Dom.* Cadretone.

CATSHILL (Bromsgrove and Walsall). Br. C. 1275 Catteshull, *a.* 1400 Cates-, Kateshull. Wa. C. *a.* 1300 Cutteslowe (see -low), *a.* 1500 Catteslowe *alias* Cattshill; also *c.* 1220 *Elect. Hugo.* Kateshill (Bury St. Edmunds). 'Hill of *Catt, Catta*, or *Ceatta.*' *Cf.* CATFOSS (Yorks), *Dom.* Catefoss, 'ditch of *Catta*,' 'Cattestone,' *sic c.* 1200 in Norfolk, CATTON and CHATHAM.

CATTAL, Magna and Little (Yorks). *Dom.* Cathale, Cathala, Catale. 'Nook of *Catt.*' See above and -hall. Magna is L. for 'Great.'

CATTERICK (Yorks). *c.* 150 *Ptolemy* Katouraktonion, *c.* 380 *Anton. Itin.* Cataractone, *Bede* Cataracta, L. for 'cataract, waterfall '— 'juxta Cataractam usque hodie cognominatur '; *a.* 900 *O.E. vers.* Bede Cetrehta, *Dom.* Catrice, 1241 Cheteriz.

CATTON (Allendale and E. Riding). E.R.C. *Dom.* Cattune, Caton, 1179-80 *Pipe* Catton. 'Village of *Ceatta* or *Catta.*' *Cf.* CHATHAM, and 1238 *Close R.* Catteshal' (Suffolk).

CAUNTON (Newark). *Dom.* Calnestone, Carleton (an error), 1166-7 *Pipe* Calnodeston, 1241 *Close R.* Calnedon. Clearly, 'town of *Ceolnoth*,' a fairly common name. CAUSTON (Rugby) is *Dom.* Calvestone, fr. a man *Ceolf.* See -don and -ton.

CAVENDISH (Suffk.). *Dom.* Kauanadisc, Kavanadis. O.E. *Ceofan, Cafan edisc*, ' park, enclosure of *Cafa.*' *Cf.* STANDISH.

CAVERSHAM (Reading). 1219 Caveresham, 1238 Cavresham. From some unknown man. CAVERSWALL (Stoke) is *Dom.* Cavreswelle, *a.* 1200 Chavereswelle, which seems clearly ' *Cœfer*'s well.' In O.E. we have *cafer-tun*, ' a hall, court, or mansion '; but this is not likely to be the origin. *Cf.* Caversfield (Oxon). *Dom.* Yorks, Caverlei is now CALVERLEY. See -ham.

CAWOOD (Lancs and Selby). La. C. 1230 Cawude, 1346 Kawode. Sel. C. not in *Dom.* (but *Dom.* Notts Cauorde, ? ' *Cawe*'s farm '). Doubtful; but prob. either, as in CAWTHORNE, 'cold, cauld wood,' or as in CAWTON, '*Ceolf*'s wood.' *Cf.* 1233 *Close R.* 'Calwodeleg' (Devon).

CAWSAND (Plymouth), more correctly Cosdon. Might be 'hill (O.E. *dún*) of *Casa*,' the only prob. name in *Onom.*

CAWSTON (Norwich) and CAXTON (Cambridge). No.C. *Dom.* Cauestuna, Caustituna, Caustuna, 1167-68 Caustona. Cam. C. *Dom.* Caustone, 1238 *Close R.* Kaxston, 1245 Caxton. The great printer's name is often spelt Causton. Difficult. Skeat conjectures, ' village of *Cah*,' gen. *Cages. Cf. K.C.D.* ii. 137 Cahing læg. But the Nor. name at least surely comes fr. *Caua* (3), *Cawe*, or *Cawo*, all names in *Onom.* See -ton.

CAWTHORNE (Barnsley). *Dom.* Caltorne, 1202 Kale-, Kaldthorn. Prob. ' cold thorn tree '; O.E. *cald,* ' cold '; *cól,* ' cool.' But CAWTON (Yorks) is *Dom.* Caluetun, which is prob. ' town of *Ceolf.' Cf. K.C.D.* 816, Ceolfestun. It may be fr. O.E. *cealf,* ' a calf.'

CEFN COCH (Newtown). W. = ' red ridge.' CEFN LLYS (Radnor). 1246 *Patent R.* Keventhles (see p. 82). W. = ' ridge with the hall or mansion.'

CEIRIOG R. (Oswestry). W. = ' abounding in trout.'

CEMAIS, incorrectly CEMMAES (N. Pembroke, Maehynlleth, and Anglesea). Pe. C. 1222 *Patent R.* Kammeis, 1298 Kemmeys, *c.* 1550 *Leland* Kemes, 1603 *Owen* 'Kemes head called Pen Kemes pointe.' W. *cemmaes* is ' a circle for games, a circus,' said to be fr. *camp,* ' a feat, a game '; and *maes,* ' a field.' But this whole derivation is disputed.

CENARTH (Caermarthen). *c.* 1130 *Lib. Land.* Cenarth Maur, *c.* 1188 *Gir. Camb.* Canarth maur. O.W. *can arth,* ' white hill or height.'

CENTURION'S COPSE (Brading). Corrup. of ' St. *Urian's* copse.' *Cf.* POLURRIAN.

CERI (Montgomery). 1298 Kery. W. *ceri,* ' medlar-trees.' For other suggestions see T. Morgan.

CERNE ABBAS (Dorchester). *Sim. Dur.* ann. 1102 Cernel, *c.* 1114 O.E. *Chron.* Cernel, *c.* 1160 *Gest. Steph.* Cernei, 1237 Cern'. CERNEY or CERNEL is also var. of R. CHURN, *c.* 800 *chart.* Cyrnea, *c.* 1130 Cirnea. Doubtful. There is an O.Nor. Fr. *kernel,* ' an embrasure in a battlement, a battlement,' which has prob. influenced the Cernel forms. But the root of Cerne Ab. is the R. Cerne, which is prob. W., as there is a R. Cerniog (Montgomerysh.) which flows into the R. Carno. W. *carn* is ' a cairn, a heap of stones,' but this can hardly be the root here; perh. it is pre-Kelt.

CERRIDGE, The (Macclesfield). W. *cerrig,* ' a rocky ridge. *Cf.* CARRICK (Sc.).

CEVNON (Cardiff). *c.* 1550 *Leland* Kevenon. W. *cefn onn,* ' ridge of the ash-tree.'

CHACOMBE (Banbury). *Sic* 1373. Not in *Dom.* or Alexander. Prob. ' valley of *Cœc, Cec, Cecca,*' a fairly common O.E. name.

Cf. CHECKLEY. See -combe. Possibly it may be '*chalk* combe.' The hard O.E. *c* as a rule becomes the softer *ch* in Southern names.

CHADDERTON (Oldham). 1190 Chaderton, 1278 Chadreton. There is no name in *Onom.* like *C(h)ader*, so this is perh. a case of a N. gen., *Chad-r*, ' of St. Chad.' Such a gen. is very rare in an Eng. place-name, but in this case it seems confirmed by CHAT-TERLEY, which *a.* 1300 is both Chadderlegh and Chaddendelle (or ' dale '). *Cf.* CHADKIRK. However, Catterton (Yorks) is *Dom.* Cadretone; so that *Chader* may be var. of *Kater*, as in CATERHAM and KETTERING.

CHADDLEWORTH (Wantage). 960 *chart.* Ceadelanwyrth, *Dom.* Cedeneord, 1291 Chadelew'rth. ' *Ceadela*'s farm.' See -worth. *Cf.* Chadshunt (Warwksh.), 1043 Chadeleshunte; Chadbury (Evesham) 714 *chart.* Chadelburi, 860 *ib.* Ceadweallan byrig; also CHADDLETON and CHALFONT.

CHADKIRK (Stockport). [*Cf. Dom.* Cheshire, ' Sco Cedde tenuit Estun.'] ' Church of St. *Chad*,' Bp. of Lichfield (d. 672). *Kirk* is the North. form of *church*, and is here near its South. limit. But CHADWICK (Birmingham) is *a.* 1200 Chadeleswiӡ, while CHADWICK (Worcstrsh.)—there are two—are both *a.* 1300 Chadeleswick or Chadleswick; the Bromsgrove one is *Dom.* Celdvic. But CHADSMOOR (Cannock Chase) is fr. ' the blessed St. Chad.' *Cf.* CHADDERTON.

CHAGFORD (Dartmoor). *Dom.* Chageforde, and still so pron. ' *Ceagga*'s ford.' *Cf. B.C.S.* 762 Ceaggan heal.

CHALE (Ventnor). *Dom.* Cela. Perh. ' cold place.' *Cf.* O.E. *cele*, ' cold, coldness '; 2-4 *chele*, mod. ' chill '; also O.E. *cald*, *ceald*, 2-4 southern *cheald*, ' cold.'

CHALFONT (Slough). O.E. *chart.* Ceadeles funtan, *Dom.* Cel-funde, 1292 Chalfount sancti Egidii (St. Giles), 1298 Chalfhunte. ' *Ceadela*'s font, fountain, or spring '; L. *fons, -tis*. *Cf.* CHADDLE-WORTH and BEDFONT, and next. But CHALFORD (Gloucestersh.) is 1297 Chalkforde.

CHALGROVE (Wallingford). 1232 *Close R.* Chaugrave, 1240 *ib.* Chalfgrave. ' Grave,' O.E. *græf*, ' of *Ceolf*,' one in *Onom.* In mod. name endings -grove often supersedes -grave.

CHALK FARM (N. London). Originally ' *Chalcot* farm '; and Upper Chalcot mansion house survived near here till recently. Chalcot is prob. *chalk cot.* 1746 Rocque's *Map of London* has ' Upper Chalk House Lane.'

CHALLOCK (Ashford). 835 *chart.* Cealf-loca. ' Calf-enclosure ' or ' lock.' *Cf.* PORLOCK.

CHALLOW, EAST and WEST (Wantage). *Chart.* Ceawan hlæwe, 1291 Westchaulawe, 1316 Estchaulo, *c.* 1540 Westchallow. ' *Ceawa*'s mound, or burial-mound.' See -low.

CHALTON (Horndean, Hants). *Dom.* Celtone, and perh. *K.C.D.* 722 Cealhtune, for O.E. *cealc tun,* 'chalk town.'

CHAPEL-EN-LE-FRITH (Stockport). 'Chapel in the wood' or 'forest.' *Frith* is some kind of a wood. See FRITH BANK and *Oxf. Dict., s.v.*

CHAPMANSLADE (Westbury). 'Lade' or 'watercourse of the chapman,' or 'pedlar.' *Cf.* 1155 *Pipe* Hants, Chepmanneshale, 1160 -essele (see -hall), and CHEPSTOW.

CHARD (Axminster). Not in *Dom.* Perh. W. *cardden,* 'a wild place, a thicket,' fr. *cardd,* 'exile.' Possibly fr. a man *Carda,* one in *Onom.,* but it is rare for a place-name to be of this pattern. *Cf.* GOODRICH and TYDD; also CHARDSTOCK, a little to the S., *Dom.* Cerdestoche. See STOKE.

CHARFORD (Salisbury). *O.E. Chron.* 508 Cerdigesford. The Saxon ealdorman, *Cerdic* or *Ceardic* came to England in 495. But Charford (Bromsgrove) is 1275 Cherleford, 1327 Charleford. O.E. *ceorla ford,* 'ford of the churl' or 'hind'; whilst CHARFIELD (Wotton-under-Edge), *Dom.* Cirvelde, *c.* 1250 Charfelde, Baddeley derives fr. O.E. *ceart,* 'rough, fern-growing ground.'

CHARING (Ashford). 799 *chart.* Ciornincge, 940 *ib.* Cirringe, *Dom.* Cheringes. This may be 'place of the sons of *Ceorra, -an,* only likely name in *Onom.* *Cf.* Cherrington (Shipston-on-Stour), no old forms. But the earliest form suggests a river-name, formed with -ing, *q.v.,* fr. a stream called Ciorn, which would be akin to CERNE, CHURN, and CIREN-CESTER (? any such name still here. Could it be an old name of the Len, on which Charing stands ?). We also have 940 *chart.* Cyrþringhyrst (Kent). CHARINGWORTH (Ebrington) is *Dom.* Chevringaurde, *c.* 1320 Chavelingworth, which Baddeley thinks may be 'farm of the sons of *Ceafhere,*' an unrecorded name.

CHARING CROSS (London). *c.* 1290 *Q. Eleanor's Executors* Crucem de la Char-rynge. Popular etymology says, '*Chère reine,*' K. Edward I.'s tribute to his Q. Eleanor; but this is absurd. Prob. it is simply a patronymic like the above.

CHARLBURY (Oxford). *Die Heilige Engl.* Ceorlingeburh, 1197-1208 Churlebiry, 1238 Cherlebir. 'Burgh, castle of (the descendants of) *Ceorl* or *Cearl,*' a common O.E. name—*i.e.,* 'the churl'; *eo* regularly becomes *a* in mod. Eng. *Cf.* next.

CHARLCOMBE (Bath). 'Valley of *Cearl* or *Ceorl,*' lit. ' of the churl, or carl, or bondman.' See -combe.

CHARLCOTE (Stratford-on-Avon). *Dom.* Cerlecote; in Salop, too. ' Cot, hut of the peasant or bondman.' See above.

CHARLTON (15 in *P.G.*). *O.E. chart.* Ceorlatun, *Dom.* Cerletone (Berks), etc. 'Village of the churls or carls.' See CHARLCOMBE, and *cf.* CHORLTON. We also have a *Dom.* Bucks Cerleslai.

CHARMOUTH (Dorset). *O.E. Chron.* 833 and *Hen. Hunt.* Carrum. R. Char is perh. the same Kelt. root as in CARRON (Sc.), and so either 'rough' or 'crooked' river. 1160-61 *Pipe* Kent, has a 'Charho.'

CHARNEY BASSETT (Wantage). *B.C.S.* i. 506 Ceornei, *Dom.* Cernei, 1291 Cernee. 'Island on R. CERNE.' See -ey. The Bassets were a Norman family who owned lands hereabouts. But CHARNES (Eccleshall) is *Dom.* Cervernest, *a.* 1200 Chavernesse, 1227 Chaunes, *a.* 1300 Chavernes, Charneves, Chaunes. O.E. *ceafor, cefer, 5 chauer,* 'a beetle'; and *nest,* 'nest,' or *næs,* 'promontory, headland, ness'—a very curious corruption.

CHARNWOOD FOREST (Leicestersh.). Not in *Dom.*, but it has Cernelega. Prob. same as CARNWATH (Sc.), which is *c.* 1165 Charnewid, W. *carn gwydd,* 'cairn, cairnlike hill, covered with shrubs or woods'; influenced, too, no doubt by the O.Dan. *wede,* Dan. *ved,* Eng. *wood.* No name like *Carn* or *Cern* in *Onom.*

CHART SUTTON (Maidstone). 838 *chart.* Cert. *Chert,* a kind of quartz, is not found in Eng. *a.* 1679, so this name is doubtful. It seems little use to compare CHERTSEY. However, CHARTLEY (Uttoxeter) is *Dom.* Certelie, *c.* 1300 Certelea, which must be '*Certe*'s' or '*Ceort*'s meadow.' We have in O.E. charters Certæcer, Ceortanstapol, etc., as well as Certham, now CHARTHAM (Canterbury). Thus the name *Certe* or *Ceorta,* though not in *Onom.*, is well established.

CHATBURN (Chitheroe). 1241-42 Chatteburn. Prob. 'brook of *Ceatta*' or '*Ceatt*,' as in next and in Chetham, *sic* 1235. But both this and CHAT MOSS may be fr. O.W. *c(h)et,* W. *coed,* 'a wood,' as in CHETWODE.

CHATHAM. *O.E. chart.* Ceattham, *Dom.* Ceteham, *c.* 1150 *chart.* Cætham. 'Home of *Ceatta*,' a Jute. *Cf.* CATTON.

CHATTERIS (Cambridge). *c.* 1080 *Inquis. Camb.* Cateriz, Catriz, Chetriz, *Dom.* Cetriz, Cietriz; *chart.* Ceatrice, Chaterik; *c.* 1120 *Hen. Hunt.* Chateric; *a.* 1153 *Lib. Eli.* Chateriz. The forms in *Ch* and *z* are all Norm. Difficult. Possibly it contains the personal name *Kater. Cf.* KETTERING. Skeat and Stevenson think not, and think it may be a Kelt. river-name, which is doubtful.

CHATTERLEY (Newcastle, Staffs). *a.* 1300 Chadderlegh, Chaddendelle. This may be 'meadow' or 'dale of St. *Chad*.' The -en is the O.E. gen. *-an,* whilst the *er* is a trace of the N. gen. in *-r.* Norse influence is common in N. Staffs. *Cf.* CHADKIRK. Great and Little CHATWELL in the same shire, *a.* 1200 Chattewelle, are also fr. *Chad.* But *cf.* Catterton, *s.v.* CHADDERTON.

CHAWTON (Alton). Not in *Dom.* It has a Caudevre (*cf.* MICHELDEVER). Old forms needed. Perh.=CHAUSON (Droitwich), *Dom.* Celvestune, 1108 Chalvestone. O.E. *Cealfes tun,* 'town of Calf,' or 'the calf.'

CHEADLE (Stoke-on-Trent and Cheshire), also C. HULME and MOSELEY (Cheshire). St. C. *Dom.* Celle (error for Cedle; *Dom.* continually has felle for felde), 1166 Chelle (repeating *Dom.*'s error), 1194 Chedele, *a.* 1300 Chedle, Dogge-Chedile. Ches. C. 1194 Chedle. This must be N. *kví dal*, ' fold-valley '; N. influence is common in N. Staffs. *Cf.* Katewell (E. Ross-shire), in G. Ciàdail, the same name. For -dale slurring into -dle, *cf.* Rodil (Harris), and the ending of MARPLE; whilst for N. *k* becoming *ch*, *cf.* -caster and -chester.

    Hulme is O.E. *holm*, ' a piece of low, flat land by a river.' *Cf.* HUME (Sc.), 1250 Home. The origin of ' Dogge-Chedile ' is unknown. Though Celle and Chelle are clearly errors here, CHELL (Burslem) is 1313 Ceolegh, or ' *Ceol*'s lea.' But Kiddal (W. Riding), *Dom.* Chidal(e), is manifestly the same name as Cheadle; plainer still is CHEE DALE, Millersdale (Derbysh.). It is worth adding as to the Celle forms that the sb. *needle*, O.E. *nédl*, whilst 3-6 *nedle* is also 3-7 *nelde*.

CHEAM (Sutton). 1018 (or later) *chart.* Cheyham. ' Home of *Ceahha*,' or some such name. *Cf. B.C.S.* 1230 Ceahhan mere. See -ham.

CHEBSEY (Eccleshall). *Dom.* Cebbesio (*o* for *e*), *a.* 1250 Chebbesey. ' Isle of *Ceobba* ' or ' *Ceob*,' 3 or 4 in *Onom. Cf. Dom.* Suffk. Cebbenhala. See -ey.

CHECKLEY (Cheadle, Herefordsh., Essex, and S. Cheshire). Che. C. *Dom.* Cedla (error), 1227 Chekkesleye, Checkele. Ches. C. *c.* 1190 *Roll* Chekelee, *later* Chackleigh. He. C. 1252 Chackileg. ' Meadow of *Cæc, Cæcca, Cec* ' or ' *Cecce*,' all forms in *Onom. Cf.* CHECKENDON (Reading), ' hill of *Cecca*,' and KEKEWICH. See -ley.

CHEDDAR (Somerset). *Exon. Dom.* Cetdre, *Chart.* Cedre, *a.* 1142 *Wm. Malmesb.* Ceddren; *later* Chedare. Kelt. *cet der*, W. *coed dwr*, ' wood on the stream.' 1158-59 *Pipe* Cedresfeld (Somerset) seems to imply a man *Ceder*, of whom we would have the patronymic in 1160-61 *Pipe* Gloucstr., Chedringwurda, ' farm of Ceder's sons.' *Cf.* CHETWODE.

CHEDDLETON (Leek). *Dom.* Celtetone, 1200 Chetilton, 1204 Cheteleton, *a.* 1400 Chetelton. Prob. not ' town of *Ceadel* ' or ' *Ceadela*,' as in CHADDLEWORTH, but ' town of *Cetel* or *Cytel*,' a common O.E. name. Change of *t* to *d*, or *vice versa*, is common. *Cf.* Catterton (Yorks), *Dom.* Cadretone, CHATTERLEY, and CHEDWORTH (Gloucstrsh.), 872 *chart.* Ceddanwyrde, fr. *Cedda*, but also 1190 Chedeleswarde, ' farm of *Ceadel*.' Caddel is still a surname.

CHELFORD (Cheshire). *Dom.* Celeford, also in Bucks, Celforde. ' Ford of *Ceolla* ' or ' *Cella*.' *Cf.* CHELSFIELD. CHELLOW (Bradford) is fr. the same name, *Dom.* Celeslau, ' *Cella*'s hill.' See -low.

CHELLASTON (Derby). Prob. *Dom.* Cellasdene. *Cf.* 939 *chart.* Ceolan hyrst (Kent). Now 'town of *Ceolla*,' but the ending seems to have been formerly -dean, *q.v.*

CHELMARSH (Bridgnorth). 1179 Cheilmarsh, 1255 Cheylmerse. Prob. contract. for '*Ceolmund's* marsh.' *Cf.* Chelmick in the same shire, 1232 Chelmundewyk; but Cheylesmore (Coventry) is *a.* 1300 Chisilmore, O.E. *ceosel mór*, 'shingly moor.'

CHELMONDISTON (Ipswich). Local pron. Chimston. Not in *Dom.* 'Village of *Chelmond* or *Ceolmund*,' a very common O.E. name. *Cf.* Cholmondestone (Cheshire), *Dom.* Chelmundestone; also CHOLMONDELEY.

CHELMSFORD. *Dom.* Celmeresfort, 1160 *Pipe* Chelmesford, 1161 *ib.* Nord chelmeresford. 'Ford of *Ceolmær*' or '*Celmar*,' 3 in *Onom.* Liquid *r* easily disappears. The name of the river Chelmer is thus a back formation fr. the ford.

CHELSEA. O.E. *Chron.* 785 Cealchype, 1465 Chalchithe, *a.* 1600 Chellsaye. The name has changed. Orig. it was 'chalkhithe' or 'landing-rise.' See HYTHE. But the present form represents O.E. *ceosel-iʒe*, 'pebble-bank isle'; O.E. *ceosel*, 'pebble or shingle.' *Cf.* Ger. *kiesel*, and Cheselhanger (Berkeley), 1368 Chisulhanger, 'shingly wooded slope.'

CHELSFIELD (Chiselhurst). Possibly by dissimilation *Dom.* Ciresfel., 1298 Chelesfelde, 'Field of *Ceolla*,' a fairly common name. *Cf.* 'Chelesbergh' in *chart.* of 935, near Shaftesbury, *Dom.* Surrey, Celesham, and Cheleswurda, 1159-58 *Pipe* Wilts. But CHELSWORTH (Bildeston, Suffk.) is 962 *chart.* Ceorlesworth, 'farm of *Ceorl*'—*i.e.*, the churl or carl—common name in *Onom.* See -worth.

CHELTENHAM. 803 *chart.* Celtanhom, *Dom.* Chinteneham, 1158-59 Chilteham. 'Enclosure on R. *Chelt*,' prob. a Kelt. word, possibly the same root as *Celtæ*. The ending here is *hamm*, not *ham*. See -ham.

CHELWOOD (Bristol). Old forms needed. (*Dom.* has only Ceol-, Celflede, fr. *Ceolf* or *Ceolwulf*.) May be '*Ceolla's* wood,' or perh. 'cold wood,' fr. 4 *cheld*, *cheald*, South. form of *cold*, O.E. *cald*.

CHENIES (Rickmansworth). ? 1131 *O.E. Chron.* (Laud.) Chinni, 1297 Cheyny. Prob. O.E. *cine*, *cyne*, 3 *chine*, 4-6 *chene*, *chyn*, 'a fissure, a crack, a chine.' *Cf.* KEMPTON. The ending is the commonly suffixed Eng. pl. But *Dom.* Yorks Chenehall is now KILLINGHALL.

CHEPSTOW. In W. Casgwent (*cas* for *castel*). *Dom.* Estrighoiel, 1228 *Close R.* Striguill; also Straguil. The *Dom.* form looks like 'dwelling, abode, W. *ystre*, of the Goidel or Gael.' But the present name is O.E. *ceap-stow*, 'market-place, place for bargaining,' as in Cheapside.

CHEQUERBENT (Bolton). *c.* 1574 *M.S.* Checkerbent. This must be 'checkered, variegated bent grass.' The vb. *chequer* is rare so early in Eng., so this seems to be formed fr. *chequer* sb. 'chess-board,' or 'chessboard pattern'; O.Fr. *eschequier ;* in Eng. 1297 *chekere.* See also BENTLEY; and *cf.* Chowbent (Lancs), 1641-42 Cholbent, ? 'bent of *Ceol.*'

CHERHILL (Calne). *Dom.* Cheurel, 1158-59 *Pipe* Ceriel. Doubtful; first part prob. as in next; -el is a very rare representative of -hill. It is conceivable that the root is O.E. *ceafor, cefer,* 4 *chauer,* ' a chafer, a beetle '; O.H.G. *chevar.*

CHERITON (4 in *P.G.*). *Dom.* Ciretona (Devon). Hardly fr. the *cherry,* O.E. *ciris, cyrs,* and then not found till *c.* 1350, *cheri, chiry.* Perh. ' village of *Ceorra* ' or ' *Cyra,*' one such of each in *Onom.* CHERRINGTON (Warwicksh.) is the same name, 1327 Chirytone. Here, and also in the case of the two Chirtons, Duignan votes for *cherry.* But Cheriton (Alresford) is prob. *Dom.* Cerewartone, fr. some man of doubtful name, (?) *Ceorl-weard,* a name not recorded, or, by dissimilation, *Ceolweard,* a fairly common name. The Kent Ch. is not in *Dom.* *Cf.* CHURSTON. However, CHERINGTON (Tetbury), *Dom.* Cerintone, *c.* 1120 Cherintone, *later* Chederintone, Baddeley thinks is, ' ton, farm-enclosure of the Ceadrings ' or ' sons of (?) *Ceadhere.*'

CHERTSEY. *Bede* Cerotæsei, id est insula Ceroti, v.r. Ceoroti [*grant of* 675 Cherteseye]. 1084 *O.E. Chron.* Ceorteseye, *Dom.* Certesy. ' Isle of *Cerot.*' See -ey.

CHERWELL R. (Oxford). 681 *chart.* Flumen quod appellatur Ceruelle. 864 *ib.* Cearwellan, 1005 Cearwylle, Cyrwylle. Possibly connected with O.E. *cyrran* ' to turn,' but prob. pre-Keltic.

CHESHAM (Bucks). *K.C.D.* 658 Cissanham. O.E. for ' home of *Cissa.*' *Cf.* CHESSINGTON, KESWICK, and *Dom.* Essex, Cesseworda, Cishelle. The names *Cis, Cisi,* and *Ciss* also occur.

CHESHUNT (Waltham Cross). *Dom.* Cistrehunt, *a.* 1300 Cesterhunt, 1402 Chesthunte, ' camp's hunt ' or ' hunting-ground.' See CHESTER. But CHESFORD (Kenilworth) is *c.* 1422 Chessford, of quite uncertain origin; perh. O.E. *ceosleg,* ' shingly.' We get the personal name *Chesney* in Sezincote (Glouc.), *Dom.* Che(i)snecote, ' cot of *Chaisne* ' or ' *Chesney,*' O.Fr. *chesnaie,* ' an oakwood.'

CHESLYN HAY (Walsall). *a.* 1300 Hay of Chistlyn, -ling, Chistling, Ches-, Chystlyn. Duignan takes this to be a dimin. of *chest,* Sc. *kist,* O.E. *cest, cist.* *Cf.* CHESTAL (Dursley), 1374 Chystelay. HAY is O.E. *hege,* ' a fenced or hedged enclosure,' here perh. round an ancient cromlech or burial-mound.

CHESSINGTON (Surbiton). *Dom.* Cisendone. ' *Cissa*'s fort '; O.E. *dún.* *Cf.* CHICHESTER. See -don and -ton.

CHESTER. *Bede,* ' Civitas Legionum, which by the English is called Legacestir, but by the Britons more rightly Carlegion,' in *c.* 810

Nennius Cair Ligion (W. *caer,* 'fort, castle') and Urbs legionis.
894 *O.E. Chron.* Anre wæstre castre, *Dom.* Cestrescire, *c.* 1097
Flor. Worc. 'Civitas quae Carlegion Britannice et Legeceaster
dicitur Saxonice.' L. *castra,* 'a camp'; O.E. *ceaster,* 'a fortified
place,' then often 'a town'; *cf.* A.S. Gospels (Luke x. 11). In
mod. W. Caerlleon Gawr, ' great fort of the legion' (? the 20th).
Cf. CAERLEON and LEICESTER; and see CAISTOR.

CHESTERFIELD (Derbysh. and Lichfield). De. C. 955 Cesterfelda,
1162-65 Cestrefelt. Li. C. 1262 Cestrefeud, Chestrefewde. See
CHESTER. Field is O.E. *feld*, 3-5 *felt(e)*. In 1262 the liquid *l* has
become *w*, as it often does, esp. in Sc., but *Oxf. Dict.* gives no
examples under *field*.

CHESTER-LE-STREET. *a.* 1130 *Sim. Dur.;* also *R. of Hexham* Cuncha
Chester; 1183 Cestria. The *street* implies a Roman road.
Cuncha is also found in the form Cununga, which suggests Icel.
konung-r, ' king.'

CHESTERTON (Cambridge, Cirencester, Bicester, Staffs, and Warwicksh.). Ci. C. *c.* 1100 Cestretone. War. C. 1043 *chart.*
Cestretune, *Dom.* Cestretone, Cestedone. O.E. *ceaster-tún,* 'town
of the fort, castle-town.' See CHESTER and -ton. Also *cf. Dom.*
Bucks Cestreham.

CHESWARDINE (Market Drayton). *Dom.* Ciseworth, *a.* 1200 Chese-
wurda, Cheswordyn, Chesewardyn, Chesew'rthin. ' Cheese-
making farm.' O.E. *cése, cýse,* 'cheese,' and -worth or its var.
-wardine, *q.v.* Similar is CHESWICK (Northumberland), *c.* 1100
Cheseuuic, 1631 Cheswick, lit. ' cheese-house.' See -wick. Also
cf. BUTTERWICK and CHISWICK.

CHETNOLE (Sherborne). (*Dom.* has Chenolle and Chenoltone and
Cnolle.) Hybrid. O. Keltic *chet ;* W. *coed,* 'a wood'; and O.E.
cnoll, ' a rounded hillock, a knoll.' *Cf.* CHETWODE, KNOWLE,
and Kits Coity House, name of a cromlech, Aylesford, Kent.
Jos. Colebroke, *c.* 1800, says Kit was an old shepherd, who fed
his flocks here; and Coity must be fr. *coed.*

CHETTLE (Blandford). *Dom.* Ceotel (*o* prob. error). 1238 *Close R.*
Chetel. O.E. *cytel, cetel ;* O.N. *cetel,* 'a kettle,' hence a valley
shaped like a kettle, a ' corrie.' *Cf.* Kettle or Kingskettle
(Fife).

CHETTON (Bridgnorth). ? *Dom.* Catinton. ' Town of *Ceatta*,' 2 in
Onom. Cf. Dom. Bucks, Cetendone.

CHETWODE (Bucks). 949 *chart.* Cetwuda, *Dom.* Cetevde, 1248 *chart.*
' Forest of Chett,' 1270 ' in Bosco (wood) de Cett,' 1290 Chet-
wood. Hybrid tautology; O.W. *coit ;* W. *coed,* ' a wood.' *Cf.*
CHUTE and the personal name Chetwynd (W. *coed gwyn*); also
Dom. Cornw. Chilcoit (Corn. for ' neck of the wood '), and Bucks,
Cetedone, though this last may be fr. O.E. *cete,* ' cot, hut.' *Cf.*
DATCHET. Also *cf.* CHETNOLE.

CHEVELEY (Newmarket). *c.* 1080 *Inquis. Camb.* Cauelei, Chauelei, Cheuelei, *Dom.* Chavelai, *a.* 1200 *chart.* Cheaflea, Cæafle, 1346 Chavele, 1426 Cheveley. ' Chaff-meadow '; O.E. *ceaf,* 2-4 *cheue,* 4 *chaue,* ' chaff.' See -ley.

CHEVENAGE (Avening). Not in *Dom.* 1626 Chavenedge. Prob. Cheven- is O.E. *Cifan,* ' Cifa's,' with the usual Norm. softening. *Cf.* Chevening, CHEVINGTON, CHIEVELEY, and *Dom.* Surrey Civentone. But it may be fr. CEFN. -age, *q.v.*, is usually a late ending, and needs old forms to interpret it.

CHEVET (Barnsley) *Dom.* Cevet; and CHEVIOT Hills. *c.* 1250 Montes chiueti, *a.* 1300 Mons chiuioth, *c.* 1500 Chevet, 1596 Cheuott. Possibly G. *c(h)iabach,* ' bushy place,' fr. *ciabh,* ' hair,' which may also be the root of CHEVY CHASE. For -ach becoming -iot, *cf.* ELLIOT {Sc.). There is also Caville (Yorks), which is *Dom.* Cevetle (see -ley). The name is very doubtful. Fr. *chevet,* ' a pillow,' seems impossible. But the CHEVIN (Otley) is plainly W. *cefn,* ' a hill ridge.'

CHEVINGTON (Acklington, Bury St. Edmunds, and Pershore). Bu. C. *Dom.* Ceuentuna. Pe. C. 972 *chart.* Civincgtune, *Dom.* Civintone, 1275 Kyvin-, Chyvintone. ' Town of the sons of *Cifa.*' *Cf.* CHEVENAGE. See -ing and -ton.

CHEVY CHASE (N. Northumberland). *Sic c.* 1650, but *a.* 1500 *ballad.* ' The hunttis of Cheuet.' See CHEVIOT and CANNOCK CHASE.

CHEWTON MENDIP (Bath). Dom. Civetune, 1230 *Close R.* Chiweton, 1238 *ib.* Chyweton. *Onom.* has no *Ciwa,* only one *Ceawa,* which may be the name here, and also in CHEW MAGNA and STOKE (Bristol). *Dom.* Chiwe. There seems no likelier origin, though it is rare for a place to be called after a man alone; but *cf.* GOODRICH, etc. Magna is L. for ' Great.'

CHICHESTER. 891 *O.E. Chron.* Cisseceaster, *c.* 1070 Ecclesia Cicestrensis, *c.* 1114 Cicestre, 1167-68 Cycestr', *c.* 1180 Cicestria, *late chart.* Chichestra, 1297 *R. Glouc.* Chichestre. ' Camp, fort of *Cissa,*' son of Ella, d. *c.* 520. See KEYNOR, and *cf.* Cissbury Camp (Worthing).

CHICH ST. OSYTH (Colchester). *c.* 1120 *Hen. Hunt.* Chicce, *Sim. Dur.* ann. 1123 Cice, 1157 *Pipe* Chich. Doubtful. None of the words spelt *chich* in *Oxf. Dict.* yield a likely origin, and there seems nothing helpful in O.E. *Cf. Dom.* Devon, Cichet. So prob. the name is Keltic, meaning some thing or place of concave or hivelike shape. *Cf.* W. *cychu,* ' to cover, to hive.' *Osyth* was a virgin martyr, of doubtful date, ? 600-800. Said to have been granddaughter of Penda of Mercia and pupil of Abbess Modwenna.

CHIDDINGSTONE (Eden Bridge). The ' chiding stone,' a sandstone boulder fr. which fractious wives used to be ' chided,' still stands at the rear of the village; O.E. *cídan,* to chide, pa. tense, *chid,* pa. pple. *chidden*. But for all that, this is prob. an example of popular etymology, and the real name will be O.E. *Cyddan stan*, ' stone of Cydda '; there are 2 of this name in Kent mentioned in *Onom*. *Cf.* KIDDINGTON (Oxon), *Dom*. Chidintone; but the Kent name is not in *Dom*.

CHIEVELEY (Newbury). *O.E. chart*. Cifan lea, 1291 Chivele. ' Lea, meadow of *Cifa*.' Not the same name as CHEVELEY (Cambs). *Cf.* CHEVINGTON, and see -ley.

CHIGWELL (Ongar). *O.E. chart* Cingwella, later Cinghewella, Chiwellia. ' King's well,' O.E. *cyning*, 1-2 *cyng, cing*. *Cf.* CHINGFORD.

CHILCOTT (Wells) and CHILCOTE (Ashby-DE-LA-Z.). Prob., as in CHILTON and CHILWELL, ' *Cilda*'s cot '; the adj. *chill* is inadmissible in all these cases, being recent. But *Dom*. Cornw., Chilcoit, will be Old Keltic, or Corn. for ' neck of the wood'; with Corn. *chil, cf.* G. *caol,* ' narrow,' and *caolas,* ' a strait, a kyle.' The Wells name could quite easily be Corn.; it is not in *Dom*. *Cf.* KILCOT.

CHILDREY (Wantage). *Chart*. Cillan rithe, Cilla rithe, *Dom*. Celrea, *a*. 1300 Celrea, Celry. *Cilla* is presumably a personal name. *Cf. B.C.S.* 1242 Cillan hrycg (*i.e.*, ' ridge '); prob. *Cille*, sister of Hean, first abbot of Abingdon. The letter *d* often suffixes itself. *Cf.* DRUMMOND (Sc.). *Rith* is O.E. for ' stream,' cognate with L. *rivus*. *Cf.* SHOTTERY. But CHILDERLEY (Cambs) is *Cildra-leáh,* ' children's ' (Sc. childer's) ' lea.'

CHILD'S WICKHAM (Broadway, Worcester). 706 *chart*. Childeswicwon, Wicwone, 972 *chart*. Vuiguuennan. The present name is a corruption; the *chart*. name may contain W. *gwig,* ' a thicket, grove, forest,' or else the name of the tribe *Huiccii*. See WORCESTER; also see WIKHAMFORD. Child is O.E. *cild,* ' a child,' not found as *child* till *c*. 1160, so that the copy of the 706 *chart*. must be late. *Cild* is also early found as a proper name.

CHILLINGHAM (Bedford). *Sic* 1595, and CHILLINGTON [Kingsbridge (Sussex), Crewkerne and Brewood (Staffs)]. Ki. and Cr. C. *Dom*. Cilletone. Br. C. *Dom*. Cillentone, *a*. 1200 Cilderton, *a*. 1400 Chilinton, ' Home, village, or town of *Cille*.' The names *Cild, Cilla, Cille*, and *Cilli* are all in *Onom*. But Sus. C. is *c*. 1060 *chart*. Cillingtun (probably), or ' village of *Cilling*,' prob. patronymic fr. above. See -ham, -ing, and -ton.

CHILTERN. *a*. 800 Chilternsaetna, *Dom*. Cilterne (Somerset), *a*. 1125 O.E. *Chron*. ann. 1009 Ciltern, *c*. 1200 *Gervase* Chiltre. *Cf.*, too, *chart Hen. I*. a ' Ciltre.' *Oxf. Dict*. says origin unknown. The name is also applied to a kind of soil. The -ern is prob. O.E. *erne,* ' a house.'

CHILTON (5 in *P.G.*). C. Poldon, Bridgewater, *Dom*. Cildetone, Steventon C. 1015 *chart*. In loco ubi solicolæ appellativo usu Cilda tun nominant, *Dom*. Cilletone, *a*. 1300 Chilton, *Dom*.

Bucks Ciltone. *Cilda,* 1015, prob. is a man's name, as the proper gen. plu. of O.E. *cild,* 'child,' is *cildra.* But Skeat says that this, like Chilford (Cambs) means 'children's.' Yet Kilton, (Yorks), *sic* 1179, is *Dom.* Chilton, which makes Skeat's assertion doubtful. *Cf.* next.

CHILVERS COTON (Nuneaton). *Dom.* Celverdestoche (see -stock), *a.* 1200 Chelverdcote, *a.* 1300 Chilverdescote, Chelverescot. '*Ceolweard's* cottages,' *coton* being an O.E. pl. of *cot.*

CHILWELL (Nottingham). *Dom.* Cilleuuelle, Cid-, Chidewelle. *Cf. Dom.* 'Cildewelle' (Cheshire). Chil- prob. represents a man *Cild, Cilla,* or *Cille;* all these forms are found in *Onom.* The Eng. adj. *chill* is not found till 1513. See, too, above, and *cf.* CHILWORTH (Romsey and Guildford), *Dom.* Leicr., Chilurda, and 1238 *Close R.* Cheleworth (Cricklade), which all must be fr. a man *Cille,* or the like. But some think Chil- is same root as in BAPCHILD. See -worth.

CHINE (in Blackgang Chine, etc., in S. and S.W.). See CHENIES. The *Oxf. Dict.* gives no quot. before 1830.

CHINGFORD (Walthamstow). The early forms vary much—*Dom.* Chilgelford, 1242 Chingel-, also Cinge-, Cinghe-, Echingels-, Schingelford. This seems to be 'Shingle-ford,' N. *singl,* 'water-worn gravel or pebbles,' M.E. *chingle;* but plainly confused with 'King's ford.' *Cf.* CHIGWELL, and 1160 *Pipe* Chingeswuda (Kingswood, ? in Surrey).

CHINNOCK, E. and W. (Somerset). *Dom.* Cinioch. Prob. Keltic. Possibly var. of CANNOCK, fr. W. *cnwc,* 'a hillock.' But also *cf.* G. *cianog,* 'a small piece of arable land.'

CHINNOR (Wallingford). 1234 *Close R.* Chynhore, Chennor. 'Bank, edge of *Cina*' or '*Cyna,*' gen. *-an. Cf.* Chinley (Stockport). See -or.

CHIPPENHAM (Wilts, Bp's. Cleeve, Cambs). Wi. C. 878 *O.E. Chron.* Cippan hamm, *c.* 900 *chart.* Cippenhamme, 1158-59 Chepeham, Bp. C. *c.* 812 *chart.* Cippanhamme, Ca. C. *c.* 1080 *Inquis. Cam.* Chipenham, *Dom.* Chipeham. 'Enclosure,' O.E. *hamm,* or 'home,' O.E. *ham,* 'of *Cippa,*' *-an,* a rare name; *Cippan* cannot be = CHIPPING. *Cf. Dom.* Essex, Kippedana, the 2 Chipsteads, and CHIPPINGHURST (Oxon), *chart.* Cibbanhyrst, '*Cibba's* wood.'

CHIPPING NORTON, ONGAR, SODBURY, etc. *a.* 1300 *Roll* Norton Mercatoria. Chipping is var. of *cheaping,* found *c.* 1200 *cheping,* 'a market, a market-place,' fr. O.E. *céap,* 'barter,' *cípan,* 'to sell,' same root as *cheap, cheapen,* etc. *Cf.* CHEPSTOW, and see NORTON, etc. The mod. Swede has the same sound and meaning, though not the same spelling. He always speaks of Copenhagen as Chippenhavn, 'merchant's haven,' though he spells it Kjöbenhavn or -hamn, whilst a name like Jönköping, 'John's market,' he pronounces Yön-

chipping. But CHIPPING (N. Lancs), *Dom.* Chipinden, is prob-
'vale of *Cipa*' or '*Ceapa*,' one in *Onom* (see -den), and CHIP-
PINGTON (Nthbld.) is *old* Cebbington, ' town of *Ceabba*,' gen. *-ban*,
one in *Onom.* See -ing.

CHIPSTEAD (Red Hill and Sevenoaks). Not in *Dom.* Prob. ' homestead of *Cyppa*.' *Cf.* CHIPPENHAM and *Dom.* Norfk. Chiptona.

CHIRBURY (Salop). 913 *O.E. Chron.* Cyricbyrig—*i.e.*, ' churchburgh '
or ' town.' See the interesting article CHURCH in *Oxf. Dict.* But
by *c.* 1120 *Hen. Hunt.* it is Cereburih, 1236 Chirebir'. See -bury.

CHIRK (Accrington and Oswestry). Acc. C. 1202 Chirche, or
' church '; but Osw. C. *a.* 1300 Cirice, *c.* 1350 Chirk, which may
not represent O.E. for ' church,' as in CHIRBURY; but, as Chirk
is on the R. CEIRIOG, it may be a corrup. of it. In W. it is
Eglwys y wæn, ' church of the moor.'

CHISELHURST. 1160 *Pipe* Chiselherst, *c.* 1380 Chesilhurst. ' Woody
place on the shingle,' O.E. *ceosel.* See CHELSEA and -hurst; and
cf. Chesil Bank, Dorset. But CHISELBOROUGH (Stoke-under-ham)
is 1236 *Close R.* Sidelberg, prob. ' burgh of *Cecil*.' The original
seat of the Cecils was in Monmouth, where the name is pron.
Seisyl; we see the same name in Isolde or Yseult of the medieval
romances and in CHISHOLM (Sc.). See -boro'. We also have
1240 *Close R.* Chiselhampt'.

CHISENBURY (Pewsey). *Dom.* Cheseberie. *Cf. Dom.* Surrey Cisendone. ' Burgh, town of *Cisi*,' one in *Onom. Cissa* is much
commoner. See -bury. Great Chishall (1597 Chishill), Royston, may be fr. the same name.

CHISLET (Canterbury). *Chart.* and *Dom.* Cistelet. Possibly O.N.
Fr. *castelet, chastelet,* dimin, of *chastel,* mod. Fr. *châtelet* and
château, ' a little castle.' We have *castelet* in Eng. *c.* 1320 and
chastelet in 1494; but the early change fr. *a* to *i* is scarcely
explained. Prof. Weekley is quite doubtful.

CHISWICK (London). Not in *Dom. c.* 1230 Chesewycke. O.E. *cese,*
cyse wic, ' dwelling, hamlet where cheese was made.' *Cf.*
BUTTERWICK and CHESWARDINE, and see -wick.

CHITTERNE (Wilts). *a.* 675 *Grant* Cyterene forde. ? *Dom.* Chetre.
Prob. ' *Cyta*'s house,' O.E. *erne.* We find both a ' Cytan ford '
and a ' Cittan den ' in early charters.

CHITTLEHAMHOLT (Chulmleigh) and CHITTLEHAMPTON (Umberleigh),
both Devon. *Dom.* Citrametona (though in MS. Curametone).
The first part must be the common O.E. name *Cytel, Chitel,* or
Ketel; the *r* in *Dom.* is due to the common interchange of
liquids. *Dom.* also has Chetelescote. *Holt* is O.E. and Icel. for
' a wood, a grove.' See HAMPTON.

CHOLDERTON (Salisbury). *Dom.* Celdre-, Celdrintone, 1287 *Close
R.* Childwarton. ' Town of *Ceolweard*,' var. ' *Kilvert*.'

CHOLLERFORD, and -TON (N. Tyne). *c.* 410 *Notit. Dign.* Cilurno, *a.* 700 *Rav. Geogr.* Celunno, 1232 *chart.* Chelreton. Cilurno suggests W. *cilwrn,* 'cauldron,' fr. the cavities in the rocky river-bed here; Sc. Rhys. But the disappearance of the *n* is curious. *Cf.* above.

CHOLMONDELEY (Cheshire). Pron. Chúmly. *Dom.* Calmundelei. '*Calmund*'s or '*Ceolmund*'s meadow.' *Cf.* CHELMONDISTON. See -ley.

CHOLSEY (Berks). 1005 *O.E. Chron.* Ceolesige, *Dom.* Celsei, *Sim. Dur.* ann. 1006 Ceolesegia, *c.* 1120 *Hen. Hunt.* Coleseige. '*Ceola*'s isle '; several *Ceolas* are known. See -ey.

CHOPPINGTON (Morpeth). *a.* 1130 *Sim. Dur.* Cebbingtun. '*Ceabba*'s village.' *Cf. B.C.S.* 282 Ceabban sol. It may be a patronymic. See -ing and -ton.

CHORLETON - CUM - HARDY (Manchester). 1296-97 Chorleton = CHARLTON.

CHORLEY (Preston). 'Meadow on the R. *Chor,*' a name prob. Keltic; ? cognate with W. *cor,* 'a circle, a crib.' *Cf. Dom.* Worcr. 'Chure.' But CHORLEY (Lichfield) is *sic a.* 1400 and *a.* 1600 Chorley *alias* Charley. 'Meadow of *Ceorl,*' or ' of the carl or churl,' O.E. *ceorl.*

CHRISHALL (Royston). Not in *Dom.* 1298 Cristeshale—*i.e.,* '*Christ*'s nook.' *Cf. Dom.* Worcr. Christetone, and Christon Bank (Northumbld.).

CHRISTCHURCH. 1058 *O.E. Chron.* Æt Christes cyrcean, *a.* 1109 Æt Xrescircean, *c.* 1160 *Gesta Steph.* Cristiciria (*sic*).

CHRISTIAN MALFORD (Chippenham). 940 *chart.* Cristemalford, 'Christ's Malford,' or 'ford of the tax or impost,' O.E. *mál,* seen in the Sc. *mailing.*

CHUDLEIGH (2 in Devon). Not in *Dom.* 'Meadow of *Cudd* ' or '*Cudda,*' names in *Onom.* See -leigh.

CHULMLEIGH (Devon). *Dom.* Calmonleuge, *Exon. Dom.* Chalmonleuge, 1242 *Close R.* Cha(u)meleg'. 'Meadow of *Ceolmund,*' a very common name; *eo* regularly becomes *a,* now slurred into *u*; and -leuge is scribe's error for -leage, dat. of *léah.* See -ley.

CHURCHHILL (4 in *P.G.*). Kidderminster C. *Dom.* Circehille, Oxf. C. 1295 *chart.* Cercelle, *later* Cherchehulle, *Dom.* Bucks Cherchehelle, also Chirchefeld; in *Dom.* Surrey it is Cercefelde. Form 1295 is only an early spelling of 'church hill.' *Cf.* the forms under CHRISTCHURCH. CHURCHDOWN (Gloustrsh.), now pron. Chosen, is already in *Dom.* Circesdune.

CHURCHINFORD (Honiton). Not in *Dom.* Perh. 935 *chart.* Chircelford. The liquids do interchange, but *l* rarely becomes *n.* The early spellings in the *Oxf. Dict.* do not encourage us to derive

Chircel fr. *circle ;* but there is a Med. L. *cercella,* O.Fr. *cercelle,* 'the teal duck,' which seems possible.

CHURCH MINSHULL (Middlewich). See MINSHULL VERNON.

CHURCHOVER (Rugby). *Dom.* Wara, 1257 Waur(e), *a.* 1300 Church Waver, 1327 Chirche-Wavre. The -overs of Warwk., Brownsover, Cester-Over, etc., are all fr. O.E. *wafre, wæfre,* 'the aspen poplar.' See WAVERTREE, etc.

CHURN, R. (Cirencester). Prob. found in *c.* 150 *Ptolemy* Corinion and *a.* 700 *Rav. Geogr.* Cironium, names for CIRENCESTER, which stands on this river; it is sometimes called the Corin. If the name is so old it cannot be O.E. *cyrin,* 'a churn,' and is prob. pre-Keltic. There is also a CHURNET, trib. of R. Dove (Staffd.), 1284 Chirnete, which *might* be dimin. of O.E. *cyrin, cirn ;* but Duignan is prob. right in connecting it with the other river. *Cf.* CERNE.

CHURSTON FERRERS (Devon). Prob. 1167-68 *Pipe* Chirestona. 'Town of *Cire,*' one *Cyra* in *Onom. Cf.* CHERITON. On Ferrers, see BEER.

CHUTE (Wilts) and CHUTE STANDEN (Andover). 1238 *Close R.* Cett, 1241 *ib.* Cet, ? which. *Cf.* 1248 *chart.* 'Forest of Chett,' 1270 in Bosco de Cett. Kelt. *chet, coit,* W. *coed,* 'a wood.' See CHETWODE.

CHYANDOUR (Penzance). Corn. = 'house on the water,' *ti, chi,* 'a house.' The G. *tigh,* 'a house,' also commonly takes the *ch* sound. *Cf.* Chysauster, Corn. *chy saws tir,* 'house on the Saxon or English land,' and Chyangwail, Lelant, 'house in the field,' *gwel, gweal,* rather than 'among the corn-stalks,' *gwail.* Also see TYWARNHAILE.

CILSAN (on R. Towy). W. *cil* is 'the back,' then 'a retreat, a place of retreat, a corner.' *Cf.* G. *cùl* and *cuil.* The -san is thought to be O.E. *segne,* L. *sagina,* Gk. σαγήνη, 'a seine (net).'

CINDERY I. (Brightlingsea). 1539 Syndry, 1674 Sinder Isle. Prob. O.E. *sunder ea,* 'isle sundered or separated' from the mainland. *Cf.* SUNDERLAND; whilst CINDERFORD, For. of Dean, is 1281 Sinderford. See -ey.

CIRENCESTER. Prob. *c.* 150 *Ptolemy* Corinion, *a.* 700 *Rav. Geogr.* Cironium, O.E. *Chron.* 628 Cirenceastre, *c.* 893 *Asser* Cirrenceastre called 'Cair ceri' in British, which is the south part of the Huiccii (see WORCESTER), 1155 Cirecestre, *c.* 1180 *Ben. Peterb.* Cirencestria, Cirecestria, 1298 Cicestre, which last is near the present pron., Sister, Sizeter. In W. Caergeri, really the same name. Usually said to be 'Ciren's camp.' There is no *Ciren* or *Cyren* in *Onom.,* though we do find *B.C.S.* 349 Cyran leah—*i.e.,* 'meadow of *Cyra.*' However, the root must be pre-Saxon, the name being 'camp on the Ciren' or 'CHURN.' See -cester.

CISSBURY (Worthing). Not in *Dom.* 'Burgh, fort of *Cissa.*' See CHICHESTER and -bury.

CLAINES (Worcester). *a,* 1100 Cleinesse, *a.* 1200 Claines. This is certainly an abnormal name, but it can hardly be aught else but O.E. *clœne, cláne næs,* 'clear, clean headland'; the orig. meaning of *clean* was 'clear.' Of course, final -ness, *q.v.,* is usually sounded; but it could easily be slurred.

CLANDOWN (Radstock) and CLANFIELD (Hants and Oxon). Ox. C. *Dom.* Clenefelde, 1216-1307 Glanfeld, 1274-79 Clanefeld. *Cf. Dom.* Clanedun (Surrey) and Clandone (Bucks). All fr. O.E. *clœne, cláne,* 'clear, clean, free from dirt or weeds.' See -don.

CLAPHAM (Westmld., London, and Beds). We. C. *Dom.* Clapeham; Lon. C. *a.* 900 *chart.* Cloppaham, Clappenham, *Dom.* Clopeham; Bed. C. 1236 Clopham. Some think Lon. C. is 'Home of the Osgod *Clapa,*' d. 1054, where Harthacnut drank himself to death; but Skeat prefers to associate both the above, and also Claphams in Yorks and Lancs, with mid. Dan. *klop,* 'a stub, a stump,' prob. allied to *clump:* so 'house in the stumpy ground.' Similarly CLAPTON (Hungerford), 1316 Clopton, and CLAPTON (Glostrsh.) *c.* 1200 Cloptune; whilst *Dom.* has a Clopcote (Berks). *Cf.* CLOPTON. Skeat does not seem to have noted the *Dom.* Westmld. form, which favours derivation fr. a man. *Cf.,* too, *Dom.* Sffk. Cleptuna.

CLARENDON (Salisbury). 1164 *Hoveden* Clarendonum, 1373 Claryndone. The adj. *clear* is not found in Eng. *a.* 1297, and there is only one obscure *Clare* in *Onom.,* so the origin of this name is doubtful. W. *clawr,* 'surface, cover,' does not seem likely; 'Hill of Clare' is more so, O.E. *dún,* 'a hill, a fort.' *Cf.* next.

CLARO (Yorks). Not in *Dom.,* though now name of a wapentake. May be 'clear, conspicuous *how*' O.N. *haug-r,* or moothill of its wapentake; only, *clear,* 3-5 *cler,* is not found in Eng. *a.* 1297. But there is also CLARETON (Yorks), *Dom.* Claretone, which favours derivation fr. a man *Clare.* *Cf.* CLARENDON, Greenho (Norfolk), and THINGOE.

CLATFORD (Andover). *Dom.* Cladford. Doubtful. No name in *Onom.* like *Clad.* Perh. fr. O.E. *cláte,* 'bur, burdock, clivers.'

CLAUGHTON-ON-BROCK (Garstang). *Dom.* Clactune, 1208 Clatton, 1241 *Close R.* Clexton, 1288 Claghton. 'Village of *Clac,*' several in *Onom.,* whilst Brock is O.E. *bróc,* 'a brook.' *Cf.* CLAXTON, Clawton, Holsworthy, and 1160-61 *Pipe* Clawurda (Notts and Derby); also *Dom.* Yorks Clactone, now Clayton West, and Cloctone now Cloughton.

CLAVERDON (Stratford, Wwk.). *Dom.* Clavendone, 1151 Claverdon, 1326 Clardon. 'Clover hill'; O.E. *clœfre.* *Cf.* next, and see -don.

CLAVERING (Newport, Essex). *Dom.* both Essex and Nfk. Clave-linga, 1241 *Close R.* Cluering, 1330 Claveryng. This cannot be the same as CLAVERLEY (Wolverhmptn.) and CLAVERHOUSE (Sc.), fr. O.E. *clafre, clœfre,* 4-7 *claver,* ' clover.' It must be, by dissimilation, fr. a man *Clavel,* prob. he who came over with Wm. the Conqueror—' place of the sons of Clavel.' See -ing.

CLAXTON (Stockton, Yorks, and Norfk.). St. C. *sic* 1344, Yo. C. *Dom.* 3 times Claxtorp (see -thorpe), Nfk. C. *Dom.* Clakestona. ' Town of *Clacc* ' or ' *Klakk-r,*' a N. name. *Cf.* Clacton and CLAUGHTON.

CLAY (Lincoln). *Sic c.* 1180 *Bened. Peterb.* The earliest instance of the form *clay,* O.E. *cláeȝ,* in the *Oxf. Dict.* is *a.* 1300.

CLAYHANGER (Devon, S. Somerset, Staffs, Essex). Dev. C. *Dom.* Clehangre, Glostr. C. Claenhangare; St. C. 1300 Cleyhunger, *later* Cleohongre; Ess. C. 1015 *O.E. Chron.* Clæighangra—*i.e.,* ' clay slope.' The prob. meaning of O.E. *hangra* is ' slope,' fr. the ob. *hang,* or perh. ' wood on a slope.' See *Oxf. Dict.* HANGER[1]. *Cf.* BIRCHANGER, HUNGERFORD, etc. In Glostr. it has now become Clinger, 1138 Cleangra.

CLAYTON (8 in *P.G.*). More than one in Yorks *Dom.* Claitone. CLAYTON GRIFFITH (Newcastle, Staffs) is *Dom.* Claitone, *a.*1300 Clayton Griffyn. O.E. *clæg-tún,* ' town in the clay.' But *Dom.* Yorks also has a Clactone = Clayton West. See CLAUGHTON. The Griffyns were lords of the manor in the 13th cny.

CLAYWORTH (Retford). *Dom.* Clauorde. 1156 Clawurda, 1202 Clawurth. ' Clayey farm.' *Cf.* above and -worth. The surname Cleworth is the same name.

CLEASBY (N. Riding, Yorks). *Dom.* Clesbi, 1202 Clasebi, 1298 Cleseby. Prob. ' Dwelling of *Clea,*' or some such name, not found in *Onom.* See -by. Hardly fr. O.E. *cleof,* later *cleo,* ' a cliff, a CLEVE ' (*q.v.* in *Oxf. Dict.*). This last is the origin of CLEE and CLEOBURY.

CLEATLAM (Barnard Castle). *a.* 1130 *Sim. Dur.* Clethinga. Doubt-ful. The -am will be -ham, ' home.'

CLEATOR (Whitehaven). *Old* Cletergh. O.N. *klett-r,* ' a cliff, a crag,' and *ergh,* N. corrup. of G. *airigh,* 'a shieling, a hut.' *Cf.* ANGLESARK.

CLEDDY R. (Milford Haven). 921 Cleðe muþan, *c.* 1120 *Hen. Hunt.* Glade mouth, *c.* 1130 *Lib. Land.* Clediv and Doncledif. Prob. O.W. *cled,* ' warm '; perh. W. *cladd,* ' a trench.' *Cf.* CLWYD. But Owen, 1603, spells it Clydagh.

CLEE HILLS (Salop). *Dom.* Clee, Cleie. O.E. *cleof,* later *cleo,* ' a cliff, a brae,' same word as CLEVE-LAND. *Cliff* in O.E. is also *clif,* N. *klif. Cf. Dom.* Lincs. Cleia, and CLEETHORPES (Grimsby), not in *Dom.*

CLENCHWARTON (K.'s Lynn). Not in *Dom*. 1234 *Close R*. Clenche-wartun. Doubtful. Hardly fr. Eng. to *clench* O.E. *clincan*, which as sb. is late. *Cf*. Clench Common (Marlboro'), which may be connected with 941 *chart*. Clinca leage, Tisted (Hants). Possibly Kelt., ? W. *clyn*, 'brake, thicket,' with 2nd syll. half lost, as in TRUNCH. See WARTON.

CLENT HILLS (Stourbridge). *Sic Dom*. Dan. and Sw. *klint*, Icel. *klett-r*, ' a hard, flinty rock,' found in Eng. as *clint a*. 1300 and as *clent a*. 1400. *Cf*. GLENTWORTH, and Clint (Ripley, Yorks), not in *Dom*. ; also Dunclent, *sic* in *Dom*., near by.

CLEOBURY MORTIMER (Salop). *Dom*. Cleberie, 1287 Cleburi Mortimer, ? 1298 Cluburi. ' Cliff-burgh ' or ' castle.' See CLEE and -bury, and MORTIMER.

CLERKENWELL (London). *Sic E.E. Wills* 1442. Very likely named ' well of the clerks ' in the time of Henry I. There is a ' Clerche-welle ' (Kent), in 1158-59 *Pipe*. Stow, *Survey*, 1598, says, the London place ' took the name of the Parish Clerks in London who, of old time, were accustomed there yearly to assemble and to play some large history of Holy Scripture.'

CLEVEDON (Somerset). 1321 Clivedon. ' Cliff-like, brae-like hill.' See CLEE, CLEVELAND, and and -don. CLEEVE PRIOR (Eves-ham) is 888 *chart*. Clife, *Dom*. Clive. 1160-61 *Pipe*, Northants has a Cliua. *Cf*. BISHOP'S CLEEVE.

CLEVELAND (N. Yorks). *Sim. Dur*. ann. 1093 Clivelande, 1209 Cliveland, 1461 Clevland. ' Cliff-land.' See CLEE. *Dom*. has only Clive in Yorks, but this 12 times = North and South Cliff, etc.

CLEWER (Windsor and Cheddar). Win. C. *Dom*. Clivore, 1291 Cliwar, Clyfwere, 1316 Clyware. Prob. O.E. *clif-wara*, ' home of the cliff-dwellers.' Such cliff-men are referred to in *B.C.S*. i. 318 (Kent). *Dom*. Somst. has only a Clovewrde, ' farm of *Clofa* '; this can hardly be Clewer, Cheddar, but ? With it *cf*. Clearwell (For. of Dean), *old* Clowerwall, fr. *clower*, ' sluice, mill-dam,' found in 1483 *clowre*, and still in North dial. *cloor*, but further S. usually *clow*. See *Oxf. Dict. s.v*.

CLIFFE. Prob. that at Selby, *c*. 890 Ælfred *Baeda* 772 Clife. O.E. *clif*, ' a cliff.' See also *s.v*. CLEVELAND.

CLIFFORD (4 in *P.G*.). Gloucester C. 922 *chart*. Clifforda, *Dom*. Clifort. ' Cliff-ford '—*i.e*., ' steep ford.'

CLIFTON (14 in *P.G*.). *Dom*. Yorks Cliftun, 14 times, *a*. 1100 *Hugo Candidus* a ' Cliftune,' Rugby C. *Dom*. Cliptone (*p* an error). CLIFTON CAMVILLE (Tamworth) is *Dom*. Clistone, another error, but 1100 Cliftun. ' Cliff town.' See above. The Camvilles were Nor. lords of the manor, who took their name fr. Canappeville, Eure, Normandy. Their name was also spelt Campville.

CLIPSHAM (Oakham) and CLIPSTON (Mket. Harboro'). *Dom.* Clipestone, 1317 Clipston. 'Clip's home' or 'village'; one *Clip* in *Onom.* *Cf. Dom.* Clipesbei, now Clixby (Norfk.).

CLITHEROE (Lancs). *Sim. Dur.* contin. ann. 1138 Clitherhou, 1175-76 Cliderhous, 1230 Cliderho, 1241 -erhow, 1501 Cliderowe. Fr. early dial. *clithers,* mod. dial. *clider,* for *clivers,* 'goosegrass,' and HOE, O.E. *hōh,* 'a height.'

CLIVE (Shrewsbury). *Sic* 1327. O.E. *clif,* 2-6 *cliue,* really a dat., 'a cliff.'

CLOPTON (Glostrsh., Thrapston, Stratford, Wwk., Woodbridge [or Clapton]). Gl. C. *Dom.* Cloptune. Thr. C. *c.* 1080 *Inquis Camb.* Clopetuna, 1210 Cloptune. Str. C. 1016 Cloptune, *Dom.* Clotone. 'Town of *Clopa*' *cf.,* CLAPTON, also 1179-80 *Pipe* Clopton (Yorks). But *cf.* CLAPHAM.

CLOSWORTH (Sherborne). Not in *Dom.* 1252 *chart.* Cloveswurthe, 1270 Clovesuude (*i.e.,* 'wood'). Prob. 'farm of *Clovis* or *Clofa,*' or some such name. The nearest in *Onom.* is *Clofena.* *Cf.* a 'Closley,' 1285 in Salop, and LOWESTOFT; and see -worth.

CLOUGHTON. See CLAUGHTON.

CLOVÉLLY (N. Devon). *Dom.* Clovelie. Doubtful; perh. Corn. *clog* (G. *cloch*), 'a steep rock' and *velen,* 'yellow.' There is also a Bratton Clovelly, near Okehampton.

CLUN (W. Salop). *Dom.* Clone, Clune. Now in W. Colunwy. [*Cf.* 1131 *O.E. Chron.* 'Prior of Clunni.'] W. *clyn,* 'a brake, a thicket.' But *cf.* CLUNIE (Sc.), and G. *cluain,* 'a meadow.' Clungunford, near by, will be W. *clyn gwyn,* 'fair, clear thicket,' whilst CLUNBURY is *Dom.* Cluneberie. See -bury; and CLUNTON is *Dom.* Clūton.

CLWYD R. (Denbighsh.). *Dom.* Cloith, Cloit. W. *clwyd,* 'warm,' also 'strong.' *Cf.* CLYDE (Sc.).

CLYDACH (Glam. and Abergavenny). Gl. C. 1207-08 Cleudach. W. *clwyd,* 'warm, comfortable, sheltering.' Some say, *ach* is 'river'; it is more prob. a suffix of place. *Cf.* Clarach, Aberystwith.

CLYST (Exeter and Topsham). Ex. C. 1001 *O.E. Chron.* Glistun, v.r. Clistun, *Dom.* Clistone, Glustone. Also *Dom.* Bucks, Worc., and Dorset Clistone, -tune. Hybrid. W. *glwys,* 'a hallowed place, a fair spot,' and -ton.

COALBROOKDALE (Salop) and COLEBROOK (Plympton). *Dom.* Colebroche, 1298 Colebroke. O.E. *cól,* 'cool, cold,' does not suit well phonetically, so it may be fr. O.E. *col,* 2-8 *cole,* 'charcoal, coal';—brook beside which charcoal was burned. *Cf. Dom.* Chesh. Colbourne, 1157 *Pipe* Northbld. Colebr'., 1107-28 *Lib. Winton.* Colobrochestrel (Winchester), and COLESHILL. See -dale.

COALEY (Frocester). *Dom.* Coeleye, *later* Covel-, Couley. Prob. '*Cofa*'s mead.' See -ley.

COANWOOD (Carlisle). 'Wood of *Coen* or *Coena*,' several in *Onom.* *Cf. B.C.S.* 313 'Cohhanleah,' date 804.

COATES (Peterboro', Cirencester). Pe. C. *Dom.* Cota, Cote. O.E. *cot, cott ;* M.E. *cotes,* ' cots, cottages.'

COBDEN HILL (Elstree). *Old* Copdene; also *cf.* 'Coppdene' 1314 in Sussex, later Cobden, now extinct. ' Hill at the head of the (wooded) valley,' fr. O.E. *cop, coppe,* 'top, summit' (*Oxf. Dict.* gives no spelling of the sb. *cop* with a *b*). See -den.

COBHAM. Surbiton C. *Grant* of *a.* 675 Chebe-, Chabbeham, *Dom.* Cebehā, 1315 Cobeham. ' Home of *Ceabba*,' one in *Onom.* But Gravesend C. 939 *chart.* Cobba hamme, ' enclosure of *Cobba.*' *Cf.* COBLEY (Alvechurch), *a.* 1200 Cobbeslee; and see -ham.

COCKERMOUTH. *c.* 1310 Cokermue, 1317 Cokermuth. Can this river's name come fr. O.E. *cocer,* M.E. *koker, cokre,* ' a quiver ' ? If not, then fr. what ? There is also COCKERHAM (Garstang), *Dom.* Cocreha, 1206 Cokerheim, which must be fr. a man *Cocker,* a surname still found. In Eng. *cocker* is ' a prize-fighter, a wrangler,' not found *c.* 1275, or ' a hay-worker,' 1st in 1393. But in our place-names Cocker- is prob. the inflected form of the N. name *Kok-r.* The river name must remain doubtful. *Cf.* next and Coker, Somst., *Dom.* Cocre.

COCKERTON (Darlington). *a.* 1130 *Sim. Dur.* Cocertune, 1183 Cokirtona. ' Town of *Cocker*,' a name not in *Onom.*, but see above, and *cf.* COCKERSAND ABBEY (Lancaster), 1213-15 Cocressand, 1236-42 Kokersond; also 1225 *Patent R.* Cokerinton, a patronymic.

COCKFIELD (Bury St. Edmunds and Durham). Bury C. *chart.* Cochanfeld. ' Field of *Cocha*' or '*Cocca.*' *Cf. B.C.S.* 246 Coccan burh. Old forms needed for Dur. C. *Cf.* 1157 *Pipe* Cochulla (? Gloster.), and *Dom.* Worc. ' Cochesie.' In Pipe Rolls of Rich. I. we also have ' Cokefeld ' (Oxfd.) and ' Cockesfeld ' (Norfk.), which seem to come fr. *cock.* See next. *Cf.* COUGHTON.

COCKLEY CLEY (Swaffham). Not in *Dom.* 1451 Cokely Clay. *Cf. Dom.* Chesh. Cocle, and 1200 *chart.* Kokedale. ' Cock's meadow '; O.E. *cocc, coc, kok,* ' a barnyard cock.' *Cf.* next and CLAY, O.E. *clǽȝ,* 4-6 *cley ;* also COXLEY. See -ley.

COCKNAGE (Trentham). 1194 Cokenache. *Ache* is not a M.E. form of *oak* (see *Oxf. Dict. s.v.*), as Duignan thinks, but is for *hatch,* O.E. *hœa*(c), gen. *hœcce,* 3-7 *hacche, bacche,* so this is ' hatch, half-door or wicket-gate of the cock,' O.E. *coc ;* or, of a man *Coc* or *Cocca,* both forms are known. *Cf.* STEVENAGE. COCKRUP (Glostr.), *old* Cocthrop, is ' *Cocca*'s farm.' See thorpe.

COCKSHOTTS WOOD (Lancs). 1377-99 Cokeshoteslacc, and COCKSHUTT (Cakemore, Halesowen, and Ellesmere). Ca. C. 1440

Kockshete. A *cockshot* is a broad way or glade through which game (*cocks*) might *shoot*, so as to be caught in nets. There are many so named in Worc.

CODNOR (Derby). *Dom.* Cotenovre. 'Bank, border of *Coda* ' or ' *Cota,* ' both on record. *Cf.* CODBARROW (Wwksh.), *a.* 1300 Codbarwe, 'Coda's mound,' and *Dom.* Kent 'Codeha.' The *n* is the sign of the O.E. gen. See -or, -over.

CODSALL (Wolverhampton). *a.* 1200 Coddeshal, *a.* 1300 Codeshale. 'Nook of *Codda* ' or ' *Coda.*' *Cf.* CODNOR, and see -hall.

COEDPENMAEN (Pontypridd). W. for ' wood of the rocky headland or height.' COED RHATH (Pembroke) 1324, Coyt rath is W. for ' wood on the mound or hill.' Coety (? Pembroke) is *old* Coetif, O.W. for ' dark wood,' W. *dy.*

COGGESHALL (Essex). *Dom.* Cogghessala, 1298 Coggeshale, ' nook of *Coga* or *Cogga.*' See *Onom.* Prob. not fr. M.E. *cogge,* ' a small ship.' *Cf.* 1183 *Boldon Bk.* Cogesalle (Durham). See -hall.

COGYROS (Cornwall). Said to be Corn. for ' cuckoo-moor.' Lit. it is ' cuckoo in the moor,' W. and Corn. *cog.*

COLCHESTER. (? 940 *chart.* B.C.S. 750, Collacestr), *Dom.* and 1160 *Pipe* Colecestra. The Camulodunum of *Tacitus—Camulos* was a Kelt. deity. An inscription shows that the Empr. Claudius founded ' Colonia Victricensis ' here, and so it may have come to be called ' Colonia castra,' *O.E. chart.* Colenceaster, in W. Caercolun. So Colchester may mean ' colony camp ' or ' city.' Only it is on R. COLNE, and so quite possibly it means only ' camp, castle on the Colne.'

COLD ASTON (Glostersh.). *c.* 955 *chart.* Æsctun—*i.e.,* ' ash-tree town.' *Dom.* Escetone. *Cf.* CALDICOT.

COLD CONISTON (Craven). *Dom.* Congehestone, Coningeston; 1202 Calde Cuningeston = Cold KINGSTON. *Cf.* CONISBOROUGH.

COLD HARBOUR (Boston, Grantham, Cambs, Glostrsh., Leith Hill). ' Cold shelter,' an ironic name, says Leo of Halle, in Ger. *Kalte-herburg.* On *harbour,* which is lit. ' a place of shelter,' see *Oxf. Dict.* *Cf. c.* 1485 *Skelton,* ' some say the devil's dead and buried in Cold Harbour.'

COLESBOURNE (Cheltenham). *c.* 800 *chart.* Colesburna, *c.* 802 *ib.* Collesburna—*i.e.,* ' burn, brook of *Colle* ' or ' *Cola,*' a common O.E. name. *Cf.* Coleby (Lincs), and COSELEY, also *Dom.* Surrey Colesdone; Nfk. Colebei. COLBOURN (Yorks) is in *Dom.* Corburne by dissimilation. There is a brook Cole (Wilts). COLECOMBE (Sevenhampton) is fr. R. COLN.

COLESHILL (Swindon, Warwksh., and Flint). Sw. C. *Dom.* Coles-elle, 1298 Coleshulle. War. C. 799 *chart.* Colles hyl, *Dom.* Coles-hille. Fl. C. *c.* 1188 *Gir. Camb.* Koleshull, but said also to be *old* Counsylht. ' Hill of *Colle* ' or ' *Cola.*'   But both the Berks and War. places are on a R. Cole, whose origin is hard to guess. It will not be O.E. *cawel, cawl,* 4 *col,* ' cole, cabbage '; nor does O.E. *cól,* ' cool,' suit well phonetically; while *cól,* ' charcoal,' does not seem likely.   *Cf.* COALBROOKDALE.

COLLINGBOURNE DUCIS and KINGSTON (Marlborough).   *Dom.* Colingeburne, 1298 Colyngborn.   ' Bourne, burn, or brook of *Colling,*' a name in *Onom.*, where also are *Collanus* and *Collinc.* It is a patronymic fr. *Coll*(*a*), a fairly common name.   *Cf. Dom.* Yorks Colingaworde, now Cullingworth, and Coneyswick (Wstrsh.), *Dom.* Colingwic.   Ducis is L. for ' of the duke.'

COLLINGHAM (Newark).   *Dom.* Colingeham, *a.* 1100 Colingham. ' Home of *Colling.*'   See above and -ing.

COLMWORTH (St. Neot's).   *Dom.* Colmeworde, -borde (*b* for *v*). ' Farm of *Colm.*'   *Cf. Dom.* Colmestan (Salop).   In Scotland *Colm* is short for *Columba.*   Here it may be for *Colman.* See -worth.

COLN R. (Glostrsh.) and COLNE R. (Herts).   Gl. C. [*c.* 740 *chart.* Cunugl ae, 855 *ib.* Cunelga, 962 *ib.* Cungle] *old* Culna, Culne, Colum; He. C. 985 *chart.* Colen, 893 *O.E. Chron.* Colne.   Prob. pre-Keltic.   A river would not be named fr. L. *colonia,* and W. *collen,* ' hazel, hazel-wood,' is scarcely likely.   In view of the undoubted early forms of both rivers, confirmed by a Devon R. Coln, found so early as 670 *chart.* Culum, it is all but certain that the Cunugl forms must have been applied to the Glo'ster river through some Saxon's error.   Phonetically they are hard to identify, and Cunugl is now represented by KNOYLE.   COLN ST. ALDWYN'S, Fairford (Glostr.), corrupt *chart.* form, dated 681 Enneglan, prob. = Cuneglan, is fr. the hermit monk *St. Ealdwine,* prob. he who d. 1085, and was founder of Malvern Priory. *Ealdwine* was a favourite name with churchmen.   See *Onom.*

COLNE (St. Ives, Hunts, and Lancs).   Hu. C. is *sic* in *Dom.*, and so prob. = above.   La. C. is 1230 Calna, 1241 *Close R.* Kaun, 1251 Caune, 1327 Coln, so must be = CALNE.   *Cf. Dom.* Nhants. Calme.

COLNEY HATCH and HEATH (St. Albans).   *O.E. chart.* Colenea— *i.e.,* ' isle on R. COLNE, *q.v.* and -ey.   *Hatch* means ' a wicket-gate.'   See ALDBOROUGH HATCH.

COLTON (Rugeley and 6 others).   *Dom.* Coltune, -tone, and so later. *Dom.* Yorks gives Coltune, Coletun, or Colletun 15 times.   Un-certain, but prob. O.E. *col tún,* ' charcoal (or coal) town.'   COL-WICH (Rugeley), 1166 Calewich, *a.* 1300 Cole-, Colwych, is also ' coal-village.'   Coal is O.E. *col,* 2-8 *cole,* 6- *coal,* but *Oxf. Dict.* gives no *cale,* and it may be an error.

COMBE (Coventry and Hungerford).   Cov. C. *old* Cumb, Combe; Hun. C. *Dom.* Comba.   O.E. *cumb,* ' a bowl, a valley, a coomb.'

Cf. W. *cwm,* ' hollow,' and COOMLEES (Sc.), also *Dom.* Worc.,
' Comble,' or ' meadow, lea, in the valley.' COMBROOKE, also
in Warwk., is ' brook in the valley.' COMBE MARTIN (N. Devon)
is fr. a Martin of Tours, who received lands here fr. Wm. Rufus.
We have a pl. form in COMBS (Stockport and Stowmarket),
the latter 1235 Cambes.

COMBERBACH (Northwich), COMBERFORD (Tamworth), and COMBER-
MERE (Nantwich). *a.* 1200 Cumbreford. 1135 Cumbermere, 1240
Cumbremer. One is tempted to derive Comber- fr. a Keltic root
meaning ' confluence,' as in CUMBERNAULD (Sc.) and in Quimper
or Kemper (Brittany). *Cf.* W. *cymmer* and G. *comar* with this
meaning. There is a ' Roger de Combre ' in Cheshire *a.* 1200,
and Comber- or Combre may be O.E. *cumbra,* gen. pl. of *cumb,*
' a valley '—at least in some cases. But COMBERTON and
COMBERWORTH almost force a derivation fr. *Cumbra,* a man's
name, lit. ' a Welshman.' The -bach is O.E. *bæc,* O.Fr. *bache,*
Nor.Fr. *bake,* M.E. *bache* (*q.v.* in *Oxf. Dict.*), ' the vale of a
stream,' same root as *beck. Cf.* BATCHWORTH, SANDBACH, and
PONTYCYMMER. *Mere* is Eng. and O.E. for ' lake.'

COMBERTON (Pershore and Cambridge). Pe. C. 972 *chart.* Cum-
brincgtune, *Dom.* Cumbri(n)tune, 1275 Cumbrintone. Ca. C.
Dom. Cumbertone, 1210 Cumbretone. ' Town of *Cumbra,*' or
' the Welshman,' or their descendants. *Cf.* CUMBERWORTH and
1157 *Pipe* Cumbremara (Staffd.); and see above and -ing.

COMBERWORTH (Lincs) and UPPER CUMBERWORTH (Huddersfd.).
1236 *Close R.* Comberworth. *Cf.* Earle *Chart.* 447 Cumbran
weorð, Pershore. ' Farm of *Cumbra,*' or ' the Welshman.' *Cf.*
above and CUMBERLAND.

COMBWICH (Bridgwater). *Dom.* Comich. O.E. *cumb wíc,* ' valley
dwelling or hamlet '; *wíc* regularly becomes *wich* in later Eng.
Cf. Combridge (Uttoxeter), *a.* 1300 Combruge.

COMPTON (16 in *P.G.*). 804 *chart.* Cumbden, Kent (-den and -ton
interchange), 962 *ib.* Cumtun (Glostr.), 990 *ib.* Cumtune
(? which), *c.* 1020 Cumtune (Guildford or Petersfield ?), *Dom.*
Cun-, Contone (Warwk.), Contone (Wolvermpton.), Cantune (I. of
Wight); 1298 Cumpton (? which), *a.* 1400 Comptone (Wolverhampton). O.E. *cumb tún,* ' valley village.' *Dom.* has 32
manors, always with *n*—Contone. *Cf.* COMBE.

COMPTON BEAUCHAMP (Berks) is named fr. Guido de *Bello Campo*
(in Fr. *Beau Champ*), Earl of Warwick, and Alicia his wife, who
held lands here 1315-16. C. SCORPION (Shipston), *Dom.* Contone parva, 1279 Compton Scorfen, which last, thinks Duignan,
may be ' track, *score* over the *fen,*' but it is quite uncertain.
Scorpion, at any rate, is popular etymology. C. WINYATES,
near by, is said to show an old form of ' vineyard.' It is *a.* 1300
C. Wyniate, Wyndyates, *c.* 1540 C. Vyneyatis.

CONBELIN (Wales). Thought to preserve the name of the early British King *Cunobellinus*.

CONDATE (Northwich). Early forms, see COUND. Old Keltic= 'confluence,' fr. *con*, 'together,' and *dhe*, 'set.' *Cf.* Condé, (France), in *O.E. Chron.* Cundoth, and Kind St., mod. name of the Roman road here. Also see Watson, *Place-Names Ross, s.v.* Contin. The streams Dane and Croco join here. *Cf.* CONDOVER and CUNLIFFE. CONGREVE (Penkridge) is *Dom.* Comegrave, *a.* 1300 Cune-, Cumgrave, where the Con- is uncertain, but it may be fr. O.E. *cumb*, 'valley,' so often in *Dom.* as Contune.

CONDERTON (Tewkesbury). 875 *chart.* Cantuaretun, 1327 Conterton. Very interesting proof of a settlement of Kent men here; for the name in O.E. means 'Kent-dwellers' town,' as in CANTERBURY. But R. CONDER (Lancaster), 1228 Gondouere, is, of course= CONDOVER. W. and H. absurdly suggest a derivation fr. *Gunnhildr !*

CONDICOTE (Stow-on-Wold). *Dom.* Condi-, Connicote, 1169 Cumdicote. Hybrid; *cond.* O.Kelt. for 'confluence,' see CONDATE, and *cf.* Fr. Condé; and O.E. *cot*, 'cottage.' Baddeley prefers to derive fr. a man. There is no *Conda*, and only one *Cunda* in *Onom.*

CONDOVER (Shrewsbury). *Dom.* Conodoure, 1228 Cunedour, 1234 Cunesdour, 1238 Cone-, Cundover. O.W. for 'the joining of the streams.' See CONDATE and DOVER. CANDOVER is prob. the same name; CONDER R. certainly is.

CONEYSTHORPE (Malton). *Dom.* Coningestorp. 'King's village.' O.N. *konung-r*, 'king,' an interesting corrup. See CONINGSBY and -thorpe. But CONEYBURY and CONEYBURROW HILL (Worc.) and CONEYGAR (Gloster.) are fr. *cony*, M.E. for 'rabbit,' while CONEYS- or CONNINGSWICK (also in Worc.) is *Dom.* Colingwic, 1275 Collingwike, 'abode of *Colling*,' or 'the sons of *Coll*.' *Cf.* COLLINGHAM, and see -wick. Coneygar is for *cony-garth*. See *Oxf. Dict. s.v.*

CONGERSTONE (Atherstone). 'Stone of *Congar*,' not in Duignan. But *cf. Dom.* Norfk. Congrethorp', and CONGRESBURY; also see -ton.

CONGLETON (E. Cheshire). *Dom.* Cogeltone. One would expect the first half to be the name of a man, but there is none likely in *Onom.* There is a *Conall*, son of *Comgal*, K. of Dabriada 563, which names might suggest an origin; but more old forms are needed. *Cf.* COLN (Glostr.), 962 Cungle; also *cogill*, found c. 1400, now dial. *coggle*, 'a water-worn or cobble-stone.'

CONGRESBURY (Weston-super-Mare). *Exon. Dom.* Cungresberia, *O.E. chart.* Congaresbyrig, which is 'burgh, town of *St. Congarus*,' who is buried here. The monastery of 'Cungresbyri' was granted by K. Ælfred to Asser. Little seems known about the saint himself. In 1155 *Pipe* it is Cungresbi. See -by.

CONINGSBY (Boston). *Dom.* Cuningesbi, 1298 Cunynggesby. 'Dwelling of the King.' O.N. *konung-r*, Dan. *konge.* See -by. *Cf.* CONNINGSBURGH (Sc.), CONINGTON (Cambs.), *B.C.S.* iii. 630 Cunningtun, *Dom.* Cunitone, 1210 Conintone, 1290 Conington, 1426 Conitone, Skeat thinks, may perh. be fr. a man, *Cuna*, gen. *Cunan.* *Cf.* Connington (Hunts), 1236 *Close R.* Conninton, Cunyton, and COLD CONISTON. CONISBURGH (Rotherham), 1240 *Close R.* Cunigeburg, is clearly = Coningsby. See -burgh.

CONISBOROUGH (Rotherham). *Dom.* Coningesburg, -borc, c. 1145 *Geoffr. Monm.* 'Kaerconan, now Cunungeburg,' 1202 Kuningbere. 'King's burgh.' See above and -burgh.

CONISCLIFFE (Darlington). *a.* 1130 *Sim. Dur.* Cingcesclife, 1202 Cuniggesclive super Teisam. The name represented in the first half is perh. doubtful. It may be *Cynegyth* or *Cynesige* (*Kinsige*). Prob. it is for *King.* *Cf.* CONINGSBY. On *cliffe*, see CLEE.

CONONLEY (Keighley). *Dom.* Cutnelai. Doubtful. Perh. corrup. of *Cutan leah*, 'Cuta's meadow.' *Cuta* and *Cutha* are both in *Onom.* See -ley.

CONSETT (Co. Durham). 1183 *Boldon Bk.* Conekesheued. Interesting corruption. *Heucd* is M.E. for O.E. *heafod*, 'head, height,' and this must be 'the height of' some quite unknown man. There is one *Cynech* in *Onom.*

CONSTANTINE (Padstow). Fr. *Constantinus*, King and martyr, a convert of St. Petrock. He died 590.

CONWAY (N. Wales). Prob. *c.* 380 *Ant. Itin.* Conovio, and *a.* 700 *Rav. Geogr.* Canubio (the river), *a.* 1196 *Gir. Camb.* Cunewe, Aberkonewe, -coneu; 1295 Aberconewey, still the proper name of the town. The R. in W. is Conwi, 'chief river,' fr. Keltic *con*, 'together,' and *gwy*, 'river,' referring to the main stream being joined by tributaries. CONWAY (Sc.) is not the same word.

COOKHAM (Maidenhead). *a.* 971 *will* Coccham, *Dom.* Cocheham, 1238 Cokh', 1241 Cocham, also Cucham. The chief evidence points to O.E. *cōc-ham*, 'cook's home'; but Cocham and the like point to O.E. *cocc*, 'a cock,' 'cock's home.' COOKRIDGE (Yorks) is *Dom.* Cucheric, ? 'cook's' or 'cock's.' COOK HILL (Inkberrow) is *a.* 1300 Cochulle, and COOKSEY (Bromsgrove) is *Dom.* Cochesei, *a.* 1300 Cokesey. The present phonetic evidence is all in favour of *cook.* *Cf.* CUXHAM.

COOKLEY (Kidderminster). 964 *chart.* Culnan clif, 1066 Cullecliffe, 1275 Coleclif. The charter name must be ' *Culna's cliff.*' The corrup. to -ley, 'meadow,' is rare. We have it the other way round in TROTTERSCLIFFE.

COOLING (Rochester). 805 *chart*. Cinges Culand, or 'King's Cow-land,' but in other charters it is 774 Colling, 778 Culinga, and 805 Culingas, as if a patronymic. The name has got mixed. There are two named *Coling* and two named *Culling* in *Onom*. This latter personal name still exists. *Cf*. COWLING.

COPDOCK (Ipswich). *Cf*. 900 in Thorpe *Diplom*. 145 On ðʒa coppedan ac. Copdock is 'copped'—*i.e*., pollarded 'oak'—O.E. *ac*, very rarely found now as *ock*. *Oxf. Dict*. gives only 3-5 *ok*. It also gives only O.E. quots. for this sense of *copped*, which is fr. *cop* sb., O.E. *cop, copp*, 'head, top.' But *Dom*. Surrey has a Copedorne, which is 1160-01 *Pipe* Coppedethorn. *Cf*. COPYTHORNE and the surname Braddock.

COPMANTHORPE (York). *Dom*. Copemantorp. 'Village of *Copman*,' N. for 'Chapman, merchant.' One in *Onom*. *Cf*. 1242 *Close R*. Copmaneford, now Coppingford (Hunts). See -thorpe.

COPPENHALL (Stafford and W. Cheshire). *Dom*. both Copehale, and *later* Copen-, Coppenhale. 'Nook of *Coppa*' or '*Copa*,' the mod. name *Cope*. *Cf*. COPGROVE (Yorks), *Dom*. Copegrave; and COPNOR (Portsmouth), *Dom*. Copenore, O.E. *Copanora*, 'Copa's bank.' See -hall and -or.

COPPLESTONE (Devon). *Cf. Dom*. Sffk. Copletuna. Prob. 'Town' or 'stone of *Cuthbeald*,' common in *Onom.; cf*. the surname Cupples. See -ton.

COPYTHORNE (Southampton). Not in *Dom*., but *cf. K.C.D*. v. 240, To ðan coppedan þorne ; also *Dom*. Surrey Copedorne and Copededorne, 1160-61 *Pipe* Coppedethorn, 'the pollarded thorn-tree.' See COPDOCK. But if this name be late, it will be fr. O.Fr. *cop-, coupp-, colpeiz*, 'a blow, a stroke, a copse'; in 5-6 *copie, copy ;* but in mod. Eng. *coppice*, 'a wood or thicket of small trees or underwood.' The earliest quot. in *Oxf. Dict*. is 1538, but *copy* is found in 1486 in *Nottingham Rec*. iii. 254.

COQUET R. (Northumbld.). *c*. 800 *Hist. St. Cuthb*. Cocwuda, *a*. 1130 *Sim. Dur*. Coqued. *Cf. c*. 1250 *Matt. Paris* Koket insula. *Cocc-wuda* is O.E. fr. ' cock's wood.'

CORBRIDGE (Hexham). *c*. 380 *Ant. Itin*. Corstopitum, *a*. 1130 *Sim. Dur*. Corebricge, 1150 Corbrig, 1157 Corebrigge. Corstopit--um is prob. G. *corr stobach*, 'hill-spur full of stumps' (*stob*), with Brythonic *p* for *b*, and *t* common scribal error for *c*. G. *corr* is lit. ' a snout, a bill, a horn '; W. *cor* is ' a circle, a crib.'

CORBY (Carlisle, Grantham, Kettering). Car. C. 1120 Chorkeby, 1222 Korkebi—*i.e*., 'dwelling by the oat-field.' N. *korki*. *Cf*. CORKICKLE. But Gr. C. is *Dom*. Corbi, and Ke. C. Carbi, ' dwelling of *Cor*' or '*Car*.' One in *Onom*. See -by.

CORFE (Taunton) and CORFE CASTLE (Wareham). Corfe *c*. 1180 *Ben. Peterb*. Chorf. C. Castle, 975 *E.O. Chron*. Corfes Geat (gate), *c*. 1160 *Gest. Steph*. Corfli castellum, 1234 Corf, 1393 *Letter*

Notre Chastelle de Corf. Prob. ' a cutting' in the Purbeck hills, in which the castle stands, fr. O.E. *ceorfan*, ' to cut.' *Cf. Dom.* Corfan (Salop), 1160 *Pipe* Corfhā, and CORTON.

CORKICKLE (Whitehaven). Prob. N. *korki-keld*, ' oat-field well.' *Cf.* Cockley Beck, also Cumbld. *old* Korkalith, O.N. *hlith*, ' a hill-slope,' and CORBY. But there is a Keekle beck near Whitehaven, and this raises uncertainty.

CORLEY (Coventry and Salop). Cov. C. *Dom.* Cornelie, 1327 Cornleye, *a.* 1400 Corley. Sal. C. *Dom.* and later Cornlie. ' Corngrowing meadow.' See -ley. We have a reverse change in Cornbrough (E. Riding), *Dom.* Corlebroc, a form of somewhat doubtful meaning.

CORNHILL (London, Sunderland, on Tweed). Lo. C. 1160-61 *Pipe* Cornhelle, 1167-68 *ib.* Cornhille, 1234 *Close R.* Cornhull, where all the endings= ' hill.' But Su. C. is 1183 Cornehall, 1322 Cornhale= -hall, *q.v.*

CORNWALL. 1047 *O.E. Chron.* Cornwalon (inflected), *Dom.* Cornvalge, *c.* 1110 *Orderic* Cornu Britanniæ, id est Cornwallia, 1189 Cornubia, *c.* 1205 *Layam.* Cornwaile, -wale. *Cf.* Cornouaille (*Rom. Rose* Cornewaile), Brittany. Earle says, ' Place of the *Walas* or strangers of *Kernyw.*' *Cf.* WALES. Others derive fr. O.Fr. *corn*, L. *cornu*, ' a horn,' fr. the shape of Cornwall.

CORNWOOD (Ivybridge). Local pron. Kernood. *Dom.* Cornehude. Looks like O.E. *corn wudu*, ' corn wood'; but wherefore such a name ? No *Corn* or the like in *Onom.* *Cf.* Cornworthy, ' corn farm' (Totnes), and Corndean (Winchcombe), 1189 Corndene. But, because of a Corne and a Cornbrook, also in Glostrsh., Baddeley thinks *Corn* must be an old stream name, and says *cf.* Abercorn. But that Sc. name is in *Bede* Æbbercurnig.

CORRINGHAM (Stanford-le-Hope and Gainsboro'). St. C. *Dom.* Coringe-, 1242 Curingeham. Ga. C. *Dom.* Currincham. Patronymic. ' Home of the sons of' some unrecorded *Cura* or *Cora.* There is one *Cyra* in *Onom.* See -ing.

CORSE LAWN (Tewkesbury). 1179 Cors. W. *cors*, ' a fen,' and *llan*, ' enclosure, then church.' *Cf.* CARSE (Sc.). There seems no authority for Duignan's assertion that *corse* is a M.E. form of *causey.*

CORSLEY (Frome) and CORSTON (Bristol). 941 *chart.* Corsantune, *Dom.* Corstune, ' mead' and ' village of *Corsa.* See -ley.

CORTON DENHAM (Sherborne). *Dom.* Corfetone, 1235 *Close R.* Corfton and Cortun. See CORFE. Denham is ' home in the dean' or ' (wooded) vale.'

CORWEN (E. Merioneth). Possibly W. *cor faen*, ' circle of stone,' or, as T. Morgan says, ' stone in a circle.' But, as likely, W. *cor gwen*, ' white, beautiful circle,' or ' choir,' or ' church.' *Cf.*

BANGOR. There is a ' Corfan ' in Salop *Dom.*, but this must be the Corfham of 1160 *Pipe* Salop.

COSELEY (Bilston). 14th to 17th cny. Colse-, Couls-, Colsley, *later* Cossley. Prob. ' meadow of *Col* ' or ' *Cola.*' *Cf.* COLESBOURNE, and see -ley.

COSGROVE (Stony Stratford). 1238 *Close R.* Couesgrave, ' grave,' O.E. *græf*, ' of *Cufa.*' *Cf.* COVENEY. The endings -grave and -grove often interchange. But COSBY (Leicester), COSFORD (Rugby), and COSHAM (Hants), 1241 Cosseby, *a.* 1200 Cosseford, and *Dom.* Cose-, Cosseham, are fr. an unrecorded man, *Cosa* or *Cosse.* See -ham.

COSHESTON (Pembroke). 1603 *Owen* Costeinston. ' Town of *Constantine.*' K. Constantine is 926 *O.E. Chron.* Cosstantin.

COSSINGTON (Bridgwater). 1237 *Close R.* Cusinton. ' Village of *Cusa,*' gen. -*an.* 3 in *Onom. Cf.* COSBY. See -ing.

COTHERIDGE (Worcester). 963 *chart.* Coddan hrycce, hrycge, *Dom.* Codrie, *a.* 1300 Coderugge. ' Ridge,' O.E. *hrycge*, *hrycce*, ' of *Codda* ' or ' *Coda.*' One each in *Onom.* In same shire is COTTERIDGE, 1275 Coderugge.

COTHERSTONE (Darlington). *a.* 1130 *Sim. Dur.* Cuthbertestun. ' St. Cuthbert's town,' an interesting corrup. The great *Cudberct* or *Cuthbert* of Melrose flourished *c.* 700. *Cf. a.* 1110 ' Cotherstoke '. (Oundle). But Cotherston (N. Yorks) is *Dom.* Codrestune, -ton, ' town of *Codra.*' *Cf. B.C.S.* 1282 Codranford.

COTON (Cambridge, 2 Warwk., Staffs, Shrewsbury). Cam. C. 1211 and 1291 Cotes, 1272 Cotun, 1296 Coton. War. C. *Dom.* and 1287 Cotes, 1327 Cottone. Staf. C. *Dom.* Cote. Skeat thinks prob. O.E. *cotum,* dat. pl. of *cot,* ' cottage.' But *coton, -un,* are regular, and *cotes* irregular nom. plurals. *Cf.* COTTON and Cotham, Notts, *Dom.* Cotun, Cotes.

COTSWOLD HILLS. 780 *chart.* Monte quem nominant in colæ mons Hwicciorum, *c.* 1188 *Gir. Camb.* Montana de Codesuualt, 1231 Coteswold, 1300 *Rolls Parlmt.* Coteswalde, *a.* 1500 Cottasowlde, *a.* 1553 *Udall* Cotssold. The present spelling may be, as *Oxf. Dict.* thinks, popular etymology; but the name prob. is ' *Code*'s, *Cota*'s, or *Cotta*'s wood.' All 3 names are in *Onom.* O.E. *wald, weald,* ' a wood,' is the origin of both *weald* and *wold. Cf.* next and CUTSDEAN, a yet older name.

COTTERED (Buntingford). *Dom.* Chodrei, 1236 *Close R.* Codreye, Coudr'. ' River, stream, brook of *Coda,*' O.E. *rith,* ' stream.' *Cf.* RYE, RYDE, CHILDREY, and Cotgrave, Notts, *Dom.* Godegrave.

COTTESBROOKE (Northampton). ' *Cotta*'s or *Cota*'s brook.' *Cf.* above, ' Coteshala,' and ' Coteslai ' (Bucks) in *Dom.*, and COTTENHAM (Cambridge), *c.* 1080 *Inquis. Camb.* Cotenham, 1283 Cotenhame. This last might mean ' cottar's home.' *Dom.* Yorks Cotesmore is now Kedmoor, so *t* here will be error for *c,* ' moor of *Coca.*'

COTTINGHAM (Hull). Prob. *O.E. Chron.* and *Sim. Dur. re* ann. 800, Cettingaham, *Dom.* Cotingeham, 1135 *O.E. Chron.* Cotingham. Patronymic. 'Home of the descendants of *Cotta* or *Cota*.' *Cf.* above, next, and also Cottingham (Market Harborough) and Cottingley (Bingley). COTTINGWITH (E. Riding) is *Dom.* Cotewid, 'Cota's wood.'

COTTON (Chesh., Derby, and Stowmarket). Ch. C. *Dom.* Cotintone, St. C. 1479 Colton (a mistake), *a.* 1490 Cotton. Some perh. O.E. *coton*, loc. plur. of *cot, cota*, 'a cot, a cottage.' But *Dom.*'s form is '*Cota's* town.' See above, and *cf.* COTON. *Dom.* Yorks has Cottun 5 times, representing Cottam, Crosby Cote, etc.

COUGHTON (Alcester and Ross, Hereford). Al. C. *Dom.* Coctune, *a.* 1200 Cocton. Either fr. a man *Cocca* or *Coche*, see COCKFIELD, or fr. O.E. *cocc, coc*, 'a cock.' See COCKLEY. For *oc* becoming *ough*, *cf.* Broughton, 1128 Broctuna.

COUND (Shrewsbury). *Dom.* Cundet, 1240 *Close R.* Cunitte. 'Confluence.' See CONDATE and next.

COUNDON (Bp. Auckland and Coventry). Bp. A. C. 1183 Condona, Coundon. Cov. C. *Dom.* Condone, Condelme, 1257 Cundulme, 1327 Cundholme. *Cond* or *cound* is O.Kelt. for 'confluence of two streams.' *Cf.* CONDATE, CONDOVER, and COUND. The -don is 'hill,' whilst -elme, -ulme, etc., represent O.E. *holm*, 'meadow by a river.' *Cf.* the early forms of DURHAM.

COURAGE (Berks). *O.E. chart.* Cusan ricge, hricge, '*Cusa's* ridge'; *Dom.* Coserige; 1147 Cuserugia; 1316 Coserugge; 1428 Currygge. The mod. form is 'a daring respelling after the Norman manner' (Skeat). It should properly be Curridge.

COURTEENHALL (Nhampton.). *Dom.* Cortenhale, -halo; 1235 *Close R.* Corten-, Curtenhal. 'Nook, corner of *Curda*,' the only name in *Onom.*, and it but once. See -hall. The abnormal -een- seems a pure freak. *Cf.* 932 *chart.* Cyrdan heal (Meon, Hants).

COVENEY (Ely). *Chart.* Coveneye, -neie, Coueneia. Skeat is sure this is 'Isle of *Cufa*,' gen. *Cufan*. *Cf. Dom.* Surrey, Covenhā. Only COVEN (Wolverhampton) is *Dom.* Cove, *a.* 1200 Covene, which must be O.E. *cofa*, gen. *cofan*, 'a cove, cave, repository.' See -ey.

COVENT GARDEN (London). The *convent* garden belonging from *c.* 1220 to the abbots of Westminster. *Convent* is always spelt *covent a.* 1550.

COVENTRY. *c.* 1043 *chart.* Couæntree, 1053 *O.E. Chron.* Cofantreo, 1066 *ib.* Couentre, *Dom.* Couentreu, *Sim. Dur.* ann. 1057 Covantreo, *a.* 1142 *Wm. Malmes.* Coventreia. *Cofan treó* (*w*) is O.E. for 'tree by the cove, cave, or chamber,' or else 'tree of

Cofa.' *Cf.* COVENEY and Covenham (Louth). The word *con-vent*, M.E. *couent*, is impossible here. It is not found in Eng. *a.* 1225.

COVERDALE (Yorks). *Sic* 1202. *Cf.* 1203 ' Couerlee ' or Coverley. Cover- here is difficult. The Eng. *cover* is fr. O.Fr., and the word is not found in Eng. till *c.* 1275; whilst in the sense of ' covert or shelter for hunted animals ' it is not found till 1719. There is a W. *cyfair*, a land measure, two-thirds of an acre, found in Eng. in 1709 as *cover*. Possibly Cover- represents some unidentified personal name, as in COVERHAM (N. Yorks), *Dom.* Covreha'.

COWBEECH (Hailsham, Sussex). Not in *Dom.* This seems the same name as COWBACH, now called Clatterbach, near Clent (Worc.), where St. Kenelm's chapel was. ? *a.* 1200 Cu-bache, *c.* 1305 Coubache, 1494 Cowbacch. See *Oxf. Dict., s.v.* BACHE, which means ' the vale of a stream or rivulet.' *Cf.* BATCHWORTH and COMBERBACH. With the first syll. *cf.* Cowick (O.E. *wic*, ' dwelling, house '), Snaith (Yorks), 1241 Cuwic.

COWBRIDGE (Glam.). Eng. translation of W. Pontyfon, where *fon* is by assimilation for *mon*, O.W. for ' cow.' Said to have been called after a cow whose horns stuck in the arch of the bridge here so firmly that it had to be shot on the spot. It is 1645 Pontyfuwch, with the same meaning. So far T. Morgan. But there is also a Cowbridge (Boston), *c.* 1280 Cubrygge, which *may be* the origin of the W. place, as the same family of Williams, *alias* Cromwell, held lands in both places in 16th cny. See Thompson, *Hist. Boston*, 616. But Cowthorp (S. Yorks) is *Dom.* Coletorp, ' village of *Cola*,' and similarly Cowsdown (Upton Snodbury) is *c.* 1108 Colleduna, 1275 Coulesdon.

COWES (I. of W.). Dates only fr. 1540. It must be a pl. form of *cove*, O.E. *cofa*, *coua*, ' an inner chamber,' only found with the meaning ' cove, inlet,' after 1590. The form *cowe* is called Sc., and the meaning, ' cave, den,' Sc. and North. The name then is ' inlets.'

COWLAM (Driffield). *Dom.* 4 times Colnun, once Coletun. Colnun is prob. an O.E. loc. ' at the tops or summits.' *Cf.* O.N. *koll-r*, ' top, summit,' and HOWSHAM, a loc. too.

COWLEY (Gnosall and W. Drayton). Gno. C. *Dom.* Covelau, *a.* 1200 Coule. W. Dr. C. *Dom.* Couelei, ' cow-meadow,' O.E. *cuu, cu, a.* 1300 *cou*. See -ley.

COWLING (Skipton and Suffolk). Skip. C. *Dom.* Collinghe, 1202 Collinge. Suf. C. 1459 Cowlynge. Patronymic, like COOLING, ' place of the sons of *Cola* or *Coll*.' See -ing.

COXLEY (Wells). Not in *Dom.* 1231 Cockesleg. ' Meadow of *Cocca*,' in *Onom.*, or else ' cock's meadow.' See COCKLEY, and *cf. Dom.* Chesh. Cocheshalle. See -ley.

CRACKENTHORPE (Westmld.). *Old* Kreiginthorpe. 'Village of'? There is no name in *Onom.* like *Creaga,* but in *Lib. Vit. Dunelm.* there is a *Craca,* gen. *-can;* also *cf.* CRAYFORD. See -thorpe.

CRACOW or -OE HILL (Craven). 1202 Craho. 'Crow how' or 'mound.' O.E. *crawe,* 'a crow.' *Cf.* CROWTHORNE, and see -how.

CRADDOCK (Cullompton). Not in *Dom.* Corruption of CARADOC. *Cf.* CRAMOND (Sc.).

CRADLEY (Stourbridge and Herefdsh.) and CRADLEY HEATH (Staffs) St. C. *Dom.* Cradeleie, *a.* 1200 Crad(e)lega, 1275 Cradeley. He. C. *Dom.* Credleia. 'Meadow of *Crada*' or '*Creda,*' or '*Creoda.*' The two latter only in *Onom.* See -ley.

CRAKEHALL (Bedale). *Dom.* Crachele. Prob. 'nook of *Craca.*' One such is named in *Liber Vitæ Dunelm.* See -hall (-ele is for -hele or -hale). *Dom.* also has a Crachetorp in E. Riding, whilst *Dom.* Crecala is said to be Crakehill in Topcliffe.

CRAMLINGTON (Northumbld.). *c.* 1141 Cranlintune. Doubtful. Perh. O.E. *cran-hlinn-tún*—*i.e.,* 'village by the torrent or linn frequented by cranes.' *Cf.* LINTON.

CRANAGE (Congleton). Prob. for an O.E. *cranawic,* 'crane's dwelling.' *Cf.* SWANAGE, O.E. Swanawic. There is a Cranswick (Driffield), *Dom.* Cranzvic (*z* = *ts*), and *a.* 1241 *Close R.* Crendon (Bucks).

CRANBORNE (Salisbury), 1241 Craneburn, and CRANBOURNE (Windsor). *Sic* 1485. 'Crane's (or heron's) burn or brook.' See above and BOURNE. The crane, now extinct, was once abundant in Britain.

CRANBROOK (Kent). It was a haunt of *cranes.* Cranbrook Castle (Dartmoor) is said to be corrup. of Cranburh, fr. O.E. *burh, burg,* 'fort, castle, burgh.' *Cf.* CRANEBROOK (Lichfield), 1300 Crone brouke, *Dom.* Norfk. Cranaworda, and CRANHAM (Painswick), 1190 *Pipe* Cronham.

CRANK (St. Helen's), CRANK HILL (Wednesbury), CRANK WOOD (Derby). See *Oxf. Dict.* crank *sb²,* 'a crook, bend, winding, a crooked path or channel.' Not found in Eng. till 1552. Duignan identifies this with a number of obscure names in Cronk, several Cronk Hills in Salop, etc. But *crank* is never spelt with *o* in Eng., and Cronk is prob. a nasalized form of crook *sb,* O.N. *krók-r.* See *Oxf. Dict., s.v.* 6 and 11.

CRANSLEY (Kettering). 956 *chart.* Cranslea. See CRANBROOK.

CRANTOCK (Newquay). Fr. St. *Carantocus,* a Welsh saint who lived *c.* 450, and who also crossed to Ireland. *Cf.* CRADOCK.

CRASWALL (Herefd.). 1237 Cressewell = CRESSWELL.

CRAVEN (Yorks) and CRAVEN ARMS (Salop). Yor. C. *Dom.* Cravescire (shire). 1202 Cravene. O.N. *kra fen,* 'nook in the fen.'

Fen is also O.E. *fen,* and is found fr. 2-4 as *ven* or *venn(e).* The name must therefore indicate a dry spot in the midst of marshes.

CRAWLEY (Winchester). All names in Craw- are fr. O.E. *crawe,* ' a crow.' *Cf. Dom.* Leicr., Crawsho.

CRAWNON (Brecon). Perh., says Anwyl, the name of the Keltic goddess of storage.

CRAYFORD (W. Kent). *Chart.* Creganford, Creacan-, Creagan-ford. ' Ford of *Creaga,*' a name not found in *Onom.* Still, as *Oxf. Dict.* says, this name has nothing to do with *creek,* and still less with crayfish ! CRAYCOMB (Fladbury), however, is 1275 Craucombe, Crowecombe, fr. O.E. *crawe,* ' a crow.' See -combe.

CRAYKE (Easingwold). *Dom.* Creic, 1197 *Rolls* Crech ; 1236 Creek, Crek. See CREECH. However, this, instead of being W. *crug,* ' stack, heap,' may be G. *crioch,* gen. *criche,* ' boundary, frontier, landmark.' Only, if so, it is very rare to find a Gaelic name so far south. *Dom.* Norfk., Kreic, must be the same.

CREDITON. 905 in *Eadmer* Ecclesia Cridiensis ; *c.* 1097 *Flor. Worc.* Cridiatunensis ; *c.* 1540 *Leland* Crideton. Also found as Kyrton. ' Town on R. *Creedy*'—739 *chart.* Cridia, *Dom.* Cridic, Credie, by some said to be fr. *Crida* or *Creoda,* grandfather of Penda, K. of Mercia, or fr. *Crioda, Creoda,* first K. of Mercia, d. 593. But it is rare to find a river called after a man. *Cf.* Credenhill (Hereford) and *Dom.* Bucks, Credendone, plainly fr. a man *Creda.* The river name may be connected with W. *cryd,* O.W. *crit,* ' to shake.'

CREECH (Wareham), *a.* 1130 *chart.* Crucha ; also CREECH HILL (Somst). 702 *chart.* Crich hulle. O.W. *cruc,* W. *crug,* G. *cruach,* ' a stack, heap, pile.' *Cf.* CRICH, CRICKHOWELL, CRICKLADE. Thus Creech Hill is a tautology. *Dom.* Somst. has Crice, Cruce, and often Cruche ; in Norfk., Kreic, Kreich.

CREECH MICHAEL (Somerset). *Chart.* of 682, ' The hill which is called in British speech Cructan, but by us (English) Crycbeorh.' Cructan is ' heap, pile, hill on the R. Tone,' while Crycbeorh is ' Stack-burgh.' 1167-68 *Pipe,* Norfk., has a Crichetot (= toft). *Cf.* EVERCREECH.

CREIGHTON (Uttoxeter). 1241 Cratton, so perh. O.E. *crœt, crat tun,* ' cart enclosure ' or ' village.' More old forms needed.

CRESSAGE (Much Wenlock). *Dom.* Cristesache, 1540 Cressege. Not ' *crest* ' (only found in Eng. fr. 1325), but ' *Christ*'s edge ' or border,' O.E. *ecg,* 1205 *agge.* It is at the foot of Wenlock Edge. *Cf.* 1494 *Fabyan,* ' in the egge of Walys.'

CRESSWELL (Norbld., Stafford, and Mansfield). Nor. C. 1235 Kereswell. Sta. C. *Dom.* Cressvale, *a.* 1300 Cresswalle. This ending is certainly ' well ' or ' spring,' O.E. *wella,* often in M.E. *wale ;* and Cress- is O.E. *cerse,* ' watercress.' *Cf. Dom.* Bucks, Cresselai, ' cress-meadow,' and CRASWALL.

CREWE. *Dom.* Crev, Creuhalle (Crewe Hall). O.W. *creu, crau,* Mod. W. *crewyn,* Corn. *crow,* ' a pen, sty, hovel.'

CREWKERNE (Yeovil). Not in *Dom.*; perh. 1160-61 *Pipe,* Devon Creueq'r. O.E. *crúc-erne,* ' cross-house,' house with the cross. *Pipes* form may refer to the Fr. family of *Crèvecœur,* often referred to in England. *Cf.* Crevequer, *c.* 1330 *chart,* Kent and Lincs.

CRICCIETH (Portmadoc). Prob. W. *crug caeth,* 'narrow hill.' *Cf.* next.

CRICH (Matlock Bath). *Dom.* Crice, and CRICK (Rugby and Chepstow). Ru. C. *Dom.* Crec. W. *crug,* ' a heap, stack, mound, hill.' *Cf.* CREECH and CRICKHOWELL and PENKRIDGE. Duignan would derive this group of words fr. G. and Ir. *crioch,* gen. *criche,* ' boundary, limit, frontier,' as in the Sc. CREICH. But this is not found in W., and the evidence given under CREECH MICHAEL and CRICKHOWELL seems practically conclusive; though *cf.* CRAYKE. There are a Crickapit and a Crickley in Cornwall.

CRICKHOWELL (Abergavenny). *c.* 1188 *Gir. Camb.* Cruco-hel. In W. Crughywel, ' Conspicuous hill,' fr. O.W. *cruc,* W. *crug,* ' a heap, a stack,' and *hywel,* ' conspicuous.' Hewell Grange (Warwick) always found *sic, may* be the same word. Baddeley thinks CRICKLEY (Birdlip), *old* Cruklea, contains O.W. *cruc.*

CRICKLADE (Wilts). 905 *O.E. Chron.* Crecca-gelade, Cricgelad; *c.* 1097 *Flor. Worc.* Criccielad; *c.* 1120 *Hen. Hunt.* Crikelade, Cricalade; *c.* 1160 *Gest. Steph.* Crichelada. *Gelad* is O.E. for ' passage,' same root as *lead* and *lode;* but the first half is doubtful. The Eng. *creek* is not found till *c.* 1250 *crike,* and *Oxf. Dict.* does not favour it here. M'Clure conjectures W. *craig,* ' a rock,' or *cruc,* ' a mound '; the latter is quite possible. *Cf.* CREECH and next. There is a *Craca,* but no nearer man's name, in *Onom.* 1160-61 *Pipe,* Surrey, has a Crichefeld.

CRICKLAS (Caermarthen). *c.* 1188 *Gir. Camb.* Cruclas. O.W. *cruc glas* (Mod. W. *crug*), ' bluish or greenish mound or stack.' *Cf.* CREECH.

CRICKLEWOOD (Middlesex). 1525 Crekyll Woddes, 1553 Crekle Woods. Doubtful; older forms needed. Prob. fr. a man *Crecel,* otherwise unknown. *Cf.* 1241 *Close R.* Krikeleston.

CROCKEN HILL and CROCKHAM HILL (Kent). Prob. ' pot-shaped ' hill, fr. W. *crochan,* O.Ir. *crocan,* G. *crogan,* O.E. *crocca, -an,* ' a crock, a pot, an earthenware dish.' *Cf. a.* 1000 ' Crocford ' in *K.C.D.,* v. 17. The -ham may be a quite late corrup.; old forms needed. *Dom.* has only Croctune.

CROCKERN TORR (Dartmoor). *c.* 1630 Crocken Torr. See CROCKEN HILL. *Torr* is a ' tower-like rock or hill,' W. *tor,* Corn. *twr, tor.*

CROCKERTON (Warminster). Not in *Dom.* ' Town of the potter '; *crocker* is first found *c.* 1315 in *Shoreham. Cf.* ' Crokerbec,' Egremont, Cumberland.

CROCKFORD WATER (Lymington). *a.* 1000 *chart.* Crocford, ? this one. Prob. hybrid. W. *crug,* O.W. *cruc,* 'a tumulus, a low hill'; *cf.* Cruckbarrow Hill (Worcester), 1275 Cruckberew, Crokeborow, a double tautology. See BARROW. It can hardly be fr. *crook,* O.N. *krók-r,* as in Le Croc du Hurté, Channel Is.

CROMER (Norfolk). Not in *Dom.* 1351 Crowemere. 'Crow (O.E. *crawa*) mere' or 'lake.' *Cf.* Bomer Pool (near Shrewsbury)— *i.e.,* 'bull lake,' and Cranmer.

CROMFORD (Derby), *Dom.* Crunforde (*m* and *n* easily interchange), and CROMHALL (Glouc.). *Dom.* Cromhal. O.E. *cromb, crumb,* 'bent, crooked, curved,' cognate with W. *crwm, crom,* G. and Ir. *crom,* O.G. *cromb,* with same meaning. *Cf.* Croome d'Abitot, Pershore, 972 Cromb, 1275 Crombe Dabitoth, 'Crook of the D'Abitots,' found in *Dom.,* who took their name fr. St. Jean d'Abbetot, E. of Havre. Earl's Croome, near by, is 969 Cromban, Cromman, *Dom.* Crumbe. There is also a Crambe (Yorks), *Dom.* Crambom, -bon, which prob. is a loc. for 'at the crooks,' fr. an unrecorded O.E. *cramb, cromb,* now represented by *crome, cromb,* 'hook, crook,' first found *a.* 1400.

CROMWELL (Newark) and CROMWELLBOTTOM (Yorks). Ne. C. *Dom.* Crunwell, 1223 Crumbwell, 1298 Cromwelle, *c.* 1340 Crumwell. Prob. 'curved or crooked well,' or 'brook,' as in CROMFORD; but *Crum* may be a man's name; it is so now. *Cf.* CROMHALL (Charfield), *Dom.* Cromale, -hal, and 1179-80 *Pipe* Yorks, Crum- wurda. Bottom is O.E. *botm,* 'the lowest part of anything,' found fr. *c.* 1325, meaning 'low-lying land, an alluvial hollow.' *Cf.* RAMSBOTTOM, etc.

CRONDALL (Farnham). *Dom.* Crundele, 1242 Crundel. See CRUNDALE.

CRONTON (Prescot). *Cf. Dom.* Bucks, Cronstone, 'Village of *Cron*,' a name not in *Onom.* CRONWARE (Pembroke) is 1603 *Owen* Cromewere, and in *c.* 1130 *Lib. Land.* Lann cronnguern, perh. W. *llan crwm gwern,* 'church on the crooked moor.'

CROOKHAM (Berks, Hants, and Northumberland). Berks C. *O.E. chart.* Croh-hamme; *Dom.* Crocheham; *a.* 1300 Crokham. 'Saffron enclosure'; *croh* being the O.E. form of the L. *crocus,* whilst the ending here is *hamme,* and not the commoner *hám,* 'home.' *Cf.* CROWLE. But CROOKS HOUSE (Yorks) is *Dom.* Croches, which will be O.N. *krók-r,* 'a crook, a bend,' with Eng. plur. The ending -hes has afterwards got turned into -house.

CROOME (three on Severn near Pershore). 969 *chart.* Cromman, Croman, Cromban, all datives, 972 *ib.* Cromb, 1038 *ib.* Hylcrom- ban (now Hill Croome), *Dom.* and 1241 Crumbe, Hilcrumbe. O.E. *cromba,* 'a crook, a bend,' cognate with O.G. *crumbadh,* as in ANCRUM (Sc.) and W. *crwm, crom,* 'crooked.'

CROPREDY (Oxon). *Dom.* Cropelie, 1109 Cropperia, ? 1275 Cro- prithi, 1291 Cropperye, 1330 Cropperdy, 1405 Croprydy, 1460

Cropredy.   Prob. '*Croppa*'s stream,' O.E. *rith*, as in RYE and RYDE; but on Crop- *cf.* next.

CROPTHORNE (Pershore).   780 Croppon-, Croppethorne, 841 Crop-panthorn, *Dom.* Cropetorn.   *Crop* sb. is found as meaning 'the head or top of a tree,' *a.* 1300.   But the early charter forms show that *Croppa* must be a man.   *Cf.* next.   CROPWELL (Notts) *Dom.* Crophelle, -hille, is fr. N. *kropp-r,* 'a hump or bunch, a hump-shaped hill.'

CROPTON (Pickering).   *Dom.* Croptun, so also in *Dom.* Suffolk. 'Village of *Croppa*.'   See above.

CROSBY (5 in *P.G.*).   *Dom.* Crosebi (Cheshire), 1189 *Pipe* Grossebi (Cumberland).   *Dom.* Yorks has Crox(e)bi, Crocsbi, and Crochesbi, representing more than one Crosby.   'Dwelling by the cross,' O.E. *cros,* 3-4 *croiz,* 4-7 *croce ;* or, at any rate in Yorks, ' dwelling of *Croc(c)*', a fairly common name.   *Cf.* CROXBY; and see -by.

CROSTWIGHT (Norfolk).   *Dom.* Crostueit, *c.* 1460 Crostweyt.   'Cross-place' or 'farm with the cross.'   This name gives a rare corrup. of -thwaite.   *Cf.* CROSTHWAITE (Kendal), 1201 Crostweit; and see -thwaite, which is very rarely found except in the North-West.

CROUCH END and HILL (London).   O.E. *cruc,* 2-3 *cruche,* 3-5 *crouch(e),* 'a cross.'   R. Crouch, Essex, may not be the same.

CROUGHTON (Brackley).   Not in *Dom.*   Curiously, this means much the same as CROSTWIGHT, ' cross town '; O.E. *cruc,* M.E. *cruche, crouche,* ' a cross.'

CROWBOROUGH (Leek and Tunbridge W.).   Neither in *Dom.*   Lee C. *a.* 1300 Crowbarwe.   Prob. ' crow's wood,' O.E. *crawe,* and *bearu,* dat. *barwe.*   *Cf.* -borough.

CROWLAND or CROYLAND (Peterborough).   806 *chart.* Croylandie; *Sim. Dur.* ann. 1075 Crulant; *c.* 1120 *Hen. Hunt.* Crulande, 1238 Croilland.   Doubtful; the first syll. may be O.E. *croh,* ' saffron.' *Cf.* CROWLE.

CROWLE (Worcester and Doncaster).   Worc. C. 836 *chart.* Croglea, 840 *ib.* Crohlea, *Dom.* Croelai, Crohlea, 1275 Crowele, O.E. *croh-leáh,* ' saffron meadow.'   Crowley is, of course, the same name. Duignan prefers the meaning ' crocus meadow,' and compares a ' Richard de Croccuswell ' found in 1332.   O.E. *croh* is just L. *crocus* in an Eng. dress.   *Cf.* CROOKHAM and CROYDON.

CROWTHORN (Berks).   *Cf. K.C.D.*, iv. 103, 'Crawan thorn,' Hants. ' Crow's thorn,' thorn-tree frequented by crows, and used as a boundary mark.   *Cf.*, too, CROWMARSH, Wallingford, *Dom.* Cravmares (O.E. *mersc, merisc,* but here rather O.Fr. *mareis, -ais,* ' a marsh '), 1242 Crawmers.

CROXBY (Lincoln).   *c.* 1180 *Ben. Peterb.* Croxebi.   ' *Crocc*'s dwell-ing '; two so named in *Onom.*   *Cf.* CROXALL (Lichfield), 773 *chart.* Crokeshalle, *Dom.* Crocheshalle, and CROSBY.

CROXTON (4 in *P.G.*). Eccleshall C. *Dom.* Crochestone, Chesh. C. *Dom.* Crostone, Cam. C. *Dom.* Crochestone, 1302 Croxtone, Thetford C. *chart.* Crochestune, 1240 Croxton, 1303 Crokeston, c. 1460 Croxeston. Also 1179-80 *Pipe* Lancs, Crokeston. ' Village, town of *Croc*,' a man; 3 in *Onom.* *Cf.* above.

CROYDON (London). 809 Monasterium quod dicitur Crogedena; *Dom.* Croindene, 1288 *Contin.* *Gervase* Croyndona. It lies on the edge of the chalk, and so is often said to mean ' chalk hill '; *cf. Oxf. Dict.* s.v. *cray* and *crayer.* Yet form 809 must mean ' dean,' (wooded) valley of the' saffron,' O.E. *croh.* *Cf.* CROWLE. But Croydon (Royston) is *Dom.* Crauuedene 1238 Craweden, 1316 Croudene, 1428 Craudene, ' DEAN, wooded vale of the crow,' O.E. *crawe.*

CRUDGINGTON (Wellington, Salop). *Dom.* Crugetune. Prob. ' town, village of *Cruga*,' gen. -*gan*, an unknown man. For *dg*, cf. *bryg* and *bridge*, *Maggie* and *Madge*. There is a surname Grudgings. See -ing.

CRUDWELL (Malmesbury). *Dom.* Credwelle. Perh. ' crypt-well,' A.Fr. *crudde*, M.E. *crowd*, ' a crypt, a vault.' See *Oxf. Dict.*, crowd *sb.*², not given there till 1399; so it may be fr. a man *Crud*. *Cf. B.C.S.* 536 Crudes silba (' wood ').

CRUG MAWR (Pembroke). *a.* 1196 *Gir. Camb.* ' Crug Maur—*i.e.*, Collis magnus,' ' big hill,' ' stacklike hill.'

CRUKERI Castle (Radnor). *Older* Cruk-keri. Prob. *a.* 810 *Nennius* Caer Ceri, ' Castle of *Ceri*.' But Cruk- must be W. *crug*, ' a heap, a stack.'

CRUMLIN (Pontypool). W. *crom llyn*, ' crooked or concave pool.'

CRUNDALE (R. Wye, Kent). O.E. *crundel, crondel*, still in South. dial., ' a cutting shaped like an open V, made by a little stream, a ravine.' *Cf. B.C.S.* 906 Abbancrundel, also 3 farms in Worcestershire called Crundel or Crundles, and CRONDALL. Baddeley says CRUNDEL (Kemble), 1280 Crondles, means ' a quarry.'

CRUTCHLEY (Northampton and Monmouth). Not in *Dom.* ' Meadow with the cross,' O.E. *crúc*, 2-3 *cruche.* *Cf.* CROUCH END and CROUGHTON, and Crutch Hill (Worcestersh.), *a.* 1200 Cruche, 1275 Cruch, Cruce.

CUB(B)INGTON (Leamington). *Dom.* Cobintone, Cubintone, *a.* 1300 Cobyngton, Cumbyngton. ' Village of *Cuba*.' See -ing. CUBBER- or COBBERLEY (Cheltenham), *Dom.* Coberleie, *later* Cuthbrightley, is ' *Cuthbert*'s mead.'

CUCKAMSLEY or -LOW (Berks). 1006 *O.E. Chron.* Cwichelmes læwe, c. 1120 *Hen. Hunt.* Chichelmes laue, 1297 Quichelmeslewe. ' Burial-mound ' or ' hill ' (O.E. *hlǽw*) of *Cwichelm* '; either he who was K. of Wessex, d. 636, or an earlier pagan king of this name, d. 593. See -low.

CUCKFIELD (Hayward's Heath). 1092 Kukefield, 1121 Cucufeld. Hardly fr. vb. *cuck* = *cucare*, not found *a*. 1440, though we have *cucking*-stool in 1308; nor likely to be fr. the *cuckoo*, which in O.E. was *géac*, Sc. *gowk*, though it is found as early as *c*. 1240 *cuccu*. Analogy, as well as other reasons, points to ' field of *Cuca* '; *cf*. *B.C.S.* 936 Cucan healas. The 1121 spelling certainly suggests the bird; if so, it is much the earliest instance known. *Cf*. next. Cooksland (Stafford) is *Dom*. Cuchesland, which Duignan takes to be ' land of *Cuca* ' or ' *Cuc*.' *Cf*. CUXHAM.

CUCKNEY (Mansfield). *Dom*. Cuchenai, 1278 Cuckenay; and NORTON CUCKNEY (Yorks). 1202 *Yorks Fines* Cucuneia. Prob. ' *Cuca*'s isle '; see above and -ey. To derive fr. *cuccu* ' cuckoo ' is forbidden by the *n*, sign of the O.E. gen.; whilst to make it O.E. *æt cucan eȝe*, ' at the running stream,' *cwicu*, *cucu*, ' living, quick,' is not in accord with analogy.

CUDDESDON (Oxford). 956 *chart*. Cupenes dune; *a*. 1200 Codesdona. ' Cuthen's dean ' or ' wooded valley.' *Cuthen* seems to be a contraction of the name *Cynethegn* or *Cythegn*; 4 in *Onom*. But *cf*. ' Cudandene,' 958 *chart*., on Stour (Staffs). There are several named *Cudd*, *Cudda*, or *Cuddi* in *Onom*.; also *cf*. CUTS-DEAN. See -den and -don.

CUDWORTH (Barnsley). Not in *Dom*. ' *Cudd*'s place or farm.' *Cf*. Cudeley, Worcester) (974 *chart*. Cudinclea, *Dom*. Cudelei, orig. a patronymic, see -ing; also *Dom*. Cornw. Cudiford. *Dom*. Yorks Cuzeworde is Cusworth.

CULCHETH (Wigan and Cmbld.). Cum. C. *c*. 1141 Culquith; also Culchet. Wig. C. 1200-1 Culchet, Kulchet, 1300 Culchyt, 1311 Culcheth. Far older is 793 *Mercian chart*. Celchyth, which seems the same name. Prob. ' strait ' or ' passage in the wood,' W. *cul*, ' a strait ' (G. *caol*, a ' kyle '), and *coed*, pl. *coydd*, ' a wood.'

CULGAITH (Penrith). This surely must be G. *cùl gaoith*, ' at the back of the wind,' or fr. G. *cùil*, ' a nook '; whilst *cul* in W. means ' a strait, a narrow place.'

CULHAM (Abingdon). 821 *chart*. Culanhom, ? 940 Culenhema, 1216 Culham. ' Enclosure of *Cula*.' *Cf*. CULWORTH; and see -ham.

CULLERCOATS (Newcastle). First syll. doubtful. It may be ' dove cots,' O.E. *culfre*, ' a dove.' If a man's name it may be *Ceolheard*, a common O.E. name, or *Ceolweard*, also common, and found once as Kilvert. *Cf*. Killirby (Durham), *sic* 1183 in Boldon Bk., but 1197 Culverdebi, plainly ' Ceolweard's dwelling '; also *Dom*. Norfk., Culuertestuna, and *c*. 1200 Culdertun, Egremont, Cumberland. There is a CULKERTON (Tetbury), *Dom*. Culcortone; if not fr. *Ceolheard*, then fr. some unrecorded name. The -coats is ' cots.' See COATES.

CULMSTOCK (Cullompton). *Dom*. Culmestoche. ' *Culm*'s, *Cylm*'s or *Cylma*'s place '; all these forms are found in *Onom*. See STOKE.

CULWORTH (Banbury). 1298 Culeworthe. '*Cula's* farm.' There is only one *Cula* in *Onom.*, but *cf.* CULHAM. See -worth.

CUMBERLAND. 945 *O.E. Chron.* Cumbraland, *c.* 960 *chart.* Cumbras (*i.e.*, 'men of Cumbria'), *a.* 142 *Wm. Malmes.* Cumberland, 1461 *Lib. Pluscard.* Cummirlandia. Now usually held to be 'land of the *Cumbri*' or *Cymry*, med. L. *Combroges*, 'fellow-countrymen.' Of course, *Cymry* is now the common name for the Welsh, whose Brythonic kingdom spread right away up to Strathclyde until the 10th cny. *Cf.* COMBERBACH and *Dom.* Worcester 'Cūbrinture,' Yorks Cu'brewrde, now Cumberworth.

CUMDIVOCK (Dalston, Cumbld.). *a.* 1080 Combeðeyfoch. *Combe* is O.E. *cumb*, lit. 'a bowl,' 'a coomb, a valley,' cognate with or loaned fr. W. *cwm*, 'hollow'; the second part may be W. *diffaith*, 'wild, uncultivated, uninhabited.' The Sc. *divot*, 'a turf,' always has *t*, and is not known *a.* 1536. But -theyfoch may well represent a man's name, as in *B.C.S.* 1237 Theofecan hyl. Only there is a Devoke Water, S. of Eskdale, in this same county. *Cf.* CUMWHINTON and 'Cumbehop,' *c.* 1200 *chart. Whalley.*

CUMNOR (Oxford). *O.E. chart.* Colmanora, Cumanora, Cumenoran; *Dom.* Comenore. '*Colman's* edge or bank,' O.E. *ora*; the liquid *l* easily disappears. *Cf.* COWDENKNOWES (Sc.).

CUMWHINTON and CUMWHITTON (Carlisle). Old forms needed, but perh. both Kelt., with Eng. -ton. The former seems to be W: *cwm gwyn*, 'clear, bright hollow.' However, LAWHITTON (Cornwall) is 'long, white town.'

CUNLIFFE (Whalley, Lancs). 1278 Gundeclyf, 1283 Cundeclive, *c.* 1300 Conlive, 1317 Cunliffe. Doubtful. W. and H.'s derivation fr. *Gunnhild-r* is little less likely here than in CONDER. Prob. hybrid, Kelt. *conde, cunde*, 'confluence,' see CONDATE, and O.E. *clif*, 'a cliff or cleve.' *Cf.* CLEVELAND, and LILLIES-LEAF (Sc.), 1186 Lillesclif, or 'Lilla's cliff.'

CUNSDINE (Durham). *Sic c.* 1200 *chart.* Prob. 'DEAN (wooded) valley of *Cuna*'; 2 in *Onom. Cf.* CUNSALL (Leek), *Dom.* Cuneshala, and Cundall (York), *Dom.* Cundel.

CURDWORTH (Birmingham). *Dom.* Credeworde, *a.* 1200 Crud-, Croddeworth, 1327 Cruddeworth. 'Farm of *Creoda*'; metathesis of *r* is common. *Cf.* Kersoe (Worcestersh.), 780 Criddesho, 1275 Crydesho.

CURRY MALLET and RIVEL (Taunton). *Dom.* and 1155 Curi (see NORTH CURRY). W. *cyri*, 'a cauldron-shaped valley,' *G. coire*; *cf.* CYRI, and Sc. CORRIE and CURRIE. Mallet denotes the name of the family to which this place once belonged. *Cf.* SHEPTON MALLET, and for Rivel *cf.* RIEVAUX.

CURY (Falmouth). 1219 *Patent R.* Egloscuri ('church of Cury'); 1445 Cury towne; also Corantyn. From St. *Corentinus,* a saint of Quimper, Brittany.

CUTSDEAN (Broadway, Worcester). 974 *chart.* and *Dom.* Codestune, 1275 Cotestone, *a.* 1500 Cotesdon, *a.* 1600 Cuddesdon. This, then, is not ' DEAN,' but ' town of *Code* or *Cota*,' perh. the same man as gave name to the COTSWOLDS. Already in 730 we find *B.C.S.* 236, æt Codeswellan.

CUXHAM (Wallingford). O.E. *chart.* Cuceshamm. ' Enclosure of *Cuc.*' *Cf.* CUCKFIELD and CUXWOLD (Lincs), 1235 Cukewald; also *B.C.S.* 936 Cucan healas (see -hall). See -ham.

CWMHIR (Radnor). *c.* 1188 *Gir. Camb.* W. *cwm hir*, ' long valley or hollow.' *Cf.* CUMDIVOCK.

CWM-LLAW-ENOG (Chirk). W. = ' valley of Enog's hand.' *Enog* was a W. chief who, it is said, had his hand cut off for being found on the E. side of Offa's Dyke.

CYCH R. (betw. Pembroke and Caermarthen). *a.* 1300 Cuch. W. *cwch*, pl. *cychod*, ' a boat.'

CYFFDY (Llanrwst). W. for ' dark, black stump.' *Cf.* Cyffylliog (Ruthin), and Cuffern (Haverford W.), *old* Coferun.

CYNON R. (Glam.) seems to be built like, and to mean the same as, the R. CONWAY (W. *con gwy*)—*i.e.*, ' chief river,' compared with the little Dare. *Con*, as in L., means ' together,' and -on is a common ending for ' river,' as in *af-on* itself, in CARRON (Sc.), etc.

CYRI (Merioneth). Name of several ' cauldron-shaped hollows,' with tarns, same as G. *coire*, ' a CORRIE ' (Sc.). *Cf. Taliesin*, ' the cauldron of Cyridwen,' and CURRY.

CYTIAU-'R-GWYDDELOD (Holyhead). W. = ' cots of the Irish.' It is a mountain, said to be the scene of a battle, *c.* 600, between the *Gwyddel* (or *Goidels*, or *Gaels*) and the Cymri, or Welsh.

DACRE (Penrith), *sic* 1353, and DACRE BANKS (Leeds). *Bede* Dacore (R. and monastery). *Dom.* Yorks, Dacre. Possibly med. L. (*e.g.*, in *Dom.*) *dicra, c.* 1300 *dacrum*, O.Fr. *dacre, dakere*, M.E. *dyker*, mod. E. *dicker*, corrup. of L. *decuria*. This number 10 was the customary unit of exchange, esp. in hides; but was it ever applied to land measurement ?

DAGENHAM (Barking). 693 *chart.* Deccan-haam; *c.* 1150 *chart.* Dechenham. ' Daecca's enclosure ' or ' pasture '; only one *Dæcca* in *Onom.* See -ham. But DAGNALL (Oxon) is *a.* 1400 Dagenhale. See -hall.

DAGLINGWORTH (Cirencester). *Feud. Aids* Dageling-; also 1240 a Dagelingstrete. ' Farm of the sons of *Dæghild*,' or ' *Dæg-weald*,' nearest names in *Onom.* See -worth.

DALDEN or DAWDEN (Sunderland). *a.* 1130 *Sim. Dur.* Daldene, O.E. *dál-denu*, ' allotment, portion, field, deal,' ' by the dean or deep, wooded vale.' See -den.

DALSTON (Carlisle). 1189 Daleston, Dalstonn. ' Town, village in the valley or dale.' O.E. *dæl*, O.N. *dal*. Possibly *Dale* may be here, as it is still, a personal name; though it is not in *Onom*, and would hardly be in use so early. *Cf.* Dalby (N. Yorks), *Dom.* Dalbi and Dalham (Newmarket), *sic* in *Dom.* Dale (Pembroke) is found in 1307 as La Dale—*i.e.*, with the Fr. art., 'the dale.'

DALTON (5 in *P.G.*). Furness D. *Dom.* Daltun. *Cf.* a 'Daltone' in *Dom.* Cheshire. 'Town, village on the allotment,' see DALDEN; in northern cases, ' village in the dale,' N. *dal.*

DANBY WISKE (Northallerton). *Dom.* and 1202 Danebi, or ' Dane's dwelling.' *Cf.* TENBY and Danemarche, Jersey; and see -by. On Wiske, see APPLETON WISKE. But DANETHORPE (Notts), *Dom.* Dordentorp, 1637 Dernthorp, is 'village of *Deorna.*' The phonetic changes are all explainable.

DANE or DAVEN R. (Chesh.); hence DAVENHAM (*sic* 1218) and DAVEN-PORT (Chesh.). *Dom.* Deveneham and Deneport, *a.* 1130 *Sim. Dur.* Devenport. Perh. W. *dain*, ' pure, pleasing, beautiful,' or else *dwfn*, ' deep.' *Cf.* DEBENHAM. Duignan suggests G. *deann*, impetuous, swift,' but that would rather yield Dann or Denn.

DARENT R. See DARTFORD.

DARLASTON (Wednesbury and Stone). St. D. 954 Deorlavestun, Derlavestone, 1004 *ib.* Deorlafestun, *Dom.* Dorlavestone. Wed. D. *a.* 1200 Derlavestone. ' Town of *Deorlaf.*' *Cf.* Darliston (Whitchurch) and DARLTON (Notts), *Dom.* Derluveton.

DARLEY (Leeds) and DARLEY Abbey and Dale (Derbysh.). Der. D. *Dom.* Dereleie. Dar- is prob. from *Deor* or *Deora*, names in *Onom.*, and phonetically possible. Darton (Yorks) is *Dom.* Dertune. In O.E. *deór* means ' any wild animal,' then ' a deer,' then used as a personal name, ' a man like a deer.' See -ley.

DARLINGTON. *a.* 1130 *Sim. Dur.* Dearningtun, Dearthingtun; but 1183 *Boldon Bk.* Derlingtona. A name which has changed. There is no trace in *Onom.* of the *Sim. Dur.* forms, and only one *Deorling* or *Derling*. As it stands, the name is ' village of the darlings,' O.E. *deórling*, a dimin. of ' dear.' ' Dearthingtun ' may possibly represent DARRINGTON. *Cf.* Derlintun in 1156 *Pipe* Notts, in *Dom.* Dallingtune and now Dalington. We have DARLINGSCOT, Shipston-on-Stour, *a.* 1300 Darlingscote.

DARNALL (Sheffield). O.E. *derne heál*, ' hidden, out of the way, dark nook.' *Cf.* Darnhall Pool (Cheshire), Dernford (Cambs), and DARNICK (Sc.); also see -hall.

DARRINGTON (Pontefract). *Dom.* Darnintone, Darnitone, 1204 Darthingtone, 1208 Dardhinton. ' Town, village of *Deorna* ' (one in *Onom.*), or possibly ' of *Deorwen*, or -*wine.*' See -ing.

DARTFORD (Kent). *a.* 1200 Derenteford, Darentford. ' Ford on R. *Darent*,' which is prob. a var. of DERWENT; it is 940 *chart.* Daerinta. *Cf.* DARWEN.

DARTMOUTH (on R. DART). *Exon. Dom.* Derta, *a.* 1130 *Sim. Dur.* Derte, 1250 *Layam.* Derte muþ. Doubtful; certainly not fr.

Eng. *dirt.* Perh. W. *dorth,* ' limit, covering,' or O.E. *daroð,* ' a dart, a spear,' though our Eng. *dart* comes to us through O.Fr. *dart.* DARTMOOR is 1228 *Close R.* Dertemor.

DARWEN R. and town (Lancs). *a.* 1130 *Sim. Dur.* Dyrwente, 1311 Derwent. W. *dwr gwen,* ' white, clear stream.' *Cf.* DARENT, DERWENT, and G. *dobhar,* ' water, river.'

DASSETT (2, Kineton, Warwick). *Dom.* Derceto, -tone, *a.* 1200 Afne Dercet, *a.* 1400 Chepyng and Great Derset. O.E. *deor,* ' deer,' and *set,* ' a place where animals are kept, a stall, fold.' See AVON, CHIPPING, DARLEY, and *r* on p. 83.

DATCHET (Windsor). *Dom.* Daceta, 1238 Dachet. A puzzling name; but all solutions fail phonetically except ' *Dacca*'s cot,' O.E. *cete,* ' cot, hut.' *Cf.* Datchworth (Stevenage), 769 *chart.* Decewrthe, *Dom.* Daceuuorde, *B.C.S.* 81 Dæccanham, and WATCHET. The O.E. *cc* normally becomes *tch.*

DAUNTSEY (Chippenham). *Dom.* Dantesie. *Cf.* 940 *chart.* Dauntesbourne (Wilts). ' Isle of *Daunt.*' See -ey.

DAVENHAM and -PORT. See DANE.

DAVENTRY (Weedon). *Dom.* Daventrei, *a.* 1124 Dauentre, *c.* 1200 *Gervase* Davintria. The present pron. is Daintry, which would suggest an O.E. *Dœfan treo,* ' tree of *Dœfa* '; *cf.* OSWESTRY. However, no *Dœfa* or *Dave* is in *Onom.,* though *cf.* 1179-80 *Pipe* Yorks Dauebi; whilst John *Dawe,* who gave name to Dawshill (Powick), was living there in 1275. In the absence of good evidence for an O.E. origin, a W. origin is not altogether to be dismissed, though a W. name would be very unlikely here. It may be ' the two summits,' fr. W. *dau,* ' two,' and *entrych,* ' summit,' as D. stands on a hill, and there is another a mile away. It may be *c.* 380 *Ant. Itin.* Devnana.

DAWLISH (S. Devon). O.E. *chart.* Doflisc, *Dom.* Dovles, *a.* 1500 Doflysch. Doubtful. The first syll. may be W. *du,* O.W. *dub,* Corn. *dew,* ' black,' or *dwfn,* ' deep.' *Cf.* DEWLISH and DOWLAIS, also R. Divelish (Dorset), which is *chart.* Deuelisc, Deflisch, Deulisc, Defelich, and *Dom.* Devon, Monlish. All these are orig. river-names. The river at Dawlish is now the Dalch. So the second syll. is prob. W. *glais,* ' stream, river,' rather than *llys,* ' court, hall,' or *glwys,* ' hallowed place, a fair spot.'

DEADWATER (N. Tyne). Perh. 1249 Dedy. Doubtful. We find ' a standing poole or dead water,' as early as 1601 Holland's *Pliny.*

DEAL. Not in *Dom.* 1160 *Pipe* Dela; *later* Dale, Dele, Dola. O.E. *dœl,* 3-6 *del,* 4-7 *dele,* ' a division, a section, a part,' a ' deal,' cognate with dale, *sb²,* ' a portion or share of land,' and with *dole,* O.E. *dál.*

DEAN, E. and W. (Eastbourne). *Asser* Dene. O.E. *denu,* ' a dean, a dell, a deep, wooded vale.' See also FOREST OF DEAN.

DEBDEN (Saffron Walden). *Dom.* Deppedana, 1228 *Close R.* Depeden—*i.e.,* ' deep, wooded valley.' See DEAN.

DEBENHAM (Framlingham, Suffk.). *Dom.* Depben-, Depbeham. 'Home on the R. Deben,' which may be W. *dwfn* 'deep.' *Cf.* DAVENHAM.

DEE R. (Cheshire). *c.* 150 *Ptolemy* Deva, 1480 Dee; but *a.* 1196 *Gir. Camb.* Deverdoeu, Deverdoe, which is just the mod. W. name Dwfr Dwy. W *dwfr* or *dwr* (O.W. *deifr*), is 'river, stream,' and *dwy* is 'two,' feminine. But *cf.* DEE (Sc.), also R. Divie, trib. of Findhorn, Moraysh.

DEERHURST (Tewkesbury). 804 *Grant* Deor -hyrst(e); *Dom.* Dere-hest, *a.* 1200 *Walter Map* Durherst. *Déor, dior* in O.E. means 'any kind of beast'; *hyrst* is 'forest.' See -hurst.

DEGANWY, DIGANWY, or DWYGANWY (N. Wales). *a.* 1145 *Orderic* Dag(e)aunoth; *Ann. Cambr.* ann. 822 Arx Deganhui. Difficult. By some connected with Ptolemy's *Dekantai;* by Rhys Jones* with the Irish Ogam form *Deccetes,* found in (?) sixth-century inscriptions in Devon, Anglesea, and Ireland. In the *Patent R. c.* 1245 it is often Gannok, which suggests a similar origin to CANNOCK.

DEIGHTON. See DITTON.

DELPH (Yorks, Rochdale, N. Staffs) and the DELVES (Wednesbury). A 'digging' (for iron ore or the like). O.E. *dælfan, delfan,* 'to dig, delve.' *Cf.* DILHORNE.

DENABY MAIN (Rotherham). *Dom.* Degenebi, Denegebi. 'Dwelling of,' it is uncertain who; perh. *Degn* or *Thegn*—i.e., 'thane, lord,' names in *Onom. Cf.* DAGENHAM; and see -by. Main meaning 'main' or 'chief vein of mineral,' seems a quite recent usage.

DENBIGH. *c.* 1350 *charts.* Den-, Dynbiegh, -eigh, 1485 Dynbigh. W. Dinbych. In W. *din bych* would mean, 'hill or fort of the wretched being.' This would be absurd. Prob. it is, as pron. in Eng., Den-by, 'dwelling of the Dane'; we have DENBY more than once in Yorks, *Dom.* Denebi, fr. O.E. *Dene,* 'Danes,' and Dene- or Den-mearc, 'Denmark.' Thus it would be the same name as DANBY and TENBY. See -by. But T. Morgan favours W. *din bach,* 'little hill,' which it is. This certainly accounts better for the final guttural -gh or -ch.

DENCHWORTH (Wantage). *O.E. chart.* Dences wyrthe, Deneces wurthe, Denices wurth; *Dom.* Denchesworde. 'Farm of *Dence,*' a name otherwise unknown; though *Onom.* has *Denisc,* or 'the Dane.' See -worth.

DENHAM (Uxbridge and Eye, Suffk.). Ux. D. *Dom.* Danehā. Eye D. *Dom.* Denham. Prob. 'home of the Dane.' *Cf.* DENTON and Den-mark.

DENNY BOTTOM (Tunbridge Wells). *Cf.* DENNY (Sc.) 1510 Dany, and *Dom.* Bucks, Danitone. Denny is a dimin. of *den* or *dean,* 'a narrow, wooded valley.' See -den.

* Cited by M'Clure, p. 94.

DENSTON(E) (Uttoxeter and Newmarket). Utt. D. *Dom.* Dene-stone, 'village of *Dene*,' 3 in *Onom.*, meaning, of course, 'the Dane.' *Cf.* above. But New. D. is *Dom.* Danardestuna, 'town of *Deneheard.*' *Cf. B.C.S.* 480 Deneheardes hegeræwe.

DENTON (8 in *P.G.*). 801 *chart.* Deantone (Sussex). *Dom.* Yorks and Lincs Dentune, 'village by the DEAN, or deep, wooded vale.' *Cf.* Denford (Berks), *Dom.* Daneford, where O.E. *dœn*, a word cognate with *den* and *dean*, means esp. 'a woodland pasture for swine.' Few Eng. names in Den- or Dane-show any connexion with the Danes; but *cf.* DENBIGH, and above.

DEPTFORD. *Sic.* 1521, but *c.* 1386 *Chaucer* Depford; not in *Dom.* 'Deep (O.E. *deóp*) ford' on the Ravensbourne, or rather, the creek at its mouth. There is another at Sunderland. *Cf.* Defford (Pershore, 972 *chart.*), Deopford, *Dom.* Depeforde, also in *Dom.* Wilts.

DERBY. 917 *O.E. Chron.* Deoraby, 1049 Deorby, 1598 Darbi-shiere. In W. Dwrgwent. 'Beasts' dwelling.' O.E. *déor, díor,* Icel. *dýr,* 'a beast'; and see -by. Derby was a Danish name; Northweorðig was the O.E. one. For its ending, *cf.* BADGEWORTHY.

DEREHAM (Norfolk). *Dom.* Dere-, Derham. *c.* 1460 Dyram, so = DYRHAM and DERBY, 'beasts' home.'

DERSINGHAM (King's Lynn). *Dom.* Dersincham, 1234 *Patent R.* Dersingham; 'home of the *Dersings.*' *Cf.* SANDRINGHAM.

DERWENT R. (Cumbld. and Yorks), also DERWENTWATER, *sic* 1298. The two rivers get a little mixed in early records—*c.* 380 *Ant. Itin.*, and *c.* 700 *Rav. Geogr.* Derventione, *Bede* Dorowensio, Deruuentis fluvius, *c.* 850 *O.E. vers.* Deorwenta, *a.* 1130 *Sim. Dur.* Dyrwenta, 1229 *Patent R.* Derewent (Yorks). W. *dwr, dwfr ywen,* 'white, clear stream.' *Cf.* DARENT and DARWEN. For suffixing of *t, cf.* LEVEN and Levant.

DESBOROUGH (Mket. Harboro'). *Dom.* Deis-, Diesburg, *c.* 1260 *Rot. Hund.* Dosteberge. Very puzzling; no name in *Onom.* seems to suit any of these forms; but it may be *Deorswith* (see DOSTHILL). 'Dais,' raised table in a hall, is O.Fr. *deis,* and not known in Eng. till 1259, so very unlikely here; but *cf.* DISS. See -burgh.

DEUDDWR (Wales). W. *dau dwr,* 'two streams.'

DEVERILL—KINGSTON DEVERILL (Bath), LONGBRIDGE DEVERILL, and BRIXTON DEVERILL (Warminster). *Dom.* Devrel, 1245 *Patent R.* Deverel (Wilts). Prob. hybrid. Devr- will be O.Kelt. for 'stream,' W. *dwfr* (see ANDOVER and DOVER); whilst -el is prob. Eng. for *hill,* or else -hale, 'nook.' See -hall. *Cf.* Derridge, Kingswood, *old* Deveridge. Possibly Devrel is Nor. for Deverèux or d'Evreux.

DEVIL'S WATER (Hexham). 1610 *Speed* Dovols fl. Thought to be corrup. of G. *dubh glas,* ' dark, peaty stream '= DOUGLAS. This is very doubtful.

DEVIZES. 1157 *Pipe* Divisis, *c.* 1160 *Gest. Steph.* Divisa, 1228 *Close R.* ad Divisas. This is corrupt L., and prob. means ' place at the division or border ' (? that between Saxon and Kelt).

DEVON. 878 *O.E. Chron.* Defenascir; *Exon. Dom.* Duuenant, 1189 Devonia; 1402 Devenshir, *c.* 1630 *Risdon,* ' Devonshire, now by a vulgar speech Denshire.' In O.W. Dyvnaint, which seems to be O.W. *dub,* W. *du nant,* ' dark ravine or valley or stream.' The Sc. DEVON, *c.* 1210 Dovan, has a similar origin, G. *dubh ān,* ' dark river.' But Rhys identifies both with the *Damnonii,* who orig. inhabited Devonshire, the *m* here being aspirated into *mh* or *v.* There is also a R. Devon, Notts.

DEVONPORT. Dates from 1689. *a.* 1130 *Sim. Dur.* Devenport is DAVENPORT. See above.

DEWCHURCH, LITTLE (Hereford). 1234 *Close R.* Deweschirch, ' Church of *Dewi,'* W. for St. David. *Cf.* Dewiston, near St. David's, LLANDEWI, and DEWSBURY; also Dowthorpe (Yorks), *Dom.* Dwetorp, 1202 Duuestorp.

DEWLISH (Dorchester). *Chart.* Diolisc, 1230 *Close R.* Deueliz, 1238 *Patent R.* Deuelis. Must be same as DAWLISH and as DEWLAS R. See DOWLAIS.

DEWSBURY (Yorks). *Dom.* Deusbereia, -berie, 1202 Deubire. ' David's burgh.' See DEWCHURCH and -bury.

DICKLEBOROUGH (Scole, Norfk.). *Dom.* Dicclesburc, 1232 *Close R.* Dikelebury. Prob. ' burgh of *Dicuil,'* a Keltic name. See -borough.

DIDCOT (Oxford). Not in *Dom. a.* 1300 Doudecote, also Dud-cote; and DIDCOTE (Beckford), 1177 *Pipe* Dudicota. *Cf. B.C.S.* iii. 101. Dyddan hamm, *ib.* 486 Dydinc cotan (dat.). ' Cot, cottage of *Dydda* or *Dudda.' Cf.* DUDLEY and Diddington (Warwk.), 1188 Didindon.

DIDMARTON (Tetbury). 972 *chart.* Dydimeretune, *Dom.* Ded-mertone, *Feud. Aids* Dudmerton. Perh. ' village of *Dudemær,'* as in 1015 *chart.* To Dudemæres hele (' nook '), Chilton (Berks). But it may be 'mere- or lake-town of *Dydda'* or ' *Dudda,'* the latter a very common name. *Cf.* DUMMER.

DIGBETH (Birmingham, Coventry, and Northfield, Worc.). Duignan thinks this may be corrup. of *dike path; dike,* O.E. *dic,* being either ' ditch ' or 'embankment.' But there are no old forms, and this is doubtful.

DILHORNE (Stoke-on-Trent). *Dom.* and till 1300 Dulverne. Duignan thinks, O.E. *dulf-, delfern,* ' place of digging or delv-ing.' *Cf.* DELPH. However, in *Dom.* Bucks we have ' Dile-herst,' and DILHAM (Norfk.) is *sic c.* 1150, fr. a man *Dela* or *Dila.*

DILSTON (Hexham). *a.* 1300 *chart.* Divelin, which looks like W. *ty Felyn,* ' house of Velyn.' *Cf.* HELVELLYN and STIRLING (Sc.) *c.* 1250 Estrivelin. But—surely very improbably—Sir H. Maxwell thinks this name is *D'Eyville's* town ' (see *Scalacronica* MS., fo. 211) ; whilst M'Clure thinks the Dils- is a corrup. of Dubglas, ' dark stream.'

DINAS (Glamorgan). W. and Corn., ' a castle,' fr. *din,* ' hill,' then ' hill-fort.' *Cf.* PENDENNIS.

DINAS EMRYS (small hill near Snowdon). 1190 *Gir. Camb.* says this means ' promontory of *Ambrosius,*' a celebrated bard of the 5th cny.

DINAS POWYS (Cardiff). 1223 *Patent R.* Dinant powis. ' Hill ' or ' fort of POWYS.' *Cf.* above.

DINEFWR CASTLE (Caermarthen). *c.* 1196 *Gir. Camb.* Dynevur, 1246 *Patent R.* Dynavor. W. *din y ffwyr,* ' castle of the onset or assault.'

DINGERREIN (Cornwall). Corn. *din Geraint,* ' fort of K. Geraint, husband of Enid, who fell at Langport, 522. *Cf.* ST. GERRANS.

DINMORE (Hereford). W. *din mawr,* ' big hill.' It is a village on the top of a high hill. *Cf.* DUNMORE (Sc.).

DINNINGTON (Newcastle-on-T. and Rotherham). Ro. D. *Dom.* Dunnitone, Dunintone, ' town of *Dun, Duna,* or *Duning,*' all in *Onom.* See -ing.

DIN-ORWIG (Caernarvon). *Old* Dinorddwig—*i.e.,* ' fort of the *Ordovices,*' a tribe of central Wales. See Tacit. *Agric.* 18. But in charters of Edw. III. it is Dynnorbin. Rhys derives Ordovices fr. O.W. *ord,* W. *gordd,* ' a hammer.'

DINTON (Aylesbury and Salisbury). Sa. D. Duntone. 1179-80 *Pipe* Yorks. Dinton, ' village of *Dynne* or *Dyne,*' a common name in *Onom.* See -ton. But DINSDALE (N. Yorks) is *Dom.* Digneshale, prob. ' *Degn's* nook (*cf.* DENABY); though Over Dinsdale is *Dom.* Dirneshala, fr. *Deorna,* or perh. *Deoring, Diring,* names in *Onom.* See -hall.

DISS (Norfolk). *Dom.* Dice. Doubtful. ? O.Fr. *deis,* found in Eng. *c.* 1259 as *deis,* ' a dais or high-table.' DISEWORTH (Derby) and DISLEY (Stockport) imply an unrecorded man *Disa. Cf.* DESBOROUGH and next.

DISSINGTON (Northumbld.). ? The Digentum in *Hexham Chrons.* Should be ' town of *Dissa* ' or the like; but there is no such name in *Onom.* Still we have Dishforth, Thirsk, *Dom.* Disforde, and the places above, suggesting such a name.

DITTON (Widnes, Bridgnorth, and Surrey) and FEN DITTON (Cambs). Cam. D. *c.* 1080 *Inquis. Camb.* Dictune, Dittune. *Dom.* Surrey and Bucks Ditone, -tune; also *c.* 1170 and 1213 *charts.* Dicton, ? which, and *c.* 1005 *chart.* Dictune, Kent,

'Town, enclosure, with the ditch,' O.E. *díc*. *Cf*. DITCHFORD (Warwk.), *Dom*. Dicforde. The names Deighton and Dighton have the same origin as Ditton. N. Yorks is *Dom*. Dictune, and Deightonby is Dictenebi, a somewhat rare hybrid.

DOCCOMBE (Newton Abbot). Not in *Dom*. 1174 Documba, 1322 Dockumbe; also corrupted into Dockham. O.E. *docce-cumbe*, 'dock-valley,' valley in which the docken weed abounded.

DODCOTT (Nantwich). 1135 Dodecotte. *Cf*. *a*. 1300 'Dodeford,' Northants. 'The cot or cottage of *Dodd, Doda*, or *Dodda*,' a very common name in *Onom*. *Cf*. DIDCOT and Dodwell, Stratford (Warwk.), close to the Doddanford of 985 *chart*.

DODINGTON (Yate and Bridgwater). Ya. D. *Dom*. Dodintone, 1170 Duddinton; and DODDINGTON (5 in *P.G*.), March D. *Dom*. Dodinton, 1302 Doddyngtone. 'Village of *Dodda*' or '*Dudda*,' gen. *-an*. *Cf*. *Dom*. Bucks and Salop, Dodintone. But DODINGTREE (Leicester) is perh. fr. *dod*, 'to clip or top,' found *a*. 1225 *dodd*; *cf*. 1440 *Prompt. Parv*., 'doddyn trees or herbys . . . *decomo*.' This tree was the meeting-place of the hundred. *Cf*. MANNINGTREE. See -ing.

DOGSTHORPE (Peterboro'). Not in *Dom*. *c*. 1100 *Grant* Dodesthorpe. Interesting corruption; 'farm of *Dodd*.' See DODCOTT and -thorpe.

DOLEBURY CAMP (Mendips). 'Burgh, fortified place of *Dola*'; one such in *Onom*. It is the site of a pre-Roman fort. See -bury.

DOLGELLY. W. *dol gelli*, 'meadow with the grove or copse,' *gelli* being var. of the commoner *celli*.

DOLLY MEADOWS (Bath). W. *Dol*. pl. *dolau* (pron. dolay), 'a meadow.' *Cf*. G. *dal*. Thus the name is a tautology.

DOLTON (Devon). *Dom*. Dueltona. 1235 *Patent R*. Dughelton. 'Town of *Dougal*' (see DUGGLEBY), only here the *h* has 'eclipsed' the *g*. *Cf*. the surname Doulton.

DON R. and DONCASTER. Prob. *c*. 380 *Ant. Itin*. Dono and *Bede* II. xiv Campodunum, *c*. 850 *O.E. vers*. Donafeld; *Nennius* Cair Daun; *Dom*. Doncastre, 1158-59 *Pipe* Dane Castre, 1202 *Fines* Danecastre, 1206 Donecastre. It cannot be the same as DON (Sc.). Perh. W. *dwn*, G. *donn*, 'brown.' See -caster.

DONNINGTON (Salop, Gloucs., and Berks). Sa. D. *Dom*. Donitone. Gl. D. 1176 *Pipe* Dunnington. Be. D. 1316 Dunyngton. 'Village of the sons of *Dunn*.' *Cf*. *B.C.S*. iii. 601 on Dunninglande. *Cf*. DUNNINGTON; and see -ing.

DONYATT (Ilminster). 1234 *Patent R*. Dunyed. O.E. *dun ʒeat*, 'hill of the gate, opening or pass.' *Yat* or *yat(t)e* has been the S.W. dial. form of *gate* since the 16th cny. *Cf*. SYMOND'S YAT.

DORCHESTER (Dorset). *c.* 380 *Ant. Itin.* Durno(no)varia, 939 *chart.* villa regalis quæ dicitur Doracestria, *c.* 1100 *Flor. Worc.* Dorsetania, 1387 Dorchestre. Durno-varia is prob. Kelt. for ' fist-plays,' there having been a Rom. amphitheatre here; W. *dwrn,* Ir. *dorn,* ' fist '; and Corn. *gware* for L. *varia,* ' a play.' Asser, ann. 875, speaks of the district (*paga*), called in British Durngueir (in MS. -eis), but in Saxon Thornsæta (*or* Dornsæta), now Dorset. In the present name there is nothing which represents *varia,* so that it really seems to mean ' fist camp.' *Cf.* CARDURNOCK; and see -chester.

DORCHESTER (Oxon). (? Durcinate in *a.* 700 *Rav. Geogr.*) *c.* 689 *Theodore* Villa Dorcacæstrensis, *Bede* Dorcic, *O.E. Chron.* 635 and 891 Dorcic-, Dorcesceaster, 905 in *Eadmer* Dorkeceastre, *Dom.* Dorchecestre. This seems either to mean ' camp of *Dorc,*' an unknown man, or, more doubtfully, ' dark camp,' O.E. *deorc,* 3 *dorc,* ' dark.' Also see DORSET.

DORDON (Tamworth). 1285 Derdon. Perh. ' hill of the deer,' O.E. *déor. Cf.* DASSETT; and see -don.

DORE R. (S. Wales). *c.* 1130 *Lib. Land.* Door ; and DORE (Hereford and Sheffield). Shef. D. *O.E. Chron.* 827 Dore, *ib.* 942 Dor. W. *dwr,* ' water, stream '; G. *dobhar. Cf.* APPLEDORE, Dour (Yorks), and Durra (Cornw.). But Plummer derives the towns fr. O.E. *duru, dor,* ' a door, an opening.'

DORSET. *a.* 900 *Asser* Thornsæta, Dornsæta, *Dom.* Dorsete, *c.* 1097 *Flor. W.* Dorsetania. Dornsæta should mean ' seat, settlement among the thorns '; but *cf.* DORCHESTER; while some connect with Ptolemy's *Durotriges,* who dwelt about here. *Cf.* SOMERSET. *Dom.* Essex has a Dorseda.

DORSINGTON (Stratford-on-A.). *Dom.* Dorsintune, and DORSTONE (Hereford), *a.* 1300 Dorsinton. ' Village of the *Dorsings,*' or ? ' sons of *Deorsige.*' *Cf.* DERSINGHAM. See -ing.

DOSTHILL (Tamworth). *Dom.* Dercelai. *a.* 1200 Dertehulla, Derchethull, *a.* 1400 Derst-, Dorsethull. The ending is clear. In *Dom.* -lai is fr. -ley, ' meadow,' *q.v.*; and *hull* is the regular Mid. form of ' hill.' Derchet or Derst prob. represents a man *Deorswith;* 2 in *Onom.* But *cf.* also *Dom.* Bucks Dusteb'ge and DESBOROUGH.

DOUGLAS (I. of Man). Local pron. Doolish. Moore says, Manx *dub glais,* ' dark stream.' *Cf.* DOUGLAS (Sc.) and DOWLAIS, pron. Dowlish. One of K. Arthur's battles, in *Nennius,* was at ' Duglas.' *c.* 1205 *Layamon* has a ' Duglas water ' too.

DOVE R. (Derby) and DOVEY or DYFI R. (S. Wales and Machynlleth). Der. D. 890 *chart.* Dufa, *a.* 1300 Duve Douve. Mach. D. 1428 Dyvi. All fr. O.W. *dubr,* W. *dwfr, dwr,* ' water, stream.' Duignan thinks Dove the ' diving ' river, O.E. *dufan.* Its tribs. certainly dive underground. DOVERDIGE (Uttoxeter) is *Dom*. Dubrige, *c*. 1300 Doubrig, ' bridge on R. Dove.'

DOVER (also near Leigh, Lancs). *c*. 380 *Ant. Itin*. Portus Dubris; *a*. 716 *chart*. Dufras, 1048 *O.E. Chron*. Dofre, *a*. 1100 *Wm Poit*. Doueria, *c*. 1097 *Flor. W*. Doru-, Doro-bernia; 1160 Doura, Dovre; *c*. 1205 *Layam*. Doure, *c*. 1275 Douere. The Kent D. is on R. Douver, W. *dwfr*., ' stream,' still correctly pron. in Fr., Douvre(s). *Cf*. above, and DOVERDALE, Droitwich, 706 *chart*. Dourdale, 817 *ib*. Doferdæl; also *Dom*. Wilts Dobrehā. There are also a R. DOVERLE (Berkeley) and a Dover Beck, 1225 Doverbec (Notts), and a Douvres on the N. coast of France.

DOVERCOURT (Harwich). *Dom*. Druurecurt (first *r* an error). ' Court on the river,' W. *dwfr*. See above. *Court*, O.F. *cort*, *curt*, L. *cohors, -tem*, ' court, poultry-yard, yard,' is not in *Oxf. Dict*. till 1297. It means ' a clear space enclosed by a wall,' then ' a large building in a yard, a castle.'

DOWLAIS (Glam.). Pron. Dowlish. Disputable; perh. O.W. *dau*, mod. W. *dou glais*, ' two streams '; but prob. = DOUGLAS. The Dewlas, trib. of Nthn. Dovey, is *sic* 1428 and locally pron. Diflas, clearly ' daik (W. *du*) stream.' DOWLISH WAKE (Ilminster) should be the same. *Cf*. DAWLISH. The Little and Great DOWARD Hills, lower Wye, were *old* Dougarth, which is O.W. for ' two garths,' or ' enclosures.'

DOWNHAM (Cambs and Norfolk). Cam. D. *K.C.D*. iv. 209 Dunham. Nor. D. 1461 Dounham. O.E. *dún-ham*, ' hill-dwelling.' *Cf*. next. DOWNHOLME (Richmond, Yorks) is in *Dom*. simply Dune. See -holm.

DOWNS, The (off Kent). *a*. 1460 *Gregory's Chron*. The Downys, 1520 The Downes. Perh. so called from the *down* or hill, O.E. *dún*, opposite the E. end of the North Downs.

DOWNTON (Salisbury). *c*. 1160 Duntuna—*i.e*., ' hill-town ' or Hilton.

DOWTHORPE (Yorks). *Dom*. Dwetorp. Prob. ' village of *Duua* ' or ' *Duha*,' names in *Onom*. See -thorpe.

DOXEY (Stafford). *Dom*. Dochesig, *c*. 1200 Dokesei, ' Isle of *Docca*,' or ' the duck,' O.E. *docce*. *Cf*. DUXFORD. In *Dom*. Salop there is Dehocsele or ' *Docca's* nook.' See -ey and -hall.

DRAKENEDGE (Warwksh.). 1251 Drakenegg. O.E. *dracan ecg*, ' devil's or dragon's edge ' or ' brink.' *Cf*. Drakelow (Derbysh.) and Wolverley, former 942 ' æt Dracan hlawen ' (see -low), also Drakestone (Gloucs.).

DRAUGHTON (Skipton). *Dom*. Dractone. Doubtful. Possibly it is ' town of the devil,' O.E. *draca*. *Cf*. above. Possibly = DRAYTON.

DRAYCOTT (Berks, Blockley, Dunchurch, Stoke-on-T.). Ber. D. *Dom*. Draicote; ·Bl. D. 1275 Draycote ; St. D. *a*. 1300 Dra- and

Draycote. This must go with DRAYTON, an even commoner name with older recorded forms. Draycott would seem to mean ' dry cot '; O.E. *drýge, dríge*, 2 *dreie*, 4 *draye, dreye,* ' dry.' Possibly it is fr. O.E. *drœge,* ' a drag-net, a dray '; but then, why so ? Certainly Skeat's derivation fr. an O.E. *drœg,* supposed to mean ' a place of shelter, a retreat ' (*cf.* mod. *dray,* ' a squirrel's nest '), seems rather laboured. But the matter is not yet settled. *Dom.* Devon has a Draheford, ? ' ford for a dray.' *Cf.* DRIG.

DRAYTON (9 in *P.G.*). *Chart.* Drægtun, *Dom.* Draitone, 1210 Drayton (Cambs). 810 *chart.* Draiton (N. Notts), 960 *chart.* Draægtun, and *Dom.* Draitone (Berks). *a.* 1100 Dræitun, *a.* 1200 Draiton (Stratford, Warwicksh.). *Dom.* Dray-, Draitone (Penkridge and Tamworth). *Dom.* Drattone (Bucks). Prob. ' dry town '; but the early forms make O.E. *drœge* ' a dray,' at least a possible origin. Skeat derives the place in Cambs and Berks fr. the O.E. *drœg,* referred to *s.v.* DRAYCOTT. The ' Cair Draithon ' of *c.* 800 *Nennius* has been identified with one of the Draytons, which is doubtful.

DRIFFIELD (Bridlington and Cricklade). Br. D. *c.* 1050 *O.E. Chron.* 705 Driffelda, *Dom.* Drifeld, -felt, 1202 Driffeld. Cr. D. *Dom.* Drifelle (common *Dom.* var.). ' Dry field,' O.E. *drige,* 3 *drigge, drie,* ' dry.' Duignan says DRIFFOLD (Sutton Colfield), is *drift fold,* ' fold into which cattle were driven.' *Cf.* next.

DRIG (W. Cumbld.). O.E. *drige,* ' dry '; *drœg,* ' a place of shelter.' *Cf.* above.

DRIGHLINGTON (Bradford). *Dom.* Dreslintone, -ingtone. The *s* in *Dom.* is to avoid the guttural *gh ;* such *Dom.* hates. Prob. ' village of the descendants of *Dryhtweald,*' or perh. ' *Drycghelm* ' (once in *Onom.*). *Cf. Dom.* Gloucs. Dricledone. See -ing.

DRINGHOE (Holderness). *Dom.* Dringolme; and DRINGHOUSES (York). Not in *Dom.* N. *dreng,* ' a free servant of the king endowed with lands.' They were found all over, N. of the Humber and Ribble. The ending -hoe is here a corrup. of -holm, *q.v.,* through the liquidity or vanishing tendency of *l* and *m,* influenced by HOE, ' height '; whilst *holm* is ' river-meadow.'

DROITWICH. 716 *chart.* In wico emptoris salis quem nos Saltwich vocamus, 888 *ib.* Saltwic, 1017 Sealtwic, 1049 *O.E. Chron.* Wic, *Dom.* Wich 24 times, Wic once, 1347 le Dryghtwych, 1469 Dertwyche. But D. is not Ptolemy's Salinai. Wich is simply O.E. *wic,* ' dwelling, village.' See -wich. True, here and in Cheshire and the neighbouring districts it is the ending of most salt-producing towns; but there is no O.E. authority for saying that *wic* or *wich* has anything to do with salt. Many—even Skeat—derive this *wich* fr. O.N. *vik,* ' a bay, a small (salt) creek '; hence, it is said, the transition is easy to ' salt or brine spring.' But that *wich* could come fr. *vik* in 716 in Worcestersh. seems simply impossible. Droit- (Fr. *droit*, ' right, privilege ') was prefixed by sanction of Edw. III., who gave the inhabitants the right to manufacture salt here *a*. 1293. The right had to be restricted in other places owing to the great waste of timber in making salt. But Edw. the Confessor already had £52 a year from the salt works. *Cf.* ' The Droits of Admiralty.'

DROMONBY (N. Riding). *Dom.* Dragmalebi, twice. A remarkable corrup. ' Dwelling of *Dragmel*,' one in *Onom.* We here see how any one liquid can become another, even *l* become *n*. See -by.

DRONFIELD (Sheffield). Not in *Dom.* ' Field of the drone-bees'; O.E. *dran*, 3-6 *dron*.

DROXFORD (Bps. Waltham). 939 *chart.* Drocenesforda; not in *Dom.* ' Ford of *Drocen*,' not in *Onom.*, but *cf.* DRAKENEDGE.

DRUID (Corwen) may be for W. *derwydd*, ' a Druid.' T. Morgan omits it. But DRUID HEATH (Warwk.) is *c.* 1400 Dru-, Drewood, fr. a family of *Dru*, or rather *Druce*, prob. taking their name fr. Dreux, Normandy.

DRYPOOL (Hull). *Dom.* Drid-, Dritpol, Dripold, ' dirty pool,' Icel. *drit*, ' dirt.'

DUDBRIDGE (Stroud). 1302 Dodebrygge; and DUDDO (Norham); 1183 Dudehowe. Named fr. some man *Dudd*, *Duda*, or *Dudda*, names very common in O.E., esp. in Mercia. *Cf.* DUDLEY and Duddeston (Birmingham), 1100 Duddestone. The -o is -howe, ' a mound,' *q.v.*

DUDDON (Tarporley) and DUDDON R. (Cumbld.). Latter thought to be *c.* 709 *Eddi* Regio Dunutinga, a name of uncertain origin. But Tar. D. may be W. *du din*, ' dark, black hill '; though *cf.* next.

DUDLEY. *Dom.* Dudelei, 1275 Duddleye, ' meadow of *Dudd*, *Dudo*, or *Dodo*,' ? the duke in Mercia, and founder of Tewkesbury Abbey, 715. *Cf.* DIDCOT and DUDBRIDGE; and see -ley.

DUFFIELD (Derby). Not in *Dom.* *c.* 1180 *Ben. Peterb.* Dufelda, ' dove field.' O.E. **dufe*, *c.* 1200 *duue*, *c.* 1300 *duu.* If this derivation be correct, we have here one of the earliest recorded examples of the Eng. word *dove.* *Cf.* Doveskar, Wensleydale, 1202 Duuesker, and Doveridge, *Dom.* Dubrige.

DUGGLEBY (Yorks). *Dom.* Dighelbi, Difgelibi. ' Dwelling of *Dougal*,' in Ir. and G. *Dubhgall*, or ' dark stranger,' the Ir. name for the Danes. This Danish Kelt prob. came from Ireland. There are other traces of such settlers. *Cf.* DOLTON; and see -by.

DULLINGHAM (Newmarket). *Dom.* Dullingeham; also *old* Dilintone. ' Home of the *Dillings*.' *Cf.* Dillington (Hunts) and

Dilham (Norfk.)—*i.e.*, 'home of *Dill*,' still a personal name, of which Dilling is the patronymic.

DULVERTON (Somerset). *Dom.* Dolvertun. The name here seems unknown. There seems trace of a N. *Tolf-r* or *Tolrius.*

DULWICH, *sic* 1606. Not in *Dom.* (There are coins with Dulwic on them, supposed to be a man's name.) Possibly 'Dola's dwelling'; one *Dola* in *Onom.* The adj. *dull* is not in Eng. *a.* 1430. *Cf. Dom.* Derby, Duluestune.

DUMBLETON (Evesham). *Sic* 1327, but 930 *chart.* Dumolan, -llan, 995 Dumbletain, *Dom.* Dunbentone. The forms are corrupt. Skeat suggested '*Domwulf's* town,' but this is doubtful.

DUMMER (Basingstoke). *Dom.* Dûmere. Prob. '*Duda's mere*' or 'lake.' *Cf. Dom.* Dodimere (Sussex) and DIDMARTON, also CROMER.

DUNCHURCH (Rugby). *Dom.* Donecerce. *c.* 1200 Dunchirch, 1444 Dunkyrke. 'Church on the hill,' O.E. *dún*, though possibly fr. a man *Donn* or *Dunn.* The 1444 -kyrke is interesting, as showing the lingering of Dan. influence, just as in Dunkirk, N. France.

DUNGENESS (Kent). 1052 *O.E. Chron.* Næss—*i.e.*, 'nose, cape, naze.' Dunge- is prob. Dan. *dynge*, 'a heap, a pile (of dung),' mod. Icel. *dyngja*, 'heap, dung,' O.E. *dung. Cf.* Dinganess, Norway.

DUNGLEDDY (Glamorgan). *c.* 1130 *Lib. Land.* Dou Clediv, 1603 Doyglethe, 'the dark (W. *du*) CLEDDY R.'

DUNHAM (6 in *P.G.*). *Sic* 1150 *chart.* K.C.D. iv. 209. *Dom.* Notts, Duneham. Norfolk D. *c.* 1460 Donham. O.E. *dún-ham*, 'hill-dwelling.'

DUNHEVED (Launceston). *Dom.* Dunhevet, *c.* 1140 Downehevede, Dunehevede, 1250 Dunhefd. Corn. *din hafod*, 'hill of the summer residence'; no doubt confused with O.E. *heafod ;* Dan. *hoved*, 'the head.'

DUNMORE (Leckhampstead). Not in *Dom. Chart.* dunn mere, which is O.E. for 'dun-coloured, brownish lake.' Perh. remodelled on DUNMORE (Sc.), 'big hill.'

DUNMOW (Essex). *Dom.* Dom(m)auua, 1160 *Pipe* Dumawa, *c.* 1386 Donmowe. Perh. tautology. W. *din*, 'a hill,' and O.E. *muga* 'a heap, a mow, a pile of hay'; found 3-7 *mowe.*

DUNNINGTON (York). *Dom.* Domni-, Donniton, also Dodinton; 1202 Dunnigton. There are several men named *Dunning* in *Onom.*, but the name here is doubtful. *Cf.* DODDINGTON.

DUNSTABLE. Not in *Dom.* 1123 *O.E. Chron.* Dunestaple, *c.* 1200 *Gervase* Dunstapele, 1433 Dunstaple. 'Hill of the market'; it

lies at the foot of Dunstable Downs. O.E. *dún-stapel*. *Cf.*
BARNSTAPLE. Dunsley (Yorks) is *Dom.* Dunesle, ' meadow on
the hill.'

DUNSTALL. Common var. of TUNSTALL.

DUNSTER (Somerset). Not in *Dom.* Prob. 1231 *Patent R.* Dintre,
which looks like W. *din tre*, ' hill with the house.' But 1243 *ib.*
Dunesterr, which may be an Eng. remodelling; O.E. *dun steor-
ra(n)*, ' hill of the star.' The common Sc. ending -ster, O.N.
staðr, ' dwelling,' is not very likely here.

DUNTISBOURNE (Cirencester). *Dom.* Tantesbourne, 1102 Dontes-,
1221 Duntesborne. ? ' Stream of.' Baddeley gives up the
implied name as hopeless. *Onom.* has a *Dunniht* and a *Thront*,
which seem at least possible. See -bourne.

DUNTON (3 in *P.G.*). *Dom.* Norfk. Dontuna. *Cf.* 672 *chart.* Dun-
tun, ? near Winchester, and *Dom.* Duntune, Salop. ' Town at
the hill '; O.E. *dún*, which also means ' a fort.'

DUNWICH (once in Suffolk, now submerged). *Bede* Domnoc, Dom-
moc, *c.* 1175 *Fantosme* Dunewiz. Doubtful. Some derive fr. W.
dwfn, ' deep.' *Cf.* DYMOCK. See -wich.

DURDANS, The (Epsom). *Sic* 1658. Said to be M.E. *durden*, ' a
coppice '; but there seems no trace of this in *Oxf. Dict.*, where the
only *durdan* is a var. of *dirdum*, ' uproar, tumult,' a Sc. and
North. dial. word found *c.* 1440 in *York Myst.* as *durdan*. This
name is prob. *Dom.* Dordnhoes, ? ' hill of *Dorda* '; the nearest
name in *Onom.* is *Durand*. See HOE. The plur. *s* often
suffixes itself.

DURDAR (Carlisle). Kelt. for ' stream with the thicket '; G. *dobhar*,
W. *dwr*, and G. *daire*; or else fr. G. *darach*, ' an oak.' The same
Dur- is seen in Durbeck or Doverbeck (Notts), 1225 Doverbec,
prob. a tautology, and in Durbridge (Worcs.). *Cf.* DOVER and
DWRBACH.

DURHAM. Founded *O.E. Chron.* ann. 995, but no name is given
there. *c.* 1070 *Wm. Jumièges* Castrum quod propria lingua
Dunelmum nuncuparunt; 1075-1128 Dunholme; *c.* 1175 *Fantosme*
Durealme; 1295 Dwreysm; *c.* 1470 *Henry* Duram; 1535 *Stewart*
Durhame. A name which has changed more than once. Dunelm
or -ealme is orig. Kelt. *dun ealm*, ' hill of the elms,' an early
loan-word. But Dunholme is O.E., meaning ' fort by the *holm*
or river-meadow '; whilst Durham should mean ' wild-beasts'
home or lair,' O.E. *deór ham*, same root as *deer;* Icel. *dýr;*
Sw. *diur*, ' a wild beast.' That the *n* should have become *r* is
but one other proof of the liquidity of the liquids. *Cf.* DEREHAM
and DYRHAM.

DURLSTONE Head (Dorset). Not in *Dom.* ' Perforated rock '; O.E.
thyrel, ' a hole,' same root as nos-*tril*. The name is perh. a
translation of TILLYWHIM near by. The Head is full of holes.

DURNFORD (Amesbury). *Dom.* Darneford. O.E. *derne, dyrne,* 'secret, hidden, obscure.' *Cf.* DARNALL and DARNICK (Sc.). Dornford (Wootton, Oxon) is the same; 1236 *Patent R.* Derneford.

DURRINGTON (Salisbury and Worthing). Sa. D. *Dom.* Derintone, Wo. D. *Dom.* Derentune. Prob. O.E. *Deoran tun,* 'town of Deora.' *Onom.* also has *Deorwen* or *Derwine. Cf.* DURSLEY (Glouc.), 1153 Duresle, also Derselega, where the name is doubtful. DURRANCE (Upton Warren) is prob. called after a Robt. *Duran,* known to be living in an adjoining manor in 1275.

DUSTON (Northampton). *Dom.* Dustone. Prob. '*Dudd's* town.' *Cf. Dom.* Dudestan (Chesh.) and DUDLEY and DUMMER.

DUTTON (Warrington). *Sic* 1302, but 1102 Dotona. Perh. 'town of *Dutta.' Cf.* 940 *chart.* Duttan hamme (Wiley, Wilts). But perh. fr. O.E. *dufe,* 'a dove'; perh. here become a proper name. *Cf.* DUFFIELD.

DUXFORD (Cambridge). *Dom.* Dochesuuorde, 1211 Dokesworth, 1284 Dukesworth, *c.* 1660 *Fuller* Dokesworth. The -ford is quite a mod. corrup. 'Farm of *Duc,'* says Skeat, and not 'of the ducks,' O.E. *dúca,* though *Duc* is an unknown personal name. *Cf.* DOXEY. See -worth. But Duxford (Berks) is *Dom.* Dudochesforde, 'Ford of *Dudoc*'; 10 such in *Onom.*

DWRBACH (Pembrokesh.). W. = 'little stream.' Durbeck or Dover Beck (Notts), 1225 Doverbec, might be the same name, but is more likely a tautology; W. *dwr* = Eng. *beck,* 'stream.'

DWYFOR and DWYFFACH (Criccieth). Prob., says Anwyl, 'great and little goddess,' L. *diva;* W. *mawr,* 'big,' and *bach,* 'little,' in both names aspirated.

DYFFRYN (Merioneth), *old* Dyffrynt. W. *dyfr-hynt,* 'water' or 'river way,' and so 'vale.'

DYM- or DIMCHURCH (New Romney, Kent). Not in *Dom.* M'Clure compares O.E. *dimhus* and *dimhof,* 'hiding or dark place.'

DYMOCK (Glouc.). *Dom.* Dimoch, 1167-68 *Pipe* Dīmoc, 1223 Dimmoc. Doubtful. It looks like an O.W. dimin. of W. *din, dyn,* 'hill' or 'fort'; *m* and *n* constantly interchange. *Cf.* Dum- or Dunbarton, and DUNWICH.

DYRHAM (Chippenham). Said to be O.E. *Chron.* 577, also 950 *chart.,* Deorham—*i.e.,* 'wild beasts' lair or home.' *Cf.* DURHAM. But *Dom.* Wilts has a Dobreham, which may be the *Chron.* place, and so a hybrid—O.Keltic *dobr;* W. *dwfr,* 'river'; and O.E. *hám,* 'home.' *Cf.* DOVER.

DYSERTH (Flint). 1245 *Patent R.* Dissard. W. form of L. *desertum,* 'a desert place,' then 'a hermit's cell,' 'a house for receiving pilgrims,' 'a church,' and so the same as the Deserts and Dysarts of Ireland and Scotland. There is a 'Desertelawa' (hill), 1156, in *Pipe* Derby.

DYVI R. (Merioneth). *c.* 1188 *Gir. Camb.* Ostium Devi. Prob. another instance of river-worship, the name prob. meaning 'goddess.' *Cf.* DWYFOR.

EAGLE STONE (Baston Edge). Local tradition says, fr. the Saxon archer god *Egil* or *Ægle.* *Cf.* AYLESBURY and EGLESBOURNE.

EAKRING (Newark). *Dom.* Aigrun, Ec(h)eringhe, 1229 *Close R.* Ekering'. 1278-1428 Aykering. This seems to be O.N. *eik-runn,* 'runlet, little stream with the oaks.' *Cf.* AIGBURTH. *Oxf. Dict.* gives *run,* sb. 9, with this meaning as North. dial., and has no quot. *a.* 1581. But the verb *run* in its earlier usages seems to have come to us chiefly through Scandinavian sources. See *Dict.* s.v. *run* vb. The later forms seem to be N. *eikar eng,* in M.E. *ing,* 'meadow of the oaks.'

EALING (London). 1245 *Patent R.* Gilling; *later* Yeling, Yealing, and Zealing (*Z* for *Y*). Evidently the same patronymic as in GIL-LINGHAM. For the falling away of *g, cf.* ILCHESTER, IPSWICH, etc., also YARMOUTH. *Onom.* has both *Gīlo* and *Gillus ;* fr. either Gilling may have come. See -ing. There are also *Dom.* Berks Elinge, and 1161-62 *Pipe* Eling, Hants. These, however, are prob. patronymics fr. *Ela,* a man's name found in *Beowulf.*

EAMONT or EAMOT Bridge (Penrith). 926 *chart.* Eamotum. M'Clure says, O.E. *ea-(ge)mot,* in 926 in a loc. plur., meaning 'river confluence' or 'meet'; the form -mont prob. showing the influence of N. *munn-r,* 'a river-mouth.' Possibly the same name as EMMET.

EARBY (Colne). *Dom.* Eurebi. Prob. 'dwelling of *Eofor.*' Eofor-mær of Driffield is found also as Euremarus. *Cf.* EVERLEY. See -by.

EARDINGTON. See ERDINGTON.

EARDISTON (Tenbury), EARDISLAND, and EARDISLEY (Herefordsh.). Ten. E. 957 *chart.* Eardufestun, *Dom.* Ardolvestone, *a.* 1100 *chart.* Eardulfestune. 'Town, land, and meadow of *Eardwulf.*' See -ley and -ton.

EARITH. See ERITH.

EARLSWOOD (Birmingham, etc.). Bir. E. in *c.* 1274 *chart.* is 'the Earl of Warwick's wood.'

EARLY (Reading). *Dom.* Erlei, 1316 Erle, Erlee, 1428 Arle. Skeat conjectures '*Earna's* lea,' or 'meadow of the eagle,' O.E. *earn,* and compares ARLEY. *Cf. Dom.* Bucks Erlai, and EARNLEY (Sussex), *B.C.S.* i. 331 Earneleagh.

EARSHAM (Bungay). Not in *Dom.* 1157 *Pipe* Eresham. 'Home of *Ere,*' one in *Onom.* *Cf.* ARRETON.

EASINGTON (4 in *P.G.*). Thame E. *Dom.* Essedene. Castle Eden E. *a.* 1130 *Sim. Dur.* Esingtun, 1183 Esyntona. 'Town, village of *Ese* or *Esne,*' both very common in *Onom.* The -ing, *q.v.,* may either represent the O.E. gen. -*an*, or be the sign of a patronymic. *Cf. Dom.* Bucks Esenberge. For interchange of -den, -don, -ton, see these endings.

EASINGWOLD (Yorks). *Dom.* Eisicewalt, Eisincewald, 1230 *Close R.* Esingewald. Prob. patronymic. ' Wold, wood of the sons of,' some man with name in Is- (*cf.* EASTOFT). Wold is O.E. *wald, weald. Cf.* EASINGHOPE (Worc.), 1275 Esighope, ' valley of the sons of *Is* or *Esi*,' and above. See -ing.

EAST BECKHAM (Norfolk). *Dom.* Becham, 1458 Est bekham. May not be ' home on the beck ' or ' brook,' see BACUP; but perh. fr. a man, as in BECKENHAM.

EASTBOURNE. *Dom.* Borne, 1114 *O.E. Chron.* Burne, *c.* 1450 *Fortescue* Borne, 1730 Eastborn or Eborn. *Burne* or *bourne* is just early Eng. for ' brook,' the Sc. burn. EASTBURN (Driffield) is actually Augustburne in *Dom.* See AUST.

EASTCOTE (Pinner). *Cf.* 958 *chart.* ' Eostacote ' on Stour, Staffs— *i.e.*, ' east cot ' or ' cottage '; also 1179-80 *Pipe* Westcotun and Oustcotun (Yorks).

EASTERTON (Market Lavington). ' Eastern village.' *Cf. Dom.* Surrey Estrehā and EASTRY.

EASTFIELD (Northampton). 963 *O.E. Chron.* Æstfeld. East-usually is ' east '; but EASTBROOK (Sutton Coldfield) is *a.* 1200 Essebrook, which is prob. ' ash-tree brook.' O.E. *œsc*, 3 *asse*, 5 *esche ; esse* for ' ash ' is found in *Dom.* EASTINGTON, 2 in Glouc., 1119 Estinthone, is prob. O.E. *eastan tún*, ' at the East village.' See -ing.

EASTOFT (Goole). Prob. 1119 *chart.* Istofte, which looks like Dan. *is-toft*, ' ice ' or ' icy field.' There is one man *Iso* in *Onom.*, and many names in Is-, *Isgod, Ishere, Iswulf*, etc., and the Is- may be a contraction of any of them. *Dom.* has only Ese-, Estorp.

EASTON (12 in *P.G.*). *O.E. Chron.* 656 Æstun, 1137 Estun (North-ampton), 796 *chart.* Eastun (Berks). *Dom.* Estune (E. Riding, Yorks), Estone (Bucks). ' East town.'

EASTRINGTON (Brough, Yorks). *Dom.* Estrincton. Perh. ' town of *Eastorwine*,' and it may be a patronymic. See -ing.

EASTRY (Dover). 788 *chart.* In regione Eastrgena, 805 *chart·* Easterege, *a.* 1000 Eastrege. The first half will mean ' Eastern '; M'Clure connects the second with the continental tribe of the *Rugii.* But in O.E. the ending *-ige* usually means ' island.' *Cf.* AUSTERFIELD. EASTREA, or ESTREA (Cambs), is prob. *B.C.S.* iii. 438, Estrey, or ' eastern isle. *Cf.* Westry farm, March, and -ey.

EASTWOOD (Nottingham). *Dom.* Estewic, error for -twit, 1166-7 *Pipe* Est Twait, 1225 Estwaite, and often so. This is now no region for -thwaite (see p. 59), hence the change.

EATHORPE (Leamington). 1327 Ethorpe. 'Village on the running water,' O.E. *éa*, O.N. *oa*. This is one of the southmost instances of -thorpe, *q.v. Cf.* EDALE, and *Dom.* Glouc. Aiforde.

EATON CONSTANTINE (Shrewsbury). *Dom.* Etone.

EATON HASTINGS (Farringdon). *O.E. chart.* Eatun, *c.* 1300 Eton.

EATON SOCON (Bedford). 1155 Eitune, 1581 Eaton Sooken. EATON WATER and WOOD (Staffs). *Dom.* Eitone, Etone. EATON (Notts) *Dom.* Etune, Ettone, Ættune. O.E. *éa-tun*, 'river-town.' *Sócn* is a district held by tenure of vocage—*i.e.*, for certain, determined service; O.E. *sóc*, 'privilege of holding a court in a district.' There are 8 Eatons in *P.G. Cf.* ETON.

EBBERSTON (Snainton, Yorks). *Dom.* Edbriztune, 1166-67 *Pipe* Edbrihteston. 'Town of *Eadbeorht*,' a very common O.E. name. *Cf. Dom.* Salop Etbretelie. But with EBBERLY (Torrington) *cf. Dom.* Hereford, Elburgelega, 'meadow of (the lady) *Elburga*.'

EBBESBOURNE (Salisbury). 672 *chart.* Ebblesburnon, *Dom.* Eblesborne. 'Elba's brook' or 'burn,' O.E. *burn(e)*. *Eabba* and *Eabe* are common in *Onom.*, and there is also one *Ebbella*. The liquid *l* would easily disappear. *Cf.* EBLEY (Glouc.), 1317 Ebbaleye, and EPSOM.

EBBSFLEET (Thanet). *O.E. Chron.* 449 Eopwinesfleot, Ypwinesfleot; also Wippedsfleot. Not in *Dom.* O.E. *fleot*, Icel. *fljót* is 'a stream' or perh. 'a creek,' same root as *fleet.* See FLEET. The first part must represent the name of some early Jutish settler. Ebbs- may be a contraction of Ypwines- or Eopwines-. There was once a channel between Thanet and Kent, and this is at the south-east mouth of it. *Cf.* IPPLEPEN.

EBCHESTER (Co. Durham). Perh. *a.* 700 *Rav. Geogr.* Ebio. 'Camp of ?.' See -chester.

ECCHINSWELL (Newbury). *Dom.* Eccleswelle. Eccles, as in next, is prob. L. *ecclesia*, W. *eglwys*, and so this name may mean 'church well.' It is a curious corrup., and shows how any one liquid may run into another, though *l* very rarely becomes *n*. There is one *Echun* in *Onom.*

ECCLES (Lancs, Attleborough, Maidstone) and ECCLESFIELD (Sheffield). Lanc. E. *sic c.* 1100. Sh. E. *Dom.* Eclesfelt, 1179 Ecclesfeld. Either L. *ecclesia*, W. *eglwys*, 'a church,' or rare case of a personal name in gen. used for a place, without suffix, '(village of) *Æcel*' or '*Æcle*,' a known O.E. name. *Cf.* BECCLES, BEEDON, and BRAILES. It is hard to be certain which alternative is right; both are contrary to the usual. *E.g.*, why should the name *Æcel* so often be used alone, when almost no other is?

ECCLESHALL (Stafford). *Dom.* Ecleshelle, 1298 Eccleshale, 1459 Eggleshal. 'Nook, corner, beside the church,' or 'of *Æcel*' (see above). See -hall. *Cf.* ECCLESHILL (S. Yorks), *Dom.* Egleshil, and ECCLESTON (Lancs), *Dom.* Eglestun.

ECCUP (Leeds). *Dom.* Echope. ' Shut-in valley of *Ecca.' Cf.*
BACUP, and see -hope.

ECKINGTON (Pershore and Sheffield). Pe. E. 972 *chart.* Eccyncgtune,
Dom. Aichintune, *a.* 1400 Ekington, Ekynton, Shef. E. ? *Dom.*
Ecinton. ' Town of the sons of *Ecca.' Cf.* next and *Grant a.* 675
' Eccantrewe ' in Surrey. See -ing and -ton.

ECTON (Northampton). *Dom.* Ecdone, 1298 Eketon. ' Ecca's
town.' *Ecca* is a very common name in *Onom.* ; -don and -ton
commonly interchange.

EDALE (N. Derbysh.). *Dom.* Aidele. ' Dale,' N. *dal-r,* ' with the
running stream.' O.E. *éa,* O.N. *áa. Cf.* EATHORPE and
EDZELL (Sc.), 1204 Edale; and see -dale.

EDDINGTON (Herne Bay). *Dom.* Eddintone. ' Town of (the sons
of) *Ede '* or ' *Eada.' Cf.* next and *Dom.* (Bucks) Eddingraue.
See -ing.

EDDISBURY (Cheshire). 914 *O.E. Chron.* Eadesbyrig, *'Eada's* or
Ede's burgh.' *Cf. Dom.* (Bucks) Eddinberge. See -bury.

EDDLETHORP (Yorks). *Dom.* Eduardestorp. ' Village of *Edward,'*
Liquid *r* has changed to liquid *l. Cf.* Eddlesborough (Dunstable)—not in *Dom.* However, in another place in *Dom.* it
is Gedwalestorp; prob. error.

EDDYSTONE LIGHTHOUSE (Plymouth). ' Stone or rock of *Eadda*
or *Æddi.'*

EDEN R. (Cumberland and Kent). Cum. E. prob. *c.* 120 *Ptolemy*
Ituna, *a.* 1130 *Sim. Dur.* Iodene and duas Geodene = Castle
Eden and Little Eden (Hartlepool); latter also occurs as Suth
Yoden. The early forms of Eden Water, a Sc. tributary of the
Tweed, are seen in those of EDNAM (Sc).; *c.* 1100 Aednaham,
1116 Edyngahum, *c.* 1120 Ednaham, *c.* 1220 Edenham. These
forms are perplexing, and it is hard to come to a verdict. The
first part possibly contains a Kelt. root meaning ' corn,' W. *yd,*
Ir. *etha,* so perh. ' river flowing through corn-lands.' On *en* or
an for ' river,' *cf.* p. 11. *Cf.* ITCHEN.

EDENHALL (Langwathby). 1158-59 *Pipe* Edenhale. ' Nook by the
Eden.' See above and -hall.

EDENSOR (Bakewell). *Dom.* Ednesoure. As this is on the R.
Derwent, it prob. means ' bank, edge of *Ædan '* or ' *Aidan.'*
See -or and -over. But Eden, see above, *may* have been another
name of the Derwent. We get the same name in BADDESLEY
ENSOR, *a.* 1300 Ednesovre, 1327 Endeshover.

EDGBASTON (Birmingham). *Dom.* Celboldstone (' *Ceolbeald's* town'),
1150 Egboldeston, *a.* 1200 Egbaldeston, Eggebaldeston.
' *Ecgbeald's* village.' We cannot now explain the change of
name. But O.E. ecg- by rule becomes edg: *e.g.,* edge is O.E.
ecg(g).

EDGEWARE (London). Not in *Dom.* *c.* 1160 Eggeswere, *c.* 1500 Eggesware. Perh. fr. an O.E. Ecgeswer, 'at the edge of the wear,' *ecg,* 2 *egge,* 'edge,' and *wer, wær,* 'a fence, an enclosure for fish.' *Dom.* also uses *wara* for 'an outlying portion of a manor,' which Round makes cognate with *wer,* 'a fence.' But the first part may be fr. a man * Æga,* in *Onom.* *Cf.* *Dom.* Norfk. Egemere and EDGWORTH (Cirencester), *Dom.* Egesuuorde, Egeiswurde, 'farm of *Æga* ' or ' *Ecg.* '

EDGTON (Aston-on-Clun, Salop). *Cf.* 1179-80 *Pipe Roll* Eggeton (Yorks). Either ' *Æga's* town,' or ' village at the edge.' See above.

EDINGLEY (Southwell). Not in *Dom.,* but *sic* 1302. *Cf.* 1005 *chart.* in Dugdale, Egæanlæa. ' *Eda's* lea ' or ' meadow.' *Cf.* EDDINGTHORPE and Edingale (Tamworth), *Dom.* Ednunghalle, *a.* 1200 Eadinghall, Edenynghal(e), which may be a patronymic, but is prob. derived fr. *Eadhun.*

E(D)DINGTHORPE (N. Walsham). Not in *Dom.* 1429 Edithorp. ' *Eada's* village.' Many of this name in *Onom.* See -thorpe.

EDINGTON (Wilts). 957 *chart.* Ethandun, *Dom.* Edintone. [879 *O.E. Chron.* Ethandun, *cf.* ASHINGTON.] ' Town of *Eda, Eada, Etha,* or *Eata* '; all these forms in *Onom.* See -ing. But Athelney E. is *Dom.* Edwinetone, 1199 Edintone.

EDLINGHAM (Alnwick). *a.* 1130 *Sim. Dur.* Eadulfingham, Eadwul-fincham. A patronymic. ' Home of the descendants of *Eadwulf,'* a common O.E. name. Similar is EDLINGTON (Horncastle). *Dom.* Ellintone, Eilintone, *c.* 1275 *Testa de Neville* Edelington.

EFFINGHAM (Leatherhead). Not in *Dom.* O.E. Effingeham, pat-ronymic; ' home of the descendants of *Effa* or *Eafa* ' *(cf.* Bede III. 24).

EGERTON (Ashford, Kent, and Bolton). Not in *Dom.* ' *Eadgar's* town.' *Cf.* Agardesley (Staffs), *c.* 1004 *chart.* Eadgares leye.

EGHAM (Surrey). *Grant* of *a.*675, and *Dom.*Egeham. ' Home of *Æga.* ' *Cf.* EDGEWARE, and Egbrough (Yorks), *Dom.* Egburg, Acheburg.

EGLESBOURNE or ECCLESBURNE (Derbysh.). Not in *Dom.* Said to be, like EAGLE STONE, fr. the archer *Egil ;* though the first syll. may be for ' church,' see ECCLES. A man's name is prob. in EGGLESTONE (Darlington), *Dom.* Eghistun (*h* error for *l*), and in 1342 ' Eglesfeld,' (Westmrld.).

EGLINGHAM (Alnwick). *a.* 1130 *Sim. Dur.* Ecgwulfingham, 1197 Eggleningeham. ' Home of the descendants of *Ecgwulf,* ' a common name in *Onom.* See -ing.

EGLOSHAYLE (The Lizard). *Sic* 1536. Corn. *eglos hayle,* ' church on the tidal river.' *Eglos* is in W. *eglwys,* G. *eaglais,* L. *ecclesia,* Gk. ἐκκλησία.

EGLOSKERRY (Launceston). Corn. *eglos,* ' church,' see above, and it is doubtful what; perh. the Corn. for ' fort,' W. *caer,* or perh.

(? Corn. and) W. *ceri*, ' medlar trees.' In *Dom*. Cornw. we have Eglosberrie, prob. fr. St. *Baire* of Cork, friend of Brendan and Cainneach.

EGLWYS NEWYDD (Cardiff), now usually called Whitchurch. *c.* 1540 Egglis Newith, which is phonetic W. for ' new church.' The usual W. for church is *llan*.

EGREMONT (Pembroke and Whitehaven). Wh. E. *a.* 1200 Egener-mot, which is clearly O.N. for ' meeting-place, court of *Egen*,' the -er being the N. gen. *Cf.* ENNERDALE. But it is 1218 Egremunde, 1246 Egremund, where the ending is O.N. *munn-r* for *mund-r*, ' mouth, river-mouth '; perh. influenced by O.E. *munt*, L. *mons, -tis*, ' hill, mountain.'

EIRL (mountains, Caernarvonsh.). W. = ' rivals.'

ELDON (Bps. Auckland). *a.* 1130 *Sim. Dur*. Elledun. Prob. ' *Ælla*'s or *Ella*'s hill,' O.E. *dún*.

ELDWICK (Bingley). *Dom*. Helguic, Helwic. O.E. *halig wic*, ' holy dwelling,' holy is 3-4 *heli, hely*. *Cf.* O.N. *heilag-r*, Sw. *helig*, and ELLOUGHTON; and see -wick.

ELFORD (Tamworth). 1004 *chart*. Elleford, *Dom*. Eleford. ' Ford of *Ælla*' or ' *Elle*,' common O.E. name. *Cf. Dom*. Essex Elefforda.

ELHAM (Canterbury). *c.* 1000 Ulaham, O.E. for ' owl village.' Not in *Dom*.

ELKINGTON, SOUTH (Louth). *Dom*. Alchinton, 1233 Suthelkinton, 1359 Elkyngton. Prob. ' town, village of *Ealhhun*,' fairly common in *Onom*., and found also as *Alchun*. But it may be ' of the sons of *Elc*.' *Cf.* next and -ing.

ELKSTONE (Cheltenham and Leek). Chel. E. *Dom*. Elchestane, 1177 *Pipe* Elkestan. Leek E. 1227 Elkesdon. *Elc* may be a man's name, otherwise unknown. *Cf.* above; Baddeley says *Ealch* for *Ealh-*, which also may be. But these are prob. ' stone ' and ' hill of the elk,' O.E. *elch, elh*, then not recorded till 1486 *elke*. See -don and -ton.

ELLAND (Halifax). *Dom*. Elant, Elont. This seems to be a var. of *island*. It stands on the R. Calder, but was it ever an island ? *Island* is O.E. *iȝland, iland, ȝillond, yllond*, 4-5 *eland*. But Ellel (Lancs.) is *Dom*. Ellhale, prob. ' *Ella*'s nook.' See -hall.

ELLASTONE (Ashbourne). *Dom*. Edelachestone, Elachestone, *a.* 1200 Adelakestone, Athel-, Ethelaxton, ' village of *Æthelac*.' There is also 1166-67 *Pipe* Adelacheston (Bucks and Beds). See -ton, which often interchanges with -stone.

ELLENBOROUGH (Maryport). *Old* Alneburg, and (prob.) Aynburg. ' Burgh, town on the R. *Ellen* or ALNE.' But ELLENHALL (Eccleshall) is *Dom*. Linehalle (an error), *a.* 1200 Ellinhale, ' nook of *Elle*.' *Cf.* ELLESHAM. And in O.E. charters we find both an Ellenbeorh and an Ellesbeorh. But ELLENTHORP

(W. Riding) is Elwinetorp and Halwidetorp (*d* error for *n*) in *Dom*—*i.e.*, ' village of *Ealhwine* or *Aluuinus*', same name as *Alcuin*. *Cf*. ELVINGTON.

ELLERBY (Holderness). *Dom*. Aluerdebi, Alwerdebi, 1179-80 *Pipe* Alwardebi. 'Dwelling of *Ealdweard*.' *Cf*. ALLERTHORPE; and see -by.

ELLERDINE (Wellington, Salop). *Dom*. Ellevrdine, 1233 *Close R*. Ele- and Ailwarthin. '*Ella*'s farm.' The ending -vrdine or -wardine (*q.v*.) is common in this region.

ELLERKER (South Cave, Yorks). *Dom*. Alrecher. Prob. O.N. *ölr* or *elrir kjarr*, ' alder copse.' *Cf*. ELLERTON and CARSWELL, also ELLERBURN (E. Riding), *Dom*. Elreburne.

ELLERTON (on Swale). *Sic* 1203, but *Dom*. Alreton, twice, Elre-ton(e), 5 times. Perh. = ALDERTON, and some cases of ALLERTON, 'town among the alders,' O.E. *alor, aler*, 5 *ellyr*, O.N. *ölr, elrir*. But it may as likely be fr. the common O.E. name *Ealhhere*, or else, *Ælfhere*, as in ALLERSTON. ELLERBY (Holderness), *Dom*. Alwerdebi, Aluerdebi, -wardebi, Elwordebi, ' dwelling of *Ealhweard*,' must be of different origin.

ELLESHAM or AILSHAM PRIORY (Lincs). *Dom*. Elesham, 1233 Ellesham. 'Home of *Ælli, Ælla*, or *Ella*.' *Cf*. 808 *chart*. Ælesbeorge, (Somerset).

ELLESMERE (Oswestry). *Sic* in *Dom*. ' Lake of *Ella* '; see above.

ELLINGHAM, GT. (Attleboro'). *Dom*. *sic* and Elincgham, and ELLINGTON (Hunts and Morpeth), Hu. E. *Dom*. Elintune, may all be patronymics; 'home, town of *Ælla*'s descendants.' But ELLINGDON (Swindon) is the Ellandune or ' Ella's fort,' of the great Mercian defeat by K. Egbert in 825; ELLINGHAM (Bungay) is *Dom*. Elminghehā, ' home of the sons of *Elm*, or *Elmund*, or *Ealhmund*'; and ELLINTHORPE (S. Yorks) is *Dom*. Adelingestorp. See ADELINGFLEET. Also see -ing and -thorpe.

ELLOUGHTON (Brough, Yorks). *Dom*. Elgendon, The Elgen- is doubtful, more old forms needed. It is not impossible it may represent *hallow*, ' a saint,' O.E. *halga, -an*, 3 *Orm*, plur. *alhen*, 4 *alwes*. *Cf*. O.N. *heilag-r*, Sw. *helig*, ' holy,' and ELDWICK. See -don and -ton.

ELM (Cambridge and Frome). Cam. E. *a*. 1154 *O.E. Chron*. 956 *Ælm*, 1346 Elm. O.E. *elm*, Dan. *œlm, alm*, ' an elm-tree.' *Cf*. ASH, POPLAR, etc. ELMBRIDGE (Glostr.) is *c*. 1210 El-brugge, but *c*. 1200 Telbrugge also Thellbruge ' bridge made of deals.' O.E. *þel, þell*. The change arose through Thel-being taken as Th'el- or ' The elm ' bridge. There is a ' Thel-brycg ' (Sandford, Devon) in 930 *chart*. On the other hand, Elmbridge (Droitwich) is *Dom*. Elmerige, *a* .1300 Elmrugge, and -brugge, which is orig. ' elm-ridge,' O.E. *hrycg*.

ELMERS END (Beckenham).   *Elmer* is a late form of *Ælfmær*, a very common O.E. name.   But ELMORE (Gloster) is 1177 *Pipe* Elmour, 1221 Elneoverc.   'Elm-tree bank,'   *Cf.* HASLER, etc., and see -over.

ELMETT.   See BARWICK-IN-ELMET.

ELMHAM (Norfolk).   ? 1038 *chart.* Ælmham.   ? O.E. = 'house built of elm-wood.'   *Cf.* ELMDON (Birmingham), *Dom.* Elmedone.

ELMSBRIDGE (Surrey).   *Dom.* Amelebrige, often; 1230 *Close R.* Emelesbrug.   'Bridge of *Æmele,*' perh. he was præfectus in Sussex in 772 (*B.C.S.* 208).   We have a similar corrup. in ELMSTONE (Kent), 1243 *Patent R.* Eylmerston—*i.e.*, 'town of *Aylmer,*' very common in O.E. as *Ælfmær.*

ELMSETT (Ipswich).   *Dom.* Elmeseta, *c.* 1210 *Jocelin* Elmset.   The meaning is a little doubtful.   *Seat,* O.N. *sæti,* is not found in Eng. till *c.* 1200, and with the meaning 'place of abode' not till *c.* 1275.   But the ending *-set* or *-sæt,* as in SOMERSET, is very old; and so the meaning here is prob. 'dwelling of a family called *Elm.*'   Trees' names often became personal names.   However, ELMSTONE HARDWICK (Cheltenham) is 889 *chart.*, Alchmundingtun, *Dom.* Almondeston, 'dwelling of *Ealhmund.*'   See -ing.

ELSLACK (Skipton).   *Dom.* Eleslac.   '*Ælla's* slack,' O.N. *slakki,* 'a small shallow dell or valley, a hollow or dip in the ground.'   *Cf.* Beeslack, Penicuik (Sc.).

ELSTON (Newark).   *Dom.* Eluestune, *c.* 1190 Elvestona, 1302 Eyliston.   *Cf. B.C.S.* 936 Ælfestun.   'Town of *Ælf.*'   *Cf.* ALVESTON and *Dom.* Dorset Ælfatune.   O.E. *ælf,* O.N. *alf-r* is 'an elf, a fairy.'

ELSTOW (Bedford).   *Dom.* Elnestou, *c.* 1160 Alnestowe, *c.* 1200 *Gervase* Helenstoe, 1233 *Patent R.* Alnestowa, 1327-1632 Elnestowe.   Perh. 'St. *Helen's* place,' O.E. *stow.*   *Cf.* MORWENSTOW.   The *Helen* is said to be Helena, mother of Constantine the Great.   But it may well be '*Ealhhun's,* *Ælhun's,* or *Ealhwine's* place.'   These are all known names.   But older forms are needed.

ELSTREE (St. Albans).   1287 Idolvestre; *later* Idelestree, Ilstrye —*i.e.*, '*Eadwulf's* tree.'   *Cf.* OSWESTRY, etc.   The form Eaglestree is a stupid invention.

ELSWICK (Preston and Newcastle).   Pr. E.   *Dom.* Edelelsuuic.   Doubtful.   Perh. '*Æthel's* dwelling.'   See -wick.

ELSWORTH (W. Cambs).   *Chart.* Elesworð, *Dom.* Elesworde, 1316 Ellesworthe.   Local pron. Elser.   '*Ella's* farm.'   *Cf.* ELLESHAM.   In O.E. charters we also have 'Ellewurthie,' now the personal name Elworthy.   See -worth, -worthy.

ELTERBURN (Nthbld.), *old* Eltheburn, and ELTERWATER (Ambleside).   Doubtful.   There is one man *Eltor* mentioned in *Dom.*

ELTHAM (Greenwich). *Sic* 1577, but *Dom.* Ealdham, which is O.E. for 'old home or house.' Another Eltham in the N. is found *sic* in 1314. *Cf.* ELTON.

ELTISLEY (St. Neot's). Not in *Dom.* 1251 Eltesle, 1302 Elteslee. The nearest name in *Onom.* is one *Eltun* or *Elstan,* a monk. Skeat conjectures '*Ælfgeat*'s lea,' but more evidence is needed.

ELTON (4 in *P.G.*). *Dom.* Derby Eltune, Hants Eltetone. Stockton E. *a.* 1130 *Sim. Dur.* Eltun; Nottingham E. *Dom.* Ailtone, *c.* 1190 Elletona. On analogy of ELTHAM one would incline to O.E. *eald tún,* 'old town.' But Elletona suggests derivation fr. a man *Ella;* whilst Mutschmann is prob. right in deriving Ailtone fr. *Ægel,* late var. of *Æthel* or *Ethel,* ' the noble-born.' *Cf.* ELLESHAM, etc.

ELVINGTON (York). *Dom.* Alvintone, '*Ealdwine*'s' or '*Ealhwine*'s town.' *Cf.* ELLENTHORP.

ELY. *Bede* iv. 19 Elge, *q.v., O.E. versn.* Elige, Elia lond; 936 *O.E. Chron.* Elig, *Die Heilige Engl.* Eligabirig, *a.* 1153 *Liber Eliensis* Ely. Anglice id est, a copia anguillarum quae in eisdem capiuntur palludibus. O.E. *el-iȝe,* 'eel-island.' *Cf.* ELIE (Sc.). But Skeat thinks that Elge represents *el-ge, ge* being a very rare and early O.E. word for 'region, district'; Ger. *gau.* See -ey.

EMBER R. (Hampton Court). Prob. same root as EMBER sb[2], *Oxf. Dict.,* which is fr. O.E. *ymb,* 'about, round,' and *ryne,* ' course, running.'

EMBORROW (Bath). Not in *Dom.* Prob. *a.* 1142 *Wm. Malmesb.* Eatumberg, 1270 *chart.* Eteneberga, 'Barrow, mound of *Eata* (*Eatan, Eathun*),' a name common in *Onom.* It is an interesting corruption. *Cf.* BARROWBY, etc.

EMBSAY (Skipton). *Dom.* Embesie, 1202 Emeseia. 'Island of *Embe.*' One monk of this name is found in *Lib. Vit. Dunelm.* See -ay.

EMLYN (Caermarthen). *c.* 1188 *Gir. Camb.* Emelin. Must surely have some connexion with W. *ymlyn, emlyn,* 'to follow, to adhere'; or perh. *emyl,* 'border, edge'; but the origin is quite doubtful. A castle was built here by Sir Rhys ap Thomas, in time of Hen. VIII.; hence it is often called Newcastle Emlyn, because built on the site of a previous castle. *Cf.* 1603 *Owen.* ' Emlyn Yskych . . . wherein newe Castle standeth.'

EMMER GREEN (Reading). *Cf. Dom.* Bucks Imere. Perh. O.E. *eá-mere,* 'lake beside the stream.' *Cf.* ETON and HAMMER.

EMMET (Northumbld. and Yorks). Perh. 926 *O.E. Chron.* Eamotum is that in Norbld.; *chart.* Emmet-roda (Yorks). M'Clure says *Eamotum* is loc. pl. of *ea-(ge)mot,* 'river confluence.'

EMNETH (Wisbech). Not in *Dom.* O.E. *emnet,* 'a plain,' fr. *emn* or *efn* or *efen,* 'even, flat, level,' with denominative suffix as in thicket, etc. The present *th* had prob. its origin with a

Norm. scribe. *Cf.* Granth for Grant (s.v. CAMBRIDGE), Thames for Tames, etc.

EMPINGHAM (Stamford). *Sic* in *Chron. Petrob.*, 1166 *Pipe* Empingehā. 'Home of the *Empings*,' an O.E. tribe. *Cf.* Impington (Cambs), *chart.* Impintun, 1210 Empintone. EMPSHOTT (Hants) is *Dom.* Hibesete, 'seat, dwelling of *Hiba*.' ? for *Himba* or *Hima*, one in *Onom. Cf.* ALDERSHOT.

EMSCOTE (Warwick). *a.* 1200 Edulfascote, *a.* 1300 Edelvecote, and Edelmescote. Two names here, '*Edulf*'s or *Eadwulf*'s' and '*Eadhelm*'s cottage.'

EMSWELL (Yorks). *Dom.* Helmeswelle, Elmeswell. 'Well of *Helm* or *Helma*.' *Cf.* EMSWORTH (Havant), 1231 *Close R.* Elmeworth. Only *Roll Rich. I.* Emeswelle, Enewelle (Herts) is now AMWELL. EMLEY (Yorks) is *Dom.* Ameleie, -lai, which, like Amwell, is fr. a man *Amma*.

ENBORNE (Berks), *c.* 1300 Enedburn, and ENFORD (Pewsey), *Dom.* and *chart.* Enedforde. Fr. O.E. *ened*, L. *anas*, *-tis*, 'a duck.' See -bourne.

ENDERBY (Leicester). *Dom.* Endrebie, 1229 *Close R.* Endredebi. 'Dwelling of *Endred*' or '*Ǣndred*,' a name not in *Onom.* See -by.

ENDON (Stoke-on-T.), *Dom.* Enedun, *a.* 1300 Hene-, Enedun, and ENFIELD (London), *Dom.* Enefelde, *later* Enfeld, Endfield, may be 'duck's hill' and 'field' too. See above, and *cf.* 1161-62 *Pipe* (Cumbld.) Endehal, 'duck's nook.' But they may be fr. a man *Ǣna*, *Ǣni*, *Eana*, or *Eni*, all forms found in *Onom.* For ENDMOOR (Kendal) we need old forms. It might be fr. O.E. *ende*, 'the end,' which in O.E. also means 'a quarter, a division,' and later, 'a boundary.'

ENGLAND. Freeman says, first in 991 *Treaty K. Ǣthelred* Englaland; 1258 *Henry III.* Engleneloande. In 975, 986, and 1002 the country is called Angel-cyn; and older is the name Saxonia. 'Land of the *Engels* or *Angles*,' who came over fr. East of the R. Elbe, where there is a Schleswig district still called Angeln. *Cf.* Freeman, *Nor. Conq.* i. 538 (3rd edit.).

ENGLEFIELD (Reading). 871 *O.E. Chron.* Englefeld, *Dom.* Englefel, Inglefelle. 'Field of the *Angles*.' *Cf.* above, and ENGLETON (Warwksh.), *sic a.* 1200.

ENNERDALE (W. Cumberland). *a.* 1200 Egenerdal, 'dale of *Egen*,' gen. case. *Cf.* EGREMONT and EYNSHAM.

ENTWISTLE (Salford). *c.* 1400 Entwisell. Perh. 'confluence of *Ena*.' See ENFIELD and TWIZEL.

ENVILLE (Stourbridge). *Dom.* Efnefeld, *a.* 1200 Efne-, Evenes-, Evene feld. 'Even field.' *Cf.*, however, EVENWOOD, which with this, may be fr. a man, though in this case prob. not.

'Even' in O.E. is *ebn, emn, efn, efen*. The -ville must be a quite mod. 'refinement.'

ENYS DODMAN (Land's End). 'Island of' prob. some unknown saint. Mr. H. Jenner spells it Dodnan, and would identify with *Donan*, perh. he after whom the Breton churches at Landonan and St. Thonan are called. This is very dubious. *Cf.* The Dodman, Fowey. Corn. *enys* is W. *ynys*, G. *innis*, 'island.' *Cf.* INCE.

EPPING (London). *Dom.* and 1229 *Close R.* Eppinges. Patronymic. 'Place of the descendants of *Eppa*,' a name of which there are several examples in *Onom. Cf.* 811 *chart.* 'Appin(c)g lond' (Kent), and *Dom.* Surrey Epingehā; also EPNEY (Glostersh.), 1252 Eppen', '*Eppa*'s isle.'

EPPLEBY (Darlington). *Dom.* Aplebi = APPLEBY.

EPSOM (Surrey). *Dom.* Ebbasham(e), 1662 Ebsham or Epsom. 'Home of *Ebbe*' or '*Æbbe*,' an abbess, early in 7th cny. *Dom.'s* Ebbas- must be an error for Ebbes-. *Cf.* Mill-om (N. of Barrow); also IPSLEY.

EPWORTH (Doncaster). Not in *Dom. c.* 1444 Eppeworth. 'Farm of *Eppa* or *Eappa*.' *Cf. B.C.S.* 253 Eppan hrycg. See -worth.

ERDINGTON (Birmingham). *Dom.* Hardintone, *a.* 1200 Erdin(g)ton, 1327 Erdyngton. 'Village of *Harding*,' once in *Dom.* Erding. *Cf.* HARDINGSTONE and EARDINGTON (Bridgenorth). This last might also be fr. *Eardwine*.

EREWASH R. (Derby). Not in *Dom. c.* 1175 Yrewis, 1637 Ar-, Erewash. Doubtful, prob. pre-Saxon. But *cf.* GUASH, IRWELL and WASH.

ERITH (London), also EARITH (St. Ives, Hunts). Lon. E. *c.* 962 *chart.* Earhyth, Earhiðe, *Dom.* Erhede, 1486 Erith, *c.* 1580 Eareth. St. I. E. *Ramsey Chron.* Herhythe, Erethe, Erithe. Dr. Morris says, O.E. *éa-rith*, 'water-channel.' But Skeat is positive that it is O.E. *ear-hythe*, 'muddy landing-place' or 'shore.' O.E. *ear* is a very rare word, Icel. *aurr*, 'wet clay, mud.' See HYTHE. Skeat is almost certainly right.

ERNLEY. See ARLEY.

ESCOMB (Bps. Auckland). *a.* 1130 *Sim. Dur.* Ediscum. '*Edda*'s or *Adde*'s valley'; but already 1183 *Boldon Bk.* Escumba. See -combe.

ESGAIR FELYN (Ogwen). W. = 'yellow scaur or cliff.' *Esgair* is same root as the Sc. *skerry*, G. *sgeir*, all borrowed fr. O.N. *sker*, N. *skjer*, 'a rugged, insulated sea rock.'

ESHER (Surbiton). *Dom.* Aissela, Aissele, *c.* 1210 Ashal, 1230-31 *Close R.* Esser, Eyser, Eiser, *c.* 1240 Assere. A curious name. It is prob. '*Ascytel's*' or '*Aschil*'s lea or meadow,' O.E. *léah;* and *l* has become *r* by dissimilation. But it is rare for the ending -lea or -ley to have wholly fallen away. In 801 *Grant* we find an Esher or Echer in Somerset, to which the above explanation could not apply; it will be= ASHER, 'ash-tree bank.' *Cf. B.C.S.* 158 Uckinge Esher.

ESK R. (S. Cumbld.). 1340 Eskheved or -head. For forms see ESK (Sc.), 3 rivers there, *a.* 800 Esce, etc. Kelt. root for 'river, water,' as in EXE, G. *uisge,* etc. Wh. Stokes cannot be right in calling Esk Pictish, when we have it in S. Cumbld.; but it may well be cognate with O.Ir. *esc,* 'a marsh, a fen,' and O.W. *uisc* or USK.

ESSENDINE or -DEAN (Stamford). *O.E. Chron.* ann. 657 Esendic, *a.* 1100 Esendike. 'Ditch,' O.E. *dic,* 'of *Esa, Ese,* or *Esi,*' all these forms are in *Onom.* The -dean is a later ending, *q.v. Cf. Dom.* Essex Lassendene, which may be La(The) Essendean (as in LASHAM), as no man *Lassa* is recorded. But by 1230 *Close R.* we get Esenden. See -dean.

ESSENDON (Hatfield). 1298 *Writ* Estdene= 'East DEAN'; but ESSINGTON (Walsall) is 994 *chart.* Esingetun, *Dom.* Eseningetone, *a.* 1300 Esynton, Esnyngton. 'Village of the descendants of *Esne,*' a common O.E. name, meaning 'servant,' or else 'of *Esa, Ese,* or *Esi,*' as above. 1160-61 *Pipe* Nthbld. has an Essinton.

ESSEX. *Nennius* Est saxum (inflected). *O.E. Chron.* 499 East Sexa, *a.* 1087 Essex, *Dom.* Exsessa, *a.* 1236 *Rog. Wendover* Est-sexia. 'Land of the East Saxons.'

ETCHELLS (Chesh., etc.). See NECHELLS. But ETCHILHAMPTON (Wilts), not in *Dom.,* is 1228 Hechelhamt, 'Homestead of ? *Heahhelm* or *Hehelm* '; one in *Onom.* See HAMPTON.

ETCHINGHAM (Sussex). 1298 Echingham. 'Home of *Ecca,*' a common name in *Onom.,* once found as *Eccha.* It may be a patronymic. See -ing. *Dom.* has only Echen-, Achintone and Achingeworde. ETCHDEN (Kent) is 1286 *Close R.* Haccheden, perh. 'woody vale entered by a *hatch* ' or half-door, or wicket; O.E. *hœc, hœcce,* 3-7 *hacche,* 5 *hetche,* 5-6 *heche ;* but it may be fr. a man *Eccha.*

ETON. *Sic* 1298, but *Dom.* Ettone, Etone. O.E. *éa-tún,* 'town on the river.' *Cf.* EATON.

ETRURIA (Burslem). The pottery works here were founded in 1769 by Josiah Wedgewood, who gave them this fanciful name ' as that of the country of old most celebrated for the beauty of its ceramic products.'

ETTINGSHAM (Shrewsbury). *Dom.* Attingehā, *a.* 1145 *Orderic* 'Apud Ettingesham in ecclesia Sancti Eattae confessoris,' abbot of Melrose, then Bp. of Lindisfarne (*Bede* iii. 26). 'Home of *Eatta*'s people '; a patronymic. *Cf.* both Etes-hale and Ettinghale in *Dom.* Cheshire, and ETTINGSHALL (Wolverhampton), 994 Ettingeshall, *Dom.* Etinghale; also

Eatington (Wwksh.), *Dom.* Etendone, and Etcloe (Awre), *Dom.*
Eteslau, ' burial mound of *Ætta* ' or ' *Eatta*.'

ETTON (Mket. Deeping and Beverley). M. D. Ett. *sic a.* 1100;
Bev. E. *Dom.* and 1202 Ettone, 1179-80 Eton. 'Town of
Eatta.' *Cf.* above.

EUSTON (Thetford). *Dom.* Eustuna, and Eusfort, 1479 Euston.
Prob. ' *Eowa's* town.' This accords with analogy better than
to derive fr. O.E. *eowu*, M.E. *ewe*, ' an ewe.' Euston Sq. is
called after the Dukes of Grafton and Earls of Euston, ground
landlords here.

EUXTON (Chorley). Pron. Allstn, Elestn. 1241 Euckeston, 1246
Eukeston, *a.* 1300 Euchestona, 1311 Huxton. ' Town of *Euca*,'
a name unrecorded, but *Huc*, *Hucco* and *Huch* are in *Onom.*

EVENLODE (Stow-on-Wold). 772 *chart* Euulangelade, 777 *ib.*
Eunlade (*u* = *v*), 969 *ib.* Eowlangelade, *Dom.* Eunilade, 1327
¶Evenlode, 1330 Eweneload. O.E. *Eowlan gelad*, ' channel of
Eowla,' *gelad* being cognate with Eng. *lade* and *lode*. Duignan
translates, ' ford, ferry.' *Eowla* is found *B.C.S.* 812 as *Eowel*,
name of a W. prince, better known to us in the form Howell.

EVENWOOD (Bps. Auckland). *a.* 1130 *Sim. Dur.* Efenwuda.
' *Eafa's* or *Eafe's* wood.' It might be fr. O.E. *efen*, *efn*, ' even,
level.' *Cf.* ENVILLE.

EVERCREECH (Bath). *Exon. Dom.* Euercriz. See next and CREECH.
Thus it is a hybrid—the ' Creech ' or ' Hill of the Boar.'

EVERLEY or -LEIGH (Marlborough and Yorks). Ma. E. *a.* 1140 *Wm.*
Malmesb. Eburleah. Yo. E. *Dom.* Eurelai, -lag. ' Meadow of
the wild boar.' O.E. *eofor*, *eofer*, 3 *eaver*, 4 *ever*, cognate with
L. *aper.* *Cf.* O.E. *seofon*, now seven. EVERSLEY (Winchfield)
is, of course, the same. But in both cases *Eofor* may be a
proper name, just as Bear, Wolf, etc., are so used. *Cf.* EVRING-
HAM and EVERTON (Notts), *Dom.* Evretone. See -ley.

EVERSDEN (Cambs). *c.* 1080 *Inquis. Cam.* Eueresdona, *Dom.*
Auresdone, 1291 Everesdon, 1316 Everesdene; and EVERTHORPE
(Yorks), *Dom.* Evertorp. ' Hill ' (or ' valley '), ' enclosure,'
and ' village of *Eofor* ' or ' of the wild boar.' See EVERLEY,
-don, -dean, and -thorpe; also *cf.* HEVERSHAM.

EVESHAM. 709 *chart.* Homme, Eveshomme, also Cronochomme,
714 *ib.* Eouesham, 716 *ib.* Cronuchhomme, 854 *ib.* Ecquines
hamme, 1045 *O.E. Chron.* (H)eofeshamme, *Dom.* Eovesham,
c. 1097 *Flor. W.* Eoveshamm. ' Enclosure of *Eof*,' herdsman
to Bp. Ecgwine, mentioned in 854 *chart.* Here, it is said, the
Virgin appeared to Eof, and a monastery was erected on the
spot. In Worcestersh. a *ham* means specifically ' riverside
meadow-land.' See -ham (2). *Cf.* Eaveston (Yorks), *Dom.*
Eveston, *Dom.* Surrey Eveshā, and 1179-80 *Pipe* Yorks Euesham.

EVINGTON (Boddington, Sussex and Leicester). Bo. E. *Dom.* Givingtune, 1303 Yivynton; and changes for Suss. name are similar. 'Dwelling of *Gefwine.*' For similar changes also see EALING; and see -ing.

EVRINGHAM (Yorks). *Dom.* Evringha', 1202 Everingeham. 'Home of the Boar's sons.' *Cf.* EVERLEY, and *Dom.* Bucks Evreham and Evringehou. See -ing.

EWELL (Epsom). 727 *chart.* Euuelle, 1160 *Pipe* Aiwella, which looks like an O.E. *eá welle,* 'river well,' ' well by the river.' But it is *Dom.* Etwelle, or ' at the well.' *Cf.* the surname Attewell. There was a well-known well here. There is also an Ewell (Kemble) whose only old form is Ewelle. *Cf.* next.

EWELME (Woodstock). *Sic* 1450. Not in *Dom.,* but *chart.* Eawylm. This last is thought to be O.E. *éa,* river; and *wielm, walm, wylm,* 'boiling, welling up.' It prob. means ' a spring.' *Cf.* EWELL, GYTING, and WALMSLEY.

EWHURST (Battle, Sussex). 822 *chart.* Iu hyrst, O.E. for ' yew-tree wood.' *Hyrst* also means ' a sandy place.'

EWYAS HAROLD (Hereford). *c.* 1130 *Lib. Land.* Eugias, 1167-68 *Pipe* Euwias, mod. W. Euas. Doubtful. Nothing in mod. W. seems to suit. EWESTON (Pembroke) is in *Black Bk. St. David's* Oweynston.

EXBOURNE (Devon). *Dom.* Echeburne. The stream here now is the Okenent. Eche- may be = EXE; and Oke- may be a var. of the same root, while -nent will be W. *nant,* 'a valley.'

EX(E) R. and EXETER. *Sic* 1485, but *c.* 380 *Ant. Itin.* Isca Dumnoniorum, *c.* 810 *Nennius* Cair Legion guar Usic (' fort of the Rom. legion on the Exe '), 877 *O.E. Chron.* Escanceaster, 893 *ib.* Exanceaster, *c.* 893 *Asser* Exceastre, *Dom.* Exonia urbs, *a.* 1130 *Sim. Dur.* Brittanice Cairwisc, Latine Civitas Aquarum, *c.* 1275 Excetre. ' Camp, town on the R. *Ex,*' in *Ptolemy* Ισκα, L. Isca, 739 *chart.* Exa, Eaxa. Same as Sc. ESK, same root as is seen in *usque-baugh* and in *whisky,* also in Ax and Usk, and prob. Ox- (in OXFORD), too, all being Keltic forms of the word for ' water, river.' The mod. W. name is Caerwysg. For Exe R., *cf.* ASHFORD.

EXHALL (Alcester). 710 *chart.* Eccleshale, *Dom.* Ecleshalle. ' Nook of Æcel or Æcle,' or possibly ' of the church. *Cf.* ECCLES, and see -hall. EXTALL (Staffs) is 1220 Hecstall, prob. ' place of the hatch ' or ' heck '; whilst EXILBY (N. Yorks) is *Dom.* Aschilebi. ' *Ascytel's* ' or ' *Askil's* dwelling.'

EXMOUTH. 1001 Exanmuðan. See EXE.

EXNING (Newmarket). *c.* 1097 *Flor. Worc.* Yxninga, 1157 *Pipe Roll* Exningis, *ib.* 1160 Exining, 1298 Ixinynge. ' Place on the water or stream.' *Cf.* EXETER. Merivale connects with the tribe *Iceni*, as in ICKNIELD. This is improbable. See -ing, as river-ending.

EXTON (Oakham, on R. Meon, Hants, Dulverton, etc.). Oa. E. 1126 Extona, Han. E. 940 *chart*. East Seaxnatune. This last is 'town of the East Saxons' or 'Essexmen.' The others *may be* 'town of *Ecca*,' a common name. *Cf. Dom.* Chesh. Exestan, which is prob. Estyn (Flint). More old forms needed. *Dom.* has Exwelle in Rutld., but no Exton there or in Somst. 1160-61 *Pipe* Kent has an Ext*nea (*cf.* Eastney, Portsmouth).

EYAM (Northants and Sheffield). Not in *Dom.* Nor. E. 1155 *Pipe* Hehham. 'High home,' O.E. *héah, héh*, 3-5 *hey*. See -ham. For EYEFORD or Heyford (Stow-on-Wold), *Dom.* Aiforde, Baddeley prefers O.E. *hege*, 'hedge'; M.E. *heie*, which is doubtful.

EYNESBURY (St. Neots). *Dom.* Einulvesberie, *c.* 1130 *Wm. Malmes.* Einulfes biri, *c.* 1136 Enesbure. 'Burgh, town of *Einwulf*,' which is contracted into '*Æna*,' '*Æne*,' or '*Ena*'; all forms are in *Onom. Cf.* next; and see -bury.

EYNSFORD (Dartford). *c.* 983 *chart*. Ænesford. 'Ford of *Æne*.' See above. *Cf. Dom.* Norfk. Ensford.

EYNSHAM (Oxford). *O.E. Chron.* 571 Egonesham, *a.* 1142 *Wm. Malmes.* Egnesham, *c.* 1450 *Bromtun* Eynesham. 'Home, house of *Egon*.' This is prob. the same name as Egensheim, old form of Ensisheim, Alsace.

EYTHORNE (Dover). 805 *chart*. Heagyðe ðorne, prob. *Dom.* Haihorne. The first part prob. represents the name of some unknown man. O.E. *giþ* is 'corn cockle.'

EYTON (Wellington, Salop). *Dom.* Aitone. Perh. 'islet' or 'ait-town.' O.E. *iggath*, 2 *eyt*, 7 *ait*, 8 *ayte*, 9 *eyot*, 'a little island.' But *cf.* AYTON. Eycote (Colesbourne), *Dom.* Aicote, is 'cot on the islet.' See -ay, -ey.

FADDILEY (Nantwich). Prob. *O.E. Chron.* 584 Fethanleag. No man *Fetha* in *Onom.*, so prob. 'meadow of the troop,' O.E. *féða.* For *th* becoming *d*, *cf. faddom* for *fathom*, *fader* for *father*, etc. *Cf.* Fiddington (Ashchurch), *Dom.* Fitentune, *a.* 1300 Fedyntone. But FADMOOR (Kirby Moorside, Yorks) is *Dom.* Fademore, where Fad- is doubtful. *Cf.*, too, *Dom.* Suss. Fodilant.

FAIRCROSS (a hundred of Berks). *Chron. Abingdon* Balliva Belle Crucis, 1428 Hundredum de Bella Cruce, of which 'fair, beautiful cross' is simply the translation.

FAIRFIELD (mtn. near Helvellyn, Cumbld.). N. *fær-fjall*, 'sheep mountain or fell.' *Cf.* FAIR ISLE (Sc.). FAIRBURN (W. Riding), *Dom.* Fareburn, prob. has a similar origin. But FAIRFIELD (Bellbroughton) is 816 *chart*. Forfeld, 'fore, front field.'

FAKENHAM (Thetford). *Dom.* Fachenhā, Fagenham. 'Home of *Facca.' Cf. B.C.S.* 1232, Faccan heah.

FAL R. (Cornwall). *c.* 1200 *Gervase* Fale, 1680 Vale. Prob. a Keltic root meaning 'moving, running, flowing.' *Cf.* G. *falbh*, 'to go, to walk.' But W. *ffal* means 'closure, or the heel of a shoe.'

FALLINGS HEATH (Wednesbury). *a.* 1200 Olde Falinge. Duignan thinks this refers to a *falling* or *felling* or clearing of timber. *Oxf. Dict.* gives no quots. illustrating such a usage, and yet it may well be. FÁLLODEN (Alnwick) is 'fallow valley,' O.E. *falu, fealo,* 'pale brownish, or yellowish coloured.' *Cf.* FALFIELD (Thornbury), 1347 Falefield.

FALMER (Lewes). *Dom.* Falemere. O.E. for 'pale brownish, or reddish-yellow mere or lake '; O.E. *falu,* 4 *fale,* now *fallow. Cf.* FOWLMERE. But FALSGRAVE (E. Riding) is *Dom.* Wal(l)esgrif, 'Welshman's or foreigner's grave,' O.E. *grœf,* O.N. *grof.* FAL-STONE (Northbld.) and 1166-67 *Pipe* Faleslea (Nhants.) seem to imply a man's name, like *Fala. Onom.* has only one *Fawle.*

FALMOUTH. *Sic* 1478, 1231 *Close R.* Falem', 1234 *ib.* Falemuth, *c.* 1450 *Fortescue* The Falmouthe; but till 1660 usually Smithwick or PENNYCOMEQUICK. See FAL.

FARCET (Peterboro'). Not in *Dom.,* but O.E. *chart.* Fearres heafod, or 'bull's head.' *Cf.* FAZELEY and Forset (N. Riding), *Dom.* Forsed, which is perh. 'head of the waterfall or force.' N. *fors.*

FAREHAM (Hants). Not in *Dom.* 1160 Ferham. 'Fair, beautiful home.' O.E. *fœger,* Icel. *fag-r,* Dan. *feir,* 'fair.'

FARINGDON (Swindon and Exeter). Swin. F. *Dom.* Ferendone, Ex. F. *Dom.* Ferentone. Doubtful at both ends. Feren- may represent a patronymic, 'town of the *Ferrings* or *Farrings.' Cf.* FARRINGFORD. Or it may be fr. O.E. *fearn,* 'ferns' (only no early spelling *feren* is recorded here); or *foera, -an,* early M.E. *fere,* 'a spouse,' a comrade, 'spouse's hill '; and the ending may either be O.E. *tún,* 'village, town,' or *dún,* 'dune, hill, hill-fort.' See FARNDON.

FARLEIGH or -LEY (Halesowen, Cheadle, Elmore, on Medway, Surrey, Salisbury). Ch. F. *Dom.* Fernlege, El. F. 1221 Farnlee, Me. F. *Text. Roff.* Fearnlega. These are all ' fern-meadow.' But Su. F. is *chart.* Fearlege, *Dom.* Ferlega; and Sa. F. *Dom.* Farlege, 1155 *Pipe* Ferlega. There is only one *Fara* in *Onom.,* so this may be fr. O.E. *fœra,* M.E. *fere,* ' spouse, comrade,' and so ' spouse's mead.' But FAREWELL (Lichfield) is *a.* 1300 Fager-, Fagre, Fayrwell, 'fair, clear spring,' fr. O.E. *fœger,* 3 *fager,* 4-7 *far(e).*

FARLINGTON (Havant and N. Riding). Hav. F. 1256 *Deed* Far-lingetone, N. Rid. F. *Dom.* Farlintun. 'Town, dwelling on the *ferling,'* O.E. *féorðling, a.* 1300 *ferlyng,* 'fourth part,' here ' the fourth part of an acre.'

FARMINGTON (Northleach). *Dom.* Tormentone, 1182 Tormer-, 1226 Thormerton, 1601 Farmington or Thormerton. Prob. ' village of *Thurmær.*' For change of early *th* to *f*, see FENGLESHAM. *Cf.* FARNINGHAM.

FARNBOROUGH (Banbury, Wantage, etc.). Ban. F. *Dom.* Fernberge. Want. F. 931 *chart.* Fearn beorg(an), *Dom.* Fermberge, 1291 Farnberg. 'Hill covered with ferns.' See FARINGDON and FARNDON; *cf.* Devon *Dom.* Ferenberga. The ending -berg(e) represents BARROW, ' mound, hill,' rather than ' burgh.' Farncote, also in Wwk., is *sic a.* 1300.

FARNCOMBE (Godalming). *Dom.* Fernecome, ' fern valley.' See -combe.

FARNDON (Newark). 924 *O.E. Chron.* Fearndune, Farndune; *Dom.* Farendune; *c.* 1140 *Wm. Malmes.* Ferenduna. This is clearly ' fern hill.' *Cf.* FARINGDON, which some hold is the place meant in these references. But FARNDON (Chester) is *Dom.* Ferentone, which may be ' town of the *Ferrings.*'

FARNHAM (Surrey, Hants, and W. Riding). Su. F. 893 *O.E. Chron.* Fearnhamm, *Dom.* Ferneham, 1297 Farnham. Ha. F. 805 *chart.* Fernham. W. Ri. F. *Dom.* Farneha.' ' Enclosure,' or ' home among the ferns.' See FARNLEY and -ham.

FARNINGHAM (Dartford). *Dom.* Fermingeha. ' Home of *Farman,*' 2 in *Onom.*, or else ' of Farman's son' (*m* and *n* often interchange). *Cf.* FARMINGTON. See -ing.

FARN ISLES (Bamborough). *Bede* Farne. M'Clure thinks this is Keltic *ferann*, Ir. *fearran*, ' land.' It may be O.E. *fearn*, ' ferns.'

FARNLEY (Leeds and Otley). Both *Dom.* Fernelie, *c.* 1200 *Gervase* Fernlege, 1202 Farnelai and Fernleie. ' Fern meadow.' *Cf. Dom.* Salop Fernelege, FARLEIGH, and FARNHAM. See -ley.

FARNSFIELD (Southwell, Notts). *Dom.* Franes- Farnesfeld, 1189 *Pipe* Farnefeld. ' Field of *Frani* or *Frano*,' a N. name. ' Field of ferns ' is not likely.

FARRINGDON (Alton, Hants). = FARINGDON.

FARRINGFORD (Freshwater). *a.* 1400 Ferringford. Prob. ' ford of the *Ferrings* or *Farrings. Cf.* FARINGDON and Ferrensby (S. Yorks), ' dwelling of *Ferren.*'

FARSLEY (Leeds). *Dom.* Fersellai. There is no likely man's name in *Onom.*, and connection with *parsley* (see *Oxf. Dict.*) hardly seems possible. Prob. it is 'furze meadow,' O.E. *fyrs*, 4-6 *firse. Cf.* 1167-68 *Pipe* Devon Far-, Fairesling. See -ley.

FARTHINGSTONE (Weedon). *Dom.* Fordinestone, 1292 Fardingeston. Prob. ' stone of *Færthegn*,' also found as *Farthain* and *Fardein*, or possibly fr. *Forthwine*, one in *Onom.* Derivation is not impossible fr. O.E. *feorðung*, 4-6 *ferdyng(e)*, 6 *farthing*, which usually means ' a farthing ' in money, but also, as early as

Exon. Dom. we find *ferdin* meaning a land-measure, ? a quarter acre. *Cf.* Ferndale. But FARTHINGHOE (Brackley) is *Dom.* and 1229 Ferning(e)ho, prob. fr. the same name as FARNINGHAM, 'height of the *Farnings.*' See HOE.

FAVERSHAM. See FEVERSHAM.

FAWLEY (Aylston, Hereford and Lambourn). Ayl. F. *c.* 1030 *chart.* Feligly. 'Meadow of one *Felig,*' or some such name. There is a *Felaga* and two anchorites called *Fel(i)geld* in *Onom.* But Lam. F. is *a.* 1300 Falelegh, 1316 Fallele, which Skeat derives fr. E. Frisian *falge,* 'fallow land.' Northants F. 1242, Falghesl', might be either, but the -es of the gen. makes it prob. fr. a man.

FAZAKERLEY (Liverpool). 1277 Fasakerlegh, 1376 Fasacrelegh. Looks as if O.E. *fas-œcer-léah,* 'border of the open-country meadow,' fr. *fas, fœs,* 'border, fringe,' and *œcer, acer,* 'open plain, field,' *mod.* 'acre.' See -ley. There is no name in *Onom.* that would suggest Fazaker-.

FAZELEY (Tamworth). 1300 Faresleye, *a.* 1400 -eslee. 'Meadow of the hill,' O.E. *fearr, -es. Cf.* FARCET, and see -ley.

FEATHERSTONE (Wolverhampton, Pontefract, Haltwhistle). Wol. F. 994 *chart.* Feother(e)stan, *Dom.* Ferdestan, 1271 Fethereston Po. F. *Dom.* Ferestane, Fredestane. 'Stone of *Fether*' or '*Feader*'—*i.e.,* 'father,' which is still dialectically pron. fether. *Cf.* also FEARBY (Yorks), *Dom.* Federbi.

FECKENHAM (Redditch). 804 *chart.* Feccanhom, 957 Feccan ham, *Dom.* and 1156 *Pipe Roll* Fecheham. 'Home of *Fecca.*' *Cf. Dom.* Surrey Fecehā. See -ham, which here may either be 'home' or 'enclosure.'

FELBRIDGE (E. Grinstead). and FELBRIGG (Norfolk and York) E. Gr. F. not in *Dom.,* but *old* Thelbrig. Yo. F. 1206 Felebrigge. No. F. 1451 Felebruge, Felbrygge. Early *th* not seldom becomes *f,* and so fel-= O.E. *þel, þell,* 'a deal, a board or plank.' Thus this name is 'bridge (O.E. *brycg*) made of boards.' *Cf.* FENGLE-SHAM, also *fill* var. of *thill,* 'the shafts of a cart,' likewise ELM-BRIDGE and THELWALL.

FELISKIRK (Thirsk). 1210 Ecclesia S. Felicis. This is the same saint as in FELIXSTOWE. However, in *Dom.* it is Fridebi, 'dwelling of *Freda.*'

FELIXSTOWE (Suffolk). Not in *Dom. c.* 1080 *chart.* 'The church of St. Felix of Walton.' Sometimes said to be 'place,' O.E. *stow,* of *Felix,* first bp. of E. Anglia, *c.* 640. But this does not agree with the form in 1318 Filthstowe, which might be 'filth place,' place full of dirt or foulness, O.E. *fýlð.* This is not likely, as there is a 'To. de Fylethe' in Kent in 1318, and a *Dom.* Felede, which is Fauld (Uttoxeter), *a.* 1300 Falede, Fauld, Felde

—*i.e.*, O.E. *fald, falœd*, ' a fold, a farmyard.' Only it is not easy to see how this last could become either Filth or Felix. The bp.'s name certainly influenced the present form.

FELMINGHAM (N. Walsham). *Dom.* Felminchā. A patronymic, otherwise unknown. See -ing and -ham.

FELSTEAD (Chelmsford). 1082 *chart.* Felstede. O.E. for ' skin, hide-place, tannery.' O.E. *fel, fell*, ' a skin.'

FELTHAM (Hampton Court). *Sic* 969 *chart.* and *Dom.* Possibly ' home of ' some man with a name like *Felgeld* or *Fildas*, the nearest in *Onom.* Prob. ' home, house in the field,' O.E. *feld*, 3-5 *felt.* The Eng. *sb. felt* already occurs in O.E. FELTHORPE (Norwich), *Dom.* Felethorp, seems to be ' village of ' some man. See -thorpe.

FELTON (Northumbld. and Bristol). Nor. F. 1242 Felton. Not in *Dom.* May be, like FELTHAM, named from some man. *Cf.* 1305 *Rougham chart.*, 'Robertus de Feletone,' E. Anglia. But Nor. F. at least may be ' town on the fell' or ' hill.' O.N. *fjall* found in Eng. as *fell a.* 1300. Also *cf.* FELSTEAD.

FEN DITTON and DRAYTON (Cambs). *Cf.* 1272 Fenne (Lincs.). O.E. *fen, fenn*, ' a marsh,' O.N. *fen*, ' a quagmire.' See DITTON and DRAYTON.

FENDRITH HILL (W. Durham). Prob. W. *ffaen d(e)rwydd*, ' rock of the magician, sorcerer, or Druid.'

FEN-, FINGLESHAM (Deal). 831 *chart.* Thenglesham. Not in *Dom.* ' Home of *Thengli*,' a name not in *Onom.* For change of early *th* into *f cf.* FARMINGTON, FELBRIDGE, and FINCHALE, and THRESHFIELD (Yorks), *Dom.* Freschefelt and Treschefelt.

FENNY COMPTON (Warwksh.). *Dom.* Contone, *a.* 1200 Cumton, *a.* 1400 Fenni Cumpton. See COMPTON, and *cf.* FENTON (Stoke), *Dom.* Fentone.

FEOCK (Devoran, Cornwall). ? *c.* 1400 Ecclesia Sancto Feoko, a saint also termed *Feoca, Fyock, Fiach ;* the name is Keltic for ' raven'; but about this person little seems known. *Cf.* Fixby (W. Riding), *Dom.* Fechesbi, which must be ' dwelling of' one of the same name.

FERNDALE (Glamorgan). M'Clure suggests that this is *ferthing-deal*, or ' fourth part.' *Cf.* FARTHINGSTONE. But old forms are needed.

FERRIBY N. and S. (Yorks). *Dom.* Ferebi. Prob. ' dwelling of the comrade or partner'; Northum. O.E. *foera*, 2-9 *fere.* See -by. But FERRYBRIDGE (Yorks) is *Dom.* Ferie—*i.e.*, ' ferry,' O.N. *ferja.* The *Oxf. Dict.* has nothing for the sb. *a.* 1425.

FESTINIOG. Fr. W. *ffestinio*, ' to hurry, hasten,' L. *festinare,* ? in allusion to the many waterfalls around.

FEV-, FAVERSHAM (Kent). 811 *chart*. Fefresham, 858 *ibid*. Febresham, *Dom*. Feversham, 1155 *Pipe* Fauresham. Some suggest from a man, or fr. L. *faber*, a ' smith,' but this seems doubtful; more prob. ' home of fever,' O.E. *fefer, fefres*. It is also said to be the Fauresfeld of 1154 *O.E. Chron.*, which is doubtful.

FEWSTON (Harrogate). *Dom*. Fostune, ' Town at the waterfall '; Dan. *fos*, O.N. *fors*. To be perh. noted also is O.Nor. Fr. *fiust*, ' lofty trees '; but Nor. Fr. names are very rare in England.

FILBY (Gt. Yarmouth). *Dom*. Filebey, *c*. 1471 Fylby. ' Dwelling of' some (Danish) man, whose name has been rubbed down into File. *Cf*. FILLEIGH, and see -by. But Baddeley says Filton (Bristol), 1340 Fyltone, is ' farm in the field,' which is doubtful.

FILEY (Yorks). *Dom*. Fiuelac—*i.e.*, ' five pools,' O.E. *fíf*, 3-9 *five*, and *lac*, ' a lake, a pool.' Camden derives fr. an early Eng. *file*, ' a thin slip of land, like a small tongue thrust out,' into the sea. The *Oxf. Dict*. does not recognize this word *file*. *Lac* for ' pool ' is very rare in O.E., and there is perh. no other instance where it has become -ley. But we have Fishlake (Doncaster) in *Dom*. Fiscelac, and also Fixca-le. *Cf*., too, BEVERLEY and FYFIELD. We may add that North Fyling (N. Yorks) is *Dom*. Nortfigelinge, a patronymic, ' place of the sons of *Fugel*,' 2 in *Onom*. See -ing.

FILLEIGH (S. Molton). *Cf*. 940 *chart*. Fileleighe (Glastonbury). ? ' meadow of *File*.' *Cf*. FILBY, and see -leigh. *Onom*. has only a *Filica*, seen in FILKINS (Lechlade), *old* Fileching, ' place of *Filica*'s sons.' See -ing.

FILLONGLEY (Coventry). *Dom*. Filung-, ingelie, *a*. 1400 Filungeye, 1475 Fylongley. Duignan cannot explain, but says *cf*. FILLINGHAM (Lincoln), *Dom*. Filingeham, Figelingeham, *c*. 1120 Figelingaham. There is no likely name in *Onom*. But we have Fyling (N. Riding), *Dom*. Figelinge, Figlinge, which must be a patronymic. *Cf*. FILBY. See -ing.

FINCHALE (on R. Weir, Durham). Thought to be *Bede*, iii., 27, Pegnaleth; 1298 Fynkhale, 1305 Fynkhalgh. O.E. *finc-halh* means ' finches' haugh ' or 'meadow by a river.' *Cf*. FINSTALL, and 1240 *Close R*. Finkel', 1241 *ib*. Finchel' (Andover). For -hale see -hall.

FINCHAM (Downham). Not in *Dom*. *c*. 1150 Fincheham, 1451 Fyncheham. ' Home of a man *Finch*,' or ' of the finches,' O.E. *finc*. *Cf*. above. Also FINCHAMSTEAD (Berks). *Dom*. Finchamstede; 1316 Fynchamsted. ' Homestead, farm with the finches.'

FINCHINGFIELD (Braintree). *Dom*. Fincinghefelde, -gefelda, 1297 Fynchingfelde. Presumably ' field for finching or hawking, or catching finches or birds in.' Only there is no *sb*. ' finching ' in *Oxf. Dict,* nor any likely man's name in *Onom.,* though *Dom.* form looks like a patronymic. See next and -ing.

FINCHLEY (London). Recorded from time of K. John. *Cf.* above. *Finch* is O.E. *finc,* 4 *finch,* some sort of small bird of the sparrow order.

FINEDON (Wellingborough). Prob. *Dom.* Tingdene, 1296 Thindon. Prob. 'hill of the *thing,*' or ' local parliament,' O.N. *þing,* N. *ting. Cf.* THINGOE. On common change of early *th* to *f* see FELBRIDGE. But FINDON (Worthing) is *Dom.* Findune, which is prob. 'hill of *Fin*' or '*Finn,*' names in *Onom.* See -don. *Cf.* FINNINGLEY (Notts). *Dom.* Feniglei, 1278 Finningelay. See -ing. *Dom.* (N'hants) also has Finemere, now FINMERE (Buckingham).

FINGHALL or FINGALL (Bedale, Yorks). *Dom.* Finegala. Perh. *O.E. Chron.* 788 Fingale (in Northumbria), which is prob. not = FINCHALE. O.E. *finnig* or *fennig halh,* loc. *hale,* 'marshy fenny nook ' or ' corner.'

FINSTALL (Bromsgrove). *a.* 1400 Fynchale. See FINCHALE.

FIRBANK (Sedbergh). *Old* Frithbank. *Frith* is some kind of a wood. See FRITH BANK. But FIRBY (Wistow, Yorks) is *Dom.* Fredebi, 1202 Fridebi, which is ' *Freda*'s dwelling.'

FISHGUARD (Pembroke). *c.* 1390 Fishgarth, 1535 Fisshecard. 'Fisher's garth or enclosure,' the -guard being but a mod. spelling of O.E. *geard,* 'yard, court, enclosure.' In W. it is Abergwaun, ' at the mouth of the level or straight river.' *Cf.* Hasguard in same shire, 1307 Huscard, where the first syll. prob. represents a man's name, now uncertain.

FISKERTON (Lincoln). *Sic a.* 1100, but *Dom.* Fiscartune. ' Town, village of the fishers,' O.E. *fiscere.*

FITTLEWORTH (Sussex). Not in *Dom,* 1167-68 *Pipe* Fitelwurða. 'Farm of *Fitel, Fitela,*' or ' *Fithele,*' all forms in *Onom.* See -worth.

FLADBURY (Pershore). 691 *chart.* Fledanburg, 714 *ib.* Fladeburi, *Dom.* Fledebirie. ' Town, castle of *Fleda* or *Flœda.*' *Cf.* Fledborough (Notts), *Dom.* Fladeburg. See -bury.

FLAMBURGH HEAD (Yorks). *Dom.* Flaneburc, -burg, *a.* 1130 *Sim. Dur.* Flamburge, *c.* 1450 *Fortescue* Flaymborough, also Flaynburg, -borght. ' Fort of *Fleinn,*' a Norseman. *Flame* (O. Fr. *flambe*) is not found in literary Eng. *a.* 1340; but doubtless it has had some influence on the present form of the name. *Cf.* Flensburg, (Schleswig). See -burgh.

FLAVELL FLYFORD (Pershore). 930 *chart.* Fleferth, 1002 *ib.* Fleferht, *a.* 1200 Flavel, *a.* 1400 Fleyford, *a.* 1600 Flyford Flavell. The two names are really a reduplication. Fle- or Fla- will be a man *Flœda, Fleda,* as in FLADBURY, and -ferth is softened form of -ford (*q.v.*). Flæferth has become Fleyferth and then Flavell, through the common dissimilation of *r* for *l.*

FLAXBY (W. Riding) and FLAXTON (York). *Dom.* Flatesbi, and Flastun, Flaxtun. The former is prob. 'dwelling of *Flœda*,' one in *Onom.*, the latter 'village among the flax,' O.E. *fleax.* See -by and -ton.

FLAXLEY ABBEY (Gloster). 1167-68 *Pipe* Flexlega, *c.* 1188 *Gir. Cambr.* Flexleia. 'Flax meadow.' *Cf.* above; also Flechham-stead (Coventry), 1327 Flechamstude, 'flax homestead.'

FLEAM DYKE and FLENDISH (Cambs). Variants of same name. *c.* 1080 *Inquis. Camb.* Flamencdic, Flamminedic, *Dom.* Flaming-dice, Flam(m)iding, 1158 Flemedich, 1279 Flemigdich, 1284 Flemesdich. 'Fleming's ditch,' of which *dyke* is the older, hard form. Fleming is O. Fr. *Flamenc*, late L. *Flamingus.* This name shows the early settlement of the men of Flanders in our midst.

FLECKNOE (Rugby). *Dom.* Flachenho, *a.* 1200 Fleckenho. Prob. 'HOE, hill of *Flecca*,' gen. -*can*, not in *Onom.*

FLEET R. (London and 2 others), also FLEET (Hants), which is *K.C.D.* 688 Fléot. O.E. *fléot*, O.N. *fljót*, 'a stream, a river, also a creek or inlet.' The root is seen in O.N. *fljót-r*, 'quick.' *Cf.* FLEET (Sc). and FLEETWOOD (Lancs), also *Dom.* (Norfk.) Fletwest and SHALFLEET.

FLEGGBURGH (Gt. Yarmouth). *Cf.* 1442 'Fleghalle,' manor in Norfolk. ? 'fort, burgh among the flags or rushes.' *Flag* is not found in Eng. till 1387, and is of doubtful etymology, but is spelt *fleg* in 5. *Flag* sb.[2] Icel. *flag*, 'the spot where a turf has been cut,' O.N. *flaga*, 'a slab of stone,' still used in E. Anglia for 'a turf, a sod,' is quite a possible origin. *Dom.* has East and West Flec and Fliceswella; but *Onom.* has no name the least likely here.

FLETCHING (Uckfield). *Dom.* Flescinge(s), 1232 *Close R.* Flescing. A patronymic; the man's name implied is unknown. See -ing.

FLETHERHILL (S. Wales). *Sic a.* 1349. A tautology; W. *llethr*, 'a hillside, a slope.' *Cf.* Shakespeare's Fluellen for Llewelyn, and p. 82.

FLETTON (Peterboro'). *Sic a.* 1100. 'Town, village on the fleet or stream,' O.E. *fléot*, in 6 *flett*. *Cf.* FLEET.

FLIMWELL-VENT (Hawkhurst). Old forms needed for Flim-; not in *Dom.*; possibly O.E. *fliema*, *flýma*, 'a fugitive, an outlaw.' A *vent* or *went* is said to be 'a place where roads meet.' The root is O.E. *wendan*, 'to go, to wend.'

FLINT. In W. Fflint, or Tegeingl. 1277 In castris apud le Flynt prope Basingwerk, 1277-8 *Welsh R.* Le Chaylou and Rothelan, where Chaylon is prob. Fr. *caillou*, 'pebble, flint.' O.E. *flint*, 'flint, rock,' fr. the rocky platform on which the castle stands. Flints are not common here. FLINTON (E. Riding) is *Dom.* Flentun, prob. 'town of the flints.' FLINTHAM (Notts) *sic* in *Dom.*, is clearly 'flint house.' See -ham.

FLIXTON (Salford). *c.* 1200 Flyxton, Fluxton. Perh. 'town of the flitch,' O.E. *flicce,* 5 *flytske,* 5-6 *flik.* There is, however, in *K.C.D.* mention of a *Flecge, Flecges,* a man otherwise unknown, and this is quite a possible origin. There is no likely name in *Onom.*

FLOCKTON (Wakefield). *Dom.* Flocheton, 1201 Floketon. 'Town of' an unrecorded *Flocca.* Hardly fr. O.E. *flocc,* O.N. *flokk-r,* 'flock.' *Cf. Dom.* (Norfk.) Flokethorp.

FLODDEN (Northumbld.). 1512 Floudane. Prob. *flood-dean—i.e.* '(wooded) glen with the stream,' O.E. *flód,* M.E. *flod,* 6 *floud,* 'a river, a flood.' See -dean.

FLOOKERSBROOK (Chester). 1340 Flokersbroke. Prob. called after some man; there is nothing in *Onom.* nor yet in the dictionaries wh. seems helpful. *Flokk-r* would be N. form of the *Flocca* of FLOCKTON.

FLUSHING (Falmouth). *Sic* 1661. Named after the Dutch port at the mouth of the Scheldt.

FOGGATHORPE (Selby). *Dom.* Fulcartorp. 'Fulchar's place or village.' In *Onom.* there are several *Folcheards,* one *Folcgaer,* and one *Fulcher.* The orig. name has had *cg* in it, and the liquid *l* and *r* easily disappear.

FOLESHILL (Coventry). *Dom.* Focheshelle, *a.* 1200 Folkeshulle, 1327 Folkeshull. O.E. *folces hyll,* 'people's hill,' which in Midland M.E. regularly is *hull.*

FOLKESTONE. *a.* 716 *chart.* Folcanstan, 1051 O.E. *Chron.* Folcstane, *Dom.* Fulchestan. 'Stone, rock of the folk or people,' or, more prob., 'of a man *Folca.*' The *Onom.* has a *Folco* and a *Fulco,* and we have FOLKTON (E. Riding), *Dom.* Fulcheton.

FONTMELL MAGNA (Shaftesbury). 939 *chart.* Funtmeales, *Dom.* Fontemale. Perh. 'Fountain of *Mœl(a),*' one in *Onom. ;* O.E. *font,* 2-6 *funt.* The order is unusual as -funt or -font usually comes last. *Cf.* BEDFONT. But -mell may be O.E. *mœl,* 'a mark, sign, cross, crucifix '—'font at the cross.' FONTLEY (Fareham), *Dom.* Funtelei, will be 'mead with the fountain or spring.' Magna is L. for 'Great.'

FORD (Shrewsbury, etc.). *Dom.* Ford. 1184 *Pipe* Devon, Ecclesia de Forda. Nothing is commoner in early Eng. names than to name a place after a ford, which was often a very important spot before bridges were made.

FORDHAM (Colchester and Soham). Colc. F. *sic* 1373, but *c.* 1080 *chart.* Fordam. Soh. F. *Dom.* Fordeham. 'House at the ford.'

FORDINGTON (Dorchester). *Dom.* Fortitone, 1156 *Pipe* Fordintune. Perh. 'village of *Forthwine,*' one in *Onom.* See -ing.

FOREST OF DEAN. *Dom.* Dene, 1160-61 *Pipe* Foreste de Dena, *c.* 1188 *Gir. Camb.* Danubiæ Sylva, which is supposed to mean 'forest of Denmark or of the Danes.' Dean here may be W. *din*, 'fort, hill-fort'; but is prob. as in DEAN.

FORMBY (Liverpool). 1203-04 Formebi, 1227 Forneby, 1269 Fornebi. 'Dwelling of *Forni*.' There are several called *Forna* or *Forne* in *Onom. Cf.* next. In Brit. names *m* and *n* are frequently found interchanging. See -by.

FORNHAM (Bury St. Edmunds). *Sic* in *Dom*. 'Home of *Forne*.' See FORMBY. There is a Forne in *Dom*. (Herefd.).

FORTON (Gosport, Newport, Staffs, N. Lancs, and 3 others). New. F. 1199 Forton, whilst for the others *Dom*. has Fortune, and Fordune (twice). Prob. 'town by the *ford*.' Of course, *dune* is 'hill.' Leland calls FORTHAMPTON (Tewkesbury) Fordhampton; but it is *Dom*. Fortemeltone, prob. '*Forthhelm*'s town.'

FOSS DYKE (Boston). 1480 Caxton *Chron. Eng.* 'Two other weyes this Belyn made . . . that one is called fosse and that other fosse dyke'—*i.e.*, a raised causeway over marshes, etc. *Fosse* sb., L. *fossa*, 'a ditch,' is first found in Eng. *a.* 1440. There is also the FOSSWAY, which stretched fr. Exeter to Lincoln, via Bath and Leicester. *Cf.* Fangfoss (N. Riding), *Dom.* Frangefos, ? 'ditch of the *Frank*.'

FOSTON (3 in *P.G.*). Foston on Wolds. *Dom*. Fodstone. 1158-59 *Pipe* Fostuna (Northants). Some may be 'town on the *foss*,' (see above); but Fodstone must be fr. some unknown man. See -ton.

FOTHERINGAY (Northampton). *Dom*. Fodringeia. *a.* 1163 Fodrigeia, 1237 Fodringh', 1434 Fotheringhey, *c.* 1460 Foodryngdre. 'Foddering-island.' O.E. *fódor*, O.N. *fóðr*, Dan. *foder*, 'fodder, food for cattle.' The vb. O.N. *fóðra*, is not found in Eng. till *a.* 1300. *Cf.* the Pile of Fotheray in FURNESS, *q.v.*; also FEATHERSTONE. See -ay, -ey.

FOULNESS (Cromer). Not in *Dom*. 'Foul, dirty cape or ness.'' O.N. *fúl næs*. Foul is also found in O.E. as *fúl*, and this is a more likely origin than O.E. *fugol*, 'fowl, bird.' *Cf.* next and FULFORD. Still *Dom*. Nfk. has a Fugalduna.

FOULSHAM (Dereham). *Dom*. and 1454 Folesham. Prob. not 'home of the fowls,' which is O.E. *fugol*. Foolston (W. Riding), *Dom*. Fugelestun, is phonetically different, and even it means the man 'Fowl's town.' Foulsham will be 'home of the man *Fula*,' seen in *B.C.S.* 1052 Fulan ea. *Cf. Dom.* (Suss.) Folsalre, or 'Fula's alder.'

FOUNTAINS ABBEY (Ripon). 1156 *Pipe* De Fontibus, *c.* 1246 de Fontanis. 'Abbey of the springs or wells.'

FOVANT (Salisbury). Not in *Dom.*, but *O.E. chart.* Fobbefunte—*i.e.*, 'font, spring of *Fobba*.' *Cf. B.C.S.* 862 Fobbanwyl (well), FONTMELL, and HAVANT.

FOWEY R. and town (Cornwall). *c.* 1200 *Gewase* Fawe fl. Town *a.* 1400 Fawi, *c.* 1450 *Fortescue*, the Ffowe; *c.* 1530 Foye, 1536 Fowey. Pron. Foy. The river, which names the town, is said to be fr. Corn. *foys* or *foy fenton*, 'walled well or fountain' (which rises near Altarnun). But it looks a little like the Corn. *foath* or *fow*, pl. *fowis*, 'cave, den.'; the W. *ffau*. FOY (Herefd.) is *c.* 1130 *Lib. Land*. Lanntiuoi. 'church of St. *Tyfai*.' *Cf.* LAMPHEY.

FOWLMERE (Royston). *Dom.* Fuglemære, Fugelesmara, which is O.E. for 'fowls' lake or mere'; 1302 Ful-, 1401 Foulmere.

FOWNHOPE (Hereford). Old forms needed. It seems a sort of hybrid; 'fawn's refuge'; O.Fr. *foun, faon*, M.E. (1369) *foun*, 'a fawn'; but very prob. Fown- is O.E. *Fornan*, 'of Forna,' a common name; and O.N. *hóp*, 'a haven, a place of refuge.' See -hope.

FOXHOLES (Yorks). *Dom.* Foxhole, Foxohole, Foxele. 1202 *Fines* Foxholeforde. *Cf.* FOXTON (Cambs)., *Dom.* Foxetune, and *B.C.S.* 750 Foxcotone. There is a FOXCOTE (Glos.), *Dom.* Fuscote.

FOX LYDIATE (Redditch). 1300 Fox huntley yates, 1377 Foxhunt Ledegate. 'Fox hunter's gate.' See LIDGATE; and *cf.* Hyett, Henbury, 1221 Hyate, 'high gate.'

FOXT (Cheadle, Staffs). 1253 Foxiate—*i.e.*, *fox-gate*, or 'opening'; O.E. *geat, get*, 6-9 dial. *yat(t)e*, (Sc.) *yett*. But in 1292 it is Foxwyst, which is inexplicable.

FRADLEY and FRADSWELL (Staffs). 1262 Foder(e)sleye, 1286 Frodeleye. *Dom.* Frodeswelle, *a.* 1300 Frotheswelle, Frodeswall, -well. Prob. all fr. a man *Frod*, which is O.E. for 'wise.' Form 1262 prob. simply illustrates the shiftiness of *r*. See -ley.

FRAMINGHAM EARL (Norwich). *Dom.* Framingahā. 1424 Framyngham. 'Home of the descendants of *Frame*,' still a surname. *Fræna* is common, and there is one *Fram* in *Onom. Cf.* FREMINGTON. See -ing.

FRAMLINGHAM (Suffolk). *Dom.* Framlingaham, 1157 *Pipe* Framingeham, 1425 Fremelyngham, *a.* 1444 Framlyngham. 'Home of the *Framlings*.' These may be 'descendants of *Frambeald*'; 2 in *Onom*. See -ing.

FRAMPTON (Boston and Dorchester). Bos. F. *Dom.* Framantune, Do. F. Frantone. 'Town of *Frama*' or '*Fram*'; 1 in *Onom*. For intrusion of *p*, *cf.* BAMPTON and HAMPTON; also *cf.* above. There is a Framwellgate, Durham, and a Framelle (? 'Fram's nook') in *Dom*. Suss. But FRAMPTON, 3 in Glos., is *Dom.* Framtone, 1221 Fremtone, 'town on R. Frame,' or 'FROME'; whilst Fraunton, same shire, is 1166 Freulinton, 1182 Froulinton, perh. fr. a man *Freo-, Freawine*.

FRANCE LYNCH (Stroud) and FRANCHE (Kidderminster). Ki. F. *Dom.* Frenesse, 1275 Frenes, Freynes. Duignan says, O.Fr.

fresne, ' ash-tree,' and that the -esse in *Dom.* is meant for O.E. *æsce,* ' ash-tree,' and so *Dom.*'s name a reduplication. He may be right.

FRANKLEY (Bromsgrove) and FRANKTON (Rugby). Br. F. *Dom.* Franchlie, *a.* 1200 Frankle, Frankeleg. Ru. F. *Dom.* Franchetone. ' Meadow' and ' town of *Franca*' or ' the *Frank.*' Origin fr. O.Fr. *franc,* ' an enclosure, esp. to feed swine in'; in Eng. *c.* 1400 as *frank, fraunke,* seems just possible.

FRECKENHAM (Ely). ' Home of *Freac* or *Frecca*'; both forms in *Onom. Cf.* 801 *chart.* Frecinghyrte (? Kent), also FRIOCKHEIM (Sc.). The root is O.E. *frec,* ' ready, quick.' We have also Frickley (Yorks). *Dom.* Frichehale, or ' Freca's nook.' See -hall.

FRECKLETON (Preston). *Dom.* Frecheltun. ' *Frecel*'s or *Freculf*'s town.'

FREEBY (Leicestersh.). *Dom.* Fredebi, 1230 *Close R.* Fretheby. ' Village' or ' dwelling of *Frith*(e)' (one in *Onom.*), or of some of the many men whose names begin with *Frithu.* But FREETHORPE (Norwich) is *Dom.* Frietorp, ' village of *Freyja,*' which was the name of a well-known Saxon goddess. *Cf.* FREYSTROP and FRITTON.

FREEMANTLE (Bournemouth and Southampton). Not in *Dom. Cf. c.* 1220 *Elect. Hugo* ' Frisomantel,' a now vanished place near High Clere House, Hants. This is a puzzling name. Friso- suggests the Frisians of N. Holland; and -mantel must surely be O.Fr. *mantel,* ' a mantle or cloak.' But how comes this in a place-name ? *Mantel* (see *Oxf. Dict.,* s.v.) in the sense of ' a fortification,' is not found in Eng. till 1475. Prob. this is one of the rare cases of a place called simply by a man's name, often referred to in 12th cny *Pipe* as Frigidum Mantellum. *Cf.* Goodrich, Snitter, etc.

FREISTON (Boston). *Sic* 1274, *Dom.* Fristune, 1381 Frestoine also Ferry FRYSTON (S. Yorks). *Dom.* Fristone. Perh. ' town of the *Frisians* or *Frieslanders*'; possibly fr. the Saxon goddess *Frea* or *Freyja.* Fraisthorp (Bridlington) is *Dom.* Frestintorp, which is puzzling.

FREMINGTON (Yorks and Devon). Yorks F. *sic* in *Dom.* The family name must be the same as in FRAMINGHAM.

FRESELEY (Polesworth). *Sic* 1256. FRIEZELAND (Walsall and Tipton) and FRISLAND (Tibberton). Duignan derives all, not fr. the *Frisians,* but fr. O.E. *fýrz,* ' furze, gorse,' dial. *freze, friez. Oxf. Dict.* gives *furse* as 4-6 *firse,* but not with transposed *r.*

FRESHWATER (I. of Wight). *Dom.* Frescewatre. Why so called is not very apparent. The usual O.E. for 'fresh'—*i.e.,* not ' salt'—is *fersc. Oxf. Dict.* says the fre- forms do not occur

till *c.* 1205 *Layamon,* and so are most likely due to adoption
fr. O.Fr. *freis, fresche.* But the much earlier *Dom.* form shows
this untenable. *Cf.* THRESHFIELD, *Dom.* Freschefelt.

FRESSINGFIELD (Harleston). Not in *Dom. c.* 1590 Fresingfield;
and FRESTON (Ipswich). *Dom.* Frise-, Fresetuna. The latter
is 'town of the *Frisians,*' who called themselves *Frise, Frese.*
The former is prob. 'field of the Frisians' descendants.' *Cf.*
FRISINGTON. See -ing.

FREYSTROP (Pembroke). '*Freyja*'s village.' She was a Norse
goddess, akin to the L. Venus. Fraisthorpe (Yorks) is *Dom.*
Frestintorp, which is puzzling; also *cf.* FREETHORPE and
FRIDAYTHORP. See -thorpe.

FRIDAYTHORP (Yorks). *Dom.* Fridarstorp, Fridagstorp, Fridaizs-
torp. 'Village of Friday,' O.E. *Frigedæg,* O.N. *Friadag-r,*
'day of *Frigg* or *Frig,*' the Norse Venus. But Friday seems to
have been used as a personal name. *Cf. B.C.S.* 1047 Frigedæges
treow. There is a Friday Street (Glouc.). See -thorpe.

FRILFORD (Berks). O.E. *chart.* Frileford, later Frylesford. Like
FRILSHAM (on R. Pang), *Dom.* Frilesham, prob. contracted fr.
Frithel, Fritholf, Frithuwolf, or some such name.

FRIMLEY GREEN (Farnborough). Not in *Dom.* 'Moist meadow,'
frim dial., O.E. *freme,* 'full of moisture, sappy.' See -ley.

FRINDSBURY (Rochester). *Dom.* Frandesberie. 'Burgh of *Frand,*'
which may be contraction of *Freomund,* likeliest name in *Onom.;*
prob. influenced by *friend,* which in Southern Eng. is 4 *vrind,*
5-7 *frind.* See -bury.

FRISINGTON (W. Cumbld.). 'Town of the *Frisings,*' or 'descendants of the *Frisians.*' See FRESSINGFIELD and -ing.

FRITCHLEY (Derby). Not in *Dom. Cf. Dom.* Nfk. Frichetuna.
'Meadow of *Fricca.*' *Onom.* has only *Frecca* and *Freca.*

FRITHAM (Lymington). Not in *Dom. Cf.* 804 *chart.* Friðesleah
(Kent). 'Home of *Frith,*' or of some man with a name beginning in Frith-; there are many in *Onom.* Frithubeorht, Frithu-
geard,' etc. The O.E. *fyrhðe,* 'a wood,' is seen in CHAPEL-
EN-LE-FRITH, and in Fretherne, Frocester, *Dom.* Fridorne,
1372 Freethorne, O.E. *frith-thyrne,* 'thorn-bush by the wood.'

FRITH BANK and FRITHVILLE (Boston). 1323 Le Frith, 1512
'The King's Frith beside Boston.' *Frith* is O.E. *fyrhðe,* 'a
wood' or 'woody pasture'; -ville is always mod.

FRITTENDEN (Staplehurst, Kent). 804 *chart.* Friðding-, Fred-
dingden, and in the same *chart.* Friðesleah. 'Dean (wooded)
valley of the descendants of *Frith.*' *Cf.* FRITHAM.

FRITTON (Long Stratton, Norfk.). *Dom.* Fridetuna, Frietuna,
'Town of *Frith* ' or ' *Fride.*' *Cf.* FREEBY.

FROCESTER (Stroud). *Dom.* Frowcester. Origin unknown; perh. pre-Keltic. See -cester.

FRODESLEY (Shrewsbury) and FRODSHAM (Retford and Warrington). Re. F. 1240 Frodesham. 'Meadow' and 'home of *Froda* or *Frod*,' common in *Onom.* *Cf.* FRODINGHAM (Yorks), *Dom.* Frotingha'. See -ham, -ing, and -ley.

FROGNAL (Windsor and 2 others). Old forms needed. The -al almost certainly represents -hall (*cf.* BIRSTALL, BRINSCALL, etc.), and the Frogn- must be some personal name. Of course, O.E. *frogga, -an* is 'a frog,' as in Frog Hall (Dunchurch), Frogham, and Frogmore (Camberley). Though there is no likely name in *Onom.*, we have 704 *chart.* Frocesburna (Middlesex), which is prob. '*Froce's*' or '*Froga's* brook.'

FROME (Somerset). Pron. Froom. 875 *O.E. Chron.* Frauu, *c.* 950 *ib.* Frome, *ib.* From (river); also FROME R. (Glouc. and Hereford), whose forms are found in FRAMPTON, Framilode, 1175-76 *Pipe* Fremelada (O.E. *gelad*, 'ferry'), and Frenchay, 1257 Fromscawe (O.E. *scaga*, 'wood'). The Gloucester R. is now rather called Frame. Dr. Bradley thinks this must be orig. Frāma, which, on Kelt lips, would aspirate and yield Frauu or Frauv. *Cf.* ABERFFRAW and BP's. FROME. Meaning doubtful; origin fr. W. *ffromm*, 'angry, fuming,' is not likely.

FROSTERLEY (Co. Durham). *Sic* in 1183 *Boldon Bk.*, but 1239 *Close R.* Forsterlegh.' 'Meadow of *Forster*' or '*Foster*'—i.e., 'the forester'—a word not in *Oxf. Dict.* till 1297, though 'Archibald Forester' occurs 1228 in *Cartul. Ross.* No name *Froster* is known, but metathesis of *r* is common. See -ley.

FROXFIELD (Hungerford and Petersfield). Pet. F. 965 *chart.* Froxafelda, 'field of the frogs,' O.E. *frox(a)*, var. of *frogga, frocga*; but also *cf.* 704 *chart.* Frocesburna (Middlesex). So perh. 'Field of *Froca*.' The name is not in *Onom.* But FROXMORE (Crowle), 1275 Froxmere, 1327 Froxemere, is plainly 'frogs' mere or lake.'

FULBECK (Lincs) and FULBOURN (Cambs). Li. F. 1202 Fulebec. Ca. F. *c.* 1080 *Inquis. Camb.* Fuleburna, *Dom.* Fuleberne, *chart.* Fuulburne. O.E. and O.N. *fúl*, 'foul, dirty'; and see -beck and -bourne. *Cf.* BACUP, *c.* 1200 Ffulebachope.

FULFORD (York, Stone, and Solihull). Yo. F. *Dom.* Fuleford and Foleford, *Sim. Dur.* ann. 1066 Fulford, St. F. *Dom.* Fuleford. 'Foul, dirty ford.' See above. *Cf.* 1183 *Boldon Bk.* Durham, Fulforth.

FULHAM (London). *Sic* 1298, but 879 *O.E. Chron.* Fullanhamme. This is prob. 'enclosure of *Fullan*.' There is one such in *Onom.* 'Home of fowls' would need a *g* in 879. O.E. *fugol*, 'a fowl.' See -ham 2.

FULNEY (Lincoln). Thought to be *B.C.S.* 1052 Fulan ea, 'isle of *Fula.'* Not in *Dom.* It has a Fulnedebi.

FURNESS. Not in *Dom.* *Old* Futherness, Fuderness, which is prob. 'fodder-ness or cape' (see FOTHERAY) ; though M'Clure ventures to identify with Pict. *fother,* 'a piece of land.' *Cf.* FORTEVIOT (Sc.). Foodra Castle, on the point at Furness, was formerly called 'the Peel of Further' (Whitaker's *Craven*).

FYFELD (Abingdon). *Dom.* Fivehide—*i.e.,* five hides of land— still 1437 Fifhide, but *c.* 1540 Ffield. Fyfeld (Essex), is also *Dom.* Fifhide, while places of the same name in Hants and Wilts were 1257-1300 *chart.* Fifhide. There are both Five Hide and Fyfield in Glouc. *Cf.* FILEY.

FYLING. See FILLONGLEY.

GAD'S HILL (Gillingham, Kent). 'Hill of *Gadd'* or '*Gaddo*,' as in GADDESBY (Leicester), *Dom.* Gadesbie, and GODSHILL. See -by.

GAERWEN (Anglesea). O.W. *gaer,* Mod. W. *caer gwen.* 'White, clear castle or fort.' *G* and *c* freely interchange in W. *Cf.* DOLGELLY, etc.

GAILEY (Cannock). 1004 *chart.* Gageleage, *Dom.* Gragelie (error). *a.* 1300 Galewey, Gaule, Gaueleye. 'Bog-myrtle meadow,' fr. O.E. *gagel,* 4 *gayl,* 5-7 *gaul*(e), 5 *gawl, gawyl,* 'the gale or sweet gale.' See -ley.

GAINFORD-ON-TEES. *a.* 1130 *Sim. Dur.* Ge(a)genforda, *c.* 1150 Gainesford, 1200 Geineford. 'Straight, direct, favourable ford.' O.N. *gegn,* found in Eng. fr. 1300 as *gain.*

GAINSBORO'. 1013 *O.E. Chron.* Gæignesburh, Gegnesburh, *Dom.* Gainesburg, *Sim. Dur.* ann. 1013 Gainesburh. May be fr. some man *Gegne* or the like; but there is no such name in *Onom.,* unless it be *Gagan-heard.* So perh. 'town, castle of gain, help, advantage,' O.N. *gagn, gegn,* found in Eng. *c.* 1200 as *ga3henn,* Mod. Eng. *gain.* *Cf.* GANSTEAD.

GALFORD (S. Devon). *O.E. Chron.* ann. 823 Gafol, Gaful forda. Not in *Dom.* 'Ford of the tribute, or payment to a superior, or *gavel.'* O.E. *gafol,* which does not mean 'a toll.' M'Clure would derive fr. a Kelt. *gabail* or *gabal,* meaning 'the fork of a stream,' G. *gabhal;* this seems doubtful, though *cf.* YEOVIL, which must be fr. O.E., rather than Kelt., *gafol, geafl,* 'a fork, a forked opening.'

GALTRES forest (Yorks). 1179-80 *Pipe* Foreste de Galtris; also Caltres. Thought to be same word as Calathros, name in the Irish Annals for CALLANDER (Sc.). The meaning is doubtful. Some identify it with 'Gerlestre Wapentac' in *Dom.* Yorks, which is possible, and may be 'tree of *Goerlaf,*' or some such name.

GAMBLESBY (Langwathby). 1179-80 Gamelobi, 1189 Gamelesbi. 'Dwelling of *Gamel*,' O.N. for 'old'; the surname now is Gamble or Gemmell. Gembling (Yorks), *Dom.* Ghemelinge, is a patronymic fr. the same name, and shows the same intrusion of *b*. *Cf.* next, Gammelspath, name of the old Rom. road, Middle March (Northumberland), and GANFIELD. See -by.

GAMLINGAY (Sandy). 1166-67 *Pipe* Gamelengeia (Essex), 1210 Gamelingehey, 1211 Gamelingeye. 'Isle of the descendants of *Gamel*.' *Cf.* above; and see -ing and -ey.

GAMSTON (Retford). *Dom.* Gamelestune. *a.* 1199 *Roll Rich. I.* Gamelesdun. 'Hill' or 'town of *Gamel*' or '*Gamall*,' names frequent in *Onom.*, being N. for 'old man.' See -don and -ton.

GANFIELD (a hundred in Berks). *Dom.* Gamesfelle, Gamenesfelle (*n* here for *l*). See above.

GANNEL (New Quay). Corn. *gan hael*, 'mouth of the saltings.' *Hael* or *hayle* means 'a tidal river.'

GANSTEAD (Hull). *Dom.* Gagenestad, 1208 Gaghenestede. The first half must be the same as in GAINSBORO'. See -stead, 'place.'

GANTHORPE (Yorks). *Dom.* Gameltorp, 1202 Gaumesthorp. 'Village of *Gamel*.' *Cf.* GAMSTON and GANTON; and see -thorpe.

GANTON (York). *Dom.* Galmetona, prob. 1179-80 *Pipe* Gonton. 'Town of *Galmund*,' one in *Onom.*, and no other likely name: But *cf.* GAMSTON and above.

GARGRAVE (Leeds). *Dom.* Geregraue, Gheregrave. 'Grave,' O.E. *græf*, 'of *Gœr*' or '*Geir*'; *cf.* next. But GARFORD (Berks) is 942 *chart.* Garanforda, 1291 Gareford, 'ford at the gore'—*i.e.* 'promontory or triangular piece of land,' O.E. *gára*. *Cf.* GAR-TREE. Yet Garforth (Leeds), *Dom.* Gereford, Ingereforde, is fr. the man *Gœr*. See -ford.

GARSTANG (Preston). *Dom.* Cherestanc, 1204-05 Geirstan, 1206 Guegrestang, 1208 Geersteng, 1230 Gerstang, 1304 Gairstang. This is a peculiar name. It seems to be, the man '*Geir*'s stang' —*i.e.*, 'spear,' or 'goad'—same root as *sting*. But *Dom.* evidently thought that the name was '*Geir*'s pool,' O.Fr. *estang*, L. *stagnum*, still used in Eng. as 'a stank.' This certainly gives a likelier sense; *cf.* Mallerstang (Cumberland), and GARGRAVE. But GARSHALL (Stone) is a much altered name, *a.* 1400 Gerynges halgh, -hawe—*i.e.*, 'river-meadow of *Gering*.' See -hall and HAUGHTON.

GARSTON (Berks and Liverpool). Ber. G. O.E. *chart.* Gærstun, Gerstun, Grestun. Also *Dom.* Garstune (Worcester). O.E. *gœrstún*, 'a grassy enclosure, a paddock,' O.E. *gœrs*, *grœs*, 'grass,' the old forms being still preserved in Sc. The orig. meaning of *ton* or *town* is 'enclosure.' But G. (Liverpool) is 1093-94 Gerstan, 1142 Gerestan(am), 1153-60 Grestan, 1205-06 Gaherstang (*cf.* GARSTANG), 1297 Garstan. 'Stone, rock among

the grass '; *cf.* the GASTONS (Tewkesbury), *old* Gerstone. GAR-
RISTON (N. Riding) is *Dom.* Gerdeston, fr. *Geard,* contracted fr.
Geardwulf, or the like. *Cf.* GREASBOROUGH.

GARTH (Bangor, etc.). W. *garth,* 'enclosure, yard '; also 'hill-
ridge, headland,' Ir. *gart,* 'a head.' If the meaning be 'yard,'
it is a loan-word in W. *Cf.* GWAELOD-Y-GARTH.

GARTREE (Leicester). *Dom.* Geretreu. 'Tree at the gore of land,'
O.E. *gára,* 4-9 *gare,* O.N. *geire.* It was the meeting-place of the
Wapentake. See GARFORD and APPLETREE.

GATCOMBE (I. of Wight). *Dom.* Gatecome. 'Valley with the
opening,' or 'gate,' O.E. *geat.* Also 2 in Glouc., no old forms.
See -combe.

GATEACRE (Liverpool). 'Field, acre,' O.E. *acer,* 'with the gate,'
O.E. *geat.* *Cf. Dom.* Bucks, Gateherst, and FAZAKERLEY.

GATESHEAD. Prob. *c.* 410 *Notit. Dign.* Gabrosenti* (Kelt. *gabar,*
'goat '). *Bede* iii. 21 Ad Murum, Æt Walle (the Roman Wall).
Sim. Dur. ann. 1080 Gotesheved id est Ad caput Caprae; also
Caput Capræ; but *Sim. Dur.* contin. *c.* 1145 Gateshevet, 1183
Gatesheued. These names, of course, all mean 'goat's head '—
i.e., the Gate- is O.E. ʒát, 'a goat,' and not ʒeat, 'a gate.' *Cf.*
GATEFORD (Notts) 1278 Gayt-, *c.* 1500 Gatford, also fr. N. *geit*
or O.E. ʒát, 'a goat.'

GAVENNY R. (S. Wales). W. Gefni. See ABERGAVENNY.

GAWSTHORPE (Macclesfield). 'Village of ?' *Cf.* Gawthorpe, Ossett,
and *Dom.* Norfk., Gaustuna, ? fr. an unrecorded *Gaha.* Gawsa
(Wales) is thought by Rhys a corrup. of causey or causeway !

GAYDON (Kineton) and GAYTON (Stafford, Blisworth, and King's
Lynn). Kin. G. 1327 Geydon, St. G. *Dom.* Gaitone, 1227 Gai-
don. Lynn G. *c.* 1150 Geitun. Prob. not fr. *gate,* but fr. a man
Gœga or *Gega,* K.C.D. vi. 137 and 148, while we get the patronymic *Gœing* in B.C.S. iii. 257. *Gay* is now a common surname.
Cf. Ginge (Berks), *Dom.* Gainʒ, 1225 Est geyng, and Gaywood,
also found near King's Lynn, likewise 940 *chart.* Gæcges stapole
(market), Hants. See -don and -ton.

GEDDINGTON (Kettering). Not in *Dom.* Said to be *c.* 1188 *Gir.*
Camb. Garcedunc. This, if the same place, must be a different
name. Prob. 'town of *Geddi,*' one such in *Onom.* *Cf.* 1363
chart. 'Wilhelmus Bateman de Giddingg,' near Kettering (which
is, of course, a patronymic), Gedney (Lincs), and Gedelega,
1157 in *Pipe* Devon.

GEDLING (Nottingham). *Dom.* Ghellinge, 1189 *Pipe* Gedlinges.
A patronymic. The same name is seen in Gillamoor (Yorks),
Dom. Gedlingsmore. Mutschmann derives fr. O.E. *gœdlingas,*
'companions in arms,' and makes GILLING the same.

* The -senti may be for -centi ; perh. the same Kelt. root as in KENT, and meaning ' head,' or ' headland.'

GEE CROSS (Stockport). An ancient cross was erected here by the *Gee* family.

GELLISWICK farm (Milford Haven). Hybrid. W. *gelli* or *celli,* 'hazel grove,' and N. *vik,* 'a bay.' *Cf.* WICK (Sc.) and Good-wick (S. Pembroke). But the Welsh tale, *Kulhwch and Oliven* (*a.* 1200), speaks of 'Gelli' or 'Kelli Wic' in Cornwall.

GENTLESHAW (Rugeley). 1505 Gentylshawe. 'Wood of *Gentle,*' a surname still in use. A John *Gentyl* is known in this district in 1341. *Dom.* Bucks, Intlesberie, may represent the same name, See -shaw.

GERRANS (Falmouth). Perh. the same as *c.* 1130 *Lib. Land.* Din-Gerein—*i.e.,* 'castle of Geraint,' K. of the Welsh in 711; 1536 Gerens. But the Welsh chronicler's castle may be in Pembroke.

GIGGLESWICK (Settle). Local pron. Gilzick. *Dom.* Ghiceleswic, Ghigeleswic. *Cf.* ICKLEFORD. 'Dwelling of *Gicel,*' now Jekyl, fr. Breton *Judicael,* which also yields Jewell, 1215 *Close R.* Gikels-wik and William Gikel. See -wick.

GILCRUX (Carlisle). Old forms needed. *Cf. Dom.* Norfk., Gillecros, Gildecros. Can it be 'cross of the guild'? O.E. *gild, gyld. Cross* was early taken into Eng. in more than one form; see *Oxf. Dict.* The M.E. *crouch* shows that late O.E. must have had a form *cruc,* L. *cruc-em,* 'cross.'

GILLING (N. Yorks). *Bede* in Gethlingum, Gætlingum. *Dom.* Gellinge(s). See GEDLING. Gilling and Gillon are still sur-names. There is a 'Gilleburc' 1160 in *Pipe* (Northants). *Cf.* EALING. See -ing.

GILLINGHAM (Dorset and Kent). Do. G. 1016 *O.E. Chron.* Gilling-ham; *Dom.* Geling(e)ham, 1160 *Pipe* Gillingehā; Ke. G. *c.* 1150 *chart.* Gyllingeham. 'Home of the *Gillings,*' a patronymic fr. *Gilo.*

GILLING-, GYLLINGDUNE, and GILLINGVASE (Falmouth). Said to be Corn. for 'William's hill,' and 'William's field,' Corn. *mœs,* here aspirated. The *William* is said to be he who was son of Henry I., drowned in the *White Ship,* crossing from Normandy to England, 1120. All this is a little doubtful.

GILSLAND (Carlisle). *Sic* 1215, but 1291 Gillesland. 'Land, terri-tory of *Giles*' or of '*Gilo,*' 2 in *Onom.*

GIMINGHAM (N. Walsham). *Dom.* Giming(h)ehā, 1443 Gymyng-ham, *c.* 1449 Gemyngham. The name or patronymic is a little uncertain here. Perh. 'Home of *Gemmund* or *Gefmund,*' the nearest name in *Onom.* See -ing.

GIPPING R. See IPSWICH.

GIRDLE FELL (Cheviots). 'Mountain with the belt or band round it.' The ending 'fell' (*q.v.*) is Norse, and so the root is quite as likely O.N. *gyrðill,* O.Sw. *giordell,* as O.E. *gyrdel.* If so, this is one of the very rare Norse names in Northumberland. *Cf.* Girdle Ness (Aberdeenshire).

GIRLINGTON (Bradford). *Dom.* Gerlinton; also *sic* in *Dom.* Somerset. 'Town of *Gerling*,' or perh. 'of *Gærland*,' one in *Onom.* See -ing.

GIRTON (Cambridge). *Dom.* Gretone, *K.C.D.* iv. 145 Gretton, 1236 Greittone, 1434 Grettone, Gyrttone. Skeat inclines to think this is not 'great town' (*cf.* the six Littletons), but prov. Eng. *gratton*, 'grass which comes after mowing, stubble,' fr. O.E. *græd*, Mercian *gréd*, 'grass.' The forms in Girton (Notts) are practically the same. Mutschmann derives, rather doubtfully, fr. O.E. *gréot*, 'sand.' *Cf.* GRETTON, which may be 'great, O.E. *great*, town.' *Great* is 3-6 *gret(e)*, 4-6 *grett(e)*. *Cf.* Girsby (Yorks), *Dom.* Grisbi.

GISBURN (Clitheroe). *Dom.* Ghiseburne, 1179-80 Giseburne, 1197 Kiseburn. ' Burn, brook of *Gisa*,' 2 in *Onom.* *Kisi* was a Norse giant. *Cf.* GUISBORO'. See -bourne.

GISLINGHAM (Eye). *Dom.* Gislingehā, -ghaham, Gissilincham. ' Home of the descendants of *Gisel* '—i.e., ' the hostage '—O.E. *ʒisel*, O.N. *gísl*. *Cf.* 1384 ' Giselyngton ' (Lincs).

GLADMOUTH (S. Wales). See CLEDDY. *Cf.* also GLADDER Brook (Worc.) 1275-1340 Gloddre, also W., -der being *dwfr*, ' stream.'

GLAMORGAN. 1242 *Close R.* Clammorgan, *c.* 1250 *Layam.* Glommorgan, 1461 Glomorganeia. Old W. name Morganwg, Mod. W. Gwlad Morgan, ' dominion of *Morgan*,' a 10th cny. prince, of which the other forms are corruptions or contractions.

GLAPTHORNE (Oundle). Not in *Dom.* *a.* 1100 Glapthorn. Prob. ' thorn-tree of *Glæppa*,' found in *Onom.* *Cf.* GLAPTON (Notts), *sic* 1216-72.

GLASBURY (Brecon). *c.* 1188 *Gir. Camb.* Glasbiria. Hybrid; W. *glas*, ' blue, green, verdancy, hence, a green spot,' and O.E. *burh*. See -bury; also *cf.* GLAZEBROOK.

GLASCOTE (Tamworth). *Sic a* 1300. ' Cot, cottage with windows of glass,' O.E. *glæs*, a very rare thing for an early cottage.

GLASTON (Uppingham). Not in *Dom.* *a.* 1100 *grant of* 664, Glathcstun. There is no name like *Glathe* in *Onom.*, though there is a *Glædwis.* So this may be ' town of gladness,' O.E. *glæd*, 4 *glathe*, but prob. not. Gleadthorpe (Notts), *Dom.* Gletorp, 1278 Gledetorp, must have the same origin.

GLASTONBURY (Somerset). *a.* 716 *Boniface* Glestingaburg; 1016 *O.E. Chron.* Glæstingabyrig; 1297 *R. Glouc.* Glastinbury. In W. Ynys Wydrin (' isle of Wydrin '); found already in *chart.* said to be of 601, Ineswytrin. Freeman thinks this a patronymic. William of Malmesbury says the name is fr. a N. Wales *Glasting*, who wandered there in search of a lost sow. The *Lib. Hymn* (Bradshaw Society), *a.* 900 calls it ' Glastimber of the Goidels ';

and *a.* 1100 *Ann. Cambr.* calls it Glastenec. M'Clure would derive fr. a somewhat dubious W. *glastan*, ' an oak '; there is certainly *glasdonen* (fr. *glas* and *tonen*), ' the scarlet oak,' a quite possible origin, though it is more prob. a patronymic, as the very early first spelling indicates. See -bury.

GLATTON (Peterborough). Not in *Dom.* 1217 Glattun. Seems to be ' glad town '; O.E. *glæd*, 3 *glað*, O.N. *glað-r*, ' bright, beautiful,' cognate with O.H.G. *glat*, ' smooth.'

GLAZEBROOK (Manchester). 1227 Glasbroc, 1303 Glasebrok. Perh. tautology. Kelt. *glas* and Eng. *brook*, both meaning the same. Glazebury is near by. *Cf. Dom.* Glese (Worc.), now Glass-hampton, and Glass Houghton (Yorks), not in *Dom.* W. and H. prefer ' glassy brook,' O.E. *glæs*, ' glass,' but are prob. wrong.

GLEASTON (Ulverston). *Dom.* Glassertun. This implies a name *Glasser*, or the like, prob. Norse. Glasserton (Wigtown), looks the same name; in early chronicles it seems to get confused with GLASTONBURY.

GLEN R. (S. Lincs and Northumberland). History wanted. Either may be Nennius § 56 Fluminis quod dicitur Glein. G. *gleann ;* W. *glyn*, ' a glen, a valley.'

GLENCUNE, GLENDHU, and GLENWHELT (all near Haltwhistle). Glencune is G. *gleann cumhann*, ' narrow glen.' *Cf.* GLENCOE (Sc.). G. *dubh* means ' black,' W. *du*, and -whelt may be W. *gwelllyn*, ' blade of grass,' or ? *ullta*, ' a crazy one, an oaf.' GLENCOIN (Ullswater) = Glencune, G. *comhann*, being var. of *cumhann*, and *mh* has become mute.

GLENDERAMACKIN R. (Keswick). Pure G., *gleann dobhair* or *doir-a-meacain*, ' glen of the stream with the roots, bulbs, or parsnips.'

GLENFIELD and GLEN MAGNA (Leicester). 1232 *Close R.* Glenesfield. Seemingly fr. a man; *Glen* may be contraction fr. *Glædwine*, 2 in *Onom.* But in *Dom.* is Glen, which surely must be G. *gleann*, W. *glyn*, ' valley,' though it, too, may be a man's name. *Magna* is L. for ' great.'

GLENTWORTH (Lincoln). *Dom.* Glenteuurde. *Cf. grant a.* 675 Glenthuþe, ? in Hants. Perh. ' farm of the hard, flinty rock '; Dan. and Sw. *klint*. See CLENT and -worth. GLINTON (Market Deeping), *sic Dom.* and *a.* 1100, would suggest a man's name like *Glent* or *Glint*. None such is recorded, but prob. must be postulated.

GLOGUE (Pembrokesh.). In W. Y Glôg, fr. O.W. *clôg*, ' a stone '; Corn. *clog*, ' a steep rock '; G. *clach*, gen. *cloiche*, ' a stone.'

GLOUCESTER. Pron. Gloster. *c.* 120 *Lat. inscr.* Glev. = Glevensis civitas, *later do.* Glevi, *c.* 380 *Ant. Itin.* Gle-, Clevo, *a.* 700 *Raven. Geog.* Glebon, 681 *chart.* Gleawceasdre, 804 *grant* Gleaw(e)ceastre, Lanfranc *Hist.* ann. 1071, Clœcistra, *ib.* 1080 Claudia Civitas, 1085 *ib.* Cleucestra, *a.*,1130 *Sim. Dur.* Glocestre,

1140 *O.E. Chron.* Gloucestre, *c.* 1160 *Gesta Steph.* Glocestrensis, 1375 *Barbour* Gloster. In W. Caerloew, as in *a.* 810 *Nennius* Cair Gloui., Saxonice autem Gloecester. Said to be called ' camp of *Gloni* ' fr. its builder, a mere guess, whilst to connect with Emperor Claudius is to make a worse guess. Many think the name Kelt., 'bright castle,' fr. W. *glaw,* 'brightness.' The forms all have the *c,* in later times the soft *c,* and not *ch* (except in *Layam.* Gleochæstre), owing to Nor. influence. See -cester.

GNOSALL (Stafford). *Dom.* Geneshale, 1199 Gnowdes-, Gnoddes- hall, 1204 Gnoweshale, 1223 Gnoushale. ' Nook, corner of ' prob. ' *Geonweald,*' one in *Onom.* Duignan suggests ' of *Cnof- wealh,*' which is very far fr. *Dom.* But older forms are needed. *Cf. Dom.* Norfk, Gnaleshala. See -hall.

GOBÓWEN (Oswestry). (1298 ' Robertus Gobyon.') W. *gob Owen,* ' heap, mound of Owen.'

GÓDALMING (Surrey). *Dom.* Godelminge, *a.* 1199 Goldhalming. Patronymic, fr. *Godhelm. Dom.* also has ' Godelannge,' Surrey; ? an error.

GODLEY (Mottram). *a.* 1250 Godelegh; also *cf. Dom.* Surrey, Godelei. Prob. not ' good meadow,' but ' meadow of *Godd, Godda,* or *Gode,*' all of them names found in *Onom. Cf.* Gode- stoch in *Dom.* Salop, and Godeston in 1155 *Pipe* Devon. See -ley.

GÓDMANCHÉSTER (Huntingdon). 970 *chart.* Guthmuncester, *Dom.* Godmundcestre, *c.* 1150-1623 Gumecestre. ' Camp of *Guth- mund,*' a name common and early, found occasionally as *Gud- mund,* which is but var. of the common *Godmund,* ' the man whom God ' (or ' a god ') ' protects,' as *guð, goð* is O.N. for ' god '; O.E. *god.* The contracted form Gume- is influenced by O.E. *guma,* 3-4 *gume,* 3-6 *gome,* ' a man,' and *Goma* occurs as a name twice in *Onom.* We have parallels in GOODMANHAM and GUMLEY. See -chester.

GODSHILL (Wroxall). 1499 Gaddishill = GAD's HILL.

GODSTOW (Oxford). Not in *Dom.* 1158-59 *Pipe* Godestov, 1161-62 *ib.* Godesto. ' Place of *Goda,*' a very common O.E. name. See STOW. *Dom.* Oxon has Godendone, ' Goda's hill.'

GOLANT, GLENT, or St. Sampson's (Par). 1507 Gullant. Prob. Keltic or Corn. *gol land,* ' holy ground.'

GOLBORN BELLOW and DAVID (Chester). *c.* 1350 Golborne, which is prob. ' gosling's burn or brook,' fr. *gull* sb.[2] in *Oxf. Dict.*, found in 4 as *goll,* ' a gosling.' Bellow is fr. the family of *Bella Aqua* or *Belleau,* ' fine water,' which once held this place.

GOLCAR (Huddersfield). *Dom.* Gudlages arc, and argo; *later,* Gouthelagh chaithes, Goullakarres. ' Shieling,' Norse Gaelic *argh,* G. *airigh,* ' of *Gudlag* ' or ' *Guthlac.*' See ANGLESARK, and *cf.* GRIMSARGH, etc. The -car comes through the influence of N. *kjarr,* ' marshy ground.'

GOLDEN VALLEY (S. Hereford). We find *c.* 1130 Richard de Aurea Valle as King's chaplain. Said to be because the French monks confused W. *dwr*, ' stream,' with Fr. *d'or*, ' of gold.'

GOLDINGTON (Bedford). *Dom.* Goldentone. 'Village of *Gold*' or '*Gould*.' *Cf. Dom.* Essex, Goldingham. See next and -ing. But GOLDICOTE (Alderminster) is 1275 Caldicote, ' cold cot.'

GOLDSBOROUGH (Knaresboro'). *Dom.* Golborg, Goldeburg, 1179-80 Goldburg. ' Burgh, castle of *Gold*,' which is still an Eng. surname. One *Golda* and one *Golde* in *Onom.* See -borough. GOLDTHORPE (Rotherham), *Dom.* Guldetorp, Golde-, Godetorp, is fr. the same name. See -thorpe.

GONALSTON (Nottingham). *Dom.* Gunnulveston, 1278 Guneliston, 1316 Gonelston. ' Town of *Gunnulf-r*.'

GOODMANHAM (E. Yorks). *Bede* Godmundigaham. *Dom.* Gudmundham, -mandham. ' Home of *Godmund* '—*i.e.*, the man whom God protects. O.E. *mund*, ' protection.' The -iga in Bede prob. represents -ing, *q.v. Cf.* GODMANCHESTER and GUMLEY.

GOODRICH (Ross, Hereford). Not in *Dom.* O.E. *Godric* (*h*), a man's name. A rare type of place-name. *Cf.* Snitter (Northumberland), also *a.* 1400 Godrichesley, now Gothersley (Stourbridge).

GOODWICK (Fishguard). Dan. and Sw. *gud vik*, ' good bay.'

GOODWIN SANDS, or THE GOODWINS (Kent). 1495 le Goodwine sandes, 1546 Goodwins sands. Said to be fr. Earl *Godwine*, so prominent in the reign of Edward the Confessor. *Cf.* The Bedwins, sands in R. Severn, perh. fr. O.E. *Beaduwine*.

GOOLE (Lincs). *a.* 1552 *Leland*, ' a place caullid Golflete'; fr. the dial. *gool*, found in Eng. in 1542 as *goole*, ' a small stream, a ditch '; O.Fr. *gole*, *goule*, ' the throat.' For -flete, see FLEET.

GOONHAVERN (Perranporth, Cornwall). Corn. *goon*, ' a down, a moorland, a marsh,' and ? some word for ' iron,' W. *haiarn.*

GOOSEY (Faringdon). O.E. *chart.* Gosige, *Dom.* Gosei, 1291 Goseye. ' Goose-isle.' See -ey. But GOOSNARGH (Preston), *Dom.* Gusansarghe, is ' shieling of *Gusan*,' an unrecorded, prob. N., name. See ANGLESARK and GRIMSARGH.

GORE (hundred of Middlesex, around Kilburn). *c.* 1134 *chart.* Gara, which is O.E. or Early Eng. for ' a wedge-shaped strip of land on the side of an irregular field.' This is a good deal earlier than any quot. in *Oxf. Dict. Cf. Dom.* Wilts, Gare.

GORLESTON (Gt. Yarmouth). *Dom.* Gorlestuna. The name is doubtful; ? fr. *Garweald*, or *Geroldus*, or *Gerbold*, as in *Dom.* Norfk., Gerboldeshā.

GORNAL WOOD (Dudley). *a.* 1500 Gwarnell, Guarnell. Prob. ' hall ' or ' nook ' (O.E. *heall* or *healh*) ' of *Garnwi* ' or ' *Geornwig*,' names in *Onom*. Duignan derives fr. O.E. *cweorn, cwearne*, 6 *quearn*, ' a quern, a hand-mill,' but this is not prob. phonetically. See -hall.

GORSLEY (Glouc.). Not in *Dom*. 1228 *Close R*. Gorstley. Prob. not ' furze-meadow,' O.E. *gors*, ' furze, whin,' but ' meadow of *Gorst*,' a name not in *Onom*., but still a surname. See -ley.

GOSFORTH (Seascale and Newcastle). Se. G. *c*. 1170 Gose-, 1390 Gosford, 1452 Gosforth. ' Goose ford,' O.E. *gós*, 3-6 *gose*, ' a goose.' But GOSCOTE (Walsall), *a*. 1300 Gorstycote, is *gorsey cot* or ' cottage among the gorse '; and GOSSINGTON (Glouc.), 1189 Gosintone, is ' village of *Gosa*,' -*an*. *Cf*. 940 *chart*. Gosanwelle (Dorset). See -forth.

GOTHAM (Notts). *Sic* 1316, but *Dom*. Gathā. O.E. *gát hám*, ' goathouse,' 4-6 *gote*, 6- *goat*. GOTHERINGTON (Bishop's Cleeve), *Dom*. Godrinton, is fr. *Godhere*. See -ing.

GOWER (S. Wales). In W. Gwyr. *a*. 810 *Nennius* Guir, *c*. 1188 *Gir. Camb*. Goer, *Ann. Camb*. 1095 Goher. Prob. W. *gwyr*, ' awry, askew '; there is a Corn. *gover*, ' a rivulet '; and W. *gwŷr* is ' fresh, verdant.' There can be no certainty as to the name.

GOWY R. (trib. of R. Mersey, Cheshire). Corrup. of W. *gwy*, ' water, river.'

GOXHILL (E. Riding and Grimsby). E. Ri. G. *Dom*. Golse (? *c*); Gr. G. Not in *Dom*., 1210 Gousele (where -ele prob. represents -hale or -hall, *q.v.*). Difficult; more old forms needed. No name like *Golc* is on record; and *gowk*, 4-6 *gok*, O.N. *gauk-r*, ' the cuckoo,' yields no *l*, nor is it found in Eng. till *c*. 1325.

GOYT R. (N.E. Chesh.). M.E. *gote*, ' a watercourse, a stream '; O.E. *gyte*, ' a flood,' fr. *géotan*, ' to pour,' still found in North. dial. as *goit, goyt*. *Cf*. W. *gwyth*, ' a conduit, a channel '; also ' Skirbeck Gowt,' *sic* 1593, near Boston, which is a watercourse or channel. Guyting-Power and -Temple (Glouc.) must be fr. same root; 814 *chart*. Gythinge, *Dom*. Getinge, 1221 Guytinge, with -ing, *q.v.*, here in its meaning of ' place on a stream.' But GOYTRE (Glamorgan) may be for W. *coed tre*, ' wood-house, dwelling in the wood.'

GRAFTON (5 in *P.G.*). Worcester G. 884 *chart*. Graftune. Two in Warwick, 710 *chart*. Graftone, 962 *ib*. Greftone, *Dom*. Grastone, 1189 Grafton. Northants G. 1166-67 *Pipe* Grafton. ' Grove town,' O.E. *gráf*. See -ton.

GRAHAM. The orig. Graham prob. was in Northumberland; *c*. 1195 a David de Grahām witnesses a charter *re* Ellingham (Belford). The surname is found *a*. 1128 as Graeme, and 1139 Grahā. O.E. *grá ham*, ' grey house.' *Cf*. 1179-80 *Pipe* Gremrig (Yorks).

GRAINTHORPE (Lincs). [*Dom*. Lincs has only Greneham.] ' Village in the forked valley '; O.N. *grein*, ' division, branch '; Sw. *gren*, 'a branch.' See -thorpe and GRAIN (Sc.), also GRAIN, sb.[2] in *Oxf. Dict.*, found in Eng. *a.* 1300. This last also means 'arm of the sea, branch of a stream,' as in Isle of GRAIN (Medway).

GRAMPOUND (Truro). Corn. *gran pont,* 'great bridge.'

GRAN(D)BOROUGH (Rugby and Winslow). 1043 *chart.* Grænesburgh, Greneburga, *Dom.* Grane-, Greneberge, 1260 Greneborwe, 'Burgh of *Grœn,*' not in *Onom.* *Cf.* GRANBY (Notts), *Dom.* Granebi, and *Dom.* Lincs., Granham. See -borough.

GRANTCHESTER. See CAMBRIDGE.

GRANTHAM. *Sic* in *Dom.* 'Home of *Granta*' or '*Grant,*' a name not in *Onom.*, but we have also GRANTLEY (Ripon), *Dom.* Grentelaia. On the meaning of *Grant,* see CAMBRIDGE.

GRASMERE (Cumberland). 'Grassy lake'; O.E. *grœs,* 3-6 *gras,* 'grass.' *Cf.* GRASELEY (Wolverhampton), *sic* 1282.

GRASSINGTON (Skipton). *Dom.* Ghersinton, 1212 Gersinton. 'Town of *Gersent*' or '*Gersendis,*' both names in *Onom.*

GRATELEY (Andover). Not in *Dom.* Prob. *a.* 941 *Lett. to Athelstan* Greatanlea. '*Greta*'s lea' or 'meadow'; but the name is not in *Onom.* *Cf.* GREETHAM and GRATWICH (Uttoxeter), *Dom.* Gratewich, which Duignan thinks 'great, large village.' O.E. *great,* 3 *grœt,* 4-6 *grait, grett.*

GRAVELEY (Stevenage and Huntingdon). Hunt. G. *chart.* Græflea, Greflea, *Dom.* Gravelei, 'grave or trench meadow.' See -ley. *Cf.* GRAVENEY (Faversham), 940 *chart.* Gravenea. See -ey.

GRAVESEND. *Dom.* Essex, Grauesanda, 1157 *Pipe* Grauesent. *c.* 1500 in Arnold's *Chron.* Gravesende—*i.e.,* 'at the end of the moat.' *Cf.* Med. Dutch *grave,* 'a trench.'

GREASBOROUGH (Rotherham). *Dom.* once Gersebroc. One would expect a man's name here, but on analogy of GARSTON this is prob. 'grassy brook,' O.E. *broc,* altered to -borough (*q.v.*). O.E. for 'grass' is *gœrs, grœs.* But it is also in *Dom.* Grese-, Gresseburg, prob. 'burgh, castle of *Grese*' or '*Grise*'—*i.e.,* 'the Pig!' See GRISTHORPE. So Gersebroc is prob. an error.

GREAT AYTON (Yorks). *Dom.* Atun, 1179-80 Atton. Perh. 'village of *Ætta, Ætte,*' or '*Ætti,*' all forms in *Onom.* If so, not = AYTON (Sc.). It may well be = ETON; O.E. *éa-tun,* 'town, village on the stream.'

GREAT BOOKHAM (Leatherhead). *Chart.* Bócham, *Dom.* Bochehā. *Cf.* 1224 *Patent R.* Bukeham (Norfk.). Prob. 'beech-built home.' See BOCKHAMPTON.

GREAT BRADLEY (Newmarket). 1341 *deed* Bradeleghe; M.E. for 'broad lea' or 'meadow.' See -ley.

GREAT KIMBLE (Bucks). *Dom.* Chenebella, *chart.* Cunebelle, 1291 Kenebelle. *Cf.* 903 *chart.* Cynebellinga-gemære. Perh., as Dr.

Birch suggests, called after *Cunobellinus*, the British King, said
to have been buried here. There is also a *Cynebill* or *Cynobill*,
brother of the Bps. Cedda and Ceadda, in *Onom.* *Cf.* Kemble
(Cirencester), *a.* 1300 Kenebelle.

GREAT TEY (Kelvedon). O.E. *tih, teah*, ' a paddock.'

GREAT WITCHINGHAM (Norwich). *Dom.* Wicinghahā, *c.* 1444
Wychyngham. ' Home of *Wiching* ' or ' *Wicing* '; three of
this name in *Onom.*, really a var. of *viking*, ' bay-man, sea-rover.'
Prob. here a patronymic. See -ing.

GREENODD (Lonsdale). O.N. *oddi, odd-r*, ' a small point of land,'
as in Odde (Norway). *Cf.* Greenhow (Pately Br.). O.N. *haug-r*,
' mound, cairn ', and *Dom.* Norfk., Grenehov.

GREENWICH. 1013 *O.E. Chron.* Grenawíc, *Dom.* Grenviz, *c.* 1386
Chaucer Grenewich. O.E. *gréne wíc*, ' green, grassy town or
dwelling.'

GREETHAM (Oakham). *Dom.* and 1292 Gretham. *Cf. Dom.* Hants,
Greteham. Prob. ' *Greta's* home,' as in GRATELEY. But it may
be ' great house '; O.E. *gréat, grécet*, 3-6 *gret*, 4-6 *greet*. GREET-
LAND (Halifax) is *Dom.* Greland.

GRENDON (Atherstone, Northampton, Aylesbury). Ath. G. *Dom.*
Grendon. O.E. *gren dún*, ' green hill.' GRINDON (Ilam and Co.
Durham), Il. G. *Dom.* Grendone, and 1183 *Boldon Bk.* Grendona
(Durham), is the same name.

GRESHAM (Norwich). *Dom.* and 1426 Gressam. Older forms
needed, but prob. 'Home of *Gressa*,' a name not in *Onom.*,
but seen in GRESSENHALL, and *cf.* GREASBOROUGH, whilst
Dom. Norfk has also Gresingahā, the patronymic form. See -ham.

GRESLEY (Burton-on-Trent). Old forms needed. Perh. ' meadow
of *Gresa* ' or ' *Gressa*.' *Cf.* GRESHAM. But also *cf.* 1179-80
Greselea, 1283 Greseleye (S. Lancs), GRIZEBECK and GRIZEDALE,
which may come fr. O.N. *griss*, ' a pig.' See -ley. Greis- or
Grassthorpe (Notts), *Dom.* Grestorp, is prob. ' grassy village ';
cf. GARSTON.

GRESSENHALL (Dereham). *Dom.* Gressenhala, *c.* 1450 Gressenhale.
Prob. as above, ' nook, corner of *Gressa*.' It does not seem prob.
that it comes fr. *grass* ; no adj. *grassen* or *gressen* is known. See
-hall.

GRETA R. (Yorks). O.N. *griót á*, ' stony, shingly river,' fr. *griót*,
O.E. *gréot*, ' gravel, sand, stones.' The name reappears in Lewis,
the R. Greeta or Creed, in G. *Gride*. We also have a R. Greet
(Notts), 958 *chart.* Greota, Great Bridge (Wednesbury) on a
stream called *a.* 1400 Grete, *a.* 1600 Greete, and GREET (Glouc.),
1195 Greta, a hamlet on a brook.

GRETTON (Kettering and Winchcombe). Ket. G. not in *Dom.*
Chron. Ramsey Gretton. Same as GIRTON. But Wi. G. is

Dom. Gretestan, or -stanes, *c.* 1175 Gretstona, prob. 'great
stone or rock.' *Cf.* GREETHAM; and see -ton, which often interchanges with -stone.

GREYSTONES (Sheffield). *Cf.* 847 *chart.* Fram Smalen cumbes heafde
to græwanstane; not this place. There is no Smallcombe in the
Gazetteers.

GRIMSARGH (Preston). *Dom.* Grimesarge. '*Grim*'s sheiling' or
'hut.' *argh* being N. corrup. of G. *airigh.* See ANGLESARK; and
cf. Sizergh (Kendal), also next.

GRIMSBY. *Dom.*, and 1156 *Pipe* Grimesbi, 1296 Grimmesby, 1297
Grymesby. '*Grim*'s dwelling.' See -by. *Grim* was a very
common O.E. name. Grimsby existed from the days of Cnut,
or earlier. Its origin is described in *c.* 1300 *Havelok.* There is a
Grimsbury (Berks) and a Grimstock (Coleshill). See -stock. But
GRIMSCOTE (Whitchurch) is said to have been Kilmescote and
Kenemyscote, which, as Duignan says, is prob. '*Coenhelm*'s' or
'*Kenelm*'s cot.' There are also several Grimstons—*e.g.*, *Dom.*
Yorks and Notts, Grimeston, Grimstun, and a Grimsbury (Glouc.).

GRIM'S DYKE, or DITCH OF GRIM, runs fr. Bradeham (High Wycombe)
to Berkhamstead (Herts). It is an ancient earthwork of unknown origin, possibly Roman. *Cf.* above and Graham's Dyke
(Falkirk), which is the old Roman Wall; also GRIME'S HILL
(Worcs.), 1275 Grimesput ('pit'). *Grim* in O.E. means 'fierce,
cruel,' common as a surname. GRIMLEY (Worcs.) is 851 *chart.*
Grimanleage, '*Grima*'s meadow.'

GRINDLETON (Clitheroe). *Dom.* Gretlintone. This seems to be a
corrup. of the common '*Grimcytel*'s town,' a name also found as
Grichetel, Grinchel, Grichel. But *cf.* next, Grindleford (Sheffield)
and Grindalythe (see HYTHE), Thirsk; neither in *Dom.*

GRINDLEY BROOK (Whitchurch). May simply be 'meadow with the
barred gate'; O.N. *grind.* See -ley. Some would compare
Grendlesmere (Wilts) fr. *Grendel,* the witch in *Beowulf.* *Cf.*
a. 1000 *chart.* Grendles bec and Grindeles pytt (Worc.), and there
is a Grindelay, or 'Grendel's isle' (Orkney); but see, too, above.
GRINDLEY (Uttoxeter) is often in 13th cny. Greneleye, as if
'green meadow.' *Cf.* Gringley (Notts), *Dom.* Grenelei.

GRINDON. See GRENDON.

GRINSHILL (Shrewsbury). Not in *Dom.* *Grin* is prob. var. of
Grim, as in GRIMSBY, etc. Grimthorpe (Yorks) is in *Dom.* both
Grim- and Grintorp; *cf.* 940 *chart.* Grinescumb (Dorset). But
GRINDALE (Yorks) is *Dom.* Grendale, 'green dale.'

GRISTHORPE (Filey). *Dom.* Grisetorp and GRISTON (Thetford).
Dom. Gris-, Grestuna. 'Village of the pigs,' or, 'of a man *Grise*';
O.N. *griss,* 'a pig.' Similar is Girsby (Yorks), *Dom.* Grisebi.
Cf. next and GREASBOROUGH; and see -thorpe.

GRITTLETON (Chippenham). 940 *chart.* Grutelingtone, *Dom.* Grete-
linton. 'Village of the sons of *Grutel,*' a name not in *Onom.*

Perhaps it is for the fairly common *Grimcytel*, var. *Grichetel*. See -ing.

GRIZEBECK (Furness) and GRIZEDALE (Cumberland). O.N. *griss*, 'a pig.' *Cf.* above. On *beck*, 'a brook,' see BECKERMET.

GROBY (Leicester). *Dom.* Grobi, 1298 Grouby. 'Dwelling by the pit.' O.N. *grof*, Ger. *grube*. See -by.

GRONANT (Rhyl). W. *gro nant*, 'sand' or 'gravel valley.'

GUASH R. (Rutland). Prob. O.W. *gwes*, 'that which moves or goes.' *Cf.*, too, G. *guaimeas*, 'quietness,' and WASH.

GUERNSEY. Possibly *c.* 380 *Notit. Dign.* 'Granona in Armorica.' If so the first part of this name must be Keltic, or pre-Keltic; perh. W. *gwern*, 'plain, moor, and alder tree,' with N. ending. But it is *a.* 1170 *Wace* Guernesi, 1218 *Patent R.* Ger(n)esie, 1219 Gernereye; 1286 *Close R.* Gennere, 1447 Guernesey, 1449 Garnyse, 1454 Gernessey. Some think it is also *a.* 1220 *Volsunga Saga* Varinsey. The name is prob. N. 'Isle of *Gœrwine*' or '*Gerinus*,' names in *Onom.*, or of an unrecorded *Gœrn*, in which case *s* in 1218 will be an Eng. gen. and *r* in 1219 a Norse one. See -ey.

GUILDEN MORDEN (Royston, Hunts) and SUTTON (Chester). *c.* 1080 *Inquis. Camb.* Mordune, 1166 Mordone, 1236 Mordene. 'Moor, down'; O.E. *dún*, changed into *denu*, '(wooded) valley.' Later, 1255 Geldenemordon, 1317 Guldenemordon, 1302 Gylden, 1342 Gilden, 1346 Gyldene. This also prob., thinks Skeat, means 'Morden of the guild-brother,' O.E. *gyldena*, gen. pl. of *gylda*, 'a guild-brother.' But further evidence is needed. It can hardly be the same as *Dom.* Goldene (Salop), with which *cf.* Goldenhill (Stoke-on-Trent).

GUILDFORD. *Dom.* Gilde-, Geldeford, *c.* 1100 *Ralph the Black* Guldedune (O.E. *dún*, 'hill, hill-fort'), 1120 Geldeforda, *a.* 1199 Goldeford, 1298 Gildeforde. 'Ford with the toll'; O.E. ȝield, ȝeld, ȝyld, 'payment, tribute.'

GUISBORO' (Yorks). *Dom.* Ghigesborg; but it is also *Dom.* Giseborne, 1151 Gyseburne. *Cf.* GISBURN, and see -bourne. It is difficult to say what name Ghige- represents, but prob. it is the same as in Ginge (Berks), which is in O.E. *chart.* Gæging, Geinge, Gainge; *Dom.* Gainz, 'place of the sons of *Gæga*'; also *cf. K.C.D.* vi. 137, Geganlege, '*Gega*'s meadow.' In Ghiges- we have a strong gen. instead of the weak -*an*, and Gise- is a contraction; also see next. See -boro'.

GUISELEY (Shipley). *Dom.* Gisele. '*Gisa*'s lea' or 'meadow.' See above, and *cf. Dom.* Norfk., Guistune. See -ley.

GULVAL (Penzance). *Sic* 1521; 1536 Gulvale *alias* Lanesleye (1222 Lanesely). Called after *Gudwal*, Bp. of St. Malo, 6th cny. But Lanesely must mean 'church of' some other saint.

GUMLEY (Leicester). *Dom.* Godmundelai, 1292 Gomundele. ' Lea, meadow of *Godmund';* 3 such in *Onom. Cf.* GODMANCHESTER and GOODMANHAM; and see -ley.

GUNNERSBURY (Kew). Not found till the 15th cny. ' Burgh, town of *Gunner,'* N. *Gunnarr,* a common name in *Onom. Cf.* next and Ballygunner (Waterford); and see -bury.

GUNNERSKELD (Shap). ' Well of *Gunner'* (see above); fr. O.N. *kelda,* ' a well, a spring.' *Cf.* Threlkeld (Penrith).

GUNNISLAKE (Tavistock). Perh. ' Lake of *Gunna';* there is one such in *Onom.* On this Norse name, which means ' war,' see the interesting discussion in *Oxf. Dict.* s.v. GUN sb. *Cf.* GUNSTON (Staffs) *a.* 1300 Gonestone, Gunstone. Gunn is still a common surname. Lake is already found in O.E. as *lac,* though rarely. *Cf.* FILEY. But *Dom.* Devon has a Gherneslete; ? this place, which may be fr. O.E. *gelœt(e),* ' open watercourse ' or ' junction of roads ' (see LEAT, sb.), and so ' leat of *Geornn'* or ' *Geornwi,'* corrupted into Gunnislake. *Cf.,* too, GURNEY SLADE.

GUNTHORPE (Nottingham and Norfolk). Not G. *Sic a.* 1100 in grant of 664, but *Dom.* Gulne-, Gunnetorp, 1278 Guntorp. Nor. G. *Dom.* Gunestorp. ' Village of *Gunna.'* See above, and -thorpe. Possibly the name embedded is *Gunhildr; cf.* GUN-THWAITE (Yorks), 1389 Gunnyldthwayt.

GUNWALLOE (The Lizard). Named fr. *Winwaloe,* son of Fragan of Brittany, *c.* 550.

GURNEY SLADE (Bath). This looks as if the same name as *Dom.* Devon, Gherneslete; see GUNNISLAKE. *Dom.* Somerset has only Gernefelle, ' *Georn's* field.'

GUYHIRN (Wisbech). ' *Guy's* nook ' or ' hiding-place '; O.E. *hyrne,* now *hern, hirn.* Guy is a common Nor. name in England. But GUY'S CLIFF (Warwick) is *a.* 1200 Gibbe- Kibbeclive, *a.* 1300 Chibbeclive—*i.e.,* ' *Gibbie's* ' or ' *Gilbert's* cliff.'

GWAELOD-Y-GARTH (Cardiff). W., ' bottom of the little corn-field.' Garth must be a loan-wood, fr. O.N. *garð-r,* ' an enclosure, a yard '; but in W. it now means ' a ridge, a hill, a promontory.'

GWAUN-CAE-GURWEN (Glam.). Looks like W. *gwaen cae gwr gwen,* ' moor with the field of the fair man '. There is also a R. Gwaun or Gwayne (Pembrokesh.) *a.* 800 Guoun, or Gvoun; W. *gwaen,* ' a (wet) moor.' *Cf.* Waunarlwydd, Glam. (W. *arglwydd,* ' a superior, a lord ').

GWEEK (Helston). Corn. *gweek;* L. *vicus,* ' town, village.' *Cf.* WEEK St. Mary, etc.

GWINEAR (Hayle, Cornwall). Not in *Dom.* 1536 Gwynner. Some would say, Corn. *gwin nor,* ' white earth.' *Cf.* ANNOR. But *Gwynear* was a saint, killed by K. Listewdrig.

GWYNFAI or -FE (Llangadock). 1317 Gwynuey. To-day W. *gwyn fai,* aspirated fr. *mai,* ' fair field.' But -uey may = *gwy,* ' river.'

GYTING and TEMPLE GUITING (Cutsdean, Worc.). 974 Gytincgas Æwelme, Gytinc, -ges. Gyting seems a patronymic, 'place of the sons of *Gytha, Gythe, Githa*,' or '*Gida*,' all forms in *Onom*. See -ing. O.E. *œwylme* is 'a spring, a well.' See EWELME.

HACHESTON (E. Suffolk). *Dom.* Haces, Hecestuna. 'Town of *Hacca*'; 2 in *Onom*.

HACKNESS (Whitby). *Bede* Haconos, Hakenes; *O.E. vers.* Hecanos; *Dom.* Hagenesse. Haco nos is O.N. for '*Haco*'s ness' or 'nose.' *Cf.* Hackthorpe (Penrith) and Haconby (Bourne). But a farm called Hack- or Ack-bury (Brewood, Staffs) is *a*. 1300 Herkebarewe and 1304 Erkebarwe, 'burial-mound of' an unidentifiable man.

HACKNEY (London). *c.* 1250 Hackenaye, Hacquenye; *temp. Edw. IV*. Hackeney or Hackney. 'Isle of *Hacca, Hacco*,' or '*Hacun*'; several so-called in *Onom*. See -ey. Nothing to do with *hackney*, the 'horse,' which is O.Fr. *haquenée*, and not found in Eng.before about 1330. *Cf.* HAGBOURNE (Wallingford), *a*. 900 *chart*. Hacca broce, *Dom.* Hacheborne, 1291 Hakeburn.

HADDENHAM (Thame and Ely). Th. H. *Dom.* Hadenā; El. H. *K.C.D.* vi. 98 Hædanham; *c.* 1080 *Inquis. Camb.* Hadenham, Hæderham, Hadreham ; *Dom.* Hadreham; 1300 Hadenham. 'Home of *Hœda*' or '*Heada*.' The forms with r pro n are due to a common confusion of liquids. *Cf.* HADEN.

HADDON HALL (Bakewell). *Dom.* Hadun(a), O.E. for 'high hill,' *heáh*, 'high.' *Cf.* a 'Hadune' (Notts), in *Roll Rich. I*.

HADEN CROSS (Dudley). Named fr. a family long resident here. A family of *Haden* is found at Rowley Regis in 1417. *Cf.* HADDENHAM.

HADFIELD (Manchester). Not in W. and H. *Cf.* 778 *chart*. 'To hadfelde ʒeate.' This cannot mean 'head field,' but will be 'field of *Hadd, Hada, Hadde*, or *Headda*,' names all found in *Onom*. *Cf. Dom.* Essex Hadfelda. Not the same as HATFIELD.

HADLEIGH (Suffk.) and HADLEY (Droitwich). Suf. H., not in *Dom*., *a*. 1200 Heddele, still the local pron. Dr. H. 1275 Hedley. Prob. '*Headda*'s meadow.' But HADLEY (Wellington, Salop) is said to be *old* Hæthleigh, O.E. *hœth*, 'a moor, a heath.' It is *Dom.* Hatlege, and in *Dom.* medial *th* regularly becomes *d*. HADSOR (Droitwich) is *a*. 1100 Headesofre, *Dom.* Hadesore, 1275 Haddesovere. 'Bank, edge of *Headda*,' O.E. *ofr, obr*, 'bank, brink, edge.' See -or.

HADSTOCK (Cambridge). 1494 *Fabyan* Hadestok. *Cf. R. Rich I*. Hadestache (Derby). Either 'place of *Hadde* or *Headda*,' see HADFIELD; or fr. *hade* sb[1] *Oxf. Dict.* 'a strip of land left unploughed, as a boundary, etc.' Found in 1523. *Stock* is the same root as *stake*.

HAGGERSTON (London). *Dom.* Hergotestane. Either 'stone of *Hœrgod, Heregod,* or *Heregyth,*' all in *Onom.*; or 'stone of the heriot,' O.E. *here-geatu,* a feudal service, now commuted to a money payment on the death of a tenant. See *Oxf. Dict. s.v.* HERIOT. But there is or was a Haggerston (Co. Durham), 1183 Agardeston, 1213 Hagardeston, which must be fr. a man *Haggard,* O.Fr. *Agard,* still a surname.

HAGLEY (Stourbridge). *Dom.* Hageleia, *a.* 1200 Hageleg. The first half is thought to be N., though such names are very rare in this shire. O.N. *hagi,* Sw. *hage,* 'enclosed field, pasture,' not found in Eng., as *hag* sb[2], until 1589. More prob. is derivation from O.E. *haga,* with the same meaning, cognate with O.E. *hege,* 'a hedge.' The -ley (*q.v.*) is 'meadow.' *Cf.* HAGLOW (Awre), *old* Hagloe. See -low. This may be fr. a man *Agga,* short for *Agamund,* a common name, as a form Aggemede is found for HAGMEDE, also in Glouc.

HAIGH and HAIGHTON (see HAUGHTON).

HAIKABLE (Westmld.). Said to be High Cop Gill or 'ravine'; fr. O.N. *há-r kopp-r,* 'high top (of a hill).' See -gill.

HAILES (Glouc.) and HALES (Mkt. Drayton). *Dom.* Hales (?), *a.* 1400 Hali, Hales. Glos. H. *Dom.* Heile, *c.* 1386 *Chaucer* Hayles. O.E. *healh,* dat. *heale,* Mercian *halh, hale,* 'a nook, corner, secret-place,' with common Eng. pl. Some make it 'meadow-land by a river, a haugh.' See -hall. HALE (Arreton, I. of W.) is *Dom.* Atehalle, 'nook of *Ata,*' 2 in *Onom.,* where the personal name has fallen away. We have the simple Hale also at Liverpool, Altrincham, Glostersh., and Chingford. The pl. *s* is usually late.

HAILSHAM (Sussex). Not in *Dom.* 1230 *Close R.* Eilesham. 'Home of *Æla,*' 1 in *Onom.*

HAINAULT FOREST (Essex). *Old* Henholt. This old form tends to bar out connection with Hainhault or Philippa of Hainhault, Germany, consort of Edward III. Some think it is, O.E. *héan* (inflected form of *héah*), *holt,* 'high wood.' As likely *hen* represents Dan. *hegna,* 'a hedge, an enclosure,' O.N. *hegna,* 'to enclose.' *Dom.* Essex has only HENHAM.

HAINTON (Lincoln), *Dom.* Hagetone, Haintone, -tun, and HAINWORTH (Yorks), *Dom.* Hageneworde. Prob. fr. same man as in Haunton (Tamworth), 942 Hagnatun, *a.* 1300 Hagheneton, and in HANYARD, 1227 Hagonegate, Hageneyate. 'Town' and 'farm of *Hagene.*' See -worth.

HAISTHORPE (Yorks). *Dom.* Aschil-, Ascheltorp, Haschetorp. 'Place of *Æs-* or *Ascytel,*' var. *Askyl, Aschil.* See ASSELBY and -thorpe.

HAKIN (Milford Haven). Sometimes thought to be fr. the Norse King *Haco(n)* (? which). Such an origin would be contrary to analogy. It may be corrup. of *haven*. *Cf.* Copen-hagen, ' merchants' haven.'

HALAM (see HALLAM).

HALE (see HAILES).

HALESOWEN (Worstrsh.). *Dom.* Halas, 1276 Halesowayn, 1286 Halesowen. See HAILES. The Owen comes fr. David ap Owen, prince of N. Wales, who married Emma, sister of Henry II., in 1174.

HALFORD (Shipston and Stourbridge). Ship. H. 950 *chart.* Halhford, 1176 Haleford. 'Ford at the meadow-land,' or 'haugh,' O.E. *healh* ; see -hale, -hall. But St. H. is 1343 Oldeforde.

HALIFAX. Curious name. It seems always (see below) to have been so spelt, since the founding of the Church of St. John the Baptist here soon after 1100. If so, it must be O.E. *hálig feax,* ' holy (2-4 *hali*) locks ' or ' head of hair,' perh. referring to some picture of the head of St. John. On the strength of a comparison with CARFAX (see *Oxf. Dict.* s.v.), it is often said to mean ' holy fork ' or ' holy roads,' converging as in a fork, L. *furca*. Carfax is first found in 1357 Carfuks, and not till 1527 as Carfaxe, so this origin seems quite untenable. Perh. the earliest *original* document which names the place is a letter, *c.* 1190, which speaks of ' ignotæ ecclesiæ de Haliflex,' where the *l* seems to be a scribe's error, and -flex must be *feax*. ' Holy flax ' would make no sense. In *Dom.* it seems to be called Feslei. Can the Fesbe *feax* too ?

HALKIN (Holywell). *Dom.* Alchene, a puzzling form. But, as the village now lies at the foot of a hill called *Helygen*, this is prob. the origin. It means in W. ' a willow-tree.'

HALLAM (Sheffield). *Dom.* Hallun. An old loc., ' on the slopes,' O.N. *hall-r*, ' a slope '; *cf.* La Haule. Jersey. HALAM (Southwell) is also in *chart.* æt Halum, 1541 Halom. For a N. word taking on an Eng. loc. form, *cf.* HOLME-ON-THE-WOLDS. HALLEN (Henbury), *old* Hel(l)en, may be fr. W. *helen*, ' salt '; but this is doubtful.

HALLIFORD (Shepperton). 969 *chart.* Halgeford, inflected form of O.E. *halig ford*, ' holy ford,' 1316 Halgheford.

HALLIKELD (Yorks). O.N. *heilag-r kelda*, ' holy well or spring.' O.E. *hálig*, ' holy.' *Cf.* GUNNERSKELD and 1202 *Fines* Helghefelde.

HALLINGBURY (Bp's. Stortford). *Dom.* Halingheberia. ' Burgh, town of the sons of ? ' Older forms needed to identify this patronymic; ? fr. *Halig* or *Healfdene*. See -ing.

HALLINGTON (Corbridge, Northumbld.). *Cf.* 806 *chart.* Halington, in the Midlands. Prob. a patronymic, '*Haling* or *Hayling*'s town.' *Cf.* HAYLING I.

HALLOUGHTON (see HAUGHTON).

HALLOW (Worcester). 816 *chart*. Heallingan, Halhegan, Halheogan, 963 *ib*. Hallege, *Dom*. Halhegan, 1275 Hallawe. A very puzzling name. It surely must be meant to represent *hallow*, ' a saint,' then, ' the shrine of a saint,' O.E. *halʒa, halʒe*, pl. *halʒan*, 2 *hale-chen ;* whilst Heall- Hal- does look as if it had something to do with -hall (*q.v.*).

HA(L)LSALL (Ormskirk). 1224 Haleshal, 1312 Halesale, 1320-46 Halsale, 1394 Halsalle. Prob. ' hall of *Hala* ' or some such name; *Halga* is the nearest in *Onom*. Were the name late it might be ' Hal's hall.' *Cf.* ' Halsam ' in a grant of *a*. 675, near Chertsey, Halstead, Halstock, and *Dom*. Halstune (Salop), also Halsham (Yorks), *Dom*. Halsam, -em. For the ending -all *cf*. WALSALL, etc., and see -hall.

HALTON (8 in *P.G.*). Leeds H. *Dom*. Halletun. Craven H. *Dom*. Haltone, Alton, 1179-80 *Pipe* Aleton. Tring H. *Dom*. Haltone. ' Village with the *hall* or mansion.' See -hall and -ton. But *Dom*. Yorks, Haltun, is now Great HOUGHTON, and 1160-61 *Pipe* Nhbld., Haulton, prob. has a similar origin.

HALTWHISTLE (Carlisle). 1178 *Arbroath Chart*. Haucwy - litle (scribe's error), 1220 *ib*. Hauetwisel; later in same *chart*. Haut-wisil, -twysill, 1553 Hawtwesyll, *a*. 1600 Hartweseil. Local pron. Haw-tessel. The first syll. is doubtful. Some say, O.E. *hawe*, ' a look-out.' The likeliest origin is O.E. *háwi twisla*, ' bluish-grey confluence,' where Haltwhistle burn joins Tyne; O.E. *háwi, héawi, hœwi*, 6-9 *haw*, ' bluish, greyish, or greenish blue,' and see TWIZEL. *Cf. chart*. ' Hocgetwisle ' (Hants), and Oswaldtwistle (Accrington).

HALVERGATE (Norwich). *Dom*. Halfriate, 1157 Halvergiata. O.N. *halfr gat* (O.E. *geat*), ' the half gate,' ? one which only closed the entrance half-way up.

HAM (Hungerford, Richmond, and Essex). Es. H. 969 *chart*. Hamme, O.E. for ' enclosure.' See -ham. But HAMBROOK (Winterbourne), *Dom*. Hambroc, may be O.E. *hean bróc*, ' at the high brook.'

HAMBLE, R. (Solent). *Bede* Homelea, *c*. 1450 *Fortescue* Hammelle Ryce and Hammelle the Hoole. M'Clure suggests that this may be an aspirated form of R. CAMEL; but the name is doubtful.

HAMBLEDON (Godalming and Cosham). God. H. O.E. *chart*. Hamælendun, *Dom*. Hameledone, ' *Hamela*'s fort.' Also HAMBLETON (Selby and Preston). Both *Dom*. Hamelton, fr. the same name.

HAMERTON (Hunts). *Dom*. Hambertune, and GREAT HAMMERTON (W. Riding), *Dom*. Hanbretune, look as if fr. an inflected form of the common name Heahbeorht—*Hanbeorht, Hanbert*, or the like. But HAMMERTON (Yorks), *Dom*. Hamereton, seems ' town of *Haimhere* or *Haimheardus* or *Haimerus*,' a name still surviving as *Hamar*. *Cf.* HAMMERSMITH and -WICH; also *Dom.* Nfk., Hameringahala.

HAMMER (Haslemere and Prescot). Not in *Dom.* O.E. *héah mere,* ' high pool ' or ' lake.' Seen inflected in the name Hanmer. *Cf.* ABINGER HAMMER and EMMER; also HAMPOLE.

HAMMERSMITH (London). Seems to have no old forms, and no history before Chas. I. 'Hermodewode,' mentioned in *Enc. Brit.*, cannot be the same name. Nor can the place be called from the artisan *hammersmith*, found in Eng. fr. 1382. There is no such place-name in England. Prob. it is '*Hamer's* smite,' O.E. *smite*, a rare word, prob. meaning ' a bog, a morass.' See SMITE, *Dom.* Smithh. It can hardly be '*Hamer's* MYTHE ' or river-mouth, as there is none such here. *Cf.* HAMERTON.

HAMMERWICH (Lichfield). *Dom.* Humerwiche, *c.* 1200 Hamerwich, *a.* 1300 Homerwich. 'Dwelling, village of *Homer* ' or ' *Hamar.*' *Cf.* HAMERTON and Homerton (E. London).

HAMOSE (Anchorage, Plymouth). 'Home (shelter) among the ooze,' M.E. *oaze, wose*, O.E. *wós*, ' juice.' See -ham.

HAMPOLE (Doncaster). *Dom.* Hanepol, which is an inflected form for O.E. *héan pol*, ' high pool.' *Cf.* HAMMER and HANLEY.

HAMPSHIRE. *O.E. Chron.* 755 Hamtúnscire, *c.* 1097 *Fhr. Worc.* Hantunscire. *Hamtún* is O.E. for ' home town,' which as a place-name is spelt HAMPTON. There is a R. HAMPS (N.E. Staffd.), but it seems impossible to guess its origin, though Duignan connects with the vb. *hamper*. It is a river so ' hampered ' that it totally disappears underground for a time. HAMPEN (Glouc.) is *Dom.* Hagenpene, ' fold of *Hagan.*'

HAMPSTEAD (London), and HAMPSTEAD MARSHALL and NORRIS (Berks). Lo. H. *Dom.* Hamestede. O.E. *hám-stede*, ' homestead, home-place or farm.' *Cf.* Ashampstead (Pangbourn), 1307 Ashamsted, and Finchamstead (Berks), *Dom.* Finchamestede, ' homestead with the finches.' Hampstead Marshall was in possession of Roger le Bygod, Earl of Norfolk and Lord Marshal of England, in 1307. Norris is fr. the Norman family of Norreys. There is also a HAMSTEAD (Handsworth), *a.* 1400 Hamp- and Hamstede, and Dunhampstead (Droitwich), 804 *chart.* Dunhamstyde, 972 Dunhæmstede. HAMPNETT (Glouc.), *Dom.* Hantone, but *Kirby's Quest*. Hamptoneth, may be for ' HAMPTON heath.'

HAMPTON and HAMPTON COURT (London; 11 Hamptons in *P.G.*). 781 *Synod of Brentford* Homtune, *Dom.* Hamntune, 1402 Hampton, 1514 *lease* Hampton Courte, also *Dom.* Hantone (Chesh.), Hantuna (Essex). O.E. *hám* has as one of its earliest, if not its earliest meaning, ' village,' so *hám-tún* will mean ' enclosed, fortified village,' or else ' house, home.' The letter *p* has a habit of intruding itself where not needed. *Cf.* BAMPTON, BROMPTON, etc.

HAMPTON-LUCY (Stratford, Wwk.). *c.* 1062 *chart.* Heamtun, *Dom.*
Hantone, and HAMPTON-IN-ARDEN, *Dom.* Hantone, *a.* 1200
Hantune in Arden, are O.E. *héan tún,* inflected form of 'high
town,' *héah,* 'high.' *Cf.* HANBURY. H.-Lucy has been held
by the *Lucy* family from the time of Q. Mary. HAMPTON GAY
(Oxon.) is also Heantun in 958.

HAMSTALL RIDWARE (Rugeley). 1004 Rideware, *Dom.* Riduare,
a. 1300 Rydewar Ham(p)stal. O.E. *hamsteall,* 'homestead.'
Cf. c. 1200 *chart. Whalley Abbey* Hamstalesclogh. Ridware
Duignan is prob. right in thinking to be *Ridwara,* 'dwellers on
the *rhyd*'; only that in W. means 'ford' not 'river.' *Cf.*
CANTERBURY, etc.

HANBURY (Droitwich, Bromsgrove, Burton-on-T., and Oxfordsh.).
Dr. H. 691 *chart.* Heanburg, 757 *ib.* Heanburh, Hanbiri, 796 *ib.*
Heanbyrig. Bro. H. 836 *chart.* Heanbyrg, *Dom.* Hambyrie.
Bur. H. *a.* 1300 Hamburi, -bury, *a.* 1400 Hanbury, 1430 Ham-
bury. Ox. H. *Dom.* Haneberge, 1495 Hanburye. O.E. *héan
byrg* is 'high burgh,' even as HAMPTON is often 'high town.'
But in both cases *ham* may be 'home'; prob. not. HENBURY
(Bristol), 691 *chart.* Heanburg, *Dom.* Henberie, is, of course =
HANBURY. *Cf.* next and HENFIELD. See -bury.

HANCHURCH (Trentham). *Dom.* Hancese (-cese for -circe), 1296
Hanchurch. O.E. *hean circe,* 'high church.'

HANDBOROUGH or HANBOROUGH (Woodstock). *Dom.* Haneberge,
prob. O.E. *hean beorge,* 'high hill'; *beorg* is 'a mountain, a hill,
a mound,' and *héah* is 'high,' gen. *héan.* It may be 'cocks'
hill,' O.E. *hana,* 'a cock,' *han-créd,* 'cock-crow.'

HANDFORTH (Manchester). Some think this is 'ford (*q.v.*) with a
hand-rail across it.' But HANDSWORTH (Sheffield) is *Dom.*
Handeswrde, fr. a man *Hand,* while Handsworth (Birmingham)
is *Dom.* Honeswrde, *a.* 1200 Hones-, Hunesworth, *a.* 1300
Hunnesworth, 'farm of *Hona*' or '*Hunna.*' See -worth.

HANGING GROVE (Hanley Child), HANGING HEATON (Dewsbury),
and HANGING HOUGHTON (Nthmptn.). Dew. H. *Dom.* Etun,
Nor. H. not in *Dom.* 1230 *Close R.* Hangadehout. Hanging
is corrup. of O.E. *hangra,* 'a wood on a sloping hill.' *Cf.*
BIRCHANGER, etc. The -dehout in 1230 seems to mean 'of
Hout,' an unrecorded name. HOUGHTON is always a difficult
name. See, too, HEATON, and *cf.* Hangerbury Hill (Glouc.).

HANKHAM (Hastings). 947 *chart.* Hanecan ham, prob. this place,
Dom. Henecha'. 'Home of *Haneca.*' *Cf. Dom.* Bucks, Hane-
chedene. 947 cannot be, as some think, HANHAM ABBOTS
(Winterbourne), *Dom.* Hanun, -on, *c.* 1170 Hanum, which seems
to be the old loc. common in Yorks, 'at *Hana's.*' See -ham.
But HANKERTON (Malmesbury) is 1282 Haneketon. fr. the same
name as Hankham.

HANLEY (3 in Worc. and Staffs). *Dom.* Hanlege, -lie (Upton-on-Severn), 817 Heanley (Tenbury), *Dom.* Hanlege, 1275 Childrehanle (Hanley Child), 1332 Hanley (Potteries). Perh. all O.E. *héan lege,* 'high meadow.' *Cf.* HANBURY. Childre- is gen. pl. of *child.* But it is to be noted that there are 2 called *Hana* in *Onom.* (*cf.* HONLEY); whilst HANNEY (Berks) is 956 *chart.* Hannige, *Dom.* Hannei, 'isle of the cock,' O.E. *hana. Cf. Dom.* Salop, Hanelev.

HANWELL (Ealing). *Dom.* Hanewelle. All these names in Hanare doubtful as to the first syll. Hanwell must be interpreted as HANLEY is, and *cf.* HANBURY. But, to show how uncertain the ground is, HANYARD (Stafford) is 1227 Hagonegate, Hageneyate, with which *cf.* Haunton (Tamworth), 942 *chart.* Hagnatun, *a.* 1300 Hagheneton, Hanneton, '*Hagene*'s gate' and 'town.'

HAPPISBURGH (Norwich). *Dom.* Hapesburc, 1450 Happysborough. Local pron. Hazeboro'. The name is sometimes spelt Haisboro' and Hazebro'. The contractions are interesting; the *z* sound is rare in such a case. 'Town of *Happi,*' though *Heppo* is the nearest name in *Onom.* See -burgh.

HARBERTON (see MARKET HARBOROUGH).

HARBLEDOWN (Canterbury). Not in *Dom.* 1360 (letter of a Fr. chaplain) Helbadonne. 'Hill, down, O.E. *dún,* of *Harble,*' which is prob. the O.E. *Heardbeald,* 1 such in *Onom.*

HARBORNE (Birmingham). *Dom.* Horeborne, *c.* 1300 Horeburn, *a.* 1400 Horbourne; -bourne (*q.v.*) is 'brook.' O.E. *hár,* M.E. *hor(e)* is 'hoar, hoary, grey, old,' but *har* or *hare* often also means 'boundary,' and this place is on the border between Staffs. and Worcestersh. *Cf.* HAROME and HOAR CROSS; also Harridge (Redmarley), 1275 Horerugge, 'ridge on the boundary' between Worcester and Hereford.

HARBOROUGH, GREAT and LITTLE (Rugby). 1004 *chart.* Hereburgebyrig, *Dom.* Herdeberge, *a.* 1300 Herdebergh, -berwe, Herburburi. '*Hereburh*'s town.' See -borough. But HARBURY (Leamington) is *Dom.* Edburberie, Erbur(ge)berie—*i.e.,* '*Eadburh*'s burgh' (see -borough); whilst HARBURSTON (Pembroke) is 1307 Herbraundyston, fr. *Herbrand,* an early Flemish settler. HARBY (Notts) is *Dom.* Herdebi, *cf.* HARDWICK.

HARBOTTLE (Rothbury). *Sic* 1595. O.E. *hár botl,* 'hoary, grey house.' *Cf.* O.N. *hár-r,* and NEWBATTLE (Sc.).

HARDEN (Walsall). *a.* 1400 Haworthyn, -werthyn, -wardyne, 1648 Harden. O.E. *héah worthyn,* 'high farm.' See -wardine. It has now the same pron., but has not quite the same meaning, as HAWARDEN. Harden (Yorks) is *Dom.* Heldetone, or 'town on the slope,' O.E. *hylde, helde.*

HARDINGSTONE ST. EDMUNDS (Northampton). *Dom.* Hardingestone, but *c.* 1123 Hardingestroona. Thought to be a corrup. of '*Harding*'s thorn.' Also HARDINGTON-MANDEVILLE (Yeovil),

Dom. Hardintone. Two *Hardings* in *Onom.*   *Cf.* ARDINGTON
and Hardington (Lamington, Sc.).   See -ton and its interchange with -stone.

HARDWICK(E).   There are said to be 26 in England.   Cambs. H.
c. 1080 *Inquis Cam.* and *K.C.D.* iv. 245 Hardwic, 1171 Herd-
wice, *Dom.* Glouc., Herdeuuic; Bucks, Harduich, -uic; Yorks,
Hardwic and Arduuic; Durham H. 1183 Herdewyk, 1197
Herdewich; Lincs. H. *Dom.* Harduic, 1204 Herduic. Also
K.C.D. iv. 288 Heordewica, perh. in Northants. Usually derived fr. *herd,* ' herd's, shepherd's dwelling.' Skeat insisted
that it could be nothing else, pointing to the form Heordewica,
and to the fact that by rule *eo* in O.E. becomes *a* in our time.
This is indisputable. There is also a word *herdwick* (see *Oxf.
Dict.* s.v.)—*Dom.* ' iii. hardvices,' ? *c.* 1150 herdewica, 1537 herd-
wyk, which is explained as ' the tract of land under the charge
of a herd or shepherd . . . a sheep farm.' But there is this difficulty, that, except occasionally in Northumbld., *herd* is never
pron. *hard ;* and according to *Oxf. Dict.* neither O.E. *heord,
hiord,* 3- *herd,* ' a flock, a herd,' nor *hirde, hierde,* ' a shepherd,'
were ever spelt *hard.* So that the name, in some of its many occurrences, must have been thought to be O.E. *heard wic,* ' hard,
solid dwelling,' *hard* being given as 2-4 *herd.* HARDWICK
PRIORS (Southam) used to belong to the monks of Coventry.
But curiously Duignan can give no early forms for either of the
Warwk. Hardwicks. He, however, gives *a.* 1300 Hordewyke
for Hardwick (Eldersfield, Worstrsh.).   See -wick.

HAREWOOD (Leeds).   *a.* 1142 *Wm. Malmesb.* Harewode.   O.E.
hara-wudu, ' hares' wood.'   *Cf.* HARWELL. But HARESFIELD
(Glouc.), *Dom.* Hersefeld, 1179 Harsefelde, is ' field of *Hersa,*'
though *Onom.* has only *Heorstan.*

HARKSTEAD (Ipswich).   *Dom.* Herchestede. ' Stead, steading, or
dwelling-place of *Heorc* ' or ' *Hark,*' still a surname.   *Onom.* has
only one *Hercus.*

HARLASTON (Tamworth) and HARLESTON (Bungay).   Tam. H.
1004 *chart.* Heorlfestun, *c.* 1100 *ib.* Heorlaveston, *Dom.* Horulve-
stune, *a.* 1200 (H)erlaveston(e), *a.* 1300 Horlaveston. Bun. H.
K.C.D. 1298 Heorulfes tun, *Dom.* Heroluestuna. ' *Heoruwulf's* '
or ' *Heorelf's* town '; 2 in *Onom.*

HARLECH (Barmouth).   W. *hardd llech,* ' beautiful rock.'   So named,
it is said, when Edw. I. built a castle here.

HARLEY (Rotherham and Much Wenlock).   Rot. H. 1179-80 Her-
lega. Mu. H. *Dom.* Harlege. Prob. North. O.E. for ' higher
meadow,' O.E. *héah, hiera,* Angl. *hera,* in 5 *har, her.*   See -ley.

HARLINGTON (Hounslow and Dunstable).   Ho. H. *Dom.* Herdington, but Du. H. *Dom.* Herlingdone. ' Town of *Harding.*' See
HARDINGSTONE. There is no name like *Harding* in *Onom.*, but
cf. HARLTON and the N. *Erling.*

HARLOW HEATH and CAR (Harrogate). Prob. 'grey, hoary-looking hill,' O.E. *hár*, O.N. *hár-r*, and see -low. Car is either O.E. *carr*, 'a rock,' or N. *kjarr*, 'copse, brush wood.' *Cf. Dom.* Essex, Herlaua.

HARLTON (Cambridge). *c.* 1080 *Inquis. Camb.* Harle-, Herletona, 1339 Harleton. Prob. ' *Herla*'s village.' *Cf.* HARLASTON and HARSTON, also Harlsey, E. and W. (N. Riding), *Dom.* Herelsaie, Herlesege, Herselaige, ' isle of *Herla*.' See -ey.

HARNHILL (Cirencester). *Dom.* Harehille, *c.* 1300 Harenhull. Prob. ' grey hill,' O.E. *har, -an,* ' grey, hoary.' *Cf.* Harridge in same shire.

HAROLD (Beds), *old* hare weald, and HAROLD WOOD (Romford). Prob. both O.E. *hara weald*, ' hare wood ' or ' forest region.' *Dom.* Beds. has only Hareuuelle, and it is not in *Dom.* Essex.

HAROME (Nawton, Yorks). *Dom.* Harem, Harun, which last must be a loc. ' at the boundaries,' O.E. *har. Cf.* HALLAM, HARBORNE, etc.

HARPENDEN (Herts). 1250 Harpendene, 1298 Harpeden, and *cf.* 966 in *B.C.S.* iii. 435 Of þære græȝan hane and lang hearpdene. ' Dean, woody vale of the harp,' O.E. *hearpe.* Skeat, however, prefers to derive fr. a man *Herp. Cf. B.C.S.* 34, Herpes ford— *i.e.,* HARPFORD (Devon). There is also a HARPSDEN (Henley-on-Thames). The differing genitives, -en and -es, are against identifying all three. Note, too, HARPHAM (E. Riding), *Dom.* Harpein, where the ending is prob. a corrupt loc. as in HALLAM, etc., and HARPLEY (Worcstrsh.), 1275 Arpeley, Harpele.

HARPERLEY (Co. Durham). 1183 Harperleia. The ' meadow of the harper,' O.E. *hearpere,* O.N. *harpari.* See -ley.

HARRINGAY (N. London). *a.* 1300 Haringee, of which HORNSEY is a corruption. As in HARRINGTON (Cumbld. and Northants) and HARRINGWORTH (Kettering), *Harring* must be, surely, a man's name, possibly a patronymic. There is one *Hæring* in *Onom.,* and *Herring* is still an Eng. surname. See -ing. The -gee in *a.* 1300 is perh. the rare O.E. *ge,* ' region,' which Skeat thought to be found in ELY, Bede's El-ge. But see also -ay. *Cf.* HERRINGBY.

HARROGATE. The original name, *a.* 1600, was Haywra or Heywray, ' hedged-in corner or landmark,' O.N. *hagi* (O.E. *hege*), ' a hedge,' and *wráa,* ' corner, turn, landmark.' *Cf.* WRAWBY. *Hay* and *haw* are very near of kin, and both mean ' hedge,' and *haw-wra* could easily refine into Harro-; while -gate is O.N. *gata,* ' a way, a road,' not the same as the common Eng. *gate,* ' a door.' Possibly the first syll. is O.E. *héah,* 3-5 *hei, hey,* ' high.' *Cf.* HAVERAH and WRAY.

HARROW-ON-THE-HILL. Perh. 767 *chart*. Gumeninga hergae. *Dom*. Herges, *later* Hareways, 1616 *Visscher* Haroue on the hill. Possibly O.E. *hœrg, hearg*, 'a heathen temple.' *Cf*. Pepper-harrow, 1147 Peper Harow. The sb. *harrow* is not found in Eng. till *a*. 1300, as *haru, harwe*, and so cannot be thought of here.

HARSTON (Cambridge and Grantham). Not in *Dom*. Camb. H. 1291 Hardeleston, 1298 Hardlistone, 1316 Hardlestone. Prob. '*Hardulf* or *Heardwulf*'s village' (Skeat).

HARSWELL (York). *Dom*. Ersewelle. More old forms needed. Perh. fr. a man *Erra*, 1 in *Onom*. Perh. fr. O.E. *har*, 'a boundary.' *Cf*. HAROME. Hardly= HARWELL.

HARTINGTON (Buxton). Not in *Dom*. ? *c*. 1150 *Grant* 'Herte-dona in Pecco (Peak).' The central *r* prob. represents a gen., 'hart's hill,' O.E. *herot, heorot*, 'a hart, a stag.' The endings -don and -ton often interchange (*q.v.*).

HARTLEBURY (Kidderminster). 817 and 980 *chart*. Heortlabyrig, 985 *ib*. Heortlanbyrig, *Dom*. Huertberie, *a*. 1200 Hertlebery, 'Burgh of *Heortla*,' otherwise unknown; but *cf*. Harford (North-leach), which is 779 *chart*. Iorotlaford, not in *Dom*.; also IRTH-LINGBORO'.

HARTLEPOOL. *Bede* Heruteu, id est, Insula Cervi; *O.E. vsn., c*. 850 Herotea. *Herot, herut*, or *heorut* is O.E. for 'hart, stag,' the ending -eu is a variant of -ey, 'island' (*q.v.*); whilst *ea* means 'a stream, water,' which points on to the later ending -pool, 1211 Hartepol, 1305 Hertelpol. The letter *l* not seldom intrudes itself. See p. 82.

HARTLEY WINTNEY (Winchfield). Prob. *Dom*. Hardelie (? fr. a man *Heard*), and prob. *Grant* of *a*. 675 Hertlys, Hertlye—a spelling which must be much later than the original grant. 'Hart's meadow.' See above, and -ley. Wintney is 'Winton's isle.' See WINCHESTER. HARTLIP (Sittingbourne) is *c*. 1250 *chart*. Hertlepe, 'hart's leap.' *Cf*. BIRDLIP.

HARTON (Yorks and S. Shields). Yor. H. *Dom*. Heretun. *Cf. Dom*. Haretone (Cheshire). Doubtful. O.E. *here* is 'an army'; but *cf*. HARWELL. HARTPURY (Glouc.), 1221 Hardpirie, Baddeley thinks 'pear-tree,' O.E. *pirige*, 'of' some unknown man. Could it not be simply fr. *hard*, as almost all its old forms seem to indicate?

HARTSHILL (Atherstone). *Dom*. Ardreshille, *a*. 1200 Hardredes-hulle, Hardreshulle. '*Heardred*'s hill,' regularly in Midland M.E. *hull*(e). This is a name to bid one beware! But HARTS-HEAD (Liversedge) is *Dom*. Horteseve, for O.E. *heortes heafod*, 'hart's head' or 'height,' while Harthill (Sheffield) is *Dom*. Hertil. With this last *cf*. Hartell or Hartle (Belbroughton), 1275 Herthulle, 'hart hill.'

HARVINGTON (Chaddesley Corbett). 1275 Herewinton, 1340 Herwynton. '*Herewine*'s town.' But H., Evesham, is 709 *chart.* Herefordtune, 963 *ib.* Herefordtun juxta Avene, *Dom.* Herferthun, 1275 Herrfortune. Here-ford-tune is, of course, 'town of the ford of the army.' The corruption is very remarkable.

HARWELL (Steventon). *O.E. chart.* Haranwylle, *Dom.* Harwelle, Harowelle. Skeat says the man '*Hare* or *Hara*'s well,' O.E. *hara* means 'a hare'; but the sign of the gen. suggests a personal name. HARE- or HARWELL (Notts) is *Dom.* Herewelle, prob. fr. O.E. *here*, 'an army.'

HARWICH. Not in *Dom. a.* 1300 Herewica, Herewyck. O.E. *here-wic*, 'army-dwelling, camp.' See -wich.

HASBURY (Halesowen). *a.* 1300 Haselburi. O.E. *hasel byrig* or *beorh*, 'hazel town' or 'hill.' *Cf.* HASLER, and Hascombe (Godalming), not in *Dom.* But HASFIELD (Glouc.), *Dom.* Has-Hesfelde, is prob. fr. O.E. *hasu, haso*, 'grey,' though *c.* 1300 we have Hersfelde. *Cf. Dom.* Wilts, Haseberie. See -bury.

HASELOR (Alcester), HASELOUR (Tamworth), and HASLER (Solent). Al. H. *Dom.* Haselove, *a.* 1300 Haselovere, Ta. H. *a.* 1300 Hazeloure, *a.* 1400 Haselovere. O.E. *haesel, haesl ofer*, 'hazel bank' or 'border.' *Cf.* HASELEY (Wwk.), *Dom.* Haseleia, and ASHER; also HASILDEN (Glouc.), *Dom.* Hasedene, 1274 Hasilton. See -over.

HASLINGFIELD (Cambridge). *Dom.* Haslingefeld, 1284 Haselingfeld. Patronymic, 'field of the *Hæslings*' or 'sons of *Hazel*,' still a personal name. O.E. *hæsel, hæsl*, 'the hazel-tree.' *Cf.* HASLINGDEN (Lancs), HASLINGTON (Chesh.), and HESLINGTON (Yorks), *Dom.* Haslinton.

HASSOCKS (Sussex). O.E. *hassuc*, 'a clump of matted vegetation,' then 'a clump of bushes or low trees.' *Cf.* (*K.C.D.* 655) 986 *chart.* On one hassuc upp an hrofan hricge.

HASTINGS. 1011 *O.E. Chron.* Haestingas, 1191 *chart.* Barones de Hastingiis. Patronymic; at first a shire distinct from Sussex, prob. called after the E. Saxon viking, *Hasten(g)*, who landed at the mouth of the Thames, *O.E. Chron.* ann. 893. *Cf.* Croix Hastain, Jersey.

HATCH BEAUCHAMP (Taunton), *Dom.* Hache, and HATCH END (Middlesex). *Cf. Dom.* Nfk. and Salop, Hach(e). O.E. *hæc* 3-7 *hacche*, 4 *hach*, 'a hatch'—*i.e.*, 'a half-door, gate, or wicket—then, any small gate or wicket.' *Cf.* COLNEY HATCH.

HATCHAM (S. London) = ATCHAM.

HATFIELD (Worcstr., Herts, Doncaster, Holderness). Wor. H. 1275 Hathfeld, Her. H. *Dom.* Hetfelle, *later* Hethfeld, Don. H. *Bede* Hethfeld, *c.* 850 *O.E. vsn.* Hæþfelda, Hol. H. *Dom.* Hedfeld. O.E. *hæþ felda*, 'heath field, open field.' But GREAT HATFIELD (Hull) is *Dom.* Haie-, Hai -feld or -felt—*i.e.*, 'hay field,' O.E. *hieȝ, héȝ*, 2-4 *hei*, 3-7 *hey(e)*, O.N. *hey*, 'hay.' *Cf.* HEATHFIELD.

HATFORD (Berks). *Dom.* Hevaford (meant for Hevadford), *a.* 1300 Havedford, 1420 Hautford. O.E. *héafod-ford,* ' head-ford, chief ford.'

HATHERLEIGH (Devon), *Exon. Dom.* Hadreleia, and HATHERLEY (Glouc.), 1022 *chart.* Hegberle (? fr. O.E. *heaȝ burh,* ' high castle lea '), *Dom.* Athelai, 1150 Haiderleia, 1177 Hedrelega, 1221 Hathirlege. All except 1022 clearly ' heather meadow.' This is interesting, as *Oxf. Dict.'s* earliest form is 1335 *hathir,* and it thinks it must be quite Northern, while postulating an orig. *hœdder, hœddre. Cf.* UTTOXETER. But HATHEROP (Fairford), *Dom.* Etherope, 1148 Haethrop, 1275 Hatrope, 1294 Haythorp, Baddeley makes ' hedged village,' O.E. *hege,* M.E. *heie,* ' a hedge.' See next, -leigh and -thorpe.

HATHERTON (Nantwich and Cannock). Can. H. 996 *chart.* Hagenthorndun—*i.e.,* ' hawthorn hill '—*Dom.* Hargedone, *a.* 1300 Hatherdone, -dene, Hetherdon. An instructive list ! See above.

HATLEY ST. GEORGE (Sandy). *K.C.D.* iv. 300 Hættanlca, *Dom.* Hatelai, Atelai, 1284 Hattele. *Cf. Dom.* Hatlege (Salop). ' *Hœtta's* lea.' See -ley.

HATTON (4 in *P.G.*). Duignan says, all Midland Hattons are O.E. *hœth-tún,* ' town on the heath.' *Cf.* HATFIELD. None in *Dom.*

HAUGHTON (Stafford), *Dom.* Haltone, *a.* 1200 Halecton, *a.* 1300 Halechtone, Haluch-, Haleg-tone; HAUGHTON GREEN (Manchester), 1314 Halghton; HAUGHTON-LE-SKERNE (Darlington), *a.* 1130 *Sim. Dur.* Halhtun, 1183 Halctona, later Halughton. This last is also the spelling of a place in Leicester, *chart.* Edw. III. Thus HALLOUGHTON (Kingsbury) is the same name, *a.* 1400 Halghton, Halugh-, Haluton ; the Notts one is 1291 Halton. O.E. *healh, halh,* 2-3 *halech,* 4-7 *hawgh,* 5-*haugh,* ' a flat meadow by a riverside.' *Cf.* Haigh (Wigan), Halugh (Bolton), Halton and Haighton (N. Lancs), *Dom.* Halctun and HOUGHTON ; also see -hall and -ton. SKERNE is a river. But HAUGHTON (Notts), *Dom.* Hoctun, 1278 Hockton, Mutschmann derives fr. a man *Hoc.*

HAUNTON. See HANWELL.

HAUXLEY-ON-COQUET. *a.* 1130 *Sim. Dur.* Hafodscalfe, which is prob. O.E. *heafodes scelfe* (O.N. *skjálf-r*), ' head, of the shelf or ledge of rock.' The corruption is curious.

HAUXTON (Cambridge). *c.* 1060 Hauekstune, *Dom.* Havochestun, 1316 Haukestone. ' Village of *Hafoc* '—*i.e.,* ' the Hawk,' still a personal name. *Cf.* Hawkesbury (Coventry), HAWKSWORTH and Hauxwell (Yorks), *Dom.* Hauocswelle.

HAVANT (Portsmouth). O.E. *chart.* Hamanfunta,. ' fountain, font, well of *Hama,*' 4 in *Onom.* The present form is simply a phonetic wearing down of the O.E. name. *Dom.* is Havehunte, where the *h* is prob. error for *f. Cf.* CHALFONT and FOVANT.

HAVERAH PARK. See HARROGATE.

HAVERFORD WEST (Pembroke). *c.* 1188 *Gir. Camb.* Itin. Haverfordia; *c.* 1200 *Gervase* Haverforde, 1603 Harford. In W. Hwlffordd or Cæralun. 'Oats-fjord,' O.N. *hafre,* pl. *hafrar,* Dan. *havre,* 'oats'; for -ford= N. *fjord, cf.* Waterford opposite, and MILFORD. The W. Hwl- must be a corrup. (? of *hywl,* 'a sail'); while *ffordd* in W. means 'a road, a passage.' The full form Haverfordwest is found as early as 1603 *Owen.*

HAVERING (Romford). *Dom.* Haveringas, 1160 *Pipe* Hauering. Prob. patronymic, 'place of the sons of *Haver*' or '*Haward.*' See HAVERSGATE, and -ing.

HAVERSGATE ISLAND (Orford). Not in *Dom.* This is prob. '*Haward's* road or way,' O.E. *geat.* Five *Hawards* in *Onom.* But HAVERTHWAITE (Ulverston), 1201 Haverthuayt, will be 'oat-place' or 'farm.' See HAVERFORD, and -thwaite.

HAWARDEN (Flintsh.). Pron. Harrden. *Cf.* CARDEN. *Dom.* Havrdin, *Inquis. p.m.* Hauwerthyn. 'Hedged farm,' Eng. *haw,* O.E. *haga,* 'a hedge,' and see -warden. *Cf.* HARDEN, which is, N.B., 'high farm.' The Mod. W. is Pennar Lag or 'high enclosure by the lake,' more correctly, *pen arth leg.*

HAWES (Kirkby Stephen). O.E. and O.N. *háls,* 'the neck, a col,' common in Northern place-names for 'the connecting ridge between two heights.' See *Oxf. Dict.* s.v. HAUSE.

HAWKSWORTH (W. Ridg. and Notts). W. R. H. *Dom.* Hauoc(h)-esorde. Not.H.*Dom.* Hochesuorde,*c.* 1190 Houkeswrthe. 'Hawk's place or farm,' O.E. *heafoc, hafoc,* 3-5 *hauk(e),* 'a hawk.' See -worth. *Cf.* Hawkridge (Berks). *O.E. chart.* Heafoc hrycg, and 940 *chart.* Hafuc cnollum (Pewsey, Wilts); also Hawkbach, *a.* 1400 Haukebache, 'hawk valley' (see COMBERBACH). Wherever you have the -s of the gen. *Hawk* will be a man's name. *Cf.* HAUXTON, Hawkswick (W. Riding), *Dom.* Hocheswic, and Hawksbury (Foleshill), *a.* 1400 Haukesbury, Hawkesbury (Wickwar.), *Dom.* Havochesberie, also *Dom.* Kent, Havochesten.

HAWNBY (Holmsley, Yorks). *Dom.* Halmebi, 1201 *Fines* Halmiby, 1298 Hainleghe. 'Meadow' or 'dwelling' of *Helm* or *Helma,*' 2 such in *Onom. Al* easily becomes *aw,* and *m* often changes into its kindred liquid *n. Cf.* HAWTON (Notts), *Dom.* Holtone, 'dwelling in the holt' or 'wood.' See -by and -leigh.

HAWSTEAD (Bury St. Edmunds). 1298 Haustede. 'Place (Sc. 'steading') with a hedge or fence,' O.E.*haga,* 4-9 *haw(e).* Haw, O.E. *haga,* and *hay,* O.E. *hege,* are, of course, cognate, and both mean 'hedge,' but they are not the same words.

HAXBY (York). *Dom.* Haxebi. 'Dwelling of *Hacca,*' 2 in *Onom. Cf.* HAXEY, Doncaster; (see -ey). See -by.

HAY (N.E. of Brecon). *c.* 1188 *Gir. Camb.* Itin. Haia, Haya. O.E. *hege,* 4-9 *hay(e),* 'a hedge, a fence,' cognate with *haw,* and *hedge. Cf.* above and OXHEY. In W. it is Tregelli, 'house among the woods.' HAYWOOD, Great (Rugeley) is *Dom.* Hai-wode.

HAYDOCK (St. Helen's). 1168-69 Hedoc, 1170-01 Heddock, 1286 Haydok, 1321 Heydok, 1565 Heghdoyk. Seems to be O.E. *hege-docce*, ' hedge of dock or docken.' *Cf.* DOCCOMBE and HAY. *Dock* for ships is a late word. W. and H. are quite uncertain, and suggest a man's name, unknown, for the first part, and O.E. *ác*,' oak,' for the second. HAYDEN (Glouc.), 1220 Heidun, 1222 Heydunn, certainly seems fr. O.E. *hege*, M.E. *heie*, ' hedge,' whilst HAYTON (Notts), 1154-89 Haythona, may be fr. O.E. *hœþ*, ' a heath.'

HAYES (Uxbridge). 793 *chart.* Hǽse, *Dom.* Hesa, *later* Hease, Heyse, Hays. Doubtful; perh. for O.E. *hasu, heasu*, ' grey or tawny-looking.' Possibly fr. O.E. *œs*, 2 *ese*, 4 *hes*, ' carrion '; for ending -a or -e= ' watery place,' see -ey.

HAYLE, THE, or SALTINGS R. (Bodmin). Corn. *hœl*, ' a tidal river.'

HAYLING I. (Portsmouth). *Dom.* Halingei. Prob. a patronymic, ' isle of the *Halings*,' though there is no such name in *Onom.* *Cf.* HALLINGTON, and -ey.

HAZLEHURST (Cobham). *Grant* of *c.* 675 Hasulhurst, *c.* 1200 *Gervase* Heselherste. ' Hazel-tree wood,' O.E. *hœsel*, and see -hurst. *Cf.* Haslewood (W. Riding), *Dom.* Heselewode.

HEADLESS CROSS (Redditch). Curious corrup. 1675 Hedley's Cross. We find a Wm. de *Hedley* in this district in 1275.

HEALAUGH (Tadcaster). *Dom.* Hailaga, Helage, O.E. *héah leah*, ' high meadow '; -laugh is a rare form of -leigh or -ley (*q.v.*). *Cf.* next and HEADON (Notts), *Dom.* Hedune.

HEALEY (Masham and Rochdale), and HEALEYFIELD (Co. Durham). Dur. H. 1183 *Boldon Bk.* Heleie, -ey. O.E. *héah léah*, ' high meadow.' *High* is 4-6 *hee, he, hie*. *Cf.* above and HEATON; and see -ley.

HEAPHAM (Gainsborough). Not in *Dom. Cf.* 1200 *chart.* Hepedale. Prob. ' home of *Heppo*,' several in *Onom.* Perh. fr. O.E. *héope*, ' the fruit of the wild rose,' a hip, 4-5 *hepe* 5 *heepe. Cf.* HEPWORTH.

HEATHFIELD (Sussex and Newton Abbot). Sus. H. not in *Dom.*, local pron. Hefful. Ne. H. *Dom.* Hetfeld, -felle—*i.e.*, ' heath field.' See HATFIELD and *cf.* ? *c.* 1150 *Grant* Hethcote, Peak District.

HEATON (7 in *P.G.*). *Dom.* Hetun, Etun (Yorks), Hetune (Salop). O.E. *héah*, 4-6 *hee, he, hie*,' high.' Similarly Headon and Hedon (Hull) are ' high hill.' *Cf.* HEALEY; and see -ton.

HEBBURN (Jarrow) and HEBBURN BELL (hill, Belford). *a.* 1130 *Sim. Dur.* Heabyrn and Hybberndune. Heabyrn is certainly Early Eng. for ' high burn or brook,' O.E. *héah, héa*. Hybbern-looks more like ' hip-burn,' brook along which the hips grow,

4-6 *heppe*, 6-7 *hep*. *Cf.* above. The personal name is usually spelt Hepburn. See HEPBORNE. *Bell*, of course, refers to the shape of the *dune* or hill; *Oxf. Dict.* gives no instances of such a usage.

HECKFIELD (Basingstoke). ' Field of *Heca* '; one was Bp. in Sussex, 1047. *Cf.* 836 *chart*. ' Heccaham.' *Dom.* has only Heceford. We get the patronymic in HECKINGTON (Lincs). *Cf. Dom.* Nfk. Hechincham.

HEDDINGTON (Calne). ' Town of *Headda* ' or ' *Hedde*,' a common O.E. name. *Cf.* 1158-59 *Pipe* Hedendon (Oxfd.), and *Dom.* Essex Hidingeforda. Perh. patronymic. See -ing.

HEDNESFORD (Cannock). *a.* 1400 Hedenesford, Edenesford. ' Ford of *Heoden*.' *Cf. B.C.S.* 544 Hednesdene, and Henshaw, Haltwhistle, *old* Hedneshalgh. See HAUGHTON.

HEDWORTH (Jarrow). *a.* 1130 *Sim. Dur.* Heathewurthe. ' Heathplace.' The *d* ending for *heath* is seen also in the Ger. and Du. *heide*, O.N. *heið-r.* See -worth.

HEELEY (Sheffield). ' High lea or meadow '; O.E. *héah*, 4-6 *hee*, *he*, *hie*. *Cf.* HEALEY ; also HEIGHLEY CAS. (Staffs). *Dom.* Heolle, *a.* 1300 Helegh, Helley. Duignan makes this a hybrid fr. W. *heol*, ' a road, a way.' See -ley.

HEIGHAM POTTER (Norfolk). *Dom.* Hecham, 1444 Heigham Porter and H. Potter. ' High home,' O.E. *héah hám*, 4-6 *heigh*, as still in Sc. *Cf.* Heighton (Sussex), and HIGHAM. Potter is a corrup. of Porter through the vanishing of the liquid *r*.

HELLESDEN (Norfolk). 1450 Heylesden, -don, Haylysdon. ' The woody vale ' or ' the hill of ' some man with a name in O.E. beginning with *Hæl-* or *Heal-*. There are several such. Possibly fr. the Scandinavian ogress *Hel*, the Northern Proserpine ; hence the Eng. *hell*. *Dom.* has only Helesham. *Cf.* HELSTON ; and see -den and -don.

HELLIFIELD (Skipton). *Dom.* Helge-, Hælgefeld. Either ' *Helgi*'s or *Helga*'s field '; or fr. O.E. *halig, haleg*, 3-4 *heli*, ' holy.' *Cf.* Helbeck (Aysgarth, N. Riding), 1230 *Close R.* Helebec. See -beck, and Hellaby (S. Yorks), *Dom.* Elgebi.

HELMDON (Brackley). ? *Dom.* Elmedene (*Oxf. Dict.* has no spelling of *elm* with *h*). Prob. O.E. *helm-dún*, ' top of the hill,' fr. *helm*, ' top, summit, then, helmet.' *Cf.* ' Helm o' the Hill ' (S. of Felton), and next.

HELMINGHAM (Stowmarket). *Sic* in *Dom.* *Cf.* 838 *chart.* Helmanhyrst. ' Home of the sons of *Helma* ' or ' *Helm*.' *Cf.* next, and *Dom.* Yorks Helmeswelle, now Emswell ; and see -ing.

HELMINGTON (Bps. Auckland). *a.* 1130 *Sim. Dur.* Helme, Healme, which is O.E. for ' top, summit '; taken later for a proper name, and -ington added. *Cf.* above.

HELMSLEY (N. Yorks). *Dom.* Elmeslac (3 times), Hamelsec (4 times) Almeslai (once). The last form is the present name, the man ' *Helm's* meadow.' *Cf.* above. But the other forms look like ' *Helm's* ' or else ' *Hamel's* oak,' O.E. *ác.* See -ley.

HELPERBY (York). *Sic* 1441, but *Dom.* Hilprebi, Ilprebi. ' Dwelling of *Helpric* or *Helpericus,*' names in *Onom.* To make it ' dwelling of the *helper* ' (a word in Eng. *a.* 1300) would be contrary to analogy. *Cf.* HELPERTHORPE (Yorks), *Dom.* Elpe-torp, and next. See -by.

HELPRINGHAM (Sleaford). *Dom.* Helperichā, -rincham. ' Home of the sons of *Helperic.*' *Cf.* HELPERBY, and see -ing.

HELPSTON (Mket. Deeping). *a.* 1100 *chart.* Helpeston. ' Dwelling, village of *Helpo,*' 2 in *Onom.* *Cf.* the mod. name Helps, and *Dom.* Bucks Helpeswrth.

HELSTON (Falmouth). *Sic* 1432, 1200 Helleston. Possibly hybrid, fr. Corn. *hellas,* ' a marsh.' But *cf.* HELLESDEN.

HELSTRY KINGSLEY (Cheshire). It prob. is the goddess ' *Hel's* tree.' *Cf.* HELLESDON, OSWESTRY, and HELSBY (Cheshire), *Dom.* Helesbe.

HELVELLYN ((Mtn., Cumberld.). Prob. Kelt. for ' yellow-looking slope,' *hel felyn,* Corn. *velen,* ' yellow.' But *hel* is a somewhat doubtful Kelt. root. There are 3 places in Wales in *P.G.* called Velindre or ' yellow house.'

HEMEL HAMPSTEAD (Herts). *Dom.* Hamelamestede, Henamestede (error), 1303 Hemelhamstead. ' Homestead, home place,' O.E. *hám-stede,* ' of *Hemele,*' several in *Onom.* *Cf.* HEMSWORTH, also HEMLINGTON (N. Riding), *Dom.* Himelintun, Himeligetun, a patronymic fr. *Hemel ; Dom.* Norfk. Hemelingetun. See -ing. HEMPSTEAD (Glouc.), *Dom.* Hechanestede, *c.* 1120-30 Heccamstede, 1230 Ehamstede, may mean ' high homestead,' O.E. *héah,* ' high,' or may be fr. *Hecca, -an,* a man. It is often found in full as Heyhamstede, etc.

HEMINGBURGH (Selby), *Knytlinga Saga* Hemingaborg, and HEMINGBY (Horncastle), *Dom.* Hamingebi. ' Fort of *Heming,*' and ' dwelling of *Heming,*' 3 in *Onom.* See -burgh and -by.

HEMPNALL (Norwich). *Dom.* Hemenhala. *Cf. c.* 1490 ' Hemnales ' (Suffolk). ' Nook of *Hemma,*' 3 in *Onom.* For intrusion of *p, cf.* BROMPTON, HAMPTON, etc. *Cf.* HEMPSHILL (Notts), *Dom.* Hamessel, *c.* 1200 Hemdeshill, Hemsby (Gt. Yarmouth), and 1166-67 *Pipe* Heimbia (Devon). See -hall.

HEMSWORTH (Wakefield). *Dom.* Hameleswrde, Hilmeword. ' Farm of *Hamele.*' *Cf.* HEMEL HAMPSTEAD ; and see -worth.

HENDON (London). O.E. *chart.* Hean dun (inflected form) *Dom.* Handune. A Keltic origin is out of the question. It is plainly ' high hill,' as it is ; or else possibly ' *Hean's* hill.' *Cf. B.C.S.*

246 Heanes pol, also HENSTILL (Sandford, Crediton), 930 *chart.*
Henne stigel, where *henne* is either O.E. for ' hen,' or inflected
form of *heáh,* ' high ' ; *stigel* is ' a step, a ladder, a stile.'   HEN-
CASTER (Wstmld.), *Dom.* Hennecastre, must be ' high camp,'
whilst HENACRE (Glouc.), *c.* 1196 Heneacre, is ' high field,' and
HENBARROW (same shire), ' high tumulus.'

HENFIELD (Sussex). *Dom.* Hamfeld. As the liquids *m* and *n* so
   often interchange, Ham- is prob. O.E. *héan,* inflected or loc.
   form of *heáh,* ' high,' so ' high field.'   *Cf.* HANBURY and Hen-
   knolle, 1183 in *Boldon Bk.*, Durham.

HENGSTON HILL (Cornwall). *O.E. Chron.* 835 Hengesterdun. ' Hill
   of *Hengest,*' but not necessarily the comrade of Horsa, A.D. 449.
   O.E. *hengest* means ' a male horse, usually a gelding.'   *Cf.*
   HINCKSEY etc. A Hengest, vassal of the Danes, is mentioned
   in Beowulf and other early O.E. poems. Baddeley thinks
   HENGASTON (Berkeley) may be for O.E. *héan gœrstun,* 'high
   grass-town.'   *Cf.* Wallgaston, near by, 1243-45 Walhamgarston.

HENHAM (Bps. Stortford). *Sic* in *Dom., c.* 1220 *Elect. Hugo*
   Hengham.   O.E. *héan hám,* ' high house,' *héan* inflected form
   of *heáh.*

HENLEY (R. Thames, and in Arden). Th. H. 727 *chart.* Henlea,
   Dom. Henlei ; Wwk. H. *a.* 1200 Henlea, *a.* 1400 Henley in Arde(r)n.
   Either O.E. *héan leáh,* 'high meadow,' *héah* being inflected, or
   henn-leáh, ' hen meadow.' There are also ' Henley ' (Ipswich)
   and ' Henlei,' *Dom.* Surrey. E. and W. HENDRED (Wantage).
   O.E. chart. Henna rith, is ' hens', water-hens' rill.'   HENWOOD
   (Solihull), *a.* 1200 Hinewud, is more likely fr. O.E. *hina,* 3 *hine,*
   5 *heynd,* 7 *hiend,* ' a hind, a servant'; but HENMARSH (Glouc.),
   1236 Hennemerse, will be ' moor-hen marsh.'

HENSALL (Whitley Br.). *Dom.* Edeshale, which seems to be for
   ' *Ædan's* ' or ' *Edan's* nook.' See -hall. But HENSHAW (Halt-
   whistle) is *c.* 1147 Hethingeshalch ; also Hedneshalgh—*i.e.,*
   ' *Heoden's* haugh ' or ' river-meadow,' influenced by North.
   Eng. *shaw,* O.E. *scaga,* ' a wood.'

HENSTRIDGE (Somerset). *Dom.* Hengesterich, O.E. *chart.* Hen-
   gestes ricg, O.E. for ' *Hengest's* ridge.'   See HENGSTON.

HEPBORNE or HAYBORNE (Wooler).   *c.* 1330 Hebhorn, 1363 Hib-
   burne, 1366 Hebburne. ' Burn, brook with the hips,' the fruit
   of the wild rose, O.E. *héope, hiope,* 4-9 *hep(e).*   *Cf.* HEBBURN.

HEPWORTH (Huddersfield). *Dom.* Heppeword. ' Farm of *Heppo.*'
   Cf. HEAPHAM ; and see -worth.

HEREFORD.   1048 *O.E. Chron.* Herefordseir, 1260 Herford. ' Fort
   of the army,' O.E. *here.* Curiously, we get much older forms,
   s.v. HARVINGTON (Evesham), which is 709 Herefordtune, etc.
   In 1161-62 *Pipe* we still read of ' Herefort in Waliis.'

HERMANSOLE (farm, Canterbury). 'Herman's pond or pool,' O.E. *sol*, 'mire, a muddy place,' now only Kent. dial. *sole*. *Cf.* Maydensole (Dover).

HERNE HILL (London) and HERNE BAY (Kent). *Cf. K.C.D.*, iii. 279. 'Earnhylle,' O.E. *hyrne*, M.E. *herne, hirn*, 'a corner, nook, hiding - place.' *Cf. Dom.* Hants Herne, and Essex Witbrictes herna.

HERRINGBY (Norfolk). *Dom.* Harringebi, *c.* 1456 Haryngby. 'Dwelling of *Herring*.' Still a surname, patronymic fr. *Heara*, gen. *Hearan. Cf.* Herringswell (Mildenhall). See -by.

HERRINGFLEET (Suffolk). *Dom.* Herlingaflet, 1361 Herlyngflet. 'River of the Herlings'; patronymic, (?) fr. *Herlewine*, 3 in *Onom. Cf. K.C.D.* 782 Herlingaham or HURLINGHAM. See FLEET.

HERSHAM (Walton-on-Thames). Not in *Dom.*, but *cf. Dom.* Norfk. Hersam. 'Home of' some one of the many men with names in *Here-, Heremod, Heresic, Hereweald*, etc.

HERSTMONCEUX (Pevensey). 'Hurst, forest (of Anderida), belonging to the Norman family *Monceaux.*' O.E. *hyrst* means 'a knoll, a hillock,' as well as 'a wood.'

HERTFORD. *Bede* Herutford, 1087 *Ordinance Wm. I.* Hertfordscire, 1258 Hurtford. 'Ford of the hart.' O.E. *heorut*, 3-6 *hert*, 'a hart.' The mod. pron. of the place-name always has the *a* sound. *Cf.* Harford (Glouc.), 743 *chart.* Heort ford, 802 *ib.* Hereforda, *Dom.* Hurford, 1221 Harford.

HESELTON, MONK and COLD (Durham). *a.* 1130 *Sim. Dur.* Heseldene. 'DEAN, den (wooded), valley with the hazels.' O.E. *hæsel.*

HESKETH BANK (Southport). 1283-92 Heskayth, 1292 Eskayth. Wyld says, O.N. *hest skeiþ*, 'race course.' It seems possibly a plural form of W. *hesg*, 'sedges.' *Cf.* WERNETH, 'place of alders'; but the ending -ayth is against this; also the rarity of W. names here.

HESLINGTON. See HASLINGFIELD.

HESSLE (Hull). *Dom.* Hasele, which must be O.E. *hæsel-léah*, 'hazel mead.' (*Cf. Dom.* Salop, Hesleie, and HESLEY, Notts, 1217 Heselay.) But it seems to be 1179-80 *Pipe* Hessewell, Hesiwald, which corresponds with an Ashwell or Heswell, 1239 in *Calend. Pap. Reg.*, i. 181, 'ash-tree well.' *Cf.* 1298 'Gerardus de Hesebrygge.'

HETTON (Skipton). *Dom.* Hetune. O.E. *héah tún*, 'high town.' *Cf.* Hewick (Yorks), *Dom.* Hawie. But HETTON-LE-HOLE (Co. Durham) seems to be 1516-17 *Durham Acc. Rolls* Hett, where Hett is doubtful.

HEVER (Eden Br.). *Sic* 1327, but 1278 Heure, also Evere. Prob. for *he-over*, or *he-oure*, 'high bank,' OE. *héah ofr. Cf.* HEELEY and WOOLER, and see= over.

HEVERSHAM or EVER- (Westmld.). *Dom.* Eureshaim, *a.* 1130 *Sim. Dur.* Hefresham. 'Home of *Eofor*'—*i.e.*, 'the wild-boar.' See -ham.

HEWORTH (Felling, Durham). 1183 Ewwrth. Prob. O.E. *iw worth*, 'yew-tree farm'; but possibly fr. a man *Eva*, *Eua*, or *Ewa*. Such names are known. See -worth.

HEXHAM. Prob. *c.* 410 *Notitia* Axelodunum, *Bede* Hagulstad, *c.* 1097 *Orderic* Haugustalda, *a.* 1130 *Sim. Dur.* Extoldesham, *a.* 1200 *John Hexham* Hestoldes-, Hextildesham, *c.* 1300 Hexelesham, 1421 Hexhamshire. A curious and difficult name. The *Notitia* name is not certainly Hexham. If it is, Axelo-dunum is certainly Kelt. for 'high hill,' and the O.E. name may be a corruption of this. But O.E. *hagosteald* is ' a young soldier, a bachelor.' *Cf. B.C.S.*, i. 97, Hægstaldes cumb (Somerset). It is often said to be ' home on the *Hestild*.' Two brooks, said once to have been called Hextol and Halgut, now the Cockshaw and Cowgarth burns, meet here.

HEXTABLE (Swanley). Not in *Dom.* Perh. '*hatch staple*,' O.E. *hæc*, -*ce*, M.E. *hec*, *hek*, 'a hatch, wicket-gate,' and *stapol*, 'a pole or pillar marking the boundary of an estate.' *Cf.* HEXTON (Bewdley), 1227 Hekstane. However, the names *Heca*, *Hecca*, and *Hecci* are common in O.E., and may well be postulated here. *Cf.* HEXTHORP (Yorks), *Dom.* Hestorp, Estorp.

HEYBRIDGE (Maldon). Prob. *Dom.* Hobruge (*cf.* HOE), ? *c.* 1250 *Visitation Churches belonging to St. Paul's* Heubrege. Prob. ' high bridge,' O.E. *héah*, 3-5 *hey*, *hei*; possibly fr. O.E. *hég*, *heg*, 3-7 *hey*, 'hay.' *Cf. Roll Rich. I.*, ' Haiscot ' (Essex). The HEYDONS (there are several) are prob. all ' high hill.' *Cf.* 1166-67 *Pipe* Hidon (Devon). *Cf.* EYAM.

HEYSHAM (N. Lancs). *Dom.* Hessam, 1094 Heseym, 1216 Hesam. ' *Hesa*'s home.' *Cf.* HESSLE, and see -ham.

HIBALDSTOW (Brigg). *a.* 1100 *Grant* of 664 Hibaltestow, 1179-80 Hybaldestow, Hibolstowe. ' Place of *Hibald* ' or ' *Hygebeald*,' common in *Onom.* See STOW.

HICKLETON (Doncaster). *Dom.* Chichelteone (*cf.* KEIGHLEY), Icheltone. ' Town of *Hicel*.' See next.

HICKLING (Melton Mowbray). *Dom.* Hechel-, Hegelinge, 1298 Hikellinge. Prob. a patronymic. *Cf. B.C.S.* 862, ' Hiceles wyrþe ' (Salisbury). ' Place of *Hicel*'s descendants.' *Cf.* above.

HIGHAM FERRERS (Northants). *c.* 1060 *chart.* Hecham, 1465 *Rolls Parlmt.* Heigham Feres. ' High house or home,' O.E. *héah*, 4-6 *heigh*. *Cf.* HEIGHAM. William *Ferrers*, Earl of Derby, became lord of the manor here in 1199. But HIGHNAM (Glouc.), *old* Hynehamme, is ' the enclosure of the hinds,' or ' servants.' See -ham.

HILBOROUGH (Norfk.) [*Dom.* Hildeburhwella] and HILLBOROUGH (Stratford, Wwk.). Str. H. 710 *chart.* Hildeburhwrthe, *later* Hildeborde, Hildebereurde; *a.* 1200 Hilburgewrth; 1317 Hildeboreworth. A very interesting corrup.—a woman, '*Hildeburh*'s farm.' *Cf.* Hilston (Holderness), *Dom.* Heldovestun, Heldeweston, ? fr. *Heldwulf,* one in *Onom.*; whilst HILCOTE (Glouc.) is *old* Hyldecote, fr. O.E. *hylde,* ' a slope.'

HILBREE I. and POINT (Cheshire). 1577 Hilbery. Possibly W. *hel bre,* ' bank on the hill or brae.' Eng. *bree* sb¹ ' eye-brow ' (*Oxf. Dict.*) never seems used for ' brae ' or hill-slope, though Skeat says it doubtless had also this sense. Of course, Hilbery could mean . ' hill-fort ' or ' burgh,' only *burgh* or *bury* very rarely becomes *bree.*

HILDENBOROUGH (Tonbridge), not in *Dom.*, and HILDENLEY (N. Yorks). *Dom.* Hildingeslei, Ildingeslei. This last is ' meadow of *Hilding,*' patronymic fr. *Hilda.*' The first name may be fr. the simple *Hilda.* HILLESLEY (Wickwar) is *Dom.* Hildeslei. See -borough and -ley.

HILDERSHAM (Cambridge). *Dom.* and *chart.* Hildricesham. ' Home of *Hilderic,*' one in *Onom.* *Cf.* HINDERWELL. HILDERTHORPE (Yorks) is *Dom.* Hilgertorp, or '*Hildegar*'s village.'

HILGAY (Cambs). *c.* 1080 *Inquis. Camb.* Helingheie, *Ramsey Chron.* Helingeye. Patronymic. ' Isle of the *Hellings.*' *Cf.* Hellingly (Sussex), and see -ay.

HIMBLETON (Droitwich). 816 *chart.* Hymeltun, *Dom.* Himeltun; and HIMLEY (Dudley), *Dom.* Himelie;, *a.* 1200 Humilileg, Humileg; *a.* 1300 Humilele, Hymele. Perh. ' town ' and ' meadow of *Hemele,*' common in *Onom.* Duignan, owing to lack of all sign of the possessive, prefers to derive fr. O.E. *hymele,* ' the hop plant,' and refers to Hemlington and HAMBLETON (Yorks), which are both fr. a man *Hamel* or *Hemel.* But there is at Himbleton a stream, 956 *chart.* hymel broc, which does seem ' hop-plant brook,' and the early spellings also favour ' the hopplant ' origin.

HINCKLEY (Leicester). *Dom.* Hinchelie. ' Meadow of *Hynca,*' one in *Onom.* See -ley. But for HINCASTER, see HENCASTER, ' high camp.' HINCHWICK, Condicote, 1294 Henewyk, 1307 Hynewyke, is perh. O.E. *henge wie,* ' steep village. *Cf.* HINKSFORD.

HINDERWELL (N. Riding). *Dom.* Heldrewelle, Hildre-, Ildrewelle; 1179-80 *Pipe* Hilder-, Hirderwalle. ' Well of *Hild* or *Held.*' The r may be the N. gen., but we also find 3 *Heldreds* and a *Hilderic* in *Onom.* The liquids *l* and *n* do interchange. *Cf.* HILDERSHAM and Hinderskelf, now Castle Howard (Yorks), *Dom.* Hildreschelf, Ilderschelf. Shelf often occurs for ' ledge of rock.'

HINDLIP, HINLIP (Worcester). 'Hind's leap,' O.E. *hlýp*, 3 *lip*, 'a leap.' *Cf.* **BIRDLIP.**

HINGHAM (Norfolk). *Dom.* Hincham, often, 1452 Hengham. Possibly contracted fr. '*Hengest*'s ham' or 'home.' Older forms needed. *Onom.* has one *Hength*.

HINKSEY (Oxford). *O.E. chart.* Hengesteseie, -ige; 1297 Hencsei. '*Hengest's* isle.' *Cf.* **HENGSTON** and **HINXWORTH.** **HINKSFORD,** Kingswinsford, is 1271 Henkeston, 1300 Hinkesford, more prob. fr. *Hynca*, as in **HINCKLEY.**

HINTLESHAM (Ipswich). *Dom.* and *sic* 1157. Puzzling. The nearest name in *Onom.* is *Hinwald* or *Hinieldus*. Possibly *Hintel* is dimin. of the known name *Hunta*. See -ham.

HINTON WALDRIST or **WALDRIDGE** (Berks; 10 Hintons besides in *P.G.*). Dorset H. *chart.* Hine-, Hyneton; Ber. H. *B.C.S.*, iii. 228, Heantunninga, *Dom.* Hentone; Cambs H. *Dom.* Hintone; Glouc. H. 1303 Henton. The *B.C.S.* form means 'dwellers in Heantun'—*i.e.*, 'high town,' O.E. *héan*, dat. of *héah*, 'high.' But the Hintons are not all the same, and come most of them fr. O.E. *hina*, gen. of *hiwan*, 'domestic servants, hinds,' or else fr. *hind*, 'a female deer.' See -ton. Waldrist is fr. O.E. *Wealdric*. He was King's Chancellor 1100-35. See *Chron. Abing.*, ii. 127.

HINTS (Tamworth and Ludlow). Tam. H. *Dom.* Hintes, *a.* 1300 Hyntes. Duignan thinks W. *hynt*, 'a road, way,' with Eng. pl. *s*.

HINXTON (S. Cambs). and **HINXWORTH** (Herts) *Ramsey Chron.* Hengestone, 1277 Hengeston, 1341 Hyngeston. *Dom.* Haingeste uuorde. '*Hengest*'s farm' and 'village.' *Cf.* **HINXTON** (Essex) and **HINKSEY,** and see -ton and -worth.

HIPPERHOLME (Halifax). *Dom.* Huperun. It seems hard to explain Huper or Hipper. There is nothing likely in *Onom.* unless it be *Hygebeorht* or *Hubert;* but it may be a dissimilated form of *hipple*, 5 *hupple*, see next, and mean 'at the little heaps,' -un being an old loc., which either becomes -holme, 'riverside meadow,' or -ham, *q.v.*

HIPSWELL (Richmond, Yorks). *Dom.* Hiplewelle, *c.* 1538 *Leland* Ipreswel. There is no name at all likely here, so this must be 'well at the *hipple*,' or 'little heap,' first recorded in *Oxf. Dict.* in 1382 as *hypil, heepil*, and derived fr. O.E. * *hiepel, hýpel*, *cf.* Ger. *haüfel*.

HIRWAIN (Aberdare). W. *hir gwaen*, 'long plain' or 'meadow.' It anciently stretched for ten miles.

HISSINGTON (Herefdsh.). *Dom.* Hesintune. Prob. 'town of *Hesa*,' a name not in *Onom. Cf. Dom.* Bucks, Hesintone.

HISTON (Cambridge). *c.* 1080 *Inquis. Camb.* Hestitona, *Dom.* Histetone, Histone, 1165 Hestona. 'Village of *Hesta* or *Hæsta*.'

HITCHIN. *Dom.* Hiz, 1210 Hiche, 1303 Huche, 1346 Hicheyn, 1541 Hechyn. *Dom.*'s Hiz = Hits. The name, it would seem, can only mean *Hicca*'s (place) ; a *Hica* and a *Hicca* in *Onom.* Had the -in been early it would prob. have represented an old loc., but it seems quite late. For similar names (which are rare), *cf.* BEEDON, BRAILES, COVEN, etc. The R. on which it stands, formerly the Hitche, seems to have been rechristened Hiz after *Dom.* HITCHAM, Ipswich and Maidenhead, ' *Hicca*'s home,' show what the normal forms of this name would have been.

HIXON (Stafford). *Dom.* Hustedone, *a.* 1300 Huntesdun, Huhtes-Hucste-, Hucces-, Huncesdon; *a.* 1600 Hickston, Hixeton. It is on a ' hill,' and the ending is clearly -don, *q.v.* The proper name which comes before is a puzzle. *Huch, Hucco,* and *Huctred,* var. of *Uhtred,* are the nearest in *Onom.* In *Dom. st* usually stands for guttural *ch* or *gh.*

HOAR CROSS (Burton-on-T.). 1248 Harecres, 1262 La Croiz, 1267 Orcross, 1268 Horecros. ' Boundary cross,' O.E. *hár.* See HARBORNE. This Hoar- in later spellings of place-names is often corrup. into Whore. *Cf.* the HOARSTONE (Bewdley), 1275 Richard o' th' horeston. Another in Glouc.

HOARWITHY (Ross). 1005 *chart.* To þam haran wiþie, ' to the old withy or willow,' O.E. *withig.*

HOBOROUGH (Kent). 838 *chart.* Holebeorh; also Holenbeorh; -beorge, ' hill, mound of *Hola.*' See BARROW.

HOBY (Leicester). *Dom.* Hobie. ' Dwelling on the HOE ' or ' hill.' *Cf.* HUBY, and see -by.

HOCKERILL (Herts and Worc.). He. H. *c.* 1250 Hokerhuka, 1491 Hokerelle. ' Hill of the *hooker,*' or ' thief who steals with a hook.' Not in *Oxf. Dict.* till 1567. So Skeat. Perh. HOCKERTON (Notts), *Dom.* Hocre-, Ocreton, may be the same, and not fr. a man *Hoc* with N. gen. *r.* All is doubtful.

HOCKLEY (Birmingham and Essex). Bi. H. 1327 Hockele, 1332 Hockelaye. *Cf. Dom.* Surrey, Hoclei. Prob. ' meadow with the hocks, holly-hocks, or mallows,' O.E. *hoc.* Skeat thought Hoc- a M.E. hardening of O.E. *hóh, hó,* ' promontory, abrupt height, HOE,' though the *Oxf. Dict.* does not confirm this. Still, next is very possibly so derived; so, too, *O.E. chart.* Hants, Hocgetwisle. See TWIZEL; also *cf. Dom.* Leicr. and Notts, Hoches, ? = ' heights,' and Beds, Hocheleia, and Hocberry (= -bury), Glouc.

HOCKLIFFE (Beds). *Old* Hocclyve. Seen also in the name of the 15th cny. poet Occleve or Hoceleve. Prob. ' promontory cliff, projecting cliff.' See above and CLEVELAND.

HOCKWOLD (Brandon). Not in *Dom. c.* 1460 Hokehold. Doubtful. It may be ' high wold '—*i.e.,* ' wood ' or ' hilly district,' cognate with *weald,* or ' high hold '—*i.e.,* ' fortress.' See

HOCKLEY. But it may be fr. a man *Hocca*. *Cf.* HOCKWORTHY (Wellington), see -worthy, 1160 *Pipe*, Hochelai (Northants) and HUCKNALL.

HODDLESDEN (Darwen). *Cf.* 1297 a ' Hodleston.' Prob. ' den or DEAN of *Holdwulf*' or '*Holdulf*,' one in *Onom*. Wyld and Hirst omit. But HODDESDON is fr. a man *Hod* or *Hoda*, both in *Onom*. *Cf.* 940 *chart*. Hoddes stoc (Wilts).

HODNET (Market Drayton). *Dom.* Hodenet. Prob. ' heath of *Hoda*,' gen. -*an*. *Cf.* Hodcot (Berks), *Dom.* Hodicote, 963 *chart*. Hodan hlæw (= -low or ' hill '), and 1160 *Pipe* Chesh., Hodeslea. For -et= heath, *cf.* HATFIELD and BASSETT. *Dom.* Salop has also a Humet. HODNELL (Southam), *Dom.* Hodenelle, -helle, is ' *Hoda*'s nook '; see -hall; while HODSOCK (Notts), *Dom.* Odesach, 1302 Hodesak, is ' *Hoda*'s oak.'

HOE, THE (Plymouth). 1590 *Spenser* The Western Hogh, 1602 *Carew* The Hawe. O.E. *hóh, hó*, ' a heel, a projection, a spur, a hill, high ground '; Sc. *heugh*. *Cf.* HOO, HOCKLEY, *Dom.* Devon, Ho (Totnes); 1160-61 *Pipe* Kent, Ho; Hoe Ford (Fareham); MORTEHOE, STAPLOW, etc. Hoe, hoo, is a common ending in Staffs and Warwk.—*e.g.*, TYSOE is *Dom.* Tiheshoche, *a.* 1300 Thysho.

HOGSTON or HOGGSTON (N. Bucks). *Dom.* Hochestone. *O.E. chart*. Hocgestán, ' stone of *Hocca*.' *Hog*, ' a pig,' is not found till 1340. *Hogge* for Hodge or Roger is found in Chaucer. *Cf.* Hogsthorpe (Lincs), not in *Dom.*, HOGSTON (Sc.), and HOXTON; also *Dom.* Lincs. Hogetune.

(La) HOGUE HATENAI (Guernsey) and HOUGUE BIE (Jersey). These names are all pure Scandinavian. Hogue is O.N. *haug-r*, ' mound, cairn.' *Cf.*, Grenehoga, -ehov, *Dom.* Norfk. See -how. Hatenai is ' isle of' some Norseman who cannot now be surely identified. See -ay. Whilst Bie is the same as the common suffix -bie or -by, ' dwelling,' *q.v.* *Cf.* Cape La Hogue (Cherbourg).

HOLBEACH (Spalding). 810 *chart*. Holebech, *c.* 1290 Holebec, 1571 Holbich. Nothing to do with *beach*. May be ' hole, hollow,' O.E. *hól*, ' with the bach or beck or brook.' Hardly ' beck of *Hola*,' a name in *Onom.*, for, if so, we should expect Holanbech in 810. *Cf.* a ' Holan bæcc,' on Stour (Staffs) in 958 *chart*. See -bach.

HOLBECK (Leeds). See above.

HOLBURN (London). *c.* 1162 Holeburn, 1513 Holborne. Pron. now clipped down to ' 'Obun.' J. R. Green says ' hollow bourne,' or burn or brook. *Cf.* Langbourne Ward in the City. O.E. *hól*, dial. *holl*, and 5-9 *hole*, ' hollow, depressed, lying in a hollow.' It may be ' *Hola*'s burn.' *Cf.* HOBOROUGH, and see -bourne. It may also be ' hole of the burn,' ' hollow with the brook,' O.E. *hól, hole*. *Cf.* the HOLBROOK (Warwk.), which Duignan says is *holh bróc*, ' hollow with the brook.' HOLBROOK (Winchcombe) certainly is *c.* 1170 Holebroc.

HOLCOMBE (Painswick and Manchester). Pa. H. 1166 Hollecumbe; Ma. H. *c.* 1215 Holcumbe hevet (head). Combe is 'valley,' *q.v.,* but Hol- must be interpreted according as one interprets HOL-BURN. *Cf.* HOLDEN (Yorks), *Dom.* Holedene; and HOLFORD (Winchcombe), *Dom.* Holeforde.

HOLCOT (Northampton). *Dom.* Holecote, ? *c.* 1220 *Elect. Hugo.* 'Philip de Holkotes.' This last prob. means 'hovel-like cottages,' fr. O.E. *hulu,* 'a husk, a hull,' found *a.* 1225 meaning 'a hut, a hovel.' *Cf.* HULL. But *Dom.*'s form points to 'cot of *Hola,*' a known name.

HOLDERNESS (E. Yorks). *Dom.* Heldrenesse, Heldernesse; *c.* 1097 *Orderic* Hildernessa; *c.* 1100 Holdernese; 1208 Holdernesse. Prob. 'cape of the High Reeve,' an officer of rank in the Dane-lagh, O.N. *hold-r,* O.E. *hold.* But in its earlier forms fr. *Held-r, Hild-r,* on which names see HINDERWELL. See -ness.

HOLKHAM (Wells, Norfk.). *Dom.* and 1157 *Pipe Roll* Holeham. Seems to be fr. O.E. *holh,* 'a hollow, a hole, a cave,' 'dwelling at or in the hollow.' See -ham.

HOLLAND (S. Lincoln). *Dom.* Hoiland, 1216 Hoyland. The Dutch Holland is prob. '*holt-land,*' woodland, see *Oxf. Dict.* s.v.; whilst the Eng. name is usually thought to be O.E. *hol land,* 'hollow or low-lying land.' But Hoiland suggests Dan. *hoi,* 'high,' which does not seem very applicable. *Cf.* HOYLAND.

HOLLINGBOURNE (Maidstone). *c.* 1018 Holingburne. 'Burn, brook of the holly-trees,' O.E. *holen, holeჳn,* 3 *holin,* 5 *holing.* *Cf.* K.C.D. 722 Holungaburna, prob. in Dorset; and *Dom.* Bucks, Holendone. We get a curious corrup. of this root in Holdfast (Upton-on-Severn), 967 *chart.* Holenfesten, prob. 'holly fastness.' *Cf.*, too, HOLLIN, Upp. and Low. (Bewdley), 1332 Holyn.

HOLLOWAY (Feckenham, London, and Matlock Bath). Lon. H. *sic* 1576, but Fe. H. *Dom.* Holewei, *a.* 1200 Holowei; Ma. H. *Dom.* Holewei. Also Holloway or Holewey (For. of Dean). 'Way which is deeply excavated or depressed, lying in a hollow,' O.E. *hol,* infl. *hole,* 4-9 *holl,* cognate with *hollow,* not found till *c.* 1205 *Layamon holh,* 3-4 *holewe,* 3-5 *holwe.* The *a.* 1200 form cited by Duignan is earlier for *hollow* than anything in *Oxf. Dict.*

HOLME (7 in *P.G.*), a very common name—found, *e.g.,* in *Dom.* Yorks 17 times as Holme or Holne. It is O.E. *holm,* 'low, flat land by a river, river-meadow.' It often interchanges as an ending with -ham, and as ending is also found as -hulme, as in Davyhulme, and as -om, in Millom (probably). HOLMFIRTH (Huddersfield) is *Dom.* Holne. The -firth is O.E. *fyrhð,* 3-*frith,* 4 *riht,* 'a wood, wooded country, unused pasture-land.' HOLME-ON-THE-WOLDS is *Dom.* Hougon, which must be a loc. 'at the hows' or 'mounds,' O.N. *haug-r.* *Cf.* Howsham, and for a Norse word taking an Eng. loc. form, *cf.* Hallam. The Nor.

family of Pierrepont or 'Perpunt' is found at HOLME PIERREPONT (Notts) in 1302. In Channel Is. holm becomes -hom, Brecqhon, Jethon (1091 *chart* 'quæ vulgo Keikhulm vocatur'), etc.

HOLMPTON (Hull). *Dom.* Holmetune. 'Town on the holm or river-meadow.' See above. For intrusion of *p*, *cf.* HAMPTON.

HOLNE (Ashburton, Devon). *Sic* in *Dom.* O.E. *holeȝn, hollen,* 'holly-tree.' *Cf.* 847 *chart.* Æthelwulf, To ðæm beorȝe ðe mon hateð 'æt ðæm holne,' also HOLLANDBUSH (Sc.).

HOLNHURST (Glouc.). 940 *chart.* Holenhyrst. 'Holly-wood.' See above and -hurst.

HOLSWORTHY (Bude). Not in *Dom.* Prob. 'farm of *Hola.*' *Cf.* HOLBEACH, and see -worthy.

HOLT (Norfolk and Worcester). *Dom.* both Holt. O.E. and N. *holt,* 'a wood, a copse.' So also HOLTON (6 in *P.G.*). Newark H. *Dom.* Holtone. 'Town by the wood.'

HOLYHEAD. Pron. Hollyhead. *a.* 1490 *Botoner* Le Holyhede. But in W. Caergybi—*i.e.,* 'fort of St. *Gybi.*' The parish church occupies an elevated site where once stood a monastery dedicated to this saint. And the 'Mountain of Holyhead' is called Pen-Caer-Gybi. *Gybi* or *Cybi* was a British saint who, after visiting Gaul and opposing Arianism, returned *c.* 380, and founded this monastic establishment here.

HOLY ISLAND (Northumbld.). *c.* 1130 Hali eland, *c.* 1330 *R. Brunne* Holy Eland. So called because the Columban monks from Iona planted the monastery of Lindisfarne here in the 7th cny. Cuthbert was its great saint.

HOLYWELL (Flint). In W. Treffynon. So called from the famous well of St. Winefride, to which many R.C. pilgrims still come. Winefride is a dubious saint, reputed to have been a noble maiden whose head was cut off by Prince Caradog because she scorned his lustful advances. The head rolled down a hill, and where it stopped this spring or well gushed forth ! She is said to have been daughter of Prince Teuyth of N. Wales in the 7th cny., but there is no mention of her doings until Robert of Shrewsbury, *c.* 1140.

HOMER (Much Wenlock). Not in *Dom.,* but *old* Holmere, which is O.E. for 'hollow lake,' lake in a hollow. *Cf.* CROMER and HOLBURN; but for HOMERTON (London), see HAMMERWICH.

HOMERSFIELD (Harleston). *Dom.* Humbresfelda, *Red Bk. Excheq.* Humeresfeld, also Humorsfeld. Doubtful. Perh. 'field of *Humberht, Humbertus,* or *Hunbeorht,*' all forms in *Onom.,* the last most correct. *Cf.* HUBBERSTONE. It might be fr. *Hormœr.* *Cf. B.C.S.* 622 Hormæres wudu. The liquid *r* could easily disappear, and a spelling Hornersfield is found. Skeat votes for a man *Hunmœr,* a name admittedly not on record.

HOMILDON (Northumbld.). *c.* 1230 Homeldun. 'Hill of *Homel.*' *Cf.* Homeliknow (Coldstream), 1198 Homelenolle. *Hommel* is still a personal name in Germany, but is not found in *Onom.* *Cf.* HUMBLETON.

HONEYBOURNE (Evesham). 709 *chart.* Huniburne, 840 *ib.* Hunig-burn, *Dom.* Huni-, Honeyburne. 'Brook with honey-sweet water,' O.E. *honig.* *Cf.* next, and see -bourne. There is a HONEYBROOK in the same shire, 866 *chart.* Hunig broc; also a HONEYBOROUGH (Pembksh.),1307 Hounteborch,1327 Honiborch. 'Burgh, castle of *Hunta*' or *Hunto,*' several in *Onom.* See -burgh.

HONEYCHURCH (Devon). *Dom.* Honecherche. The connexion between a 'church' and 'honey,' O.E. *huniȝ,* 4-7 *honi,* is not very obvious, and this is prob. 'church of *Huna.*' *Cf.* HONILEY (Warwk.), *a.* 1200 Hunilegh, plainly fr. *honey,* even as is HON-NINGTON (same shire), 1043 *chart.* Huniton, *Dom.* Hunitone. On HONEY CHILD (Romney Marsh), 1227 Honi Child, see BAPCHILD.

HONICKNOWLE (Crown Hill, Devon). Prob. 'knoll, hill of *Honoc,*' a name in *Onom.* *Cf. Dom.* Devon, Honecherde (-erde prob.= -worth, 'farm), and KNOWLE.

HONING (Norwich). HONINGHAM (Norwich), and HONINGTON (3 in *P.G.*). *Dom.* has only Honincgetoft. Honing is *c.* 1150 Haninges, 'place of the sons of *Hana*' or '*Hona.*' *Cf. Dom.* Kent, Honinberg. See -ing. But HONLEY (Huddersfield) is *Dom.* Haneleia, prob. 'mead of *Hana,*' 2 in *Onom.* *Cf.* HANLEY.

HOO (Rochester). *c.* 700 *chart.* Hogh, *Dom.* Hou, How= HOE. Stanhoe was orig. Stanhoghia. There is also a HOO FARM (Kidderminster), 1275 John de la Ho.

HOOK (7 in *P.G.*). Where these are fr. *hook,* O.E. *hóc,* 'a hook,' then 'an angle or bend' in a river, etc., they must be late, as *Oxf. Dict.* has nothing in this sense till late in 16th cny. But some of the Hooks (those in Norse regions) are prob. of the same origin as the Hog and Hough of Lincs, and Hook (Goole). See HOUGHTON. The numerous Hooks in Pembk. will have this origin. 1603 *Owen,* 'South hooke,' etc., and in older *charts.* Hoch.

HOOK NORTON (Banbury). 917 *O.E. Chron.* Hocneratun, Hoc-ceneratun; *late chart.* Hokenarton; *c.* 1115 *Hen. Hunt.* Hoche-neretune. An interesting and puzzling corrup. *Hocnera* must surely be a gen. pl., and the name mean 'town of the *Hocs*' or 'sons of *Hoc.*'

HOOLE (Chester). *Sic* 1340. O.E. *hól,* 5-6 *hoole,* 'a hole, a hollow.' *Cf.* 'Hammelle the Hoole,' s.v. HAMBLE R.; also *cf.* MUCH HOOLE.

HOOTON PAGNELL and ROBERTS (Doncaster and Rotherham). Dom. H. *Dom.* Hotun, 1203 Hoton. 'Village on the HOE' or 'hill.' Hoton is very frequent in *Dom.* Yorks, usually for some HUTTON.

HOPE (4 in *P.G.*). *Dom.* Hope (Salop). This is HOPE sb² in *Oxf. Dict.*, 'a place of refuge,' O.E. *hóp*, 'a piece of enclosed land, an enclosed little valley '; O.N. *hóp*, 'a small, land-locked bay, an inlet,' as in St. Margaret's Hope (Sc.). *Cf.* HOPEHOUSE (Martley), 1275 'John de Hope.' Hope (Denbigh) is now in W. Yr Hob, ' the hope,' or Hoben, ' 2 hopes.' HOPE-MANSEL (For. of Dean) is 1263 Hope Maloysell, an O.Fr. proper name.

HOPTON (Mirfield and Great Yarmouth). Mi. H. *Dom.* Hoptone; Ya. H. *sic c.* 1080. The plant *hops* is not found till *c.* 1440. This is prob. for *hope*, as above; or it may be, like HOPWOOD (Alvechurch), 848 *chart.* Hopwuda, fr. O.E. *hop*, ' the privet.'

HOPWAS (Tamworth). *a.* 1100 Hopewaes, *Dom.* Opewas, *a.* 1200 Hopwas. O.E. *hóp wase, wæs*, ' valley of the swamp or marsh.' *Cf.* ALREWAS ; and see -hope.

HORPURY (Wakefield). *Dom.* Orberie. Doubtful. There seems no likely name in *Onom.* It may be as next. See -bury. HORFIELD. (Bristol), *Dom.* Horefelle, Baddeley derives fr. O.E. *horh*, M.E. *hore*, ' mire.' *Cf.* Hormead, same shire.

HORHAM (Eye, Suffolk). *Sic c.* 1150, but *Dom.* Horam, -an. Prob. like HOREHAM (Sussex), ' home of the whore ' or ' harlot,' O.E. *hór*, O.N. *hóra. Dom.*'s Horan may be an old loc., ' at the whore's.' See -ham.

HORNBLOTTON (E. Somerset). *Dom.* Horblawctone, *a.* 1145 *Wm. Malmesb.* Hornblawerton, ' Horn-blower town.' Already in the *Corpus Glossary, c.* 725, we find *horn blauwere.*

HORNBY (Lancaster). *Dom.* Hornebi, 1278 Horneby; also more than one in Yorks, *Dom.* Hornebi. ' Dwelling of *Horn.*' *Cf.* Horncastle, and King Horn, perh. orig. *Horm*, a Dan. Viking of the 9th cny., who fought for the Ir. King Cearbhall. But Hornby in Smeaton (Yorks) is *Dom.* Horenbodebi, Horebodebi, where the man's name is now hardly recognizable. See -by.

HORNCASTLE (Lincs). *Dom.* Hornecastre, 1161-62 *Pipe* Hornecastra. ' Camp of *Horn.*' See above. The ending -caster, *q.v.*, rarely becomes -castle.

HORNINGSEA (Cambridge). *c.* 1080 *Inquis. Camb.* Horningeseie. ' Isle ' and ' home of the *Hornings* ' or ' descendants of *Horn. Cf.* Hormer (Berks), *B.C.S.*, iii. 520, Horninga mære (lake, mere), *Chron. Abing.* Hornigmere; also HORNINGLOW (Burton-on-T.), *sic a.* 1300, See -low, ' burial-mound.' *Cf.*, too, *Dom.* Essex Horminduna, and Norfk. Hornincgetoft; also HORNINGTON (Ainsty), *Dom.* Horninc-, Hornin-, Horni- tone. See -ing. On *Horn*, see above.

HORNINGSHAM (Warminster). *Dom.* Horningeshā. ' Home of the sons of *Horn.*' See above, and -ing.

HORNSEY (N. London). *a.* 1300 Haringee, with the hard *g* still preserved in HARRINGAY. Hornsea is a corrup. which has arisen through softening of the *g* into Hārnjy, and then Hornsea. But HORNSEA (E. Riding) is *Dom.* Hornesse, ' isle, peninsula of *Horn.*' See HORNBY and -ay.

HORRIDGE (Glouc.). Prob. ' hoar, grey ridge,' O.E. *hár,*' hoary, grey, old,' 3-5 *hor.* But *cf.* HORTON. *Dom.* Glouc. has only Horedone.

HORSFORD (Norwich) (*Dom.* Hosforda, also Horshā) and HORS- FORTH (Leeds). Le. H. *Dom.* Horseforde, Hoseforde. There are coins of K. Alfred which seem to read Orsnaforda as well as Oksnaforda (OXFORD). ' Horse ford.' See -forth.

HORSHAM (Sussex). Prob. ' home of *Horsa*'; perh. the Jute who came over with Hengest, 449 A.D. There is also one in Worstrsh. *sic.* 1275, which may be the same, or else ' horse's enclosure '; O.E. *hors hamm.* See -ham 2, and *cf. Dom.* Bucks Horsedene. *Dom.* Sussex has only Horselie and Horstede.

HORSLEY (8 in *P.G.*). Leatherhead H. perh. 871-89 *chart.* Horsa leh, *Dom.* Horslei, *ib.* Derby, Glouc. and Sussex Horselei. Rather ' *Horsa*'s ' than ' horse meadow.' See above, and -ley.

HORSMONDEN (Kent). Not in *Dom.* 1570-76 *Lambarde* Hors- mundene. ' The DEAN or (woody) vale of the ward of Horsa.' O.E. *mund,* ' protection.'

HORSTED KEYNES (E. Grinstead). *Dom.* Horstede. Prob. as in HORSHAM, ' *Horsa*'s place '; O.E. *stede.* Keynes is the Nor. family, *de Cahanges.*

HORTON (10 in *P.G.*). 972 *chart.* Horton (Worc.), *Dom.* Yorks, Salop, Worcr., Bucks, Hortone, -tune; *a.* 1130 *Sim. Dur.* Hore- tun. Doubtful. It might be ' hoary, grey-looking town.' See HORRIDGE. Duignan prefers O.E. *horh tun,* ' dirty, muddy town,' and says *cf.* HORMEAD (Herts), which Skeat makes ' muddy mead.'

HORWICH (Bolton and Stockport). *Cf. Dom.* Worc. Horwich. = HORTON. See -wich.

HOTHAM (Yorks). *Dom.* Holde twice, Hode 5 times. O.E. *heald* is only found in sense of ' holding, keeping, possessing.' *Holde,* ' a lair, lurking-place,' is not found recorded till *c.* 1205, and as ' fort, fortress ' not till *a.* 1300. The -ham has been added after *Dom.* But *Dom.* has once Hodhu'. With *Dom.*'s Hode *cf.* the Sc. *haud, hod,* for ' hold.'

HOUGHTON (11 in *P.G.*). A difficult name, with several origins. Those in the N. seem often to be fr. North. Eng. *how,* ' hill, hillock, tumulus, barrow '; O.N. *haug-r,* ' cairn, mound,' in 7 *hough. E.g.,* H., Heddon-on-the-Wall, is 1200 *Yorks Fines* Houton, while H. (E. Riding) is *Dom.* Houe-, Oueton. *Cf.,* too, Hougon, a loc., ' at the mounds,' name in *Dom.* for Holme on

the Wolds. Glass Houghton (S. Yorks), *Dom.* Hoctun, Hough-
ton-le-Side, 1200 *Yorks Fines* Hoctona, H. (K's. Lynn) *Dom.*
Hodtune, and the many Hohtones in *Dom.* Northants, are
prob. fr. HOE, ' height, promontory,' 3-6 *hogh.* See HOCKLEY.
Houghton (Beds and Hants) will be the same, being both
Houston(e) in *Dom., st* being *Dom.'s* regular ' avoidance ' of
guttural *gh.* Great Houghton (Barnsley) is *Dom.* Halton, and
so = HOUGHTON or *halhtun,* ' river-meadow town'; whilst HANGING
HOUGHTON may possibly be fr. a man *Hout.* Old forms are
always needed.

HOUNSLOW (London). *O.E. chart.* Hundeshlæw, *Dom.* Honeslowe.
' Burial-mound of *Hund* ' or ' *Hunda.*' See -low. But HOUND-
HILL (Uttoxeter) is *a.* 1300 Hogenhull, *a.* 1400 Howenhull, as
well as Hunhyle, Hounhull, suggesting origin fr. a man *Hoga,*
-an, ' the prudent.'

HOWDEN-LE-WEAR (Co. Durham). 1130 Houendena, and HOWDEN
and HOWDEN DYKE (Yorks), *Dom.* Houeden, *c.* 1200 Hoveden,
1635 Hovenden (prob. not *a.* 1130 *Sim. Dur.* Offedene). Doubtful. Very likely fr. an unrecorded *Hofa. Cf.* HOVINGHAM
(Yorks), *sic.* in *Dom.,* giving its patronymic; only *Offa* and *Ofa*
in *Onom.* It might be ' wooded vale of the plant *hove* ' (spelt
so *c.* 1440), O.E. *hofe,* which may be the violet or ground ivy.
A Roll of Rich. I. has Houedensir', or Howdenshire. Of course,
in North. Eng. *how* is ' a hill,' found in Eng. fr. *a.* 1340 (see
-how), whilst HOWTHORP (Yorks), *Dom.* Holtorp, is ' village in
the hollow ' or ' hole.' See -den.

HOWLE HILL (Ross, Hereford). W. *hywel,* ' conspicuous.' *Cf.*
CRICKHOWELL.

HOWSHAM (E. Riding and Lincoln). E. Ri. H. *Dom.* Huson, O.E.
loc. *huson,* ' at the houses.' *Cf.* HALLAM and NEWSHAM.
Housen (Cotheridge) is just the M.E. pl. ' houses.' See -ham.

HOWTEL (N.W. of Wooler). 1525 Howtell Swyre (O.E. *swira*
' neck'; *cf.* MANOR SWARE, Sc.). How will be O.N. *haug-r,*
' mound, hill '; the -tel must remain doubtful. *Cf.* HOUGHTON.

HOXNE (Eye, Sfk.). *Dom.* Hoxana, *Hund. Roll* Hoxene, 1473
Hoxon. Doubtful. O.Fris. *hoxene, hoxne* is ' a hamstring '
(see *Oxf. Dict.* s.v. hox *sb.*); but this seems unlikely. Skeat
adopts the suggestion of Mr. Anscombe, that here we have an
O.E. *Hoxena,* gen. pl. of *Hoxan,* possibly the name of some small
tribe of settlers, just as we find mention of the tribe *Wixan*
and the famous tribe of *Seaxan* or ' Saxons.' The name in any
case seems abnormal.

HOXTON (London). *Dom.* Hochestone, *c.* 1350 Hoggeston, later
Hogston, 1610 *B. Jonson* Hogsdon. ' Town of *Hocca* ' (H*oga* is
found once). *Cf. Dom.* Bucks Hochestone, and 1179-80 *Pipe*
Hokesgarth (Yorks).

HOYLAKE (Birkenhead). *Dom.* Hoiloch. The 'Hoyle Lake' was formed by the 'Hoyle Bank,' *sic a.* 1600, still visible at certain states of the tide. Hoyle is an inflected form of O.E. *hól,* 'hole, hollow place,' given in *Oxf. Dict.* as 5-6 *hoil*(e), and Yorks dial. *hoil.* The *Oxf. Dict.* calls *lac* 'lake' early M.E., but it is found in *O.E. Chron.* ann. 656, and once or twice in *Dom.* The Sc. form *loch* is not recorded till *Barbour,* 1375.

HOYLAND (Barnsley). *Dom.* Hoiland, Holant (another in Derby), 1242 Hoyland. *Cf. a.* 1100 *chart.* 'Hoylandia' (Lincs). 'Hollow, low-lying land.' See HOYLAKE and HOLLAND. HOYLAND SWAINE (Sheffield) is *Dom.* Holan and Holande; but *Dom.* Holun and Holam is Hollym (Yorks), an O.E. loc. *hólun,* 'at the holes.'

HUBBERHOLME (W. Riding) and HUBBERSTONE (Milford Haven), *Dom.* Yorks Huburgheha' (for -ham, which often interchanges with -holm). 'River-meadow' and 'stone of *Hunbeorht, Humberht, Hunburh,* or *Hubert,*' all names on record. The *Hubber* in Pembroke is said to have been the viking who with his brother Hingua led the great invasion of 866. But this can hardly be the same, for the 866 man is in *O.E. Chron.* Hubba or Ubba. There is a Hubberst' recorded in Derbyshire, and a Hobrichtebi in 1167-68 *Pipe* Cumbld.

HUBY (Leeds and Easingwold). *Dom.* Hobi. 'Dwelling on the HOE' or 'hill.' *Cf.* HOBY; and see -by.

HUCCLECOTE (Glouc.). *Dom.* Hochilicote, 1221 Hukelingcote, *later* Hokelin- and Hokelcote. 'Cot of *Hocel*' or his sons. *Onom.* has only *Hicel* (see HICKLING); and *cf.* 1231-34 *Close R.* Hukels-, Hucliscot (Leicester). See -ing.

HUCKNALL TORKARD (Nottingham). *Dom.* Hochenale, 1160 *Pipe* Hochenhala, 1287 Hokenale Torkard. O.E. *Hoccan heal,* 'nook of Hocca.' *Cf.* HOCKWOLD, and *Dom.* Bucks Huchdene and Huchehā. The Nor. family of *Torkard* is found here in 1284. See -hall.

HUDDERSFIELD. *Dom.* Oderesfelte, Odresfeld. 'Field of *Odhere*' or '*Oderus,*' one such, and one Northern *Udardus,* 12th cny., are found in *Onom.* HUDSWELL (Richmond, Yorks), *Dom.* Hudreswelle, is prob. fr. the same name. But HUDDIKNOLL (Glouc.), *old* Hodenknole, is fr. *Hoda* or *Hudda.*

HUISH CHAMPFLOWER (Wiveliscombe, Smst.). Huish is O.E. *hig-, hiwisc,* 'a household, then, a hide of land.' *Cf.* K.C.D. 107. On Cotenes felde an hywysce, and Melhuish. Champflower is a Nor. name, Fr. *champ fleuri,* 'flowery field.' We find Richard de Hywis of Lod Hywis (Smst.), in time of K. John; 1253 Hywish, 1298 Hyuhyshe.

HULAM (Hartlepool). *a.* 1130 *Sim. Dur.* Holum, a loc., 'at the holes,' O.E. *hól. Cf.* HALLAM.

HULL (formerly KINGSTON-ON-HULL). Name of a small river. Prob. connected with O.E. *hól,* mod. dial. *holl, howl*(e), 'hollow, depressed, lying in a hollow.' Named Kingston-on-H. by Edw. I. 1299; in *a*. 1552 *Leland* simply Kingston.

HUMBER. *Bede* Humbra, Hymbra, *c*. 890 *Alfred* Humbre (in *Lat. vsn.* Abus fl.). Prob. aspirated form of *cumber*, 'confluence' of Ouse and Trent, W. *cymmer*, G. *comar ;* the -ber is prob. the same root as in ABER. *Cf.* COMBERBACH, etc., also CUMBERNAULD (Sc.), and *Dom*. Sffk. Humbresfelda. This last, with HUMBERSTONE (N. Lincs and Leicstr.), will be fr. *Humbert* or *Hunbeorht*. See HOMERSFIELD and HUBBERSTONE.

HUMBLETON (Hull). *Dom*. Humeltone. 'Town of *Humel*,' var. of *Homel* (see HOMILDON). The letter *b* readily intrudes itself. *Cf. Dom*. Norfk. Humiliat (-iat = yet, 'gate ').

HUNCOAT (Accrington), *Dom*. Hunnicot, and HUNDCOT (Leicester). *Dom*. Hunecote, 1124 *O.E. Chron*. Hundehoge (see -how). 'Cot, dwelling of *Hunda*' or '*Huna*.' O.E. *hund* means, of course, 'a hound.' *Cf.* 'Hunditone' (Cheshire) in *Dom*.

HUNGERFORD. The oldest (14th-15th cny.) forms all have Hunger-, Hungre-, but this can have nothing to do with Eng. *hunger*. It is O.E. *hongra, hangra*, ' a hanging wood on a hillside.' *Cf.* CLAYHANGER (1300 Cleyhunger), Hungerfield (Glouc.), *old* Hanger-, HUNGERHILL, and also 'Hungrewenitune' (Chesh.) in *Dom*.

HUNGERHILL (Nottingham, Henley - in - Arden, and Somerset). Nott. H. *old* Hongerhill. O.E. *hangra, hongra*, ' a wood on a hill slope.' *Cf.* BIRCHANGER, CLAYHANGER, and above. There are also 2 HUNGRY HILLS in Worc., and a Honger Grove (Puddleston).

HUNMANBY (Yorks). *Dom*. Hundemanebi, 'Dwelling of *Huneman*,' one in *Onom*. See -by.

HUNNINGHAM (Leamington). *Dom*. Huningeham, *a*. 1200 Honyngham. ' Home of the sons of *Huna* ' or ' *Hun*,' a common name in *Onom. Cf.* HUNNINGTON (Halesowen), 1402 Honyngton. See -ing.

HUNSINGORE (Wetherby). *Dom*. Holsingoure. More old forms needed; but the liquids *l* and *n* not uncommonly interchange. The ending is prob. not GORE, ' triangular wedge of land,' but rather ' bank,' O.E. *ofr, obr*, M.E. *oure* (see -over), ' of *Hunsige*,' a common O.E. name.

HUNSLET and H. CARR (Leeds). *Sic Dom*., but 1202 Hunesflet. ' River of *Huna*.' See above and FLEET. The same man's name is seen in HUNSHELF (S. Yorks), *Dom*. Hunescelf. *Shelf* in names often has the meaning ' ledge of rock.' For Carr ' rock,' *cf*. REDCAR; also *cf*. HUNSCOTE (Wwksh.), 1327 Hunstanscote, *a*. 1400 Huntscote. But HUNSLEY (N. Yorks) is *Dom*. Hundeslege, ' meadow of *Hund* ' or ' the Dog.'

HUNSTANTON (The Wash). 1038 and *c*. 1150 *chart*. Hunstanestun. Local pron. Hunston. ' Town of *Hunstan*.' There are 5 such in *Onom*.

HUNTINGDON (also near Chester, *Dom.* Hunditone.) *O.E. Chron.* ann. 656, Huntendune, 921 *ib.* Huntandune, 1011 *ib.* Huntadunscir, *c.* 1175 Huntedune. 'Hill, down, of the hunter,' O.E. *hunta,* 2-6 *hunte. Cf.* HUNTINGTON (Cannock), 1262 Huntingdon, 1300 Huntyndon, and *Dom.* Yorks Huntindune. *Hunta* and *Hunting* were also men's names. See -ing, -don, and -ton.

HUNTINGTRAP COMMON (Hadsor, Worc.). *a.* 1300 Huntingthrope, Huntingdrope, 'hunting village.' See -thorpe.

HUNTON (Bedale and Maidstone). Be. H. *Dom.* Huntone. 'Town of *Huna.*' See HUNSLET and next. So HUNWORTH (Melton Constable), *Dom.* Huneworda. See -worth, 'farm.'

HUNTSPILL (Highbridge). *Dom.* Hunespil, *a.* 1500 Honys-, Honspill. 'Pool of *Huna,*' as above. Pill is often found in S. Wales for 'pool,' and the *Dom.* form here shows it is an O.E. variant, and not W. *Cf.* HUNTSHAM (For. of Dean), *c.* 1145 Honsum, *c.* 1200 Hunstone, 1298 Hondsum. '*Huna*'s home.' See -ham.

HURLEY (Atherstone and Marlow). Ath. H. *chart.* Hurnlega, 1199 Hurnlege, -lei. Mar. H. *Dom.* Herlei, 1316 Hurle. Skeat derives both fr. O.E. *hyrne,* 'a corner, a nook.' The Marlow H. is doubtful. See -ley. HURCOT (Kidderminster) is also puzzling. *Dom.* Worcote (W for H), *a.* 1200 Hurchote, -cote, 1275 Horecote, *a.* 1600 Hurdcote. Here Duignan prefers 'cot of the herd or shepherd,' O.E. *hyrde.* Much more likely is O.E. *horh* or *hore,* 'dirt, filth,' 4 *hoore,* here used adjectivally as in HORTON.

HURLINGHAM (Putney). *K.C.D.* 782 Herlinga ham. 'Home of the Herlings.' ? descendants of *Herlewin. Cf. Roll. Rich. I.* Hurlingebure (Notts).

HURSTBOURNE (3 in Hants). Not in *Dom.* Winchester H. 961 *chart.* Hysseburna. 'Brook of *Hyse,*' 3 in *Onom.,* var. of *Husa;* the corrup. is unusual. Of course, Hurst is O.E. *hyrst,* 'a wood, a grove, and also a sandy place.' See -bourne.

HURWORTH-ON-TEES. 1183 Hurdewurd, 1344 Hurreworth. 'Farm of *Hyrde*' or '*Hirde,*' 2 in *Onom.* See -worth.

HUSTHWAITE (Easingwold). Not in *Dom.* Prob. 'farm, croft of *Husa,*' or '*Husi,*' names in *Onom. Cf.* Huthwaite (Mansfield), no old forms, and *Dom.* Bucks Huscott. See -thwaite.

HUTTON (13 in *P.G.*). *Dom.* Somst. Hutone, *Dom.* Yorks Hoton, Hottune over 40 times, nearly all for some Hutton, while 1202 *Yorks Fines* has Hoton, Hottun, *a.* 1130 *Sim. Dur.* Hotun, 1183 Hotona—*i.e.*, Hutton Henry. 'Town, village on the HOE or projecting height.' *Cf.* HOOTON and SHERIFF HUTTON. HUTHWAITE (Mansfield and Sheffield) prob. has the same origin; but perh. fr. a man *Huti* or *Hutto,* seen in 'Hutisted' (Staffs), *Roll. Rich. I.* The Sheff. H. is not in *Dom.* See -thwaite.

HUXLEY (Chester).   Said to be *chart*. Hodeslea.   ' Meadow of *Hod* '
or ' *Hoda*.'   *Cf*. *B.C.S*. 1282 Hodes ac.   But this is abnormal.
The names *Huc, Huch,* or *Hucco,* all in *Onom.,* seem more likely
origins.   See -ley.

HYDE (Cheshire, Staffs, Wwksh., and Glouc.).   HYDE HEATH (Bucks),
and HYDE PARK (London).   O.E. *higid,* later *hid, hide, hyde,*
an O.E. measure of land, orig. as much as would support one
family and their dependents.   The spelling of the place-name
seems almost always Hyde, and the London H. goes back to
Dom.   The *hida* or ' hide ' is often referred to in *Dom*.

HYDON HEATH (W. Surrey) is wrongly spelt High Down, as it is
1453 Hyddeneshethe, ' heath of ? *Hyddan*.'   *Onom*. has only
Hidda and *Hiddi*.   On the Heath is Hydons Ball.

HYLTON (Sunderland).   Prob. ' town on the slope or incline.'   O.E.
hylde, helde, cognate with *hyll,* ' a hill.'

HYTHE (Kent).   1051 *O.E. Chron*. Hiðe, 1228 *Close R*. Heth, Heia,
1234 *ib*. Hee.   A *hithe* is ' a landing-rise, a quay,' *a*. 700 *hydde,*
later *hyð*.   *Cf*. ROTHERHITHE, etc.   The old forms are exactly
paralleled by those of O.E. *rith,* ' a stream.'   See RYE, RYDE, etc.

IBSTONE (Wallingford).   *Dom*. Ypestan.   Prob. ' *Ipa's* stone.'
Onom. gives *Ibba, Ibe, Ipa, Ipo, Ippa*.   Possibly ' look-out
stone, fr. O.E. *yppe,* ' a raised or look-out place.'   *Cf*. Ibstock
(Leicester)—see STOKE—and IPSTONES.   See -ton.

ICKENHAM (Uxbridge).   *Dom*. Ticheham, also Tykenham.   ' Home
of *Tica* ' or ' *Tican*,' a name in *Onom*.   O.E. *ticcen,* Ger. *zieke,*
is ' a goat, a kid.'   *Cf*. TITCHBORNE.   The loss of the initial *t* is
curious; but Norm. scribes regularly softened *c* into *ch*.   But
ICOMBE (Stow-on-Wold) is 781 *chart*. Icancumb, ' *Icca's* valley.'

ICKHAM (Canterbury).   785 *chart*. Ioccham, *Dom*. Gecham.   ' Home
of *Iocca*,' a name not in *Onom.,* but *Ica, Icca,* and *Ycca* are.
The O.E. charter name of R. OCK (Berks) is Eoccen.

ICKLEFORD (Hitchin) and ICKLETON (S. Cambs).   *Ramsey Chart*.
Icklingford, *Rams. Chron*. Iclesforde.   *B.C.S*. iii. 630 Icelingtun.
Dom. Hichelintone, Inchelintone, 1210 Iclintone.   Patronymics.
' Ford and village of the sons of *Icel*.'   *Cf*. next and GIGGLES-
WICK.   We get the same name in ICKLESHAM (Winchelsea),
1160-61 *Pipe* Icheleshā, ' home of *Icel*.'   Kickle (Bucks) was
1236 *Close R*. Ykel'.   See -ham, -ing, and -ton.

ICKNI(E)LD STREET or WAY runs fr. ICKLINGHAM (Bury St. Edmunds) to Wantage.   854 *chart*. Icenhilde weg, 903 *ib*. Iccen-
hilde wege, *a*. 1200 Ad regalem viam quae vocatur Ikenhilde-
strete; Stratam regiam quae appellatur Ykenild; via regia vel
le Ricnelde strete, *a*. 1300 Rikelinge strete, *a*. 1400 Rykenylde-
strete.   Also *a*. 100 *chart*. Cinges stræte.   Commonly said to
come fr. the tribe *Iceni* (Ικηνοὶ), who occupied all E. Anglia in
1st cny. A.D.   This is denied by Duignan in his full and valuable

arts. s.v. The ending -hylt, -hilde, -ild may be O.E. *hylde*, ' the slope of a hill.' The rest of the name must remain doubtful. ICKWORTH (Bury St. E.) will be like ICKHAM (Canterbury), ' farm of *Ica*,' not fr. the *Iceni* ; whilst Icklingham will be ' home of the sons of *Icel*.' See above.

IDDESLEIGH (Winkleigh, Devon). *Dom*. Edeslege. ' Meadow of *Eda* ' or ' *Ida*,' or ' *Iddi*,' all in *Onom*. *Cf*. 836 *chart*. Iddeshale (*i.e.*, nook), and IDBURY (Oxon), *Dom*. Ideberie. See -bury and -leigh.

IDLE R. (Notts, trib. of Trent). *Bede* Idla, *c*. 1120 *Henry Hunt*. Idle, 1200 *chart*. Yddil. There seems no likely W. root, so possibly it may be fr. O.E. *idel*, ' idle,' in its orig. meaning, ' empty.' *Cf*. ELSTREE. There is also an Idle (Bradford), not in *Dom*. IDLICOTE (Shipston) is actually *Dom*. Etelincote, or ' *Æthelwyn*'s cot ' ! IDELSBURY (Pinswick), *a*. 1125 Idelberge, is fr. a man *Idel* ; the name is found in 1199, and Rhys thinks it may be orig. W. *Ithel* for Juddhael, found on one of the Llantwit stones as Juthahels. Thus the man's name will be the same as in GIGGLESWICK and ICKLEFORD.

IEITHON R. (Radnorsh.). Anwyl thinks this is perh. the Keltic goddess of speech.

IFFLEY (Oxford). 1004 *chart*. Gifetelea, *Dom*. Givetelei, 1165 Ivittelai, 1233 Iftel', 1234 Ghyftele, 1316 Yiftele. H. Alexander says origin unknown. Certainly it is not likely to be ' gift-meadow,' O.E. *gift, gyft*. Curiously there is in *B.C.S*. 834 an ' Yffeles leah.'

ILAM (Ashbourne). 1006 *chart*. Hilum, *Dom*. Ylum, *a*. 1300 Hylum, Illum. Prob. O.E. loc. *Ylon*, ' at the Yl,' old name of the brook Manifold, trib. of R. Dove, on which it stands. Perh. same root as R. ISLA (Sc.), which Whitley Stokes thought perh. cognate with Old High Ger. *ilen*, mod. Ger. *eilen*, ' to hurry.' However, Duignan thinks Ilam is O.E. *hyllum*, ' at, among the hills.' ' The whole manor is hill and dale.' *Cf*. HALLAM, HULAM, etc. *Oxf*. *Dict*. gives only one reference to a spelling of *hill* without *h*, and that *c*. 1580; so Duignan's origin is doubtful. ILLEY (Halesowen), *a*. 1200 Hilleley, Yleley, 1250 Hilleleye, is prob. ' mead of *Ylla*,' one such known. *Cf*. an Illeyge or Illanley in Kentish charters, and MONKS ELEIGH.

ILCHESTER (Taunton). Perh. *Ptolemy*'s Iskalis. *Dom*. and 1155 Givelcestre, *c*. 1097 *Flor*. *W*. Givelceastra, 1158 Iuelcestre. ' Camp on the R. Ivel, Ile, or Isle,' O.E. *geafol, geafl*, G. *gabhal*, ' a fork ' (of a river). *Cf*. YEOVIL. Contraction began early, because already in *Dom*. we have Ivle, and even Ile-minstre. See -chester.

ILFORD (Essex). *Dom*. Ilefort, 1166-67 *Pipe* Ileford. Prob. ' ford of *Illa, Illo*,' or ' *Ilo*,' all names in *Onom*. Ile= isle, O.Fr. *ile*, is not in Eng. till 1290. But see above; it may be ' ford at the fork.'

ILFRACOMBE (N. Devon). *Dom.* Alfreincome, 1233 *Close R.* Affride-, Aufredecumbe, 1234 *ib.* Alfridecumbe. 'Valley of *Ealhfrith*,' a common O.E. name, spelt later *Alfrith* and *Alfrid*. See -combe.

ILKERTON (Devon). *Dom.* Incrintona. Prob. 'village of *Ilgær*,' one in *Onom.* The Inc- in *Dom.* will be due to the common interchange of liquids.

ILKETSHALL (Bungay). *Dom.* Ilchesteshala. M'Clure thinks '*Ulfketel's* hall or mansion.' More old forms needed. It may be 1225 *Patent R.* Kilketeleshal. ? *Ki* error for *U* or *Wi*.

ILKLEY (Yorks). Thought to be *Ptolemy* Olicana. *Dom.* Illicleia, Illiclei, Illeclive (*i.e.*, 'cliff'). 'Meadow of ?' If the name be O.E. it may be fr. *Ulfach, Ulfeg, Willac* or *Willoc*, all these are in *Onom.* See -ley.

ILMINGTON (Shipston-on-Stour). *c.* 1010 *chart.* Ylmandune, *Dom.* Edelmitone, Ilmedone, *a.* 1200 Illamedone, 1326 Ilmyndon. 'Hill, down of *Eadhelm*,' though some of the forms suggest *Ælmin*, also in *Onom.* Endings -don and -ton often interchange, *q.v.*

ILMINSTER (Somerset). *Dom.* Ileminstre. 'Church on the *Ile*' or '*Isle*.' See ILCHESTER and -minster.

ILSINGTON (Newton Abbot). *Dom.* has only Ilesham. *Cf. Dom.* Nfk. Ilsinghetuna. 'Town of the *Ilsings*,' ? 'sons of *Ylla*,' one in *Onom. Cf.* ELSING and next. See -ing.

IL(S)TON (Swansea). 1340 Iltwiteston; in W. Llanilltyd, *a.* 1400 Lanyltwyt, -iltwyt. 'Town' or 'church of *St. Illtyd*,' 5th cny. *Cf.* LLANTWIT. But ILSLEY (Berks) is *Dom.* Hildeslei, '*Hild's* mead,' and ILTON (N. Yorks) is *Dom.* Ilche-, Hilchetun, where the man's name seems already corrupted beyond recognition.

IMMINGHAM (Grimsby). *Dom.* Imungehā. Patronymic. 'Home of the sons of *Imma*.' See -ing. The same man's name is seen in IMPNEY (Droitwich), *a.* 1200 Imney, *a.* 1300 Ymenege, Imeneye, 'Isle of *Imma*.' See -ey.

INCE (S. of R. Mersey). *Dom.* and *c.* 1380 Inise, *a.* 1200 Ynys, W. *ynys*, 'an island';, or, as it does not seem ever to have been an island, G. *innis*, 'an inch,' 'a meadow by a river.' It seems to have this meaning in W. too, though not in the ordinary dictionaries. *Cf.* 'Ynichebeche' (For. of Dean), cited by Baddeley, s.v. INCHBROOK, which has no old forms.

INGATESTONE (W. Essex). The original name in *Dom.* is simply Ginge, Ing. It is regular for initial *g* to fall away (see I *passim*). Thus originally this must be the same as Ginge (Hendred, Berks), *B.C.S.* iii. 257 Gæging, later *ib.* iii. 173 Gainge, iii. 67 Gaincg, i. 506 Geinge, *Dom.* and *Pipe* (1155-56) Gainȝ, 1125 Estgeyng. Patronymic. 'Place of the sons of *Gæga*.' *Cf.* GAYDON. Gate is presumably O.E. *geat*, 'gate.' See -ing. Inglestone

(Hawkesbury) is also spelt Ingateston, and 1610 Inguston. Older forms unknown.

INGBIRCHWORTH (Sheffield). *Dom.* Berceworde, which also stands for Rough Birchworth. ' Farm of *Ingebiorg,*' or ' *Ingelbeorht.*' Long names readily contract. See -worth.

INGESTRE (Stafford). *Dom.* Gestreon, *a.* 1300 Ing-, Yngestre, Inge-straund, -trent. Prob. ' *Inga*'s tree,' O.E. *treo, treow. Cf.* OSWESTRY. But -straund is O.E. *strand,* ' shore, bank of a river,' here the Trent, which accounts for Ingestrent. The *Dom.* form is corrupt, but represents a pl. of *treo.*

INGHAM (Lincoln and Norwich), INGWORTH (Norwich). *Dom.* Lin. Ingehā; Nfk., Ingewrda. ' Home ' and ' farm of *Inga,*' 2 in *Onom.* See -ham and -worth. Duignan thinks INGON (Stratford, Wwk.), 704 *chart.* Ingin, must be O.E. *in gin,* ' in the gap '; while INGTHORP (Yorks) is *Dom.* Ucnetorp, or ' *Ycca*'s village '; the -ne represents the O.E. gen. *-an, ne* sounding *en.* See -thorpe.

INGLEBOROUGH (hill, W. Yorks). Said to be ' beacon-borrow or hill.' Only *ingle,* ' fire,' is not found till 1508, and in the 16th cny. only in Sc. Ingle -is prob. for Angle, O.E. *Engle,* ' barrow of the Angle,' or ' English ' man. *Cf.* next. -borough is O.E. *biorg, beorh,* 2 *beoruh,* 4 *borw, burgh,* 7 *barrough,* ' hill, mound-like hill, barrow. *Cf.* BARROW and Whitbarrow (N. Lancs).

INGLEBY CROSS and GREENHOW (Yorks) and INGLETON (Darlington and Kirby Lonsdale). *Dom.* Englebi, 1179-80 Ynglebi. Dar I. *a.* 1130 *Sim. Dur.* Ingeltun. ' Abode of the Angle,' O.E. *Engle,* or ' Englishman.' See -by and -ton. The -how will mean ' hill.' See HOUGHTON. *Cf.* Inglestone (Hawkesbury).

INGLEWHITE (Preston). This must surely be the same name as *Dom.* Yorks Ingulfvestuet, ' *Ingulph*'s village' or -thwaite, *q.v.*

INGOLDISTHORPE (King's Lynn), *a.* 1300 *chart.* Ingoldesthorp, and INGOLDSBY (Grantham). *Dom.* Ingoldesbi. ' Village ' and ' dwelling of *Ingold,*' in *Onom.* See -thorpe and -by.

INKBERROW (Worcester). 789 *chart.* Intanbeorgas, 803 *ib.* Intan-bergum, Intanbeorgan, Intebeorgas, *Dom.* Inteberge, 1275 Inkbarewe. ' BARROW, mound-like hill of *Inta,*' 3 in *Onom. Cf.* INGLEBOROUGH.

INKPEN BEACON (Hungerford). 931 *chart.* Ingepenne, *Dom.* Hinge-pene, 1298 Ingepenne, 1316 Inkepenne. ' *Inga*'s pen,' O.E. *penn,* ' a fold for cattle.' *Cf.* Inkford (Worc.) and PAMBER.

INLADE R. (N. Kent). *Bede* Genlade. ? W. *gwen, gwyn lloed,* ' white, clear place.'

INSKIP (Preston). *Dom.* Inscip. Prob. ' *Ine*'s or *Ini*'s hut,' Da. *kippe,* ' hut, low alehouse.' *Oxf. Dict.* does not give *kip,* ' a sharp-pointed hill,' before 1815. Possible also is ' *Ine*'s skep ' or ' beehive.' O.N. *skeppa,* ' a basket,' is found once in O.E., and, after 1225, is common as *skep*, also 4-9 *skip(pe)*, though not found for ' beehive ' till 1494. *Cf.* MINSKIP.

INSTOW (N. Devon). Old forms needed; not in *Dom*. Perh. ' place,' O.E. *stow*, ' of *Ine* or *Ini*.' *Cf. Dom*. Bucks Instofald.

IPPLEPEN (Newton Abbot). *Dom*. Iplepene, 1230 Ipelepenn. Prob. ' pen, enclosure (O.E. *penn*) of *Ipele*,' var. of *Ypwine*, the base name of EBBSFLEET, called in *Life of St. Mildred* Ypples fleet. The liquids *l* and *n* not seldom interchange.

IPSLEY (Redditch). 963 *chart.* Æps leage, *Dom*. Epeslei, *a.* 1200 Ippeslei. Either ' aspen-tree (O.E. *æps*) meadow '; *cf.* APPS COURT and APSLEY. Or perh. '*Æppa*'s mead.' *Cf.* EPSOM.

IPSTONES (Cheadle). *a.* 1200 Yppestan, *a.* 1300 Ippestanes. May be fr. a man as above. Duignan prefers ' look-out stones,' fr. O.E. *yppe*, ' a raised or look-out place.' *Cf.* IBSTONE.

IPSWICH. 993 *O.E. Chron.* Gipeswic, *Dom*. Gyppeswik, Guppewicus, *c.* 1097 *Orderic* Gepesuicum, 1455 Yepiswiche, 1463 Ipysweche, ' Dwelling of *Gipa* or *Gyppa*.' The name of the R. *Gipe* or *Gipping* is a back-formation. For loss of initial *g cf.* ILCHESTER and ISLEHAM; also *cf.* ISLIP and Gibsmere (Notts), *Dom*. Gipesmare, 1302 Gyppesmere. See -wich.

IRBY (Yorks, Burgh, and Birkenhead) and IREBY (Kirkby Lonsdale and Carlisle). Yo. I. *Dom*. Irebi, 1202 *Yorks Fines* Yrebi. Kir. I. *Dom*. Irebi. ' Dwelling of *Ira*.' *Cf. B.C.S.* 1297 Yran ceaster, now IRCHESTER (Wellingborough) and IRTON (E. Riding), *Dom*. Iretune. See -by and -ton.

IRELETH (Askam, Lancs). *Dom*. Gerleuuorde. ' Farm of '? The old ending is clear (see -worth), but the man's name quite doubtful. Perh. it is *Girweald* or *Giroldus*, perh. *Gerl*, implied in the patronymic *Gerling*, of which *Onom.* has one case. The present ending -leth has been influenced by N. *hlith*, ' a slope.' *Cf.* Holleth, also Lancs.

IRT R. and IRTLING R. (Cumbld.). ? W. *iarth*, ' a long rod, a goad.' *Cf.* next.

IRTHLINGBOROUGH (Northampton). *a.* 1100 *chart.* Irtelingburge, 1135 *O.E. Chron.* Hyrtlingberi. Presumably a patronymic; nothing likely in *Onom. Cf.* above and HARTLEBURY. See -borough.

IRWELL R. (S. Lancs). *c.* 1200 Irewill. Doubtful, prob. Keltic. Perh. ' vigorous river,' W. *ir gwili. Cf.* ABERGWILI and EREWASH.

ISHAM (Kettering). *Sic a.* 1100; not in *Dom*. It is uncertain what man's name Is- will represent. The R. Isborne (Evesham) is 709 *chart.* Esigburn, 777 Esegburn, ' brook of *Esig, Ese*, or *Esi*,' all forms are found; and Isham may come fr. this name too, as certainly does 1160-01 *Pipe* Sussex, Eisewrda (*Dom*. Isiwirde), ' farm of *Ese*.' *Cf.* Isfield, Uckfield (not in *Dom*.), and ESSENDON.

ISIS R., name of R. Thames above Oxford. *Sic* 1537 *Leland,* but *c.* 1387 *Higden* Ysa, 1603 Yshnyver (see NEVERN). It is almost certain that this is a Keltic name for ' river ' or ' water,' as in OUSE, and G. *uisge. Cf.* WISBEACH and the Wissey, trib. of Ouse. Skeat thinks that Ismere House, Kidderminster, *c.* 757 *chart.* Usmere, may show the same root. H. Alexander asserts that Isis is merely a ' fanciful separation ' of the L. name for Thames —Tam -esis. This is contrary to our evidence, esp. that of Higden; and the form Esis never seems to occur.

ISLEHAM (Soham) and ISLEWORTH (R. Thames). Pron. I-zelworth. *Dom.* Gisleham, 1284 Isilham, 1321 Yeselham. *Dom.* Ghistel-worde, *later* Yhistelworth, Istelworth, *c.* 1600 Thistleworth. ' Home ' and ' farm of the hostage,' O.E. *gisel.* ISLEBECK (N. Yorks), *Dom.* Iselbec, is presumably ' brook of the hostage ' too. But Islehampstead is prob. 1230 *Close R.* Ysenhamested, ' homestead of Isen-.' There are several possible names, Isenbard, Isengrim, etc. See -worth.

ISLE OF DOGS (London). Formerly Stepney Marsh. 1588 *Ames' Map,* Ile of Dogges; 1593 *Norden's Map,* ' Isle of Doges Ferme.' The origin of the name is quite unknown to history. See Thornbury and Walford's *Greater London,* i. 535-37. Possibly because so many dogs were drowned in the Thames here.

ISLINGTON (London). *Old* Isendune. The *l,* as in *island,* is said to be quite mod. Prob. ' hill of *Isena.' Cf. B.C.S.* 144 Isenan æwylm (' spring '); and see -ing, -don, and -ton.

ISLIP (Oxford and Thrapston). Ox. I. *a.* 1100 *chart.* Githslep. Thr. I. *Dom.* and *c.* 1240 Islep. ' *Githa's* leap,' O.E. *hlýp,* 3 *leep, lip,* 4-6 *lepe.* There are 4 *Githa's* in *Onom. Cf.* BIRDLIP.

ITCHEN R. (Hants and Warwick). Ha. I. 961 *chart.* Icena; Wa. I. 998 *chart.* on Ycænan, 1001 *ib.* on Ycenan. Some identify the Hants R. with Ytene, which *Flor. W., c.* 1097, says is the Angles' name for the New Forest. If so, we prob. have the common scribe's error *t* for *c*; and origin fr. O.E. *etan,* 3rd sing. pres. *ytt,* ' to devour, consume,' is not to be thought of. Prob. both rivers are pre-Kelt. *Cf.* R. ITHON (Radnor), R. Ythan (Aberdeensh.), Ythancæstir (Essex) in *Bede* iii. 22, BP'S ITCH-INGTON, and ICKNIELD ST. LONG ITCHINGTON (Southam) is 1001 *chart.* Yceantune, *Dom.* Icentone, ITCHINGTON (Thornbury), is 967 *chart.* Icenantune, *Dom.* Icetune; whilst ITCHINGTON (Suffolk) is also fr. a R. *Icenan. Cf. K.C.D.,* iii. 316.

ITTERINGHAM (Norfolk). *Sic* 1504, also Iteryngham. ' Home of *Wihthering, Withering,* or *Witherwine,'* all names in *Onom. Dom.* has only a Witeingeham. *Cf.* WITHERNSEA. See -ing.

IVEL (or ILE) R. (Somerset, and trib. of Great Ouse). See IL-CHESTER.

IVER (Uxbridge). *a.* 1300 Evere, Evre. Not in *Dom.* *Ivor* is an old Brit. name found in Geoffrey of Monmouth and Giraldus Cambrensis. But here it is prob. O.E. *ifig ofr*, M.E. *ivi-over*, 'ivy bank.' It is on a bank. *Cf.* Asher, Beecher, Hasler, etc.; and see -over.

IXHULL (Oakley, Bucks). Not in *Dom.* 1240 *Close R.* Yxenhull. Prob. 'hill of *Ycca*,' 2 in *Onom.* *Cf.* IXWORTH (Bury St. E.). *Dom.* Icsewurda', '*Icca*'s farm.' *Hull* is regular Midland Eng. for *hill*.

JACKMENTS BOTTOM (Kemble, Cirencester). *Old* Jakemans, Jacumans, called fr. a man. A Walter *Jakemans* is known in 1355. Bottom is O.E. *botm*, found with the secondary meaning, 'dell, low-lying land,' fr. *c.* 1325.

JACOBSTOW (Cornwall). 'Place (O.E. *stow*) of *Jacob*,' brother of Winwaloe. See GUNWALLOE.

JARROW, on Tyne. *Bede* In Gyrvum, Gyrwum; *a.* 1130 *Sim. Dur.* Girva, 1593 Southe Yarowe. W. *garw, geirw*, 'rough'; also 'a torrent.' *Cf.* G. *garbh*, 'rough,' and YARROW (Sc.). But M'Clure thinks fr. Kelt. *gyrwe*, 'fen, marsh.' *Cf.* WEAR.

JERSEY. *c.* 380 *Anton. Itin.* Cæsarea, *c.* 1070 *Wm. Jumièges* Gersus, *a.* 1170 *Wace* Gersui, 1218 *Patent R.* Geresye, 1219 *ib.* Gerese, 1447 Jersey, 1454 Gersey, 1587 Iarzie. Caesarea is 'place named in honour of *Cæsar*,' the ending being L. -ea, and not N. -ey. The present form is due to N. influence, and may be meant for O.N. **gers*-ey, 'grass-covered isle'; O.E. *græs, græs*; O.Fris. *gers*; Dan. *græs*, 'grass.' But, all the same, it must be corrup. of Caesarea. Cherburg, close by, is 1237 *Close R.* Cesariburg; whilst Caithness—*i.e.*, Norse-blooded—lips to-day always call Jews Chews. *Cf.* JERBOURG, Guernsey. See -ey.

JERVAULX or JOREVAL (Yorks, N. Riding). Pron. Jarvis. 1297 Jerovalle. Fr. *val*, mod. pl. *vaux*, is 'a valley'; but Jer(o)- is doubtful. *Cf.* JARROW. The Cistercian abbey was founded here in 1156. For the ending -val, *cf.* the name Furnivall, found fr. 13th cny., from Fournival, Normandy.

JESMOND (Newcastle). *Sic a.* 1270. As above, the latter half seems clear enough, Fr. *mont*, 'mount, hill,' but the former is quite doubtful. *Cf.* RICHMOND.

JOHNSTON (Pembroke). *Sic* 1603. Founded by Flemish settlers early in the 12th cny. *Cf.* Jameston, JORDANSTON (1516 Jordanyston, W. Tref Wrdan), and Williamston, in same shire.

JUMP (Barnsley). Modern. The word *jump* is not found in Eng. till 1511.

KEDINGTON (Haverhill, Suffolk). *Dom.* Kidituna. *Cf. Dom.* Kedington (Worc.). 'Town of *Cedd, Cedda*, or *Ceadda*,' gen. -*an*. *Cf.*, too, *Dom.* Cedeslai (Worc.). Kedsley is still a surname. See -ing.

KEEL (2 in Montgomery) and KEELE (Newcastle-under-L.). New. K.
a. 1200 Kiel. Duignan is prob. right in calling all these Keltic.
G. *cille,* 'graveyard, church,' comes very near in sound; but G.
words are unknown hereabouts, so it is prob. W. *cil,* 'a corner,
a nook.' But KEELBY (N. Lincs) must be fr. a man, as in
KELMARSH, KELLOE, etc.; so also Nun Keeling (Yorks), *Dom.*
Chelinge, plainly a patronymic fr. a man, *Keel* or *Cele.*

KEEVIL (Trowbridge). *Dom.* Chivele, 1217 *Patent R.* Kivele. The
ending -ley, *q.v.,* very rarely falls away to *l* only. But this is
prob. 'meadow of *Cifa.*' *Cf.* CHEVENAGE, Kiveton Park,
Sheffield, etc.

KEGWORTH (Derby). Not in *Dom.* 'Farm of *Ceagga.*' *Cf. B.C.S.*
762 Ceaggan heal, and 939 *chart.* Cagbroc (Shaftesbury). See
-worth.

KEIGHLEY (Yorks). Now pron. Keithly. *Dom.* Chichelai, 1300
Kighelye, 1303 Kighley. This is the same name as the well-
known Abp. Chichele (*c.* 1362-1443), and must be 'meadow of
Cykell' (var. of *Cytel* or *Ketel,* a common name), a name found
once in *Sim. Dur.* The present pron. curiously confirms the
fact that *Cykell* is var. of *Cytel.* See -ley.

KEKEWICH or -WICK (Runcorn). See KENSWICK, and *cf.* CHECKLEY,
and 1286 *Close R.* Kekaller, '*Cec*'s alder-tree.'

KELD (Richmond, Yorks). O.N. *kelda,* 'a well, a spring.' *Cf.*
GUNNERSKELD, Threlkeld, etc.; also *Dom.* Worc. 'Celdeslai,'
and *ib.* Bucks, Celdenuella and Celdestone.

KELFIELD (York). *Dom.* Chelchefeld. The name represented by
Chelche- is doubtful. It may be *Ceollach* or *Cellah,* found once
in *Onom.*

KELLET, OVER and NETHER (Carnforth). *Dom.* Chellet, *a.* 1400
Keldelith. O.N. *kelda-hlith,* 'spring, well on the hill-slope.'
How early the name contracted, yet how late the true form
lingered !

KELLINGTON (Normanton). *Dom.* Chellinctone, Chelintune. 'Town
of *Celling,*' a recorded name, or ' of the sons of *Ceolla.*' See
-ing.

KELLOE (Coxhoe, Durham). 1522 Kellowe. Prob. ' *Ceol*'s hill ' or
'how,' O.N. *haug-r,* 'a mound, a cairn,' found in Eng. as *how*
a. 1340. See -how.

KELMARSH (Northampton). *Dom.* Keilmersc. 'Marsh,' O.E.
mer(i)sc, ' of *Ceol.*' *Cf.* Kelby (S. Lincs), *Dom.* Chelebi, and
above.

KELSTON (Bath). Old forms needed. Not in *Dom.* But *cf. Dom.*
Bucks Celdestane—*i.e.,* ' stone at the well ' or ' spring,' O.E.
celde, O.N. *kelda.* *Cf.* KILHAM, also KELMSTOW, Halesowen,
1327 Kelmestowe, ' place ' of a chapel to St. *Kenelm* or *Coenhelm.*

KELVEDON (Essex). 998 *chart.* Cynlaue dyne, *Dom.* Keluenduna, 1298 Kelwendon. Prob. ' hill of *Cynelaf,*' 6 in *Onom.* The change here is unusual. See -don.

KEMERTON (Tewkesbury). Said to be 840 *chart.* Cyneburgincgtun (*B.C.S.* 430), ' dwelling of the sons of *Cyneburh,*' a woman. See -ing. But *Dom.* Chin-, Chenemertune, ' dwelling of *Cynemær.*'

KEMMAES HEAD. See CEMMAES.

KEMPLEY (W. Glouc.). *Dom.* Chenepelei, 1221 Kenepelege, 1239 -pelega. Some think, O.E. *cyne-æppel-léah,* ' royal apple-meadow,' an interesting corruption. Norm. scribes, esp. in *Dom.,* have a habit of turning *c* into the softer *ch.* But it is already 1195 Kempelee, and Baddeley may be right in making it ' *Cnapa*'s lea.'

KEMPSEY (Worcester). 799 *chart.* Kemesei, 977 *ib.* Cymesige, *Dom.* Chemesege (Norm. spelling), 1275 Kemesey. Prob. ' isle of *Ceomma.*' A *p* often intrudes, *cf.* BAMPTON, BROMPTON, etc. See next and -ey.

KEMPSFORD (Glouc.). *O.E. Chron.* 800 Cynemæresford, 1236 Kynemeresford, 1541 Kamyseford. ' Ford of *Cynemær.*' But KEMPSTON (Bedford), *Dom.* Cameston (4 times), 1242 *Close R.* Kemes-, Kemstun, is prob. fr. a man *Ceomma,* in *Onom.* The letter *p* is a common intruder.

KEMPTON (Sunbury). *Dom.* Chenetone; 1222 *Patent R.* Kenintun; 1238 Kenni-, Kenyton, Kenet'; 1331 Kenyngton. Prob. ' town of *Coen* or *Coena,*' both in *Onom.*

KENCHESTER (Hereford). *c.* 380 *Anton. Itin.* Magnis, *Dom.* Chenecestre. O.E. *cyne ceaster,* ' royal camp or town.' *Cf.* KEMPLEY.

KENDAL. *a.* 1199 Kirkeby in Kendal, 1303 *Brunne* Kendale, 1575 Kirkbie Kendall. ' Dale, valley of R. *Kent,*' which must be the same as R. KENNET—at least so thinks Skeat. This K. is not in *Dom.,* but we have there a ' Cheldale '—*i.e.,* Kendall Farm (Driffield)—on the R. Kell, trib. of the Hull. The liquids *l* and *n* occasionally interchange. Kell may be W. *celli,* ' a wood, a grove.' See -dale and KIRKBY.

KENFIG HILL (Bridgend, Glam.). *Chart.* Kenefeg. W. *cefn y ffyg,* ' at the head of the swamp,' now mostly buried in the sand, but once famous. Caen or Ken Wood (Hampstead) might be fr. *cefn* too; but it does not seem mentioned till 1661, which is far too late for us to be sure of anything.

KENILWORTH (Warwick). *Dom.* Chinewrde, *a.* 1199 *Roll. Rich. I.* Kenilleworhe, 1229 Kenillewurth, 1297 *R. Glouc.* Keningwrthe, Kiningwurthe, 1298 Kenilworthe. The true form is found only in the other and now defunct Kenilworth, near Worcester, 974 *chart.* Cynelde weorthe, 980 *ib.* Cinilde wyrthe. ' Farm of *Cynehild,*' a woman. *Cf. Dom.* Salop Cheneltone. The word *kennel* is fr. Nor. Fr., and not found in Eng. till *c.* 1350. See -worth.

KENLEY (Shrewsbury and Surrey). Shr. K. *Dom.* Chenelie. '*Coena*'s meadow.' Several of this name in *Onom.* See -ley. But KENNERLEY (Oswestry) and KENNERSLEY (Wellington, Salop, and Hereford), *Dom.* Chenardelei, Oswestry, are fr. *Coenweard.* The surname Kenward is still in use.

KENNET R. (Berks) and town and R. (Newmarket); also old name of Marlboro, which is 1223 Kenet. Be. K. is *c.* 380 *Ant. Itin.* Cunetio, 1006 *O.E. Chron.* and *B.C.S.*, ii. 367, Cyneta; Ne. K. *c.* 1080 Kenet, *Dom.* Chenet. Keltic root of unknown meaning. *Cf.* KENNET (Sc.), KENT R. (Wstmld.), Kentford (Sussex) (*Chron. Ramsey* Chenetheford), and KINTBURY.

KENNINGTON (London and Berks). Lo. K. *Dom.* Chenintone, *c.* 1390 Kennyngton. Be. K. *O.E. chart.* Cenintune, Cenigtune; *later* Chenig-, Chenitun; *c.* 1290 Keninton. Seems to be O.E. *Coenantun*, ' town of *Coena* ' (3 in *Onom.*, and 1 *Coen*), or else ' of Coena's descendants.' Skeat prefers to derive fr. *Keen* or the *Keenings*, O.E. *cene*, ' bold, valiant, keen.' *Cf. Dom.* Devon, Chenigedone, ' Keening's hill,' and Kensworth (Beds). KENNINGHALL (Thetford), *Dom.* Cheninchala, Chenighehala, has prob. the same origin. The -ighe- is the common -incg, sign of the patronymic. See -ing and -hall.

KENSINGTON (London). *Dom.* Chenesitune. Prob. ' town of *Coensige* ' or ' *Censige* ' (2 in *Onom.*). See -ing.

KENSWICK (Worcester). *Dom.* Checinwiche, *a.* 1200 Checkingwic, *a.* 1400 Kekingwik, Kekingewyke, Kekeswych. Prob. ' dwelling of the sons of *Cecca*,' *cf.* CHECKLEY, or ' of *Cygincg*,' one in *Onom. Cf.* KEKEWICH and Kensworth, Beds (not in *Dom.*), and see -wick.

KENT. 55 B.C. *Jul. Cæsar* Cantium, *c.* 30 B.C. *Diod. Sicul.* Καντιον, ? *a.* 600 *Gregory Tours* Cantia, *Bede* Cant-uarii, *a.* 810 *Nennius* Chent, *O.E. Chron.* 676 Centlond, *Dom.* Chent; also *c.* 930 *Lett. to Athelstan* Cantescyre. E. Nicholson conjectured an O.Kelt. root meaning ' white,' fr. the chalk cliffs. *Cf.* W. *gwyn*, *gwen*. Possibly it means ' headland.' *Cf.* G. *ceann*, ' head,' and Gabrosenti, O.Kelt. form of GATESHEAD. For R. KENT see KENDAL and KENNET.

KENTCHURCH and KENDERCHURCH (Hereford) are only 1 mile apart. Not in *Dom.* Prob. both are = LLANGYNIDR.

KENTISBURYFORD (Barnstaple). *Dom.* Chentesberie, *Exon. Dom.* Chentisberia. The Kenti- may represent some such O.E. name as *Centwine* or *Cintswine*, a common name, or perh. *Coenstan* or *Chenestan. Cf.* KENTCHURCH. 1160-61 *Pipe* Glouc. has a Cantebohhan, which may be for ' *Canta*'s bow ' or ' arch.' O.E. *boʒa* has this sense. There is a *Canta* in *Onom.*, and this may be the name in Kentisbury too. *Cf.* KENTISBEARE (Cullompton), *Dom.* Chentesbere. See BEER, 'a wood.'

KENTISH TOWN (London). *Old* Kanteloues Town, *later* Kentestowne. Named fr. the family of *Cantlow,* formerly *Kaunteloe,* Norm. Chanteloup, or *champ de loup,* 'wolf's field.' Interesting example of 'popular' etymology.

KENTON (Exeter and 2). *Dom.* Devon and Bucks Chentone, Sffk. Kenetona; 1157 *Pipe* Chenton (Devon). Older forms needed. May be fr. a man *Coen,* in *Onom.* Perh. fr. the common name *Centwine,* contracted.

KERESLEY (Coventry). 1275 Keresleye. 'Meadow of the watercress,' O.E. *cærse, cerse.* *Cf.* CRESSWELL and ABBOT'S KERSWELL; also Kersewell (Wstrsh.), 1275 Kersewelle.

KERSEY (Suffolk). O.E. *chart.* Caersige, 1342 Kersey; also 1262 'panni cersegi,' Kersey cloths. 'Isle of watercresses.' See above and -ey. *Dom.* has only Keresfelda and -halla.

KESSINGLAND (Lowestoft). *Dom.* Kessinga-, Kessingeland; 1225 *Patent R.* Cassinge-, Casingland. 'Land of the sons of *Casa,*' one in *Onom.* *Cf. B.C.S.* 341 Kasingburne and CHESHAM. See -ing.

KESTEVEN (E. Lincs). *Dom.* Chetsteven, *a.* 1200 *chart.* Ketstefena, 1242 Ketsteven'. Looks like '*Cetta*'s stem or stock,' O.E. *stefn, stemn.* But for Chet- *cf.* also CHETWOOD.

KESTLE MILL (St. Columb Minor, Cornwall). There is in *Dom.* Salop a Cestulle, or 'hill of *Cest,*' an unknown man. But it is quite uncertain if this is the same.

KESWICK (Cumberland, and Taverham, Norfolk); also EAST KESWICK, near Leeds (*Dom.* Chesuic). Tav. K. *Dom.* Kesewic, *c.* 1150 Casewic, and so = CHESWARDINE and CHISWICK, '*cheese* farm,' 'house where cheese is made.' See -wick. KESTON (Hayes, Kent), *Dom.* Chestan, may be similarly 'cheese stone' or 'cheese-press'; otherwise it will be 'stone of *Cis,*' a name in *Onom.*

KETLEY (Wellington, Salop). Not in *Dom.* *Cf.* 1158-59 Chateleia, *Pipe* Norfk. and Suffk., 'Meadow of *Cetil, Chetel,*' or '*Ketil*'; all forms in *Onom.* The seat of the Curzons of Keddleston was *a.* 1400 Ketilston. See -ley. But KETFORD (Dymock), *Dom.* Chitiford, is fr. a man *Cyta.*

KETTERING. 963 O.E. *Chron.* Ketering, 1125 Kateringes (pl.), and KETTERINGHAM (Norwich), 956 *chart.* Æt Cytringan, *Dom.* Ketrincham. Patronymics. 'Abode of the sons of *Kater,*' still in use as a surname. See -ing and -ham (where the -an of 956, a possible loc., will be found referred to).

KETTLEBURGH (Wickham Mket.). 1224 Ketelbergh. 'Burgh, castle of *Cetel* or *Cytel*'; a common name. See -burgh.

KETTON (Stamford). Not in *Dom.* *Cf.* 1183 *Boldon Bk.* Kettona (Durham). Prob. 'village of *Cetta*'; one in *Onom.* *Cf.* KETFORD; see -ton.

KEVERNE (Cornwall). Not in *Dom.* 1536 Keweyn. Prob. fr. St. *Keynwen* or *Kenew*, daughter of Brychan of Brecknock, and aunt of St. Cadoc. KENWYN is the name of the parish of which Truro stands. *Cf.* St. Keyne (Cornwall), but not KEYNSHAM.

KEW (London). Old Kayhough, Kayhoo, Keye; 1749 Kew. 'Promontory, point of land at the quay or wharf'; O.Fr. *kay, cai ;* in Eng. 4 *keye*, and see HOE, HOO.

KEWSTOKE (Weston-super-Mare). *Dom.* Chiwestoch. Said to be 'place of St. *Kew.*' St. *Ciwg* or *Cwick* was patron saint of Llangwick, on R. Taff, possibly *Exon. Dom.* Lancichuc. There is also a St. *Kywa* or *Ciwa* in the *Exeter Martyrology*, Feb. 8. *Cf. Roll Rich. I.*, 'Kiweshope' (Hereford).

KEYHAM (Leicester and Devonport). Lei. K. *Dom.* Caiham and Caitorp. *Cf. Dom.* Surrey and Salop Ceihā. 'Home of ?' perh. *Ceawa. Cf. B.C.S.* 833 Ceawan hlæw. There is a well-known Pict. name *Ce* or *Keth*, now *Kay. Cf.* Keyworth (Notts), *Dom.* Caworde, 1200 Kye-, *c.* 1294 Keword, which Mutschmann takes for O.E. *cý worth*, 'cow farm,' O.E. *cú*, pl. *cý*, Sc. *kye.*

KEYMER (Hassocks, Sussex). *Dom.* Chemere. Prob. '*Ceomma*'s mere' or 'lake.' *Cf.* CROMER, etc.

KEYNOR (Selsea). *O.E. Chron.* 477 Cymenesore, '*Cymen*'s shore,' *Dom.* Coonore, -nare; where the Saxon Ælle and his 3 sons, Cissa, Cymen, and Wlencing, landed in 477. *Cf.* the Cumensora near W. Wittering (Sussex), mentioned in a spurious charter. See -or.

KEYNSHAM (Bristol). *c.* 990 *Ethelweard re* 871 Cœginesham, *Dom.* Cainesham, 1223 *Patent R.* Keinesham. 'Home of *Keigwin*,' a surname, prob. Cornish, still in use. *Cf.* CANWELL.

KEYNTON (Dorset, Wilts, Salop). Do. K. formerly Chintone, Con-, Cuntone; Wi. K. Contone; Sa. K. Cantune. *O.E. Coenantun,* 'town of *Coena*' (3 in *Onom.*).

KIBWORTH (Leicester). *Dom.* Chiburde. *Cf.* 1208 *Yorks Fines* Kybbewordhe. 'Farm of *Cybba.*' *Cf. B.C.S.* 1002 Cybban stan. See -worth.

KIDDAL. See CHEADLE.

KIDDERMINSTER. *Dom.* Chideminstre, 1223 Kideminstre, *a.* 1300 Kyder-, Kydelminstr, *c.* 1350 Kiderminestere. In a grant of 736 lands at 'Chideminstre' (Norm. scribe's spelling) are given by K. Æthelbald to Earl Cyneberght on which to build a monastery (see -minster). So the name is 'Monastery, monastery-church of *Cydda.*' There are 3 in *Onom.*, also a *Cyda*, a *Cydd*, and a *Cyddi*. The *r* is a later insertion, so M'Clure's derivation fr. O.W. *cyddwfr* (= *cyn-dwfr*), 'confluence of the rivers,' is barred out. Besides, the confluence of Stow with Severn is 4 miles away. But there is a Kiddermore Green (Wolverhampton), which *may* have a W. origin. For ' cockney ' insertion of *r cf.* TATTERSHALL.

KIDLINGTON (Oxon). *Dom.* Chedelintona, Cedelintona (also in Devon), 1149 Cudelyngton, 1214 Kedelinton, 1227-28 Cudelinton, Kedelyngton. ' Town of the sons of *Cydel,*' or perh. ' of *Ceadela.*' But KIDDINGTON (Oxon.) is *Dom.* Chidintone, ' town of *Cydda.*' See KIDDERMINSTER.

KIDSGROVE (Stoke-on-T.). No old forms; but *cf. Dom.* Northants Chidesbi. ' Grove, wood of *Cydda.*' *Cf.* above.

KIDWELLY (Cærmarthen). *a.* 810 *Nennius* and *a.* 1130 *Lib. Landav.* Cetgueli; *Brut y Twys.* ann. 991 Cydweli; *Ann. Cambr.* Kedweli; 1401 Kedewelly. In mod. W. Ced-, Cadweli. A little doubtful; prob. a tribal name fr. a chief *Cadwal.*

KIELDER (Cheviots). G. *caol dobhar* (W. *dwr*). ' Narrow stream.' In G. *ao* is pron. *ü,* but on Eng. lips varies greatly in sound; with the sound in Kielder *cf.* EDDRACHILIS (Sc.) = G. *eadar-a-chaolais,* and pron. by English people Eddrahéelis.

KILBURN (London). *c.* 1134 *chart.* Kuneburna, Keneburna; *later,* Kele-, Keeleburn, Caleburn; 1536 Kilnborne. ' Burn, brook of *Cuna* or *Coena* or *Coen* '; several in *Onom.* But later forms indicate some comparison with O.E. *céol,* ' a keel, a ship.' As we often see, any liquid may interchange with any other; hence the *n* becoming *l. Cf.* KILLINGHALL.

KILCOT (Gloucester). *Dom.* Chilecot, 1307 Kulkotte. Prob. = CHILCOTT (Wells), and so Keltic for 'narrow wood.' It is difficult to account for the Chile- otherwise, unless it be similar to KILHAM, with *chile* for O.E. *celde,* ' a spring.' *Cf.* Killpeek (Herefd.), 1219 Kilpec. However, there is one *Killa,* or *Cylla,* in a Mercian chart.

KILHAM (Driffield). *Dom.* Chillon (6 times), 1179-80 *Pipe* Chillum. An old loc., *chillon* or *cyllum,* ' at the sources or springs ' of R. Hull; O.E. *celde,* O.N. *kelda,* ' a spring, a well.' *Cf.* Kelham (Notts), *Dom.* Calun, 1189 *Pipe* Kelum, and WELHAM. There is another near Coldstream (Sc.).

KILLINGHALL (Harrogate). *Dom.* Chenehalle, Chilingale. ' Nook of *Coena* ' or ' *Cilla,*' with gen. -*an. Dom.* is perpetually inter-changing *l* and *n. Cf.* CHILLINGHAM, KILBURN, etc. See -hall.

KILLINGWORTH (Newcastle). *c.* 1330 *R. Brunne* Kilyngworth, 1424 Kyllynworth, and KILWORTH, South (Lutterworth), 1288 *Close R.* Suth-Kevelingwrth, 1307 Kivelingworth. The ending, of course, is ' farm.' See -worth. The prefix seems a patrony-mic otherwise unrecorded, perh. fr. vb. *kevel,* O.N. *kefla,* ' to bit or bridle,' and so this might be ' bridling-place.' *Cf.* above. But Kilworth is in *Dom.* Chivelesworde, which postulates a man *Cifel,* or the like.

KILMINGTON (Bath and Axminster). *Dom.* Chelmetone, *Ex. Dom.* Chilmatona. Ax. K. 1219 *Patent R.* Kelmeton. 'Town of *Celm*,' one in *Onom.*, or ' of *Celm*'s sons.' See -ing.

KILNSEA (Spurn Hd.). *Dom.* Chilnesse. Perh. 'isle, peninsula of the kiln '; O.E. *cyline, cyln*, O.N. *kylna.* *Cf.* Kilnhurst (Rotherham). The sign of the gen. in Kilnsea suggests a man's name, but there is nothing in *Onom.* except *Cylm* ; *Cyln* might be a variant. KILNWICK (Beverley) is *Dom.* Chelingewic, Chilewid, a patronymic fr. *Cil* or *Cele,* the name seen in Kelby (S. Lincs), *Dom.* Chelebi. See -wick, 'dwelling.'

KILSBY (Rugby). Not in *Dom.* 1155-62 *chart.* Kylesbya. 'Dwelling of *Cille* or *Cilla* ' ; several in *Onom.* *Cf.* 1155 *Pipe* Cheleswurda, ' *Cille*'s farm,' and Kelby (S. Lincs), *Dom.* Chelebi. See -by.

KILVINGTON (Thirsk). *Dom.* Cheluintun, *c.* 1190 Kilvingtone, 1200 Kilvintone. Prob. ' town of *Ceolwynn* '; one in *Onom.* But KILVINGTON (Notts), *Dom.* Chilvintun, Chelvinctun. Mutschmann would make 'home of the sons of *Cylfa* ' ; one in *Onom.*) See -ing. KILVE (Bridgwater), not in *Dom.*, 1221 *Patent R.* Kelve, seems to be one of the rare cases, like GOODRICH, etc., where a place-name is simply a man's name, here *Ceolf,* short form of the common *Ceolwulf.*

KIMBERLEY occurs 3 times, each a different name, and none fr. KIMBER, name of R. Pang (Berks) near its source, Kelt. *cumber,* W. *cymmer,* 'a confluence.' K., Nottingham, is *Dom.* Chinemar(e)lie, '*Cynemœr*'s mead.' K., Warwksh., is 1311 Cynebaldeleye, '*Cynebald*'s mead '; and K. near R. Yare (Norfk.) is *Dom.* Chineburlai, 1237 Kyneburl', 'mead of *Cynebeorht,*' a very common O.E. name. *Cf.* Kilmersdon (Bath), 1235 Kynemerdon, and Kimsbury (Gloster), *c.* 1230 Kinemeresbur.

KIMBOLTON (Hunts and Leominster). Hu. K. *Dom.* Chenebaltone, 1297 Kynebauton. ' Town of *Cynebald* ' ; *m* and *n* often interchange. *Cf.* GREAT KIMBLE, and Kilmeston (Southampton), *Dom.* Chenelmestune, '. *Kenelm*'s town.'

KIMPTON (Andover and Welwyn). An. K. *Dom.* Chementune. We. K. *Dom.* Kamintone, 1210 Kentone, *later* Kymi-, Kemitone, 1346 Kumynton. Skeat is clear that this last is O.E. *Cyman tun,* ' town of Cyma.' It is on the R. Kime, but this must be a back formation. *Cf.* KYME and *Dom.* Devon Chiempabera, perh. fr. *Cempa—i.e.,* ' warrior.'

KINDER SCOUT (The Peak). Scout is *Oxf. Dict.* sb[1], fr. O.N. *skute,* ' a high, overhanging rock.' Kinder is doubtful; old forms. needed. It looks like G. *cinn dobhair* (W. *dwr*), ' at the head of the stream,' but this would be a very rare type of name for this region. So prob. it is fr. *kind. sic* in O.E. and O.N., in mod. Icel. *kind-r,* ' sheep,' though in older usage it seems to mean only ' kind, sort.'

KINETON or KINGTON (Warwksh.). 969 *chart.* Cyngtune, *Dom.*
Cintone. Plainly ' royal town, town of the king '; O.E. *cyning.*
Cf. Dom. Lincs Chinetorp, O.E. *cyne,* ' royal ' village.

KINGSBURY (Tamworth). *Dom.* Chinesburie, *a.* 1200 Kinesburi,
1322 Kinesbury. ' Burgh, town of *Cyne* '—*i.e.,* ' the royal.' Said
to have been a residence of the Mercian kings. See -bury.

KINGSCLERE (Newbury). See BURGHCLERE.

KINGSCLIFFE (Wansford, Northants). 1202 *Yorks Fines* Cuniggesclive super Teisam, must be the same name.

KING'S LANGLEY (Herts). ' King's long meadow '; O.E. *lang léah.*
The land here was in royal possession from Hen. I. to Cromwell,
and a house was built here by Hen. III. KINGSNORTON (Birmingham), *Dom.* Nortune, also belonged to the Crown from
the Conquest to Hen. III.

KING'S LYNN. *Dom.* Lena, *c.* 1100 Lun, 1314-15 Lenne, 1450
Lynne. O.E. *hlynn* means usually ' a torrent running over
rocks,' which does not exist here. Its later meaning, ' a pool,'
is not recorded till 1577-87, Holinshed's *Chron.* Cognate with
W. *llyn,* Corn. *lin,* G. *linne,* ' a pool '; so the origin here may be
Keltic. The town's history goes back at least to 1100, prob.
earlier. Originally it was a fief of the Bp. of Norwich, and so
called Lynn Episcopi; but it was emancipated by Hen. VIII.,
and at that time received its present name, Lynn Regis or
King's Lynn.

KINGSLEY (Cheshire and Hanley). Ches. K. *sic a.* 1128. Han.
K. *Dom.* Chingeslei, *a.* 1300 Kynggesley. ' King's meadow.'
See -ley.

KING'S NYMPTON (Chulmleigh). 1287 Kingesnemeton. Hybrid.
See NYMPHSFIELD.

KINGSTHORPE (Northampton). *Dom.* Chingestorp. ' King's village.' See -thorpe.

KINGSTON (13 in *P.G.*). Surrey K. 619 Cingestun, 838 Cyningestun.
Camb. K. *Dom.* Chingestone, 1210 Kingestone. Notts K. *Dom.*
Chinestan, 1291 Kynstan. Warwk. K. 1327 Kyngestone. ' King's
town.' Sur. K. was the usual place for the consecration of the
Saxon Kings. The Notts name is O.E. *cyne stan,* ' royal stone.'
KINGSTON LISLE (Wantage), 1288 Kingeston Lisle, was called
after William *de Insula* or De L'Isle, in the time of Hen. II.

KINGSTONE BAGPUIZE (Berks). *Dom.* Chingestune in Merceham
(Marcham); also in *chart.* Kingestun, Cingestun. Called after a
Norman Bachepuiz (Chron. Abingdon, *temp.* Wm. II.), 1316
Bakepus, 1428 Bagepuys. Prob. fr. O.Fr. *bache,* ' a gulley, a
watercourse,' *cf.* Eng. *bach,* and O.Fr. *puz, puiz,* Fr. *puits,* L.
puteus, ' a well.' The Fr. place is now Bacquepuis, Eure.

KINGSWINFORD (Dudley). 1023 *chart.* Swinford, *Dom.* Suinesford.
' Ford of the swine '; O.E. *swin.* It was a royal manor in *Dom.*

KINGSWOOD (5 in *P.G.*). 1160 *Pipe* Chingeswuda, Kent. *Dom.*
Glouc. has only Chingescote, now Kingscote.

KINGWESTON (Somerset). *Dom.* Kenwardston, an interesting corruption. *Cyneweard* is a very common O.E. name.

KINNERLEY (Oswestry) and KINNERSLEY (W. Hereford, Severn-
Stoke, and Wellington, Salop). 1223 *Patent R.* Kinardeseia
(see -ey), ? which. Wel. K. *Dom.* Chinardelei, Chinardeseie.
'Meadow of *Cyneheard*,' a common O.E. name. *Cf.* next and
1155 *Pipe* Oxon. Chenewardberge, 'hill of *Coenweard*' or
'*Kenward*'; also KINGERBY (Lincs), 1218 *Patent R.* Kyngorby,
prob. 'dwelling of *Cynegar*'; one in *Onom.* See -by and -ley.

KINNERTON (Cheshire). *Dom.* Cinbretune. '*Cynebeorht*'s town.'
Cf. above.

KINTBURY (Hungerford). *Dom.* Cheneteberie, *chart.* æt Cynetan
byrig, 1316 Kenetbury. 'Burgh on the R. KENNET.' See -burgh.

KINTON (Hereford and Salop). He. K. *Dom.* Chingtune; also
KINGTON (Worcester). *Dom.* Chintune, 1275 Kyngton, 1340
Kynton, which Duignan renders O.E. *cyne tun*, 'royal town.'
Cf. 1167-68 *Pipe* Sussex Cunton.

KINVER FOREST (Stourbridge). 736 *chart.* 'the wood called
Cynibre,' 964 Cynefare, *Dom.* Chenefare, 1222 Kenefer, *Testa
de Nevill* Kinefar, 1282 Kynefare. M'Clure thinks this may
represent an early *Cunobriga*, 'high burgh.' The origin is quite
uncertain. It is very likely Kelt., ? W. *cwn y bre*, 'height, top
of the brae' or 'slope.' O.E. *cyne* means 'royal,' and *cyne
fare* (or *fær*) 'royal road'; but this may have been a Saxon
corrup. of a W. name.

KIPPAX (Pontefract). *Dom.* Chipesch. The local pron. is Kippis.
O.E. *ceap-æsc*,'market ash-tree.' *Cf.* CHEPSTOW and BORROWASH.

KIRBY (11 in *P.G.*). *Dom.* Leicr. Cherchebi. Contracted fr.
KIRK-BY, 'dwelling by the church.' KIRBY WISKE (Thirsk)
is 1212 Kirkeby super Wisc. See APPLETON WISKE.

KIRBY CROSS and KIRBY-LE-SOKEN (Walton-on-Naze). See above.
Not in *Dom.* These are among the most southerly of names
in -by. Soken is a district held by socage, in O.E. *sócn*, fr.
soc, 'the right of holding a court in a district.' All dwellers in a
soken were under the jurisdiction of the lord of the manor there.

KIRDFORD (Petworth). Not in *Dom. Cf. c.* 1030 'Cyrdeslea,'
Hereford. 'Ford of *Cyrd*,' contraction of *Ceolred*, a common
O.E. name.

KIRKBRIDE (Carlisle). 1189 Kirkebride. 'Church of St. *Bride*,'
or Bridget or Brigida of Kildare.

KIRKBY (16 in *P.G.*). *Dom.* Yorks Chirchebi or Cherchbi 35 times,
and Kirkebi once, all for some Kirkby or Kirby—*i.e.*, 'dwelling
by the church.' *Cf.* KENDAL; see -by.

KIRKHAM (N. of R. Ribble). *Dom.* Chicheham (*r* omitted by error), *c.* 1141 Chircheham, the name as written by a Norman or Southern scribe. 'Home, house by the *kirk*,' N. Eng. and Sc. for *church*.

KIRKLINGTON (Bedale and Southwell). Be. K. *Dom.* Cherclinton, Cherdinton, 1212 *Yorks Fines* Kertlinton. So. K. *Dom.* Cherlinton, Cherluintone, 1291 Kirtelyngton. These may be same as KIRTLINGTON; but prob. they are mostly Kirk-linton, 'the LYNTON by the church.' However, KIRKLINTON (Carlisle) is *c.* 1120 Kirklevington, prob. 'church of the village of *Lewine*' or '*Leofwine*,' or his descendants. *Cf.* LIVINGSTONE (Sc.); and see -ing.

KIRKOSWALD (Cumbld.). 1166-67 *Pipe* Karcoswald. 'Church of *Oswald.*' *Cf.* OSWESTRY.

KIRKSTALL ABBEY (Leeds). Founded 1147-52. 1237 *Close R.* Kirkestal. *c.* 1540 *Leland* Christal. 'Kirk' or 'church place.' O.E. *stœl.*

KIRTLING (Newmarket) and **KIRTLINGTON** (Oxford). *c.* 1080 Curtelinge, *Dom.* Chertelinge, 977 *O.E. Chron.* Kyrtlingtune, *a.* 1130 *Sim. Dur.* Cirtling, 1230 *Close R.* Kurt-, Kertlinton, 1241 *ib.* Curlinton. This must be a patronymic, 'place of the sons of *Cyrtel,*' though no name like this is given in *Onom.* *Cf.* KIRKLINGTON; and see -ing.

KIRTON LINDSEY (Lincs). 1156 *Pipe* Chirchetune. 'Kirk or church town of the Lindsays.' *Cf.* KIRKHAM. Randolph de Limesay or Lindeseye—*i.e.,* 'isle of lime-trees'—came over with the Conqueror.

KNAPTON (York and N. Walsham) and **KNAPWELL** (Suffk.). Yo. K. *Dom.* Cnapetone, others not in *Dom.,* 'town of *Cnapa*'; whilst Suf. K. is *sic* 1230, 'well of *Cnapa.*' *Cf.* Knapthorpe (Caunton), *Dom.* Chenapetorp. But Knap Farm, Cold Knap Wood, etc. (Wstrsh.), are fr. O.E. *cnœp,* M.E. *knap,* 'a hillock.' So also KNAPPE (Sussex), 1218 Cnappe.

KNARESBOROUGH. *Dom.* Chenaresburg (5 times). 1155 *Pipe* Chanardesburc, 1156 Canardsburc, 1158 Cnardesburc, 1179-80 Cnarreburi, *c.* 1180 *Ben. Peterb.* Cnaresburgus. The orig. name was 'burgh, castle of *Kenward*' or '*Cyneweard.*' But as it stands on a rocky slope it seems early to have been thought 'fort of the rugged rock,' M.E. *knarre,* found *a.* 1250.

KNAVES CASTLE (Lickfield). *a.* 1300 'a place called Cnaven castle,' now a small mound. O.E. *cnafa,* 'a boy, a servant '; later, 'a knave, a rogue.' *Cf.* KNAVENHILL (Alderminster).

KNAYTON (Thirsk). *Dom.* Cheneve-, Chenivetune, Chennieton, 1235 Cneveton. 'Town of *Coengifu,*' a woman's name, only found here. *Cf.* Kneveton (Notts), *Dom.* Chenivetone, *c.* 1190 Chnivetun, which Mutschmann prefers to derive from O.E. *cniht,* 'a servant,' which explains the Kn-, but not the -ev.

KNEBWORTH (Stevenage). *Dom.* Chenepeuorde, *a.* 1300 Kenebbes-wrth, 1303 Knebbeworth. '*Cnebba*'s farm.' See -worth.

KNEESWORTH (Royston, Herts). 1276 Knesworth, 1346 Knees-worthe. 'Farm of *Knee*'; O.E. *cneo,* 'a knee'; not recorded as a personal name. *Cf.* KNEESALL (Notts), *Dom.* Cheneshale, 1189 *Pipe* Cneeshala. See -hall.

KNIGHTON (4 in *P.G.*) Lei. K. *Dom.* Cnihtetone. K.-on-Teme 957 Cnihtatune, *Dom.* Cnistetun (*Dom.* almost regularly has *st* for *gh*), 1108 Cnihtetun, 1218 Cnigheton. 'Servants' town.' On *Knight* see next. *Cf.* KNIGHTWICK (Worcester), 738 *chart.* Cnihtwic. See -wick, 'dwelling.'

KNIGHTSBRIDGE (London). *c.* 1150 Cnihtbriga; later, Knyghtsbrigg. O.E. *cniht* meant orig. 'a boy, a lad, an attendant, a servant.' Its mod. usage as 'knight' is not recorded till *O.E. Chron.* 1086.

KNOCKIN (Salop). Prob. dimin. of W. *cnwc,* G. *cnoc,* 'a hillock.' *Cf.* KNOOK and KNUCKLAS. One would like to see the old forms of Knock holt or 'wood' (Sevenoaks). It is not in *Dom.*

KNODDISHALL (Saxmundham). *Dom.* Chenotessala, 1225 *Patent R.* Kenodeshal. 'Nook, corner of *Cnod, Cnut,*' or '*Canute.*' *Cf.* KNOTTINGLEY and KNUTSFORD. See -hall.

KNOLTON BRYN (Ellesmere). Tautological hybrid. 'Town on the knoll.' O.E. *cnoll,* Dan. *knold,* W. *cnol,* Sc. *knowe,* and W. *bron,* Corn. *bryn,* 'a hill.' *Cf.* KNOWLE and NOTTING HILL. But Kinoulton (Notts), *Dom.* Chineltune, 1152 Cheneldestōa, is '*Cyneweald*'s town.'

KNOOK (Wilts). *a* 800 *chart.* Nox gaga, *Dom.* Cunuche, 1236 Cnuke. W. *cnuch,* 'a junction'; or *cnuwch,* 'a junction, a bush.'

KNOTTINGLEY (Yorks). *Dom.* Notingelai, 1202 Cnottinglai. Patro-nymic. 'Meadow of the sons of *Cnot*' or '*Cnut.*' See -ley. But KNOTT in Cumbld. and Westmld. means 'a hill,' as in Arnside Knott, Hark Knot, Scald Knot, etc. O.E. *cnotta,* see *Oxf. Dict.,* knot sb. 14.

KNOWL(E) (Birmingham, Bristol, etc.). Bir. K. *Dom.* Gnolle, *a.* 1300 La Cnolle, *a.* 1400 Knole. Wednesfield K. *a.* 1300 le Knolle. Alvechurch K. 1275 la Cnolle. O.E. *cnoll,* 'a round-topped hillock' or 'hill,' a knoll; Sc. knowe. Two 'Cnolle' in *Dom.* Dorset.

KNOWSLEY (Liverpool). *Dom.* Phenulweslei (*P* error for *C*). 'Lea, meadow of *Coenwulf,*' a name common in *Onom.* See -ley.

KNOYLE (Salisbury). 948 *chart.* Cunugl, Cnugel, 1228 Stepel Knoel. *Cf. B.C.S.* i. 240 Cunugl-ae (= 'isle'), which Birch identifies with COLNE (Glouc.), *q.v.* This cannot be the same as *knoll,* O.E. *cnoll,* 'hill-top, hillock,' though M'Clure declares that the *Oxf. Dict.* says this is the origin of Knoyle. Where does it say that? Nor is it likely to be O.E. *cnucel,* 'knuckle, hill like a knuckle.' This would not have become Knoyle. Cunugl looks like W. *cwn uchel*, ' lofty height ' or ' hill-top,' the O.W. *ugl* thus being cognate with OGLE, and Sc. *Ochils*, and *Ogil-vie*. It is only fair to add that the Gazetteers speak of no hill here, so the name may be pre-Kelt.

KNUCKLAS (Radnor). In W., Cnwcglas, 1246 *Patent R.* Cnuclays. ' Green hill,' fr. W. *cnwc*, ' lump, hillock,' and *glas (llas)*, ' green, blue.' *Cf.* KNOCKIN and KNOOK.

KNUTSFORD (Cheshire). *Dom.* Cunetesford. ' Ford of K. *Cnut* or *Canuti*.' *Cf.* KNUSTON (Northants), *Dom.* Cnutestone, and KNODDISHALL.

KNUTTON (Newcastle, Staffs). *Dom.* Clotone (error), *a.* 1300 Cnot(t)on, Knotton. ' Village on the hillock '; O.E. *cnotta*, ' a knot,' found fr. 14th cny. used as ' a hill.' See KNOTT.

KYLOE (Belford). 1272 Kilei, 1561 Kilhowe, Killowe, 1636 Kilo. Hybrid. G. *cill(e)*, ' church, churchyard,' and *howe*, O.N. *haug-r*, ' mound, cairn '; in Eng. as *how*, *a.* 1340, ' a hill, a hillock.' *Cf.* TYSOE, etc.

KYME (Lincoln). *Sic* 1136, 1233 Kima. O.E. *cyme* vbl. sb. means ' coming.' But this seems to be the W. *cyme*, ' lovely, beautiful.' Skeat thinks that this Kyme and others must all come fr. a man *Cyma*, 5 in *Onom.*, but this type of name is rare. *Cf.* KIMPTON. There is also a R. Kym, trib. of the Gt. Ouse.

KÝNANCE COVE (The Lizard). Corn. *Kyne sans*, ' holy Kyne,' a Corn. saint who lived *c.* 490. *Cf.* KEVERNE and PENZANCE.

KYNDELYN (Wales). Prob. not same word as *Cunobellinus* (see KIMBLE), though M'Clure thinks so. Much more likely W. *cwn Velyn*, ' height of Velyn,' aspirated form of Melyn. *Cf.* HELVELLYN. *Cwn* is cognate with the G. *ceann*, loc. *cinn*, ' head, height,' so often found in Sc. names as Ken-, Kin-. *Cf.* KINVER and KNOYLE.

KYRE WYRE (Tenbury). *Dom.* Cuer, Chuer, 1108 Cyr, 1275 Cure Wyard. W. *cwr*, ' border, edge, limit '; it is on the border between Worcester and Hereford. The Wyards were its early Nor. lords.

LACEBY (Grimsby). *Dom.* Levesbi, 1234 Lesseby. ' Dwelling of *Lefa* ' or ' *Leofa*,' common in *Onom.* See -by.

LACKENBY (Redcar). *Dom.* Lachenebi, Lachebi, 1202 Lackenbi. ' Dwelling of *Lacen*,' a name still found as Laking. See -by.

LACKFORD (Bury St. Edmunds). *Dom.* Lacforda, Lacheforda. Prob. ' ford at the pool '; O.E. *lace*. *Cf.* MORTLAKE, *Dom.* Suffk. Lacheleia, and Hants Lacherne.

LADBROKE (Southam, Wwksh.). 980 *chart.* Hlodbroce, *Dom.* Lodbroc, *a.* 1200 Lodebroc(h). Looks like ' brook of *Hlod* ' or ' *Hloth* '; but *Lodbroc* or *Lothbroc* is name of a well-known hero of the Sagas. *Cf. Dom.* Chesh. Latbroc.

LADOCK or LANDOC (Grampound Rd., Cornwall). 'Church,' Corn. *lan*, W. *llan*, ' of St. *Cadoc.*' See CARADOC and LLANGADOC.

LALEHAM (Staines). *Dom.* Leleham, 1237 Estlalham. 'Home of *Lela*' or '*Lilla.*' *Cf.* LAWFORD, and Laleston (Bridgend). See -ham.

LAMBETH (London). 1041 *O.E. Chron.* Lambhythe, 1088 Lamhytha, *c.* 1130 *Eadmer* Lambetha, -beta, 1217 Lamheye, -heth, 1588 Lambehith. *O.E. lamb-hiðe,* 'landing-place for lambs.' See HYTHE. Derivation fr. O.E. *lám,* 'loam,' is inadmissible. *Cf.* next and Lamcote (Notts), *Dom.* Lanbecote.

LAMBOURN (Berks). *K. Alfred's Will* Lamb-burna, 943 *chart.* Lamburna. 'Lamb's burn or brook.' See -bourne.

LAMORNA COVE (Penzance). Corn. *lan mornader,* 'enclosure for the lampreys ' or ' pilchards '; L. *murœna.*

LAMPETER (Cardigan). In W. Llanbedr Pont Stephan. The W. Llan bedr is ' church of *Peter.*' *Cf.* next. On *llan cf.* LLANAFAN. We find the Lam- very early—*e.g.,* *Dom.* Glouc., ' In Wales sunt iii hardvices (herds' farms), Lamecare (? *llan y caer,* 'church by the castle '), & Porteschivet (Portskewett) & Dinan.'

LAMPHEY (Pembroke). *Old* Llandyfei, 1603 Lantfey; forms Llanfaith and -feth are also found, as *if* W. *llan ffydd,* ' church of faith.' But the name is ' church of St. *Tyfai,*' seen also in Foy (Herefd.), *Lib. Land.* Lanntiuoi, and in Lampha (Glam.).

LAMPORT (Northampton). 1158-59 *Pipe* Lāport, *Cf. Dom.* Kent Lamport. The Lam- is doubtful, but is prob. O.E. *lamb,* as in LAMBETH; and so ' lamb's gate,' L. *porta,* in Eng. as *port,* fr. *c.* 950. See also *Oxf. Dict.* port sb², ' a town.'

LANARTH (Cornwall). 1285 *Close R.* Lannarth. Corn.= ' high enclosure.' The orig. meaning of *lan, llan, lam, lann,* in all Kelt. languages is ' enclosed place.' ' Church ' is a later meaning.

LANCARF (Cornwall). Corn.= ' graveyard '; Corn. *corf,* L. *corpus,* ' a body, a corpse.'

LANCAREOW (Cornwall). Corn.= ' deerpark,' *carw,* ' a hart '; L. *cervus,* ' a stag.' *Dom.* has a Lancharet.

LANCASTER. *Sic* 1399, but *Dom.* and 1198 Loncastre, 1161-62 Lancastria. ' Camp on the R. LUNE.' See -caster. Lancashire is first mentioned in 1169; in 1523 we have it in its mod. form, ' Lancasshyre.' Till after *Dom.* Lancashire S. of the Ribble was in Cheshire, and Lancaster itself in Yorks.

LANCAUT (Chepstow). 956 *chart.* Landcawet, 1221 Langcaut. The 956 form is O.Kelt for ' enclosed land,' W. *llan cauad.* Kelt *lan,* W. *llan,* means ' enclosure,' and is cognate with Eng. *land.*

LANCHERLY (Somerset). Perh. 801 *chart.* Lancherpille. *Lancher* is ' land share '; *K.C.D.* 706 Brisnodes Land-share; *ib.* 419 Hebelmes Landschere. The ledges at Worth Maltravers (Dorset) are also called Lanchers.

LANCHESTER (Durham). 1183 *Boldon Bk.* Langchestre, 'long camp.' O.E. and N.Eng. *lang,* 'long.' See -chester.

LANCING (Sussex). *Dom.* Lancinges. Named fr. *Wlencing,* son of Ælla, *O.E. Chron.* 477. *Cf.* KEYNOR, and *Dom.* Surrey Lanchei. See -ing.

LANDARE (Cornwall). *Dom.* Lander. Corn. *lan dar,* ' enclosure of the oaks.' *Cf.* O.G. *dair,* ' an oak.'

LANDBEACH (Cambridge). *Dom.* Utbech—*i.e.,* a little farther away or *out* from the old shore of the Wash than WATERBEACH— 1235 *Close R.* Londbech'. *Beach* is a curious word. It must mean ' shingle ' or simply ' shore,' but is not recorded in *Oxf. Dict.* till the 16th cny. *Cf.* WISBECH.

LANDEWEDNACK (The Lizard). *Dom.* has Langenewit, and Lan wenehoc. Corn. = ' church of *St. Devinicus,*' said to be a con- temporary of St. Columba. *Cf.* BANCHORY DEVENICK (Sc.).

LANDICAN (Wirral). *Dom.* Landechene. Prob. ' church of the deacon,' referring to Woodchurch near by. W. *diacon,* in Eng. *a.* 1300 *deken,* ' a deacon,' one not in full orders.

LANDICLE (Cornwall). *Sic* in *Dom.* Corn. = ' Church of St. *Teela.*' *Cf.* ' Lantocal,' *B.C.S.* 47. Tecla was a Roman abbess in the days of Gregory the Great. LANDKEY (Barnstaple) seems to be 1235 *Close R.* Landegeye; *cf.* KEVERNE.

LANDOC. See LADOCK.

LAND'S END. 997 *O.E. Chron.* Penwiht Steort; *a.* 1130 *Sim. Dur.* Penwithsteort. *Welsh Triads* Penbryn Penwaeth, *Wdsh Laws* Pengwaeth or -waed, *Myrv. Archaeol.* Penwedic yng Ngherniw. Pen is Keltic for ' head, headland '; wiht, with, or waᵹth must be W. *gwydd,* Corn. *gwedh,* ' woods,' while *steort* is O.E. for ' tail.' *Cf.* START Point. The name Penwith is still applied to this whole district.

LANDUE (Cornwall). Corn. *lan dew,* ' black, dark church.'

LANDUFF (Cornwall). Corn. = ' church of *Ulf* ' or ' St. *Olaf,*' one of the most saintly of the Norse Kings, 995-1030, patron saint of Norway.

LANDYWOOD (Walsall). No old forms. Duignan thinks ' launde i' th' wode,' M.E. *launde,* O.Fr. *land, launde,* ' a plain sprinkled with bush or tree,' then ' a lawn.'

LANGFORD (Oxford). 1155-58 *chart.* Langeford. ' Long ford.' Similarly there are 6 LANGTONS in *P.G.*, *Dom.* Yorks Langeton and Lanton, Lincs Langtone. There are also several LANGDALES; one in 1160-61 *Pipe* Notts and Derby, has the curious reduplica- tion Langedala Dala.

LANGLEY (Bromley). 862 *chart.* To langan leaᵹe. ' Long meadow.' So Langley, Henley-in-Arden, 1150 Langelleie, *a.* 1200 Langeleg, *a.* 1300 Langele. But LANGLEY Park (Cumberland) is old Lang-

lif erga, ' shieling, dairy hut of *Langlif*,' a N. woman. For erga
see ARKLID. See -ley.

LANGPORT (Central Somerset). Prob. *Llywarch Hen* Llongborth,
1160-01 *Pipe* Lāport. As it stands, ' Long Harbour,' O.E. *lang,
long*, also 4-5 *lang*, ' long,' while *port* is a very early loan fr. L.
portus. But evidently the orig. name was Keltic, the common
Ir. *Longphort*, ' ship's harbour,' then ' encampment,' seen about
20 times in Ireland to-day as Longford, and also, says K. Meyer,
in the Sc. LUNCARTY, 1250 Lumphortyn. Ir. and G. *long, luing*
is ' a ship,' also a loan fr. L. *longa (navis)*, ' a war-ship.' The
meaning in Somerset must be ' encampment.'

LANGRIGG (Aspatria). 1189 Langrug. *Cf.* 896 ' Langenhrycge '
(Glouc.); this is O.E. for ' long ridge '; in North. Eng. and Sc.
lang rigg. There is a Longridge (Preston).

LANGTHORPE (Yorks). *Dom.* Lambetorp, La'betorp, Lanbetorp.
' *Lambi*'s place.' No *Lambi* in *Onom.*, but *m* and *n* often inter-
change; *cf.* KIMBOLTON. But LANGTHWAITE (Yorks) is *Dom.*
Langetouet, Langetouft, ' long place.' See -thwaite and TOFT.

LANGWATHBY (Cumberland). 1189 Langwadebi. ' Dwelling by
the long ford.' *Cf.* LANGWITH (Notts), 1291 Langwaith, and
WADEFORD. See -by.

LANTERN MARSHES (Orford). Dangerous to mariners, and so a
lantern was once placed here, whilst now there are two light-
houses.

LAPLEY (Frocester and Stafford) and LAPWORTH (Birmingham).
Fr. L. 1315 Lappeleye. St. L. *Dom.* Lepelie, *a.* 1200 Lapelie,
Lappely. 816 *chart.* Hlappawurthin (*cf.* -warden), *Dom.* Lape-
forde, ' *Hlappa*'s lea ' and ' farm.' See -ley and -worth.

LARKBEARE (Exeter). *Dom.* Laurochebere, *Exon. Dom.* Lauroca-
bera, 1237 Laverk ber, ' Lark wood,' O.E. *láwerce* or *láferce bearu*.
Cf. BEER, and the personal name Conybeare; also 1160 *Pipe*
Lauerchestoc (Essex), and LARKBOROUGH (Worcestersh.), 709
chart. Lauerkeboerge—*i.e.*, ' lark hill.' See BARROW. LARK-
FIELD (Maidstone) is *Dom.* Laurochesfel'. The R. LARK, Suffk.,
is a back-formation fr. LACKFORD.

LARTINGTON (Barnard Castle). *a.* 1130 *Sim. Dur.* Lyrtingtun. *Cf.*
B.S.C. Lortan hlæw. ' Town of' some unknown man, *Lurta,
Lorta*, or *Larta*. Very prob. a patronymic. See -ing.

LASHAM (Alton, Hants). *Dom.* Esseham'. ' Home, house by the
ash-trees.' *Cf.* ASHBY, etc. The L. comes fr. the Fr. *la*, ' the,'
prefixed by a Nor. scribe, 1284 L-asham. *Cf.* Lappal, Halesowen, 1335 Lappole, ' the pool,' 1342 Thomas atte Pole, also *Dom.*
Essex, Lassendene, where the La- prob. has the same origin.
There is both an Essendine (Stamford), and an Essendon (Hatfield).

LASKET (Cumberland) and LASKET GROVE (Monmouth). Perh. W.
glas coed, ' green wood '; *cf.* CHETWOOD. But Lasboro' (Glouc.),

c. 1220 Lasseberewe, is ' lesser mound ' or ' tumulus,' O.E. *læssa,* M.E. *lasse,* ' less.'

LASTINGHAM (Cleveland). *Bede* iii. 23 Lestingau, but in pref. Læstinga ea. *Dom.* Lestingeham. Patronymic; ' home of the *Lestings* '; *éa* is O.E. for ' river.'

LATCHFORD (Warrington). Fr. *letch* sb [1], *Oxf. Dict.* 6-9 *lache.* 9 *latch,* ' a muddy ditch, a stream through a bog, a bog,' cognate with *leach* v., ' to water, to wet,' prob. fr. O.E. *leccan,* ' to water.' *Cf.* 1138 *Newminster Cart.* ' Appeltreleche,' and see LECHLADE.

LATHOM (Ormskirk). *Dom.* Latune, 1201-56 Lathun, 1225 *Patent R.* Lathum, 1535-43 Latham, Latheham. This is a corrupt loc., ' at the barns,' O.N. *hlaða,* loaned in O.E. *Cf.* HALLAM, KIL-HAM, etc., also the common and puzzling Sc. LETHAM, *sic a.* 1200, 1284 Latham. Horsfall Turner gives Latun in *Dom.* for Amounderness as now LAYTON, Ladon in E. Riding as now Lathom, and Ladon in Cave Hundred (Yorks) as LAYTHAM. All these names may have a similar origin to what Wyld and Hirst give above. *Cf.* LATTON. But LATHBURY (Bucks), 1225 Late-biry, is fr. a man *Leot ;* that and *Leotan* are in *Onom.*

LATIMER (Chesham). Not in *Dom., a.* 1440 Latemer. It would be a very unlikely thing if formed fr. the personal name Latimer, *sic* in Eng. *c.* 1205, fr. O.Fr. *Latim(m)ier,* ' an interpreter,' corrup. of *latinier* or Latiner. The sb. *latimer* is already found in *Dom.* It may be ' mere, lake of *Leot,*' a man in *Onom.*

LATTON (Swindon). *Dom.* Latone; *cf. Dom.* Essex Lattuna. It may be ' village of *Leot,*' one in *Onom. ; eo* regularly becomes *a.* As likely = LATHOM, *Dom.* Latune, ' at the barns.'

LAUGHARNE (W. of Caermarthen). Pron. Larn, 1603 Talagharn. In W. Tallacharn or Talycoran, ' at the end of R. *Coran,*' ? W. *corafon,* ' a rivulet.' The origin of Laugharne is doubtful. One might guess, ' the low alder tree '; see *Oxf. Dict.* s.v. *low* (early M.E. *lah,* 4 *lagh,* 5 *lawghe*), and *arn ;* but prob. it is corrup. fr. the W. name. There is a R. LAUGHERN (Worcestersh.), 757 *chart.* Lawern(e). This is O.W. *llawern,* Corn. *lowern,* ' a fox.' Lavernock (Cardiff), *old* Llywernog, is the dimin., ' little fox.'

LAUGHTON (Rotherham, and 3). Ro. L. *Dom.* Lastone (*Dom.* regu-larly replaces a guttural by *st*). Prob. ' low town,' fr. O.N. *lag-r* ' low,' early M.E. *lah,* 3-4 *laȝh,* 4 *laghe, loghe,* 5 *lough,* Sc. *laigh. Cf. Dom.* Hereford Lautone. Lastun in *Dom.* Yorks also stands for W. LAYTON.

LAUNCESTON. *Dom.* Lanscavetone, Lancauetone, 1154-89 Lan-ceston, 1199 Lanstaveton, 1220 Lanzavetun, 1224 Lancaveton, 1227 Lanstone (the mod. pron.; how early it was reached !), 1245 Lanstaueton, Lanceueton, 1260 Launcetton; also said to be *a.* 1176 *chart.* ' The town of St. Stephen at Lanstone.' Commonly said to be ' church (Corn. *lan*) of St. Stephen,' but this seems far fr. certain. *Scave* or *Stave* could with difficulty represent *Stephen,* a name always spelt in *O.E. Chron.* Stephne, and prob. represents some Corn. word now lost. An older name was DUNHEVED. Lansdown (Glouc.) is a doubtful name; some of its old forms (Launtes-, Lantesdon) look as if they might orig. be something similar to Launceston.

LAUNTON (Bicester). *Dom.* Lantone, 1274 Langetun, 1525 Lawnton. O.E. *lang tún,* ' long village.'

LAVAN SANDS (Conway). A tautology. W. *llafan,* ' a strand, a sandy beach.'

LAVENHAM (Suffolk). *Dom.* Lauenham. *Cf. B.C.S.* 1288-89 Lauan ham. 'Village, dwelling of *Lafa, Leofe,* or *Lawa,*' all forms are known. *Cf. Dom.* Norfk. Lawendic, and LAVINGTON.

LAVERSTOCK (Salisbury). *Dom.* Lawrecestokes and Lavertestoch, 1221 *Patent R.* Laverkestok. ' Place of *Lawerce*'—*i.e.,* ' the lark.' See STOKE.

LAVERTON (Yorks and Broadway, Worcestersh.). Yo. L. *Dom.* Laureton, Lavretone. Br. L. *c.* 1240 Lawertune. Prob. ' town of *Leofgar* or *Leuegarus,*' or ' of *Leofweard,*' a common name. More old forms needed. *Cf.* Laverhay, Wamphray (Scotland).

LAVINGTON (Chichester). 725 *chart.* Lavingtune, *Dom.* Laventone. Patronymic. ' Town, village of the descendants of *Lafa* ' or ' *Leofa.*' *Cf. Dom.* Bucks Lauuendene, and LAVENHAM.

LAWFORD (Manningtree and Rugby). Man. L. *Dom.* Laleforda. Ru. L. *Dom.* Leile-, Lelle-, Lilleford, 1086 Ledleford, 1161 Ledesforde, 1236 Lalleford. Fine proof of the liquidity of *l.* 'Ford of *Lil* ' or ' *Lilla,*' names in *Onom. Cf.* LALEHAM.

LAWHITTON (Launceston). *Dom.* Longvitetone, *Ex. Dom.* Languitetona, which is simply ' long white town,' O.E. *hwit,* O.N. *hvit-r,* ' white.' *Cf.* CUMWHITTON.

LAWRENNY (Pembrokesh.). *c.* 1190 *Gir. Camb.* Leurenni, -eni, 1603 *Owen* Lawrenny. The first syll. is W. *llawr,* ' floor, bottom,' but *Enni* is unknown. *Cf.* Ystrad Enni on the Ithon.

LAXFIELD (Framlingham). *Dom.* Suffk. and Essex, Laxefelda. ' Field of *Leaxa.*' Similarly, LAXTON, Howden and Newark, *Dom.* Yorks and Notts Laxintun, New. L. 1278 Lexington. See LEXDEN.

LAYCOCK (Keighley). *Dom.* Lacoc, 1237 *Close R.* Lacok.' Prob. ' low cock ' or ' heap,' O.N. *lag-r kökk-r,* Norw. *kok,* ' a heap.' *Cock* in the sense of hay-cock, etc., is not found in *Oxf. Dict.* till 1598. On Lay- *cf.* next, LAUGHTON, and the mod. surname Locock.

LAYER MARNEY (Essex). *Dom.* and *a.* 1300 *chart.* Legra, which is gen. plur. of O.E. *leger,* ' a lair, a camp,' in M.E. ' a place for animals to lie down in '; *cf.* 1573 Tusser *Husband,* 'Borne I

was . . . in Essex laier, in village faier, that Riuenhall hight.'
Marney is fr. Marigny in Normandy. There are also LAYER
BRETON and LAYER DE LA HAYE, near Colchester. One of
these is 1217 *Patent R.* Lawefare, 1235 *Close R.* Laghefar, which
must be 'low road.' See LAUGHTON and *cf.* thorough*fare.*

LAYTON (N. Riding). East and West. *Dom.* Lastun, Lattun. As
Dom. regularly replaces a guttural by *st*, prob. ' low town,' Sc.
laigh toun, and so = LAUGHTON (*q.v.*). But LAYTON (Amounderness) is *Dom.* Latun, and so it may be = LATHOM, ' at the barns.'

LAZONBY (Cumberland and Northallerton). No. L. *Dom.* Lesingebi,
Leisenebi, Lesinghebi, Leisingbi, 1179-80 *Pipe* Lagenebi, 1203
Fines Leysingeby. ' Dwelling of the *Les(s)ings*,' a patronymic;
one *Lesing* in *Onom.* See -by.

LEA R. (Essex). 891 *O.E. Chron.* Lyga, 913 *ib.* Lygea(n), Ligene,
c. 1120 *Hen. Hunt.* Luye. M'Clure connects with the Keltic
river-name Logana, but the origin is quite doubtful. *Hen. Hunt.*
gives another R. Luye near Hereford; there is to-day a village,
Lea, near Ross, but very likely this is the common O.E. *léah*,
' meadow.' *P.G.* has 6 places called Lea; For. of Dean L. 1195
La lega.

LEADENHAM (Lincoln). *a.* 1150 Lang ledenham. ' Home of *Leda*,'
one such in *Onom.* *Cf.* LEDBURY.

LEA MARSTON (Coleshill). Two hamlets, 1257 Waure Merston,
1573 Waver Merstone. The Wavers were lords of this ' marsh
town,' O.E. *mersc tún*, for a considerable time. For Lea, see -ley.

LEAMINGTON. *Dom.* Lunintone (*un* error for *em*), 1242 Leminton.
' Town on R. *Leam*,' which may be O.E. *leom(a)*, ' a flash, a
gleam,' less likely fr. O.E. *lám*, ' mud,' Du. *leem*, Eng. *loam*.
LEAMINGTON PRIORS (of Kenilworth) is *Dom.* Lamintone, 1327
Lemynton Prioris. Lemington (Moreton-in-Marsh), *Dom.* Lemin-
ingtune, Limen-, Lemintone, is ' town of (the sons of) *Leofman*,'
common name, found shortened to *Leman.* See -ing.

LEATHERHEAD (Surrey). *Sic c.* 1670. *Dom.* Lered, a puzzling
form. *Leather* is the O.E. *leðer*, Icel. *leðr*, O.Fris. *leer*, Breton
ler; but it is doubtful if this is the real origin of the name. More
old forms are needed. There is an O.E. *læfer*, ' a plant,' see
Oxf. Dict. s.v. LEVERS ; and LIVERPOOL is 1222 Litherpool,
whilst Larford (Stourport), was 706 Leverford; so the name is
prob. ' head, height with the rushes or sword-bladed plants,'
O.E. *læfer, leber.* It may be fr. *Leod-, Leothere*, a well-known
name, cognate with Luther, *cf.* Leatherbarrow. Also *cf.*
LETHERINGSETT.

LEATHLEY (Otley). *Dom.* Ledelai (*Dom.* regularly makes *th* into *d*).
' Meadow on the slope,' O.E. *hlith.* *Cf.* LEITH Hill, and Kirkleatham (N. Yorks), *Dom.* Westlidu'.

LEAVEN R. See LEVEN.

LEAVENING (York). *Dom.* Ledlinghe, -inge. *Dom's* forms seem corrup. of ' place of *Leofwine's* or *Leofwynn's* sons.' See -ing.

LEBBERSTON (Filey). *Dom.* Ledbeztun, -bestun, 1206 Ledbrizton, 1208 Ledbristone. ' *Leodbeorht's* town '; this is prob. the origin of Liberton (Midlothian). *Dom.* prefers to use *z* and *st* instead of a harsh guttural.

LECHLADE (Glouc.). 872 *chart.* Lecche, *Dom.* Lecelade, 1221 Liche-lade. 'Way, path,' O.E. *gelád,* 'by or over'—*i.e.,* ferry over 'the R. Leach,' whose old forms are seen also in Eastleach, *Dom.* Lece, 1347 Estlecche, and Northleach, *Dom.* Lecce. This is prob. O.E. *lœce,* ' a stream,' fr. *leccan,* ' to water.' *Cf.* LATCH-FORD.

LECK (N. Lancs). *Dom.* Lech. Prob. N. *loeck-r,* ' a brook.' *Cf.* LEEK and LUCKER. It may be Eng. *Cf.* LATCHFORD.

LECKFORD ABBAS (Stockbridge, Hants). 947 *chart.* Legh-, Leaht-ford. Prob. 'ford in the meadow,' O.E. *léah.* See -leigh.

LECKHAM(P)STEAD (Berks and Bucks). Ber. L. *B.C.S.* ii. 534 Leachamstede; *Dom.* Lecanestede, Lekehamstede, 1316 Leck-hampsted. *Dom.* Bucks Lechāstede. 'Homestead, HAMP-STEAD, with a kitchen-garden.' O.E. *léac, 3 lec,* is ' a leek,' then, any garden herb. *Cf.* LEIGHTON. Similarly, LECKHAMP-TON (Glouc.) is *Dom.* Lechantone. See HAMPTON.

LECONFIELD (Beverley). *Dom.* Lachinfeld, -felt. ' Field of ' some unknown man, ? *Lecca, -can. Laking* is a personal name to-day.

LEDBURY (Malvern). *Dom.* Liedeberge, 1235 Lidebir; *cf. Dom.* Salop Ledewic. ' *Leoda's* burgh.' *Cf.* LEADENHAM, also LAT-COMBE, *Dom.* Bucks Ledingberge, a patronymic, and *ib.* Surrey Ladesorde. Duignan derives Ledbury fr. the R. *Leaden,* 972 *chart.* and *Dom.* Ledene, on which it stands, is also does Up-leadon (N.-W. Glouc.). This is doubtful, and the origin of Leaden is unknown. Perh. connected with W. *lledan,* ' breadth,' or *lliad,* ' flooding, streaming.'

LEEDS. *Bede* Loidis, *Dom.* Ledes. Doubtful; ? W. *lloed,* ' a place.' There are also Lede Chapel (Tadcaster), *Dom.* Lede, and a Leeds (Maidstone), 1235 *Close R.* Lhedes. *Lede* or *lead=* ' water-course,' is not found till 1541.

LEEK (Staffs). *Dom.* Lec, *a.* 1200 Lech, 1284 Leyc. Prob. N. *lœck-r,* ' a brook.' *Cf.* LECKFORD. Leake (Boston), *Dom.* Leche, 1216 Leake, 1313 Lek, 1320 Leek, and E. and W. Leake (Notts), *Dom.* Lec(c)he, *a.* 1277 Leyk, must be the same name. It may be Eng.; see LECHLADE. For Leek Duignan prefers W. *llech,* ' a flagstone.' LEEK WOOTTON (*q.v.*) (Kenilworth), is 1327 Lekwottone. There is also a Lec in 1183 *Boldon Bk.,* Durham. All these names are doubtful. The forms in *Oxf. Dict.* s.v. *lea* sb[1] do not encourage us to call them hardened forms of O.E. *léah,* ' meadow.'

LEICESTER, pron. Léster. *a.* 800 Legoracensis civitas, *c.* 800 *Nennius* Caer Lerion, 918 *O.E. Chron.* Legraceaster, Ligranceaster, 980 *ib.* Legeceasterscir (here, as in several other places, this means Cheshire, *q.v.*), 1120 Legrecestrie, *c.* 1145 *Geoffr. Mon.* and *c.* 1175 *Fantosme* Leircestre, 1173 Leicestria, *c.* 1205 *Layamon* Leirchestre, but *c.* 1275 Leycestre, 1258 *Henry III.* Leirchestr. 'Camp, fort on R. Leir,' old name of R. Soar (1253 Sor). Leir may be the same as LAYER, but this is quite doubtful. Connexion with K. *Lear* is even more so. In *Mabinogion* he is Llyr, and he is first named in Geoffr. Mon. Possible is a connexion with W. *llithro*, 'to slip, to glide.' See -caster.

LEIGH (12 in *P.G.*). *Dom.* Lecie (prob. near Cricklade) and Lege (Salop and Worcester). O.E. *léah*, dat. *léage*, 'a piece of cultivated land, a meadow,' so common in the ending -ley, *q.v.*

LEIGHTERTON (Tetbury) *c.* 1140 Letthrinton, 1273 Lettrinthone. Perh. 'village of' (the sons of) '*Leothere.*' See -ing.

LEIGHTON (Hunts, Salop, Welshpool). 956 *chart.* Wilmanlehtune (see WORMLEIGHTON). Hun. L. 1260 Lechton, 1291 Legheton, but men of the name Leighton lived in this barony *a.* 1066. *Cf.*, too, 1154-61 *chart.* Lectona (Lincs), and *a.* 1199 Lecton (Beds). O.E. *léahtun, lehtune,* 'a herb garden,' fr. *léac,* 'a leek.' See LECKHAMSTEAD; and *cf.* next.

LEIGHTON BUZZARD. 917 *O.E. Chron.* Lygtun; later, Lygetun; *a.* 1700 L. Beaudezert. See above. The Norm. family *Beaudesert* or *Bosard* were influential here in 14th cny. *Cf.* Beaudesert (Henley-in-Arden), *c.* 1135 Beldesert, and in Cannock Chase.

LEINTWARDINE (N. Hereford). *Dom.* Lentevrde (Salop), which is 'farm of *Lenta,*' an unknown man. See -wardine.

LEITH HILL (S. Surrey). Tautology. O.E. *hlíth,* 'a slope, a hillside.' *Cf.* LYTHAM.

LENBOROUGH (Bucks). *O.E. Chron.* 571 Liggeanburh, Lygeanbirg; not in *Dom.* Prob. the burgh or fort of some man, whose name is now unrecognizable.

LENHAM, West (Maidstone). 804 *chart.* Westra Leanham. 'House, home given as a reward or gift,' O.E. *lean.*

LEOMINSTER. 1046 *O.E. Chron.* Leomynstre, *Dom.* Leominstre, 1233 Leminstr', *c.* 1600 *Camden* Lemester; in W. Llanllieni. Said to be 'church of *Leof*' or '*Leofric.*' It is doubtful who he was; perh. the W. Mercian earl, husband of Lady Godiva, *c.* 1030.

LEONARD STANLEY (Stonehouse, Glouc.). Not in *Dom.*, but *cf. Dom.* Linor = a Leonard in Devon. Doubtful. There is a Burton Leonard in S. Yorks. St. *Leonard* was a confessor of the 6th cny. at Corbigny (Autun, France), a reputed miracle-worker, but not otherwise famous, and not likely to be denoted in our Eng.

names. These may be connected with W. *llenu,* 'to veil or envelope.'

LEPTON (Huddersfield). *Dom.* Leptone. 'Town of *Leppa,*' 3 in *Onom.*

LESNEWTH (Camelford). Corn. *les newydh,* 'new hall.' W. *llys,* 'court, hall,' G. *lios. Dom.* has a Lisniwen.

LETCOMBE REGIS and **BASSET** (Wantage). *Dom.* Ledencumbe, Ledecumbe, 1161-62 *Pipe* Ledccūba; later Letecoumb. 'Deep valley of *Leoda.*' *Cf.* LEDBURY, and see -combe. The Bassets were a Norman family of many possessions. *Cf.* BASSETT.

LETHERINGSETT (Holt, Norfk.), *a.* 1300 *Eccleston* Leveringsot. Prob. 'seat, residence,' O.E. *sæt,* 'of the descendants of *Leofgar.*' For *f* or *v* becoming *th, cf.* LIVERPOOL. See -ing. But LETTERSTON (Pembroke), *c.* 1300 Letarston is prob. fr. the name *Leodheard* or *Leothere,* in *Onom.* However, in 1516 it is Littardiston, and was then held by a John *Littard.*

LETTON (Hereford). *Dom.* Letune. Prob. 'town on the leat,' 7 *let,* O.E. *gelæt,* 'an open conduit, a water channel'; but it may be = LATHOM.

LEVEN (N. Yorks), *Dom.* Levene, **LEVEN R.** (N. Lancs), and **LEAVEN R.** (Yorks); and prob. same name, **LEVANT R.** (S. W. Sussex), as *t* would easily suffix itself. *Cf.* DARWEN and DERWENT, both the same root. W. *llevn,* 'smooth'; also *cf.* LEVEN (Sc.). But LEVEN (Hornsea), old forms needed, is prob. an O.E. gen. *Leofan* 'Leofa's' place; *cf.* BEEDON, 'Leventon' (Cumberland) in 1189 *Pipe,* and LEVENHULL. LEVENS (Milnthorpe, Westmorland), *Dom.* Lefuenes, looks like another gen., '*Lefwen's,* or *Leofwen's*' (place), 4 of this name in *Onom.*

LEVENHULL (Leamington). A curious name, not in Duignan. Its form suggests W. *llevn hel,* 'smooth bank.' But -hull in Midlands stands for *hill,* 2-5 *hull(e); cf.* ASPULL and SOLIHULL; so that this should be 'hill of *Leofa,*' gen. *-fan;* several named Leof, Leofa, and Leofe in *Onom. Cf.* above.

LEVERINGTON (Wisbech). 1285 Liverington, 1302 Leveryngtone. Patronymic. 'Village of the sons of *Leofere* or *Leofhere.*' *Cf.* LIVERPOOL. See -ing.

LEVERTON (Boston) may be fr. *Leofhere* or *Lifere,* 2 such in *Onom.* LEVERTON N. and S. (Notts) is *Dom.* Legretune, 1189 Leirton, *c.* 1200 Legherton, and Mutschmann doubtfully derives fr. LEOFHERE; *cf.* LAYER and LIVERPOOL. But GREAT and LITTLE LEVER (Bolton) will prob. be fr. O.E. *læfer,* some plant, now 'levers,' a rush, an iris, or the like. The forms are *a.* 1200 Leuer, 1212 Little Lefre, 1227 Leoure, 1326 Great Leure.

LEVERTON (Boston). *Dom.* Levretune. Said to be fr. *Leofric,* seneschall of Earl Algar the younger, who d. fighting the Danes in 870. But more prob. fr. *Leofhere; cf.* LIVERTON. Kirk

Levington (N. Riding) is *Dom.* Levetona, 'town of *Leofa*.' *Cf.*
Dom. Devon, Levestone.

LEWAN(N)ICK (Launceston). 'Church (Corn. *lan*) of St. *Wethenoc*'
or '*Winoch*,' brother of Winwaloe. See GUNWALLOE.

LEWDOWN (N. Devon). Prob. Keltic *leu dyn*, 'lion hill,' hill like a
lion, such as Arthur's Seat (Edinburgh).

LEWES. *Sic Dom. O.E. chart.* Loewas; *a.* 1200 *Lib. de Hyda* Leu-
wias; also Loewen, Leswas, Laquis. Perh. fr. an O.E. **hleow*, M.E.
lewe, 'warm, sunny '; found as sb in *hus-hleow*, 'house-shelter.'
The variants are somewhat puzzling; in the last *qu* will stand for
w, as in old Scots.

LEWISHAM (Surrey). *O.E. chart.* Liofshema. 'Enclosure of' some
man with a name beginning *Leof-* or *Leofw-*. There were many
such. See -ham, 'enclosure.' But LEVISHAM (Yorks) is *Dom.*
Lewe-, Levecen, where the ending is prob. a corrupt loc., 'at
Leoveca's,' a known name; *cf.* HALLAM and -ham, also next.
LEWSTON (Pembrokesh.) is 1324 Lewelestoun, prob. '*Leofweald's*
town.'

LEWKNOR (Wallingford). *Dom.* Levecanol, -chanole, 1154-89 Leo-
vecachanoran (inflected), 1178 Levechenore, -eckenore, 1224
Leuekenor. 'Shore, bank of *Leofeca*,' only one in *Onom.; O.E.
ora*, 'bank, edge '; *cf.* WINDSOR, etc. The -ol(e) in *Dom.* is but
another instance of its constant confusion of the liquids.

LEXDEN (Colchester). *Dom.* Laxendena, 1157 *Pipe* Lexeden(e).
'The den' or 'DEAN of *Leaxan*.' *Cf.* LAXFIELD and *O.E. chart.*
Leaxanoc.

LEYBURN (Yorks). *Dom.* Leborne. *c.* 1330 Leyborne. Prob. 'sheltered brook,' O.E. *hléo*, 'protection, shelter,' 4-6 *le*, 7 *ley, lay*, our
word 'lee '; it is not recorded as an adj. till *c.* 1400. *Cf.* Libbery
(Worcestersh.), 972 *chart.* Hleobyri, 'refuge, shelter town.'

LEYLAND (Preston). *Dom.* Lailand, 1140-49 Leilande. O.N. *lág-r*,
early M.E. *lah*, 3 *laih*, Sc. *laigh*, 'low land.'

LEYTON (Essex). ? *Dom.* Leiendune. 'Town on R. LEA.' Leyton-
stone seems modern.

LICHFIELD. *Bede* Lyceitfeldensis, *a.* 900 *O.E. vers.* Liccetfelda,
c. 800 *Nennius* Licitcsith, 803 *chart.* Liceidfeld; *O.E. Chron.*
731 Licetfelda, 1053 *ib.* Licedfelde, *c.* 1120 *Hen. Hunt.* Lichfeld;
perh. also *a.* 700 *Rav. Geogr.* Le(c)tocetum, and *c.* 800
Nennius Cair Luit Coyt, mod. W. *caer llwyd coed*, 'fort in the
grey wood.' This, however, was prob. near Welshpool. The
popular derivation, 'church-yard,' lit. 'field of corpses,' fr. O.E.
lic, 4-5 *liche*, fails to explain the early *t*. But *lic-cet-feld* is O.E.
for 'corpse-hut-field,' field with the mortuary, O.E. *cete*, 'a cot,
a hut,' as in DATCHET, WATCHET, etc.

LICKEY HILLS (BIRMINGHAM). 1330 Leckheye. W. *llechau*, pron.
leckay, plur. of *llech*, 'a flag or flat stone,' G. *leac*.

LIDFORD or LYDFORD (Bridestowe, Devon). 997 *O.E. Chron.*
Hlidaford, 1018 *chart.* Lidauorde, *Exon. Dom.* Lidefort, *a.* 1130
Sim. Dur. Lideforda. ' Ford on *R. Lid*,' W. *llêd*,' ' broad.'
There is no O.E. *hlida*, whilst *hlid* means ' a lid '; but *lípe* means
' gentle,' which is not impossible.

LIDGATE (Newmarket). Not in *Dom.* O.E. *hliʒeat*, ' a postern,'
fr. *hlid*, ' a gate, a lid.' *Cf.* LUDGATE and FOXLYDIATE. There
is a Hlidgeat in 963 *chart. re* Wasing (Berks).

LIFTON (Devon). 1157 *Pipe* Liftuna, 1283 Lyfton. ' Town of *Leof* '
or ' *Leofa* ' ; common in *Onom.* *Dom.* has only Levestone. *Cf.*
Kirk LEVINGTON.

LIGHTHORNE (Warwick). *Dom.* Listecorne (*Dom.* scribes hated a
combination like *ght*), 1252 Lychtehirn, *c.* 1300 Liththorn,
1327 Lighttethurne, O.E. *leoht thorn* or *thyrne*, ' light thorn.'
? Thorn-bush with a lamp hung on it. But Duignan derives LIGHT-
WOOD (Cotheridge) fr. O.E. *hlith*, M.E. *lith, lyth*, ' a slope, a hill-
side.'

LILLESHALL (Newport, Salop). *Dom.* Linleshalle. It is difficult
to say what name is represented here. There is one *Lunling*
in *Onom.* But *Dom.* may be in error, and the man's name be
Lilla, as in next and in LILLIESLEAF (Sc.), 1116 Lillescliva,
' Lilla's cliff.'

LILLINGTON (Sherborne and Warwicksh.). War. L. *Dom.* Lillin-
tone, *later* Liletun. ' Village of *Lilla*.' *Cf.* LALEHAM and 2 Lil-
lingstones in Bucks; also LILLING (Yorks), *Dom.* Lil(l)inge,
patronymic fr. *Lilla*. See -ing and -ton.

LIMEHOUSE (Stepney). 1536 Limehowse Reche. Said to be corrup.
of *lime-oast*, O.E. *ást*, 4-7 *host*, 8 *oust*, ' a kiln.' Older forms
needed. *Cf. Dom.* Surrey Limevrde (= -worth).

LIMEN R. (Kent). *Sic* 893 *O.E. Chron.*, but *a.* 716 *chart.* Limming,
? W. *llym*, ' sharp, keen,' from the air there. It can hardly be
llyman, ' naked one.' There is also a R. LIMIN (Hunts), seen in
Limining, old form of Lymage, where -ing (*q.v.*) will have its
meaning, ' place on a stream '; -age is usually late and trouble-
some.

LIMPLEY STOKE (Bath) and LIMPSFIELD (Surrey). Not in *Dom.*
' Meadow, field of *Limpa*,' an unrecorded man; but *cf. Dom.*
Norfk. Limpeho (ho = ' height ') and *Dom.* Essex Limpwella;
also see STOKE and -ley.

LINCOLN. *c.* 150 *Ptolemy* Lindon; *c.* 380 *Ant. Itin.* Lindum;
Bede Lindocolina civitas, *a.* 900 *O.E. tr.* Lindcylene; 942 *O.E.*
Chron. Lindcylene, Lindcolne, 1093 *ib.* Lincolne; *Dom.* Lincolia,
Lincolescire; *c.* 1100 *Flor. Worc.* Lindicolinensis; 1461 Linde-
colnea. In W. Caer lwydgoed (' castle of the grey wood ').
Lindum colonia, says Freeman, is a unique name for England.
As Lindon is found in Ptolemy, it cannot be, as is often said,

fr. O.E. *lind*, 'lime tree,' but is prob. fr. a Keltic *lind*, 'water.'
W. *llynn*, G. *linne*, ' a pool, a lake '; and the name will mean
' Roman settlement by the pool.' *Cf*. next.

LINDISFARNE or Holy Island (Northumberland). *Bede* Provincia
Lindisfarorum, Lindisfarnenses incolæ; *a.* 800 *chart*. Lindes-
farona. Doubtful. M'Clure thinks fr. Celt. *lind*, ' water ' (see
above and next), and, perh., fr. same root as Lombardic *fara*,
' race, family '—' dwellers in the water.' The rivulet opposite
is still called Lind or Lindis. The -farne may come fr. G. *fearann*,
' land, estate, farm.'

LINDSEY (Lincs). *Bede* Lindissi; *c.* 1000 *Ælfric* Lindesig, *c.* 1190
Gir. Camb. Lindeseia; *c.* 1300 Lindeseye. Quite possibly this
may contain the same root as **LINCOLN**, and so be ' isle in the
water '; see -ay. But here it is more likely to be ' isle of the
lime-tree, or linden,' O.E. and O.N. *lind*. **LINDLEY** (Huddersfield) is *Dom*. Lillai, prob. a corrupt form. But **LINDRIDGE**
(Tenbury) is *Dom*. Linde, 1275 Linderugge.

LINFORD (Stanford-le-Hope). Not in *Dom*., but *cf. Dom*. Bucks
Linforde. This must go with **LINTON**.

LINKINHORNE (Callington, Cornwall). Not in *Dom*. Said to be
corrup. of *lan tighern*, Kelt. for ' church of the King' or ' lord '—
i.e., St. Melw, son of Melyan, prince of Devon. One would like
a little more proof of this.

LINTON (5 in *P.G.*). *K.C.D.* iii. 368 Lin tun, *Dom*. Yorks Linton,
Devon Lintone. Prob. *O.E. lin tún*, ' flax-enclosure.' L. *linum*.
Cf. Eng. *lin-seed*; also **LINFORD**, Linehill Green, Penkridge,
a. 1300 Lynhull, and **LINTON** (Sc.)., 1127 Lintun.

LISKEARD (Cornwall). *Dom*. Liscarret, *a.* 1199 Liscaret, -chared,
1474 Leskirde, 1536 Lyscarde. Les-, Lis-, or Lys- is Kelt. for
' court, hall, enclosure '; the second part is doubtful, but *cf*.
W. *cariad*, ' a lover, a sweetheart,' G. *caraid*, ' a friend, a rela-
tion.' G. *càraid* is ' a pair, a couple.' The meaning quite
possibly is ' lover's hall.'

LITHERSKEW (N. Riding, Yorks). Not in *Dom*. Lither- is perh.
Eng. adj. *lither*, O.E. *lýðre*, ' bad, foul, pestilential,' while -skew
is fr. O.E. *sceaga* or O.N. *skóg-r*, ' a wood, a copse.' *Cf*. Askew,
' ash-wood,' now only a personal name, and **SHAW**. Lither- is as
likely to be O.E. *læfer*, ' any sword-bladed plant.' *Cf*. **LIVER-
POOL**, etc.; *v* can become *th*.

LITLINGTON (Royston, Herts). *c.* 1080 Lidlingtone, Litlingtona,
Dom. Lidlintone, 1316 Lutlingtone. ' Village of the *Littlings*,'
or sons of the ' little ' (O.E. *lytel*) ' man.'

LITTLE BREDY. See **BRIDPORT**.

LITTLEBURY (Saffron Walden and Notts). Saf. L. *Dom*. Litelbyria.
Not. L. *Dom*. Litelburg, ' Little burgh.' See -bury.

LITTLE HAY (Lichfield). *a.* 1300 Luttelhay, 'little hedge,' or 'fence.' See HAY.

LITTLEPORT (Ely). *Dom.* Litelport. O.E. *port* is rarely fr. L. *porta,* 'a gate,' generally as here fr. L. *portus,* 'a harbour.' The sea once came right up past here.

LITTLE RIBSTON (Wetherby). *Dom.* Ripestain, -sten, *c.* 1505 Rybstone. 'Stone of *Rippa,*' one in *Onom.* See -ton.

LITTLE SALKELD (Cumberland). 1167-68 *Pipe* Alde (Old) Sale-child, 1189 Salekil. The latter part is O.N. *kelda,* 'a spring.' *Cf.* Threlkeld (Penrith); the former perh. represents some man's name in Sele- or Sal-; there are several such in *Onom.* But it may be O.E. *sœl, sal,* 4-7 *sale,* O.N. *sal-r,* 'a hall, spacious chamber, castle.' Sale- could hardly represent *salt.*

LITTLE SNORING. See SNOREHAM.

LITTLETON (7 in *P.G.*). *Dom.* Surrey Liteltone. 'Little village.'

LITTLEWORTH (Faringdon, Wstrsh., and Staffs), no old forms in Duignan, is presumably 'little farm.' But L. in S. Yorks is *Dom.* Scitelesworde, 'farm of *Scytel*' or '*Sceotweald*'; 1 in *Onom.* See -worth.

LITTON (Bath, Buxton, Skipton). *a.* 1067 *chart.* Hlytton (? Bath), *Dom.* Yorks Litone. 'Town on the slope' or 'hill-side.' O.E. *hliδ.* But Litton Cheney (Dorset) is 940 *chart.* Lidentune, 'town of *Lida*'; 1 in *Onom.*

LIVERMERE PARVA and MAGNA (Bury St. Edmunds). 'Rushy lake.' See next. Parva and Magna are L. for 'Little' and 'Great.'

LIVERPOOL. 1189-99 Leverpol, 1190-94 Liuerpul, 1222-26 Litherpol, 1229 Leverpul. In W. Llerpwll. Nothing to do with any imaginary bird called *liver.* Not impossibly W. *llyvr pwl,* 'expanse or confluence at the pool.' But it is prob. Eng., meaning 'rushy pool'; fr. O.E. *lœfer, leber,* 'any rush-like or sword-bladed plant.' See *Oxf. Dict.* s.v. LEVERS. This is confirmed by LIVERMERE, also by Larford (Stourport) in 706 *chart.* (of really later date) Leverford, and by LEATHERHEAD, *Dom.* Lered, which gives the same contraction as W. Llerpwll, whilst in its mod. form we get a *th* corresponding to 1222 Litherpol (*cf.* LITHERSKEW). W. and H. are confident it is 'pool of *Leofhere,*' which is certainly possible, and is confirmed by LEVERINGTON; prob. also by LEVERTON and LIVERTON. *Cf. K.C.D.* vi. 243 Leofereshagan, near the Thames. But this cannot be the same as LIVERSEDGE (Yorks), *Dom.* Livresec and -sech. This last must be simply (place of) 'rushy sedge,' O.E. *sœcg, secg, sech, seic;* 1222 *Patent R.* has a Livredal.

LIVERTON (Newton Abbot) and LIVERTON MINES (Loftus, Yorks). Lo. L. *Dom.* Livreton, Liureton, 1179-80 *Pipe* Liuerton.

'Village of *Leofhere.' Dom.* Devon, has only Leovricestone, somewhere in the S., fr. *Leofric,* but prob. not Liverton. See above, LEVERTON and -ton.

LIZARD PT. *Dom.* Lisart. Corn. *lis arth,* 'court, hall on the height.' *Cf.* W. *llys,* G. *lios;* also WESTON-UNDER-LIZARD.

LLANAFAN (Aberystwith). W. *llan Afan,* 'church of St. Afan Buallt, disciple of St. Padarn, 6th cny., and himself a bp. and brother of King Dogged. W. *llan, O.W. lan,* 'enclosure,' then 'church.' Corn. *lan,* Ir. *land, lann,* G. *lann* (*cf.* LHANBRIDE, Sc.), is the same root as Eng. *land* and Bret. *lann,* 'a heath,' seen also in the Fr. *Landes.* The earliest instance we have noted in England is in a Grant of 680 (copy later), to the Abbot of Glastonbury, *B.C.S.* 47 'Lantocal,' ? = 'church of St. *Tecla.' Cf.* LANDICLE, also LAMPETER. In some W. names *llan* or *lan* is for *glan,* 'a bank,' as in Llanhaithog (Kentchurch, Hereford), which is prob. *lan haiddog,* 'bank of oats.'

LLANARMON (Ruabon) and LLANARMON-YN-YALE (Mold). W. *llan Garmon,* 'church of St. Germanus,' Bp. of Auxerre, sent to Britain by Pope Celestine, *c.* 430. *Cf.* MAES GARMON. The yn Yale is better *yn Ial,* fr. *ial,* 'an open space or region.' *Cf.* YALE.

LLANBABO (Anglesea). 'Church of St. *Pabo.' Cf.* M'Clure, pp. 57 and 59. Pabo Post Prydain was a great warrior, who latterly became very devout.

LLANBADARN (Aberystwith and Radnor). 'Church of St. *Padarn,'* a Breton, companion of St. David. *Cf.* LLANAFAN. L. in Radnor is L. Mawr, 'the great L.'; there are at least 2 others.

LLANBERIS (Caernarvon). 'Church of St. *Peris,'* said to have been a cardinal sent as a missioner from Rome in 6th cny. Close by there are Llyn Peris and Llyn Padarn. *Cf.* LLANBADARN.

LLANBOL (Anglesea). *Old* Llanvol. 'Church of St. *Bol.' Cf.* Cors y Bol ('marsh of Bol') and Rhos y Bol ('heath of Bol') near by. The *Dict. Christ. Biog.* records only a *Bolcan,* who was baptized by St. Patrick, and was one of his helpers.

LLANCARFAN (Cowbridge). *c.* 1145 *Geoffr. Mon.* epil. Lancarvan. 'Church of St. *Carfan* or *Corbagni';* said to be corrup. of *Germanus,* who is said to have built the first monastery in Britain here. *Cf.* LLANARMON. The church is now dedicated to St. Cadoc.

LLANDAFF. *c.* 1130 *Lib. Land.* Landavia. 'Church on the TAFF.'

LLANDDEWI (4 in *P.G.*). 1346 Llandewivrevi, or L. Brefi (Cardigansh). 'Church of St. *David,'* Bp. of St. David's, d. 601, patron St. of Wales. *Cf.* DEWCHURCH.

LLANDDOGGET (Denbighsh.). Founded by K. *Dogged,* who died *c.* 542. See *Mabinogion,* and *cf.* LLANAFAN.

LLANDDUW or -DDEW (Brecon). c. 1180 *Gir. Camb.* Landu. W. *llan duw*, ' dark church,' and not ' church of St. David ' or *Dewi.*

LLANDEGFAN (Menai Br.). Fr. St. *Tegfan,* of whom little seems known.

LLANDEILO (Caermarthensh.). c. 1130 *Lib. Land.* Lanteliau Penn litgart (' head, end of the grey ridge,' now LLWYDARTH). ' Church of St. *Teilo,*' Bp. of Llandaff in 7th cny.; also called *Tiliaus*; a very popular saint. *Cf.* LLANTILIO, also Llandeilo Tref y Cernyw (*Lib. Land.* Cerniu), where the latter part means ' house of Cornishmen.'

LLANDOVERY (Caermarthen). c. 1550 *Leland* Llanameueri. In W. *llan ym Ddyfri*, ' church beyond or among the waters.'

LLANDRINDOD WELLS. W. = ' church of the Trinity.' It was dedicated in 1603.

LLANDUDNO. ' Church of St. *Tudno,*' son of Seithengu; he was a W. saint early in the 6th cny.

LLANDYSSUL (Cardigan). *Lib. Communis* Llandowssuld, -dussuld. See ST. ISSELL'S, and *cf.* Llandyssil (Mont.).

LLANELIAN (Colwyn Bay). Here also is Elian's Well. *Elian Geimiad* was a saint of 6th cny.

LLANELLY (Caermarthen and Brecknock). Caer. L. 1788 Llanelliw. From St. *Elliw,* granddaughter of Brychan of Brycheiniog. There is also a Llanelieu (Breck.).

LLANERCHYMEDD (Anglesea). This has nothing to do with church, though there has long been a church here. It is W. *llanerch y medd*, ' forest glade or clearing where they drank mead.' *Cf.* LANARK (Sc.).

LLANFAIR (8 in *P.G.*). ' Church of *Mary,*' the Virgin. Such churches show the rise of Latin influence. *Cf.* BUILTH.

LLANFIHANGEL DIN SYLWY (Anglesea). The first part is ' church of the Archangel' (Michael). The second seems to mean ' on the hill of the wide view,' fr. *syllu*, ' to gaze.'

LLANGADOC (Caermarthen). 1285 *Close R.* Lancaddok. ' Church of St. *Cadoc,*' c. 500, who lived on an islet in the Bristol Channel, but d. in Brittany. *Cf.* CARADOC.

LLANGEFNI (Anglesea). ' Church on R. Cefni,' prob fr. W. *cefn*, ' a ridge.'

LLANGOLLEN. ' Church of St. *Collen,*' son of Gwynawc, abbot of Glastonbury, and then an austere hermit; 7th cny.

LLANGOVAN (Monmth.). Fr. St. *Cofen,* of whom little seems known.

LLANGROVE (Ross, Herefd.). A post-office and ignorant local corruption. In all old documents ' Long grove,' which exactly describes the place as seen from a distance.

LLANGRWYNEY (Crickhowell). 1603 *Owen* llon y grwyne. 'Church of *Grewyn.*' But who was he? ? Gwrwan or Gurvan, bp. of Llandaff, who excommunicated Tewdwr, K. of Dyfed.

LLANGYNIDR (Crickhowell). It has an Eng. form Kenderchurch; 'church of St. *Gynidr,*' or in O.W. Lanncinitir. The saint was of the 5th cny. Also *old* Lannicruc, W. *llan y Crug,* 'church at the heap or barrow.'

LLANILLTY (Glamorgan). *c.* 1150 *chart.* Landiltwit, *c.* 1350 *ib.* Launlltwyt. 'Church of St. *Illtyd,*' or *Iltutus,* orig. a Breton knight, who came over to the court of K. Arthur, and nephew of St. Garmon. *Cf.* ILSTON and LLANTWIT. Llantyd (Pembroke) gives the same name in a contracted form.

LLANOVER (Monmouth). 'Church of St. *Govor*' or Gower, a W. saint, of whom little seems known.

LLANRHIAN (Pembroke). *c.* 1190 *Gir. Camb.* Lanrian. 'Church of St. *Rhian,*' who seems unknown. Can it be fr. *Reathun* or *Hrethun,* abbot of Abingdon and bp. of Leicester, who died *c.* 835 ?

LLANSAINTFRAIDD (Monmouth). 'Church of Saint *Bride,*' or Bridget of Kildare, 453-523.

LLANSTADWELL (Pembroke). *Sic* 1594, but *c.* 1190 *Gir. Camb.* Lanstadhewal. W. *llan ystad hywel,* 'church of the conspicuous stadium or furlong,' which seems a curious name. More explanation is needed. *Cf.* St. Tudwall's I., Caernarvon.

LLANSTINAN (Letterston, Pembroke). *Sic* 1594. 'Church of St. *Justinian,*' said to have come fr. Brittany to Wales in the time of St. David.

LLANTHONY (Abergavenny). *a.* 1196 *Gir. Camb.* Lanthotheni. He also says: 'The English corruptly call it Lanthoni, whereas it should either be called Nanthodeni—*i.e.,* the brook Hodeni— or else Lanhodeni, the church upon the Hodeni,' now the Hondu, origin unknown. For change of *nant* to *llan* see NANTWICH. The other old forms intermingle with those of the offshoot from this priory, at Gloucester—1160-61 *Pipe* Lantoeni, 1221 Launtoney, 1223 Lantonay, 1225 Lantoeny.

LLANTILIO CROSSENNY (Abergavenny). Prob. 1285 *Close R.* Lanthelyou, 'church of St. *Teiliaw,*' of the 6th cny.; same as in LLANDILO.

LLANTRISANT (Glamorgan). W.= 'church of the three saints,' —viz., Illtyd, Tyfodwg, and Gwynno.

LLANTWIT MAJOR (Cardiff) or in W. Llanilltud Fawr. 'Church of St. Illtyd.' *Fawr* or *mawr,* 'big,' is the tr. of Major, L. for 'the greater.' There are 2 other Llantwits in Glam., as well as LLANTOOD (Kemes), *Valor. Eccl.* Llantwyd. See ILSTON and LLANILLTY.

LLANWEYNO (Herefordsh.). Fr. St. *Beuno*, contemporary of Kentigern, who founded a religious society at Clynnog Fawr, Carnarvon, *c.* 616. Eleven churches are dedicated to him.

LLAN-Y-GWYDDEL (Holyhead). ' Church of the (Irish) Gaels.' *Gwyddel* lit. means ' dwellers in the forest, or, among the shrubs,' *gwydd*. *Cf.* TRWYN-Y-GWYDDEL.

LLITHFAEN (Pwllheli). ? W. *llithr*, ' a slide or glide,' and *ffaen*, ' a stone.' T. Morgan says *llith* implies attraction, and that there is a stone near here of the nature of a loadstone.

LLIW R. (Bala and Loughor). Doubtfully derived fr. W. *llw*, ' an oath.'

LLWYDARTH (Glamorgan). *c.* 1130 *Lib. Land.* Litgart, 1603 *Owen* Lloydarch. W. *llwyd garth*, ' grey ridge ' or ' cape.'

LLYNCAWS (Denbighsh.). W. = ' pool like a cheese '; while LLWYN-CELYN (Rhondda) is, ' lake of the holly.' Sometimes *llyn* becomes *llan*, ' church,' as in Llangwathan or LLYN GWAEDDAN, in *c.* 1130 *Lib. Land.* Luin Guaidan. This is perh. *Gwarthan*, who helped to establish the monastery at Bangor Iscoed, 6th cny.

LLYN CYRI (Cader Idris). W. ' pool of the cauldron or Corrie '; *cyri* is hardly a Welsh word, yet see CYRI.

LLYN-YR-AFRANGC (pool on R. Conway). W. = ' pool of the beaver.'

LLYSFAEN (Abergele). W. = ' hall, court made of stone.' W. and Corn. *maen*, here aspirated; *f = v* or *mh*.

LLYS HELIG (now a sandbank off Conway). ' Palace of *Helig*,' now submerged. He was a great Cymric lord of the Middle Ages.

LOCKINGTON (Derby and Beverley). *Dom.* Yorks Lochetun, Lecheton. *Cf. Dom.* Essex Lochintuna. ' Town, village of *Loc*,' 1 in *Onom*. *Cf.* next. See -ing and -ton.

LOCK'S BOTTOM (Orpington, Kent). A *bottom*, O.E. *botm*. is ' a low-lying valley.' *Cf.* RAMSBOTTOM. Lock is the O.E. name *Loc*, and is still a surname. *Cf.* above, 1158-59 *Pipe* Loches-wella (Wilts), and LOXWOOD.

LOFTHOUSE (Pateley Br. and Wakefield). *Dom.* Lofthuse, -tose, Lot- and Loct -huse. ' House with an upper room or garret,' O.N. and O.E. *loft*. This name has also become LOFTUS, in the same county.

LOLWORTH (Cambridge). *Chart.* Lulleswyrð, Lollesworth. *Dom.* Lolesuuorde, 1284 Lulleworth. ' Farm of *Lull*.' *Cf.* Lulworth (Dorset). The patronymic is seen in Lullington (Burton), and *Dom.* Kent Lolingestone.

LONDESBOROUGH (Mket. Weighton). *Dom.* Lodenesburg, ' Burgh of *Lothan* or *Lothen*,' both in *Onom.* The *o* has been nasalized; whilst *Dom.* regularly makes medial *th* into *d*. See -burgh.

LONDON. *c.* 100 *Tacitus* Londinium, *c.* 360 *Amm. Marcell.* Londinium vetus oppidum quod Augustam posteritas appellavit; *c.* 610 *E. Saxon coin* Lundonia, *a.* 810 *Nennius* Cair Londein. *O.E. Chron.* 457 Lundenbyrig (= Londonburgh), *c.* 1175 *Fantosme* Lundres, *c.* 1250 *Layamon* Lundene, but ' Frensca Lundres heo hehten '; 1258-1450 Lunden, 1298 London, *a.* 1300 *Mabinogion* Lwndrys (*q.v.* p. 89, Everyman's Libry., for an early legend *re* the origin), *c.* 1460 Londyn; also 1140 *O.E.Chron.* Lundenisce folc. Commonly derived fr. a Keltic *lon din,* ' marsh or pool with the fort,' W. *llyn,* ' pool, lake,' G. *lòn,* ' a marsh,' and W. *din,* G. *dùn,* gen. *dùin,* ' a hill, a fort.' This is quite possible. W. J. Watson identifies it with Sc. LUNDIN and the commoner Lundy, G. *lunndan,* ' a green spot,' strictly ' green, wet place,' fr. a nasalized form of *lod,* ' a puddle,' which he thinks is prob. same root as Lutetia Parisiorum. If so, it is very remarkable that both London and Paris should originally have names practically the same. The Saxons, at any rate, early made Lon- into Lun-, which, in pron., it has remained ever since. For this there is abundant analogy. The *o* sound is retained in Fr. Londres. *Cf.* LUDGATE and LUNE.

LONGMYND RANGE (Salop). *c.* 1285 *Testa de Neville* Foresta de Longe Munede. The -mynd seems W. *mynydd,* ' hill ': the name may be a hybrid and the Long- be the common Eng. adj. O.E. *lang, long.* But *Oxf. Dict.* mentions a doubtful O.Ir. or Keltic *long-* in combinations, also meaning ' long.' But *cf.* MUNET, and MINDTON. LONGDON (Upton-on-Severn) is 972 *chart.* Langdune, ' long hill.' LONG EYE (Bromsgrove) is 972 *chart.* Longaneye (dat.), ' long island.' See -ey. LONGTHWAITE (Cockermouth) *may* be translation of Longovicium in *c.* 400 *Notit. Dignit.* See -thwaite.

LONGNOR (Buxton, Shrewsbury, Leek, and Penkridge). Pen. L. *Dom.* Longenalre, 1223 Langenalre, 1327 Longenolre. Le. L. *a.* 1300 Longenorle. Sh. L. *a.* 1300 Longenholre, Langenalre, Longenolre, Longnore. O.E. *lang alor, alr,* ' long, tall alder-tree.' LONGNER-on-Severn is also the same. Longboro' (Moreton-in-Marsh), *Dom.* Langeberge, is ' long tumulus.' See BARROW; whilst LONGNEY (Gloster), 972 *chart.* Longanege, is ' long island.' See -ey.

LONGSDON (Stoke-on-T.) *a.* 1300 Longesdon. ' Hill of *Lang* ' or ' *Long,*' which have always been Eng. personal names. See -don.

LONGSHIP (off Land's End). 1667 ' the rock called the Longship.'

LOPPINGTON (Shrewsbury). *Dom.* Lopitone. ' Town of *Loppa* ' or ' *Loppo,*' both in *Onom. Cf.* South LOPHAM (Thetford), 1225 Luppeham.

LOSTOCK GRALAM (Nantwich), LOSTOCK HALL (Preston). Pres. L. 1205 Lostok, 1296 Loes, -Lestok. Wyld thinks fr. an unrecorded O.E. *hlos,* same root as *lot,* O.E. *hlot ;* and so perh. ' place where lots used to be cast; ' O.E. *stoc, stocc,* lit. ' a block or stake *stuck* into the ground.' *Cf.* Hlosstede (*B.C.S.* iii. 449) and

Loscombe (both Dorset). This is doubtful. In *Dom.* Surrey
we have Losele, which rather suggests ' mead of ' an unrecorded
man ' *Losa*,' though it may be ' lot-nook.' See -hall. Gralam
was son of Hugh de Bunchamp, *c.* 1080.

LOSTWITHIEL (Cornwall). Pron. Los-wíthi-el. 1485 Lestwithiell,
1536 Lostuthyell. Many absurd derivations have been given.
It is quite simple, Corn. *lost withell*, ' rump of the lion,' referring
to the shape of a hill here. *Cf.* WITHIEL.

LOTHBURY (London). *c.* 1515 *Cock Lorells Bk.* Lothe bery.
' Sheltered town,' fr. O.E. *hléowþ*, 1554 *lothe*, ' shelter, warmth.'
Cf. L. Lothing, Lowestoft, and LOUTH. But, as we already have
Lothingland in *Dom.*, see LOWESTOFT, Loth- may well be the
contracted form of a man's name.

LOTHERSDALE and LOTHERSDEN (Craven). *Dom.* Lodresdene, 1202
Lodderesden. A *Lothewardus*, or *Lodewardus*, or *Hrothweard*
was Abp. of York *c.* 925-930. See -dale and -den.

LOTHINGLAND (Suffolk). *Dom.* Ludingalanda, 1158-59 *Pipe* Loinge-
land, 1237 *Patent R.* Luddinglond, Ludingeland, 1459 Lodyng-
lond. ' Land, territory of the sons of *Luda* ' or ' *Loda*.' See -ing.

LOUGHBOROUGH. *Dom.* Lucteburne, and -burg, 1298 Luhteburge.
Possibly this may be the same name as LOTHBURY. Or more
prob. fr. a man's name, ' burgh, castle of *Luhta* ' or ' *Luhha*,' the
latter a known form. See -borough.

LOUGHOR (Glamorgan). Possibly *c.* 380 *Anton. Itin.* Leucaro. In
W. Cas llywchyr. The *Cas* is said to be for *castell*, and *llwchyr*
a word for a lake = G. *loch*. There is a lakelike expanse of water
here, and a R. Llwchwr or Llychwr. Certainly W. *llwch* is ' pool.'

LOUND (Lowestoft and Retford). *Dom.* both Lund(a). Re. L.
1302 Lound. O.N. *lund-r*, ' grove, wood.' But possibly, fr.
phonetic reasons, same as *lown* or *lound*, ' calm, sheltered
place'; also of N. origin. See *Oxf. Dict.* s.v. LUND (Beverley),
Dom. Lont, 1179-80 *Pipe* Lund, is the same name. *Cf. Dom.*
Lincs Lund.

LOUTH (Lincs). *Dom.* Ludes, 1154-65 *chart.* Luda. *Croxden Chron.*
re 1210 Percolude—*i.e.*, ' park of Louth,' 1225 Louth. Perh. fr.
O.E. *hlúd*, ' loud,' ' noisy place.' Much more likely, O.E.
hléowþ, 1554 *lothe*, now in *dial. lewth*, ' shelter, warmth '; and
so, ' sheltered, warm place.' The letters *d* and *th* very often
interchange in old charters, through Norm. scribes.

LOWDHAM (Notts). *Dom.* Ludhā, *c.* 1170 Ludam, 1302 Loudham.
(It is near Ludcerce in *Dom.*). ' Home of *Luda* or *Lude*,'
several in *Onom.*

LOWESTOFT. *Dom.* Lothuwistoft, *later* Lowistoft, Loistoft. 1455
Leystoft, *c.* 1600 *Camden* Lestoffenses. The curious *Dom.* form
must represent ' toft ' or ' field of *Hlothewig*,' a name found as
that of a port reeve in Kent, *B.C.S.* 1212, same name as that of

the famous K. of the Franks, O.Ger. *Chlodwig*, Ger. *Ludwig*, Fr. *Lewis* or *Louis*. This name exactly suits the phonetics of all the forms given above. *Toft* is O.N. *topt*, N. *toft*, *tuft*, 'a homestead, a house-site, a holding.' L. Lothing, *Dom.* Lothing-land, beside Lowestoft, shows us a patronymic fr. *Hlothewig*, with its ending dropped, as often happens. *Cf.* CLOSWORTH.

LOWESWATER (Cumbld.). 1189 Laweswater. Perh. 'water, lake of *Hlæwa*'; 1 in *Onom.*

LOWTHER R. (Westmorland). Perh. connected with O.Ir. *lóthur*, 'canalis,' Bret. *laouer*, 'a trench.' *Cf.* Sc. LAUDER and LOWTHER.

LOWTHORPE (Driffield). *Dom.* Loghetorp, Logetorp, 1161-62 *Pipe* Leu-, Luitorp, 1179-80 Luuetorp. Prob. fr. *low* adj., early M.E. *láh* (O.N. *lág-r*), 2-3 *lah*, *laȝe*. 'Low-lying village.' See -thorpe. *Oxf. Dict.* has no example of *low*, *a.* 1150.

LOXLEY (Warwick, Uttoxeter, and Sheffield). Wa. L. *Dom.* Loches-lei, 1151 Lochesle. Ut. L. *Dom. ib.*, *a.* 1300 Lockesleye. A Warwick *chart.* of 985 also speaks of 'Locsetena gemære,' 'boundary of the Loc dwellers or settlers,' here in gen. pl. *Cf.* DORSET, etc. This is 'meadow of *Loc*.' *Cf.* next, and 1161-62 *Pipe* Locheswell (Wilts). See -ley.

LOXWOOD (Billingshurst). Not in *Dom.*, but *cf. Exon. Dom.* Lochesbera, where *bera* is 'wood.' Perh. 'wood of *Loc*.' There is one *Loc*, and there are two *Lucas* in *Onom. Cf.* LOCK'S BOTTOM and above.

LUCKER (Belford). 1152 Lucre. This must simply be N. *loeck-r*, 'a brook,' a very rare type of name in Northumberland. *Cf.* LECKFORD and LEEK.

LUDCHURCH (Narberth, Pembroke). 1353 Londeschirch, 1377 Londchirch; but in *Myv. Archaeol.* Yr Eglwys Lwyd, 'the grey church.' The *n* is a common intrusion in the early spellings, due to the nasalizing of the *w* or *u* sound, a proceeding not rare. Some hold that Llwyd means 'the adorable, the blessed one.'

LUDDINGTON (Stratford-on-A. and Garthorpe). St. L. *c.* 1000 *chart.* Ludintune, *Dom.* Luditone, *a.* 1100 Ludintune. Ga. L. *Dom.* Ludintone. 'Village, town of *Luda*.' *Cf.* LUTTON and 947 *chart.* Ludanbeorh (Wilts). There are also LUDBOROUGH, Louth, and LUDHAM, Gt. Yarmouth, *sic* 1262.

LUDGARS- LUDGERSHALL (Andover, Aylesbury, Gloster). An. L. *a.* 1200 Lutgershal. Ay. L. 1232 *Close R.* Lutegare-, Lutte-gartshal. Gl. L. 1220 Lutegares-, 1280 Letegareshale. 'Nook of *Leodgœr*, *Liutger*, *Ludegar*,' the name occurs in many forms. See -hall.

LUDGATE (London). *Sic* 1585. It may possibly, though not prob., be O.E. *hlidgeat*, 6 *lydyate*, 'a postern, a swing-gate, a gate between meadow and ploughed land.' Lydiate Lane (Hales-owen) is *a.* 1300 Nonemonnes Lydegate, 'no man's gate.'

But c. 1145 *Geoffrey Monm.*, c. 1205 *Layamon*, and a. 1300 *The Brut* tell that *Lud* or *Lludd* was a British king, brother of Cassibelaunus, and that London was called from him Caerlud; also that he was buried near this gate which now bears his name, called in the British language Porthlud, and in Saxon Ludesgate. Good authorities hold that *Lludd* was a Celtic deity. See, too, *Mabinogion* (Everyman's Libry.), p. 89.

LUDLOW. Not in *Dom.*, unless it be one of the Ludes—*i.e.*, Lud's (place), there; 1223 *Patent R.* Ludelawe, 1497 Ludlowe. In W. Llwydlo. 'Hill of *Lud*.' See LUDGATE and -low.

LUFWICK (Northants). *O.E. Chron.* 675 (late MS.) Lufgeard, which is 'yard, court of *Lufa*,' 2 in *Onom.* But *Dom.* Luhwic, 1166-67 *Pipe* Luffewich, fr. O.E. *wic*, 'dwelling.' *Cf. K.C.D.* iv. 288 Lofintune, prob. Northants; and Luffenham (Stamford), 1166 Luffenhā.

LUGG R. (Leominster). c. 1097 *Flor. Worc.* Lucge. Perh. connected with W. *llwch*, 'a lake, a pool.' As likely this is another case of river-worship. A god *Lugus*, Ir. *Lug*, seems to have been one of the ancient deities of the Kelt. family. *Cf.* CARLISLE. For LUGWARDINE 1233 *Patent R.* Lugwurthin, on this river, see -warden—*i.e.*, 'farm.'

LUNDY I. (Bristol Channel). Not in *Dom.* Doubtful. May be same as Sc. LUNDY; see LONDON. This scarcely suits the site, so prob. Norse *lund-ey*, 'puffin island,' N. *lunde*, Icel. *lundi*. See -ey. For LUND see LOUND.

LUNE R. (Lancaster and N. Yorks). Lan. L. prob. c. 150 *Ptolemy* Alona; also see LANCASTER. Said to be fr. a Keltic *louno*, 'mud'; on Keltic *lon* and *lod*, see LONDON.

LUSTON (Leominster). *Dom.* Lustone. 'Town of *Lusa*.' *Cf.* 940 *chart.* Lusebeorg (Wilts) and Lustleigh (Newton Abbott); the latter prob. fr. a man *Lustwine*; 3 in *Onom.*

LUTON (Beds and Chatham). Bed. L. *sic* a. 1199, but *Dom.* and 1157 Loitone, 1155 *Pipe* Luitune. Prob. 'village, town of *Luha*,' a name in *Onom.* But LUTLEY (Staffs), c. 1300 Lutteleye, and LUTLEY (Halesowen), *Dom.* Ludeleia, is 'mead of *Luda*' or '*Luta*.' Lutley may be fr. O.E. *lýt*, 3-4 *lut*, 3-5 *lute*, 'little,' as in Luthebury, old form of Littlebury (Saffron Walden).

LUTTERWORTH (Leicester). *Dom.* Lutresurde; also LUTRINGTON (Co. Durham), 1183 Lutringtona. This must be 'farm' and 'village of *Lutter*' or '*Luther*,' or '*Lutter*'s descendants'; but there is no such name in *Onom.*, only one *Lothewardus*, also a *Leutherius* or *Hlothhere*. See -ing, -ton, and -worth.

LUTTON (Yorks, Oundle, and Wisbech). *Dom.* Yorks Ludton; not in others. 'Town of *Luda*' or '*Lud*.' *Cf.* LUDDINGTON.

LUXULYAN (Lostwithiel). *Sic* 1536; also called LAN SULIAN. Said to be corrup. of Corn. *Lan Iulian*, 'church of St. Julian';

which of this name is doubtful. There are 115 Julians in *Dict. Christ. Biogr.* It is now dedicated to Julitta; hence the parish of St. Juliot, Cornwall. The story of Julitta and her child Cyric was very popular, and St. Basil wrote in praise of her.

LYDBURY NORTH (Salop). *Dom.* Lideberie. Prob. ' *Lida*'s burgh.' See LYDNEY and -bury. But LYDEARD ST. LAWRENCE (Taunton) seems to be fr. a man *Lidgeard. Dom.* Lidegar, 1285 Lydeyarde. *Cf.* 963 *chart.* Lidgeardes beorge, *re* Wasing, Berks. Only, of course Lidgeard will itself mean ' *Lid*'s yard ' or ' garth.' LYDBROOK-on-Wye is *a.* 1300 Luddebrok, and there is a *Dom.* Glouc. Ludebroc: perh. fr. a man *Lydda ;* but Baddeley suspects the first part to be a pre-Saxon river name.

LYDD (Kent). 774 *chart.* Hlid; *later,* Lyde, Lide. O.E. *hlid,* ' a cover.'

LYDFORD (N. Devon). See LIDFORD.

LYDIARD. There are places of this name at Wootton Basset and Swindon (Wilts). *Dom* Lidiarde, Lediar, also Lydeard St. Lawrence (Somst.), and Bp.'s Lydeard (Taunton). *Dom.* Lidiard, Lediart. 1224 *Patent R.* Lidiard is in Wilts. The name might be ' *Lida*'s yard,' or ' enclosure ' (O.E. *geard*); but is prob. O.E. *lid-geard,* ' boat, ship-yard '—at least in some cases.

LYDNEY (on Severn). 972 *chart.* Lidan ege, 1224 Lideneia, 1230 Lideneya. ' Isle on R. *Leden.*' See LEDBURY and -ey.

LYDSTEP (Penally, Pembk.). 1603 *Owen* Ludsopp, ' *Lud*'s place of refuge.' See LUDGATE and -hope.

LYE (Cradley). *Old,* Leeh, Lyegh, Lyghe, Lye, Lee, which show it var. of *lea,* ' meadow.' See -ley. Lye (Glouc.) has similar old forms.

LYME REGIS. Mentioned in 774. *Dom.* and 1234 Lym, 1184 *Hist. Selby* Luma, which last suggests a possible derivation fr. O.E. *leóma,* ' a ray of light, a flash, a gleam '; 4 *lewme, lime, lym.* But both here and in N. Staffs there is a R. Lyme, the latter *a.* 1200 Lima (other forms see BURSLEM), which seems to be simply O.E. *hlimme,* ' a stream, a river '; and this is quite possibly the origin of this town too. Regis is L. for ' of the King.' Lyme received a royal charter from K. Edward I. in 1316, when it was surrendered to the Crown. *Cf.* KING'S LYNN.

LYMINGE (Shorncliffe). 804 *chart.* Limming, *Dom.* Leminges. Doubtful; prob. patronymic. There are two named *Luning* in *Onom. Cf.* next; and see -ing.

LYMINGTON (Hants). Not in *Dom.* c. 1450 *Fortescue* Limyngton. The man's name here is prob. *Leofman,* var. *Leman* and *Lowman. Cf.* above, and see -ing.

LYNDHURST (Hants). *a.* 1100 *chart.* Lindhyrst, which is O.E. for ' forest, wooded place with the limes or lindens.' *Cf.* LYNDON

(Warwk.), *a*. 1300 Lynden, possibly fr. O.E. *lín*, ' flax,' as in Lyncroft (Lichfield). See -den and -don.

LYNNE or LYMNE or LYMPNE (S. Kent). 77 *Pliny* Limnus, *c*. 150 *Ptolemy* Portus Lemanis ; *Dom*. Lymne, 1392 Linne. Prob. Kelt. *linn*, ' pool, lake '; but for Lemanis *cf.* LOMOND (Sc.) and L. Leman or L. of Geneva. LYNN (Lichfield), however, is *c*. 1300 la Lynd, Lynde, O.E. *lind*, ' the linden ' or ' lime-tree.'

LYTHAM (Preston). *Dom*. Lidun. Prob. loc. of O.E. *hlið*, ' on the slopes or hill-sides.' *Cf.* HALLAM, KILHAM, etc.; also LYTHE (N. Yorks), *Dom.* Lid. The LYTH (Ombersley) is the same.

MABLETHORPE (Lincs). *Dom*. Malb'torp. 1202 Mapertorp, Maupertorp, Mautorp, 1318-1469 Malberthorpe, 1591 Mabberthorp. An interesting corrup., ' village of *Malber*,' or some such name. The nearest in *Onom*. are *Marbert* and *Mœthelbeorht* or *Madalbert*. See -thorpe.

MACCLESFIELD. *Dom*. Maclesfeld, 1297 Makelesfelde, 1503 Maxfeld. Looks like ' Matchless, peerless field,' fr. *makeless, a*. 1225 *makelese*, ' matchless,' fr. O.E. *gemaca*, ' a peer, equal, match, a make.' There seems no name in *Onom*. which would yield *Makele*, but MALTON (Cambs) is 1282 Makelton; and so it is prob. derived from a man's name, as all analogy suggests.

MACHYNLLETH (Aberdovey). W. *ma Chynlleth*, ' field of Cyn lleith,' in *Geoffr. Mon*. Kinlith map Neton. *Cf.* Mallwyd (Merioneth), field of Llywd '; Manest, ' field of Nest,' etc.

MACKNEY (Wallingford). 957 *chart*. Maccanige, 1428 Mackeney. ' Island of *Macca*.' See -ey.

MADEHURST (Sussex), not in *Dom*., and MADELEY (Salop and Staffs). Sa. M. *K.C.D.* iii. 123 Madan leage, *Dom*. Madelie. St. M. 975 *chart*. Madanlieg. *Cf. Dom*. Suss. Medelei. ' Wood ' and ' meadow of *Mada* '; O.E. *hyrst*, ' a wood '; and see -ley. MADELEY ULFAC (Uttoxeter) is named fr. its Saxon possessor in *Dom*.

MADINGLEY (Cambridge). *Dom*. Madingelei, 1284 Maddingele. ' Meadow of the descendants of *Mada*.' *Cf.* above, and Maddington (Wilts); and see -ley.

MADLEY (on Wye, Hereford). *c*. 1130 *Lib. Landav*., pp. 323, 324, Madle, *q.v.*, W. *mad lle*, ' good place.' Though, of course, some will hold it must be the same as MADELEY.

MADRESFIELD (Worcester). *a*. 1200 Medeleffeld, 1275 Madresfelde. Skeat thinks, ' *Mœth-here*'s field '; *Dom*. regularly writes *th* as *d*.

MADRON (Penzance). Fr. St. *Maternus* of Treves, in *Chaucer* Madryan; also Medhran, disciple of St. Piran or Kieran.

MAER (Newcastle, Staffs). *Dom*. and later Mere, O.E. for ' mere, lake.'

MAES GARMON (Mold). W.= ' (battle)field of St. *German*,' Bp. of Auxerre, France, who came to Britain in 429. We find a 'Maisbeli' as early as *c.* 1145 *Geoffr. Monm.* ?= MAESBURY (Oswestry). *Cf.* LLANARMON.

MAGOR (Newport, Mon.). W. *magwyr*, 'a wall'; also found in Cornwall as MAGOR and MAKER, *old* Macuir.

MAIDENHEAD. 1297-98 Mayden heth, *c.* 1350 Magdenhithe, 1538 Maidenhedde. 'Maiden's hythe' or 'landing-place'—*i.e.*, one very easy to land at, fr. O.E. *hydde*, later *hyð*, 'a haven, a landing-place.' *Cf.* HYTHE. MAIDEN CASTLE (Dorchester), not in *Dom.*, is claimed as a Keltic name, which is quite unlikely. *The* Maiden Castle is Edinburgh, found *c.* 1150 as 'Castellum puellarum.' Dorset also has MAIDEN NEWTON.

MAIDSTONE. *Dom.* Medwegestun; 1245 *Patent R.* Maidenestan; *later* Meddestane, Maydestan, which will mean 'rock' rather than 'town on R. MEDWAY,' though its W. name is said to be Caer Meguaid or Medwig, 'fort on the Medway.' See -ton.

MALDEN (Kingston, Surrey). *Dom.* Meldone, prob. 'sword hill' or 'dune,' O.E. *dún;* fr. O.E. *mæl*, 'sword, mark, ornament.' This will be the root also of MALDON (Essex), 993 *O.E. Chron.* Mældún, 1472 Malden, rather than O.E. *mál*, 3 *male*, 'tax, tribute.' But *cf.* CHRISTIAN MALFORD. A man *Mal*, or the like, seems implied in such names as Malshanger and Malsworth. See BIRCHANGER and -worth.

MALHAM (Leeds). *Dom.* Malgon, -un. These are clearly old locatives of the common Yorks *Dom.* type. But there seems no O.E. word to give us *malg-;* *mœle*, *mele*, 'a cup, a basin,' seems the nearest—' among the cup-shaped hollows.' But, then, the *g* must be an error. See -ham.

MALLING, SOUTH (Sussex). *Sic* 838, *a.* 1200 Mellinges, 1288 *Contin. Gervase* Suthmallinges. Patronymic. *Cf.* MELLING.

MALLWYD (Dinas Mawddy). W. *ma llwyd*, 'grey plain' or 'district.'

MALMESBURY. *Bede* v. 18, Monasterium quod Maildulfi urbem nominant, *O.E. vers.* Maldulfesburh, 940 *chart.* Matelmesburg, 1015 *O.E. Chron.* Ealdelmesbyrig; but, in latest MSS., Mealdelmesbyri, where the M. prob. stands for In. *Cf.* Inhrypum= RIPON. *Dom.* Ecclesia Malmsburiensis, *c.* 1097 *Flor. Worc.* Malmesbyriensis, *c.* 1160 *Gesta Steph.* Malmesbiria. 'Burgh of *Maldulf*,' 7th cny. abbot and teacher here. He was succeeded by *Ealdhelm;* hence arose a very curious confusion.

MALPAS (Chesh. and Truro). Former pron. Morpus, latter Mohpus. Same as the Fr. *Mauvais pas* (O.Fr. *mal pas*), or 'bad path,' alongside the Mer de Glace.

MALTBY (Rotherham). *Dom.* and 1179-80 Maltebi, 1442 Mauteby. Perh. 'Malt town,' O.E. and O.N. *malt*, north dial., etc., *maut*. But more likely it is 'dwelling of *Malte*,' 2 in *Onom*. *Mallt* is W. for 'Matilda.' See -by.

MALTON (Yorks). *Dom.* Maltun, *Contin. Sim. Dur.* ann. 1138 ᴇ.ʀ Maaltun, 1202 Melton. Doubtful. Might be 'malt town' (*cf.* MALTBY), but prob. 'tax, tribute town,' O.E. *mál, 3 male.* See MALDEN. However, MALTON (Cambs) is 1279 Malketon, 1282 Makelton, and may come fr. the same man's name as is prob. seen in MACCLESFIELD.

MALVERN. *Dom.* Malferna, *Ann. Worc.* 1085, Major Malvernia ('Great Malvern') fundata est per Alwium' or Ealdwine, 1156 *Pipe* Maluerna, 1362 Maluerne, W. *moel gwern,* 'hill of alders,' or 'hill over the moor or plain.'

MAMBLE (Worc.). 957 *chart.* Momela (gen. pl.). *Dom.* Mamele. Keltic *mam,* 'round, rounded,' G. *màm,* 'a round, breastlike hill'; the ending is uncertain. *Cf.* MAMBEG (Sc.).

MAMHILAD (Monmouthsh.). *c.* 1130 *Lib. Landav.* Mamheiliad. *Cf.,* in same book, Mamilet forest (Herefordsh.), evidently the same name; and also MANCHESTER. *Mam* will mean 'round, rounded'; and there is a W. *heledd,* 'a salt-pit'; but the name seems more likely to be W. *maen heiliad,* 'stone, rock for the serving [of liquor],' referring to some custom now forgotten.

MAN, I. OF. *J. Cæsar* Mona, *c.* 77 *Pliny* Monapia, *c.* 150 *Ptolemy* Μοναρίνα, v.r. Μονάοιδα (former = Μονάπνα, Nicholson, and same as Ptol.'s Μανάπιοι, near Wicklow), *Bede* Mevaniæ Insulæ, *a.* 810 *Nennius* Eubonia, id est Manau, 1000 *O.E. Chron.* Mon ege (= Mona's Isle), *c.* 1110 *Orderic* Insula Man; in Manx Eilan Mhannin. Doubtful. Earle thought O. Kelt. *man,* 'a place.' *Cf.* Akemanchester, old name of Bath, Akeman Street, Aylesbury, and MANCHESTER.

MANACLES (rocks near Lizard). Corrup. of Corn. *men, mœn eglos,* 'rocks of the church,' perh. fr. the Church of St. Keverne on the high ground behind.

MANCETTER (Atherstone). 1251 Mancestre. An old Rom. station, and = next. See -caster.

MANCHESTER. *c.* 380 *Ant. Itin.* Mancunio, v.r. Mamucio; 923 *O.E. Chron.* Mameceaster; *Dom.* and on to 1421 Mamecestre. Perh. a hybrid, 'round hill camp' (see MAMBLE and -chester); but it may be fr. Kelt. *man, maen,* 'stone.' *Cf.* above and MANSFIELD, and Maumbury Rings, Dorchester.

MANEA (March). This, says Skeat, must be '*Manna's* isle,' as it once was an island. *Cf.* Manley (Warrington) and Manton (Marlborough); and see -ey.

MANGOTSFIELD (Bristol). *Dom.* Manegodes felle. 'Field of *Mangod, Mangold,* or *Managolt,*' all forms in *Onom.*

MANNINGTREE. Not in *Dom.* 'Tree of,' *Mann, Manna, Manne, Manni, Manno, Mannig,* or *Manning.* All, except the two last, common names in *Onom. Cf.* BRAINTREE, OSWESTRY, etc.; and see -ing.

MAN OF WAR (rock, Scilly). Corrup. of Corn. *men, maen an vawr*, run into one word, Menavawr or Menawore, 'big rock.' *Cf.* MANACLES.

MANORBIER (Pembrokesh.). *c.* 1188 *Gir. Camb.* says it is 'Mansio Pyrri,' manor, estate, mansion-house of a man *Pyrr. Cf.* CALDY. Some think the ending is the N. *bœ-r*, 'dwelling' (see -by), and so the name a tautology. *Cf. c.* 1130 *Lib. Landav.* Mainaur Garth Benni, and MANOR FABON, 'manor of *Mabon*,' Cmrthnsh. Note, W. *mœnor*, 'district,' has nothing to do with Eng. *manor*.

MANSERGH (S. Westmorld.). *Dom.* Manzserge. 'Hut, shieling of *Mann*,' here a proper name. On -ergh see ANGLESARK. *Cf.* MANSTON.

MANSFIELD (Notts). *Dom.* Mamm-, Mamesfelde, 1162-65 *chart.* Mameffellt, 1189 *Pipe* Mamefeld, 1278 Man'efeld, Maunsfewd, 1291 Mannesfeld. Difficult. It is on R. Man or Maun, which may be a back formation, but not certainly, for we get it 1300 Mainesheued (*in* prob. error for *m*), 1332 Mammesheued, 'head of R. Mam.' It may then be 'field on the Man, Maun, or Mam,' which according to all analogy will be Kelt., either W. *mawn*, 'a bog,' or, transferred by some ignorant Saxon fr. some neighbouring hill, and so fr. *mam*, now only in G. *màm*, *maim*, 'a low, rounded hill, like a *mamma* or breast.' But it may be fr. some man, unrecorded in O.E.; *cf.* Mammendorf, Bavaria, Mansfeld, Saxony, and MANCHESTER.

MANSTON (W. Riding and Sturminster Newton). *Dom.* Yorks Maines-, Manestun. 'Town of *Man, Mana*, or *Mœna*,' all in *Onom. Cf.* MANSERGH.

MAPLEDURHAM (Reading). 1217 *Patent R.* Mapeldureham. We have *mapuldur* as O.E. for 'maple-tree' as early as *c.* 725 *Corpus Gloss. Cf.*, too, MAPLEBOROUGH (Alcester), *Dom.* Mapelberge, 940 *chart.* Mapildore (Wilts), and 1282 *Close R.* Mapeltreham (Chesh.); also MAPLEBECK (Notts), *Dom.* Mapelbec, and *Dom.* Kent Mapledescam. See next, and -ham.

MAPLEDURWELL (Basingstoke). Grant of *a.* 675 Mapeldure—*i.e.*, 'maple-tree.' *Cf.* the name Rowantree, and above.

MAPPLETON (Hull and Ashbourne). Hu. M. *Dom.* Mapleton. 'Town of a man called *Maple*,' O.E. *mapel.* Men are often called after trees—Ash, Birch, Beech, etc. It may be fr. the tree alone.

MARAZION (Penzance). 1250 Marhasgon, 1309 Marhasyon, 1313 Marhasion; *c.* 1470 Markysowe, Marchasyowe, *c.* 1540 *Leland* Markesju, 1595 Marghas-iewe (often to-day Market Jew—a curious example of popular etymology). The name is Corn. *marhas Diow* (fr. *De Yew*), 'market on Thursday.' But *Diow* must have had an older form *Dion*.

MARCHAM (Abingdon). *B.C.S.* iii. 427 Merchamme, *Dom.* Merceham. 'Enclosure,' O.E. *hamme*, 'on the march or boundary,' O.E. *merc, mearc.* MARCH itself is *c.* 1080 Merc, 1169 Merch.

Cf. next. But the cognate Eng. *march* is O.Fr. *marche,* first in Eng. *c.* 1290 in ' The Marche of Walis.' *Cf.* MARK and Markham (Notts). *Dom.* Marcham.

MARCHINGTON (Uttoxeter). 951 *chart.* Mærcham, 1004 Merchamtune, *Dom.* Marchamtone, *a.* 1300 Marchynton upon Nedwode. ' Town with the house on the march ' or ' boundary,' between Staffs and Derby. See above and -ing.

MARDEN (Hereford). *Dom.* Mawrdine, 1232 *Close R.* Maw-, Mauworthin. ' Farm of '? perh. *Maw,* one in *Onom.* See -warden.

MARGATE. 1225 *Patent R.* Meregate; also Mergate; prob. ' road,' O.E. *geat,* ' by the *mere* ' or ' lake ', now drained. For *e* become *a* *cf.* Derby, pron. Darby. *Cf.* MARFLEET (Hull), *Dom.* Mereflet, ' river by the mere.' See FLEET.

MARK (Highbridge), MARK BEECH (Eden Bridge), etc. O.E. *mearc,* Anglian *merc,* 2 *marc,* 4- *mark,* ' boundary, frontier, limit, later, landmark.' *Cf.* 847 *Grant* (Dorset), on merce cumb, and MARCHAM. Markyate (Beds) is ' the boundary gate ' between Beds and Herts.

MARKET DEEPING (Peterboro'). *a.* 1100 *Grant* of 664 Depingge, *c.* 1200 *Gervase* Dieping. There seems no Eng. sb. ' deeping ' or ' dippimg ' which will suit; but *cf.* ' Depenbech ' in Cheshire *Dom.,* now Malpas. There seems no helpful name in *Onom.*; but see -ing as denoting a place on a stream. The ' Market ' in all names with this prefix seems a late addition, though NEWMARKET goes back to the 12th cny.

MARKET HARBOROUGH. Not in *Dom. a.* 1300 Haverberg, 1517 Harborow. The *Oxf. Dict.* says = Market *Harbour (q.v.,* s.v.). But *a.* 1300 shows this cannot be; it must be fr. Dan. *havre,* ' oats.' See HAVERFORD and -burgh. HARBERROW (Hagley) is *a.* 1200 Hardberwe, *a.* 1300 Herdeberue, O.E. *hierdan beorge,* ' herdsman's barrow or burial mound '; also *cf.* Harberton (Totnes).

MARKET WEIGHTON (Yorks). Pron. Weeton. *Dom.* Wicstun. 1298 Wighton, Wyhton, Wyghton. From some man; *Weah, Wigheah,* and *Wiht* are possible names in *Onom. Dom.* regularly changes guttural *ch* or *gh* into *st.*

MARKINGTON (Leeds). *Dom.* Merchintone. ' Town of *Mearca,*' not in *Onom.,* or, of one of the many names in *Mearc-.*

MARKS TEY (Colchester). J. H. Round has shown that Marks involves the name of the village of *March,* Pas de Calais, borne by Adelolf de Mark, owner of Marks Tey district in *Dom.* So this name means ' Mark's paddock,' O.E. *tih, teah, teag. Cf.* GREAT TEY.

MARLBOROUGH. *Dom.* Marleberge, 1110 *O.E. Chron.* Mærlebeorg, 1158 Merleb'ga. *Marl,* O.Fr. *marle,* is not found as an Eng. word till 1372, nor *merle,* ' blackbird,' till 1450. So this is prob. ' BARROW, tumulus of *Mœrle,*' short form of *Mœrleswegen,* 4 in

Onom. Cf. Dom. Worc. Merleberg. MARL CLIFF (Wstrsh.), *c.* 872 *chart.* Marnan Clive, *later* Maranclive, Mearnanclif, *a.* 1790 Mar Cleeve, is ' marble cliff,' fr. O.E. *marma,* here perh. rather with its meaning ' stiff clay,' which is the meaning of O.Fr. *marne, marle.* MARLEWOOD (Thornbury), in its old forms, 1221 to *Leland,* is always Morle-, and so prob. fr. O.Fr. *morele,* ' nightshade,' found so spelt in Eng. fr. *c.* 1265. ..

MARLEY (Bingley) and MARLEY HILL (Swalwell, Durham). Sw. M. 1183 Merleia and Bin. M. 1202 Merlegh, which is prob. ' meadow by the *mere* ' or ' lake.' *Cf.* MARLOW, etc. But Marley (W. Riding) is *Dom.* Mardelei, Merdelai, prob. ' marten's mead,' O.E. *mearð. Dom.* regularly makes *th* into *d. Cf.* MARTLEY.

MARLINGFORD (Norwich). *Dom.* Merlingeforda, 1161-62 Merlingef'-, 1454 Marlynferthe, 1482 Marlyngforthe. ' Ford of *Merlin,*' or perh. of his descendants. See CAERMARTHEN and -ing. The -ferthe or -forthe for -ford (*q.v.*) is due to Norse influence.

MARLOES (Milford Haven). *Tax. Eccl.* Malros, 1603 *Owen* Marlasse. Evidently =MELROSE (Sc.), O.W. *mœl rhos,* ' bare moor.'

MARLOW (Maidenhead). *Dom.* Merlawe. ' Hill by the lake or mere,' O.E. *mere,* 2-3 *mœre,* 4 *marre,* 5 *mer. Cf.* MARLEY and MARTIN. See -low.

MAROWN (I. of Man). Named fr. St. *Runy* or *Ronan,* Bp. of Sodor A.D. 600. *Ma-* is the common Kelt. endearing prefix, ' my own.'

MARPLE (Manchester). Not in *Dom.* Prob. corrup. of *merc- pool,* or ' pool, lake at the boundary.' See MARWOOD.

MARR (Doncaster). *Dom.* Marra, 4 times, Marle once (error). Perh. fr. *mar* sb. ' a hindrance, obstruction,' found first in *Oxf. Dict.* in *a.* 1300 *Cursor Mundi,* fr. O.E. *merran,* ' to mar.'

MARRICK (Richmond, Yorks). *Dom.* Marige, Mange (*n* for *ri*). Prob. ' isle in the mere.' *Cf.* MARGATE; but -ey (*q.v.*) is rarely seen as -ick.

MARSHAM (Norwich). *Dom.* Marsam. *Cf. B.C.S.* 496 Mærsa ham. Perh. ' home of *Mœrsa.*' See -ham. On *marsh* see next. MARSTON Moor (Yorks) is *Dom.* Merstone, prob. fr. same name.

MARSKE (2 in Yorks). *Dom.* Mersc, Mersch. O.E. *merisc, mersc,* ' a marsh.' Seen also in Little Marsis (Yorks) *Dom.* Parvo Merse, and Pickering Marishes, *Dom.* Oudulvesmersc, etc. But Baddiley derives MARSHFIELD (Box), *Dom.* Meresfelde, fr. a man *Mœrwine.*

MARSTON (12 in *P.G.*). Warwk. M. *c.* 1000 Merston juxta Avonam, *Dom.* Mers(e)ton, two, also near Penkridge *ib.,* 1327 Mershton. Glouc. M. *Dom.* Merestune. *Cf.* 774 *chart.* ' Mersctun,' (Rochester). ' Town, dwelling by the marsh '; O.E. *mersc, mœrsc, merisc,* 4 *merss,* 5- *marsh. Cf.,* too, *Dom.* Meresberie (Salop). Duignan gives 5 Marstons in Warwksh. alone.

MARTIN (Lincs, Dover, Salisbury). Sa. M. (prob. 871 *O.E. Chron.*
Meretune), *Dom.* Mertone, 1227 Meretone. ' Town on the
mere.' See MARLOW; and *cf.* MEERTON. MARTIN (Notts), *Dom.*
Martune, on the borders of Yorks, is prob. O.E. *mearc tún*,
' boundary town.' MARTON (7 in *P.G.*), *Dom.* Lincs Martone,
Yorks ₁Martun, -tone, 21 times, Mereton 4 times, may not
always be₁ the same. That near Leamington, 1327 Merton,
seems to be; but in 1179-80 *Pipe* Yorks we have a ' Mareton,'
which *might* be fr. O.E. *mare*, ' a goblin ' (*cf.* nightmare). In
1157 *Pipe* Cheshire we have a ' Monte Martin,' prob. fr. St.
Martin of Tours, 4th cny.

MARTLETWY (Pembksh.). 1603 *Owen* Marteltwy. The first part is
corrup. of W. *merthyr*, ' a martyr,' the second doubtful.

MARTLEY (Worcester). *Dom.* Mertelai. 1275 Mertelee. No likely
name in *Onom.*, nor can it be fr. *mart*, ' market,' or *mart*, ' an
ox ' (see *Oxf. Dict.*, *s.v.*), so prob. ' meadow of the *mart*,' dial.
name of the marten, O.E. *meardð, merð*. *Cf.* foumart and
MARLEY (W. Riding); see -ley. But MARTHRY (Pembk.) *c.* 1130
Lib. Land. Mathru, some think to be W. *mai* or *ma thru*,
' field of woe ' (*tru*). Prob. it is fr. MERTHYR.

MARWOOD (Barnard Castle). *a.* 1130 *Sim. Dur.* Marawude. Marais doubtful. It may represent a proper name clipped down. *Cf.*
Onom. under Mar-, Marc-, Mear-, Mearh-. Prob. it is fr. O.N.
mara, O.E. *mare*, ' a goblin.' *Cf.* nightmare.

MARY-LE-BONE (London). 1742 St. Mary at the Bourne, or brook—
i.e., the Tyburn. The Cockney has caused the liquid *r* to
vanish.

MARYPORT. Where, or near where, Q. *Mary* landed in her flight
from Scotland, 1568; but till 1750 called Ellenfoot.

MASBOROUGH (Rotherham). Not in *Dom.* Prob. contraction of
' *Mœssa's* ' or ' *Masso's* burgh '; both forms in *Onom.* *Cf.*
next, and Maisemore (Glouc.), 1221 Meismore, *later* Meyesmora,
which is prob. ' *Mœg's* moor '; one in *Onom.*

MASHAM (Yorks). *Sic* 1296, but *Dom.* Massan. Prob. as above,
' *Massa's* home '; only *Dom.'s* form will be an irregular
loc., such as *Dom.* Yorks is full of, ' at Massa's.' *Cf.* HAL-
LAM, etc.

MATHERN (Chepstow). Addit. *Lib. Land.* Martharne, -erne, *later*
Matharn; prob. W. *ma theyrn*, ' field of the king or lord ' (*G.*
tighearn), and not fr. *merthyr*, ' martyr.'

MATHON (Gt. Malvern). *Dom.* Matma, 1275 Mathine, *a.* 1500
Mathan. O.E. *maðum, maðm*, ' a precious thing, a valuable
gift '; *m* and *n* easily interchange. *Cf.* MEDOMSLEY.

MATLASK (Norfolk). *Dom.* Matelasc. 1453 Matelask. Curious
name; looks like O.E. *mæte*, ' small, poor, bad,' and *lisk*, a M.E.

word of prob. Scandinavian origin, *a.* 1200 *lesske,* 5-6 *laske,* ' the flank or loin.' *Cf.* next.

MATLOCK. Not in *Dom.* ? O.E. *mǽte loca,* ' small enclosure.' *Cf.* PORLOCK and above. But Matford (Berkeley) is *c.* 1270 Mathford, whilst MATSON, same shire, is *c.* 1121 Matesdona, 1199 Metteresd', showing that this is for ' *Mæthhere's* down.' See -don.

MATTISHALL (Dereham). *Dom.* Mateshala, 1484 Mateshal(l)e. ' Hall ' or ' nook of *Mata.'* See -hall.

MAUGHOLD Hd. (I. of Man). St. *Maughold* was chief of an Irish band of robbers converted by St. Patrick and, next to St. German, patron saint of the Isle.

MAUNBY (Thirsk). *Dom.* Mannebi, Mannesbi, 1202 Magnebi, 1204 Mageneby. ' Dwelling of ' some man with a name in Magen- or Mægen-. There are many in *Onom.,* Mægenfrith, Mægenheard, etc. It can hardly be fr. the simple *Mann,* as in MANSERGH, etc. See -by.

MAYFIELD (4 in *P.G.*). Ashbourne M. *Dom.* Madevelde, *a.* 1300 Mathelefell, Matherfield, *a.* 1400 Mathefeld, Mayfield. Prob. O.E. *mæthel felda,* ' field of the meeting ' or ' council.' *Cf.* *K.C.D.* 1339 Metheltun. Old forms needed for the other names; not in *Dom.* They may be fr. *may,* ' the hawthorn,' found so used *a.* 1548. Meaburn (E. Cumbld.) is 1120 Maiburn; ? meaning.

MAYFORD (Woking). 955 *chart.* Mæȝðe forda. ' Virgin's ford.' O.E. *mæȝð* or *mæȝeð,* ' a maid, a virgin.'

MEAS-, MEESDEN (Herts). *a.* 1300 Mesdune. O.E. *méos dún,* ' mossy hill.'

MEASE R. (Derbysh. and Warwick) and MEES R. (Staffs). O.E. *méos ;* O.N. *mose,* ' moss,' found in Eng. *c.* 1639 *meese,* and still in S.W. dial. *meesh.* So, ' mossy ' river. MEASHAM (Atherstone) is *Dom.* Messeham, and MILL MEESE (Stone) is *Dom.* Mess, *a.* 1400 Mulneme(e)s, which gives us the old forms of both river names. *Cf.,* too, MEASDEN and MISSENDEN.

MEDMENHAM (Marlow). *Dom.* Medemehā. ' Home of ' prob. ' *Mæthhelm,'* one in *Onom. Dom.* regularly makes *th* into *d,* and liquid *l* easily vanishes. *Cf.* next.

MEDOMSLEY (Co. Durham). 1211 Madmesl'. Prob. ' Meadow of the valuable gift,' see MATHON; it is found in *c.* 1200 *Ormin.* in pl. as *maddmess.* If a man's name be preferred, it *may* be found in *Mældomen* or *Meldum,* var. of *Mailduf,* or in *Mæthhelm,* as above. See -ley.

MEDWAY R. *a.* 1000 *chart.* Mædwæȝa, 1016 *O.E. Chron.* Medewæȝa, *a.* 1130 *Sim. Dur.* Meodewage, 1215 *Mag. Chart.* Medewaye. Perh. O.E., fr. *mæd,* ' a meadow,' and *waga,* ' deep waters ' (M'Clure). But some think, W. *med gwy,* ' water, river which is extended or full.' *Cf.* R. WEY and MAIDSTONE.

MEEDHAM (Rochester). 774 *chart.* Mædham. 'Home on the meadow'; O.E. *mœd,* 'a mead'; though *Dom.* Kent Meddestan suggests a man's name. See -ham. Meeth (Devon) *may* also be fr. *mœd,* but is doubtful.

MEERBROOK (Leek). 'Brook on the boundary'; O.E. *mœre ;* M.E. *mœr, mer. Cf.* 1241 *Newminst. Chart.* Usque ad Merethorne. But MERESBROOK (Sheffield) and *Dom.* Meresbroc (Salop) *may* be fr. O.E. *mere,* 'a lake.' *Cf.* 940 *chart.* Mærhlinc, Wiley (Wilts), 'links at the boundary.' MEERING (Notts), *Dom.* Meringe, is a patronymic.

MEIFORD (Welshpool). Prob. W. *mai fod,* aspirated fr. *bod,* 'field with the house or hut in it.'

MELBOURNE (Cambs, Derby, and E. Riding). Cam. M. *chart.* Meldeburne, *Dom.* Melleburne, 1661 *Fuller* Meldeburn. 'Brook of *Melda.' Cf.* MELDRETH. De. M. *Dom.* Mileburne (3 times), Somerset Meleburne. There are also 1157 *Pipe* Meleburna (Northumberland), and another in 1158 in Wilts. But M., E. Riding, is *Dom.* Middelburne, Midelborne, 'middle brook.' *Cf.* MELTON. See -bourne.

MELDRETH (Royston, Herts). *c.* 1080 *Inquis. Camb.* Meldrethe, *Dom.* Melrede. '*Melda's* enclosure.' See MELBOURNE, and SHEPRETH near by.

MELKSHAM (Wilts). *Dom.* Melcheshā, 1155 *Pipe* Melchesham, 1223 Melkesham. 'Home of *Melc,*' or the like. No such name in *Onom.* See -ham.

MELLING (Carnforth). *Dom.* Mellinge. *Cf.* MALLING. Prob. a patronymic.

MELLIS (Eye, Suffolk). *Dom.* Melles, and MELLS (Frome), ? *Dom.* Mulle. *Cf. Dom.* Melas and Mele (Chesh.). W. *melys,* 'sweet,' is not likely; prob. all are fr. O.N. *mel-r,* 'a sandbank,' also 'bent grass.' *Meals* or *miols* are the common name for 'sand-dunes' on the shores of Norfolk, Lancs, etc. See *Oxf. Dict.,* s.v. MEAL sb[5]. *Cf.* MELFORD (Sc.) and MEOLS. Duignan thinks MELLY (Halesowen), *a.* 1200 Melley, to be a form of *mill,* O.E. *mylen,* 1 *myll,* 4-6 *melle ;* if so the -ey must be a dimin. *Cf.* MILWICH.

MELLOR (Blackburn and Stockport). Not in *Dom.* W. *maelawr,* 'a place of traffic,' *cf.* Maelor, a hundred in Flint, is conceivable. But prob. O.N. *mel-r,* 'a sandbank,' or 'bent grass.' The N. nominative ending *r* seldom survives in a name.

MELMERBY (E. Cumberland and N. Yorks). *Dom.* Yorks Mal-, Melmerbi; 1202 *Yorks Fines* Melmorbi. 'Dwelling of *Melmor' ;* one is known in the days of K. Eadred, *c.* 950. See -by.

MELSONBY (Darlington). *Dom.* Malsenebi. 'Dwelling of' some unknown man, perh. *Mœrleswegen* or *Merleswain.* See -by.

MELTON (Brough, Yorks, and Woodbridge). *Dom.* Yorks Medeltone —i.e., 'middle town.' M. CONSTABLE (King's Lynn), *Dom.*

Meltuna, was held under the Bps. of Thetford by their hereditary constables, the de Lyons or de Meltons. Little Melton (Norwich) is *Dom.* Meltun parva. M. MOWBRAY, *Dom.* Medeltun, is called after the family who once held lands here. Roger de *Moribray,* or *Moubray,* is on the Roll of Battle Abbey (1066, or later), *c.* 1175 *Fantosme* Munbrai, 1179-80 *Pipe* Molbrai, *a.* 1200 *Wm. Newbury* Monbrai; origin doubtful. There is a Mowbray south of Silloth. Some of the Meltons—*e.g.,* in Norfolk—may possibly be as in MELLIS, ' village on the sand-dune.' *Cf. Dom.* Surrey Meldone. MELTONBY (E. Riding) is *Dom.* Meltebi, ' dwelling of *Melte* ' or ' *Malte* '; 2 in *Onom.* The *n* is sign of the gen. *Cf.* MELTHAM (Huddersfield).

MELVERLEY. See MILVERTON.

MELYNLLYN (Llanrwst). W. ' yellow lake '; W. *felyn,* ' yellow,' unaspirated. *Cf.* DUNFERMLINE (Sc.).

MENAI Straits (Bangor). There is a Menei in *Taliessin,* but the name here seems to date only from the construction of the great bridge. It is supposed to be W. *main gwy,* ' narrow water ' or ' strait.'

MENDHAM (Harleston). *Dom.* Mendaham. *Cf.* 1179-80 *Pipe* Mendham (Lancs). This must be ' home of *Menda,*' an unrecorded name. See -ham.

MENDIP Hills (Somerset). *a.* 1100 *chart.* in *Wm. Malmesb.* Mons Munidop, 1284 *Close R.* Munedep, 1290 *chart.* Menedipp. Prob. not fr. W. *mynydd;* Corn. *menit, menyth,* ' a hill.' ' Munidop' prob. means, ' enclosed land in a privileged district '; see MINETY and -hope. Menith Wood, Lindridge (Worc.), is 1718 Meneth, but *a.* 1300 Menhey wood, so that the mod. form must be corrupt.

MENHENIOT (Liskeard). 1536 Menhynyott. Corn. *maen hen Neot,* ' old rock of Neot,' eldest brother of K. Alfred. *Cf.* ST. NEOTS.

MENSTON (Leeds). *Dom.* Mersintone. ' Town of *Mœrsa* '; gen. *-san. Cf.* MARSHAM. The liquid *r* has disappeared !

MENTMORE (Leighton Buzzard). *Dom.* Mentemore. It looks Kelt. = W. *mynydd mawr,* Corn. *menit meur* or *mur,* ' big hill.' *Cf.* MENDIP and PENMAENMAWR. There is no name like *Mente* in *Onom.,* but an origin fr. O.E. *minte,* 3-7 *mente,* ' mint,' any plant of the aromatic genus *Mentha,* is quite possible, and so ' mint moor.' Duignan derives Monmore (Wolverhampton) fr. W. *mawn mawr,* ' great bog,' but it is 1327 Monnemere, which must mean ' lake of *Monne, Monna,*' or ' *Monn,*' all fairly common names in *Onom.*

MEOLE BRACE (Shrewsbury), MEOLS (Wirral), and MEOLS COP (Southport). *Dom.* Salop Melicope, Melela. Prob. not fr. W. *moel,* ' a conical hill,' with Eng. plur. *s,* but fr. O.N. *mel-r,* ' a sand dune,' a ' meal.' See MELLIS. As Mielle it is common in Channel Is. *Brace* is a mining term for ' the mouth of a shaft,' and Cop is O.E. *cop, copp,* ' top, summit.'

MEON R. (S. Hants), and MEONSTOKE (Bp's. Waltham). 932 *chart.*
To Meóne. Thought to contain the same root as Bede's province
of the *Meanuari*, O.E. vers. Meanwara, 'dwellers in Mean.' We
can say no more. See STOKE. There is also Meon (Glouc.), 1164
Muna, 1221 Meen, which must be the same.

MEOPHAM (Gravesend). 940 *chart.* Meapeham, Meapham; *Dom.*
Mepeham. 'Home of *Meapa.*'

MEPAL (Ely). 1302-1428 Mephale. 'Nook or corner of *Meapa.*'
Cf. above and -hall.

MERE (Wilts and Knutsford). Wilt. M. *Dom.* Mere, Mera; 1155
Pipe Mera. O.E. *mœre, ʒemœre,* 'a boundary, a landmark,'
or else *mere,* 'lake'; these have often been drained of recent years.

MERIDEN (Coventry). 1398 Muridene, 1440 Meryden, *c.* 1550
Alspathe, *alias* Myredene. Prob. not 'merry vale,' but fr. *miry,*
4-6 *myry,* 6-7 *myrie,* 6 *myerry,* 7 *merie,* fr. *mire ;* O.N. *mýrr,* 4-6
myr, 4 *mure, muyre,* 'boggy, swampy ground.' *Cf.* MIRFIELD
and the name Merrylees. See -den. Merry Brook, Cropthorne
(Worc.), may have a similar origin.

MERIONETH. Named after *Merion,* grandson of Cunedda Wledig;
the -eth or -ydd is an enclitic particle, with no very clear
meaning.

MERRIOTT (Crewkerne). *Dom.* Merret. [? *cf.* 859 *chart.* Meritie
stret to Senfeling forde.] Perh. 'island in the lake' or *mere,*
fr. AIT (*q.v.* in *Oxf. Dict.*), 2-8 *eyt,* 'island.'

MERSEA (Essex). 895 *O.E. Chron.* Meresig; O.E. = 'isle in the mere'
or 'lake'; *Dom.* Meresai. *Cf. Dom.* Merssse (Salop), Merse
(Bucks), and Merestone, now MERSTON (I. of Wight); also
Merstowa (Somerset), 1231 *Patent R.* See -ea.

MERSEY R. *a.* 1100 Mærse. Doubtful. Prob. 'river of the
boundary,' from O.E. (*ge*)*mære,* 'boundary, march,' and *éa, é,*
1-3 *œ,* 'river.' The Mers- may be fr. 'marsh,' O.E. *mersc,*
merisc. Cf. Dom. Cheshire Mersham, also name of a village near
Ashford, and 1179-80 *Pipe* Mershon (Yorks). *Cf.,* too, the
Mearse (Bromsgrove), ? 'the boundary,' of which name there are
no old forms; and see MERSEA and MERSTHAM.

MERSTHAM (Red Hill and Ashford). Red. M. *Dom.* Merstan. Prob.
'stone at the boundary'; O.E. *mœre* (*gemœre*) *stan ;* -an easily
becomes -ham (*q.v.*).

MERTHYR TYDVIL or TYDFIL. W. for 'martyr Tydvil.' She was
daughter of Brychan, Keltic chief in S. Wales in 5th cny. With
her father and brother she was murdered here, and a church
was erected in her memory. *Cf.* Merthyr Cynog (Brecon).
C., son of Brychan, was murdered by the Saxon pagans. The
same root is prob. found corrupted to Marthrey (Pembrk.), *c.* 1130
Lib. Land. Marthru, Mathru; *c.* 1190 *Gir. Camb.* Martru.

MERTON (Surrey and Dolton, Devon). Sur. M. *O.E. Chron.* 755 Merantun, is 'town of the mare'; O.E. *mere, -ran*; *Dom.* Meretoni. Other Mertons—*e.g.*, *Dom.* Devon Mertone—will be= MARTON.

MESSINGHAM (Brigg). *Sic a.* 1100 *chart.* A patronymic, as shown by MESSING (Kelvedon). There is one monk *Messa*, gen. *-san*, in *Onom.* *Cf.* Great Massingham (King's Lynn), 1179-80 *Pipe* Mesington (Yorks), and *K.C.D.* 721 Mæssan wyrth. Also *cf.* MISSENDEN.

MESTY CROFT (Wednesbury). Prob. 'field, little farm of *Meste*.' *Cf. Dom.* Derby Mestesford.

METHLEY (Leeds). *Dom.* Medelai. As *Dom.* for Middleton is Medeltone, this is prob. 'middle meadow,' the Meth. being influenced by O.N. *mith-r*, 'mid.' *Cf.* Middop ('mid hope,' *q.v.*), Craven; *Dom.* Mithope; and *Dom.* Yorks 'Mith Hundret' —*i.e.*, 'Middle Hundred.' See -ley.

MEXBOROUGH (Rotherham). *Dom.* Mechesburg. Prob. 1202 *Yorks Fines* Merkis-, Morkisburg; 1206 Merkesburgh. 'Burgh, fort of,' it is not certain what; perh. some name in Mearc- or Marc-, if the latter identification be right. But if *Dom.* is right, then fr. some man *Mecca, Mecco*, or *Mecga*, all names in *Onom.* See -boro'.

MICHELDEVER (Winchester). *Dom.* Miceldevre. Looks like O.E. *micel*, 'great'; Sc. *muckle*; and Kelt. *dever*, 'water, river.' *Cf.* DOVER. There is no river nearer than the Itchen. *Cf.* 1322 'le Mikeldor de Yowberg' (Wastwater), and 1160-61 *Pipe* Hants Micheldene. There is another MICHELDEAN, *old* Mucheldene (Forest of Dean).

MICHELNEY or MUCHELNEY (Somerset). *Dom.* Michelniu, *a.* 1130 *Sim. Dur.* Micelnei, *c.* 1114 *O.E. Chron.* Myclaniȝe. O.E.= 'great island,' O.E. *iȝ.* The *n* is the accus. inflexion.

MICKLEBY (Yorks). *Dom.* Michelbi. MICKLEHAM (Dorking). *Dom.* Michelham. MICKLETHWAITE (W. Riding). *Dom.* Mucheltuoit, -tuit, 1202 *Fines* Micle-, Mikelthwaite. MICKLETON (Campden, Glouc.). 1005 *chart.* Micclantun, *Dom.* Muceltune; whilst M. (Yorks) is *Dom.* Micleton. All fr. O.E. *micel, micle, mycel*, 'great'; in Sc. *muckle.* See -by, -ham, -thwaite, and -ton.

MIDDLESBOROUGH. *Sic* 1586. Prob.'*Mailduf*'s town.' *Cf.* MALMESBURY; and see -borough. But, of course, Middleham (Yorks), *Dom.* Middelha', is 'middle house,' and MIDDLEWICH (Chesh.) the same, though, by a scribe's freak, *Dom.* spells it Mildestvic.

MIDDLESEX. 1011 *O.E. Chron.* Middelseaxe, 1087 *ib.* Middelsex. 'Land of the Middle Saxons.' *Cf.* ESSEX, SUSSEX, Wessex.

MIDDLETON (21 in *P.G.*). Tamworth M. *Dom.* Mideltone, King's Lynn M. *Dom.* Middeltona, etc. *Cf.* MILTON. We find Midel-, Middeltun, 19 times in Yorks *Dom.*, whilst Middleton (Morley) is *Dom.* Mildentone, ' town of *Milda.*' *Cf.* MELBOURNE.

MIDGHAM (Berks). *K.C.D.* iii. 193, 196 Mieghæma gemæra; *Dom.* Migeham, 1316 Migham. *Cf.* 1161-62 *Pipe* Migehal close by. ' Home of the midges '; O.E. *mycg, micg.* See -ham.

MIDGLEY (Luddenfoot, Yorks). *Dom.* Micleie. O.E. *micel,* ' great ledge ' and *léah,* ' meadow.' MIGLEY (Co. Durham) 1183 Migleia, is prob. the same name. *Cf.* MITCHAM. The *dg* is palatalized *c, cf.* BADGEWORTHY.

MILDENHALL (Suffk. and Marlbro'). Suf. M. *Dom.* Mildentune and Mitdenehalla (*t* for *l*), 1158-59 *Pipe* Mildehala. Ma. M. *Dom.* Mildenhalle. ' Corner of *Milda,*' one such woman in *Onom.* See -hall.

MILES PLATTING (Manchester). *Miles* is presumably a man's name. Platting is ' a small foot-bridge.' See *Oxf. Dict.* (*s.v.*).

MILFORD HAVEN. *c.* 1190 *Girald.* Milverdicus portus (harbour), *c.* 1425 Melyford, *c.* 1450 Mylford, 1593 Millford Havon. Milford is prob. = MELFORD (Sc.), ' sandy bay ' or ' fjord,' N. *mel-r,* ' a sand-dune ' or ' sandbank,' and *fjord.* *Cf.* Waterford. The *-icus, c.* 1190, is adjectival. There was a *Rhyd y felin,* or ' ford of the mill,' only a mile away, but this cannot be the origin of the present name. North Milford (Tadcaster) is *Dom.* Mileford, ' ford at the mill '; O.E. *mylen* and *myll.*

MILLBANK (London). *Sic a.* 1560.

MILLINGTON (Yorks). *Dom.* Mileton, 1206 *Fines* Milington. ' Town of *Mile* ' or ' *Milo* '; 4 of the latter in *Onom.* See -ing.

MILLOM (S. Cumberland). Old forms needed. Perh. *mill-holm,* a ' holm,' O.E. and Dan. *holm,* O.N. *holm-r,* is a small island in a river, and also a flat meadow near a river or the sea, easily flooded.

MILTON (20 in *P.G.*). Some of these are prob. ' mill-town,' but M. Kent or Essex is 893 *O.E. Chron.* Middeltûn, *c.* 1120 *Henr. Hunt.* Middletune. MILTON ABBEY (Dorset) is also *old* Middletune, so is Milton (Cambs), while Milton (Abingdon) is *Dom.* Middeltune, 1291 Middelton, *c.* 1540 Milton. Milton (Cumbld.) is 1230 Muleton, which is O.E. *mylen,* 3-4 *mulle,* ' a mill.' Milburn (Pontefract) is 1201 Milneburn, or ' mill-brook.' *Cf.* MIDDLETON.

MILVERTON (Warwick and Somerset). Wa. M. *Dom.* Malvertone, *a.* 1200 Melv-, Mulvertone. Som. M. *c.* 1043 *chart.* Milferton, *Dom.* Milvertone. ' Village, town of *Milfer.*' *Cf.* Melverley (Salop).

MILWICH (Stone). *Dom.* Melewiche, *a.* 1200 Mulewich. ' Village, dwelling with the mill.' See MILTON and -wich.

MIMMS (Herts). *Dom.* Mimmise, 1278 Mymmys. This is simply 'abode of the *Mimmas.*' *Onom.* has only *Minna.* This is an abnormal name.

MINARD (St. German's). Corn. *min arth,* ' edge of the height.' *Cf.* Miniard (Worcs.), where the central *i* will be the *y* of the W. article. Not the same as MINARD (Sc.).

MINCHINHAMPTON (Stroud). *Dom.* Hantone, *a.* 1300 Munnechen-, Monneken-, Mynchyn-, Munchun- hampton—*i.e.,* HAMPTON— 'home-town of the monks '; O.E. *monec, munec,* here gen. pl. *Cf.* Grant *a.* 675, Menechene Rude or Monk's Cross, on borders of Hants and Surrey.

MINDRUM or -DRIM (N. Northumberland). *Old* Minethrum, 1324 Mundrum. Seems a curious hybrid and tautology. W. *mynydd ;* Corn. *menit,* ' hill '; and G. *druim,* ' hill-ridge.' Drum is very common in Sc. place-names, cognate with L. *dorsum,* ' back.' *Cf.* next.

MINDTON or MINTON (Salop). *Dom.* Munetune. Prob. not hybrid, ' town beside the hill ' (the Longmynds); W. *mynydd ;* Corn. *menit,* ' a hill.' But, like MINETY (Wilts), not in *Dom.* and not in a Kelt. region, it will prob. go with Meend, a name common in Forest of Dean, 1263 Mihinde, 1281 La Munede, 1303 Miinde, now derived by Rev. A. L. Mayhew fr. an O.E. or rather Anglo-Nor. form of low L. *munita,* for *immunitas,* ' privileged district, one free from seignorial rights.' *Cf.* Mint (Westmld.), *Dom.* Munet, and MUNET.

MINSHULL VERNON (Cheshire). *Dom.* Manessele, -shale. ' Nook, corner of *Manne* ' or ' *Man(n)a,*' a common name in *Onom.* This is one of the very rare cases where -hull is really -hall (*q.v.*).

MINSKIP (York). *Dom.* Minescip. Must be rendered like INSKIP.

MINSTERLEY (Shrewsbury). *Dom.* Menistrelie. ' Church meadow.' *Cf.* MINSTERWORTH (Glouc.), 1221 Munstreworthe, and *Dom.* Notts Ministretone, now and since 1316 Misterton. See -ley, -minster, and -worth.

MINWORTH (Birmingham). *Dom.* Meneworde, *a.* 1200 Muncworth, *a.* 1400 Myneworth. No name *Mene, Mine* known; and O.E. *mene, myne* is ' a necklace, an ornament '; but there is a name *Manne ;* see MINSHULL. See -worth.

MIRFIELD (Yorks). *Dom.* Mirefeld, -felt; 1202 Mirfeld; ? 1297 *R. Glouc.* 520. ' The churche founded in a miry place, called mury felde '; fr. Icel. *mýrr, mýri,* ' swamp, fen, a (quag)mire.'

MISSENDEN, GREAT and LITTLE (Bucks). *Dom.* Missedene and Missevorde. Perh. ' Vale of *Missa* ' or ' *Messa* '; one in *Onom.* *Cf.* MESSINGHAM; and see -den. However, they are on a little R. Mise, which, if not a back formation, is prob.= MEES. There is also a MISSON (Bawtry), *Dom.* Notts Misne, 1278 Misin,

which is prob. an old loc. ' at *Missa*'s ' (place). MISSERDEN
(Glouc.), *old* Musardere, -ader, seems to be fr. a foreign family
of *Musard*.

MITCHAM (Surrey). *Dom.* Michleham, *later* Miecham, Micham.
O.E. *micel hám*, ' large house.' *Cf.* MICKLEHAM, MIDGLEY, and
Mitcheldean (Glouc.). See -dean.

MITCHELL (New Quay). *Old* Modishole. A curious corruption;
certainly nothing to do with St. *Michael*. Prob. 'Hole of
Modred,' a Corn. name, also spelt *Medraut*, and name of K.
Arthur's treacherous nephew. But Mitchel (Wolverhampton)
is 1332 Mucheale, 'great hall' or 'big nook.' See -hall. *Much*
in M.E. was used for ' great, large,' as in Much Wenlock.

MITE R. Prob. = MYTHE.

MITFORD (Morpeth). Prob. ' ford at the water's meet.' See next;
and *cf.* MUTFORD and 940 *chart.* Myþford (Wilts).

MITTON (Blackburn, Warwick, Penkridge, Stourport, Tewkesbury).
St. M. 841 *chart.* Mythun, *Dom.* Methune, 1275 Mutton. Tew.
M. 964 *chart.* Myttunc, 965 *ib.* Muctone (*c* common error for *t*),
1033 Mytune. Wa. M. *Dom.* Mutone, *a.* 1300 Mutton. Pe. M.
Dom. Mui-, Moitone; also *Dom.* Salop Mutone. O.E. (ge)*mythan*
or (ge)*mythe*, ' junction of streams or roads, waters' meet.'
Penk. M. is at the junction of Avon and Leam. The root is the
same as (river's) *mouth*. *Cf.* MITFORD, MYTHE, and MYTON;
also see -ton.

MIXEN (Leek), 1219 Mixne, and MIXENDEN (Halifax), not in *Dom.*
O.E. *mixen*, -*ne*, ' a dunghill, a midden.' *Cf.* MIXERNE (Winchcombe), 1300 Blakemixerne (O.E. *ern*, ' house '). See -den.

MOBBERLEY (Knutsford). *Dom.* Motburlege. ' Meadow of *Mod-
beorht* '; 2 in *Onom.* See -ley.

MOCHDRE (Conway). W. (and Corn.) *moch*, pl. of *mochyn*, ' a sow ';
dre must be for W. *tre*, ' house, shed.'

MODBURY (Ivybridge). *Cf. Dom.* Devon Modlei. ' Burgh of *Mod*,'
or some of the many names in *Mod*-. *Onom.* has one *Moding*,
the patronymic.

MODDERSHALL (Stone). *Dom.* Modredeshale. ' Nook of *Modred*,'
a well-known name. See -hall.

MOELFRE (Menai and Oswestry). W. = ' bald hill '; *moil*, ' bald,'
like a bald head, hence *moel*, ' a conical hill.' *Fre* is for *bre*, ' a
hill, a brae.'

MOLD (Flint). Mold is contracted fr. mo -alt; Norm. Fr. *Mont haut*
or *Monthault*. The Norman Roger de Montalto is found here in
1244. L. *mons altus* means ' high hill.' *Cf.* MELTON MOWBRAY,
and MONTGOMERY. The name prob. is a translation of the
W. name Gwyddgrug, ' conspicuous hill.' Also *cf.* HAINAULT.

MOLE R. (S. tributary of Thames). It is a river that burrows like a *mole*; M.E. *mulle, molle*; M.Du. *mol*. Not found in Eng. till 1398. But MOLE COP, hill, N. Stafford, is prob. tautology; W. *moel*, 'a bare, rounded hill'; and O.E. *cop*, 'a summit.' See CASSOP. It *may* be *Dom*. Melicope (Salop).

MOLESWORTH (Hunts). *Dom*. Molesworde. 'Farm of *Moll* '; four in *Onom*. *Cf*. *Dom*. Essex Molesham, *ib*. Bucks Moleshov, *ib*. Yorks Molescroft; and see -worth.

MOLLAND BOTREAUX (S. Molton). *Exon. Dom*. Mollanda. Prob. 'Land of *Moll*' or '*Mole*.' See above. The lords of Bottreaux lived near Tintagel. Moleston or MOLLESTON (Narberth), 1283 Moylhistonne, may be fr. a man of similar name. Certainly it can have nothing to do with moles!

MOLLINGTON (Banbury and Cheshire). Ban. M. *a*. 1000 *chart*. Mollintun; Ches. M. *Dom*. Mol-, Mulintone; also *K.C.D*. 759 Mulantun. 'Town of *Moll, Mollo, Mul*,' or '*Mula*'; several persons of these names in *Onom*. *Cf*., too, MOLESWORTH and 1179-80 *Pipe* Molebi (Yorks). But Moilgrove (Pembroke) is for *Mallt's—i.e.,* '*Matilda's* grove.'

MOLTON, SOUTH (Devon). *Dom*. Sudmoltone. 'Town of *Moll*.' See above. *Exon. Dom*. also gives 'Molacota.' *Cf*. MOULTON.

MONKS ELEIGH (Bildeston, Suffk.). 958 *chart*. Illeyge, 972 *ib*. Illan lege, 990 *ib*. Illege. 'Mead of *Ylla*'; one in *Onom*. *Cf*. ILLEY; and see -leigh.

MONKSILVER (Taunton). *Dom*. Selvra, Selva. Curious name, prob. fr. L. *silva*, 'a wood.' MONK'S KIRBY (Lutterworth) is *Dom*. Chirchberye or 'Churchbury,' but, through Danish influence, changed by 1198 into Kirkebi. See -by. The monks of Angiers (Normandy) had property here.

MONKTON (Jarrow). *a*. 1130 *Sim. Dur*. Munecatun. 'Town of the monks' (of Jarrow); O.E. *monec, munec*, 'a monk.' *Cf*. BISHOP MONKTON and Monkwick (E. Riding), *Dom*. Moncwic. *Oxf. Dict*. does not give the contracted form *monk* or *munc* until the 13th cny. *Dom*. has the full form in Monechetune or Moor Monkton (Ainsty), and Monuchetone—*i.e.*, Monkton (Barkston Ash), whilst another, spelt as last, is Nun Monkton (York).

MONMORE. See MENTMORE.

MONMOUTH. *Dom*. (Hereford) Monemuta. 1298 Monemuthe. 'At the mouth of the R. *Monnow*'; W. Mynwy, ? *myn gwy*, 'kid river.' *Cf*. also W. *mawn*, 'a bog.' The shire only dates fr. 1536; before that it was part of the Welsh region of Gwent.

MONTACUTE (S. of Somerset). 1160-61 *Pipe* Monte Acuto. Built by and called after Drogo of Montacute ('sharp hill') in Normandy, *temp*. Wm. the Conqueror.

MONTGOMERY. *Dom.* Castellum de Montgomeri, also Muntgumeri; *c.* 1130 *Eadmer* de Monte Gummeri, *c.* 1145 *Orderic* Mons Gomerici, Rogerius de Monte Gomerici. 'Hill' (L. *mons, -tis;* Fr. *mont*) 'of *Gomeric,*' a Norman; this name is unique as an Eng. or W. county name. In W. it is Trefaldwyn, 'house of Baldwin,' its Norman founder. His castle was taken by Roger Montgomery *a.* 1086, and thereafter called by his name.

MONTON (Eccles, Lancs). 1478 Mawnton. Prob. O.E. *Mawan -tún,* 'town of *Mawa*'; 2 of that name in *Onom.*

MOORSHOLM, Great and Little (Boosbeck, Yorks). *Dom.* Morehusun, 1179-80 *Pipe* Morhuse. The *Dom.* form is an O.E. loc., 'at the moor houses.' The -holm (*q.v.*), 'meadow,' must be late. We have the simple MOOR (Worc.), *Dom.* More.

MORCHARD and NORCHARD (Forest of Dean). No old forms. Baddeley thinks the *m* and *n* relics of the O.E. article, 'at the orchard'; O.E. *æt thæm ortgearde.* *Dom.* has an Orcartone (Devon), and *Exon. Dom.* an Orcerdleia. But MORCHARD BP. (Crediton) seems *Dom.* and *Exon. D.* Morcet(h), -chet, which looks like Kelt. for 'big wood'; Corn. *meur, mer;* W. *mawr,* 'big'; and W. *coed,* pl. *coydd;* O.W. *cet, chet,* 'a wood.'

MORDEN (Cambs, Wimbledon, and Wareham). War. M. *K.C.D.* 722 Mordun; O.E. for 'moor hill.' Cam. M. *c.* 1080 *Inquis. Camb.* Mordune, 1166 Mordone, 1236 Mordene, where -dene is O.E. *denu,* 'valley.' *Cf.* MOORSHOLM, and Moreby (Yorks), *Dom.* Morebi.

MORECAMBE. *c.* 150 *Ptolemy* Μορικαμβη, which would be Keltic for 'crooked sea' or 'bay.' *Cf.* CAMBO (Sc.) and next. But no other early forms seem known, so this is prob. an antiquary's name.

MORETON (10 in *P.G.*). Wallingford M. 962 *chart.* Mordun, O.E. for 'moor hill'; but *Dom.* Mortune, *c.* 1290 Morton. *Dom.* Surrey has Moriton, Warwick and Glouc. Mortone, while *Dom.* Yorks has Mortun 17 times. See -don and -ton.

MORFA BYCHAN, NEVIN, and WAEN (all N. Wales), and MORFE (Bridgnorth). *Dom.* Staffs Morve. W. *morfa,* 'a marsh.' W. *bych* means 'a wretched being,' and *gwaen,* 'a plain, a meadow.' *Cf.* NEVERN.

MORGANSTOWN (Cardiff). Morgan is Pict. Morcunn; O.Bret. *mor cant,* 'sea bright.' *Cf.* TILLYMORGAN. The man referred to here is Morgan Thomas, on whose land the village was built.

MORLEY (5 in *P.G.*). Leeds M. *Dom.* Moreleia, -lege, Morleia, 'Moorland meadow.' *Cf.* MORDEN. See -ley.

MORNINGTHORPE (Norfolk). *Dom.* Maringathorpe. *Maringa* must be a patronymic. See -ing and -thorpe.

MORPETH. Contin. *Sim. Dur.* ann. 1138, Morth path; so not, as often said, 'moor path,' O.E. *pæð*, but 'murder-road,' fr. O.E. *morð*, 4-5 *morth, murth,* 'murder.'

MOR ROS (The Lizard). Corn. = 'sea heath, or moor.'

MORT HOE (N. Devon). *Dom.* Mortehov, *c.* 1190 *Letter in Canterb. Regist.* Moreth'. Prob. as above, 'murder hill.' *Cf.* O.Fris. *morth, mord,* 'murder.' Similar must be Mortham (Yorks), *sic* in *Dom.* and MORTLAKE. See HOE.

MORTIMER (Reading). 1258 Mortemer. Fr. Ralph de *Mortuo Mari* ('of the Dead Sea '), or *Morte mer* (a castle and abbey near Rouen), who came over with Wm. the Conqueror. He is mentioned in *Dom.* The 'Dead Sea' origin is a myth.

MORTLAKE (London). *Dom.* Mortelega, -lage, *c.* 1130 *Eadmer* Murtelac. 'Murder lake.' See MORPETH. Not prob. fr. O.Fr. *lac,* though *lace,* 'pond, pool,' is found in O.E., but fr. O.E. *lagu,* gen. *lage,* 3 *laȝe,* 4-5 *laye,* 'a lake, a pool.' *Cf.* LACKFORD.

MORTON. See MORETON.

MORVILLE FELL (hill, Kirkby Stephen). Looks like a reduplication, 'moor' (O.E. *mór*), 'fell.' See -fell.

MORWINSTOW (Bude). 1536 Morwynstow. 'Placc,' O.E. *stow,* 'of *Morwine*'; one such in *Onom. Cf.* PADSTOW.

MOSELEY (Birmingham and Worcester). Wo. M. 816 *chart.* Mose-leage, 851 *ib.* Mosleage. Bi. M. *Dom.* Museleia. O.E. *mose* or *meós léah,* 'moss' or 'mossy lea.' *Cf. Dom.* Bucks Moslei, Muselai, and Mossley Hill (Liverpool).

MOSTYN (Flint). Prob. 1301 *chart.* Moston. Can it be W. *mws twyn,* 'foul, stinking hillock'? T. Morgan suggests, corrup. of W. *maes ddin,* 'field of the fortress.'

MOTTINGHAM (Eltham, Kent). O.E. *chart.* Modingahema and -hamme. 'Enclosure of *Moding*,' one such in *Onom.,* or 'of the sons of *Mod*' or '*Mot*.' See -ing and -ham, 'enclosure.'

MOTTISFONT (Romsey). *Dom.* Mortesfunde. 'Spring or fountain.' L. *fons, -tis,* 'of *Morta*'; one in *Onom. Cf.* BEDFONT.

MOULIN HUET (Guernsey). Eng. pron. moolin whet. It is Fr. for 'mill of the little grey owl'; or, as likely, Huet is dimin. of Hugh, hence our name Hewett.

MOULSFORD (Wallingford). *Chart.* Mullesford. 'Ford of *Mul* or *Mula*'; 4 in *Onom.*

MOULTON (8 in *P.G.*). Middleton Tyas M. *Dom.* Moltun. North-ampton M. *Dom.* Moltone. Spalding M. 1272 Muleton. 'Village of *Mula*' or '*Mola*.' See above.

MOUNTAIN (Bradford and Pembroke). Pe. M. is 1603 Muncton, 'monk town.' *Dom.* Yorks has many 'Monuchetones,' but J. H. Turner identifies all with various MONKTONS.

MOUSEHOLE (Penzance). *c.* 1600 *Carew* Mowgehole. If the name has ever been different from what it now is, it is hard to say what it can be corrup. of. There is nothing like *mowge* in *Oxf. Dict.*, nor any spelling of *mouse* with *g.*

MOWL COP (Cheshire). Tautological hybrid. W. *moel*, G. *maol*, ' a rounded or conical hill '; and O.E. *cop, copp,* ' head, summit, hill.'

MOWSLEY(Rugby). Prob. ' *Mula*'s mead.' *Cf.* Mowthorp (Yorks), *Dom.* Muletorp; see -thorpe; and MOULTON.

MOXHULL (Coleshill) and MOXLEY (Wednesbury). *a.* 1300 Mukeshull, *a.* 1400 Mockeslowe, Mox(e)lowe. ' Hill ' and ' burial-mound of *Morc.*' Hull is regular in Mid. names for ' hill '; and see -low and -ley. But MOXBY (Yorks) is *Dom.* Molzbi, Molscebi, 1158-59 *Pipe* Molesbi, 1183 Molseby, ' dwelling of ' some un-recorded ' *Molsc.*'

MOYE (Channel Isles). Common name for ' a dangerous point.' Fr. *moie* is lit. ' a mass of stones.'

MUCH WENLOCK (Salop). *Dom.* Wenloch, *a.* 1130 *Sim. Dur.* Waneloc. ' Much ' is early M.E. *muche, moche, meche, miche,* short form of *muchel* or *michel,* Sc. *mickle, muckle,* and is frequent in early use for ' great, large.' *Cf.* MUCH DEWCHURCH, MUCH HOOLE (Preston), MUCH MARCLE (Glouc.), ' boundary (O.E. *mearc*) hill,' etc. Much Wenlock in 17th cny. is also More Wenlock. ' Waneloc ' is O.E. *wœn* (short for *wœȝen*) *loca,* ' waggon, wain enclosure.' *Cf.* MATLOCK.

MUCKLESTONE (Mket. Drayton). *Dom.* Moclestone, 1253 Muklestone. Prob. ' big stone '; O.E. *micel, mycel,* ' great, large '; possibly fr. a man *Mucel. Cf.* MICHELDEVER, etc. MUCKLEY CORNER (Lichfield) is *a.* 1600 Mucklow, which *may* mean ' great mound.' See -low; *cf.* MUCKLOW Hill (Halesowen), 1424 Moke-lowe, Moghlowe.

MUMFORDS (S.E. Bucks). Not in *Dom.* The personal name *Mumford* is corrup. of the Norm. *Montfort,* but this may not be the same. *Cf.* MUNDFORD.

MUNCASTER (Ravenglass). *Old* Meolcaster, 1290 Mulcaster. Good illustration how almost any of the liquids, like *l* and *n*, may interchange. The first syll. might be W. *moel,* ' a conical hill,' but it is prob. fr. O.N. *mel-r,* ' a sand dune,' a ' meal.' See MELLIS, and -caster, ' fort '; also *cf.* next.

MUNDESLEY (Norfolk). *Dom.* Muleslai, *c.* 1150 Mulesle, 1444 Moneslee. An exact parallel to the above; and *d* readily suffixes itself. The orig. name seems to have been ' *Mul*'s meadow.' *Onom.* gives us *Mon, Monn, Mouna, Mul, Mula, Mund,* and *Munda,* any of which may have had influence here. There is a Moundesley Hall (King's Norton); no old forms; but a Mundes dene is found in 972 *chart.* near by. *Cf.*, too, *Dom.* Kent Mundingeham. See -ley.

MUNDFORD (Norfolk). *Dom.* Mundeford. Prob. 'protected ford,' fr. O.E. *mund*, 'protection.' But *cf.* MUMFORDS and MUNDES- LEY.

MUNDHAM (Norfolk). *Chart.* Mundan ham, 'home of *Munda*.' *Cf. B.C.S.* 1282 Mundes den, and above.

MUNET (Clun, Salop). *Dom.* Munete. Perh. Corn. *menit*, W. *mynydd*, 'hill.' *Cf.* Mynyd Eidden, O.W. for Edinburgh; but more prob. it is fr. *Munita*, as in MINDTON. Mynytho (Carnvnsh.) is corrup. of W. *mynyddoed*, 'mountains.'

MUSTON (Filey and Nottingham). Fi. M. *Dom.* Mustone, 4 times. No. M. not in *Dom.* Prob. 'town of *Mus*,' 1 in *Onom.* But N. and S. MUSKHAM (Newark), *Dom.* Muschā, 1314 Suthe Muskham, must be fr. a man *Musca*, or the like. *Onom.* has only *Mocca*; but *cf.* Muschenheim, *old* Muscanheim, Hesse.

MUSWELL HILL (N. London). *Old* Mustwell, O.E. *must*, L. *mustum*, 'new wine.' There is one *Mus* in *Onom.* But MUSTERS (Co. Durham) is 1130 de Monasteriis—*i.e.*, 'monasteries.'

MUTFORD (Beccles). *Dom.* Mitteforda, *c.* 1460 Motford. = MIT- FORD, 'ford at the waters' meet'; O.E. *(ge)mythe. Cf.* MITTON.

MYDDLE (Shrewsbury). Not in *Dom.* Perh. W. *midd dol*, 'en- closed place in the meadow.' W. also has *midlan*, 'enclosed place, lists,' and *middi*, 'a pit in a river.'

MYTHE, The (Tewkesbury). Not in *Dom.* Prob. O.E. *(ge)mypa*, 'place where 2 rivers meet,' here the Avon and Severn. M'Clure prefers to derive fr. O.E. *muth*, dat. *mythe*, cognate with O.N. *munn-r*, Dan. *mund*, 'mouth, river-mouth.' The R. Mite (Eskdale, Cumbld.) is prob. the same word. *Cf.* MITFORD and MITTON. MYTON-ON-SWALE is *Dom.* Mitune, O.E. *mythan* (see MITTON); and Myton (Hull), *Dom.* Mitune, will prob. be the same, though some derive fr. O.N. *my*, 'a midge,' so 'tiny town.'

NABURN (York). *Dom.* Naborne, 4 times. The Na- is doubtful; it seems to be O.N. *ná*, 'nigh,' 'the nigh or near brook'; only *ná* is found only in comb., as *ná-bui*, 'neighbours,' etc. Kneeton (Yorks) is *Dom.* Naton, which also seems 'nigh town,' O.N. *ná*, or rather, O.E. *neáh*, *néh*, 3-4 *nei*, 4 *neie*, 'nigh, near.' See -burn.

NACTON (Ipswich). *Dom.* Nachetuna, 1455 Nakton. Doubtful. No very likely name in *Onom.*, so perh. 'town at the neck'; O.E. *hnecca*, in 4 *nak*, O.N. *hnakki*, Da. *nakke*, mid. Du. *nac*, 'neck.' 'Neck of land' is not found till 1555. See NECTON for possibility of being fr. an unrecorded man *Nece*.

NAFFERTON (Driffield). *Dom.* Nadfartone. *Nadfar* must represent some unrecorded man's name. *Onom.* has a *Nothfrith* and
a *Nothbeorht,* which are conceivable as origins.

NAILBOURNE (Canterbury). *B.C.S.* ii. 172 Næglesburna, *c.* 1480
Warkworth Naylborne. '*Nail*'s brook,' the sb. *nail,* O.E. *nægel,*
here being used as a personal name, as in Nælesbroc and Nægles-
cumb, in *B.C.S. Cf.* NAILSLEA (Bristol), 740 *chart.* Negles-
leah, Nailstone (Nuneaton), and Nailsworth (Stroud). See -ea
and -worth; also EYLEBOURN in *Oxf. Dict.,* where a ' Nailbourne ' is interpreted in several quotations as a sort of inter-
mittent spring or stream.

NANTWICH. Hybrid. ' Dwelling by the stream '; O.E. *wíc,* L.
vicus, ' a village,' and W. *nant,* ' stream, valley.' In W. it is
Yr heledd Wen., ' the clear or white place for making salt.' *Cf.*
NENE and DROITWICH. In W. names *nant* often changes to
llan, ' church,' as in Nanhyfer (Nevern), now Llanhyfer,
Nant Carfan, now LLANCARVAN, NANTYAN (Cornwl.), now
LANTYAN, etc.

NANTYFFIN (Crickhowell). W. = ' brook of the boundary '; L.
finis. See above. It is close to the boundary of Wales.

NANTYMWYN (Carmarthen). W. = ' brook of the mine.' Lead-
mines abound here.

NANTYSAESON (Montgomy.). W. = ' brook of the Saxon,' or
Englishman. G. *Sassanach.*

NAPTON (Rugby). *Dom.* Neptone. ' Town on the crest of the hill ';
O.E. *cnæp,* the Bible *knop,* ' a knob, protuberance, button ';
Icel. *knapp-r,* Dan. *knap, knop.*

NAR R. and NARBOROUGH (Swaffham). *Dom.* Nereburh, *c.* 1150
Nereburg. ' Burgh, fort on the *narrow* river '; Fris. *nār,* O.E.
neara, neare, 3-4 *nare,* var. of *nearu,* ' narrow.' There is also a
Narborough (Leicester) on R. Soar; not in *Dom.*

NARBERTH (Pembroke). 1248-49 Nerberd, but *Mabinog.* Arberth—
i.e., ' slope abounding in bushes,' W. *perthi.* The *n* comes from
the prep. *yn,* ' in,' which was commonly used before the name.
Cf. Nangle and Nolton (' old town ') in the same shire.

NASEBY (Rugby). *Dom.* Navesberie, '*Burh*' or ' burgh,' now
changed to ' dwelling, of *Hnæf,*' a known Dan. name, in *Onom.*
See -by.

NASH (Stony Stratford, Glouc.) and NASH MILLS (Hemel Hempstd.).
All prob. for M.E. *atten ashe,* ' at the ash-tree.' *Cf.* Prinknash,
(Painswick), 1121 Prinkenesche. But NASH (Newport, Mon.),
and prob. once in Glouc. too = NASS on Severn, O.E. and Dan.
næs, O.N. *nes,* ' promontory, headland.'

NAWTON (Helmsley). *Dom.* Naghelton, Nageltone, Nagletune, 1202
Nawelton. Prob. not ' Town in the centre ' or ' at the central

point of the district.' O.E. *nafela*, 3-4 *nauele*, 5 *nawelle*, ' the navel '; used of the central point of a district from Wyclif's time. Prob. fr. a man *Nagel;* see NAILBOURNE.

NAZE, The (N. Sussex). 14 . . . *Sailing Directions* The Naisse, the Nasse. It may also be Eadolfes næsse in 1049 *O.E. Chron.*, or that may be Dungeness, called Næsse a few years later. The word is almost certainly contained in *Dom.* Essex Nessetocham, Nasestocā, or Ness STOKE. *Oxf. Dict.* derives fr. O.E. *næs, nes,* O.N. *nes,* Sw. *näs,* ' promontory, headland,' related to O.E. *nasu,* M.E. *nase,* ' nose.' But it is prob. fr. *nasu,* found 1390 *nase, c.* 1407 *nasse.* O.E. *næs* gives ' ness,' which is so common in this quarter—Orford Ness, Eastness, Foulness, etc. *Cf.* TOTNESS, 1297 Tottenays, NESSCLIFFE, and Gronez, Rouge Nez, etc., Channel Is.

NEASHAM (Darlington). 1203 Nesham; *cf. Dom.* Salop Nessham. Prob. ' home on the ness ' or ' naze.' O.E. *næs,* O.N. *nes,* ' a promontory,' cognate with *nose. Cf.* above.

NEATH. Perh. *c.* 380 *Ant. Itin.* Nido. In W. *Nedd*—*i.e.* ' nest ' L. *nidus. Cf.* NEDD (Sc.) and NEEDWOOD. The root idea seems to be ' place of rest, abode.'

NECHELLS (Birmingham and Wolvermptn.). In both cases *a.* 1300 de Echeles, les Echelis, *c.* 1500 Nechels, later ' Echells otherwise Nechells.' This seems O.Fr. *echelles,* ' ladders, stairs,' implying a two-storied house, ? with outside stair. The *n* is fr. the old art. *atten,* ' at the,' as Nash is *atten Ash,* etc. There are several other Etchells in Chesh. and elsewhere in Midlands.

NECTON (Swaffham). *Dom.* Neketuna, 1160-61 *Pipe* Necheton, 1167-68 *ib.* Neketona, 1298 Neketon, 1472 Neyghton. Seems to be ' town at the neck or pass '; O.E. *hnecca,* ' neck.' *Cf.* NACTON. But though there is no likely name in *Onom.*, it is prob. fr. some man. *Cf.* 1179-80 *Pipe* Neckesford and Nekesfeld (Yorks).

NEEDLES, The (I. of Wight). *c.* 1400 *Anc. Pet.* Les nedeles del Isle de Wight. O.E. *nædl, nédl,* ' a needle.' This is the earliest known instance of the word used for ' a sharp rock '; as ' a pillar or obelisk ' it is found in 1387.

NEEDWOOD (Burton-on-T.). *a.* 1200 Nedwode. Prob. ' wood of *Nedda.' Cf. K.C.D.* 624 Neddan leah. Duignan suggests W. *nedd, nydd,* ' a dingle, a resting-place.' *Cf.* Nidd (Ripon), *Dom.* Nit.

NEEN SOLLARS (Cleobury Mortimer) and NEENTON (Bridgnorth). *Dom.* Nene. Doubtful; perh. same as next. It can hardly be fr. *Neavana,* or *Nafana,* d. 1016. See *O.E. Chron.*

NEN(E) R. *c.* 950 Nyn, Nen. Local pron. Néan. Also called in early times—*e.g.,* by Leland, *c.* 1542—the Avon or ' river.'

It must be a form of W. *nant,* inflected *nentydd, neint,* ' a ravine, dingle, or brook.' There is also *nennig,* ' a small brook.'

NESSCLIFFE (Shrewsbury). Fr. *ness* or NAZE, ' promontory.' Such may be far inland, as in Great and Little Ness, in same shire. *Cf. Dom.* Nessham. In Yorks we have the simple NESS, *Dom.* Nesse, and also NESWICK, *Dom.* Nessewic; see -wick. But NESTON (Chesh.), *Dom.* Nestone, might perh. be fr. *Nest,* found, *e.g.,* as name of a daughter of Gruffydd, K. of Wales.

NETHERTON (5 in *P.G.*). Pershore N. 780 *chart.* Neotheretune. Persh. and Dudley N. *Dom.* Neotheretune. Rothbury N. *a.* 1130 *Sim. Dur.* Nedertun. ' Lower town '; O.E. *nioþerra, niþera,* 3 *neothere,* 5-6 *neder,* ' nether.'

NETLEY (Southampton). *O.E. Chron.* 508 says called Natanleaga (' Natan's meadow '), after a British K. *Natanleod,* slain near there in 508; *Dom.* Nataleie. *Cf.* 1161-62 *Pipe* Nethā (Hants).

NETTLESTEAD (Maidstone). 939 *chart.* Netles stede, O.E. for ' nettles' place.' *Onom.* gives no personal name *Nettle,* yet *cf.* Nettleham (Lincs), NETTLESTONE, and Nettlesworth (Chester-le-Street), also NETTLEWORTH (Notts), *c.* 1300 Nettelwurd. But the plant seems plain enough in Nettlebed (Henley) and ' Netelcumb,' *Dom.* Devon.

NETTLESTONE (Ryde). *Dom.* Hotelstone, error for Notel-. ' Stone,' or more prob., ' town of *Nothhelm,*' a name fairly common in *Onom.* See -ton.

NEVERN R. (N. Pembrokesh.). 1603 *Owen.* Ysh nyver. In Bain says = NAVER (Sc.), fr. Kelt. *nav, snav,* G. *snàmh,* ' to flow, swim.'

NEWARK. 1066 *chart.* Newarcha, *Dom.* Newerche, Newerca, 1154-66 *chart.* Niwerca, Newerc. ' New work or fort.' *Cf. bulwark, outwork,* and WARK.

NEWBALD (Yorks), *Dom.* Niwebolt; NEWBOLD (Tredington), 991 *chart.* Nioweboldan; and NEWBOLD ABBEY (Congleton), *Dom.* Newbold. There are 4 other Newbolds in Warwk., *Dom.* Newe-, Niwebold, and several elsewhere. Newbold-on-Stour is 991 *chart.* Niowebolda, *a.* 1200 Newebolt, 1275 Newebold. New-bold (Kinoulton) is *Dom.* Neubold. O.E. *niwe bold,* ' new dwelling.' *Cf.* N. *bol,* O.E. *botl,* ' house,' and NEWBIGGIN.

NEWBIGGIN (5 in *P.G.*). 1183 Newbiginga (Darlington). ' New building.' *Biggin* is N. Eng. and Sc. for ' building '; O.N. *bygging,* ' a building.' *Cf.* NEWBIGGING (Sc.). But, as *new* is Eng., not Norse, all these names must have been given by Angles or Englishmen.

NEWBOTTLE (Fence Houses, Durham). 1183 Newbotill. O.E. *niwe botl,* ' new dwelling.' *Cf.* Harbottle (Rothbury) and NEW-BATTLE (Sc.).

NEW BRIGHTON (Birkenhead). It was founded *c.* 1845.

NEWBURN (Northumbld.). *a.* 1130 *Sim. Dur.* Nywe burne. ' New brook.' *Cf.* NEWBURN (Sc.). See -bourne.

NEWBURY (Berks). *a.* 1135 *Chron. Abingd.* Niuuberia, 1310-11 Newburye. ' New burgh or castle.' See -bury.

NEWCASTLE-ON-TYNE. *c.* 1097 *Flor. Worc.* Novum Castellum, *c.* 1175 *Fantosme* Noef-Chastel-sur-Tine, *a.* 1200 *Wm. Newbury* Castellum Novum super fluvium Tinum. *Sim. Dur.* tells us it was so named when built by Robert, son of Wm. the Conqueror, in 1081. In *c.* 410 *Notit. Dignit.* it is Pons Ælii, and in 1073 Munechecaster or ' monks' castle.' NEWCASTLE-UNDER-LYME is 1166 Novum Oppidum (= New-town), *a.* 1200 Novum Castrum super Limam, which is L. for the present name. NEWCASTLE (Pembk.) is 1594 Newcastell.

NEW CROSS (London). 1675 *Evelyn's Diary* ' New Crosse.' There used to be a famous inn here called ' the Golden Cross.' In 1160-61 *Pipe* Mdsex. we have a Noua firma, or New Farm.

NEWENT (Glouc.). *Sic* 1228 in *Close R.*, but *Dom.* Noent. Doubtful. Possibly W. *newydd gwent,* ' new clearing '; as likely Eng. fr. *new,* O.E. *niowe, neowe,* and *went,* M.E. and dial. for ' path,' fr. root *wend. Cf.* Nether- and Over-went.

NEW FOREST. *c.* 1097 *Flor. Worc.* In Nova Foresta, quae lingua Anglorum Ytene nuncupatur. Freeman thought *Ytene* must be connected with *Jutes.* 1155 *Pipe* ' Censu Noue foreste.' 1297 *R. Glouc.* The nywe forest þat ys in Souþamtessyre. Wm. the Conqueror cleared away several hamlets to make this Forest in 1079.

NEWHAVEN (Sussex). *Sic* 1563. In the 16th cny. this was also the Eng. name of Havre.

NEW HEY (Rochdale). ' New hedge.' See HAY, and *cf.* 1330 ' Neweheye ' (Staffs).

NEWINGTON (Glouc., London, and 2 in Kent). Gl. N. *Dom.* Neweton, also *ib.* Yorks, Chesh., Worc., Newentune. O.E. *Niwan tún,* a dat. ' at the new town.' In Glouc. it also becomes Naunton, *Dom.* Niwetone, *later* New-, Nawenton. *Cf.* NEWNHAM.

NEWLYN (Penzance). *Sic* 1536. St. *Newlyna* (? Kelt. for ' white cloud '), a Kelt of noble birth, went to Brittany, and is there commemorated at *Noualen,* the same name.

NEWMARCH (Yorks). 1161-62 *Pipe* de Nouom̄cato, 1179-80 *ib.* De Novo Mercato; and NEWMARKET (Cambs, Louth, Stroud, Flint). Ca. N. 1219 Novus Mercatus, 1383 Newe market. The two names are thus the same. *Market* is O.Nor.Fr., not found in Eng. till *c.* 1120, whilst *march* here is mod. Fr. *marché,* with the same meaning. We also find *a.* 1161-62 *Pipe* de Nouom̄cato, Hants.

NEWNHAM (7 in *P.G.*). Monk's Kirby N. *Dom.* Niweham, *a.* 1300 Newnham. Cam. N. *chart.* Niwanham, *later* Newenham, 1436

Newynham. Tenbury N. 1007 *chart.* Neowanham, 1043 Neowenham. Severn N. *Dom.* Nuneham. This is an O.E. dat., ' at the new home.' *Cf.* Newington, also 1160 *Pipe* Niweham (Hereford). N. Padox (Warwksh.) is for *paddocks,* a late addition.

Newport (10 in *P.G.*). N. Pagnell is *Dom.* Nevport, 1297 Neuport, 1571 N. Pannel. O.E. *port.,* L. *porta,* lit. ' gate,' comes to mean ' a town, a market-town.' But see *Oxf. Dict.* s.v. Port sb[1], [2], and [3]. Pagnell is fr. the Norm. family of *Pagenel,* now Paynell. Ralf Pagenel is found in *Dom.* in Somerset.

New Quay (N. Cornwall) is of 19th cny. origin.

Newsham. At least 4 places so called. Kirby Wiske (Yorks) N. is *Dom.* Newehusu', Neuhuson, 1201 Newesum. *Newe huson* is a late O.E. loc., of the type very common in Yorks, ' at the new houses.' *Cf.* Hallam, Howsham, etc. There are also Newsham in Leckonfield and Newsham in Spofforth, both Yorks, and both *Dom.* Neuson(e), an early contraction; whilst Newsham, or Newsome, (N. Lancs) is *Dom.* Newhuse.

Newstead (Notts) is 1189 de Novo Loco, ' new place ' or ' dwelling.'

Newton (40 in *P.G.*). Cambs N. *chart.* Neutun. Lancs and Norwich N. *Dom.* Neweton(a), N. Reigney (Penrith) 1189 *Pipe* Niweton, *Dom.* Yorks Neutun, Neweton, 43 times. ' New town.' *Cf.* Newington. Newton Abbot (S. Devon), *Dom.* Niueton, was given by Ld. Brewer to the abbot of Tor.

Nocton (Lincoln). 1233 Noketon. Doubtful, but it must be fr. some man named *Nok* or the like, though *Onom.* has none such. *Oxf. Dict.* has more than one *nock* sb., but none are likely here; nor does there seem anything in O.E. which would yield Noke-.

Noe. R. (trib. of Derwent, Derbysh.). Perh. *a.* 900 *Rav. Geogr.* Anava. *Cf.* Navione, a place given as near. ? some connexion with G. *naomh* (nüv), ' holy.'

Norbiton (Wimbledon). Name invented *c.* 1840 as a contrast to Surbiton. The parent town is Kingston.

Norbury (E. Salop). *Dom.* Cheshire Nor(d)berie, *a.* 1300 Northbyri. ' North town '; O.E. *norð.* See -bury.

Nore, The (Essex). 1049 *O.E. Chron.* Innan Norðmuðan, ' In North mouth ' of Thames. But Nore is N. *nór,* ' a bay with a narrow entrance.' There seems to be a White Nore near Lulworth, Weymouth.

Norfolk. *Dom.* Nordfolc, Norf', 1160 *Pipe* Norfolch, 1258-1658 Northfolk, 1397 Norfolk. ' Land of the north folk.' *Cf.* Suffolk—*i.e.,* the North and South Angles.

Norham-on-Tweed. *Sic* 1183, 1461 Norame. ' North home '; O.E. *hám,* on the Northern border of England. *Cf. c.* 1100 *chart.* Norhamscire.

NORMACOTT (Longton, Staffs). *Dom.* Normanescote, 1242 Normancote. 'The Norman's cottage.' See next. *Cf.* the name Westacott.

NORMANBY (Doncaster, Middlesbrough, and 2 others). *Sic* in spurious grant of 664 (*a.* 1100). Mid. N. *Dom.* Normanebi, *a.* 1130 *Sim. Dur.* Northmann-bi, 1179-80 *Pipe* Normannesbi. 'Dwelling of the Northmen' or 'Normans,' who in Flodoard of Rheims, d. 966, are Nortmanni; but already in *chart.* of 963-84 (*B.C.S.* iii. 367) 'Into Normannes cros.'

NORMANTON (6 in *P.G.*). Yorks N. *Dom.* Norma'tune, Normetune. Grantham N. *Dom.* Norman-, -entone. 'Town of the *Normans*,' or the '*Northmen*,' the Scandinavians. See above and -ton.

NORTHALL or NORTHOLT (Southall). *Dom.* Nort hala. 'North hall' or 'corner,' as opposed to 'South hall.' But *holt* is O.E. and N. for 'a wood, a copse.' See -hall.

NORTHALLERTON. *Dom.* Alvretune, 1298-1538 North alverton. See ALVERTON.

NORTHAMPTON. 1088 *O.E. Chron.* Norðamtune, *c.* 1097 *Flor.* W. Northamtunensis, *a.* 1145 *Orderic* Northantonia, 1373 Northamptonia. 'North home-town.' See HAMPTON, and *cf.* SOUTHAMPTON and Northam (N. Devon and Southampton).

NORTHAW (Potter's Bar), also *old* Northall; but 1539 Northawe. 'North haw' or 'hedge'; O.E. *haʒa*.

NORTHCOTE (S. Devon) and NORTH COTES (Lincs). Dev. N. *Dom.* Norcote. 'North cot or cottage'; O.E. *cot, cott,* 'a chamber, a hut.'

NORTH CURRY (Taunton). 1155 *Pipe* Nordcuri, 1161 *ib.* Norcuri. See CURRY MALLET.

NORTH HYLTON (Sunderland). ? *a.* 1000 *chart.* Does clifes norð hyldan. Corrup. of O.E. *hylda, dan,* 'a slope.'

NORTHLEW (Beaworthy). 1219 *Patent R.* Lyu. Doubtful. ?= LLIW.

NORTHOWRAM (Halifax). *Dom.* Oure, Ufron, 1202 Northuuerum. Ufron is the common Yorks O.E. loc., 'on the river-banks'; O.E. *ofer,* Ger. *ufer.* See OVER, HALLAM, etc., and -ham. NORTHOVER (Somst.) is 1219 Northovre.

NORTH STAINLEY (Ripon). *Dom.* Nordstanlaia, which is meant to be O.E. for 'north stony meadow.' *Cf.* STANLEY. The *stain* is a sign of Dan. influence. See -by.

NORTH STOKE (Wallingford). *a.* 1087 *chart.* Norð stoke; late O.E. for 'north place.' *Cf.* STOKE.

NORTHUMBERLAND. *Sic c.* 1175 *Fantosme,* but *Bede* Nordanhymbri, *c.* 890 *Ælfred* On Norþanhymbra þeode, 898 *O.E. Chron.* Norþhymbre, *c.* 1000 *Ælfric* Norðhymbralande. This name for a district far ' North of Humber ' came early into use. Deira, to the S., became largely Danish; but Bernicia, to the N., was never so. *Cf.* 1065 *O.E. Chron.* Worc., ' In Yorkshire and in Northumberland.' *Sim. Dur.* ann. 883 already distinguishes Eboracum and Northimbri; and even more noteworthy is his ' Solius Northumbriae Comitatum.' *c.* 1097 *Flor. W.* has ' Suthymbria '= Deira.

NORTHWICH. *Dom.* Norwich. ' North dwelling '; O.E. *wic.* In W. it is *Yr Heledd ddu,* ' the dark place for making salt.' *Cf.* DROITWICH and NORWICH.

NORTHWOLD (Stoke Ferry, Norfk.). *a.* 1200 Nordwolde, *c.* 1220 Norwolde, *c.* 1225 Northwaude. O.E. *norð wald,* ' north wood ' or NORWOOD.

NORTON (22 in *P.G.*). Often in *Dom.* Nortone. ' North town.' Eleven times in *Dom.* Yorks alone.

NORWICH. 1004 *O.E. Chron.* Norðwic, *Dom.* Norwic, 1297 Norwiche. O.E. *norð wíc,* ' northern dwelling ' or ' village.' See -wich. NORWELL (Newark) is *Dom.* Nortwelle.

NORWOOD (London). *a.* 1697 Aubrey *Perambltn. Surrey,* ' The great wood called Norwood,' or ' north wood.' *Cf.* NORTHWOLD.

NOSTELL (Pontefract). *a.* 1114 *chart.* Ecclesia sancti Osuualdi, 1119 *chart.* Nostell, *c.* 1160 Nostl'. Here was the priory of *Saint Oswald,* so that the corrup. is a very early one. *Cf.* OSWESTRY and ST. AUSTELL'S, pron. St. Ossle's. The *n,* of course, comes fr. the prefixed *saint.* Horsfall Turner identifies Nostell with *Dom.* Osele (p. 37b), but this seems doubtful. Noverton (Worcestrsh.) is really Overton; it also appears as Nurton (Abberley), which in 1327 is given both as Noverton and Overton.

NOSTERFIELD (Cambs). *c.* 1080 *Inquis. Camb.* Nostresfelda. Skeat derives fr. a tenure by saying *Paternosters,* and compares the name of an Alice Paternoster, who held lands at Pusey (Berks).

NOTTINGHAM. *Asser* ann. 868, ' Scnotingaham quod Britannice Tigguocobauc interpretatur, Latine Speluncarum domus,' or ' house of caves.' Tigguocobauc is prob. Kelt. for ' house in the little cave '; *cf.* W. *ty,* G. *tigh,* ' a house,' Corn. *ogo,* ' a cavern,' and W. *bach,* O.W. *becc,* ' little.' *Dom.* Snotingeham, *a.* 1190 *Walter Map* Notingam, 1461 Snotingham. ' Home of the *Snotinga,*' a patronymic. *Onom.* gives *Snoding* and *Snot.* Snoddy is still used as a personal name. *Cf.* SNEINTON. There are also 2 Nottinghams in Gloster. See -ing.

NOTTING HILL (London) is said to have been formerly ' Knolton Barn Hill.' *Cf.* KNOLTON BRYN.

NOTTON (Barnsley). *Dom.* Notone. 'Nut town,' O.E. *hnut.*
Cf. NUTTLES, *Dom.* Notele.

NUNBURNHOLME (York). *Dom.* Brunha', but 1206 Brunnum, a
loc. 'At the burn' or 'bourne,' O.N. *brunn-r.* See -bourne
and -holme ('a meadow by a river'). -ham and -holme often
interchange, and many Yorkshire places in -ham or -am are
orig. locatives.

NUNEATON (Warwicksh.). *a.* 1200 Etone, O.E. *éa-tun,* 'town on
the river' Anker, where the nuns live. A Benedictine nunnery
was built here in the 12th cny. *Cf.* EATON. Similarly NUN
KEELING (Yorks) is in *Dom.* simply Chelinge, Chilinghe, 'place
of the sons of *Cille*' or '*Cilla.*' See -ing.

NUNNEY (Frome). *Dom.* Nonin. 'Nun's isle'; L. *nunna,* O.E.
nunne, 3-6 *nonne,* 'a nun.' See -ey.

NUNNINGTON (York). *Dom.* Nonninctune, Noningtune, Nunnige-
tune. Patronymic. 'Town of the sons of *Nun*' or '*Nunna,*'
several in *Onom.* *Cf.* ALTARNUN. See -ing and -ton.

NURSLING (Southampton). Dom. Notesselinge, *later* Nutshalling.
A curious and unexplainable corrup.; prob. patronymic fr. some
unrecorded man. See -ing.

NURTON. See NOSTELL.

NUTFIELD (Redhill). *Dom.* Notfelle. 'Field of nuts,' O.E. *hnut.*

NUTHURST (Horsham). *Cf.* 704-9 *chart.* Hnuthyrste (Warwicksh.),
O.E. for 'nut wood.' See -hurst. NUTTLES (Holderness) is
Dom. Notele, 'nut meadow'; see -ley. *Cf.* NUTTALL (Notts),
Dom. Nutehale; see -hall. But Notgrove (Stow-on-Wold) is
743 *chart.* Natangraf, 'trench, ditch of *Nata.*'

NYMPHSFIELD (Stonehouse). 872 *chart.* and 1280 *Close R.*Nymdes-
feld, *Dom.* Nimdesfelde (1287 Kingesnemeton, see KING'S
NYMPTON). W. and Bret. *nemet,* also aspirated in W. *nevet,*
'a wood,' then prob. 'a sacred grove,' and then 'a temple.'
There are several Nymets in Devon, as well as 3 Nymphs near
Tawton. It will be noted that *p* after *m* is almost always a
mod. intrusion; *cf.* BAMPTON, BROMPTON, HAMPTON, etc.

OAKEN (Wolverhampton). *Sic* 1398, but *Dom.* Ache, *a.* 1300 Ake,
Oce, Oken. Prob. an old loc., O.E. *acon* or *acum,* 'at the oaks.'
Cf. HALLAM, etc.

OAKFORD (Bampton). 1174 *chart.* Acforde. O.E. *ác,* 'an oak.'

OAKHAM. Local pron. Yekkm. 1298 Okham. This will prob.
mean 'home, house built of oak.' OAKHAMPTON (Astley,
Wstrsh.) is 1275 Okhamtone.

OAKHANGER (Berkeley, Alton, and Dorset). Be. O. 1250 Ochungre;
chart. ? where, Achangra (*c.* 1350 Akhangre), which is O.E. for
'oak-tree slope.' *Cf.* CLAYHANGER. There is also 961 *chart.*

Geoc hangra (at Hurstbourne, Winchester), but this is fr. O.E. *geoc*, ' a yoke,' or ' as much land as a pair of oxen can plough in a day.'

OAKINGTON (Cambridge). *c.* 1080 *Inquis. Camb.* Hokintona, Hoc-chintona, Hockingtona, *Dom.* Hochintone, 1284 Hokingtone, Hoggitone. Patronymic. ' Village of the *Hockings* '—*i.e.*, sons of *Hoc* or *Hoca*, both known names.

OAKLEY (Rochester, Bp's. Stortford, and 4 others). Roch. O. *chart.* of date 774 Acleag. Staffs O. 1004 *chart.* Acclea, *Dom.* Aclei. Beds. O. 1166 *Pipe* Achelai. Bp's. S. O. 1474 Ocle Magna and Parva; 958 *chart.* Acleg, -lea, on Stour, Staffd. O.E. *ác léah*, ' oak meadow.' Similarly OAKWORTH (Keighley) is *Dom.* Acewrde, Acurde, ' oak farm.' See -worth.

OARE (Chieveley, Berks, Wilts, Faversham, N.W. Somerset). Ch. O. *B.C.S.* iii. 509 Ora, 1316 Ore. O.E. *ora*, ' bank, shore, edge,' cognate with L. *ora.* *Cf.* BOGNOR, etc. But Som. O. is 1264 Ar, perh. same root as ARROW, or ? N. *aa-r*, ' river.' It is on the East Lynn R., whilst Fav.O. is on a creek of the R. Swale.

OBY (Norfolk). 1479 Owby. ' Dwelling of *Oba, Ova, Oua*,' a name common in *Onom.* See -by.

OCK R. (Abingdon) and OCKBROOK (Derby). *Dom.* Ochebroc. O.E. *chart.* Eoccen, and in late copy of *chart.* of 955 Occen. Skeat cannot suggest any meaning for the Berks river; and the Derby name is presumably the same, though some think it a tautology, making Ock Kelt. for ' water.' This last is some-what confirmed by *Geoffr. Mon.* iv. 12, who tells us that ' Ridoc ' is the British name of Oxford (W. *rhyd*, O.W. *rit*, ' a ford,' whilst *oc* is certainly not W. for ' ox '). *Cf.* 1201 ' Yockflet '—*i.e.*, Yokefleet (Howden). There is also an OCTON (E. Riding), *Dom.* Ocheton, which seems fr. the same root.

OCKER HILL (Tipton). *Cf. Dom.* ' Ocretone ' (Notts). Perh. fr. M.E. (*a.* 1225) *oker*, O.N. *okr*, ' increase of money, usury '; but Duignan, more prob., suggests W. *ochr, ochren*,' a side, a shelving locality.' But OCKERIDGE WOOD (Little Witley, Worcstr.), 1332 Ocrugge, is ' oak-tree ridge,' O.E. *ác*, 3-5- *ok*.

OCKLEY (Dorking) = OAKLEY.

ODELL (Sharnbrook, Beds). Said to be *old* Wode-hul or ' wood-hill.' Not in *Dom.*, but it has Odecroft. *Cf.*, too, 941 *chart.* Odden-heal, ' nook of *Odda*,' Hants. See -hall.

ODIHAM (Winchfield). 1116 *O.E. Chron.* Wudiham. ' Home in the wood,' O.E. *wudu.* For change of *w* to *o cf.* Wodin and Odin, also *Dom.* Essex, Oddesforda, fr. the common *Odda* or *Oda*, which gives name to ODDINGTON (Moreton-in-Marsh). Oddingley (Droitwich), 816 *chart.* Oddingalea, is a patronymic fr. *Odda.* See -ing. *Cf.*, too, ODCOMBE (Somerset), 1167-68 *Pipe* Devon Odecūba.

OFFCHURCH (Leamington). . 1300 Ofechirche, 'church of *Offa*,' ? the K. of Mercia in 8th cny. OFFLEY, in the same county, is *Dom*. Offeleia.

OFFENHAM (Evesham). 714 *chart*. Vffaham, 860 *ib*. Uffenham, *Dom*. Offenham. ' Home of *Uffa* ' or ' *Offa*.'

OFFERTON (Durham). *a*. 1130 *Sim. Dur*. Uffertun. Prob. ' town on the bank,' O.E. *obr, ofr*, Ger. *ufer;* see -over. But Offerton (Hindlip) is 972 *chart*. Ælflædetun, ? *Dom*. Alcrintune, 1275 Alfverton, *a*. 1600 Alcrinton, now called Alfreton, *a*. 1800 Affreton. A most remarkable corrup. 'Town of *Ælflæd*,' perh. she who was daughter of K. Offa, 757-786. Duignan suggests that *r* came in through similarity of Ælflæd to Ælfred.

OFFORD (Warwksh.). *Dom*. Offeworde, *a*. 1200 Offorde. This is ' *Offa*'s farm.' *Cf*. OFFMOOR (Halesowen), 1288 Offemore, and PAMPISFORD; and see -worth.

OGLE (Newcastle-on-Tyne). Prob. O.W. *ugl*, W. *uchel*, ' high '; same root as OCHILS, OGILVIE, and GLEN OGLE (Sc.). *Cf*. KNOYLE. But OGLETHORP (W. Riding) is *Dom*. once Ocelestorp and 4 times Oglestorp, ' village of ' some man, the nearest in *Onom*. seems *Ugelbert;* the -bert may easily have dropped. See -thorpe.

OGO DOUR (the Lizard). Corn.= ' cave by the water.'

OKMENT HILL (Devon). W. *uch mynydd* (Corn. *menit*), ' high hill.' *Cf*. LONGMYND and OCHILS (Sc.).

OLD MAN OF CONISTON. Supposed to be W. *allt maen*, ' cliff-like ' or ' high rock.' *Cf*. ALLTWEN. As curious a corrup. is OLD-BARROW (Henley in Arden), 709 *chart*. Ulenbeorge, ' hill, barrow of the owl,' O.E. *ula, -an*. See BARROW.

OLDSWINFORD (Stourbridge). *Dom*. Suineford, 1275 Swyneford, 1340 Oldeswynesford. O.E. *swin ford*, ' swine's ford.'

OLNEY (Bucks and Coventry). *Dom*. Olnei, Bucks; Cov. O. 1349 Olneie. *Cf*. *K.C.D*. 621 Ollan eg, O.E. for ' *Olla*'s isle.' Also 1016 *O.E. Chron*. Olanige, *c*. 1097 *Flor*. W. Olanege, an islet in the Severn near Deerhurst. See -ey.

OLTON (Hampton-in-Arden). 1295 Oulton, *c*. 1450 Oulton alias Ulverton—*i.e.*, ' *Ulfr*'s town.' *Cf*. Sc. *oo* for *wool*, and Oldcoates or Ulcoates (Notts), *Dom*. Caldecotes, but 1269 Ulcotes, 1302 Ulecotes. ' Cots of the owl,' O.E. *ūla*. But OLVESTON, close to ALVESTON, is 1303 Olveston, 1515 Olston, and is orig. the same name, ' *Ælfe*'s town.'

OMBERSLEY (Droitwich). 706 *chart*. Ambreslege and Ombreswelle, 714 *ib*. Ambresleie, *Dom*. Ambreslege. May be fr. O.E. *amber, omber*, ' a pitcher.' See AMBERGATE and AMBERLEY. Or perh. it is fr. a man *Amber, Ambre*. See AMBROSDEN and AMESBURY. See -ley.

OMILY R. (Hereford). Prob. W. *amwyll*, 'shady, gloomy on all sides.'

ONECOTE (Leek). 1199 Anecote, 1285 Onecote—*i.e.*, 'one cottage,' as ONEHOUSE (Suffk.) is *chart*. Anhus. But ONESACRE (S. Yorks) is *Dom*. Anesacre, 'field of *Anna*' or '*Onna,*' a common name in *Onom*.

ONGAR (Essex) or CHIPPING ONGAR. *Dom*. Angra, O.E. *hangra*, 'a wooded, hill-slope.' *Cf*. CLAYHANGER, and see CHIPPING.

ONIBURY (Craven Arms). *Dom*. Aneberie. 'Burgh, town on R. Onney or OUNY.' See -bury. But High and Little ONN (Staffs). are *Dom*. Otne (error) and Anne, which Duignan derives fr. W. *onn*, 'ash-trees.' There is an ONNELEY also in Salop, *Dom*. Anelege; and an Oney Coppice (Lindridge). *Cf*. ONECOTE.

ORBY (Burgh, Lincs). *Cf*. Arbury (Nuneaton), *a*. 1200 Ordburi, Erdbury, 1235 Orbyri, which is prob. '*Eardulf's* burgh.' See -ly.

ORCHESTON (Devizes). Must be fr. some man. *Cf*. 1298 'Willelmus de Orkesleghe.' The nearest in *Onom*. is Oric, a dux in Kent, of 9th cny. There is an *orc, orke, orch*, 'an ogre,' but it is not found in Eng. *a*. 1598.

ORETON (Wolvermptn.). *Dom*. Overtune, *a*. 1300 Overton, Orton. O.E. *ofer-tun*, 'upper town.' *Cf*. Orgrave (N. Lancs), *Dom*. Ourgreve, prob. 'bank'; O.E. *obr, ofr*, 'of the grave.' See OVER. Orgrave (S. Yorks) is *Dom*. Nortgrave.

ORFORD (Suffolk and Warrington). Suff. O. not in *Dom*. 1166-67 *Pipe* Oreford, *c*. 1450 *Fortescue* Orford havyn. Like ORWELL, near by, prob. corrup. fr. N. *aar fjord*, 'river' or 'river-like firth or bay.' In N. *aa* sounds *o*. *Cf*. HAVERFORD, Waterford (Ireland), etc. Warr. O., *sic* 1511, may be fr. a man Ord, or contracted fr. one of the many names in Ord-.

ORLETON (Tenbury). *Dom*. Alretune, 1275 Olretone, 'alder town.' See ALLERTON, etc. *Alder* is O.E. *alor, aler*, 3 *olr*, 7 *owler, ouller*. The ORLS (Mathon) is fr. same root. Alder is still pron. *orl* in S. Salop. But OLLERTON (Newark), *Dom*. and 1190 Alretun, 1278 Alverton, is perh. fr. *Ælfweard* or *Ælfhere*.

ORLINGBURY (Northants). *c*. 1190 Orlingberge. 'Town or fort of *Eorlwine,*' 3 in *Onom*. See -bury.

ORMESBY (Yorks and Gt. Yarmouth). *Dom*. both Ormesbi. 'Dwelling of *Orm.*' See -by.

ORM'S HEAD (Llandudno). *a*. 1145 *Orderic* Horma heva, a N. form of Ormes heafod or Orm's Head, or WORM'S HEAD. *Orm* or *Orma* is a common name in *Onom*.

ORMSKIRK. 1285 Ormeskirke. See above. The *Orm* here is not the monk who wrote the *Ormulum*, but a Saxon noble who gained large estates near here through marrying a Norman heiress. The place is not in *Dom*., but is referred to *temp*. Rich. I., d. 1199.

ORRELL (Wigan). *Dom.* Olegrimale, Olringemele, 1201-02 Horhill, -hull; 1205-06 Orhille; 1320 Orell. Even though *Dom.* is so clumsy, it gives the clue to a most interesting corrup. The first part is the N. name *Authgrimr*, later *Udgrim.* An *Oudgrim* is actually found in *Dom.* Notts. The second part is either -hall (*q.v.*) or -hill, regular W. Midl. *hull.*

ORSLOW (Staffs). 1203 Horselawe, *a.* 1400 Orselow—*i.e.*, 'Horsa's mound.' See -low. Orsett (Grays) (-sett= 'seat') prob. has a similar origin. *Cf. Dom.* Surrey, Orselei.

ORSTON (Nottingham). *Dom.* Oschintone, 1242 Orskinton, 1284 Orston. Mutschmann thinks, 'Ordric's town,' as in Ordsall, *Dom.* Ordeshale. *Dom.* confuses with OSSINGTON.

ORWELL R. (Suffolk). 1015 *O.E. Chron.* Arwa, Arewe; *Dom.* Ordewelle; *c.* 1386 *Chaucer* Orewell; *c.* 1450 *Fortescue* Orwell havyn. The 1015 forms suggest, and ORFORD near by confirms, that this must be a corrup. fr. N., akin to that of KIRK-WALL (Sc.), *c.* 1225 Kirkiuvagr, 1438 Kirkwaw, *c.* 1500 Kirk-wall. The Ar- will be N. *á*, gen. *aar*, 'river,' *aa* in mod. N. being pron. *o*. The wa- will be O.N. *vagr*, 'bay, voe,' the liquid *r* having early become *l*, or else disappeared. So the name is 'bay of the river.'

ORWELL (Royston, Herts). *c.* 1080 *Inquis. Camb.* Oreuuella, *Dom.* Oreuuelle, Orduuelle (a mistake), 1210 Norwelle (for 'atten Orewelle '), 1284 Orewelle. O.E. *oran wella*, 'well at the edge or brink.' *Cf.* Orton (Tebay).

OSCOTT (Birmingham). *a.* 1300 Oscote, *c.* 1615 *Camden* Auscote, Perh. 'East cottage,' O.N. *aust-r*, 'east.' *Cf.* AUSTWICK. But Duignan prefers some name in Os-, Osbeorn, Oswald, etc., which may well be.

OSGATHORPE (Loughborough). 'Village of *Osgar* or *Osgeard*,' common in *Onom.* See -thorpe.

OSGODBY (E. Riding and Market Rasen). E. R. O. *Dom.* Ansgo-tesbi, -gotebi, Asgozbi (*z=ts*); 1204 *Fines* Angodeby; 1206 An-goteby. M. R. O. *a.* 1100 *chart.* Osgoteby, 1298 Osgodeby. *Cf. Dom.* Osgotcros, 1179-80 *Pipe* Osegotecros, now Osgoldcross (Wapentake), Yorks. 'Dwelling of *Osgod*' or '*Osgot*,' common names in *Onom.*, which also has the Norm. forms *Ansgod* and *Ans-got. Cf.* next, and Ansthryth, var. of name Osthryth. *Osgod*, in N. *Asgod*, seems to mean 'the good '—*i.e.*, 'the property, of the gods.' See -by.

OSMOTHERLEY (Lancs and Northallerton). Lan. O. 1260-72 Osmunderlawe, 1269 Asemunderlai, 1276-79 Asmunderlauue, 1588 Estmotherlie, 1667 Osmonderley, 1670 Osmotherlow. Nor. O. *Dom.* Asmundrelac, 1197 *Rolls* Hosmundeslea, *a.* 1300 Osmunderley. Instructive forms. 'Meadow of *Asmund*' or '*Osmund*' ('the protected' or else 'the mouth of the gods'). *Cf.* Osborne, N. *Asenbjörn*, 'bear of the gods or demigods.'

The ending is often -low (*q.v.*) or -lawe, ' hill.'   *Cf.* ASPATRIA, and AMOTHERBY, and MYTHE; also Osmondthorpe (Notts), 1331 Osmundthorp.

OSNEY (Oxford).   1155 *Pipe* Osineia, 1161 *ib.* Oseneia, *c.* 1200 *Gervase* Osneye. ' Island of *Osa*,' gen. ' *Osan*,' common name in *Onom.* See -ey.

OSSETT (Yorks).   *Dom.* Osleset. ' Seat, abode,' O.N. *sæti*, ' of *Osla*,' 2 in *Onom.*   Liquid *l* easily vanishes.

OSSINGTON (Newark).   *Dom.* Oschintone, 1162-65 *chart.* Oschintona, 1278 Oscington, ' Town of *Osecg*,' a name in *Onom.* Mutschmann derives fr. a dubious *Osketin*, var. of the common *Asketill.* See -ing and -ton.

OSWALDTWISTLE (Accrington).   1241 Oswaldtuisil. ' *Oswald*'s confluence.' See TWIZEL; and *cf.* Birtwistle, ENTWISTLE, Tintwistle. In E. Yorks we also have OSWALDKIRK, *Dom.* Oswaldes cherca.

OSWESTRY.   *c.* 1190 *Gir. Itin. Camb.* Osewaldstreu, id est Oswaldi arborem, or ' tree of *Oswald*,' K. of Northumbria, d. 642. He was prob. slain here by Penda, K. of Mercia. 1603 *Owen* Osestree. In W. Croesoswallt, ' cross of Oswald.' *Cf.* Brentry (Glouc.), 1247 Bernestre, ' tree of *Beorn*.'

OTFORD (Sevenoaks).   O.E. *Chron.* 774 Ottanford, *a.* 1130 *Sim. Dur.* Ottaforda, 1160-61 *Pipe* Otteford. ' Ford of *Otta* ' or ' *Otto*.' *Cf.* OTHAM (Maidstone).

OTHERTON (Penkridge and Worcester) and OTHERY (Bridgwater). Pe. O. *Dom.* Orretone, *a.* 1200 Oderton, *a.* 1300 Otherton, which, like Otherton (Wrcstrsh.), is prob. ' *Ohthere*'s or *Othere*'s or *Otre*'s town.' All these forms are in *Onom.* Othery is prob. similar, with ending -y or -ey, ' islet.' But *cf.* OTTERY.

OTLEY (W. Riding and Ipswich).   W. Rid. O. *Dom.* Othelai, *a.* 1130 *Sim. Dur.* Oteleia. ' *Otta*'s lea ' or ' meadow.' See above and -ley.

OTTERY ST. MARY (Exeter).   963 *chart.* Otheri, *Dom.* Otri, *c.* 1200 *Gervase* Oteri, 1460 Otryght. ' Isle,' O.E. *iʒe, iʒ*, ' on R. *Otter*,' which is prob. O.E. *otr, oter, otor*, ' an otter.' *Cf.* Otterburn (Craven and Northumbld.), *Dom.* Yorks and Hants, Otreburne, 1160-61 *Pipe* Devon has a Fenotri, ? Fen Ottery.

OTTRINGHAM (Hull), OTTERINGTON (N. Yorks), and OUGHTRINGTON (Warrington).   *Dom.* Otringeha', Otrege, Otrinctune, Otrintona. Wyld and H. connect these Ottring- names with the N. *Authgrimr* or *Oudgrim* (see ORRELL), which certainly seems the origin of the Warr. name, which Wyld and H. omit. But the Ottring- names prob. are patronymics fr. *Othhere, Otre*, or perh. *Othgœr*, all found in *Onom.* *Cf. Dom.* Otringeberge and Otringedene (Kent), which is by no means a specially N. region. See -ing.

OULTON (6 in *P.G.*).   Stone O. *a.* 1300 Oldeton, Oldington. Possibly O.E. *Ealdantun*, ' Ealda's town,' or else ' old town.' But *Dom.* Norfolk Oulstona—*i.e.*, Oulton, Aylsham—will be

' *Ulf*'s town.' It is in 1477 Owstoonde. Possibly it is ' town of *Ule* '—*i.e.*, ' the owl.' *Cf.* Ouston and Outchester (Bamboro') 1242 Ulecestr.

Oundle (Northampton). *Bede* Undalum, *a.* 1000 Undola, *a.* 1100 *chart.* Undale, 1542 *Leland* Oundale. Thought to be a contracted form of Avon + dale, O.E. *dœl*. But the contraction seems almost too early to be found in Bede. Avon means ' river,' here the Nen. For a similar contraction, *cf.* Dunoon (Sc.).

Ouny or **Onney** R. (Salop and Hereford). Seen in Onibury, *Dom.* Aneberie, and also in Anelege. Must be Keltic for ' river.' The G. *abhuinn* or *amhuinn*, ' river,' is in certain districts pron. ŏwn. *Cf.* Oundle and Avon.

Ouse Great, Ouse R., and **Ouseburn** (York). Gr. O. 905 *O.E. Chron.* Wusa, 1010 *ib.* Usa, *a.* 1130 Use, 1330 Ouse. York O. *Dom.* Useburne, 1237 Usus. Perh. connected with O.E. *wáse*, 4-6 *wose*, 6 *oous, ouse*, ' wet mud, ooze.' The name occurs all over England—in Essex and Sussex, as well as in the cases above—and very possibly it is Keltic. See p. 12. Isis, *c.* 1350 Ysa, must surely be a cognate root. See -burn.

Ousel R. (trib. of Great Ouse). Presumably O.E. *ósle*, old name of the blackbird, the ouzel; but old forms needed.

Ousethorp (Howden). *Dom.* Owestorp, Dwestorp (D error for O). Not fr. R. Ouse, but ' village of *Oua, Ova*, or *Oba*,' forms all in *Onom.* See -thorp.

Ouston (Stamfordham, Birtley, Durham; and Coxwold, N. Riding). St. O. 1201 *Yorks Fines* Hulkeleston—*i.e.*, ' *Hulfcytel* ' or ' *Ulfcytel*'s village.' But Cox. O. *Dom.* Ulvestone, 1201 Ulveton, ' village of *Ulf*,' ' Ulf's town.' Now also called Oulston. But Ouston (Coleshill) is *old* Oustherne, Owsthirn, which is prob. ' east nook.' East Riding in *Dom.* is Oust redenc; and see Herne. *Cf.* Oulton and Owston.

Ovenden (Halifax). *Sic Sim. Dur.* contin. ann. 1147. O.E. *Ofandenu*, ' den, cave of *Ofa*,' or possibly ' of *Owen*.'

Over (Glouc., Cambridge, and Winsford, Chesh.). Gl. O. 804 *chart.* Ofre ad Gleawecestre. Cam. O. *Dom.* Ovre, Oure; 1210 Overe. Chesh. *Dom.* Ovre. O.E. *ofre*, dat. of *ofer*, ' a shore of a sea or bank of a river.' *Cf.* Ger. *ufer ;* and see -over.

Overton (9 in *P.G.*). *Dom.* Ovretone, Chesh. and Worcr. ' Upper town,' O.E. *ufera*, 3-5 *ouere*, ' over.' *Cf.* Overbury, Tewkesbury, 875 *chart.* Uferebiri, Vfera birig, *Dom.* Oureberie, with the same meaning. See -bury.

Owersby (Market Rasen). 1233 Orresby. Prob. corrup. of ' *Ordgœr*'s or *Ordgar*'s dwelling.' The name is very common in *Onom.* See -by.

Owslebury (Winchester). Not in *Dom.* *Cf.* Ozleworth (Charfield), *Dom.* Osleworde, *c.* 1220 Hoheleswordi, *later* Wozel-,

Owselworth. The man's name is uncertain. *Cf. B.C.S.* 764 Oslan wyrth, ' *Osla*'s farm.' It might be *Oshelm,* 4 in *Onom.,* or *Oswulf,* as in OWSTON. Also *cf.* ST. AUSTELL'S. See -bury and -worth.

OWSTHORP (Pocklington). *Dom.* Ianulfestorp, 1203 Ulnestorp, *a.* 1400 Ulvesthorpe. Very curious corruption. ' Village of *Eanwulf,*' very common in *Onom.* In *a.* 1400 the Ean- has dropped away. With the present form Ows-, *cf.* Ooston, mod. pron. of ULVERSTON; also *cf.* next. OWTHORP (Notts), *Dom.* Ovetorp, *c.* 1190 Hustorp, is ' village of *Ufi* or *Uvi.*' See -Thorpe.

OWSTON PRIORY (Leicester) is 1233 Osulveston, ' town of *Oswulf,* a name common in *Onom.* But OWSTON (Doncaster), *Dom.* Ulsitone, 1179-80 *Pipe* Ouston, is prob. = OUSTON (Coxwold), *Dom.* Ulvestone, ' town of *Ulf.*' Only it seems to be in *Dom.* also Austun and Austhu', which may be an O.E. loc., ' in the east places,' *oust* and *aust* being early forms of ' east,' and loca tives in -un or -on are not uncommon; only they usually turn into -ham. See HALLAM, etc., and next.

OWSTWICK (Hull). *Dom.* Ostewic. Prob. ' eastern dwelling,' just as East Riding is in *Dom.* Oust redenc, and in the Yorks *Pipe Rolls* we have ' Oustcotun ' and ' Westcotun,' or Eastcott and Westcott. *Cf.* above; and see -wick.

OXENHOLME (Westmld.). ' Oxen's meadow.' See -holm. *Cf.* OXLEY (Wolverhampton), *Dom.* Oxelie, and OXNAM (Sc.). Oxcliff (N. Lancs) is *Dom.* Oxeneclif.

OXFORD. *a.* 900 *coins of K. Alfred* Oksnaforda, but some read Orsnaforda, which conceivably represents a ' Horse-ford '; 912 *O.E. Chron.* Oxnaforda; *c.* 1000 *chart. K. Æthelred* Oxonaforda; 1011 *O.E. Chron.* Oxenafordscire; *c.* 1160 Oxenefordia; 1479 Oxenford. O.E. *oxena ford,* ' ford for the oxen.' *Cf. Grant* of *a.* 675 Oxelake (on the Thames). The regular W. name is Rhyd ychen, which also means ' ford of the oxen.' It is agreed that this W. name is very old, and that there is no recorded spelling for ' ox ' other than *ych,* unless it be a dial. *wch.* However, *c.* 1145 *Geoffrey of Mon.,* iv. 12, speaks of ' Boso of Ridoc, that is Oxford.' It seems unlikely that this 12th cny. name Ridoc is meant for *rhyd ychen,* though *rid* is clearly O.W. for ' ford.' It seems more prob. that in -oc we have O.Kelt. for ' water.' See OCK. So that, while the Anglo-Saxons thought the name was their own *ox,* it orig. was Keltic, and cognate with Ax, Ex, USK, and Ux- bridge. *Cf.,* too, ISIS. But for two or three centuries the Kelt. name must have been quite lost, and the Welsh would coin a new name when they began to frequent the University. Before the 14th cny. Oxford would prob. be of too little importance to the Welsh to have a W. name of its own. As to forms *a.* 900, curiously enough for OXENHALL (Dymock), *Dom.* writes Horsenehal, prob. an error; *c.* 1230 Oxonhale. *Cf.* also the curious form Tweoxn eam, s.v. TWYNING.

OXHEY (Watford). 1007 *chart.* Oxangehæge—*i.e.*, O.E. for ' oxen's enclosure ' or ' hedge,' O.E. *hege.* *Cf.* HAY and Oxenhay (Berkeley), 1243 Oxhaye.

OXNEAD (Norfolk). 1420 Oxenede. The ending is difficult. There seems nothing likely in *e* or *n* (no *ede* or *nead* or the like), so this may be ' oxen-head,' where *head* is used in the sense of ' a pond or body of water dammed up.' Caxton, 1480, speaks of ' fissh-ponde hedes,' and *head* is spelt 3-6 *heed,* 4-7 *hede.*

OXSTED (Reigate). *Dom.* Acstede, O.E. for ' oak-place ' *Cf.* homestead, etc.

OXTON (W. Riding, Birkenhead, and Southwell, Notts). W. R. O. *Dom.* Oxetone and Ossetone. So. O. *Dom.* Oxetune. ' Village of the oxen.' *Cf.* Oxspring (Sheffield), *Dom.* Osprinc, and Oxenton (Tewkesbury), *Dom.* Oxendone.

OYSTERLOW (Pembroke). *c.* 1200 *Girald.* Oisterlaph, -laf, *c.* 1210 Osterloyth, 1325 Oystrelof, 1541 Usterloys. This is the O.W. Esterlwyf, W. Ysterlwyf, or *ystre lwyf,* ' dwelling in the elm-wood,' influenced, of course, by Eng. *oyster,* O.Fr. *oistre,* not found in Eng. till 1357. OYSTERMOUTH (Glam.), said to be *old* Ostremuere (prob. error for -muue, M.E. for ' mouth '), may have a similar origin, only here it will be a hybrid.

PACKINGTON (Tamworth and Ashby-de-la-Zouch). Ta. P. *Dom.* Pagintone, *a.* 1200 Pakintone. Ash. P. 1043 *chart.* Pakinton, *Dom.* Patitone (error). *Cf. Dom.* Essex, Pachenduna, and Packwood (Warwk.). The nearest name in *Onom.* is one *Pæcga ;* so prob. ' village of *Pæcga.* ' See -ing and -ton.

PADBURY (Bucks). *B.C.S.,* ii. 377, Padde byrig, *Dom.* Pateberie, ' Burgh, town of *Padda,*' 3 in *Onom. Cf.* PADDINGTON, London, (1167-68 *Pipe* Padinton, 1439 Paddyngton) and Warrington, and *Dom.* Surrey, Padendene; also PADWORTH.

PADSTOW (N. Cornwall and Devon). Corn. P. 981 *O.E. Chron.* See Petrocstow, 1536 Padstowe. Dev. P. *Dom.* Petroches stow, *later* Petrockstow. ' Place of St. *Petroc,*' an interesting corruption. The ending -stow, found already in 981 in Cornwall, is an early proof of Anglo-Saxon influence there.

PADWORTH (Theale, Berks). *O.E. chart.* Peadan wurth, *Dom.* Peteorde, *c.* 1280 Paddewurth. ' Farm of *Peada.* ' See -worth.

PAGHAM (Bognor). *a.* 1130 *Sim. Dur.* ann. 1108 Paggaham, 1298 Pageham. ' Home of *Paga,*' only one in *Onom.*, and he at Carlisle. But Paythorne (W. Riding), *Dom.* Pathorme, prob. contains the name *Pæga* or *Paga* also; 2 *Pægas* in *Onom. Cf.* PAGANHILL (Stroud), 1346 Paganhulle, and PAINLEY.

PAILTON (Rugby). *a.* 1300 Paylynton, Pailinton. ' Village of *Pælli,*' one in *Onom.*

PAINLEY (Craven). *Dom.* Paghenale, possibly a gen. pl. ' lea of the
pagans.' Oxf. Dict. has no instance of *pagan, a.* 1375 ; but *Pagan,
Paganus,* and *Pagen* are all names in *Onom. Paine* and *Payne*
are surnames fr. *pagan.* PAINSWICK (Stroud) is *Dom.* Wyke,
but *later* Wyke Pagani, Payneswyke, called after *Pain Fitzjohn,*
Justiciar Sheriff, who seems to have built his castle here during
the wars of Stephen. Similarly PAINSTHORPE (E. Riding) is in
Dom. simply Thorf. Paghenale may also stand for ' nook of
Paga,' gen. *-an.* If so, the ending must have changed. See
-hall, -ley, -thorpe (' village '), and -wick (' dwelling ').

PALFREY GREEN (Walsall). *a.* 1600 Palfraye Green. A *palfrey* or
(lady's) riding-horse was a common fine or payment to a King
or superior for land. Sometimes it was an annual or periodical
payment. For the word, which is O.Fr., see *Oxf. Dict.*

PALGRAVE (Diss). 962 *chart.* Palegrave, *Dom.* Pag(g)raua, *c.* 1210
Jocelin Palegrava, *c.* 1430 Pagrave. Prob. ' *Pallig's* grave,'
O.E. *græf.* A *Pallig,* a Danish earl, is mentioned 1001 in *O.E.
Chron. Pale* sb. is Fr., and not in Eng. till *c.* 1330; *pale* adj. is
also Fr., and not in Eng. *a.* 1300. *Cf.* Orgrave (Yorks), etc.

PALLINSBURN (N. Northumbld.). ' Burn, brook of *Paulinus,'* who
prob. preached and baptized here. See Bede.

PAMBOROUGH (Glastonbury). 956 Pathenebergh. Prob. ' burgh,
castle of *Patta,'* gen. *Pattan. Cf.* ' Pattnaden,' *B.C.S.* 1307.
See -burgh. But PAMBER (Hants) is 1217 *Patent R.* Penbere,
1225 Pen-, Pember. Prob. O.E. *penn bearu,* ' fold in the wood.'
Cf. PENN and BEER, also PAMINGTON (Ashchurch), *Dom.* Pamin-
tone, fr. an unrecorded *Pama.*

PAMPISFORD (Cambridge). *Dom.* Pampesuuorde, even as late as
1851 Pampsworth. ' Farm of *Pamp,'* an unknown name. *Cf.*
Dan. dial. *pamper,* ' a short, thick-set person.' The local pron.
is Paanza, which Skeat says is ' regularly shortened from
Pamp's'orth.' See -worth.

PANGBOURN (Berks). 833-34 *chart.* Peginga-, Pægeinga- burnan,
956 Pangan-burnan. ' Burn, brook of *Pæginga '—i.e.,* ' son of
Pæga,' 2 in *Onom.* The river is now called simply the Pang,
and nearer its source the Kimber. *Cf.* PENISTONE.

PANNAL (Harrogate). *Dom.* Paghenhale, 1315 Pattrehall, *later*
Panhale, 1448 Pannal. ' Hall of *Paga* or *Pæga,'* gen. *Pagan.*
Both forms in *Onom.*

PANTSAESON (Wales). W.= ' glen of the Saxon ' (G. *Saisneach*) or
' Englishman.'

PANTYCELYN (Breconsh.). W.= ' glen, hollow of the holly.' *Cf.*
LLWYNCELYN.

PAPCASTLE (Cockermouth). From a local L. inscription, *c.* 200, it is
known that Pap- represents Abalabba, site of a Roman fort.

PAPWORTH EVERARD (Cambridge). Local pron. Parpor. *Dom.* Papeworde, *Ramsey chart.* Pappenwrthe, Pappeworthe. ' Place of *Pappa.*' *Papo* is the only name in *Onom.* See -worth.

PAR (Cornwall). ? = W. *pawr,* ' pasture.'

PARCANSCALLI (Cornwall). Corn. = ' park, field of the bats.'

PARFORD (Moreton Hampstead). Prob. 1174 *chart.* Pirforde. Prob. fr. O.E. *piriʒ,* ' a pear-tree.' *Cf.* PARHAM (Berkeley), 1264 Perham, and PIRBRIGHT.

PARRET R. (Somerset). *O.E. Chron.* 658 Pedrida, *ib.* 893 Pedrede, Pedret. W. *pedryd,* ' a square,' perh. referring to the piece of land enclosed by the river bend near Pawlett.

PARTNEY (Spilsby, Lincs.). *Bede* Peartaneu. ' Isle of *Peartan,*' O.E. *eu* var. of *iʒ, iʒe,* ' island,' see -ey. *Peartan* may be a personal name. Nothing like it in *Onom.* Perh. W. *partyn,* ' a smart little fellow,' or *perthen,* ' a bush.'

PASSENHAM (Northants). 921 *O.E. Chron.* Passanhamm. ' Enclosure, O.E. *hamm,* of *Passa,*' only one in *Onom.,* in Kent. But *cf.* next. See -ham.

PASSFIELD (Liphook). *Cf. Dom.* Essex, Passefelda. ' Field of *Passa,*' one in *Onom.*

PASTON (N. Walsham). *a.* 1150 *chart.* Pastun. Contraction for ' *Passa*'s town.' See above. But PASTON or Pawston (Wooler) is for Pollokston.

PATCHAM (Brighton) and PATCHING (Worthing). 947 *chart.* Peccinges and Pettingas (*tt* for *cc.*). ' Home of *Pecca, Pecga,* or *Pacca,*' and ' place of the sons of Pecca.' *Cf. Dom.* Surrey, Pachesham, Paxford, Campden, *sic* 1275 and Paxton (Berwick), *c.* 1098 Paxtun. The only name in *Onom.* is *Pecga.* See -ham and -ing.

PATNEY (Devizes). *B.C.S.* iii. 354, Peatanige. O.E. for ' Isle of *Peata, Peatta,* or *Peada,*' all 3 forms are known. Peat and Pate are both still in use as surnames. *Cf.* PATTISHALL and *Dom.* Patintune, Salop.

PATRINGTON (Hull). *Dom.* Patrictone. ' Town of *Patrick*' ; the -ick has become -ing, because -ing is so much commoner in place-names. See -ing.

PATTINGHAM (Wolverhampton). Pron. Pattinjem, *cf.* BIRMINGHAM. *Dom.* Patingham, *a.* 1200 Pattingeham, *a.* 1500 Patincham. ' Home of the sons of *Patta* ' or ' *Peatta.*' *Cf.* PATTON (Salop), prob. *B.C.S.* 77 Peattingtun, and *Dom.* Essex, Patenduna. Patton (Kendal) is *Dom.* Patun. See -ing and -ham.

PATTISHALL (Towcester). 1207 Pateshill, 1236 Pateshull (*cf.* ASPULL, etc.). ' Hall of *Peata* ' ; *cf.* PATNEY, Patshull (Wolverhampton) is *Dom.* Pecleshella, *a.* 1300 Petles- Patleshull—*i.e.*, either '*Pœcgel*'s or *Pyttel*'s hill.' PEGGLESWORTH *Cf.*

PAULERSPURY (Towcester). 'The *pury* of (Robert de) *Paveli*,' an early owner. The name ' Pury end ' still survives; it is in *Dom.* Pirie, O.E. *pirʒe, piriʒe, pirie,* ' a pear-tree.' *Cf.* PIRBRIGHT.

PAULL (Hull). *Dom.* Paghel, Pagele: *later* Pagula. Contraction for ' nook of *Paga* or *Pæga*,' both in *Onom.* See -hall.

PAVENHAM (Sharnbrook, Beds.). ' Home of *Paba* or *Peabba*,' a name not in *Onom.*, but *cf.* Pebworth, Stratford-on-Avon. 848 *chart.* Pebeworthe, *Dom.* Pebevorde. See -worth, ' farm.'

PAVEY ARK (hill, Grasmere). Said to be ' shieling, dairy hut of *Pavia*.' See ARKLID.

PAWLETT (Bridgwater). *c.* 705 *chart.* Pouelt: *later* Pouholt. Perh. ' village in the holt or wood.' Pou is said to be = L. *pagus*, as often in Brittany. Pouelt, however, prob. represents an O.W. *pwl allt,* ' pool by the cliff.' But PAWTON, St. Breock, Cornwall, is *c.* 988 *chart.* Polltun, ' village by the pool or stream.'

PEAK, The (Derbyshire). *a.* 800 *chart.* Pecsætna (*i.e.*, dwellers in the Peak), 924 *O.E. Chron.* Peac-lond; *Dom.* Pechesers, now ' Peak's Arse'; *c.* 1120 *Hen. Hunt.* In monte vocato Pec, *a.* 1135 *chart.* dominium de Pecco, 1173-4 Pech. *Oxf. Dict.* says ' origin unknown, perh. British,' and not connected with the Eng. *peak* sb. *Cf.* PECKHAM, PEGSDON, etc. It may be the name of a demon or spirit. *Cf.* Puck.

PEAKIRK (Peterboro'). *c.* 1015 *chart.* Pegecyrcan, *a.* 1100 *Grant* Pei-, Peychirche. ' Church of *Pega* or *Pæga*,' both in *Onom.* This is far south to find a ' kirk ' !

PEASEMORE (Leckhampstead). *Chron. Abing.* Pesimara, *a.* 1224 Pesemere, *c.* 1540 Peysmer. ' Land for growing pease,' O.E. *pise.* The ending is a little unsettled; O.E. *mere,* ' marsh, fen ' seems scarcely prob., yet we have Peasemarsh (Sussex), as well as Peasenhall (Saxmundham). It may be O.E. *mór,* ' a moor '; (Peasbrook, Broadway, Worcester), in 972 *chart.* Pisbroc, is also fr. O.E. *pise,* ' a pea.'

PECKHAM (London) and PECKHAM BUSH (Tonbridge). ? *c.* 1130 *Eadmer* Petteham; but *Dom.* Pechehā, 1278 Pecham. ' Home of *Peca* or *Pecha*,' possibly the same name as PEAK, if it mean a demon or sprite, or Puck. *Cf.* too *Dom.* Surrey, Pechingeorde, ' farm of the sons of Peca.'

PEDMORE (Stourbridge). A name which has curiously changed. *Dom.* Pevemore, *c.* 1200 Pebbemore, 1340 Pebmore. ' Moor of *Peuf*' or ' *Peufa*,' both in *Onom.*, or rather fr. *Peobba*, a dimin. form of *Peof* or *Peuf.* ' Moor ' is O.E. *mór.*

PEEL (I. of Man) and PEELE HALL (Tarvin, Cheshire). I. of M. P. 1399 *chart.* Pela, 1656 Peel-Town, mentioned with Castle-

Town. The Eng. *peel* is not found till *c.* 1330, and meant originally ' a palisade or fence of stakes,' then ' a castle.' Its history is rather curious. See *Oxf. Dict.* s.v. There was formerly a moated tower at Peele Hall. But the Manx name of Peel is Port-na-hinsey, ' port of the island' (now connected by a narrow breakwater with the mainland). It was also called Holmtown.

PEGSDON (Bedfordsh.). *Dom.* Pechesdon, ' hill of PEAK,' *q.v.*

PEGSWOOD (Morpeth). Prob. ' wood of *Pecge;*' *cf.* 958 *chart.* Pecges ford, on Stour, Stafford, 740 *ib.* Peginhullis (Wilts), and above. PEGGLESWORTH (Dowdeswell) *Dom.* Peclesurde, is prob. fr. a man *Peohtgils.* See -worth, ' farm.'

PELSALL (Walsall). 994 *chart.* Peolshale, *Dom.* Peleshale, *a.* 1400 Peoleshale. ' Nook, corner of *Peola.*' *Cf. Dom.* Surrey, Peleforde, and see -hall.

PELUTHO (Abbey Town, Cumbld.). Prob. G. *poll uchdaich,* ' pool by the ascent.' In any case the name is much corrupted.

PEMBERTON (Wigan). *Sic* 1323, but 1200-1 Penberton, 1202 Penbreton. Perh. hybrid, W. *penn brc,* ' head of the hill' (there is a Pembrey in Wales) + -ton, *q.v.* But quite possibly fr. a man, as *Pember,* though not in *Onom.,* is still a surname.

PEMBRIDGE (Herefordsh.). *Dom.* Penebruge. Prob. hybrid as above, W. *penn,* ' head, height,' + bridge.

PEMBROKE. *c.* 1180 *Gir. Camb.* Pembrochia caput maritimae sonat, 1297 *R. Glouc.* Penbroc, *c.* 1350 Pembrok, 1450 Pembroke. O.W. *pen broc,* mod W. *penfro,* head of the sealand.' O.W. and Bret. *bro,* O.Ir. *brog,* country, land (vale).' There is also Penbro, or -fro, near the Lizard; 1219 *Patent R.* Eglospenbroc (*eglos,* ' church '). *Cf.* Pentire (Cornwall) and KINTYRE (Sc.).

PENALLY (Pembk.). *Old* Pen Alun, which is perh. O.W. for ' beautiful height,' G. *aluinn,* ' fair, lovely.'

PENARTH (Glamorgan). W. *penn arth,* ' head of the height,' or ' high headland.' *Cf.* LANARTH, and KINNAIRD (Sc.).

PENBERRY HEADLAND (St. David's). May be hybrid, W. *penn,* ' head, headland,' and -berry, = -burgh, *q.v. Cf.* TURNBERRY (Sc.). But it prob. is fr. W. *beri,* ' a kite, a glede.' PENBURY (Gloster.) must be at least half Eng., perh. wholly so.

PENCARROW (Bodmin). Corn. *pen caerau,* ' height of the forts,' Corn. and W. *caer,* G. *cathair,* ' a castle, a fort.'

PENCOYD (Ross, Herefd.). = Pencoed (Glam.), W. for ' head of the wood,' *coed,* pl. *coydd.*

PENDENNIS (Falmouth). *Sic* 1567. Corn. *pen dinas,* ' headland with the castle.'

PENDLETON (Manchester). *Dom.* Peniltune. Prob. ' town of *Pendwulf* ' or ' *Penweald*,' both names in *Onom.; *older forms needed. But Pendle (*sic* 1612) Hill, Clitheroe, is 1344 Penhull, a tautology, W. *penn*, ' height,' and *hull*, regular old Midl. for ' hill.' Pendle Hill is therefore a triple tautology. *Cf.* Penhull (Lindridge), *sic c.* 1300.

PENDOCK (Tewkesbury). 877 and *Dom.* Pene-, Peonedoc, 1275 Penedoch. Prob. W. *penn y dych*, ' height of the groan or sigh,' Pensax (Stourport), in the same shire, will also be W., fr. W. *Sais*, ' a Saxon, an Englishman.' It is found *c.* 1400 as Pensax, -sex.

PENDRAGON (Westmld.), ' head, height of the dragon,' was a castle of Wm. Rufus. *Oxf. Dict.*, does not give *dragon* in Eng. till *c.* 1220, and says, fr. Fr. *dragon*, L. *draco, -nem.* It certainly was adopted in the Keltic tongues too.

PENENDEN HEATH. *Dom.* Pinnedenna, *c.* 1200 *Gervase* Pin- nindene. O.W. *pinn, penn eiddyn*, ' head of the hillslope.'

PENGE (Sydenham). 957 *chart.* ' Se wude þe hatte Pœnge, 1067 *chart.* ' Penceat Wood in Battersea Manor '; 1308 *chart.*, ' Penge in parochia de Badricheseye.' M'Clure thinks this a worn-down form of Kelt. *penceat*, ' chief wood ' = PENKETH.

PENISTONE (Sheffield). *Dom.* Peng-, Pangeston, 1551 Pennystone. ' Town of *Panga*,' or ' of (nasalized) *Pæga*,' both names in *Onom.; Cf.* PANGBOURN and Pendeford (Wolverhampton), *a.* 1400 Penneford.

PENKETH (Warrington). *Sic* 1292, but 1296 Penket; prob. as in PENGE. *Cf.* 1166-7 *Pipe*, Devon, Morchet, prob. O.Kelt. for ' great wood.'

PENKHULL (Stoke-on-T.). *Dom.* Pinchetel, a hybrid, ' height,' W. *penn*, ' of *Cytel* or *Ketel*,' a common O.E. name. But *a.* 1200 Pencul, which looks like W. *penn cul*, ' slender height ' or ' head '; while the present form has been influenced by *hull*, W. Midl. form of *hill*. *Cf.* PENKRIDGE.

PENKRIDGE (Stafford). *c.* 380 *Ant. Itin.* Penno Crucis, 958 *chart.* Pencric, *Dom.* Pancriz, 1158 *Pipe* Peincrig, 1160 *ib.* Peincriz, 1297 Pen-, Pemcriche, *a.* 1400 Penk rich. W. *penn crych*, ' wrinkled, rumpled height.' But M'Clure and Rhys connect with CREECH. The R. PENK seems to be a back formation or contraction fr. Penkridge—*a.* 1300 ' the river of Pencriz,' *a.* 1400 ' River Penk.' *Cf.* PENTRICH. Duignan's art. is very full; with Penkridge he classes Penncricket Lane, Oldbury, no old forms.

PENLLYN (Cowbridge). Prob. W. *penn llwyn*, ' head, height with the grove.'

PENN (Wolvermpton). *Dom.* Penne. O.E. *penn*, ' a pen, a fold.' There is also PEN MILL (Yeovil), prob. *Dom.* Penne too.

PENNARD, E. and W. (Somerset). *Spurious chart.* of 681 Pengerd. Corn. *pen gerd,* 'height with the hedge,' Corn. *gerd, gard,* G. *garradh,* Eng. *garth, yard.*

PENNI-, PENNEGANT (N.W. Yorks). W. *penn y gwant,* 'height of the butt or mark,' or perh. '*y gwynt*' 'of the wind.' The name 'Pennine Range' seems to have no ancient history.

PENNINGTON (Lymington and Ulverston). Ul. P. *Dom.* Pennegetun. This must be fr. O.E. *penning, pœnig,* or *penig,* 'a penny,' 'penny town,' referring to some tax or impost. *Cf.* PENNY 4 e in *Oxf. Dict.* Pennyland, 'land valued at 1d. a year,' is not given in *Dict.* till a Glouc. *chart. a.* 1300, Penilond.

PENNYCOMEQUICK (old name of Falmouth). Corn. *pen comb ick,* 'height of the narrow valley or combe,' though others say, '*y cum cuig,* 'of the valley of the cuckoo.'

PENPONT (Altarnon). *Dom.* Penponte. Corn. = 'at the head of the bridge.' *Cf.* PENPONT (Sc.). We have the dimin. in PENPWNTAN (Knighton, Radnor), which means 'little milldam'; but *pont,* L. *pons, -tis,* is regular W. and Corn. for 'bridge.'

PENRITH. 1166-7 *Pipe* Penred, 1461 Penreth. W. *penn rhydd,* 'red, ruddy height'; though some say, 'head of the ford,' W. *rhyd,* O.W. *rit.* But what ford? The Eamont is a good bit away. Quite possible is an Eng. origin, fr. *pen* for cattle, and *rith* 'stream,' as in COTTERED, RYDE, etc., so 'cattle-fold by the stream.' But against an Eng. origin is the parish of Penrith, *sic* 1603, in Pembroke, 1594 Penrythe.

PENRUDDOCK (Penrith). Prob. W. *penn rhuddog,* 'reddish, russet-coloured height.' There is also *rhodog,* 'a little circle.'

PENRYN (Falmouth). *Sic* 1536. Corn. *pen ryn,* 'at the head of the promontory or peninsula,' lit. 'nose .' *Cf.* RHYNNS (Sc.). The three places called PENRHYN in Wales are, of course, of similar origin, W. *penn rhyn.*

PENSELWOOD (Gillingham). *Nennian Catalogue* Pensauelcoit. W. *penn sawell coed.* 'Wood of the height like a chimney or smokehole.' Near by are the Pen pits, prob. *O.E. Chron.* 658 'Æt Peonnum,' *ib.* 1016 Peonnan.

PENSNETT (Kingswinford). 1248 Peninak, *c.* 1300 Penniak, *a.* 1400 Pensyned, Pensned chace. Clearly W., *penn sinach,* 'head of the ridge'; it is on high land. But PENSHAM, Pershore, is 972 *chart.* Pedneshamme, 'enclosure of *Peden.*' See -ham.

PENT R. (Essex), and on it PENTLOW, or 'hill, mound on the Pent.' See -low. *Bede* Penta. Prob. W. *pant,* 'a hollow, a dingle.' On its lower reaches it is called the Blackwater.

PENTNEY (Swaffham). 1451 Penteney. Prob. O.E. *Pendan iȝe,* 'Penda's isle.' See -ey.

PENTREATH (Cornwall). Corn. = 'at the head of the sands or strand.' Cf. Pentraeth, Menai Br. and PORTREATH. Treath is the G. *traigh*.

PENTRICH or -RIDGE (Derby and Dorset). De. P. *Dom.* Pentric; Do. P. 958 *chart.* Pencric. Prob. both = PENKRIDGE.

PENTYRE (Padstow). Corn. *pen* or *pedn tir*, 'head, end of the land,' Brythonic form of KINTYRE (Sc.).

PENWORTHAM (Preston). *Sic* 1343, but 1140-9 Penuerthan, 1201-2 Pelwrdham, 1204 Penwrthan, 1242 Penwirtham, 1305 Penwurtham. No likely name in *Onom.*, so this is prob. W. *penn gwrthan*, 'at the head of the dell or corrie,' the -an being corrupted, very naturally, on Eng. lips into -am or -ham, *q.v.*

PENZANCE. Corn. *pen* or *pedn sans* (L. *sanctus*), 'holy headland.'

PEOPLETON (Pershore). 972 *chart.* Piplincgtune, *Dom.* Piplintune, 1275 Pyplinton. A curious and not easily explained corruption. Perh. Piplin- is a corrup. of *Pippen*, one in *Onom.*, the only likely name on record. But 972 is certainly a patronymic, and points to an unrecorded *Pipel*, 'town of the sons of Pipel.' See -ing.

PEPPARD COMMON (Henley-on-T.). Prob. fr. some man not in *Onom.* Cf. *Dom.* Surrey, Pipereberge. We also have PEPPER NESS (Sandwich), which is 1023 *chart.* Piperneasse, and must surely be fr. a man too, and not fr. O.E. *pipor, peppor,* and *piper,* 'pepper.' PEPPER WOOD (Bellbroughton) is 1242 Purperode, which is perh. 'wood (O.E. *wudu,* of which -ode is corrup.) of *Purper* or *Purperd.*' A Robt. *Pippard* is found here in 1294, and *Pippard* may be fr. *Purperd*, a name otherwise unknown.

PERANZABULOE (Cornwall). *Dom.* Lanpiran ('church of Piran'), 1536 Vicaria sancti Perani in Zabulo, 'of St. P. on the sands,' L. *sabulum* or *sabulo*, 'coarse sand, gravel.' *Peran* is Bryth. form of *Kieran*, founder of Clonmacnoise monastery, famous Ir. saint, d. 545. Cf. Perranporth and Perranuthnoe in Cornwall, and PERANWELL (Sc.); also PERAN TOWANS (New Quay), *temp.* Hen. I. Perran Tohod, *temp.* Hen. III. Pyran Thohon. See TOWAN Hd.

PERRY BARR and HALL (Staffs.). Barr P. *Dom.* Pirio, *a.* 1200 Piri, Pirie, Pirye, *a.* 1300 Pyrie; Hall P. *a.* 1300 Pyrye. O.E. *pirige,* M.E. *pirie,* 'a pear-tree.' Cf. 1160-1 *Pipe* Somst., Perretona.

PERSHORE (Worcester). 972 Perscoran, 1056 *O.E. Chron.* On Perscoran, *Dom.* and 1298 Persore, 1102 *Eadmer* Perscore. O.E. *persoc ora*, gen. *-an*, 'peach-growing bank or shore.' Cf. KEYNOR, WINDSOR, etc. *Shore* is prob. Du., and only found in M.E.

PETERBOROUGH. Its old names were Burh = 'burgh,' and Medehamstede. It received its present name, in honour of St. *Peter,* fr. K. Edgar. See *O.E. Chron.* 963.

PETERSHAM (Richmond). 727 *chart.* Pitericheshame, *Dom.* Patri-cesham (*cf.* BATTERSEA), 1266 Petrichesham. 'Home of *Patricius*' or '*Patrick,*' which to this day, in Scotland, is con-stantly interchanged with *Peter.*

PETRIDGE (Tunbridge). O.E. *Pedan hrycg,* 'Peda's ridge.' *Cf.* Petham, Canterbury and *Dom.* Petelie (Salop). These may be fr. *Peatta. Cf. K.C.D.* 949 Peattan ig. There is also a Pedewrde in *Dom.* Salop. See next.

PETTAUGH (Stowmarket). *Dom.* Pete-, Pette haga. 'Meadow, haugh of *Piot*' or '*Peott,*' O.E. *halech, halh,* which in endings is usually found in its dat. *hale;* see -hall. But *Dom.*'s form -haga is very rare, and is O.E. *haga,* 'fenced-in place, enclosure.'

PETWORTH (Sussex). 1199 Pitteworth. O.E. *chart.* Peartinga-wyrth is thought by Birch to be P., but more early forms are needed. The Pet- may be the same as in PETRIDGE. But it should be noted that *pet* is regular Kentish for *pit,* O.E. *pytt,* O.Fris. *pet.* So Petham, Canterbury, is prob. 'house beside the (gravel) pit.'

PEULINIOG (C'marthen). W. = 'land of *Paulinus,*' the well-known missionary in Bede. *Cf.* Capel Peulin.

PEVENSEA. 1049 *O.E. Chron.* Pefenasæe, later MSS. Peuenesea, 1088 *ib.* Pefensea, *c.* 1097 *Flor. W.* Pevanessa, but *Dom.* Pevene-sel, *c.* 1160 *Gest. Steph.* Pevenesel. 'Island of *Pefen,*' perh. a British not an O.E. name. The -ea is O.E. *iʒ, iʒe,* O.N. *ey,* 'island'; what -el represents is not so certain. Certainly -*esel* cannot represent *isle* or *island.* See these words in *Oxf. Dict.*

PEWSEY (Wilts). *a.* 1400 Pevesey, = PUSEY, 'Pefi's isle.'

PHEPSON or FEPSTON (Himbleton, Worcester). 956 *chart.* and *Dom.* Fepsetnatun(e), 1108 Fepsintune. 'Town of the dwellers in *Fep,*' an unknown name. *Cf.* 'Petsætna,' s.v. PEAK.

PICKERING (E. Yorks). *Dom.* Pickeringa, Pickeringe. 'Home of *Pichere*'s sons.' *Cf. B.C.S.* 125 Pickeresham; and Pixham Ferry, Worcester, 1275 Pykerham, Pykresham. See -ing.

PICKHILL (Thirsk). *Dom.* Picala, -ale. 'Nook of *Picc.*' *Cf.* next, and see -hall, which is rarely corrupted into -hill.

PICKTON (Chester). 1340 Pykton, and PICKWORTH (Rutland), *K.C.D.* 812 Piccingawurth. *c.* 1460 Pykeworth. 'Town of *Picc,*' and 'farm of the descendants of *Picc.*' See -ton and -worth. Also PICTON (Stockton). 1179-80 Piketon, fr. the same name. *Cf. Dom.* Pichetorne (Salop). '*Picc*'s thorn'; also PICKBURN (Brodsworth, Yorks), *Dom.* Picheburne, 1202 Pikeburn, PICK-TREE, Co. Durham, 1183 Piktre, and *Dom.* Norfk, Pichenha'.

PICKWELL (Devon). *Exon. Dom.* Pedicheswell. As *Pedich* is not in *Onom.*, it may be corrup. of *Patrick.* See PETERSHAM.

PIDDLE R. and hamlet (Pershore), and PIDDLETOWN (Dorchester). Pe. P. 963 *chart.* Pidele, *Dom.* Pidele, Pidelet, 1275 Pydele North. Do. P. *K.C.D.* 522 and 656. Pyedele, *Dom.* Pydele. It may be cognate with the Eng. *piddle* and *puddle*, but these appear late in recorded Eng. See *Oxf. Dict.* There is no W. sb. like *pydel.* Duignan thinks it means ' a small stream.' *Cf.* next, AFFPIDDLE and TOLPIDDLE.

PIDDLETRENTHIDE (Dorchester). A difficult name needing further light thrown on it. On PIDDLE see above. The rest is doubtful. W. *tren* is ' impetuous,' and the R. TRENT in W. is Trin., while W. *hydo* is ' sheltering, apt to cover.' But all this is groping in the dark. Possibly -trent- may represent *thirteen*, O.N. *prettan*, Dan. *tretten*, Sw. *tretton*, nasalized; and *hide* may be the well-known land measure. See HYDE.

PIDLEY (Huntingdon). Not in *Dom.* Perh. ' *Peda's* mead; the name is in *Onom.* But PIDSLEY (Devon) is 930 *chart.* Pidersleage, where *Pider* is a name hard to identify; in *Dom.* it has become Pidelige.

PIERSE BRIDGE (Darlington). *a.* 1130 *Sim. Dur.* Perse brycg. *Perse* is not in *Onom.*; but it is the Fr. *Piers.* Cannot be connected with *pierce*, which is Fr., and not in Eng. *a.* 1297.

PILKINGTON (Prestwich). 1301 Pylkington. A patronymic, which seems otherwise unknown.

PILL (Bristol) and WEST PILL (Pembroke). Pe. P. *c.* 1550 *Leland* Pille. *Pill* in these cases, in E. Cornwall and S.E. Ireland, is a var. of *pool*, and generally means ' a tidal creek '; also ' a running stream.'

PILLERTON HERSEY (Kineton). *Dom.* Pilarde-, -dintun (e). 1176 Pilardintone, 1327 Pylardynton, 'village of *Pilheard*,' a rare name. *Bilheard* is also found. The Herce family held the manor in Nor. days.

PILLEY (Lymington and S. Yorks). Yor. P. *Dom.* Pillei. Prob. ' isle of *Pila* ' or ' *Pilu.* ' See next, and -ey.

PILSLEY (Chesterfield). *Cf. a.* 1100 *chart.* ' Pilesgate,' Melton Mowbray. ' Meadow of *Pilu* or *Pilwine.* ' There is a ' Pileford ' in *Dom.* Yorks. See -ley.

PILTON (N. Devon and Shepton Mallet). Dev. P. *c.* 1130 *Wm. Malmesb.* Piltune. Shep. P. 1233 Pilton. *Peel* sb[1], ' a palisade or fence,' is not in Eng. *a.* 1300; so this is prob. ' *Pilu's* town.' See above, also PILL. But Pilland is Pelland in *Exon. Dom.*

PIMLICO (London). So spelt from 1598; first found as a place in 1614. *Cf. Pymlyco or Runne Red Cap*, 1609, a pamphlet on London life. See, too. *N. and Q.*, 21 Nov. 1908. It seems to be a personal name, ' old Ben Pimlico ' being referred to in 1598.

PIMPERNE (Blendford). 935 *chart.* Pimpern welle. A puzzling name. O.W. *pimp*, W. *pump* is ' five,' but W. *ern* is ' a pledge ';

O.E. *erne* is 'house,' but there seems no O.E. name or word *Pimp*.
Connexion with *pimpernel* seems impossible. See *Oxf. Dict. s.v.*

PINCHBECK (Spalding). 810 *chart.* Pyncebek, *Dom.* Picebech.
1290 Pyncenbent (? error). O.E. *pynce* or *pinca* is 'a point';
but here it is quite as likely to be name of a man. *Cf. Dom.*
Norfk, Penkesford, and PINKNEYS GREEN; and see -beck,
'brook.'

PINCHFIELD (Hertford). 796 *chart.* Pinnelesfeld. 'Field of *Pinnel*,'
no other known.

PINHOE (Exeter). 1001 *O.E. Chron.* Peonnho, *a.* 1130 *Sim. Dur.*
Penho. Tautology. Corn. *pen*, W. *pinn, penn*, 'a height,'
and O.E. *hóh. Cf.* HOE. PINDRUP (Gloster), *old* Pinthrup, may
be similar, with its ending a rare var. of -thorpe, 'village.'

PINKNEYS GREEN (Maidenhead). *c.* 1160 *Gest. Steph.* Pinchenei,
1161-2 *Pipe* Pinchenni, 1298 Pynkeny. 'Isle of *Pinca*,' gen. *-an*.
Cf. B.C.S. 665 Pincan ham, 1160-1 *Pipe* Pinchinei (Hants), and
PINCHBECK. See -ey.

PINNER (Harrow). Named in 1336 *chart.* Prob., like ASHER,
Beecher, HASLER, etc., O.E. *pin-ofr*, 'pine-tree bank'; *cf.*
WOOLER. The name of the rivulet Pin here will be a back
formation. PINLEY (Warwksh.), *a.* 1200 Pinelei, is also fr.
O.E. *pín*; see -ley. We read in *c.* 1205 *Layamon* 4057, 'In Logres
was King Piner'; but this can have no connexion here. PINNAR
PIKE (Yorks) will be W. *pinn arth*, 'head of the height,' or 'high
headland.' *Cf.* PENARTH and RED PIKE. Baddeley derives
PINNOCK, Hailes, *Dom.* Pignocsire, *later* Pinnoc, (prob.) fr.
pinnock sb[1], found *a.* 1250, as name for the hedge-sparrow or
some other bird. The -sire in *Dom.* is for 'shire.' *Exon. Dom.*
also has a Pinnoc, prob. Kelt. for 'little hill.'

PIPE (Lichfield, Hereford) and PIPE GATE (Mket. Drayton). Pi. P.
a. 1200 Pype, Pipe, which is O.E. for 'pipe.' The city water
has for long been conveyed by pipe from here. Her. P. is also
Dom. Pipe. *Cf.* Pipe Hayes ('hedges'), Erdington.

PIPEWELL (Kettering). *Sic Dom.* and 1160 *Pipe Roll.* 'Well with
a pipe from it,' O.E. *pipe*.

PIRBRIGHT (Woking). 1300-1400 Pirifrith, Pirifirith, Pirifright,
Purifright. O.E. *piriȝ-fyrhðe*, 'pear-tree-wood.' *Cf.* PAULERS-
PURY, PIREHILL, Stone, *Dom.* Pirehel, Pireholle, and POTTERS-
PURY, also next.

PIRTON (Hitchin, Worcester, and Awre). Wor. P. 766 *chart.*
Pirigton, Pyrigtun, 972 Pyritune, *Dom.* Peritune. Aw. P. *Dom.*
Peritone, 'pear-tree village.' *Cf.* Perton or Purton (Wolver-
hampton), *c.* 1060 Pertune, *Dom.* Pertone.

PITCHCOMBE (Stroud), 1253 Pychencombe; and PITCHFORD (Shrewsbury). 1238 *Close R.* Pycheford, 1298 Redulphus de Picche-

forde.' Prob. fr. a man *Picc, Pic,* or *Picco.* See *Onom.,* and *Cf.* PEGSWOOD. The verb *pitch,* ' to throw,' is not found in Eng. till *c.* 1205. See -combe, ' valley.'

PLAINANGUARE (Cornwall). ' Plain for theatrical plays.' *Plain* is O.Fr., L. *planus,* but *guare* is late Corn., L. *varia. Cf.* DORCHESTER.

PLAISTOW (London, Sussex, Selborne). Lo. P. *old* Plegstow, Se. P. 1271 La Pleystow, now called Plestov. O.E. *plegstow,* 'play-place, playground.' *Cf.* Plestins (Warwksh.), *a.* 1300 Pleystowe, Pleistouwe. See STOW.

PLASHETTS (Northumbld). Dimin. of *plash* sb[1], O.E. *plæsc, plesc,* ' a marsh, or marshy pool.' *Plashet* is also an Eng. word, found from fr. 1575, and given in *Oxf. Dict.* as fr. O.Fr. *plassiet plaschet,* dimin. fr. *plascq,* ' a damp meadow.'

PLECK (Gloster and Walsall). Gl. P. 1220, Plocke. M.E. (found *c.* 1315) *plecche,* ' a small enclosure or plot of ground,' cognate with Du. *plecke* with same meaning; but there is no O.E. *plæcca,* as Baddeley thinks.

PLEMONSTALL or PLEMSTALL (Chester). 1340 Plemondstow. ' *Plegmund's* place.' See STOW. But -stall is O.E. *steall, stœl,* also ' a place,' then ' a stall.'

PLUMPTON (Penrith, Preston, Yorks, and Lewes). Pr. P. *Dom.* Pluntun. Yor. P. *Dom.* Plontone, 1206 Plumton, 1490 Plompton. Prob. ' plum-village.' O.E. *plume.* No name like *Pluma* in *Onom.* For the intrusion of *p cf.* BAMPTON, BROMPTON, etc.

PLUMSTEAD (Woolwich and Norwich). Wool. and Nor. P. *Dom.* Plumestede; Nor. P. 1450 Plumbsted. O.E. *plume-stéd,* ' plum-place.' *Cf.* PLUMPTREE (Notts), *Dom.* Pluntre.

PLYMOUTH. *Sic* 1495, but 1231 *Close R.* Plimmue, 1234 *ib.* Plime-muth, *c.* 1450 *Fortescue,* The Plymouthe. PLYMPTON, *Dom.* Plintone, *c.* 1160 Plintona, 1218 Plinton. PLYMSTOCK, *Dom.* Plemestoch. All on R. Plym. W. *plym,* L. *plumbum,* is ' lead '; but some think the root simply means here ' river.'

PLYNLIMMON MOUNTAIN (Wales). 1603 *Owen* Penplymon. W. Pumlumon; *c.* 1200 *Gir. Camb.* Montana de Elenit or Elennith. *Pum llumon* seems to be W. for ' five beacons.' O.W. *pimp,* W. *pum, pump,* ' five,' and *llumon,* ' beacon.' *Cf.* BEN LOMOND (Sc.), G. Laomuinn.

POCKLINGTON (York). *Dom.* Poclinton, 14 times, 1202 Pokelinton. 1298 Pokelington. Prob. ' town of *Puccla,*' gen. *-lan,* fr. O.E. *púcel,* ' a goblin,' prob. connected with *puck,* ' a fairy.' *Cf.* PUCKLECHURCH, and Pockley, E. Riding, *Dom.* Pochelac (for this ending, *cf.* FILEY). Possibly this last is fr. *Poha* or *Pohha,* names in *Onom. Cf.* 1161-2 *Pipe* Pocheslea, Northants.

POLDHU (the Lizard). Corn. = ' black pool.'

POLESWORTH (Tamworth). *Old* Polles-, Polsworth, 'farm of *Pol.*' *Cf. Dom.* Bucks, Policote, and *K.C.D.* 641 Polesleah.

POLLINGTON (Wellingboro'). *Cf. Grant* of *a.* 675 'Poddenhale,' Winchester. O.E. Poddantun, 'town of *Podda,*' in *Onom. Cf.* PODMORE (Eccleshall) *Dom.* Podemore ('moor'), and Poden (Worc.), 860 *chart.* Poddan-, -denho. See HOE.

POLURRIAN (the Lizard). Corn. *pol yrhian,* 'pool at the boundary,' or else, 'pool of St. *Urian.*' *Cf.* CENTURION'S COPSE. Others say fr. St. *Ruman* or *Ruan,* whose bones were translated to Tavistock Abbey in 960. St. Ruan's, Major and Minor, are near.

PONSONBY (Whitehaven). 'Dwelling of *Punzun,*' in Fr. *Ponson,* on record *c.* 1300, whilst another *Punzun* is named 1179-80 in *Pipe,* Yorks. See -by.

PONTEFRACT. *Sic* 1608, *c.* 1097 *Orderic* Fractus Pons, 1120 *Bull* Pontefractum, *c.* 1160 *John Hexh.* Pontifractus. L. *ponte fracto,* 'broken bridge,' a rare type of Eng. name, prob. referring to the bridge broken down by Wm. I., 1069. Remains of a Roman bridge were still visible in Leland's time. *Cf.* CATTERICK.

PONTESBURY (Shrewsbury). Prob. *O.E. Chron.* 661 Posentesbyrg, 'Burgh, castle of *Posente.*' See -bury.

PONTRILAS (Hereford). W. *pont tri glas,* 'bridge over three streams.' It is so still. Pontfadoc (Chesh.), is for Pont Madoc, 'son of Owain Gwynedd,' who, the natives say, discovered America ! *F* is aspirated *m.*

PONTYPOOL (Monmouth). As it stands, W. *pont y pwl,* 'bridge at the pool,' but commonly held to be *pont ap Howel,* 'Powell's bridge.'

PONTYPRIDD (Glamorgan). *c.* 1540 *Leland* Pont Rherhesh, W. *pont yr hesg,* 'bridge of the rushes.' But renamed *pont y pridd,* lit. ' bridge of clay,' for *pont yr hen dy pridd,* 'bridge of the old house of earth,' erected by Wm. Edwards, 1755.

POOLE. 1234 *Close R.* La Pole, *c.* 1450 *Fortescue* Polle havyn. O.E. *pól,* Corn. *pol,* 'a pool.' But POOL, W. Riding, is *Dom.* Pouele, which may be 'pool-nook.' See -hall.

POPLAR (London). *c.* 1350 Popler. There is no reason to doubt Dr. Woodward, writing in 1720, 'Popler or Poplar is so called from the multitude of poplar-trees (which love a moist soil) growing there in former times.' The Manor of Poplar belonged to Sir John de Pulteney, *temp.* Edw. III., which gives about the earliest mention of the name of the tree in England (see *Oxf. Dict.*), O.Fr. *poplier,* L. *populus.*

POPPLETON (York). *Dom.* Popletune, Popletunis, pl. for P. Upper and Nether. 'Poplar-tree town,' late O.E. *popul,* dial. *popple.* But Papplewick, Nottingham. *Dom.* Paplewic, is fr. O.E. *papol,* 'pebble.'

POR(T)CHESTER (Fareham). *c.* 150 *Ptolemy* Μέγας Λιμην, the Rom. Portus Magnus, 'great harbour,' *c.* 1170 *Wace* Porecester, *c.* 1205 *Layam.* Port-chæstre. L. *portus,* 'harbour,' and *castrum,* 'camp.' See CHESTER, and *cf.* PORTSMOUTH. Identification with Cair Peris in *Nennius* is very doubtful.

PORCUIL (Falmouth). Local form Perkil. Corn. *porth chil,* 'harbour on the neck of land,' which it is. *Chil* is same as G. *caol,* 'narrow, a strait, a kyle.'

PORINGLAND (Norwich). *Dom.* Porringelanda. *Porring* is an otherwise unknown patronymic.

PORLOCK (Somerset). 1052 *O.E. Chron.* Portlocan, 1275 Porlok. *Port-loca* is 'enclosed harbour,' *loca,* 'an enclosure.' *Cf.* MATLOCK.

PORTHCAWL (Glamorgan). W. *porth cawell,* 'harbour of the weir '; or 'of the hampers or baskets.' Corn. dial. *cawel, cowel,* ' a fish creel,' O.E. *cawl, ceawl,* ' a basket.' *Cf.* CALBOURNE.

PORTH GAVERNE, ISAAC, QUIN (Padstow). Corn. *porth,* ' harbour,' L. *portus,* ' of the goat,' *gavern,* ' of the corn,' *iz,* with its adj. *izick,* ' of corn,' and ' white,' *gwin.*

PORTHMEAR (Cornwall). Corn. = ' great harbour,' *Mear* is cognate with Eng. *more,* L. *major,* G. *mór,* as well as W. *mawr.*

PORTINSCALE (Keswick). *Old* Portingscale. Thought to be ' the harbour or ferry by the hut,' of the viking, O.N. *skali,* ' a shieling, a hut.'

PORTISHAM (Dorchester). *a.* 1250 *Owl and Night.* Porteshom. ' Home on the harbour.' See above and -ham.

PORTISHEAD (Bristol). Pron. Posset. ' Head, headland at the port or harbour.'

PORTLAND. *Sic a.* 1130 *Sim. Dur.*; *O.E. Chron.* 837 Port, v.r., Portlande—*i.e.,* ' land forming a harbour or shelter.'

PORT LLANW (S. Wales). Thought to be *c.* 150 *Ptolemy* Louentinon. Doubtful.

PORTREATH (Redruth). Corn. *porth treath,* ' harbour on the strand or sands.' *Cf.* PENTREATH.

PORTSKEWETH (Chepstow). 1065 *O.E. Chron.* Portascihð, *Dom.* Porteschiwet, *c.* 1130 *Lib. Land.* Porthisceuin, *a.* 1130 *Sim. Dur.* Portascith, *Gir. Camb.* Itin. Eskewin. Doubtful. Perh. W. *porth yscuit,* ' harbour at the shoulder.' But the W. name is said to be Porthiscoed, ? *ysgoad,* ' a thrusting aside.' See M'Clure, p. 300, *note.*

PORTSMOUTH. *O.E. Chron.* 501 refers to *Port,* and to a chief *Port* who landed here. *c.* 1097 *Orderic* Portesmude, 1203 Portesmuthe, 1213 Portesmue. Very likely it is simply L. *portus,* ' harbour,' but we have PORTINGTON (Yorks) *Dom.* Portiton,

-inton, which must be fr. a man *Port*. In 1160-1 *Pipe* Hants, we have Portesdon or PORTSDOWN.

POSTWICK (Norwich). 1452 Possewyk. Nothing likely in *Onom.* so prob. O.E. *post-wic*, ' house, dwelling with the posts.' But, POSTLIP (Gloster), *Dom.* Poteslepe, 1175 Postlepa, is prob. ' *Potta's* leap.' *Cf.* BIRDLIP.

POTTON (Sandy). *a.* 1130 Pottona. Possibly ' pot-town,' O.N. *pott-r*, ' a pot.' Perh. fr. a man *Pohta* or *Poto*, names in *Onom. Cf.* 1179-80 *Pipe*, Potton (Yorks), not in *Dom.*, but there we have POTTERTON, *Dom.*Potertun; this is as early as, or earlier than, any quot. for *potter*, in *Oxf. Dict.* POTTERSPURY (Stony Stratford) is, however, in 1229 simply Estpirie. See Paulerspury. POTTERNE (Wilts) is *Dom.* Poterne, where *erne* is certainly O.E. for ' house.'

POULTON LE FYLDE (Preston) and POULTON (Fairford and Birkenhead). Pr. P. *Dom.* Poltun, O.E. for ' village by the pool.' Fa. P. 1303 Polton.

POWICK (Worcester). *Chart.* Poincgwic, *Dom.* Poiwic, 1275 Poyswyke, *a.* 1300 Poywick. Poincg- is clearly a patronymic, fr. *Po* or *Poha*, see -ing; so this is ' dwelling-place of Poha's descendants.' See -wick.

POWYS (this includes Flint, Montgomery, Merioneth), also POWYS CAST. (Welshpool). *c.* 1200 *Gir. Camb.* Powisia, *Ann. Camb.* 828 Poywis, 1297 Powys. W. *powys*, ' a state of rest.'

POYNINGS (Hurstpierpoint, Sussex). *Dom.* Poninges. A patronymic. Nothing in *Onom.* POYNTON (Stockport) is *Dom.* Pontone; so evidently *Pon* was a man's name.

PRAZE (Camborne). Corn. *pras*, L. *pratum*, ' a meadow.'

PREES (Whitchurch) and PREESE (Lytham). Ly. P. *Dom.* Pres. W. *prys, pres*, ' copse, shrubs.' *Cf.* DUMFRIES (Sc.). PREESALL (Preston) is *Dom.* Pressouede, where the ending is doubtful; prob. it is for ' wood,' and so a tautology. Also see -hall.

PRENDERGAST (Haverford W.). *Sic* 1603 *Owen*. The name is also found with same spelling in Berwicksh., 1100 Prenegest, 1451 Prendregest, also Plenderguest; whilst in Roxburghsh. is Plenderleith, 1587 Prenderleith. A puzzling name. The first part may be for O.W. *premter*, found in Ir. as *prenter*, ' a presbyter, a priest,' and the second may be, W. *gest, cest*, ' a deep glen between two hills.' Fris. *gaast*, ' a morass,' seems also possible.

PRESCOT. ' The cot or cottage of the priest.' O.E. *préost*, O.N. *prest-r*.

PRESTEIGN (Radnor) and PRESTON (19 in *P.G.*). *Dom.* Yorks, Bucks, and Salop, Prestone, -tun; *ib.* Warwk., Prestetone. All = ' priest's town.' In W. Presteign is Llanandras or ' church of St. Andrew.'

PRESTWICH (Manchester). 1301 Prestwyche. O.E. *préost-wíc*, 'priest's dwelling.' *Cf.* PRESTWICK (Sc.) and Prestwood (Stourbridge), *a.* 1200 Prestewude; also Prestbury (Cheltenham), *Bede* Preosdabyrig, *Dom.* Presteberie. See -bury.

PRICKWILLOW (Ely). Called fr. a willow, used for making *pricks* or skewers. *Cf.* the 'spindle-tree.'

PRINCE- or PRINSTHORPE (Rugby). *a.* 1300 Prenesthorpe. 'Village of *Preon*'—i.e., 'the pin' or 'brooch,' Sc. *preen.* *Cf.* Preen (Salop).

PRIORS HEYS (Tarvin, Cheshire). An 'extra-parochial liberty' of 1,100 acres, with houses. See *Oxf. Dict.* hay sb², O.E. *hege*, 3 *heie*, 4-7 *hey(e)*, 'a hedge.'

PRIVETT (Alton). Prob. *O.E. Chron.* 755 Pryfetes floda. Prob. a personal name of unknown origin. The shrub *privet* is not surely known in Eng. *a.* 1542, and its etymology is very doubtful. Can Pryfet be for *prefect*, L. *præfectus?*

PRUDHOE or -HOW (Bywell, Northumbld). *c.* 1175 *Fantosme* Prudhame (= ham), *a.* 1200 Prudchou. Prob. 'Prud's height.' There is one *Prud* in *Onom.* in Cornwall, while 'proud' (O.E. *prút, prúd*) is not used *re* things till *c.* 1290. See HOE.

PUCKERIDGE (Ware). This is a name of the night-jar. See *Oxf. Dict.* But the place-name is prob. '*Pucca*'s ridge.' *Cf.* Pouke Hill and Powke Lane (Staffs.), Puckington (Ilminster) and a 'Pokebrook,' 1274 in Lincs. Old forms needed. They may all come fr. *puck* or *pook*, O.E. *púca*, O.N. *púki*, 'a sprite, demon, fairy.' See *Oxf. Dict., puck* sb.¹

PUCKLECHURCH (Bristol). 946 *O.E. Chron.* Puc(e)lan cyrcan, *Dom.* Pulcrecerce, *Sim. Dur.* ann. 946, Puclecirce. O.E. for 'church of the goblin,' *púcel*, prob. connected with *puck*, 'a fairy.' *Cf.* POCKLINGTON and Puckle- or Picklenash (Gloster), 'fairies' ashtree.' Gloster also has a PUCKSHOLE.

PUDSEY (Leeds). *Dom.* Podechesaie, 1183 Puteaco, 1203 Pudeckshee, 1213 Picteaceo. 'Isle of *Podeca*' (? = *Bodeca*, 1 in *Onom.*). See -ey. 'Poody-Crofte' *sic* 1423 *Coventry Leet Bk.*, seems to be fr. the same name. It is not in Duignan.

PULLOXHILL (Beds). *c.* 1200 Polochessele. 'Hill of *Poloc*.' This can hardly be the same name as POLLOCK (Renfrewsh.), 1158 Pollock, Pullock, though it may. The -ele may be for *hale*, 'nook'; see -hall; or -sele may be O.E. *sele*, 'a hall, a house.'

PUNCKNOLL (Dorchester). 'Knoll, hillock of *Punt*,' 1 in *Onom.*, short form of *Puntel.* *Cf.* 940 *chart.* Punteles treow (Dorset).

PUNSBORNE (Hatfield). Not in *Dom.*, *c.* 1495 Pamsborow. It must be fr. the same name as Panshanger, also in Herts, no old forms, 'wooded slope of *Pan*.' The ending -borne is -bourne, 'brook,' while -borow is -burgh or -boro', *q.v.* PUNCHESTON (Letterston,

Pembk.) is 1603 *Owen* Pontchardston, a name not in *Onom.;* but *Punchard* is common in medieval France.

PURBECK. 1205 Purbice, 1410 Purbrick. ' Brook of the ram, or wether lamb,' O.E. *pur* found only in *pur lamb;* or ' of the snipe or bittern,' also O.E. *pur.* *Cf.* PURFLEET and PURTON, and see -beck.

PURFLEET (Essex). O.E. *pur-fléot,* ' snipe or bittern creek or inlet.' *Cf.* FLEETWOOD.

PURLEIGH (Maldon) and PURLEY (Reading and Surrey). Read. P. *Dom.* Porlei, *a.* 1290 Purle. Ma. P. prob. 998 *chart.* Purlea. Thought by Skeat to be, like PURTON, ' pear-tree meadow '; but old forms are against this, and prob. these names are to be taken as in PURBECK.

PURSTON (Pontefract). *Dom.* Prestun, and so = PRESTON. But PUR-SHALL, (Bromsgrove) is *a.* 1300 Pershull, ' hill of *Piers,*' *Cf.* ' Piers Plowman.'

PURTON (Swindon and Berkeley). Sw. P. 796 *chart.* Perytun, Puritun, *later* Pyryton, pear-tree town.' O.E. *pirige,* ' pear-tree,' *peru,* ' a pear.' *Cf.* PAULERSPURY.

PUSEY (Berks). *a.* 900 *Ælfred's Will* Pefesigge, *later* Peuesige; 1066-87 *Chron. Abingdon,* Pusie, *Dom.* Pesei, *a.* 1290 Pesey. O.E. *Pefes -iȝe,* ' isle of Pefi,' an unknown man. *Cf.* PEWSEY.

PUTLOE (Standish). *a.* 1200 Puthleleye, 1274 Potteley; PUTNEY (London) *old* Putton -heath; and PUTTENHAM (Guildford). All fr. the common O.E. name *Put(t)a, -an.* In the first case -ley, ' meadow,' has varied with -loe or -low, ' burial mound.'

PWLLHELI. Pron. pool-thelly. W. for ' brine pool.' *Cf.* Treheli, ' house of brine,' ' salt-house,' in Carnarvon also.

PWLL CROCHAN (Fishguard), 1377 Porttraghan, *Tax. Eccl.* Port-crachan, and PWLL Y CROCHAN (Colwyn Bay). Prob. not ' pool of the pot ' for drawing water, or ' like a cauldron,' same as Eng. *crock;* but fr. W. *clochan,* ' a little bell '; the liquids *l* and *r* easily interchange. There is another Pwll Crochan, N. of Llanrian.

PYTCHLEY (Kettering). *Dom.* Pihteslea, ' meadow of *Piht,*' or ' *Peoht.*' See -ley.

QUADRING (Spalding). *a.* 1100 Quadaveringge. Seemingly a patronymic; possibly fr. *Wadbeorht* or *Vadipert,* or fr. *Wad-weard,* names in *Onom.* But this is quite uncertain. See -ing.

QUANTOCKS (Somerset) and EAST QUANTOXHEAD. *Chart.* attrib. to 681 Cantuc-uudu (' wood '). *Dom.* Cantocheheve' (' head,' O.E. *heafod*). W. *cant uch,* ' upper, higher circle.' W. *uch* is same root as OCHILS (Sc.) and G. *uachdar,* ' the top, upper part,' so common in Sc. place-names as Auchter-.

QUARLTON (Bolton). 1292 Quelton. Prob. 'town of the quarry,'
still in north dial. *quarrel*, O.Fr. *quarriere*. See *Oxf. Dict.* s.v.
quarrel and *quarry* sbs.[2] We find in 1298 'Thomas de Querle,'
now Quarrell (Kinnaird, Stirlingsh.).

QUARNFORD (Buxton). 1227 Querneford. 'Ford of the quern'
or 'handmill,' O.E. *cweorn, cwyrn. Cf.* QUARNDON (Derby),
'hill like a quern,' Quernhowe (Yorks) and QUORN. However, Baddeley thinks the Querns (Cirencester) corrup. of
Crundles, *sic* 1286, see CRUNDALE.

QUARRINGTON (Coxhoe, Durham). *a.* 1130 *Sim. Dur.* Queorming-
tun, 1183 Querindune, Queringdona. Seemingly patronymic,
fr. O.E. *cweorn,* 'a quern, a handmill.'

QUATBRIDGE (Bridgenorth). 895 *O.E. Chron.* Cwatbrýcge; *Dom.*
Quatford and Quatone, *c.* 1097 *Orderic* Quatfort now Quatford
Castle; *c.* 1120 *Hen. Hunt.* Quadruge, Quathruge. Some think
fr. O.W. *coit,* W. *coed,* 'a wood,' which is not very likely. There
is an obscure *quat,* 'a pimple, a boil,' found fr. 1579. The
Quat- is quite doubtful. *Cf.* QUOTHQUHAN (Sc.).

QUEDGELEY (Gloster). *c.* 1142 Quedesley, *c.* 1155 Quedesleg;
also perh. 1136 Quadresse. Prob. 'mead of (an unrecorded)
Cwed.' Baddeley says, *cf.* Quither (Tavistock), 1286 Quedre;
but it is prob. Kelt. *Cf.* W. *cwthr,* 'excretory orifice, anus.'

QUEENBOROUGH (Chatham). *c.* 1460 Queneborow. Called after
Philippa, Queen of Edward III., who d. in 1369. Edward built
a castle here. See -burgh.

QUEEN'S CAMEL (Cadbury, Somerset). See CAMEL.

QUEMERFORD (Calne). Thought to be Kelt. *cumber,* 'confluence.'
Cf. the Breton Quimper and COMBERBACH.

QUINTON (Birmingham and Gloster). Bi. Q. 840 *chart.* Cwentune,
1275 Quintone. Gl. Q. 848 *chart.* Cwentone, *Dom.* Quenintune.
O.E. *cwœn, cwén(n), tun,* 'woman's' or 'queen's village.'
This is the same name as QUEMINGTON, also in Gloster, *Dom.*
Quenintone.

QUOISLEY MERE (Cheshire). Perh. 'meadow of the heifer or
quey,' 6-9 *quoy,* only in North dial.; fr. O.N. *kvíga,* 'a heifer.'

QUORN (Loughborough). See QUARNFORD.

QUY (Cambs). *c.* 1080 *Inquis. Cambs.* Coeie, Choeie, *Dom.* Coeia,
1210 Cueye, 1261 Queye, 1272 Coweye, Cowye, O.E. *cu -ege,*
'cow island.' *Cf.* SHEPPEY, and *quey* (Sc.) for 'a heifer, a
young cow,' O.N. *kvíga,* also *Dom.* Devon, Coie. See -ey.

RABY (Cheshire and Darlington). Ches. R. *Dom.* Rabie. Dar. R.
a. 1130 *Sim. Dur.* Rabi, -by; this might be O.N. for 'dwelling
made with poles or stakes,' *rá;* but this last also means 'a roe-
deer.' See -by.

RADCLIFFE (4 at least). Devon R. *Exon*. *Dom*. Radcliva. Manchester R. 1343 Radclive, -cliffe. Also *Dom*. Bucks Radeclive. ' Red cliff,' O.E. *réad* (3 *ræd*) *clif*. *Cf*. Ratcliffe-upon-Soar, *Dom*. Radeclive. RADBROOK (For. of Dean), is 1204 Redebroc.

RADFIELD (Cambs). *c*. 1080 *Inquis*. *Camb*. Radefelde, Radesfeld, *Dom*. Radefelle, 1284 Radefeld, 1302 Radfelde. Prob. ' *Ræda*'s field '; though here and in other names in Rad-, as Skeat admits, an origin fr. O.E. *réad*, 3 *ræd*, ' red,' is always possible. *Cf*. 1158-9 *Pipe* Rademora (Staffs). RADHOLME (Yorks), is *Dom*. Radun, an old loc. ' on the roads,' O.E. *rad*. See -ham with which -holme often interchanges.

RADFORD (Wrcstrsh. and Leamington). Wor. R. 1275 Radeford. Le R. *Dom*. Redeford, *a*. 1189 Radeford. Perh. ' red, reddish ford,' O.E. *réad*, 3 *ræd*, ' red '; but perh., as in Radbourne, ' reedy ford '; O.E. *hréod*, (*h*) *réad*, ' a reed.' Also *cf*. two next. RADHAM (Gloster) is 955 *chart*. Hreodham.

RADLETT (Herts). No old forms. Skeat thinks, O.E. *rad* (*ge*) *lœt*, ' road meeting-point.' But *Dom*. Herts has Radeuuelle, which is prob. ' well of *Rada*.' *Cf*. next; and 1161-2 *Pipe* Raden -heoh', ? ' height of *Rada*,' Bucks and Beds.

RADLEY (Abingdon). *a*. 1290 Radeley, *c*. 1520 Raydeley. Prob. ' red meadow,' as in RADCLIFFE; see -ley. But Skeat compares *B.C.S*. iii. 85 ' Radeleage ' (Wilts), which he derives fr. *Rada* or *Ræda*, a pet form of one of the many names in Ræd-; whilst Radbourne (Southam.), is 980 *chart*. Hreodburne or ' reedy brook.'

RADNOR (Wales, and old hamlet near Congleton). *Dom*. Raddrenore (prob. the central *r* is an error). O.E. *raden ora*, ' edge of the road or ride '; prob. in the first case the Rom. road which ran fr. Wroxeter to Abergavenny and Cærleon. The W. name is Maesyfed or -hyfed, prob. for *hyfaidd*, ' field of the dauntless one.'

RADSTOCK (Bath). Looks like O.E. *rád -stoc*, ' place on the road.' *Cf*. STOKE. But it may be fr. a man, as in next. *Cf*. too Radway, Banbury, *Dom*. Rad- Rodeweie, which Duignan thinks ' red way,' because the soil here is reddish marl.

RADSTON (Northants). *c*. 1275 Radistone; also Rodeston. Prob. ' town of *Rada* or *Rodo*,' names in *Onom*. There is also a ' Radeston,' ? Salop, *c*. 1205 in *Layam*. But RADWICK (Gloster) is *c*. 955 *chart*. Hreodwica, ' reed-built ' or ' thatched dwelling.'

RAINFORD and RAINHILL (St. Helens). 1189-98 Raineford, 1202 Reineford; 1190 Raynhull, 1246-56 Reynhill, 1382 Raynhull. Fr. some man with a name in Rægen- or Regen-. They are very common, see *Onom*.—Regenbeald, Regenhild, etc. Rainors (Cumbld.) is said to have been formerly pron. Renneray, which is pure N. See -ay. RAINES BROOK (Warwksh.), *a*. 1200 Reynesbroc, is known to be fr. *Rainald*, the *Dom*. tenant of the manor.

RAINHAM (Chatham). 811 Roegingaham. Evidently a patronymic, fr. *Rœgen* or *Regen*, a name generally found in one of its numerous combinations, *Regenburh, -frith, -heard*, etc. RAINTON Thirsk, *Dom.* Rainincton 1183 Rayntona, will have a similar origin; only here it is a patronymic. *Dom.* also calls it Raininge-wat, where -wat will be O.E. *wœd*, 'ford.' Cf. WATH.

RAISTHORPE (Yorks). *Dom.* Redrestorp. '*Rether*'s place.' There is one *Regðer* and one *Ratherus* in *Onom.* See -thorpe.

RAKE (East Liss), RAKE END, and the RAKES (Staffs). O.N. *rák*, 'a stripe, streak,' Norw. dial. *raak*, 'footpath,' found in 14th cny. Eng. as *rake*, 'a way, a (rough) path'; still dial. and Sc.

RAMPTON (Cambridge). c. 1080 *Inquis. Camb.* Ramtune, *Dom.* Rantone, 1210 Ramptone. 'Village of rams,' O.E. *ramm.* Cf. FOXTON and SHEPTON.

RAMSBOTTOM (Manchester). A 'bottom,' O.E. *botm*, north. E. *bodome*, is 'a valley, a fertile valley.' Cf. BODDAM (Sc.) and STARBOTTOM. As to the Ram- *cf.* next and Ramsley (Salop), *a.* 1100 Hremesleage, *Dom.* Rameslege, '*Hrœm*'s or *Ram*'s lea.'

RAMSBURY (Hungerford). c. 988 *chart.* Hremnesburg, c. 1097 *Flor. W.* Reamnesbyrig. 'Town of *Ramni*,' a Saxon name found also in RAMSHORN (Sc.). The root is O.E. *hremn*, 'raven.' *Cf.* next, and 1179-80 *Pipe* Rammesberia (Yorks).

RAMSDEN (Charlbury, Oxfd). O.E. *chart.* Remnesdún. 'Hill of *Remni*,' see above. Perh. it is c. 1450 *Oseney Reg.* 134 Ramme dune. But Ramsden Heath, Billericay, is *Dom.* Ramesdana, 'Dean, valley of *Ramni*.' See -den.

RAMSEY (Hunts). *K.C.D.* iv. 300 Hrames ege, *Dom.* Ramesy, c. 1097 *Flor. W.* Ramesia. c. 1130 *Eadmer* Rammesei, *a.* 1150 *chart.* Ramesige. Not orig. 'isle of rams,' O.E. *ram(m)*, but 'isle of *Hrœm*' or 'the Raven,' O.E. *hrœm*, var. of *hrœmn, hrafn*, 'raven.' *Cf.* Hremmesden, now, says Kemble, Ramsdean (Hants).

RAMSGATE. c. 1540 Ramesgate, 'Road,' O.E. *geat*, 'of *Ram*,' a fairly common name. *Cf.* 940 *chart.* Hremnes geat (Wilts), *B.C.S.* 356 Rames cumb, near Hallow on Severn, and RAMSDEN.

RANBY (Lincoln and Retford). Both *Dom.* Randebi, '*Rand*'s dwelling.' *Cf.* RANWORTH (Norwich), O.E. *chart.* Randworth. See -by and -worth. But all names in Rand-, like these and RANDWICK (Stroud), 1120 Randwyke (O.E. *wíc* 'dwelling'), may be fr. O.E. *rand, rond*, 'brink, bank,' O.N. *rönd*, 'shield rim, stripe,' Sw. and Dan. *rand*, 'rim, border,' also in Du., seen in the famous Rand (Johannesburg). *Cf. Dom.* Lincs, Rande.

RAPES of Sussex. *Dom.* In Rap de Hastinges. One of six districts into which Sussex is divided. *Oxf. Dict.* says *rape* may mean 'land measured by the rope,' O.E. *ráp*, O.N. *reip* ; but that there is no positive proof. Yet *cf. Orderic* 678 *c.*, Omnes carucatas quas Angli hidas vocant funiculo [Randolf Flambard] mensus est et descripsit. *Cf.* ROPE.

RASKELF (Easingwold). *Dom.* Raschel. O.E. *rá-scelfe,* ' roe-deer's shelf of rock.'

RASTRICK (Brighouse). *Dom.* Rastric. O.E. *rœst hryeg,* O.N. *rast hrygg-r,* ' rest ' or ' resting ridge.'

RATHMELL (Settle). *Dom.* Rodemele. ' Sand-dune of the rood,' or ' cross,' O.E. *ród,* with the North. *a.* A ' mell ' is O.N. *mel-r;* see MEOLE.

RATLEY (Banbury). *Dom.* Rotelei, *a.* 1200 Rottelei, *a.* 1300 Rotley. ' Good, excellent meadow,' O.E. *rót;* or fr. *rót,* ' a root, an edible root.' See -ley.

RATTLESDEN (Bury St. E.). 1161-2 *Pipe* Radleston, *c.* 1420 *Lydgate* Ratlysdene. Older forms needed. ' Wooded valley of.' ? *Rœdweald* var. *Radoald, Rœdwealh* var. *Ratuvalah,* or *Rœdwulf* var. *Rathwulf* or *Radulf,* all forms in *Onom.* See -den and -ton.

RAUGHTON HEAD (Dalston, Cumbld.). 1189 Rachton. Doubtful; no likely name in *Onom.*, and it is phonetically difficult to derive fr. *rache,* O.E. *rœcc,* 3-6 *racch,* 4-5 *rach,* ' a hunting-dog '; so prob. named fr. some unknown man. See -ton.

RAVENGLASS (S. Cumbld.). Prob. W. *yr afon glas,* ' the greenish or bluish river,' *afon* pron. as in Stratford on Avon. All other explanations seem to break down. But we have 1189 *Pipe* ' Ravenewich,' (Cumbld.), dwelling of *Raven* ' or ' *Hrafn.*' See next.

RAVENINGHAM (Norwich). *a.* 1300 *Eccleston* Ravingham. A patronymic. Prob. most names in Raven-, like RAVENSTONE (Bucks), etc., come fr. a man, as in Hrafnsaust and Hrafnseyri (Iceland), known to be called fr. a settler. See, too, RAMSBURY, RAMSEY, and RENHOLD, and *cf.* 1189 *Pipe* ' Ravenewich ' (Cumbld.).

RAVENSTHORPE (Dewsbury and Northmpton). De. R. *Dom.* Rag(h)enel -torp. No. R. *Grant of* 664 Ragenildetorp. ' Village of *Ragenald*' or *Regenweald*, mod. *Reginald.* Ragh- has become Raw- and then Rav-. There is also in N. Yorks a RAVENTHORP, *Dom.* Ravenetorp, fr. a man *Raven.* See above, and see -thorpe.

RAVENSTONE (Olney and Ashby de la Z.). Oln. R. *Dom.* Raveneston. The man ' *Raven*'s village '; and RAVENSWORTH (Richmond, Yorks, and Chester-le-Street). Ri. R. *Dom.* Raveneswet. Ch. R., *a.* 1130 *Sim. Dur.* Raveneswurthe. The man ' *Raven*'s farm.' See above and -worth.

RAWDON (Leeds). *Dom.* Rodum, -un. Old loc. ' at the roods ' or ' crosses.' But W. and H. derive RAWCLIFF and -FOLD (Lancs), fr. O.N. *rauð-r,* ' red.'

RAWMARSH (Rotherham). *Dom.* Rodemesc (*for* -mersc), 1206
Rumareis. Prob. ' rough marsh,' O.E. *ruw,* 3 *ru,* 3-5 *rowe,* now
row, var. of *rough.* *Dom.*'s Rode- may be an error; or fr. a man
Roda, 2 in *Onom.* *Marsh* is O.E. *mersc, mœrsc,* but *-mareis* is
rather the now almost obs. *marish,* O.F. *marais, -eis,* as in
BEAUMARIS.

RAWNSLEY (Hednesford). Duignan says modern, and prob. named
fr. Rawnpike Oak half a mile away. See RIVINGTON PIKE.

RAWTENSTALL (Rossendale). *Sic* 1585, but 1465 Rowtanstall.
It was on a ' Rowtan clough,' and so prob. means ' roaring,
noisy, boisterously windy place.' It is *Oxf. Dict.*'s *rout* vb[2]
fr. O.N. *rjóta,* N. *ruta,* ' to roar,' in Eng. 3 *rute,* 4 *route, rowte.*
Cognate with *rout* vb[3], O.N. *rauta,* Sw. *röta,* ' to bellow or roar.'
1513 *Douglas* speaks of ' rowtand Caribdis,' and ' a haly routand
well,' while Carlyle in his *Reminiscences* speaks of ' a rowting
Brig.' It is possible, however, that the first part is the name
Hrothwine or *Rothin,* of whom there are 3 in *Onom.*; -stall is
O.E. *steall, stœl,* ' place, stable.' *Cf.* Rowten or Routen Cave
(Ingleboro'), and Ratten, *older* Routand Clough (Thieveley Pike).

RAYLEIGH (Essex). Perh. ' meadow on the stream.' Ray or
Rea is a frequent name for ' a small river,' the *r* coming on by
attraction fr. the preceding O.E. art.—' *on thœre éa,*' ' on the
river.' *Cf.* NECHELLS, 1161-2 *Pipe* Raelega (Devon), and RYE.
But Sir H. Maxwell thinks = Raelees (Selkirk), O.E. *rá-leáh,*
' roe meadow.' This is confirmed by Raygill, Craven, *Dom.*
Roghil. See -gill, ' ravine.'

REACH (Swaffham, Cambs). 1279 Reche, a ' reach ' or extension
of land, O.E. *rœcan,* ' to reach.' The earliest quot. for the sb.
in *Oxf. Dict.* is 1536, Limehowse Reche.

READING. Pron. Redding. 871 *O.E. Chron.* Readingas, 1006 *ib.*
Rædingan (late dat. pl.), *Dom.* Redinges, 1254 *chart.* Rading.
Patronymic. ' Home of the descendants of *Réada,*' or the Red,
now found spelt as a surname Reid, or Reade.

RECULVER (N. Kent). *c.* 410 *Not. Dign.* Regulbi, *a.* 716 *chart.*
Ræulf, *Bede* Racuulfe, Raculph. *O.E. Chron.* 679, Ra-, Reculf'
811 *chart.* Reacolvensa ecclesia, 1241 Racolor; also Raculfs
Cestre, where *Raculf* is imagined to be a man's name. The root
is unknown, but the present form has been influenced by O.E.
culfre, culfer, ' a culver dove or wood-pigeon.'

REDANNICK (the Lizard). Corn. = ' place of ferns.' *Cf.* W. *rhedyn*
Ir. *raithneach,* G. *raineach,* ' fern.' The -ick is the same ending
as Ir. and G. -ach, ' place of,' or ' abounding in.' *Cf.* Trelissick,
etc.

REDBRIDGE (Southampton). Perh. *Bede* iv. 16. ' A place called
Hreutford, v.r. Reodford '—*i.e.,* ' ford with reeds '; but *cf.*
RETFORD.

REDCAR (Whitby). Not in *Dom.* 1179-80 Redkier. ' Red rock,' O.E. *carr*, cognate with or derived fr. Keltic *car*, ' a rock.' See CARR ROCKS (Sc.).

REDCLIFFE (Bristol). *Dom.* Redeclive. O.E. for ' red cliff.' *Cf.* CLEVELAND. There is another ' Redeclive ' in Cheshire *Dom.*

REDDITCH. (843 *chart.* in readan sloe, ' to the red slough '). 1300 Redediche, 1642 Red ditch, Reddiche, ' red ditch '; but REDDISH (Stockport) is 1296-97 Radish, which is quite doubtful. The vegetable *radish* is found in O.E. as *redic*, 3 *redich*, 5 *radish*.

REDESDALE (Mid-Northumbld.). 1421 Redes-, Rydes-, Ridesdale, *a.* 1600 Risdale. On R. *Rede,* which may be O.E. *hreut, hréod,* or *réad,* 4-5 *red,* ' a reed.'

REDMARLEY D'ABITOT (Newent). 963 *chart.* Reode mære leage, and 978 *ib.* Rydem-, *Dom.* Redmerleie, Ridmerlege, 1275 Rudmereley, Redmereligh, Rudmareligh. Prob. O.E. *hréod mere ¹eah,* ' reedy lake meadow'; see -ley. But it may be as in ROD-MARTON. *Urse d'Abitot* held lands here under the Bps. of Worcester, in *Dom.*'s time.

REDMIRE (Yorks). *Dom.* Ridemare, Rotmare. Prob. ' reedy lake,' O.E. *hréod, réad,* ' a reed,' and *mere.* *Mire* is O.N. *mýr-r,* ' swamp, bog,' and not found in Eng. *a.* 1300. *Cf.* above.

REDNAL (Bromsgrove). 730 *chart.* Wreodan hale, 1275 Wredin-hale. ' Nook of *Wreoda,*' not in *Onom.* See -hall.

RED PIKE (Wastwater). 1322 le Rede Pike. Pike, *Oxf. Dict.* sb², is the North. Eng. name for a pointed or peaked hill or mountain, and is chiefly found in Nthn. Lancashire, Westmorland, Cumberland, and the Sc. borders. The earliest case cited is *c.* 1250 *Lanc. Charters,* ' Ad Winterhold pike.' The furthest S. cases seem to be Thieveley Pike, Rossendale, Rivington Pike, Mid-Lancs, and Backden, Haw, and Pinnar Pikes in Yorks. The range is much the same as the kindred *fell,* and confirms the suggested deriv. fr. N. or West N. dial. *pik,* '.a pointed mountain,' *piktind,* ' a peaked summit.' There is one curiously corrupted example in Northbld., WANSBECK, which is orig. Wannys pike.

REDRUTH (Cornwall). Corn. *rhe Druth,* ' stream, swift current of the Druids.'

RED SWIRE (Nthbld.). *c.* 1375 Red Swyre, O.E. *swíra,* 'neck, pass.' *Cf.* MANOR SWARE (Sc.).

REEDHAM (Norfolk). *c.* 1300 Redhamme, 1424 Redeham, 1460 Redham, ' enclosure,' O.E. *hamm,* ' among the reeds.' See REDESDALE, and -ham.

REEPHAM (Lincoln). *a.* 1100 *chart.* (dated 664). Refham. Perh. ' home on the rock.' O.N. *rif,* ' a rock, a reef.' Change fr. *f* to *p* is very rare. It may be fr. *Ræfen,* a name 3 times in *Onom.*

REETH (Richmond, Yorks). *Dom.* Rie. O.E. *rið, riðe,* ' a stream.' *Cf.* RYE.

REIGATE. 1199 Regat, *later* Reygate. ' Gate, opening (O.E. *geat,* 2-6 *gat*) on the ridge,' O.E. *hrycg,* 4 *reg,* 4-5 *regge,* 5 *ryge.* Its pre-Conquest name was Cherchefelle, ' church-field.'

REIGHTON (Bridlington). *Dom.* Rictone. Prob. ' town of *Rica,*' one in *Onom.*

REMENHAM (Henley). *Dom.* Rameham, *a.* 1290 Remeham, 1316 Remenham. Prob. ' home of the Raven.' O.E. *hræfn,* late O.E. *hræmn, hremn,* here a man's name. *Cf.* RAMSBURY.

REMPSTONE (Loughboro'). *Dom.* Repestone, *c.* 1180 *chart.* Rempeston. Prob. fr. some unknown man. The nearest in *Onom.* are *Hrambertus* and *Hramfridus.* Mutschmann prefers *Hrafn* or *Raven,* which is at least possible.

RENDLESHAM (Suffolk). *Bede* iii. 22 Rendlaesham, id est Rendili mansio, 1459 Rendelesham. ' Home of *Rendil.*' But REND-COMB, Cirencester, *Dom.* Rindcumbe, perh. contains an old river-name. See -combe.

RENHOLD (Bedford). *Old* Ren-, Ranhale (see -hall); but *Abbey chart.* Ravenshold, ' hold, fort of a man *Raven* or *Hremn.*' *Cf.* REMENHAM. A man *Rauan or Raven* is found in *Dom.* at Beeston, 6 mls. to S.E.

RENNINGTON (Alnwick). *a.* 1130 *Sim. Dur.* Reiningtun. ' Town of the descendants of ? *Hranig.*' See *Onom.,* and -ing.

REPTON (Derby). 874 *O.E. Chron.* Hreopodune. Prob. fr. some unknown man, ' *Hreopa*'s hill.' *Cf. B.C.S.* 216 Hroppan broc.

RESTORMEL (Cornwall). *Old* Lestormel. All the liquids may interchange. *Corn.* = ' court of *Tormel.*' *Cf.* Listewdrig, called after the king who killed St. Gwynear.

RETFORD. *Sic* 1225, but *Dom.* Redforde, ' red ford.' Perh. *Bede* iv. 16 Hreutford, Hreudford, ' reedy ford.' *Cf.* REDBRIDGE.

RETTENDON (Chelmsford). ? 1298 Johannes de Ratingden. Prob. ' hill, fort, O.E. *dún,* of *Reathun* or *Rethhun,*' in *Onom.*

REVESBY (Boston). 1156 *Pipe* Reuesbi, *c.* 1275 Righesbey, 1498 Resbie. ' Dwelling of *Rewe,*' one in *Onom.* See -by.

REYNOLDSTON (Glamorgan). *Reynold* is the common O.E. *Regenhild* or -*weald.* *Cf.* RAVENSTHORPE.

RHAYADER (Radnor). W. *rhaiadr Gwy,* ' waterfall on the Wye.'

RHIWLAS (Bangor and Herefordsh.). W. *rhiw glas,* ' green slope.'

RHOS (Denbigh and Pembrksh.). Per. R. now pron. Roose. *c.* 1190 *Gir. Camb.* and 1297 Ros, 1603 Rose. W. *rhos,* Corn. *ros,* ' a dry meadow, a moor, heath.' *Cf.* ROOSE and ROSS.

RHOSCROWTHER (Pembroke). 1324 Restrouthur, *Tax. Eccl.* Rostruther; also Rustruthur, Ruscrouthur, Rescorthurg, 1594

Rosgrothor. W. *rhos* is 'moor.' See above. The second part is doubtful. The early forms remind of ANSTRUTHER (Sc.), *c.* 1205 Anestrothir, 1231 Anstrother, fr. G. *srathair,* ' a cart-saddle,' also ' a swamp, a bog.' The latter sense is found in Eng. dial.

RHUDDLAN (Flints and Cardigan). Flint R. 1063 *O.E. Chron.* Rudelan. *Dom.* Roelent. *a.* 1130 *Sim. Dur.* Rudelant. W. *rhudd llan,* ' red enclosure ' or ' church '; or more prob. *rhydd y llan,* ' ford by the church.'

RHYD ORDDWY (Rhyl). W. = ' ford of the *Ordwi,*' or ' Ordovices,' a tribe whose name is derived from O.W. *ord,* ' a hammer.' *Cf.* DINORWIG.

RHYD-Y-GROES (Upton-on-Severn). In *Drayton* Crossford. W. = ' ford of the cross,' W. *croes.* It was the scene of one of Gruffydd's battles in 1039; and it still retains its old name.

RHYFONIOG (Denbigh). *Ann. Cambr.* 816 Roweynauc. Said to have been given to *Rhufawn,* son of Cunedda Wledig, for his gallantry in driving the Picts out of N. Wales. The -iog seems to be here simply a suffix of place; whilst *Rhufawn* is thought to be the W. form of *Romanus.*

RHYL. Either W. *yr hal* or *haleg,* ' the salt marsh,' or *yr hel*(*a*), ' the hunting-ground ' (of Rhuddlan).

RIBBLE R. (Preston). *c.* 150 *Ptolemy* Belisama, ' most warlike one,' another case of river-worship. The Beli- is of course the same root as L. *bellum,* ' war.' *Ptol.*'s river may be the Mersey. *c.* 709 *Eddi* Rippel, *Dom.* Ribel, *a.* 1100 Ribbel. The first part may be W. *rhe,* ' swift motion or current,' and the second is as in Beli-sama. The Eng. *ripple* is onomatopoeic and quite recent. *Cf.* RIPPLE.

RIBCHESTER (Preston). Perh. *Not. Dign.* Bremetonaci. *Dom.* Ribelcastre. ' Camp on the RIBBLE.' See -chester.

RIBSTON (Wetherby). *Sic* 1527, but *Dom* Ripestan, 1202 Ribbestain, ' Stone of *Ribba,*' or ' *Rippa,*' only the latter in *Onom.* See -ton. But Ribbesford, Bewdley, is 1023 *chart.* Ribbedford, *a.* 1100 Ribetforde, where the meaning of the first part is quite unknown. It may be a man's name.

RICCAL (Selby). *Dom.* and *c.* 1097 *Flor.* W. Richale—*i.e.,* ' nook of *Ricca.*' *Cf. K.C.D.* 713 Rican forda; and see -hall.

RICHBOROUGH (Thanet). *a.* 65 *Lucan* Rutupina litora, *c.* 100 *Juvenal* Rutupinus fundus, *c.* 150 *Ptolemy* Ρουτούπιαι, *Bede,* ' The city of Rutubi Portus, by the English corrupted into Reptacestir; *c.* 1550 Leland *Itin.* Ratesburgh, 1758 *Thorn.* Retesburgh. ' Burgh, fort or camp or harbour (*portus*) of *Rutub,*' an unknown man.

RICHMOND (Yorks and Surrey). Yor. R. (*Dom.* Hindrelache). *a.* 1130 *Sim. Dur.* Richmundia, *c.* 1175 *Fantosme* Richemunt,

c. 1250 *M. Paris* Richemund. Fr. *riche mont,* 'rich, fertile hill.'
Named by the Breton Alan, who built a castle here on lands
given him by William I. R. in Surrey was orig. Shene, and was
changed to R. out of compliment to Hen. VII., 'Henry of
Richmond,' his father being Edmund Tudor, Earl of Richmond.

RICKERSCOTE (Staffd.). *Cf. Dom.* Recordine, Salop (-dine prob.
= wardine, 'farm,' *q.v.*). 'Cot, cottage of *Ricard, Ricred,
Reccaredus, Richere* or *Ricerus'*; all these forms are in *Onom.*

RICKINGHALL (Diss) and RICKNALL (Co. Durham). Dur. R. 1183
Rikenhall. 'Hall' 'of (the decsendants of) *Rica.*' *Cf. chart.*
of 679 Ricingahaam, Essex, and RICCAL. See -hall. RICKE-
STON, Pembksh., is 1324 Ricardyston, '*Richard*'s town.'

RICKMANSWORTH (Herts). *Dom.* Ricemareworde, 1303 Rikemares-
worth, '*Ricmœr*'s farm.' There is an 'Ikemaneswurda' in
1167-68 *Pipe* Devon. See -worth.

RIDDLESDEN (W. Riding) and RIDDLESWORTH (Thetford). *Dom.*
Redelesden, 'wooded vale' and 'farm of *Rœd-* or *Redwulf.*'
Cf. Riddlecombe, Chulmleigh. See -combe, -den, and -worth.

RIDGEWAY or RUDGEWAY (Bristol, Pershore, Staffs, Sheffield).
Br. R. 950 *chart.* Hricweg, Per. and St. R. O.E. *chart.* Hrycg-,
Ricweg, -weye, 1300 Reggewey. 'Way, road on the ridge,'
O.E. *hrycg,* 3 6 *rugge.* The Rom. road fr. Chester to Worcester
is called 'la Rugge,' but all Ridgeways are not Roman. *Cf.
Grant* of *a.* 675 Ruggestrate (-street), Hants.

RIDING (one of the 3 divisions of Yorks). In *Dom.* we have 'Est
Treding and Reding,' Yorks, also 'Nort-trading, West-reding,
and Sudt-reding' of Lincolia, also edit. 1783, p. 375, 'Treding
dicit quod non habet ibi nisi ix acras et dimid.' 1295-96 *Rolls
Parlt.* West redyng, Est-redyng, North redyng; also 'In Comi-
tatu Ebor.' . . . 'et in supradictis tribus Trithing.' Late O.E.
þriding or þriding, fr. O.N. þriðjung-r, 'third part,' fr. O.E.
þridda, O.N. þriðe, 'third.' There is a RIDING MILL, Northbld.,
and a Riding burn, *c.* 1250 Revedeneburne, ? 'valley of *Refa,*'
an unrecorded name. See -dean.

RIEVAULX (Helmsley, Yorks). 1132 Rievalle, 1156 *Pipe* Rieuall,
1200 Riuille, *c.* 1246 Ryeualle, 1394 Reival. 'Vale of the R. RYE,'
fr. O.Fr. *valle,* Fr. *val,* 'a valley'; -vaulx is an old plur. form.

RILLINGTON (York). *Sic* 1391, but *Dom.* Redlinton, Renliton.
The name is very corrupt; orig. it may have been 'town of
Hredle,' a name in *Onom.*

RIMINGTON (Clitheroe). *Dom.* Renitone. More old forms needed,
? fr. a man, *Hrani.*

RINGLAND (Norwich), RINGLEY (Manchester), RINGSTEAD (King's
Lynn), RINGWAY (Cheshire), RINGWOOD (Hants). They are on
the rivers Wensum, Irwell, Nene, Bollin, and Avon, so none can

be connected with the river in *c.* 1169 *chart.* Ad sicam (brook, syke) Polterkeved quae cadit in Ring.' All prob. come fr. O.E. *wring,* O.N. *wring-r,* ' a ring.' See -ley, -stead, etc. There is also a RINGBURGH (Holderness). *Dom.* Ringheborg, Ringeburg, ' burgh, castle of *Hring,*' contracted form of Hringweald or -wulf; whilst Rangeworthy (Gloster), 1303 Ryngeworth, is prob. fr. a similar name. See -worth, ' farm.'

RINGMER (Lewes). *Saga Olaf Har.* Hringamara. Said to be corrup. of Regin-mere, ' lake of *Regnum,* or *Regno,*' name of Chichester in *Ant. Itin., c.* 380. *Cf.* above.

RIPLEY (Leeds, Derby, Woking). Leeds R. *Dom.* Ripeleia, 1202 Rippeleg; Wo. R. *K.C.D.* 1361 Rippan leah, ' Meadow of *Rippa.* See -ley.

RIPON. *Sic* 1386, but *c.* 709 *Eddi* Hrypi, *Bede* In hrypum, *c.* 1050 *O.E. Chron.* ann. 769 Ripum, 948 *ib.* Rypon, *Dom.* Ripum. Prob. fr. L. *ripa,* ' bank '; it is on the bank of the Ure. It can hardly be fr. O.E. *hrópan,* ' to howl or scream.' The -um and -on are loc. endings—' on the banks ' of the Ure.

RIPPINGALE (Bourne). 806 *chart.* Repingale, *Dom.* Repinghale. Patronymic; ' Nook, corner of the *Repings,*' a name not in *Onom.*; but *cf. a.* 1100 Hrepingas in S. Lincs. For *hale,* ' nook,' see -hall.

RIPPLE (Tewkesbury and Deal). Tew. R. 680 *chart.* Rippell, later Ryppel, *Dom.* Rippel. Skeat thinks this must be a personal name, because of next; if so, this is very exceptional. Some think it = RIBBLE; anyway, it is on a long stream, trib. of Severn. The Eng. *ripple* is quite a recent word. *Dom.* Kent has only Ripe.

RIPPLESMERE (Windsor). *Dom.* Riplesmer(e), 1316 Ripplesmere, ' Lake of ' an unknown man ' *Rippel.*' *Cf.* RIPPLINGHAM (E. Riding), *Dom.* Riplingha', 1179-80 *Pipe* Ripplingeham Arches. See -ing.

RISBY (York and Bury St. E.). Yo. R. *Dom.* Risbi, ' Dwelling of *Risa* ' or ' *Rhys,*' a W. name. *Cf.* RESTON (Sc.), 1098 Ristun, next, Long Riston (Yorks), *Dom.* Ristun, and Princes Risboro' (Bucks), *Dom.* Riseberge, Risberg.

RISELEY (Bedford and Reading). *Cf. Dom.* Bucks Riseberge, and Northants Ristone. ' Meadow of *Risa.*' *Cf.* above. See -ley. But RISE (Holderness), *Dom.* Risun, and RISE CARR (Darlington), seem to be fr. *rise,* ' a hill, rising ground.' The vb. is O.E., though the sb. is only recorded late. The -un in Risun is a common loc. in Yorks *Dom.* See CARR, ' rock.'

RISHANGLES (Thorndon, Suffk.). *Dom.* Ris angra, late O.E. for ' rush-covered slope,' O.E. *rise,* M.E. *rishe,* ' a rush,' and *hanȝra,* ' hill-slope.' *Cf.* CLAYHANGER. The mod. ending -les shows how easily the liquid *r* slides into *l*.

RISHTON (Blackburn). ' Rush -town.' See above, and *cf.* ' Rise-
tone' in Cheshire *Dom.* ; it may be this same place; also RISSING-
TON (Gloster), *Dom.* Risendune, ' rushen down.' See -don, -ing,
and -ton.

RIVINGTON PIKE (Mid Lancs). *Sic* 1588, but *a.* 1290 Roinpik,
a. 1552 Rivenpike, 1588 Ryven pyke, 1673 Riving Pike. The
meaning seems, ' riven, cloven pike or PEAK '; though no form
of *rive* (vb. in *Oxf. Dict.*) exactly explains Roin (*a.* 1290). The
vb. *rive* is O.N. *rifa*, found in Eng. *a.* 1300. *Cf.* RED PIKE, and
Rawnpike Oak (Warwksh.), which Duignan says is *dial.* for ' a
stag-headed tree,' one with dead branches on its top, also spelt
Ranpike, Rampick.

ROBIN HOOD'S BAY (Whitby). *c.* 1550 *Leland* Robyn Huddes
Bay. The legendary *Robin Hood* is first found in 1377 *Piers
Plowman*, and his name is commemorated in cairns, crosses,
caves, oaks, etc., as far S. as Somerset, and as far N. as this.

ROBOROUGH (2 in Devon). S. Torrington R. *Dom.* Raweberge,
also *old* Rougaburga. Doubtful; either ' burgh of *Ruga* ' (see
ROUTON), or ' rough burgh or fort ' (see ROWINGTON), and *cf.*
Roughcastle (Falkirk), and Rowberrow (Axbridge). See -borough.
ROEL or Rowell (Notgrove), *Dom.* Rawelle, is ' roe-deer's well,'
O.E. *ráh*.

ROCESTER (Uttoxeter). *Dom.* Rowecestre, *a.* 1200 Roffecestre,
' *Hrof*'s ' or ' *Ralph*'s castle,' and so = ROCHESTER. See -cester.

ROCHDALE. *Dom.* Recedam (see -ham), 1241-92 Rachedale, 1286
Rached. Must be fr. a man *Rached* or *Reced*, which may be
contracted fr. *Reccared* or *Riccared*, names in *Onom.* The *d* has
become merged in the -dale, hence later confusion with *Hroche*
or *Roche*, who give name to ROCKBEARE, ROXBURGH (Sc.), etc.
The nouns *roach* and *rock*, M.E. *roche*, are both fr. Fr., and not
found in Eng. *a.* 1250. The R. Roch on which the town stands
is plainly a back-formation. *Cf.* PINNER, YEOVIL, etc. See -dale.

ROCHESTER. *c.* 380 *Ant. Itin.* Durobrevis; *Tabula Peutinger.*
perh. earlier than *Itin.*, Roribis, 604 *chart.* Hrofibrevi, *Bede*
Hrofescæstir, 762 *chart.* In civitate Hrofi; O.E. *Chron.* ann. 604
Hrofesceaster, *Dom.* Rouescestre, *c.* 1386 *Chaucer* Rowchestre.
A name that has changed. Durobrevis is said to mean ' fort at
the bridges,' *duro* being perh. cognate with Eng. ' door,' and
brivo is said to be O.Kelt. for ' bridge.' The Peutinger form is a
scribe's corruption. How Duro- became Hrofi- we cannot tell; but
already Bede believed that *Hrof*, Norm. Fr. *Rou*, was a man, formerly *primarius* in this town. See -chester, ' a camp.' There
is a Rochester (Otterburn), and a Rochecestre, *Dom.* Salop,
which might be fr. a Norman *Roche*, *cf.* next and ROXBURGH
(Sc.), but more prob. fr. O.E. *roh*, M.E. ro3, *roch*, ' rough,' prob,
same as RUGBY, in *Dom.* Rocheberie. *Cf.* ROCESTER and
ROWINGTON.

ROCHFORD (Essex and Tenbury). Ess. R. *Dom.* Rochesfort. 'Ford of *Roc.*' *Cf.* ROXBURGH (Sc.), and Ruxford (Devon), 930 *chart.* Hrocesford; also Rokeby (Yorks), *Dom.* Rochebi.

ROCKBEARE (Exeter). *Dom.* Rochsbere. 'Wood of *Roche.*' See above. O.E. *bearu,* 'a wood.' *Cf.* BEER and the personal name Conybeare, also ROXBURGH (Sc.) and Rookwith (Yorks), *Dom.* Rocuid, where the ending also means 'wood.'

ROCKCLIFFE (Carlisle). 1595 Rowclif. Possibly mod. corrup. for 'cliff of *Rou*' or '*Rolls.*' *Cf.* ROCHESTER, in *Chaucer* Row-chestre. As likely fr. O.E. *ruh, rug,* 4-6 *rogh,* 5-7 *roche* (Sc.), 6 *rowch* (Sc.), 'rough, shaggy.' ROCKHAMPTON (Thornbury), *Dom.* Rochemtune, *later* Rokampton, is thought to be 'rooks HAMPTON,' O.E. *hróc.*

ROCKING (Kent). 785 *chart.* Hroching. Patronymic. 'Place of the descendants of *Hroche.*' *Cf.* ROCKBEARE and next.

ROCKINGHAM (Uppingham). *Dom.* and 1160 *Pipe* Rochingeham, 1135 *O.E. Chron.* Rogingham, 1482 Rokyngham. 'Home of the *Rockings,*' or 'descendants of *Roche.*' See above, and -ham.

ROCK SAVAGE (Frodsham). A splendid mansion was erected here by Sir John *Savage* in 1565.

RODEN R. (Wroxeter), RODING R. (central Essex), and RODINGTON (Shrewsbury). Roden is perh. *c.* 380 *Ant. Itin.* Rutunio. R'ton is *Dom.* Rodintone. There are 2 called *Roda,* gen. -*an,* in *Onom.,* and R'ton might be 'town of *Roda,*' and Roding a patronymic. See -ing. This is unlikely for a river, and both rivers are prob. Keltic; whilst R'ton will be 'village near the Roden.' The root might be W. *rhudden,* 'a red streak, a ruby,' fr. *rhudd, rhydd,* 'red'; or these river names might be connected with W. *rhwtioni,* 'to produce dregs'; but the origin—like that of so many river names—is quite doubtful. There is a 'Gibbe Ruydinges' found in Staffs in 1309, a name which might well be fr. *rhudd* or *rhydd.*

The Essex R. gives name to quite a number of places—Abbot's Roding, Leaden Roding, White Roding, etc.

RODBORO' (Stroud). *c.* 740 *chart.* Roddenbeorgh, is 'BARROW of *Rodda.*' RODLEY, same shire, is *Dom.* Rodele, but 1163-64 Radelea, and often, later, Rad- and Rud-; so it may either be fr. a man *Rodda,* or 'red lea.' See -ley. RODMARTON (Tetbury), *Dom.* Redmertune, is '*Rœdmœr*'s town.' *Cf.* RED-MARLEY.

ROLLESTON (Burton-on-T. and 3). Bur. R. 942 *chart.* Rothulfeston, 1004 *ib.* Rolfestun, *Dom.* Rolvestune. '*Hrothwulf*'s town.' All the others may not be the same. R. (Notts) is *Dom.* Roldestun, Rollestone, 1346 Roldeston, 'town of *Rold,*' 2 in *Onom.*

ROLVENDEN (Ashford, Kent). Perh. 'den or DEAN or wooded valley of *Roland.*' The famous R. is in Eginhard, ' Hruodlandus Brittanici limitis praefectus.'

ROMAN WALL, The (R. Tyne). *a.* 1500 *Black Bk. Hexham* Murus Romanorum.

ROMNEY Marsh (Kent). 697 *chart.* Rumin -ing, 1052 *O.E. Chron.* Rumenea, 1228 Rumenal, 1288 *Contin. Gervase* In marisco de Romenal. Rumin or Rumen quite possibly represents *Roman,* as this district is so full of connexion with Rome. The -ey, *q.v.,* means 'island.' But form 697 seems more like a patronymic, 'place of the sons of *Ruma*'; and this is the most prob. origin. ROMANBY (Yorks) is *Dom.* Romundebi, ' dwelling of *Hrothmund*' or ' *Rodmund.*' See -by.

ROMSEY (Hants). Pron. Rúmsey. *a.* 1142 *Wm. Malmesb.* Rumesium, *a.* 1160 *Gest. Steph.* Abbas Rumensis, 1298 Romeseie. 'Isle of *Rum.*' *Cf.* RUMHOLT and RUMNEY.

ROOMFIELD (Todmorden). 1314 Romesgrene, close by—*i.e.,* ' Green of *Roma* ' or ' *Ruma,*' one in *Onom.*

ROOS(E) (Hull and Furness). Both in *Dom.* Rosse. As RHOS (Pembroke) is to-day pron. Roose, these are clearly the same name, W. *rhos,* ' a moor, heath, marsh.' There is also a Roose (Portkerry, Glam.).

ROPE (Nantwich). This is an old place, and prob. means, ' a piece of land meansured by a rope.' See RAPES and next.

ROPLEY (Alresford). 972 *chart.* Ropleah. O.E. for ' lea, meadow, measured by a rope.' *Cf.* RAPES.

ROSEMARKET (Neyland, Pembk.). 1603 *Owen* Rosmarken. Rose- is W. *rhos,* ' a moor,' and the present ending is mod. *Cf.* Rhosmarket, or Rhos y Farket, Nevern, same shire, *old* Rosavarken. The name must surely be the same as ROSEMARKIE (Fortrose, Sc.), *c.* 1228 Rosmarkensis Episcopus, 1510 Rosmarky, where W. J. Watson takes the ending for G. *marcnaidh,* or *maircnidh,* old gen. of *marcnach,* 'place of horses.' No likely W. origin seems forthcoming; so this may be a rare Gadhelic survival.

ROSER CASTLE (Carlisle). 1272 Rosa. Named by its builder, Bp. Manclerk, *c.* 1240, fr. the *rose,* symbol of the Blessed Virgin. The change of -a to -er denotes a ' Cockney ' pronunciation. *Cf.* KIDDERMINSTER.

ROSS (Hereford). In W. Rhossan ar Wy. W. *rhos,* ' a moor, a heath.' *Cf.* RHOS. Ros- is common in Corn. names; we have already Roscarel in *Dom.* Lord de Ros is fr. Ros, Holderness, *Sic. a.* 1130.

ROSSALL (Fleetwood). *Dom.* Rus-hale, 1228 Roshale, -hal, 1265 Rossale. ' Nook, enclosure of the horse,' O.N. *hross,* O.E. *hors.* See -hall.

ROSSENDALE (N.E. Lancs). *Sic c.* 1230, 1294 Roscyndale, 1296 Rosendale. ' Valley of *Roschil,* or ' *Roscytel,*' nearest name in *Onom.* The liquids *l* and *n* interchange without much difficulty. See -dale.

ROSSETT (Wrexham). *a.* 1700 Yr orsidd; besides the village 2 or 3 fields in this district are now called Rossett. The W. name means ' the throne,' or ' high seat,' and must refer to some mound in, or once in, the field. T. Morgan says it is corrup. of *rhosydd,* pl. of *rhos,* ' a moor.' Rosset (W. Riding) is *Dom.* Rosert, a name of doubtful meaning.

ROSTHERNE MERE (Altrincham). Looks like ' roost,' O.E. *hróst,* ' of the *hern* or *heron,*' O.Fr. *hairon,* Fr. *héron,* in Eng. fr. 1302. But it may also be fr. O.E. *hyrne,* M.E. *herne,* ' a nook, a hiding-place.' *Cf.* HERNE HILL.

ROTHERHAM (Yorks and Surrey). Yo. R. *Dom.* Rodreha, 1242 Roderham. Some say, ' home on the R. Rother,' Icel. *rauð-r,* ' red.' Others derive fr. O.E. *hríðer, hrýðer,* 3- *rother,* 5 *rodder,* ' an ox.' *Cf.* RUTHERFORD (Sc.). But this occurrence of the name in Sussex makes it prob. that the river-name is a back formation (*cf.* Rochdale), and that the name of the town is ' home of *Hroðhere,*' a known name. But Ryther (W. Riding), *Dom.* Ridre, must be O.E. *rið ofer,* ' brook bank '; *cf.* RYDE, WOOLER, etc. ROTHERFIELD GREYS (Henley-on-Thames) is 1237 Retherefeld, 1242, Retheresfeld, prob. ' ox's field.'

ROTHERHITHE (London). 1298 Retherhethe, 1460 Redre, 1660 *Pepys* Redriffe (a plain corruption). Looks like, not ' red HYTHE ' or ' harbour,' but rather ' ox-harbour ' or ' landing-place.' See above. But *cf.* ? *a.* 1100 *Hugo Candidus* In Londone . . . juxta portum qui vocatur Etheredishythe, ' harbour of *Ethered,*' var. of the common O.E. *Æthelred.*

ROTHWELL (Leeds, Kettering, and Caistor, Lincs.). *Dom.* Leeds and Ket. Rodewelle, Caist. Rodowelle. Ket. R. 1360 *Pipe* Rothewelle, now pron. Rówell, while Ruthwell (Dumfries) is pron. Rivvel. ' Well of the rood ' or ' cross,' O.E. *ród.*

ROTTINGDEAN (Brighton). Old forms needed. Referred to *c.* 1380. It may be ' rotten,' O.N. *rotinn,* or ' rotting (Icel. and N. *rot,* vb.) valley.' The *rotten* has as one pretty early sense, ' of ground, soil, etc., extremely soft . . . friable.' This suits the site. But perh., as in RAWTENSTALL, ' routing valley '—*i.e.,* one ' making a roaring noise, boisterously windy.' See *Oxf. Dict.* s.v. *rout* vb[2] and vb[3], both of Norse origin. No spelling *rotting* or *rot* is given s.v., but we do find *rote, rawt,* and *raut.* See -dean.

ROUGHAM (Norfolk). *Dom.* Ruhham, *c.* 1280 *chart.* Rucham. O.E. *ruh hám,* ' rough, shaggy-looking house.'

ROUTH (Beverley). *Dom.* Rute, Rutha. O.N. *ruð,* ' a clearing in a wood,' a rare word.

ROUTON (Norfolk). *Sic* 1451, but 1477 Rowton; also ROWTON (E. Yorks and Chester). Yo. R. *Dom.* Rugheton, Rugeton. All prob. ' town of *Ruga.*' See ROWNER, and *cf.* ROBOROUGH.

ROWINGTON (Warwick). *Dom.* Rochintone, *a.* 1200 Rokintun, *a.* 1400 Rouhinton, 1378 Rochinton. Doubtful; Duignan prefers 'rough town,' O.E. *roh.* See ROCHESTER and RUGBY, -ing and -ton.

ROWLANDS CASTLE (Havant) and GILL (Newcastle). Rowland or Roland is the O. Teut. *Rodland* or *Hruodland*, fr. *hrod*, 'famous.' *Cf.* ROLVENDEN. Gill is Icel. *gil*, 'a gap.' *Cf.* fish-gill. In names it means either 'a little bay' or 'a ravine.' *Cf.* AUCHIN GILL (Sc.).

ROWLEY WATER (N. of Hexham). *a.* 1300 *chart.* Ruleystal (= O.E. *stœl*, 'stall, place'). Perh. 'rest-meadow,' O.N. *ró*, Eng. *c.* 1200 *ro*, 4-5 *roo*, 4 *rou*, 5 *rowe*, 'rest, repose, peace.' There are other Rowleys. *Cf. Dom.* Bucks, Rovelai, which suggests some man's name, ? what, whilst ROWLEY REGIS (Dudley) is *a.* 1200 Rohele, Rueley, Roele, *a.* 1300 Rueleg, which is prob. 'rough lea,' O.E. *ruh.* See RUGBY. It belonged to the King in *Dom.*, hence Regis, 'of the King.' See -ley.

ROWLSTON (Yorks). *Dom.* Roolfestone, Rolvestun. 'Town of *Hrolf.*' *Cf.* ROCHESTER.

ROWNER (Gosport). *Dom.* Ruenore, 1114 *O.E. Chron.* Rugenor. O.E. *Rugan ora,* ' shore of Ruga.' *Cf.* WINDSOR, etc. Also *cf. B.C.S.* 699 Rugan dic (' dyke '), *ib.* ii. 516 Ruwanbeorg (Berks), *ib.* i. 545 Ruganbeorg, *Dom.* Norfk. Ruuenore. But ROWNALL (Cheadle) is *Dom.* Rugehala, *a.* 1300 Roughenhale, Rowenhale. These last Duignan thinks oblique cases of O.E. *ruh*, in its weak declension, *ruwa, -an*, 'rough nook.' *Cf.* RUGBY, and see -hall.

ROXBY (Doncaster) and ROXTON (St. Neot's). *Dom.* Rozebi, a spelling which *Dom.* Yorks also gives to Rousby. *Dom.* Roche-stone. Prob. 'dwelling' and 'town of *Roc*' or '*Rocga*,' names in *Onom. Cf.* ROXBURGH (Sc.) and ROCKBEARE. See -by and -ton.

ROYSTON (Herts and Barnsley). Her. R. *c.* 1220 *Elect. Hugo* Crux Roies, 1263 Croyrois, 1298 Villa de Cruce Roisia, v.r. Rohesia, Rosia; 1428 Roystone. Said to be called fr. a Lady *Roysia*, or *Roese*, about whom nothing is known. A lady called *Rohais* is known in 1156, and there is a Roese de Lucy, temp. Hen. II. *Crux* is L. and *croy* is O.Fr., Mod. Fr. *croix*, ' cross.'

RUÁBON (Denbigh). W. *rhiw Mabon*, ' slope of Mabon,' *M* eclipsed by aspiration. Mabon was a saint who founded a church here.

RUAN MAJOR and MINOR (The Lizard). For this saint, see POLUR-RIAN.

RUBERY HILL (King's Norton). No old forms. Duignan says O.E. *ruh beorh* (M.E. *berg*), 'rough hill.' But *cf.* 947 *chart.* Rugan

beorh (Wilts), fr. a man *Ruga,* as in *B.C.S.* 699 Rugan dic.
Cf. ROWNER. RUARDEAN-on-Wye, 1281 Rowardin, *later* Ruworthyn, exhibits a rare var. of -worthy or -wardine, ' rough farm.'

RUDDINGTON (Nottingham). *Dom.* Roddintone, Rodintun. 1261
Rotinton, 1287 Rotyngton; also Rodington, Rutyngton. 'Town
of *Hroda, Rudda,* or *Ruta,'* all names found in *Onom. Cf.* Hutton
RUD(E)BY (Yorks), *Dom.* Rodebi, 1179-80 *Pipe* Rudebi (see
HUTTON), and RUDEFORD (Glouc.), *Dom.* Rudeford.

RUDGE (Stroud and Salop). Str. 1179 Rugge, Sal. R. *Dom.*
Rigge—*i.e.,* ' ridge.' See RIDGEWAY.

RUDSTON (Birchington). *Dom.* Rodestan, 1206 Ruddestain, which
is prob. not *rood-stone,* O.E. *ród,* but ' stone ' or ' town of *Roda* '
or ' *Rudda.*' Two of each so named in *Onom.* See -ton.

RUFFORD (Ormskirk and Notts). Or. R. 1318 Roughford, 1332
Rughford, which explains itself. No. R. *Dom.* Rugforde, 1161-
62 *Pipe* Rucford, 1198 Rocheforde. Thus this cannot be the
same as 1160 *Pipe* Runfort (Notts and Derby). But it is prob.
the same as Rufford (Holderness), *Dom.* Ruforde, and RUFFORTH
(York), *Dom.* Ruford. See -forth.

RUGBY. *Dom.* Rocheberie, *a.* 1300 Rokeby, *a.* 1500 Rukby. Very
likely fr. a man, ' dwelling of *Roc* ' or ' *Hroca,*' both in *Onom. ;*
and *cf.* ROXBURGH (Sc.), also ROCHFORD and ROCKBEARE, in
the early forms of which we find a plain gen. But Duignan
prefers here, as in ROWLEY, ROWNALL, RUGELEY, and RUDGE-
WAY, O.E. *ruh, hruh,* 3 *ruhe,* 4 *roh,* 5 *rouh, rowh (Oxf. Dict.* gives
also many forms in *-euch, -och, -uch,* but calls them all Sc.), also
4 *rug(g),* 4-6 *rughe, rogh(e),* 4-5 *rouȝ, rowȝ,* ' rough.' See -by.

RUGELEY (Staffs). *Dom.* Rugelei, *a.* 1200 Ruggeley, Ruggleg, 1217
Rugeleg. ' Rough lea ' (see above), or, quite possibly, ' meadow
of *Ruga* ' or ' *Rugga,*' both in *Onom. Cf.* ROWNER and RYTON.
See -ley.

RUISLIP (Uxbridge). *Old* Ryselippe. Prob. ' leap of ' some man;
more old forms needed to tell whom, ? *Ruga. Cf.* HINDLIP.

RUMHOLT (Norfolk). *Sic* 1293. O.E. *rúm holt,* ' roomy, spacious
wood.' *Cf.* RUMWORTH (Bolton). ' Roomy farm,' 1205 Rumworth. In either case they may come fr. a man *Rum. Cf.* next.
Onom. gives one *Ruma.*

RUMNEY (Cardiff). *c.* 1330 *R. Brunne* Chron. 35. ' The abbey
of Rumeye,' ? this place. ' Isle of *Ruma* -gen, -an (*cf.* ROMNEY),
of ' of *Rum.*' *Cf.* Rumburgh, Halesworth, and above. See -ey.

RUNCORN. 913 *O.E. Chron.* Rumcofan, v.r. Romicofan, *a.* 1200
chart. Runcofa, 1377 Runnkorn. O.E. *rúm cofa,* gen. *-an,*
' roomy, spacious cave or chamber.'

RUNCTON HOLME (Downham). *Dom.* Runghetuna. 'Town of
Runca,' or some such unrecorded name. See HOLME.

RUNHALL (Attleborough). *Dom.* Runhala. *Cf. Dom.* Bucks Ruenhale, which, on analogy of ROWNER, *Dom.* Ruenore, will be ' *Ruga's* nook ' or ' corner.' See -hall.

RUNHAM (Yarmouth). 1285 Runham, 1475 Runnham; and RUNTON (Sheringham), *c.* 1460 Runeton. Prob. both fr. a man *Run* or *Runa*, not in *Onom.* Not likely fr. O.E. *rún,* 1-4 *run,* ' a rune, counsel, speech.' *Cf. Dom.* and 1179 Runtune, now Rounton (Yorks), 1160-61 *Pipe* Notts and Derby, Runfort, and above. See -ham and -ton.

RUNNYMEDE (R. Thames). *c.* 1220 *Elect. Hugo* Runemad. ' Mead, meadow (O.E. *mæd, mædu*) of rune '—*i.e.*, counsel or speech. Here Magna Charta was signed in 1215.

RUSCOMBE (Twyford and Cainscross). Tw. R. *c.* 1520 Ruscombe; also Roscombe, Ruscamp. ' Rush valley.' See -combe and next; also *cf.* 1202 ' Risewich '= Ruswick (Bedale).

RUSHALL (Pewsey, Scole, Nfk., and Walsall). Pe. R. (or another) 967 *chart.* Rischale, 972 *ib.* Hrischeale, Wa. R. *Dom.* Rischale, *a.* 1200 Ruissale, Rushale. ' Rushy nook.' O.E. *hrise, risc(e),* 4-7 *rish,* 5-*rush,* ' a rush.' See -hall. The RUSHTONS will be similar, *Dom.* Staffs Riseton, also RUSWICK (Yorks), *Dom.* Risewic (see -wick); but RUSTON PARVA (N. Yorks), is in *Dom.* not only Roxtun but five times Roreston, which looks as if fr. an unknown man *Rora,* ? G. and Ir. *Ruairidh* or *Rory.* Liquid *r* when medial readily disappears.

RUSHOCK (Droitwich). *Dom.* Russococ (mid. *o* an error), *a.* 1300 Rushoke. The ending is doubtful, ? *cock,* ' a heap,' N. *kok,* not in *Oxf. Dict.* till 1398, but we have 1086 *Dom.* Yorks Lacoc, now Laycock, ' low heap.' On rush- see RUSHALL. Rushock (Herefd.) is *Dom.* Ruiscop, fr. O.E. *cop(p),* ' top, summit, covered with rushes.'

RUSHOLME (Manchester). ' Rushy meadow by the river.' O.E. *holm,* Icel. *holm-r* has this meaning. *Cf.* HOLM (Sc.).

RUSWARP (Whitby). Pron. Rússarp. Not in *Dom.* Prob. ' rushy heap,' fr. O.E. *geweorp,* ' that which is cast or thrown up.' hence ' a heap,' same root as in ' warp and woof.' *Cf.* SALWARPE. For the Rus- see RUSHALL. But a man *Rust(a)* is seen in RUSTINGTON (Worthing) and RUSTALL (Tunbridge Wells). *Cf. Dom.* Wilts Rusteselle, ' Rusta's nook.' See -hall.

RUTHIN (Denbigh). 1399 *Writ* Ruthyn. Looks like W. *rhudden,* ' a red streak, a ruby,' fr. *rhudd,* ' red.' The prevailing soil here is red.

RUTLAND. As a shire later than *Dom.,* where it is Roteland, 1156 *Pipe* Rotelanda, 1298 *Close R.* ' Vic. Northampt., Vic. Rotel.' *c.* 1500 Rutland. Prob. ' land full of roots,' O.N. and late O.E. *rót,* 3-6 *rote,* 4 *rotte,* 6 *rott,* 9 *rut,* ' a root,' though often derived fr. Icel. *rauðr,* ' red.'

RUYTON - ELEVEN - TOWNS (Shrewsbury). *Dom.* Rutune. Perh. 'town of *Ruta,*' 3 in *Onom.* But it is quite possibly Rutunium, *c.* 380 in *Ant. Itin.* There are Rom. remains here. As for 'the eleven towns,' there are still five townships in the parish. Also *cf.* Rotsea (Driffield), *Dom.* Rotesse, and RYTON.

RYDAL (Windermere) and RYDAL BECK. 'Rye-dale,' O.E. *ryʒe,* 4-6 *ry. Cf.* 1179-80 *Pipe* Ridala (Yorks). For *beck,* 'a brook,' see BECKERMET.

RYDE. 1377 La Rye, La Riche; it was then destroyed by the French. Riche would be *reach* sb., 'a bay,' 'the portion of a channel between two bends.' But La Riche is certainly an error for Rithe, *c* for *t* being a very common error in old MSS., they are so alike. *Cf.* SHOTTERY. Rithe is O.E. *rith(e),* Firs. *ryd, ride,* in Eng. 8-9 *ride ;* also in Sussex and I. of W. dialect *rithe, rythe,* 'a small stream, a brook.' W. *rhyd,* 'ford,' is phonetically inadmissible; it would never yield the mod. pron. Ryde any more than Riche; and there is no ford here. *Cf.* SHEPRETH (Cambs) in *Dom.* Escepride, REETH, and RYE.

RYE (Kent) (*c.* 1060 Ria, 1230 Rya, *later* la Rie) and RYE R. (Yorks) (1132 Rie, 1200 Ri, 1394 Rei, forms taken from RIEVAULX). Not fr. *rye,* see RYDAL. The same as RYDE, fr. O.E. *rithe,* 'a small stream'; not cognate with *ree* sb., 'a stream, channel, river' (not found till 1422), which *Oxf. Dict.* thinks may be O.E. *éa,* 'stream,' with *r* fr. the fem. art. as in 'on thære éa '; but cognate, prob. with Flem. *reie, rui,* N.Fris. *ride, rie,* 'streamlet, rill.' *Cf.* REETH and HYTHE; also Ryther (W. Riding), *Dom.* Rie, and Peckham Rye.

RYHALL (Stamford). 963 *O.E. Chron.* Rihala, *a.* 1100 *chart.* Rihale, 1528 Ryall. 'Nook, enclosure with the rye,' O.E. *ryʒe. Cf.* RYDAL. RYHILL (Wragby, Yorks), *Dom.* Rihella, is exactly the same name. See -hall. But Ryall (Worcsr.) is 1275 Ruhale, and may either be the same, or fr. O.E. *ruh,* 'rough.'

RYHOPE (Wearmouth). *a.* 1130 *Sim. Dur.* Reofhoppas, 1183 *Boldon Bk.* Refhope, 1197 Riefhope. Perh. 'hope '—*i.e.,* 'piece of enclosed land,' with a roof to part of it '—O.E. *hróf,* 1-5 *rof,* Sc. *rif,* 'a roof '; and see -hope. *Reef,* 'a rock,' is not in Eng. till 1584. But the phonetics of the first half are very unsatisfactory with the present evidence. It may represent a contracted form of some man's name in *Rœf-, Rœfmœr, Rœfwine,* or the like. But *Boldon Bk.* also has the v.r. Resehoppe and Roshepp, which only makes confusion worse confounded.

RYTON (Co. Durham, and 2 in Warwk.). War. R. *Dom.* Rietone, *a.* 1300 Ruyton, Rugintune, Rutune; Dur. R. 1183 Ritona. As with RUGELEY, '*Ruga*'s town,' or 'rough town '; but this last does not sound a prob. name. In 1183 Ritona the *i* is sounded as *y.*

SACOMBE (Herts). *Dom.* Sueuecamp, -champ, Seuechampe. An interesting name and change. 'Camp or field,' Fr. *champs* ' of *Swœf,*' a name in *Onom.*; or, says Skeat, ' of the *Suevi,*' a tribe of N.E. Germany.

SAFFRON WALDEN. 'Wooded region in which saffron (Fr. *safran*) grew.' Walden is a derivative of O.E. *weald,* 'forest.' *Cf.* 1577 Harrison *England,* 'Their saffron is not so fine as that of Cambridgeshire and about Walden.'

SAIGHTON (Chester). Perh. *Dom.* Saltone. 'Willow' or 'saugh town,' O.E. *salh,* north. dial. *saugh,* 'a willow.' *Cf.* SAUCHIE and SAUGHTON (Sc.).

SAINTBURY (Honeybourne). *Dom.* Svineberie, *Hund. R.* Seynburie, 1345 Seynesbury. Nothing to do with a *saint,* but, ' town of *Svein*' or ' *Swegen,*' a Dan. name, common in old England, now *Swayne.* See -bury.

ST. ALBAN'S. *Dom.* de Sco Albano, *c.* 1114 *O.E. Chron.* St. Albanestow (= place), 1148 *chart.* Apud Sanctum Albanum. The Roman Verulamium. *Alban,* England's protomartyr, was beheaded here, *c.* 303, and an abbey was built in his honour, *c.* 796. *Cf.* VERULAM.

ST. ANTHONY-IN-MENEAGE and ST. ANTHONY'S HEAD (Falmouth). Churches were built at both these places by Normans soon after the Conquest in honour of the famous *St. Anthony,* Egyptian hermit, in the time of Athanasius.

ST. ASAPH. 1373 'Evesque de Saint Assaphe.' A bishopric, it is said, was founded here by St. Kentigern, *c.* 560, in honour of *Asaph,* his favourite disciple. The W. name is Llanelwy, ' church on R. Elwy.'

ST. AUSTELL'S (Cornwall). Local pron. St. Ossles. The saint was a disciple of Sampson of Dol, Brittany. Austell is var. of *Osweald* or *Oswald.* *Cf.* NOSTELL.

ST. BREOCH (Cornwall). He was a disciple of St. German of Auxerre, *c.* 500. *Cf.* St. Brieux (Brittany).

ST. BRIAVELS (Glouc.). 1131 *Pipe* St. Briavellus. Prob. fr. St. *Eberulphus, c.* 600, who also gives name to the Norm. Evroult.

ST. BRIDE BAY (Pembroke). 1603 Bridbay. 'Bay of St. *Brigada,*' the famous *Bridget* of Kildare, A.D. 453-523.

ST. BURIAN or BURYAN (Penzance). *Buriena* was the pretty daughter of Aengus, K. of Munster, in time of St. Patrick. Said to have lived here in 6th cny.

ST. DAVID'S. *Dewi* or *David* was first Bp. of Menevia (St. David's), grandson of Ceredig, d. 601. The W. name is Ty Ddewi, ' house of David.' Owen, 1603, calls it Mynyw.

ST. ERTH (Hayle, Cornwall). 1536 Ergh. St. *Erc* was one of the earliest saints to come over fr. Ireland, *c.* 500. He was a disciple of Brendan and father of St. Enny.

ST. FAGAN'S (Cardiff). He was reputed a missionary sent by Pope Eleutherus to Britain late in the 2nd cny., on the urgent invitation of Lleurwg.

ST. GERMAN'S (Cornwall and King's Lynn). *Dom.* Devon Germani Sⁱ. He was Bp. of Auxerre, France, and is said to have come to Britain in 429. *Cf.* LLANARMON and WEEK.

ST. GOWAN'S HEAD (Pembroke). 1603 St. Govens pointe. St. *Cofen, Govein*, or *Goven*, was an early W. saint, wife of Tewdrig and mother of Mewrig, Kings of S. Wales. We find her name also in Llangovan (Mon.), and St. Goven's chapel (Pembk.).

ST. HELIER (Jersey). Named fr. St. *Helerius* or *Hilary*, one of the earliest Breton monk missionaries, who settled in Jersey.

ST. HERBERT'S ISLE (Derwentwater). Bede tells of a presbyter *Herebeorht* or *Heriberct*, who lived here as a hermit.

ST. ISHMAEL'S (Milford Haven). *a.* 1200 *Gir. Camb.* Apud Sanctum Hysmaelem, Sancto Ysmaele, 1603 *Owen* St. Ismells. This saint was prob. nephew of St. Teilo; certainly he had nothing to do with the son of Abraham. In *Lib. Land.* the name is Lanyssan, where Yssan is derived fr. *Ysfœl.* In *Tax. Eccl.* it is Ecclesia Sancti Wynnoci, ' church of St. Winnoc ' or Wymocus or Winelle, as in the 2 Trewinnows (Cornwl.). There are also in this shire two ST. ISSELL'S, that at Tenby in W. Llan Usyllt or Hussillt, ' church of St. *Ussille* ' or ' *Usyllt,*' same name as Yseult or Isolde of the medieval romances. This one is a man, father of St. Teilo. See LLANDEILO, and *cf.* LLANDYSSUL.

ST. IVE (pron. Eve, Liskeard), ST. IVE'S (Cornwall and Hunts). Hun. C. *c.* 1200 *Gervase* Seint Ive. Some derive the Corn. names fr. St. *Ia,* an Irish virgin and princess, martyred at Hayle A.D. 450. Others derive all fr. *Ivo* or *Yvo,* a Persian bp. said to have come over fr. Ireland, and to have d. at Hunts St. I., *c.* 590. They are prob. all too old to be derived fr. *Yves,* Bp. of Chartres, in the time of our Henry I.

ST. JUST (Falmouth and Land's End). He was deacon of St. Patrick and tutor of St. Kieran, *c.* 430. On the meaning of St. Just ' in Penwith ' see LAND'S END. There are 45 saints called *Justus* or *Just* in *Dict. Christ. Biogr.*

ST. MARTIN LE GRAND (London). 1285 *Stat. London* ' Seint Martyn le Graunt.' This is the great *Martin,* Abbot of Tours, *c.* 350.

ST. MAWES (Falmouth). An Irish saint, who perh. came with Ruan. See POLURRIAN.

ST. MICHAEL'S MOUNT (Penzance). *a.* 1066 *chart.* Sanctum Michælum qui juxta marc, 1474 The Mounte. Called after *Michæl* the archangel. *Cf.* Mont St. Michel (Normandy), right opposite, *c.* 1205 *Layam.* Mihæles munte.

ST. NEOT (Liskeard) and ST. NEOT'S (Hunts). Hun. St. N. 1132 *O.E. Chron.* 'Prior of St. Neod,' 1161-62 *Pipe* de sancto Neoto. He was the eldest brother of Ælfred the Great. His relics were translated from Cornwall to Hunts, and a Benedictine monastery founded for them in 974.

ST. OSYTH (Clacton-on-Sea). 14 . . . *Sailing Directns* Seint Hosies. This is prob. *Hosius,* Bp. of Cordova, famous adviser of Emperor Constantine, and prominent figure in the Council of Nicæa, A.D. 325.

ST. PANCRAS (London). *Dom.* Pancratius S'. *Pancratius,* a Roman boy of fourteen, was one of Diocletian's martyrs, *Bede* iii. 29. *Cf.* WEEK ST. PANCRES.

ST. PETER PORT (Guernsey). 1286 *Close R.* St. Peter in Portu ('harbour').

SALCOMBE (Glouc. and Devon). Gl. S. 1121 Salcumbe, De. S. O.E. *chart.* Sealtcumb—*i.e.,* 'salt valley'; but O.E. *sealh,* M.E. *salwe,* 'willow' is possible in the first case. See -combe.

SALE (Manchester). Prob. *Dom.* Salhale—*i.e.,* 'nook among the willows,' O.E. *salh. Cf.* SALTON, and Saul (Stonehouse), *c.* 1120 Salle, prob. 'willow lea.' See -hall.

SALFORD (Manchester). *Sic* in *Dom.* 1588 Sallford. 'Ford at the willows.' See above. *Cf.* WELFORD. But there are also Salford (Beds) (old forms needed), and 3 in Warwk., of which Salford Abbots and Priors (Evesham) are 714 *chart.* Saltford (Major et Minor), *Dom.* Salford, *a.* 1300 Saltford, Salford, Sauford, '*salt* ford,' fr. an ancient salt spring once near the ford on the Arrow there. Then Salford or Safford Br. on Tame is *a.* 1300 Scraford, Schrafford Brugge, plainly fr. O.E. *scræf,* 'a cave.' *Cf.* SHRAWARDINE.

SALISBURY and SALISBURY PLAIN. *O.E. Chron.* 552 Searobyrig, *ib.* 1086 Searebyrig, *Dom.* Sarisborie, *c.* 1110 *Orderic* Salesburia, 1232 Sarresbere, 1294 Saresbury, 1297 *R. Glouc.* The plein of Salesbuary. *c.* 380 *Ant. Itin.* Sorbiodoni (= -dunum) is old Saresbury. M'Clure conjectures that Sorbio may be Ir. *soirb,* 'easy' and perh. earlier, 'level.' But the Saxons prob. thought *Searo* or *Sar* was a forgotten man, and the liquid *r* easily becomes *l. Cf.* Saredon (Warwksh.), *Dom.* Sardone, Seresdone, *a.* 1300 Saredune. In *Nennius* S. is called Cair Caratauc. See -bury.

SALOP. See SHREWSBURY.

SALT (Stafford). 1004 *will* Halen, *Dom.* Selte, *a.* 1300 Saut (the Sc. and local pron. to-day). O.W. *halen,* O.E. *sealt,* 'salt.' There were saltworks two miles away; ? any nearer.

SALTASH (Plymouth). 1279 Esshe—*i.e.*, 'ash-tree.' *Cf.* ASH. But it is difficult to see the relevance of the Salt-. Prob. it is a man's name, as prob. in SALTNEY. *Salt* is still an Eng. surname. There is a SALT BOX (Ebbworth) where perh. Glastonbury Abbey kept a store of salt.

SALTERFORD (Notts), SALTERFORTH (Colne), SALTERHEBBLE (Halifax), SALTERSFORD (Worcestersh.), and SALTERS BR. (Alrewas). No. S. *Dom.* Saltreford. Al. S. *a.* 1400 Salte-, Salterbrugge. *Cf. c.* 1200 *chart. Whalley* Saltergat, 963 *chart.* Sealter ford. O.E. *sealtere*, 'a salt-dealer or carrier, a (dry) salter'; this part of Staffs is quite a salt district. On -forth see -ford. -Hebble seems to be var. of *Abele*, 'the aspen tree,' found *c.* 1440 *Promp. Parv.* as 'Awbel or ebelle tree,' v.r. 'ebeltre'; whilst 1830 Forby, *East Anglian Glossary*, gives 'Ebble, the asp tree.'

SALTFLEETBY (Louth). 1229 *Close R.* Saltfleteby. 'Dwelling by the salt river.' See FLEET and -by.

SALTNEY (Chester). *Cf.* 810 *chart.* Salteney (Lincs), which prob. means 'isle of a man *Salt*.' *Cf.* SALTASH and -ey. SALTON (York), *Dom.* Saleton, is prob. 'willow town.' *Cf.* SALE and SALWARPE. But SALTMARSH (Yorks), *Dom.* Saltemerse, is, of course, as it says.

SALWARPE R. and Village (Worcester). 770 *chart.* Saluuerp, *later* Salewearpe, *Dom.* Salewarpe, which looks like O.E. *salh-gewearp*, 'willow-heap.' *Cf.* SALFORD and RUSWARP. *Salt* fr. the earliest times always has a *t*, and so cannot be admitted here. *Cf.*, too, SALTLEY (Birmingham), *a.* 1300 Salughtley, Salegl', Salutely, Salua *alias* Salegh, plainly fr. O.E. *salh, sealh*, M.E. *salugh, salwe*, 'the willow or saugh.' Similar is SALWICK (Preston), *Dom.* Saleuuic. See -wick.

SAMBOURNE (Alcester) and SAMBROOK (Newport, Salop). 714 Samburne (recent copy of O.E. *chart.*), *Dom.* Sandburne, 1327 Sombourne. These both must be '*sandy* brook,' O.E. *sand; m* and *n* often interchange. *Cf.* BAMPTON, etc.; and see -bourne.

SAMPFORD (6 in *P.G.*, Devon and Somerset). *Cf.* 1157 *Pipe* Samford (? Norfolk) and 1158 Samfort (? Staffs). Doubtful. Nothing likely in *Onom.* Sam- in O.E. and M.E. is a common prefix for 'half' = semi. But 'half ford' does not seem a very prob. origin, so these too are prob. for '*sandy* ford.' See above. Letter *p* is a very common intrusion, as in HAMPTON, etc.

SAMPSON (Scilly). Called after St. S., the Bp. of Dol, Brittany, b. in Glamorgan in 5th cny., and earlier Abbot of St. Peirio's, Llantwit. Also commemorated in Guernsey.

SANCTON (Yorks). *Dom.* Santune, 1202 Santona. 'Saint's town.' 'Saint' is found in Eng. as early as *c.* 1175 *seint*, L. *sanctus*, O.Fr. *saint, seint*, Eng. 3-5 *sant*, 4 *san*, 4-8 *sanat*, 'holy.' *Cf.* SANTON and BISHOP'S BURTON, orig. Sanctuary Burton.

SANDAL (Wakefield). *Dom.* Sandala, -alia, -ale, 'sandy nook.' See -hall.

SANDBACH (Cheshire). *Dom.* San bec. 'Sandy beck or brook.' O.E. *sand.* See COMBERBACH. SANDGATE (Sandbridge, Kent) is 862 chart. *sænget hryc,* 'sandy road ridge,' O.E. *geat,* 'a way.' Saundby (Notts) is *Dom.* Sandebi. See -by.

SANDHURST (Glouc., Berks, and Kent). Glo. S. *Dom.* Sanher, 1167-68 *Pipe* Sandherst. Ken. S. *O.E. chart.* Sandhyrst. *Cf.* 858 *chart.* Illa sylva sandhyrst nominatur. 'Sandy, woody region,' 'forest with sandy bottom.'

SANDLEFORD PRIORY (S. Berks). *a.* 1190 *Pipe* Sandlesford, 1291 Sandelford. 'Ford of a man *Sandle,'* in O.E. *Sandwulf, Sandolf.*

SANDON (Chelmsford, Royston, and Stone) and SANDOWN (I. of W.) Sto. S. *Dom.* Sandon, Scandone (error); *a.* 1200 Sandone. O.E. *sand dún,* 'sand hill.'

SANDRINGHAM (King's Lynn). *Dom.* Santdersincham. Curious corruption. This is 'holy Dersingham,' as compared with the next parish, DERSINGHAM. Fr. *saint,* L. *sanctus,* 'holy.'

SANDWICH. 993 *O.E. Chron.* Sandwíc, c. 1300 *Becket* Sandwych. 'House, dwelling, O.E. *wíc,* among the sand.' But quite possibly the name is N. *sand-vík,* 'sandy bay,' as in Sandwick (E. Ross). Saints Bay, Guernsey. 1309 Saynte, may be a corrup. of this last. See -wich.

SANDY. *Dom.* Sande, also in Hants. 'Sandy isle.' See -ay.

SANFORD (Glouc.) (1230 Sam-, *later* Saunforde) and SANFORD BRET (Somerset). 'Sandy ford.' *Cf. B.C.S.* i. 490 Sandforda—*i.e.,* Sandford (Berks). In Scotland and Ireland we have the name as Sandyford. *Cf. Dom.* Salop Sanford. The family of *Bret* or *Brito*—*i.e.,* 'the Breton'—is very old. Richard le Bret was one of Beckett's murderers.

SANTON BRIDGE (Cumberland). *Cf. Dom.* 'Santune' (Cheshire). 833 *chart.* Sandtun is SAMPTON (West Hythe), where, for change of *n* to *mp, cf.* BAMPTON. The meaning of Santon may either be 'sand-town,' 'village on the sand,' as above; or 'saint's town,' as in SANCTON. Kirk Santon (N. Lancs) is *Dom.* Santacherche, 'holy church.' *Cf.* Saintbridge (Glouc.), 1245 Sondebrugge, *later* Send-, Senbridge, which must have come orig. fr. O.E. *sand, sond,* 'sand '; *sond* is found as late as 1512.

SAPCOTE (Hinckley), perh. like SAPEY PRITCHARD (Bromyard), 781 *chart.* æt Sapian, *Dom.* Sapie, fr. O.E. *sœpige,* 'fir, spruce fir '; -cote is 'cot, cottage.' *Cf.* c. 1130 *Wm Malmesb.* Sapwic, ? N. Devon. All of them may be fr. an unknown man *Sap* or the like. Salperton and SAPPERTON (Glouc.), the former 969 Saper(e)tune, *Dom.* Salpretune, the latter *Dom.* Sapletorne, 1221 Sapertone, are both, doubtfully, derived fr. O.E. *sœp,* 'sap,' and so perh. 'sapling pear enclosure.' *Cf.* PERRY.

SARK (Channel Islands). 1218 *Patent R.* Serk and 1219 Serck. Perh. fr. its supposed shape, fr. O.E. *serc*, O.N. *serk-r*, ' a shirt.' Sc. ' sark.'

SATTERTHWAITE (Ulverston). ' Place of the *sæter.*' N. for ' summer farm, log hut used by dairy farmers then.' See -thwaite.

SAVERNAKE (Marlboro'). Not in *Dom.* 1161-62 *Pipe* Sauernac, 1222 *Patent R.* Savernac. Perh. 1298 ' Bertramus de Savynaco.' More old forms needed. Possibly ' *Sæffa*'s oak,' O.E. *ác. Cf.* *K.C.D.* 550 Sæffan mor. For *a* becoming *er, cf.* KIDDERMINSTER. It might perh. be ' *Severn*'s oak.' SEVERN is still found as a surname, but only recently.

SAWBRIDGE (Daventry) and SAWBRIDGEWORTH (Herts). Dav. S. *Dom.* Salwebrige, 1327 Salebrugge, 1598 Salbridge. ' Bridge of withies' or ' willows,' O.E. *salh.* See SALWARPE. But the latter is *Dom.* Sabrixtewoode, 1166 Sabrihtesworth, 1428 Sabrige-worth. ' Farm of *Sæbeorht,*' later ' *Sabriht,*' ' the sea-bright.' See -worth.

SAWLEY (Ripon, Clitheroe, Derby). Ri. S. *Dom.* Sallaia. Prob. ' willow or saugh meadow,' O.E. *salh. Cf.* SALE, and above; and see -ley.

SAWSTON (Cambridge). *c.* 1080 *Inquis. Camb.* Salsintona, *Dom.* Salsiton, 1210 Sausintone, 1284 Sausitone; also *Chron. Ramsey* Salsingetun, Selsingetona, which shows the name is orig. a patronymic, ' village of the *Sælsings,*' an unknown family. But we have *Dom.* Sawesberie (Salop), which suggests some name in Saw- or Sæw-; there are several.

SAWTRY (Peterboro'). *Cart. Rames.* Saltreche, ' salt reach.' See REACH.

SAXMUNDHAM. Prob. ' house, home under the protection, O.E. *mund,* of the Saxons,' O.E. *Seaxe.* No name *Seaxmund* in *Onom.* See -ham, and *cf.* GOODMANHAM. There is a MUNDHAM (Norfolk), prob. fr. a man . *Cf.* Saxon Street (Cambs).

SAXTON (Tadcaster). *Dom.* Saxtun, 1119 *chart.* Saxtona—*i.e.,* ' town, settlement of Saxons,' O.E. *Seaxe,* in this Anglian region. *Cf.* Saxby (Melton Mowbray). There was also a Saxton (Wood Ditton, Cambs.), *Dom.* Sextone, 1284 Saxtone, which Skeat prefers to derive fr. a man *Saxa. Cf.,* too, *Dom.* Essex Saxendena, and SAXONDALE (Notts), *Dom.* Saxeden, 1291 Saxndal. See -den and -dale.

SCAGGLETHORPE (Malton). *Dom.* Scachetorp, -ertorp, Scarchetorp; 1207 *Fines* Scaketorp. The orig. man's name must be repre-sented by *Dom.*'s Scacher- (*r* easily becomes its kindred liquid *l*) but in *Onom.* we only find *Scacca* or *Scœcca. Cf.* SCACKLETON (Yorks), *Dom.* Scacheldene, evidently fr. the same name; so is Skeckling (Holderness), *Dom.* Scachelinge, ' place of the sons of *Scacel.*' To derive fr. O.N. *skagi,* ' low cape, ness,' accounts for neither the -le nor *Dom.*'s -er.

SCALBY (Yorks). *Dom.* 1178-80 Scallebi, Scalebi. ' Hut or shiel-ing-abode,' O.N. *skale. Cf.* SKELBROOKE, and see -by.

SCAM(P)STON (Yorks). *Dom.* Scameston, 4 times, 1202 *Fines* Scameliston. ' Village of *Scamel.*' *Onom.* has only *Scamma* and *Sceomma. Cf.* SCAGGLETHORPE.

SCARBOROUGH. Not in *Dom.* 1179-80 *Pipe* Scardeburc, 1194 *Rog.* Hoveden Scardleburg, 1297 Schardeburghe, 1436 Scarborough; also Scarhburge. ' Burgh, castle on the sherd or shard,' O.E. *sceard*—*i.e.,* piece ' sheared off.' SCARGILL (N. Yorks) is in *Dom.* Scacreghill, which can hardly be fr. O.N. *sker,* ' a rock, a scaur.' See -gill.

SCAWBY (Lincs). ' Dwelling on the promontory,' O.N. *skage. Cf.* next. But SCAWSBY (Brodsworth, Yorks) is *Dom.* Scalchebi, 1205 Scauceby, ' dwelling of *Scealc,*' 2 in *Onom.* SCAWTON (Yorks), *Dom.* Scaltun, is a little doubtful. *Cf.* SCALBY.

SCAWFELL and S. PIKES (Cumbld.). O.N. *skage,* ' a promontory,' and *fjall,* N. *fjeld,* ' a mountain, a hill.' *Cf.* The Skaw (Den-mark) and The Scaw of Unst. On Pike, see RED PIKE.

SCILLY ISLES. *c.* 400 *Sulpicius Sev.* Sylinancis (insula), *c.* 1200 *Gervase* Insula Suilli, *Sagas* Syllingar, 1345 Insula de Scilly, 1592 Silley (so now pron.), 1603 *Owen* Sorlinges commonly cleped Syllie. In Mod. Fr. Les Iles Sorlingues. A little diffi-cult. The early references are to an *insula,* or ' island,' and may refer to the tiny islet of Scilly, in the N.W. of the group, which has given its name to the whole. The *c* in the name is plainly an intrusion; and the form Sorlinges plainly represents the name as known to the Romans; the liquids *l* and *r* readily interchange. What the *c.* 400 ending -nancis represents it is hard to say. But prob. the Syli- or Suilli is Corn. *silli, selli,* Bret. *sili,* ' a (conger) eel '; so ' isle of eels.' But it might be fr. Corn. *syll, sull,* ' a view, a prospect.' *Cf.* SULLY (Cardiff), and see -ey. The earlier name Cassiterides, ' tin-islands,' must have included part of Cornwall. Κασσιτερίδες goes back to *Herodotus, c.* 450 B.C., and to *Strabo.*

SCORTON (Garstang and Darlington). Da. S. prob. *Dom.* Scortone (Yorks). Prob. ' town of *Scorra*' or ' *Scorta,*' both in *Onom. Cf. Dom.* Norfk. Scartune. But SCOREBY (Pocklington), *Dom.* Scornesbi, must be ' dwelling of ' ? *Sceorfwine.* See -by.

SCOTBY (Carlisle). *c.* 1139 Scotebi, 1189 Scottebi. ' Dwelling of the *Scots*' *:* one cannot be quite sure who are meant. Duignan construes the SCOTLANDS (Bushbury), as O.E. *sceat landes,* ' corner lands.' But Scotforth (Lancaster), *Dom.* Scozford, must be ' Scots' ford ' (*z* = *ts*). See -forth.

SCOTTER (Lincoln). *a.* 1100 *chart.* Scotere. Prob. ' spit of land, Icel. *eyri,* inhabited by Scots.' *Cf.* Scottow (' Scot's how ' or ' hill ') (Norwich), and *Dom.* Norfk. Scottesā.

SCOTTON (Yorks and Lincs). Yor. S. *Dom.* Scotton, -tune. ' Town of the *Scots.*' *Cf.* above.

SCOULTON (Attleborough). *Dom.* Sculetuna. ' Town of *Skuli,*' a N. name.

SCRAYINGHAM (York). *Dom.* Screngha'. Prob. ' home of the sons of *Scræwa,*' 1 in *Onom.* See -ing and -ham.

SCREMERSTON (Berwick). 1197 Schermereton, *later* Screm'ston. Older forms needed. Possibly ' village of *Scealdamer.*' *Cf.* SKELMERSDALE.

SCRIVEN (Knaresboro'). *Dom.* Scravinge. ' Place of the sons of *Scræf*' or ' *Sceorf,*' only the latter in *Onom.* *Cf.* Scarle (Notts), *Dom.* Scorvelei. See -ing and -ley.

SCRUTON (Bedale). *Dom.* Scuruetone. ' Town of *Scurua*' or ' *Scyrua,*' a monk, or perh. of ' *Scurfa,*' a Danish jarl, in *Onom.* *Cf.* SHERATON and Screveton (Notts), *Dom.* Scrivetone, 1284 Scrouton. SCROOBY (Notts) is *Dom.* Scrobi.

SEACOURT (Oxford). *c.* 957 *chart.* Seofecan wyrthe, *Dom.* Seuacoorde, *c.* 1130 *Chron. Abingd.* Seovecwurde, 1401-02 Seokeworthe. A most instructive and warning corruption. ' *Seofeca*'s farm '; whilst SEABRIDGE (Staffs) is *a.* 1300 Sheperugge, ' sheep ridge ' ! See -worth.

SEACROFT (Leeds and Skegness). Le. S. *Dom.* Sacroft, 1199 Secroft. O.E. *sæ,* ' sea,' was also applied to a lake like the Sea of Galilee; but there is no trace of such here. So prob. ' sedgy croft ' or ' farm,' O.E. *sæcg, secg,* 5 *sege,* 7 *sage,* 9 dial. *seag,* ' sedge.' *Cf.* SEAGRY, SEATON, and *Dom.* Northants Sewelle; also see ANCROFT.

SEAFORD (Sussex). 1234 *Close R.* and *c.* 1450 *Fortescue* Seforde. ' Ford, passage, by the sea.'

SEAGRY (Chippenham). *Dom.* Segrie, 1225 *Patent R.* Seggreye. O.E. *secg rithe,* ' sedge-grown strem.' *Cf.* SEDGEFIELD and RYE.

SEAL (Sevenoaks) (*c.* 1250 *chart.* La Sele), and SEALE (Farnham). Neither in *Dom.* O.E. *sœl, sele,* ' a house, a hall.'

SEAMER (Yorks) and SEMER (Ipswich). Yo. S. *Dom.* Semers, Semær, -mer. Prob. O.E. *sem, sam* (ge)*mære,* ' half boundary.' But Sea- seems often doubtful in Eng. place-names. See above *Cf. Dom.* Salop Semebre, ? ' half bank ' (O.E. *obr*). There are 3 men in *Onom.* called *Sœmer* or *Semer.*

SEASALTER (Whitstable). Old forms needed. It may, as some think, be partly of Brythonic orig.; but this is doubtful.

SEASCALE (Cumbld.). ' Dwelling by the sea,' O.N. *skáli,* found in Eng. *a.* 1300 as *scale,* ' a hut, a shed '; same root as *sheal* and *shieling.* *Cf.* GALASHIELS (Sc.) and Bowscale (W. Cumbld.), which is fr. N. *bol skali,* ' hut, shed dwelling.'

SEATON (9 in *P.G.*). *Dom.* and 1179-80 *Pipe* Setton (Yorks); also *Dom.* Seton= Seaton Ross. 1298 'Simon de Seyton,' ? which. Not all are on the sea—*e.g.*, Seaton (Uppingham). So Sea- may represent some of the many O.E. names in Sæ- or Sea-, 'town of ?' The Sc. SEATON is called after the *De Sey* family. But Setton looks like *seat-town*, with *seat* in the sense of 'settlement,' country 'seat,' O.E. *sæt*, as in SOMERSET.

SEATON CAREW (W. Hartlepool). Said to be *a*. 1130 *Sim. Dur.* Ceattune, 'town of *Ceatta*.' The hard O.E. *c* very rarely becomes *s*. The Carew may be fr. Henry *Carey* or *Carew* (the names are the same), first Baron Hunsdon, who received lands in Yorks fr. Q. Elizabeth in 1571.

SECKINGTON (Tamworth). *O.E. Chron.* 755, Secggandune, Sæcandune—*i.e.*, 'hill' or 'hill-fort of *Secca* or *Seccga*'; several in *Onom.*

SEDBERGH (Yorks). *Dom.* Sedberge, 1549 Sedberg. O.E. *sæd*, 3 *sed*, 'sad,' often in early use 'massive, solid,' also, fr. 1412 'dark, deep in colour'; -bergh is a M.E. var. of BARROW, O.E. *beorh, berh*, 'a hill.' *Cf. Dom.* Roeberg hundred, *later* Rugheberg, Rubergh, name of a now defunct 'hundred' in Berks.

SEDGEBERROW (Evesham). 771 and 964 *chart.* Secgesbearwe, *Dom.* Seggesbarve, 1275 Seggesberrow. Prob. 'BARROW, hill or tumulus of *Secg*.' SEDGELEY (Wolverhmptn.) is *c*. 1006 *chart.* Secges lea, *Dom.* Segleslei (*l* for *c*), *a*. 1300 Seggesleye, clearly '*Secg*'s' or '*Segge*'s lea,' though the name is not in *Onom.* Also *cf.* SEDGEMOOR.

SEDGEFIELD (Ferryhill). Said to be *a*. 1130 *Sim. Dur.* Ceddesfeld—*i.e.*, '*Ceadda*'s' or '*Chad*'s field.' Note the corruption. *Cf.* SHADWELL. Only in 1183 *Boldon Bk.* it is Seggesfeld, and 1197 *Rolls* Secchefeld, plainly fr. O.E. *secg*, 'sedge, rushes'; see next. So that the identification of *Sim. Dur.*'s name is prob. wrong.

SEDGEMOOR (Somerset). It cannot be *K.C.D.* iii. 386 Seзes mere. O.E. *secg*, 5-*sedge*, is applied to various coarse, rush-like plants; *mere*, of course, is 'lake.' *Cf.* above.

SEDLESCOMBE (Battle). 'Valley of *Sedel*'; *cf. B.C.S.* 997 Sideleshham, and *Dom.* Kent Sedlinges, the patronymic. See -combe.

SEFTON (Liverpool). *Dom.* Sexton (*x* an error), 1236 Ceffton, 1249 Cefton, 1318 Sefton. Either fr. a man *Sæffa* (*cf. Dom.* Leics. Sevesbi) or fr. O.N. *sef*, 'sedge.'

SEIGHFORD (Stafford). *Dom.* Cesteford, *a*. 1400 Sesteford. In *Dom.* often *st= ht*, as *Dom.* hates gutturals, so this is prob. O.E. *seohtre ford*, 'brook, ditch ford.'

SEINT or SEOINT (Carnarvon). Prob. *c*. 380 *Ant. Itin.* Segontium. Also called Caer Seoint; prob. the same as Cair Segeint in list appended to Nennius. The *Segontiaci* were a British tribe who prob. dwelt near Silchester.

SEISDON (Wolverhmptn.). *Dom.* Seis-, Saisdone, *a.* 1300 Seisden. Duignan is puzzled here. Seis- prob. is a contraction of some man's name, ? *Siward, Sœwulf, Seulf;* it might be W. *Sais,* 'a Saxon.' See -don.

SELBY. *Sic* 1483; not in *Dom. a.* 1130 *Sim. Dur.* Selebi. May be ' dwelling of ' a man with one of the many O.E. names in Sele-, Seleforth, Selewig, etc. But Sel- may also be Icel. *sel,* ' a shed at a mountain-farm,' a *sœtor,* or else O.N. *sœll,* ' happy.' See -by.

SELLACKS MARSH (Ross, Herefd.). Prob. 1160-61 *Pipe* Salceia. Prob. ' isle of *Seolca* ' or ' *Seoloce,*' names in *Onom.;* -eia = -ey, *q.v.* Sellacks is for *Seoloce*'s. It might be fr. L. *salic(e)tum,* ' a willow grove '; hence the Fr. name Saussaie.

SELLAFIELD (Whitehaven). Hybrid. N. *selja,* ' a dairy.'

SELLY OAK (Birmingham). *a.* 1200 Selleg', Selley. Doubtful. Sell- or Selle- prob. represents a man's name, a contraction of one of the many in Sele-, Seleburh, Selered, etc. The ending may either be -ey or -ley, *q.v.*

SELSEA. *Bede* Selaeseu, Selesei (in *a.* 900 O.E. *versn.* Sylesea), quod dicitur Insula vituli marini (' isle of the sea calf '). Seal-island,' O.E. *siol, seol ;* Icel. *sel-r.* See -ea.

SELSTON (Nottingham). *Dom.* Salestune, 1284 Seliston. Perh. same name as 1160 *Pipe* Selveston (Northants). ' Village of *Selua,*' 2 in *Onom.* Also *cf. Dom.* Kent Selesburne and Selinge, which postulate a man *Sele,* and a patronymic. See -ing.

SELWOOD (now Frome or Frome Selwood). 878 O.E. *Chron.* Seal-wudu, *c.* 893 *Asser* ' Selundu—i.e., sylva magna in Latin, Coit maur in British.' O.E. *sél,* ' good.' *Cf. Dom.* Hants, Seldene.

SEMER (Ipswich). See SEAMER.

SEMLEY (Shaftesbury). ' Half-meadow '; O.E. *sam, sem. Cf. Dom.* Bucks Senlai. See -ley.

SEMP(E)RINGHAM (Bourne). O.E. *Chron.* 852 Sempiȝaham, 1156 Shim-, Shempingeham, ? *c.* 1290 The Ermitage of Sempling-ham, *c.* 1330 Sempyngham. A patronymic. See -ham; and *cf.* SHIMPLING. *Semple* is still a common surname, but it is for *St. Paul.*

SENNEN (Land's End). From *Senan,* b. Co. Clare, *c.* 488, Bp. near Kilrush, and friend of St. David.

SESSAY (Thirsk). *Dom.* Sezai. Doubtful. In *Dom. z* usually = *ts;* ? ' isle of *Sœgeat* ' or ' *Saietus,*' names in *Onom.* See -ay.

SETHAR (Lizard). Corn. for ' gull, sea-mew.'

SETTLE (Yorks). *Dom.* Setel. O.E. *setl,* ' a seat, a resting-place.' *Cf.* 939 *chart.* ' Fram Setle to netles stede,' near Maidstone.

SETTRINGTON (Malton). *Dom.* Sendriton, *c.* 1100 Seteringetun, 1179-80 Setrinton. Might be ' abode of the *sœtor* (N.) or sum-mer-farm dwellers.' Only *Dom.*'s form must then be a mistake. There is no name in *Onom.* like *Sender.* See -ing and -ton.

SEVENOAKS (Kent and Northwich). J. R. Green thought prob. a sacred group of trees forming an ancient boundary-mark. Snooks is a corrup. of this word. The town in Kent does not seem to go back much before 1400. There is a Sevenstorp in *Dom.* Yorks. SEVENHAMPTON (Glouc. and Wilts) is *Dom.*, both, Sevenhamtone. See HAMPTON. Sennington, close by the former, is a corrup. of the same name.

SEVERN R., in W. Hafren. *c.* 90 *Tacitus* Sabrina, 893 *O.E. Chron.* Sæfern, *Dom.* Saverna, *c.* 1190 *Gir. Camb.* Haveren, 1297 *R. Glouc.* Seuerne, *c.* 1450 Saverne. Name prob. pre-Keltic; change of Kelt. *h* to Rom. *s* is according to rule.

SEWERBY (Bridlington). *Dom.* Siward-, Siwarbi. ' Dwelling of *Sigeweard* ' or ' *Siward.*' See -by.

SHACKERSTON (Atherstone). 1298 ' Ricardus de Shakelston.' Prob. ' town of *Sæcol* ' or ' *Sæcolf*,' in *Onom.* The liquids *l* and *r* readily interchange. *Cf.* the common surname Shackleton.

SHADFORTH (Durham). 1183 Shaldeford, Shadeford. O.E. *sceald ford*, ' shallow ford.' See SHALCOMBE, SHALFORD, and -forth.

SHADWELL (E. London). Said to be ' St. *Chad's* well.' *Cf.* SEDGE-FIELD ; but see above.

SHAFTESBURY. *c.* 893 *Asser* Sceftesburg, 935 *chart.* Scheftesburi, 982 *O.E. Chron.* Sceaftesbyrig, 1156 Shaftesbiria, 1228 Saftesbir.' Prob. not fr. O.E. *sceaft*, ' a spear, dart, pole,' but fr. a man so-called. *Cf.* next and *B.C.S.* 629 Sceaftes hangra (wooded slope), also Scaftworth (Notts), *Dom.* Scafteorde; and see -bury and -worth.

SHAFTON (Barnsley). *Dom.* Sceptone, -tun. ' Village with the sheep '; O.E. *sceap*. *Cf.* SHEFFORD.

SHALBOURNE (Hungerford). *B.C.S.* iii. 404 æt Scealdeburnan; *Dom.* Eseldeborne (a Norm. addition of *e*, as they could not pro-nounce our *sh* ; *cf.* SHEFFIELD), 1316 Shaldeburne, *c.* 1540 Shalborne. O.E. *sceald burna*, ' shallow brook or burn.' See next and SHELFORD.

SHALCOMBE (I. of W.). *Dom.* Eseldecome (on E- see above); and SHALFLEET (I. of W.). 838 *chart.* Scealdan fleote, *Dom.* Selde flet. ' Shallow valley,' see -combe, and ' shallow river,' see FLEET. O.E. *sceald*, ' shallow' (in Barbour *schald*, same root as *shoal*), curiously enough is not in O.E. dicts. Form 838, also 939 *chart.* Scealdan forð, Shaftesbury, suggest derivation fr. a man *Scealda*. Skeat does not favour this, but it is quite possible; *cf.* SHALSTONE (Bucks), *Dom.* Scaldetone. *Cf.* also SHADFORTH and next.

SHALFORD (Braintree and Guildford). Br. S. *Dom.* Escaldeforde, Scaldefort. Gu. S. *Dom.* Scaldeford. O.E. *sceald ford*, ' shallow ford.' See above.

SHANKLIN (I. of W.). *Dom.* Sencliz. The *z* prob. represents a nasalized *g* or *ng*, and so this is prob. O.E. *sc(e)anca hlinc*, ' rising

ground, ridge, like a man's *shank*' (M.E. *sanke*), or 'legbone.'
Cf. Oxf. Dict. shank sb. 8. *Hlinc* is, of course, the mod. *links*.

SHAPCOMBE (Devon). *Dom.* Scobacoma. 'Valley of *Scoba*.' There
is a *Scobba* and a *Scoppo* in *Onom.* *Cf.* Shapwick (Bridgewater),
and see -combe. But SHAPRIDGE, (For. of Dean) is 1281-82
Sheepridge; O.E. *sceap*.

SHAP FELL (Westmorld.). Prob. 'hill shaped like a bushel.'
O.N. *skjappa*. Shap Abbey dates *a.* 1200. *Cf.* SCAWFELL.

SHARESHILL (Wolverhmptn.). *Dom.* Servesed, *a.* 1200 Sareshulf,
a. 1300 Sarnesculf, Sarneshull, Sharnshull, S(h)areshull. A
much altered name. *Dom.* is prob. '*Sceorf*'s head,' and Sareshulf or -sculf, '*Sceorf*'s shelf' of land. *Cf.* SHELFANGER, etc.
Hull is common midl. M.E. for *hill*.

SHARNBROOK (Beds), *Dom.* Sernebroc, and SHARNFORD (Hinckley).
Dom. Scerneford. *Cf.* 792 *chart.* Scranaburna (belonging to
St. Albans). These all seem to come fr. O.E. *scearn*, O.N. *skarn*,
O.Fris. *skern*, N.Fris. *sjaarn*, 'dung, esp. dung of cattle,' still
in dial. as *sharn*.

SHARPNESS (Berkeley, Glouc.). 956 *chart.* On scearpan nesse.
O.E. for 'sharp, pointed headland'; perh. not this one. It is
1349 Sharpenesse. The Berkeley MSS. forms—Shopenash,
Shobenasse, etc.—prob. refer to another place.

SHATTERFORD (Bewdley). 996 *chart.* Sciteresford, 1286 Sheteresford.
'Shooter's, archer's ford'; O.E. *scytere, sceótere*.

SHAVINGTON (Nantwich). 1298 Shaventon. 'Town of *Sceafa*' in *Onom.*

SHAW (Melksham and Lancs). Mel. S. *Dom.* Essages (*cf.* SHAL-
BOURNE), 1291 Schawe, 1316 Shaghe. O.E. *scaga*, 'thicket,
wood.' Shaw is common in Sc. names.

SHEEN (Surrey and Longnor). Sur. S. O.E. *chart.* Sceon; Lon. S.
Dom. ib. Prob. O.E. *scine, scene, sceone*, 'beautiful.' Its use as
sb. seems late. There is also a Sheen Hill (Worcs).

SHEERNESS. O.N. *skœrr nes*, or M.E. *scere næs*, 'bright, clear
headland.' The adj. *sheer* is very puzzling; see *Oxf. Dict.* The
town is comparatively recent.

SHEFFIELD. *Dom.* Scevelt, Scafeld, Escafeld; 1298 *Writ* Shefelde;
c. 1386 *Chaucer* Sheffeld. 'Field on the R. Sheaf'; O.E. *scéaf*,
'a sheaf.' On Norm. prefixing of E- in *Dom.*, see SHALBOURNE.
But SHEFFORD on R. Lambourne (Berks), *Dom.* Siford, is O.E.
Scypford, 'sheep ford.' *Cf.* SHAFTON.

SHELDON (Birmingham) and SHELFIELD (Henley-in-Arden). *a.* 1200
Scheldon, 1370 Scheldone, *a.* 1300 Scelefhull, 1322 Schelfhull.
Prob. both fr. O.E. *scelfe*, 'shelf-like' or 'shelving hill,' and
'field.' *Cf.* SHELFANGER, SHELTON (Staffs), *Dom.* Scelfitone,
a. 1350 Selfton, *a.* 1400 Schelton; also *Dom.* Bucks Skeldene,
and SHILDON; and see -don and -ton.

SHELF (Halifax). *Dom.* Scelf. O.E. *scelfe*, 'shelf' (of rock, etc.). *Cf. Dom.* Scelves (Worc.) and SHELFIELD (Walsall); *Dom.* Scelfeld, *a.* 1300 Schelfhul.

SHELFANGER (Diss). 1291 Shelfangel. O.E. *scelfe-angra*, 'shelf-like, wooded slope.' *Cf.* BIRCHANGER.

SHELFORD (Cambridge and Stoke Ferry, Notts). Cam. S. *c.* 1080 *Inquis.* Camb. Esceldford, Sceldford; *Dom.* Escelforde, 1210 Selford; *cf. K.C.D.* iv. 157 Scealdeforda. O.E. *sceald*, M.E. *schald*, *scheld*, 'shallow.' *Cf.* SHALBOURNE, SHALFORD, and Shallowford (Stone), *a.* 1300 Schaldeford. The initial E- is a Norman euphonic prefix, and quite according to rule.

SHELLINGFORD (Faringdon). *B.C.S.* ii. 373, Scaringaford, but p. 372 Xalingeford (*X* for *Sh*); *Dom.* Serengeford, 1291 Schalinge-ford, 1316 Shallingford. Curious corrup. ' Ford of the *Scarings* ' or ' sons of *Scara.*' *Cf. Kent. chart.* Scarendene.

SHELSLEY BEAUCHAMP and WALSH (R. Teme, Worcester). *Dom.* Caldeslei, 1275 Sceldeley Walleys, 1346 Sheldesleye. Prob. fr. some man *Sceld* or *Sceald*, rather than fr. O.E. *scyld*, and so 'island like a shield.' See -ey. B. and W. were former owners. 1275 *Subsidy Roll* says: ' Quod Henricus le Waleys quondam tenuit.' Waleys, Wallace, Walsh, and Welsh are all the same name, and mean ' the Welshman.'

SHENBORO' and SHENINGTON (Glouc.). *Sic* 1293, but *Dom.* Senen-done, 1263 Schenedon. ' Hill ' or ' town of the beautiful man '; O.E. *scén*, Ger. *schön*, 'fair, beautiful,' also used as a personal name, now spelt Chiene, but pron. sheen. We get the patrony-mic in SHEN-, SHINGAY (Cambs), *c.* 1080 *Inquis. Camb.* Sceningei, 1276 Schenegeye, ' *Shening*'s isle.' *Cf.* SHEEN, Shenfield (Brent-wood), Shenley (Barnet), Skinflats (Grangemouth), and next.

SHENSTONE (Lichfield and Hartlebury). Li. S. *a.* 1100 Scenstan, *Dom.* Seneste, *a.* 1200 S(h)enestan, *a.* 1300 Schenestane; Ha. S. 1275 Scheneston, 1327 Shenston. O.E. *scene stan*, 'beautiful, bright rock' or ' stone.' *Cf.* SHEEN.

SHEPLEY = SHIPLEY, and SHEPTON = SHIPTON.

SHEPPERTON (Middlesex). *Dom.* Scepertone. No likely name in *Onom.*, and *skipper*, which is Du. or Low Ger., is not in Eng. *a.* 1390; so prob. ' Ship's host or army town,' fr. O.E. *scip-here.* Possibly, not prob., fr. Corn. *sciber*, W. *ysgubor*, in Eng. 1567 *skipper*, ' a barn.'

SHEPPEY (Kent). *a.* 716 *chart.* Scepeis, O.E. *Chron.* 832 Sceap ige— *i.e.,* ' sheep island '; also 1229 *Close R.* Shipweya, 1230 Sypweya. There is also a Sheppy or Sheepway near Bristol. See -ey.

SHEPRETH (Royston, Herts). *c.* 1080 *Inquis. Camb.* Scepereie *Dom.* Escepride, 1302 Scheperethe. Not ' sheep stream,' O.E. *rith, ride*, says Skeat, because of the long *i*, whilst here we have only a short *e*. Prob. fr. O.E. *wræð, wræd*, ' a wreath, a ring, a

bandage, then a fence of twisted or wreathed hurdles.' *Cf.*
MELDRETH, near by.

SHEPSHED (Loughboro'). 1245 Shepesheved. 'Headland like the
head of a sheep'; O.E. *héafod*, 2-5 *heved*; Dan. *hoved*, 'head.'
But SHEPSCOMBE (Painswick), 1263 Sebbescombe, is 'valley of
Sceobba.'

SHERATON (Castle Eden). 1183 Shurutona. 'Village of *Scurua*'
or '*Scyrua,*' a name in *Onom. Cf.* SCRUTON.

SHERBORNE. 671 Scireburnensis ecclesia, *O.E. Chron.* 860 Scira-
burna, 905 Scireburnensis, *c.* 1130 *Wm. Malm.* Schireburnensis.
O.E. *scire burna*, 'brook, burn at the shire or division.' SHER-
BOURN (Warwick) is also *Dom.* Scireburne, the boundary between
the hundreds of Barlichway and Kineton. And SHERBURN
(Durham) is 1183 Sirburne, prob. the same root; whilst SHER-
BORNE (Glouc.), *Dom.* Sareburne, is doubtful. There is an O.E.
scir, 'bright, pure.'

SHERIFF-HUTTON (Yorks). 1398 Schiref hoton. 'Village, enclosure
on the *hoe.*' See HUTTON. Presumably a sheriff lived here.

SHERINGHAM (N. Norfk.). *Dom.* Sc(h)erninga', '1351 Shiryng-, *c.* 1460
Sheringham.' Prob. O.E. Sciranham. 'Home of *Scira,*' 2 in
Onom. Prob. here a patronymic. SHERINGTON (Newport Pag-
nell), *Dom.* Serintone, is prob. fr. same name. No *Sera* in
Onom. See -ing.

SHERSTONE (Wilts). 1016 *O.E. Chron.* Sceorstan, *c.* 1100 *Encom.*
Emmae Scorastan, *a.* 1130 *Sim. Dur.* Scearstan. Prob., though
not certainly, fr. late O.E. *scoru*; O.N. *skor*, 'a notch, a tally,
a score,' same root as *shear*; O.E. *sceran.* Thus the name may
mean 'stone, rock with the notch or crevice,' or 'boundary
stone,' or 'a standing stone with a sharp edge' (M'Clure).

SHERWOOD FOREST (Notts). 1189 *Pipe* Schirewude, 1237 Shirewud
—*i.e.*, 'wood at the shire or boundary.' *Cf.* SHERBORNE.

SHEVINGTON MOOR (Wigan). 1200-33 Shefinton, 1268-79 Shevinton,
1322 Skeventon. 'Town, village of *Sceafa,*' gen. -*an. Cf.*
Scevintone, *Dom.* Salop.

SHIDE (Newport, I. of W.). *Dom.* Side. Prob. aspirated form of
O.E. *side*, 'a side,' found in Eng. with the meaning 'slope of a
hill' as early as *c.* 1250. For similar aspiration *cf.* Shareshill
(Wolverhmptn.), *Dom.* Servesed, *a.* 1200 Sareshulf, also, in same
district, the Showells, *a.* 1300 Sewalle, Sewale.

SHIFFORD (Oxford). 'Sheep ford' = SHEFFORD.

SHILDON (Co. Durham). 1211 Selvedon. Prob., as in SHELDON,
O.E. *scelfe dún*, 'shelf-like hill.' See -don.

SHILLINGSTONE (Blandford), also called SHILLING OCKFORD (*cf.*
OCKBROOK). *Old* Ockford Eskelling, fr. a man *Schelin* or

Eschelinus in *Dom.* On the E- prefixed by *Dom.*, see SHAL-BOURNE. But SHILLINGTON (Hitchin) is *c.* 1080 Schitlingedune, *Dom.* Sethlindone, *Rams. Hist.* Schitlingdone, fr. an unrecorded patronymic *Scitling. Onom.* has nothing but *Sceaftweald* and *Scilling.* See -ing, -don, and -ton.

SHILSTON (several farms, Devon). Said to be ' shelf stone '—*i.e.*, the site of a dolmen; O.E. *scelfe, scylfe,* ' a shelf.'

SHIMPLING (Bury St. Edmunds). *Dom.* Sempingaham; see SEMP-RINGHAM. On the dropping of the -ham, *cf.* Woking and Wokingham.

SHINFIELD (Reading). *Dom.* Scanesfelt, 1316 Shenyngfelde; also Senefeld, Schunnyngfeld. Skeat thinks the *Dom.* form a scribal error, and says this is ' field of the *Scienings* ' or ' sons of *Sciene.*' *Cf.* the mod. name Chiene, pron. Sheen, and next.

SHINGAY (Cambs). *Old* Shening-ay. ' Isle of the *Scienings.*' See above.

SHIPLEY (Leeds and Salop) and SHIPTON (10 in all). *Dom.* Warwk. Sciplea (in Salop), Yorks Scipeleia. ' Sheep meadow ' and ' sheep village '; fr. O.E. *scéap, scép,* ' a sheep,' and so = Shepley (Huddersfield), *Dom.* Seppeleia, and the Sheptons. See also -ley and -ton. SHEPTON MALLET (Somerset) has added to it the name of its former owners; Malet is still a surname. SHIPTON-UNDER-WYCHWOOD (Oxford) is *c.* 1450 Schiptone under Whic-wode. See WYCHWOOD; and *cf.* RAMPTON.

SHIPPEN (W. Riding), *Dom.* Scipen, and SHIPPON (Abingdon). *c.* 1100 *Chron. Abing.* Scippene, Scipena; 1316 Shupene. O.E. *scypen,* ' a cow-house '; dial. Eng. *shippen, shuppen.*

SHIPSTON-ON-STOUR. 770 *chart.* Scepeswasce, 957 *ib.* Scepwæsctun. *Dom.* Scepwestun. A curious contraction. ' Town of the sheepwash.' SHIPTON OLIFF (Glouc.), *Dom.* Scip(e)tone, is ' sheep-town.' Oliff is the family name Olive.

SHIRLEY (Solihull, Derby, and Southampton). Sol. S. *a.* 1300 Schirley. Der. S. *Dom.* Sirelei. Doubtful. There is no likely name in *Onom.*, and no O.E. *sire.* Prob. O.E. *scir léah,* ' shire meadow '; *cf.* SHERBORNE and Shirbourne (Coventry) (*a.* 1300 Shirburne), which mean ' shire ' or ' boundary brook '; also SHIREOAKS (Notts) and SKIRLAUGH.

SHOBDON (Herefordsh.) and SHOBNALL (Burton-on-T.). *a.* 1300 Sco-, Shobenhale. ' Hill ' and ' nook of *Sceoba,*' gen. -*an.* See -don and -hall.

SHOBROOKE R. (Devon). 930 *chart.* Sceocabroc; O.E. for ' brook of *Sceocca* '—*i.e.*, the devil, Satan ! *Cf.* SHUCKBURGH.

SHOCKLACH (Malpas). *Dom.* Socheliche. The first syll. must be as above, and the second is a rare variant of O.E. *léah,* ' a meadow.' *Cf.* SKIRLAUGH and STUBLACH; and see -leigh.

SHOEBURY (Essex). 893 *O.E. Chron.* Sceoburg, 994 *ib.* Sceobyrig. Hardly fr. O.E. *sceó,* ' a shoe '; prob. ' burgh, fort of *Sceoba* ' or ' *Sceobba,*' in *Onom.*

SHOOTER'S HILL (London). 1549 *Latimer,* Shooters hyll. Prob. a resort for archery.

SHOREDITCH (London). *K.C.D.* index, a ' *Sordic.*' *c.* 1360 Soerditch, 1597-98 Shorditch. *Stow,* 1598, says he had evidence that 400 years before his day it was called Soersditch. *Soer* prob. is the name of a man. There are in *Onom. Soart* and *Sogor. Cf.* next. *Shore* meaning ' sewer ' is not found till 1598.

SHOREHAM (Sussex, Sevenoaks). Not in *Dom.* Sus. S. 1234 *Close R.* Shor-, 1238 *ib.* Sorham; but *c.* 1120 *Hen. Hunt.* Cymensore, ' shore, border of *Cymen,*' now represented by KEYNOR. Thus it would seem the *Cymen* has been dropped, and the ending -sore treated as if it were a proper name, and the common -ham added. Shoreham (Kent) is *sic a.* 1300, and can have nothing to do with *shore* either. The last is prob. fr. Du., and not found in Eng. till 14th cny. Shore- here must be a name, as in Jane *Shore,* famous mistress of Edw. IV. The only likely name in *Onom.* is one *Scorra. Cf.* next, and 1231 *Close R.* Sorham (Suffk).

SHORNCLIFFE (Folkestone), ? *Dom.* Soaneclive (*a* error for *r*), and SHORNE (Gravesend). 1160-61 *Pipe* Shorna. The root seems to be O.E. *scieran,* ' to sheer, cut off '; pa. pple. *scoren,* ' shorn, cut short off, precipitous.' O.E. *scearn,* O.N. *skarn,* ' sharn, dung of cattle,' 6-9 *shorn,* and *a.* 1300 *chart.* schorn-penny, does not seem likely.

SHORWELL (Newport, I. of W.). *Dom.* Sorewella. ' Well of *Sor(r)a* ' (not recorded), or ' *Scorru.*' See SHOREHAM.

SHOTOVER (Oxford). *Dom.* Scotorne (error for -ovre), *Close R.* 1229 Sothore, 1230 Shotor', 1231 Shotovr'. Not *chateau vert!* but ' *shot,* division of land on the bank or brink '; O.E. *obr, ofer;* M.E. *overe.* See ALDERSHOT and -over.

SHOTSWELL (Kineton). 1123 Soteswalle, -welle; *a.* 1300 S(c)hoteswell. ' Well '; O.E. *wella,* ' of *Scot* ' (in *Onom.*) or ' the Scot.' *Cf.* next.

SHOTTERY (Stratford-on-Avon). 704-09 *chart.* Scottarith, O.E. for ' stream of the *Scots.*' How came they here ? 1016 ' on Scotrithes gemæro,' *a.* 1400 Shoteriche, Shotrech. *Cf.* next. On *rith cf.* CHILDREY.

SHOTTESBROOKE (Bray). *Dom.* Sotesbroc, 1189 Schottesbroch, 1316 Sotesbroke. ' *Scot*'s brook.' *Cf.* 958 *chart.* Scotteshealh (haugh), and above.

SHOTTON (Wooler, Castle Eden, and Flint). Wool. S. *a.* 1130 *Sim. Dur.* Scotadun, but *c.* 1230 Schottun; Cas. S. *a.* 1130 *Sim. Dur.* Sceottun, 1183 Siottona and Shotton. This name represents two, or rather three, different meanings: (1) Scots' ' down or hill,' (2) ' Scots' town,' and (3) ' town, village on which is levied a scot or tax '; O.E. *sc(e)ot*, *gesc(e)ot*, same words as in ' paying your shot.' Without old forms the Flint name is uncertain.

SHOTWICK (Chester). 1340 Shotwyk. Prob. ' dwelling ' (O.E. *wíc*) ' of a *Scot* '; but *cf.* above.

SHRAWARDINE (Shrewsbury). Prob. *Dom.* Salevrdine (*cf.* SALFORD Br.), where we have a Nor. scribe making exactly the same phonetic change as SALOP for Shropshire; 1318 Luytel (Little) Shrowardyn. The Shra- may either mean ' cave ' or a man's name *Scrawa*; see next. The ending means ' farm, holding '; see -wardine. We also have a Stavrdine in *Dom.* Salop.

SHRAWLEY (Stourport). 804 *chart.* Scræfleh, *a.* 1200 Escreælei (Norm. spelling), 1275 Schreweley. And SHREWLEY (Warwick) *Dom.* Servelei, *a.* 1300 Screweley, Shreueley, Schreule, *a.* 1400 Sravesle, Shreussle. Both may be ' meadow with the cave '; O.E. *scræf.* But Duignan thinks the forms of the latter all point to a worn-down form of O.E. *scír gerefa*, ' shire reeve, sheriff.' Also *cf.* *B.C.S.* 723 Scræwanleah, near Exeter, which must represent a man's name. See -ley.

SHREWSBURY, also SALOP and SHROPSHIRE. 901 *chart.* In civitate Scrobbensis, 1007 *O.E. Chron.* Scrobbesbyrg, 1083 *chart.* Salopesberia, *Dom.* Sciropesberie, *c.* 1097 *Flor. Worc.* Scrobbesbyria, *a.* 1145 *Orderic* Scrobesburia, *c.* 1190 *Gir. Camb.* Solopusburia, 1271 Salopseburi, 1283 Slopesbiry, 1387 Schroysbury, 1461 Schrevisbery, 1485 Shrewsbury; also 1088 *O.E. Chron.* Scrobscyre. Shrewsbury is O.E. *scrobbes byrg*, ' burgh, castle among the shrubs,' Shropshire is simply Scrobscire, whilst Salopesbury is supposed to be the nearest that the Norman could come in pron. to Scrobbesbury. Then the -bury was dropped, and we get Salop. No Norman could pron. Sc-. *Cf.* SHRAWARDINE.

SHRIVENHAM (W. Berks). *K.C.D.* vi. 131 Scrifenan hamm; *O.E. chart.* Scrivenanhom, *Dom.* Scrivenham, 1316 Shrivenham. ' Enclosure of *Scrifena*,' an unknown man. *Scrivein—i.e.*, scrivener —is found in Eng. *a.* 1300. *Cf.* SCRUTON; and see -ham.

SHUCKBURGH (Southam) and SHUCKNALL (Hereford). *Dom.* Socheberge, *a.* 1300 Suckeberge, Shukborow, Schuckborough. Shucknall will be O.E. Scuccan heal. ' Nook ' and ' castle of the Devil '; O.E. *scucca*, ' Satan, a demon, evil spirit.' *Cf.* SHUGBOROUGH (Staffs), *a.* 1400 Shokke-, Shukburgh, and SHOBROOKE. See -burgh and -hall.

SHUSTOKE (Coleshill and Walsall). Col. S. *Dom.* Scotescote, 1256 Schuttestok, 1290 Schustoke. *Dom.* is ' *Scot*'s cottage '; as to the *Scot*, *cf.* SHOTTERY. But STOKE is ' place.'

SHUTTINGTON (Tamworth). *Dom.* Cetitone, 1165 Sheftintone, *a.* 1300 Schetynton, 1327 Schutinton. *Dom.*'s form is abnormal, and prob. represents a deliberate change fr. the original O.E. *Sceaftingtun* (as it would seem), 'village of Sceaft's descendants.' SHURDINGTON (Leckhampton), 1148 Schurden-, 1157 Scherdyntone, is thought to be fr. *Scirgeard* or *Scirierd*, one in *Onom.* See -ing.

SIBLE HEDINGHAM (Essex). *Dom.* Hedingham, but 1488 Henyngham, 1489 Hevenyngham. It is not easy to explain the change of *n* to *d* after 1489. The name is a patronymic, 'home of the sons of *Hœdda*' or '*Headda*,' a very common name. See -ing.

SIBSTONE (Atherstone). 'Stone of *Siba*' or '*Sibba.*' *Cf. Dom.* Sibetune (Salop), and Sibetorp, now SIBTHORPE (Notts).

SICKLINGHALL (Wetherby). *Dom.* Sichingal, Sidingale (*d* error for *cl*), *c.* 1150 Sieclinhale. 'Nook of the *Sicklings,*' an unrecorded patronymic, though we do have Suckling. It is prob. 'sons of *Sœcol*' or '*Sœcolf*'; 1 in *Onom.* See -ing and -hall.

SIDCUP (Kent). Old forms needed, not in *Dom.* Prob. '*Sida*'s cop' or 'hill'; O.E. *cop, copp,* 'head, summit, hill.' *Cf. B.C.S.* 159 Sidan ham. The first syll. might be O.E. *sœd,* 3 *sed,* 4-5 *said,* 'sad,' often in early use 'massive, solid,' and also fr. 1412 'dark, deep in colour.' *Cf.* SEDBERGH, and SIDDINGTON (Cirencester), *Dom.* Sudin-, Suditone, plainly fr. *Syda* or *Sida.*

SIDDICK (Workington). This is said to be O.E. *Scidwíc,* 'dwelling at the *shed*' or 'divide'; O.E. *scéadan,* 'to separate.' But this is doubtful; more prob. fr. some man *Sida* or *Side.* *Cf.* SIDENHALL (Tamworth), *a.* 1300 Sydenhale. Sidnall (Cherbury) is orig. the same. In later North. MSS. of *Layamon* the Wall of Severus is Sid-wall. Side sb., O.E. *side,* is 4-5 *sid,* and this quite possibly gives the origin, its root being possibly O.E. *sid,* 'ample, spacious, extensive.' *Sid wic,* 'ample dwelling,' is a very likely name.

SIDLESHAM (Chichester). *B.C.S.* 997 Sidelesham. *Cf. Exon. Dom.* Sidelham. 'Home of *Sidel.*'

SID R. and SIDMOUTH (S.E. Devon). *Dom.* Sedemude. Sidmouth *may* be Ptolemy's Dunion. The root of Sid may be W. *sid,* 'a round, a circling.'

SILCHESTER (Reading). *c.* 1205 *Layam.* Selechæstre. *c.* 150 *Ptolemy* Caleva, which may be caled-va, with *caled = silva* or 'wood.' *Cf.* the name Caledonia in Tacitus *Agricola.* But Sil- or Silechester is also derived fr. L. *silex, -icis,* 'flint,' and the first syll. is really quite doubtful. Quite possibly the name is 'good camp,' fr. O.E. *sél,* 'good.' Eng. names in -chester, *q.v.,* almost never have a L. word like *silva* or *silex* as the first part.

SILKMORE (Stafford), SILKSTONE (Barnsley), and SILKSWORTH (Sunderland). *Dom.* Selchmore, *a.* 1400 Selke-, Silkemor; *Dom.*

Silchestone. ' Moor,' ' town,' and ' farm of *Seolca*.' *Cf.* Silkby (S. Lincs). See -ton and -worth.

SILLOTH (Cumbld.). Perh., as Dr. Guest thinks, same word as SOLWAY. Prob. N. *söl wath*, ' muddy ford '; O.E. *sol*, ' mud,' that which ' sullies.'

SILSDEN (Keighley). *Dom.* Siglesdene. The name is a little uncertain; more old forms needed. It may be ' *Sigelac*'s ' or ' *Silac*'s,' or else ' *Sigefugul*'s dean ' or ' woody vale.' See -den. Sigglesthorne (Hull), *Dom.* Siglestorne, is fr. the same name.

SILTON (York). ? *O.E. Chron.* 779 Seletun, prob. ' village by the hall '; O.E. *sele*. But it is *Dom.* Silftune, Silvetune, which seems to be ' town of *Seulf*,' short form of *Sæwulf*.

SILVERDALE (Carnforth), *chart.* Siuerdale, '*Sigeweard*'s dale. SILVER How (see -how), and SILVERSIDE (*cf.* Ambleside), Lake District, are thought to be fr. *Selver*, gen. of the O.N. personal name *Sölvr*. This will do for North. names, but hardly for SILVER STREET, a common name for old roads in the South.

SILVERLEY (Cambs). *c.* 1080 *Inquis. Cambs.* Seuerlaio, also Seiluerleia; *Dom.* Severlai, 1284 Silverle. ' Silver-like meadow.' *Cf.* Silverdale (Newcastle, Stafford), Silverhill (St. Leonard's), Silverton (Devon); but *cf.* above. SILVERTON (Devon) is *Dom.* Sulfretone. ' Silver town.' *Cf.* SWINNERTON.

SINDER-. See SUNDER-.

SINGLETON (Chichester), Great SINGLETON (Preston). Pr. S. *Dom.* Singletun, 1168-69 Schingeltona. Our adj. *single* is Fr. and late, so this must be M.E. *scincle*, L. *scindula*, a ' shingle,' or thin piece of wood used as a house-tile, seen also in *Dom.* Bucks Sincleberia. *Oxf. Dict.*'s earliest quot. is *c.* 1200.

SINNINGTON (Yorks). *Dom.* Sevenictun, Siuenintun, Siverinctun, Siuerintun. Perh. ' town of the sons of *Siferth*,' short form of the common *Sigefrith*. Sifer- has become Siven- and then Sinn-; liquids *r* and *n* easily interchange. SINWELL (Wotton-under-Edge) is *c.* 1220 Sienewell, ' beautiful well '; see SHEEN.

SINODUN, -don Hill (Wallingford). Old forms unknown. But Skeat thinks there is no reason why it should not mean ' synod down.' The word, in the forms *sinoth, synoth, senoth*, is often found in *O.E. Chron.* for ' a council.'

SISLAND (Norfk.). *Dom.* Sislanda, 1450 Cyselond. Prob. ' land of *Sysilt*,' a Nor. family, now *Cecil*. *Cf.* CHISHOLM (Sc.) and *Dom.* Kent Siseltre. But SISTON (Bristol) is *Dom.* Sistone, 1240 Sixtune, and Syston (Leicester) is *old* Syche-, Syeston, which both may be ' town of *Sica* '; 1 in *Onom.*

SITTINGBOURNE (Kent). Not in *Dom.* 1360 S'Eborne, *c.* 1386 *Chaucer* Sydingborne. Prob. ' brook, burn of *Sida* '; gen. -*an*. *Cf.* SYDENHAM. It may be a patronymic. *Cf. Dom.* Sethlindone (Beds) and Settintone (Leics). See -bourne.

SKEFFINGTON (Leicester). ? 822 *chart.* Sciofingden, 1298 Skefting-
ton. The charter form is ' dean, wooded den,' or ' valley of the
descendants of *Skiofa* or *Skioba*'; latter name only in *Onom.*
See -ing.

SKEGNESS (Lincs) is tautological. O.N. *skagi,* ' a promontory,'
with the English later addition -ness, O.E. *næs. Skagi* is fr. O.N.
skaga, ' to stand out.' *Cf. skegg,* ' a beard.' SKEGBY (Notts),
Dom. Schegebi, is fr. a man *Skeggi,* ' the bearded.' See -by.

SKELBROOKE (Doncaster). *Dom.* Scalebro. ' Brook by the hut ' or
' shireling '; O.N. *skali. Cf.* SCALBY.

SKELLINGTHORPE (Lincoln). *a.* 1100 *chart.* Scalðorpe, which will
mean ' village of *Skald* ' or ' *Skealda.*' But SKILLINGTON
(Grantham) shows that prob. both these names are patronymics,
' dwelling of the sons of Skeald.' A ' Skekelinge ' is mentioned
in Lincs in 1528; and *Scilling* is common in *Onom.* See -thorpe.

SKELMANTHORPE (Huddersfield). *Dom.* Scemel-, Scelmertorp.
' Village of *Skelmer* ' or ' *Scealdamer,*' as in next. The liquids
n and *r* often interchange. See -thorpe.

SKELMERSDALE (Ormskirk). *Dom.* Schelmeresdale. *Cf.* 901-09
chart. Scealdæmeres hamme. ' *Scealdamer*'s dale.' *Cf.* SKEL-
MORLIE (Sc.) and above.

SKELTON (4 in *P.G.*). Leeds S. *Dom.* Sceltune, 1179-80 Scelton.
Penrith S. 1189 Schelton. Prob. ' town, village of huts or
booths '; O.N. *skali. Cf.* SCALBY and SKELBROOKE.

SKERNE R. (Durham). Perh. fr. O.N. *Skernir,* ' the Bright,'
messengre of Frey, god of light, fr. *skirr,* ' clear, pure, bright.'
Cf. Scarning (Dereham), prob. patronymic fr. Skernir, and
SHARNBROOK.

SKERTON (Lancaster). *Dom.* Schertune. ' Town on the rock ' or
' scaur '; O.N. *sker ;* so hybrid. Escrétons, Jersey, shows the
same root.

SKETTY (Glam.). For W. *ynys Ketti,* ' isle of *Ketti,*' which may
be = COETY (see COED). There is a Maen, or rock, Ketti on a
hill here.

SKIDDAW (Cumbld.). Old forms needed. Perh. W. *ysgeth,* pl.
-thau, ' a spear, spears,' fr. its supposed shape; *y* would soon
drop, and *th* easily harden into *d.* The mountain has 3 peaks
or ' spear-heads.'

SKIPTON. *Dom.* Scipton, Schipetune, *a.* 1130 *Sim. Dur.* Scipe-
tuna. ' Town, village with the sheep '; O.E. *scép, scéap.*

SKIPWITH (Selby). *Dom.* Schipewic, 1200 Scippewic. This seems
to be unlike SKIPTON, and to mean ' dwelling of *Scippa* ';
though *Onom.* has only *Sceobba* and *Scepius.* The -with is
var. of -wich, *q.v.,* O.E. *wíc,* ' dwelling, house.' This is a very
rare variant.

SKIRBECK (Boston). *Dom*. Schirebec, 1216 Scirbec. ' Beck, brook at the shire ' or ' dividing-line '; O.E. *scír*. Possibly fr. O.N. *skirr*, ' clear, pure, bright.' *Cf*. SKERNE. See -beck.

SKIRLAUGH (Hull). *Dom*. Scirelai, Schirle, Schirelai; = SHIRLEY. For meaning see above. With -laugh *cf*. SHOCKLACH. SKIRLINGTON (E. Riding) is *Dom*. Schereltun, 1179-80 *Pipe* Sirlinton; prob. fr. a man *Scirold* or *Scirweald*.

SKIRPENBECK (York). *Dom*. Scarpenbec. ' Brook of *Sceorfa* ' or ' *Scurfa* ' ; perh. the Danish jarl in *Onom*. *Cf*. *Roll Rich*. *I*. Scurpige, Beds. See -beck.

SKYRACK (a Yorks wapentake). *Dom*. Siraches wapentac. O.E. *scír-ác*, ' shire oak,' meeting-place of the hundred. *Cf*. APPLE-TREE.

SLAD (Stroud) and SLADE (Gower). O.E. *slæd, sled*, ' a valley, dell, forest glade,' still in use. *Cf*. SLEDMERE. But SLAIDBURN (Clitheroe), *Dom*. Slateborne, is prob. fr. O.N. *sletta*, ' a flat piece of land.' *Cf*. SLEAT (Sc.).

SLAITHWAITE (Huddersfield). Not in *Dom*. Now pron. Slówat. ' Sloe-covered farm ' or ' field '; O.E. *sla*(*h*), 3-7 *slo*, 6-9 *slae*, ' a sloe, the fruit of the blackthorn.' See -thwaite.

SLAPTON (Leighton Buz., Nottingham, and Kingsbridge). Not. S. *sic* 1287. Lei. S. *Dom*. Slapetone. *Cf*. *Dom*. Devon Slape-forda. Cannot be fr. Eng. *slap*, ' an opening,' a late word, but fr. a man *Slapa*, not in *Onom*.

SLAUGHTERFORD (Glouc.). 779 *chart*. Sloh tranford, 1154-61 Slaforda. Interesting corrup. ' Ford of the sloe-tree '; O.E. *sloh-treo*, gen. pl. *tran*. An older form of *sloe* is found in the Glossaries, *slach-thorn*—i.e., ' sloe ' (or ' black ') ' thorn.' We also have an Upper and Lower SLAUGHTER, Stow-on-Wold, *Dom*. Sclostre, 1183 Sloctre, ' sloe-tree '—a curious corruption !

SLEAFORD. O.E. *Chron*. 852 Sliowaforda. Prob. O.E. *sleow, sliw éa*, ' tench ' or ' mullet river,' and not O.E. *sláw*, Icel. *sljó-r*, ' slow.' The brook here is still called the Slea. But it is also thought to be the ' Lafford ' in *Patent R*. for 1217 and 1218. Initial *s* does sometimes disappear in Gaelic names. See LEVEN (Sc.).

SLEDMERE (York). *Dom*. Slidemare. ' Mere, lake in the valley, dell, or bit of boggy ground '; O.E. *slæd, sled*, now *slade*. *Cf*. SLADE.

SLINDON (Eccleshall, Arundel). Ecc. S. *Dom*. Slindone, *a*. 1300 Slyndon. Doubtful. *Slim* adj. is not in Eng. till 17th cny. Prob. fr. O.E. *slim*, ' slime, ooze, soft mud '; *m* and *n* often interchange. *Cf*. SLINFORD (Sussex) and SLYNE; also Slimbridge (Coaley), *Dom*. Heslinbruge (Nor. scribes often prefix E-, seldom He-), 1166 Slimbergge, 1224 Slymbrugge.

SLINGSBY (York). *Dom.* Sehingesbi, Eslingesbi (Nor. spelling), 1202 Slingebi. ' Dwelling of ' a man unknown, ? *Selewine.* See -by.

SLOLEY (Cromer, Arley). Ar. S. *a.* 1200 Slalei, *a.* 1300 Sloley. Cro. S. *a.* 1300 *Eccleston* Sloler (the *r* a scribe's or Cockney's error). ' Slough-meadow '; O.E. *slóh.* See -ley.

SLYNE (Lancaster). *Dom.* and 1176 *Pipe* Sline, 1272 and 1310 Scline. Prob. O.E. and O.N. *slim,* ' slime, soft mud, alluvial ooze '; *m* and *n* often interchange. *Cf.* SLINDON.

SMEETON WESTERBY (Leicester) and GREAT SMEATON (Northaller- ton). Nor. S. *Dom.* Smidetune, Smet(t)on, 1183 Smetheton, 1211 Smitheton. ' Smooth, level village '; O.E. *sméthe. Cf.* SMETHWICK.

SMESTER (Worcestersh.). M'Clure thinks that this place on the little R. Smestow *(stow,* ' place '), a trib. of the Stour, is ' sma ' ' or ' small STOUR.' Icel. *smá-r,* Dan. *smaa,* O.E. *smœl,* ' small.' In Sc. the common ending *-ster* is always for N. *staб-r,* ' steading, farm-place.' Duignan has neither Smester nor Smestow.

SMETHWICK (Birmingham). *Dom.* Smedewich, *a.* 1250 Smeythe- wick, Smethewyke. O.E. *sméthe wíc,* ' smooth dwelling.' *Cf. Dom.* Norf. Smethedune. It is on a plain, and so may be ' village on the plain,' as there is a Smeath (Kent), the Smeath (K.'s Lynn), and Markham Smeath (Swaffham). But *Oxf. Dict.* gives for *smethe* sb. only one quot., *c.* 1440, and E. Anglican dial. See -wick.

SMITE (Coventry and Droitwich). Co. S. *Dom.* Smithh, 1251 Smite. Wo. S. 978 *chart.* Smita, 1275 Smite. O.E. *smita,* which prob. means ' bog, morass, foul place.' There is also a R. Smite (Notts), in *Leland* Myte, *c.* 1613 Snite.

SMITHFIELD (London). *c.* 1425 ' The Priory of seynt Bartholomew yn Smythfyld.' Referred to early, ? 1154, as ' the smooth field.' O.E. *sméбe,* ' smooth.' SMITHDOWN (Liverpool) is ' smooth hill.'

SNAILWELL (Cambs). *c.* 1080 *Inquis. Camb.* Snegeluuelle, *Dom.* Snellewelle, *chart.* Sneillewelle, 1169 Sneilwella, 1316 Sneylewelle. O.E. *snœgel, snœgl, snœl,* Dan. *snegl,* ' a snail.'

SNEATON (Whitby). *Dom.* Sneton. Perh. ' town of *Snet* ' or ' *Snat.*' *Cf.* SNETTISHAM.

SNEINTON (now part of Nottingham). *Dom.* Notintone, 1168-9 *Pipe* Snotinton; so the first part of the name represents the same family as in NOTTINGHAM. But SNAINTON (N. Yorks) is *Dom.* Snechin- tune, ' town of *Snecca* ' or ' *Snocca* '; only the latter in *Onom.*

SNELLAND (Lincoln). Thought to be Norse, ' *Snel's* wood '; O.N. *lund-r,* ' a grove.' 3 *Snels* in *Onom. Cf.* SNELSTON (Ash- bourne) and TIMBERLAND.

SNETTERTON (Norfolk). 1455 Snyterton. 'Town of *Snoter*' or '*Snothere*,' in *Onom*. *Cf. Dom*. Derby Esnotrewic (with Nor. E.). We have also SNITTERFIELD (Warwk.), *Dom*. Snitefeld, 1151 Snitenesfeld, *a.* 1300 Snitenefeld; fr. a man *Snite* or *Sniter*, seen also in Snitterby (Lincs), and *Dom*. Yorks Snitertun. The liquids *n* and *r* often interchange.

SNETTISHAM (King's Lynn). *Cf. a.* 1199 Snetesham (Salop) and 804 *chart.* Snattingden (Kent). 'Home of *Snat*, or *Snet*.'

SNEYD GREEN (Hanley). 1410 Snede. O.E. *snæd*, O.N. *sneith*, 'a small piece, a piece cut or "sned" off, an outlying portion of a manor.' *Cf*. Halsnead (Lancs), Snead Common, Stourport and Mamble (Salop), Snaith (Yorks), *Dom*. Esneid, Esnoid. The E- is fr. a Nor. scribe, a common prefix for him; and SNYDALL (Yorks), *Dom*. Snitehala. Duignan says Snead is a common Midlands name.

SNODLAND (Kent). 838 *chart.* Snoddingland. 'Land of the *Snodings*' or ' descendants of *Snodda* or *Snodd*.' All these names are in *Onom.*; and Snody is still a surname. *Cf. Dom*. Snodesbyrie (Worcs.), now Upton Snodsbury, in 840 *chart.* Snoddes lea; also 940 *chart.* Snodesdelle (Dorset).

SNOOK. See BLYTH-SNOOK.

SNOREHAM (Essex) and LITTLE SNORING (Fakenham). *Dom*. Snaringa, 1454 Litel Snoring. The name *Snor*, and the patronymic *Snoring*, are not in *Onom*. But *Snorri* is a well-known N. name. It has nothing to do with Eng. *snore*, not found *a.* 1330.

SNOWDON. *a.* 1145 *Orderic* Mons Snaudunus, *c.* 1200 Snaudune, id est, Mons Nivis, *a.* 1235 *Rog. Wendover* Snauduna, 1461 Snauwdon. A 'Snowdenhill' is mentioned near Cambridge in 1447. O.E. *snáw dún*, 'snow-capped hill.' In W. it is Y Wyddfa, ' the tomb' or ' tumulus.'

SOAR R. (Leicester). Welsh *Red. Bk. of Hergest* Sorram, *c.* 1145 *Geoffr. Monm.* Sore, 1253 *chart.* Sor. Perh. N. *saur*, 'mud, swamp,' perh. Keltic.

SOCKBRIDGE (R. Eamont). ? the 'Soccabyrig' in *O.E. Chron.* 780. It may be Sockburn-on-Tees. There is one *Soca* in *Onom*.

SODBURY (Yate). *c.* 900 *chart.* Soppanbyrig, *Dom*. Sopeberie, 1224 Sobbiri. ' Town of *Soppa*.' See -bury.

SOHAM (Cambs). *Dom*. Saham, *a.* 1200 *chart.* Sægham, *Chron. Ramsey* Seham. 'Home in the hollow,' fr. O.E. *sigan*, pa. tense *sag*, ' to sink down, to sag'; Bavar. *saig*, Tyrol. *sege*, *söga*, ' a depression, a swamp.' There was once a large mere at Soham. *Cf. Dom*. Norfk. Sahā.

SOHO (London). *Sic* 1632. Said to be fr. the cry of the huntsmen calling off the harriers—'So-hoe!' Stow speaks of hunting in this very district in 1562.

SOLENT. *Bede* Solente. Breton *sol*, ' the tide.' Can the -ent be a Kelt. suffix cognate with the common Teut. *end; cf.* W. *entrych, entyrch*, ' top, summit ' ? Thus the name might mean, ' head, end of the tide.'

SOLIHULL (Warwicksh.). *Dom.* Ulverlei—*i.e.*, Wolverley—but *a.* 1300 Soly-, Sulihull. ' Muddy hill '; O.E. *sol*, ' mud, that which *sullies*,' *syla*, ' wallowing places.' *Layamon* always has *hull* for *hill*, and he belongs to this region; O.E. *hill, hyll*, 2-5 *hull. Cf.* ASPULL, LEVENHULL, etc.; also SOILWELL, Lydney), also spelt Sully, 1281 Sollewalle, ' muddy spring.'

SOLWAY FRITH. *c.* 1300 Sulway, 1682 Sulloway; also Sulliva. Likewise called Tracht-Romra, fr. G. *tràghadh*, ' ebbing,' and Scottwade or Scottiswathe—*i.e.*, ' Scots' ford,' N. and Dan. *wath.* O.N. *söl-vag-r*, ' muddy bay '; O.E. *sol*, ' mud,' that which ' sullies.' For *vag-r* becoming -way, *cf.* SCALLOWAY and STORNOWAY (Sc.). *Cf.* SILLOTH, SOLENT, and SOLIHULL. Firth or frith is Icel. *fjörð-r*, N. *fjord*, ' bay, inlet of the sea.' There is a R. Salwey near Kidderminster, for which old forms are needed.

SOMERBY (Grantham and Oakham). Gr. S. *Dom.* Sumerlede, Sumerdebi, Sumertebi. ' Dwelling of *Somarled* ' or ' *Sumarliði*.' The most famous of this name was regulus of Argyll, d. 1166, ancestor of the Lords of the Isles. See -by.

SOMERFORD (Staffs), SOMERFORD KEYNES (Swindon), and GT. SOMERFORD (Chippenham). Sta. S. *a.* 1300 Somerford. ' Ford usable only in summer.' There are 37 Sumor- or Sumrefords in *Dom.*

SOMERSET. 878 *O.E. Chron.* Sumor sæt, 1204 *chart.* Sumerset, 1443 Somerset. ' Seat, dwelling of the family *Sumor*,' seen also in SOMERTON in this shire.

SONNING (Reading). *B.C.S.* i. 56 Sunninges, *Dom.* Soninges, *c.* 1280 Sunninge, 1316 Sonnynge. ' Place of the descendants of *Sunna.*' *Sunna, Sunno*, and *Suno* are all in *Onom.* Normans wrote *on* for O.E. *un.* Skeat is doubtful of connexion with sun-worship. *Cf.* SUNDON and SUNNINGHILL.

SOTWELL (Wallingford). *Dom.* Sotwelle, *c.* 1280 Sottewell. ' Well of *Sota* '—*i.e.*, the foolish man, the ' sot.' *Sota, Soto*, and *Sotus* are all in *Onom.* The sb. *sot* is in Eng. *c.* 1000, but is fr. O.Fr. *sot*, of unknown origin.

SOULBURY (Leighton Bzd.) and SOULBY (Kirkby Stephen). Prob. ' burgh ' and ' dwelling of *Sola*,' 2 in *Onom.* See -bury and -by, and *cf. Dom.* Bucks Solintone. But SOULEY END (Bedworth), *Dom.* Soulege, is ' meadow on the R. Sow.' See -ley.

SOURBY (N. Lancs). *Dom.* Sorbi = SOWERBY.

SOUTHACRES (Ripley, Yorks). *Dom.* Sotesac', Sosacre. ' Acre, field of *Sota*,' a man in *Onom.*

SOUTHALL (Middlesex). Modern, after NORTHALL, which is ancient.

SOUTHAM (Warwksh.). 980 *chart*. Sutham, 1043 *ib*. Southam, Suoham, *Dom*. Sucham. 'South house ' or 'home.'

SOUTHAMPTON. *O.E. Chron*. 837 Hamtun, *c*. 1100 *Flor. Worc*. Suthamtone, -enses, *a*. 1145 *Orderic* Suthamptona, *c*. 1175 *Fantosme* Suhantune. 'South HAMPTON ' or 'home-town ' or 'home-stead.' *Cf*. NORTHAMPTON.

SOUTH LEIGH (Axminster). *c*. 1305 *St. Kinelm* Souþ leȝ. 'South meadow.' *Cf*. Leigh and -ley.

SOUTHMINSTER (Essex). *a*. 716 *chart*. Suðmynster—*i.e.*, 'south church.' See -minster.

SOUTHROP (Lechlade). *Cf. a*. 1100 *chart*. Suthorpe, in the Midlands. 'South *thorpe*,' *q.v.*, also found in the form *throp*.

SOUTH SHIELDS. 'South huts or shielings.' The root is Icel. *skjól*, O.N. *skali*, 'a shelter '; Icel. *skjold-r*, 'a shield.' *Cf*. SHIELDHILL (Sc.).

SOUTHWARK. 1023 *O.E. Chron*. Suðgeweorc, *Dom*. Sudwerche, 1160-61 *Pipe* Sutwerc, *Sagas* Sydvirke, *c*. 1386 *Chaucer* Southwerk. 'South work ' or 'fort '; same root as in *bulwark* and WARK.

SOUTHWELL (Notts). 958 *chart*. at Suthwellan, *Dom*. Sudwelle.

SOW R. (Staffs and Warwk.). War. S. *O.E. chart*. Sowa, Sow, *Dom*. Sowa, Sou. St. S. *a*. 1200 Sowe. Origin unknown; not O.E. *sugu*, *c*. 1150 *suwa*, ' a sow.'

SOWERBY (2 in Yorks) and SOWERBY Row (Carlisle). Yor. S. *Dom*. Sourebi, Sorebi, 1179-80 Sourebi. Car. S. 1189 Sourebi. 'Dwelling amid the mud ' or 'swamp '; N. *saur*. *Cf*. SOURBY, also SORBIE and SOROBA (Sc.). See -by.

SOWLEY (now a lake near Lymington). Prob. 'South meadow.' See -ley.

SPALDING. *Dom*. Spallinge, *a*. 1100 *chart*. Spalda, 1154 *O.E. Chron*. Spaldelyng. 'Place of the descendants of *Spalda* '; a patronymic. *Cf*. next. SPALDINGTON (E. Riding) is *Dom*. Spellinton, 4 times, so that a var. name *Spalla* or *Spella* must have existed.

SPALDWICK (Hunts). *Cf. Dom.*, Spaldes forde, now SPALFORD, Notts. 'Dwelling,' O.E. *wíc*, 'of *Spalda*.' See above.

SPARKFORD (Bath). 1298 Sparkeforde. Older forms needed. Prob. 'ford of *Spearhafoc* ' or '*Sperauoc*,' 2 in *Onom*. Prob. not 'sparkling ford,' fr. O.E. *spœrca*, *spearca*, 'a spark.' SPARKHILL (Yardley) is fr. a family of *Spark*, known here in 1275.

SPARSHOLT (Winchester). 963 *chart*. Spheresholt; also *chart*. Spæresholt, *Dom*. This is prob. 'holt, wood of *Spere*,' a man; *cf*. SPERNAL, (Alcester) *Dom*. Spernore ('bank of *Spera* '); but it may be 'wood for spear shafts,' O.E. *spere*, 'a spear.'

SPEEN (Newbury). Supposed to be *c.* 380 *Ant. Itin.* Spinis (locative), 821 *Grant* Spene, *Dom.* Spone, 1316 Spene. Usually said to be L. *spinae*, ' thorns,' and Newbury, the ' new burgh,' as contrasted with the old Rom. Spinae. But Skeat says the vowel sounds make this impossible, because O.E. *Spene* would not be pron. Speen, but Spainĕ(*r*). He says *Spene* is an adj. fr. O.E. *spon,* 'a chip, thin plank,' hence, he supposes, ' a wooden tile for roofing '; and so Speenham, a form also found, would be ' shingled house.' Skeat's case is not fully demonstrated; but *cf.* SINGLETON.

SPEETON (Bridlington). *Dom.* Specton, Spetton, Spreton. ' Town of ?' *Onom.* has a *Spieta.* It may be as next.

SPEKE (Liverpool). Prob. called after Walter *L'Espec* (Nor. Fr. for ' a woodpecker '), who founded Kirkham, Rievaulx, and Warden Abbeys, *temp.* Hen. I.

SPELSBURY (Charlbury). *Dom.* Spelesberie. ' Burgh of *Spila,*' one in *Onom. Cf.* SPILSBY; and see -bury.

SPETCHLEY (Worcester). 816 *chart.* Spæcleahtun, 967 *ib.* and *Dom.* Speclea, 1275 Spechesleye. Duignan thinks ' vegetable garden of ' an unrecorded ' *Spæc.*' See LEIGHTON, or *leah tun.*

SPILSBY (Lincs.), also SPILSBURY (Mamble). 1275 Spelebury, 1327 Spellesbury. ' Dwelling ' and ' town of *Spila* ' or ' *Spille.*' See -by and -bury.

SPINNEY (Cambs). Prob. O.Fr. *espinaye,* L. *spinetum,* ' place of thorns, a small wood,' fr. O.F. *espine,* L. *spina,* ' a thorn.' But SPENNITHORNE (Leyburn) is *Dom.* Spennigetorp, which must be a patronymic, fr. *Spen,* or *Spens,* a name still in use.

SPOFFORTH (Harrogate). *Dom.* Spoford. ? ' ford of *Spot,*' a recorded name. See -forth.

SPONDON (Derby). Prob. O.E. *spón dún,* ' hill like a spoon,' which was orig. a chip of wood, O.N. *spónn. Cf.* SPEEN, *Dom.* Sponelege (Salop) and Spon End (Coventry). There is no name like *Spon* in *Onom.,* but we have 1231 *Close R.* Sponton, (Suffk.) as well as SPOONLEY (Sudeley), 1320 Sponley.

SPREYTON (Bow, Devon). *Dom.* Spreitone. ' Town of *Sprae,*' shotr form of *Spraecaling,* 2 in *Onom.* It also has *Spœr, Sperri,* and *Sperus.*

SPROATLEY (Hull), *Dom.* Sprotelei, and SPROTBOROUGH (Doncaster), *Dom.* Sproteburg. ' Meadow ' and ' Burgh, castle of *Sprot(t),*' 3 in *Onom.* See -burgh and -ley.

SPROWSTON (Norwich). ' Town, village of *Sprow,*' 3 in *Onom. Cf. Dom.* Sprostune (Cheshire), and SPROUSTON (Sc.), *Dom.* Yorks Sprostune is now SPROXTON; and there is another Sproxton near Melton Mowbray.

SPURSTOW (Tarporley). *Dom.* Spurstone. Prob. 'stone' or else 'stow' (O.E. for 'place') 'of *Spor* or *Sporri*,' one in *Onom.* Perh. fr. O.E. *spura, spora*, Icel. *spori*, 'a spur.'

STACKPOLE (Pembroke). 1594 Stacpoll, -pole, 1603 Stackpoole. Hybrid. O.N. *stak*, 'a cliff, an isolated rock,' common in N. of Scotland, and W. *pwl*, 'a pool, a small inlet of the sea.' But STACKHOUSE (Yorks), *Dom.* Stacuse, is prob. 'house like a stack'; O.N. *stakk-r*, Sw. *stack*, and Dan. *stak*. The -house here will be O.N. too—*hús*. Stakesby (Whitby), *Dom.* Staxebi, and Stakes Hill (Cosham), seem to imply an otherwise unknown man, *Stœcc.*

STADDLE BRIDGE (Northallerton). *Cf.* 838 *chart.* 'Estre Stadelham' (Limming, Kent). *Stadel* seems to be the name of a man not in *Onom.*

STADMENT (Hereford). M'Clure derives -ment fr. O.Corn. *menedh*, also *menit, menyth*, 'a hill.' *Cf.* LONGMYND. Stad- is uncertain; it may be for O.E. *strœt*, L. *stratum*, 'a (Roman) road.' *Cf.* Stradfeld for STRAFFIELD, in *Dom.* The liquid *r* could easily drop out. As likely it is W. *ystad*, 'a furlong, a stadium.'

STAFFORD. 1016 *O.E. Chron.* Stæfford, 1071 Staffordescir, *Dom.* Stat-, Stadford. 'Ford which needs a staff'; O.E. *stœf.* M'Clure thinks it here means 'a guiding rail.' This town is mentioned earlier on coins, as early as Edgar (958-75)—Stæth, which is O.E. for 'bank, shore, waterside' (*cf.* STATHAM); so Stæth or Stathe may have been the orig. name, and -ford a later additon.

STAINDROP (Darlington) and STAINFORTH (Doncaster). *Dom.* Stainforde. 'Stone-built village' and 'stoney ford.' O.N. *steinn*, 'stone, rock.' See -thorpe and -forth.

STAINER KER (Selby). *Sic* 1259. St. may be, as it still is, a man's name. It may be O.E. *stan* (or rather O.N. *steinn*) *ofer*, 'stone, bank, rocky bank.' *Cf.* STAINBURN (Yorks), *Dom.* Stain-, Stanburne, and STAINLAND (Halifax), *Dom.* Stanland. Ker is var. of Carr, 'a rock.' See REDCAR.

STAINE, STANE (Cambs), and STAINES (R. Thames). Cam. S. *Dom.* Stanes. Tham. S. 969 Stana, 993 *O.E. Chron.* Stane., *Dom.* and 1228 Stanes. O.E. *stán*, 'a stone, a rock.' Skeat points out that the mod. spelling, Staines, not Stones, shows Scandinav. influence. *Cf.* Icel. *steinn*, 'a stone.' *Cf.* too *Dom.* Stanes (Worc.), now STONE.

STAINTON (5 in *P.G.*). Rotherham S. *Dom.* Stantone, 1179-80 Steinton. 'Stone-built village'; Icel. *steinn*, Dan. and Sw. *sten*, O.E. *stan*, 'stone, rock.' *Cf.* STAINLAND (Halifax), *Dom.* Stanland, and STENTON (Sc.), and above.

STAITHES (Yorks). Not in *Dom.* O.E. *Stœþ*, 'shore, river-bank,' with the common pl. -es. *Cf.* **STAFFORD**, and Stath (Glouc.), 1304 Staith.

STALEYBRIDGE. 'Bridge at the stall'; O.E. *stœl, steall,* 'place, stall, stable.'

STALISFIELD GREEN (Faversham). Local pron. Starchfel, an example of the common change of liquid *l* into *r.* In *Dom.* it seems to be Stanefelle, an instructive instance how all the liquids, here *l, n,* and *r,* can interchange. Thus the name orig. is 'stoney field.'

STALMINE (Preston). *Sic Dom.* and 1212. Hybrid. O.E. *steall,* 'place,' and O.N. *minni,* 'meeting of two roads' or 'rivers.' *Cf.* **AIRMYN.**

STAMFORD. *Bede, Dom.,* and *Pipe* Stanford, 922 *O.E. Chron.* Steanford, Steamfordd. O.E. for 'ford with the stones'; O.E. *stán.* Interchange of *m* and *n* is common. Prob. *stone* and *stem* are the same in root. *Cf.* **STANFORD** (Berks and Notts), *Dom.* Stanford. There are 7 Stanfords in *P.G.*

STAMFORDHAM (Newcastle-on-T.). 1201 Stanfordeham. See above and -ham.

STANDISH (Glouc. and Wigan). Gl. S. 872 *chart.* and *Dom.* Stanedis (also Stanhus—*i.e.,* 'Stone house'; *cf.* **STENHOUSEMUIR,** Sc.). Wi. S. 1177-78 Stanesdis, 1180-1206 Stanedis, 1211-13 Stanedich, 1332 Standissh. O.E. *stán edisc,* 'enclosure, park, enclosure with the stone wall.' The -isc has become -ish just as in dish, O.E. *disc.* Skeat derives this and Farndish (Beds), *Dom.* Fernadis, fr. O.E. *disc,* 'dish, cup, hollow, concave place in a field'; but for these latter meanings *Oxf. Dict.* gives nothing *a.* 1810. *Cf.* **CAVENDISH.**

STANDON (Eccleshall). *Dom.* Stantone = **STANTON;** whilst **STANDHILL** (Oxon) is *a.* 1300 Standelf, 'stone-delf'—*i.e.,* quarry. See *delf* sb[1], fr. vb. *delve,* 'to dig.'

STANHOE (King's Lynn). 14 ... *Liber Sharbur,* Edwinus ... vocavit Mam Stanhoghiam, quae postea vocabatur Stanhowe. 'Rocky point of land.' See **HOE.** ? What Edwin is referred to. *Cf.* 1179-80 *Pipe* Stangaho (Yorks).

STANLEY (5 in *P.G.*). *c.* 938 *chart.* Stanleaȝe, ? which; 940 *chart.* Stanleyghe (Wilts); *Dom.* Yorks Stanlei, 12 times; 1156 *Pipe* Stanlega (Warwick); 1369 *Mem. Ripon* Staynlay (Wakefield). O.E. *stan leaȝe,* locative, nom. *léah,* 'stony meadow.' See -ley.

STANMER (Sussex). *Dom.* Stan mere—*i.e.,* 'stony lake.' *Cf.* the name Cranmer—*i.e.,* 'crane lake.'

STANSTED (Wrotham, Kent). 810 *chart.* Stanham stede—*i.e.,* 'stone house place.'

STANTON (20 in *P.G.*). *Dom.* Stantun(e) (Yorks, Salop, Notts, and Staffs). 'Stone-built town' or 'village'; O.E. *stán,* 'stone.'

STANWAY (Colchester, Toddington, and Winchcombe). *Cf. Dom.*
Staneweie (Salop), and 1189 *Pipe* Stanwega (Cumbld.). ' Way,
road paved with stone '; O.E. *stán. Dom.* Yorks Stenweghe(s),
Steinuege, is now STANWICK. Stein- is clearly fr. O.N. *steinn,*
not O.E. Stawell (Leach and Bridgwater) is *Dom.* Glouc.
Stanewell.

STANWELL (Middlesex). *Dom.* Stanwelle. ' Stone well '—*i.e.,*
prob. ' well surrounded by a stone wall.' *Cf.* STONEWELL.

STAPENHILL (Burton-on-T. and Stourbridge). Bu. S. *Dom.* Stapen-
hille. St. B. 1342 Stapenhull. ' Hill of *Steapa, -an,*' one in *Onom.*

STAPLEFORD (7 in *P.G.*) and STAPLETON (4 in *P.G.*). Romford S.
Dom. Staplefort. Cam. S. *B.C.S.* iii. 687 Stapelford, *Dom.* Staple-
ford (also Notts). ? *c.* 1150 *Grant* Stapelfordia, Notts. 1179-80
Pipe Stapleton (Yorks). O.E. *stapul, stapol,* ' a stake, an up-
right post, a pillar '; then ' a market.' STAPLOW, -LOE (Cambs),
is *Dom.* Staplehou, 1428 Stapulho; O.E. *hoh,* ' heel, projection.'
See HOE. Curiously, Stapleton (Yorks) is in *Dom.* both Staple-
tone and Staplendun, ' hill of the staple '; while Stapleton (N.
Lancs) is in *Dom.* Stopeltierne, ' market of the lord,' G. *tighearna.*
Cf. THRIMBY.

STARBECK (Harrogate). *Old* Osbern-stahbec. ' Rushy brook ';
Sw. *starr,* a ' rush '; Icel. *bekk-r,* ' a brook.' *Cf.* STAR (Sc.).

STARBOTTOM (Skipton). *Dom.* Stamphotne (plainly an error).
Prob. ' rushy bottom ' or ' valley '; O.E. *botm.* See above; and
cf. RAMSBOTTOM.

START POINT (S. Devon). O.E. *steort,* ' a tail, a promontory.' *Cf.*
LAND'S END. For STARTFORTH, a corrupt form, see STRAD-
BROKE. *Steort* reappears in many names—Stert (Devizes,
Glouc., and Somerton), Stert I. and Point (Bridgwater, perh.
1184 *Pipe* Sterte), Stirtloe (see -low) (Hunts), etc.; also STARDENS
(Newent), 1301 Styrtesden. For STARTON see STAVERTON.

STATHAM (Warrington), not in W. and H., and STATHERN (Melton
Mow.). Prob. both fr. O.E. *stæth,* ' bank, waterside, shore.'
O.E. *erne* is ' house.' *Cf.* STAITHES.

STAUNTON (5 in *P.G.*). 1297 *Scotch Roll* (Chancery) Steynton, 1302
Staunton (Notts). O.E. *stan tun,* ' stone-built village.' *Cf.*
STANTON and STENTON (Sc.).; but the *u* here shows Nor. influence.

STAVELEY (Knaresboro', Kendal, and Chesterfield). Kn. S. is
prob. *Dom.* Stanleia (*n* for *u*), p. 65*a. Dom.* has nothing else
for the first two, and for Ch. S. Stavelie. The Stave- is doubtful; prob. it is, like STAFFORD, which was orig. not fr. *staff,* but
fr. O.E. *stæth,* ' bank, shore, waterside,' mod. dial. *staithe,* ' a
river landing-place '; *th* has also become *v* in STEVENAGE.
See -ley.

STAVERTON (Daventry, Cheltenham, Totnes). Da. S. 1156 Stauer-
tun. Ch. S. *Dom.* Starventon, 1230 Stauerton. *Cf.* Starton

(Coventry), 1163 Stauerton, and *Dom.* Staurecote (Salop). These all may be 'town of *Stanhart*,' var. of *Stanheard* or *Stanhere.* But at any rate To. S. is *a.* 1100 *chart.* Stofordtune, *Dom.* S(t)overton, which looks like ' STAFFORD town.'

STAXTON (York). *Dom.* Stacstone, Stactone. No man *Stac* in *Onom.*, so this is perh. a tautology; O.N. *stak,* ' a cliff, isolated rock,' and O.E. *stán,* 'stone, rock.' But see Stakesby s.v. STACKPOLE, and -ton.

STECHFORD (Birmingham). 1242 Stichesford, *a.* 1300 Stichford, Stycchefford. *Stetch* is dial. for ' a ridge between two furrows in ploughed land '; perh. cognate with *stake* and *stick.* But this also may be fr. *Stifec. Cf.* STETCHWORTH, Stivichall (Coventry), and STEWKLEY.

STEEPLE (Southminster). *Cf. Dom.* ' Steple ' (Cheshire). O.E. *stépel,* ' a church steeple,' same root as *steep.* There are six places in *P.G.* like Steeple Ashton, Steeple Claydon, etc. We already have ' Stepelknoel ' in 1228 *Close R.*

STEETON (Keighley). *Dom.* Stivetune, 1298 Stiveton. ' Town of *Styfa.*'

STEPNEY (London and Hull). Lon. S. *old* Stebenhythe, Stibenhede, Stebunhethe, 1503 Stepney. On the analogy of STEVENAGE, which has much earlier attestation (there is no trace, it seems, of Stepney till 1299), almost certainly O.E. *æt stithan hydde,* ' at the stout, strong landing-stage,' or HYTHE. But the name has certainly been influenced by thoughts of *Stephen,* a name which, however, *O.E. Chron.* always spells *Stephne,* and no spellings with *b* seem to occur. The form Stepney (see -ey) is quite late; so presumably is the name at Hull.

STETCHWORTH (Newmarket). *K.C.D.* iv. 245 Steuichesworðe, 269 Steuecheworde, *Dom.* Stiuicesuuorde, Stuuicesworde, 1235 Stivecheswrthe, 1383 Stewcheworthe. ' Farm of *Styfec* ' or ' *Stifec.' Cf.* STECHFORD and STUKELEY. But Stitchbrook (Lichfield) is *Dom.* Tichebroc and *a.* 1300 Sichelesbroc, Stichelesbroc, ' brook of *Sticcele.*'

STEVENAGE (Herts). *K.C.D.* iv. 176 Stichenæce, Stithenæce, *Dom.* Stigenace, 1199 Stivenach, *a.* 1199 Stiphenage, *c.* 1250 Stitenache, *Hundred R.* Stepenacth, 1303 Stivenhach. O.E. *æt stithan hœcce,* ' at the strong hatch ' or ' gate '; influenced by the name *Stephen* or *Steven,* for which the first part was mistaken by Nor. scribes. *Cf.* COCKNAGE, STAVELEY, and STEPNEY.

STEVENTON (Berks, Whitchurch, and Beds, where also spelt STEVINGTON). *Dom.* Stivetune, 1291 Stiventon, 1316 Styvington, *c.* 1540 Stevynton. The name has been influenced by *Stephen,* but orig. it must have been *Styfan tún,* ' Stifa's village.' *Cf.* STEETON.

STEWKLEY (Leighton Buz.). 974 *chart.* Stiveclei, 1040 *ib.* Styve-clea; *later* Stiucle. Prob. not ' *Styfec*'s meadow ' (*cf.* STETCH-WORTH), but ' meadow in the clearing in the wood '; O.E. *styfec* is said to mean this. *Cf.* STUKELEY.

STEYNING (Sussex). *Dom.* Staninges. ' Place of the descendants of *Stan* ' or ' *Stein.*' Patronymic.

STICKLEPATH (Okehampton). Dev. dial. *stickle,* ' steep.' Prob. same root as in *stickleback ;* O.E. *sticle,* ' a prickle.' We get the sb. in Harrison STICKLE, a hill near Windermere.

STILLINGFLEET (York). *Dom.* Steflingfled, Steflinflet, also Steflinge-feld (error). *Stefling* must be a patronymic, perh. fr. *Stefan* or its dimin. See -ing; -fleet is ' river '—see FLEET. We get the same name in STILLINGTON (Easingwold), *Dom.* Stivelinctun.

STILTON (Helmsley and Peterboro'). He. S. *Dom.* Tilstun, 3 times. ' *Tila*'s town.' Pe. S. not in *Dom.* It seems a case of meta-thesis.

STINCHCOMBE (Dursley). 1150-60 Stintescombe, 1220-89 Stinctes-cumb. Prob. ' valley of *Stinta* '—*i.e.,* ' the stinted, or stunted one.' *Cf. Dom.* Norfk. Stinckai, and STINSFORD (Dorset), *old* Styntes-, Stinchefford.

STIRCHLEY (Birmingham and Shifnal). *B.C.S.* 71 Stercan lei. *Cf.* STRICKLAND and 1155 *Pipe* Sterchelai (Wilts). ' Meadow of *Sterca* ' or ' the stirks.' See -ley.

STISTED (Braintree). *Dom.* Stiestedā. This must be the same as 1231 *Close R.,* Stisted', Tystede. It seems to be ' sty-stead ' or place; O.E. *stige,* Dan. *sti,* ' a sty, a pen.' But TISTED is ' *Ticca*'s stead.'

STOCKINGFORD (Nuneaton). 1155 Stoccingford, *a.* 1300 Stockeford. Duignan says *stocking* means ' a grubbing-up of woodland or waste, and preparing it for cultivation.' *Cf.* STOCKING (Hares-feld), 1205 Stockem putte, ' pit at the tree-stocks '; an O.E. loc., *stoccan.*

STOCKPORT. 1488 *Will* Stopforde, *a.* 1600 Stoppord, -ort, and still locally pron. Stoppert. Prob. not fr. O.E. *stoppian,* ' to stop,' but ' ford of *Steapa* '; one in *Onom.* The orig. ending might be -worth, ' farm,' *q.v.* The form Stock- seems quite recent.

STOCKTON-ON-TEES. 1183 Stoktona, 1208 Stocton. O.E. *stoc, stocc,* means ' a stock, stem, stick, block.' The meaning here is ' fenced-in village.' *Cf.* next. There are 7 Stocktons in *P.G.* STOCK-TON-ON-THE-FOREST (York) is *Dom.* Stocthun, while St. near Harewood is Stochetun, and STOCKTON-ON-TEME is 958 *chart.* Stoctune.

STOCKWELL and STOCKWELLFLAT, or S. GREEN (Lambeth). 1296 Stokwelflatte. Prob. ' well with the stocks or stakes around it.' *Cf.* above and the Stockwell (Glasgow).

STODMARSH (Canterbury). Perh. fr. an unknown man *Stod*. *Cf*. *Dom*. Essex Stodfelt, Norfk. Stodeia (see -ey), and Salop Stodes-done. Most of these may be fr. *stud*. See STOODLEIGH.

STOKE (many). *E.g.*, 808 *chart*. Norðstoc (Somerset), *Dom*. Stoca, Stocha (St.-on-Trent). O.E. *stoc*, ' place,' lit. what is *stuck* in or down, a stake. *Dom*. has 31 cases of Stoche (*ch*= *k*) and 32 of Stoches.

STOKE BRUERN (Towcester). 1370 Stoke Brewerne—*i.e.*, ' brew house.' *Cf*. WHITHORN (Sc.). O.E. *hwit erne*.

STOKE POGES (Bucks). *Sic* 1612, but *Dom*. Stoches. Amica, heiress of this Stoke, married Robt. *Pogis*, knight, in the 12th cny.

STOKESLEY (Yorks). *Dom*. Stocheslage, ' Meadow of the STOKE ' or ' place.' *Cf*. Stokesby (Gt. Yarmouth); and see -ley.

STONE (Kent and Kidderminster). Kent S. 993 *O.E. Chron*. Stane See M'Clure, p. 280. Kidd. S. *Dom*. and 1275 Stanes, 1327 Stone. See STAINE. Stone (Staffs) is *a*. 1300 both Stane and Stanes.

STONEHAM (Winchester). *Bede* iv. 16, ' The place called Ad Lapidem '; *O.E. vers*. Æt Stane. See -ham, and *cf*. STONE-HOUSE (Stroud), 1229 Stanhus, and STONELEIGH (Coventry), *Dom*. Stanlei.

STONEHENGE (Salisbury). *Sic* 1529, but *c*. 1120 *Hen. Hunt*. Stanenges, *c*. 1145 *Geoffrey Mon*. Stanheng, *c*. 1205 *Layam*. Stan-henge, 1297 *R. Glouc*. Ston heng, and -hyngel. M'Clure thinks of O.E. *Stan hange*, ' sloping stones '; *hange*= *hangra* or *angra*. *Cf*. CLAYHANGER, etc. There is an early tradition that the circle was erected at the instigation of Merlin the enchanter, in memory of 460 nobles slain by *Hengist* the Saxon in 472. But the W. bard Aneurin says it existed even before the time of Ambrosius, the opponent of Hengist.

STONEWELL (Lancaster). 1418 Stanewelle, and STONEYWELL (Lich-field), *a*. 1300 Stoniwelle, *a*. 1400 -walle. = STANWELL.

STONNALL (Walsall). *a*. 1200 Stanhale, Stonhale. See -hall. *Cf*. STANCIL (Yorks), *Dom*. Steineshale. Prob. ' stoney corner.'

STOODLEIGH (Tiverton) and STUDLEY (Warwksh. and W. Riding). Wa. S. *Dom*. Stodlei, *a*. 1300 Stodelegh. W. Rid. S. *Dom*. Stollai (5 times), 1202 *Fines* Stodlee. ' Meadow of the breed-ing stud '; O.E. and O.N. *stód*. *Cf*. STOTFOLD, but also STOD-MARSH. See -leigh. Duignan says the Stude, Ch. Lawford, *a*. 1300 de la stude, is a var. of *stead*, ' homestead '; but prob. it is fr. *stód* too.

STOPHAM (Pulboro'). *Sic* 1238 *Close R*. Prob. ' home of *Steapa*,' 2 in *Onom*.

STORT R. (Essex). See BP'S. STORTFORD.

STOTFOLD (S. Yorks and Baldock). Yo. S. *Dom.* Stod-, Stotfald. Ba. S. 1007 *chart.* Stodfald. O.E. for ' enclosure, fold for the breeding stud.' *Cf.* STOODLEIGH, and Stodfauld burn (*sic* 1542), near Cullen (Banffshire).

STOTTESDON (Cleobury Mortimer). *Sic* 1160 *Pipe.* ' Hill of *Stotta* ' (not in *Onom.*) or ' *Stut.*' *Cf. B.C.S.* 787 Stutes hyl; and see -don.

STOULTON (Worcester). 840 *chart.* Stoltun, *Dom.* Stotune, 1275 Stoltone, 1332 Stotton. O.E. *stól-tun,* ' stool town,' a unique name, perh. referring to some seat of civil or ecclesiastical authority, now forgotten. Stutton (Ipswich) may be fr. *Stut.* *Cf. B.C.S.* 787 Stutes hyl.

STOUR R. (Kent, Dorset, Worcester, Staffs). Ke. S. *a.* 700 *chart.* Sturia, 839 Stura. Wo. S. 757-985 *chart.* Sture. St. S. 781 *chart.* Sture, and so *Dom.* Skeat inclines to associate with Eng. *stir.* Perh. cognate with Bret. *ster, steir,* ' river.' There is a tiny R. Stour (Cambs), on which is STUR- or STOURBRIDGE; but it must be an invented name, for we have, 1199-1200 Steresbrig, 1201-02 Steresbreg, 1418-19 Sterrebridge, ' bridge of *Steer*,' a personal name fr. O.E. *stéor,* ' steer, ox.' *Cf.* Bull, and Stearsby (Yorks), *Dom.* Estiresbi, Stirsbi. STOURBRIDGE (Worcester) is 1333 Sturbrugg, and STOURTON is 1227 Sturton.

STOW (7 in *P.G.*). *Dom.* Bucks Stov. Lichfield S. 1221 Stowe. O.E. *stow,* ' a place, village, town.' *Cf.* CHEPSTOW, etc.; STOWICK (Henbury) is 1316 Stokewicke.

STRADBROKE (Suffolk). 13 . . . in *Matt. Westmr.* Strodbrocke. ' Brook '; O.E. *bróc,* ' on the (Roman) road or street '; O.E. *strœt.* *Cf.* next. *Dom.* Yorks Stradford has now become Startforth. Stroat (Tidenham) is 956 *chart.* Strœt.

STRAFFIELD or STRATFIELD MORTIMER (Reading). *Dom.* Stradfeld; later, Stratfeld. ' Field on the street or Roman road '; O.E. *strœt.* *Cf.* next, STREATLEY, and 1160-61 *Pipe* Northants Strafford.

STRAMSHALL (Uttoxeter). *Dom.* Stagrigesholle (a bad shot !), *a.* 1300 Strangricheshull, -hall, Strangeshull, *a.* 1400 Strongeshull. The first part is ' *Stranglic*'s ' or ' *Stronglic*'s ' (both in *Onom.*)— *i.e.,* ' the stronglike's '—while the second varies between -hall, *q.v.,* and -hill, midl. *hull.*

STRANGEWAYS (Manchester). 1326 Strangwas. Popular etymology ! Orig. O.E. *strang wáse,* ' strong, stiff ooze ' or ' mud.' *Cf.* ALREWAS, etc. W. and H. prefer to derive fr. O.E. *wœsc,* ' washing up ' of water. But none of our names in -was ever show a trace of a final *c.*

STRATFORD, STONY, on AVON, and 3 others. Avon S. 691 *chart.* æt Stretfordæ, 714 *ib.* Straetforda. *O.E. Chron.* 675 Stretford (Lincs). *Dom.* Essex and Warwk. Stradford. They all mean ' ford on the *stratum* ' or ' Roman road,' O.E. *strœt. Cf.* STRAFFIELD. There is a Straford in *Dom.* (Salop), and a Strafford in 1160 *Pipe* Northants; whilst Straf(f)ord or Strafforth is name of a wapentake in *Dom.* Yorks.

STRATHFIELDSAYE and STRATFIELD or STRAFFIELD MORTIMER (Reading). *Dom.* Stradfeld in Redinges hundred—*i.e.*, ' *street*-field,' or field near the Roman way. The -saye is the *s* of the gen., and -ay, ' islet ' or ' watery spot.' See above.

STRATTON (7 in *P.G.*). *Dom.* Stratun (Salop), Strattone (Bude), 1156 Strattun (Leicester). ' Town, village on the street ' or ' road.' Prob. they all stood on Roman roads. See above. *P.G.* has also 10 cases of STRETTON, and there are 4 in Warwk. alone, 2 in *Dom.* as Stratone, and, of course, all the same name. S.-on-Fosse and S.-under-Fosse refer to the Rom. Fossway or road fr. Lincoln to Exeter; L. *fossa*, ' a ditch.' It is called in O.E. *chart.* Fos and Foss. Stretton (Burton-on-T.) is found so spelt as early as a charter of 942; also *cf.* STURTON.

STREATLEY (Reading). *B.C.S.* i. 108 Stræt-leah, Stretlea. *Cf. c.* 700 *Kent chart.* Stretleg. ' Meadow on the street or *stratum.*' See STRATFORD, and *cf.* STRETHAM (Cambs), *c.* 1080 Streatham, and STRELLEY (Notts), *Dom.* Straleia, 1166 *Pipe* Stratlega, and so the name as Streatley. But STREETTHORP (S. Yorks) is *Dom.* Stirestorp, ' village of *Stir* '; ? the majordomo of Harthacnut. The same name recurs in Stearsby (Yorks), *Dom.* Stirsbi.

STRENSALL (N. Riding). *Dom.* Strenshale. Perh. ' nook of *Streon.*' See -hall. But STRENSHAM (Pershore) is 972 *chart.* Strengesho, ' hill ' (see HOE) ' of *Streng* '—*i.e.*, ' the strong.' Strong and Strang (Sc.) are still common surnames. By 1275 it is Strenge-sham.

STRICKLAND (Westmorld.). *Dom.* Stercaland. ' Stirk land '; O.E. *styrc, styric,* ' a young bullock or heifer.'

STROOD (Rochester). 1160 *Pipe* Stroda; and STROUD (Glouc.), 1200 La Strode. O.E. *strod(e)*, a common charter word for ' marshy land.' *Cf.* Stretaston (Monks Kirby), *a.* 1400 Strodaston, ' East town in the marshy land,' and STROUD GREEN (N. London), which has no old history.

STRUMPSHAW (Norfolk). *Dom.* Stromessaga, 1452 Stromsaw, 1454 Strumpeshawe. Doubtful. There is no likely name in *Onom.*, yet *Strome-* prob. represents a man. The ending may either be *shaw*, ' a wood ' *q.v.*, or ' *haw*, ' a hedge '; O.E. *haga.*

STUBHAM (Ilkley). *Dom.* Stube (-e ?= -ey, *q.v.*), and STUBHOUSE (Harewood), *Dom.* Stubhuṣon (a loc.). O.N. *stubb-r, stobbi,* O.E. *styb,* ' a stump, a stub.' Here ? ' house made of stumps,' or ' beside the stump.' See -ham.

STUBLACH (Middlewich). Not in *Dom.* But there were orig. two hamlets, Stubs (prob. O.E. *styb,* ' a stub ' or ' stob ' or ' stake,' Icel. *stubbi, stobbi, stubbr,* Dan. *stub,* ' a stump ') and Lache (*Dom.* Leche—*i.e.*, O.E. *léah, léaʒ,* ' meadow ').

STUDLEY. See STOODLEIGH.

STUKELEY, GREAT and LITTLE (Hunts). *Chart.* Styvec lea, Stivec-lea, *Dom.* Stivecle. ' *Styfec*'s meadow.' *Cf.* STETCHWORTH. On *styfec* see STEWKLEY. See -ley.

STUNTNEY (Ely). *c.* 1080 *Inquis. Camb.* Stuntenei, ' Isle of the weak or foolish man '; O.E. *stunta, stunt.* See -ey.

STURTON (2 in Lincs, Retford, and Cambridge). Re. S. *Dom.* Estre-tone, *c.* 1200 Strattone; also STURTON GRANGE (Yorks), *Dom.* Stretun, = STRATTON. Old forms needed for the others.

STURRY (N.E. Kent). 679 *chart.* Sturia. See STOUR and -ey.

STUTTON (Ipswich and Tadcaster). Ta. S. *Dom.* Stutone, Stouetun. ' Town of *Stut,* one in *Onom.,* contracted fr. *Stutheard* or *Stuthere. Cf. B.C.S.* 787 Stutes hyl, and 1160-61 *Pipe* Somst. Stuttevill.

SUCKLEY (Worcester). *Dom.* Suchelei, 1275 Sukkeleye. ' Meadow of *Succa* ' or ' *Sucga.*' *Cf. B.C.S.* 1234 Succan pyt, 958 *chart.* Sicanbyrig, on R. Stour (Stafford), and SUGWORTH. See -ley.

SUDBROOK (Grantham, Chepstow, and Glouc.). Like next, these may all be ' south brook '; O.E. *súð,* O.N. *suð-r,* Dan. *syd,* ' south.' But *cf.* Sotebroca, *Dom.* Devon, ' brook of *Sota,*' 2 in *Onom.*

SUDBURY (Worcester and Suffolk). Wo. S. 963 *chart.* Suthan byrig. Su. S. *O.E. Chron.* 798 Sudberi; also Suthberi; *a.* 1200 Sudbiri, 1471 Sudberrye. ' South burgh ' or ' fort.' *Cf.* SUDELEY (2 in Glouc.), *Dom.* Sudlege, 1250 Suthlege. See -bury.

SUFFIELD (N. Riding, Aylsham, Cromer). York S. *Dom.* Sudfelt. ' South field.' See next.

SUFFOLK. Orig. the southern part of East Anglia. 1076 *O.E. Chron.* Suðfolc, *c.* 1175 *Fantosme* Sufolke, 1478 Suffolk. ' The South folk.' *Cf.* NORFOLK. Earlier—*e.g.,* 1010 *O.E. Chron.*—it was Eastengle or Engla, now East Anglia.

SUGNALL (Eccleshall). *Dom.* Sotehelle (error), *a.* 1200 Sogenhull, *a.* 1300 Suggenhale, -hille; and SUGWORTH (Sunningwell, Berks), *Dom.* Sogorde. *Cf.* 1293-94 ' Suggeden ' (Salop). ' Farm of *Sucga.*' See SUCKLEY and -worth. In Sugnall the ending varies between -hall, *q.v.,* and -hill, midl. *hull,* as often.

SULHAM (Reading) and SULHAMPSTEAD (Berks). Skeat says not the same names. *Dom.* Soleham, *c.* 1130 *Chron. Abingd.* Sule-ham, also Soulham, which is prob. ' home of *Sula.*' *Cf.* Sulan-broc, -ford, and -graf, all in O.E. charters, and *Dom.* Suletune (Salop), and *ib.* Soleberie (Bucks). But *c.* 1290 Sylhamsted, 1402 Syllampstede, 1428 Silhamsted, *c.* 1540 Sulhampsted Banaster (now Bannister, fr. a Norman*), and S. Abbatis, now

---

* A Robert Banistre was Nor. lord of Prestatyn, Flint, in 1164.

S. Abbots. These persistent *y* forms must represent an O.E. *ū*, and not *u*, so this is prob. ' homestead in a miry place,' O.E. *sylu*. *Cf*. Sowlk- or Sookholme (Notts), 1189 *Pipe* Sulcholm, 1230 *Close R.* Sulgholm, ' miry meadow,' fr. O.E. *sulig, sulh*, ' miry, wet '; and see -holm. Soulby (Cumbld.) is ' dwelling of *Solva*.' *Cf*. HAMPSTEAD.

SULLY (isle off Glamorgan). *a*. 1300 *Taxatio* Sulleye, 1610 Sylye. M'Clure's suggested connexion with *Silures* seems very doubtful. More likely ' Isle of *Sulf*,' 2 in *Onom*. See -ey. However, it lies at the mouth of the rivulet *Sili*, which T. Morgan says may mean ' hissing water.' It may contain the same root as SCILLY. Curiously SULLEY (Lydney) is 1281 Sollewalle, ' muddy spring.' See above.

SUNBURY (Hampton Court). *a*. 962 *chart*. æt Sunnanbyrg, *Dom*. Suneberie; also Sunnabyri. ' Burgh, castle of *Sunna*'—*i..e*, ' the sun '; O.E. *sunne* fem., Icel. *sunna*. *Cf*. SUNDON.

SUNDERLAND. The orig. town was Wearmouth. This ' Sunderland ' occurs first in 1183 *Boldon Bk.* as, presumably, land *sundered* from Bp's and Monk's Wearmouth, land specially privileged, fr. O.E. *sundor*, ' apart, special '; *sun-*, *syndrian*, ' to separate.' *Cf*. SUNDERLANDWICK (Driffield), *Dom*. Sundrelanwic (see -wick), *Dom*. Chesh. Sundreland, and perh. Sinderhope (Allendale). But Sinderby (Thirsk), *Dom*. Senerebi, is perh. ' dwelling of *Sind-*, *Sundbeorht*,' an old Teutonic name. See -by and -hope. There was also a ' Sunderland ' found in Wstrsh. charters. On it now stands SUNDAY's HILL (Spetchley), a curious example of popular etymology.

SUNDON (Dunstable). *K.C.D.* 920 Sunnan dun, which may be ' hill of the sun,' but quite as likely ' fort of *Sunna*.' See SUNBURY.

SUNNINGHILL and -WELL (Berks). *Old* Suninghull, Sunningehulle (hull= hill; *cf*. SOLIHULL, etc.). *B.C.S.* i. 506 Sunningauuille, *ib*. iii. 108 Sunninga wylle, *Dom*. Soningeuuel, *c*. 1290 Sunningewell. ' Hill ' and ' well of the *Sunnings*.' See SONNING.

SURBITON. See NORBITON.

SURLINGHAM (Norwich). *Dom*. Sutherlinga-, Suterlinge-ham. ' Home of the dwellers in the South '; a patronymic. See -ing. *Cf*. Easterling, ' a dweller in East Germany,' etc., and SUTHERLAND (Sc.).

SURREY. *Bede* iv. 6 In regione sudergeona; *O.E. vers*. Suthrigra lande, 838 Suthreie, 1011 *O.E. Chron*. Suthrige, *c*. 1175 *Fantosme* Surrei, *c*. 1386 *Chaucer* Surrye. ' Southern kingdom '; O.E. *ric, rige*—*i.e.*, south of the Thames.

SURTEES (Co. Durham). 1211 Super Teisam. L. *super*, Fr. *sur*, ' on the TEES.'

SUSSEX. *c.* 800 *Nennius* Sutsaxum (inflected), *O.E. Chron.* 449
Suð Sexa, 891 *ib.* Suðseaxas, *c.* 1330 *R. Brunne* Southsex.
(Land of) ' the South Saxons.' *Cf.* ESSEX, and Wessex, or
' the West Saxons.'

SUTTERTON (Boston). *Sic* in *chart.* of ? 810. The *Onom.* has only
a *Sutta,* so this will be ' town of the *soutar*' or ' tailor '; O.E.
sutere, O.N. *sutar.*

SUTTON (38 in *P.G.*). *B.C.S.* ii. 224 Suðtun, *Dom.* Sudtone; *later*
Suthtun, Suttone (Berks); *Dom.* Suttone (Surrey and Cambs.);
1160 *Pipe* Sutton (Kent). ' South town.' But 825 *chart.*
Suthtune has, in one case, in Worcestersh., become Sodington.
Dom. Yorks has Sudtun or -tunen 23 times, and Sutun 10 times.

SUTTON COLDFIELD. *Dom.* Sutone, *a.* 1200 Sutton Colmesfeld,
Colnes field, *a.* 1400 Sutton in Colfield. ' South town ' (see
above) ' in *Colm's* field.' *Colm* is short form of *Columba* or
Colum, as in INCHCOLM (Sc.); and the liquids *m* and *n,* though
not so commonly as *l* and *r,* tend to disappear. Cold- is a late
and ill-informed corruption.

SWAFFHAM (Cambridge) and SWAFFHAM BULBECK. *K.C.D.* iv. 245
Suafham, *Dom.* Suafam, 1210 Swafham. ' Home of *Swœf.*' *Cf.*
SWAVESEY. SWAFIELD (Norfk.) is *c.* 1150 Suathefeld, which
may be for ' *Swœf's* field ' too. *Onom.* has nothing nearer.
For a similar change *cf.* STEVENAGE.

SWAINSTHORP (Norfolk). 1451 Sweynnysthorp, 1458 Sweynsthorp.
' Village of *Swegen* ' or ' *Sweyn,*' or ' of the swain or herd or
swineherd.' *Cf.* SWAINBY (Yorks), *Dom.* Suanebi, and SWAINSET
(N. Lancs), *Dom.* Suenesat, ? ' seat of the swain.' *Cf.* SOMERSET.
See -by and -thorpe.

SWALE R. (Yorks and Kent). Yor. S. *Bede* Sualua, *O.E. vers.*
Swalwa, 1155 *Pipe* Svaledale. Kent S. is a salt-water strait.
M'Clure thinks connected with O.E. *swellan,* ' to swell,' and
compares the numerous Ger. Schwal-bachs. *Cf.* SWALWELL.

SWALLOWFIELD (Berks). *Dom.* Solafel, *c.* 1290 Swalefeld; *later*
Swaleewefeld. O.E. *swealwe, swalwe,* ' a swallow.'

SWALWELL (Co. Durham). 1183 *Boldon Bk.* Sualwels. Perh.
' *Sualo's* well,' 1 such in *Onom.* As likely fr. same root as SWALE.

SWANAGE (Bournemouth). *O.E. Chron.* 877 Swana-, Swanewic,
O.E. for ' swans' dwelling.' It might also be *swāna wic,* ' swine-
herds' dwelling.' For the phonetic changes involved in the
change of -wic into -age *cf.* the forms of KNOWLEDGE v. in
Oxf. Dict. Cf., too, Cranage, ' cranes' dwelling ' (Congleton).
Greenwich to-day is pron. Greenage. But SWANBORO' TUMP
(Pewsey, Wilts) is *a.* 900 *K. Alfred's Will* Swinbeorg, ' *swine's*
mound ' or ' BARROW.' Thus Tump is but a tautology.

SWANLAND (Brough). 1298 Swanelond. *Cf.* above.

SWANSEA. 1188 Sweynsei, *c.* 1190 *Gir. Camb. Itin.* Sweineshe quod et Kambrice Abertawe ('mouth of R. TAWE') vocatur; 1210 Sueinesheia, 1234 Sweinesheie, 1298 Sweynese. 'Isle of K. *Swegen*' or '*Sweyn*,' d. 1014, who thrice invaded England from Denmark. *Cf.* SWAINSTHORP, and Swancote (Worc.), 1275 Swanecote, 'cot of the swain' or 'swineherd.' See -ea.

SWARDESTON (Norwich). 'Town of *Swearta*,' 3 in *Onom.*, or 'of *Sweorda*.' *Cf. B.C.S.* ii. 174 Sweordestan (Glouc.).

SWARLING (Kent). 805 *chart.* Sueordhlincas. 'Links for sword-play'; O.E. *sweord. Cf.* SWERFORD, and 941 *chart.* Suuyrdling (Twickenham).

SWARTH (Ulverston). *Dom.* Warte; but the other *Dom.* Yorks Warte is Warter Hundred. ? fr. O.E. *sweart*, 'swart, swarthy, black, dark' (place), or *sweard*, O.N. *svörd-r*, 'sward, turf.'

SWAVESEY (Cambridge). *Dom.* Svavesye, 1266 Suauiseye, 1346 Swafsey. 'Isle of *Swæf*,' lit. one of the tribe *Suevi*, now the Swabians. *Cf.* SWAFFHAM and SWAYTHORP (E. Riding), *Dom.* Suauetorp. See -ey.

SWERFORD (Oxford). Perh. *a.* 800 *chart.* Sweord ora, O.E. for 'sword bank'—*i.e.*, level bank fit for fighting with swords. *Cf.* SWARDLING.

SWETTENHAM (Congleton). 'Home of *Sweta*,' gen. -*an*, or 'of *Swet*.' *Sweting* is also in *Onom. Cf. Dom.* Norfk. Suatinga, patronymic, and SWETTON (W. Riding), *Dom.* Suatune.

SWINBROOK (Burford, Oxon). 'Swine's brook'; O.E. *swin*, O.N. *svin. Cf. Dom.* Bucks Svene-, Sueneborne, or 'Swinburne'; see -bourne. SWINDON—there are 3, *Dom.* Wilts and Glouc. Suindone—is, of course, 'Swine's hill.' SWILLAND (Ipswich) is *c.* 1330 *chart.* Swinnlonde.

SWINE (Hull). *Dom.* Swine, Suine. 'Swine island,' with -e = -ey. O.E. *swin*, 'swine.'

SWINESHEAD (Boston, Hunts, Eccleshall, and Spetchley). Bos. S. 786-96 *chart.* Suinesheabde, *a.* 1100 *ib.* Swyneseheved. Ecc. S. *Dom.* Sueneshed. Sp. S. 989 *chart.* Swinesheafod, *a.* 1300 Swynesheved. Prob. 'height of the swine'; O.E. *swin;* but possibly fr. a man *Sigewine*, which would contract into *Swine;* so Duignan.

SWINFORD (Rugby). *Cf.* 808 *chart.* Swinford (Somerset), and 958 *chart.* Swinforda (on R. Stour, Staffd.). 'Swine's ford.'

SWINNERTON (Staffs). *Dom.* Sulvertone, 1205 Silverton, 1206 Soulverton, 1298 Swynnreton, *a.* 1300 Swinaferton, Swyne-farton, *a.* 1500 Swynerton. A name which has changed; orig. 'Silver town'; O.E. *seolfor*, *siolfor*, 2-7 *siluer*, 3-4 *suluer ;* ? why so called. *Cf.* SILVERTON. But its present form is fr. some unrecorded man with a name like *Swinafer*, or ? fr. *swine ford.*

SWINTON (3 in Yorks, and Manchester). *Dom.* Yorks, Suintun 5 times. 1179-80 *Pipe* Suineton (Yorks). Prob. 'town of *Swegen* (also *Suen, Svein*),' a very common name in *Onom.* There is also SWINDEN (Craven), *Dom.* Suindene, prob. fr. O.E. *swin,* 'swine.' See -den.

SYDENHAM (S. London and Wallingford) and S. DAMAREL (Tavistock). *B.C.S.* 759 Sidanham. O.E. for 'home of *Sida.*' The London S. is 1675 *Evelyn* Sydnam. The Tav. S. at first belonged to the Damarels.

SYMOND'S YAT (Hereford). ' Opening, pass, gate ' (O.E. *geat*) ' of *Simund* ' or ' *Sigemund.*' *Cf.* Yatton (Bristol), and YETHOLM (Sc.).

SYRESCOTE (Tamworth). 1100 Siricescotan, *a.* 1200 Sirichescote, Sirescote, but *Dom.* Fricescote (*F* error for *S*). Form 1100 is O.E. for ' cots, cottages of *Sigeric* ' or ' *Siric*,'—*i.e.,* ' the victorious.' SYERSTON (Notts), *Dom.* Sirestune, and SYRESHAM (Brackley), *Dom.* Sigres-, Sigreham, are fr. the same name. *Cf. Dom.* Salop Sireton, and Syreford (Glouc.).

TACHEBROOK, BISHOP'S, and T. MALLORY (Warwick). *K.C.D.* 751 Tæcelesbroc, *Dom.* Taschebroc, Tacesbroc, *a.* 1200 Tachelesbroc. ' Brook of *Tæcel.*' *Cf.* TACKLEY (Oxford), *Dom.* Tachelie. The Mallorys were old lords of the manor here. Sir Thos. Malory of the *Morte d'Arthur* prob. belonged to this shire.

TADCASTER. 1066 *O.E. Chron.* Taða, *Dom.* Tatecastre. Prob. ' Camp of *Tada.*' *Cf. B.C.S.* 1152 Tadan leah—*i.e.,* TADLEY (Basingstoke), and TODWICK; also TADLOW (Cambs), *Dom.* Tadelai, and *Dom.* Surrey, Tadforde. See -caster.

TAFARN SPITE or TAVERNSPITE (Whitland, Caermthnsh.); also TAFARNAUBACH (Tredegar). Tafarn is just the W. form of L. *taberna,* Eng. *tavern.* Spite is a corrup. of L. *hospitium* ' hospice,' the ' hospital.' *Cf.* Llanspyddyd (Brecon) and YSPYTTY YSTWYTH. *Tafarnau* is the plur., and *bach* means ' a hook,' prob. for attaching horses; but the meaning of the name is not very clear.

TAFF R. (S. Wales). *c.* 1540 *Leland* Thave. Its oldest recorded form is found *c.* 1130 in Landavia—*i.e.,* LLANDAFF; it is very doubtful if also in the early forms of CARDIFF. Prob. Keltic, aspirated form of Tam or Tame (see TAMWORTH), meaning ' quiet ' or perh. ' wide ' river.

TALKE (Stoke-on-T.). *Dom.* Talc, *a.* 1300 Talk; now called more fully ' Talk o' the Hill.' As *talc,* ' mica,' is quite late in Eng., this last may be a tautology, like Barrhill (Sc.), fr. W. *twlch,* ' a height, a hill,' the G. *tulach,* which gives us many Sc. names in Tilly- and Tullie-. *Cf.* TALKIN (Brampton), which may be a dimin., and also TALOG, which may be the origin here.

TALOG (Caermarthen). W. *talawg*, 'high-fronted' or 'high house,' not a thatched cottage.

TALSARN (Lampeter). Prob. 'the end of the road,' W. *tal*, 'forehead, front,' and *sarn*, 'road.' It is at the end of Sarn Helen, an old Roman road.

TAMAR R. (S. Devon). *c.* 150 Ptolemy Ταμαρος, *c.* 988 *chart*. Tamur, 997 *O.E. Chron.* Tamer. Prob. same Kelt. root as TAFF and Tam. See below. The -ar will be terminational.

TAMERTON FOLIOT (Crown Hill, Devon). ? *Dom.* Tanbretone. 'Town on R. TAMAR.' Gilbert *Foliot*, Bp. of Hereford, 1149-63, was a native of this place. In *Exon. Dom.* we also find a 'Tamerlande.'

TAMWORTH. 840 *chart*. Tomeworðig, *later chart.* Tamanworðig, 913 *O.E. Chron.* Tamaweorðige, 918 *ib.* Tamanweorðe, 943 *ib.* Tamwurth, *a.* 1130 *Sim. Dur.* Tameweorde. 'Farm on R. *Tame*,' which is Kelt. for 'quiet, calm,' mod. W. *taw* (*w* = aspirated *m*), G. *tàmhach*, same root, and THAMES. M'Clure derives fr. a man *Toma* or *Tuma*; but Eng. rivers are not called in this way after a man; and there is no *Toma* or *Tama* in *Onom.*, only one *Tomus* and *Tuma*, while the place is never found with a *u*. Connection with O.E. *tam, tom*, 'tame,' is quite conceivable. Tamhorn, near by, is *Dom.* Tamahore, *a.* 1200 Tamenhorn, 'horn, hornlike bend of the Tame.' See -worth and -worthy.

TANFIELD (Ripon). Doubtfully thought to be K. Alfred's Donafelda. *Dom.* Tanefeld. It may be 'field of *Teona*.' Cf. *B.C.S.* 801 Teonan hyl; *eo* regularly becomes *a*. Certainly nothing to do with tanning.

TANKERVILLE (once in Warwick). 1120 Tanc' villa, 1157 Tancharuille, *c.* 1175 Tankarvile. Really a Norm. name, 'town,' Fr. *ville*, 'of *Tancred, Tancrad*, or *Thancred*,' a name common enough in O.E. There is now no Tankerville in England, but there is a TANKERSLEY (Barnsley), *Dom.* Tancresleia.

TANSHELF (Pontefract). *Sic* in 1257 *chart.*, but 947 *O.E. Chron.* Taddenes scylfe—*i.e.*, '*Tadden*'s shelf' or 'ledge,' O.E. *scelfe, scylfe*. There is a *Tada*, gen. -*an*, in *Onom.*, but no *Tadden*. The form in *Dom.*, Tatessella, only puzzles us a little more. It is the same name as TATTERSHALL.

TANSLEY (Matlock and Dudley) and TANWORTH (Birmingham). These all postulate a man *Tan* or *Tana*, not in *Onom.*, but *cf.* TANWORTH. We must not invoke W. *tan*, 'fire.' However, Duignan says, the Dudley name is rightly Tansy Hill, fr. the wild *tansy*, or potentilla. See -ley and -worth, 'farm.'

TANTON (Stokesley, Yorks). *Dom.* and 1209 Tameton. It is on a R. THAME; also see TAUNTON. Similarly TANWORTH-IN-ARDEN, *a.* 1200 Taneworth, *a.* 1500 T(h)oneworthe, is 'farm on ' a little river, which Duignan thinks would once be called Tan or Tone. See -worth.

TAPLOW (Maidenhead). *Dom.* Thapeslav. ' Burial mound of *Tapa*;' the *h* in *Dom.* is a Nor. insertion. *Cf. B.C.S.* 993 Tapan hal. See -low.

TARANNON R. (Wales). This, says Anwyl, may be the Keltic goddess of Thunder, W. *taran.*

TARDEBIGGE (Bromsgrove). *c.* 1000 *chart.* Tærdebicga, *a.* 1000 Terde bicg, *Dom.* Terdeberie, 1158-59 *Pipe* Terdebigga, 1283 Tyrdebigg. There is nothing likely in *Oxf. Dict.* to give origin to -bigge, though it surely must be = the Norse BIGGIN or 'building.' For the first half we must postulate a name *Terde* or *Tarde* ; only a rare *Tyrd(d)a* seems known.

TARN WADING (little lake, Hesket, Penrith.) 1089 *chart.* Tarnwadelyn, *c.* 1360 Terne Wathelyne. O.N. *tjörn*, ' a tarn, a mountain lakelet.' Many *Wada*s in *Onom.*, but nothing nearer in the way of a man's name.

TARRANT KAINES or KEYNSTON (Blandford). 935 *chart.* Terenta, *a.* 1225 *Ancren Riwle* Tarente. Prob. = TARANNON. *Cf.* 1160 *Pipe* Tarenteford (Kent).

TARRINGTON (Ledbury). Not in *Dom.* Hardly fr. W. *taran,* ' thunder.' No likely man's name in *Onom.*, unless it be *Tora*, gen. -*an.*

TARRING (Worthing). 941 *chart.* Terring. ' Place of the sons of *Terr*,' a name not in *Onom.* See -ing.

TASS R. (Norfolk). Prob. W. *tas*, ' what binds, a band.'

TATENHILL (Burton-on-T.). 771 *chart.* Taten hyll, ' hill of *Tate*,' fem. of *Tata.* See next, and *cf.* TATTENHALL (Chester), *Dom.* Tatenale, and Tatworth (Somst.). TATHAM (N. Lancs). *Dom.* Tathaim, is fr. the same name in its male form.

TATTERSHALL (Boston). *Dom.* Tateshale, 1161-62 *Pipe* Tateshal, 1249 Tateshall, *a.* 1450 Tatessall. ' Nook of *Tata*.' The *r* results fr. a ' Cockney ' pron. *Cf.* KIDDERMINSTER. See -hall.

TATTINGSTONE (Ipswich). 1199 Tatingetun. ' Village of the descendants of *Tata*,' a common O.E. name. *Cf.* above. See -ton.

TAUNTON. *Sic* 1499, but *O.E. Chron.* 722 Tantun (so pron. still), *Dom.* Tantone. ' Town on the R. *Tone*,' prob. same root as Tame, THAMES, etc, the liquids *m* and *n* not rarely interchanging, and so ' quiet ' river. *Cf.* TANTON. Not prob. are derivations fr. W. *tan*, ' fire,' or *tonn*, ' unploughed land.' Taynton (Newent) is *Dom.* Tet-, Tatinton, ' town of *Tetta* ' or ' *Tata*.' See above.

TAVERHAM (Norwich). *Sic* in *Dom.* Taver- may stand for *Tathere* or *Tatbeorht*, names in *Onom.* ; *th* often becomes *v*. *Cf.* STEVENAGE, etc. See -ham.

TAVISTOCK. 997 *O.E. Chron.* Tefingestoc, Tæfingstoc, *Dom.* Taue-stoch, *c.* 1130 *Eadmer* Tavestoc, *c.* 1145 *Wm. Malmes.* Tavis-tokium, 1155 Tauistoche. Tefingestoc is an O.E. patronymic, ' place of the *Tæfings*,' but, as it is on R. Tavy, these will mean, ' dwellers on the *Tavy*,' a Keltic root same as Tame and THAMES, only aspirated. *Cf.* G. *tàmh*, ' rest, quiet.' See STOKE, and *cf.* next; also 1179-80 *Pipe* Taueston (Yorks).

TAW R. (N. Devon). *Sic* 1068 *O.E. Chron. c.* 1097 *Flor. W.* Tavus, 1166-67 *Pipe* Taui. Also TAWE R. (Swansea), *c.* 1190 *Gir. Camb.* Tawe; also said to be *old* Tafwy (W. *gwy*, ' river '). W. *taw*, ' silent, quiet,' same root as Tame (see TAMWORTH), Tavy (see TAVISTOCK), THAME, etc., the *m* here being aspirated.

TAWTON (Devon). *Dom.* Tavvetone, 1157 *Pipe* Tautun. See above.

TAYNTON (Burford). = TEIGNTON, also see TAUNTON.

TEAN R. and hamlet (Staffs). *Dom.* Tene, *a.* 1400 Teyne. Like so many river names, doubtful. *Cf.* TEIGN and TYNE. TAIN (Sc.) is 1223 Tene, and generally thought fr. N.; but fr. what ?

TEDDINGTON (R. Thames and Warwk.). Th. T. *sic* 1427, but 969 *chart.* Tudintun, 1279 Todington, Wa. T. 969 *chart.* Tidinctune, 1016 *ib.* Tiddingtun. ' Town of the sons of *Tidda* ' or ' *Tuda*,' gen. *-an*, a common O.E. name. Grave scientific men in the 20th cny. have actually thought it meant ' Tide-end-town.' ! *Cf. Dom.* Tedenesvlle (for -hulle) (Salop), which is ' hill of ' ? ' *Teden*,' whilst *Dom.* Bucks Tedinwiche suggests a man *Teda* or *Teoda*, 1 in *Onom.* There is also TEDDESLEY (Penkridge). *Sic a.* 1300. See -ley. But TEDDINGTON (Tewkesbury) is 780 *chart.* Teottingtun, 977 *ib.* Teodintun, Tidingctun, *c.* 1046 Theotinctun, *Dom.* Teotin tune. 1275 Tedinton. ' Town of the sons of *Teotta* ' or ' *Tette* ' (this is common). See -ing.

TEES R. *a.* 1130 *Sim. Dur.* Tesa, 1387 Teyse. Perh. fr. W. *tesach*, ' wantonness,' fr. *tes*, ' heat of the sun.' The R. Test (Hants) is sometimes called Tees, and the Teise, trib. of R. Medway, will be the same name. They may all be pre-Keltic.

TEIGN R. Mod. pron. Tinn. 739 *chart.* Teng. *Dom.* Taigne, Teigne; and DREWS TEIGNTON (S. Devon). 1001 *O.E. Chron.* Tegntun, *Dom.* Teinton, Taintone. Perh. fr. W. *teneu* or O.E. *þynne*, W. Fris. *ten, tin*, ' thin, slender.' The Drews comes fr. *Drewe* de Teignton, landholder *temp.* Hen. II. *Cf.* Taynton (Burford), *Dom.* Tentone.

TELPEN PT. (Amroth). W. *telpyn*, ' a lump.'

TEME R. (Worc.). O.E. *chart.* Temede, once Tamede. Seems the same as THAMES; but it is said to be in O.W. Tefaidd, Tefedd (*f* = *v*, and *v* = aspirated *m*). On it was Tempsiter. *Cf.* TEMPSFORD.

TEMPLE EWING, GRAFTON, etc. Such names indicate lands of the Knight Templars.

TEMPSFORD (Sandy). 921 *O.E. Chron.* Tamese-, esaforda, *Dom.* Tamiseford. There was another R. THAMES here; the form Temps is said to come through the Norse sagas. *Cf.* TEME.

TENBURY (Worc.). *Dom.* Tametde-, Tamedeberie. ' Burgh, fort on the R. *Teme,*' which is the same root as TAM-WORTH and THAMES. See -bury.

TENBY. 1248-49 Tinbegh, 1325 Tyneby, 1350 *chart.* Tynby, in W. Dinbych y Pysgod. See DENBIGH. There are a good many traces of the Norseman hereabouts; and there is little doubt that Tenby is corrup. of Den-by, ' Danes' dwelling.' *Cf.* DANBY, and see -by.

TENDRING (Weeley, Essex). *Dom.* Tendringa, and Ten-, Tonderingae (ae = ' isle,' ; see -ey). A patronymic, ? fr. *Tondheri,* 2 in *Onom.* See -ing.

TENTERDEN (Ashford). *Sic* 1439; so now meant for ' DEAN, wooded valley where *tenters* were spread for stretching cloth.' This word in English goes back to the 14th cny. *Cf.* 1408 *Nottingham Rec.* ii. 60 ' Johannes London occupat unum croftum cum taynters.' But in *Dom.* it is Tintentone, fr. some unknown man, *Tinta* or *Tenta.*

TERN R. (W. Staffs). *a.* 1200 Tirne, Tyrne, Turne. Prob. M.E. *terne* (found in Wstmld. in 1256). Dan. *tjern,* N. *tjörn,* ' a tarn, a small hill lake.' *Cf.* TIRLEY.

TERRINGTON (York, K.'s Lynn, and Wisbech). Yo. T. *Dom.* Teurinc-, Teurintone, 1202 *Yorks Fines* Theverington. Doubtful. Wis. T. *Dom.* Terintune. Patronymic, ? fr. *Theodhere* or *Teherus* or *Theudor,* names in *Onom.* See -ing.

TETBURY (S. Glouc.). 680 *chart.* Tettan Monasterium, *c.* 1000 *ib.* Tettanbyrig, *Dom.* Teteberie. ' Burgh of *Tetta.*' *Cf.* next, TATENHILL, Tetsworth (Oxon), and TITTESWORTH. See -bury.

TETTENHALL (Wolverhampton). *O.E. Chron.* 593 Teotanhealh, *ib.* 910 Teotanheale, *Dom.* Totehala, *c.* 1120 *Hen. Hunt.* Totanhale, *a.* 1300 Tetenhale. ' Nook, enclosure of *Teota* or *Tetta.*' Skeat thinks *Teota* a form of O.E. *tota,* ' a spy, a look-out,' a tout ! *Cf.* TOTLEY; and see -hall.

TETTON (Sandbach). *Dom.* Tedtune. May be ' *Tette*'s town.' See above; but perh. ' people's town.' *Cf.* THETFORD, *a.* 1200 Tedford.

TEVERSHALL (Mansfield). *Dom.* Tevreshalt, 1284 Teversalt, and TEVERSHAM (Cambridge). *Dom.* Teuresham, Teuersham, 1210 Teuersham. ' Holt, wood,' and ' home of *Tefere,*' an unknown name. See too -hall.

TEWIN (Welwyn). *Dom.* Teuuinge, and Theunge, 1166 Tiwinge. ' Place of the sons of *Tiw.*' He was the Teutonic Mars, or god of war. See -ing.

TEWKESBURY. *Dom.* Teodechesberie, *c.* 1145 *Wm. Malmesb.*
Theochesberia, 1157 Tiochesbiria, 1201 Teokesberi, *c.* 1350
Teukesbury. 'Burgh of *Teodeca,*' or '*Theoc,*' a Saxon hermit,
settled here; soon after a monastery was here founded by Odo
and Dodo, dukes of Mercia, 715. *Cf.* 963 *chart.* Teodeces leage,
near Redditch, now TIDSLEY.

TEY R. (Essex). *Chart.* Tiga(n). May be same as GREAT TEY, O.E.
tih, teah, teag, 'a paddock.' *Cf.* O.E. *léah,* 'meadow,' often
found as *leaʒ,* and to-day usually -ley in names. Or fr. O.E.
tyge, 'a diverting' (of a water-course).

TEYNHAM (Faversham). 801 *chart.* Tenham. Prob. 'home of
Thegn' or '*Degn,*' the nearest forms in *Onom.* Derivation fr.
O.E. *tén,* 'ten,' can hardly be thought of; but possibly the name
is = TWYNHAM. It is now in a marshy region, near a creek of
the Swale.

THAME R. (trib. of Thames, Aylesbury, also N. Yorks, 1209 Tame)
and THAMES R. Latter is *c.* 50 B.C. *J. Cæsar* Tameses, *c.*100
Tacitus Tamesa, *c.* 893 *Ælfred* and 1297 *R. Glouc.* Tamese; v.r.
in *Ælf.* Temes, 1377 *Langland* Themese, 1503 Thamyse, 1649
Thames. Keltic root, meaning 'quiet, silent,' or perh. 'wide
river.' W. *taw* (aspirated form), 'still,' G. *tàmh,* 'rest, quiet,'
tàmhach, 'quiet, dull, heavy.' Same root as Tamar, Tame,
Tavy, Taw, Teme, etc. Skeat, however, declares the origin
quite unknown. The initial Th- is a Norm. innovation, which
it is really absurd to retain. On the -eses *cf.* ISIS and OUSE; it
must be Kelt. for 'river.'

THANET. 80 *Solinus* Ad-Tanatos, 679 *chart.* Tenid, *Bede* Tanet,
a. 810 *Nennius,* Tanet, 1461 Thenede. Thought to be Keltic
for 'fire,' O.Ir. *teine,* gen. *tened,* W. and Corn. *tan.* But *tann*
also seems to be Kelt. for 'an oak.' If the former, it will prob.
mean 'place of beacon-fires.'

THATCHAM (Berks). *B.C.S.* iii. 432 Thæcham, *Dom.* Taccham,
Taceham. The charter name is O.E. for 'thatched house,' or,
more exactly, as in Sc., 'a thack hoose.' Norman scribes often
wrote *t* for *th,* as to them the *h* was mute. *Cf.* THAXTED.

THAXTED (Dunmow). 1528 Thackstedd. *Cf.* 1298 Thaxton. O.E.
thæc stede, 'thatched,' lit. 'roofed place, steading, or farm.'
Cf. above.

THELWALL (Warrington). 923 *O.E. Chron.* Ðelwæl—*i.e.,* 'wall,
rampart made of *deals,* boards, or planks,' O.E. *þel, þell.* *Cf.*
Theale (Reading), which Skeat thinks must have meant a place
where a plank was thrown over a stream; also *cf.* ELMBRIDGE
and FELBRIDGE, and Tilbridge (Upton-on-Severn), 1275 Tel-
drugge (*d* for *þ*), plainly from same root.

THEMELTHORPE (Norfolk). Not in *Dom.* 1477 Thymbilthorpe.
Prob. not 'village where thimbles were made,' O.E. *thýmel,* fr.

thúma, ' the thumb'; see -thorpe. It is fr. a man *Tymbel,* in *Onom.,* also seen in Thimbleby (Yorks), *Dom.* Timbelbi. But Great Timble (Yorks) is *Dom.* Timble, Timbe, and is perh. ' mound, hill like a thimble '; only *Oxf. Dict.* gives no form with *b* till 15th cny.

THENFORD (Banbury). Not in *Dom.* 1298 Teneford; perh. ' ford of harm '—*i.e.,* where some grave accident took place, O.E. *téona,* 3-6 *tene,* ' harm, injury.' There was in 958 *chart.* a ' Theonfan-forth,' on R. Stour (Stafford), but this cannot be the same name. *Dom.* Oxon. has Tentone, now Taynton (Burford), also Teigtone; this suggests a first syll. = TEIGN.

THERFIELD (Royston, Herts). 796 *chart.* Thyrefeld. Prob. ' *Thyra*'s field.' *Cf. B.C.S.* 702 Thyrran mere. *Thyra* is still a woman's name in Denmark.

THETFORD (Suffk. and Ely). Suf. T. *O.E. Chron.* 870 Theodforda, 1094 *ib.* Theotforda, *Dom.* Tetford, *c.* 1120 *Hen. Hunt.* Tedforde (*cf.* note on THATCHAM), 1237 Thefford. Ely T. *Dom.* Tedford, *Lib. de Hydh* Theedford, 1157 *Pipe Roll* Tetforð. ' Ford of the people,' O.E. *þeód*—*i.e.,* ' large, wide ford ' (Skeat).

THINGOE (Suffolk). *Dom.* Thingehov, Tingehv. ' How or mound of the *thing* ' or provincial assembly. *Cf.* DINGWALL and TING-WALL (Sc.). The ending -oe is O.N. *haug-r,* ' mound, cairn, how.' See HOWDEN.

THIRKLEBY (Thirsk). *Dom.* Torchilebi, Turchilebi, Turgilebi, Turgislebi, -gisbi. ' Dwelling of *Thurkill* ' or ' *Turchill,*' contracted fr. *Thurcytel,* a common name. See -by.

THIRSK (Yorks). *Dom.* Treske, *c.* 1150 Trescs, 1202 Tresc, Tresch, *c.* 1350 Thresk. Prob. Keltic *tre esk,* ' house on the water ' (G. *uisge*)—*i.e.,* the Codbeck. Sec ESK, USK, etc. If it be Keltic, it is a very exceptional name in these parts. *Cf.* THRESHFIELD.

THIXENDALE (New Malton, Yorks). *Dom.* Sixtendale, Sixtedale. ' *The sixteen dales,*' which go to form the township.' O.E. *syx-, sixtyne,* ' 16 '; there is no form in *Oxf. Dict.* without *t.*

THOLTHORPE (York). *Dom.* Turulfestorp, Turolvestorp. ' Village of *Thurwulf* ' or ' *Turolf,*' 3 in *Onom.* See -thorpe.

THORALBY (Aysgarth). *Dom.* Turoldesbi, Turodes-, debi, ' Dwelling of *Thurweald* ' or ' *Turold,*' several in *Onom. Cf.* Tharles-thorp (Yorks), *Dom.* Toruelestorp, and Thorlby (Yorks), *Dom.* Toreddereby, Torederebi, prob. fr. *Thurweard* or *Toruerd;* also Tarleton (Preston), *old* Thurweald -tun. In O.N. the name is *Thórvaldr; cf.* Trodais, Jersey. See -by.

THORMANBY (Easingwold). *Dom.* Tormozbi, Turmozbi (*z*= *ds* or *ts*). ' Dwelling of *Thurmund, Thurmod,* or *Thurmot,*' all names in *Onom.; so* = next. *Cf.* THORMARTON, now usually FARMING-TON, and Thrumpton (Notts), *Dom.* Turmodestun.

THORNABY - ON - TEES. *Dom.* Thormozbi ($z = ds$). ' Dwelling of *Thurmod* ' or ' *Thurmund*.' *Cf.* above; and see -by.

THORNBURY (Glouc.)—896 *chart.* Thornbyrig, *Dom.* Turneberie—and **THORNCOMBE** (Chard). 1417 Thornecombe. Prob. ' burgh,' and ' valley with the thorn-trees '; but former may be fr. a man *Thorn*, still a personal name. *Cf.* **THORNTON.** Thornholme (Yorks) is *Dom.* Thirnon, also Tirnu', a loc. ' at the thorns.' See -ham and -holme. *Cf.*, too, Thirntoft (N. Yorks), *Dom.* Tirnetoft, ' croft, farm with the thorn-tree.'

THORNER (Leeds). *Dom.* Tornoure, -eure. ' Thorn-tree bank,' O.E. *ofr.* See -over.

THORNEY (Chichester and Cambs). Chi. T., 1048 *O.E. Chron.* Thornege, 1066 *ib.* Thurneie. Cam. T., *Dom.* Torny, 1158 Torneya, 1169 Thorneia. There is also one on R. Thames near London. *O.E. Thorn-ege* is, of course, ' thorn isle.' See -ey. *c.* 1170 Wace, *Roman de Rou*, 1065, writes of the London T.: ' *Ee* est isle, *Zon* est espine, seit rainz, seit arbre, seit racine, Zonée ço est en engleiz, Isle d'espine en franceiz.' This is another illustration how hard a Norman found it to reproduce our Eng. *th.*

THORNGUMBALD (Hull). *Dom.* Torne. ' Thorn-tree of *Gumbeald* ' or ' *Gundbeald*,' both names in *Onom.*

THORNHAM (King's Lynn). *a.* 1300 *Eccleston* Turnham (which is now the Norfolk pron.). *Th* again ! See above and -ham.

THORNTHORPE (Yorks). *Dom.* Torgrimestorp. ' *Thorgrim-r*'s place. See -thorpe. But **THORNINGTON** (Nhbld.) is said to be *old* Thoburnham, or ' *Thorburn*'s ' or ' *Thorbeorn*'s home.' The latter is found in *Lib. Vit. Dunelm.*

THORNTON (15 in *P.G.*). In *Dom.* Yorks it occurs 34 times as Torneton, Tornitun, Torentun, Tornenton. Either ' village with the thorn-trees,' O.E. *thorn*, or ' of *Thorn*,' a man. *Cf.* **THORNBURY.**

THORP ARCH (Boston Spa, Yorks). *Dom.* Torp. ' Village by the shieling or summer-farm,' Norse G. *argh*. See **ANGLESARK** and -thorpe.

THORPE AUDLIN(G) (Pontefract). *Old* Audelin, *cf.* **AUDLEM**, *Dom.* Aldelime; and see -thorpe, ' village, (little) farm.'

THORPE CONTSANTINE (Tamworth). *Dom.* Torp, *a.* 1300 Thorp Constantin. A family so called fr. *Constantine*, Normandy.

THRAPSTONE (Oundle). Prob. ' Thorpe on the rock.' See **THORPE.** *Cf.* **THROAPHAM** (Yorks), *Dom.* Trapun, a loc., ? ' at the village.' See -ham.

THRELKELD (Penrith). *Cf. Dom.* Trelefelt—*i.e.*, Threlfalds (N. Lancs). The Threl- is uncertain. It may be contracted fr. *Thorkell.* Thurkleby (Yorks) is *Dom.* Turchilebi. -keld is ' well, spring.' See **KELD.**

THRESHFIELD (Skipton). *Dom.* Treschefelt, Freschefelt. A little doubtful. The Thresh- may be Keltic, as in THIRSK. But *th* does interchange with *f*, as in FENGLESHAM, and so it may be ' fresh.' See FRESHWATER.

THRIMBY (Shap). *Dom.* Tiernebi. ' Dwelling of *Tierne*,' the mod. name Tierney. *Onom.* has one *Thrim*, but nothing like *Tierne*, which is the almost exact phonetic representative of G. *tighearna*, ' lord,' O.W. *tern;* and this may be the word here. *Cf.* STAPLEFORD, but also THURNE. See -by.

THROCKENHOLT (Wisbech). *O.E. Chron.* 657 (late MS.) Throkonholt. ' Wood for sharebeams or plough-heads,' O.E. *throc. Cf.* HOLT. THROCKMORTON (Fladbury), *c.* 1200 Troche-, *c.* 1220 Trokemertum, -mardtune, 1275 Throkemorton, can hardly be fr. the same root. The ending will be ' mere-town,' ' moortown,' or perh. ' boundary-town,' O.E. (*ge*)*mære;* whilst *Throc* will be a personal name. *Cf.* 939 *chart.* Throcbryge, Hants, Throcking (Herts) (patronymic), and Throckley (Northbld.).

THROWLEY (Ham), T. FORSTAL (Faversham), and THROWLEIGH (Okehampton). Il. T., *a.* 1300 Truleg. ' Meadow of the coffin, tomb, or grave,' O.E. *thruh, thru(u)ch,* 5 *throh, throw,* and still in Sc. and N. dial. *Cf.* THROUGHAM (Glouc.), pron. Druffum, *Dom.* Troham, *later* Truham. See -ham and -ley.

THROOP (Christchurch) and THRUPP (Mid Oxon and S. Northants) = THORPE.

THRYBERGH (Rotherham). *Dom.* Triberga, -ge. Prob. ' three barrows ' or 'mounds,' O.E. *pri;* and see BARROW. *Cf.* SEDBERGH.

THUNDERSLEY (Rayleigh). *Dom.* Thunreslau. ' Meadow (or ' mound,' see -low) of the god *Thunor* ' or ' *Thor*.' See -ley.

THURGOLAND (Sheffield). *Dom.* Turgesland. Prob. ' land of *Thurgod* ' or ' *Turgot*,' a common O.E. name. THURGARTON (Notts) is *Dom.* Turgarstune.

THURLASTON (Dunechurch and Hinckley). Dun. T. *Dom.* Torlavestone, *a.* 1300 Thurlaveston. ' Village of (an unknown) *Thurlaf*'; but Hin. T. *c.* 1190 *chart.* Thurkeleston, ' village of *Thurkill* ' or ' *Thurcytel*.' Old forms needed for THURLESTONE (Kingsbridge) and THURLSTONE (Sheffield). THURLSTON (S. Yorks) is *Dom.* Turulfestone, Turolveston, ' *Thurwulf*'s ' or ' *Turolf*'s town '; while THURSTASTON (Birkenhead) is *Dom.* Turstaneton, ' *Thurstan*'s town.' It is now pron. Thirsaston.

THURLBY (Bourne). *a.* 1100 *chart.* Thurleby. ' Dwelling of *Thurkill* ' or ' of *Thurlac*.' See -by.

THURLEIGH (Bedford) and THURLOW (Suffolk). ' Meadow ' and ' hill of the god *Thor* ' or ' *Thunor*,' an old Scandinavian and Saxon deity. *Cf.* Thursday; and see -leigh and -low.

THURMASTON (Leicester). *c.* 1200 Turmotestona. ' *Thurmod*'s ' or ' *Thormood*'s town.'

THURNE (Yarmouth). 1477 Thirne. There is in Eng. *c.* 1300 *therne,* ' a girl, a maid,' fr. O.N. *þerna ;* but this will not suit for Thurne. THURNHAM (Lancaster) is *Dom.* Tiernun. It is prob. that these names come fr. *thorn,* the tree, even though it is never found with an *i* or *u* in *Oxf. Dict.* But ' Thorne ' is found alone as a place-name in *Dom.* Yorks. Tiernun, according to all analogy, should be an old loc. (see -ham), ' at the thorn-trees '; and will be the same name, originally, as Thornholme (Yorks), which is in *Dom.* Thirnon and Tirnu'. *Cf.* THORNBURY and next.

THURNSCOE (Rotherham). *Dom.* Ternusc, -usche, which must be Kelt. either for ' chief, head stream,' O.W. *tern.* *Cf.* TINTERN, or for ' vehement stream,' W. *tern.* Also see USK; and *cf.* THIRSK. But the present name, a Norse corrup., is ' thorn-tree wood,' O.N. *skóg-r.* *Cf.* BURSCOUGH. It is now pron. Thrunsker.

THURROCK (Grays). *Dom.* Thurrucca. O.E. *þurruc* is ' the bilge of a ship,' in mod. dial. ' a heap of dirt,' and ' a drain.' This place must surely have been orig. one where filth and dirty water gathered. *Cf.* WEST THURROCK.

THURSFORD (Dereham) and THURSLEY (Godalming). 1305 Thyrs-forde. ' Ford ' and ' meadow of *Thor,*' the thunder god. For spelling with *u, cf. Dom.* Essex, Turestapla, and Thursday; and see -ley. There is a now obs. THURSFIELD (Newcastle-under-L.), which was *Dom.* Turvoldes feld, *a.* 1300 Thurfredesfeld, and Torvedeston. ' Town of *Thurweald* ' or ' *Thorold.*' *Cf.* Thoresby (Notts), *Dom.* Turesbi.

THURSTON (Bury St. E.). *Dom.* Turstanestuna. ' Town of *Thur-stan.*' *Cf.* THURSTASTON (Birkenhead), pron. Thursiston, *Dom.* Turstaneton. There is also a Thurstonland (Huddersfield), *Dom.* Tostenland, prob. a scribe's error.

THUXTON (Attleboro'). *Dom.* Thustuna. The man's name here is uncertain. The nearest in *Onom.* is *Thochi,* var. of *Tokig ;* but we have also several called *Toc(c)a,* a *Toce,* and a *Tocga.*

THWAITE (Eye). *c.* 1150 *chart.* Thwete. O.N. *thveit,* lit. ' a piece cut off,' fr. *thvíta,* ' to cut,' then ' a small bit of land.' *Cf.* CROSSTHWAITE, etc. Thwaite End (Irton, Cumbld.) is actually said to have been corrupted into Ayners !

THWING (Hunmanby, Yorks). *Dom.* Twenc, Tuinc, Tuenc; 1206 Twenge. Seems to be the rare O.E. *twing,* ' a mass, a lump,' lit. what is pressed together, fr. *twengan,* ' to pinch, squeeze, twinge.' *Cf. Dom.* Salop Tuange.

TIBBERTON (Salop, Droitwich, and Glouc.). Dr. T., 978 *chart.* Tidbriht - ingctun, *Dom.* Tibbertun, 1275 Tybrytone. Gl. T. *Dom.* Tebristone (on *st,* see p. 26), *later* Tyber-, Typertone. ' Town of *Tidbeorht* ' or ' *Tidburh.*' On 978 see -ing.

Tibthorpe (Driffield). *Dom.* Tibetorp, Tipetorp. ' Village of *Tiba* ' or ' *Tibba.*' *Cf. Dom.* Tibetune (Salop), and also **Tipton**. See -thorpe.

Tich-. See **Titch-**.

Tickhill (Rotherham). *c.* 1097 *Flor. W.* Tyckyll, 1119 *chart.* Tykyll, *Sim. Dur.* ann. 1102 Tychill, 1194 *Hoveden* Tikehil. ' Hill of the tike,' Icel. *tik,* ' a bitch, a cur,' Sw. *tik,* ' a boor.' But *Dom.* Tichele-vorde (Salop) must be ' farm of *Ticel,*' an unknown man; and **Ticknall** (Derby), *chart.* Ticcenheal, is ' *Tica's* nook.' *Cf. Dom.* Bucks Tichesla and Ticheforde; also **Titchborne** and **Tixall**.

Tickton (Beverley). *Dom.* Tichetone. ' Town of *Tica* ' or ' *Ticca.*' *Cf.* above; also 1166-67 *Pipe* Tichesoura (Rutld.), and 1460 *Paston* Tychewell.

Tidmarsh (Pangbourn). 1316 Thedmersshe, 1428 Tydemershe, *c.* 1540 Tedmarsh. ' *Tydda's* marsh,' 6 Tidas or Tydas in *Onom. Cf.* **Tidenham** (on Wye), 956 *chart.* Dyddan-hamme, ' enclosure of *Dydda,*' but *Dom.* Tideham, 1253 Tudenham. See -ham. **Tidsley** or Teddesley Wood (Pershore) is 963 *chart.* Teodeces-leage, ' *Teodec's* lea.' *Cf.* **Tewkesbury**.

Tidnock (Cheshire). Prob. dimin. of W. *tyddyn,* ' a farm.'

Tidwell (E. Budleigh, Devon). *a.* 1300 Todewil, Toddville, Tode-vil, Tudewille, Toudeville. ' *Tuda's* ' or ' *Todea's* pool,' O.E. *wœl,* ' a whirlpool, an eddy, a fish-pool.' *Cf.* **Maxwell** (Sc.). The name prefixed occurs in a great variety of forms—Tida, Toda, Tuda, Tudda, Tydda. *Cf.* **Tidmarsh**.

Tilbrook (St. Neots). Prob. ' Brook of *Tila* or *Tile,*' 4 in *Onom. Cf.* **Tilford**, and 1179-80 *Pipe,* Tillul (? ' *Tila's* hill ') (Yorks). But some think of W. *twll,* ' a hole.' This is not prob.

Tilbury. *Bede* Tilaburg, *Dom.* Tilleberie, *c.* 1120 *Hen. Hunt.* Tilaburh, *c.* 1200 Westilleberie (West Tilbury), 1278 Tillebury. ' *Tila's* fort or burgh.' See above, and -bury.

Tilehurst (Reading). *K.C.D.* iv. 157, Tigelhyrste, 1316 Tyghel-hurst, *c.* 1540 Tylehurst. This must mean ' tile wood or copse,' O.E. *tigel,* L. *tegula,* ' a tile.' They may have been made here.

Tilford (Farnham, Surrey). *c.* 1160 Tileford. ' *Tila's* ' or ' *Tile's* ford.' *Cf.* **Tilbrook**. **Tiln**(e) (Notts), *Dom.* Tilne, Tille, 1189 *Pipe* Tilnea, is ' *Tila's* isle.' See -ay.

Till R. (Northumbld.). *a.* 1130 *Sim. Dur.* Tillemuthe, W. *twll,* ' a hole,' or perh. *tyle,* ' a steep, an ascent.'

Tillingham (Southminster). *B.C.S.* 8 Tillingeham, and **Tilling-ton** (Petworth and Stafford). Pet. T., *Dom.* Tellingedone and Tedlinghā (*d* prob. error). St. T. *Dom.* Tillintone. ' Home ' and ' village of the sons of *Tila.*' *Cf. Dom.* Bucks Telingham. See -don, -ham, -ing, and -ton.

TILLY WHIM CAVES (Swanage). M'Clure says Corn. *toulen veyn,* ' holes in the rocks.' *Cf.* DURLSTONE. But one may also conjecture W. *tuell gwyn,* ' clear, bright covert.'

TILMANSTONE (Dover). 1298 Tilmanneston. ' Town of *Tilman,*' 3 in *Onom.* A ' tillman ' is a ploughman or peasant, found as an Eng. word as early as *Cursor Mundi. Cf.* 940 *chart.* Tilmannes dene.

TIMBERHANGER (Bromsgrove). *Dom.* Timbrehangre; TIMBERLAND (Lincoln), 1204 Timberlun; TIMBERLEY (Cas. Bromwich), 1301 Timberweissiche (timber-way -syke, O.E. *sic, sice,* ' rivulet, ditch '). All fr. O.E. *timber,* O.N. *timbr,* ' timber, wood for building purposes.' -hanger is O.E. *hangra,* ' wooded slope.' *Cf.* CLAYHANGER, and -land here is O.N. *lund-r,* ' grove, wood.' *Cf.* TOSELAND. Also see -ley.

TINGEWICK (Buckingham). *Dom.* Tedinwiche, *a.* 1199 Tingwic. Seems to be ' dwelling of *Teda, -an, Tigga, -an,* or *Thegn,* all in *Onom.* More old forms needed. See -wick.

TINSLEY (Sheffield). *Dom.* Tinestawe, Tirneslawe; also Tineslege (under Derby). ' Meadow of *Tinna*' (*cf. Roll Rich. I.,* ' Tinneston,' Kent); or, rather, as the liquid *r* has early disappeared, ' meadow of the thorn-tree,' O.E. *þorn,* Da. and Sw. *torn. Cf.* THORNBURY. On -lawe see -low, ' mound,' which is not= -ley.

TINTAGEL (Camelford). *c.* 1205 *Layamon* Tintageol, edit. *c.* 1275 Tyntagel, 1536 Tyndagell; also Dundagel. Corn. *dun, din diogl,* ' safe fort ' or ' castle.'

TINTERN (Chepstow). O.W. for ' castle of the chief.' *Cf.* above and K. Vor-*tigern,* and Caer Guor-thigirn, *Nennius ;* also G. *tighearna,* ' lord,' and THRIMBY.

TIPTON (Staffs). *a.* 1300 Tibinton, Tybeton. ' Village of *Tiba.*' St. Tibbe, or Tybba, was patroness of hunting and hawking. *Cf.* TIBTHORP.

TIRLE BROOK (Tewkesbury). 780 *chart.* Tyrle, 785 *ib.* Tyrl. Prob. fr. E. Fris. *tirreln, tirlen,* ' to turn about quickly,' the Sc. *tirl.* But TIRLEY (Market Drayton) is *Dom.* Tireleye, Tyrlegh, ' meadow on the R. TERN,' the liquid *n* having disappeared; whilst TIRLEY (Tewkesbury), formerly Trinley, is *Dom.* Trinleie, *c.* 1220 Trinlega, where the Brook name has got confused with the name of some man. *Trimma* and *Trumwine* are nearest in *Onom.* See -ley.

TISBURY (Salisbury). *a.* 716 *chart.* Dyssesburg. ' Castle of *Tisa* ' or ' *Tiso,*' both in *Onom.* See -bury.

TISTED (Hants). 941 *chart.* Ticcestede, *Dom.* Tistede. ' Homestead, farm of *Ticca.*' But *cf.* STISTED.

TI(T)CHBORNE (Alresford), TITCHFIELD (Fareham), TITCHMARSH (Thrapston), and TITCHWELL (Norfolk). 909 *chart.* Ticceburna, 1298 Tycheburn; O.E. *chart.* Ticcenesfeld; 1298 Tychemershe; 1450 Tichewill. ' Burn or brook,' ' field,' ' marsh ' and ' well of *Ticca, Tica,* or *Ticcea,*' all names in *Onom.* But any of them might also come fr. O.E. *ticce(n),* Ger. *zieke,* ' a kid.' *Cf.* TIXALL and Tickenhill (Bewdley). See -borne.

TITTENSOR (Stoke-on-Trent). *Dom.* Titesoure, *a.* 1200 Titesoura, Titnesovre, *a.* 1300 Titneshovere. ' Bank, brink, edge,' O.E. *obr, ofr, ofre, ora,* ' of *Tita,*' -*an,* or ' *Titel,*' both in *Onom.* *Cf.* BOLSOVER, EDENSOR, TITTLESHALL, etc. TITTESWORTH (Leek) is *a.* 1300 Tet(t)esworth, ' farm of *Tette* ' or ' *Teta,*' both in *Onom.* See -worth.

TITTLESHALL (Swaffham). 1425 Titeleshale, *c.* 1471 Tytlyshall. ' Nook of *Tyttla* ' or ' *Titillus,*' both in *Onom.* See -hall.

TIVERTON (Chesh. and Devon). Ch. T. *Dom.* Tevretone. De. T. *Dom.* Tovretone, *Exon. Dom.* Touretona, Tuuertone, 1166-67 *Pipe* Tuuerton, *later* Tuyverton. Thought also to be *a.* 900 *K. Alfred's Will* Tuiford = TWYFORD and -ton, O.E. *twi,* ' double, *twá, tú,* ' two,' and so ' double-ford-town.' In *Dom.* re is regu-larly = er; and in W. still *f* is pron. *v.* So the *vret* or *vert* is O.E. *ford,* 3 *vord.* *Cf. c.* 1190 *Gir. Camb.* Milverd-icus for Milford. The *d* of *ford* has in Tiverton become merged in the *t* of -ton. *Cf.* TWERTON and TEVERSHALL.

TIVY R. (Cardigan). *c.* 800 *Nennius* Tivis, or Teibi; and see ABERTEIVI. Prob. = TOWEY.

TIXALL (Stafford). *Dom.* Ticheshale, *a.* 1200 Tikeshale. ' Nook of *Tica.*' *Cf.* TICKNALL and *Dom.* Bucks Tichesla. See TITCH-BORNE and -hall.

TOCKENHAM (Swindon) and TOCKINGTON (Glouc.). *B.C.S.* 481 Toccanham, *Dom.* Tochintune, 1298 Tokynton. ' Home ' and ' town of *Tocca.*' *Cf.* TOCKETTS (Yorks), *Dom.* Tocstune, also Toscotune; and TOCKWITH, *Dom.* Tocvi, ' *Tocc*'s wood,' O.N. *Tóki- vith-r,* Dan. *ved.* *Cf.* Le Van Tocque, Jersey.

TODENHAM (Chipping Norton). *c.* 804 *chart.* Todanhom. ' En-closure of *Toda* ' or ' *Tuda.*' Of the latter, there are many in *Onom.* *Cf. Dom.* Bucks Todeni. There are also 3 Todding-tons, *Dom.* Todintun (Glouc.), 1314 Todinton (Lancs). See -ham and -ton.

TODMORDEN. ' The *Morden* of the *tods* or foxes.' *Tod,* common still in Sc., is fr. Icel. *toddi,* ' a bunch of wool,' referring to the fox's tale. *Cf. c.* 1170 *Newminster Cartul.* Todholes. There are 2 Mordens, at Mitcham and Wareham. This is O.E. *mór, denu,* ' moorland valley.'

TODWICK (Sheffield). *Dom.* Tatewic. ' Dwelling of *Tata.*' *Cf.* TADCASTER. See -wick.

TOFT (Dunchurch, Beccles, and Cambridge), TOFT HILL (Bp. Auckland), TOFTWOOD (Dereham). Ca. T., *Dom.* Tofth, 1302 Thofte. O.N. *topt*, adopted into O.E., 'cleared space for the site of a house,' then 'homestead, (small) farm'; also sometimes 'a knoll or hillock.' J. H. Turner gives 5 places ending in -toft in Yorks—Altofts, Arnoldstoft, Langtoft, Thirntoft, Willitoft. In these cases *Dom.* spells -toft or -tot. In the defunct Elestolf it inserts an *l.* Duignan records none fr. Staffs or Worcester. It recurs in Ametot, Jersey.

TOLLESBURY (Witham). 'Burgh of *Tolla.*' *Cf.* Tolesby (N. Riding) *Dom.* Tollesbi. TOLLERTON (York), *Dom.* Tolentun, Tolletun, is also *Tollantun*, the *n* of the gen. being changed to its kindred liquid *r*, perh. through Norse influence. Tolthorp (Yorks), *Dom.* Toletorp, is fr. the same name. *Cf.* Tolworth (Surbiton). See -worth. TOLLERTON (Notts), *Dom.* Troclauestone, 1166 *Pipe* Turlaueston, 1294 Thorlaxton, *c.* 1500 Torlaston, is difficult. The forms represent either *Thurlac* or *Thorlaf*.

TOLPIDDLE (Dorchester). Prob. 'clump of trees beside the small or puddly stream,' fr. TOLL sb,[4] which *Oxf. Dict.* says is now dial. fr. Kent to Hants. This *toll*, first found in 1644, is of unknown origin. See PIDDLETOWN. TOLLERDINE (Worc.), 1327 Tolwardyn, means, thinks Duignan, not 'toll-farm,' but 'farm free fr. toll or tax,' O.E. *toll* has this meaning. See -wardine.

TONBRIDGE or TUNBRIDGE. *Dom.* Ton(e)bridge, *c.* 1097 *Flor. Worc.* Tunebrycgia. Prob. 'bridge of *Tuna*,' common in *Onom.* A little stream called the Tun here joins the Medway. It may be a later back formation, or ? W. *tonn*, 'land unploughed.' *Cf.* 1303 R. Brunne *Handl. Synne* 10586: 'So long he [*Tumna*] leuede yn that estre (place) that for hys name he hyȝt (was called) Tuncestre.' This last name seems now lost.

TONG (Bradford and Shifnal). Br. T. *Dom.* Tuinc. TONGE (Middleton, Manchester), 1227 Tonge, 1285 Toung, Tong, 1551 Tongue. TONG PARK (Shipley). O.E. *tunge*, O.N. *tunga*, Dan. *tunge*, 'tongue, tongue of land, promontory.' *Cf. Dom.* Worc. Tonge, and TONGUE (Sc.). TONG FOLD (Bolton) is now pron. Tomfont.

TOOLEY STREET (London). *c.* 1650 St. Tulie's Street. Corrup. of 'St. *Olave*'s Street.' The Danes were settled here, and *Olaf* was patron saint of Norway. *Cf. tawdry*, fr. St. Audrey's or Ethelreda's fair.

TOOTHILL (Ongar, Alvanley, Chesh.). It may be a tautology, as *toot* or *tote* is found in Eng. for 'an isolated, conspicuous hill, a look-out hill,' fr. 1387. The O.E. *tótian* is found only once, meaning 'to protrude, peep out'; but the vb. *tote*, 'to peep out, peer, gaze,' is common fr. *a.* 1225. There is also O.E. *tota*, 'a spy, a look-out, a tout,' often a proper name. See next.

Tooter, too, is found as a sb. fr. Wyclif, 1382, ' one who gazes, a watchman,' as in TOOTER HILL (S. Lancs). *Cf.* TOTHILL, and Cleeve Toot (Bristol). The name *toot* to-day seems chiefly S. Wstn.; but we have a Tote-hill, Hartington (Northumbld.), and a Tuthill stairs (Newcastle).

TOOTING (London). 727 *chart.* Totinge, *Dom.* Totinges, 1228 Toting', 1229 Thotinges. Patronymic. ' Place of the sons of *Tota.*' Four called *Tota* and 2 *Tuta* in *Onom.* For pl. ending in *Dom. cf.* BARKING, WOKING, etc.; and see above. But TOTON (Notts), *Dom.* Tolvestune, 1189 *Pipe* Turuerton, is fr. a man *Thorolf.*

TOPCLIFFE (Thirsk). *Dom.* Topeclive, 1301 Topclive. ' Cliff of *Topa, Tope,* or *Topp,*' all forms in *Onom. Cf.* CLEVELAND.

TOPPESFIELD (Halstead). 1298 Toppesfelde. ' Field of *Toppa.*' See above.

TOPSHAM (S. Devon). *c.* 1072 Toppeshamme, 1297-98 Topesham. ' Enclosure of *Toppa* or *Topa.*' See above. The -ham here is O.E. *hamm,* ' enclosure, place hemmed in.'

TORCROSS (Kingsbridge), TORPOINT (Cornwall), etc. Tor or TORR must be Kelt., though already found as *torr* in an O.E. Dorset *chart.* of 847. As a name, it is chiefly confined to Cornwall, Devon, and Peak (Derby) district. Corn. *toor, tor,* ' hill, prominence ' (though this form is denied existence by *Oxf. Dict.*), W. *twr,* O.W. *twrr,* ' heap, pile,' as in Mynydd Twrr, old name of Holyhead Mtn., G. *tòrr,* ' a heap, a pile, then, a hill, lofty or conical, a mound, a heap of ruins.'

TORKSEY (Lincoln). 873 *O.E. Chron.* Turces ig(e), Turices ige, *a.* 1130 *Sim. Dur.* Torchasia. ' Isle of *Turca* or *Turc,*' but hardly of ' the *Turk.*' *Cf. B.C.S.* 165 Turcan den. See -ey.

TORPENHOW (Wigton, Cumbld.). *c.* 1200 Thorphinhow. ' Mound, cairn,' O.N. *haugr,* ' of *Thorfinn,*' a common name in Cumbld. in 12th cny. *Cf.* BRANT How and MAESHOW (Sc.).

TORQUAY. Kelt. *tor cau* (in W. pron. kay). ' Hill by the hollow.' See TORCROSS. *Quay* is a quite recent spelling of *kay* or *key,* ' a wharf,' and the pron. key instead of kay is recent, too. Of course, Torquay really has nothing to do with *quay.*

TORRINGTON (Devon). 1156 *Pipe* Torentun, 1219 Torintun. Perh. ' town of *Tora,*' gen. *-an,* one in *Onom.* But Torentun in *Dom.* Yorks, 1179-80 *Pipe* Torenton, always seems for THORNTON. *Cf. Dom.* Chesh., Torentune.

TORRISHOLME (Morecambe). *Dom.* Toredholme. ' Meadow by the sea of *Thored,*' a common O.E. name. See -holm. *Cf.* TORT-WORTH (Glouc.), *Dom.* Torteuord, 1364 Tortheworth, where the name seems to be *Torth* or *Torht,* which is var. of *Thored ;* also found in *Onom.* as *Thord, Thorth,* and *Tori.*

TOSELAND (Hunts). *Dom.* Toleslund. 'Grove,' O.N. *lund-r,* ' of *Toli,*' a N. name. *Cf.* TIMBERLAND. But TOSTOCK (Bury St. E.) and 1167-68 *Pipe* Devon, Tosby, imply a man's name like *Tos.* See -by and STOKE.

TOTHILL (London). 1250 *Patent R.* Tothull, *c.* 1590 Totehill, 1598 *Stow* the Tuthill, 1665 Tuttle, 1746 Toote Hill= TOOTHILL. Wyclif, 2 Sam. v. 7, has ' the tote hill Syon.'

TOTLAND BAY (I. of Wight). ' Look-out land.' See TOOTHILL.

TOTLEY (Sheffield). *Dom.* Totele. The site is so commanding it is prob. O.E. *totan léah,* ' meadow of the spy ' or ' look-out,' the ' tout.' *Cf.* TETTENHALL and next; also Totenhull *sic a.* 1600, now Tutnell, Tardebigge.

TOTNESS (Devon). 930 *chart.* Tottaness, *c.* 1205 *Layam.* Tottenæs, 1250 Totenas, 1297 Tottenays. ' Cape of the look-out ' or ' coastguardsman,' O.E. *tota, -an.* See TOOTHILL and -ness.

TOTTENHAM (London). *Dom.* Toteham, *a.* 1124 Totenham, 1479 Totnam (the mod. pron.). ' Home of *Tota* ' or ' *Totta.*' *Cf.* above, and TOTTNO (Oundle), 1229 *Close R.* Toteho. ' HOE, hill of *Tota.*' See -ham.

TOTTERIDGE (S. Herts). Not in *Dom.,* unless it be there Torinch, ? an error. 1291 Tatterigg. ' Ridge of *Tata* ' or ' *Totta,*' both names common in *Onom*; but *cf.* TOTHILL. Ridge is O.E. *hrycg,* Icel. *hrygg-r,* Dan. *ryg,* ' a ridge of land,' lit. ' the back.'

TOTTINGTON (Bury and Thetford). *Cf. Dom.* Teotintune (Worc.). ' Village of *Teta, Tetta, Tetto, Teotta,*' all forms in *Onom.* See -ing.

TOWAN HEAD (New Quay). *c.* 1130 Tohod (an error), *c.* 1180 Thohon. Corn. *towan,* W. *tywyn,* ' seashore.' The th- in *c.* 1180 will come fr. a Norm. scribe. *Cf.* TOWYN. Jago, in *Cornw. Gloss,* gives *towan, towin, tewen, tuan,* or *tyen,* as ' Cornish words for a dune or heap of sand.'

TOWCESTER (Northants). 921 *O.E. Chron.* Tofeceaster, *Dom.* Tovecester. ' Camp, settlement of *Tofig* ' or *Tof* or *Toui,* all forms in *Onom.,* and Tofig very common. It now stands on the R. Tove, but this name seems to be a late back formation. TOWTHORP (Yorks), *Dom.* Tovetorp, is ' village of *Toui.*' Similar is TOWTON (S. Yorks), *Dom.* Touetun.

TOWY R. (S. Wales). *c.* 1130 *Lib. Landav.* Tywi (so still in W.), *Ann. Cambr.* 1095 Stra tewi. Perh. same root as W. *tywio,* ' to spread out.' *Cf.* TIVY.

TOWYN (Abergele and Merioneth). W. *tywyn,* Corn. *towan,* ' seashore, place of sands.' *Cf.* TOWAN.

TRAFFORD (Manchester). *Sic* 1292. Wyld and H. conjecture ' trough-like ford.' O.E. *tróh.*

TRAWSMAWR (Caermarthen). W. *traws* is 'across,' and *mawr*, G. *môr*, 'big.' *Cf.* TRAWSFYNYDD (Merioneth), 'across the mountain,' W. *mynydd*. *Traws* is L. *trans*. But here it must be W. *trawst*, 'rafter'—'the big beam.' ? why.

TREALES (Preston). *Dom.* Treueles. Seems Kelt. ? 'house in the field,' W. and Corn. *tre*, 'house,' and Corn. *gwel, gweal*, 'field.' 1160-61 *Pipe* Hereford, Trivel, must be the same. W. has also *tra* for 'house,' as in *Pipe ib.*, Trawent, ? 'windy house,' W. *gwynt*, 'wind.'

TRE ASSER (Pembroke). W. *tre* or *tref*, 'house of *Asser*.' It was the birthplace of Asserius Menevensis, friend and biographer of Alfred the Great.

TRECASTLE (Brecon). 1298 *Close R.* Tria Castra—*i.e.*, 'three camps.' But, of course, W. *tre* is 'house, village.'

TREDINGTON (Shipton-on-Stour, and Tewkesbury). Sh. T. 757 *chart.* Tredingctun, 964 *ib.* Tyrdintune, 991 *ib.* Tredintune, *Dom.* Tredinctun. Te. T., *Dom.* Trotintune, 1221 Tredigtone. 'Town of the sons of *Tyrdda*,' a *comes* or earl, its known early owner. Transposition of *r* is common. 1280 *Close R.* Tradington, now Trotton (Sussex), will rather be fr. *Treda*, given in *Onom.* as abbot in Worc., Mercia, *c.* 775; so might the other place, too. But TREDWORTH (Glouc.), 1284 Truddeworth, is also fr. *Tyrdda.* See -ing and -worth.

TREETON (Rotherham). *Dom.* Trectone. ? 'town of *Trecca*,' a Yorks name in *Onom.* Or, as it is also *Dom.* Treton, it may simply be fr. *tree*, O.E. *tréo*. *Cf.* Tresham (Hawkesbury), *sic* in 972 *chart.*

TREFECCA (Talgarth, Brecknockshire). W.='house of *Rebecca*' or '*Becky*.' The mod. W. *tra, tre*, or *tref*, is 'house, village, town,' in O.W. *trev*. Seen in 1324 Traueger, now TREFGARN (Pembk.). For this, *cf.* TREGAER.

TREGAER (Monmouth). 1325 Tregeyr, and TREGEARE (Egloskerry, Cornwall). Prob. 1285 *Close R.* Tregear. 'House, settlement by the castle,' O.W. *gaer*, W. *caer*, Bret. *ker*. *Cf.* TREFGARN and Treflerw (Pembk.), 'nice, delicate house.' But TREGARON (Cardingsh.) is fr. *Caron*, a saint of unknown history.

TRE-GWENGN (Cornwall). Corn.='house, village of bees.'

TRELAWNE INLET (West Looe). Corn. *tre lawn*, 'clear, open townlet'; *lawn* is cognate with Ir. and Brit. *lann*, W. *llan*, Corn. *lan*, 'enclosure, open space among woods,' seen also in Eng. *lawn*, found earlier as *laund*.

TRELLECK (Monmouth). 1347 *Rolls Parlmt.* Trillek. W. *tre llech*, 'house made of flags or flagstones.'

TREMAINE (Launceston). Corn. *tre meini*, 'house of the stones,' or 'of the dolmen,' *maen*.

TRENANS (St. Austell). Corn.='house in the valley,' W. *nant*.

TRENT R. and TRENTHAM (Stone). *Bede* and *O.E. Chron.* 633 Treanta, 924 *ib.* Treonta, *c.* 900 *Asser* Terente, *Dom.* Trenta; also a R. 'Trent' in Worc., *K.C.D.* iii. 396. *Dom.* Trenham, 1156 *Pipe* Trentham. H. Bradley's ingenious conjecture, that in Tacitus *Ann.* we should read 'Trisantonam' *pro* 'castris Antonam,' and make Trisantona the orig. form of Tre(h)anta, seems far-fetched. The origin seems unknown. It cannot be the same as the famous counsel of Trent (Tyrol), which is the L. Tridentum.

TRERYN DINAS (Land's End). Corn. = 'castle of the fighting-place,' *treryn,* now pron. treen. *Cf.* 1268 *Norwich Assize Rolls* Treneham. There is no name like *Trena* in *Onom.*

TRESCO (Scilly) and TRESCOWE (Marazion). *Dom.* Trescau. Corn. for 'house beside the elder-tree,' still called *scaw* in Cornwall, Corn. *scawen,* as in BOSCAWEN, Bret. *scao, scav, scaven.*

TRESILLIAN R. (Truro) seems to be Corn. for 'house of eels,' *silli,* 'an eel'; but if so the ending is unexplained.

TRE SPIRIDION (The Lizard). Corn. = 'house of spirits or ghosts.'

TREVINE (Letterston, Pembroke). *Black Bk. Carm.* Trefdyn, -dun, W. *tref ddin,* 'house, village on the hill.' TREVETHIN (Mon.) is the same name, 1285 *Close R.* Trevedyn. W. *tref y din.* But TREVEAN (Cornwall) is *Dom.* Trebihan, Corn. *tre bean* or *vean* (W. *bian, bihan*), 'little house.'

TRIMDON (Co. Durham). 1183 Tremeldon. A curious contraction; older forms needed. Perh. 'hill of *Trumweald,*' the nearest name in *Onom.*

TRIMPLEY (Suffolk and Bewdley). Su. T. *Dom.* Tremelaia, Tremlega; Be. T. *Dom.* Trinpelei; 1275 Trympeleye. 'Meadow of' some unknown man. There is one *Trimma,* a Mercian monk, in Bede. See -ley.

TRING (N. of London). *Dom.* Trevinga, Trevng, Treunge; 1211 Traynge; 1313 Trehynge. 'Place of the sons of *Tryg.*' See -ing. Thring is still a common surname (de Thring is found 1273), and the Th- may have been orig. Norm., and so the *h* would then be mute.

TRITTON (E. Kent ? now). *a.* 1200 Tritton. Said to be fr. *Trithona* (or *Frithona*) 5th Abp. of Canterbury, and first English one.

TROEDYRHIW (Glam.). W. = 'base of the slope.' *Cf.* Troedybryn.

TROON (Camborne). W. or Corn. *trwyn* = G. *sròn,* 'a nose, point, cape.' *Cf.* TROON (Sc.).

TROSTON (Bury St. E.). *Dom.* Trostuna. On analogy of next this may be '*Trota's* town.' *Onom.* has nothing likelier. *Cf. Dom.* Chesh. Trosford.

TROTTERSCLIFFE (W. Malling). Pron. Trosley, which shows -cliffe to be a recent 'improvement'; so is Trotter-; the man here recorded is prob. *Trota,* one in *Onom.* 'Trota's mead.'

TROUTBECK (Penrith and Windermere). *c.* 1080 Bek Troyte. It may be fr. a man *Trota* in *Onom*. *Trout* is fr. Fr. *truite*, and would hardly be looked for in Cumberland *c.* 1080; whilst *Troyte* is still an Eng. surname. TROUTSDALE (E. Riding) is *Dom*. Truzstal. Here also *trout* is doubtful; it may be fr. *Truthec*, a name in *Onom*. In *Dom*. *z* is for *ts* or *tcs*; while -stal will be O.E. *stcall*, *stœl*, 'place.'

TROWBRIDGE (Wilts). [*Dom*. has a **Troi** near here.] *c.* 1160 *Gest. Steph*. Trobriga, 1212 Trobrigge. Unless fr. a man *Trota*, this is prob. fr. W. *tro*, 'a turn'; the river on which it stands is called the Biss. But the name may be a hybrid. TROWELL (Notts), *Dom*. Trowalle, Mutschmann derives fr. O.E. *tréow*, 'a tree.'

TRUMPET (Ledbury) and TRUMPINGTON (Cambridge). *K.C.D.* iv. 245 Trumpintun, 1270 Trumpington, 1297 Trumpiton. The latter name is perh. corrup. of *Trumbeorht's* or *Trumberct's* town.' Any such name as *Trump* or *Trumping* is unknown. But the former is prob. W. 'hill-ridge with the croft or land-portion on it.' W. *trum*, G. *druim* and *peth*, Pict. *pit, pet*, 'a portion.'

TRUNCH (N. Walsham). *Dom*. Trunchet, Truchet; 1426 Trunche. A rare case in this region, plainly W. *trwyn chet*, 'point' lit. 'nose of the wood,' O.W. *chet, cet, coit*, mod. W. *coed*. *Cf*. CHETWOOD. *Cf*. TROON (Sc.), and 1179-80 *Pipe* Yorks Trunfield, not in *Dom*. This last may be contracted fr. '*Trunwinc's* field.' Fr. *tranchet*, 'paring-knife, chisel-shank,' seems out of the question for *Dom*.'s Trunchet. The TRUNCH (Oakridge) seems to have as old form The Trench, here in its oldest meaning, 'lane through a wood.' *Oxf. Dict*. gives no spelling of *trench* with *u*.

TRURO. *Old* Treuru, Triueru, 1536 Truroo. Corn. *tre vuru* (pl. of *vor*), 'three ways'; 3 main roads meet here.

TRUSHAM (Chudleigh) and TRUSTHORPE (Mablethorpe). The man's name here is uncertain. *Cf*. Trewsbury (Cirencester), *Dom*. Tursberie, *c.* 1300 Trussebyry. W. H. Stevenson inclines to connect this with O.E. *trús*, 'brushwood.' *Cf. Dom*. Norfk. Treus. See -bury, -ham, and -thorpe.

TRWYN-Y-GWYDDEL (Cardigan Bay). W. = 'cape of the Gael.' *Cf*. TROON (Sc.) and Murian-'r-Gwyddel (Harlech), name of ancient fortifications. W. *trwyn* is same as G. *sròn*, lit. 'nose.'

TRYSULL (Wolvermptn.). Pron. Treezle. 984 *chart*. and *later*, Tresel, *Dom*. Treslei. It means *trestle*. This occurs in O.Fr. *trestel*, but that is fr. Bret. *treustel*, fr. *treust, trest*, 'a beam,' found also in W. *tresll*, fr. *trawst*, so the root is Keltic, though very early in O.E.—*e.g.*, Trescot near by is 1006 Treselcote, 'hut built in trestle fashion.'

TUBNEY (Mareham). *c.* 1290 Tubbeney, 1316 Tobbeney, *c.* 1540 Tubney. *Cf. B.C.S.* ii. 514 Tubban ford. 'Isle of *Tubba*.' See -ey.

TUDDENHAM (2 in Suffolk). 1298 Tude'ham, 1450 Tudenham, 1477 Todenham. ' Home of *Tuda* ' or ' *Tudda*,' names common in *Onom*. *Cf.* TUDHOE (Spennymoor), Tudhope and Tudworth (Yorks), *Dom*. Tudeworde.

TUGBY (Leicester) and TUGGAL (Alnwick). *a.* 1130 *Sim. Dur.* Tugga- and Tughala. *Cf.* 958 *chart.* Tigwella, on Stour (Staffd.). ' Dwelling' and ' nook of *Tuga* '; one in *Onom*. See -by and -hall.

TUNBRIDGE WELLS dates from 1606. See TONBRIDGE.

TUNSTALL (Kirby Lonsdale, Yorks, Stoke-on-T., Suffolk). Kir. T. Dunstall; Yor. T. *Dom.* Tonnestale, 1179-80 Tunstale; Sto. T. 1272 Tunstall; Suff. T. *c.* 1460 Tonstale; also *B.C.S.* iii. 605 ' the old Tunsteall '—*i.e.*, Brockley Hall. O.E. *tún steall,* ' en-closed place '; a *stall* is properly ' a farm-yard.' The name is always changing into Dunstall; in Staffs we find it so on four occasions. *Cf. Dom.* Norfk. Tonstede. See -don and -ton.

TURNANT BROOK (S. Wales). *c.* 1130 *Lib. Landav.* Nant tri neint —*i.e.*, ' valley of the three valleys.'

TURVEY (Bedford). *Dom.* Toruei, -ueie; ? *a.* 1153 *Lib. Eliensis* Torneia. *Cf. Dom.* Bucks Turvestone. ' Isle of *Turf*,' or ' of *Turfida*,' nearest name in *Onom*. See -ey.

TUSMORE (Oxon.). *Dom.* Toresmere, 1216 Thuresm'e, 1274-79 Tursmer. ' Lake, mere of the god *Thor*.' The liquid *r* has vanished.

TUTBURY (Burton-on-T.). *Dom.* Toteberie, *a.* 1200 Tuttebury, Stuteberie,; *a.* 1300 Tuttesbiri, Tutesbury. ' Burgh of *Tota*,' or else, ' look-out castle '; the castle commands a wide prospect. *Cf.* TOOTHILL and TOTTENHAM, also TUTNALL CROSS (Broms-grove), *Dom.* Tothehel, *a.* 1300 Tot(t)enhull, ' *Tota's* hill.'

TUXFORD (Notts). *Sic c.* 1350, but *Dom.* Tuxfarne (error). 1454 Tux-forthe. ' Ford of *Tucca, Tuca*, or *Tucu*,' all in *Onom*. See -ford and -forth.

TWEED R. and TWEEDMOUTH. ? *a.* 600 *Avellanau* Tywi; *Bede* Tuidus, Twidus; *a.* 800 *Hist. St. Cuthbt.* Tweoda; *c.* 966 *Pict. Chron.* Tede; *a.* 1130 Tweda; *a.* 1150 Thveda; 1211 Tydemue. Perh. fr. W. *twyad*, 'a hemming in,' fr. *twy*, ' to check, to bound.'

TWERTON-ON-AVON (Bath). *Dom.* Twertone= TIVERTON.

TWICKENHAM. Prob. 704 *chart.* Twicanhom, and 793 *chart.* Twit-tanham, with *t* for *c*, 948 Twiccanham, *c.* 1200 *Gervase* Twiccen-ham. Prob. ' home of *Twica* ' or ' *Twicga*,' in *Onom*.; or fr. O.E. *twicen*, ' place where two roads meet.' The derivation of M'Clure, p. 214, seems far-fetched. TWIGWORTH (Glouc.), 1242 Twyggenwrthe, is plainly ' farm of *Twicga*.'

TWISTON (Clitheroe). Prob. 1318-19 Twysdenne, which is a hybrid; W. *twys*, ' top, tuft, head,' and O.E. *denu* ' (wooded) valley.'

Twizel (Norham), Twizel House (Bamboro'), and Twysell (N. Durham). Nor. T. *c.* 800 *Hist. St. Cuthbt.* Twisle, 1183 Tuisela. Dur. T. 1183 Tuisill. O.E. *twisla,* 'confluence,' fr. *twislian,* 'to fork, to split.' The pron. to-day is Twy-zel. *Cf.* Haltwhistle and *Dom.* Yorks Tuislebroc.

Twyford (5 in *P.G.*). Northumb. T. *Bede* Ad tuifyrdi quod significat 'ad duplex vadum.' [Evesham T. 714 *chart.* Tuiforde, *a.* 1000 Twyfyrde.] 956 *chart.* Twyfyrd (Glouc.), *Dom.* Bucks Tveverde, *ib.* Oxon. Tuiforde, 1298 Twyforde (prob. Herts); also 1160 *Pipe* Twiuerð (Kent). O.E. *twi ford,* 'double ford.' *Cf.* Tiverton and Twerton. But Twiver (Glouc.) is for 'the Weaver' river.

Twynham (Christchurch). *Sic* in *Dom.* O.E. *tweon éan,* 'between the rivers,' O.E. *éa.* Twynholm (Sc.), *c.* 1200 Twenham, is the same name. *Cf.* the Rom. Interamna and *Dom.* Hants Tuina.

Twi-, Twyning (Tewkesbury). 814 *chart.* Bituinæum, *Dom.* Tveninge, Tuninge; 1221 Tweninges. This is O.E. *betwynum, betweonan éas,* 'between streams,' *éa* being later supplanted by *-ing* with same meaning (see p. 56). *Cf.* Twynham and 902 *O.E. Chron.* Tweoxn eam, Tweoxnam, ? = Twyning.

Tyburn (London). *Dom.* Tiburne, *c.* 1420 *Lydgate* Tyburne. Prob. 'two burns' or 'brooks,' O.E. *twi,* 'two.' See -bourne.

Tydd or Tid St. Giles (Wisbech). 1293 Tyd. Perh. W. *tuedd,* 'a region, a coast.' Skeat says fr. a personal name *Tidi,* and compares Tidmarsh, Tidworth, etc. But this is abnormal.

Tyddyn Wysgi (Anglesea). W.= 'farm by the water.' *Cf.* Tidnock and Usk, and 'whisky.'

Tyldesley (Manchester). *Sic c.* 1430. 'Meadow, lea of the tent,' O.E. *tyld, teld.* Weekley suggests '*Tilda's*' or '*Matilda's* lea.'

Tyne, R. etc. *Bede* Tinus, Tyne; *a.* 1130 *Sim. Dur.* Tina and Tynemuthe; *c.* 1145 *Wm. Malmes.* Tinemuthe; 1157 *Pipe* Tindala; 1178 Tyndale. Ptolemy's Tίνα is prob. the Haddington Tyne (Sc.). Perh. fr. W. *tynu,* 'to draw, pull,' G. *teanu,* 'to move, stir, proceed,' or fr. W. *tyno,* 'a green plot, a dale.'

Tysoe (Warwicksh.). *Dom.* Tiheshoche; *a.* 1200 Tiesoch, Thiesho, Thisho, Tyeso; *a.* 1300 T(h)ysho. 'Height of *Tihha*' or '*Tih.*' See Hoe.

Tytherington (Thornbury). *Dom.* Tidrentune, *c.* 1170 Tidrington, 'town of the sons of *Tidhere.*' See -ing and -ton.

Tywarnhaile (Cornwall). Corn. *ty war an hayle,* 'house on the tidal river.' *Cf.* Hayle. We get this *ty* or *ti* (G. *tigh*) in such *Dom.* Cornw. names as Ticoith, 'house in the wood,' Tiwarthel, etc. *Cf.* Chyandour.

UCKFIELD (Sussex). Not in *Dom.*, but 1240 *Close R.* Quicfeld. Perh. ' Field of *Ucca* ' or ' *Ucco*,' both in *Onom. Cf. B.C.S.* 158 Uckinge esher, UCKINGTON (Glouc.), *Dom.* Hochinton, 1221 Uchintone, and UCKINGHALL (Worc.), 1275 Hugingehale, where we get the patronymic; also UPTON (Pembk.), in *Gir. Camb.* Ucketune, Uccetuna. 1240 Quic- looks like O.E. *cwicu, c(w)ucu*, ' moving, shifting, alive,' as in *quicksand;* but this sense is not in *Oxf. Dict. a.* 1340.

UFFINGTON (Berks). *B.C.S.* ii. 376 Uffentune, *Dom.* Offentone. 1291 Offingtone, Offentone; also about same date, Uffinton, ' Town, village of *Uffa*,' a common name in *Onom. Cf.* Uffnell (Pershore), and next.

UFFORD (Melton). *Sic a.* 1100. ' Ford of *Ufa*,' a common name in *Onom. Cf.* above.

UFTON (Southam and Theale, Berks). So. U. *c.* 1000 Ulfetune; *Dom.* Ulchetone (error); *a.* 1300 Ulston, Oluston, Oulfton, Oluf-, Oloughton; Th. U. 1317 Uftone. The latter may be fr. *Ufa*, as above; it is now called U. Newet (prob. = NEWENT). *Cf. Dom.* Somt. Vfetone. But all the other forms point to ' town of *Ulf*,' Nor. Fr. form of the common *Wulf*.

UGBOROUGH (Ivybridge). *Dom.* Ulgeberge. ' Town, burgh of ' ? *Onom.* has one *Olfgeat* or *Oluiet;* and *cf.* UGTHORPE. See -borough.

UGGLEBARNBY (Sleights, Yorks). *Dom.* Ugleberdsbi, 1179-80 Vgulbardebi. ' Dwelling of *Ugelbert* '; one in *Onom.* See -by.

UGTHORPE (Grosmont, Yorks). *Dom.* Ugetorp, Ughetorp. Prob. ' village of *Huga* ' or ' *Hug*,' both names in *Onom. Cf.* Ughill (Yorks), *Dom.* Ughil; and see -thorpe.

ULCEBY (Alford and Lincs). *Dom.* Uluesbi. ' Dwelling of *Ulf*.' *Cf. Dom.* Bucks Vlchestone. See -by.

ULEY (Dursley). *Dom.* Euulege, *later* Huelege. ' Yew-tree meadow,' O.E. *iw, eow.* See -ley.

ULGHAM (Morpeth). ' Home of ?' *Cf. Dom.* Bucks Oilgi, and Chesh. Ulchenol (? *Ulca's knoll* '). No *Ulga* in *Onom.* It may be like the next, ' home of the *Owl*,' nickname of some man, O.N. *ugla*, O.E. *úle.* ULCHESTER, or Outchester (Belford), may have a similar origin. Some identify it with *a.* 700 *Rav. Geogr.* Oleiclavis.

ULLENHALL (Henley-in-Arden). *Dom.* Holehale, *a.* 1200 Hulehale, 1257 Hunhal, 1326 Ulnhale, Ulehale, Holenhale. ' Nook of the owl,' O.E. *úle, -an*, 5-6 *howle*, 6 *houle*, 7 *oole;* O.N. *ugla.* And ULLSWATER, as well as ULDALE (Cumberland), are, of course, fr. the same bird; prob. through N. rather than Eng. Ullett Rd. (Liverpool) is for *owlet*, 1542 *oulette. Cf.* 1211 Ulecote (? Co. Durham) and Oubrough (Yorks), *Dom.* Uleburg,

Ulenburg, also Ulcombe (Maidstone), with which prob. goes 940 *chart*. Olencumb (Dorset). But ULLINGWICK (Glouc.), *a*. 1200 Ollinggewike, 1212 Wyllynwyck, is 'dwelling of the sons of *Willa*.' See -ing and -wick.

ULLESKELF (York). *Dom*. Oleslec, Oleschel. 'Ledge of *Olla*' or '*Ula*,' both forms in *Onom*. O.E. *scelfe, scylfe*, 'a shelf.' ULLEY (Sheffield), *Dom*. Ollei, is fr. same man's name. See -ey.

ULROME (Yorks). *Dom*. Ulfram, Ulreham. 'Home of *Ulfarr*,' N. form of the common O.E. *Wulfhere*. See -ham.

ULVERSTONE. Local pron. Ooston. *Dom*. Vluerston, 1196 Olues-ton, 1202 Vlveston, 1230 Ulveston. Prob. 'town of *Wulfhere*,' a very common name. *Cf. Dom*. Chesh. Ulvre, Bucks Vlfre-stone; also ULVERLEY (Acock's Green), *Dom*. Uluerlie, *a*. 1200 Hulferle. *Cf*. OWSTHORPE with Ooston; also *cf*. Woolverstone (Ipswich). ULMSTON (Nthbld.) is *c*. 1316 Ouston, prob. fr. a man *Ulfhelm*.

UMBERLEIGH (Devon) is var. of AMBERLEY and OMBERSLEY, 'pitcher meadow,' while UMBERSLADE (Henley-in-Arden), *a*. 1200 Ombreslade, is 'channel, watercourse,' O.E. (*ge*)*lád*, 'of the pitcher,' O.E. *amber, omber*. *Cf*. CRICKLADE.

UNCLEBY (Yorks). *Dom*. Unchelsbi, Unglesbi, Unchelfsbi. Prob. 'dwelling of *Wuncild*,' one in *Onom*., which also gives one *Hun-chil*, or *Huncytel*, seen in *Dom*. Yorks Hunchilhuse. Eng. *uncle* is fr. Fr. See -by.

UNSTONE (Sheffield) (not in *Dom*.) and UNSWORTH (Manchester). 1522 Undesworth. There are 2 *Unas* but no *Unda* in *Onom*. See -stone and -worth.

UNTHANK (Alnham and Haltwhistle, Northumbd., and 3 in Cumbld.). Common, too, in Sc. (*q.v.*), where found 1228 Vnthanc. O.E. *un- anc* means 'ingratitude,' and the reference may be to the barrenness of the soil. But Canon Taylor says it denotes a piece of ground on which some squatter had settled 'without leave' of the lord.

UPHILL (Weston-s.-M.). *Dom*. Opopille. Doubtful. Perh. 'hill of *Oppo*' or '*Oppa*,' both in *Onom*.

UPLEATHAM (Redcar). *Dom*. Upelider, 1204 Uplium. The *Dom*. is plainly O.N. *upp a hlíðar*, 'up on the slope or hill-side.' *Hlíð* is also O.E. for 'slope,' *cf*. LEITH HILL; and 1204 is an old loc. from it, now, like all these Yorks locatives, turned into -ham (*q.v.*). Kirkleatham is *Dom*. Westlidu'. But UPLEADON (N.W. Glouc.) is 'upon the R. *Leadon*.' See LEDBURY.

UPMINSTER (Romford). *a*. 716 *chart*. Upmynster, *Dom*. Upmon-stra. 'Upper' or 'high-up church.' *Cf*. UPTON and Upthorp (Shipston-on-Stour), 990 *chart*. Uppsthrop.

UPPER WYCHE (Malvern). O.E. *wíc*, ' dwelling-place.' *Cf. Dom.* Wiche (Salop), and **DROITWICH**.

UPSALL (Thirsk). *Dom.* Upesale, Upsale, Upeshale; 1179-80 Hupsale. This is prob. O.E. *up sœl*, ' upper hall,' 4-7 *sale*, 5 *sall*. Thus the ending, unlike most old names in -ale or -all, is not -hall (*q.v.*). *Cf.* **UPMINSTER**.

UPTON (24 in *P.G.*). 962 *chart.* Uptun (on Severn), *Dom.* Yorks and Salop Uptune, -tone, Berks, Glouc., and Warwk. Optone, Bucks Opetone, Suffk. Opituna. O.E. *up tún*, ' upper, high-up village.' Oldest of all perh. is Upton Warren (Bromsgrove), 714 *chart.* Uptone. The *Warins* and Fitz-Warins owned the manor in the 13th cny. Upton (Pembk.), 1603 *Owen* Vpton, is *c.* 1190 *Gir. Camb.* Ucketune, Uccetuna, fr. a man *Ucca*, as in **UCKFIELD**.

UPWARE (Cambs). 1349 Upwere. O.E. *up wœr*, ' upper weir ' or ' fish pool.' *Cf.* **UPWELL** (Wisbech).

UPWOOD (Huntingdon). *Cf.* 1060 *chart.* ' Uppwude cum Ravelaga berewico suo.' ' Upper wood.' *Cf.* above.

URE, R. See **YORK**.

USK R. In W. Wysc. *c.* 380 *Ant. Itin.* Isca, 1050 O.E. *Chron.* Wylisce (' in Welsh ') Axa, *Dom.* Huscha, *c.* 1130 *Lib. Landav.* Huisc, *c.* 1250 *Layam.* Uske. Kelt. *uisc*, ' water, river,' same root as G. *uisge*, ' whisky,' **AXE**, **OUSE**, and **UX-BRIDGE**.

USWORTH (Washington, Co. Durham). 1183 Useworth. ' Farm of *Osa*,' a common name; no *Usa* is recorded. *Cf.* **OUSE**. See -worth.

UTLEY (Keighley). *Dom.* Utelai. ' Meadow of *Uta*.' *Cf.* 839 *chart.* Uhtlufe (Kent). There are 2 *Utas*, and also 4 *Utels* in *Onom.* See -ley.

UTTOXETER. Pron. Úxeter. *Dom.* Wotocheshede (*d* for *th* as usual, medially, in *Dom.*); *a.* 1200 Uttockeshedere, Uttoxeshather, Huttokeshagh, Ottokeshather; *a.* 1400 Uttoxhather, Uttoxeshather, Uttoxatre, Uttockcestre; *a.* 1600 Utcester, Utseter, Uttecester. The analogy of **EXETER** tempts one, and Chambers's *Encycl.* actually invents an O.E. Uttocceaster; but the name has nothing to do with -cester or ' camp.' The first half must represent an unrecorded man *Wotoc* (*ch* in *Dom.* is the usual Norm. softening), or *Uuottok*. *Cf.* the mod. names Whittock and Whytock. The second half, -hedere or -hather, must surely be Norse, the O.N. *heith-r*, ' a heath, a moor.' Eng. *heath* would yield no *r*, and ' Wotoc's heather ' is a very unlikely name, though *heather* is a much earlier and wider spread Eng. word than *Oxf. Dict.* knows. See **HATHERLEIGH**.

UXBRIDGE (Middlesex). Not in *Dom.*, but it has an Exeforde near Bedfont. 1139 Oxebridge; later Woxbridge. It is on the

R. Colne, so Ux- or Oxe- here may be = Usk, ' river, water.'
Oxf. Dict. gives no case of *ox* becoming *ux* in Eng.; but O.N. for
' ox ' is *uxe* or *oxe*. This is to be viewed as one views Oxford.

Valle Crucis Abbey (Llangollen). L. = ' in the valley of the
Cross.' Cistercian abbey founded here, *c.* 1200, by Madoc ap
Gruffydd. In W. it is Llan Egwest. Le Clos du Valle, Guernsey,
1135 Wallus, however, is fr. O.N. *völl-r*, 'a field.'

Vauxhall (Lambeth). 1363 ' Faukeshalle juxta London.' *Fawkes*
was a powerful baron, in the reign of K. John, who built ' La
Salle' (the hall) ' de Fawkes.'

Ventnor (I. of Wight). Ventanora must mean ' shore, edge,
brink of the *Venta*.' Venta is common in Eng. place-names of
Roman times, Venta Belgarum, Icenorum, Silurum, etc. (*i.e.*,
Winchester, Caistor near Norwich, Chepstow, etc.). M'Clure
(pp. 32-33) shows that Venta is not Keltic but late Latin, the
meaning being ' market, place where things are sold,' L. *vendere*,
venditum. *Cf*. Wentnor.

Verulam = St. Albans. *Bede* ' Verulamium ' or in Eng. ' Verla-
macæstir or Vætlinga-cæstir,' v.r. Væclinga-Cæstir. In Bede's
O.E. versn., over 100 years later, Werlameceaster or Wæclinga-
ceaster. *c.* 1205 *Layam*. Verolam or Verolamestun. Verlam
or Werlame seems to have been a river name, about which
M'Clure has some conjectures, drawn fr. Whitley Stokes (see
his p. 40). Vætlinga reminds of Watling Street.

Verwood (Wimborne). Old forms needed. But *cf.* 1179-80 *Pipe*
Verli (Yorks), which *may* be ' lea, meadow of *Verca* ' or ' *Werca*.'
There was one, abbess at Tynemouth. *Dom.* Wilts has a
Vergroh (S.W. of Dorchester).

Vradden or Braddn (Cornwall). To guess, as some do, ' chough's
abode,' and derive fr. Corn. *vran*, Ir. and G. *bran*, ' a crow,
chough, Cornish crow,' is to leave the *d* quite unaccounted for.
Braddan was a Keltic St. of the 7th cny. *Cf.* Kirk Braddan
(I. of Man).

Vyrnwy (Montgomerysh.). Perh. W. *bryn* (*b* aspirated) *gwy*,
' hill with the stream.' But Vreny or Breni Vawr (Pembroke), is not ' big hill ' (W. *mawr*, ' big '), but prob. ' big
prow,' O.W. *breni.*

Waberthwaite (Millom). ' Place, farm of ' ? Old forms needed.
Perh. fr. a *Wyberth* in a Cumbld. charter, *c.* 1080, or fr. *Wac-*
beorht or *Weardbeorht*, names in *Onom*. Perh. fr. *Walbert* or
Wealhbeorht, as in Walberswick (Sfk.). See -thwaite.

Wadborough (Pershore). 972 *chart.* Wadbeorh, *Dom.* Wadberge.
These are just O.E. for ' woad-hill,' *woad* being a plant for dyeing
blue. See -burgh.

WADDINGTON (Lincoln). *c.* 1300 Widdindune—*i.e.,* O.E. *Wyddan dùn,* 'hill of Wydda.' *Cf. B.C.S.* 960 Wyddan beorh. The name *Wada* is also common in *Onom.,* and *Wid* and *Wida* are also found. For the tale of the mythic *Wade* and his boat, see Kemble *Saxons in Engld.* I., 420.

WADDON (Croydon). Prob. *a.* 900 *B.C.S.* ii. 196 Hwæte dun, *Dom.* Watendone, Wadone, 1287 Whatdon; and WADDON Hill (Shipston-on-Stour), *chart.* Hwætdune, both being O.E. for 'wheat hill.' *Cf.* WHADDON and *Dom.* Bucks Wadruge, 'wheat ridge.'

WADEFORD (Chard). Tautology. O.E. *wœd,* dial. *wath,* Icel. *vað,* 'a ford.' *Cf.* Langwade (Cambs), 1210 Landwath, 1284 Landwade. *Cf.* WATH. Wassand (Yorks), *Dom.* Wadsande, is prob. fr. the same root.

WADENHOE (Oundle). 1166-67 *Pipe* Wadeho. 'Hill, height of *Wada.*' *Cf. B.C.S.* 50 Wadan hlæw, WADDINGTON, and next; and see HOE.

WADSWORTH (Hebden Br.) (*Dom.* Wadeswrde) and WADWORTH (Doncaster) (*Dom.* Wadewrde). 'Place, farm of *Wad, Wada,*' or '*Wade.*' See WADDINGTON, and *cf.* WADSLEY (Sheffield), *Dom.* Wadesleia, Wadelei; only in *Dom.* Derby it seems given as Wodnesleie, 'meadow of *Woden*' (*cf.* WANBOROUGH); also *cf.* 940 *chart.* Wadleaʒe (Wilts). See -worth.

WAINFLEET (Lincs). 1396 Waynflete. FLEET is 'river,' Wain is not the Rom. Venonio, which is High Cross; it may be W. *gwaen,* 'plain, meadow,' as in WAENFAWR, 'big plain,' Carnarvon. But WAINLODE-on-Severn, 1424 Waynelodus, is 'wain, wagon ferry,' O.E. (*ge*)*lád.*

WAKEFIELD. *Dom.* Wachefeld, *c.* 1350 Wakefeld. Perh. 'field of the vigil or *wake*'; O.E. *wacu,* so Skeat. But *cf.* 1332 *Rolls Parlmt.* 'Le Seigneur de Wake,' which suggests 'field of a man *Wake.*' In *Onom.* are *Wacca, Wacco,* and *Wach,* whilst *Wac* is common in early Rolls.

WALBROOK (London). Perh. *c.* 1140 Walebroc. See *Oxf. Dict.* s.v. HUSTING. 'Brook by the (London) Wall.'

WALCOT (Pershore, Alcester, Norwich), WALCOTE (Lutterworth), and WALCOTT (Lincoln). Pe. W. *a.* 1200 Walecot, *Dom.* Warwk. and Salop Walecote. 'Cot, cottage by the wall,' O.E. *weall;* though perh. *wale* is dat. of O.E. *wealh,* 'stranger, foreigner, Welshman.' *Cf.* WALSALL.

WALDEN STUBBS (Pontefract). Perh. 1179-80 *Pipe* Yorks Alanus de Stublis. Doubtful. Stubbs is prob. fr. Sc. and G. *stob,* 'a stake, a stump.'

WALDRINGFIELD (Suffolk). Local pron. Wunnerful! Waldring-prob. means 'the descendants of *Wealdhere,*' a common name in *Onom.* See -ing.

WALES. 922 *O.E. Chron.* On Norþ Wealum, Eall Norþ Weallcyn;
as name of the country perh. first in 1046 *O.E. Chron.* Into
Wealan; *Dom.* Rex de Nort-Wales; *c.* 1160 *Gest. Steph.* Walonia;
c. 1175 *Fantosme* North Wales. In 1055 *O.E. Chron.* also called
Brytland or ' Britons' land '; whilst in *O.E. Chron.* the people
are called Wealas, *passim.* O.E. *weal, wealh,* fem. *wylen,* is ' a
stranger, a foreigner,' then, ' a slave '; so Wales is ' land of the
strangers,' from the Anglo-Saxon point of view. Earle thinks
we get the same root not only in the Ger. *Welsch,* but in Wal-
loons, Wallachia, and canton Wallis in Switzerland. We get
the older name in *c.* 1145 *Geoffr. Monm.* ' Kambria, in their
British tongue Kambri.' The mod. W. name is Cymru or
Kymru, fr. *cym -bro,* ' the compatriot, the native of the country.'
WALES (Sheffield), *sic Dom.* also Walis, seems to be an inflected
form of O.E. *weall,* ' wall, rampart.' But WALESBY (Newark),
Dom. Walesbi, is fr. *wealh.* See -by.

WALFORD (Ross) and WALFORD Heath (Shrewsbury). ' Ford at
the wall,' or possibly ' the well,' O.E. *weall* or *well(a).* *Cf.*
Dom. Surrey Walforde. WALHAM (Berkeley) is *old* Waleham,
prob. fr. O.E. *wealh.* See above.

WALK MILL (Burnley and Cannock), WALKER BARN (Macclesfd.),
WALKFORD (Christchurch). All fr. to ' walk,' Sc. *wauk,* ' to full
cloth,' O.E. *wealcan,* ' to turn about,' *wealcere,* ' a fuller.'

WALKINGHAM (Knaresboro'). *Dom.* Walchingha', and WALKING-
TON (Beverley), *Dom.* Walchinton. ' Home ' and ' village of the
sons of *Wealh* ' or ' the foreigner.' See WALES, and -ing. But
WALKERINGHAM (Gainsboro'), *Dom.* Walcheringeham, is ' home
of the sons of *Walchere.*'

WALL HEATH (Dudley). 1332 Kingswallhuth (= heath). Ancient
earthworks near by. There is a fort near Wolverhampton, ' The
Walls.'

WALLINGFORD. *c.* 893 *chart.* Welinga ford, 1006 *O.E. Chron.*
Wealinga ford, 1216 *ib.* Walinge ford, 1298 Walinford, 1373
Walyngforde. ' Ford of the *Wealings* ' or ' sons of *Wealh,*' or
' sons of the foreigner.' See WALES. We get a Norm. spelling
in *Wm. of Poitiers* Guarenford. *Cf.* WALLINGTON (Surrey),
Dom. Wallingehā, and *Dom.* Walitone (Salop). But WALLING-
WELLS (Notts), 1278 Wellandwell, is fr. O.E. *weallende,* ' boiling,
bubbling up.'

WALLSEND (Newcastle). 1382 *Dur. Halm. Rolls* Campus de Wal-
leshond. ' End of the (Roman) Wall,' whose other end is
Bowness (Cumbld.), built by Hadrian, *c.* 130. WALLOP (Stockbridge), *Dom.* Wallope, -lop; 1217 *Close R.* Welhop, prob. means
' piece of land enclosed with a wall,' O.E. *weall,* Fris. *wal.* See
-hope.

WALMERSLEY (Bury). ' Meadow of *Waldemar* ' or ' *Wealdmœr,*'
this only, and this but once, in *Onom.* *Cf.* 1220-51 *Cockersand*

Chart. Waldemurfeld. Wyld and H. omit both this and Walmer Br. (Preston). See -ley.

WALMESFORD (Northants). *O.E. Chron.* 657 Welmesford. Perh. ' Ford of '? some unknown man. But both it and WALMLEY ASH (Sutton Coldfield), *a.* 1300 Warmleye, are more prob. fr. O.E. *walm, wielm,* ' a boiling or bubbling up, a spring.' *Cf.* EWELM and Walmgate (York).

WALNEY I. (Barrow). 1127 Wagneia, 1189-94 Wageneia, 1227 Wagneia. ' Isle of *Waga,*' gen. -*an.* The *l* must be a mod. intrusion. See p. 82, and -ey.

WALPOLE HIGHWAY and ST. ANDREW (Wisbech). ? *a.* 1244 *Anct-deed* Villa de Walepol. ' Pool at the wall,' O.E. *weall,* ' a wall, a rampart.' There seem to have been men named Walpole in Norfk., *a.* 1200.

WALSALL. 1004 Walesho (see HOE), *a.* 1100 Waleshale, *a.* 1300 Wales-Walsale. ' Nook, corner of the Welshman.' See WALCOT.

WALSHAM, North and South. *Dom.* Walessam, -eshā; 1373 *Will Edw. Black Pr.* ' Robert de Walsham.' Prob. ' home of *Wale,*' 2 in *Onom.* See WALCOT and -ham.

WALSINGHAM (Norfolk). *K.C.D.* 782 Wælsinga-, *Dom.* Walsinga-, *a.* 1340 Walsyngham. A patronymic, fr. *Wæls,* a name in *Beowulf.* See -ing.

WALTHAM (9 in *P.G.*) and WALTHAMSTOW. Kent. W. 727 *chart.* Waltham, 1001 *O.E. Chron.* Wealtham, Essex and Berks *Dom.* (and *chart. a.* 1067) Waltham. ' Home of *Wealt* ' ; *Weald* and *Wealda* are also in *Onom.* As the spelling is always with *t* it is not at all likely to be ' home in the *weald,*' O.E. for ' wood,' same root as *wold.* Skeat, because we never find any sign of a gen. in even the earliest charters, thinks it cannot be from a man, and conjectures an O.E. *wealt,* ' unsteady, ill-built, de-cayed,' comparing the known *unwealt,* ' steady, firm,' and Icel. *valt-r,* ' easily upset.' See -stow.

WALTON (21 in *P.G.*). Carlisle W. *Bede,* ' The royal vill called Ad murum ' (' at the Wall '); Suffk. W. 1046 *chart.* Wealtun; Blackburn, Stone, and Epsom W. *Dom.* Waletone. Two in Warwk., *Dom.* Waltone. Peterboro' W. 1147 *chart.* Walton. ' Town with or at the wall or rampart,' O.E. *weall.* There are prob. over 50 Waltons in England; some may be fr. O.E. *weal,* ' stranger, foreigner, Welshman,' dat. *wale.* *Cf.* WALCOT. *Dom.* varies all through between Wal- and Wale-. In *Dom.* Yorks Walton, Waleton, or Waliton occur 10 times. White Walton (Berks) is *B.C.S.* 762 Wealtun, whilst Bps. Walton (Hants) is 909 *chart.* Wealtham. See above.

WALWORTH (S. London). *Dom.* Waleorde. ' Farm of *Wale.*' *Cf.* above; and see -worth, regularly -orde in *Dom.* WALSWORTH (Glouc.), *old* Wale-, Wallesworthe, is the same name.

WAMBROOK (Chard). Said to be ' *Woden's* brook.' *Cf.* WAN-BOROUGH. Old forms needed; it is not in *Dom.* It might be ' *Wamba's* brook.'

WAMPOOL R. (N.W. Cumbld.). *c.* 1080 *chart.* Pollwathoen; also Wathanpol. W. *pwl,* G. *poll* is our Eng. *pool,* but all these words tend to mean ' a stream,' in Sc. a *pow,* also. Wathan may perh. be the same root as W. *gwydden,* Corn. *gwedhen,* ' a tree.'

WANBOROUGH (Swindon and Guildford). Neither will be *O.E. Chron.* 591 Wodnesbeorge, Woddesbeorg, fr. the god *Woden.* But Sw. W. is *Dom.* Wemberge, 1245 Wamberge, and Guil. W. is 1147 Wenebergia. This seems to be ' burgh, fort of *Wana,*' 2 in *Onom.* There is a Wodnesborough (Kent), *a.* 1300 Wodnes-berge, but this cannot be the *O.E. Chron.* name either. *Cf.* WEDNESBURY. But WANDALE, which occurs several times in Cumbld. and Yorks, is prob. fr. O.N. *vang-r,* ' field '—*i.e.,* valley partly cultivated.

WANDSWORTH (S. London). *Dom.* Wendelesorde, Wandesorde. ' Farm on the R. *Wandle,*' prob. W. *gwen dol,* ' fair, beautiful mead.' Connexion with the Teutonic *Vandals,* whose homes was between Vistula and Oder, or with the Slavic *Wends,* who dwelt nearer Britain, in the same latitudes, is quite doubtful. *Cf. K.C.D.* 1283 Wændlescumb, 1223 *Patent R.* Notts Wandles-legh, and Hutton Wandesley (Yorks), *Dom.* Wandeslage, all of which point to a man *Wandel* or *Wanda.* There is one *Wandel* in *Onom. Cf.* WENDLEBURY and WINDSOR. See -worth.

WANSBECK R. (Northumbld.). *a.* 1700 Wannys pike water. This, then, is a corrup. of ' Wanny's peak.' There are no genuine *becks* in Northbld., they are all *burns.* For *pike* see RED PIKE; but who or what is *Wanny?* Perh. the same as the Sc. *wannis* in Bellenden's *Livy,* which is ' scars, wens,' O.E. *wenn.*

WANSBOROUGH (N. Devon). Not in *Dom.* The associating with *Woden,* seeing that it fails of proper authentication in some other cases, is uncertain here also. Prob.= WANBOROUGH, though the ending may be = BARROW. *Cf.* WANSFORD (Driffield and Northants). But also see next.

WANSDYKE, The (Bath). *a.* 1145 *Wm. Malmes.* Wodnesdic—*i.e.,* ' dyke or rampart of *Woden,*' the famous Saxon god, also called Odin. But WANSWELL (Berkeley), 1170-90 Weneswell, is fr. a man *Wene.*

WANTAGE (Berks). O.E. *chart.* Waneting, Wæneting; 1238 Wanet-ing; *c.* 1540 Wanting; so the ending -age seems quite modern. Patronymic. ' Place of the *Wanetings,*' an unknown family. See -age and -ing.

WAPENBURY (Leamington) (*Dom.* Wapeberie, 1198 Wapenbiri), WAPLEY (Yate) (*Dom.* Wapelei, 1163-64 *Pipe* Wappelai), and WAPPENHAM (Towcester) (*Dom.* Wapeham). ' Burgh, mead, and home of *Wap(p)a,*' an unrecorded name. *Cf.* WAPLING-

TON (Yorks), *Dom.* Waplinton, which gives an extended form. See -bury, -ham, and -ley.

WARBLETON (Heathfield Tower, Sussex). *Dom.* Warblitetone. *Cf. Dom.* 'Werblestun' (Chesh.). Prob. corrup. of 'town of *Wernbeald*,' 3 in *Onom.*

WARBOROUGH (Wallingford). 913 *O.E. Chron.* Weardbyrig, O.E. *chart.* Weardburh. 'Guard -burgh or fort,' O.E. *weard,* 'a guard, a watch, a ward.'

WARBOYS (Hunts). *Dom.* Wardebusc. A little doubtful. It seems to be 'guard bush,' 'bush of the watch,' fr. O.E. *weard* and O.N. *busk-r,* 'bush, wood,' not found in *Oxf. Dict.* till *c.* 1250. *Cf.* Dan. *varde,* 'a beacon, a landmark.' But the ending has certainly been influenced by Fr. *bois,* 'a wood.' *Cf.* p. 64.

WARBURTON (Altrincham). *Dom.* Wareburgetun, *a.* 1200 Werburton. 'Town of St. *Werburga*,' daughter of Wulfhere, K. of Mercia, Abbess of Ely and then of Chester (d. *c.* 875), where a monastery was dedicated to her, *c.* 1057.

WARDEN (Hexham). *a.* 1130 *Sim. Dur.* Waredun, 1183 Wardona. Possibly 'sentry hill,' O.E. *wær,* Dan. *var,* 'wary, on guard.' Or fr. a man *Ware*, one in *Onom.* See -don.

WARDLE (Nantwich). 1602 Woodhull. *Cf. Dom.* Yorks Wardille, now Warthill, and *Dom.* Worcr. Warthuil. 'Ward or guard hill,' which often becomes *hull* in this region and to the S. of it. *Cf.* ASTLE, SOLIHULL, etc. See, too, WARBOROUGH.

WARE (London). *a.* 900 Guare, *Dom.* Waras, 1210 Wares (? 1304 *Rolls Parlmt.* I. 163. 1, In Villa Warr). Perh. O.E. *wær, wer,* 'a fence, a wear, an enclosure for fish.' However, Skeat is confident it is simply O.E. *waras,* 'dwellers'; a very bald and curious name. *Cf.* CANTERBURY; also *Dom.* Wwk. Wara, and WARTON. *Dom.* uses *wara* for 'the outlying part of a manor,' prob. fr. same root as *ward—i.e.,* 'defence.'

WAREHAM. *O.E. Chron.* 876 Werham, 978 *ib.* Wærham. 'House at the wear.' See above. But *cf.* WARDEN, WARLEY, and UPWARE.

WARESLEY (Hartlebury). 817 *chart.* Wæresleye, 980 *ib.* Wereslæge, *c.* 1108 Wæresley, *a.* 1200 Wareslei. 'Meadow of *Wær*.' But Waresley (Sandy) is '*wether*'s lea,' 'ram's meadow.'

WARGRAVE (Berks, on Thames). 1061-65 *chart.* Weregravæ, *Dom.* Weregrave, *later* Wergrave. O.E. *wera græf,* 'grave of the men'; *wer,* 'a man,' and *graf, græf,* 'a trench, a grave.' *Cf.* GARGRAVE, etc.

WARHAM ALL SAINTS (Wells, Norfk.). *Sic c.* 1160 *Gest. Steph.* Either = WAREHAM, 'home at the wear,' or fr. a man *Warr* or *Ware.* Skeat derives WARFIELD (Berks), *Dom.* Warwelt, fr. O.E. *wær,* 'a weir.' *Cf.* WARLEY and WHARRAM.

WARK (Northumbld.).   1157 *Pipe* Werch, *c.* 1175 *Fantosme* Werc, lit. 'work,' hence 'fortification.' *Cf.* bulwark, outwork, etc., and next.

WARKWORTH (Northumbld.).   *u.* 1130 *Sim. Dur.* Werceworde. 1150 Werkewurthe, *c.* 1175 Werkewde, *c.* 1460 Warcorth. 'Place, manor with the work or rampart.' *Cf.* above, Warkleigh (N. Devon), 796 *chart.* Wrkeleye (Wilts), and **WARKWOOD** (Redditch), 1242 Werewode (prob. *re* for *rc*).

WARLEY (Halifax) (*Dom.* Werla) and **WARLEY COMMON** (Brentwood) (*Dom.* Wareleia). Doubtful. See **WAREHAM, WARHAM,** and -ley. **WARLEY WIGORN** (Halesowen) is *Dom.* Werwelie, *a.* 1400 Werulege, Wereulegh, Werweleye, which Skeat thinks prob. '*Wœrwulf*'s mead.' Wigornia is the common L. for **WORCESTER.**

WARMINGTON (Oundle and Banbury).   Oun. W. 963 *O.E. Chron.* Wermingtun. Ban. W. *Dom.* Warmintone. A patronymic; there are no likely names in *Onom.*, unless it be *Wœrmœr* or *Wœrmann.* But **WARSMSWOTH** (Doncaster) is *Dom.* Wermes-, Wemesford, which implies a man *Werm* or *Weorm*; so does **WARMFIELD** (W. Riding), *Dom.* Warnesfeld, and **WARNDON** (Worc.), *Dom.* Wermedun, 1275 Warmdone. *Cf.* **WORM'S HEAD.** See -ing, -ton, and -worth.

WARMINSTER (Westbury).   *Dom.* Guerminstre, 1165 *Pipe* Warmenist', *a.* 1228 Wermenistr'.   The War- may be as in **WARHAM,** but as *Dom.* has no dislike for initial O.E. *w,* Guer- may be for W. *gwerdd, gywrdd,* 'green, verdant,' and so 'green-looking church'; *dd* easily disappears. See -minster.

WARRENTON (N.E. Northumbld.).   *Old* Warndham. Doubtful. There are 2 called *Wœrin* or *Warin* in *Onom.* *Cf.* Warrenby (Redcar), not in *Dom.*, and next. John, earl of Warrenne (b. *c.* 1240), is 1297 'erl of wareine,' O.Fr. *warene, -enne,* 'a piece of ground or preserve for breeding rabbits.'

WARRINGTON.   *Dom.* Walintune, 1175-82 W'linton, 1255 Wherinton, 1277 Werington.   Orig. 'town of *Waling*,' or ' the foreigner.' See **WALLINGFORD.**   But early the liquid *l* dissimilated into *r,* and the name became ' town of *Warin*,' of whom there are several in *Onom.* *Cf.* Warenberie, *Dom.* Cheshire, and the personal names Warren and Waring, prob. fr. O.N. *vœringi,* 'a confederate.'

WARSASH (Southampton).   Perh. contracted fr. ' *Wœrstan*'s ash,' the man's name is fairly common.   *Cf. Dom.* Hants Warschessele (= -hale or -hall, *q.v.*) and next, and **BORROWASH.**

WARSOP (Notts).   *Sic* 1230, but *Dom.* Wareshope, Warsope. 'Valley of *Wœr*' or ' *Ware*'; Icel. *hóp,* 'a haven, a place of refuge.' *Cf.* Sc. **HOBKIRK;** also **WARSLOW** (Leek), *Dom.* Wereslie, 1300 Werselow. See -hope, -low, and -ley.

WARSTOCK (Birmingham).   Duignan says, *a.* 1500 *har stóc,* 'hoar stoke' or ' boundary place,' and says **WARRIDGE** (Bromsgrove) shows the same change. Old forms seem lacking.

WARTER (York). *Dom.* Wartre (*re* sounded *er*). Doubtful. *Cf.* -er. Possibly 'ward, guard, sentry bank.' Wassall Grove (Halesowen), 1275 Warselde, seems to have been similarly, 'wardsettle' or 'watch-tower' (O.E. *seld* or *setl*, synonyms).

WARTON (Carnforth, Preston, Atherstone, and Staffs). Ath. W. 1285 is Wavertone (still sometimes so called) and St. W. 1272 Wavertune. 'Aspen-tree town.' See **WAVERTREE.** But Pres. W. is *Dom.* and later Wartun, which points to some man *War*(*r*). *Cf.* **WARE** and **WARDLE.**

WARWICK. 915 *O.E. Chron.* 'This year was Wærinwic built,' yet 701 *chart.* 'in Wærincwicum,' also *chart.* Wæringwic, *Dom.* Warwic, *a.* 1145 *Orderic* Guarewicum, 1258 Warewik. 'Dwelling of the *Wærings*.' Waring is still a common name. *Cf.* **WARRINGTON.** There was said to be a tribe of that name on the S.W. coast of the Baltic (Shore's *Origin of A.-S. Race*, p. 36). However, **WARWICK** (Carlisle) is 1120 Warthewic, 'dwelling of *Wearda*,' nearest name in *Onom.* See -wick.

WASH, The (Lincs), and **WASH** or **GUASH** R. (Rutland). Often said to be Kelt. for 'water'; but almost certainly O.E. *wáse*, 'ooze, soft mud,' as in **WASHFIELD** (Tiverton), 1166 *Pipe* Wasfeld, **ALREWAS,** etc. *Cf.* O.N. *veisa*, 'stagnant pool, puddle.' The Wash at low water looks like a collection of muddy sandbanks. *Cf.* next and Wass (York). *Dom.* Worc. and Glouc. has Waseburne, -borne, the latter now **WASHBOURNE** (Beckford).

WASHFORD (Somerset). *Exon. Dom.* Wasforda. Perh. 'ford of *Wassa*' or '*Wasa*.' *Cf.* next. More likely fr. O.E. *wáse*, 'ooze, soft mud,' O.N. *vás*, 'wetness,' as above. *Cf.* Vason, Guernsey.

WASHINGBOROUGH (Lincoln). *a.* 1100 *Grant of* 664 Wassingburge. 'Burgh, castle of the descendants of *Wassa*.' *Cf. B.C.S.* 236 Wassanburn. But Skeat says **WASING** (Berks), *Dom.* Walsinge, *a.* 1290 Wawesenge, 1316 Wausynge, is 'home of the *Wælsings*' or 'sons of *Wæls*,' a name found as early as *Beowulf*. **WASHINGTON** (Co. Durham) is 1183 Wassyngtone, 1197 Wessinton, plainly a patronymic fr. *Wassa*. See -ing.

WASKERLEY (Darlington). Mawer thinks this a hybrid; N. *was*, 'hardship, toil, danger,' and *kjær, kjerr*, 'marsh, wet copse,' so 'dangerous, marshy ground,' as it is still; and -ley (*q.v.*). *Cf.* Wasdale (Cumbld.).

WASPERTON (Warwick). 1043 *chart.* Waspertone, as also in *K.C.D.* 939. Duignan says, O.E. *wáse- perig- tún*, 'mud or fen, peartree town.' This looks peculiar. It is prob. fr. some unrecorded man; at any rate *Vosper* is still a known Cornish surname. *Cf. Dom.* Devon Wasberlege.

WATCHET (Somerset). 915 *O.E. Chron.* Weced, 988 *ib.* Wecedport. *Dom.* Wacet, *a.* 1300 Wechet. O.E. *wœcce*, 'a watch,' fr. *wacan*, 'to watch, wake,' and *cete*, 'cot, hut'; so 'watch-cot, outlook hut.' The hard O.E. *c* normally becomes *tch* in mod. Eng., as in BLETCHLEY, etc. *Cf.* DATCHET.

WATCHFIELD (Shrivenham). 931 *chart.* Wæclesfeld, Wachenesfeld, *later* Uacenesfeld. 'Field of *Wacol* '—*i.e.,* ' the wakeful one,' early confused, says Skeat, with O.E. *wacen,* ' vigilance, keeping watch.'

WATERBEACH (Cambridge). *Dom.* Bech, Bece. See LANDBEACH.

WATERLEY (Rochester). 774 *chart.* Wæterlea, ' meadow by the water.' WATERLOO (London) has perh. the same meaning, -loo being the Flem. equivalent of O.E. *léah.* See *Oxf. Dict.* s.v. *lea* sb[1].

WATER ORTON (Coleshill). *a.* 1300 Overton. ' Upper town on the river ' Tame.

WATFORD (Herts, Rugby, Shenstone). He. W. 946 *will* Watford, *chart.* Watforda, 1390 Wathford. Ru. W. *Dom.* Wat- and Wad-ford. Prob. ' ford of *Wata* ' or ' *Wada,*' both in *Onom.,* the latter very common; but the absence of all trace of the gen. is not usual. Weddington (Hinckley) is *Dom.* Watitune. *Cf.* WATTON and Watnall (Notts), *c.* 1200 Wattenhou.

WATH-ON-DEARNE (Rotherham). *Dom.* Wat, Wate. Wath is a common Eng. or Scandinavian name for ' a ford.' See WADE-FORD, and *cf.* Watlas (Yorks), *Dom.* Wadles (? O.N. *lest,* ' a burden, a last '). The R. Dearne is fr. O.E. *derne, dyrne,* O.Fris. *dern,* ' hidden, obscure, secret.'

WATLING ST. (Roman road ' fram Dovere in to Chestre,' *R. Glouc.* 174). 880 *chart.* Wætlinga stræt, 926 *ib.* Wæc-, Wæxlinga stræte, 1013 *O.E. Chron.* Wætlinga Stræte, v.r. Wat-, Wæc-, *Sim. Dur.* ann. 1013 Wætlinga strete, 1387 *Trevisa* Watlynge strete. Orig., some say, the name of the Milky Way, by which the hero-sons of *Wœtla* were supposed to march across the sky. But it seems really to have been orig. the road N. fr. London to VERULAM or Wætling cæster. *Cf.* M'Clure (pp. 40-41), and next. For Street, *cf.* Birchley Street (Atherstone), *a.* 1300 Birchelei stret. In W. it is *Hynt St. Ialm,* ' St. James's Way.' See Duignan, s.v., and next.

WATLINGTON (Battle, Wallingford and Downham). Ba. W. *Dom.* Watlingtone, Wa. B. *ib.* Watelintune, in O.E. *chart.* Wæclinctune, Hwætlinga tune, Wætlinc-, Wætlingtune. ' Town of the *Wat-lings.'* See above and *cf. Dom.* Watelintune (Berks) and Watlingeseta (Norfk.). Who *Wœtla* or *Watla* really was is quite unknown. This is evidently a patronymic. See -ing.

WATTLESBOROUGH (Wroxeter). It stands on WATLING STREET. See -borough.

WATTON (3 in *P.G.*). Yorks W. *Bede* Wetadun, O.E. for ' wet hill,' *Dom.* Wattune, Waton. But W. Herts is *K.C.D.* vi. 212 Wad-tune, *Dom.* Watone, 1210 Wattone. 'Town of *Wada*' or '*Wade*,' still a common surname. *Cf.* WATFORD.

WAUN. See GWAUN. WAWNE (Hull), not in *Dom.*, must be the same.

WAVENDON (Woburn Sands). *Dom.* Wauuendone. 'Hill of *Waga, Wagan*' or '*Vagan*,' all names in *Onom.* See -don.

WAVENEY R. (S. Norfolk). As rivers are nearly all Kelt. this is prob. a form of W. *afon*, 'river,' pron. as in Stratford-on-Avon, with the Eng. ending -ey. For a somewhat similar prefixing of *w, cf.* WEMYSS (Sc.), from G. *uamh;* also Wodin and Odin, and our pron. of *one*.

WAVER R. (Cumberld.). *c.* 1080 Wafyr. ? fr. W. *gwefr*, 'amber,' fr. its colour; but prob. O.E. *wœfre*, 'wandering, restless.'

WAVERLEY (on R. Wey, Farnham). 1155 *Pipe* Wauerle. Abbey founded here 1128. WEY *might* be contract. of WAVER (*q.v.*) and -ley. There is also possible O.E. *wœferlice*, 'belonging to theatres,' though one would need evidence to vote for such an origin. More likely is the supposed O.E. *wœfre*, 'the aspen-poplar.' See WAVERTREE. There are also 2 Wavertons (Chesh. and Cumbld.). and see WARTON.

WAVERTREE (Liverpool). Pron. Wartree. *Dom.* Wauretreu (Chesh.), O.E. *wœfre*, 'restless.' This must refer to some trembling tree like the aspen. Duignan holds that there must be an O.E. *wœfre*, 'the aspen poplar.' *Cf.* above.

WEAR R. and WEARMOUTH (Durham). *Bede* Were, *c.* 800 *Hist. St. Cuthbt.* Wirra. Possibly *c.* 150 *Ptolemy* Οὐέδρα; also *Bede* Viurae muda or Wiremuth, *a.* 1130 *Sim. Dur.* Weremuthe, Giuramuthe. M'Clure connects with Kelt. *gyrwe*, 'fen, marsh,' and with JARROW. This is uncertain. In 1160-61 *Pipe* Nthbld. is a Werewurda, ? 'farm of a man called *Weir*.' See -worth.

WEAVER R. and WEAVERHAM (Cheshire). *Dom.* Wevre, Wivre, Wivreham. The root must be Keltic; perh. W. *gwyf*, 'that yields, is smooth, is drawn out,' hence *gwyfr*, 'a wire'; possibly W. *gwefr*, 'amber,' fr. the colour of the water. *Cf.* WAVER and WYRE. See -ham.

WEAVERTHORPE (York). *Dom.* Wilfretorp, Wifretorp, 1206 Wyuer-torp. 'Village of *Wiferth*,' var. of *Wilfrith*, a very common O.E. name. See -thorpe.

WEDMORE (Weston-s.-M.). *Sic* in *Dom.*, but O.E. *Chron.* 878 Weðmor. 'Moor of the agreement or pledge,' O.E. *wedd-mór*. A treaty was signed here in 878. *Cf.* wedder and wether and wadset in Sc.

WEDNESBURY and WEDNESFIELD (Wolvermptn.). (? *O.E. Chron.* 592 and 715 Wodnesbeorge, -beorh, -byri; *cf.* WANBOROUGH); *Dom.* Wadnesberie, *a.* 1200 Wodnesbyrg, -beri, Wodenesbeorh. 994 and *Dom.* Wodnesfeld. 'Burgh, fort' and 'field of the god *Woden'* (Ger.) or *'Odin'* (N.). There is said to have been a temple of Woden at Wednesbury. See -bury.

WEEFORD (Lichfield) (*Dom.* and *later* Weforde) and WEETON (Leeds) (*Dom.* Widetun). The North and Sc. *wee* is late, and not to be thought of. Both are fr. O.E. *wid* (pron. weed), 'wide'; the *d* was bound to disappear before *f* and *t*. Wideton, in *Dom.* Yorks, also represents WEIGHTON and Wyton (E. Riding), where *wíd* has taken on its mod. pron. wyde, our 'wide.'

WEEK St. Germans and St. Pancras (Devonsh.) and St. Mary (Bude). Perh. *a.* 800 *chart.* East and West Wixna (Devonsh.). Corn. *gweek,* fr. L. *vicus,* 'a town, village,' O.E. *wíc,* 'a dwelling.' See St. GERMANS and St. PANCRAS.

WEIGHTON (E. Yorks). Little W. is *Dom.* Widetone, O.E. *wíd tun,* 'wide village.' *Cf.* WEETON. But 'Widetona' (W. Riding) is now WIDDINGTON, and WEIGHTON MARKET is *Dom.* Wicstun, '*Wicga*'s or *Wyga*'s village'; it is now pron. Weeton.

WELBOURN or -BURN (Lincs and Yorks). Lin. W. *O.E. Chron.* 675 (late MS.) Wætelleburne—*i.e.,* 'burn, brook of *Weatla*'; one in *Onom. Cf.* WATLING ST. But W. Yorks, *Dom.* Wellebrune, is 'brook which comes out of a spring'; *well* has this meaning. See -bourn. *Cf.* WELBECK (Worksop), 1189 Wellebec, 1290 Welbec.

WELDON (Kettering). 1363 *chart.* Weldone. O.E. *wella-dún,* 'well hill.' Similar is WELBURY (Northallerton), *Dom.* Welleberge. See -bury.

WELFORD (on Lambourn, Bucks). 949 *chart.* Weligforda, *c.* 1540 Welleford. 'Ford at the willows,' O.E. *welig. Cf.* SALFORD, which also means 'willow ford.' But WELFORD (Stratford-on-A.) is *Dom.* Welleford, *a.* 1200 Walleford, 1221 Welneforde; prob. 'ford of the Welsh.' See WALES.

WELHAM (Mket. Harboro', E. Retford, and New Malton). Ret. and Mal. W. *Dom.* Wellon, -un, O.E. loc. 'at the wells.' But M. Har. W. *Dom.* Welehā, prob. 'home of *Wale*' or '*Wealh*'; several in *Onom. Cf.* WALES. See -ham.

WELLAND R. (Northants). 921 *O.E. Chron.* Weolud, which looks like W. *gwælod,* 'base, bottom.' The -ud has now been nasalized into -and. But WELLAND (Upton-on-Severn) is 1196 Weneland, 1297 Wenlond, 1461 Wenelond. 'Land of *Wenna.*' *Cf.* WALLINGWELLS.

WELLESBOURNE (Warwick). 862 *chart.* Welesburn, *Dom.* Waleborne. Doubtful. Duignan prefers, 'brook of the stranger, serf, or Welshman,' O.E. *wealh,* dat. *wale. Cf.* WALCOT, and see -bourne.

WELLINGBORO', WELLINGORE (Lincoln), and WELLINGTON (Hereford). 1154-61 *chart.* Wellingoura, *c.* 1030 *chart.* Weolintun. The Welling- will prob. represent the same name as in WAL-

LINGFORD. The ending -gore or -ore may either be O.E. *gára*, 4 *goore*, 4-9 *gore*, ' a triangular or wedge-shaped piece of land at the side of a field ' (*cf.* Kensington Gore), or fr. O.E. *ora*, ' edge, brink, border.' See -boro'.

WELLOW (Newark, Bath, and Yarmouth I.W.). Bath W. *Dom.* Wilege, Yar. W. *Dom.* Welige, O.E. *welig, wilig,* ' a willow-tree ' here prob. in loc. But W. (Newark) 1278 Welhagh, 1302 -hawe, is prob. *well-haugh.* See HAUGHTON.

WELLS (Somerset and Norfolk). Som. W. 1087 *O.E. Chron.* Wellensis æcclesia, 1231 Welles. Nor. W. *a.* 1200 Welle, 1298 Wells. O.E. *wella.* ' a spring, a well,' with mod. Eng. plur. Som. W. was founded in A.D. 704, and called from 3 springs in the garden of the bishop's palace.

WELNEY (Wisbech). O.E. *wellan ig,* ' isle of the well or spring.'

WELSHPOOL. *c.* 1530 *Rolls Papers,* ' the Welshe poole.' On the adj. Welsh, O.E. *wylisc,* see WALES. It is said to have been called Welshpool to distinguish it fr. Poole (Dorset). The W. name is Trallwm, whose traditional meaning, ' the greedy swallow,' seems very doubtful.

WELTON (Lincoln; 7 in *P.G.*). *Dom.* Welleton, ' village by the well.' *Cf.* WELHAM. Welleton occurs 10 times in *Dom.* Yorks.

WELWYN (Herts). O.E. *chart.* On Weligun—*i.e.,* ' at the willows,' a loc. *Cf.* HALLAM, KILHAM, etc., and WELLOW.

WEM (Shrewsbury). *Dom.* Weme. O.E. *wenn,* ' a swelling, a wart, a wen '; often in 14th cny. *wem—m* and *n* readily interchange.

WEMBURY (Plymouth). 951 *O.E. Chron.* Wicgan beorge, *c.* 1120 *Hen. Hunt.* Wienbeorhe. ' Burgh of *Wicga* '; several in *Onom.* *Cf. K.C.D.* 1296 Wicgan dic. There is a ' Weneberge ' in *Dom.* Surrey.

WENDLEBURY (Bicester), *Dom.* Wandesberie, 1216-1307 Wendebur, Wendlebur, 1274-79 Wendelbur, and WENDLING (Dereham), *Dom.* Wenlingā. Said to be fr. the *Vandals,* a doubtful statement. The name *Wendel,* and other such as *Wendelburh,* are to be found in *Onom.,* so that connexion with the Vandals could at most be indirect. The -ing is the sign of a patronymic. See WANDSWORTH, WINDSOR, and -bury.

WENDON or WANDON (Northbld.). *c.* 1300 *Egilsaga* Vinheide (-heide is O.N. *heið-r,* ' a heath '); also Weondun, which seems to be O.E. *Weohhan dún,* ' hill of *Weohha* ' or ' *Wehha* '; 1 in *Onom.*

WENDOVER (Bucks). *K.C.D.* 593 Wændofron, *Dom.* Wendovre, 1155 *Pipe* Wendoura. *Cf.* 958 *chart.* Windofere, near R. Stour (Staffd.). O.W. *gwen dubr,* mod. W. *gwyn dwfr,* ' clear river.' *Cf.* ANDOVER, DOVER, etc., also DEVERON (Sc.). Connexion with the *Wends* (see WINDSOR) is very unlikely.

WENDY (Royston, Herts.). *c.* 1080 Wendeie, *Dom.* Wandei, Wandrie; 1316 Wendye. ' Isle of *Wenda.*' *Cf. a.* 1199 ' Wend ' (Norfk.) in *Roll. Rich. I.* This may refer to a *Wendish* settler. *Cf.* WANDSWORTH. See -ey.

WENLAS R. W. *gwen glas,* ' white ' or ' fair stream.'

WENLOCK, MUCH and LITTLE (Salop). *Dom.* Wenloch, *a.* 1163 Wenlock. W. *gwen llwch,* ' clear lake ' or ' pool.' But in W. it is Llan Meilien, ' church of St. Milburga,' or simply Llane. On this use of Much, see *Oxf. Dict.,* s.v.

WENNINGTON (Lancaster and Rainham, Essex). La. W. *Dom.* Wininctune, Ra. W. 961 *chart.* Winintune. ' Town, village of the *Winings,*' or ' sons of *Wine.*' *Cf. Dom.* Sussex, Venningore, and Wen-, Wincote (Glouc.), *Dom.* Wenecote, 1175-76 Winecota, ' cot of *Wine* ' or ' *Wynna.*'

WENSLEY (Leyburn, Blackburn, Matlock). Le. W. *Dom.* Wendreslaga, Wentreslage; 1204 Wandeslei. Not in W. and H. The name here is uncertain; it may be that of *Wendretha,* saint and virgin, but more old forms needed. *Cf.* 1223 *Patent R.* Wandleslegh (Notts), and *Dom.* Bucks Weneslai (prob. fr. *Wenna* or *Wenni* in *Onom.*). See -ley.

WENSUM R. (Yarmouth). *Cf. Bede* Wantsumu, Thanet. M'Clure thinks this is a Teutonic *want* or *went,* ' a way,' common in dial., and -sonu a qualifying adj., as in winsome, etc. *Cf.* next.

WENTBRIDGE (Pontefract). *Went,* ' a way or a ford '; see above. But WENTWORTH (Cambs and Rotherham) is Cam. W. *Dom.* Winteworde, 1291 Wynteworth, ' farm of *Winta,*' in *Onom.* But Ro. W. is *Dom.* Wintre-, Winteworde. ' Farm of the man *Winter.*' *Cf.* WINTERINGHAM. See -worth.

WENTNOR (Bp.'s Castle, Salop). *Dom.* Wantenoure. ' Bank, brink, edge,' O.E. *ofer, obr;* M.E. *overe,* ' of *Want*'; 1 in *Onom.* Also *cf.* VENTNOR.

WENVOE (Cardiff). Said to be Norm. corrup. of W. *gwyn fa,* ' blessed place '; *gwyn, gwen* orig. means ' white, clear,' and Gwynfa is now popular W. for ' Paradise.' The -voe rather suggests Norse influence, it being Norse Eng. for ' bay '; O.N. *vag-r,* Icel. *vö-r. Cf.* Van Rouget, Jersey.

WERGS, The (Wolverhmptn.). *a.* 1300 Wytheges, *a.* 1400 Wytheges, Withegges, Wyrges. ' Wythy hedges,' fr. O.E. *withig,* ' a willow,' and *hecg*(e), ' a hedge.' A curious corruption. *Dom.* Hants Wergeborne is prob. fr. a man. *Cf.* O.E. *dweorg, duerg,* ' dwarf.'

WERNETH (Stockport and Oldham). St. W. *Dom.* Warnet. Old W. 1558-59 Wyernyth, 1572 Wyreneth. Perh. ' place of alders '; W. *gwern,* old pl. *gwernedd.* Same root common in Sc. names as FEARN.

WERRINGTON (Peterboro' and Stoke-on-T.). Prob. ' village of a man *Wera.*' *Cf. Dom.* Bucks Verendone: and see -ing and -ton.

Werwick. c. 380 *Ant. Itin.* Viroviacum. Doubtful. Wer- might be W. *gwyr,* ' pure, fresh.' *Cf.* Warwick and Winwick, and above; also Wervin (Chesh.). ? *Dom.* Wiveorene, 1387 *chart.* Wyrvyn, a puzzling name. See -wick.

Wesenham Heath (Norfk.). *Dom.* and 1245 Wesenham. ' Home of *Wesa* '; not in *Onom.,* but *cf.* Wessington (Alfreton).

Wesham (Preston). 1235 Westhus, 1262 Westesham, 1524 Wessom. It has varied between O.E. *west hús* and *west hám,* both meaning ' west house ' or ' home.' *Cf. Dom.* Wesberie (Salop). There is an unidentified ' Westhuse ' in *Dom.* Yorks, near Maunby.

Westbury (Bucks, Glouc., and Wilts). Glo. W. 793-96 Uuestburg, Wil. W. 794 Westbyri, 1053 *O.E. Chron.* Wæstbyrig, *Dom.* Bucks and Wilts Westberie. ' West burgh ' or ' town.' *Cf. Dom.* Wesberie (Salop).

Westcote (Chipping Norton) and **Westcott** (Dorking and Ayles- bury). Dor. W. *Dom.* Wescote. *Cf.* 1179-80 *Pipe* Westcotun (Yorks), the latter a loc. ' West cots ' or ' huts.'

Westerdale (Grosmont, Yorks). 1179-80 Westerdale. ' Western dale '; Icel. *vestr.,* ' the West.' *Cf.* Westerdale (Caithness).

Westminster. 1040 *O.E. Chron.* Westmynstre, *Dom.* abbas West- monasteriensis. This means the *minster* or abbey church West of London. See -minster.

Westmorland. 966 *O.E. Chron.* (MS. of ? *a.* 1200) Westmoringa- land, ' land of the dwellers in Westmor ' (see *infra*), as yet only the barony of Appleby; 1131 *Pipe* Westmarieland, *c.* 1175 *Fantosme* Westmari(e)lande, 1194 *Hoveden* Westmerilande, 1200 Westmerland (often later Westmari-), 1461 Westmurland. Prob. not ' west moor land,' but ' land on the West border of England,' the land to the W. of this not being English till late. O.E. *(ge)mǽre,* ' boundary, border.'

Weston (33 in *P.G.*). In *Dom.* always Weston(e). ' West town ' or ' village.' *Dom.* Bucks, Westone = W. Turville.

Weston-under-Lizard (Shifnal). *Dom.* Westone, *a.* 1400 Weston- under-Lusyerd, *a.* 1500 Weston-subtus-Luceyord. Lizard is *a.* 1100 Lusgerd, *a.* 1200 Luseiard, *a.* 1300 Lusyard. Duignan thinks this is *luce-yard* or ' fish-pond '; only *luce,* ' a pike,' O.Fr. *lus, luis,* is not found in Eng. *a.* 1338. *Lizard,* the animal, is not found till 1377, but then as *lusarde,* O.Fr. *lesarde,* L. *lacerta.* It is not likely to be the origin. It might be *louse-yard,* ' court- yard full of lice '! O.E. *lús, luus,* 3 *luse.*

Westow (York). Not in *Dom.* Said to be O.E. *wíf-stow,* ' woman's place.' ' Wifestede,' in *Dom.* Yorks, is now Winstead.

West Thurrock (Grays). *c.* 1460 Westthirrok. ' Thurrock ' is O.E. *þurruc,* ' a small ship (?), the bottom of a ship, the bilge.' Hence it comes to mean, as it does still in several county dialects, ' a heap, esp. of mud.' In Kent it means ' a covered drain.'

WETHERAL (Carlisle) and WETHERBY (Tadcaster). c. 1120 Weder-
hal, *Dom.* Wedrebi. ' Hall ' and ' dwelling among the *wethers*
or rams.' O.E. *wether*, Sc. *wedder*. Cf. WEDDERBURN (Sc.).
Or else *Wedr* may be a man's name, as in next. Skeat prefers
the ' sheep ' origin for WETHERLEY (Cambs), c. 1080 *Inquis.*
Camb. Wederlai, Weðerlai; *Dom.* Wederlai; 1166 Wederleah;
1284 Wetherle.

WETHERINGSETT (Stowmarket). *K.C.D.* 907, 932 Wederinge sete.
Cf. 1298 ' Johannes de Wethering'ton.' ' Seat, abode of the
descendants of *Wedr.*' Cf. above.

WETWANG (York). *Dom.* Wetwangham. Curious name. O.N.
voett or *vett vang-r*, used in Iceland for ' place of summons,' fr.
vett-r or *voetti*, ' a witness,' and *vang-r*, ' a field.' The -ham
rarely drops off; but perh., as *hám* is O.E., it never should have
been on. Cf. Lingwang, ' heather field,' *sic* in Notts *chart.*,
c. 1160, and Goldswong Terrace, Nottingham.

WETWOOD (Eccleshall, Staffs). 1298 Wetwude. O.E. *wæt wudu*,
' wet wood.' But Wetmoor (Burton) is *a.* 1100 Withmere or
' withy lake.' Cf. Westwood (Yorks), *Dom.* Westude.

WEY R. (Surrey). *a.* 675 *Grant* Waiemuþe, where it joins the
Thames (late MS.). Kelt. *gwy*, ' river,' esp. a slow-flowing one.
Cf. WYE and Suthld. G. *uidh*, ' slow-flowing water.' Also
WEYBRIDGE, *a.* 675 Waigebrugge, 727 *chart.* Weibrugge, *Dom.*
Webruge. Cf. WEYMOUTH. This Wey may also have con-
nexion with the *waga*, ' deep waters ' of the *O.E. Glosses, a.* 900;
and the O.E. and Kelt. words may be cognate.

WEYMOUTH. c. 1450 *Fortescue* the Weymouthe. There is another
little R. WEY here.

WHADDON (Cambs, Bletchley, and Glouc.). Ca. W. c. 1080 *Inquis.*
Camb. Phwaddune, *Dom.* Wadone, -dune; 1210 Waddon; 1302
Whaddone. Gl. W. *Dom.* Wadune, 1221 Waddone. O.E.
hwǽte dún, ' wheat hill.' Cf. WADDON and WHATCOMB and
Whatton (Nottingham), *Dom.* Watone.

WHALLEY (Blackburn). *O.E. Chron.* 798 Hwælleage, Hweallæg;
Dom. Wallei; c. 1120 *Hen. Hunt* Wellehaie; *a.* 1400 Whalleye;
a. 1130 *Sim. Dur.* Walalege. Prob. ' whale island '; O.E. *hwæl*,
O.N. *hval-r*, or rather ' marshy region called after *Whale.*' But
how comes such a name here ? Prob. ' whale ' was the name of
a man, a viking. Two *Hwalas* in *Onom.;* there is also a Whaley
Br. (Stockport). W. and H. prefer to derive fr. O.N. *hwall*, ' a
hill.' But it is to be remembered that *whale* can certainly
become *whall* on Northern tongues. O.N. *hwall* is a very rare
word. See -ey.

WHAPLODE (Holbeach, Lincs). 810 *chart.* Cappelad, 1236 Quappelode, c. 1275 Quappelade. There is one *Cape*, but no other name
likely in *Onom.*, and it is hard to see how the name could be fr.
O.E. *cæppe*, ' cap, cope.' There is an O. Du. *quappa*, ' a toad,'

a possible origin. Aspirated *c* often turns to *wh*- in Gaelic place-names. *Cf.* COLQUHOUN, DALQUHARRAN, DALWHINNIE, etc., in Sc. The -lode is O.E. *lád*, ' a lode, a canal, a waterway, a lead '; in Sc. ' lade.'

WHARFE R. and WHARFEDALE (Yorks). *a.* 1130 *Sim. Dur.* Hwerf, Hwerverdale (-er shows a gen.). Prob. Icel. *hvarf*, ' a turning, a shelter '; O.E. *hweorfan*, ' to turn.' *Cf.* QUARFF (Sc.).

WHARRAM (York). *Dom.* Warron, -an; 1199 Warham. *Warron* seems to be loc. of O.E. *wær*, ' a weir,' ' at the weirs.' *Cf.* WARFIELD and HALLAM; and see -ham.

WHATCOMB or WATCUMBE (Berks). *Dom.* Watecumbe, O.E. *hwæte cumb*, ' wheat valley.' *Cf.* WHATCOTE (Kineton), *Dom.* Quater- cote (error), 1183 Quatcote, 1301 Wathcote (perh. fr. a man), Whatfield (Suffk.), and Whetecombe (Dorset), also WADDON and WHADDON.

WHATLEY (Frome). ' Wheat meadow.' *Cf. Dom.* Essex Wateleia, Whateley Hall, Cas. Bromwich, 1278 Wateley, Wheatley (Tam- worth), *a.* 1600 Whateley, and Wheatley (Doncaster and Notts), *Dom.* Watelage and Wateleia. But Wheatenhurst (Glouc.), *Dom.* Witenher(s)te, is ' wood of *Hwita*,' gen. -*an*.

WHEAL (common in Cornwall). Corn. *huêl*, ' a mine,' or, at times, *gwel*, ' a field.' There is a ' Hvele ' in *Dom.* Salop, and R. WHEELOCK (Sandbach) may be the same root, or at any rate Keltic, the -lock being perh. W. *llwch*, ' a lake, a pool.'

WHELDRAKE (York). *Dom.* Coldrid (3 times). *Dom.*'s form prob. means ' cold ' or ' cool stream '; O.E. *cól ríth*. The *th* has become *d* also in COTTERED, RYDE, etc, and it is quite in accord with rule for *c* to aspirate and become *wh*. *Cf.* WHAPLODE. WHELDALE (W. Riding) is *Dom.* Queldale (*qu = w*), fr. O.E. *ceald, cald*, ' cold.' But the present ending -drake needs more old forms to explain it.

WHENBY (Easingwold). *Dom.* Quennebi, 1202 Quenebi. ' The woman's house '; O.N. *kvenna*, ' a woman, a quean.' See -by.

WHERNSIDE (W. Yorks). Hybrid. W. *gwern*, ' plain, moor.' On -side, see AMBLESIDE.

WHERWELL (Hants). 1048 *O.E. Chron.* to Hwerwillon (*loc.*), *c.* 1145 *Wm. Malmes.* Werewelle. O.E. *hwer-willa*, ' pot or cauldron well.'

WHICHFORD (Shipton-on-Stour). 1128 Wicheford. ' Ford of the wych '; O.E. *wice*, M.E. *wiche*, prob. ' the wych elm ' or ' hazel.' *Cf.* WICHFORD and WYCHWOOD. But WHICHCOTE (Wootton Bassett) is *old* Wykles-, Wikeles-, Wyghelscote. ' Cot, cottage of *Wicel*,' a name not in *Onom.*, perh. contraction of *Wichelm* or *Wichelinus*, known forms.

WHICKHAM (Swalwell, Durham). 1183 Quykham. Fr. O.E. *cwicu*, 1-3 *cwic*, 3-6 *quik, quyk*, 5 *whik, whyk*, lit. ' living, endowed with life,' but here in sense 2, *Oxf. Dict.*, ' consisting of animals, livestock,' as in ' quick stock,' ' quick goods,' etc., found fr. O.E. on to 18th cny. O.E. *hám* must here mean ' farm.' See -ham.

WHINLATTER (hill, Bassenthwaite). W. *gwyn llethr* (G. *leitir*), ' fair, clear slope.' *Cf*. DULLATUR (Sc.) and all the Ir. names in Letter-. **WHINFELL** (Shap), *sic* in 1203 *chart.*, is prob. fr. the common name *Wine*. *Whin*, the rock, is late. See -fell.

WHIPPINGHAM (Newport, I. of W.). *Dom*. Wipingeham. ' Home of the descendants of *Wippa* '; 1 in *Onom*. *Cf*. WHIPLEY in Clint, *Dom*. Wipeleie. See -ing and -ham.

WHISSENDINE (Oakham). *c.* 1230 *Rob. Grossesteste* Wissenden. ' The dean of ' prob. ' *Hwithyse*,' the nearest name in *Onom*., and common there. The -dine or -den will be O.E. *denu*, M.E. *dene*, *dane*, ' a valley deep and wooded.'

WHISTLEY (Reading). *B.C.S.* iii. 511 Wiscelea, *c.* 1130 *Chron. Abing*. Wisseleia, Wischeleia; *c.* 1400 Wirselay. Skeat says ' meadow lea '; E. Fries. *wiske*, ' a small meadow '; Ger. *wiese*, ' a meadow '; in Eng. usage, moist or low-lying. *Cf*. WISHFORD.

WHISTON (Worstrsh., Penkridge, Cheadle, Prescot, Rotherham). Pe. W. 1004 *chart*. Witestun, *Dom*. Witestone; Wo. W. 1262 Wytstan, Wystan, *a.* 1400 Wyston, Whiston; Che. W. *Dom*. Witestone; Pr. W. 1190-1292 Quistan, 1385 Whistane; Ro. W. *Dom*. Widestan, Widestha'. Perh. all O.E. *hwit stan*, ' white stone ' or ' rock '; though some may be ' town of *Hwit* '—*i.e.*, the white man—and Widestan looks like ' wide, broad stone.'

WHITACRE, Over and Nether (Coleshill), *Dom*. Witacre (also *sic* in Nthants), *a.* 1300 Wythacre, Wytacer, *a.* 1400 Whitacre, is either ' white (O.E. *hwit*) field,' or ' withy field '; O.E. *withig*, ' a willow ' or ' withe.' But 1289 contin. *Gervase* Whetekre, prob. in Hants, is ' wheat-field '; O.E. *hwæte*. *Acre* is adopt. of L. *ager*, ' field.' *Cf*. Birkacre (Chorley), WHATCOMB, Wetmoor (Burton), *a.* 1100 Withmere, etc.

WHITBY. *Dom*. and *a.* 1130 *Sim. Dur*. Witebi, 1298 Wythby. ' Dwelling of *Hwita*.' *Cf. B.C.S.* 724 Hwitan beorh. But in *Bede* Streonshalh, Streoneshalch—*i.e.*, it is said—' sinus fari,' ' bay of the lighthouse.' Streonshalh suggests a G. *sròn shealg*, ' nose, point of the hunt.' See -by.

WHITCHURCH (12 in *P.G.*). 1001 *O.E. Chron*. Hwitciricea, ? Hants, *Dom*. Warwk. Witecerce, 1326 Whitcherche, 1166-67 *Pipe* Devon Wicherche. In *Tax. Eccl*. Album Monasterium is the name of several Whitchurches. ' White church.' *Cf*. WHITFORD (Surrey), *Dom*. Witford, and Whitkirk (W. Riding).

WHITEHAVEN. *Sic* 1300. From O.E. *hæfen*, O.N. *höfu*, ' a haven, harbour, 'or ' sheltered inlet of the sea.' The ending is rare in Eng., and prob. denotes Norse influence. *Cf*. MILFORD HAVEN and STONEHAVEN (Sc.). The name seems sometimes to have been contracted into Whitton.

WHITEWELL (Dore, Sheffd.).   942 *O.E. Chron.* Hwitan Wylles geat.
The *Hwita* or ' White ' here is prob. a man.   *Cf.* WHITBY.   There
is another Whitewell Bottom (Manchester), whilst *P.G.* has 5
WHITWELLS, or ' white wells,' *Dom.* Yorks Witeuella, etc.

WHITLAND Abbey (Caermarthensh.).   *c.* 1190 *Gir. Camb.* Alba
Landa, or ' white land.'   Its old W. name was BANGOR y Ty
Gwyn ar Dāv, or ' Bangor of the White House on the R. Taff.'

WHITLEY (S. Northbld., 2 in York, and 2 in Warwk.).   Nor. W.
1322 Whiteley; Yo. W. *Dom.* Witelaia; War. W. *Dom.* Witeleia,
1376 Whyteleie.   ' White meadow.'   See -ley.

WHITMINSTER (Stonehouse).   *c.* 1188 *Gir. Camb.* Album monasterium.   ' White abbey ' or ' abbey church.'   See -minster.

WHITMORE (Newcastle-under-L.).   *Dom.* Witemore, 1242 Wyte-
more.   ' White moor '; O.E. *hwit mór.*

WHITNASH (Leamington).   *Dom.* Witenas, 1327 Whitenasshe.
' White ' or ' whiten ash-tree '; O.E. *hwit,* in dat. *-an.*   ' Ash '
is O.E. *œsc.*

WHITSTABLE (Kent).   *Dom.* Witenestaple.   ' Market of *Wita,*' or
' the wise,' gen. pl. *witena.*   *Cf.* BARNSTAPLE and Witenagemot.

WHITSUNBROOK (Worc.).   *K.C.D.* 570 Wixenabróc.   Prob. ' brook
of the *Huiccii.*'   See WORCESTER.   *Wicga* is a very common
name in *Onom.*   It is a curious corruption.

WHITTINGHAM (Alnwick and Preston).   Pr. W. *Dom.* Witingheham,
Witingha; *Sim. Dur.* ann. 883 Hwitingaham (? that near N.
Berwick); Al. W. 1160-61 *Pipe* Witingehā.   ' Home of the
Whitings ' or ' sons of White ' or ' *Hwita* '—*i.e.,* the white man.
There is one Hwiting, found in Kent and Wessex, in *Onom.*   *Cf.*
WHITTINGHAM (Sc.) and *Dom.* Salop Witentrei, and next.   WHIT-
TINGE (Hartlebury), 1325 Whyteling, *may* mean ' white heather,'
as Duignan thinks.   Prob. it is a patronymic fr. *Witulf* or *Wit-
beald,* or some such name.   See -ing.

WHITTINGTON (8 in *P.G.*).   Carnforth, Gloucester, and Oswestry W.
Dom. Witetone; Lichfield W., 925 *chart.* Hwitantone, -tune;
Stourbridge W. *a.* 1300 Whytynton, Whitenton.   ' Town of
Hwita, Wita,' or ' *Witta* '—*i.e.,* the white man.   *Cf.* above and
-ing.

WHITTLEBURY (Towcester).   Not in *Dom.*   1284 *Close R.* Wytle-
bery.   ' Burgh of *Witla.*'   See next and -bury.

WHITTLESEAMERE (now drained).   *O.E. Chron.* 657 (late MS.)
Witlesmere.   ' Lake of *Witla,*' a name not in *Onom.*   *Cf. K.C.D.*
iii. 101 Insulam quae Witlesig nuncupatur, now WHITTLESEA
(Peterboro'), *c.* 1080 Witleseie, *Dom.* Witesie, 1394 Witleseye.
The *Witla* or *Witol* may be fr. O.E. *witol,* ' wise,' or else short
for *Witwulf.*   *Cf.,* too, WHITTLESFORD (Cambridge), *Dom.*
Witelesford.

WHITTON (3 in *P.G.*). Perh. 1156 *Pipe* Wihtuna (Yorks) may be Whitton (Doncaster). There is one *Wiht* in *Onom.* But these names should prob. all be ' white town.' *Cf.* WHITCHURCH, etc.

WHITWELL (5 in *P.G.*). *Dom.* Norfk. Witewell, Yorks Witeuella. O.E. *hwit wella,* ' the white well.'

WHITWORTH (Rochdale and Co. Durham). Dur. W. 1183 Whit-wortha. O.E. *hwit worth,* ' white-looking farm.'

WHIXLEY (York). *Dom.* Crucheslaga, Cucheslaga (twice); 1281 *Close R.* Quixeley; *c.* 1300 Quixley (*qu* = *w*). ' Meadow of ' prob. ' *Cuca* ' ; one in *Onom.* On aspirated *c* = *wh, cf.* WHAPLODE; and see -ley.

WHORLTON (Barnard Cas.). *Dom.* Wirveltun, 1202 Wher-, Whor-uelton. Obscure. Perh. fr. a man *Wernweald* or *Wernwulf,* names in *Onom.*

WIBSEY (Bradford) (*Dom.* Wibetese) and WIBTOFT (Lutterworth) (1004 Wibbetoft, *Dom.* Wibetot). ' Isle ' and ' farm of ' prob. not *Wibba* but ' *Wigbeorht, Wihtbeorht,* or *Wibert,*' all forms in *Onom. ; r* readily disappears. See -ey and -toft.

WICAUGH (Malpas). *Old* Wichenhalgh, *later* Wycough. ' Haugh, river-meadow,' O.E. *halech, halh,* of some kind of tree, O.E. *wice,* M.E. *wiche, wyche.* *Cf.* the wych elm and hazel; or else, ' of *Wicga,*' a common name in *Onom.* WICHENFORD (Wor-cester) being 1007 *chart.* Wiceneford, confirms derivation fr. *wice,* ' ford of the wych elms.'

WICHFORD (Ely). *a.* 1200 Wycheford. See above. Possibly fr. O.E. *wicce,* ' a witch '; but *cf.* WHICHFORD. Whilst WICHNOR (Lichfield), *a.* 1100 Hwiccen ofre, *Dom.* Wicenore, *a.* 1200 Whichnore, Wytchnor, *a.* 1300 Wychenovere, is prob. ' bank, edge of the hutch,' O.E. *hwiccen ofr* or *ofer,* where *hutch* is not the same as, but is often confused with, the O.E. *hwicce,* M.E. *whicche,* mod. dial. *whitch.* *Cf.* EDENSOR. There was also a tribe *Huiccii* (see WORCESTER), from which prob. comes WICH-BOLD (Droitwich), 692 *chart.* Uuicbold, or ' house, royal dwell-ing of the *Huiccii.*'

WICK (Littlehampton, Pershore, Bristol, Cowbridge). *Dom.* Wiche, Wicha, *passim.* Like Wyck (Rissington, Glouc.) and WYKE, prob. all the Eng. names are O.E. *wic,* ' dwelling, village,' L. *vicus,* not N. like the Sc. WICK, ' a bay,' and the Jersey Vicqs. The Cow. W. is said to be orig. W. *y wig fawr,* ' the great wood ' or ' thicket.' Similar is WICWER (Denbigh). See -wick.

WICKEN (Soham and Stony Stratford). So. W. 1210 and 1284 Wykes, 1395 Wykyne. Wykes is M.E. pl. of O.E. *wic,* ' dwell-ing, village,' and form 1395 is a M.E. loc. for O.E. *wicum,* ' at the villages.' But in some cases, and in Wykin (Coventry), *a.* 1300 Wykene, the name may be = *quicken* sb[1], *Oxf. Dict.,* found fr. 1387, in 6 *whicken,* 9 *wicken, wiggin,* ' the rowan or mountain ash.' *Cf.* ROWANTREE (Sc.).

WICKENBY (Lincoln). *Cf.* 605 *chart.* Wycingesmarce (? near Canterbury). ' Dwelling of *Wicing,*' 3 in *Onom.,* prob. same word as *viking,* O.E. *wicing,* ' a sea-rover.' *Cf.* WIGANTHORPE, *Dom.* Bucks Wichendone, and above.

WICKERSLEY (Rotherham). *Dom.* Wincreslei, Wicresleia. ' Mead of *Wingœr* or *Winegœr.*' See -ley.

WICKFORD (Essex). *Dom.* Wicfort, later Wykeford. Either fr. O.E. *wic,* ' village,' as next, or fr. a man *Wicga* or *Wyga ;* prob. the former, as we have Wicford in *Dom.* Salop.

WICKHAM (Berks, Hants, Herts, Banbury) (Be. W. *B.C.S.* i. 506 and 1154-58 Wicham) and West WICKHAM (Cambs) (*K.C.D.* vi. 98 Wicham). Skeat in his *Berks,* but not in his *Cambs,* says this name is also in *chart.* Wichamm. Either ' village enclosure ' or ' village home.' See -ham and -wick. WICKHAMBREAUX (Canterbury) is *chart.* Wichæma. *Cf. Dom.* Norfk. Wichhātun and WYKEHAM. However, CHILD'S WICKHAM is different, and WICKHAM FORD (Evesham), near by, is 709 Wicwon, 792 Wigwenn; *K.C.D.* iii. 396 on Wicweoniga, *Dom.* Wiquene, 1275 Wike Waneford, 1332 Wykewane; a difficult name, which must go with CHILD'S WICKHAM. WICKWAR (Chipp., Sodbury), *Dom.* Wichen, is ' village of John La *Warre,*' to whom K. John gave it.

WICKLEWOOD (Wymondham, Norfk.). *Cf. a.* 1100 Wecelle burne, which cannot have been far away, and *Dom.* Surrey Wachelestede. The name *Wecela* or the like is not in *Onom.,* nor is there anything like it in the *O.E. Dict.*

WIDDINGTON (W. Riding, Newport, Essex). *Dom.* Yorks Widetona. *Cf. Dom.* Glouc. Widindone, and Surrey Wdintone. ' Town of *Wida, Widda,* or *Widia,*' all in *Onom.* It may be a patronymic. But WIDDIAL (Herts) is *Dom.* Widihale, ' withy nook,' O.E. *withig,* Dan. *vidie,* ' a willow, a withe.' See -hall.

WIDECOMBE (Ashburton, Devon). *B.C.S.* 164 Widan cumban, *Wessex chart.* Wídcumb, O.E. *wíd cumb,* ' wide valley.' But WIDFORD (on Windrush). *Dom.* Widiforde, 1231-34 Wythiford, is ' withy ford,' O.E. *withig.*

WIDNES (Liverpool). 1241 - 42 Wydenes, 1256 Wydnes. O.N. *vid-r nœs* (O.E. *wíd nœs*), ' wide nose or ness or promontory.'

WIFOL or WIFORD (Berks). *Dom.* Wiford, which Skeat thinks prob. the orig. name and = O.E. *wic-ford,* ' ford by the village.' *Cf.* WICKHAM. It is not easy to explain the form WIFOL without further old forms, though *r* easily replaces *l.*

WIGAN. 1245 Wygayn, Wigayn; *a.* 1281 Wygan, Wigan. Said commonly to be Kelt. for ' battle, beating, wigging ' ! and to

be the only Kelt. town-name in Lancs, which is nonsense. Freeman thought the very old church of St. Mary le Wigford (Lincs)
was the site of a battle. But the only likely origins in W. are
gwig, ' a grove, a nook, a cove,' or *gwyg*, ' a vetch'; whilst
gwegio is ' to totter, to wag.' The -an or -ayn (*cf.* Gavin and
Gawayne) will be terminational. To derive fr. W. *gwig* is more
likely than to make the name O.E. *Wicgan*, a gen. ' *Wiga*'s '
(Sc. town). This would be abnormal; but *cf.* BEEDON, COVEN,
etc., and the two next, also Waghen (Yorks), *Dom.* Wagene,
1179-80 Wagane. There are 2 men *Wighen* in *Onom.*, 4 called
Wagan, and 1 *Wagene*. More illuminating is WIGANTHORPE
(York), *Dom.* Wichingastorp, ' village of the *Wicings*.' See
WICKENBY. But if Lancs Wigan is for Wicing, a patronymic,
it is once again quite abnormal.

WIGBOROUGH (Somerset). 1408 *chart.* Wiggebeare, which looks
like a tautology, W. *ywig*, ' a grove,' and O.E. *bearo*, ' a wood,'
as in BEER, Conybeare, etc. But if this is *O.E. Chron.* 851
Wicganbeorg, as it may be, then it is ' BARROW of *Wicga*,' a
common name in *Onom.* *Cf.* *Dom.* Essex Wicghebgā, and
Wigwold (Cirencester), *old* Wygewold, ' wold, high moor of
Wicga.' See -boro'.

WIGGINTON (Yorks, Tamworth, Banbury, and Tring). Yo. W.
Dom. Wichistun; Tam. W. *a.* 1100 Wicgintun, *Dom.* Wigetone;
Tr. W. *Dom.* Wigentone, 1303 Wygentone. ' Town, village of
Wicga, -*an*,' common in *Onom.*, which has also 2 *Wighens*.
Cf. WIGGINS HILL (Sutton Coldfield), *a.* 1300 Wygeneshul,
Wiginghul.

WIGGLESWORTH (Long Preston). *Dom.* Wiclesforde and Win-
cheleswrde. ' Farm of *Wincel*.' *Cf.* WINCHELSEA. On the
interchange of ending, see -worth.

WIGHILL (Tadcaster). *Dom.* Wicheles. Doubtful; *Dom.*'s form
may be for ' *Wicga*'s nook '—*i.e.*, fr. hale or -hall (*q.v.*) rather
than -hill.

WIGHT, I. of. 77 *Pliny* Vectis, *c.* 110 *Suetonius* Vectis Insula,
Bede Vecta, *a.* 810 *Nennius* Inis gueith, *O.E. Chron.* 449 Wiht,
a. 1200 Gueid vel Guith, quod Latine *divortium* dici potest,
c. 1400 *Anct. Pet.* Isle de Wight. Prob. O.W. *gueid, gueith*,
' division '; there is also a W. *gwth*, ' rage, violence, also a
channel, a conduit.' *Cf.* CARISBROOKE, WINWIDFIELD, and
WYTHBURN. Of course, *Insula* in L., *inis* in O.W. (mod. W.
ynys), and *isle* in Fr. all mean ' island.'

WIGHTON (Walsingham). *c.* 1426 Wyghton. ' Town of *Wiht*,'
one in *Onom.* So WIGHTWICK (Wolvermptn.), though *Dom.*
Wistewic, *a.* 1300 Wystewyk and Wytewyk, is plainly ' *Wiht*'s
village.' *Dom.* often has *st* for *ht*; it so hates gutturals *Cf.*,
e.g., WILBRIGHTON.

WIGMORE (Herefordsh.). *Dom.* Wigemore, 1283 Wygemor. Prob. 'moor,' O.E. *mór*, ' of *Wiga* ' or ' *Wicga* or *Wigga*,' all common in *Onom*. *Cf.* WIGBOROUGH. But it may be W. *gwig mawr*, 'great thicket.'

WIGSTON (Leicestersh.). *Dom.* Wichingestone. 'Town of the viking,' O.N. *viking-r*, O.E. *wicing*.

WIGTOFT (Boston). *Sic* 1484 Prob. 'farm of *Wiga* '; but *cf.* above, and see -toft. *Cf.* WIGSLEY (Notts), *Dom.* Wigeslei.

WILBRAHAM (Cambs) and WILBURTON (Ely). 1156 Wilbureham, 1302 Wilburham, *K.C.D.* vi. 98 Wilburhton. ' Home ' or ' town of *Wilburh*,' a woman. But WILBRIGHTON (Gnosall), *Dom.* Wilbrestone, *a.* 1300 Wylbricton, is ' *Wilbriht*'s town.'

WILDEN (Stourport and Bedford). St. W. 1275 Wybeldone—*i.e.*, ' hill of *Wigbeald, Widbeald, Wilbeald*, or *Wibald*,' all forms in *Onom*. See -don. But Bed. W. is *Dom.* Wildene, O.E. *wild denu*, ' wild, waste valley.' See -den.

WILEY or WIL R. (Wilts). *a.* 800 *chart*. East and West Willa, *c.* 893 *Asser* Guilou, 940 *chart.* Wilig. This last is O.E. *wilig*, ' willow,' but the root is prob. W. *gweilgi*, ' a torrent.' *Cf.* ABERGWILI; or possibly O.W. *gwyll*, ' a fairy,' and so this would be a haunted stream.

WILLENHALL (Coventry and Walsall). Wal. W. prob. the *c.* 732 *chart.* Willanhalch, 996 Willanhale, *Dom.* Winehala, Winenhale, *a.* 1200 Willenhal(e); Cov. W. *a.* 1400 Wilnehale, Willenhale. ' Nook ' or ' meadow, haugh, of *Willa*.' See -hall.

WILLERBY (Scarboro' and Hull). *Dom.* Wilgardi (for -debi), Hull. ' Dwelling of *Wilgeard*,' one in *Onom*. See -by. WILLERSEY (Honeybourne), *c.* 850 *chart.* Wylleressie, *Dom.* Willersei, is fr. the same name. See -ey.

WILLESDEN (London). *Dom.* Wellesdone, 1561 Wilsdone. *Dom.* might be O.E. *welles dún*, ' hill of the well ' (*cf.* WHERWELL); but *Willa* is a common man's name in *Onom*. The -den is evidently a late corruption. But there is a Wilsden (Craven), which is *Dom.* Wilsedene.

WILLEY (Lutterworth). *Dom.* Welie, 1129 Wilee. Prob. ' meadow of the willow,' O.E. *welig, wilig*. *Cf.* Willitoft (E. Riding), *Dom.* Wilgetot, ' willow farm.'

WILLINGHAM (Cambridge and Gainsboro'). Cam. W. *K.C.D.* iv. 245 Uuuilingeham, *Dom.* Wiuelingehem, 1750 Wivelingham; Gain. W. 1301 Wyvelingham. Patronymic. ' Home of the *Wifelings* ' or ' sons of *Wifel*,' a known name. *Cf.* WIVELIS-COMBE. See -ing.

WILLINGTON (Bedford and Durham). Bed. W. *Dom.* Welitone, Dur. W. *a.* 1130 *Sim. Dur.* Twilingatun, Twinlingtun. In both cases a patronymic. In the former. ' town. village of the sons of *Willa* ' (*cf.* above); in the latter, fr. some unknown man and his sons. *Onom.* gives one *Tulling* at Exeter, but nothing nearer. It might be ' village of the twins '; *cf.* Ger. *zwilling.* But WILLINGTON (Shipston-on-S.) is *Dom.* Ullavintone, *a.* 1300 Wolyngton, 1327 Wolamynton, which is prob. a patronymic, ' village of the sons of *Wulflaf.*' See -ing.

WILLOUGHBY (4 in *P.G.*), Rugby W. *Dom.* Wilebere (-bury), Wilebei, -bee, *a.* 1300 Wilibi, 1327 Wylughbi. Also 1298 Wylgheby, 1419 Wylleby, perh. Lincs. Notts W. *Dom.* Wilgebi. Perh. ' dwelling of *Willech,*' 2 in *Onom. ;* more prob. fr. O.E. *welig, wilig,* ' a willow.' See -by.

WILMCOTE (Stratford-on-Avon) and WILNECOTE (Tamworth). Str. W. 1016 *chart.* Wilmundigcote, *Dom.* Wilmecote, *a.* 1200 Wilmunde-, *a.* 1400 Wilmoncote. Ta. W. *Dom.* Wilmundecote, 1224 Wilmecote, *a.* 1300 Wilmondecote, 1356 Wylmyncote. Both are ' *Wilmund*'s cottage.' The -ig- in 1016 is a remnant of the patronymic -ing.

WILMINGTON. See WIMBLINGTON.

WILSHAMSTEAD (Bedford). 1327 Wilsamstede. ' *Will*'s HAMP-STEAD ' or ' home-place.' *Willa* is common in *Onom.*

WILTON (3 in *P.G.*). O.E. *Chron.* 871 Wiltun, prob. near Salisbury. ' Town of the tribe *Wilsœtas.*' *Cf.* next. But Wilton (Ross), like Bishop's Wilton (York), *Dom.* Wiltone, is ' town of *Willa,*' a name common in *Onom.*

WILTS. 1011 *O.E. Chron.* Wiltunscir, 1298 Wiltesh. (*sic*). Wilts is a contraction of *Wilsœtas,* ' sitters, dwellers on the R. WIL.' So says Asser.

WIMBLEDON. *O.E. Chron.* 568 Wibbandune, ' *Wibba*'s hill,' *Cf,* WIBSEY. The *b* has been nasalized. But it may be fr. *Winebeald.*

WIMBLINGTON (Manch.). 1387 Wilmyngton, 1539 Wymelington. Willmington. Patronymic. ' Town of the *Wilhelmings* ' (Skeat). *Cf.* Wilmington (Honiton and Dartford).

WIMBORNE (Poole). *O.E. Chron.* 718 Wimburn, *ib.* 871 Winburna mynster. *Cf. Dom.* ' Wimberie ' (Chesh.). Doubtful. Perh. ' burn, brook of the battle,' O.E. (*ge*)*winn,* ' battle, strife.' But WIMPOLE (Cambs) is *Dom.* Winepole, 1302 Wynepol, 1346 Wympole. ' Pool of *Wina,*' a known name; the pool is still there. Wimborne very likely has a similar origin.

WINCANTON (Somerset). *a.* 800 *chart.* Hwinca. Prob. a man's name, nasalized form of *Hwicca. Cf.* WHIXLEY, and see -ton.

WINCHAM (Northwich). *Dom.* Wimundisham, *later* Wymincham. ' Home of *Wymund.*' *Cf.* WYMONDHAM.

WINCHCOMBE (Glouc.). 803 *chart.* Wincelcumba, 1053 *O.E. Chron.* Wincelcumbe, *a.* 1130 *Sim. Dur.* Wincencomb, Wincelcumb. *c.* 1305 *St. Kenelm* Wynchecumbe. Perh. ' valley of *Wincel* ' (not in *Onom.*) or ' *Winca.*' *Cf.* WINCHELSEA. But O.E. *wincel,* ' a corner,' is as likely. See -combe.

WINCHESTER. *c.* 150 *Ptolemy* Venta, *Bede* Ventæ Civitas, *O.E. vers.* Wintancestir, *O.E. Chron.* 755 Wintanceastre, *ib.* 1036 Winceastre, *c.* 1100 *Flor. W.* Wintonia, *c.* 1175 Wincestre, 1297 *R. Glouc.* Winchestre. In W. Cær Gwent—*i.e.,* 'fort, castle on the plain, clearing or open country.' See -chester.

WINCHELSEA (S.W. Kent). (*Dom.* Winchelesmere), 1288 contin. *Gervase* Winchelese, 1297-98 Wynchelese, -chilse. ? 'Isle of *Wyncel.*' See WINCHCOMBE and WINKLEIGH and -ea.

WINCLE (Cheshire). *Dom.* Winescol, *a.* 1200 Winchal. Prob. 'hill of *Wina,*' 3 in *Onom.* O.E. *hyll,* 'hill,' regularly became *hull* in the Midlands fr. 2 on. *Cf.* ASPULL.

WINCOMBLEE (Northumbld.). *Old* Wynkhamlea. Doubtful. Perh. O.E. *Wincan léah,* 'meadow of *Winca,*' one in *Onom. Cf.* Wincolmlee (Hull).

WINDERMERE. *a.* 1130 *Sim. Dur.* ann. 791 Wonwaldremere (a corrupt reading), 1157 Winendemere, 1196 Winendremer, 1196-1748 Winandermere. More and better old forms needed. The first part may be Kelt. and contain W. *gwyn,* 'clear, white, beautiful'; -mere is O.E. *mere,* 'lake.' W. and H. derive fr. a hypothetical Norseman *Vignandr,* a name, they say, exactly equivalent to the known O.E. Wignoþ. This is ingenious, but our verdict must be 'not proven.' There is a WINDER (Frizington, Cumbld.) which certainly looks like W. *gwyn dwr,* 'clear stream.' WINDERTON (Warwksh.) is 1327 Wyntertone.

WINDRUSH R. (Oxford). 779 *chart.* Uuenrisc, *Die Heilige Engl.* Wenrisc. Prob. Keltic. *Cf.* W. *gwyn,* fem. *gwen,* 'fair, clear,' and *rhysgiad,* 'an overgrowing.' The ending is plainly influenced by O.E. *risc,* 'a rush.'

WINDSOR. [*K.C.D.* iv. 165 Wendles ore], *Dom.* Windesores, 1096 *O.E. Chron.* and *Eadmer* Windlesora, *a.* 1145 *Ord. Vit.* Windressoris, 1297 *R. Glouc.* Windelsore; also Wyndelshore. 'Bank, border, shore,' O.E. *ora,* 'of *Wendel* or *Windel.*' The liquids *l* and *r* easily interchange. The O.E. name *Wendel* or *Wœndel,* thinks Skeat, is akin to the Teutonic tribe, the *Vandals.* Connexion with the *Wends,* a Slavic race, cannot be thought of. *Cf.* WENDLEBURY and Windlesham (Camberley); also BOGNOR, CUMNOR, etc.

WINFARTHING (Diss). *Dom.* Wineferthinc, *later* Wynneferthing. Prob. patronymic, 'place of the sons of *Winefrith.*' See -ing. But perh. 'the *ferding*' (common *Dom.* term), or quarter of a hide of land, 'of *Wynne,*' the common O.E. *Wine. Cf.* Pinfarthing (Amberley); Pin- ? = O.E. *penn,* 'sheep-fold.'

WINFORD EAGLE. See AQUILATE; and *cf.* next.

WINFRITH (Dorset). *Chart.* Wenfrut. W. *gwen ffrwdd,* 'white, clear stream.'

WINKLEIGH (N. Devon). *Dom.* Wincheleie. *Cf.* 1298 'Thomas de Wyncelade.' '*Winca's* meadow,' or, as likely, '*Wincel's* meadow.' *Cf.* WINCHCOMBE, WINCHELSEA, *Dom.* Northants Winewincle, etc. See -leigh. WINKSLEY (Yorks), *Dom.* Wichingeslei, is a patronymic, 'meadow of the sons of *Winca.*'

WINNINGTON (Mket. Drayton). *Dom.* Wennitone. 'Town of *Wenna,*' -*an,* or '*Wenni.*'

WINSLOW (Bucks). *Chart.* Uines hlau, '*Wine's* hill'; *Wine* is common in *Onom.* See -low. *Cf.* WINSLEY (Bradford-on-Avon), *Dom.* Wineslei (Salop), and 792 *chart.* Uuineshauue (belonging to St. Albans), also WINSON (Bibury), *Dom.* Wines-tune, '*Wine's* town.'

WINSTER R. (Derby and Westmld.). W. *gwyn,* 'white, clear,' and. thinks M'Clure, *ster,* common river name in Brittany, of which the many British cases of STOUR may be another form.

WINTERBORNE (14 in Dorset; also Berks, Wilts, and Glouc.). 1155 *Pipe* Winterburne (Glouc.). Presumably, 'bourne, burn,' O.E. *burna,* 'stream, which runs only in winter,' O.E. *winter.*

WINTERHOLD PIKE (N. Lancs). *Sic c.* 1250 in *chart.* Either 'hold for dwelling in in winter,' O.E. *winter,* or '*Winter's* hold'; the name is still a personal one. *Cf. B.C.S.* 761 Wintres hlæw. Hold is O.E. *heald,* 3-*hold,* found fr. *c.* 1205 in the sense of 'lair, den, place of refuge.' *Cf.* SCAWFELL PIKES.

WINTERINGHAM (Doncaster). *Dom.* Wentrigha', -rigena; 1298 Wyntringham. Patronymic. 'Home of the sons of *Winter* or *Wintar,*' both forms in *Onom. Cf.* above, and see -ham. WIN-TERTON (3 in *P.G.*), *Dom.* Norfk. Wintretuna, is fr. the same name; so is WENTWORTH.

WINTON (N. Yorks, Kirby Stephen, Patricroft, Bournemouth). Yo. W. *Dom.* Winetune. 'Town of *Wine,*' a common O.E. name. But WINTHORPE (Newark) is *Dom.* Wimuntorp, 'village of *Winemund.*' See -thorpe.

WINWICK (Warrington). ? the Cair Guinntguic of *a.* 810 *Nennius,* which will be Kelt for 'fair, clear village,' W. *gwyn,* Corn. *gwin,* and Corn. *gwek,* L. *vicus,* 'village.' But all analogy would lead one to say, 'dwelling of *Wine,*' a common name in *Onom.* See -wick.

WINWIDFIELD. Freeman thinks = Wingfield (Derbysh.). On the R. Uinuaed, says *Bede* iii. 24, which will be Kelt. *Vindo,* W. *gwyn,* 'clear, white,' and ? O.W. *gueid, gueith,* 'division, channel.' If so this may now be represented by the R. Went or Wynt, a trib. of R. Don.

WIRKSWORTH (Derbysh.). 835 *chart.* Wyrceswurthe. This may be the 'farm of a man *Weorc.*' *Cf. B.C.S.* 1282 Weorces mere, and *Dom.* Bucks Wirecesberie. Or it may be, 'farm with the

fortification or outwork or bulwark,' O.E. *weorc*. *Cf.* WARK,
c. 1175 Werk and *Dom*. Wirceshel, now Worsall (N. Riding),
and Wircesburg, now Worsbrough (S. Yorks). It is prob. fr. a
man's name. See -worth.

WIRRAL (Birkenhead). 895 *O.E. Chron.* Wir heala, *Dom.* Warhelle,
a. 1100 Wirhalas. The name has a Keltic look (*cf.* W. *gwyr*,
'pure, fresh,' and Corn. *hal*, 'a moor'); but Sir E. Anwyl does
not favour this. The W. name used to be Cilgwri, 'retreat of
Gwri.' If the present name were 'Gwri's hall,' O.E. *heall*, we
should have prob., though not certainly, had a gen. sign in 895.
So we must leave the name doubtful. See -hall. Wyrley
(Walsall) is *Dom.* Wireleia, *a.* 1200 Wirlege, which Duignan
derives fr. O.E. *wir*, 'the wild myrtle.' This may be the root
of Wirral, too. *Cf.* WORRALL.

WISBECH. *O.E. Chron.* 657 Wisebece, *K.C.D.* v. 4 Wisebeche, 1298
Wysebeke. 'Beach of *Uui*,' 4 men called *Uui* or *Uvius* in
Onom., all East Anglians too. *Cf.* WISLEY. *Beach* is not found
in *Oxf. Dict.* till *c.* 1535. *Cf.* LANDBEACH. Skeat derives Wis-
fr. O.E. *Wis-ea*, ' Ouse stream,' as the OUSE once flowed past
here. The early spellings of Ouse do not support this, and the
pronunciations seem always to have been distinct.

WISHAW (Tamworth). *Dom.* Witscaga, *a.* 1200 Witteshage, *a.* 1300
Wissawe, *a.* 1400 Wyschawe, -shawe. '*Wita*'s wood,' O.E.
scaga, ' a small wood, a grove.' *Cf.* Wishaw (Lanarksh.).

WISHFORD (Salisbury). 'Ford on the meadow,' E. Fries. *wiske*,
Low. Ger. *wische*, Ger. *wiese ;* in Eng. *wisce* seems to mean a
small meadow, moist and low-lying. *Cf.* WHISTLEY, and next;
also the Wysshes (Siddington).

WISKE MOOR (Northallerton). Might be Kelt. = G. *uisge*, ' water,'
or *whisky!* More likely, ' meadow moor.' See WISHFORD.
Cf. APPLETON WISKE.

WISLEY (Worcester). 759 *chart.* Uuisleag. ' Meadow of *Uui.*'
Cf. WISBEACH.

WISTANSTOW (Craven Arms). *Cf. Dom.* Wistanestune (Chesh.).
' Place' (O.E. *stow*) 'of *Wistan*' or '*Wigstan*,' '*Wihstan*,' or
'*Winestan*'—all forms in *Onom.*

WISTON (Pembk. and Steyning). Old forms needed for Stey. W.
? *Dom.* Wistanestun. *Cf.* WISLEY. Pem. W. is *old* Castell
Gwis, in W. Cas Gwys, ' castle of *Gwys*'—i.e., *Wiz*, the Norm.
knight who built it.

WITCHAM (Ely). *Dom.* Wiceham, 1302 Wychham. ' Home of
Wica,' or ' by the witch-elm,' O.E. *wice*. *Cf.* WITCHFORD, near
by, *Dom.* Wiceford.

WITHAM (several). Somerset W. *Dom.* Witeham, *c.* 1170 Witte-
ham, now pron. Wít-am; O.E. *hwít hám*, ' white house.' Essex
W. *Dom.* Witham is pron. Wít-ham, and is on a R. Guith; while

R. Witham (Lincs) is pron. Wídh-am. It is said to be 1115 *chart.* Witham; but *c.* 1190 *Gir. Camb.* Widhema, *Die Heilige Engl.* Withma, 1240 Wima, 1281 Wyme. *Leland* says it takes name fr. the place Witham, where it rises 8 miles beyond Grantham. But very likely both these last are Keltic, ? with the root O.W. *gueid, gueith,* ' division, separation, a channel.' 941 *O.E. Chron.* Hwitanwyllesgeat is the mouth of R. Witham. There is a ' Wyþie ' in 796 *chart.* Wilts.

WITHERIDGE (Devon). *Dom.* Wederige, *Exon. D.* Wedreriga. Perh. *a.* 800 *chart.* Widerigge. ' Ridge' or ' rigg' (as in Sc. and N. Eng.) ' of *Widr* ' or ' *Wither.*' *Cf.* WITHERSFIELD.

WITHERNSEA (Hull) (*Dom.* Widfornessei, Wilfornes) and WITHERN-WICK (Hull) (*Dom.* Widfornewic). The *Dom.* forms seem erroneous, or *f* has replaced *th* (see FENGLESHAM); and both names are prob. patronymics—' peninsula ' and ' dwelling of the sons of *Wihthere,*' 3 in *Onom.,* whilst we have *Wihthering* in *B.C.S.* 779. See -ea and -wick.

WITHERSFIELD (Newmarket). ' Field of *Wither,*' 4 in *Onom.* *Cf.* *a.* 1100 *Grant* of 664 ' Wytherington,' near Peterboro'.

WITHIEL (Bodmin) and WITHIEL FLOREY (W. Somerset). Corn. *withell,* ' a lion,' fr. the supposed look of the place. *Cf.* LOST-WITHIEL.

WITHINGTON (4 in *P.G.*). Cheltenham W. 736-37 *Grant* Wudiandune, *Dom.* Widendune. ' Hill (O.E. *dún*) of *Widia* or *Wudga,*' 3 in *Onom.* *Cf. Dom.* Bucks Withungraue.

WITHYBROOK (Brinklow) is 1198 Widebroc, which should mean ' *wide* brook'; but the mod. pron. shows it is only the common Nor. *d* for *th* medial, and the name really is fr. O.E. *withig,* ' a willow, a withe.' So is Witcombe (Birdlip), 1330 Wydycoumbe, *later* Wydecombe; though Baddeley thinks it, ' wide valley.'

WITLEY (Godalming, Halesowen, Worcester). Ha. W. *a.* 1500 Whiteley. Wo. W. 964 *chart.* Wittleage, 969 *ib.* Witleag, *Dom.* Witlege. *Cf. Dom.* Chesh. and Devon Witelei. Either O.E. *hwít léah,* ' white mead,' or ' meadow of *Wita,*' 3 in *Onom.,* as in WITNEY (Oxford), ' isle of *Wita.*'

WITSON (Newport, Mon.). Old forms needed. We may *cf.* 1157 *Pipe* Witsand, or ' white sand ' (Beds.).

WITTENHAM (Abingdon). *B.C.S.* ii. 224 Wittanhamme, *c.* 1540 Whittenham Comitis (' of the count or earl ') and Wittenham Abbatis (' of the abbot'). ' Enclosure ' (O.E. *hamm*) ' of *Witta.*'

WITTERSHAM (Peasmarsh, Sussex). ' Home of *Wither,*' 3 in *Onom.* *Cf. B.C.S.* 60 Uuidringa muth—*i.e.,* West Wittering (Sussex), patronymic fr. *Wither* or *Widr.* *Cf.* WITHERIDGE.

WITTON (7 in *P.G.*). Droitwich W. **714** *chart.* Wittona, **1043** Hwitona; Birmingham W. *Dom.* Witone, *a.* **1400** Wytton; Norwich W. *Dom.* Witona, **1179-80** *Pipe* Witeton (Yorks). Prob. all O.E. *hwít tun,* ' white village '; but *cf.* WITLEY and WITTENHAM.

WITTON-LE-WEAR (Bp. Auckland). *a.* **1130** *Sim. Dur.* Wudu-, Wudetun—*i.e.,* 'Wood-town,' See WEAR.

WIVELISCOMBE (Somerset). *Cf.* **941** Wifeles cumbe (Sussex). 'Valley of *Wifel.*' *Cf.* also *B.C.S.* **699** and **1067** Wifeles ford and ham, *Dom.* Chesh. Wivelesde, and Yorks Wifleshale, now Wilsill (see -hall), WILLINGHAM and WORSTON. See -combe.

WIVENHOE (Essex). *c.* **1452** Whevenho, Wevenho, Wefnow. 'HOE, height of *Wifa,*' gen. *-fan.*

WIVETON (Norfolk). *Dom.* Wiuetona, **1482** Wyveton, Weveton. 'Village of *Wifa.*' *Cf.* above. WIVERTON (Notts), *Dom.* Wivretune, is fr. *Wigferth* or *Wifare.*

WOBURN Sands (Bletchley). **969** *chart.* Woburninga (ʒemære)— *i.e.,* 'district of the dwellers on the Woburn.' **1155** Wobburne, O.E. *wó, wóh burna,* 'crooked stream or bourne or burn.' *Cf. a.* **675** *Grant* 'Woburne brugge' (Surrey), and **796** *chart.* Woburne (Wilts). There are, or were, also several Womeres in England—'crooked lakes.'

WODNESBOROUGH (Kent). *a.* **1300** Wodnesberge. 'Burgh or BARROW of the god *Wodin* or *Odin.*' *Cf.* WANBOROUGH.

WOKING. *a.* **715** *chart.* Wocchingas, O.E. *Chron.* **777** Wocingas, *Dom.* Wochinges. Patronymic. 'Place of the sons of *Wocc,*' one in *Onom.* Also WOKINGHAM or OAKINGHAM or OCKINGHAM (Berks), *c.* **1280** Wokingham, *c.* **1540** Okyngham, **1568** Okingham. 'Home of the *Woccings.*' See -ham and -ing.

WOLLASTON (Stourbridge and Wellingboro'). St. W. **1327** Wolarston, prob. '*Wulfgar*'s town'; the name is common. But WOLLASHILL in same shire is **1275** Wollaueshull, 'hill of *Wulflaf,*' a still commoner name. Similar is WOLLATON (Notts), *Dom.* Olavestune. Welling. W. seems to be *Dom.* Walesdone, 'hill of *Wale,*' 2 in *Onom.* See -don and -ton.

WOLSELEY (Rugby). *Dom.* Ulslei, *a.* **1200** Wulfsiesleg, *a.* **1300** Wulseleye. 'Meadow of *Wulfsige* or *Wulfsie,*' a very common name in *Onom.,* and a fuller form of WOLSEY (King's Lynn), **1166** *Pipe* Wulsi—*i.e.,* 'wolf's isle,' O.E. *wulfes ige.* See -ley and -ey.

WOLSINGHAM (Co. Durham). *Sic* **1183.** 'Home of *Wolsin,*' var. of the very common name *Wulfsige.* See -ham.

WOLSTANTON (Stoke-on-Trent). *Sic c.* **1350,** but *Dom.* Wistanetone, **1198** Wulstanestone. 'Village of *Wulfstan,*' a common O.E. name. *Cf. Dom.* Salop Vlestanesmude. However, *Dom.*'s form will rather represent *Wigstan* or *Wistan,* also a very common name. WOLSTROP (Glouc.) is *old* Wulvesthrop, 'thorpe, village of *Wulf.*'

WOLVERHAMPTON. 985 *chart.* Heantune, 994 *chart.* of *Wulfrun* (corrupt copy), Hamtune, Hantone, 1006 *chart.* Heantun, *Dom.* Hantone, -done, *Dom.* Worc. Wrehantone, *a.* 1200 Wulfrune-hanton, -nhamtun, Wolvernehampton. Héan túne is the inflected form of O.E. *héah tún,* 'high town,' which not seldom gets confused with HAMPTON. This, then, has become 'the hampton of *Wulfrun,*' daughter of K. Edmund. She founded a college here, and endowed the church with great possessions, in 994.

WOLVERLEY (Kidderminster) and WOLVERTON (Warwick). 866 *chart.* (late copy) Wulfferdinleh, Wulferdinlea, 1046 *ib.* Wulf-weardiglea, *Dom.* Ulwardlei, 1275 Wolffardeleye, *Dom.* Ulwardi-tone, 1150 Wlwarditone. 'Meadow of the sons of' and 'town of *Wulfweard* (*cf.* -ing). But WOLVERSHILL (Nuneaton), *a.* 1300 Wulfareshull, and WOLVERTON (Pershore), 977 Wulfringetune, 984 Wulfrinton, *Dom.* Ulfrinton, 1275 Wolfertone, are 'hill of' and 'town of the sons of *Wulfhere,*' a very common name. *Cf.* 854 *chart.* 'Of Wulfherescumbe on Wulfheres clif,' and WORDSLEY. From *Wulfhere* also is WOLVERTON (Basingstoke), *Dom.* Ulvretune, Vluretune; whilst WOLVERTON (Bucks) in *Dom.* has the patronymic -ing—Wluerintone.

WOLVEY (Nuneaton). *a.* 1200 Wulfeia, 1251 Wolveye. 'Isle of *Wulf*' or '*Wolf.*' See -ey. But with WOLVISTON (Stockton-on-Tees), *cf. Dom.* Suffk. Wluerthestuna, which is prob. '*Wulfheard*'s town.'

WOMBLETON (Nawton). *Dom.* Winbeltun, Wilbetun, 1235 Wim-bleton. 'Town of *Winebeald.*'

WOMBOURNE (Wolvermptn.). *Dom.* and later Wamburne, *a.* 1300 Wombeburne, Wamburn. Prob. 'brook in the hollow,' lit. 'womb,' O.E. *wambe, womb*(*e*). *Cf.* Wombridge (Salop) and WOMBWELL (Barnsley), *Dom.* Wanbuelle, -la. See -bourne.

WOMERSLEY (Pontefract). *Dom.* Wilmereslege. 'Meadow of *Wulfmœr*' or '*Ulmar,*' a very common name.

WONERSH (Guildford). Old forms needed. Won- may be for '*Wana*'s,' a name in *Onom.* ; -ersh is almost certainly *ersh* or *arrish,* both forms in *Oxf. Dict.* as var. of *eddish* (*q.v.*), O.E. *edisc,* of obscure origin, 'a wheat-stubble, a cleared corn-field,' found in dial. fr. Devon to Sussex. *Cf.* CAVENDISH.

WOODCHESTER (Stroud). 740 *chart.* Wuduceastre, *Dom.* Wide- and Udecestre. 'Fort, town in the wood,' O.E. *wudu.* See -chester.

WOODCOTE (Warwick, Bromsgrove, and Reading). Wa. W. *Dom.* Widecote, 1165 Wudcote; Br. W. *Dom.* Udecote, 1275 Wodecote. 'Cot, cottage in the wood,' O.E. *wudu.*

WOODCROFT (Chepstow). (*Cf. a.* 1100 *Grant* of 664 'Wodecrofte,' near Market Deeping.) O.E. *croft,* 'a field, a small farm.'

WOODEND (Shipley, Towcester, etc.). There are 3 in Staffdsh., which mark the bounds of the Forest of Arden.

WOODHAY (Kintbury, Berks). 1316 Wydehay, c. 1540 Woodhay. ' Wood fence or hedge,' O.E. *hege* (also *haga* and *hecg*, but these are distinct words). *Cf.* OXHEY.

WOODSTOCK (Oxford). *Dom.* Wodestok, -stock; 1154-71 Wudes-toca, c. 1160 *Gest. Steph.* Wodestoc, 1163 Wdestoke. ' Place, settlement in the wood.' *Cf.* STOKE, Hadstock (Cambs), etc.; whilst WOODMANCOTE (3 in Glouc.) is 1230 Wdemenecote, ' woodman's cot.'

WOOKEY and WOOKEY HOLE (Wells). 1231 *Patent R.* Woky. Prob. O.W. *guocov*, mod. W. *gwcof*, ' a cave.'

WOOLACOMBE TRACY (N. Devon). *Dom.* Olecūbe, *Exon. D.* Vla-cumbe; *Dom.* also has Wolnecome. *Cf.* 941 *chart* Uulecumb, (Twickenham). ' Valley of *Wola*,' one in *Onom.* ' Willelmus de Traci ' (*sic chart.* 1174) lived here. He was one of the murderers of Beckett.

WOOLAVINGTON (Bridgwater). O.E. *chart.* Wulflafing tun. ' Village of *Wulflaf*'s children.' *Cf.* WOOLLASTON (Staffd.), *Dom.* Ullavestone, and Woollavington (Sussex); also WOOLASTON-on-Severn, *Dom.* Odelaweston, 1218 Wolaveston, where Baddeley postulates an unknown *Wudelaf*. See -ing and -ton.

WOOLER (N. Northumbld.). Local pron. Oolor. 1197 *Rolls* Wel-loure, *Testa de Nevil* Willore. ' Well on the bank or edge,' O.E. *ofer, obr*, now usually -over, as in Ashover, Shotover, etc., but often contracted as in Asher, HADSOR, HASLER, etc. In more recent times the vowel sounds have been transposed, and the name now is locally suppoed to denote ' a wool market '; and, indeed, W. was a great wool centre. But, as will be seen, Eng. place-names in Wool- very seldom have any connexion with *wool*. *E.g.*, WOOLDALE (S. Yorks) is *Dom.* Ulvedel, ' dale of *Ulf*' or ' the Wolf,' etc.

WOOLHAMPTON (Berks). *Dom.* Ollavintone, c. 1280 Wulavinton, 1428 Wolamptone. A name which has changed. Not orig. the HAMPTON or ' home town,' but the ' town, village of *Wullaf* or *Wulfflaf*' or rather ' of the *Wulflafings*,' or ' sons of Wulflaf.' *Cf.* the N. Olaf and *K.C.D.* vi. 243 Wullafingland and WOOLAVINGTON.

WOOLLEY (Wakefield). *Dom.* Wiluelai. ' Meadow of the willows,' O.E. *wilig, welig. Cf.* WILLEY.

WOOLMER GREEN (Stevenage). *Chart.* Wulfmær. ' Boundary, district,' O.E. (*ge*)*mære*, ' of a man *Wulf*.'

WOOLNOTH St. Mary (parish, London). Prob. fr. *Wulfnoth*, brother of K. Harold (d. 1066).

WOOLPIT (Bury St. Edmunds). *Dom.* Wlfpeta. ' Wolf-pit,' O.E. *wulf-pyt. Cf.* 1148 *Glouc. chart.* Wlpitta.

WOOLSTONE (Shrivenham, Berks). *Dom.* Olvricestone, *c.* 1280 Wulfricheston, Wulvricheston, 1316 Wolfricheston. ' Town, village of *Wulfric.*' See -ton. This name shows how hopeless it is to try to guess origins ! WOOLSCOTT (Warwk.) is equally hopeless, for it is *Dom.* Werlavescote, ' *Wærlaf*'s cottage.' WOOLSTON (Bp's. Cleeve) is simpler—*Dom.* Olsendone, 1316 Wolsiston—*i.e.,* ' *Wolsi*'s,' fuller, ' *Wulfsige*'s town.'

WOOLWICH. *Dom.* Hulviz (Norman phonetics !), *Text. Roffensis* Welwic, *a.* 1400 Wolwiche. The O.E. form is said to be Wule-wic, prob. ' dwelling, house for wool,' O.E. *wul, wull,* Icel. *ull,* ' wool,' and O.E. *wic.* See -wich.

WOORE (S. Chesh.). *Dom.* Waure. *Cf.* Brownsover (Rugby), *Dom.* Gaura, *a.* 1300 Waure, Bruneswaure, -wafre, which Duignan derives fr. a supposed O.E. *wæfre* or *wafre,* ' the aspen poplar.' *Cf.* WAVERTREE.

WOOTTON (13 in *P.G.*) and WOTTON (2). *Dom.* Vdetune (Salop), Wodetone (Staffs), Wotone (Warwk.), Utone (Glouc.). WOOT-TON RIVERS (Marlboro'), *c.* 680 *chart.* Wdetun, *B.C.S.* i. 506 Uudetun (Berks). ' Wood-town,' ' dwelling in the wood.' HILL WOOTTON (Leamington) is *Dom.* Hille, 1327 Hull wottone; while WOOTTON WAWEN (Henley-in-Arden) goes back to 723 *chart.* Widu tún, 1043 Wagene de Wotton, *c.* 1350 Wawenes and Waunes Wotton. Wawen, O.E. *Wahgene,* was a great local proprietor before the Conquest.

WORCESTER. 691 *chart.* Weogorna civitas, *Bede* Provincia Huic-ciorum, *O.E. vsn.* Hwicna Gemære (territory), *a.* 810 *Nennius* Huich, *c.* 800 *chart.* Hicca, *c.* 802 *ib.* Wegoranensis civitas, Wigornensis ecclesia, 804 *ib.* Wigornacestre, 836 *ib.* Weogur-nacestre, *c.* 897 *Ælfred* Wiogora ceastre, *c.* 1075 Wigraceastre, *c.* 1100 *Flor. Worc.* Episcopatus Wigornensis, 1274 Wirecestre, *c.* 1290 Wyricestre, 1297 *R. Glouc.* Wurcetre, 1666 *Merrett* Wostershire. Mod. pron. Wū-ster. Some think it is the ʻCær Guiragon or Guveirangon of *Nennius. Cf.* WROXETER. ' Fort of the *Huiccii* ' or ' *Wigorna* '—*i.e.,* prob. ' the forest men,' O.W. *guig, gwig,* ' a grove.' See M'Clure (p. 165), and *cf.* WHICHFORD, and the WYRE forest once in this shire. Hu- and Gu- both equal W.

WORD (Kent and Sussex) and WORTH (Eastry, Kent, and Ware-ham). O.E. *worth,* ' a farm,' in *Dom.* always -word(e), -vord(e), -orde. See -worth. The people at the Kent Word always call it Worth.

WORDSLEY (Stourbridge). *a.* 1200 Wuluardeslea, *a.* 1300 Wol-wardele. ' Meadow of *Wulfweard.*' *Cf.* WOLVERLEY. See -ley.

WORKINGTON (W. Cumbld.). 1300 Werkenton. ' Town of (the sons of) *Weorc,*' one in *Onom.* See -ing.

WORKSOP (Retford). *Dom.* Werchesope, 1189 *Pipe* Worcheshope, 1285 Wyrkesop, 1456 Worsop. Prob. 'Hope, harbourage, or valley of *Worc*.' *Cf.* WORSLEY and WARSOP; but also *cf.* WARK. See -hope.

WORLESTON (Nantwich). Not in *Dom.*, but *cf. Dom.* Bucks Vorlsdone. 'Town, village of *Worla*,' a name not in *Onom.* *Cf.* WHORLTON.

WORLINGHAM (Suffk.), WORLINGTON (Soham), and WORLINGWORTH (Framlingham). All three in the same county, and yet in each the Worling- has a different origin. They are in *Dom.* War-, Werlingahā, 'home of the sons of *Warl*'; Wirilintona, where the name is doubtful, *Onom.* has one *Wernweald*; and Wyrlingwortha, 'farm of the *Wyrlings*.' See -ing and -worth.

WORMEGAY (King's Lynn). c. 1150 Wirmegeie, 1232 Wurmegaye, *Red Book* Wirmingai. Patronymic. 'Isle of the *Wyrmings*,' or 'sons of *Wyrm*,' the Snake. *Cf.* Worminghall (Thame). See -ay.

WORMINGFORD (Essex). *Dom.* Widemondefort, *later* Withermondford, 1481-90 *Howard Bks.* Wyrmyngforde. 'Ford of *Withermund*,' an unrecorded name, but *Onom.* has *Widmund* and *Witherwine*. *Withermond* could easily become Wyrmyng-, and *wyrm* is O.E. for 'worm,' hence the confusion and present spelling. WORMINGTON (Glouc.), *Dom.* Wermetun, is simply 'town of *Wyrme*' or '*Wurm*.' See -ing.

WORMLEIGHTON (Southam). 956 *chart.* Wilmanlehtune, *Dom.* Wimeres-, menestone, *a.* 1200 Wilmelathune (*t* for *c*), 1327 Wilmeleghtone, *a.* 1400 Wormleytone. '*Wilman*'s LEIGHTON,' a very remarkable corruption; 2 *Wilmans* in *Onom.* The *Dom.* forms show how unreliable *Dom.* may be.

WORM'S HEAD (Pembrokesh.). Low Dutch, prob. Flemish form of ORM'S HEAD. See p. 79.

WORRALL (Sheffield). *Dom.* Wihala, -hale. Possibly 'wild myrtle nook'; O.E. *wir.* See WIRRAL and -hall.

WORSBORO' (Barnsley). *Dom.* Wircesburg. 'Burgh, town of *Wirc*' or '*Worc*.' *Cf.* next, and see -burgh.

WORSLEY (Manchester and Abberley). Ma. W. 1296-97 Werkslegh, 1293 Workellegh. 'Mead of *Werc*.' *Cf.* above and WORKSOP. But Ab. W. *a.* 1200 Wermeslai, Wervesleye, 1275 Worvesle, 1327 Werwesle, 1332 Worsley. Prob. 'mead of *Wœrwulf*.' See -ley.

WORSTEAD HALL (Walsall). *a.* 1560 Walstede, -stode. 'Stead, steading, farm of *Wealh*'—*i.e.*, 'the stranger.' WORSTON (Stafford) is *c.* 1300 Wiveleston, Wyverstone, Wyfridestone, Worflestone. The name shows variations, but prob. is 'town of *Wifel*.' *Cf. B.C.S.* 699 and 1067 Wifeles ford and ham, and WIVELISCOMBE.

WORTH. See WORD and -worth.

WORTHING, also **WORTHEN** (Shrewsbury, perh. *c.* 1350 *chart.* Worthyn). Prob. the dat. of O.E. *worþig,* ' enclosed farm.' *Cf.* TAMWORTH and WORTHY (Winchester), which is the same name, 1001 *O.E. Chron.* Worthige. See -worth.

WORTLEY (2 in Yorks and Wotton-under-Edge). Yo. W. *Dom.* Wirtleie, Wirlei, Wrleia, 1298 Wurtele. Wo. W. *old* Wurthelye, Worteley. Prob. O.E. *wyrt léah,* ' field for growing roots '— turnip or suchlike. **WORTON** (Yorks and Potterne), *Dom.* Yorks and Wilts, Werton(e), is prob. the same.

WOULDHAM (Rochester). *c.* 970 *chart.* Wuldaham. Prob. ' home of ' an unrecorded man.

WRANGLE (Boston). *Dom.* Weranghe, 1276 Wrangle, 1396 Wranghill, Wrangel. Prob. O.E. *wer, waer,* ' a fence, enclosure for fish, a weir,' and *angel,* ' fish-hook '; so, ' weir for fishing in.'

WRATHING (Cambs and Suffolk). Cam. W. *Dom.* Waratinge, *chart.* Wrættincge, 1167 Wreting, 1210 Wrotinge, 1302 Wrattinge. ' Home of the sons of *Wrætta* ' or ' the man with the *wart* '; E. Anglian *wret.* *Dom.* inserts an *a,* and makes it Warat-, to help a Norman's pronunciation. See -ing.

WRAWBY (Brigg) and **WRAY** (Lancaster and Windermere). *Cf.* 1612-13, in *N. Riding Rec.,* ' A parcell of meadow called the Wraie '; N. *wraa,* ' a corner, a landmark.' *Cf.* Capernwray (Lancs), ' chapman's, merchant's corner,' HAVERAH, and WRAE (Sc.) See -by.

WRAYSBURY (Staines). Not in *Dom.,* but *old* Wyrardisbury, ' Town, burgh of *Wœrheard* ' or ' *Werardus,*' a common name in *Onom.* See -bury.

WREKIN, The (Salop). ? *a.* 600 *Llywarch Hen.* Dinnle Wrecon, *a.* 900 *chart.* Wreocensetun. Prob. same root as WROXETER, *q.v.* Possibly same root as W. *gwrechyn, gwrachin,* ' a crabbed fellow,' but this is doubtful.

WRELTON (Pickering). *Dom.* Wereltun. More old forms needed; ? fr. *Werdwulf* or *Wernbeald.* *Cf.* WRESSEL, also E. Riding, *Dom.* Weresa. This may be the same name as *Dom.* Worc. Weredshale, interpreted by Skeat as ' O.E. weoredesheale, " a place occupied by a host," wherein a set of men squatted in company.'

WREXHAM. In W. *Gwrecsam,* corrup. of the Eng. name. In Saxon days it was in Mercia, not Wales. 1160-61 *Pipe* Chesh. Wristlesham, 1222 *chart. Madoc ap Gruffith* Wrechceosam, 1236 Wreccesham, Wrettesham (*t* common error for *c*), 1291 Wyrcesson, 1316-17 Wrightlesham, *c.* 1620 *Beaumont and Fletcher* Rixum. Prob. ' home of *Wryhtsleof,*' one in *Onom. ;* 1160 has the regular Nor. *st* for guttural *h,* which the Norman could not abide. See -ham.

WRIBBENHALL (Bewdley). *Dom.* Gurbehale, *a.* 1100 Wrbenhala, 1240 Wrubenhale. ' *Wrobba*'s nook.' See -hall.

WRITTLE (Chelmsford). Prob. 692-93 *chart.* Writolaburna (brook), 1234 *Close R.* Writel. Perh. Keltic; *cf.* W. *gwrthol,* ' backwards.' WRITHINLGTON (Bath) is *Dom.* Writelinctune,' a patronymic, prob. based on the same root. See -ing.

WROCKWARDINE (Wellington, Salop). 'Farm of *Wrocc.*' *Cf.* WROXALL, and see -wardine.

WROTHAM (Kent) and WROTTESLEY (Wolverhampton). *Dom.* Wrotolei, *a.*1200 Wrotelei, Wroteslea. ' Home ' and ' meadow of *Wrot.*' See -ham and -ley.

WROXALL (Ventnor and Warwk.). Ve. W. 1038-44 *chart.* Wroccesheale binnan Wiht. War. W. *a.* 1200 Wrocheshal(e), Wrokeshal. ' Nook of *Wrocc.*' *Cf.* Wroxhill (Beds) and Wroxton (Oxon). See -hall.

WROXETER (Shrewsbury). *c.* 150 *Ptolemy* Urioconio, *c.* 380 *Ant. Itin. ibid.,* also Virocono. Prob. also *a.* 810 *Nennius* Caer Guiragon or Guoricon, or Urnahc, *Brut y Tywysogion* Caerwrangon. Wroxeter is for *Wrocn*'s caster. *Cf.* EXETER, and see -caster. It may contain the same root as WREKIN. M'Clure thinks Virocono may contain the name of *Verica,* son of the Keltic King Commios.

WYCHWOOD (W. Oxon.). *O.E. Chron.* 841 Huicceuudu, *Dom.* Huchewode, 1284 Whyche-, Whucchewode. ' Wood of the *Huiccii.*' It formerly belonged to the bishops of this tribe, who perh. took their name fr. O.E. *wice,* M.E. *wiche,* ' a tree,' prob. the wych elm, or hazel. See also WORCESTER and WICHFORD.

WYCLIFFE (Teesdale). *Dom.* Witclive—*i.e.,* ' white cliff,' O.E. *hwit clif*; there is one here; but *a.* 1130 *Sim. Dur.* Wigeclif—*i.e.,* ' cliff of *Wiga,*' 4 in *Onom.*

WYCOMBE (Bucks). *Dom.* Wicombe, *c.* 1350 Wycombe, 1387 *Trevisa* Wycomb malban. Mod. pron. Wick-am. ' Valley of the WYE,' a little trib. of R. Thames. *Cf.* 1160-61 *Pipe* Sussex Wicumba. See -combe.

WYE, R. *Dom.* Waia, *c.* 1097 *Flor. Worc.* Weage, *Latin Chrons.* Vaga, *c.* 1130 *Lib. Landav.* Gwy, which is W. for ' river, stream.' *Cf.* WEY and WYCOMBE.

WYKE (Bradford) and W. REGIS (Weymouth). *Dom.* Wiche. ' Dwelling.' See -wich. Regis, L. ' of the king.'

WYKEN. See WICKEN.

WYLAM (Northumbld.). 1201 Wilum; a loc., as in KILHAM, etc., ' at the wells '; O.E. *wiell(a),* ' a spring, a fountain.' See -ham.

WYLE COP (Shrewsbury). M'Clure thinks Wyle is same as *Wyla,* prob. gen. pl. of *wygel,* both words in the early O.E. glossaries,

with the meaning ' cave.' Cop is O.E. *cop, copp,* ' top, summit.'
See *Oxf. Dict.*, cop sb².

WYMONDHAM (Norfk. and Oakham). No. W. *c.* 1150 Wimundehame.
' Home of *Wimund,*' a common O.E. name. *Cf. Dom.* Wimun-
disham (Chesh.), now WINCHAM, and Wimuntorp (Notts), now
Winthorpe. See -ham, here prob. ' enclosure.'

WYRE, R. (Lancs). *Sic a.* 1300. WYRE FOREST (Wstrsh.).
Always Wyre. There is also WYRE PIDDLE (Pershore), *Dom.*
Pidele, 1290 Wyre Pidele. Any of these may be fr. W. *gwŷr,*
' oblique, sloping, bending,' or *gwyre,* ' pure, fresh, lovely.'
But all is doubtful. *Cf.* 1235 *Close R.* Wirburne. Duignan
cites the rivers Wyre Fawr and Fach (W. *mawr* and *bach*),
' great and little spread,' fr. Cardigansh.

WYSALL (Nottingham). *Dom.* Wisoc, 1302 Wishow, 1637 Wysshaw.
' Hill,' O.E. *hóh,* ' of *Uui* '; *cf.* WISLEY. *Onom.* has only 1 *Wizo.*
The present ending is quite recent; *cf.* WATNALL.

WYTHAM (Oxford). *O.E. chart.* Wihtham, *c.* 1130 *Chron. Abing.*
Uuihteham, Wictham, *c.* 1540 Wightham. ' Home of *Wihta* '
or ' *Wiht.* WYTHBURN (Keswick) may be fr. the same man's
name, but is prob. = WIGHT, a Kelt root.

YALDING (Maidstone). Not in *Dom.* 1230 *Close R.* Ending.
More evidence needed. Possibly patronymic fr. *Gelda,* 1 in
Onom. See -ing.

YALE (Derbysh.). W. *ial,* ' open land.' *Cf.* LLANARMON-YN-
YALE (Mold).

YANWORTH (Hazleton). *Dom.* Teneurde, 1221 Jeanworth, 1251
Zaneward. ' Farm of *Ean,*' short for *Eanbeorht,* or the like.
See -worth.

YAPHAM (E. Riding). *Dom.* Iapun, 1230 Japun. Perh. a loc.,
' at the gaps '; O.N. *gap,* ' chasm '; Sw. *gap,* Da. *gab,* ' open
mouth.' *Gap* is not found in Eng. till *c.* 1380. See -ham.
But YAPTON (Arundel), not in *Dom.*, will be fr. a man *Geppa ;*
2 in *Onom.*

YAR R. (I. of Wight) and YARE R. (Gt. Yarmouth). Forms see
YARMOUTH. The Yare is perh. *c.* 150 *Ptolemy* Gariennos, *c.*
380 *Notit. Dign.* Garianno, whilst the earliest sure form is
Dom.'s Gerne. M'Bain held that Yare is = YARROW (Sc.),
which is G. *garbh,* ' rough). So Garianno will be Kelt. for
' rough river '; the -enn- or -ann- or -ne representing a Kelt. word
for ' river,' like G. *abhuinn.* *Cf.* the rivers, Gar-onne, Guadi-ana,
etc. The Yar may represent the simple Kelt. adj. for ' rough,'
its earliest known form being *Dom.*'s Er. However, ARNCLIFFE
(Skipton) is once in *Dom.* Gerneclif, where Gerne must be O.E.
earn, ' an erne ' or ' eagle.'

YARDLEY (Birmingham). 972 *chart.* Gyrdleahe, *Dom.* Gerlei, 1275 Jerdeleye. YARDLEY HASTINGS (Northants), *a.* 1124 Jerdelai. ' Enclosed meadow,' fr. O.E. *geard,* ' a yard, a court.' See -ley.

YARKHILL (Hereford). 811 *chart.* Geard cylle, which is O.E. for ' Yard vessel,' a strange name for a place. O.E. *geard* is ' yard, enclosure, dwelling.' Kiln is O.E. *cylene,* and not to be thought of here. In any case the corruption is notable. Yartledon (Glouc.), *old* Yarcledon, Yacledon, and Zarkley, Baddeley derives fr. the dial. *yark,* ' ragwort.'

YARLETT (Stone). *Dom.* 1300 Erlide, *a.* 1500 Erlid, *a.* 1600 Yerlett. Doubtful; an abnormal name. Duignan's O.E. *geard lyt,* ' little yard,' seems out of the question. The name seems Norse; O.N. *earl-* or *iarl- hlíth,* O.E. *eorl-hlith,* ' earl's ' or ' jarl's slope.' *Th* certainly could harden into *t* or *d*—medially it often does in *Dom.*—and the Eng. *earl* is 6-7 *yerle.* The Sc. -lets seem generally to have been orig. -leth, as in Cromlet, HURLET, and Passelet, old form of PAISLEY.

YARM (N. Riding). *Dom.* Iarun, Gerou (*u* error for *n*). Iarun looks like an O.E. loc.; see -ham. But the name is prob. O.E. *gerúm,* ' room, space,' or *gerúma,* ' a place '; *gerúme,* ' roomy.'

YARMOUTH, Great. *Dom.* Gernemua, *c.* 1130 *Eadmer* and 1167 *Pipe* Gernemutha, 1223 Jernemue, 1278 Magna Jernemouth, 1461 Yarmouth. YARMOUTH, LITTLE (Suffolk) is 1229 *Close R.* Parva Gernem'. YARMOUTH (I. of Wight) is *Dom.* Er mud, 1231 *Close R.* Erem'. *Oxf. Dict.'s* earliest quot. for *mouth* in the sense of ' river mouth ' is *a.* 1122.

YARNFIELD (Stone and Somerset). 1266 Ernefeld, 1327-79 Ernefen, *a.* 1600 Yernfyn, Yarnefylde. Som. Y. *Dom.* Gernfelle (*ll* as often for *ld*), O.E. *gearn feld,* ' yarn field,' or else ' fen.' *Cf.* YARNWICK (N. Riding), *Dom.* Gernwic, ' house for making yarn.' See -wick.

YARWELL (Wansford, Northants). Not in *Dom.* 1238 Jarewell. Doubtful. Possibly fr. O.N. *jara,* poetic word for ' a fight, a combat.'

YATESBURY (Calne). *Cf. Dom.* Bucks Iateberie. ' Town, burgh of *Geat* ' or ' *Geot.*' See -bury. But YATE (Bristol), 778 *chart.* Gete, *Dom.* Giate, is O.E. *æt Geate,* ' at the gate.'

YATTENDEN or -DON (Berks). *Dom.* Etingedene, 1316 Yatindene, 1365 Yatyndene, 1428 Yatendene. ' Dene, valley (O.E. *denu,* often confused in names with O.E. *dún,* ' hill, down ') ' of the *Geatings* ' or ' sons of *Geat.*' *Cf. B.C.S.* iii. 68 Geates cumb (Cumnor), and YATTING (Kent), 1235 *Close R.* Jatingden.

YAXHAM (Norfolk) and YAXLEY (Peterboro'). 1477 Yeaxham. 940 *chart.* Geakeslea, 1235 *Close R.* Jakesli. There is also one at Eye (Suffolk). ' Home ' and ' meadow ' of *Yeaca,*' not in *Onom.* See -ham and -ley.

YEADON (Leeds). *Dom.* Iadun. Prob. an old loc., ' at the roads,' or ' on the way,' fr. O.N. *gata*, Da. *gade*, ' a road, a way '; the Sc. *gate*. We see *t* become *d* also in Yokefleet (N. Yorks), *Dom.* Iucu-, Iugufled. See FLEET.

YEARSLEY (Yorks). *Dom.* Eureslage, O.E. *eofors léah*, ' wild-boar's field '= EVERSLEY. *Cf.* YEVERING.

YEDDING or YEADING (Middlesex). 793 *chart.* Geddingas. Patronymic, ' Home of the sons of *Geddi*,' one in *Onom*. *Cf.* the mod. surname Giddings.

YELVERTON (Norwich and Dartmoor). No. Y. prob. *Dom.* Ailuertun, ' town of *Ælfweard*,' a common name. Da. Y. is doubtful. Said to be *Elford-town*, as the Elfords once had a seat here. This is phonetically very doubtful. Perh. it is *Dom.* Utvretone (*Ut-* error for *Ul-*), and so ' town of *Ulfheard*' or ' *Ulfard*,' var. of the very common *Wulfheard*. There is an Elforde in *Dom.* Devon.

YENLET (several at mouth of Thames). 789 *chart.* Iaegnlaad, 808 *chart.* Genlad (Kent), *Bede* Genlada, said to be O.E. *gegn*, ' opposite, over against,' and *lada* (*gelad*), ' way, passage.' Perh. one origin of Eng. *inlet*. *Cf.* 1570-76, Lambarde *Peramb. Kent* (1826) 234, ' A thing yet well known in Kent and expressed by the word yenlade or yenlet, which betokeneth an Indraught or Inlett of water into the land.' Inlet is found as early as *a.* 1300 *Cursor Mundi*, In-late.

YEO, R. There are 3, one in N. Devon, 2 in Somerset. The one near Crediton is 739 *chart.* Eowe. Possibly fr. Ir. *eó*, ' yew-tree' river. W. J. Watson, ' with hesitation,' derives the R. Ewe (Ross-shire) from this root. *Cf.* next.

YEOVIL and YEOVILTON. *a.* 800 *chart.* Gifla, *Dom.* Givele, Ivle, *chart.* Gavylton. Though Yeovil is on R. YEO, it orig. had nothing to do with Yeo. Gifla or Gavyl seems to be O.E. *gafol*, *geafl*, ' a fork, a forked opening '; cognate with G. *gabhal* or *gobhal* (*bh*= *v*), ' a fork,' as in Gavell (Kilsyth). The mod. name is made up of *Yeo* and Fr. *ville*, a truly modern compound ! There is also said to be a St. *Ivel*, fr. whom the town took its name. No such name appears in the *Dict. Christ. Biogr.* *Cf.* GALFORD, ILCHESTER, and YIELDEN.

YEVERIN(G) (Wooler). *Bede* Ad gefrin, *a.* 1120 *Hen. Hunt.* Adgebrin. Doubtful. ? containing W. *gwefr*, ' amber,' ' amber-coloured.' Yaverland (I. of Wight) is *Dom.* Evreland, fr. the name *Eofor*, *Eofer*, or *Ever*, *i.e.*, ' the Boar.' *Cf.* EVERSLEY, etc.

YEWBARROW (hill, Wastwater). 1322 Yowberg. ' BARROW mound-like hill, with the yews '; O.E. *iw*.

YIELDEN (Beds). *Dom.* Giveldene. ' Dean, wooded vale at the forked opening '; O.E. *geafl*. See YEOVIL and -den. YIELDING TREE (Broom, Worc.) *may* have the same root, but it is 1275 Gyldintre, which looks like ' tree of *Gilda*,' gen. -an. *Onom.* has only *Gildewine*.

YNYS GLANACH (Anglesea). *a.* 1190 *Gir. Camb.* Enislannach. W. = ' island of *Glanach*,' or perh. ' isle of the landing or going ashore '; W. *glaniad.* Also called Priestholme (O.E. and Dan. *holm,* ' a small, low island ') and Puffin Isld. But T. Morgan says the W. name now is Ynys Seiriol, fr. a saint who erected his cell here in 6th cny.

YOCKLETON (Shrewsbury). *Dom.* Loclehuile, error for Geochulle, just as *Dom.* has Locheshale for YOXALL. This seems to be ' village of the *yokel*,' at least, there seems no likely man's name; only *yokel*, ' a boor, a country lout,' is, so far as records go, a recent and dial. word, for which we can find nothing earlier than Jamieson's *yochel*, ' a big, stupid person.' Prob. it is derived fr. *yoke,* and meant orig. ' a ploughman.' But *cf.* GIGGLES-WICK.

YORK. *c.* 380 *Ant. Itin.* Ebur-, Eboracum, *Bede* Ecclesia Eboracensis, *c.* 780 *Alcuin,* a resident there, Euborica civitas, *O.E. Chron.* 738 Eoforwic, *a.* 998 *Richer* Eurvich, *c.* 1000 *Ælfric* Eferwíc, *Dom.* Euruic, 1198 *Hoveden* Everwic, *c.* 1205 *Layam.* ' icleped Eborac, seoðð en Eoverwic,' 1275 *ib.* Euerwich. *Layam.* 2666 says the name used to be Caer Ebrauc, fr. the good K. Ebrauc, 1298 Everwyke, 1479 *Surtees Misc.* York. Also YORK-SHIRE, 1065 *O.E. Chron.* Eoforwicscire, *c.* 1386 *Chaucer* Yorkshire. The name orig. was the Kelt. Ebur-, Eborach, which Gluck says is Ir. *ebrach,* ' muddy,' fr. *abar,* Ir. and G., ' a marsh,' with the common ending *-ach,* ' place of.' But the Angles may have taken it to be ' town, dwelling,' O.E. *wic,* ' on the R. *Ure* ' or ' *Eure*,' which looks like G. *iubhar,* Ir. *ibar,* ' a yew.' *Cf.* the *Eburones,* a tribe in Belgium, Caesar *B.G.* 2. 4. 4, *Eborius,* Bp. of York, at the Council of Arles, A.D. 314, and the *Eburovices,* the tribe who have given name to Evreux. The mod. W. name is Caerefrog, the descendant of Layam.'s Caer Ebrauc, ' castle of Ebrauc.' The present pron. York comes through the influence of the Danes, who called it Jorvik—*j* = *y.*

YOULGRAVE (Bakewell), *Dom.* Giolgrave, and YOULTON (N. Riding), *Dom.* Ioletune. Prob. ' yellow grave ' and ' town '; O.E. *geolo, -lu,* ' yellow '; but Iole- may represent a man *Gola,* 2 in *Onom.*

YOULTHORPE (Pocklington). *Dom.* Aiultorp. Doubtful; hardly fr. O.E. *úle,* Mid High Ger. *iuwel, iule,* ' an owl '; prob. ' village of *Howœl, Howel, Huwal,* or *Owel*,' recorded names of British princes. But *cf.* above. See -thorpe.

YOXAL (Burton - on - T.). *Dom.* Iocheshale (see YOCKLETON). *a.* 1300 Yoxhal(e), Jokesal, *a.* 1400 Yokeshale, Joxhale. No likely name in *Onom.*, so prob. ' nook ' or ' meadow of the *yoke*.' O.E. *geoc, gioc, ioc*—*i.e.*, as much as could be plowed by a yoke or pair of oxen in one day. See -hall. Similarly YOXFORD (Saxmundham) is *Dom.* Gokesford.

YR ARAN, etc. See ARAN, etc. *Yr* or *y* is the W. article ' the,' *yr* being used bef. a vowel or *h*.

YSPYTTY (Betws y Coed) and YSPYTTY YSTWYTH. Corrup. not of L. *hospitium*, ' a hospice, a hospital,' but of L. *hospes, -itis*, ' a guest,' and W. *ty*, ' house,' and so, ' an inn.' *Cf.* TAFARN SPITE and ABERYSTWYTH.

YSTALYFERA (Glam.). *Old* ynys tal fera (perh. for *furiau*), ' meadow at the foot of the high walls '—*i.e.*, ' hills.' But W. *ystal* is ' a stall,' and *fera* or *bera*, ' a stack of hay or corn.'

YSTRAD MYNACH (Cardiff). W. = ' monk's meadow.' W. *ystrad* is same as G. *srath* or ' strath,' but in W. means rather ' a meadow ' or ' rich lowland.' However, the original name is said to have been Y-Maenarch, named after one of the Earls of Hereford.

ZENNOR (St. Ives). There seems to be no saint of this name. Perh. Corn. and W. *iender*, ' cold, coldness,' Corn. *iein*, W. *iain*, ' cold.' *Cf.* the personal name Jenner.

ZOY (Somerset). *c. 725 chart.* Soweie, *Dom.* Sowi. O.E. *su iʒe*, ' sow isle.' Initial *s* regularly becomes *z* in this region. *Cf.* Chedzoy, Bridgwater, 1257-1300 *chart.* Chedeseye, ' *Cedda*'s isle.' See -ey.

BIBLIOGRAPHY

H. ALEXANDER: Place-Names of Oxfordshire. 1912.
H. ALEXANDER: Place-Names and Dialect Study (Yorks Dialect Socy.). 1911.
E. ANWYL, Celtic Religion. 1906.
W. ST. CLAIR BADDELEY: Place-Names of Gloucestershire. 1913.
BJÖRKMAN: Nordische Personennamen in England. 1910.
DICTIONARIES:
  A New English Dictionary, edited by Sir J. A. H. Murray, etc. Oxford. 1888 *sq*
  Dialect, Joseph Wright. 6 vols.
  Anglo-Saxon, Bosworth-Toller.
  Cornish, R. Williams, Lexicon Cornu-Britannicum. 1865.
  Gaelic, Macleod and Dewar. 1853.
  Icelandic, R. Cleasby and G. Vigfusson. 1874.
  Welsh, W. O. Pughe and R. T. Pryse. 2 vols.
W. H. DUIGNAN: Place-Names of Staffordshire. 1902.
W. H. DUIGNAN: Place-Names of Worcestershire. 1905.
W. H. DUIGNAN: Place-Names of Warwickshire. 1912.
ENCYCLOPÆDIA BRITANNICA. 11th edit.
E. FREEMAN: History of the Norman Conquest. 4 vols.
E. FREEMAN: History of William Rufus. 2 vols. 1882.
GAZETTEERS:
  Cassell's, of Great Britain and Ireland. 6 vols. 1900.
  Comprehensive, of England and Wales, edited by J. H. Brabner. 6 vols.
A. GOODALL: Place-Names of South-West Yorkshire. 1913.
G. DE GRUCHY: The Settlement of Normandy [and Channel Islands], 1911.
J. S. HILL: Place-Names of Somerset. 1913.
J. B. JOHNSTON: Place-Names of Scotland. 2nd edit. 1903.
W. L. JONES: King Arthur in History and Legend. 1911.
A. MAWER: The Vikings. 1913.
E. M'CLURE: British Place-Names in their Historical Setting. 1910.
F. W. MOORMAN: Place-Names of the West Riding. 1910.
T. MORGAN: Place-Names of Wales. 2nd edit. 1912.
H. MUTSCHMANN: Place-Names of Nottinghamshire. 1913.
G. OWEN: Description of Pembrokeshire, edited by H. Owen. 2 vols. 1892-1897.
W. G. SEARLE: *Onomasticon Anglo-Saxonicum.* 1897.
W. W. SKEAT: English Dialects. 1911.
W. W. SKEAT: Place-Names of Cambs. 1901.
W. W. SKEAT: Place-Names of Hunts. 1902.
W. W. SKEAT: Place-Names of Herts. 1904.
W. W. SKEAT: Place-Names of Bedford. 1908.
W. W. SKEAT: Place-Names of Berks. 1911.
W. W. SKEAT: Place-Names of Suffolk. 1913.
W. THORNBURY and E. WALFORD: Old and New London, also Greater London.
  2 vols. 1898.
J. H. TURNER: Yorkshire Place-Names in Domesday Book (Bingley).
H. C. WYLD AND HIRST: Place-Names of Lancashire. 1911.
ZACHRISSON: A Contribution to the Study of Anglo-Norman Influence on English
  Place-Names. 1909.
The History of Northumberland, by C. J. Bates, 1895; of Cumberland and of
  Westmorland. by R. S. Ferguson, 1890 and 1894.
O.E. Charters in Birch, and Kemble, and in A. S. Napier and W. H. Stevenson,
  Anecdota Oxoniensia. 1895.

For those who wish to continue their researches in the original sources, the early
Charters, Rolls, and Chroniclers, much useful guidance will be found from the
Bibliography in Searle.

The above list simply contains the modern books found most useful by the writer,
together with several others which proved inaccessible to him in Scotland, or which
have been published so recently that he has been able to consult them very im-
perfectly or not at all, but which will be found—all of them—very useful by the
student. The Isle of Man has been barely touched in the preceding pages,
because the ground has been so well covered already in A. W. Moore's 'Surnames and Place-Names of the Isle of Man,' 1890.

INDEX TO PLACES NOT DEALT WITH IN THEIR ALPHABETICAL ORDER

INDEX OF SUBJECTS AND PERSONAL NAMES

531